ELLIOTT AND WOOD'S

CASEBOOK
ON
CRIMINAL LAW

Sixth Edition

by

D. W. ELLIOTT, LL.B.
Solicitor, Emeritus Professor of Law, University of Newcastle upon Tyne

and

MICHAEL J. ALLEN, LL.M.
Barrister, Senior Lecturer in Law, Newcastle Law School

LONDON
SWEET & MAXWELL
1993

D. W. Elliott & J. C. Wood, First Edition 1963
Second Impression 1967
D. W. Elliott & J. C. Wood, Second Edition 1969
Second Impression 1971
D. W. Elliott & J. C. Wood, Third Edition 1974
D. W. Elliott & Celia Wells, Fourth Edition 1982
D. W. Elliott & Michael J. Allen, Fifth Edition 1989
D. W. Elliott & Michael J. Allen, Sixth edition 1993

Published by
Sweet & Maxwell Limited of
South Quay Plaza, 183 Marsh Wall, London E14 9FT
Computerset by P.B. Computer Typesetting, Pickering, N. Yorks.
Printed in England by Clays Ltd., St. Ives plc

A CIP catalogue record for this book
is available from The British Library

ISBN 0421 466 502

PREFACE

End paragraph

In the four years since the last edition, there has been considerable judicial activity in many areas of criminal law. However it must be said that the continuing urgent need for a Criminal Code has not been at all reduced by this activity. Particularly in the House of Lords, the quality of the decisions has often been open to question because of a failure of the majority to go back to first principles, even where those principles have been persuasively articulated in the minority speeches. In this respect *Gotts* on duress, *Gomez* on appropriation in theft and *Brown* on consent in assaults are notable. In other instances—*Savage and Parmenter* on "Caldwell" recklessness and offences against the person, and *In Re F.* on necessity—some problems were cleared up but others remain because of a failure to articulate coherent principles.

The Court of Appeal has also been active, generally carrying greater conviction, on Causation, Insanity, Accessoryship, Attempts, Provocation and Theft. Their output, together with that of the House of Lords, has required extensive revision of the relevant chapters. All chapters have needed some revision and in most, the revised draft of the Criminal Code has been extensively quoted, along with the Law Commission's own Commentary.

In general we have not included anything published after July 31, 1992, but notable exceptions to this are the House of Lords decisions in *Brown* and *Gomez*. Again we have to thank the many persons and bodies who kindly allowed us to reproduce copyright material. We must also thank the publishers for providing what we hope will be an attractive typographical style.

D. W. ELLIOTT
M. J. ALLEN

April 1993

CONTENTS

Preface   v
Table of Cases   xiii
Table of Statutes   xxxiii
Table of Reports and Official Proposals   xxxix
Abbreviations   xli
Acknowledgments   xliii

1. INTRODUCTORY   1
   1. The Concept of Crime   1
   2. The Form of English Criminal Law   8

2. ACTUS REUS   12
   1. Elements of Crime   12
   2. Voluntariness   14
   3. Omissions   18
      i. Breach of Duty to Act   20
      ii. Commission by Omission   21
   4. Causation   33
      i. Sine Qua Non   34
      ii. Imputability   36
      iii. An Alternative Approach   55
   5. Coincidence of Actus Reus and Mens Rea   56

3. MENS REA   64
   1. The Requirement of Mens Rea   64
   2. The Meaning of Mens Rea   68
      i. Intention   70
      ii. Motive and Intention   97
      iii. Knowledge   102
      iv. Recklessness   106
      v. Wilfulness   128
      vi. Proposals for Reform   137
   3. Mistake   140
      i. Relevant Mistakes   141
      ii. Irrelevant Mistakes   169
   4. Strict Liability   182
      i. The Evolution of Strict Liability   182
      ii. The Present Uncertainty   183
      iii. Critique   206
      iv. Proposals for Reform   210

4. MENTAL INCAPACITY   214
   1. Insanity   215
      i. Disease of the Mind   219
      ii. The Nature and Quality of the Act   223
      iii. Uncontrollable Impulse   226

2. Automatism 226
3. Proposals for Reform 237
4. Intoxication 246
   i. Specific and Basic Intent 246
   ii. Becoming Intoxicated With Intent—the "Dutch Courage" Problem 265
   iii. Intoxication and Defences 268
   iv. Proposals for Reform 273

5. DEFENCES 280
1. Defences in General 280
2. Duress 281
   i. An Imminent Threat of Death or Serious Injury 282
   ii. The Test for Duress 284
   iii. Voluntary Association with Criminal Organisation 287
   iv. Duress and Murder 292
3. Necessity 314
   i. A Defence of Necessity 314
   ii. Duress of Circumstances 319
   iii. Necessity, Duress of Circumstances and Homicide 321
   iv. A Common Law Defence of Necessity 324
4. Self-Defence and Kindred Defences 330
   i. Scope of the Defences 331
   ii. The Issues of Imminence and the Pre-emptive Strike 339
   iii. Is there a Duty to Retreat? 342
   iv. Unknown Circumstances of Justification 345
   v. To Which Offences do the Defences Apply? 346
   vi. Reasonable Force 347
   vii. Mistake 350
   viii. Excessive Force 350
5. Proposals for Reform 353
   i. General Principles 353
   ii. Duress 355
   iii. Necessity 358
   iv. Self-Defence and Kindred Defences 360

6. DEGREES OF RESPONSIBILITY 366
1. Accomplices 366
   i. Principles and Accessories 366
   ii. Innocent Agency 368
   iii. Aids, Abets, Counsels or Procures 374
   iv. Mens Rea of an Accessory 379
   v. Accessory Not Convictable as a Principle 402
2. Vicarious Liability 408
3. Corporations 413

7. INCHOATE OFFENCES 424
1. Attempts 424
   i. Mental Element 426
   ii. Actus Reus 437

2. Conspiracy 451
    i. Statutory Conspiracies 451
    ii. Common Law Conspiracies 462
    iii. Jurisdiction 467
3. Incitement 473
4. Impossibility in Relation to Inchoate Offences 478
    i. Attempt 478
    ii. Conspiracy 490
    iii. Incitement 491

8. HOMICIDE 495
1. The *Actus Reus* of Homicide 495
2. Murder 497
    i. The Penalty for Murder 497
    ii. The Mental Element in Murder 497
    iii. Proposals for Reform 505
3. Special Defences 513
    i. Provocation 513
    ii. Diminished Responsibility 528
4. Involuntary Manslaughter 545
    i. Unlawful Act Manslaughter 546
    ii. Reckless Manslaughter 557
5. Other Unlawful Homicides 568
    i. Infanticide 568
    ii. Child Destruction 568
    iii. Abortion 568
    iv. Suicide 575
    v. Causing Death by Driving 576
6. Reform of the Law of Homicide 577

9. NON-FATAL OFFENCES AGAINST THE PERSON 581
1. Assault and Battery 581
    i. *Actus Reus* 582
    ii. *Mens Rea* 586
    iii. Justifications 587
2. Assault Occasioning Actual Bodily Harm 622
3. Malicious Wounding and Wounding with Intent 622
    i. Malicious Wounding 622
    ii. Wounding with Intent 629
4. Sexual Offences 632
    i. Rape 632
    ii. Other Offences Involving Sexual Intercourse 644
    iii. Indecent Assault 647

10. THEFT AND ROBBERY 660
1. Theft 660
    i. Appropriation 662
    ii. "Property" 679
    iii. "Belonging to Another" 692
    iv. "With the Intention of Depriving Permanently" 717
    v. "Temporary Deprivation" 727
    vi. "Dishonesty" 733

2. Robbery   744

11. FRAUD   749
    1. Obtaining Property by Deception   751
        i. Obtaining Property Belonging to Another with
           Intention Permanently to Deprive   751
        ii. Deception   751
        iii. The Obtaining must be by the Deception   762
        iv. Dishonesty   774
    2. Obtaining Pecuniary Advantage by Deception   776
    3. Obtaining Services by Deception   777
    4. Evasion of Liability by Deception   778
    5. Making Off Without Payment   784

12. BLACKMAIL   789
        i. Demand with Menaces   789
        ii. Unwarranted   793
        iii. With a View to Gain, etc.   799

13. HANDLING   803
        i. Stolen Goods   804
        ii. Otherwise than in the Course of Stealing   814
        iii. Forms of Handling   817
        iv. Knowing or Believing them to be Stolen Goods   822
        v. Dishonesty   826

14. BURGLARY AND KINDRED OFFENCES   828
    1. Burglary   828
        i. Entry   829
        ii. As a Trespasser   831
        iii. Buildings or Parts of Buildings   838
        iv. Intent to Commit an Offence in the Building   839
        v. The Ulterior Offence   845
    2. Aggravated Burglary   846
    3. Going Equipped   848
        i. Has with Him   848
        ii. When not at his Place of Abode   849
        iii. Any Article   850
        iv. For use in the Course or in Connection with any
            Burglary, Theft or Cheat   851

15. CRIMINAL DAMAGE   853
    1. Destroying or Damaging Property   853
        A. The Simple Offence   857
        i. Belonging to Another   857
        ii. Without Lawful excuse   860
        iii. Intending to Destroy or Damage any such Property   864
        iv. Being Reckless as to whether any such Property
            would be Destroyed or Damaged   867

B. The Aggravated Offence 868
2. Other Offences 870

Index 873

TABLE OF CASES

[Page refs. in **bold** indicate the page upon which an extract from the report appears.]

Abbott v. R. [1977] A.C. 755 .... 288, **295**, 297, 298, 301, 305, 307, 309, 311, 312
Abraham [1973] 1 W.L.R. 1270; 117 S.J. 663; [1973] 3 All E.R. 694; [1974] Crim.L.R.
    246; sub nom. R. v. Abraham (Alan), 57 Cr.App.R. 799, C.A. 331
Ackroyd v. Barett (1894) T.L.R. 115 586
Advocate (H.M.) v. Braithwaite 1945 S.C. (J.) 55 534
—— v. Ritchie 1926 J.C. 45 232
Ahluwalia [1993] Crim.L.R. 63 514
Airedale N.H.S. Trust v. Bland, *The Times*, February 5, 1993 26
Albert v. Lavin [1982] A.C. 546; [1981] 1 All E.R. 628 .... 152, 155, 157, 158
Allan [1966] A.C. 1; [1965] 1 Q.B. 130; [1963] 3 W.L.R. 677; 127 J.P. 511; 107 S.J. 596;
    [1963] 2 All E.R. 897; 47 Cr.App.R. 243, C.C.A. 380
Allen [1985] A.C. 1029; [1985] 3 W.L.R. 107; (1985) 129 S.J. 447; [1985] 2 All E.R.
    641; (1985) 81 Cr.App.R. 200; [1985] Crim.L.R. 739; *affirming* [1985] 1
    W.L.R. 50 .... **785**, 788
Alphacell v. Woodward [1972] A.C. 824; [1972] 2 W.L.R. 1320; [1972] 2 All E.R.
    475; 116 S.J. 431; 70 L.G.R. 455; [1972] Crim.L.R. 41, H.L. 196
Anderson [1986] A.C. 27; [1985] 3 W.L.R. 268; (1985) 129 S.J. 522; [1985] 2 All E.R.
    961; (1985) 81 Cr.App.R. 253; [1985] Crim.L.R. 651, H.L.; *affirming* (1984) 80
    Cr.App.R. 64 .... **452**, 457
Anderson and Morris [1966] 2 Q.B. 110, [1966] 2 W.L.R. 1195; 130 J.P. 318; 110 S.J.
    369; [1966] 2 All E.R. 644; 50 Cr.App.R. 216 .... 394, 395
Anderton v. Burnside. *See* Morris [1984] A.C. 320.
—— v. Ryan [1985] A.C. 560; [1985] 2 W.L.R. 968; (1985) 129 S.J. 362; (1985) 81
    Cr.App.R. 166; [1985] Crim.L.R. 503, H.L.; *reversing* (1984) 128 S J
    850 .... 485, 486, 487, 488, 489, 490
Andrews v. D.P.P. [1937] A.C. 576; 106 L.J.K.B. 370; 53 T.L.R. 663; 101 J.P. 386; 81
    S.J. 497; [1937] 2 All E.R. 552; 26 Cr.App.R. 34; 35 L.G.R. 429; sub nom. R. v.
    Andrews, 156 L.T. 464; 30 Cox 576 .... 135, 550, 551, 558, 559, 560, 566
Andrews-Weatherfoil; R. v. Sporle; R. v. Day [1972] 1 W.L.R. 118; (1971) 115 S.J.
    888; 56 Cr.App.R. 31; sub nom. R. v. Andrews-Weatherfoil [1972] 1 All E.R.
    65, C.A. 458
Andrews & Hedges [1981] Crim.L.R. 106 783
Appleyard (1985) 81 Cr.App.R. 319, C.A. 859
Applin v. Race Relations Board [1975] A.C. 259; [1974] 2 W.L.R. 541; 118 S.J. 311;
    [1974] 2 All E.R. 73; 72 L.G.R. 479, H.L.; *affirming sub nom*. Race Relations
    Board v. Applin [1973] 1 Q.B. 815; [1973] 2 W.L.R. 895; 117 S.J. 417; [1973] 2
    All E.R. 1190, C.A. 474, 475
Argyll (Duchess) v. Argyll (Duke) [1967] Ch. 302; [1965] 2 W.L.R. 790; [1965] 1 All
    E.R. 611 690
Arrowsmith v. Jenkins [1963] 2 Q.B. 561; [1963] 2 W.L.R. 856; [1963] 2 All E.R. 210;
    127 J.P. 289; 107 S.J. 215; 61 L.G.R. 312; 79 L.Q.R. 330, D.C. **128**, 130
Ashford and Smith (unreported) decided on May 26, 1988 .... 862, 863
Assistant Recorder of Kingston-upon-Hull, ex p. Morgan [1969] 2 Q.B. 58; [1969] 2
    W.L.R 246; (1968) 133 J.P. 165; 112 S.J. 1005; [1969] 1 All E.R. 416; 53
    Cr.App.R. 96, D.C. 474
Att.-Gen. v. Able and Others [1984] 1 Q.B. 795; [1983] 3 W.L.R. 845; (1983) 127 S.J.
    731; [1984] 1 All E.R. 277; (1984) 78 Cr.App.R. 197; [1984] Crim.L.R. 35 576
—— v. Whelan [1934] I.R. 518 .... 282, 286, 293
Att.-Gen.'s Reference (No. 1 of 1974) [1974] Q.B. 744; [1974] 2 W.L.R. 891; 118 S.J.
    345; [1974] 2 All E.R. 899; 59 Cr.App.R. 503; [1974] Crim.L.R. 165, C.A. **809**
—— (No. 1 of 1975) [1975] Q.B. 773; [1975] 3 W.L.R. 11; 119 S.J. 373; [1975] 2 All
    E.R. 684; 61 Cr.App.R. 118; [1975] R.T.R. 473; [1975] Crim.L.R. 449,
    C.A. 366, **374**

Att.-Gen.'s Reference (Nos. 1 and 2 of 1979) [1980] Q.B. 180; [1979] 3 W.L.R. 577;
    (1979) 123 S.J. 472; [1979] 3 All E.R. 143; (1979) 69 Cr.App.R. 266; [1979]
    Crim.L.R. 585, C.A. 692, 719, **839**
—— (No. 4 of 1979) (1980) 71 Cr.App.R. 341; [1981] Crim.L.R. 51, C.A. **805**, 823
—— (No. 4 of 1980) [1981] 1 W.L.R. 705; (1981) 125 S.J. 374; [1981] 2 All E.R. 617;
    (1981) 73 Cr.App.R. 40; [1981] Crim.L.R. 492, C.A. **61**
—— (No. 6 of 1980) [1981] 3 W.L.R. 125; (1981) 125 S.J. 426; [1981] 2 All E.R.
    1057; [1981] Crim.L.R. 553; [1981] 1 Q.B. 715; (1981) 73 Cr.App.R. 63,
    C.A. 597, 601, 602, 603, 605, 613
—— (No. 1 of 1982) [1983] Q.B. 751; [1983] 3 W.L.R. 72; [1983] 2 All E.R. 721; [1983]
    Crim.L.R. 534, C.A. 458, 470
—— (No. 2 of 1982) [1984] 2 Q.B. 624; [1984] 2 W.L.R. 447; [1984] 2 All E.R. 216;
    [1985] Crim.L.R. 241 .... 677, 678, 692
—— (No. 1 of 1983) [1985] Q.B. 182; [1984] 3 W.L.R. 686; [1984] 3 All E.R. 369;
    (1984) 79 Cr.App.R. 288; [1984] Crim.L.R. 570, C.A. 682, 717
—— (No. 2 of 1983) [1984] A.C. 456; [1984] 2 W.L.R. 465; [1984] 1 All E.R. 988;
    (1984) 78 Cr.App.R. 131; [1984] Crim.L.R. 289 .... **339**
—— (No. 1 of 1985) [1986] Q.B. 491; [1986] 2 W.L.R. 733; [1986] 2 All E.R. 219;
    (1986) 83 Cr.App.R. 70; [1986] Crim.L.R. 476 .... 702, 704, **707**, 715
Att.-Gen. for Hong Kong v. Nai Keung [1988] Crim.L.R. 125 .... 688, 816
Att.-Gen. for Northern Ireland's Reference (No. 1 of 1975) [1977] A.C. 105, H.L.
    (N.I.) **349**, 352
Att.-Gen. for Northern Ireland v. Gallagher [1963] A.C. 349; [1961] 3 W.L.R. 619;
    105 S.J. 646; [1961] 3 All E.R. 299; 45 Cr.App.R. 316; [77 L.Q.R. 457; 25
    M.L.R. 238; 111 L.J. 751; 97 I.L.T. 57], H.L. 249, **265**
Att.-Gen. for South Australia v. Brown [1960] A.C. 4 32; [1960] 2 W.L.R. 588; 104
    S.J. 268; [1960] 1 All E.R. 734; 44 Cr.App.R. 100 .... 226, 228
Austin [1981] 1 All E.R. 374; *sub nom.* R. v. Austin, Withers, Fieldsend and
    Trigwell (1981) 72 Cr.App.R. 104, C.A. 368, **371**, 373
Australasian Steam Navigation Co. v. Morse (1872) L.R. 4 P.C. 222 318
Ayres [1984] A.C. 447; [1984] 2 W.L.R. 257; [1984] 1 All E.R. 619; (1984) 78
    Cr.App.R. 232; [1984] Crim.L.R. 353, H.L. 466

B. (A Minor) (Wardship: Sterilisation), *Re* [1988] A.C. 199; [1987] 2 W.L.R. 1213;
    [1987] 131 S.J. 625; [1987] 2 All E.R. 206; [1987] 2 F.L.R. 314; (1988) 86 L.G.R.
    417; (1987) 17 Fam.Law 419; (1987) 84 L.S.Gaz. 1410; (1987) 137 New L.J.
    432; (1987) 151 L.G.Rev. 650; [(1987) 151 L.G.Rev. 764], H.L. 594
B. and S. v. Leathley [1979] Crim.L.R. 314 839
Bailey (1818) R. & R. 341 829
—— (1977) 66 Cr.App.Rep. 31n. 227, 233, 535, 536
—— [1983] 1 W.L.R. 760; (1983) 147 J.P. 558; (1983) 127 S.J. 425; [1983] 2 All E.R.
    503; [1983] Crim.L.R. 533, C.A. 217, 218, **234**, 237, 260, 262
Bainbridge [1960] 1 Q.B. 129; [1959] 3 W.L.R. 656; 123 J.P. 499; [1959] 3 All E.R. 200;
    43 Cr.App.Rep. 194 .... 376, 389, 390, 391
Baker (1875) *The Times*, July 31, 1875 655
Bank of England v. Vagliano Bros. [1891] A.C. 107 .... 446, 447
Bank of New South Wales v. Piper [1897] A.C. 383; 66 L.J.P.C. 73; 76 L.T. 572; 13
    T.L.R. 413; 61 J.P. 660 .... 142, 148, 194, 195
Barker v. R. [1983] 57 A.L.J.R. 426 838
Barr [1978] Crim.L.R. 244 731
Barrow (1868) L.R. 1 C.C.R. 156; 38 L.J.M.C. 20; 19 L.T. 293; 17 W.R. 102; 11 Cox
    C.C. 191 618
Bashir (1983) 77 Cr.App.R. 59 641
Bateman (1925) 94 L.J.K.B. 791; 133 L.T. 730; 41 T.L.R. 557; 89 J.P. 162; 69 S.J. 622;
    28 Cox C.C. 33; 19 Cr. App.R. 8 .... 558, 564, 566
Beal v. Kelley [1951] 2 All E.R. 763 .... 652, 655
Becerra; R. v. Cooper (1975) 62 Cr.App.R. 121, C.A. **398**, 402
Beckford v. R. [1988] 1 A.C. 130, P.C. 157, 272, 342, 350, 495
Bedder v. D.P.P. [1954] 1 W.L.R. 1119; 98 S.J. 556; [1954] 2 All E.R. 801; 38
    Cr.App.R. 133 .... 266, 518, 519, 521
Beecham (1851) 5 Cox C.C. 181 725
Belfon [1976] 1 W.L.R. 741; [1976] 3 All E.R. 46 C.A. 81

Belmont Finance Corporation Ltd. *v.* Williams Furniture Ltd. [1979] Ch. 250;
  [1978] 3 W.L.R. 712; (1977) 122 S.J. 743; [1979] 1 All E.R. 118 677
Bembridge (1783) 22 State Tr. 1; 3 Doug. K.B. 327; 99 E.R. 679 21
Benge (1865) 4 F. & F. 504 22
Bentley (1850) 4 Cox 406 .... **630**
Bernhard [1938] 2 K.B. 264; 107 L.J.K.B. 449; 159 L.T. 22; 54 T.L.R. 615; 102 J.P. 282;
  82 S.J. 257; [1938] 2 All E.R. 140; 31 Cox C.C. 61; 26 Cr.App.R. 137; 36 L.G.R.
  333 795
Betts *v.* Stevens [1910] 1 K.B. 1; 79 L.J.K.B. 17; 101 L.T. 564; 73 J.P. 486; 26 T.L.R. 5;
  22 Cox C.C. 187; 7 L.G.R. 1052 130
Bevans (1987) 87 Cr.App.R. 64; [1988] Crim.L.R. 236, C.A. 799, 800
Bird [1985] 1 W.L.R. 816, C.A. **342**, 365
Bishop (1880) 5 Q.B.D. 259; 49 L.J.M.C. 45; 42 L.T. 240; 28 W.R. 475; 44 J.P. 330; 14
  Cox C.C. 404 184
Black-Clawson International *v.* Papierwerke Waldhof-Aschaffenburg Aktienge-
  sellschaft [1975] A.C. 591; [1975] 2 W.L.R. 513; 119 S.J. 221; [1975] 1 All E.R.
  810; [1975] 2 Lloyd's Rep. 11, H.L. 672
Blake *v.* Barnard (1840) 9 C. & P. 626 585
Blakely *v.* D.P.P., *The Times,* June 12, 1991; *The Guardian,* July 11, 1991 .... 377, 388
Blaue [1975] 1 W.L.R. 1411; 119 S.J. 589; [1975] 3 All E.R. 466; *sub nom.* R. *v.* Blaue
  (Robert Konrad) (1975) 61 Cr. App.R. 271; [1975] Crim.L.R. 648,
  C.A. 40, 42, 47, 54
Bloxham [1981] 1 W.L.R. 859; [1981] 2 All E.R. 647; (1981) 72 Cr.App.R. 323; [1981]
  Crim.L.R. 337; [1981] R.T.R. 376, C.A. 817, **821**
Board of Trade *v.* Owen [1957] A.C. 602; [1957] 2 W.L.R. 351; 121 J.P. 177; 101 S.J.
  186; [1957] 1 All E.R. 411; 41 Cr.App.R. 11; [102 S.J. 189], H.L. 451, **467**
Boggeln *v.* Williams [1978] 1 W.L.R. 873; (1978) 122 S.J. 94; [1978] 2 All E.R. 1061;
  (1978) 67 Cr.App.R. 50; [1978] Crim.L.R. 242, D.C. 743
Bolam *v.* Friern Hospital Management Committee [1957] 1 W.L.R. 582; 101 S.J.
  357; [1957] 2 All E.R. 118; [101 S.J. 291] 593
Bolton, H.L. (Engineering) Co. Ltd. *v.* T. J. Graham and Sons Ltd. [1957] 1 Q.B.
  159; [1956] 3 W.L.R. 804; 100 S.J. 816; [1956] 3 All E.R. 624; [[1957] J.B.L. 14;
  73 L.Q.R. 16, 21 Conv. 77], C.A. 416
Bonner [1970] 1 W.L.R. 838; [1970] 2 All E.R. 97n.; 114 S.J. 188; 54 Cr.App.R. 257,
  C.A. **698**
Bonollo [1981] V.R. 633 744
Bourne [1939] 1 K.B. 687; 108 L.J.K.B. 471; [1938] 3 All E.R. 615 ...... 100, 316, 319, **570**
—— (1952) 36 Cr.App.R. 125 .... 368, 371, 373, 568
Boyea (January 28, 1992) [1992] Crim.L.R. 23 .... 603, 617
Boyle (1954) 2 Q.B. 292; [1954] 3 W.L.R. 364; 118 J.P. 481; 98 S.J. 559; [1954] 2 All
  E.R. 721; 38 Cr.App.R. 111 836
Boyle and Boyle (1987) 84 Cr.App.R. 270, C.A. 445
Bradshaw (1878) 14 Cox 83 .... 126, 586, 627
Brain (1834) 6 C. & P. 349 497
Bratty *v.* Att.-Gen. for Northern Ireland [1963] A.C. 386; [1961] 3 W.L.R. 965; 105
  S.J. 865; [1961] 3 All E.R. 523 .... 16, 219, 220, 221, 222, **227**, 230, 232, 249
Brend *v.* Wood (1946) L.T. 306; 110 J.P. 317; 62 T.L.R. 462 .... 188, 192
Briggs [1977] 1 W.L.R. 605; [1977] 1 All E.R. 475; (1976) 63 Cr.App.R. 215,
  C.A. 113, 114, 116, 120
Brooks & Brooks (1983) 76 Cr.App.R. 66 .... 784, 785
Brow [1981] V.R. 783 744
Brown (1899) 63 J.P. 790 482
—— [1970] 1 Q.B. 105; [1969] 3 W.L.R. 370; [1969] 3 All E.R. 198; 133 J.P. 592; 113
  S.J. 639; (1969) 53 Cr.App.R. 527, C.A. 818
—— [1972] 2 Q.B. 229; [1972] 3 W.L.R. 11; [1972] 2 All E.R. 1328, C.A. **525**
—— [1985] Crim.L.R. 212, C.A. 830
—— (1993) Official Transcript House of Lords **595**, 617
Brown and Morley (1968) S.A.S.R. 467 308
Brutus *v.* Cozens [1973] A.C. 854; [1972] W.L.R. 521; [1972] 2 All E.R. 1297 735
Bryan (1857) D. & B. 265 .... 759, 760
Bryson [1985] Crim.L.R. 669 629
Buck & Buck (1960) 44 Cr.App.R. 213; [1960] Crim.L.R. 730 550

Buckingham (1976) 63 Cr.App.R. 159, C.A. 871
Buckoke v. G.L.C. [1971] Ch. 655; [1971] 2 W.L.R. 760; [1971] 2 All E.R. 254; 115
    S.J. 174; [1971] R.T.R. 131; 69 L.G.R. 210, C.A. 314, 321
Bullock [1955] 1 W.L.R. 1; 119 J.P. 65; 99 S.J. 29; [1955] 1 All E.R. 15; 38 Cr.App.R.
    151 383
Bullock v. Turnbull [1952] 2 Lloyd's Rep. 303 141
Bundy [1977] 1 W.L.R. 914; [1977] 2 All E.R. 382, C.A. 849
Burgess [1991] 2 Q.B. 92; [1991] 2 W.L.R. 1206; [1991] 2 All E.R. 769, C.A. 222
Burles [1947] V.L.R. 392; [1918] A.L.R. 460 147
Burns (1984) 79 Cr.App.R. 173 459
Button (1848) 11 Q.B.D. 929; 18 L.J.M.C. 19; 12 L.T.O.S. 309; 13 J.P. 20; 12 Jur.
    1017; 3 Cox C.C. 229; 116 E.R. 720 465
—— [1900] 2 Q.B. 597; 69 L.J.Q.B. 901; 83 L.T. 288; 16 T.L.R. 525; 48 W.R. 703; 64
    J.P. 600; 44 S.J. 659; 19 Cox C.C. 568 .... 770, 774
Byrne [1960] 2 Q.B. 396; [1960] 3 W.L.R. 440; 104 S.J. 645; [1960] 3 All E.R. 1; 44
    Cr.App.R. 246 .... 226, 529, **530**, 535, 536, 540
—— v. Kinematograph Renters Society [1958] 1 W.L.R. 762; 102 S.J. 509; [1958] 2
    All E.R. 579; [102 S.J. 645; 103 S.J. 65, 84; [1959] C.L.J. 30; 21 M.L.R. 661] 836

C. v. Eisenhower [1984] Q.B.331 623
Caldwell [1982] A.C. 341; [1981] 2 W.L.R. 509; [1981] 1 All E.R. 961; (1981) 73
    Cr.App.R. 13, H.L. 116, 118, 119, 120, 121, 122, 123, 124, 126, 127, 128, 237,
                  257, 260, 261, 262, 560, 561, 563, 564, 623, 643, 867, 868
Calhaen [1985] Q.B. 808; [1985] 2 W.L.R. 826; [1985] 2 All E.R. 226; (1985)
    Cr.App.R. 131; [1985] Crim.L.R. 303 377
Callender [1992] 3 All E.R. 51 .... 774, 777
Callow v. Tillstone (1900) 83 L.T. 411 388
Cambridgeshire and Isle of Ely County Council v. Rust [1972] 2 Q.B. 426; [1972] 3
    W.L.R. 226; 116 S.J. 564; [1972] 3 All E.R. 232; 70 L.G.R. 444; [1972]
    Crim.L.R. 433, D.C. 866
Campbell [1991] Crim.L.R. 268 447
Camplin [1978] A.C. 705; [1978] 2 W.L.R. 679; (1978) 122 S.J. 280; (1978) 67
    Cr.App.R. 14; [1978] 2 All E.R. 168, H.L. 122, 123, 285, 515, **517**, 522,
                                           527, 528
Carter [1959] V.R. 105 232
Carter v. Richardson [1974] R.T.R. 314; [1974] Crim.L.R. 190 388
Cascoe [1970] 2 All E.R. 833; 54 Cr.App.R. 401, C.A. 513
Case (1850) 1 Den. 580; T. & M. 318; 4 New Sess.Cas. 347; 19 L.J.M.C. 174; 15
    L.T.(o.s.) 306; 14 J.P. 339; 14 Jur. 489; 4 Cox C.C. 220 .... 645, 647
Cassady v. Morris (Reg) (Transport) [1975] R.T.R. 470; [1975] Crim.L.R. 398 382
Cato; R. v. Morris; R. v. Dudley [1976] 1 W.L.R. 110; 119 S.J 775; [1976] 1 All E.R.
    260; [1976] Crim.L.R. 59; *sub nom.* R. v. Cato (Ronald Philip); R. v. Morris
    (Neil Adrien); R. v. Dudley (Melvin) (1975) 62 Cr.App.R. 41, C.A. **34**, 551
Cattell v. Ireson (1858) E.B. & E. 91; 27 L.J.M.C. 167; 4 Jur.(N.S.) 560 2
Chan Man-sin v. Att.-Gen. of Hong Kong [1988] 1 All E.R. 1; 86 Cr.App.R. 303,
    P.C. 662, 682, 687, 726
Chan Wing-sui v. R. [1985] A.C. 168; [1984] 3 W.L.R. 677; [1984] 3 All E.R. 877;
    (1984) Cr.App.R. 117; [1984] Crim.L.R. 849 .... 394, 395, 396, 398
Chandler v. D.P.P. [1964] A.C. 763; [1962] 3 W.L.R. 694; 106 S.J. 588; [1962] 3 All
    E.R. 142; 46 Cr.App.R. 347 .... **97**, 101, 863
Chapman v. D.P.P. (1988) 89 Cr.App.R. 190; [1988] Crim.L.R. 843, D.C. 345
Charlson [1955] 1 W.L.R. 317; 119 J.P. 283; 99 S.J. 221; [1955] 1 All E.R. 859; 39
    Cr.App.R. 37; [73 S.A.L.J. 90] 228
Chase Manhattan Bank v. Israel-British Bank [1981] 1 Ch. 105; [1980] 2 W.L.R. 202;
    (1979) 124 S.J. 99; [1979] 3 All E.R. 1025 .... 703, 704, 716
Cheshire [1991] 1 W.L.R. 844; [1991] 3 All E.R. 670; 93 Cr.App.R. 251, C.A. **48**, 51
Chief Constable of Avon and Somerset Constabulary v. Shimmen (1986) 84
    Cr.App.R. 118
Chisham (1963) 47 Cr.App.R. 130, C.A. 337
Church [1966] 1 Q.B. 59; [1965] 2 W.L.R. 1220; [1965] 2 All E.R. 72; 109 S.J. 371;
    J.P. 366; 49 Cr.App.R. 206 .... 58, 59, 60, 62, 63, **547**, 551, 553, 556, 561
Churchill v. Walton [1967] 2 A.C. 224; [1967] 2 W.L.R. 682; 131 J.P. 277; 111 S.J.
    112; [1967] 1 All E.R. 497; 51 Cr.App.R. 212 389

City of Sault Ste Marie (1978) 85 D.L.R. (3d) 161 .... **202**, 206
Clarence (1888) 22 Q.B.D. 23; 58 L.J.M.C. 10; 59 L.T. 780; 5 T.L.R. 61; 37 W.R. 166;
   53 J.P. 149; 16 Cox C.C. 511 .... 608, **617**, 619, 623, 624, 638
Clarkson [1971] 1 W.L.R. 1402; [1971] 3 All E.R. 344; 115 S.J. 654; 55 Cr.App.R. 445,
   Cts.-Martial App.Ct. **379**
Clear [1968] 1 Q.B. 670; [1968] 2 W.L.R. 122; [1968] 1 All E.R. 74; 132 J.P. 103; 112
   S.J. 67; 52 Cr.App.R. 58, C.A. 790, 791, 792
Clouden [1987] Crim.L.R. 56, C.A. 748
Clucas [1949] 2 K.B. 226; L.J.R. 1571; 65 T.L.R. 346; 113 J.P. 355; 93 S.J. 407; [1949] 2
   All E.R. 40; 33 Cr.App.R. 136; 47 L.G.R. 563 .... **769**, 774
Codere (1916) 12 Cr.App.R. 21 .... **223**, 225
Cogan and Leak [1976] 1 Q.B. 217; [1975] 3 W.L.R. 316; 119 S.J. 473; [1975] 2 All
   E.R. 1059; [1975] Crim.L.R. 584; *sub nom.* R. *v.* Cogan (John Rodney); R. *v.*
   Leak (Michael Edward) (1975) 61 Cr.App.R. 217, C.A. 366, **369**, 373, 640
Cole *v.* Turner (1705) 6 Mod. 149; 876 E.R. 907; Holt K.B. 108 591
Coleman [1986] Crim.L.R. 56, C.A. 826
Collins (1864) L. & C. 471; 4 New Rep. 299; 33 L.J.M.C. 177; 10 L.T. 581; 12 W.R.
   886; 28 J.P. 436; 10 Jur.(N.S.) 696; 9 Cox C.C. 497 .... 481, 482, 487
—— [1973] 1 Q.B. 100; [1972] 3 W.L.R. 243; [1972] 2 All E.R. 1562; 113 S.J. 897; 54
   Cr.App.R. 19, C.A. 829, 830, **831**, 836, 837, 838
—— *v.* Wilcock [1984] 3 All E.R. 374 .... 587, 590, 603, 605, 612
Collins & Fox *v.* Chief Constable of Merseyside [1988] Crim.L.R. 247 368
Collis-Smith [1971] Crim.L.R. 716 762
Collister and Warhurst (1955) Cr.App.R. 100 793
Comer *v.* Bloomfield [1971] R.T.R. 49; (1970) 55 Cr.App.R. 305, D.C. 440, 441
Commissioner of Police for the Metropolis *v.* Charles [1977] A.C. 177; [1976] 3
   W.L.R. 431; [1976] 3 All E.R. 112, H.L. 766, 768
Coney (1882) 8 Q.B.D. 534; 51 L.J.M.C. 66; 46 L.T. 307; 30 W.R. 678; 46 J.P. 404; 15
   Cox C.C. 46 .... 379, 380, 385, 596, 601, 604, 605, 612, 613, 614
Conway [1988] 3 All E.R. 1025 .... 284, 319, 320, 321, 360
Cook (1963) 48 Cr.App.R. 98, C.A. 439
Cooke [1986] A.C. 909; [1986] 2 All E.R. 985 .... 768, 852
Cooper & Cooper [1991] Crim.L.R. 524 854
Coppen *v.* Moore (No. 2) [1898] 2 Q.B. 306 410
Corbyn *v.* Saunders [1978] 1 W.L.R. 400 787
Corcoran *v.* Anderton (1980) 71 Cr.App.R. 104; [1980] Crim.L.R. 385, D.C. 744
Coroner for Inner West London *ex p.* De Luca [1989] 3 All E.R. 414 496
Cottle [1958] N.Z.L.R. 999 .... 232, 233, 235
Court [1989] A.C. 28; [1988] 2 W.L.R. 1071; [1988] 2 All E.R. 221; 87 Cr.App.R. 144,
   H.L. **649**
Cox (18818) R. & R. 362 500
—— [1968] 1 W.L.R. 308; [1968] 1 All E.R. 386; *sub nom.* R. *v.* Cox (Maurice George)
   (1967) 111 S.J. 966; 52 Cr.App.R. 130, C.A. 538
—— *v.* Riley (1986) 83 Cr.App.R. 54 .... 855, 856
Cozens *v.* Brutus. *See* Brutus *v.* Cozens.
Croft [1944] 1 K.B. 295; 88 S.J. 152; [1944] 2 All E.R. 483; 113 L.J.K.B. 308; 170 L.T.
   312; 60 T.L.R. 226; 29 Cr.App.R. 169, C.C.A. 400
Crutchley (1837) 7 C. & P. 814 497
Cugullere [1961] 1 W.L.R. 858; 125 J.P. 414; 105 S.J. 386; [1961] 2 All E.R. 343; 45
   Cr.App.R. 108 .... 105, 106, 847
Cullen (1974), unreported 714
Cullum (1873) L.R. 2 C.C.R. 28; 42 L.J.M.C. 64; 28 L.T. 571; 21 W.R. 687; 37 J.P.
   422; 12 Cox C.C. 469 .... 709, 710
Cundy *v.* Le Cocq (1884) 13 Q.B.D. 207; 53 L.J.M.C. 125; 51 L.T. 265; 32 W.R. 769;
   48 J.P. 599 .... **183**, 196
Cunliffe *v.* Goodman [1950] 2 K.B. 237; 66 T.L.R. 109; [1950] 1 All E.R. 720; 94 S.J.
   179, C.A. 79, 431
Cunningham [1957] 2 Q.B. 396; [1957] 3 W.L.R. 76; 121 J.P. 451; 101 S.J. 503; [1957]
   2 All E.R. 412; 41 Cr.App.R. 155 .... 109, 112, 113, 114, 118, 126, 127,
   128, 237, 260, 327, 629
—— [1981] 3 W.L.R. 223; [1981] 2 All E.R. 863; (1981) 125 S.J. 512; [1981] Crim.L.R.
   835; (1981) Cr.App.R. 253, H.L. 262, **503**

Curley (1909) 2 Cr.App.R. 96, 109 .... **38, 53**
Curr [1968] 2 Q.B. 944; [1967] 2 W.L.R. 595; 131 J.P. 245; 111 S.J. 152; [1967] 1 All
E.R. 478; 51 Cr.App.R. 113 .... **475**

D. [1984] A.C. 778; [1984] 3 W.L.R. 186; [1984] 2 All E.R. 449; 79 Cr.App.R. 313,
H.L. 621
D. (A Minor) (Wardship: Sterilisation), *Re* [1976] Fam. 185; [1976] 2 W.L.R. 279;
(1975) 119 S.J. 696; [1976] 1 All E.R. 326; [126 New L.J. 104] 594
Dadson (1983) 127 S.J 306; (1983) 77 Cr.A..R. 91; (1983) Crim.L.R. 540, C.A. 345
Dalby (1982) 74 Cr.App.R. 348 .... 552, 557
Dalloway (1847) 2 Cox 273 .... 18, 36
Dalton. *See* Percy Dalton Ltd.
Daly [1968] V.R. 257 .... 143, 144
Davenport [1954] 1 All E.R. 602 681
Davey *v.* Lee [1968] 1 Q.B. 366; [1967] 3 W.L.R. 105; 131 J.P. 327; 111 S.J. 212; [1967]
2 All E.R. 423; 51 Cr.App.R. 303 .... 443, 445
Davidge *v.* Bunnett [1974] Crim.L.R. 252 715
Davies [1975] Q.B. 691; [1975] 2 W.L.R. 586; [1975] 1 All E.R. 890; 69 Cr.App.R.
253, C.A. 516
——— [1983] Crim.L.R. 741 246
——— *v.* Flackett [1973] R.T.R. 8 762
——— *v.* Harvey (1874) L.R. 9 Q.B. 433; 43 L.J.M.C. 121; 30 L.T. 629; 22 W.R. 733; 38
J.P. 661 184
——— *v.* Leighton (1978) 68 Cr.App.R. 4 695
Davis (1881) 14 Cox 563 267
Dawson (1976) 64 Cr.App.R. 170 .... **747**, 748
——— (1985) 81 Cr.App.R. 150 .... 552, **554**
Day (1841) 9 C. & P. 722 .... 634, 637
Dee (1884) 14 L.R. Ir. 486; 15 Cox C.C. 579 618
De Freitas *v.* R. (1960) 2 W.I.R. 523 352
Dent [1955] 2 Q.B. 590, C.A. 759
Denton [1982] 1 All E.R. 65 .... **857**, 859
Devlin *v.* Armstrong [1971] N.I. 13, C.A. 330, 333, **336**, 339
Dicken (1877) 14 Cox 8 .... 646, 647
Diplock, *Re* [1948] Ch. 465 705
D.P.P. *v.* Beard [1920] A.C 479; 89 L.J.K.B. 437; 122 L.T. 625; 36 T.L.R. 379; 84 J.P.
129; 64 S.J. 340; 26 Cox C.C. 573; 14 Cr.App.R. 159 .... 228, 248, 249, 251,
252, 253, 254, 266, 267
——— *v.* Bell [1992] Crim.L.R. 176 319
——— *v.* Camplin. *See* Camplin.
——— *v.* Daley [1980] A.C. 237; [1979] 2 W.L.R. 239; [1979] Crim.L.R. 182; *sub nom.*
D.P.P. *v.* Daley; D.P.P. *v.* McGhie (1978) 69 Cr.App.R. 39; *sub nom.* D.P.P.
v. Daley and McGhie (1978) 122 S.J. 861, P.C. 39
——— *v.* Doot; [1973] A.C. 807; [1973] 2 W.L.R. 532; [1973] 1 All E.R. 940; 57
Cr.App.R. 600, H.L. 471, 472
——— *v.* Head [1959] A.C. 53; [1958] 2 W.L.R. 617; [1958] 1 All E.R. 679, H.L. 483
——— *v.* K. (A Minor) [1990] 1 W.L.R. 1067 126
——— *v.* Kent and Sussex Contractors Ltd. [1944] K.B. 146 416
——— *v.* Majewski [1977] A.C. 443; [[1977] Crim.L.R. 532; 3 Crim.L.J. 13], H.L.;
[1976] 2 W.L.R. 623; 120 S.J. 299; [1976] 2 All E.R. 142; (1976) 62 Cr.App.R.
262; [1976] Crim.L.R. 374, H.L. 120, 126, 235, **246**, 255, 256, 257, 258, 259,
260, 261, 262, 264, 265, 268, 269, 271, 272, 273
——— *v.* Morgan; Same *v.* McDonald; Same *v.* McLarty; Same *v.* Parker [1976] A.C.
182; [1975] 2 W.L.R. 913; 119 S.J 319; 61 Cr.App.R. 136; *sub nom.* D.P.P. *v.*
Morgan [1975] 2 All E.R. 347; [1975] Crim.L.R. 717, H.L. 8, 141, **142**, 148,
149, 150, 151, 152, 153, 154, 155, 157, 158, 159, 164,
171, 247, 251, 252, 268, 633, 640, 642, 643
——— *v.* Newbury; D.P.P. *v.* Jones [1977] A.C. 500; [1976] 2 W.L.R. 918; [1976] 2 All
E.R. 365; 62 Cr.App.R. 291, H.L. **552**, 556, 557
——— *v.* Nock [1978] A.C. 979 .... 451, 490, 491, 492, 843, 844
——— *v.* Ray [1974] A.C. 370; [1973] 3 W.L.R. 359; [1973] 3 All E.R. 131; 117 S.J.
663 .... **752**, 758, 759, 761, 787

D.P.P. *v.* Shannon [1975] A.C. 717; [1974] 3 W.L.R. 155; 118 S.J. 515; 59 Cr.App.R. 250; *sub nom.* R. *v.* Shannon [1974] 2 All E.R. 1009; [1975] Crim.L.R. 703, H.L. **458, 459**

—— *v.* Smith [1961] A.C. 290; [1960] 3 W.L.R. 546; 124 J.P. 473; 104 S.J. 683; [1960] 3 All E.R. 161; 44 Cr.App.R. 261 .... 83, 84, 85, 87, 250, **500**, 501, 502, 503, 504, 505, 623

—— *v.* Stonehouse [1978] A.C. 55; [1977] 3 W.L.R. 143; (1977) 121 S.J. 491; [1977] 2 All E.R. 909; (1977) 65 Cr.App.R. 192; [1977] Crim.L.R. 544, H.L. 437, 438, 439, 443, 445

—— *v.* Sykes. *See* Sykes *v.* D.P.P.

—— *v.* Turner [1974] A.C. 357; [1973] 3 W.L.R. 352; 57 Cr.App.R. 932, H.L. 776

—— *v.* Withers [1975] A.C. 849; [1974] 3 W.L.R. 751; 118 S.J. 862; [1974] 3 All E.R. 984; 60 Cr.App.R. 85; [1975] Crim.L.R. 95, H.L. 467

D.P.P. for Northern Ireland *v.* Maxwell (1978) 122 S.J. 758; [1978] 3 All E.R. 1140; [1978] Crim.L.R. 40; *sub nom.* Maxwell *v.* D.P.P. for Northern Ireland (1978) 68 Cr.App.R. 128, *sub nom.* D.P.P. *v.* Maxwell [1978] 1 W.L.R. 1350, H.L. 366, 379, **388**

—— *v.* Lynch [1975] A.C. 653; [1975] 2 W.L.R. 641; 119 S.J. 233; 61 Cr.App.R. 6; *sub nom.* Lynch *v.* D.P.P. for Northern Ireland [1975] 1 All E.R. 913; [1975] Crim.L.R. 707, H.L.; [1975] N.I. 35 .... 68, 285, 286, 288, 289, 290, **292**, 295, 296, 297, 298, 300, 302, 303, 304, 306, 307, 309, 312, 313, 323

—— *v.* Taylor and Little [1992] 1 All E.R. 299 125

Dobson *v.* General Accident Fire and Life Assurance Corporation plc [1990] 1 Q.B. 274 .... 669, 670, 672, 675, 676

Doherty (1887) 16 Cox C.C. 306 248

Dolan (1855) Dears. 436; 24 L.J.M.C. 59; 1 Jur.(N.S.) 72; 3 W.R. 177; 6 Cox C.C. 449 .... 483, 810, 812

Donnelly [1970] N.Z.L.R. 980 .... 480, 481, 483

Donovan [1934] 2 K.B. 498; 103 L.J.K.B. 683; 152 L.T. 46; 50 T.L.R. 566; 98 J.P. 409; 78 S.J. 601; 30 Cox C.C. 187; 25 Cr.App.R. 1; 55 L.G.R. 439 .... 5, 597, 601, 603, 613

Doughty (1986) 83 Cr.App.R. 319, C.A. **514**

Doukas [1978] 1 W.L.R. 372; (1978) 122 S.J. 30; [1978] 1 All E.R. 1061; (1977) 66 Cr.App.R. 228; [1978] Crim.L.R. 177, C.A. **763**, 852

Downes (1875) 1 Q.B.D. 25 135

—— (1983) 77 Cr.App.R. 260; [1983] Crim.L.R. 819, C.A. 724

Du Cros *v.* Lambourne [1907] 1 K.B. 409 382

Dudley [1989] Crim.LR. 57 870

Dudley and Stephens (1884) 14 Q.B.D. 273; 54 L.J.M.C. 32; 52 L.T. 107; 1 T.L.R. 118; 33 W.R. 347; 49 J.P. 69; 15 Cox C.C. 624 .... 297, 298, 299, 300, 303, 305, **321**, 323

Duffy [1949] 1 All E.R. 932n. 337, 513, 514, 532

—— [1967] 1 Q.B. 63, C.A. **332**

Dunbar [1958] 1 Q.B. 1; [1957] 3 W.L.R. 330; 121 J.P. 506; 101 S.J. 594; [1957] 2 All E.R. 737; 41 Cr.App.R. 182 529

Duru and Asghar [1974] 1 W.L.R. 2; (1973) 117 S.J. 7; *sub nom.* R. *v.* Duru [1973] 3 All E.R. 715; (1973) 58 Cr.App.R. 151; *sub nom.* R. *v.* Asghar [1973] Crim.L.R. 701, C.A. 685, 687, 688, 721, 724

Dyson [1908] 2 K.B. 454; 77 L.J.K.B. 813; 99 L.T. 201; 24 T.L.R. 653; 72 J.P. 303; 52 S.J. 535; 221 Cox C.C. 669; 1 Cr.App.R. 13 .... **495**

Dytham [1979] Q.B. 722; [1979] 3 W.L.R. 467; (1979) 123 S.J. 621; [1979] 3 All E.R. 641; (1979) 69 Cr.App.R. 387; [1979] Crim.L.R. 666, C.A. **20**

Eagleton (1855) Dears. 376, 515; 24 L.J.M.C. 158; 26 L.T.(o.s.) 7; 4 W.R. 17; 19 J.P. 546; 1 Jur.(N.S.) 940; 6 Cox C.C. 559 .... 437, 443, 444, 445, 446

Easom [1971] 2 Q.B 315; [1971] 3 W.L.R. 82; [1971] 2 All E.R. 945; 115 S.J. 485; 55 Cr.App.R. 410 .... **717**, 721, 841, 842, 844, 845

Eaton *v.* Cobb [1950] 1 All E.R. 1016; (1950) 114 J.P. 271 .... 129, 141

Eckman *v.* Midland Bank Ltd. [1973] Q.B. 519; [1973] I.C.R. 71; [1973] 3 W.L.R. 284; (1972) 117 S.J. 87; [1973] 1 All E.R. 609; *sub nom. Re v.* Goad, *Re v.* Amalgamated Union Engineering Workers (Engineering Section); Eckman *v.* Midland Bank and Hill Samuel & Co. [1973] 1 Lloyd's Rep. 162, N.I.R.C. 684

Edmeads and Others (1828) 3 C. & P. 390 399
Edwards v. R. [1973] A.C. 648; [1973] 1 All E.R. 152 .... 527, 528
—— v. Ddin [1976] 1 W.L.R. 942; 120 S.J. 587; [1976] 3 All E.R. 705; [1976] 63
    Cr.App.R. 218; [1976] R.T.R. 508; [1976] Crim.L.R. 580, D.C. 693, 762
Eldershaw (1828) 3 C. & P. 396 405
Eldredge v. U.S. 62 F. 2nd 449 (1932) 401
Ellames [1974] 1 W.L.R. 1391; 118 S.J. 578; [1974] 3 All E.R. 130; [1974] Crim.L.R.
    554; sub nom. R v. Ellames (Charles John) (1974) 60 Cr.App.R. 7, C.A. **851**
Elliot (1889) 16 Cox 710 22
Elliott v. C. (A Minor) [1983] 1 W.L.R. 939; [1983] 2 All E.R. 1005, D.C. 117, **119**,
                                                                         123, 261, 642, 867
Ellis, Street and Smith (1986) 84 Cr.App.R. 235 105
Emary v. Nolloth [1903] 2 K.B. 264; 72 L.J.K.B. 620; 89 L.T. 100; 67 J.P. 354; 52 W.R.
    107; 19 T.L.R. 530; 47 S.J. 567; 20 Cox C.C. 507 412
Evans [1986] Crim.L.R. 470 474
Evans and Gardiner (No. 2) [1976] V.R. 523 49
Evans v. Dell (1937) 156 L.T. 240; 53 T.L.R. 310; 101 J.P. 149; 81 S.J. 100; [1937] 1 All
    E.R. 349; 30 Cox C.C. 558; 35 L.G.R. 105 102
—— v. Hughes [1972] 3 All E.R. 412 341
—— v. Wright [1964] Crim.L.R. 466 341

F. (Mental Patient: Sterilisation), Re [1990] 2 A.C. 1 .... **317**, 320, **587**
Fagan v. Metropolitan Police Commissioner [1969] 1 Q.B. 439; [1968] 3 W.L.R.
    1120; 133 J.P. 16; 112 S.J. 800; [1968] 3 All E.R. 442; 52 Cr.App.R.
    700 .... 29, 33, 56, **582**, 586
Fairclough v. Whipp [1951] W.N. 528; [1951] 2 T.L.R. 909; 115 J.P. 612; 95 S.J. 699;
    [1951] 2 All E.R. 834; 35 Cr.App.R. 138 .... **584**, 648, 775
Farrance [1978] R.T.R. 225; (1977) 67 Cr.App.R. 136; [1978] Crim.L.R. 496, C.A. 484
Faulkner (1877) 13 Cox C.C. 550; I.R. 11 C.L. 8 109
—— v. Talbot [1981] 3 All E.R. 468 648
Feely [1973] Q.B. 530; [1973] 2 W.L.R. 201; [1973] 1 All E.R. 341; 117 S.J. 54; [1973]
    Crim.L.R. 193; 57 Cr.App.R. 312, C.A. **734**, 738, 741, 744, 774
Fegan [1972] N.I. 80 340
Fenton (1830) 1 Lew. 179 547
—— (1975) 51 Cr.App.R. 261 .... 540, 541
Ferguson v. Weaving [1951] 1 K.B. 814; [1951] 1 T.L.R. 465; 115 J.P. 142; 95 S.J. 90;
    [1951] 1 All E.R. 412; 49 L.G.R. 339 .... 366, 378, 379, **387**, 398, 410
Figures [1976] Crim.L.R. 744 679
Firth [1991] Crim.L.R. 326 759
Fisher (1865) L.R. 1 C.C.R. 7 855
Fitzmaurice [1983] Q.B. 1083; [1983] 2 W.L.R. 227; [1983] 1 All E.R. 189; (1983)
    Cr.App.R. 17, C.A. 491
Fitzpatrick [1977] N.I. 20, C.C.A. 290
Flannery and Prendergast [1969] V.R. 31 .... 146, 148
Flattery (1877) 2 Q.B.D. 410; 46 L.J.M.C. 130; 36 L.T. 32; 25 W.R. 398; 13 Cox C.C.
    388 .... 618, 646, 647
Ford (1976), unreported 537
Francis [1982] Crim.L.R. 363, C.A. 846
Franklin (1883) 15 Cox 163 .... **546**, 550, 551
Fraser v. Evans [1969] 1 Q.B. 349; [1968] 3 W.L.R. 1172; 112 S.J 805; [1969] 1 All E.R
    8, C.A. 690
Fretwell (1862) L. & C. 161; 31 L.J.M.C. 145; 6 L.T. 333; 10 W.R. 545; 26 J.P. 499; 8
    Jur. (N.S.) 466; 9 Cox C.C. 152 384

Gammon (Hong Kong) Ltd. and Others v. Att.-Gen. of Hong Kong [1984] 2 All
    E.R. 503 .... **198**
Garlick [1981] Crim.L.R. 178 255
Garrett v. Churchill (Arthur) (Glass) Ltd. [1969] 2 All E.R. 1141 386
Garwood [1987] 1 All E.R. 1032 791
George [1956] Crim.L.R. 52 .... 652, 657
—— (1960) 128 Can.Crim.Cas. 289 252
Ghosh [1982] Q.B. 1053; [1982] 3 W.L.R. 110; [1982] 2 All E.R. 689, C.A. **736**, 774,
                                                                              775, 798

Gilks [1972] 1 W.L.R. 1341; [1972] 3 All E.R. 280; 116 S.J 632; 56 Cr.App.R. 734;
    [1972] Crim.L.R. 440, C.C.A. 714, 741, 743
Gillick v. West Norfolk and Wisbech Area Health Authority [1986] A.C. 112; [1985]
    3 W.L.R. 830; [1985] 3 All E.R. 402; [1986] Crim.L.R. 113; (185) 135 New L.J.
    1055 .... 313, 314, 316, 319, 386, 621
Gittens [1984] Q.B. 698 541
Golechha and Choraria (1990) 90 Cr.App.R. 241 .... **800**
Gomez [1993] 1 All E.R. 1 .... **663**, 693, 696, 750, 846
Goodfellow (1986) 83 Cr.App.R. 23, C.A. 545, **556**, 562
Goss (1990) 90 Cr.App.R. 400 659
Gotts [1992] 2 W.L.R. 284 .... **306**, 313
Gould [1968] 2 W.L.R. 643; 132 J.P. 209; [1968] 2 Q.B. 65; [1968] 1 All E.R. 849; 52
    Cr.App.R. 152 .... 142, 162, 172, 194
Governor of Holloway Prison, *ex p.*Jennings [1983] 1 A.C. 624 .... 559, 564
Graham (1981) 74 Cr. App.R. 235, C.A. **166**, 167
—— [1982] 1 W.L.R. 294, C.A. **284**, 301, 304, 305
Grant v. Borg [1982] 1 W.L.R. 638 174
Gray v. Barr [1971] 2 Q.B. 554; [1971] 2 W.L.R. 1334; [1971] 2 All E.R. 949; 115 S.J.
    364; [1971] 2 Lloyd's Rep. 1, C.A. 553, 556, 559
Greenstein; R. v. Green [1975] 1 W.L.R. 1353; 119 S.J. 742; [1975] 1 All E.R. 1; *sub*
    nom. R. v. Greenstein (Allan); R. v. Green (Monty) (1975) 61 Cr.App.R. 296;
    [1975] Crim.L.R. 714, C.A. 736, 738, 739, 742
Gregory (1867) L.R. 1 C.C.R. 77; 36 L.J.M.C. 60; 16 L.T. 388; 15 W.R. 774; 31 J.P.
    453; 10 Cox C.C. 459 473
—— (1981) 77 Cr. App.R. 41 .... 679, 826
Grieve v. Macleod 1967, S.L.T. 70 341
Griffiths (1974) 60 Cr.App.R. 14, C.A. 823, 825
—— v. Studebakers Ltd. [1924] 1 K.B. 102; 93 L.J.K.B. 50; 130 L.T. 215; 40 T.L.R.
    26; 87 J.P. 199; 68 S.J. 118; 27 Cox C.C. 565; 21 L.G.R. 796 186
Grundy [1977] Crim.L.R. 543, C.A. 401
Gullefer (1986) [1990] 3 All E.R. 882, C.A. **442**, 446, 447
Gush [1981] N.Z.L.R. 92 397

H.M. Coroner for East Kent, *ex p.* Spooner (1989) 88 Cr.App.R. 10 420
Haggard v. Mason [1976] 1 W.L.R. 187; (1975) 120 S.J. 7; [1976] 1 All E.R. 337;
    [1976] Crim.L.R. 51, D.C. 497
Hale (1978) 68 Cr.App.R. 415; [1979] Crim.L.R. 596, C.A. 679, **745**
Hall (1849) 2 C. & K. 947; 1 Den. 381; T. & M. 47; 3 New Sess.Cas. 407; 18 L.J.M.C.
    62; 12 L.T.(o.s.) 383; 13 J.P. 55; 13 Jur. 87; 3 Cox C.C. 245 .... 725, 727
—— (1961) 45 Cr.App.R. 366 550
—— [1973] 1 Q.B. 126; [1972] 3 W.L.R. 381; [1972] 2 All E.R. 1009; 116 S.J. 598;
    [1972] Crim.L.R. 453; 56 Cr.App.R. 547, C.A. **705**, 714, 715, 716
—— (1985) 81 Cr.App.R. 205 .... **824**, 826
Hallett (1841) 9 C. & P. 748 634
Halliday (1889) 61 L.T. 701 624
Hancock and Shankland [1986] 1 A.C. 455; [1986] 2 W.L.R. 357; [1986] 1 All E.R.
    641; 82 Cr.App.R. 264, H.L. **86**, 90, 91, 395
Hardie [1985] 1 W.L.R. 64; [1984] 3 All E.R. 848, C.A. **260**, 261, 262
Hare [1934] 1 K.B. 354 648
Hargreaves [1985] Crim.L.R. 243 852
Harris [1964] Crim.L.R. 54, C.C.A. 382
Harrow Justices [1985] 3 All E.R. 185 622
Harry [1972] Crim.L.R. 32 791
Haughton v. Smith (R.D.) [1975] A.C. 476; [1974] 2 W.L.R. 1; [1973] All E.R.
    1109 .... 478, **479**, 484, 485, 489, 490, 491, 492, 812, 817, 823, 824
Hayes (1976) 64 Cr.App.R. 82 715
Hayward (1908) 21 Cox 692 37
Hector (1978) 67 Cr.App.R. 224, C.A. 842 842
Henderson and Batley (unreported, November 29, 1984) 855
Hennessy [1989] 1 W.L.R. 287 223
Henshall, John (Quarries) Ltd. v. Harvey [1965] 2 Q.B. 233; [1965] 2 W.L.R. 758;
    129 J.P. 224; 109 S.J. 152; [1965] 1 All E.R. 725, D.C. 409, 417

Hensler (1870) 11 Cox C.C. 570 481
Hibbert *v.* McKiernan [1948] 2 K.B. 142; [1948] L.J.R. 1521; 64 T.L.R.256; 112 J.P.
    287; 92 S.J. 259; [1948] 1 All E.R. 860; 46 L.G.R. 238 697
Hickey [1976] 68 D.L.R. (3d) 88 205
Hicklin (1868) L.R. 3 Q.B. 360; 37 L.J.M.C. 89; 18 L.T. 395; 16 W.R. 801; 11 Cox C.C.
    19; *sub nom.* Scott *v.* Wolverhampton Justices, 32 J.P. 533 .... **99**
Higgins (1801) 2 East 5; 102 E.R. 269 .... 405, 474
Hill (1988) 89 Cr.App.R. 74 .... 860, **861**
—— *v.* Baxter [1958] 1 Q.B. 277; [1958] 2 W.L.R. 76; 102 S.J. 53; [1958] 1 All E.R.
    193 .... 227, 231
Hillen and Pettigrew *v.* I.C.I. (Alkali) Ltd. [1936] A.C. 65 .... 836, 837
Hills *v.* Ellis [1983] Q.B. 680; [1983] 2 W.L.R. 234; [1983] 1 All E.R. 607; (1983) 76
    Cr.App.R. 217; [1983] Crim.L.R. 182 .... 130, 131
Hinchcliffe *v.* Sheldon [1955] 1 W.L.R. 1207; 120 J.P. 13; 99 S.J. 797; [1955] 3 All
    E.R. 406; [19 M.L.R. 411], D.C. 131
Hobbs *v.* Winchester Corporation [1910] 2 K.B. 471; 79 L.J.K.B. 1123; 102 L.T. 841;
    74 J.P. 413; 8 L.G.R. 1072; 26 T.L.R. 557 188
Hoffman *v.* Thomas [1974] 1 W.L.R. 374; (1973) 118 S.J. 186; [1974] 2 All E.R. 233;
    [1974] R.T.R. 182; [1974] Crim.L.R. 122, D.C. 316
Holland (1841) 2 Mood. & R. 351 41
Holloway (1849) 2 C. & K. 942; 1 Den. 370 727
Holmes *v.* D.P.P. [1946] A.C. 588 .... 518, 519, 521
Holt and Lee [1981] 1 W.L.R. 1000; (1981) S.J. 373; (1981) 2 All E.R.854; [1981] 73
    Cr.App.R. 96; [1981] Crim.L.R. 499, C.A. **780**
Hope *v.* Brown [1954] 1 W.L.R. 250 .... 443, 445
Howard [1965] 3 All E.R. 684 634
Howe (1858) 100 C.L.R. 448; 32 A.L.J.R. 212 .... 287, 352, 357
Howe and Bannister [1987] 1 A.C. 417; [1987] 2 W.L.R. 568; [1986] Q.B. 626; [1986]
    2 W.L.R. 294; (1986) 130 S.J. 110; (1986) 150 J.P. 161; [1986] 1 All E.R. 833;
    (1986) 83 Cr.App.R. 28; [1986] Crim.L.R. 331 .... 166, **296**, 306, 308, 309, 310,
    312, 319, 379
Howells [1977] Q.B. 614; [1977] 2 W.L.R. 716; (1977) 121 S.J. 154; [1977] 3 All E.R.
    417; (1977) 65 Cr.App.R. 86; [1977] Crim.L.R. 354, C.A. 170, 172, 196
Hudson and Taylor [1971] 2 Q.B. 202; [1971] 2 W.L.R. 1047; [1971] 2 All E.R. 244;
    115 S.J. 303; 56 Cr.App.R. 1; 21 New L.J. 845, C.A. **282**, 303
Huggins (1730) 2 Strange 869; 1 Barn.K.B. 358; Fitz-G. 177; 2 Ld.Raym. 1574; 17
    State Tr. 309; 94 E.R. 241 408
Hughes (1785) 1 Leach 406 .... **829**
—— (1857) Dears. & B. 248; 26 L.J.M.C. 202; 29 L.T.(o.s.) 266; 5 W.R. 732; 21 J.P.
    438; 3 Jur.(N.S.) 696; 7 Cox C.C. 301 22
Hulbert (1979) 69 Cr.App.R. 243, C.A. 822
Hunt (1978) 66 Cr.App.R. 105 .... 862, 863
Hunter [1974] Q.B. 95; [1973] 3 All E.R. 286; C.A. 72
Hurley and Murray [1967] V.R. 526 .... 283, 284, 289, 293, 308
Hussey (1924) 41 T.L.R. 205; 89 J.P. 28; 18 Cr.App.R. 160 .... 333, 334
Husseyn (1977) 67 Cr.App.R. 131n.; *sub nom.* R. *v.* Hussein [1978] Crim. L.R. 219,
    C.A. 840, 841, 842, 843, 844
Hyam *v.* D.P.P. [1975] A.C. 55 ... 71, **78**, 81, 82, 83, 84, 85, 87, 88, 145, 428, 429, 431, 501,
    503, 504, 506
Hyde [1990] 3 All E.R. 892; [1990] 3 W.L.R. 1115; [1990] 3 All E.R. 892; 92
    Cr.App.R. 131, C.A. 396

I.C.R. Haulage Ltd. [1944] K.B. 551 416
Ibrams and Gregory (1981) 74 Cr.App.R. 154, C.A. 513
Ilyas (1983) 78 Cr.App.R. 17 .... 441, 442, 443, 445
Instan [1893] 1 Q.B. 450; 62 L.J.M.C. 86; 68 L.T. 420; 9 T.L.R. 248; 41 W.R. 368; 57
    J.P. 282; 37 S.J. 251; 17 Cox C.C. 602 .... 22, **23**, 30
Invicta Plastics *v.* Clare [1976] R.T.R. 251 474

J. *Re* [1992] 4 All E.R. 614 621
Jackson [1983] Crim.L.R. 617 782
—— [1985] Crim.L.R. 442 458

Jaggard *v.* Dickinson [1981] 2 W.L.R. 118; (1980) 124 S.J. 847; [1980] 3 All E.R. 716;
   [1980] Crim.L.R. 717, D.C. **268**, 278, 861, 867
Jakeman (1982) 76 Cr.App.R. 223, C.A. **56**
James & Son Ltd. *v.* Smee [1955] 1 Q.B. 78; 104 L.J. 730; 218 L.T.J.O. 251; 118 J.P.
   536; 98 S.J. 771; [1954] 3 All E.R. 273; 52 L.G.R. 545 .... 188, 409
Johns *v.* R. (1980) 143 C.L.R. 108 .... 396, 397
Johnson [1989] 1 W.L.R. 740, C.A. **526**
—— *v.* Phillips [1976] 1 W.L.R. 65; 119 S.J. 645; [1975] 3 All E.R. 682; [1976] R.T.R.
   170; [1975] Crim.L.R. 580, D.C. 315
—— *v.* Youden [1950] 1 K.B. 544; [1950] 1 All E.R. 300; 60 T.L.R. (Pt. 1) 395; 114
   J.P. 136; 94 S.J. 115; 48 L.G.R. 276 .... 389, 391
Johnston *v.* Wellesley Hospital (1980) 17 D.L.R. (3d) 139 621
Jones (1986) 83 Cr.App.R. 375 447
—— [1990] 3 All E.R. 886, C.A. **444**
Jones and Smith [1976] 1 W.L.R. 672; [1976] 3 All E.R. 54; *sub nom.* R. *v.* Jones
   (John) and Smith (Christopher), 120 S.J. 299; *sub nom.* R. *v.* Smith
   (Christopher) R. *v.* Jones (John) (1976) 63 Cr.App.R. 47, C.A. **835**, 838
Jordan (1956) 40 Cr.App.R. 153 .... 41, **44**, 45, 47, 48, 49, 51
Julien (1969) 1 W.L.R. 839; [1969] 2 All E.R. 856; 133 J.P. 489; 113 S.J. 342; 53
   Cr.App.R. 407 .... 343, 344

Kaitamaki [1985] A.C. 147; [1984] 3 W.L.R. 137; [1984] 2 All E.R. 435, P.C. 57
Kanwar [1982] 2 All E.R. 529 .... **819**
Kaur *v.* Chief Constable of Hampshire [1981] 1 W.L.R. 578; (1981) 125 S.J. 323;
   [1981] 2 All E.R. 430; (1981) 72 Cr.App.R. 359; [1981] Crim.L.R. 259, D.C. 711
Kay *v.* Butterworth (1942) 173 L.T. 191; 62 T.L.R. 452; 110 J.P. 75; 89 S.J. 381 231
Kelly, *The Times,* December 2, 1992 847
—— *v.* Solari (1841) 9 M. & W. 54 703
Kelt (1977) 3 All E.R. 1099 847
Kemp [1957] 1 Q.B. 399; [1956] 3 W.L.R. 724; 120 J.P. 457; 100 S.J. 768; [1956] 3 All
   E.R 249; 40 Cr.App.R. 121 .... **219**, 221, 227, 228, 231
Khan and Others [1990] 1 W.L.R. 813; [1990] 2 All E.R. 783, C.A. **429**, 457
Kilbourne [1972] 3 All E.R. 545 649
Kilbride *v.* Lake [1962] N.Z.L.R. 590 18
Kimber [1983] 1 W.L.R. 1118 .... 125, **153**, 156, 157, 158, 643, 649, 656
King [1938] 2 All E.R. 662; (1938) 82 S.J. 569 812
—— [1964] 1 Q.B. 285; [1963] 3 W.L.R. 982; 107 S.J. 832; [1963] 3 All E.R. 561; 48
   Cr.App.R. 141 142
—— [1987] Q.B. 547; [1987] 2 W.L.R. 746; [1987] 1 All E.R. 547
   C.A. **771**, 773, 774
Knuller (Publishing, Printing and Promotions) Ltd. *v.* D.P.P. [1973] A.C. 435;
   [1972] 3 W.L.R. 143; 116 S.J. 545; 56 Cr.App.R. 633, H.L. 467
Kohn (1979) 69 Cr.App.R. 395; [1979] Crim.L.R. 675, C.A. 662, 682
Kong Cheuk Kwan *v.* R. (1985) 82 Cr.App.R. 18, P.C. 562, **563**, 567
Kyslant [1932] 1 K.B. 442 758

La Fontaine *v.* R. (1976) 136 C.L.R. 62 504
Lamb [1967] 2 Q.B. 981; [1967] 3 W.L.R. 888; 131 J.P. 456; 111 S.J. 541; [1967] 2 All
   E.R. 1282; 51 Cr. App.R. 417 .... **550**, 553, 558, 567
Lambert *v.* California 355 U.S. 225 (1957) 175, 638
Lambie [1982] A.C. 449; [1981] 3 W.L.R. 88; [1981] 2 All E.R. 776; 73 Cr.App.R. 294,
   H.L. **765**, 784
Landy; R. *v.* White; R. *v.* Kaye [1981] 1 W.L.R. 355; (1981) S.J. 80; [1981] 1 All E.R.
   1172; (1981) 72 Cr.App.R. 237; [1981] Crim.L.R. 326, C.A. 736, 737, 738, 840
Lang (1975) 62 Cr.App.R. 50 634
Larkin (1944) 29 Cr.App.R. 18; [1943] 1 K.B. 174 .... 545, 550, 553, 556
Larsonneur (1933) 149 L.T. 542; 97 J.P. 206; 77 S.J. 486; 29 Cox C.C. 673; 24
   Cr.App.R. 74; 31 L.G.R. 253 .... **16**, 17
Latimer (1886) 17 Q.B.D. 359; 55 L.J. 135; 54 L.T. 768; 51 J.P. 184; 16 Cox C.C.
   70 .... 109, **176**, 177, 178, 393
Latter *v.* Braddell (1880) 50 L.J.K.B. 166 .... 619, 634
Laverty [1970] 3 All E.R. 432; 54 Cr.App.R. 495, C.A. 762, 769

Lawrence [1982] A.C. 510; [1981] 2 W.L.R. 524; (1981) 125 S.J. 241; [1981] 1 All
    E.R. 974; (1981) 73 Cr.App.R. 1; [1981] R.T.R. 217; [1981] Crim.L.R. 409,
    H.L. 84, 117, 118, 119, 120, 123, 124, 125, 127, 560, 563, 564, 567, 642
—— *v.* Metropolitan Commissioner of Police [1972] A.C. 626; [1971] 3 W.L.R. 225;
    [1971] 2 All E.R. 1253; 115 S.J. 565; 55 Cr.App.R. 471; *sub nom.* Lawrence *v.*
    Commissioner of Police for the Metropolis [1971] 2 All E.R. 1253; [[1971]
    C.L.J. 185], H.L. 663, 664, 666, 669, 670
Lawrence and Pomroy (1971) 57 Cr.App.R. 64; [1971] Crim.L.R. 645, C.A. **790**
Le Brun [1992] 1 Q.B. 61; [1991] 3 W.L.R. 653; [1991] 4 All E.R. 673,
    C.A. **60,** 61, 63
Lederer *v.* Hutchins [1961] W.A.R. 99   115
Lemon; R. *v.* Gay News [1979] A.C. 617; [1979] 2 W.L.R. 281; (1979) 123 S.J 163;
    [1979] 1 All E.R. 898; [1979] Crim.L.R. 311; *sub nom.* Whitehouse *v.* Gay
    News; Whitehouse *v.* Lemon (1978) 68 Cr.App.R. 381; [143 J.P.N. 300],
    H.L. 77, 81
Lennard's Carrying Co. Ltd. *v.* Asiatic Petroleum Co. Ltd. [1915] A.C. 705; 84
    L.J.K.B. 1281; 113 L.T. 195; 31 T.L.R. 294; 59 S.J. 411; 13 Asp.M.L.C. 81; 20
    Com.Cas. 283 .... 415, 416
Lesbini [1914] 3 K.B. 1116; 84 L.J.K.B. 1102; 122 L.T. 175; 24 Cox C.C. 516; 11
    Cr.App.R. 7 .... 519, 523
Lester and Byast (1955) 39 Cr.App.R. 157   848
Lewis (January 1922, unreported) 771, 772, 774
Lewis *v.* Cox [1985] Q.B. 509 .... **129,** 132
—— *v.* Dickinson [1976] Crim.L.R. 442   132
Lim Chin Aik [1963] A.C. 160; [1963] 1 All E.R. 223 .... 17, 174, **187,** 194, 199
Lince (1873) 12 Cox 451   762
Linneker [1906] 2 K.B. 99   445
Linnett *v.* Metropolitan Police Commissioner [1946] K.B. 290; 115 L.J.K.B. 513; 174
    L.T. 178; 62 T.L.R. 203; 110 J.P. 153; 90 S.J. 211; [1946] 1 ALl E.R. 380; 44
    L.G.R. 95   387
Lipman [1970] 1 Q.B. 152; [1969] 3 W.L.R. 819; [1969] 3 All E.R. 410; 133 J.P. 712;
    113 S.J. 670; 53 Cr.App.R. 600, C.A. 232, 235, 260, 272
Lister & Co. *v.* Stubbs (1890) 45 Ch.D. 1   712
Little [1992] 1 All E.R. 708   581
Lloyd [1985] Q.B. 829; [1985] 3 W.L.R. 30; [1985] 2 All E.R. 661; (1985) 81
    Cr.App.R. 182; [1985] Crim.L.R. 518, C.A. **721,** 726
Lloyd *v.* D.P.P. [1992] 1 All E.R. 982   861
Lockyer *v.* Gibb [1967] 2 Q.B. 243; [1966] 3 W.L.R. 84; 130 J.P. 306; 110 S.J. 507;
    [1966] 2 All E.R. 653 .... 208, 698
Lolley's Case (1812) R. & R. 237   185
Lomas (1913) 110 L.T. 239; 30 T.L.R. 125; 78 J.P. 152; 58 S.J. 220; 9 Cr.App.R. 220;
    23 Cox C.C. 765   383
London and Globe Finance Corporation Ltd., *Re* [1903] 1 Ch. 728 .... 463, 752, 754
Lord [1905] 69 J.P. 467, C.C.R.   715
Low *v.* Blease (1975) 119 S.J 695; [1975] Crim.L.R. 513, D.C. 691, 846
Lowe [1973] 1 Q.B. 702; [1973] 2 W.L.R. 481; [1973] 1 All E.R. 805; 117 S.J. 144;
    [1973] Crim.L.R. 238; 57 Cr.App.R. 365, C.A. 136, 561
Lynch *v.* D.P.P. for Northern Ireland. *See* D.P.P. for Northern Ireland *v.* Lynch.

McCarthy [1954] 2 Q.B. 105; [1954] 2 W.L.R. 1044; 98 S.J. 356; [1954] 2 All E.R. 262;
    38 Cr.App.R. 74   266
McCrowther (1746) Fost. 13   282
McCullum (1973) 117 S.J. 525; [1973] Crim.L.R. 582; 57 Cr.App.R. 645, C.A.   822
McDavitt [1981] Crim.L.R. 843   785
McDonough (1962) 106 S.J. 961; 47 Cr.App.R. 37   492
McGregor [1962] N.Z.L.R. 1069 .... 522, 523, 524
McHugh [1988] 88 Cr.App.R. 385   677
McInnes [1971] 1 W.L.R. 1600; 115 S.J. 655; [1971] 3 All E.R. 295; *sub nom.* R. *v.*
    McInnes (Walter), 55 Cr.App.R. 55, C.A. 339, 344, 352
McIvor [1982] 1 W.LR. 409; [1982] 1 All E.R. 491; [1982] Crim.L.R. 312; [1982] 74
    Cr.App.R. 74, C.A. 736, 737, 738, 739, 740
McKechnie [1992] Crim.L.R. 194   51
Mcleod *v.* Att.-Gen. for New South Wales [1891] A.C. 455; 60 L.J.P.C. 55; 65 L.T.
    321; 7 T.L.R. 703; 17 Cox C.C. 341, P.C.   467

M'Naghten (1843) 10 Cl. & F. 200; 8 E.R. 718; 4 St.Tr.(N.S.) 847; 1 Town St.Tr. 314; 1
    C. & K. 130n. **215**, 218, 219, 222, 223, 224, 226, 229, 241, 251, 252, 531, 532, 533
McPherson (1857) Dears. & B. 197; 26 L.J.M.C. 134; 29 L.T.(O.S) 129; 5 W.R. 525; 21
    J.P. 325; 3 Jur.(N.S.) 523; 7 Cox C.C. 281 .... 481, 482, 691, 719
McPherson, Farrell and Kajal [1980] Crim.L.R. 654 169
McShane (1977) 66 Cr.App.R. 97; [1977] Crim.L.R 737; (1977) 121 S.J 632, C.A. 575
Machent v. Quinn [1970] 2 All E.R. 255 691
MacKay [1957] V.R. 560 352
Mackie (Robert) (1973) 57 Cr.App.R. 453; [1973] Crim.L.R 438, C.A. **38, 42**
Magna Plant v. Mitchell (unreported) April 27, 1966 417
Maher v. Musson (1934) 52 C.L.R. 100 194
Mainwaring (1981) 74 Cr.App.R. 99 715
Malcherek & Steel [1981] 1 W.L.R. 690; (1981) 125 S.J. 305; [1981] 2 All E.R. 422;
    [1981] 73 Cr.App.R. 173; [1981] Crim.L.R. 401 .... **46**, 48, 49, 496
Mancini v. D.P.P. [1942] A.C. 1; 111 L.J.K.B. 84; 165 L.T. 353; 58 T.L.R. 25; [1941] 3
    All E.R. 272; 28 Cr.App.R. 65 .... 518, 519, 520, 521, 524, 525, 526
Manning (1852) Dears. 21 727
—— (1871) L.R. 1 C.C.R. 338; 41 L.J.M.C. 11; 25 L.T. 573; 36 J.P. 228; 20 W.R. 102;
    12 Cox C.C. 106 838
Mansfield [1975] Crim.L.R. 101, C.A. 852
Marshall v. Curry (1933) 3 D.L.R. 260 592
Martin (1832) 5 C. & P. 128 40
—— (1867) L.R. 1 C.C.R. 56 773
—— (1881) 8 Q.B.D. 54; 51 L.J.M.C. 36; 45 L.T. 444; 30 W.R. 106; 46 J.P. 288; 14 Cox
    C.C. 633 .... **176**, 177, 624
—— [1989] 1 All E.R. 652; [1989] R.T.R. 63; 88 Cr.App.R. 343, C.A 284, 319,
                                                                                 320, 321
Matheson [1958] 1 W.L.R. 474; [1958] 2 All E.R. 87; 42 Cr.App.R. 145 .. 530, 535, 536,
                                                                                 537
Matthews (1950) 66 T.L.R (Pt. 1) 153; 114 J.P. 73; [1950] 1 All E.R .137; 34 Cr.App.R.
    55; 48 L.G.R. 190 827
Maxwell v. D.P.P. for Northern Ireland. *See* D.P.P. for Northern Ireland v.
    Maxwell.
Mayers (1872) 12 Cox C.C. 311 634
Meade [1909] 1 K.B. 895; 78 L.J.K.B. 476; 25 T.L.R. 359; 73 J.P. 239; 53 S.J. 378; 2
    Cr.App.R. 54 .... 254, 266
Mearns [1991] 1 Q.B. 82 581
Meredith [1973] Crim.L.R. 253 702
Merriman. *See* D.P.P. v. Merriman.
Metharam (1961) 125 J.P. 578; 105 S.J. 632; [1961] 3 All E.R. 200; 45 Cr.App.R. 304 .. 623
Metropolitan Police Commissioner v. Streeter (1980) 71 Cr.App.R. 113 814
Millard and Vernon [1987] Crim.L.R. 393 430
Miller [1954] Q.B. 282; [1954] 2 W.L.R. 138; 118 J.P. 340; 98 S.J. 62; [1954] 2 All E.R.
    529; 38 Cr.App.R. 1 .... **622**
—— [1975] 1 W.L.R. 1222; 119 S.J. 562; [1975] 2 All E.R. 974; [1975] R.T.R. 479;
    [1975] Crim.L.R. 723; *sub nom.* R. v. Miller (Robert) 61 Cr.App.R. 182,
    C.A. 169, 172
—— (1980) 55 A.L.J.R. 23 397
—— [1983] 2 A.C. 161; [1983] 2 W.L.R. 539; [1983] 1 All E.R. 978; (1983) 77
    Cr.App.R. 17; [1983] Crim.L.R. 466 .... 13, **26**, 29, 123, 305
Mills (1857) 8 Cox 263; D. & B. 205; 26 L.J.M.C. 79; 29 L.T.(O.S.) 114; 21 J.P. 294; 3
    Jur.(N.S.) 447; 5 W.R. 528 762
Minister of Pensions v. Chennell [1947] K.B. 250; [1946] 2 All E.R. 719 45
Minor v. D.P.P. (1987) 86 Cr.App.R. 378 852
Mitchell [1983] 2 W.L.R. 938 176
Moberley v. Alsop (1991) *The Times*, December 13, 1991 784
Mohan [1967] 2 A.C. 187; [1967] 3 W.L.R. 676; 111 S.J. 95; [1967] 2 All
    E.R. 58 .... 366, **367**
—— [1976] Q.B. 1; [1975] 2 W.L.R. 859; 119 S.J. 219; [1975] 2 All E.R. 193; [1975]
    R.T.R. 337; [1975] Crim.L.R. 283; *sub nom.* R. v. Mohan (John Patrick) 60
    Cr.App.R. 272, C.A. 81, 366, **367**, **426**, 431
Moloney [1985] 1 A.C. 905; [1985] 2 W.L.R. 648; (1985) 129 S.J. 220; [1985]
    Crim.L.R. 378; (1985) 81 Cr.App.R. 93 ...... **81**, 86, 87, 88, 89, 90, 91, 313, 395, 429

Moore (1852) 3 C. & K. 153; 2 Den. 522; 21 L.J.M.C. 199; 16 J.P. 744; 16 Jur. 621; 5
    Cox C.C. 555 266
Moore v. Green [1983] 1 All E.R.663 130
Moore and Dorn [1975] Crim.L.R. 229 60
Morgantaler v. The Queen [1976] 1 S.C.R. 616 .... 324, 325, 326, 327, 328
Morphitis v. Salmon [1990] Crim.L.R. 48 856
Morris v. Tolman [1923] 1 K.B. 166; 92 L.J.K.B. 215; 128 L.T. 118; 39 T.L.R. 39; 86
    J.P. 221; 67 S.J. 169; 27 Cox C.C. 345; 20 L.G.R. 803 368
Morris; Anderton v. Burnside [1984] A.C. 320; [1983] 3 All E.R. 288 ...... 663, 666, 667,
    669, 670, 672, 684, 685, 695, 826
Most (1881) 7 Q.B.D. 244; 50 L.J.M.C. 113; 44 L.T. 823; 29 W.R. 758; 45 J.P. 696; 14
    Cox C.C. 583 474
Mousell Bros. v. London and North Western Railway [1917] 2 K.B. 836; 27 L.J.K.B.
    82 118 L.T. 25; 81 J.P. 305; 15 L.G.R. 706 .... 409, 412
Mowatt [1968] 1 Q.B. 421; [1967] 3 W.L.R. 1192; 131 J.P. 463; 111 S.J. 716; [1967] 3
    All E.R. 47; 51 Cr.App.R. 402 .... 127, 128, 628, 629
Moynes v. Copper [1956] 1 Q.B. 439; [1956] 2 W.L.R. 562; [1956] 1 All E.R. 450;
    120 J.P. 147; 100 S.J .171; 40 Cr.App.R. 20; [1956] Crim.L.R. 516 716
Muir v. H.M. Advocate, 1933 S.C.(J.) 46 534
Mulcahy (1868) L.R. 3 H.L. 306 451
Murray v. McMurchy (1949) 2 D.L.R. 442 592
Myers v. D.P.P. [1965] A.C. 1001; [1964] 3 W.L.R. 145; [1964] 2 All E.R. 881,
    H.L. 311

National Coal Board v. Gamble [1959] 1 Q.B. 11; [1958] 3 W.L.R. 434; 102 S.J. 621;
    [1958] 3 All E.R. 203 .... 379, **382**, 410
Navvabi [1986] 1 W.L.R. 1311; [1986] 3 All E.R. 102; (1986) 83 Cr.App.R. 271; [1987]
    Crim.L.R. 57, C.A. 682
Nedrick [1986] 1 W.L.R. 1025; [1986] 3 All E.R. 1, C.A. **90**, 92, 93
Newell (1980) 71 Cr.App.R. 331; [1980] Crim.L.R. 576, C.A. 285, **522**
Nicholls (1875) 13 Cox 75 .... 22, 25
Nichols v. Hall (1873) L.R. 8 C.P. 322; 42 L.J.M.C. 105; 28 L.T. 473; 21 W.R. 579; 37
    J.P. 424 185
Norwich Union Fire Insurance Society Ltd. v. Wiliam H. Price Ltd. [1934] A.C.
    455 704

O'Connor (1980) 54 A.L.J.R. 349 .... 262, 264, 265, 273
—— [1991] Crim.L.R. 135 350
O'Grady [1987] 3 W.L.R. 321, C.A. 157, **270**, 272, 273, 278
O'Leary (1986) 82 Cr.App.R. 341 847
Olugboja [1982] Q.B. 320; [1981] 1 W.L.R. 1382; [1981] 3 All E.R. 443; (1981) 73
    Cr.App.R. 344, C.A. 620, **633**, **639**, 640, 647
Oropesa, The [1943] P. 32; 112 L.J.P. 91; 168 L.T. 364; 59 T.L.R. 103; [1943] 1 All
    E.R. 211 43
Orpin [1980] 1 W.L.R. 1050; (1980) 124 S.J. 271; [1980] 2 All E.R. 321; (1980) 70
    Cr.App.R. 306; [1980] Crim.L.R. 304, C.A. 258, 259
Ortiz (1986) 83 Cr.App.R. 173 284
Osborn (1919) 84 J.P. 63 483
O'Shay (1898) 19 Cox 76 .... 645, 646
Osman, Re [1989] 3 All E.R. 701, D.C. 662, 682, 688
Ostler v. Elliot [1980] Crim.L.R. 585, D.C. 141
O'Toole (1971) Cr. App.R. 206 316
Owens v. H.M. Advocate 1946 S.C.(J.) 119 337
Oxford v. Moss (1978) Cr.App.R. 183; [1979] Crim.L.R. 119, D.C. **689**, 690, 731

Pagett (1983) 76 Cr.App.R. 279, C.A. 48, **51**
Pallante v. Stadiums Pty. Ltd. (No. 1) [1976] V.R. 331 614
Palmer v. R. [1971] A.C. 814; [1971] 2 W.L.R. 831; [1971] 1 All E.R. 1077; 115 S.J.
    264; 55 Cr.App.R. 223, P.C. 344, 347, 348, **350**, 352
Papadimitropoulos v. R. (1957) 98 C.L.R. 249 638
Pappajohn (1980) 111 D.L.R. 1 151
Park [1988] Crim.L.R. 238, C.A. 817

Parker (1910) 74 J.P. 208 794
—— (Daryl) [1977] 1 W.L.R. 600; (1977) 121 S.J. 353; [1977] 2 All E.R. 37; (1976) 63
    Cr.App.R. 211; [1977] Crim.L.R. 102, C.A. 113, 114
Parkes [1973] Crim.L.R. 358 799
Parmenter. *See* Savage.
Pawlicki & Swindell [1992] 3 All E.R. 902 847
Pearce *v.* Brooks (1866) L.R. 1 Ex. 213; 4 H. & C. 358; 35 L.J.Ex. 134; 14 L.T. 288; 14
    W.R. 614; 30 J.P. 295; 12 Jur.(N.S.) 342 385
Pearson [1992] Crim.L.R. 193 514
Pembliton (1874) L.R. 2 C.C.R. 119; 43 L.J.M.C. 91; 30 L.T. 405; 22 W.R. 553; 38 J.P.
    454; 12 Cox C.C. 607 .... 109, **175**, 176, 177, 178
People *v.* Jaffe (1960) 185 N.Y. 496 483
—— *v.* Rojas (1961) 10 Cal.Rptr. 465 483
Percy Dalton (London) Ltd. [1949] L.J.R. 1626; 65 T.L.R. 326; 93 S.J. 358; [1949]
    W.N. 198; (1949) 33 Cr.App.R. 102 483
Perka et al *v.* R. (1984) 13 D.L.R. (4th) 1 .... **324**, 330
Peter Pan Manufacturing Corp. *v.* Corp *v.* Corsets Silhouette [1964] 1 W.L.R .96;
    108 S.J .97; [1963] 3 All E.R. 402; [1963] R.P.C. 45 690
Pharmaceutical Society of Great Britain *v.* Storkwain Ltd. [1986] 1 W.L.R. 903;
    [1986] 2 All E.R. 635, H.L. 163, **196**
Phekoo [1981] 1 W.L.R. 1117, C.A. 151, 154
Philippou (1989) 89 Cr.App.R. 290 .... 678, 693
Phillips (Glasford) *v.* R. [1969] 2 A.C. 130; [1969] 2 W.L.R. 581; 53 Cr.App.R. 132,
    P.C. 525, 526
Pierce Fisheries [1970] 12 D.L.R. (3d) 1591 204
Pierre [1963] Crim.L.R. 513 847
Pigg [1982] 1 W.L.R. 762 .... 125, 430, 433, 561, 642
Pike [1961] Crim.L.R. 114 559
Pinney (1832) 3 B. & Ad. 947; 5 C. & P. 254; 3 State Tr.(N.S.) 11; 1 Nev. & M.M.C.
    307; 110 E.R. 349 339
Pitchley (1972) 57 Cr.App.R. 30; [1972] Crim L.R. 705, C.A. **817**
Pitham & Heyl (1976) 65 Cr.App.R. 45; [1977] Crim.L.R. 285, C.A. 678, **814**, 815,
                                                                            816, 817
Pitts (1842) C. & M. 284 53
Pittwood (1902) 19 T.L.R. 37 .... **22**, 30
Plummer (1844) 1 C. & K. 600; 8 J.P. 615; 8 Jur. 921 40
Podola [1960] 1 Q.B. 325; [1959] 3 W.L.R. 718; 103 S.J. 856; [1959] 3 All E.R. 418; 43
    Cr.App.R. 220 227
Poulton [1832] 5 C. & P. 330; 172 E.R. 997 .... **496**
Prager *v.* Blatspiel Stamp & Heacock Ltd. [1924] 1 K.B. 566 318
Price (1989) 80 Cr.App.R. 409, C.A. 743
——, *The Times*, December 22, 1971 539
Pratt [1984] Crim.L.R. 41 .... 653, 656
Prince (1875) L.R. 2 C.C.R. 154; (1875) 13 Cox C.C. 138; 44 L.J.M.C.122; 32 L.T.
    700; 24 W.R. 76; 39 J.P. 676 .... 146, 147, 159, 161, 162, 169, 172, 183, 184, 195
Proprietary Articles Trade Association *v.* Att.-Gen. for Canada [1931] A.C. 324;
    100 L.J.P.C. 84; 144 L.T. 577; 47 T.L.R. 250 21
Proudman *v.* Dayman (1941) 67 C.L.R. 536 .... 170, 172, 191, 195, 204

Quick; R. *v.* Paddison [1973] Q.B. 910; [1973] 3 W.L.R. 26; [1973] 3 All E.R. 347; 117
    S.J. 371; 57 Cr.App.R. 722; [1973] Crim.L.R. 434, C.A. 221, 223, **230**, 234,
                                                                            235, 236, 369

R. *v.* R. (Stephen Malcolm) (1984) 79 Cr.App.R. 334, C.A. **122**, 867
—— *v.* —— [1992] A.C. 599; [1991] 3 W.L.R. 767; [1991] 4 All E.R. 481,
    H.L. 311, 371, 633, 640
Race Relations Board *v.* Applin. *See* Applin *v.* Race Relations Board.
Ram (1893) 17 Cox C.C. 609 405
Rank Film Distributors Ltd. *v.* Video Information Centre [1982] A.C. 380; [1981] 2
    W.L.R. 688; [1981] 2 All E.R. 76 723
Ransford (1874) 31 L.T. 488; 13 Cox C.C. 9 474
Rashid [1977] 1 W.L.R. 298; [1977] 2 All E.R. 237; (1976) 64 Cr.App.R. 201; [1977]
    Crim.L.R. 237, C.A. 764, 765

Reading v. Att.-Gen. [1951] A.C. 507 711
Reed [1982] Crim.L.R. 819, C.A. 458
Reeves (1839) 9 C. & P. 25 497
Reid [1992] 1 All E.R. 673, H.L. 117
Renouf [1986] 1 W.L.R. 522, C.A. 346
Reynolds, *The Times*, April 23, 1988 539
—— v. G. H. Austin & Sons Ltd. [1951] 2 K.B. 135; [1951] 1 T.L.R. 614; 115 J.P. 192;
    95 S.J. 173; [1951] 1 All E.R. 606; 49 L.G.R. 377 .... **185**, 188
Rice v. Connolly [1966] 2 Q.B. 414; [1966] 3 W.L.R. 17; 130 J.P. 322; 110 S.J. 371;
    [1966] 2 All E.R. 649; [82 L.Q.R. 457; 29 M.L.R. 682], D.C. 131
Richards [1974] Q.B. 776; [1973] 3 W.L.R. 888; 117 S.J. 852; *sub nom.* R. v. Richards
    (Isabelle) [1973] 3 All E.R. 1088; *sub nom.* R. v. Richards (Isabelle Christina)
    (1973) 58 Cr.App.R. 60; [1974] Crim.L.R. 96, C.A. 379
Ring, Atkins and Jackson (1892) 61 L.J.M.C. 116; 66 L.T. 300; 56 J.P. 552; 8 T.L.R.
    326; 17 Cox C.C. 491 .... 482, 718
Roberts [1986] Crim.L.R. 188, C.A. 626, 627, 628, 826
Robertson [1977] Crim.L.R. 629 715
Robinson [1915] 2 K.B. 342; 84 L.J.K.B. 1149; 113 L.T. 379; 31 T.L.R. 313; 79 J.P. 303;
    58 S.J. 366; 24 Cox C.C. 726; 11 Cr.App.R. 124 .... 439, 440, 441, 445, 448
—— [1977] Crim.L.R. 173, C.A. 744
Roe v. Kingerlee [1986] Crim.L.R.735 857
Roffel [1985] V.R. 511 .... 677, 678
Roper v. Taylor's Central Garages [1951] 2 T.L.R. 284 102
Rose (1884) 15 Cox 540 331
Rouse, William v. Bradford Banking Co. Ltd. [1894] A.C. 586 684
Royal College of Nursing of the United Kingdom v. D.H.S.S. [1981] 2 W.L.R. 279;
    (1981) 125 S.J. 149; [1981] 1 All E.R. 545; [1981] Crim.L.R. 322,
    H.L. 572, 574
Royle [1971] 1 W.L.R. 1764 740
Russell [1933] V.L.R. 59 382
——, [1985] Crim.L.R. 231 .... 105, 847
—— v. H.M. Advocate 1946 S.C.(J.) 37 227

S. v. Goliath 1972 (3) S.A. 1 286
—— v. Masilela 1968 (2) S.A. 558 591
—— v. Nkosiyana (1966) (4) S.A. 655 405
St. George (1840) 9 C. & P. 483; 173 E.R. 921 .... 583, **585**
St. Margaret's Trust Ltd. [1958] 1 W.L.R. 522; 102 S.J. 348; 122 J.P. 312; [1958] 2 All
    E.R. 289; 42 Cr.App.R. 183 188
Salisbury [1976] V.R. 452 .... 623, 625
Salvador et al (1981) 59 C.C.C. (2d) 521 .... 325, 328, 329
Salvo [1980] V.R. 401 744
Sanders (1982) 75 Cr.App.R. 84, C.A. 819, 821
Sansom (1990) 92 Cr.App.R. 115 .... **470**
Sangha [1988] 2 All E.R. 385 .... **124**, 867
Satnam and Kewel (1984) 78 Cr.App.R. 149; [1985] Crim.L.R. 236, C.A. 125, **641**
Saunders and Archer (1573) 2 Plowden 473; 75 E.R. 706 .... **392**, 399, 400
Savage, R. v. Parmenter [1992] A.C. 699; [1991] 4 All E.R. 698, H.L. **625**,
    626, 629
Savage 1923 S.C.(J.) 49 .... 126, 634, 587, 622
Sayce v. Coupé [1953] 1 Q.B.1; [1952] W.N. 473; [1952] 2 T.L.R. 664; 116 J.P. 552; 96
    S.J. 748; [1952] 2 All E.R. 715 .... **402**, 407
Schloendorff v. Society of New York Hospital 105 N.E. 92 (1914) 591
Schmidt (1866) L.R. 1 C.C.R. 15; 55 L.J.M.C. 94; 13 L.T. 679; 30 J.P. 100; 12
    Jur.(N.S.) 149; 14 W.R. 286; 10 Cox C.C. 172 .... 811, 812
Scott v. Metropolitan Police Commissioner [1975] A.C. 819; [1974] 3 W.L.R. 741;
    [1974] 3 All E.R. 1032; 60 Cr.App.R. 124; *sub nom.* R. v. Scott, 118 S.J. 863;
    [1975] Crim.L.R. 94, H.L. **463**, 466, 727, 731, 737
Scully (1824) C. & P. 319; 171 E.R. 1213 331
Seager v. Copydex Ltd. [1967] 1 W.L.R. 923; 111 S.J. 335; [1967] 2 All E.R. 415; 2
    K.I.R. 828; [1967] F.S.R. 211; [1967] R.P.C. 349, C.A. 690
Secretary of State for Trade and Industry v. Hart [1982] 1 All E.R. 817 ...... **172**

Senior [1899] 1 Q.B. 283; 68 L.J.Q.B. 175; 79 L.T. 562; 63 J.P. 8; 47 W.R. 367; 15
T.L.R. 102; 43 S.J. 114; 19 Cox C.C. 219 .... 135, 136, 550
Seymour [1983] 2 A.C. 493; [1983] 3 W.L.R. 349; [1983] 2 All E.R. 1058; (1984)
Cr.App.R. 215; [1983] Crim.L.R. 742 .... 125, **559**, 562, 564, 565, 567
Shadrakh-Cigari (1988) (unreported) **703**, 716
Shama [1990] 2 All E.R. 602 759
Shannon (1980) 71 Cr.App.R. 192; (1980) 124 S.J. 374; [1980] Crim.L.R. 438, C.A. .. **347**
Sharp [1987] 1 Q.B. 833, [1987] 3 W.L.R. 1; [1987] 3 All E.R. 103, C.A. **287**
Sharpe [1980] 1 W.L.R. 219 .... **711**
Shaw v. D.P.P. [1962] A.C. 220; [1961] 2 W.L.R. 897; 125 J.P. 437; 105 S.J. 421;
[1961] 2 All E.R. 446; 45 Cr.App.R. 113 4
Sheaf (1927) 134 L.T. 127 707
Sheehan [1975] 1 W.L.R. 739 246
Shepherd (1988) 86 Cr.App.R. 47, C.A. **291**
Sheppard [1980] 3 W.L.R. 960; (1980) 124 S.J. 864; [1980] 3 All E.R. 399,
H.L. 23, 32, **132**
Sherras v. De Rutzen [1895] 1 Q.B. 918; 64 L.J.M.C. 218; 72 L.T. 839; 11 T.L.R. 369;
43 W.R. 526; 59 J.P. 440; 39 S.J. 451; 18 Cox C.C. 157 ..... **184**, 187, 189, 191, 651
Shippam [1971] Crim.L.R. 434 17
Shivpuri [1987] A.C. 1; [1986] 2 W.L.R. 988; (1985) 130 S.J. 392; (1986) 150 J.P.
353; [1986] 2 All E.R. 334; (1986) 83 Cr.App.R. 178; [1986] Crim.L.R.
536; (1986) 150 J.P.N. 510; (1986) 136 New L.J. 488; (1986) 83 L.S.
Gaz. 1896; 105, 456, **485**, 720, 817
Shoukatallie [1962] A.C. 81; [1961] 3 W.L.R. 1021; 105 S.J 884; [1961] 3 All E.R.
966 547
Sibartie [1983] Crim.L.R. 470 782
Sidaway v. Board of Governors of the Bethlem Royal Hospital and The Maudsley
Hospital [1985] A.C. 871; [1985] 2 W.L.R. 480; [1985] 1 All E.R. 643, H.L. 591
Silverman [1987] Crim.L.R. 574 .... **760**
Simpson [1983] 3 All E.R. 789 847
Sinclair; R. v. Queenswood (Holdings); R.v. Smithson (Frederick William) [1968]
1 W.L.R. 1246; sub nom. R. v. Smithson; R. v. Queenswood (Holdings), R.
v. Sinclair, 112 S.J 703; sub nom. R. v. Sinclair, 132 J.P. 527; [1968] 3 All
E.R. 241; sub nom. R. v. Sinclair (William Vernon Squire); R. v. Queens-
way (Holdings); R. v. Smithson (Frederick William), 52 Cr.App.R. 618,
C.A. 465
Siracusa (1989) 90 Cr.App.R. 340 455
Sirat (1985) 83 Cr.App.R. 41 474
Skivington [1968] 1 Q.B. 166; [1967] 2 W.L.R. 665; 111 S.J. 72; 131 J.P. 265; [1967] 1
All E.R. 483 .... 744, 802
Slack [1989] Q.B. 775; [1989] 3 W.L.R. 513; [1989] 3 All E.R. 90,
C.A. 379, **393**, 396
Smith [1959] 2 Q.B. 35; [1959] 2 W.L.R. 623; 123 J.P. 295; 103 S.J. 353; [1959] 2 All
E.R. 193; 43 Cr.App.R. 121 .... 40, 41, **44**, 47, 49, 51
—— [1961] A.C. 290 .... 79, 172
—— Re (1858) 3 H. & N. 227 .... 366, 378
—— v. Land and House Property Corp. (1884) 28 Ch.D. 7, 15 760
Smith (Charlotte) (1865) L. & C. 607; 34 L.J.M.C. 153; 12 L.T. 608; 13 W.R. 816; 29
J.P. 532; 11 Jur.(N.S.) 695; 10 Cox C.C. 82 23
Smith (David) [1974] Q.B. 354; [1974] 2 W.L.R. 20; [1974] 1 All E.R. 632,
C.A. 141, 142, 146, 268, 269, **864**
Smith (Donald) [1973] Q.B. 924 56
Smith (William) (1826) 2 C. & P. 449; 172 E.R. 203 .... 24, 25, 48, 49
Smith & Smith [1986] Crim.L.R. 166, C.A. 719
Sockett (1908) 24 T.L.R. 893; 72 J.P. 428; 52 S.J. 729; 1 Cr.App.R. 101 569
Sodeman [1936] 2 All E.R. 1138; [1936] W.N. 190 .... 218, 226
Somchai Liangsiriprasert v. The Government of The United States of America
and Another [1990] 3 W.L.R. 606 472
Southern Portland Cement Ltd. v. Coooper (Rodney John) (an Infant by his next
friend Peter Alphonsus Cooper) [1974] A.C. 623; [1974] 2 W.L.R. 152; sub
nom. Southern Portland Cement v. Cooper (1973) 118 S.J. 99; [1974] 1 All
E.R. 87, P.C. 84

Southwark London Borough Council *v.* Williams [1971] Ch. 734 .... 315, 316, 326
Sperotto and Salvietti (1970) 71 S.R.(N.S.W.) 334 148
Spratt [1991] 2 All E.R. 210; [1990] 1 W.L.R. 1073 .... 126, 626, 627
Spriggs [1958] 1 Q.B. 270; [1958] 2 W.L.R. 162; 102 S.J 89; [1958] 1 All E.R. 309; 42
    Cr.App. 69 .... 533, 534
Srinivas Mall Bairoliya *v.* King Emperor (1947) I.L.R. 26 Pat. 460 187
Staines (Linda Irene) (1974) 60 Cr.App.R. 160; [1975] Crim.L.R. 651, C.A. 759
Stanley, October 19, 1990 420
Stapleton (1952) 86 C.L.R. 358 225
Stapylton *v.* O'Callaghan [1973] 2 All E.R. 782 816
Stark (unreported) October 5, 1967 .... 718, 812
Steane [1947] K.B. 997; 61 L.J.R. 969; 117 L.T. 122; 63 T.L.R. 403; 111 J.P. 337; 91 S.J.
    279; [1947] 1 All E.R. 813; 32 Cr.App.R. 61 .. 75, 77, 81, 85, 86, 145, 252, 313, 384
Steele (1977) 65 Cr.App.Rep. 22, C.A. 640
Steer [1988] A.C. 111; [1987] 3 W.L.R. 205; [1987] 2 All E.R. 833, H.L. **868**
Stephens (1866) L.R. 1 Q.B. 702; 7 B. & S. 710; 35 L.J.Q.B. 251; 14 L.T. 593; 14 W.R.
    859; 30 J.P. 822; 12 Jur.(N.S.) 961; 10 Cox C.C. 340 203
Stephenson [1979] Q.B. 695; [1979] 3 W.L.R. 193; (1979) 123 S.J. 403; [1979] 2 All
    E.R. 1198; (1979) 69 Cr.App.R. 213; [1979] Crim.L.R. 590, C.A. 110, 114,
                                                                             116, 268, 269
Stevens *v.* Gourlay (1859) 7 C.B.(N.S.) 99 838
Stewart (1983) 149 D.L.R. (3rd) 583; *reversed* (1988) 50 D.L.R. (4th) 1 690
Stone [1977] 1 Q.B. 354; [1977] 2 W.L.R. 169; (1976) 121 S.J. 83; [1977] 2 All E.R. 341;
    (1976) 64 Cr.App.R. 186; *sub nom.* R. *v.* Stone and Dobinson [1977]
    Crim.L.R. 166, C.A. **24**, 31, 559
Stones (1989) 89 Cr.App.R. 26 847
Strasser *v.* Roberge (1980) 103 D.L.R. (3d) 193 206
Stratton (1779) 1 Doug. K.B. 239; 99 E.R. 156; 21 State Tr. 1045 338
Subramaniam *v.* Public Prosecutor [1956] 1 W.L.R. 965; 100 S.J. 566, P.C. 283
Sullivan (1945) 30 Cr. App.R. 132 769
—— [1981] Crim.L.R. 46, C.A. 629
—— [1984] A.C. 156; [1983] 3 W.L.R. 123; (1984) 148 J.P. 207; (1983) 127 S.J .460;
    [1983] 2 All E.R. 673; [1984] 77 Cr.App.R. 176; [1983] Crim.L.R.
    740 .... 217, 218, **220**, 222, 223, 237
Surujpaul [1958] 1 W.L.R. 1050 808
Sweet *v.* Parsley [1970] A.C. 132; [1969] 2 W.L.R. 470; 113 S.J 86; [1969] 1 All E.R.
    347 .... 102, 106, 136, 142, 143, 170, 171, 183, **190**, 195, 197, 200, 204, 206, 651

T., *Re* [1992] 4 All E.R. 649 621
Taafe [1984] A.C. 539; [1984] 2 W.L.R. 326; (1984) 128 S.J. 203; (1984) 148 J.P.
    510; [1984] 1 All E.R. 747; (1984) 78 Cr.App.R. 301; [1984] Crim.L.R.
    356 .... **103**
Tacey (1821) R. & R. 452 855
Tandy [1989] 1 W.L.R. 350 .... **539**
Tarling *v.* Government of Singapore (1978) 70 Cr. App.R. 77; [1978] Crim.L.R. 490,
    H.L. [[1979] Crim.L.R. 220] 712, 715
Taylor (1869) L.R. 1 C.C.R. 194 624
Terry [1961] 2 Q.B. 314 541
Tesco Supermarkets Ltd. *v.* Nattrass [1972] A.C. 153; [1971] 2 W.L.R. 1166; [1971] 2
    All E.R. 127; 115 S.J. 285; 69 L.G.R. 403, H.L. **413**
Thabo Meli *v.* R. [1954] 1 W.L.R. 228; 98 S.J. 77; [1954] 1 All E.R. 373 .... **58**, 59, 62
Thomas (1983) Cr.App.R. 63 .... 641, 642
—— *v.* The King (1937) 59 C.L.R. 279 .... 142, 153, 194
Thompson (1869) 21 L.T. 397; 33 J.P. 791; 11 Cox C.C. 362 .... 848, 849
Thorne *v.* Motor Trade Association [1937] A.C. 797; 106 L.J.K.B. 495; 157 L.T. 399;
    53 T.L.R. 810; 81 S.J. 476; [1937] 3 All E.R. 157; 26 Cr.App.R. 51 789
Thornhill (1981) (unreported) May 15, 1981 819
Thornton [1992] 1 All E.R. 306 514
Thornton *v.* Mitchell (1940) 162 L.T. 296; 56 T.L.R. 296; 104 J.P. 108; 84 S.J. 257;
    [1940] 1 All E.R. 339; 38 L.G.R. 168 .... **368**, 373, 409
Tideswell [1905] 2 K.B. 273; 74 L.J.K.B. 725; 93 L.T. 111; 69 J.P. 318; 21 T.L.R. 531;
    21 Cox C.C. 10 691

Tolson (1889) 23 Q.B.D. 168; 58 L.J.M.C. 97; 60 L.T. 899; 5 T.L.R. 465; 37 W.R. 716;
    54 J.P. 4, 20; 16 Cox C.C. 530 .... 27, 142, 143, 145, 146, 147, 159, 163, 164,
                                    171, 183, 191, 193, 194, 195, 196, 247, 251
Tomlin [1954] 2 Q.B. 274; [1954] 2 W.L.R. 1140; 118 J.P. 354; 98 S.J. 374; [1954] 2 All
    E.R. 272; 38 Cr.App.R. 82, C.C.A. 692
Traill v. Baring (1864) 4 De G.J. & Sm. 318 757
Treacy v. D.P.P. [1971] A.C. 537; [1971] 2 W.L.R. 112; 115 S.J 12; [1971] 1 All E.R.
    110; 55 Cr.App.R. 113, H.L. 791, 792, 830
Tuberville v. Savage (1669) 1 Mod.Rep. 3; 86 E.R. 684; 2 Keb. 345 .... 584, 585
Turner (No. 2) [1971] 1 W.L.R. 901; [1971] 2 All E.R. 441; [1971] R.T.R. 396 . 700, 702
Twose (1879) 14 Cox C.C. 327 866
Tyrell [1894] 1 Q.B. 710; 63 L.J.M.C. 58; 70 L.T. 41; 10 T.L.R. 167; 42 W.R. 255; 38
    S.J. 130; 17 Cox C.C. 716 .... 403, 406, 407, 467

United States v. Bank of New England 821 F. 2nd 844 (1987) 420
—— v. Holmes 26 Fed.Cas. 360 (1842) 322

Valderrama-Vega [1985] Crim.L.R. 220 284
Vane v. Yiannopoulos [1965] A.C. 486; [1964] 3 W.L.R. 1218; 129 J.P. 50; 108 S.J.
    937; [1964] 3 All E.R. 82; 63 L.G.R. 91 .... 409, 411, 417
Venna [1976] Q.B. 421; [1975] 3 W.L.R. 737; 119 S.J. 679; [1975] 3 All E.R. 788;
    [1975] Crim.L.R. 701; *sub nom.* R. v. Venna (Henson George) (1975) 61
    Cr.App.R. 310, C.A. 125, 126, 250, 586, 626, 627
Vickers [1957] 2 Q.B. 664; [1957] 3 W.L.R. 326; 121 J.P. 510; 101 S.J. 593; [1957] 2 All
    E.R. 741; 41 Cr.App.R. 189 .... 84, 498, 500, 501, 502, 503, 504, 505
Villensky [1892] 2 Q.B. 597; 61 L.J.M.C. 218; 8 T.L.R. 780; 41 W.R. 160; 56 J.P. 824;
    36 S.J. 745 .... 483, 871
Vinagre (1979) 69 Cr.App.R. 104, C.A. 530, 537, 539
Viro v. R. (1978) 141 C.L.R. 88 352

W. (A Minor) v. Dolbey [1983] Crim.L.R. 681; 88 Cr.App.R. 1 126
Wai Yu-Tsang v. R. [1991] 3 W.L.R. 1006; [1991] 4 All E.R. 664, P.C. 466
Waite [1892] 2 Q.B. 600 483
Waites [1982] Crim.L.R. 369, C.A. 776
Wakely [1990] Crim.L.R. 119 396
Walker [1984] Crim.L.R. 112 695
Walker and Hayles (1990) 90 Cr.App.R. 226 921
Walkington (1979) 1 W.L.R. 1169; (1979) 123 S.J. 704; [1979] 2 All E.R. 716; (1979) 68
    Cr.App.R. 427; [1979] Crim.L.R. 526, C.A. 839, 842, 843, 845
Wall (Geoffrey) [1974] 1 W.L.R. 930 561
Walters v. Lunt [1951] W.N. 472; 115 J.P. 512; 95 S.J. 625; [1951] 2 All E.R. 645; 35
    Cr.App.R. 94; 49 L.G.R. 809 .... 369, 373
Walton v. The Queen [1977] 3 W.L.R. 902; (1977) 121 S.J. 728; [1978] 1 All E.R. 542;
    [1978] A.C. 788; (1978) 66 Cr.App.R. 25; [1977] Crim.L.R. 747, P.C. ... 530, 535
Ward (1836) 4 A. & E. 384; 1 Har. & W. 703; 6 Nev. & M. 38; 5 L.J.K.B. 221 2
—— (1872) L.R. 1 C.C.R. 356; 41 L.J.M.C. 69; 26 L.T. 43; 20 W.R. 392; 36 J.P. 453;
    12 Cox C.C. 123 .... 126, 177, 627
—— (1986) 85 Cr.App.R. 71 395
Warner (1970) 55 Cr.App.R. 93, C.A. 148, 171, 192, 721, 723, 724, 725
—— v. Metropolitan Police Commissioner [1969] 2 A.C. 256; [1968] 2 W.L.R.
    1303; 132 J.P. 378; 112 S.J. 378; [1968] 2 All E.R. 356; 52 Cr.App.R.
    373 .... 142, 190, 847, 870
Waterfall [1970] 1 Q.B. 148; [1969] 3 W.L.R. 947; [1969] 3 All E.R. 1048, C.A. 740
Watkins [1976] 1 All E.R. 578 777
Watmore v. Jenkins [1962] 2 Q.B. 572 232
Watson [1989] 2 All E.R. 865 .... 37, 555
Welsh (1869) 11 Cox C.C. 336 518
West (1848) 2 Car. & Kir. 7884; 11 L.T.(o.s.) 49; 2 Cox C.C. 500 497
Westminster City Council v. Croyalgrange Ltd. [1986] 1 W.L.R. 674; [1986] 2 All
    E.R. 353, H.L. 103
Wheat and Stocks [1921] 2 K.B. 119; 90 L.J.K.B. 583; 124 L.T. 830; 37 T.L.R. 417; 85
    J.P. 203; 65 S.J. 554; 26 Cox C.C. 717; 15 Cr.App.R. 134 194

Table of Cases

Wheeler [1967] W.L.R. 1531; 132 J.P. 41; 111 S.J. 850; [1967] 3 All E.R. 829; 52
    Cr.App.R. 28 330
Whitchurch and Others (1890) 24 Q.B.D. 420; 59 L.J.M.C. 77; 62 L.T. 124; 6 T.L.R.
    177; 54 J.P. 472; 16 Cox C.C. 743 .... 403, 459, 569
White (1859) 1 F. & F. 665 823
—— [1910] 2 K.B. 124; 79 L.J.K.B. 854; 102 L.T. 784; 26 T.L.R. 466; 74 J.P. 318; 54
    S.J. 523; 22 Cox C.C. 325; 4 Cr.App.R. 257 482
Whitefield (1983) 79 Cr.App.R. 36, C.A. 402
Whitehead [1977] Q.B. 868 474
Whitehouse [1977] Q.B. 868; [1977] 2 W.L.R. 925; 121 S.J. 171; [1977] 3 All E.R. 737;
    (1977) 65 Cr.App.R. 33; [1977] Crim.L.R. 689, C.A. **404**, 407
Whitehouse (alias Savage) (1941) 1 W.W.R. 112 399
Whiteley (1991) 93 Cr.App.R. 25 .... **854**
Widdowson (1986) 82 Cr.App.R. 314; [1986] Crim.L.R. 233; (1986) L.S.Gaz. 288,
    C.A. 441, 445, 778
Wille (1988) 86 Cr.App.R. 296 726
Willer [1987] R.T.R. 22 .... 319, 320
Williams [1893] 1 Q.B. 320 483
—— [1923] 1 K.B. 340; 92 L.J.K.B. 230; 128 L.T. 128; 39 T.L.R. 131; 87 J.P. 67; 67 S.J.
    263; 27 Cox C.C. 350; 17 Cr.App.R. 56 .... 495, **645**
Williams (Gladstone) (1984) 78 Cr.App.R. 276; [1984] Crim.L.R. 163; (1984) 81
    L.S.Gaz. 278, C.A. 155, 157, 158, 167, 271, 287, 336, 350
Williams and Davis [1992] 1 W.L.R. 380 39
Williamson (1977) 67 Cr.App.R. 35, C.A. 847
Willmott v. Atack [1977] 1 Q.B. 498; [1977] Crim.L.R. 187] 130, 131, 141
Wilson [1984] A.C. 242; [1983] 1 W.L.R. 356; (1983) 127 S.J. 187; (1983) 147 J.P. 344;
    [1983] 1 All E.R. 993; (1983) 76 Cr.App.R. 255 .... **623**, 629
—— v. Inyang [1951] 2 K.B. 799; [1951] 2 T.L.R. 553; 115 J.P. 411; 95 S.J 562; [1951]
    2 All E.R. 237; 49 L.G.R. 654 .... 141, 146, 385
—— v. Pringle [1986] 3 W.L.R. 1; (1986) 130 S.J. 469; [1986] 2 All E.R. 440; (1986)
    136 New L.J. 416; (1986) 83 L.S.Gaz. 2160, C.A. 591, 603
Wimpey (George) & Co. Ltd. v. B.O.A.C. [1955] A.C. 169; [1954] 3 W.L.R. 932;
    [1954] 3 All E.R. 661, H.L. 676
Windle [1952] 2 Q.B. 826; [1952] 1 T.L.R. 1344; 116 J.P. 365; 96 S.J. 379; [1952] 2 All
    E.R. 1; 36 Cr.App.R. 85 .... **224**, 225
Winzar v. Chief Constable of Kent (1983) *The Times*, March 28, 1983 17
With v. O'Flanagan [1936] Ch. 575; 105 L.J.Ch. 247; 154 L.T. 634; 80 S.J. 285; [1936]
    1 All E.R. 727, C.A. 757
Wollaston (1872) 72 Cox C.C. 180 615
Woodman [1974] Q.B. 758; [1974] 2 W.L.R. 821; 118 S.J. 346; [1974] 2 All E.R. 955;
    [1974] Crim.L.R. 441; *sub nom.* R. v. Woodman (George Eli) (1974) 59
    Cr.App.R. 200, C.A. **696**, 698
Woodrow (1846) 15 M. & W. 404; 2 New Mag.Cas. 1; 2 New Sess.Cas. 346; 16
    L.J.M.C. 122; 10 J.P. 791 203
Woods (1981) 74 Cr.App.R. 279
Woods v. Richards [1977] R.T.R. 201 316
Woolmington v. D.P.P. [1935] A.C. 462; 104 L.J.K.B. 433; 153 L.T. 232; 51 T.L.R.
    446; 79 S.J. 401; 25 Cr.App.R. 72 .... 171, 191, 194, 195, 204, 227
Woolven (1983) 77 Cr.App.R. 231 .... **775**
Wright (1866) 4 F. & F. 967 634
Wyat (1705) 1 Salk. 380; 2 Ld.Raym. 1189; 11 Mod.Rep. 53; 88 E.R 880 21

Yeandel v. Fisher [1966] 1 Q.B. 440; [1965] 3 W.L.R. 1002; 129 J.P. 546; 109 S.J. 593;
    [1965] 3 All E.R. 158 190
Young [1984] 1 W.L.R. 654; (1984) 128 S.J. 297; (1984) 148 J.P. 492; (1984) 78
    Cr.App.R. 288; [1984] 2 All E.R. 164; [1984] Crim.L.R. 363 .... 270, 279
Yule [1964] 1 Q.B. 5; [1963] 3 W.L.R. 285; 127 J.P. 469; 107 S.J. 497; [1963] 2 All E.R.
    790; 47 Cr.App.R. 229, C.C.A. 706

Zecevic v. D.P.P. for Victoria (1987) 61 A.L.J.R. 375 352

TABLE OF STATUTES

[Page references in **bold** indicate the page upon which the section is set out.]

1803 Lord Ellenborough's Act (43
    Geo. 3, c. 58) 501, 502,
                503, 504
1842 Tobacco Act (s. 13) 403
1855 Metropolitan Building Act ... 839
1861 Accessories and Abettors
    Act (24 & 25 Vict.
    c. 94)—
    s. 8 .... 366, 367, 370, 374, 375,
                378
    Larceny Act (24 & 25 Vict.
    c. 96) 681
    s. 3 464
    s. 68 709
    s. 82 .... 464, 737
    s. 83 .... 464, 737
    s. 84 464
    s. 97 803
    Malicious Damage Act (24 &
    25 Vict. c. 97) ... 112, 113, 128,
                178, 838, 853
    s. 3 858
    s. 13 .... 858, 866
    s. 14 855
    s. 51 .... 175, 858
    Forgery Act (24 & 25 Vict.
    c. 98)—
    s. 3 749
    Offences Against the Person
    Act (24 & 25 Vict. c.
    100) 403, 581, 605, 607,
                615, 616
    s. 4 474
    s. 18 .... 127, 128, 222, 234, 235,
        252, 256, 257, 296, 298, 306,
        313, 341, 346, 500, 605, **629**,
                630, 631
    s. 20 .. 22, 126, 127, 128, 176, 178,
        179, 234, 251, 253, 335, 341,
        346, 586, 595, 600, 601, 604,
        605, 607, 608, 610, 617, 618,
        622, 623, 625, 626, 628, 629,
                631
    s. 23 .... 109, 110, 552
    s. 24 .... 179, 617
    s. 25 617
    s. 35 427
    s. 47 .... 125, 126, 251, 587, 595,
        598, 600, 604, 605, 607, 608,
        609, 610, 617, 618, **622**, 625,
            628, 629, 631
    s. 49 161
    s. 55 .... 147, 162, 169

1861 Offences Against the Person
    Act—*cont.*
    s. 56 .... 161, 372, 460
    s. 57 .... 147, 159, 161, 193
    s. 58 .... 316, **568**, 570, 572,
                573, 575
    s. 59 .... **569**, 573
1868 Larceny and Embezzlement
    Act (31 & 32 Vict.
    c. 116) 669
1869 Debtors Act (32 & 33 Vict.
    c. 82)—
    s. 13 749
1872 Licensing Act (35 & 36 Vict.
    c. 94)—
    s. 12 17
    s. 13 183
    s. 14 184
    s. 16 184
       (1) 184
       (2) 184, 185
1874 False Personation Act (37 &
    38 Vict. c. 36)—
    s. 1 749
1875 Explosives Act (38 & 39 Vict.
    c. 17) 341
    Falsification of Accounts Act
    (38 & 39 Vict c. 24) ... 464, 738
1882 Bills of Exchange Act (45 &
    46 Vict. c. 61)—
    s. 84 704
1883 Explosive Substances Act (46
    & 47 Vict. c. 3)—
    s. 4 .... 339, 340, 341
    Trial of Lunatics Act (46 & 47
    Vict. c. 38)—
    s. 2 220
1885 Criminal Law Amendment
    Act (48 & 49 Vict c.
    69) 161, 618, 635, 639, 645
    s. 3 (2) 646
    s. 4 .... 161, 403
    s. 5 .... 161, 403, 645
    s. 6 161
    s. 7 161
    s. 16 .... 646, 647
1893 Sale of Goods Act (56 & 57
    Vict. c. 71) 694
    s. 18 .... 383, 694
    s. 19 694
1907 Criminal Appeal Act (7 Edw.
    7, c. 23)—
    s. 5 (4) 223

1911 Official Secrets Act (1 & 2
        Geo. 5, c. 28)—
      s. 1 97
      Maritime Conventions Act
        (1 & 2 Geo. 5, c. 57)—
      s. 6 (1) 19
1915 Indictments Act (5 & 6 Geo.
        5, c. 90)—
      s. 5 719
1916 Larceny Act (6 & 7 Geo. 5,
        c. 50) 660, 700, 709, 717
      s. 1 .... 717, 796
        (1) 665, 733, 735
      s. 17 709
      s. 20 (1) (iv) 706, 707
      s. 25 828
      s. 26 828
      s. 27 828
      s. 28 848
      s. 29 (1) 789, 793
      s. 30 793
      s. 32 749
        (1) 739, 740, 749, 770, 774
      s. 33 803
        (1) 369
      s. 40 (4) 699
1921 Licensing Act (11 & 12 Geo.
        5, c. 74)—
      s. 4 387
1929 Infant Life (Preservation)
        Act (19 & 20 Geo. 5,
        c. 34)—
      s. 1 .... **568**
        (1) 570
      Age of Marriage Act (19 & 20
        Geo. 5 c. 36)—
      s. 1 648
1930 Road Traffic Act (20 & 21
        Geo. 5, c. 43)—
      s. 72 186
1933 Children and Young Per-
        sons Act (23 Geo. 5,
        c. 12) 23, 32, 132
      s. 1 .... 132, 133, 137
        (1) 134, 135, 136
        (2) (a) 134
1934 Road Traffic Act (24 & 25
        Geo. 5, c. 50)—
      s. 25 (1) (b) 186
1936 Public Order Act (1 Edw. 8 &
        1 Geo. 6, c. 6)—
      s. 5 735
1938 Infanticide Act (1 & 2 Geo. 6,
        c. 36)—
      s. 1 .... **568**
1945 Family Allowances Act (8 &
        9 Geo. 6, c. 41)—
      s. 9 476
        (b) 475, 476
1948 Companies Act (11 & 12
        Geo. 6, c. 58)—
      s. 161 (2) 172

1948 Companies Act—*cont.*
      s. 455 172
1949 Wireless Telegraphy Act (12,
        13 & 14 Geo. 6, c. 54) 475
      Marriage Act (12, 13 & 14
        Geo. 6. c. 76)—
      s. 2 648
1951 Rivers (Prevention of Pollu-
        tion) Act (14 & 15 Geo.
        6, c. 66)—
      s. 2 (1) (a) 196
1952 Magistrates' Courts Act (15
        & 16 Geo. 6 & 1 Eliz. 2,
        c. 55)—
      s. 35 378
      Sched. 1, para. 20 475
1953 Prevention of Crime Act (1 &
        2 Eliz. 2, c. 14) .. 105, 341, 851
      s. 1 847
      Post Office Act (1 & 2 Eliz. 2,
        c. 36)—
      s. 53 730
1954 Protection of Birds Act (2 & 3
        Eliz. 2, c. 30) 681
1956 Road Traffic Act (4 & 5 Eliz.
        2, c. 67)—
      s. 8 559
      Sexual Offences Act (4 & 5
        Eliz. 2, c. 69) **143**, 430, 601,
                          635, **644**, 647
      s. 1 .... 143, **632**, 634, 635
        (1) 142
      s. 2 640
      s. 3 .... 636, 640
      s. 6 .... 314, 403
      s. 10 .... 404, 406, 407
      s. 11 .... 404, 405, 406, 407
        (1) 404
      s. 14 .... 125, **647**
        (1) 647, 651
        (2) 647, 656
      s. 15 .... 125, **648**
      Sched. 2 648
      Copyright Act (4 & 5 Eliz. 2,
        c. 74) 722
1957 Homicide Act (5 & 6 Eliz. 2,
        c. 11 ...... 88, 254, 300, 497, 504,
                          519, 532
      s. 1 .... 136, **498**, 502
        (1) 498, 501
      s. 2 .. 268, 507, 528, 531, 534, 535,
                          543, 544
        (1) 528, 531, 532, 540, 542
      s. 3 .. **513**, 515, 516, 518, 520, 521,
                          524, 525
      s. 4 .... **575**
      s. 5 (2) 501
      s. 18 300
1959 Highways Act (7 & 8 Eliz 2,
        c. 15)—
      s. 121 (1) 129, 130, 132

1959 Mental Health Act (7 & 8
Eliz. 2, c. 72) 244
s. 4 .... 243, 543, 544
s. 60 .... 544, 545
1960 Road Traffic Act (8 & 9 Eliz.
2, c. 16)—
s. 217 729
Indecency with Children Act
(8 & 9 Eliz. 2, c. 33) 584,
648

Administration of Justice
Act (8 & 9 Eliz. 2,
c. 65)—
s. 1(2) 664
1961 Criminal Justice Act (c. 39)—
s. 66(2) 397
Suicide Act (9 & 10 Eliz. 2,
c. 60) 495, **575**
s. 2(1) 382, 575, 576
(4) 576
Licensing Act (9 & 10 Eliz. 2,
c. 61)—
s. 22(1) 411
(a) 412
Offices, Shops and Railway
Premises Act (c. 41)—
s. 67 206
1964 Police Act (c. 48)—
s. 51 .... 154, 179
(1) 130, 179
(3) 129, 130
Criminal Proceedings
(Insan-
ity) Act (c. 84)—
s. 5 215
s. 6 .... **528**
1965 Dangerous Drugs Act
(c. 15)—
s. 5 192
(b) 190
Law Commissions Act
(c. 22) 9
Murder (Abolition of Death
Penalty) Act (c. 71) 497
s. 1(2) 497
1967 Road Traffic Regulation Act
(c. 21)—
s. 79 315
Criminal Law Act (c. 58)—
s. 1 .... 370, 374
s. 2 .... 345, 730
s. 3 .... 54, 156, 363
(1) 337, 339
(c) 364
s. 4 .... 367, 827, 852
(1) 424, 451
s. 5 827
(1) 424, 451
s. 6 719
(3) 623, 625
s. 8 .... 136, 247, 253

1967 Criminal Law (Northern Ireland) Act (c. 58)—
s. 3 345
(1) 346, 347
Sexual Offences Act (c. 90)—
s. 1 .... 598, 601, 605, 607
s. 1 (1) 598, 604
Criminal Justice Act (c. 80)—
s. 8 .... 85, 88, 89, 116, 250, 428
Abortion Act (c. 87) **569**, 572
573, 580
s. 1 .... 573, 574
s. 5 (2) 573
Criminal Appeal Act
(c. 19)—
s. 2(1) 148, 798
(3) 369
s. 3(2) 629
Firearms Act (c. 27)—
s. 1 .... 170, 342
s. 16 869
s. 58(2) 170
Trade Descriptions Act
(c. 29) 413, 414
s. 11(2) 414
s. 24(1) 413, 414
(a) 414
(b) 414
(2) 414
(3) 206
Theft Act (c. 60) 9, 10, 473, 661,
717, 747
s. 1 .. 466, **661**, 677, 699, 737, 738,
741, 742, 746
(1) 464, 664, 665, 666, 670,
671, 672, 673, 674, 675,
676, 677, 689, 733, 735,
737, 840, 844
(3) 664, 671
s. 2 .... 671, **733**, 737
(1) 665, 734, 735, 775
(a) 667, 775
(b) 677
(c) 734
(2) 734
s. 3 .... **662**, 663, 671, 699, 746
(1) 662, 664, 665, 666, 667,
668, 669, 732, 816
(2)–(4) 671, 751
s. 4 .... 671, 677, **679**, 854
(1) 664, 673, 677, 681, 751,
807
(2) 671, 677
(3) 716
s. 5 .. 466, 671, 677, **692**, 694, 695,
699, 709, 711, 712, 713
(1) 671, 677, 696, 700, 704,
708, 710, 714, 722
(2) 702
(3) 682, 705, 707, 708, 709,
710
(4) 682, 704, 723

1967 Theft Act—*cont.*
s. 6 .... 671, **720**
    (1) 671, 718, 720, 722, 723,
        724, 725, 727
s. 7 664
s. 8 .... 679, **744**
s. 9 .... **828**, 832, 834, 840, 746
    (1) 833, 842
      (a) 555, 840, 843, 844,
        845, 846
      (b) 661, 835, 836, 837,
        845, 846
s. 10 .... **846**
    (1) 848
s. 11 .... 728, **729**, 731
    (1) 677, 729
    (2) 729
    (3) 729
s. 12 .... 728, **730**, 731
    (1) 677, 848
s. 13 677
s. 15 .... 670, 671, 676, 677, 685,
    736, 737, 738, 739, 742, 750,
    751, 768, 775, 778
    (1) 664, 666, 670, 673, 724,
    733, 739, 760, 774, 804
    (3) 724
    (4) 751
s. 16 .... 740, 766, 768, 772, **776**,
    787, 802
    (1) 765
      (a) 777
    (2) 772, 774
      (a) 740, 752
      (b) 777
    (3) 751
s. 17 .... 462, 465, 737, 738, 801
    (1) 800
s. 21 .... **789**
    (1) 790, 796, 799
      (a) 795, 796
      (b) 790
s. 22 .... 479, 483, 678, **803**, 807,
    820, 821, 826
    (1) 479, 480, 817
s. 23 827
s. 24 .... 480, **804**, 806, 807
    (2) 804, 806, 808
      (a) 806, 807, 808
    (3) 480, 804, 809, 810, 813
    (4) 671, 804, 806
s. 25 .... 763, **848**, 851, 852
    (1) 849, 851
    (3) 851
s. 28 (6) 671
s. 32 (2) (a) 799
s. 34 .... **799**, 804
    (1) 677, 751
    (2) 807
      (a)(i) 799
      (b) 804, 805, 806
Sched. 1 681

1967 Medicines Act (c. 67)—
s. 45 (2) 197, 206
s. 46 (1) 197, 206
    (2) 197, 206
    (3) 197, 206
s. 63–65 .... 197, 206
s. 121 .... 197, 206
Race Relations Act (c. 71) 474
1971 Misuse of Drugs Act (c.
    38) 103, 195
s. 3 (1) 485
s. 4 493
s. 28 (3) 270
Criminal Damage Act (c.
    48) 9, 10, 107, 110, 111, 112,
    146, 642, 853
s. 1 ...... 26, 81, 564, **853**, 854, 865,
    868
    (1) 27, 111, 115, 119, 120,
    125, 141, 258, 259, 268,
    269, 565, 853, 854, 855,
    856, 858, 859, 860, 862,
    864, 865, 867, 868
    (2) 111, 115, 116, 124, 257,
    258, 260, 853, 860, 868, 869
      (a) 870
      (b) 112, 122, 124, 258,
      259, 868, 869, 870
    (3) 26, 259, 860, 861
s. 2 .... 858, **870**
s. 3 .... 858, 861, **870**
s. 4 .... **853**
s. 5 ... 858, 859, **860**, 865, 867, 868
    (2) 268, 269, 270, 363, 858,
    862, 865
      (a) 866, 867
      (b) 861, 862
        (i) 862
    (3) 268, 269, 865
    (5) 861, 865
s. 10 .... **854, 857**
    (1) 680, 856
Immigration Act (c. 77)—
s. 24 (1) (b) (i) 174
1972 Road Traffic Act (c. 20) 19, 376
s. 1 346
    (1) 559
s. 2 346
s. 6 (1) 372, 484
s. 99 (6) 169
Criminal Justice Act (c. 71)—
s. 36 .... 374, 707, 809, 810
    (1) 806
Northern Ireland
    (Emergency Provisions)
    Act (c. 53) 392
1974 Trade Union and Labour
    Relations Act (c. 52) 452
1975 Conservation of Wild Crea-
    tures and Wild Plants
    Act (c. 48) 681
Salmon and Freshwater
    Fisheries Act (c. 51) 681

1975 Poisons Act (c. 66)—
    s. 8 (2) (a) 206
          (b) 206
  European Communities Act
    (c. 68)—
    s. 2 (1) 353
    s. 4 (4) 353
1976 Companies Act (c. 69)—
    s. 13 (5) 172, 173
        (6) 172, 173
  Sexual Offences (Amend-
    ment) Act (c. 82) .. 8, 148, 153,
             601, 635, 640, 642
    s. 1 .... 371, 643
        (1) 430, **632**, 633
        (2) 641
1977 Patents Act (c. 37)—
    s. 30 (1) 688
  Protection from Eviction Act
    (c. 43)—
    s. 1 334
  Criminal Law Act (c. 45) **459,**
                462, 473
    s. 1 334
        (1) 455, 457, 473, 497
        (2) 456
        (4) 470
    s. 2 .... **460,** 647
        (1) 407, 461
    s. 3 .... **334,** 335
        (1) 334
        (2) 462, 463
        (3) (a) 462
          (b) 462
        (7) 462, 474
    s. 6 334
    s. 50 559
    s. 54 406
    Pt. I 424
  National Health Service Act
    (c. 49) 570
1978 National Health Service
    (Scotland) Act (c. 29) 570
  Interpretation Act (c. 30)—
    s. 5 413
    Sched. 1 413
  Theft Act (c. 31) 10, 473, 751
    s. 1 .... 661, 733, **777**
    s. 2 .... **778,** 779, 802
        (1) 780, 781
          (a) 779, 781, 782
          (b) 778, 779, 780, 781,
                782, 783
          (c) 778, 779, 781, 782
        (2) 778
        (3) 784
    s. 3 .... **784,** 786, 787
        (1) 784, 785, 786
    s. 5 (1) 752
        (5) 776
  Consumer Safety Act (c.
    38)—
    s. 2 (6) 206

1979 Customs and Excise Man-
    agement Act (c. 2)—
    s. 170 (1) (b) 485
        (2) 56, 103, 104, 105
    s. 2 (b) 456
  Sale of Goods Act (c. 54) . 456, 695
1980 Magistrates' Courts Act (c.
    43)—
    s. 44 .... 366, 367
  Highways Act (c. 66)—
    s. 137 (1) 132
  Deer Act (c. 49) 681
1981 Forgery & Counterfeiting
    Act (c. 45) 473
  Criminal Attempts Act (c.
    47)—
    s. 1 .... **424,** 429, 430, 432,
                433, 485, 487
        (1) 57, 430, 431, 442, 445,
                486
        (2) 486, 491
        (3) 489
        (4) 474
    s. 3 (4) 425
        (5) 425
    s. 4 (3) 425, 442, 448
        (5) **424**
    s. 5 493
        (1) 452, 491
    s. 6 (1) **424,** 425, 449, **486**
    s. 10 462
  Wildlife and Countryside
    Act (c. 69)—
    s. 13 681
1982 Criminal Justice Act (c. 48)—
    s. 37 581
1983 Mental Health Act (c. 20)—
    s. 1 (2) 245, 543
    s. 12 240
    s. 37 214
    s. 41 241
    Pt. IV 588
  Copyright (Amendment)
    Act (c. 42) 722
1984 Police and Criminal Evi-
    dence Act (c. 60) 363, 364
    s. 24 (4) 345
    s. 28 (3) 346
1985 Sexual Offences Act (c. 44) ... 601
    s. 3 (3) 648
1987 Criminal Justice Act (c. 38) ... **462**
    s. 12 .... 462, 466
1988 Criminal Justice Act (c. 33)—
    s. 12 726
    s. 39 .... 125, **581**
    s. 40 581
  Road Traffic Act (c. 52)—
    s. 1 .... 576, 577
    s. 2 .... 576, 577
    s. 4 .... 576, 577
    s. 5 17
    s. 7 .... 576, 577

1988	Road Traffic Act—*cont.*	
	s. 103	103
1990	Food Safety Act (c. 16)—	
	s. 21 (2)	206
	Computer Misuse Act (c.18)—	
	s. 3 (1)	857
	s. 3 (4)	856
	Human Fertilisation and Embryology Act (c. 37)—	
	s. 37	**569**
1991	Criminal Procedure (Insanity and Unfitness to Plead) (c. 25)—	
	s. 3	215
	s. 5	215
	(1) (*a*)	215

1991	Criminal Procedure (Insanity and Unfitness to Plead)—*cont.*	
	s. 5—*cont.*	
	(1)(*b*)	215
	(2) (*a*) (i)	215
	(*b*) (ii) (iii)	215
	(3)	215
	Sched. 1	215
	Sched. 2	215
	Road Traffic Act (c. 26)–	
	s. 1	117, 563, **576**
	s. 3	**576**
	Criminal Justice Act (c. 53)—	
	s. 24 (4)	750
	s. 25 (1)	750
	s. 26	664, 750
	s. 26 (2)	**828**

REPORTS AND OFFICIAL PROPOSALS

Law Commission Reports
No. 76: Conspiracy, 457
102: Attempts, etc., 425, 437, 439, 484
177: A Criminal Code for England and Wales: Vol. 2, Commentary on Draft Criminal Code Bill, 102, 137, 167, 180–182, 238, 241–246, 276, 353–365, 373, 411, 433, 511

Criminal Law Revision Committee Reports
8th: Theft and Related Offences, 689, 704, 717, 719, 741, 759, 777, 785
13th: S.16, Theft Act 1968, 787
14th: Offences against the Person, 508–511, 543–545
15th: Sexual Offences, 640

Draft Criminal Code Bill
Cl. 6: (General Interpretation), 137
14: (Proof of States of Mind), 167
16: (Omissions), 31
17: (Causation), 31, 55
18–21: (Fault), 138, 139, 140, 167
22: (Intoxication), 274
23, 24: (Supervening and Transferred Fault), 32, 274
25–27: (Parties and Accessories), 373, 407
29: (Vicarious Liability), 410
30, 31: (Corporations), 421–423
33: (Automatism and Physical Incapacity), 237
34–40: (Mental Disorder Verdict), 239–241
41–45: (Defences), 167, 354, 355, 358, 360–362
47–50: (Inchoate Offences), 450, 461, 477, 478
54–57: (Murder, Manslaughter), 511, 577, 578
62–64: (Suicide, Infanticide), 579
65: (Threat to Kill), 580
66–69: (Abortion, etc.), 560

Draft Criminal Law Act (1992)
Cl. 4, 5,
6, 8: Assaults, 631
147: Burglary with Intent, 846

American Law Institute: Model Penal Code (1985)
s. 1.04 (Classification of Crimes), 212
2.03 (Causation), 36
2.05 (Culpability), 212
2.08 (Intoxication), 250
3.02 (Necessity), 324
5.01 (Attempts), 449

British Reports and Official Proposals reproduced by permission of The Controller of H.M.S.O.

ABBREVIATIONS

Blackstone	*Commentaries on the Laws of England*, by Sir William Blackstone (1765) (Chitty's ed., 1826).
Butler Committee	Report of The Committee on Mentally Abnormal Offenders, Cmnd. 6244, 1975.
C.L.J.	*Cambridge Law Journal.*
C.L.R.C.	Criminal Law Revision Committee.
Col. L.R.	*Columbia Law Review.*
Crim. L.Q.	*Criminal Law Quarterly.*
Crim.L.R.	*Criminal Law Review.*
Fletcher	*Rethinking Criminal Law*, by George P. Fletcher (1978).
Glazebrook	*Reshaping the Criminal Law*, P. Glazebrook (ed.) (1978).
Griew	*The Theft Acts 1968 and 1978*, by Edward Griew (6th ed., 1990).
Hale	*Pleas of the Crown*, by Sir Matthew Hale (1682).
Hall	*General Principles of Criminal Law*, by Jerome Hall (2nd ed., 1960).
Harv. L.R.	*Harvard Law Review.*
Kenny	Kenny's *Outlines of Criminal Law* (19th ed., by J. W. C. Turner, 1966).
L.Q.R.	*Law Quarterly Review.*
M.L.R.	*Modern Law Review.*
Model Penal Code	American Law Institute, *Model Penal Code* (1962).
Russell	*Russell on Crime* (12th ed., by J. W. C. Turner, 1964).
Smith	*The Law of Theft*, by J. C. Smith (6th ed., 1989).
Smith and Hogan	*Criminal Law*, by J. C. Smith and Brian Hogan (7th ed., 1992).
Stephen, H. L. C.	*A History of the Common Law of England*, by Sir James Fitzjames Stephen (1883).
Williams, C. L. G. P.	*Criminal Law, The General Part*, by Glanville Williams (2nd ed., 1961).
Williams, Proof of Guilt	*The Proof of Guilt, A study of the English Criminal Trial*, by Glanville Williams (3rd ed., 1963).
Williams, T. C. L.	*Textbook of Criminal Law*, by Glanville Williams (2nd ed., 1983).

ACKNOWLEDGMENTS

Grateful acknowledgment is made to the following authors and publishers for permission to quote from their works:

ALLDRIDGE, P.: "The Coherence of Defences" [1983] Crim.L.R. 665–666.

ASHWORTH, A.J.: "Self-defence and the Right of Life" [1975] C.L.J. 282. (© Cambridge University Press).

BARLOW, N.L.A.: "Drug Intoxication and the Principle of Capacitas Rationalis" (1984) 100 L.Q.R. 639, 646–652.

BEAN, PHILIP AND WHYNES, D. (eds.): *Wootton, Essays in Her Honour* (1986, Tavistock Publications).

BRETT AND WALLER: *Criminal Law Text and Cases* (4th ed., Butterworths).

COWLEY, D.: "The Retreat from Morgan" [1982] Crim.L.R. 198, 206–208.

CROSS, PROF. SIR RUPERT: "Centenary Reflections on Prince's Case" (1975) 91 L.Q.R. 551; "Murder under Duress" (1978) 28 U.T.L.J. 369.

DELL, S.: "Diminished Responsibility Reconsidered" [1982] Crim L.R. 809, 813–814.

DENNIS, I.: "The Elements of Attempt" [1980] Crim.L.R. 758–768.

DUFF, R.A.: "The Circumstances of an Attempt" [1991] C.L.J. 100 (© Cambridge University Press).

FIELD, S. AND JÖRG, N.: "Corporate Liability and Manslaughter: should we be going Dutch?" [1991] Crim.L.R. 157.

FITZGERALD, P.J.: "A Concept of Crime" [1960] Crim.L.R. 257, 259.

FLETCHER, G.P.: *Rethinking Criminal Law* (1978, Little, Brown & Co., Boston).

GALLIGAN, D.J.: "The Return to Retribution in Penal Theory—Crime, Proof and Punishment," *Essays in Memory of Sir Rupert Cross* (1981, Butterworths).

GLAZEBROOK, P.R.: "Criminal Omissions: The Duty Requirement in Offences against the Person" (1960) 76 L.Q.R. 386, 387.

GLAZEBROOK, P.R. (ed.): *Reshaping the Criminal Law* (Essays in honour of Glanville Williams) (1978, Stevens & Sons):
Griew, E.J.: "Consistency, Communication and Codification: Reflections on Two *Mens Rea* Words"
Smith, A.T.H.: "On *Actus Reus* and *Mens Rea*"
Smith, J.C.: "Aid, Abet, Counsel or Procure"
Thomas, D.A.: "Form and Function in Criminal Law."

GRIEW, E.: *The Theft Acts 1968 and 1978* (6th ed., Sweet & Maxwell).

HAMMOND: "Theft of Information" (1984) 100 L.Q.R. 252, 263.

HART, H.L.A.: *Punishment and Responsibility* © Oxford University Press, 1968), by permission of Oxford University Press.

HUTCHINSON, A.C.: "Note on Sault Ste. Marie" (1979) *Osgoode Hall Law Journal* 415, 429, footnote 78.

JUSTICE: "Breaking the Rules" (1980), § 4.12.

KENNY: *Freewill and Responsibility* (1978, Routledge & Kegan Paul Ltd.).

LEIGH, L.H.: *Strict and Vicarious Liability* (1982, Sweet & Maxwell).

LLOYD, D.: *Introduction to Jurisprudence* (4th ed., Stevens & Sons).

MACKENNA, SIR BERNARD: "Blackmail: A Criticism" [1966] Crim.L.R. 466.

MODERN PENAL CODE (© American Law Institute, 1985), reprinted with the permission of The American Law Institute.

NORRIE, A.: "Oblique Intention and Legal Politics" [1989] Crim.L.R. 794–796.

PATIENT, I.H.E.: "Transferred Malice—A Misleading Misnomer" (1990) 54 J.C.L. 116–124 (Pageant Publishing).

PAULUS, I.: "Strict Liability: Its Place in Public Welfare Offences" (1978) 20 Crim.L.Q. 445, by permission of author and Canada Law Book Inc.

R. V. SHADRAKH-CIGARI (1988) (Lexis Legal Research).

SAYRE, F.B.: "Public Welfare Offences" (1933) *Columbia Law Review* 55 (© Directors of the Columbia Law Review Association, Inc., 1933).

SMITH, PROF. J.C.: "Comment on Olugboja" [1981] Crim.L.R 718; Commentary [1983] Crim.L.R. 471; Commentary (1984) Crim.L.R. 290; Commentary [1986] Crim.L.R. 123; Commentary [1987] Crim.L.R. 483–484; "Criminal Damage" [1981] Crim.L.R. 393; "Intent: A Reply" [1978] Crim.L.R. 14; Note [1981] Crim.L.R. 401, 403; "A Note on Intention" [1990] Crim.L.R. 85; *The Law of Theft* (6th ed., Butterworths).

SMITH AND HOGAN: *Criminal Law* (7th ed., Butterworths).

SMITH, K.J.M.: "Proximity in Attempt: Lord Lane's Midway Course" [1991] Crim.L.R. 576, 577.

SMITH, P. (ed.): *Criminal Law Essays in Honour of J. C. Smith* (1986, Butterworths):
Griew, E.: "States of Mind, Presumptions and Inferences"
Hogan, B.: "Omissions and the Duty Myth."

SPENCER, J.R.: "The Theft Act 1978" [1979] Crim.L.R. 24; "The Metamorphosis of section 6 of the Theft Act" [1977] Crim.L.R. 653.

WALKER, N.: *Crime and Punishment in Britain* (1965, Edinburgh University Press).

WASIK, M.: "Duress and Criminal Responsibility" [1977] Crim.L.R. 453; "*Mens Rea*, Motive and the Problem of 'Dishonesty' in the Law of Theft" [1979] Crim.L.R. 543.

WELLS, C.: "Swatting the Subjectivist Bug" [1982] Crim.L.R. 212–213; "Whither Insanity?" [1983] Crim.L.R. 787–788, 793–794.

WILLIAMS, PROF. GLANVILLE: *Textbook of Criminal Law* (2nd ed., Stevens & Sons); *Criminal Law: The General Part* (2nd ed., Stevens & Sons); "The Definition of Crime" (1955) *Current Legal Problems* 107; "Appropriation: A Single or Continuous Act?" [1978] Crim.L.R. 69; "Assault and Words" [1957] Crim.L.R. 219, 220; "Temporary Appropriation should be Theft" [1981] Crim.L.R. 129, "The Theory of Excuses" [1982] Crim.L.R. 739; "Criminal Law—Causation" (1976) C.L.J. 15; "Oblique Intention" (1987) C.L.J. 417, 420; "Finis for Novus Actus" [1989] C.L.J. 39 (© Cambridge University Press); "Wrong Turnings in the Law of Attempt [1991] Crim.L.R. 418, 419.

WOOTTON, B.: *Crime and the Criminal Law—Reflections of a Magistrate and Social Scientist* (2nd ed., Sweet & Maxwell).

CHAPTER 1

INTRODUCTORY

PAGE   PAGE
1. The Concept of Crime   1   2. The Form of English Criminal Law 8

THIS chapter is concerned briefly to sketch some of the assumptions underlying criminal law, and then to look, equally briefly, at the present form of English criminal law. As will be seen, in form it is a mixture of common law and statutory rules, with some progress discernible in the direction of complete codification.

1. THE CONCEPT OF CRIME

Williams, "The Definition of Crime" (1955) Current Legal Problems 107

"Is the effort [to define crime] worth making? The answer is that lawyers must try to clarify the notion of 'crime,' because it suffuses a large part of the law. For example: there is generally no time limit for criminal proceedings, whereas civil proceedings are commenced differently, and often in different courts. A criminal prosecutor generally need not be the victim of the wrong, and a private criminal prosecutor is for many purposes not regarded as a party to the proceedings; he is certainly not 'master' of the proceedings in the sense that he can drop them at will; these rules are different in civil cases. The law of procedure may generally be waived in civil but not in criminal cases. There are many differences in the law of evidence, and several in respect of appeal. . . .
. . . The common-sense approach is to consider whether there are any intrinsic differences between the acts constituting crimes and civil wrongs respectively. It is perhaps natural to suppose that since 'a crime' differs from 'a civil wrong,' there must be something *in* a crime to make it different from a civil wrong.

As everybody knows, there is one serious hindrance to a solution of this kind. This is the overlap between crime and tort. Since the same act can be both a crime and a tort, as in murder and assault, it is impossible to divide the two branches of the law by reference to the type of act. So also it is impossible to divide them by reference to the physical consequences of the act, for if the act is the same the physical consequences must be the same.

It has occurred to some that there is a possible escape from this difficulty. Although the act, and its consequences, are the same, the act and consequences have a number of different characteristics or aspects; and it may be possible to identify some of these characteristics as criminal and some as civil. Pursuing this line of thought, two separate aspects have been seized upon as identifying crime: the aspect of moral wrong and the aspect of damage to the public. . . .

The proposition that crime is a moral wrong may have this measure of truth: that the average crime is more shocking, and has graver social consequences, than the average tort. Yet crimes of strict responsibility can be committed without moral wrong, while torts and breaches of trust may be, and often are, gross moral wrongs.

1

Even where a forbidden act is committed intentionally, a court deciding that it is a crime is not committed to the proposition that it is a moral wrong. Thus in holding that a summary proceeding for an offence under the Game Act was criminal in character, Lord Campbell C.J. said: 'It is our business, not to estimate the degree of moral guilt in the act of the appellant, but to see how such act is treated by the legislature. ... I cannot be bound by any opinion that I may form of the morality of that act: but I must see what it is that the legislature has chosen to punish': *Cattell* v. *Ireson* (1858) E.B. & E. at pp. 97–98. There are crimes of great gravity in the legal calendar, such as mercy-killing and eugenic abortion, which are disputably moral wrongs, though they are indisputably crimes. The same is true of numerous summary offences. Lord Atkin put the situation pungently. 'The criminal quality of an act cannot be discerned by intuition; nor can it be discovered by reference to any standard but one: is the act prohibited with penal consequences? Morality and criminality are far from coextensive; nor is the sphere of criminality necessarily part of a more extensive field covered by morality—unless the moral code necessarily disapproves of all acts prohibited by the state, in which case the argument moves in a circle': *Proprietary Articles Trade Association* v. *Att.-Gen. for Canada* [1931] A.C. 324 (P.C.).

The second intrinsic difference between crimes and civil wrongs found by some writers is in respect of the damage done. In tort there is almost invariably actual damage to some person, whereas in crime such damage is not essential, the threat being to the community as a whole. ... Again there are formidable objections. Some torts do not require damage (such as trespass and libel), while many crimes do involve private damage. Some crimes are punished as an affront to the moral feelings of the community although they cause no damage to the community as a whole. This is true of the group of crimes having in differing degrees a religious aspect: blasphemy, attempted suicide, abortion, bigamy. It is also largely true of obscenity and adult homosexuality. Even murder need not cause public damage: for example, when a mother kills her infant child. This creates no general sense of insecurity; the only material loss to society is the loss of the child, and whether that is economically a real loss or a gain depends on whether the country is under- or over-populated at the time. Evidently, the social condemnation of infant-killing rests on non-utilitarian ethics. Some forms of public nuisance, too, are crimes although they positively benefit the community: *Ward* (1836) 4 Ad. & El. 384.

Even where an act injures the community, it need not be exclusively a crime. Thus some crimes, as has already been pointed out, may be made the occasion either of a criminal prosecution or of a civil action (generally a relator action) for an injunction by the Attorney-General; in the latter event the crime is treated not as a crime but as a civil wrong to the public. There are civil public wrongs that are not crimes, for which there is no remedy, but a relator action as where statutory powers are being exceeded. Indeed, an ordinary tort to property may be committed against public property and so become a public wrong.

We have rejected all definitions purporting to distinguish between crimes and other wrongs by reference to the sort of thing that is done or the sort of physical, economic or social consequences that follow from it. Only one possibility now remains. A crime must be defined by reference to the *legal* consequences of the act. We must distinguish, primarily, not between crimes and civil wrongs but between criminal and civil proceedings. A crime then becomes an act that is capable of being followed by criminal proceedings, having one of the types of outcome (punishment, etc.) known to follow these proceedings. ...

As stated at the outset, there are many differences of procedure between crimes and civil wrongs. Often these differences are of no help in distinguishing between the two, because they are consequential differences—it is only when you know that the act is a crime or a civil wrong respectively that you know which procedure to select. However, some elements in procedure do assist in making the classification. When Parliament passes a statute forbidding certain conduct, it may refer in terms to certain procedural matters—such as trial on indictment, or summary conviction—which indicate that the act is to be a crime. Again, when it is disputed whether a given proceeding, such as a proceeding for a penalty, is criminal or civil, a point can be scored by showing that this proceeding has been held in the past to be governed by some procedural rule which is regarded as indicative of a criminal or civil proceeding, as the case may be. For example, the fact that a precedent decides that a new trial may be granted in a particular proceeding indicates that the proceeding is civil, since new trials are not granted in criminal cases. On the other hand a precedent deciding that evidence of character is admissible in a certain proceeding indicates that it is criminal, since evidence of character is not admissible in civil cases, apart from certain quite definite exceptions.

Since the courts thus make use of the whole law of procedure in aid of their task of classification, an attempt to define crime in terms of one item of procedure only is mistaken. This remark applies to the test of crime adopted by Kenny, following Austin and Clark, which links crime with the ability of the Crown to remit the sanction. This test tells you whether an act is a crime only if you already know whether the sanction is remissible by the Crown. Almost always, however, the latter has to be deduced from the former, instead of vice versa. Thus Kenny defines *ignotum per ignotius*. This objection would not be open if Kenny's chosen procedural test were made available *along with all the others*. The procedural test does not give full assistance unless one is allowed to use the whole law of procedure.

... In short, a crime is an act capable of being followed by criminal proceedings having a criminal outcome, and a proceeding or its outcome is criminal if it has certain characteristics which mark it as criminal. In a marginal case the court may have to balance one feature, which may suggest that the proceeding is criminal, against another feature, which may suggest the contrary."

P. J. Fitzgerald, "A Concept of Crime" [1960] Crim.L.R. 257, 259

"In the question what is a crime there seems to be entangled three different though related questions.

1. The question may be simply the request of the non-lawyer as to how he is to tell whether an act is a crime or not. Here we may give an imperative definition by saying that a crime is a breach of the criminal law. Though dismissed by Glanville Williams as circular, such a definition is useful firstly in emphasising that a crime is not necessarily a moral wrong and vice versa. Secondly, its value is that it directs attention away from abstract speculation on the nature of the act and focuses it on the need to study the provisions of the criminal law itself. ...

2. The request for a definition of crime may be the request of the non-lawyer to be told what it means for the law to lay down that certain conduct shall be criminal. In other words he may want to know the effect of the law providing that an act is a crime. Here lies the usefulness of the definition proposed by Glanville Williams which distinguishes criminal wrongs from other legal wrongs. ...

3. The quest for a definition of crime may be a more sophisticated question, of a lawyer reflecting on the criminal law, namely, what have all crimes in common other than the fact that they are breaches of the criminal law? In so far as the motive behind such a question is the desire for a simple test to decide whether conduct is criminal or not without reference to the provisions of the law, Glanville Williams' discussion is helpful and illuminating in demonstrating that this is a search for the unattainable. But what may lie behind the question 'What is a crime?' may be the idea that Parliament and still more the courts have not created crimes arbitrarily or irrationally. Given that the aim of the criminal law is to announce that certain acts are not to be done, and to bring about that fewer of these acts are done, what is the principle or principles that have led the criminal law to prohibit the acts it has prohibited? ... "

Lloyd, Introduction to Jurisprudence (4th ed., 1979) pp. 54–59

"A good deal of controversy has arisen in recent years as to whether the fact that conduct is, by common standards, regarded as immoral, in itself justifies making that conduct punishable by law. This controversy was set off by the opinion expressed in the Wolfenden Committee Report on Prostitution and Homosexuality (Cmnd. 247, 1957), which in effect reasserted the answer given by John Stuart Mill, that legal coercion can only be justified for the purpose of preventing harm to others. Accordingly, on this view, there is a moral or ethical limit beyond the appropriate reach of the law. Mill's thesis had been attacked by the great Victorian judge, Stephen, in his *Liberty, Equality and Fraternity*, and the issue was now rekindled by Lord Devlin's critique of *Wolfenden* in a lecture called 'The Enforcement of Morals' delivered in 1959. Lord Devlin has subsequently returned to this theme a number of times [see Devlin, *The Enforcement of Morals*, O.U.P., 1965]. He has argued that there is a public morality which provides the cement of any human society, and that the law, especially the criminal law, must regard it as its primary function to maintain this public morality. Whether in fact in any particular case the law should be brought into play by specific criminal sanctions must depend upon the state of public feeling. Conduct which arouses a widespread feeling of reprobation, a mixture of 'intolerance, indignation and disgust,' deserves to be suppressed by legal coercion in the interests of the integrity of society. For this purpose, Lord Devlin has recourse to the common law jury idea, the notion that the 'man in the jury-box' supplies an adequate standard of current morality for the purpose of assessing the limits of legal intervention. The juryman after all does not give a snap judgment; his verdict is the outcome of argument and deliberation after, perhaps, listening to expert evidence and receiving guidance from an experienced judge. And as for reliance upon feeling, this was the ordinary man's best guide where a choice had to be made between a number of reasonable conclusions. He therefore stigmatises as an 'error of jurisprudence' the view in the Wolfenden Report that there is some single principle explaining the division between crime and sin, such as that based upon Mill's notion of what may lead to harmful consequences to third persons.

Devlin concluded that if vice were not suppressed society would crumble: 'The suppression of vice is as much the law's business as the suppression of subversive activities.'

Such a thesis appears to have received some support from the remarkable decision of the House of Lords in the so-called *Ladies' Directory Case* (*Shaw* v. *D.P.P.* [1962] A.C. 220), but has been strenuously opposed by Professor Hart (H. L. A. Hart, *Law, Liberty and Morality*, O.U.P., 1963). Hart has outlined (35 Univ. of Chicago Law Review 1, 11–13), in the first place, 'the types of evidence that might conceivably be relevant to the issue.' One could examine 'crude historical evidence,' look at disintegrated societies and enquire whether disintegration was preceded by a malignant change in their common morality, considering further any 'causal connection.' Such a survey would have formidable difficulties for, even supposing, which is most unlikely, that moral decadence was responsible for the decline of Rome, would such evidence be persuasive in considering modern technological societies? Hart puts his faith rather in the evidence of social psychology. Depending on one's idealogy, the way of viewing the alternatives to the maintenance of a common morality, this could take one of two forms. One view would be *permissiveness*: one would show how this led to a weakening of individual capacity for self-control and contributed to an increase in violence and dishonesty. But the other side of the coin is *moral pluralism*. Would this lead to antagonism, to a society in the state of nature depicted by Hobbes [see *Leviathan*, Pt. 1, Chap. 13 (' . . . the life of man, solitary, poor, nasty, brutish, and short').] or rather to mutual tolerance, to co-existence of divergent moralities? What evidence there is comes down firmly in favour of co-existence. Having removed the foundations of Devlin's thesis, Hart then sets about to demolish the structure erected upon them. He dismisses as fantastic the notion that all morality forms 'a single seamless web' so that deviation from any one part will almost inevitably produce destruction of the whole. The mere fact that conventional morality may change in a permissive direction does not mean that society is going to be destroyed or subverted. Again, Lord Devlin assumes a degree of moral solidarity in society, which may have existed in mid-Victorian England, but is hardly discernible at the present time. Hart goes on to point out that the real solvent to social morality is not the failure of the law to endorse its restrictions, but rather the operation of free critical discussion, and he goes on to point out the dangers to democracy which might flow from the notion that free discussion should be prohibited on account of its impact on the prevalent social morality. That the moral notions of the majority are matters to which the legislature must pay close account seems beyond question, but what Mill had in mind was that at all costs the idea that the majority had a moral right to dictate how everyone else should live, was something which needed to be resisted. It is essential, therefore, from a libertarian point of view, that public indignation, while given due weight, should be subject to the overriding tests of rational and critical appraisal.

Nevertheless, Hart accepts the need for the law to enforce some morality and the real area of dispute is where the line should be drawn. Mill drew it at harm to others. Hart extends the role of the law by his acceptance of 'paternalism,' in addition to Mill's reliance on harmful consequences to others (*Law, Liberty and Morality*, pp. 30–34). So, where Devlin justified *R. v. Donovan* [1934] 2 K.B. 498, (see, *post*, p. 601) as enforcement of morality, Hart sees the decision as a concession to paternalism. Hart never defines paternalism and Devlin has been critical of its vagueness. 'What, also, I did not foresee was that some of the crew who sail under Mill's flag of liberty would mutiny and run paternalism up the mast.' (*The Enforcement of Morals*, p. 132.) Although Devlin is unable to distinguish paternalism and the enforcement of morals, there is a distinction which centres on the decision-making process of those who are subject to the law. Paternalism thus may intervene to stop self-inflicted harm such as the results of drug-taking or cigarette smoking or of the refusal to use crash helmets or seat belts, not because of a wish to enforce conventional morality, but because of doubts as to the capacity of the 'victim' to make a rational decision, especially where he is mentally disturbed (according to conventional morality) or physically ill.

But Hart goes further than this. He admits, with Devlin, that some shared morality is essential to society, what he calls 'universal values' (*Law, Liberty, and Morality*, p. 71). If *any* society is to survive, if any legal system is to function, then there must be rules prohibiting, for example, murder. But is abortion or euthanasia murder? The standard case remains uncontroversial, the marginal situation is no nearer solution. Hart further argues, in a later formulation (35 Univ. of Chicago Law Review, p. 10), that rules essential for a *particular* society (monogamy might be an example) might be enforced. 'For any society there is to be found ... a central core of rules or principles which constitutes its pervasive and distinctive style of life.' And he continues: 'it then becomes an open and empirical question whether any particular moral rule is so organically connected with the central core that its preservation is required as a vital bastion.' At this stage a point has been reached where there is not much to choose between the two main contestants. (For further viewpoints in this controversy see E. Rostow [1960] C.L.J. 174, reprinted in *The Sovereign Prerogative* (1962); Hughes, 71, Yale L.J. 662, reprinted in Summers, *Essays in Legal Philosophy* (1968), p. 183; Summers (1963) 38 N.Y.U.L. Rev. 1201; Henkin (1963) 63 Col.L.Rev. 393; Samek, 49 Can. Bar Rev. 188.)''

Note

Quite apart from this quarrel about what the criminal law should prohibit, there is another controversy about what should be done with individuals who defy such prohibitions as the criminal law has.

Galligan, "The Return to Retribution in Criminal Theory" in "Crime, Proof and Punishment"; Essays in Memory of Sir Rupert Cross (1981), pp. 144, 146 et. seq.

"If one were to attempt to explain the principal functions of that complex amalgam of institutions, persons, rules, and practices which we loosely refer to as the system of criminal justice, then two particular things would seem to call out for special attention. First, criminal justice is concerned centrally with trying, convicting and punishing those who are guilty of breaking the criminal law. Secondly, such systems are concerned to punish those who are convicted with a view to upholding the authority and effectiveness of the criminal law by sanctions that seek to deter, to prevent, to reform, or to incapacitate. These two tasks will often, but not necessarily, be compatible with each other. One view of criminal justice is to emphasise the forward-looking or utilitarian functions while another view sees the backward-looking or retributive aspect as primary. How one perceives the system will largely determine how one explains it and the kind of justifications that one finds acceptable. ...

Utilitarian accounts usually begin with the assumption that the central purpose of criminal justice is to reduce crime. This purpose is achieved by taking coercive action against selected individuals, usually those who have broken the law and who can be held personally responsible for so doing. There is an increasing body of offences which do not require responsibility in the usual legal sense, but nevertheless, with respect to the main corpus of criminal laws there is still a meticulous concern to be sure that before a person is punished he is guilty in the sense that he is responsible. But why should this be so? It is an important aspect of forward-looking explanations of criminal justice that the punishment of wrong-doers is not itself part of the general aim or purpose. Rather, confinement of impositions to the guilty law-breaker is a costly constraint on pursuit of the general reductivist aim. One approach faces this problem by suggesting that these constraints are misguided, in that inquiries into matters of personal responsibility are inevitably very crude, and unfairly selective in that there are large areas where action is taken without the requirement of responsibility. According to this view criminal justice should not be thought of as significantly different from other methods of social protection, such as confining dangerous mental defectives. Society has an interest in protecting itself from the person who has or is likely to commit serious crime and may legitimately take whatever preventive action is necessary. Although such an understanding of criminal justice has been anathema to most, a few modifications show it in a much better light. A modified approach might see considerable advantages such as economy, humanitarianism and the reduction of suffering in retaining the basic constraints of the aim of reducing crime, but since these would be conditional they could be departed from if to do so would provide better service to the general aim. It is worth noting that much of the practice of criminal justice is indeed compatible with this position for while coercion is normally based on responsibility, it is also often departed from if we bear in mind the preventive powers of the police and courts, the areas of strict and vicarious liability and the means available for confining mental defectives.

Views of this kind, however, have never dominated explanations of criminal justice. Most forward-looking accounts of criminal justice, no matter how different in other respects, seek to show that while the general purpose of criminal justice is forward looking, the responsibility constraints on that purpose are explicable, justifiable and necessary. Since Bentham's famous but flawed defence of punishing only those responsible for their actions, a range of increasingly subtle and sophisticated explanations have been advanced. There is, for example, the pragmatist argument that as a matter of practicalities it would be virtually impossible to design an efficacious system of criminal justice that did not limit the distribution of sanctions to the responsible offender. Alternatively there is the suggestion that the purpose of criminal justice is not only reduction-through-deterrence, but also reduction-through-respect for the law. Unless the administration of criminal justice is in accordance with values esteemed in the community then respect for law is hardly to be earned and naturally most people think that a man should only be punished if he is guilty. There is much to be said for this view; notice however that it puts forward the responsibility constraint not as an independent value in itself, but of value because it maximises the efficacy of law. . . .

Finally, it is a frequently heard criticism of utilitarian accounts that since the aim is crime control, there are difficulties in finding principles that limit the amount of punishment that may be inflicted on any offender. To the practical reformer this is the central issue, for recent penal history has shown the difficulty of controlling punishment distributed according to forward-looking goals. Retributive accounts, with their emphasis on punishment according to deserts, is naturally an attractive alternative to the unruly policies of rehabilitation and deterrence. . . .

Retributive explanations emphasise the concern of the criminal justice system to punish those who break the law. The core of the idea of retribution is the moral notion that the wrongdoer ought to be punished.

Thus a system that is centrally concerned with punishing offenders is retributive. In explaining the practice of criminal justice in this way, the retributive approach avoids the difficulties in explanation that beset forward-looking accounts. There is no need to distinguish between aim and distribution since the aim provides the criterion of distribution. The person who has not broken the law, or who could not help breaking it, or who can offer some other acceptable excuse is not a wrongdoer and is not liable for punishment. In other words within the context of criminal justice as we know it, punishment means inflicting sanctions on wrongdoers. This does not imply that coercion is never used against people in other ways; all it claims is that the reasons for coercing wrongdoers are different from the reasons that would explain other areas of coercion.

Put in this bald way, retribution includes both a description of criminal justice and a justification. Just as the utilitarian sees criminal justice as primarily concerned with reducing crime, so the retributivist sees the punishment of offenders as the dominant purpose. The logic of punishment consists in singling out an offender, condemning him for his offence and imposing punitive treatment upon him. The retributivist sees these three elements as part of one unified and justifiable social process: the offender has done wrong which, by punishment, is somehow righted. In short, the distinctive feature of retribution as a justifying principle, is that it provides a basis not just for singling out and condemning the offender, but also for inflicting punitive treatment. .... "

2. THE FORM OF ENGLISH CRIMINAL LAW

In some Commonwealth jurisdictions, *e.g.* Queensland, the criminal law is in the form of a code. In England and Wales, despite an attempt in that direction in nineteenth century, no general criminal code has reached the statute book.

Law Com. 177: A Criminal Code for England and Wales

Vol. 1: Report and Draft Criminal Code Bill

1.3 English criminal law is derived from a mixture of common law and statute. Most of the general principles of liability are still to be found in the common law, though some for example, the law relating to conspiracy and attempts to commit crime have recently been defined in Acts of Parliament. The great majority of crimes are now defined by statute but there are important exceptions. Murder, manslaughter and assault are still offences at common law, though affected in various ways by statute. There is no system in the relative roles of common law and legislation. Thus, incitement to commit crime—though closely related to conspiracy and attempts—is still a common law offence. Whether an offence is defined by statute has almost always been a matter of historical accident rather than systematic organisation. For example, rape is defined in the Sexual Offences (Amendment) Act 1976 because of the outcry which followed the decision in *Morgan* v. *D.P.P.* (*post*, p. 142) and led to the subsequent Heilbron Report. The legislation in force extends over a very long period of time. It is true that only a very small amount of significant legislation is earlier than the mid-nineteenth century, but that is quite long enough for the language of the criminal law and the style of drafting to have undergone substantial changes.

1.4 There has been a steady flow of reform of the criminal law in recent years but it has been accomplished in somewhat piecemeal fashion. Some of it is derived from our own reports, where in recent years we have been pursuing a policy of putting common law offences into statutory form, and some from reports of the Criminal Law Revision Committee and committees, like the Heilbron Committee, appointed to deal with particular problems. Other reforms have resulted from the initiative of Ministers or private Members of Parliament in introducing Bills. As there is no authoritative statement of general principles of liability or of terminology to which we or these other bodies, or their draftsmen, can turn it would be surprising if there were not some inconsistencies and incongruities in the substance and language of the measures which are proposed and which become law.

Further inconsistencies and incongruities result from the very fact that the law is a mixture of statute and common law, and the difficulty in discovering the law on any point in this mixture can be formidable. Moreover, the continuing influence of unelected judges, while it is sometimes defended as securing a desirable flexibility in the law, offends constitutional susceptibilities. These perceived disadvantages have, since the middle of the present century, produced a sustained movement for systematic change and restatement. In English law, criminal law is peculiar in having had two standing bodies actively devoted to its reform. The Criminal Law Revision Committee was set up in 1959 by the Home Secretary as a standing committee to examine such aspects of the criminal law as he might refer to it and to make recommendations for revision if thought necessary. This committee of part-time lawyer members has made no pretentions, nor indeed has it had the power, to examine the criminal law as a whole. However it has produced a number of reports on particular areas, usually resulting in legislation, *e.g.* the Theft Act 1968. In 1965 the Law Commissions Act established a permanent body of salaried Commissioners to keep the whole of the law, civil and criminal, under review "with a view to its systematic development and reform, including in particular the codification of such law, the elimination of anomalies, the repeal of obsolete and unnecessary enactments, the reduction of the number of separate enactments and generally the simplification and modernisation of the law" (s.3). In pursuance of this remit, the Law Commission announced an ambitious programme for the codification of criminal law, but in the event soon found itself examining and reporting on particular areas of the law, which reports have sometimes resulted in legislation, *e.g.* the Criminal Damage Act 1971. Commonly the Law Commission sets up a Working Party to make a preliminary examination of a topic and produce a Working Paper. The Law Commission's Report usually endorses the conclusions in the Working Paper, but not always, *e.g.* Law Com. No. 102 on attempts. Since after 1965 in practice both bodies were considering and making proposals about particular areas of the law, it might have been decided that the Criminal Law Revision Committee was redundant. However the Home Secretary continued to refer matters to it. Both bodies continued to produce reports on particular areas. For a fair idea of their work so far, see Table of Reports. The criminal law is the better for their efforts, and would be further improved if Parliamentary time were found to embody all their reports in legislation.

However, codification has still not been achieved. Reforming particular parts of the law before producing a code covering general principles may seem like putting the cart before the horse, but this way of proceeding proved inevitable. The Law Commission was not able to find the great amount of time needed to think about general principles. Recognising this, in 1981 the Commission set up a small team of senior academics to undertake the necessary preliminary work. That team reported with a first draft of a Criminal Code Bill in 1985 (Law Com. No. 143). After wide consultation, the Law Commission in 1989 recommended to Parliament a Draft Criminal Code Bill, founded on this first draft. Frequent extracts from this Draft Bill appear throughout this book.

When considering these extracts, the reader must bear in mind that the draftsmen did not consider their task as law reform, but as restatement of the law. When the law is clear, the Draft Code restates it, except where the reports of the Law Commission or other public bodies have recommended changes. In such places, the Draft almost always incorporates the proposals. Where the present law exhibits a plainly indefensible inconsistency, the Draft eliminates it. In other cases of law which has attracted criticism, the Draft nevertheless reproduces it as it is thought to be, *e.g.* the part of the Code on Theft and related offences reproduces the Theft Acts 1968 and 1978, with changes only of arrangement and lay-out to conform with the style of the Draft Code. In one case, however, the Law Commission refuses to incorporate the effect of House of Lords decisions. This is as to "Caldwell recklessness" (see, *post*, p. 111). The Draft reproduces the wording of the Criminal Damage Act 1971, but subjects it to the Code's own definition of recklessness, taking no account of the House of Lords' definition of that word in that statute.

The bulk of the Draft Code is taken up with Part I: General Principles of Liability. Part II is concerned with specific offences and deals with Offences against the Person, Sexual Offences, Theft, Fraud and Related Offences, Other Offences relating to Property and Offences against the Public Peace and Safety. It is envisaged that some other offences will be collected in the Code in due course, *i.e.* Offences against the International Community, against the State, relating to the Administration of Justice, against Public Morals and Decency. But it is not envisaged that all offences will eventually find a home in the Criminal Code. Technical complexity, triviality, and convenience of the users of the law, who need a "dedicated" statute to refer to (*e.g.* the Road Traffic or Health and Safety legislation) mean that some offences will continue to be excluded from the Criminal Code. But as a general rule, the Principles in Part I are to apply to all offences created after the enactment of the Code, whether or not they are incorporated in it. As to existing offences the Code's principles of substantive law, *e.g.* as to fault terms or vicarious liability, are not to apply, because to allow the Code to govern these would be to work many unconsidered changes into the law. But the Code's principles on procedural matters, such as alternative verdicts or double jeopardy, are to apply to all offences whenever created and whenever committed.

The problem remains of engaging the legislators' attention for long enough to translate proposals into actual law. Some proposals from, *e.g.* the Criminal Law Revision Committee, which have been included in the Draft Code, have been waiting for Parliamentary attention for many years, and are now regarded as urgent, notably those on Non-Fatal Offences against the Person. The prospects of the Draft Criminal Code Bill reaching the statute book in the near future are regarded as slim enough for the Law Commission to produce a separate Criminal Law Bill dealing specifically with that subject, in the hope that a limited Bill has a better chance of early enactment than the full Criminal Code Bill.

CHAPTER 2

ACTUS REUS

	PAGE		PAGE
1. Elements of Crime	12	4. Causation	33
2. Voluntariness	14	i. *Sine Qua Non*	34
3. Omissions	18	ii. Imputability	36
i. Breach of Duty to Act	20	iii. An Alternative Approach	55
ii. Commission by Omission	21	5. Coincidence of *Actus Reus* and	
		Mens Rea	56

1. ELEMENTS OF CRIME

THE terms *actus reus* and *mens rea* when used to describe the elements of a criminal offence are deceptively simple. Not only is there a host of conceptual pitfalls concealed within each, but there is also no agreement amongst lawyers as to the precise divide between them.

A. T. H. Smith, "On Actus Reus and Mens Rea" in Reshaping the Criminal Law (ed. Glazebrook), pp. 95–107

"As the elliptic statements of the basic ingredients of criminal liability that they are frequently taken to be, both expressions [*actus reus* and *mens rea*] are incomplete and misleading. While the term *mens rea* is used in at least three distinct senses, so that failure to distinguish clearly between them leads inevitably to confusion, the terminology of *actus reus* tends to conceal the important principles that are at stake when the courts are deciding what sorts of conduct deserve condemnation as criminal. I do not mean to suggest that the traditional terminology should be abandoned; rather I would argue that a sharper awareness of its limitations might help us to see more clearly what the preconditions to criminal liability really are, and how far they really reflect the principles they are commonly supposed to encapsulate. . . .

This division of crime into its constituent parts is an exercise of analytical convenience: the concepts of *actus reus* and *mens rea* are simply tools, useful in the exposition of the criminal law. Great care should, therefore, be taken to avoid determining questions of policy by reference to definition and terminology. Such observations as that the maxim *actus non facit reum nisi mens sit rea* serves the 'important purpose of stressing two basic requirements of criminal liability,' make *actus reus* and *mens rea* seem rather more than analytical tools. They have been converted from the descriptive to the normative: to propositions that criminal liability *should* be based on harmful conduct, and *should* require a mental element. . . .

The raw material of any crime is the particular social mischief that the legislator is seeking to suppress. But for ascertaining the *actus reus* of any given offence, the starting point for the courts is the statute, or, as it may still be, the common law definition. Questions of statutory interpretation must be solved before the exact scope of the proscribed activity can be known. Where the defendant's conduct can fairly be described as coming within the terms of the proscribed activity, an offence has, prima facie, been committed: liability will ensue unless he advances some explanation of his conduct which shows that it was justified, in which case there is no *actus reus*. As one writer puts it, 'the *actus reus* is a defeasible concept.' But some lawyers are content to say that the requirements of *actus reus* are satisfied whenever the terms of the definition are fulfilled. The danger of taking such a very limited view of what is entailed in the *actus reus*, is that it may too readily be concluded that the harm that the law seeks to prevent has occurred. Much depends on the view taken of the role of defences. ...

Glanville Williams [C.L.G.P., p. 20] inclines to the view that all the elements of a crime are divisible into either *actus reus* or *mens rea* and holds that the *actus reus* includes absence of defence. By implication, therefore, all defences are a denial that the prosecution has proved a requisite part of its case. Although they nowhere clearly articulate the point, Professors Smith and Hogan seem to prefer the view that the constituent ingredients of crime are threefold, and include defences which are themselves composites of physical (or external) and mental elements. This mode of analysis is becoming increasingly widespread amongst academic writers, and has been carried furthest by Professor Lanham [[1976] Crim.L.R. 276]. He says that:

> as a matter of analysis we can think of a crime as being made up of three ingredients, *actus reus, mens rea* and (a negative element) absence of a valid defence. Some defences (*e.g.* alibi) negative the *actus reus*. Some defences (*e.g.* I did not mean to do it) negative the *mens rea*. A third group of defences (*e.g.* self-defence) operate without negativing either positive element, in effect as a confession and avoidance. But there is a fourth kind of defence (*sic*) which is perfectly capable of standing as a confession and avoidance but which normally will negative one or other (or both) of the *actus reus* and *mens rea*.

According to this view, then *actus reus* and *mens rea* do not encapsulate all the ingredients of a crime."

Notes

1. The use of Latin terminology is not without its critics; Lord Diplock stated in *Miller* [1983] 2 A.C. 161, 174.

> "My Lords, it would I think be conducive to clarity of analysis of the ingredients of a crime that is created by statute, as are the great majority of offences today, if we were to avoid bad Latin and instead to think and speak ... about the conduct of the accused and his state of mind at the time of that conduct, instead of speaking of *actus reus* and *mens rea*."

This counsel has been adopted by the Draft Criminal Code Bill (Law Com. No. 177, 1989) which uses the term "act" to describe the external elements of offences in preference to "*actus reus*" in the narrow sense as used by Lanham (*ante*). For "*mens rea*" the draft uses the phrase "fault element."

2. Most writers seem agreed that the "act" implied in the phrase "*actus reus*" does not stop at bodily movements or overt acts. "Some acts can only be engaged in, some can only be performed,

some only are done, and there are even some that can only take place; and this suggests the richness and variety of those bits of the world that we may choose to regard as acts." (Gross, p. 133). Williams takes the view that "the proposition that an offence requires an act requires to be so qualified by exceptions that its utility comes to seem doubtful. . . . It is therefore less misleading to say that a crime requires some *external state of affairs* that can be categorised as criminal." (T.C.L., p. 31).

(The normal mode of definition of offences is *result-oriented* requiring proof of an act or omission and usually proof that the conduct caused a specified result. This mode of definition is backed up with the law of attempts to cover cases where the intended result does not occur. An alternative mode of definition is that which concentrates on conduct, the *inchoate mode*, making it an offence to do certain acts in order to produce a certain outcome; the offence is committed whether or not the outcome results. An example of a result crime is murder where it must be proved that the deceased died as a result of the accused's conduct. An example of a conduct offence is perjury where the relevant conduct is the making of a statement on oath which the maker does not believe to be true; it is not a requirement of the offence that anyone else should believe the statement. For further discussion of result and conduct crimes see: Smith and Hogan, pp. 33–34; Smith, "The Element of Chance in Criminal Liability" (1971) Crim.L.R. 63; Ashworth, "Defining Criminal Offences Without Harm" in *Criminal Law: Essays in Honour of J. C. Smith* (1987, ed. P. Smith).)

2. VOLUNTARINESS

H. L. A. Hart, "Act of Will and Responsibility" in Punishment and Responsibility (1968), p. 90

"The General Doctrine
In this lecture I propose to air some doubts which I have long felt about a doctrine, concerning criminal responsibility, which has descended from the philosophy of conduct of the eighteenth century, through Austin, to modern English writers on the criminal law. This is the doctrine that, besides the elements of knowledge of circumstances and foresight of consequences, in terms of which many writers define *mens rea*, there is another 'mental' or at least psychological element which is required for responsibility: the accused's 'conduct' (including his omissions where these are criminally punishable) must, so it is said, be voluntary and not involuntary. This element in responsibility is more fundamental than *mens rea* in the sense of knowledge of circumstances or foresight of consequences; for even where *mens rea* in that sense is not required, and responsibility is 'strict' or 'absolute' . . . , this element, according to some modern writers, is still required. . . .

In many textbooks there are general assertions that for *all* criminal responsibility conduct must be 'voluntary,' 'conduct [must be] the result of the exercise of his will' there must be an 'act with its element of will,' 'an act due to the deliberate exercise of the will.' Yet, surely, even if there is any such general doctrine, these phrases are very dark. What does doctrine mean? What after all is the will? . . .

We know now what the general doctrine means: it defines an act in terms of the simplest thing we can do: this is the minimum feat of contracting our muscles. Conduct is 'voluntary' or 'the expression of an act of will' if the muscular contraction which, on the physical side, is the initiating element in what are loosely thought of as simple actions, is caused by a desire for the same contractions. This is all the mysterious element of the 'will' amounts to: it is this which is the minimum indispensable link between mind and body required for responsibility even where responsibility is strict. . . .

. . . The . . . theory that has got into our law books through Austin is first, nonsensical when applied to omissions, and secondly cannot characterise what is amiss even in involuntary interventions; for the desire to move our muscles, which it says is missing there, is not present in normal voluntary action either."

Consider Hart's alternative definition under which he seeks to classify those acts generally regarded as not voluntary:

" . . . We could characterise involuntary movements such as those made in epilepsy, or in a stroke, or mere reflex actions to blows or stings, as movements of the body which occurred although they were not appropriate, *i.e.*, required for any action (in the ordinary sense of action) which the agent believed himself to be doing."

Williams, Textbook of Criminal Law, p. 148

"Lawyers sometimes speak of a voluntary act meaning only that it was willed. Since every act is by definition willed, there is no need to call it voluntary.

The element of volition in an act has greatly exercised the philosophers. I can look at my hand, say to myself 'Hand, move to the left,' and then cause it to move to the left. But that is not the way in which I usually live and move. I do not consciously direct orders to my muscles. Two philosophers, Ryle and Melden, have attempted to argue away the notion of will. They build their case upon the difficulty of identifying conscious volitions accompanying bodily movement. Certainly it would be false to assume that every act is the result of deliberation: I may scratch my nose while thinking, without knowing I am doing it or recollecting I have done it. Even when the act is conscious, introspection does not show a conscious exercise of will preceding conduct. When I move my arms, say in writing a letter, I do not consciously decide to move them before moving them. It is true that electrical impulses run from the motor nerve cells in the spinal cord through the nerve fibres to the muscles; and these muscles are under the control of my brain. But the mental functioning that controls movement is not conscious determination, and it takes place at practically the same time as the movement. Will is the mental activity accompanying the type of bodily movement that we call an act. It is, of course, possible to will the absence of an act, as when we sit still.

A bodily movement is said to be willed, generally speaking, when the person in question could have refrained from it if he had so willed, that is, he could have kept still. Movements that are the result of epilepsy, for example, are involuntary or unwilled because the person concerned cannot by any mental effort avoid them. Whatever the difficulties in explaining what we mean by volition, everyone realises the important difference between doing something and having something happen to one; and this distinction is a basic postulate of a moral view of human behaviour."

Note

Voluntariness and consciousness

It is not *necessary* for a person to be unconscious before his or her acts are said to be involuntary. A person suffering from St. Vitus Dance, or having a muscle spasm, is acting involuntarily under either the Hart "inappropriateness" formula, or the Williams "inability to refrain" test. Nor is unconsciousness in itself *sufficient* to avoid liability. As Lord Denning said in *Bratty* v. *Att.-Gen. for Northern Ireland* [1963] A.C. 386, 410: "It is not every involuntary act which leads to a complete acquittal." This dictum applies in particular where the defendant is responsible for his or her own incapacity. A separate defence of automatism has thus developed with its own limitations. There is also a connection between some instances of automatism and insanity. For these two reasons automatism is dealt with below in Chapter 4. But what happens when the defendant is conscious but still claims he or she acted involuntarily? Does the concept of voluntariness cover more than muscle twitches? The following case has often been criticised for ignoring the requirement of a voluntary act.

R. v. Larsonneur
(1933) 97 J.P. 206
Court of Criminal Appeal

The defendant, a French subject, landed in the United Kingdom with a French passport. This was indorsed with conditions prohibiting her employment here. On March 22 these conditions were varied by a condition requiring her to leave the United Kingdom that day. This she did, going to the Irish Free State. The Irish authorities ordered her deportation and she was brought to Holyhead in the custody of the Irish police and she was there handed over to the English police. She was charged that "she being an alien to whom leave to land in the United Kingdom has been refused, was found in the United Kingdom contrary to Articles 1(3) (*g*) and 18 (1) (*b*) of the Aliens Order, 1920, as amended by S.R. & O. No. 326 of 1923 and 715 of 1931." She was convicted at London Sessions and appealed.

LORD HEWART C.J.: The fact is, as the evidence shows, that the appellant is an alien. She has a French passport, which bears this statement under the date March 14, 1933. "Leave to land granted at Folkestone this day on condition that the holder does not enter any employment, paid or unpaid, whilst in the United Kingdom," but on March 22 that condition was varied and one finds these words: "The condition attached to the grant of leave to land is hereby varied so as to require departure from the United Kingdom not later than March 22, 1933." Then follows the signature of an Under-Secretary of State. In fact, the appellant went to the Irish Free State and afterwards, in circumstances which are perfectly immaterial, so far as this appeal is concerned, came back to England. She was at Holyhead on April 21, 1933, practically a month after the day limited by the condition of her passport. . . .

Appeal dismissed

Notes

Part of the problem with this case is that the prohibition related to a state of affairs rather than a physical act. One way of solving the apparent injustice is by the implication of *mens rea* into the offence: as in *Lim Chin Aik* v. *R.*, *post*, p. 187. But it may still be possible to reconcile the case with the doctrine of a voluntary act. Lanham defends the decision, though not the reasoning, in "Larsonneur Revisited" [1976] Crim.L.R. 276. He suggests that Miss Larsonneur was herself responsible for her seemingly unfortunate fate, and no more deserved acquittal than a person who becomes an automaton through drink or drugs. It appears from a confession which she made to the police that Miss Larsonneur had gone to Ireland to arrange a marriage between herself and an Englishman, and had been told by the Irish police to leave by April 17: "Miss Larsonneur's story . . . reveals that the defendant brought upon herself the act of compulsion which led to her being charged. . . . No-one could claim that *Larsonneur* stood as a shining example of jurisprudence. But it can hardly be regarded as the last word in judicial depravity. If Miss Larsonneur had been dragged kicking and screaming from France into the United Kingdom by kidnappers and the same judgment had been given by the Court of Criminal Appeal, the defence of unforeseeable compulsion would truly have been excluded and the case would be the worst blot on the pages of the modern criminal law. But she wasn't and it wasn't and it isn't."

Even if Miss Larsonneur's conviction was not in accordance with the doctrine of voluntary conduct, it may be questioned whether the doctrine is the appropriate instrument with which to apportion criminal responsibility. A driver whose drinks have, unbeknown to him or her, been "laced," resulting in an excessive blood-alcohol concentration will not avoid conviction under the Road Traffic Act 1988, s.5; *R.* v. *Shippam* [1971] Crim.L.R. 434. The rationale here does not seem to be that the drinking was not self-induced (*cf.* "involuntary" intoxication as a defence to non-alcohol-related crimes, *post*, p. 246) but that the "driving" was voluntary. This suggests that the doctrine is still a little unpolished.

See also *Winzar* v. *Chief Constable of Kent*, *The Times*, March 28, 1983. The appellant had been brought to hospital on a stretcher. He was diagnosed as being drunk and was asked to leave. When he was later found slumped on a seat in the corridor the police were called. They removed him to the highway and then placed him in the police car charging him with being drunk on the highway contrary to section 12 of the Licensing Act 1872. The Queen's Bench Divisional Court upheld his conviction on the basis that as the purpose of the offence was to deal with the nuisance of public drunkenness, it was sufficient to establish guilt to prove that the person was drunk while in a public place; how he came to be there was considered to be irrelevant.

Compare *Kilbride* v. *Lake* [1962] N.Z.L.R. 590. Kilbride's conviction for failing to display a current warrant of fitness was quashed by the New Zealand Court of Criminal Appeal on the ground that the omission was not within his conduct, knowledge or control, since the warrant was there when he parked his car and inexplicably not there when he returned.

The critics of Larsonneur might be expected to welcome this display of antipodean juristic maturity but an argument is put forward by Budd and Lunch, in "Voluntariness, Causation and Strict Liability" [1978] Crim.L.R. 74 that "it is a form of involuntariness quite unlike those forms usually referred to in the Law. ... If one believes that strict liability, although entailing the conviction of the morally blameless, is nevertheless beneficial to society, then there is no purpose in excluding from its ambit those who can demonstrate that some unforeseeable intervening event produced the result, or those who can show that they lacked the physical 'opportunity to act otherwise,' whether on the extended *Kilbride* v. *Lake* definition or in the more limited sense of their being in a state of automatism."

It seems that "voluntariness" is a slippery concept which raises, but does not answer, all sorts of questions about culpability.

For further exploration of the utility of strict liability, see Chapter 3, p. 182.

3. OMISSIONS

P. R. Glazebrook, "Criminal Omissions: The Duty Requirement in Offences Against the Person" (1960) 76 L.Q.R. 386 at 387

"Although a failure to act may have as serious consequences as an act, and although any difference between acts and omissions is often denied, the distinction is deeply embedded in the law. This fact is no less inescapable because there is no precise test for distinguishing an act from an omission. Human conduct may often be described in either positive or negative terms, though usually one way rather than the other will appear more natural. ... But difficult cases there will be, and their very existence leads to the imposition of liability for omissions. A man is in his spring cart; the reins are not in his hands, but lying on the horse's back. While the horse trots down a hill a young child runs across the road in front of the cart, is knocked down and killed. Had the man held the reins he could have pulled the horse up. Did he kill the child by driving the cart recklessly, or by recklessly failing to drive the cart?"

The facts of the case cited in the last sentence are those of *R.* v. *Dalloway* (*post*, p. 36).

One distinction which is important is that between offences whose essence is an omission and those which, though usually committed by a positive act, can also be committed by omission. The former are *conduct* crimes while the latter are *result* crimes.

Fletcher, Rethinking Criminal Law (1978), p. 421

"Both 'acts' and 'omissions' can be brought under the general rubric of 'conduct'. . . . If there is a special problem in punishing omissions, we can learn what it is only by examining the contexts in which lawyers conventionally talk about 'omissions' or 'failing to act.' In fact, there is a radical cleavage between two forms of liability for 'omissions.' According to one type, the focus of liability is a breach of statutory obligation to act [appropriate English examples would be failure to display a vehicle tax disc, failure to report an accident]. . . . We shall call this the field of liabiity for 'breach of duty to act.' The contrasting field is the imposition of liability for failing to intervene, when necessary, to prevent the occurrence of a serious harm such as death or the destruction of property . . . we shall refer to this second type of liability as 'commission by omission.' The substantive difference [between the two] is that liability for breach of a statutory duty does not presuppose the occurrence of harm. . . . In contrast, the death of the victim is essential for committing homicide by omission. . . . The gravamen of liability for 'breach of duty' is the breach itself; for commission by omission, the occurrence of a particular result."

B. Hogan, "Omissions and the Duty Myth" in Criminal Law: Essays in Honour of J. C. Smith (1986, ed. P. Smith).

"[T]here is no way you can *cause* an event by doing nothing (or is it, more precisely, by not doing anything?) to prevent it . . .

But we immediately encounter the problem of what is meant by doing nothing, or, rather, not doing anything. The vexing problem of the distinction between act and omission. And 'although my difference between act and omission is often denied,' wrote Mr. Peter Glazebrook, 'the distinction is deeply embedded in the law.' True enough, but my own view is that the distinction is at best unhelpful and at worst misleading. It is, however, well entrenched, has found its way into the Draft Criminal Code Bill and, whatever I say, is likely to stay entrenched for some time yet. But that does not deter me from putting another view which I believe to be more logically attractive and even to express more accurately the common law. . . .

[I]t would be much more conducive to clarity of thought if we spoke of conduct and causation. If any proposition is self-evident (and, arguably, none is) it is that a person cannot be held to have caused an event which he did not cause. . . .

This is not to say that I am against liability for omissions. . . . There are of course numerous instances where Parliament (and a handful where the common law) has penalised omissions but what is noteworthy is that the defendant is penalised for the omission but not visited with liability for the consequences of that omission. Thus it is an offence under s.6(1) of the Maritime Conventions Act 1911, punishable with two years' imprisonment on indictment, for the master of a vessel to fail to render assistance to anyone in danger of being lost at sea. Fair enough, but it is to be noted that the master is made liable in respect of the omission; he is not, rightly enough, made liable in respect of any death or injury for any such death or injury is not of his doing. Exceptionally a statute may punish an omission as severely as the completed offence. A well-known example arises under the Road Traffic Act 1972, as amended, under which the punishment for a failure to provide a specimen is the same as for driving with an excessive blood-alcohol concentration. The driver is, however, convicted and punished in respect of the omission; he is not convicted and punished for the separate offence of driving etc. since this has not been proved. In these circumstances it is entirely acceptable to punish the motorist for his omission as severely as for the driving offence but it would be wrong to convict him for the driving offence and unnecessarily grotesque to deem him to have driven over the prescribed limit. ...

[I]n no sense am I against liability for omissions. I would ask only two conditions of a law punishing omissions. One is that it be clearly articulated and the other is that it seeks to punish the defendant for his dereliction and does not artificially treat him as a cause of the event he has not brought about by his conduct."

While Hogan's arguments are persuasive they do not yet represent the law which still speaks in terms of duties. Accordingly, Fletcher's two-fold classification will be used as a framework for considering the cases in this area.

i. Breach of Duty to Act

Note

Williams' T.C.L., p. 148 states: "a crime can be committed by omission, but there can be no omission in law in the absence of a duty to act. The reason is obvious. If there is an act, someone acts; but if there is an omission, everyone (in a sense) omits. We omit to do everything in the world that is not done. Only those of us omit in law who are under a duty to act.

When a statute expressly or impliedly creates an offence of omission, it points out the person under the duty by the wording of the offence."

The common law rarely imposed liability purely for omissions; an example was misprison of felony. Occasionally an indictment has been found to lie at common law for neglect of a duty imposed by common law or statute; see the following case.

R. v. Dytham
[1979] 3 All E.R. 641
Court of Appeal

The defendant, a police constable, was on duty in uniform near a club when a man was ejected from the club and kicked to death by a "bouncer." D. took no steps to intervene and drove off. He appealed against conviction for misconduct whilst acting as an officer of justice.

LORD WIDGERY C.J.: ... [T]he argument ... ran deep into constitutional and jurisprudential history. The effect of it was that not every failure to discharge a duty which devolved on a person as the holder of a public office gave rise to the common law offence of misconduct in that office. As counsel for the appellant put it, non-feasance was not enough. There must be a malfeasance or at least a misfeasance involving an element of corruption. In support of this contention a number of cases were cited from 18th and 19th century reports. It is the fact that in nearly all of them the misconduct asserted involved some corrupt taint; but this appears to have been an accident of circumstances and not a necessary incident of the offence. Misconduct in a public office is more vividly exhibited where dishonesty is revealed as part of the dereliction of duty. Indeed in some cases the conduct impugned cannot be shown to have been misconduct unless it was done with a corrupt or oblique motive. ...

[I]n Stephen's Digest of the Criminal Law are to be found these words:

"Every public officer commits a misdemeanour who wilfully neglects to perform any duty which he is bound either by common law or by statute to perform provided that the discharge of such duty is not attended with greater danger than a man of ordinary firmness and activity may be expected to encounter."

In support of this proposition *R.* v. *Wyat* (1705) 1 Salk. 380 is cited as well as *R.* v. *Bembridge* (1783) 3 Doug.K.B. 327, a judgment of Lord Mansfield. The neglect must be wilful and not merely inadvertent; and it must be culpable in the sense that it is without reasonable excuse or justification.

In the present case it was not suggested that the appellant could not have summoned or sought assistance to help the victim or to arrest his assailants. The charge as framed left this answer open to him. Not surprisingly he did not seek to avail himself of it, for the facts spoke strongly against any such answer. The allegation made was not of mere non-feasance but of deliberate failure and wilful neglect. This involves an element of culpability which is not restricted to corruption or dishonesty but which must be of such a degree that the misconduct impugned is calculated to injure the public interest so as to call for condemnation and punishment. Whether such a situation is revealed by the evidence is a matter that a jury has to decide.

Appeal dismissed

Question

Did the officer's failure to act cause the death of the victim of the bouncer's assault?

ii. Commission by Omission

Note

An alternative heading would be *"liability for failing to intervene."* Offences are usually worded in terms requiring active conduct; can liability arise from causing the prohibited result by omitting to act? It is generally recognised that the attitude adopted by the common law is well summarised in the passage below.

Lord Macaulay's Works (ed. Lady Trevelyan), Vol. VII, p. 497

"It is, indeed, most highly desirable that men should not merely abstain from doing harm to their neighbours, but should render active services to their neighbours. In general, however, the penal law must content itself with keeping men from doing positive harm, and must leave to public opinion, and to the teachers of morality and religion, the office of furnishing men with motives for doing positive good. It is evident that to attempt to punish men by law for not rendering to others all the service which it is their duty to render to others would be preposterous.

We must grant impunity to the vast majority of those omissions which a benevolent morality would pronounce reprehensible, and must content ourselves with punishing such omissions only when they are distinguished from the rest by some circumstance which marks them out as peculiarly fit objects of penal legislation."

Not all offences are susceptible of commission by omission. Most of the cases concern murder or manslaughter although liability could arise in a similar way for causing grievous bodily harm under section 20 of the Offences Against the Person Act 1861.

Not all omissions give rise to liability; liability depends on there being a duty, recognised by the law, to act or intervene in the circumstances. There are four situations in which such duties have been recognised: duties arising out of contract, duties arising out of relationship, duties arising from care of the helpless and infirm, duty arising from creation of a dangerous situation.

(a) *Duty arising out of contract*

R. v. Pittwood
(1902) 19 T.L.R. 37
Taunton Assizes

The defendant was a gatekeeper on the Somerset and Dorset Railway. He had to keep the gate shut whenever a train was passing during the period 7 a.m. to 7 p.m. One afternoon the gate was open and a hay cart which was crossing the line was hit by a train. One man was killed and another was seriously injured. Witnesses testified that the road was an accommodation road and not a public road. The accused was charged with manslaughter.

WRIGHT J., without calling upon the prosecution, gave judgment. He said he was clearly of opinion that in this case there was gross and criminal negligence, as the man was paid to keep the gate shut and protect the public. In his opinion there were three grounds on which the verdict could be supported: (1) There might be cases of misfeasance and cases of mere nonfeasance. Here it was quite clear there was evidence of misfeasance as the prisoner directly contributed to the accident. (2) A man might incur criminal liability from a duty arising out of contract. The learned judge quoted in support of this *R.* v. *Nicholls* (1875) 13 Cox 75; *R.* v. *Elliott* (1889) 16 Cox 710; *R.* v. *Benge* (1865) 4 F. & F. 594; *R* v. *Hughes* (1857) Dears. & B. 248. The strongest case of all was, perhaps, *R.* v. *Instan*, [*post*, p. 23] and that case clearly governed the present charge. (3) With regard to the point that this was only an occupation road, he clearly held that it was not, as the company had assumed the liability of protecting the public whenever they crossed the road. ...

Verdict: Guilty

(b) *Duty arising out of relationship*

Note

The existence of close relationships can give rise to a duty to act, such as that owed by parents to their children or spouses to each other. There is little common law authority on the point although it is generally accepted that there is such a duty. Statute has largely intervened in the case of parents' duty to their children. For a case on wilful neglect under the Children and Young Persons Act 1933 see *Sheppard, post*, p. 132.

(c) *Duty arising from the assumption of care for the helpless and infirm*

R. v. Instan
[1893] 1 Q.B. 450
Court for Crown Cases Reserved

The defendant lived with her aunt who was 73 years old. The aunt was healthy until shortly before her death. During the last 12 days of her life she had gangrene in her leg and could not fend for herself, move about nor summon help. Only the defendant knew of this condition. She appeared not to have given her aunt any food nor did she seek medical or nursing aid. She was charged with manslaughter and convicted.

LORD COLERIDGE C.J.: We are all of opinion that this conviction must be affirmed. It would not be correct to say that every moral obligation involves a legal duty; but every legal duty is founded on a moral obligation. A legal common law duty is nothing else than the enforcing by law of that which is a moral obligation without legal enforcement. There can be no question in this case that it was the clear duty of the prisoner to impart to the deceased so much as was necessary to sustain life of the food which she from time to time took in, and which was paid for by the deceased's own money for the purpose of the maintenance of herself and the prisoner; it was only through the instrumentality of the prisoner that the deceased could get the food. There was, therefore, a common law duty imposed upon the prisoner which she did not discharge.
Nor can there be any question that the failure of the prisoner to discharge her legal duty at least accelerated the death of the deceased, if it did not actually cause it. There is no case directly in point; but it would be a slur upon and a discredit to the administration of justice in this country if there were any doubt as to the legal principle, or as to the present case being within it. The prisoner was under a moral obligation to the deceased from which arose a legal duty towards her; that legal duty the prisoner has wilfully and deliberately left unperformed, with the consequence that there has been an acceleration of the death of the deceased owing to the non-performance of that legal duty. It is unnecessary to say more than that upon the evidence this conviction was most properly arrived at.

Conviction affirmed

Note

Consider the two following cases in the light of the following extract from the judgment of Erle C.J., in *R. v. Charlotte Smith* (1865) 10 Cox 82, where a master was charged with the homicide of his servant by, amongst other things, neglecting to give her sufficient food or wholesome lodgings. "The law is undisputed that, if a person having the care or custody of another who is helpless, neglects to supply him with the necessaries of life and thereby causes or accelerates his death, it is a criminal offence. But the law is clear, that if a person having the exercise of free will, chooses to stay in a service where bad food and lodging is provided, and death is thereby caused, the master is not criminally liable."

R. v. William Smith
(1826) 2 C. & P. 449; 172 E.R. 203
Gloucester Assizes

The defendants were two brothers and a sister. They had lived with their mother and with a helpless idiot brother. The mother died and it was alleged that the idiot brother was neglected and suffered in health. The defendants were charged with assault and false imprisonment.

BURROUGH J.: I am clearly of opinion that on the facts proved there is no assault and no imprisonment in the eye of the law, and all the rest of the charge is nonfeasance. In the case of *Squires* and his wife for starving the apprentice, the husband was convicted, because it was his duty to maintain the apprentice, and the wife was acquitted, because there was no such obligation on her. I expected to have found in the will of the father that the defendants were bound, if they took the father's property, to maintain his brother; but, under the will, they are only bound to pay him £50 a year, and not bound to maintain him. William Smith appears to have been the owner of the house, and Thomas and Sarah were mere inmates of it, as their idiot brother might be; as to these latter, there could clearly be no legal obligation on them: and how can I tell the jury that either of the defendants had such a care of this unfortunate man as to make them criminally liable for omitting to attend to him. There is strong proof that there was some negligence; but my point is, that omission, without a duty, will not create an indictable offence. There is a deficiency of proof of the allegation of care, custody and control, which must be taken to be legal care, custody and control. Whether an indictment might be so framed, as to suit this case, I do not know; but on this indictment I am clearly of opinion that the defendants must be acquitted.

Verdict: Not guilty

R. v. Stone and Dobinson
[1977] 1 Q.B. 345
Court of Appeal

S, who was 67, partially deaf, nearly blind and of low intelligence, cohabited with D, aged 43, who was described as ineffectual and inadequate. Also living with them was S's mentally subnormal son. S's younger sister, F, came to live there in 1972, suffering from anorexia nervosa. She stayed in her room most of the time though she was known to creep down and cook herself something to eat when S and D went to the pub.

S and D attempted to find her doctor in spring 1975 though she refused to tell them his name. In July, D and a neighbour washed F who, by this time, was confined to bed and lying amidst her own excrement. The defendants were unable to use the telephone and a neighbour was unsuccessful in getting a local doctor to visit F No one was informed of F's condition, even though a social worker came to the house from time to time to visit S's son. F died in August. The pathologist's report suggested that she had been in need of urgent medical attention for days, if not weeks. S and D appealed against their convictions for manslaughter.

GEOFFREY LANE L.J.: There is no dispute, broadly speaking, as to the matters on which the jury must be satisfied before they can convict of manslaughter in circumstances such as the present. They are (1) that the defendant undertook the care of a person who by reason of age or infirmity was unable to care for himself; (2) that the defendant was grossly negligent in regard to his duty of care; (3) that by reason of such negligence the person died. . . .

[Counsel for the appellants] submitted that the evidence which the judge had suggested to the jury might support the assumption of a duty by the appellants does not, when examined, succeed in doing so. He suggests that the situation here is unlike any reported case. Fanny came to this house as a lodger. Largely, if not entirely due to her own eccentricity and failure to look after herself or feed herself properly, she became increasingly infirm and immobile and eventually unable to look after herself. Is it to be said, asks Mr. Coles rhetorically, that by the mere fact of becoming infirm and helpless in these circumstances she casts a duty on her brother and the appellant Dobinson. . . . ? The suggestion is that, heartless though it may seem, this is one of those situations where the appellants were entitled to do nothing; where no duty was cast upon them to help, any more than it is cast upon a man to rescue a stranger from drowning, however easy such a rescue might be.

. . . Whether Fanny was a lodger or not she was a blood relation of the appellant Stone; she was occupying a room in his house; the appellant Dobinson had undertaken the duty of trying to wash her, of taking such food to her as she required. There was ample evidence that each appellant was aware of the poor condition she was in by mid July. It was not disputed that no effort was made to summon an ambulance or the social services or the police. . . .

This was not a situation analogous to the drowning stranger. They did make efforts to care. They tried to get a doctor; they tried to discover the previous doctor. The appellant Dobinson helped with the washing and the provision of food. All these matters were put before the jury in terms which we find it impossible to fault. The jury were entitled to find that the duty had been assumed. They were entitled to conclude that once Fanny became helplessly infirm, as she had by July 19, the appellants were, in the circumstances, obliged either to summon help or else to care for Fanny themselves. . . .

Appeal dismissed

Questions

1. Can this case be distinguished from *R. v. William Smith, ante,* p. 24? Does the following statement of principle by Brett J. in *R. v. Nicholls* (1875) 13 Cox 75 help?

"If a grown up person chooses to undertake the charge of a human creature helpless either from infancy, simplicity, lunacy or other infirmity, he is bound to execute that charge without (at all events) *wicked* negligence."

2. Would Stone and Dobinson have been liable if F. was Stone's sister-in-law (*i.e.* his brother's wife)?

3. Would they have been liable if they had made no efforts to help at all?

4. Did Stone and Dobinson *cause* F.'s death? Farrier's Note at (1978) 41 M.L.R. 211, n. 6 raises the question whether the restrictive policy adopted in *Blaue, post,* p. 40 should apply where the causal conduct consists of an omission.

Note

Where a doctor is treating a patient there is no absolute obligation on him to prolong the life of the patient regardless of the circumstances; the question is what is in the best interests of the patient (see *Airedale NHS Trust* v. *Bland, The Times,* February 5, 1993). Treatment which artificially prolongs life will not be appropriate where it has no therapeutic purpose, which will be the case where it is futile because the patient is unconscious and has no prospect of any improvement in his condition. In such circumstances discontinuance of treatment, although an omission, will not be unlawful as it would not breach any duty owed by the doctor to the patient; there is no duty to continue life supporting treatment which is not in the patient's best interests. Similar principles apply when deciding whether to place a patient on life supporting treatment in the first place. In the instant case the House of Lords declared that it would not be unlawful for doctors to withdraw life supporting medical treatment, including artificial feeding through a nasogastric tube, from a patient in one of the Trust's hospitals who was in a persistent vegetative state due to injuries sustained four years previously in the Hillsborough Football Stadium disaster, as there was no prospect of recovery or any improvement in his condition.

(d) *Duty arising from creation of a dangerous situation*

R. v. Miller
[1983] 2 A.C. 161
House of Lords

M a vagrant who lived in an unoccupied house, awoke to find that a cigarette he had been smoking had set fire to the mattress on which he was lying. He did not attempt to extinguish the fire but moved to another room. The house caught fire. M was convicted of arson contrary to section 1 (1) and (3) of the Criminal Damage Act 1971. The Court of Appeal dismissed his appeal against conviction and he appealed to the House of Lords.

LORD DIPLOCK: [T]he Court of Appeal certified that the following question of law of general public importance was involved:

"Whether the actus reus of the offence of arson is present when a defendant accidentally starts a fire and thereafter, intending to destroy or damage property belonging to another or being reckless as to whether any such property would be destroyed or damaged, fails to take any steps to extinguish the fire or prevent damage to such property by that fire?"

The question speaks of "actus reus." This expression is derived from Coke's brocard in his *Institutes*, Part III (1797 ed.), c. 1 fo. 10: "et actus non facit reum, nisi mens sit rea," by converting, incorrectly, into an adjective the word "reus" which was there used correctly in the accusative case as a noun. As long ago as 1889 in *R. v. Tolson* (1889) 23 Q.B.D. 168, 185–187, Stephen J. when dealing with a statutory offence, as are your Lordships in the instant case, condemned the phrase as likely to mislead, though his criticism in that case was primarily directed to the use of the expression "mens rea." In the instant case, as the argument before this House has in my view demonstrated, it is the use of the expression "actus reus" that is liable to mislead, since it suggests that some positive act on the part of the accused is needed to make him guilty of a crime and that a failure or omission to act is insufficient to give rise to criminal liability unless some express provision in the statute that creates the offence so provides.

The first question to be answered where a completed crime of arson is charged is: "Did a physical act of the accused start the fire which spread and damaged property belonging to another (or did his act cause an existing fire, which he had not started but which would otherwise have burnt itself out harmlessly, to spread and damage property belonging to another)?" I have added the words in brackets for completeness. They do not arise in the instant case; in cases where they do, the accused, for the purposes of the analysis which follows, may be regarded as having started a fresh fire.

The first question is a pure question of causation; it is one of fact to be decided by the jury in a trial upon indictment. It should be answered "No" if, in relation to the fire during the period starting immediately before its ignition and ending with its extinction, the role of the accused was at no time more than that of a passive bystander. In such a case the subsequent questions to which I shall be turning would not arise. The conduct of the parabolical priest and Levite on the road to Jericho may have been indeed deplorable, but English law has not so far developed to the stage of treating it as criminal; and if it ever were to do so there would be difficulties in defining what should be the limits of the offence.

If on the other hand the question, which I now confine to: "Did a physical act of the accused start the fire which spread and damaged property belonging to another?" is answered "Yes," as it was by the jury in the instant case, then for the purpose of the further questions the answers to which are determinative of his guilt of the offence of arson, the conduct of the accused, throughout the period from immediately before the moment of ignition to the completion of the damage to the property by the fire, is relevant; so is his state of mind throughout that period.

Since arson is a result-crime the period may be considerable, and during it the conduct of the accused that is causative of the result may consist not only of his doing physical acts which cause the fire to start or spread but also of his failing to take measures that lie within his power to counteract the danger that he has himself created. And if his conduct, active or passive, varies in the course of the period, so may his state of mind at the time of each piece of conduct. If at the time of any particular piece of conduct by the accused that is causative of the result, the state of mind that actuates his conduct falls within the description of one or other of the states of mind that are made a necessary ingredient of the offence of arson by section 1 (1) of the Criminal Damage Act 1971 (*i.e.* intending to damage property belonging to another or being reckless as to whether such property would be damaged) I know of no principle of English criminal law that would prevent his being guilty of the offence created by that subsection. Likewise I see no rational ground for excluding from conduct capable of giving rise to criminal liability, conduct which consists of failing to take measures that lie within one's power to counteract a danger that one has oneself created, if at the time of such conduct one's state of mind is such as constitutes a necessary ingredient of the offence. I venture to think that the habit of lawyers to talk of "actus reus," suggestive as it is of action rather than inaction, is responsible for any erroneous notion that failure to act cannot give rise to criminal liability in English law.

No one has been bold enough to suggest that if, in the instant case, the accused had been aware at the time that he dropped the cigarette that it would probably set fire to his mattress and yet had taken no steps to extinguish it he would not have been guilty of the offence of arson, since he would have damaged property of another being reckless as to whether any such property would be damaged.

I cannot see any good reason why, so far as liability under criminal law is concerned, it should matter at what point of time before the resultant damage is complete a person becomes aware that he has done a physical act which, whether or not he appreciated that it would at the time when he did it, does in fact create a risk that property of another will be damaged; provided that, at the moment of awareness, it lies within his power to take steps, either himself or by calling for the assistance of the fire brigade if this be necessary, to prevent or minimise the damage to the property at risk.

My Lords, in the instant case the prosecution did not rely upon the state of mind of the accused as being reckless during that part of his conduct that consisted of his lighting and smoking a cigarette while lying on his mattress and falling asleep without extinguishing it. So the jury were not invited to make any finding as to this. What the prosecution did rely upon as being reckless was his state of mind during that part of his conduct after he awoke to find that he had set his mattress on fire and that it was smouldering, but did not then take any steps either to try to extinguish it himself or to send for the fire brigade, but simply went into the other room to resume his slumbers, leaving the fire from the already smouldering mattress to spread and to damage that part of the house in which the mattress was.

The recorder, in his lucid summing up to the jury (they took 22 minutes only to reach their verdict) told them that the accused having by his own act started a fire in the mattress which, when he became aware of its existence, presented an obvious risk of damaging the house, became under a duty to take some action to put it out. The Court of Appeal upheld the conviction, but their ratio decidendi appears to be somewhat different from that of the recorder. As I understand the judgment, in effect it treats the whole course of conduct of the accused, from the moment at which he fell asleep and dropped the cigarette on to the mattress until the time the damage to the house by fire was complete, as a continuous act of the accused, and holds that it is sufficient to constitute the statutory offence of arson if at any stage in that course of conduct the state of mind of the accused, when he fails to try to prevent or minimise the damage which will result from his initial act, although it lies within his power to do so, is that of being reckless as to whether property belonging to another would be damaged.

My Lords, these alternative ways of analysing the legal theory that justifies a decision which has received nothing but commendation for its accord with commonsense and justice, have, since the publication of the judgment of the Court of Appeal in the instant case, provoked academic controversy. Each theory has distinguished support. Professor J. C. Smith espouses the "duty theory"; Professor Glanville Williams who, after the decision of the Divisional Court in *Fagan* v. *Metropolitan Police Commissioner* (*post*, p. 582) appears to have been attracted by the duty theory, now prefers that of the continuous act. When applied to cases where a person has unknowingly done an act which sets in train events that, when he becomes aware of them, present an obvious risk that property belonging to another will be damaged, both theories lead to an identical result; and since what your Lordships are concerned with is to give guidance to trial judges in their task of summing up to juries, I would for this purpose adopt the duty theory as being the easier to explain to a jury; though I would commend the use of the word "responsibility," rather than "duty" which is more appropriate to civil than to criminal law, since it suggests an obligation owed to another person, *i.e.* the person to whom the endangered property belongs, whereas a criminal statute defines combinations of conduct and state of mind which render a person liable to punishment by the state itself.

So, while deprecating the use of the expression "actus reus" in the certified question, I would answer that question "Yes" and would dismiss the appeal.

Appeal dismissed

Questions

1. Was M found guilty because he had fallen asleep while smoking a cigarette or because, when he awoke, he failed to take reasonable steps to put out the fire caused by his lighted cigarette?

2. The facts in the case involved damage to property; would M have been guilty of manslaughter if a fellow squatter sharing the mattress with him had died as a result of asphyxiation?

3. Would M have been liable for arson/manslaughter if the fire had been caused by an electrical fault? Would it make any difference if the fellow squatter was his eight-year-old son?

4. What is the general principle for which *Miller* is authority?

B. Hogan "Omissions and a Duty Myth" in Criminal Law: Essays in Honour of J. C. Smith (1986, ed. P. Smith)

"*R.* v. *Miller* holds, and with respect rightly, that one who inadvertently (or otherwise faultlessly, presumably) starts a chain of events causing harm may be properly held liable if, having become aware that he was the cause, he fails to take steps reasonably available to him to prevent or minimise the damage that will ensue. ...

Miller is interesting. One analysis of the case is to say that when the defendant became aware that he had caused (albeit inadvertently) the fire he was under a duty to take steps reasonably available to him to prevent or minimise further harm. Lord Diplock, with whom all their lordships agreed, expressed some support for the duty theory as having the merit of being easier to explain to the jury but then added that he would prefer 'responsibility' instead of duty. He thought that 'duty' was:

" ... more appropriate to civil than to criminal law since it suggests an obligation owed to another person, *i.e.* the person to whom the endangered property belongs, whereas a criminal statute defines combinations of conduct and states of mind which render a person liable to punishment by the state itself."

Quite what Lord Diplock is getting at here is not perhaps as clear as crystal, but two things may be said. The first is that he was right to say, if this is what he was saying, that there is no general duty to intervene to prevent or minimise harm to another's property. The second is, in the context of his speech read as a whole, that, having addressed his mind to the question whether it could be said that the defendant caused the fire and inevitably concluding that he did, he sees that it can make no sensible difference that mens rea was formed after the first event in the chain of events leading to the damage. Nor, with respect, can I. The defendant's causal contribution did not end when he inadvertently dropped the lighted cigarette. The fire was causally attributable to him from start to finish; he can hardly be heard sensibly to say that the only damage he caused was the scorch hole in the mattress. When he became aware that steps reasonably available to him would prevent further harm he was still causing the damage. The only difference between the damage caused before and after his awareness was that he was not criminally liable for the damage occurring before his awareness since he lacked mens rea but was liable for the damage he caused after his awareness since he now had mens rea. . . .

So in *R. v. Pittwood* it becomes fruitless to debate whether leaving open the level-crossing gates is to be characterised as omission or commission. The court characterised the conduct as misfeasance and in so doing, though the report is brief, appears to have looked at the totality of the defendant's conduct. And looking at the totality of his conduct it can easily be said that he created a situation of danger which caused harm to the victim.

It is true that in *R. v. Pittwood* the court also said that a duty might arise out of a contract and the cases on 'omissions' are certainly littered with references to 'duty.' In my view these references to duty are unhelpful. The issue in *R. v. Pittwood* was simply whether the defendant had *caused* the deaths of the victims with the relevant mens rea. Most assuredly he had no duty to take employment as a level-crossing keeper but once he did so he must not perform the office (in the same way as one must not drive a car or handle a gun) in such a way as to cause harm to others. No one has a duty to buy a car or a gun, or to obtain employment as a level-crossing keeper, or even to walk down the road to post a letter. But if they choose to do any of these things they must so conduct themselves so as not to cause harm, and if their conduct causes harm with the relevant mens rea they will fall foul of the criminal law. There is no need to complicate such cases by the search for duty.

There is perhaps a stronger case for imputing the duty concept in connection with domestic and similar relationships. So in *R. v. Instan* where the niece failed to summon medical assistance for her aunt who died of gangrene, the court talks of a duty founded in moral obligation. In law, of course, and now as much as then, the niece had no duty whatever to look after her aunt. Had she been paying a casual visit to her aunt, noticed that her aunt would die without prompt medical attention, but had left without taking any measures of assistance then surely the case would have been decided differently. What was determinative in *R. v. Instan* was that the niece had taken it upon herself to look after her aunt. She had no duty to do so, any more than the defendant in *R. v. Pittwood* had any duty to take the job of level-crossing keeper, but having undertaken a certain task (and it is essentially on all fours with driving a car or using a gun or walking down the road to post a letter) it must be performed properly. If it is performed improperly and, with the relevant mens rea, causes harm to another, then criminal liability follows.

I see nothing wrong with the principle in *R. v. Stone* which I take to be that if one chooses to assume the care and control of another then the self-imposed responsibility must be carried out with reasonable care and skill and that liability for manslaughter (or even murder) may be incurred if that responsibility is discharged in a grossly negligent (now reckless) manner. What is disturbing about *R. v. Stone* is that the evidence hardly supported the inference that these two elderly incompetents had taken it upon themselves to discharge the onerous task of looking after the sister. Did they really *kill* the sister?

I am unhappy about the duty concept in the context of 'omission.' It is likely to mislead a jury into thinking of duties in other than legal terms; into a consideration of the immorality of particular conduct; into convicting the defendant merely for his callousness. Better to put the issue as simply one of causation. For this purpose it is proper to look not merely at the last link in the causal chain, be it commission or omission, but all the relevant conduct of the defendant. The questions then become whether the *conduct* of the defendant caused the actus reus and whether he did so with mens rea. To introduce an imprecise, ill-defined concept of "duty" into the equation only serves to confuse the issue."

Draft Criminal Code Bill

Offences of omission and situational offences

16. For the purposes of an offence which consists wholly or in part of an omission, state of affairs or occurrence, references in this Act to an 'act' shall, where the context permits, be read as including references to the omission, state of affairs or occurrence by reason of which a person may be guilty of the offence, and references to a person's acting or doing an act shall be construed accordingly.

Causation

17.—(1) Subject to subsections (2) and (3), a person causes a result which is an element of an offence when—

(a) he does an act which makes a more than negligible contribution to its occurrence; or

(b) he omits to do an act which might prevent its occurrence and which he is under a duty to do according to the law relating to the offence.

Notes

1. Clause 16 is an interpretation clause which instructs the user of the Code *inter alia* that the requirement of proof of an "act" in Code offences may be satisfied "where the context permits" with proof of an omission. This will be appropriate where there is a recognised duty to act. The Code does not specify when there is such a duty relying on the situations which have already been recognised by the courts. This hardly makes for clarity in the law.

2. Clause 17(1)(b) represents a radical change in the law of causation. It seems that as it is difficult to establish that a

consequence has occurred as the result of an omission, the Law
Commission is proposing to make it easier to establish causation
(or, to be precise, their version of causation) in the case of
omissions. Causation will be established where the prosecution
prove that the consequence might not have occurred had D acted
in performance of his duty to act. By contrast, where an offence of
commission is involved, the prosecution must prove that the
consequence would not have occurred "but for" D's act. This
appears to make criminal liability more stringent in the case of
those who omit to act. The Law Commission provides the
following illustration of the operation of clause 17(1)(b)—

> 17(ii)   D, E's mistress, lives with E and P. E's child by his wife. While E is
> away P falls seriously ill. D, wishing P to die, fails to call a doctor. P
> dies. P's life might have been prolonged by medical attention. If D was
> under a duty to obtain medical attention for P she is guilty of murder.
> She has caused P's death intending to cause death."

Questions

1. Is D guilty of murder because of the possibility that medical
assistance might have prolonged P's life?

2. If the expert medical evidence was to the effect that swift
medical attention might have prolonged P's life for an hour, will D
be liable for murder?

3. In the above example if, instead of failing to call a doctor D
had done so but the doctor was delayed and P was dead on his
arrival, what was the cause of P's death? How does this differ from
the situation where D fails to call a doctor? Would D's culpability
not be adequately reflected in a conviction under section 1 of the
Children and Young Persons Act 1933 of wilfully neglecting a child
in a manner likely to cause injury to his health? (See *Sheppard, post,*
p. 132).

4. Is it not the case that the current law imposing liability for
omissions in respect of "result crimes" represents a policy decision
whereby the existence of a duty combined with a failure to prevent
a consequence occurring is treated as equivalent to causing that
consequence?

Draft Criminal Code Bill

Supervening fault

23. Where it is an offence to be at fault in causing a result, a person who
lacks the fault required when he does an act that causes or may cause the
result nevertheless commits the offence if—

(a)   he becomes aware that he has done the act and that the result has
occurred and may continue, or may occur; and

(b)   with the fault required, he fails to do what he can reasonably be
expected to do that might prevent the result continuing or
occurring; and

(c)   the result continues or occurs.

Note

This clause restates and generalises the principle applied by the House of Lords in *Miller*. The clause also covers the facts of *Fagan* v. *Metropolitan Police Commissioner, post,* p. 582.

4. CAUSATION

Brett and Waller, Criminal Law Text and Cases (4th ed., 1978), p. 145

"Many philosophers have devoted great effort to elucidating the notion of causation. In particular, Hume and Mill have made great contributions in this field of enquiry, and from time to time one finds echoes of or borrowings from their work in judgments and legal writings. It is fair to say, however, that their views (and those of other philosophers also) are concerned with causal statements of general application, such as scientific laws. They are thus of comparatively slight value to lawyers, who are concerned with isolated events in the past which cannot be reproduced in the present or future. . . .

For our purposes it is enough to say that when the law treats a particular act or omission as the cause of an event it makes a choice. It does so for the purpose of attributing the responsibility for that event to a particular person, or of denying that he is responsible for it.

This, however, leaves unanswered the question: how is the choice made? The currently fashionable answer (in many other legal contexts as well as in this) is that the judges resort to considerations of 'policy.' But that tells us very little, and it may indeed be positively misleading. For it conjures up a picture of the judge consciously considering various possible choices and selecting what he thinks to be the 'best' one ('best' here having some rather vague reference to notions of supposed social utility). And it is reasonably clear that this is not what the judge does, either consciously or (as some would argue) unconsciously.

We think that a more accurate way of answering the question is to say that the judges make use of the common sense notions of the ordinary man (Hart and Honoré, in their *Causation in the Law* (1959), adopt broadly the same view). Nor indeed, is there any good reason why they should not do so. The ordinary common sense notions of causation and responsibility can be shown to have, in most respects, a sound moral basis. . . .

The cases and books make use of a number of phrases in the attempt to clarify these common sense notions. Many of these, however, do little more than state a conclusion which has been reached rather than the reasons for reaching it—as when it is said that the law looks to 'proximate' causes as opposed to 'remote' causes, the notions of proximity and remoteness being taken as self-explanatory, likewise it is sometimes said that the law seeks for the 'primary' cause, or even the 'legal' cause, or that it seeks for the *causa causans* (causing, or operative cause)."

Williams (T.C.L., pp. 379–382) elucidates the meaning of some of these phrases:

"A convenient English equivalent of the term causation *sine qua non* is but-for causation (properly speaking, but-for . . . not causation). For a factor to be a but-for cause, one must be able to say that *but for* the occurrence of the antecedent factor the event would *not* have happened. . . .

When causation is in issue, the defendant's act (or omission) must be shown to be not only a but-for cause but also an imputable or legal cause of the consequence. Imputable causes are *some* of the but-for causes. In other words, the defendant's act, being a but-for cause, must be sufficiently closely connected with the consequence to involve him in responsibility. The lawyer is interested in the causal parentage of events, not in their causal ancestry. ...

Several attempts have been made to find a suitable name for this second notion of cause. To call it the 'direct' or 'proximate' cause (as is often done) is misleading, because several stages may intervene between the so-called direct cause and the effect. D may send poisoned chocolates to V, who lives at the other side of the world; if V eats the chocolates and dies, the law will certainly regard D as responsible for the death, though his act was far removed in space and considerably removed in time from its effect. To call D's act the 'effective' cause is unhelpful because every cause must by definition be effective—if an act is not effective to produce a given result, it is not a cause of it. 'Substantial' is a less misleading adjective, but it is not illuminating.

Sometimes (looking at the situation backwards instead of forwards) imputable causation is stated in terms of 'remoteness of consequence.' To say that a particular consequence is 'too remote' is only another way of saying that the defendant's act (or omission) is not an imputable cause.

... When one has settled the question of but-for causation, the further test to be applied to the but-for cause in order to qualify it for legal recognition is not a test of causation but a moral reaction. The question is whether the result can fairly be said to be imputable to the defendant. If the term 'cause' must be used, it can best be distinguished as the 'imputable' or 'responsible' or 'blamable' cause, to indicate the value-judgment involved. The word 'imputable' is here chosen as best representing the idea. Whereas the but-for cause can generally be demonstrated scientifically, no experiment can be devised to show that one of a number of concurring but-for causes is more substantial or important than another, or that one person who is involved in the causal chain is more blameworthy than another."

The remainder of the discussion of causation is divided as follows:

    i.   *Sine qua non*
    ii. Imputability
            (a) Fright and flight
            (b) Weak or intractable victims
            (c) Intervening causes
    iii. An alternative approach

i. Sine qua non

R. v. Cato
[1976] 1 W.L.R. 110
Court of Appeal

C and his victim F, were friends. F invited C to have a "fix" of his heroin. Each filled his own syringe and then asked the other to inject it into him. This procedure was repeated several times during one night.

F died the next morning. One of the grounds on which C appealed against his conviction for manslaughter concerned causation.

LORD WIDGERY C.J.: ... It seems to us that the first and most important single factor to which counsel for the appellant directed our attention was concerned with causation, that is to say with the link alleged to exist between the injection of heroin and the death of Farmer. ...

He pointed out that the medical evidence did not at any point say "This morphine killed Farmer"; the actual link of that kind was not present. The witnesses were hesitant to express such a view and often recoiled from it, saying it was not for them to state the cause of death. It is perfectly true ... that the expert evidence did not in positive terms provide a link, but it was never intended to. The expert witnesses here spoke to factual situations, and the conclusions and deductions therefrom were for the jury. The first question was: was there sufficient evidence upon which the jury could conclude, as they must have concluded, that adequate causation was present?

When one looks at the evidence it is important to realise that no other cause of Farmer's death was supplied. Dr. Robinson thought that there might have been another drug, and she said at one stage it might have been cocaine, but there was never any cocaine found in the body. The only cause of death actually supplied by the evidence was morphine. No natural disease was present and no other drug was identified. Furthermore, the symptoms and the external appearance of the body, and the nature of the final terminal cause, was consistent with poison by the administration of heroin in the way which was described. ...

Of course behind this whole question of the sufficiency of evidence of causation is the fact that it was not necessary for the prosecution to prove that the heroin was the only cause. As a matter of law, it was sufficient if the prosecution could establish that it was *a* cause, provided it was a cause outside the de minimis range, and effectively bearing upon the acceleration of the moment of the victim's death. When one has that in mind it is, we think, really possible to say that if the jury had been directed to look for heroin as a cause, not de minimis but a cause of substance, and they came back with a verdict of not guilty, the verdict could really be described as a perverse one. The whole background of the evidence was the other way and there certainly was ample evidence, given a proper direction, upon which a charge of manslaughter could be supported.

But what about the proper direction? [the jury had been asked: "Did [the] injection of heroin by [the appellant] cause, contribute to or accelerate the death of Farmer?"] It will be noted that in none of the versions which I have quoted of the judge's direction on this point, nor in any of those which I have not quoted which appear in the summing up, is there any reference to it being necessary for the cause to be a substantial one. It is said in clear terms ... that the jury can consider whether the administration of the heroin was a cause or contributed to or accelerated the death, and in precise terms the word "contributed" is not qualified to show that a substantial contribution is required. ...

Before pursuing that, it is worth reminding oneself that some of the more recent dicta in the textbooks about this point do not support as strongly as was once the case the theory that the contribution must be substantial. In Smith and Hogan, *Criminal Law*, 3rd ed. (1973), p. 217 there is this rather interesting extract:

"It is commonly said by judges and writers that, while the accused's act need not be the sole cause of the death, it must be a substantial one.

This appears to mean only that a minute contribution to the cause of death will not entail responsibility. It may therefore be misleading to direct a jury that D is not liable unless his conduct was a 'substantial' cause. Killing is merely an acceleration of death and factors which produce a very trivial acceleration will be ignored."

Whether that be so or not, and we do not propose to give that passage the court's blessing today at all events, if one looks at the circumstances of the present case with any real sense of reality, we think there can be no doubt that when the judge was talking about contribution the jury knew perfectly well that he was talking about something more than the mere de minimis contribution. We have given this point particular care in our consideration of the case because it worried us to some extent originally, but we do feel in the end, having looked at all the circumstances, that there could not have been any question in this case of the jury making the mistake of thinking that the contribution would suffice if it were de minimis. ...

Appeal dismissed

Model Penal Code

"S.2.03(1) Conduct is the cause of a result when:

(a) it is an antecedent but for which the result in question would not have occurred; and

(b) the relationship between the conduct and result satisfies any additional causal requirements imposed by the Code or by the law defining the offence."

ii. Imputability

The *Model Penal Code* continues:

"S.2.03(2) When purposely or knowingly causing a particular result is an element of an offence, the element is not established if the actual result is not within the purpose or the contemplation of the actor unless: ...

(b) the actual result involves the same kind of injury or harm as that designed or contemplated and is not too remote or accidental in its occurrence to have a just bearing on the actor's liability or on the gravity of his offence."

S.2.03(3) contains a similar provision "when recklessly or negligently causing a particular result is an element of an offence."

R. v. Dalloway
(1847) 2 Cox 273
Stafford Assizes

A child ran in front of the defendant's cart and was killed. The reins were not in the defendant's hands but loose on the horse's back.

ERLE J., in summing up to the jury, directed them that a party neglecting an ordinary caution, and, by reason of that neglect, causing the death of another, is guilty of manslaughter; that if the prisoner had reins, and by using the reins could have saved the child, he was guilty of manslaughter;

but that if they thought he could not have saved the child by pulling the reins, or otherwise by their assistance, they must acquit him.

Not guilty

Note

This case could also be seen as illustrating the but-for principle. The difficulty here is that the presence of the cart *was* a *sine qua non* of the child's death but D's negligent driving was not.

Problems can also arise where D's act was not the direct cause of death (where, for example, fright exacerbates a medical condition or V dies escaping from D), or where D's act does not cause instantaneous death and a complex chain of causation develops (through, for example, negligent medical care).

(a) *Fright and flight*

Note

Death may ensue as a result of fright caused by D bringing about a physiological reaction in V, such as a heart attack, or it may occur where V, because he is frightened by D, seeks to flee from him and dies in the process. In *Watson* [1989] 2 All E.R. 865 the Court of Appeal accepted that a jury, properly directed, could have found that the appellants' acts of burgling V's house, wakening and verbally abusing him, V being a frail 87-year-old, caused his death when he died ninety minutes later from a heart attack. See further Busuttil and McCall Smith, "Fright, Stress and Homicide" (1990) 54 J. Crim. L. 257.

R. v. Hayward
(1908) 21 Cox 692
Maidstone Assizes

The defendant returned home in a state of violent excitement. He was heard to express the intention of "giving his wife something" when she came in. When she did arrive there were sounds of an altercation and shortly afterwards the woman ran from the house into the road, closely followed by the defendant. She fell into the roadway and the accused kicked her on the left arm. She died and a medical examination showed that the bruise on her arm, caused by the kick, was not the cause of death. The deceased woman was in good health apart from a persistent thyrus gland. Medical evidence was given that a person subject to this condition might die from a combination of fright or strong emotion and physical exertion. The defendant was charged with manslaughter.

RIDLEY J.: . . . directed the jury that if they believed the witnesses there was a sufficient chain of evidence to support a conviction of manslaughter. He pointed out that no proof of actual physical violence was necessary, but that death from fright alone, caused by an illegal act, such as threats of violence, would be sufficient. The abnormal state of the deceased's health did not affect the question whether the prisoner knew or did not know of it if it were proved to the satisfaction of the jury that the death was accelerated by the prisoner's illegal act.

Verdict: Guilty

R. v. Curley
(1909) 2 Cr.App.R. 109
Court of Criminal Appeal

The appellant had been indicted for murder and convicted of manslaughter. He was heard to be quarrelling with the woman with whom he lived. She was heard to cry from her bedroom "Let me out," "murder" and "police." The appellant was heard to go into the room, the window was thrown up. It appeared that the woman jumped from the window.

JELF J.: Appellant told the officer, "I ran at her to hit her. I didn't quite touch her. Out she jumped." On that statement a verdict of murder might well have been returned, but it was mercifully reduced to one of manslaughter. The jumping out of the window was contributed to by the appellant's unlawful act. ...

Appeal dismissed

R. v. Mackie
(1973) 57 Cr.App.R. 453
Court of Appeal

M was convicted of the manslaughter of a boy aged three whom he was looking after. It was alleged that the boy fell downstairs while running away in fear of being ill-treated.

STEPHENSON L.J. read the judgment of the court:

Where the injuries are not fatal, the attempt to escape must be the natural consequence of the assault charged, not something which could not be expected, but something which any reasonable and responsible man in the assailant's shoes would have foreseen. Where the injuries are fatal, the attempt must be the natural consequence of an unlawful act and that unlawful act "must be such as all sober and reasonable people would inevitably recognise must subject the other person to, at least, the risk of some harm resulting therefrom, albeit not serious harm": *Church* (*post*, p. 000) ...

In this case there were two complications: (1) the victim was a child of three and regard must be had to his age in considering whether his reaction was well-founded or well-grounded on an apprehension of immediate violence (in the language of the old cases appropriate to adults) and therefore reasonably to be expected. (2) This defendant was in the position of a parent, which may have entitled him to "assault" the child by smacking or threatening him without breaking the law, and it was not every act which might be expected to cause slight harm to the boy that would be unlawful for a man in his parental position; he might have to do some act in the interests of the boy's own safety, for instance, to keep him away from the upstairs window. The purpose of correcting the child—and perhaps the sole justification for correcting a young child—is to deter; how else can the kind parent of a nervous child save it from danger than by in some degree hurting or frightening it? How far was it reasonable, and therefore lawful, for the appellant to go in punishing this child was one of the questions the jury had to decide. Whether the boy "over-reacted" (as Mr. Back put it) in a way which the appellant could not reasonably be expected to have foreseen was another.

... At the end of the summing-up the judge came back to these questions in suggesting what the vital points might be: 'First, was the boy in fear of Mackie? Secondly, did that cause him to try to escape? Thirdly, if he was in fear, was that fear well-founded? If it was well-founded, was it caused by the unlawful conduct of the accused, that is, by conduct for which there was no lawful excuse even on the part of a man in the position of a father. ...

We think that the judge directed the jury clearly and correctly as to the law laid down in the cases. ...

Appeal dismissed

Note

This approach to "manslaughter by 'flight' " was confirmed by the Privy Council in *D.P.P.* v. *Daley* [1979] 2 W.L.R. 239. Lord Keith of Kinkel summarised it thus:

"[T]he essential ingredients of the prosecution's proof of a charge of manslaughter, laid upon the basis that a person has sustained fatal injuries while trying to escape from assault ... are: (1) that the victim immediately before he sustained the injuries was in fear of being hurt physically; (2) that this fear was such that it caused him to try to escape; (3) that whilst he was trying to escape, and because he was trying to escape he met his death; (4) that his fear of being hurt there and then was reasonable and was caused by the conduct of the defendant; (5) that the defendant's conduct which caused the fear was unlawful; and (6) that his conduct was such as any sober and reasonable person would recognise as likely to subject the victim to at least the risk of some harm resulting from it, albeit not a serious harm. Their Lordships have to observe that it is unnecessary to prove the defendant's knowledge that his conduct was unlawful."

Daley was further considered in *Williams and Davis* [1992] 1 W.L.R. 380. V was a hitch-hiker who had been picked up by a car driven by W in which D was also a passenger. After about five miles, while the car was travelling at 30 miles per hour, V jumped from the car and died from head injuries. It appeared that he had been threatened if he did not hand over his money. The Court of Appeal quashed W's convictions for manslaughter and robbery because of misdirections on evidence, and quashed D's convictions as it regarded a direction based on *Daley* as insufficient where there was a real issue as to causation. Stuart-Smith L.J., after referring to the six ingredients in *Daley*, stated:

"Where the unlawful act was a battery, there was no difficulty with the second ingredient. However, where the unlawful act was merely a threat unaccompanied and not preceded by actual violence, the position might be more difficult. The nature of the threat was important in considering both the foreseeability of harm to the victim from the threat and the question whether the deceased's conduct was proportionate to the threat, that is to say that it was within the ambit of reasonableness and not so daft as to make it his own voluntary act which broke the chain of causation. The jury should consider two questions: first whether it was reasonably foreseeable that some harm, albeit not serious harm, was likely to result from the threat itself; and second, whether the deceased's reaction in jumping from the moving car was within the range of responses which might be expected from a victim placed in his situation. The jury should bear in mind any particular characteristic of the victim and the fact that in the agony of the moment he might act without thought and deliberation."

(b) *Weak or intractable victims*

It is a general rule of criminal liability that defendants take their victims as they find them. Thus in *R. v. Plummer* (1844) 1 C. & K. 600, where a husband had denied shelter to his wife who died soon afterwards, Gurney B. said, "It does not appear in evidence what her disease was, or that she was afflicted with that mortal illness under which she laboured, or that she was suffering from diarrhoea which caused her death; but he was, nevertheless, informed that she was very ill, and had no shelter. If you should be of opinion that her death was caused or accelerated by his conduct you will say that he is guilty (of manslaughter)." And in *R. v. Martin* (1832) 5 C. & P. 128 Parke J. said, "It is said, that the deceased was in a bad state of health; but that is perfectly immaterial, as, if the prisoner was so unfortunate as to accelerate her death, he must answer for it." This principle applies where, for religious or other reasons, the victim refuses medical help.

R. v. Blaue
[1975] 1 W.L.R. 1411
Court of Appeal

The appellant stabbed a woman; the wound penetrated her lung. At the hospital she was told that a blood transfusion and surgery were necessary to save her life. She refused to have a transfusion as it was contrary to her beliefs as a Jehovah's Witness. She died the next day. Medical evidence indicated that she would not have died had she accepted the medical treatment.

LAWTON L.J.: . . . Towards the end of the trial and before the summing up started counsel on both sides made submissions as to how the case should be put to the jury. Counsel then appearing for the defendant invited the judge to direct the jury to acquit the defendant generally on the count of murder. His argument was that her refusal to have a blood transfusion had broken the chain of causation between the stabbing and her death. As an alternative he submitted that the jury should be left to decide whether the chain of causation had been broken. Mr. Herrod submitted that the judge should direct the jury to convict, because no facts were in issue and when the law was applied to the facts there was only one possible verdict, namely, manslaughter by reason of diminished responsibility.

When the judge came to direct the jury on this issue he did so by telling them that they should apply their common sense. He then went on to tell them they would get some help from the cases to which counsel had referred in their speeches. He reminded them of what Lord Parker C.J. had said in *R. v. Smith* [1959] 2 Q.B. 35, 42 and what Maule J. had said 133

years before in *R.* v. *Holland* (1841) 2 Mood. & R. 351, 352. He placed
particular reliance on what Maule J. had said. The jury, he said, might find
it "most material and most helpful." He continued:

> "This is one of those relatively rare cases, you may think, with very
> little option open to you but to reach the conclusion that was reached by
> your predecessors as members of the jury in *R.* v. *Holland,* namely, 'yes'
> to the question of causation that the stab was still, at the time of the
> girl's death, the operative cause of death—or a substantial cause of
> death. However, that is a matter for you to determine after you have
> withdrawn to consider your verdict."

Mr. Comyn has criticised that direction on three grounds: first, because *R.*
v. *Holland* should no longer be considered good law; secondly, because *R.*
v. *Smith,* when rightly understood, does envisage the possibility of
unreasonable conduct on the part of the victim breaking the chain of
causation; and thirdly, because the judge in reality directed the jury to find
causation proved although he used words which seemed to leave the issue
open for them to decide.

In *R.* v. *Holland,* 2 Mood. & R. 351, the defendant in the course of a
violent assault, had injured one of his victim's fingers. A surgeon had
advised amputation because of the danger to life through complications
developing. The advice was rejected. A fortnight later the victim died of
lockjaw. Maule J. said, at p. 352: "the real question is, whether in the end
the wound inflicted by the prisoner was the cause of death." That
distinguished judge left the jury to decide that question as did the judge in
this case. They had to decide it as juries always do, by pooling their
experience of life and using their common sense. They would not have
been handicapped by a lack of training in dialectic or moral theology.

Maule J.'s direction to the jury reflected the common law's answer to the
problem. He who inflicted an injury which resulted in death could not
excuse himself by pleading that his victim could have avoided death by
taking greater care of himself: see *Hale's Pleas of the Crown* (1800 ed.), pp.
427–428. The common law in Sir Matthew Hale's time probably was in line
with contemporary concepts of ethics. A man who did a wrongful act was
deemed *morally* responsible for the natural and probable consequence of
that act. Mr. Comyn asked us to remember that since Sir Matthew Hale's
day the rigour of the law relating to homicide has been eased in favour of
the accused. It has been—but this has come about through the
development of the concepts of intent, not by reason of a different view of
causation. Well known practitioner's textbooks, such as *Halsbury's Laws of
England,* 3rd ed., vol. 10 (1955), p. 706 and *Russell on Crime,* 12th ed.
(1964), vol. 1, p. 30 continue to reflect the common law approach.
Textbooks intended for students or as studies in jurisprudence have
queried the common law rule; see Hart and Honoré, *Causation in Law*
(1959), pp. 320–321 and Smith and Hogan, *Criminal Law,* 3rd ed. (1973), p.
214.

There have been two cases in recent years which have some bearing
upon this topic: *R.* v. *Jordan* (1956), [*infra*] and *R.* v. *Smith,* [*infra*]. The
physical cause of death in this case was the bleeding into the pleural cavity
arising from the penetration of the lung. This had not been brought about
by any decision made by the deceased but by the stab wound.

Mr. Comyn tried to overcome this line of reasoning by submitting that
the jury should have been directed that if they thought the deceased's
decision not to have a blood transfusion was an unreasonable one, then
the chain of causation would have been broken. At once the question
arises—reasonable by whose standards? Those of Jehovah's Witnesses?

Humanists? Roman Catholics? Protestants of Anglo-Saxon descent? The man on the Clapham omnibus? But he might well be an admirer of Eleazar who suffered death rather than eat the flesh of swine (2 Maccabees, ch. 6, vv. 18–31) or of Sir Thomas More who, unlike nearly all his contemporaries was unwilling to accept Henry VIII as Head of the Church of England. Those brought up in the Hebraic and Christian traditions would probably be reluctant to accept that these martyrs caused their own deaths.

As was pointed out to Mr. Comyn in the course of argument, two cases, each raising the same issue of reasonableness because of religious beliefs, could produce different verdicts depending on where the cases were tried. A jury drawn from Preston, sometimes said to be the most Catholic town in England, might have different views about martyrdom to one drawn from the inner suburbs of London. Mr. Comyn accepted that this might be so: it was, he said, inherent in trial by jury. It is not inherent in the common law as expounded by Sir Matthew Hale and Maule J. It has long been the policy of the law that those who use violence on other people must take their victims as they find them. This in our judgment means the whole man, not just the physical man. It does not lie in the mouth of the assailant to say that the victim's religious beliefs which inhibited him from accepting certain kinds of treatment were unreasonable. The question for decision is what caused her death. The answer is the stab wound. The fact that the victim refused to stop this end coming about did not break the causal connection between the act and death. . . .

Appeal dismissed

Williams, Note (1976) C.L.J. 15

"Although the case follows the precedents, . . . it fails to notice that all of them dated from a time when medical science was in its infancy, and when operations performed without hygiene carried great danger to life. It was therefore open to the court for the benefit of the defendant to consider the question afresh, and there were several reasons for doing so.

It had been held in the law of tort that the test of reasonable foresight applies to facts like those in *Blaue*, but the court refused to bring the criminal law into line. The criminal law should avoid the appearance of harshness, and to make it more stringent than the civil law in the matter of causation is surprising. Lawton L.J., speaking for the court, explained the difference between crime and tort by saying that 'the criminal law is concerned with the maintenance of law and order and the protection of the public generally.' This overlooks that Blaue was in any event punishable severely for wounding with intent. What social purpose is served by giving an attacker *extra* punishment because the person attacked unreasonably refused treatment?"

Note

The Court of Appeal's objection to a test of reasonable refusal was countered by K. J. M. Smith, Note (1976) 92 L.Q.R. 30 at 31: " . . . [It] might be contended that this problem arises when an objective test is applied in the criminal law, yet it does not prevent the courts arriving at an appropriate standard. . . . " The same writer also suggests that the Court of Appeal is inconsistent in allowing an unreasonable "flight" to break the chain of causation (see *Mackie* and *Daley, ante,* p. 39) and asks "Is there some essential distinction to be drawn between passive and active behaviour by a victim?"

(c) *Intervening causes*

G. Williams, *"Finis* for *Novus Actus"* [1989] C.L.J. 391

"A person is primarily responsible for what he himself does. He is not responsible, not blameworthy, for what other people do. The fact that his own conduct, rightful or wrongful, provided the background for a subsequent voluntary and wrong act by another does not make him responsible for it. What he does may be a but-for cause of the injurious act, but he did not do it. His conduct is not an imputable cause of it. Only the later actor, the doer of the act that intervenes between the first act and the result, the final wielder of human autonomy in the matter, bears responsibility (along with his accomplices) for the result that ensues. . . .

The autonomy doctrine, expressing itself through its corollary the doctrine of *novus actus interveniens*, teaches that the individual's will is the autonomous (self-regulating) prime cause of his behaviour. Although this may sound unbelievably metaphysical, the doctrine is supported because it accords with our ideas of moral responsibility and just punishment, and serves social objectives. The first actor who starts on a dangerous or criminal plan will often be responsible for what happens if no one else intervenes; but a subsequent actor who has reached responsible years, is of sound mind, has full knowledge of what he is doing, and is not acting under intimidation or other pressure or stress resulting from the defendant's conduct, replaces him as the responsible actor. Such an intervening act is thought to break the moral connection that would otherwise have been perceived between the defendant's acts and the forbidden consequence.

Policy arguments in favour of novus actus

(1) The law should not saddle a person with liability for consequences that not only he but also the general public would blame on someone else. The intervention of the responsible actor diverts our retributive wrath from the first actor, who may, in the event, appear to be so much less culpable than the later actor; and this switching of retributive feeling from the first actor to the later actor is expressed in causal language.

(2) Sometimes we may feel that making people responsible for the subsequent behaviour of others, merely because they foresaw or could have foreseen that behaviour, would be too great a restriction upon liberty. . . .

(3) The rule has the beneficial effect of restricting the number of persons made liable for a particular occurrence. Part of the object of the criminal trial is to dramatise society's rejection of the deed, and, generally speaking, this is adequately done by prosecuting the immediate author and his accomplices. No pressing necessity exists to regard more remote authors as responsible for causing the harm . . . though some of them may well be prosecuted for other offences, such as attempt, or in appropriate circumstances as accessories."

Note

A problem which has arisen in several cases is that of medical treatment of wounds inflicted by D on V. If the medical treatment is negligent will this break the chain of causation? Will D only be liable where the original wound is not healed and V dies from it? What happens if the original wound is healed and the medical treatment itself is the immediate cause of death; as D's wounding of V. caused him to undergo medical treatment, can it be said that this was still a substantial cause of V's death?

R. v. Jordan
(1956) 40 Cr.App.R. 153
Court of Criminal Appeal

The appellant stabbed the deceased in the abdomen. The deceased was taken promptly to hospital and the wound was stitched. A few days later he died. Jordan was convicted of murder at Leeds Assizes and on appeal sought to adduce further medical evidence. This evidence disclosed that the wound, which had penetrated the intestine in two places, was mainly healed at the time of death. At the hospital terramycin was administered to prevent infection. The deceased was found to be intolerant to this antibiotic. A doctor who was unaware of this ordered its continuance. Two fresh witnesses also testified that abnormal quantities of liquid had been given intravenously. This caused the lungs to become waterlogged and pulmonary oedema was discovered.

HALLETT J.: ... We are disposed to accept it as the law that death resulting from any normal treatment employed to deal with a felonious injury may be regarded as caused by the felonious injury, but we do not think it necessary to examine the cases in detail or to formulate for the assistance of those who have to deal with such matters in the future the correct test which ought to be laid down with regard to what is necessary to be proved in order to establish causal connection between the death and the felonious injury. Not only one feature, but two separate and independent features, of treatment were, in the opinion of the doctors, palpably wrong and these produced the symptoms discovered at the post-mortem examination which were the direct and immediate cause of death, namely, the pneumonia resulting from the condition of oedema which was found.

Conviction quashed

R. v. Smith
[1959] 2 Q.B. 35
Courts-Martial Appeal Court

The appellant, a soldier, was charged with, and convicted of, the murder of a fellow soldier during the course of a fight between the men of two regiments who shared the same barrack room. The deceased received two bayonet wounds, one in the arm and one in the back which pierced the lung and caused haemorrhage. Another soldier tried to carry the wounded man to the medical reception station. He twice dropped him on the ground. At the station the medical officer and his orderly were extremely busy. There were two other stabbed men to deal with as well as others with minor injuries. The medical staff did not know of the haemorrhage nor was the serious nature of the injury realised. A transfusion of saline solution was tried but failed and when breathing seemed impaired, oxygen and artificial respiration were given. This treatment was "thoroughly bad" and might well have affected his chance of recovery. There was medical evidence at the trial that haemorrhage of this type tends to stop. Had there been a blood transfusion available chances of recovery were assessed as high as 75 per cent. by a medical witness for the defence.

LORD PARKER C.J.: In these circumstances Mr. Bowen urged that not only was a careful summing-up required, but that a correct direction to the court would have been that they must be satisfied that the death of Private Creed was a natural consequence and the sole consequence of the wound sustained by him and flowed directly from it. If there was, says Mr. Bowen, any other cause, whether resulting from negligence or not, if, as he contends here, something happened which impeded the chance of the deceased recovering, then the death did not result from the wound. The court is quite unable to accept that contention. It seems to the court that if at the time of death the original wound is still an operating cause and a substantial cause, then the death can properly be said to be the result of the wound, albeit that some other cause of death is also operating. Only if it can be said that the original wounding is merely the setting in which another cause operates can it be said that the death did not result from the wound. Putting it another way, only if the second cause is so overwhelming as to make the original wound merely part of the history can it be said that the death does not flow from the wound.

There are a number of cases in the law of contract and tort on these matters of causation, and it is always difficult to find a form of words when directing a jury or, as here, a court which will convey in simple language the principle of causation. It seems to the court enough for this purpose to refer to one passage in the judgment of Lord Wright in *The Oropesa* [1943] P. 32, 39, where he said: "To break the chain of causation it must be shown that there is something which I will call ultroneous, something unwarrantable, a new cause which disturbs the sequence of events, something which can be described as either unreasonable or extraneous or extrinsic." To much the same effect was a judgment on the question of causation given by Denning L.J. in *Minister of Pensions* v. *Chennell* [1947] K.B. 250.

Mr. Bowen placed great reliance on a case decided in the Court of Criminal Appeal, *R.* v. *Jordan* [*ante*, p. 44] and in particular on a passage in the headnote which says, " . . . that death resulting from any normal treatment employed to deal with a felonious injury may be regarded as caused by the felonious injury, but that the same principle does not apply where the treatment is abnormal." Reading those words into the present case, Mr. Bowen says that the treatment that this unfortunate man received from the moment that he was struck to the time of his death was abnormal. The court is satisfied that *Jordan's* case was a very particular case depending upon its exact facts. It incidentally arose on the grant of an application to call further evidence, and leave having been obtained, two well-known medical experts gave evidence that in their opinion death had not been caused by the stabbing but by the introduction of terramycin after the deceased had shown that he was intolerant to it, and by the intravenous introduction of abnormal quantities of liquid. It also appears that at the time when that was done the stab wound which had penetrated the intestine in two places had mainly healed. In those circumstances the court felt bound to quash the conviction because they could not say that a reasonable jury, properly directed, would not have been able on that to say that there had been a break in the chain of causation; the court could only uphold the conviction in that case if they were satisfied that no reasonable jury could have come to that conclusion.

In the present case it is true that the judge-advocate did not in his summing-up go into the refinements of causation. Indeed, in the opinion of this court he was probably wise to refrain from doing so. He did leave the broad question to the court whether they were satisfied that the wound had caused the death in the sense that the death flowed from the wound, albeit that the treatment he received was in the light of after-knowledge a bad thing. In the opinion of this court that was on the facts of the case a perfectly adequate summing-up on causation; I say "on the facts of the case" because, in the opinion of the court, they can only lead to one conclusion: a man is stabbed in the back, his lung is pierced and haemorrhage results; two hours later he dies of haemorrhage from that wound; in the interval there is no time for a careful examination, and the treatment given turns out in the light of subsequent knowledge to have been inappropriate and, indeed, harmful. In those circumstances no reasonable jury or court could, properly directed, in our view possibly come to any other conclusion than that the death resulted from the original wound. Accordingly the court dismisses this appeal.

Appeal dismissed

R. v. Malcherek
R. v. Steel
[1981] 2 All E.R. 422
Court of Appeal

These two cases raised the same question. M stabbed his wife with a kitchen knife causing a deep abdominal wound. S was accused of attacking a girl causing grave head injuries. Both victims were put on life support machines during normal courses of treatment. In each case the machines were switched off after a number of tests indicated that brain death had occurred. Both M and S were convicted at their trials for murder. The ground of M's appeal and S's application for leave to appeal was that the judge should not have withdrawn the question of causation from the jury. S also sought leave to adduce further medical evidence that the doctors in each case had not complied with all the Royal Medical College's suggested criteria for establishing brain death.

LORD LANE C.J.: [After stating the facts] ... This is not the occasion for any decision as to what constitutes death. ... There is, it seems, a body of opinion in the medical profession that there is only one true test of death and that is the irreversible death of the brain stem, which controls the basic functions of the body such as breathing. When that occurs it is said the body has died, even though by mechanical means the lungs are being caused to operate and some circulation of blood is taking place. ...

The question posed for answer to this court is simply whether the judge in each case was right in withdrawing from the jury the question of causation. Was he right to rule that there was no evidence on which the jury could come to the conclusion that the assailant did not cause the death of the victim?

The way in which the submissions are put by counsel for Malcherek on the one hand and by counsel for Steel on the other is as follows: the doctors, by switching off the ventilator and the life support machine, were the cause of death or, to put it more accurately, there was evidence which the jury should have been allowed to consider that the doctors, and not the assailant, in each case may have been the cause of death.

In each case it is clear that the initial assault was the cause of the grave head injuries in the one case and of the massive abdominal haemorrhage in the other. In each case the initial assault was the reason for the medical treatment being necessary. In each case the medical treatment given was normal and conventional. At some stage the doctors must decide if and when treatment has become otiose. This decision was reached, in each of the two cases here, in circumstances which have already been set out in some detail. . . .

There are two comparatively recent cases which are relevant to the consideration of this problem. [His Lordship then considered *R. v. Smith, ante*, p. 43 and *R. v. Jordan, ante*, p. 43].

In the view of this court, if a choice has to be made between the decision in *R. v. Jordan* and that in *R. v. Smith*, which we do not believe it does (*R. v. Jordan* being a very exceptional case), then the decision in *R. v. Smith* is to be preferred.

The only other case to which reference has been made, it having been drawn to our attention by counsel for Steel, is *R. v. Blaue*, [*ante*, p. 40] . . .

The passage . . . is the last paragraph of the judgment of Lawton L.J. [1975] 1 W.L.R. 1411 at 1416:

"The issue of the cause of death in a trial for either murder or manslaughter is one of fact for the jury to decide. But if, as in this case, there is no conflict of evidence and all the jury has to do is apply the law to the admitted facts, the judge is entitled to tell the jury what the result of that application will be. In this case the judge would have been entitled to have told the jury that the appellant's stab wound was an operative cause of death. The appeal fails."

There is no evidence in the present case here that at the time of conventional death, after the life support machinery was disconnected, the original wound or injury was other than a continuing, operating and indeed substantial cause of the death of the victim, although it need hardly be added that it need not be substantial to render the assailant guilty. There may be occasions, although they will be rare, when the original injury has ceased to operate as a cause at all, but in the ordinary case if treatment is given bona fide by competent and careful medical practitioners, then evidence will not be admissible to show that the treatment would not have been administered in the same way by other medical practitioners. In other words, the fact that the victim has died, despite or because of medical treatment for the initial injury given by careful and skilled medical practitioners, will not exonerate the original assailant from responsibility for the death. It follows that so far as the ground of appeal in each of these cases relates to the direction given on causation, that ground fails. . . . Where a medical practitioner adopting methods which are generally accepted comes bona fide and conscientiously to the conclusion that the patient is for practical purposes dead, and that such vital functions as exist (for example, circulation) are being maintained solely by mechanical means, and therefore discontinues treatment, that does not prevent the person who inflicted the initial injury from being responsible for the victim's death. Putting it in another way, the discontinuance of treatment in those circumstances does not break the chain of causation between the initial injury and the death.

Although it is unnecessary to go further than that for the purpose of deciding the present point, we wish to add this thought. Whatever the strict logic of the matter may be, it is perhaps somewhat bizarre to suggest, as counsel have impliedly done, that where a doctor tries his conscientious best to save the life of a patient brought to hospital in extremis, skilfully using sophisticated methods, drugs and machinery to do so, but fails in his attempt and therefore discontinues treatment, he can be said to have caused the death of the patient. . . .

Appeal and applications dismissed

Note

In *Jordan* the original wound had healed whereas in *Smith* and *Malcherek* the original wounds were still operating at the time of death. In the case which follows the Court of Appeal had sought to move away from the simplistic analysis of whether or not the original wound had healed at the time of death, as concentration on this may lead to the wrong conclusion. The issue is whether D has caused the death of V not whether the wound D inflicted caused V's death. Even though the actual wound may have healed, D's act may still be an operating and substantial (in the sense of "more than minimal") cause of death.

R. v. Cheshire
[1991] 1 W.L.R. 844
Court of Appeal

In December 1987 D shot V in the leg and the stomach. V underwent surgery and when respiratory complications arose a tracheotomy was performed, the tube remaining in place until early January 1988. In February V developed difficulty in breathing which was diagnosed as being due to anxiety. On February 14, V complained of further problems with breathing. His condition deteriorated and despite attempts at resuscitation V died early on February 15. The cause of death was given as cardio-respiratory arrest due to a condition produced as a result of provision of an artificial airway in treatment of gunshot wounds. At D's trial for murder the defence presented expert medical evidence that the gunshot wounds no longer threatened V's life and that the cause of death was the failure to correctly diagnose and treat the cause of V's breathlessness which was due to a narrowing of V's windpipe near the site of the tracheotomy scar. The trial judge directed the jury that in order to find that the chain of causation between the original wounding and V's death had been broken, they had to be satisfied that the medical treatment or lack of it was not merely negligent but reckless in the sense that the doctors had acted or failed to act "careless of the consequences, careless of the comfort and safety of another person."

BELDAM L.J.: In the criminal law, and in particular in the law of homicide, whether the death of a deceased was the result of the defendant's criminal act is a question of fact for the jury, but it is a question of fact to be decided in accordance with legal principles explained to the jury by the judge. We think the matter cannot be better put than it was by Robert Goff L.J. in *R. v. Pagett* (1983) 76 Cr.App.R. 279, 288 (*post*, p. 51) . . .

Since the apportionment of responsibility for damage has become commonplace in the civil law, judges have sought to distinguish the blameworthiness of conduct from its causative effect. Epithets suggestive of degrees of blameworthiness may be of little help in deciding how potent the conduct was in causing the result. A momentary lapse of concentration may lead to more serious consequences than a more glaring neglect of duty. In the criminal law the jury considering the factual question, did the defendant's act cause the deceased's death, will we think derive little assistance from figures of speech more appropriate for conveying degrees of fault or blame in questions of apportionment. Unless authority suggests otherwise, we think such figures of speech are to be avoided in giving guidance to a jury on the question of causation. Whilst medical treatment unsuccessfully given to prevent the death of a victim with the care and skill of a competent medical practitioner will not amount to an intervening cause, it does not follow that treatment which falls below that standard of care and skill will amount to such a cause. As Professors Hart and Honoré comment, treatment which falls short of the standard expected of the competent medical practitioner is unfortunately only too frequent in human experience for it to be considered abnormal in the sense of extraordinary. Acts or omissions of a doctor treating the victim for injuries he has received at the hands of a defendant may conceivably be so extraordinary as to be capable of being regarded as acts independent of the conduct of the defendant but it is most unlikely that they will be.

[His Lordship referred to the cases of *Jordan*, *Smith* and *Malcherek*. Referring to the latter case he continued].

[I]t was not suggested that the actions of the doctors in disconnecting the life support machines were other than competent and careful. The court did not have to consider the effect of medical treatment which fell short of the standard of care to be expected of competent medical practitioners.

A case in which the facts bear a close similarity to the case with which we are concerned is *R. v. Evans and Gardiner (No. 2)* [1976] V.R. 523. In that case the deceased was stabbed in the stomach by the two applicants in April 1974. After operation the victim resumed an apparently healthy life but nearly a year later, after suffering abdominal pain and vomiting and undergoing further medical treatment, he died. The cause of death was a stricture of the small bowel, a not uncommon sequel to the operation carried out to deal with the stab wound inflicted by the applicants. It was contended that the doctors treating the victim for the later symptoms ought to have diagnosed the presence of the stricture, that they had been negligent not to do so and that timely operative treatment would have saved the victim's life.

The Supreme Court of Victoria held that the test to be applied in determining whether a felonious act has caused a death which follows, in spite of an intervening act, is whether the felonious act is still an operating and substantial cause of the death.

The summing up to the jury had been based on the passage already quoted from Lord Parker C.J.'s judgment in *R. v. Smith* [1959] 2 Q.B. 35 and the Supreme Court endorsed a direction in those terms. It commented upon the limitations of the decision of *R. v. Jordan*, 40 Cr.App.R. 152 and made observations on the difference between the failure to diagnose the consequence of the original injury and cases in which medical treatment has been given which has a positive adverse effect on the victim. It concluded [1976] V.R. 523, 528:

"But in the long run the difference between a positive act of commission and an omission to do some particular act is for these purposes ultimately a question of degree. As an event intervening between an act alleged to be felonious and to have resulted in death, and the actual death, a positive act of commission or an act of omission will serve to break the chain of causation only if it can be shown that the act or omission accelerated the death, so that it can be said to have caused the death and thus to have prevented the felonious act which would have caused death from actually doing so."

Later in the judgment the court said, at p. 534:

"In these circumstances we agree with the view of the learned trial judge expressed in his report to this court that there was a case to go to the jury. The failure of the medical practitioners to diagnose correctly the victim's condition, however inept or unskilful, was not the cause of death. It was the blockage of the bowel which caused death and the real question for the jury was whether that blockage was due to the stabbing. There was plenty of medical evidence to support such a finding, if the jury chose to accept it."

It seems to us that these two passages demonstrate the difficulties in formulating and explaining a general concept of causation but what we think does emerge from this and the other cases is that when the victim of a criminal attack is treated for wounds or injuries by doctors or other medical staff attempting to repair the harm done, it will only be in the most extraordinary and unusual case that such treatment can be said to be so independent of the acts of the defendant that it could be regarded in law as the cause of the victim's death to the exclusion of the defendant's acts.

Where the law requires proof of the relationship between an act and its consequences as an element of responsibility, a simple and sufficient explanation of the basis of such relationship has proved notoriously elusive.

In a case in which the jury have to consider whether negligence in the treatment of injuries inflicted by the defendant was the cause of death we think it is sufficient for the judge to tell the jury that they must be satisfied that the Crown have proved that the acts of the defendant caused the death of the deceased adding that the defendant's acts need not be the sole cause or even the main cause of death it being sufficient that his acts contributed significantly to that result. Even though negligence in the treatment of the victim was the immediate cause of his death, the jury should not regard it as excluding the responsibility of the defendant unless the negligent treatment was so independent of his acts, and in itself so potent in causing death, that they regard the contribution made by his acts as insignificant.

It is not the function of the jury to evaluate competing causes or to choose which is dominant provided they are satisfied that the defendant's acts can fairly be said to have made a significant contribution to the victim's death. We think the word "significant" conveys the necessary substance of a contribution made to the death which is more than negligible.

[His Lordship concluded that although the judge erred when he invited the jury to consider the degree of fault in the medical treatment rather than its consequences, no miscarriage of justice had occurred as he had correctly directed the jury that the prosecution did not have to prove that the bullets were the only cause of death but that they were one operative and substantial cause of death.]

Appeal dismissed

Questions

1. In *Smith* Lord Parker C.J. stated:

"Only if it can be said that the original wounding is merely the setting in which another cause operates can it be said that the death did not result from the wound. Putting it another way, only if the second cause is so overwhelming as to make the original wound merely part of the history can it be said that the death does not flow from the wound."

Is there any essential difference between this statement of principle and the following from Beldam L.J. in *Cheshire*?:

"Even though negligence in the treatment of the victim is the immediate cause of his death, the jury should not regard it as excluding the responsibility of the defendant unless the negligent treatment was so independent of his acts, and in itself so potent in causing death, that they regard the contribution made by his acts as insignificant."

2. If the facts of *Jordan* were to recur how might the question of causation be decided?
3. What would have happened in *Cheshire* if the doctor, having misdiagnosed V's condition, rather than giving no treatment had gone on to give him drugs which exacerbated his condition?

Note

In *McKechnie* [1992] Crim.L.R. 194, the Court of Appeal upheld D's conviction of manslaughter on the grounds of provocation, D having caused serious head injuries to V. V died not from the head injuries but five weeks later from a burst duodenal ulcer. When V was first admitted to hospital unconscious from the head injuries, the doctors decided that they dare not operate on the ulcer. V would not have died had he had an operation on the ulcer. D's act therefore did not cause V to undergo medical treatment but rather prevented him undergoing treatment that would have saved his life. The decision not to operate was not to be judged on its correctness but its reasonableness. On this basis it could not be considered "extraordinary and unusual" and was not "so independent of the acts of the accused that it could be regarded in law as the cause of the victim's death."

R. v. Pagett
(1983) 76 Cr.App.R. 279
Court of Appeal

P, while hiding behind V whom he was holding against her will and whose body he was using as a shield, fired a shotgun at police officers who were attempting to arrest him. The officers returned P's fire killing V. P was charged, *inter alia*, with murder. On the issue of causation the judge directed the jury that they had to be sure that P had fired first at the officers and that that act caused the officers to fire back with the result that V was killed, and that in doing so they had to be satisfied that the police acted reasonably either by way of self-defence or in the performance of their duties as police officers. If they were not sure of those facts then they should acquit P because the chain that linked his deliberate and unlawful acts to V's death would be broken. The jury acquitted P of murder and convicted him of manslaughter. P appealed.

ROBERT GOFF L.J.: (for the court) ... [Two of the] three specific points raised on behalf of the appellant were as follows (we quote from the grounds of appeal):

(1) The learned judge erred in law in directing that the jury must as a matter of law find that the appellant caused the death of the deceased, if they were satisfied as to the four matters of fact which he set out. The learned judge ought rather to have left it to the jury to determine as an issue of fact whether the defendant's act in firing at the police officers was a substantial, or operative, or imputable, cause of the death of the deceased.

(2) In the alternative, if the learned judge was correct in himself determining as a matter of law what facts would amount to causation of the death by the appellant, he ought to have held that the appellant had not in the circumstances of this case caused the death of the deceased. The learned judge, in directing himself upon the law, ought to have held that where the act which immediately resulted in fatal injury was the act of another party, albeit in legitimate self-defence, then the ensuing death was too remote or indirect to be imputed to the original aggressor. ...

The argument addressed to this Court by Lord Gifford on behalf of the appellant was concentrated primarily on the first and second grounds of appeal, and was as presented concerned with the issue of causation. We find it convenient to deal first with the second ground of appeal. ...

[I]t was pressed upon us by Lord Gifford [for the appellant] that there either was, or should be, a ... rule of English law, whereby, as a matter of policy, no man should be convicted of homicide (or, we imagine, any crime of violence to another person) unless he himself, or another person acting in concert with him, fired the shot (or, we imagine, struck the blow) which was the immediate cause of the victim's death (or injury).

No English authority was cited to us in support of any such proposition, and we know of none. So far as we are aware, there is no such rule in English law; and, in the absence of any doctrine of constructive malice, we can see no basis in principle for any such rule in English law. ...

In our judgment, the question whether an accused person can be held guilty of homicide, either murder or manslaughter, of a victim the immediate cause of whose death is the act of another person must be determined on the ordinary principles of causation, uninhibited by any such rule of policy as that for which Lord Gifford has contended. We therefore reject the second ground of appeal.

We turn to the first ground of appeal, which is that the learned judge erred in directing the jury that it was for him to decide *as a matter of law* whether by his unlawful and deliberate acts the appellant caused or was a cause of Gail Kinchen's death. It is right to observe that this direction of the learned judge followed upon a discussion with counsel, in the absence of the jury. ...

In cases of homicide, it is rarely necessary to give the jury any direction on causation as such. .... [H]ow the victim came by his death is usually not in dispute. ....

Even where it is necessary to direct the jury's minds to the question of causation, it is usually enough to direct them simply that in law the accused's act need not be the sole cause, or even the main cause, of the victim's death, it being enough that his act contributed significantly to that result. ....

Occasionally, however, a specific issue of causation may arise. One such case is where, although an act of the accused constitutes a *causa sine qua non* of (or necessary condition for) the death of the victim, nevertheless the intervention of a third person may be regarded as the sole cause of the victim's death, thereby relieving the accused of criminal responsibility. Such intervention, if it has such an effect, has often been described by lawyers as a *novus actus interveniens*. ....

[The phrase is] a term of art which conveys to lawyers the crucial feature that there has not merely been an intervening act of another person, but that that act was so independent of the act of the accused that it should be regarded in law as the cause of the victim's death, to the exclusion of the act of the accused.

.... Professors Hart and Honoré, *Causation in the Law* ... consider the circumstances in which the intervention of a third person, not acting in concert with the accused, may have the effect of relieving the accused of criminal responsibility. The criterion which they suggest should be applied in such circumstances is whether the intervention is voluntary, *i.e.* whether it is "free, deliberate and informed." We resist the temptation of expressing the judicial opinion whether we find ourselves in complete agreement with that definition; though we certainly consider it to be broadly correct and supported by authority. Among the examples which the authors give of non-voluntary conduct, which is not effective to relieve the accused of responsibility, are two which are germane to the present case, *viz.* a reasonable act performed for the purpose of self-preservation, and an act done in performance of a legal duty.

There can, we consider, be no doubt that a reasonable act performed for the purpose of self-preservation, being of course itself an act caused by the accused's own act, does not operate as a *novus actus interveniens*. If authority is needed for this almost self-evident proposition, it is to be found in such cases as *R. v. Pitts* (1842) C. & M. 284, and *R. v. Curley* (1909) 2 Cr.App.R. 96. In both these cases, the act performed for the purpose of self-preservation consisted of an act by the victim in attempting to escape from the violence of the accused, which in fact resulted in the victim's death. In each case it was held as a matter of law that, if the victim acted in a reasonable attempt to escape the violence of the accused, the death of the victim was caused by the act of the accused. Now one form of self-preservation is self-defence; for present purposes, we can see no distinction in principle between an attempt to escape the consequences of the accused's act, and a response which takes the form of self-defence. Furthermore, in our judgment, if a reasonable act of self-defence against the act of the accused causes the death of a third party, we can see no reason in principle why the act of self-defence, being an involuntary act caused by the act of the accused, should relieve the accused from criminal responsibility for the death of the third party. ....

No English authority was cited to us, nor we think to the learned judge, in support of the proposition that an act done in the execution of a legal duty, again of course being an act itself caused by the act of the accused, does not operate as *novus actus interveniens*. .... Even so, we agree with the learned judge that the proposition is sound in law, because as a matter of principle such an act cannot be regarded as a voluntary act independent of the wrongful act of the accused. A parallel may be drawn with the so-called "rescue" cases in the law of negligence, where a wrongdoer may be held liable in negligence to a third party who suffers injury in going to the rescue of a person who has been put in danger by the defendant's negligent act. Where, for example, a police officer in the execution of his duty acts to prevent a crime, or to apprehend a person suspected of a crime, the case is surely *a fortiori*. Of course, it is inherent in the requirement that the police officer, or other person, must be acting in the execution of his duty that his act should be reasonable in all the circumstances; see section 3 of the Criminal Law Act 1967. . . .

The principles which we have stated are principles of law . . . It follows that where, in any particular case, there is an issue concerned with what we have for convenience called *novus actus interveniens*, it will be appropriate for the judge to direct the jury in accordance with these principles. It does not however follow that it is accurate to state broadly that causation is a question of law. On the contrary, generally speaking causation is a question of fact for the jury. . . .

But that does not mean that there are no principles of law relating to causation, so that no directions on law are ever to be given to a jury on the question of causation. On the contrary, we have already pointed out one familiar direction which is given on causation, which is that the accused's act need not be the sole, or even the main, cause of the victim's death for his act to be held to have caused the death.

[His Lordship then cited the principle in *R.* v. *Blaue, ante*, p. 40, as an example of a *statement legal of principle* on causation.]

Likewise, in cases where there is an issue whether the act of the victim or of a third party constituted a *novus actus interveniens*, breaking the causal connection between the act of the accused and the death of the victim, it would be appropriate for the judge to direct the jury, of course in the most simple terms, in accordance with the legal principles which they have to apply. It would then fall to the jury to decide the relevant factual issues which, identified with reference to those legal principles, will lead to the conclusion whether or not the prosecution have established the guilt of the accused of the crime of which he is charged.

In the light of these principles, we do not consider that any legitimate criticism can be made, on behalf of the appellant, of the direction given by the learned judge to the jury on the issue of causation in the present case. . . .

For these reasons, we are unable to accept Lord Gifford's argument based on the first ground of appeal.

Appeal dismissed

Questions

1. Would the outcome have been the same if the victim had been an innocent passer-by?

2. Would P have been guilty of wounding if V had not died?

3. Would P have been guilty if V had escaped from his hold and run in the line of police fire?

iii. An Alternative Approach

Fletcher, Rethinking Criminal Law, pp. 362, 368

"It would be plausible to define a law protecting life in terms that made the occurrence of death irrelevant. The critical issue would be an act endangering life. An attempt to kill, particularly if manifested unequivocally in the actor's behaviour, would be treated the same as an actual killing. Conduct highly dangerous to human life would be treated as equivalent to reckless homicide. The rationale for eliminating the issues of causation and death would be that the purpose of the law should be to punish and to deter blameworthy assaults on the interest in life. The actual occurrence of death and its causal attribution are irrelevant to the sets of acts that should be deterred, and it is also irrelevant to the criteria rendering the accused blameworthy for his conduct. The man who shoots at an apparently alive but dead patient, is arguably no less blameworthy than the assassin who has the bad luck to shoot and kill a living patient. . . .

There is no easy solution to the problem of causation. The metaphysics of proximate cause, degrees of contribution and intervening causes will continue to affect even the most rational penal system. The reasons are several. First, the inquiry into causation is categorical. A death is attributable to someone or it is not. There is no room for a compromise verdict as there is in the assessment of culpability for criminal homicide. Secondly, the issue of causation, along with the elements of acting and the occurrence of death, goes to the foundation of liability. . .

A third significant factor is that the courts are bound to render these appellate decisions in an all-or-nothing fashion without having a general theory to guide their assessment whether in close cases they should find for the defendant or the prosecution. . . .

Rooted in the practice of tainting, the causal inquiry bears neither on the definition of conduct that should be deterred nor on the criteria for justly blaming someone who endangers human life."

Question

Consider whether any of the above cases would have been decided differently had the question not been one of causation but of an act endangering life, as suggested by Fletcher.

Draft Criminal Code Bill

Causation

17.—(1) (See *ante*, p. 31).

(2) A person does not cause a result where, after he does such an act or makes such an omission, an act or event occurs—

   (a) which is the immediate and sufficient cause of the result;
   (b) which he did not foresee, and
   (c) which could not in the circumstances reasonably have been foreseen.

(3) A person who procures, assists or encourages another to cause a result that is an element of an offence does not himself cause that result so as to be guilty of the offence as a principal except when—

(a)   section 26(1)(c) applies; or
(b)   the offence itself consists in the procuring, assisting or encouraging
      another to cause the result.

5. COINCIDENCE OF ACTUS AND MENS REA

Note

Where an offence requires *mens rea* the prosecution must prove
that D had *mens rea* at the time he did the act which caused the
actus reus.

R. v. Jakeman
(1982) 76 Cr.App.R. 223
Court of Appeal

J booked two cases containing cannabis on a flight from Accra to Rome
and from there to London. The flight was diverted from Rome to Paris. J
did not claim her cases in Paris but flew on to Rome and then to
London. Officials in Paris sent the cases to London where they were not
collected. The cannabis was discovered and J was charged with being
knowingly concerned in the fraudulent evasion of the restriction on the
importation of cannabis contrary to section 170(2) of the Customs and
Excise Act 1979. J's defence was that on boarding the aircraft she
repented of her original intention and tore up the baggage tags. The
judge ruled that this provided no defence. J appealed.

WOOD J.: Mr. Mansfield . . . submits that for the offence under section
170(2) of the 1979 Act, the participation of the applicant and her *mens rea*
must continue throughout the offence—in this case at least until the
wheels of the aircraft touched down at Heathrow Airport. . . .

The following propositions are supported by decisions of this court.
First, that the importation takes place when the aircraft bringing the goods
lands at an airport in this country, see *R. v. Smith (Donald)*; [1973] Q.B.
924, 935G. Secondly, acts done abroad in order to further the fraudulent
evasion of a restriction on importation into this country are punishable
under this section, see *R. v. Wall (Geoffrey)* [1974] 1 W.L.R. 930, 934C.

For guilt to be established the importation must, of course, result as a
consequence, if only in part, of the activity of the accused. If, for example,
in the present case the applicant had taken her two suitcases off the
carousel at Charles de Gaulle airport in Paris, removed all the luggage
tags, placed the suitcases in a left luggage compartment and thrown the
key of that compartment into the Seine, and then subsequently, in a
general emergency, all left luggage compartments had been opened, a
well-known English travel label had been found on her suitcase and those
suitcases had been sent to the Travel Agents' agency, care of Customs and
Excise at Heathrow, then that undoubted importation would not be the
relevant one for the purposes of a charge against the applicant. . . .

Although the importation takes place at one precise moment—when the
aircraft lands—a person who is concerned in the importation may play his
part before or after that moment. Commonly, the person responsible for
despatching the prohibited drugs to England acts fraudulently and so does

the person who removes them from the airport at which they have arrived. Each is guilty. . . .

There is no doubt, that . . . the applicant had a guilty mind when at Accra she booked her luggage to London. By that act, she brought about the importation through the instrumentation of innocent agents. In this way, she caused the airline to label it to London, and the labels were responsible for the authorities in Paris sending it on to London.

What is suggested is that she should not be convicted unless her guilty state of mind subsisted at the time of importation. We see no reason to construe the Act in this way. If a guilty mind at the time of importation is an essential, the man recruited to collect the package which has already arrived and which he knows contains prohibited drugs commits no offence. What matters is the state of mind at the time the relevant acts are done, *i.e.* at the time the defendant is concerned in bringing about the importation. This accords with the general principles of common law. To stab a victim in a rage with the necessary intent for murder or manslaughter leads to criminal responsibility for the resulting death regardless of any repentance between the act of stabbing and the time of death, which may be hours or days later. This is so even if, within seconds of the stabbing, the criminal comes to his senses and does everything possible to assist his victim. Only the victim's survival will save him from conviction for murder or manslaughter.

The applicant alleged that she repented as soon as she boarded the aircraft; that she deliberately failed to claim her luggage in Paris, that she tore up the baggage tags attached to her ticket and so on, but none of this could have saved her from being held criminally responsible for the importation which she had brought about by deliberate actions committed with guilty intent. Thus, the learned judge was right in the ruling he made.

Appeal dismissed

Questions

1. If checking in the cases at Accra amounted to an "act which is more than merely preparatory to the commission of the offence" (s.1(1) Criminal Attempts Act 1981), would removal of the luggage in Paris, in the manner suggested by the judge, have provided an answer to a charge of attempted fraudulent evasion of importation restrictions?

2. If checking in the cases at Accra did not amount to "an act which is more than merely preparatory to the commission of the offence," should such an intention be sufficient for conviction of the completed offence which unexpectedly occurs at a time when *mens rea* no longer exists?

Note

Where an *actus reus* may be brought about by a continuing act, it is sufficient that the accused had *mens rea* during its continuance even though he did not have *mens rea* at its inception (see *Fagan* v. *Metropolitan Police Commissioner, post,* p. 582; see also *Kaitamaki* [1985] A.C. 147). A problem which has arisen in relation to homicide, is that of death resulting from a series of acts performed by the accused only some of which were performed with *mens rea*.

Thabo Meli v. The Queen
[1954] 1 W.L.R. 228
Privy Council

The deceased was taken to a hut by the appellants where he was struck over the head with intent to kill him. His unconscious body was then rolled over a small cliff to make the death appear to be an accident. Medical evidence indicated that the appellants had not succeeded in killing the deceased in the hut but that he had died from exposure.

LORD REID: The point of law which was raised in this case can be simply stated. It is said that two acts were necessary and were separable: first, the attack in the hut; and, secondly, the placing of the body outside afterwards. It is said that, while the first act was accompanied by *mens rea*, it was not the cause of death; but that the second act, while it was the cause of death, was not accompanied by *mens rea*; and on that ground it is said that the accused are not guilty of any crime, except perhaps culpable homicide.

It appears to their Lordships impossible to divide up what was really one transaction in this way. There is no doubt that the accused set out to do all these acts in order to achieve their plan and as parts of their plan; and it is too refined a ground of judgment to say that, because they were under a misapprehension at one stage and thought that their guilty purpose had been achieved before in fact it was achieved, therefore they are to escape the penalties of the law. . . .

Note

1. In the next chapter the issue of mistake will be considered. In *Thabo Meli* the appellants made a mistake; they thought they were disposing of a corpse when they threw the victim over the cliff. An intention to destroy or dispose of a corpse is not sufficient *mens rea* for murder; what is required is an intention to kill or to cause grievous bodily harm. Thus, in strict legal principle, the appellants' mistake meant that they did not have the *mens rea* of murder at the time they caused death. If they were to be convicted of murder, the court would have to extend the law on policy grounds to cover this situation where there was no contiguity between the *actus reus* and *mens rea*. As Williams states (C.L.P.G. pp. 174–175):

"In [this case of *Thabo Meli*] the accused intends to kill and does kill; his only mistake is as to the precise moment of death and as to the precise act that effects death. Ordinary ideas of justice and common sense require that such a case shall be treated as murder. If so it is necessary to make an exception to the general principle [that mistake as to an element of the *actus reus* negatives *mens rea*], and to hold that although the accused thinks that he is dealing with a corpse, still his act is murder if his mistaken belief that it is a corpse is the result of what he has done in pursuance of his murderous intent. If a killing by the first act would have been manslaughter, a later destruction of the supposed corpse should also be manslaughter."

2. In the case of *Church* [1966] 1 Q.B. 59 *post*, p. 547, the problem of the supposed corpse arose in relation to a conviction of

manslaughter. The appellant struck and attempted to strangle a woman. She fell unconscious and the appellant, believing her dead following his extremely cursory examination of her, threw her into a river where she drowned. He was convicted of manslaughter and on appeal that conviction was upheld. The Court of Criminal Appeal appears to have upheld the conviction on the basis of gross negligence manslaughter (now referred to as reckless manslaughter) although it also made comments on the "series of acts" doctrine in *Thabo Meli*. It adopted "as sound" Williams's view as expressed in the final sentence of the passage above. The court was of opinion that the judge should have directed the jury that—

" ... they were entitled (if they thought fit) to regard the conduct of the appellant in relation to Mrs. Nott [the deceased] as constituting throughout a series of acts which *culminated in her death,* and that, if that was how they regarded the accused's behaviour, it mattered not whether he believed her to be alive or dead when he threw her in the river." (emphasis added) (at p. 71).

The problem with this approach is that it begs a question; was it such a series of acts that would have led to conviction under the *Thabo Meli* approach? In *Thabo Meli* the acts of attack and disposal were part of a concerted plan to kill the accused and then dispose of the corpse. There was no such plan in *Church* (nor could there be in a case of manslaughter unless it arose as a result of a plea of diminished responsibility), so were the acts of original attack and the act of disposal part of a series? In *Thabo Meli* the acts formed a series, not because the act of disposal followed sequentially on the attack, but because they were concerted acts in pursuance of a plan. In speaking of *Thabo Meli* the Court of Criminal Appeal stated that, with regard to the charge of murder against *Church* (of which he was acquitted),

" ... the jury should have been told that it was still open to them to convict of murder, notwithstanding that the appellant may have thought his blows and attempt at strangulation had actually produced death when he threw the body into the river, if they regarded the appellant's behaviour from the moment he first struck her to the moment when he threw her into the river as a series of acts designed to cause death or grievous bodily harm." (at p. 67)

This statement talks of a "series of acts designed to cause death" whereas, in respect of manslaughter, the court talked of a "series of acts which culminated in ... death." It is difficult to follow the court's reasoning when it talks of a series of acts designed to cause death as the act of disposal is for the purpose of disposing of a *body,* it being the actor's belief that death had occurred already. Such a direction would be inherently illogical.

In *S.* v. *Masilela* 1968 (2) S.A. 558 the Supreme Court of South Africa (Appellate Division) held that a conviction of murder could be returned where death resulted from the act of disposal by the assailant even though there was no preconceived plan. In the case which follows there was neither a preconceived plan nor did the accused believe he was dealing with a corpse.

R. v. Le Brun
[1991] 3 W.L.R. 653
Court of Appeal

D and W (his wife) argued in the street, W refusing to go home. D struck W rendering her unconscious. He dragged her from the street either to get her into the house where she did not want to go or to conceal his previous assault and in so doing W's head struck the pavement, fracturing her skull and death resulted. D was convicted of manslaughter and appealed.

LORD LANE C.J.: ... The question can be perhaps framed in this way. There was here an initial unlawful blow to the chin delivered by the appellant. That, again on what must have been the jury's finding, was not delivered with the intention of doing really serious harm to the wife. The guilty intent accompanying that blow was sufficient to have rendered the appellant guilty of manslaughter, but not murder, had it caused death. But it did not cause death. What caused death was the later impact when the wife's head hit the pavement. At the moment of impact the appellant's intention was to remove her, probably unconscious, body to avoid detection. To that extent the impact may have been accidental. May the earlier guilty intent be joined with the later non-guilty blow which caused death to produce in the conglomerate a proper verdict of manslaughter?

It has usually been in the previous decisions in the context of murder that the problem has arisen. We have had our attention directed to a Privy Council case, *Meli* v. *The Queen* [1954] 1 W.L.R. 228. ... That decision of course is not binding upon us. It is of very persuasive authority and it was adopted by another division of this court in 1975 in *R.* v. *Moore* [1975] Crim.L.R. 229.

However, it will be observed that the present case is different from the facts of those two cases in that death here was not the result of a preconceived plan which went wrong, as was the case in those two decisions which we have cited. Here the death, again assuming the jury's finding to be such as it must have been, was the result of an initial unlawful blow, not intended to cause serious harm, in its turn causing the appellant to take steps possibly to evade the consequences of his unlawful act. During the taking of those steps he commits the actus reus but without the mens rea necessary for murder or manslaughter. Therefore the mens rea is contained in the initial unlawful assault, but the actus reus is the eventual dropping of the head on to the ground.

Normally the actus reus and mens rea coincide in point of time. What is the situation when they do not? Is it permissible, as the prosecution contend here, to combine them to produce a conviction for manslaughter?

The answer is perhaps to be found in the next case to which we were referred, and that was *R.* v. *Church* [1966] 1 Q.B. 59.

[His Lordship quoted Edmund Davies J.'s judgment where he stated that a manslaughter verdict would have been returned on the basis of a "series of acts which culminated in death," and continued.]

It seems to us that where the unlawful application of force and the eventual act causing death are parts of the same sequence of events, the same transaction, the fact that there is an appreciable interval of time between the two does not serve to exonerate the defendant from liability. That is certainly so where the appellant's subsequent actions which caused death, after the initial unlawful blow, are designed to conceal his commission of the original unlawful assault. ...

In short, in circumstances such as the present, which is the only concern of this court, the act which causes death, and the necessary mental state to constitute manslaughter, need not coincide in point of time. ...

[His Lordship concluded that the judge's direction to the jury was satisfactory in so far as it related to manslaughter.]

Appeal dismissed

Questions

1. In all the earlier cases D killed in the course of covering up the homicide he mistakenly believed he had already committed. Is the true principle either of the following alternatives: that D is liable for homicide (murder or manslaughter depending on his *mens rea*) where he performs a series of acts which culminate in death, *mens rea* existing either (a) at the time of the initial act, or (b) at some stage during the transaction? (see *Att.-Gen.'s Reference (No. 4 of 1980), infra*).

2. Lord Lane C.J. also sought to support the conviction of manslaughter in *Le Brun* on the basis of causation. He stated:

"It would be possible to express the problem as one of causation. The original unlawful blow to the chin was a cause sine qua non of the later actus reus. It was the opening event in a series which was to culminate in death: the first link in the chain of causation, to use another metaphor. It cannot be said that the actions of the appellant in dragging the victim away with the intention of evading liability broke the chain which linked the initial blow with the death."

Was the initial assault a substantial cause of death? Could the conviction be supported solely on this causation basis without the "series of acts" doctrine being applied? If it can be supported solely on causation what was the *mens rea* at the time of "the later *actus reus*"?

Note

A problem which the Court of Appeal did not address in *Le Brun* is that which arose in the following case where it was impossible to tell which act caused death.

Attorney-General's Reference (No. 4 of 1980)
[1981] 2 All E.R. 617
Court of Appeal

D and V were arguing. D slapped V causing her to fall backwards down a flight of stairs head first onto the floor where she lay motionless. D tied a rope around her neck and dragged her upstairs, placed her in the bath, cut her throat to let out her blood, and then cut her up and disposed of the pieces. The body was never found so the cause of death could not be determined. V died either from the fall, from being strangled by the rope or from having her throat cut. The defence submitted that there was no case to go to the jury and the judge withdrew the case directing an acquittal on the basis that the Crown had failed to prove the cause of death. The Attorney-General sought the court's opinion on the following point of law: whether a person who has committed a series of acts against another culminating in the death of that person, each act in the series being either unlawful and dangerous or an act of gross criminal negligence, is entitled to be acquitted of manslaughter on the ground that it cannot be shown which of such acts caused the death of the deceased.

ACKNER L.J.: On the above facts this reference raises a single and simple question, *viz.*, if an accused kills another by one or other of two or more different acts each of which, if it caused the death, is a sufficient act to establish manslaughter, is it necessary in order to found a conviction to prove which act caused the death? The answer to the question is No, it is not necessary to found a conviction to prove which act caused the death. No authority is required to justify this answer, which is clear beyond argument, as was indeed immediately conceded by counsel on behalf of the accused.

What went wrong in this case was that counsel made jury points to the judge and not submissions of law. He was in effect contending that the jury should not convict of manslaughter if the death had resulted from the "fall," because the push which had projected the deceased over the handrail was a reflex and not a voluntary action, as a result of her digging her nails into him. If, however, the deceased was still alive when he cut her throat, since he then genuinely believed her to be dead, having discovered neither pulse nor sign of breath, but frothy blood coming from her mouth, he could not be guilty of manslaughter because he had not behaved with gross criminal negligence. What counsel and the judge unfortunately overlooked was that there was material available to the jury which would have entitled them to have convicted the accused of manslaughter, whichever of the two sets of acts caused her death. It being common ground that the deceased was killed by an act done to her by the accused and it being conceded that the jury could not be satisfied which was the act which caused the death, they should have been directed in due course in the summing up, to ask themselves the following questions: (i) "Are we satisfied beyond reaonable doubt that the deceased's 'fall' downstairs was the result of an intentional act by the accused which was unlawful and dangerous?" If the answer was No, then they would acquit. If the answer was Yes, then they would need to ask themselves a second question, namely: (ii) "Are we satisfied beyond reasonable doubt that the act of cutting the girl's throat was an act of gross criminal negligence?" If the answer to that question was No, then they would acquit, but if the answer was Yes, then the verdict would be guilty of manslaughter. The jury would thus have been satisfied that, whichever act had killed the deceased, each was a sufficient act to establish the offence of manslaughter.

The facts of this case did not call for "a series of acts direction" following the principle in *Thabo Meli* v. *R.* [*supra*]. We have accordingly been deprived of the stimulating questions whether the decision in *R.* v. *Church* [*post*, p. 547] correctly extended that principle to manslaughter, in particular to "constructive manslaughter" and if so whether that view was part of the ratio decidendi.

Determination accordingly

Questions

1. If the jury are satisfied that D, with *mens rea*, committed an unlawful and dangerous act in hitting V, could they, applying *Le Brun* (which approved the direction on manslaughter in *Church* based on a series of acts culminating in death), convict of manslaughter even though the cause of death is not determined? Has *Le Brun* rendered nugatory the decision in *Att.-Gen.'s Reference*?

2. Should the dual test articulated by Ackner L.J. be applied if the charge is one of murder or should the "series of acts" doctrine in *Le Brun* be extended to cover murder?

CHAPTER 3

MENS REA

	PAGE		PAGE
1. The Requirement of *Mens Rea*	64	3. Mistake	140
2. The Meaning of *Mens Rea*	68	i. Relevant Mistakes	141
i. Intention	70	ii. Irrelevant Mistakes	169
ii. Motive and Intention	97	4. Strict Liability	182
iii. Knowledge	102	i. The Evolution of Strict Lia-	
iv. Recklessness	106	bility	182
v. Wilfulness	128	ii. The Present Uncertainty	183
vi. Proposals for Reform	137	iii. Critique	206
		iv. Proposals for Reform	210

1. THE REQUIREMENT OF MENS REA

Williams, Criminal Law: The General Part, p. 30

"Nature of the requirement of mens rea
There is no need to go into the remote history of *mens rea*; suffice it to say that the requirement of a guilty state of mind (at least for the more serious crimes) had been developed by the time of Coke, which is as far back as the modern lawyer needs to go. 'If one shoot at any wild fowl upon a tree, and the arrow killeth any reasonable creature afar off, without any evil intent in him, this is *per infortunium.'*
It may be said that any theory of criminal punishment leads to a requirement of some kind of *mens rea*. The deterrent theory is workable only if the culprit has knowledge of the legal sanction; and if a man does not foresee the consequence of his act he cannot appreciate that punishment lies in store for him if he does it. The retributive theory presupposes moral guilt; incapacitation supposes social danger; and the reformative aim is out of place if the offender's sense of values is not warped.
However, the requirement as we have it in the law does not harmonise perfectly with any of these theories. It does not fit the deterrent theory, because a man may have *mens rea* although he is ignorant of the law. On the deterrent theory, ignorance of the law should be a defence; yet it is not. Again, the requirement does not quite conform to the retributive theory, because the *mens rea* of English law does not necessarily connote an intention to engage in moral wrongdoing. A crime may be committed from the best of motives and yet remain a crime. (In this respect the phrase *mens rea* is somewhat misleading). There are similar difficulties with incapacitation and reform.
What, then, does legal *mens rea* mean? It refers to the mental element necessary for the particular crime, and this mental element may be either *intention* to do the immediate act or bring about the consequence or (in some crimes) *recklessness* as to such act or consequence. In different and more precise language, *mens rea* means intention or recklessness as to the elements constituting the *actus reus*. These two concepts, intention and recklessness, hold the key to the understanding of a large part of criminal

law. Some crimes require intention and nothing else will do, but most can be committed either intentionally or recklessly. Some crimes require particular kinds of intention or knowledge.

Outside the class of crimes requiring *mens rea* there are some that do not require any particular state of mind but do require negligence. Negligence in law is not necessarily a state of mind; and thus these crimes are best regarded as not requiring *mens rea*. However, negligence is a kind of legal fault, and in that respect they are akin to crimes requiring *mens rea*.

Yet other crimes do not even require negligence. They are crimes of strict or vicarious responsibility, and, like crimes of negligence, they constitute exceptions to the adage *Actus non facit reum nisi mens sit rea.*"

Note

Williams regards intention and recklessness as basic *mens rea* in that a defendant's culpability should be dependent on his awareness of the relevant circumstances surrounding, and consequences of, his conduct. The Law Commission in their Draft Criminal Code Bill recognise recklessness as the "presumed minimum requirement for criminal liability" and by clause 20(1) create a presumption for Code offences and offences created subsequent to the Code's enactment:

"Every offence requires a fault element of recklessness with respect to each of its elements other than fault elements, unless otherwise provided."

Is *mens rea* a merely descriptive term or does it serve other purposes? The extracts which follow address this problem.

A. T. H. Smith "On Actus Reus and Mens Rea" in Reshaping the Criminal Law (ed. Glazebrook), p. 103

"The idea that *mens rea* is in some sense a basic or indispensable ingredient of criminal liability is deeply rooted. For example, Stroud stated that:

the guilt of an act charged against a prisoner must always depend upon two conditions ... [which] ... may be called the condition of illegality (*actus reus*) and the condition of culpable intentionality (*mens rea*). (*Mens Rea* (London, 1914), p. 7.)

Kenny's view was that:

no external conduct, however serious or even fatal its consequences may have been, is ever punished unless it is produced by some form of *mens rea*. (*Outlines of Criminal Law* (2nd ed.) (Cambridge, 1904), p. 39).

These writers explicitly discount the phenomenon of strict liability, and they should not be taken to task for failing to elucidate matters with which they were not concerned. Nevertheless, by insisting that *mens rea* is a necessary constituent of crime, they distort the function that that concept really performs. A fully descriptive account of criminal responsibility would be forced to acknowledge that there are many instances where liability is imposed without proof of *mens rea* as to at least some elements in the *actus reus*.

It may be helpful to identify three of the purposes for which the expression *mens rea* is used. It is, first, an expositional tool, when used in sentences such as 'the *mens rea* of X offence is Y,' where Y might be (depending on the offence in question) intention, recklessness, malice, dishonesty, an intent to defraud or deceive. We could substitute the expression 'mental element' without any change of meaning. This is the use to which Stephen referred when he said that

> the maxim about '*mens rea*' means no more than that the definition of all or nearly all crimes contains not only an outward and visible element, but a mental element, varying according to the different nature of different crimes. (*A History of The Criminal Law of England* (London, 1883), vol. ii, p. 95).

In addition the term is used, as has already been seen, to denote traditional *mens rea*, a catalogue of more or less blameworthy mental states of intention, recklessness and negligence from which the legislator, in defining crime, is free to pick and choose to suit his requirements.

The expression *mens rea* performs, however, another function by acting as an ideal towards which the legal system should evolve. A balance of modern opinion favours imposing liability on the basis of fault, subjectively assessed, and a considerable body of literature criticises such strict liability and constructive liability for deviating from this ideal. Such criticisms are premised on a view of criminal responsibility which has fault as its basis. But when traditional *mens rea* is referred to as the 'fault' element, this fault principle and a purely technical usage are conflated. The two by no means necessarily coincide, since traditional *mens rea* refers only to awareness of circumstances and to the contemplation of particular results. It does not follow that, because a person foresees or intends he is necessarily at fault: the intention may have been formed in a variety of exculpating circumstances such as under provocation, duress or necessity. As the expression of a fault principle, then, traditional *mens rea* is no more than a rule of thumb. Even as a description of the present law, it is necessary to look for a more embracing fault principle within which the existing excuses can be subsumed. This more fundamental principle has been formulated by Professor Hart in these terms:

> unless a man has the capacity and a fair opportunity or chance to adjust his behaviour to the law its penalties ought not to be applied to him. (*Punishment and Responsibility* (Oxford, 1968), p. 181).

This, he argues, is not only a rationale for most of the excuses which the law already admits; it might also act as a critical principle to ask of the law more than it already concedes.

An account of criminal liability that treats traditional *mens rea* as a necessary fault requirement is thus deficient in two respects. It overlooks the phenomenon of strict liability, and it takes no account of a number of efficacious excuses which do not negative the element of awareness or cognition."

Fletcher, Rethinking Criminal Law, pp. 396–397

"Descriptive and Normative Uses of the Same Terms
One of the persistent tensions in legal terminology runs between the descriptive and normative uses of the same terms. Witness the struggle over the concept of malice. The term has a high moral content, and when it came into the law as the benchmark of murder, it was presumably used

normatively and judgmentally. Yet Fitzjames Stephen and succeeding generations of English jurists have sought to reduce the concepts of malice to the specific mental states of intending and knowing. California judges, in contrast, have stressed the normative content of malice in a highly judgmental definition, employing terms like 'base, anti-social purpose' and 'wanton disregard for human life.' For the English, malice is a question of fact: did the actor have a particular state of consciousness (intention or knowledge)? In California, malice is a value judgment about the actor's motives, attitudes and personal capacity.

If the English have tried to reduce the normative concept of malice to a state of fact, other commentators and courts seek to invest nominally descriptive terms with moral force. Though the terms 'intent,' 'state of mind,' and 'mental state' appear to be descriptive, legislators and courts use these terms to refer to issues that require normative judgment. ...

The confusion between normative and descriptive language is so pervasive in Anglo-American criminal law that it affects the entire language of discourse. There appear to be very few terms that are exempt from the ambiguity. The term 'intent' may refer either to a state of intending (regardless of blame) or it may refer to an intent to act under circumstances (such as failing to inquire about the age of a sexual partner) that render an act properly subject to blame. The term 'criminal intent' does not resolve the ambiguity, for a criminal intent may simply be the intent to do the act, which, according to the statutory definition, renders the act 'criminal,' *i.e.* punishable under the law. There may be nothing morally blameworthy in keeping a pair of brass knuckles as a conversation piece, yet that intent renders the act punishable and, in this sense, is a criminal intent.

It is obvious that the very word 'criminal' is affected by the same tension between descriptive and normative illocutionary force. When used normatively, 'criminal' refers to the type of person who by virtue of his deeds deserves to be branded and punished as a criminal. When used descriptively, as in the phrase 'criminal act' it may refer simply to any act that the legislature has declared to be 'criminal.' Thus the term 'criminal intent' may mean the intent to act under circumstances that make it just to treat the actor as a criminal in the pejorative sense. ... But it is equally plausible to use the term 'criminal intent' to refer to the intent or knowledge sufficient to commit a crime as defined by the legislature. The adjective 'criminal' in this context simply means that the intent is sufficient to render the act punishable under the statute. ...

There is no term fraught with greater ambiguity than that venerable Latin phrase that haunts Anglo-American criminal law: *mens rea*. Glanville Williams defines *mens rea* to mean 'the mental element necessary for the particular crime.' Of course, the term 'mental element' may be employed either descriptively or normatively, yet in this context it seems clear that Williams means to refer to a factual state of affairs. Intent, used descriptively, is an example of a required 'mental element.' In another passage, Williams argues that the issue of duress should not be seen as negating either intention or *mens rea*. Thus he would conclude, ... that someone who was acquitted on grounds of duress nonetheless acted with *mens rea*. However prestigious this line of analysis might be, the courts fortunately remain unimpressed. Engaged as they are in the processes of judgment and condemnation, the courts repeatedly stress the normative content of *mens rea*, ...

This tension between descriptive and normative usage carries significance for the structuring of issues in the criminal law. Descriptive theorists, like Stephen, Turner, Williams and others in the English tradition, are apt to see problems of insanity, duress and mistake as extrinsic to the analysis of *mens rea* and criminal intent. Normative theorists, in contrast, are able to integrate these 'defensive' issues into their formulation of the minimum conditions for liability. If *mens rea* raises a normative issue of just and appropriate blame, then there is no *mens rea* or 'criminal intent' when the intentional commission of the offence is excused by reason of duress, insanity, or reasonable mistake about an attendant circumstance (*e.g.* the age of the girl in statutory rape)."

2. THE MEANING OF MENS REA

Note

While there may be differences in theoretical approach, a more pressing problem for any student of criminal law is the bewildering array of words and phrases with which the mental element in offences may be indicated. Lord Simon of Glaisdale in *D.P.P. for Northern Ireland* v. *Lynch* [1975] A.C. 653, 688, speaking in a wider context than the issue of duress, with which the case was primarily concerned, said:

"A principal difficulty in this branch of the law is the chaotic terminology, whether in judgments, academic writings or statutes. Will, volition, motive, purpose, object, view, intention, intent, specific intent or intention, wish, desire; necessity, coercion, compulsion, duress—such terms which do indeed overlap in certain contexts, seem frequently to be used interchangeably, without definition, and regardless that in some cases the legal usage is a term of art differing from the popular usage. As if this were not enough, Latin expressions which are themselves ambiguous, and often overlap more than one of the English terms, have been freely used—especially animus and (most question-begging of all) mens rea."

For this obfuscation of the law the judges must carry a large share of the blame.

E. Griew, "Consistency, Communication and Codification: Reflections on Two Mens Rea Words" in Reshaping the Criminal Law (ed. Glazebrook), pp. 57–59.

"A striking feature of English criminal law has been the casual, erratic quality of the use of key terms in its technical language. This has been most marked in the case of important words that Parliament or the judges have used to express aspects of the mental element of crimes: words like 'malice' and 'maliciously' (examples of ancient casualness), 'wilfully' (a once-popular statutory adverb that has left a legacy of confusion), 'intention' and 'recklessness' (the most discussed of the criminal 'states of mind'). Judges in particular, but Parliament as well, have on the whole seemed to care little about achieving consensus or consistency in this department of the legal vocabulary. This indifference in the matter of language has been part of a larger indifference to criminal law analysis as a whole. . . .

There has recently arisen a judicial practice of disposing of problems in the criminal law—some would say, of escaping from them—by explicit reliance on the linguistic competence of the common man. To the extent that consensus about the meaning of a word in a particular context is in the nature of language possible, it can arise in two broad ways. One of these occurs when, as it might be put, 'everyone knows what the word means.' If, however, there is no such spontaneous consensus, or if a special use is to be made of the word, the required consensus must be imposed by authority. The authority stipulates a meaning. Legal authority in this connection is legislature or court. In relation both to general concepts in the criminal law and to words in particular contexts, the courts have tended to make a virtue of refraining from 'stipulative definition' —from imposing consensus by saying what words are to be understood to mean. This tendency has been reinforced by the proposition, which has recently enjoyed a powerful vogue in appellate criminal courts, that the meaning of an ordinary word of the English language is not a question of law. Those courts have been very ready—though not consistently so—to find that statutory words whose application is in question before them are 'ordinary words,' and have approved of trial judges' restraint in the explication of the words for their juries' assistance. ... The result is that even though there is in fact no spontaneous consensus about the meaning of a word, the courts proceed on the fiction that 'everyone knows what it means.' Parliament too has so far been silent in this field. In short, authority has not yet asserted itself in the stipulation of criminal law definitions. ...

Concern for language, whether as an aspect of the criminal law as a whole or in the expression of particular rules, is a concern for principle and for substance. If lawyers are not involved in understanding and expounding the theory of the criminal law, their operations will tend towards mere ritual. Theory depends upon the development and accurate deployment of a self-consistent language, through the medium of which legal statements may tellingly respond to discriminations of policy and to the relationships between relevant concepts. The theory and its servant language are not matters for the legislator alone. Lawyers and judges are vital participants in the business of communication by which legislative intention is translated into acts of adjudication. Where legislation is wanting, or where it lacks 'definition,' the task of making or clarifying the law is with the courts. That task has, by its nature, to be performed as occasion arises and only to the extent demanded by the occasion. When occasion does not arise, the court's contribution ought to be made with two considerations (among others) in mind. One is the larger picture—the total body of criminal law theory into which the court's decision and the language that embodies it must fit; indifference to theory and principle involves the danger of particularistic decision and in the long run of incoherence. The second consideration is that criminal law rules are of general application. To deny explanation of them as required, on the ground that it is not the court's job to explain 'ordinary words,' is to risk all upon the assumption that the word, being ordinary, is within the lexical equipment of the adult population at large and understood (if not used) by everyone in the same sense. This is in fact a set of uniformly unsafe assumptions about people's linguistic competence, about the sociology of language, and about the composition of tribunals of fact. The assumptions upon which, for safety, we should proceed, are: that very low levels of linguistic competence are quite general in the adult population; that even 'ordinary' words (and especially abstract words) are variously understood—everyone may 'know what they mean' but, without knowing it, use them with different meanings; and that the decisions of two benches or juries could depend upon quite different collective senses of how the law is using the same undefined abstract word."

i. Intention

"Intention" is the *mens rea* term which conveys the highest level of culpability of an offender. If a person intends to cause a result he is more culpable than a person who acts recklessly, that is, who acts recognising that the result might occur. It is important to define the boundary between intention and recklessness not only to determine the degree of culpability of the offender for sentencing purposes, but also to determine in many cases whether the offender is liable to conviction where the offence charged is one which requires intention to be proved. The *Concise Oxford Dictionary* defines "intend" as "have as one's purpose" and "intention" as "intending, one's purpose ... object ... ultimate aim." The law, however, does not always attribute to words their dictionary meaning. "Intention" is such a word.

G. Williams, "Oblique Intention" (1987) 46 *C.L.J.* 417

"WHY is it that intention, or intent, one of the basic concepts of the criminal law, remains so unclear? Judges decline to define it, and they appear to adjust it from one case to another.

Part of the trouble is the disagreement on the subject of intention among jurists generally. The philosophers who have lately arrived on the scene, hoping to help the lawyers to solve their legal problems, in fact give only limited assistance. Their philosophical interest stems from the fact that intention is an important ethical concept, but they do not relate their discussions to any particular ethical theory, and they do not sufficiently consider the specific requirements of the criminal law. Indeed, they mix up the ordinary meaning of the word 'intention' with its desirable legal meaning. To be sure, the meaning of intention as a technical term of the law ought to be close to the literary and popular one, but there are sound reasons for saying that the two should not always be identical.

Added to the confusion of counsel is the fact that judges sometimes wrap up excuses into the meaning of intention, though rationally excuses should have nothing to do with the matter.

Judges reject the proposition that the legal concept of intention in relation to the consequences of action necessarily involves desire of the consequence. This is quite right, and a useful beginning; but the recent pronouncements of the lords get no further. They do not acknowledge the truth that intention generally does involve desire, and they do not say when it does not."

Note

What, then, is the possible meaning of "intention" in the criminal law? Does "doing an act with foresight of its consequences" amount to the same as "doing an act intending to bring about that consequence"? To answer this question it is necessary to examine the various states of mind that might constitute intention. The states of mind competing to be included within the compass of the term *intention* may be illustrated as follows—

Scenario

D has insured V's life. He decides to kill V in order to obtain the insurance moneys. D's *desire* is to kill V and his *motive* is to obtain the insurance moneys. What is his *intention*?

Case (a) D intends a consequence if it is his *aim* or *objective*. If D shoots at V in order to kill him, the consequence, V's death, is both desired and *intended* by D.

Case (b) D intends a consequence if he foresees it as certain to result from his conduct.

So D wishing to kill V shoots at V who is standing behind a window.

In this case D knows that in order to kill V the bullet must pass through the window. With regard to the window, D intends to break it although he does not desire to do so for its own sake; breaking the window is a necessary precondition to shooting V, that is, it is a means to that end. As Lord Hailsham said in *Hyam* [1975] A.C. 55, 74, "intention [includes] the means as well as the end and the inseparable consequences of the end as well as the means." In the circumstances as they exist, it is not possible for D to kill V without breaking the window. Thus it can be said that D has a *direct* intention regarding V and an *oblique* intention regarding the window; breaking the window is his subsidiary or secondary aim which must be achieved if he is to achieve his ultimate or primary aim.

Does D *desire* to break the window? This depends on the width of the definition of desire. Duff, "The Obscure Intentions of the House of Lords" [1986] *Crim.L.R.* 773, argues that a person may intend to do various unpleasant things without desiring them. For example, a person with toothache visits the dentist; he does not like visiting dentists and thus does not want or desire to go but he does go intentionally. Williams questions this conclusion.

G. Williams, "Oblique Intention" (1987) 46 *C.L.J.* 417–421

"What the courts ought to hold appears to me to be clear. (1) Except in one type of case, intention as to a consequence of what is done requires desire of the consequence. Of course, intention, for the lawyer, is not a bare wish; it is a combination of wish and act (or other external element). With one exception, an act is intentional as to a consequence if it is done with (motivated by) the wish, desire, purpose or aim (all synonyms in this context) of producing the result in question. (2) The one type of case in which it is reasonable to say that an undesired consequence can be intended in law is in respect of known certainties. A person can be held (but will not always be held) to intend an undesired event that he knows for sure he is bringing about.

(1) The first proposition is disputed by some writers, particularly the two philosophers, [Alan White and R. A. Duff], who have taken an interest in the English criminal law. Their principal argument is that one can intend to do various unpleasant things, *e.g.* visiting the dentist; therefore intention need not involve desire. I would have thought that the error in this is too obvious to need stating. The premise is true, but the conclusion does not follow. Obviously, people go to the dentist in order to get certain

benefits (relief from pain or the preservation of the teeth). To get these benefits, the possibility of pain or discomfort is accepted. It is accepted not as an end in itself but as part of the package, and the package as a whole is desired—otherwise one would not go to the dentist. The pain taken by itself is not desired, but the proposition was not that the patient intends the pain but that he intends to visit (intentionally visits) the dentist.

The writers who deny the relevance of desire replace it with the word 'purpose.' But does not purpose imply desire? One can have an undeclared purpose, but not a undesired purpose. 'Undesired purpose' is a contradiction in terms.

(2) The second proposition seemed to be on its way to legal acceptance until recent pronouncements of the lords. Perhaps the lords intended to negative it. Or perhaps they did not. More of this later.

In one application, at least, the second proposition is accepted as almost universally true. Where the defendant desires result x, and anyone can see, by merely considering x, that another result, y (forbidden by law), will also be involved, as the direct consequence of x and almost as part and parcel of it, then the defendant will be taken to intend both x and y.

Three men accidentally killed a girl in horseplay. Being frightened, they hid the body under a pile of stones. It was held that they were guilty of conspiracy to prevent the burial of a corpse [*Hunter* [1974] Q.B. 95]. The Court of Appeal upheld a direction that 'if the defendants agreed to conceal the body and the concealment in fact prevented burial, then the offence was made out, although prevention of burial was not the object of the agreement.'

A result that is either witnessed or foreseen as certain is almost always regarded as sharing the intentional nature of an act where it is either the contemporaneous (concurrent) result or the immediate consequence of the act. A person will normally be taken to intend something that he is consciously doing, or that follows under his nose from what he is then doing. . . .

Using the word 'intention' in this way admittedly involves an extension beyond its normal meaning in the language. The normal meaning connotes desire. [White] writes: 'What I do knowing I am doing it need not be done intentionally, as when I know that I am hurting your feelings but not doing so intentionally.' The remark is true for ordinary speech, and true in law for offences involving the 'hurting of feelings'; but the law is much more concerned with hurting bodies than with hurting feelings. If I drive over you because I am in a hurry and you will not get out of the way, I drive over you intentionally, and it would be no use my saying that my sole intention was to make progress. For legal purposes the meaning of intention has to be widened to this extent.

Similarly, a surgeon intentionally wounds his patient when he inserts the scalpel. He does not, of course, commit a crime of intention, but that is because he has the justification of consent. Lord Hailsham on one occasion denied this, and put the surgeon's defence on lack of intent; this is an example of the judicial tendency already mentioned, to bring in defences under the heading of lack of intention. In the unlikely case of a surgeon kidnapping his recalcitrant patient and making various incisions in him, entirely for the patient's benefit, the surgeon would be guilty of the offence of wounding with intent; yet his intention to make the incisions would be the same as in an ordinary medical operation.

The law should generally be the same where the defendant is aware that a consequence in the future is the certain (though undesired) result of what he does. He is liable for a crime of intention if the foreseen though undesired consequence is inseparably bound up with the desired consequence. This opinion has been supported by some writers, though not all. More importantly, it has been accepted by several of the major reform bodies of the common-law world. If such a variety of intention is accepted we need a name for it, the best being Bentham's coinage of 'oblique intention'. Direct intention is where the consequence is what you are aiming at. Oblique intention is something you see clearly, but out of the corner of your eye. The consequence is (figuratively speaking) not in the straight line of your purpose, but a side-effect that you accept as an inevitable or 'certain' accompaniment of your direct intent (desire-intent). There are twin consequences of the act, x and y; the doer wants x, and is prepared to accept its unwanted twin y. Oblique intent is, in other words, a kind of knowledge or realisation.

When one speaks of the unwanted consequence as being 'certain', one does not, of course, mean certain. 'Nothing is certain save death and taxes.' For example, a person who would otherwise have been the victim of the criminal's act may be warned in time, or providentially happen to change his plans, and so escape what would otherwise have been his fate. Certainty in human affairs means certainty as a matter of common sense—certainty apart from unforeseen events or remote possibilities. Realisation of practical certainty is something higher in the scale than appreciation of high probability."

Case (c) D intends a consequence if it is a virtual, practical or moral certainty that it will result from his actions—in other words, he intends a result where he acts being aware that the result will occur in the ordinary course of events.

So D places a bomb under V's seat timed to kill him in mid-flight as he pilots a plane.

In this case D does not desire to kill the crew or passengers but if he realises that their deaths are a *virtual, practical* or *moral certainty*, that is, that they will die in the ordinary course of events, he obliquely intends their deaths. The deaths of the crew or passengers are not a pre-condition to killing V but, in the ordinary course of events, they are the inevitable *by-product* of D's killing V; they are an inseparable consequence of that end. If, miraculously, the crew and passengers survive, D will not have failed in achieving his purpose, that is, killing V. This does not necessarily mean that D did not desire their deaths, if desire is given a wider meaning. Norrie is a supporter of the view that an act is intended where it is seen by the actor as having some "desirable characteristic." While agreeing that "intention" should include oblique intention he disagrees that obliquely intended consequences are undesired; this conclusion involves attributing a wider meaning to "desire."

A. Norrie, "Oblique Intention and Legal Politics" [1989] *Crim.L.R.* 793, 794–796

"2. Defining oblique intention

I agree with Williams that intention ought to be defined to include desire but, so long as it is so defined, disagree with his claim that the concept of oblique intention 'involves an extension beyond its normal meaning in the language.' That is not to say that the legal usage of oblique intention corresponds wholly with the ordinary usage.

Intention and desire

Duff argued, I believe correctly, in an earlier paper that the idea of an intended act includes the notion of a desire to bring the act about, using the term 'desire' (or 'want')

'as the most general term of volition, covering attitudes normally contrasted with "wanting," like seeing an action as a duty, as the lesser of two evils, or as an unpleasant but necessary means to a desired end. To intend an action is to see it as having some "desirable characteristic" ... '

But he later rejected this view:

'It is unnecessary, since it adds nothing to an analysis which talks only of the agent believing that her action might bring X about, and acting because of that belief. Indeed we may ascribe a desire for X to the agent only *because* we realise she intends to bring X about, rather than taking her to intend it because we realise that she desires it. It may be misleading, since it may lead us to treat desire as an independent ingredient or criterion of intention. We may then forget to distinguish the philosophers' use of "desire" (according to which it is an empty truism that all intended results are desired) from its ordinary use (according to which intention need not involve desire).'

The 'philosphers' use,' however is not an empty truism. Desire is analytically distinct from the narrow view of intention proposed by Duff. We may understand that the agent intended to bring X about either by deduction from the patterns of her action *or* by reference to her expressed wishes prior to the action or her *post facto* explanation of why she did it. Desire need not simply be tacked onto an already pre-established deduction of intention. Secondly, it is a moot point whether what Duff regards as ordinary use is not rather narrowly conceived. Take the standard illustration of the person with toothache who, in Duff's view, intends but does not want to go to the dentist. As Williams points out, there is no logical barrier to saying in a real (not technical) sense that the person *does* more broadly want to go to the dentist—as a means to an end, as part of a 'package' which has the ultimate end of removal of the pain at its heart. There seems no objection to saying both 'I didn't want to go to the dentist, but ... ' and 'I wanted to go to the dentist (but only) in order to ... ' Duff's original conception of a 'desirability characteristic' is valuable, and while the recognition of narrow and broader definitions of desire may entail complexity, it does not thereby entail confusion.

Intention, desire and oblique intention

The relevance of this philosophical discussion becomes apparent when we consider the rationale for a doctrine of oblique intent. Oblique intention only becomes a problem for ordinary usage if one separates intention from desire, for one then loses the possibility of seeing what was intended as being that which possesses a 'desirability characteristic,' as being part of a 'package' of desires. Williams is wrong to say that oblique intention involves a departure from the ordinary usage of 'intention,' for oblique intention can quite naturally be seen as a species of intention once one realises that what is intended is that which is desired in the broad 'package' sense of the term. Williams writes: 'If I drive over you because I am in a hurry and you will not get out of the way, I drive over you intentionally, and it would be no use my saying that my sole intention was to make progress.' Indeed not, but Williams gives the example to illustrate a situation where desire does not go with intent, whereas given his espousal of the 'package' view of desire, it does. I want to drive over you as part of a package which includes my making progress. Your injury is not my direct desire, but it has a 'desirability characteristic' in the broader context. Oblique intention, which includes the intention of means necessary to ends and of necessary side consequences to ends, connotes desire in the broad sense outlined above.

Two further points may be made. First, to identify oblique intention with desire in this way makes good sense for it does away with the need for alternative artificial strategies to cover what normal usage requires. Duff suggests that obliquely intended actions may be intentional but not intended. He writes that 'if I know that my action will cause death, I surely cause that death intentionally, even if I do not act with the intention of causing it: for I voluntarily make myself its agent.' This circuitry could have been avoided had he followed the logic of the broad 'philosophers' sense of desire outlined earlier in the same article, for his definition of 'intentional' action corresponds to the 'philosophers' usage, rendering this distinction unnecessary.

Secondly, the so-called 'test of failure' is only relevant to the narrow sense of intention outlined above and has the effect of artificially constricting commonsensical usage. Where I intend to bring X about and am sure that Y is a necessary corollary, but it turns out that X happens without Y, I have failed to produce the necessary corollary but not failed in my intention. Therefore Y was not part of my intention. But Y *was* part of my intention in that I was prepared to accept its necessity as a means to my end or as a side-consequence of it. I may not directly have wanted Y to happen, but I wanted X sufficiently to will the existence of Y too. I may be quite happy that X occurs without Y, but that does not mean to say the bringing about of Y was not part of my initial intention. . . .

The 'test of failure' is too constricting because it only tests direct intention, and not surrounding circumstances, means to ends, and necessary side-consequences. . . . [It] is only relevant if one has already defined intention in the narrow direct sense, and constrains commonsensical usage."

Case (d) D intends a consequence if he foresees it as a probable or likely consequence of his actions.

So D shoots at V, while he is driving a bus, in order to kill him. D foresees that it is probable that the passengers on the bus or other road users will also be killed.

In this case D does not desire the deaths of the passengers or other road users and will have been successful in his objective if only X dies. Does his foresight of their probable death amount to *intention* or does it only constitute *recklessness*?

If there are different states of mind which may be classed as *intention* or *intentional* (as the examples above illustrate), how have the courts dealt with this definitional problem.

Their approach has been far from consistent.

R. v. Steane
[1945] K.B. 997
Court of Criminal Appeal

The appellant, a British film actor, was employed in Germany when war broke out. He was arrested and entered the service of the German

broadcasting system reading news bulletins and helping to produce
films. He gave evidence that this was done under the pressure of
beatings and of threats and with a view to saving his wife and children
from a concentration camp. After the war he was convicted of doing acts
likely to assist the enemy, with intent to assist the enemy, contrary to
Regulation 2A of the Defence (General) Regulations 1939. On appeal it
was argued by the Crown that the saving of his wife and children from
a concentration camp might have been the motive for his act, but that
this was irrelevant on the issue whether he acted with the intent
alleged.

LORD GODDARD C.J.: The difficult question that arises, however, is in
connexion with the direction to the jury with regard to whether these acts
were done with the intention of assisting the enemy. The case as opened,
and indeed, as put by the learned judge appears to this court to be this: A
man is taken to intend the natural consequences of his acts; if, therefore,
he does an act which is likely to assist the enemy, it must be assumed that
he did it with the intention of assisting the enemy. . . .

While no doubt the motive of a man's act and his intention in doing the
act are, in law, different things, it is, none the less, true that in many
offences a specific intention is a necessary ingredient and the jury have to
be satisfied that a particular act was done with that specific intent,
although the natural consequences of the act might, if nothing else were
proved, be said to show the intent for which it was done. To take a simple
illustration, a man is charged with wounding with intent to do grievous
bodily harm. It is proved that he did severely wound the prosecutor.
Nevertheless, unless the Crown can prove that the intent was to do the
prosecutor grievous bodily harm, he cannot be convicted of that felony. It
is always open to the jury to negative by their verdict the intent and to
convict only of the misdemeanor of unlawful wounding. Or again, a
prisoner may be charged with shooting with intent to murder. Here again,
the prosecution may fail to satisfy the jury of the intent, although the
natural consequence of firing, perhaps at close range, would be to kill. The
jury can find in such a case an intent to do grievous bodily harm or they
might find that if the person shot at was a police constable, the prisoner
was not guilty on the count charging intent to murder, but guilty of intent
to avoid arrest. The important thing to notice in this respect is that where
an intent is charged in the indictment, the burden of proving that intent
remains throughout on the prosecution. No doubt, if the prosecution
prove an act the natural consequence of which would be a certain result
and no evidence or explanation is given, then a jury may, on a proper
direction, find that the prisoner is guilty of doing the act with the intent
alleged, but if on the totality of the evidence there is room for more than
one view as to the intent of the prisoner, the jury should be directed that
it is for the prosecution to prove the intent to the jury's satisfaction, and if,
on a review of the whole evidence, they either think that the intent did
not exist or they are left in doubt as to the intent, the prisoner is entitled
to be acquitted. . . .

In this case the court cannot but feel that some confusion arose with
regard to the question of intent by so much being said in the case with
regard to the subject of duress. Duress is a matter of defence where a
prisoner is forced by fear of violence or imprisonment to do an act which
in itself is criminal. If the act is a criminal act, the prisoner may be able to
show that he was forced into doing it by violence, actual or threatened,
and to save himself from the consequences of that violence. There is very
little learning to be found in any of the books or cases on the subject of

duress and it is by no means certain how far the doctrine extends, though we have the authority both of Hale and of Fitzjames Stephen, that while it does not apply to treason, murder and some other felonies, it does apply to misdemeanors; and offences against these regulations are misdemeanors. But here again, before any question of duress arises, a jury must be satisfied that the prisoner had the intention which is laid in the indictment. Duress is a matter of defence and the onus of proving it is on the accused. As we have already said, where an intent is charged on the indictment, it is for the prosecution to prove it, so the onus is the other way.

Now, another matter which is of considerable importance in this case, but does not seem to have been brought directly to the attention of the jury, is that very different considerations may apply where the accused at the time he did the acts is in subjection to an enemy power and where he is not. British soldiers who were set to work on the Burma road or, if invasion had unhappily taken place, British subjects who might have been set to work by the enemy digging trenches would undoubtedly be doing acts likely to assist the enemy. It would be unnecessary surely in their cases to consider any of the niceties of the law relating to duress, because no jury would find that merely by doing this work they were intending to assist the enemy. In our opinion it is impossible to say that where an act was done by a person in subjection to the power of others, especially if that other be a brutal enemy, an inference that he intended the natural consequences of his act must be drawn merely from the fact that he did it. The guilty intent cannot be presumed and must be proved. The proper direction to the jury in this case would have been that it was for the prosecution to prove the criminal intent, and that while the jury would be entitled to presume that intent if they thought that the act was done as the result of the free uncontrolled action of the accused, they would not be entitled to presume it, if the circumstances showed that the act was done in subjection to the power of the enemy, or was as consistent with an innocent intent as with a criminal intent, for example, the innocent intent of a desire to save his wife and children from a concentration camp. They should only convict if satisfied by the evidence that the act complained of was in fact done to assist the enemy, and if there was doubt about the matter, the prisoner was entitled to be acquitted.

Appeal allowed
Conviction quashed

Questions

1. Is it true to say that Steane had no intention to assist the enemy, or is it not the case that he intended to assist the enemy in order to save his family from the concentration camp? (see A. K. W. Halpin, "Intended Consequences and Unintended Fallacies" (1987) 7 O.J.L.S. 104, 110–111) 2. Is Glanville Williams correct when he states that "a more satisfactory way of deciding the case would have been to say that the accused did in law intend to assist the enemy but that duress was a defence?" (See Williams, C.L.G.P. section 18.)

Note

Steane is the leading authority against the view that intention includes foresight of certainty. There are authorities, however, that suggest the opposite. In *R.* v. *Lemon* [1979] A.C. 617, 638 Lord

Diplock, although dissenting on the question whether blasphemous libel required a mental element beyond the intention to publish, stated:

"The fear that, by retaining as a necessary element of the mens rea of the offence the intention of the publisher to shock and arouse resentment among believing Christians, those who are morally blameworthy will be unjustly acquitted appears to me to manifest a judicial distrust of the jury's capability of appreciating the meaning which in English criminal law is ascribed to the expression 'intention' of the accused. When Stephen was writing in 1883, he did not then regard it as settled law that, where intention to produce a particular result was a necessary element of an offence, no distinction is to be drawn in law between the state of mind of one who does an act because he desires it to produce that particular result and the state of mind of one who, when he does the act, is aware that it is likely to produce that result but is prepared to take the risk that it may do so, in order to achieve some other purpose which provided his motive for doing what he did. It is by now well-settled law that both states of mind constitute 'intention' in the sense in which that expression is used in the definition of a crime whether at common law or in a statute. Any doubts on this matter were finally laid to rest by the decision of this House in *R. v. Hyam* [1975] A.C. 55."

But did *Hyam* settle the meaning of intention? See *infra*.

Hyam v. D.P.P.
[1975] A.C. 55
House of Lords

Mrs Hyam's lover became engaged to be married to Mrs Booth. Being jealous of this and wishing to frighten Mrs Booth from the neighbourhood, Mrs Hyam went to her house in the early hours of the morning, poured petrol through the letterbox, stuffed newspaper through it and lit it. Mrs Booth escaped but her two daughters were suffocated by the fumes from the fire. Mrs Hyam was charged with their murder. The question before the House of Lords was whether the mens rea required for murder was established where the accused knew that it was highly probable that her act would result in death or serious bodily harm. The question was not whether foreseeing a consequence as highly probable was the same as intending that consequence, but in the course of their judgments, their Lordships did deliver some dicta on intention.

LORD HAILSHAM OF ST. MARYLEBONE: My Lords, in my view the one point in this case is the intention which it is necessary to impute to an accused person in order to find him guilty of the crime of murder. Is it simply the intention to kill or cause grievous bodily harm (in the sense of really serious injury) as is commonly assumed, or is it enough that he intends wilfully to expose another to the risk of death or grievous bodily harm in the sense of really serious injury? I do not believe that knowledge or any degree of foresight is enough. Knowledge or foresight is at the best material which entitles or compels a jury to draw the necessary inference as to intention. But what is that intention? It is acknowledged that intention to achieve the result of death or grievous bodily harm in the sense of really serious injury is enough to convict. But may the intention wilfully to expose a victim to the serious risk of death or really serious injury also be enough? It is upon the answer to this question that, in my view, depends the outcome of the present appeal. . . .

I know of no better judicial interpretation of "intention" or "intent" than that given in a civil case by Asquith L.J. (*Cunliffe* v. *Goodman* [1950] 2 K.B. 237) when he said, at p. 253:

> "An 'intention' to my mind connotes a state of affairs which the party intending . . . does more than merely contemplate: it connotes a state of affairs which on the contrary, he decides, so far as in him lies, to bring about, and which, in point of possibility, he has a reasonable prospect of being able to bring about, by his own act of volition."

If this be a good definition of "intention" for the purposes of the criminal law of murder, and so long as it is held to include the means as well as the end and the inseparable consequences of the end as well as the means, I think it is clear that "intention" is clearly to be distinguished alike from "desire" and from foresight of the probable consequences. As the Law Commission pointed out in their disquisition on *Smith* [1961] A.C. 290 [Law Commission Report No. 10], a man may desire to blow up an aircraft in flight in order to obtain insurance moneys. But if any passengers are killed he is guilty of murder, as their death will be a moral certainty if he carries out his intention. There is no difference between blowing up the aircraft and intending the death of some or all of the passengers. . . .

No doubt foresight and the degree of likelihood with which the consequences are foreseen are essential factors which should be placed before a jury in directing them as to whether the consequences are intended.

I do not, therefore, consider . . . that the fact that a state of affairs is correctly foreseen as a highly probable consequence of what is done is the same thing as the fact that the state of affairs is intended. . . .

I do not think that foresight as such of a high degree of probability is at all the same thing as intention, and, in my view, it is not foresight but intention which constitutes the mental element in murder. It is the absence of intention to kill or cause grievous bodily harm which absolves the heart surgeon in the case of the transplant, notwithstanding that he foresees as a matter of high probability that his action will probably actually kill the patient. It is the presence of an actual intention to kill or cause grievous bodily harm which convicts the murderer who takes a very long shot at his victim and kills him notwithstanding that he thinks correctly as he takes his aim that the odds are very much against his hitting him at all.

I, therefore, propose the following propositions in answer to the question of general public importance.

(1) Before an act can be murder it must be "aimed at someone" . . . and must in addition be an act committed with one of the following intentions, the test of which is always subjective to the actual defendant:

(i) The intention to cause death;

(ii) The intention to cause grievous bodily harm in the sense of that term explained in *Smith*, at p. 335, *i.e.* really serious injury;

(iii) Where the defendant knows that there is a serious risk that death or grievous bodily harm will ensue from his acts, and commits those acts deliberately and without lawful excuse, the intention to expose a potential victim to that risk as the result of those acts. It does not matter in such cir-

cumstances whether the defendant desires those consequences to ensue or not, and in none of these cases does it
matter that the act and the intention were aimed at a
potential victim other than the one who succumbed.

(2) Without an intention of one of these three types the mere fact that
the defendant's conduct is done in the knowledge that grievous bodily
harm is likely or highly likely to ensue from his conduct is not by itself
enough to convert a homicide into the crime of murder.

VISCOUNT DILHORNE: . . . A man may do an act with a number of
intentions. If he does it deliberately and intentionally, knowing when he
does it that it is highly probable that grievous bodily harm will result, I
think most people would say and be justified in saying that whatever
other intentions he may have had as well, he at least intended grievous
bodily harm. . . .

LORD DIPLOCK: . . . This appeal raises two separate questions. The first is
common to all crimes of this class. It is: what is the attitude of mind of the
accused towards the particular evil consequence of his physical act that
must be proved in order to constitute the offence? . . .
    Upon the first question I do not desire to say more than that I agree
with those of your Lordships who take the uncomplicated view that in
crimes of this class no distinction is to be drawn in English law between
the state of mind of one who does an act because he desires it to produce
a particular evil consequence, and the state of mind of one who does the
act knowing full well that it is likely to produce that consequence although
it may not be the object he was seeking to achieve by doing the act. What
is common to both these states of mind is willingness to produce the
particular evil consequence: and this, in my view, is the mens rea needed
to satisfy a requirement, whether imposed by statute or existing at
common law, that in order to constitute the offence with which the
accused is charged he must have acted with "intent" to produce a
particular evil consequence. . . .

LORD CROSS OF CHELSEA: . . . Counsel for the appellant argued . . . that
unless the accused believed that the consequences in question were certain
to ensue, one ought not to equate mere foresight of consequences with an
intention to produce them. Even if one views the matter simply from the
point of view of linguistics I am not sure that the ordinary man would
agree. If, for example, someone parks a car in a city street with a time
bomb in it which explodes and injures a number of people I think that the
ordinary man might well argue as follows: "The man responsible for this
outrage did not injure these people unintentionally; he injured them
intentionally. So he can fairly be said to have intentionally injured
them—that is to say, to have intended to injure them. The fact that he was
not certain that anyone would be injured is quite irrelevant (after all, how
could he possibly be certain that anyone would be injured?); and the fact
that, although he foresaw that it was likely that some people would be
injured, it was a matter of indifference to him whether they were injured
or not (his object being simply to call attention to Irish grievances and to
demonstrate the power of the I.R.A.) is equally irrelevant." But I can see
that a logician might object that the ordinary man was using the word
"intentionally" with two different shades of meaning, and I am prepared
to assume that as a matter of the correct use of language the man in
question did not intend to injure those who were in fact injured by his
act. . . .

LORD KILBRANDON: ... If murder is to be found proved in the absence of an intention to kill, the jury must be satisfied from the nature of the act itself or from other evidence that the accused knew that death was a likely consequence of the act and was indifferent whether that consequence followed or not. ...

Appeal dismissed

Note

The judgments in *Hyam* do not appear to have been as certain and emphatic regarding intention as Lord Diplock suggested in *Lemon*. This, doubtless, was due to the fact that their Lordships were directly concerned with the mens rea for murder rather than a definition of intention. Several cases have suggested a narrower meaning of *intention* somewhere between that adopted in *Steane* and that declared by Lord Diplock in *Lemon*.

In *Mohan* (*post*, p. 426), a case on attempt, the Court of Appeal rejected the argument that in *Hyam* the House of Lords had given intention a meaning which was to be generally applicable in the criminal law. In *Belfon* [1976] 1 W.L.R. 741, a case of wounding with intent where the trial judge had directed the jury that foresight of grievous bodily harm was enough to convict the accused, the Court of Appeal quashed the conviction, Wien J. stating:

" ... we do not find ... in any of the speeches of their Lordships in *Hyam's* case anything which obliges us to hold that the 'intent' in wounding with intent is proved by foresight that serious injury is likely to result from a deliberate act. There is certainly no authority that recklessness can constitute an intent to do grievous bodily harm. Adding the concept of recklessness to foresight not only does not assist but will inevitably confuse a jury. Foresight and recklessness are evidence from which intent may be inferred but they cannot be equated either separately or in conjunction with intent to do grievous bodily harm."

Both *Mohan* and *Belfon* sought to distinguish intent from evidence from which intent may be inferred. Thus evidence of foresight of likely consequences is not intent but is evidence pointing towards the existence of intent. This point is reiterated in *Moloney* (*infra*), a murder case, where the House of Lords repudiated the definition of intention derived from *Hyam*.

R. v. Moloney
[1985] 1 A.C. 905
House of Lords

The appellant, a soldier, and his step-father had been drinking heavily. His step-father challenged him to a competition to see who could load, draw and fire a shotgun in the shortest time. The outcome was that the appellant shot his stepfather and was charged with murder. The appellant testified that he had no intention to kill and had not aimed his gun at his stepfather. In summing-up the judge gave the following direction on intent: "When the law requires that something must be proved to have been done with a particular intent it means this: a man intends the consequences of his voluntary act (a) when he desires it to happen, whether or not he foresees that it will probably happen; and (b) when he foresees that it will probably happen, whether he desires it or not." He appealed against conviction of murder.

LORD BRIDGE OF HARWICH delivered the following opinion with which the remainder of their Lordships agreed: ... The fact that, when the appellant fired the gun, the gun was pointing directly at his stepfather's head at a range of about six feet was not, and could not be, disputed. The sole issue was whether, when he pressed the trigger, this fact and its inevitable consequence were present to the appellant's mind. If they were, the inference was inescapable, using words in their ordinary, everyday meaning, that he intended to kill his stepfather. The undisputed facts that the appellant loved his stepfather and that there was no premeditation or rational motivation, could not, as any reasonable juror would understand, rebut this inference. ...

The definition of intent on which Stephen Brown J. based his initial direction to the jury in this case and which first appeared in the 40th edition but now appears virtually unchanged in the 41st edition of *Archbold Criminal Pleading Evidence & Practice* published in 1982, is, as previously stated, clothed with the spurious authority of quotation marks. I will repeat it here for clarity (para. 17–13, p. 995):

"In law a man intends the consequence of his voluntary act, (a) when he desires it to happen, whether or not he foresees that it probably will happen, or (b) when he foresees that it will probably happen, whether he desires it or not."

Although in its terms applicable to any offence of specific intent, this so-called definition must be primarily derived from *R. v. Hyam* [1975] A.C. 55. The text embodies a reference to Viscount Dilhorne's opinion, implicit in the passage cited above from p. 82 of the report, that in *R. v. Hyam* itself, as in the vast majority of cases, an explanation of intent was unnecessary and notes the endorsement of this view to which I have already referred in *R. v. Beer*, 63 Cr.App.R. 222. Apart from copious references to *R. v. Hyam*, the ensuing citation in support of the claim that the definition "is in accordance with the great preponderance of authority," refers to many decided cases in which there are to be found obiter dicta on the subject. But looking on their facts at the decided cases where a crime of specific intent was under consideration, including *R. v. Hyam* itself, they suggest to me that the probability of the consequence taken to have been foreseen must be little short of overwhelming before it will suffice to establish the necessary intent. Thus, I regard the *Archbold* definition of intent as unsatisfactory and potentially misleading and one which should no longer be used in directing juries.

The golden rule should be that, when directing a jury on the mental element necessary in a crime of specific intent, the judge should avoid any elaboration or paraphrase of what is meant by intent, and leave it to the jury's good sense to decide whether the accused acted with the necessary intent, unless the judge is convinced that, on the facts and having regard to the way the case has been presented to the jury in evidence and argument, some further explanation or elaboration is strictly necessary to avoid misunderstanding. In trials for murder or wounding with intent, I find it very difficult to visualise a case where any such explanation or elaboration could be required, if the offence consisted of a direct attack on the victim with a weapon, except possibly the case where the accused shot at A and killed B, which any first year law student could explain to a jury in the simplest of terms. Even where the death results indirectly from the act of the accused, I believe the cases that will call for a direction by reference to foresight of consequences will be of extremely rare occurrence. I am in full agreement with the view expressed by Viscount Dilhorne that, in *R.* v. *Hyam* [1975] A.C. 55, 82 itself, if the issue of intent had been left without elaboration, no reasonable jury could have failed to convict. I find it difficult to understand why the prosecution did not seek to support the conviction, as an alternative to their main submission, on the ground that there had been no actual miscarriage of justice.

I do not, of course, by what I have said in the foregoing paragraph, mean to question the necessity, which frequently arises, to explain to a jury that intention is something quite distinct from motive or desire. But this can normally be quite simply explained by reference to the case before the court or, if necessary, by some homely example. A man who, at London Airport, boards a plane which he knows to be bound for Manchester, clearly intends to travel to Manchester, even though Manchester is the last place he wants to be and his motive for boarding the plane is simply to escape pursuit. The possibility that the plane may have engine trouble and be diverted to Luton does not affect the matter. By boarding the Manchester plane, the man conclusively demonstrates his intention to go there, because it is a moral certainty that that is where he will arrive.

I return to the two uncertainties by the Criminal Law Revision Committee in the Report referred to above as arising from *R.* v. *Hyam*, which still remain unresolved. I should preface these observations by expressing my view that the differences of opinion to be found in the five speeches in *R.* v. *Hyam* have, as I believe, caused some confusion in the law in an area where, as I have already indicated, clarity and simplicity are, in my view, of paramount importance. I believe it also follows that it is within the judicial function of your Lordships' House to lay down new guidelines which will achieve those desiderata, if we can reach broad agreement as to what they should be.

In one sense I should be happy to adopt in its entirety the qualified negative answer proposed by my noble and learned friend on the Woolsack to the certified question in *R.* v. *Hyam* because, if I may say so, it seems to me to be supported by the most convincing jurisprudential and philosophical arguments to be found in any of the speeches in *R.* v. *Hyam*. But I have to add at once that there are two reasons why I cannot regard it as providing practical guidance to judges who have to direct juries in the rare cases where foresight of probable consequences must be canvassed with the jury as an element which should affect their conclusion on the issue of intent.

First, I cannot accept that the suggested criterion that the act of the accused, to amount to murder, must be "aimed at someone" as explained in *D.P.P.* v. *Smith* [1961] A.C. 290 by Viscount Kilmuir L.C., at p. 327, is one which would be generally helpful to juries. The accused man in *D.P.P.* v. *Smith* was driving a car containing stolen goods. When told to stop by a police constable he accelerated away. The constable clung to the side of his car and the accused, in busy traffic, pursued an erratic course in order to shake the constable off. When finally shaken off, the constable fell in front of another car and was killed. In this context it was, no doubt, entirely apposite to say, as Viscount Kilmuir L.C. did, at p. 327: "The unlawful and voluntary act must clearly be aimed at someone in order to eliminate cases of negligence or of careless or dangerous driving." But what of the terrorist who plants a time bomb in a public building and gives timely warning to enable the public to be evacuated? Assume that he knows that, following evacuation, it is virtually certain that a bomb disposal squad will attempt to defuse the bomb. In the event the bomb explodes and kills a bomb disposal expert. In our present troubled times, this is an all too tragically realistic illustration. Can it, however, be said that in this case the bomb was "aimed" at the bomb disposal expert? With all respect, I believe this criterion would create more doubts than it would resolve.

Secondly, I believe that my noble and learned friend, Lord Hailsham of St. Marylebone L.C.'s inclusion in the mental element necessary to a conviction of murder of "the intention to expose a potential victim," *inter alia*, to "a serious risk that . . . grievous bodily harm will ensue from his acts" ([1975] A.C. 55, 79) comes dangerously near to causing confusion with at least one possible element in the crime of causing death by reckless driving, and by inference equally of motor manslaughter, as identified by Lord Diplock in the later case of *R.* v. *Lawrence* (*post*, p. 117), where the driving was such "as to create an obvious and serious risk of causing physical injury to some other person" and the driver "having recognised that there was some risk involved, had nonetheless gone on to take it." If the driver, overtaking in a narrow country lane in the face of an oncoming cyclist, recognises and takes not only "some risk" but a serious risk of hitting the cyclist, is he to be held guilty of murder?

Starting from the proposition established by *R.* v. *Vickers* [1957] 2 Q.B. 664, as modified by *D.P.P.* v. *Smith* that the mental element in murder requires proof of an intention to kill or cause really serious injury, the first fundamental question to be answered is whether there is any rule of substantive law that foresight by the accused of one of those eventualities as a probable consequence of his voluntary act, where the probability can be defined as exceeding a certain degree, is equivalent or alternative to the necessary intention. I would answer this question in the negative. Here I derive powerful support from the speech of my noble and learned friend. Lord Hailsham of St. Marylebone L.C., in *R.* v. *Hyam* [1975] A.C. 55. He said, at p. 75:

"I do not, therefore, consider, as was suggested in argument, that the fact that a state of affairs is correctly foreseen as a highly probable consequence of what is done is the same thing as the fact that the state of affairs is intended."

And again, at p. 77:

"I do not think that foresight as such of a high degree of probability is at all the same thing as intention, and, in my view, it is not foresight but intention which constitutes the mental element in murder."

The irrationality of any such rule of substantive law stems from the fact that it is impossible to define degrees of probability, in any of the infinite variety of situations arising in human affairs, in precise or scientific terms. As Lord Reid said in *Southern Portland Cement Ltd.* v. *Cooper* [1974] A.C. 623, 640:

"Chance probability or likelihood is always a matter of degree. It is rarely capable of precise assessment. Many different expressions are in common use. It can be said that the occurrence of a future event is very likely, rather likely, more probably than not, not unlikely, quite likely, not improbable, more than a mere possibility, etc. It is neither practicable nor reasonable to draw a line at extreme probability."

I am firmly of opinion that foresight of consequences, as an element bearing on the issue of intention in murder, or indeed any other crime of specific intent, belongs, not to the substantive law, but to the law of evidence. Here again I am happy to find myself aligned with my noble and learned friend, Lord Hailsham of St. Marylebone L.C., in *R.* v. *Hyam*, where he said, at p. 65: "Knowledge or foresight is at the best material which entitles or compels a jury to draw the necessary inference as to intention." A rule of evidence which judges for more than a century found of the utmost utility in directing juries was expressed in the maxim: "A man is presumed to intend the natural and probable consequences of his acts." In *D.P.P.* v. *Smith* your Lordships' House, by treating this rule of evidence as creating an irrebuttable presumption and thus elevating it, in effect, to the status of a rule of substantive law, predictably provoked the intervention of Parliament by section 8 of the Criminal Justice Act 1967 to put the issue of intention back where it belonged, viz., in the hands of the jury, "drawing such inferences from the evidence as appear proper in the circumstances." I do not by any means take the conjunction of the verbs "intended or foresaw" and "intend or foresee" in that section as an indication that Parliament treated them as synonymous; on the contrary, two verbs were needed to connote two different states of mind.

I think we should now no longer speak of presumptions in this context but rather of inferences. In the old presumption that a man intends the natural and probable consequences of his acts the important word is "natural." This word conveys the idea that in the ordinary course of events a certain act will lead to a certain consequence unless something unexpected supervenes to prevent it. One might almost say that, if a consequence is natural, it is really otiose to speak of it as also being probable.

Section 8 of the Criminal Justice Act 1967 leaves us at liberty to go back to the decisions before that of this House in *D.P.P.* v. *Smith* and it is here, I believe, that we can find a sure, clear, intelligible and simple guide to the kind of direction that should be given to a jury in the exceptional case where it is necessary to give guidance as to how, on the evidence, they should approach the issue of intent.

I know of no clearer exposition of the law than that in the judgment of the Court of Criminal Appeal (Lord Goddard C.J., Atkinson and Cassels JJ.) delivered by Lord Goddard C.J. in *R.* v. *Steane* [1947] K.B. 997 (*ante*, p. 75) where he said, at p. 1004:

> "No doubt, if the prosecution prove an act the natural consequence of which would be a certain result and no evidence or explanation is given, then a jury may, on a proper direction, find that the prisoner is guilty of doing the act with the intent alleged, but if on the totality of the evidence there is room for more than one view as to the intent of the prisoner, the jury should be directed that it is for the prosecution to prove the intent to the jury's satisfaction, and if, on a review of the whole evidence, they either think that the intent did not exist or they are left in doubt as to the intent, the prisoner is entitled to be acquitted."

In the rare cases in which it is necessary to direct a jury by reference to foresight of consequences, I do not believe it is necessary for the judge to do more than invite the jury to consider two questions. First, was death or really serious injury in a murder case (or whatever relevant consequence must be proved to have been intended in any other case) a natural consequence of the defendant's voluntary act? Secondly, did the defendant foresee that consequence as being a natural consequence of his act? The jury should then be told that if they answer yes to both questions it is a proper inference for them to draw that he intended that consequence. . . .

Appeal allowed

Questions

1. Lord Bridge spoke of a result being a "natural consequence." Does this mean that a consequence must be substantially more likely than one which is described as being probable if the inference of intention is to be drawn; or does this phrase create an ambiguity in that a consequence may be considered a *natural consequence* by the fact that it causally follows on directly from the original act?

2. Lord Bridge stated with regard to the term "natural consequences" that "the probability of the consequence taken to have been foreseen must be little short of overwhelming before it will suffice to establish the necessary intent." Was Lord Bridge really speaking of "oblique" intention in the sense in which Glanville Williams uses this term? (see *ante*, p. 70).

3. Lord Bridge sought to distinguish *intention* from *foresight of consequences*; the latter is relevant only as *evidence* of intention. Lord Bridge also sought to distinguish *intention* from *motive* or *desire*. J. Stannard in "Mens Rea in the Melting Pot" [1986] 37 N.I.L.Q. 61, accordingly concludes that *intention* must be equivalent to *purpose*. He states that the "failure test" distinguishes intended consequences from those that are merely foreseen. In the Manchester plane example, if the plane had been diverted from Manchester to Leeds, would the escapee have failed in his purpose?

4. Lord Bridge declared that he knew no clearer exposition of the law than that in *Steane*. Given his Manchester plane example and the expressed outcome, should Lord Bridge not regard *Steane's* intention as having been to assist the enemy?

5. In the terrorist example does Lord Bridge not incorrectly make the assumption that the terrorist is guilty of murder? If the terrorist has no desire to kill anyone, can it be said that death is virtually certain to ensue?

Note

The judgment in *Moloney*, far from clarifying the law, created its own problems which quickly surfaced in the following case.

R. v. Hancock and Shankland
[1986] 1 A.C. 455
House of Lords

The appellants, who were striking miners, were charged with the murder of a taxi-driver who was killed when taking a miner to work. The appellants pushed a concrete post and concrete block from a bridge on to the taxi travelling along the road below. The appellants' plea of guilty to manslaughter was not accepted and they were tried for murder. Their defence was that they had intended to block the road or frighten but they had no intention to kill or cause serious bodily harm. The judge gave a direction to the jury based on Lord Bridge's speech in *Moloney* (above). The jury convicted but the Court of Appeal substituted convictions of manslaughter holding that the *Moloney* guidelines were misleading and their use by the trial judge may well have misled the jury. The Crown appealed to the House of Lords.

LORD SCARMAN delivered the following opinion with which the remainder of their Lordships agreed: ... The question for the House is ... , whether the *Moloney* guidelines are sound. In *Moloney's* case the *ratio decidendi* was that the judge never properly put to the jury the defence, namely that the accused was unaware that the gun was pointing at his stepfather. The House, however, held it necessary in view of the history of confusion in this branch of the law to attempt to clarify the law relating to the establishment of the mental element necessary to constitute the crime of murder and to lay down guidelines for assisting juries to determine in what circumstances it is proper to infer intent from foresight. The House certainly clarified the law. First, the House cleared away the confusions which had obscured the law during the last 25 years laying down authoritatively that the mental element in murder is a specific intent, the intent to kill or to inflict serious bodily harm. Nothing less suffices: and the jury must be sure that the intent existed when the act was done which resulted in death before they can return a verdict of murder.

Secondly, the House made it absolutely clear that foresight of consequences is no more than evidence of the existence of the intent; it must be considered, and its weight assessed, together with all the evidence in the case. Foresight does not necessarily imply the existence of intention, though it may be a fact from which when considered with all the other evidence a jury may think it right to infer the necessary intent. Lord Hailsham of St. Marylebone L.C. put the point succinctly and powerfully in his speech in *R.* v. *Moloney*:

"I conclude with the pious hope that your Lordships will not again have to decide that foresight and foreseeability are not the same thing as intention although either may give rise to an irresistible inference of such, and that matters which are essentially to be treated as matters of inference for a jury as to a subjective state of mind will not once again be erected into a legal presumption. They should remain, what they always should have been, part of the law of evidence and inference to be left to the jury after a proper direction as to their weight, and not part of the substantive law."

Thirdly, the House emphasised that the probability of the result of an act is an important matter for the jury to consider and can be critical in their determining whether the result was intended.

These three propositions were made abundantly clear by Lord Bridge of Harwich. His was the leading speech and received the assent of their other Lordships, Lord Hailsham of St Marylebone L.C., Lord Fraser of Tullybelton, Lord Edmund-Davies, and Lord Keith of Kinkel. His speech has laid to rest ghosts which had haunted the case law ever since the unhappy decision of your Lordships' House in *D.P.P.* v. *Smith* and which were given fresh vigour by the interpretation put by some upon the speeches of members of this House in *R.* v. *Hyam*.

It is only when Lord Bridge of Harwich turned to the task of formulating guidelines that difficulty arises. It is said by the Court of Appeal that the guidelines by omitting any express reference to probability are ambiguous and may well lead a jury to a wrong conclusion. The omission was deliberate. Lord Bridge omitted the adjective "probable" from the time-honoured formula "foresight of the natural and probable consequences of his acts" because he thought that "if a consequence is natural, it is really otiose to speak of it as also being probable." But is it?

Lord Bridge of Harwich did not deny the importance of probability. He put it thus:

> "But looking on their facts at the decided cases where a crime of specific intent was under consideration, including *R.* v. *Hyam* itself, they suggest to me that the probability of the consequence taken to have been foreseen must be little short of overwhelming before it will suffice to establish the necessary intent."

In his discussion of the relationship between foresight and intention, Lord Bridge of Harwich reviewed the case law since the passing of the Homicide Act 1957 and concluded:

> "foresight of consequences, as an element bearing on the issue of intention in murder, or indeed any other crime of specific intent, belongs, not to the substantive law, but to the law of evidence."

He referred to the rule of evidence that a man is presumed to intend the natural and probable consequences of his acts, and went on to observe that the House of Lords in *Smith's* case had treated the presumption as irrebuttable, but that Parliament intervened by section 8 of the Criminal Justice Act 1967 to return the law to the path from which it had been diverted, leaving the presumption as no more than an inference open to the jury to draw if in all the circumstances it appears to them proper to draw it.

Yet he omitted any reference in his guidelines to probability. He did so because he included probability in the meaning which he attributed to "natural." My Lords, I very much doubt whether a jury without further explanation would think that "probable" added nothing to "natural." I agree with the Court of Appeal that the probability of a consequence is a factor of sufficient importance to be drawn specifically to the attention of the jury and to be explained. In a murder case where it is necessary to direct a jury on the issue of intent by reference to foresight of consequences the probability of death or serious injury resulting from the act done may be critically important. Its importance will depend on the degree of probability: if the likelihood that death or serious injury will result is high, the probability of that result may, as Lord Bridge of Harwich noted and the Lord Chief Justice emphasised, be seen as overwhelming evidence of the existence of the intent to kill or injure. Failure to explain the relevance of probability may, therefore, mislead a jury into thinking that it is of little or no importance and into concentrating exclusively on the causal link between the act and its consequence. In framing his guidelines Lord Bridge of Harwich emphasised that he did not believe it necessary to do more than to invite the jury to consider his two questions. Neither question makes any reference (beyond the use of the word "natural") to probability. I am not surprised that when in this case the judge faithfully followed this guidance the jury found themselves perplexed and unsure. In my judgment, therefore, the *Moloney* guidelines as they stand are unsafe and misleading. They require a reference to probability. They also require an explanation that the greater the probability of a consequence the more likely it is that the consequence was foreseen and that if that consequence was foreseen the greater the probability is that that consequence was also intended. But juries also require to be reminded that the decision is theirs to be reached upon a consideration of all the evidence.

Accordingly, I accept the view of the Court of Appeal that the *Moloney* guidelines are defective. I am, however, not persuaded that guidelines of general application, albeit within a limited class of case, are wise or desirable. Lord Lane C.J. formulated in this case [1986] 1 A.C. 416 guidelines for the assistance of juries but for the reason which follows, I would not advise their use by trial judges when summing up to a jury.

I fear that their elaborate structure may well create difficulty. Juries are not chosen for their understanding of a logical and phased process leading by question and answer to a conclusion but are expected to exercise practical common sense. They want help on the practical problems encountered in evaluating the evidence of a particular case and reaching a conclusion. It is better, I suggest, notwithstanding my respect for the comprehensive formulation of the Court of Appeal's guidelines, that the trial judge should follow the traditional course of a summing up. He must explain the nature of the offence charged, give directions as to the law applicable to the particular facts of the case, explain the incidence and burden of proof, put both sides' cases making especially sure that the defence is put; he should offer help in understanding and weighing up all the evidence and should make certain that the jury understand that whereas the law is for him the facts are for them to decide. Guidelines, if given, are not to be treated as rules of law but as a guide indicating the sort of approach the jury may properly adopt to the evidence when coming to their decision on the facts.

In a case where foresight of a consequence is part of the evidence supporting a prosecution submission that the accused intended the consequences, the judge, if he thinks some general observations would help the jury, could well, having in mind section 8 of the Criminal Justice Act 1967, emphasise that the probability, however high, of a consequence is only a factor, though it may in some cases be a very significant factor, to be considered with all the other evidence in determining whether the accused intended to bring it about. The distinction between the offence and the evidence relied on to prove it is vital. Lord Bridge's speech in *Moloney* made the distinction crystal clear: it would be a disservice to the law to allow his guidelines to mislead a jury into overlooking it.

For these reasons I would hold that the *Moloney* guidelines are defective and should not be used as they stand without further explanation. The laying down of guidelines for use in directing juries in cases of complexity is a function which can be usefully exercised by the Court of Appeal. But it should be done sparingly, and limited to cases of real difficulty. If it is done, the guidelines should avoid generalisation so far as is possible and encourage the jury to exercise their common sense in reaching what is their decision on the facts. Guidelines are not rules of law: judges should not think that they must use them. A judge's duty is to direct the jury in law and to help them upon the particular facts of the case. ...

Appeal dismissed

Questions

1. In *Moloney* Lord Bridge, while declining to define what *intention* means, did provide guidelines for the jury on how to discover it. Lord Scarman deprecated the use of such guidelines because of the danger that they would be followed slavishly. He opined that the jury should "exercise practical common sense" and

base their decision upon a consideration of all the evidence, stating
that whereas the law is for the judge to define, the facts are for the
jury to decide. But what is the law in relation to intention? Is
intention an ordinary word with an ordinary meaning known to all?
If, rather, it is a word with a technical meaning, what is that
technical meaning?

2. If foresight of the probability of a consequence is simply
evidence from which intention may be inferred, what is the further
mental element the jury must find before they can conclude that
the accused intended that consequence? (see R. A. Duff "The
Obscure Intentions of the House of Lords" [1986] *Crim.L.R.* 771,
772).

Note

In *Nedrick* (below) the Court of Appeal sought to draw together
various threads contained in the speeches in *Moloney* and *Hancock
and Shankland* to provide some guidance for trial judges.

R. v. Nedrick
[1986] 1 W.L.R. 1025
Court of Appeal

The appellant had a grudge against a woman. He poured paraffin
through the letter box and on to the front door of her house and ignited
it without giving any warning. A child died in the ensuing fire. The
appellant admitted starting the fire but claimed he only wished to
frighten the woman and did not want anyone to die. He was convicted
of murder following a direction to the jury which equated foresight with
intention.

LORD LANE C.J. read the following judgment of the court: ... That
direction was given before the publication of the speeches in the House of
Lords in *R. v. Moloney* and *R. v. Hancock*. In the light of those speeches it
was plainly wrong. The direction was based on a passage in *Archbold
Criminal Pleading Evidence & Practice*, 41st ed. (1982), p. 994, paragraph
17–13, which has been repeated in the 42nd ed. (1985), p. 1162, paragraph
17–13. That passage was expressly disapproved in *R. v. Moloney*, in that it
equates foresight with intention, whereas "foresight of consequences, as
an element bearing on the issue of intention in murder ... belongs, not to
the substantive law, but to the law of evidence," *per* Lord Bridge of
Harwich, at [1985] A.C. 928. The judge was in no way to blame of course
for having directed the jury in this way.

What then does a jury have to decide so far as the mental element in
murder is concerned? It simply has to decide whether the defendant
intended to kill or do serious bodily harm. In order to reach that decision
the jury must pay regard to all the relevant circumstances, including what
the defendant himself said and did.

In the great majority of cases a direction to that effect will be enough,
particularly where the defendant's actions amounted to a direct attack
upon his victim, because in such cases the evidence relating to the
defendant's desire or motive will be clear and his intent will have been the
same as his desire or motive. But in some cases, of which this is one, the
defendant does an act which is manifestly dangerous and as a result

someone dies. The primary desire or motive of the defendant may not have been to harm that person, or indeed anyone. In that situation what further directions should a jury be given as to the mental state which they must find to exist in the defendant if murder is to be proved? ...

It may be advisable first of all to explain to the jury that a man may intend to achieve a certain result whilst at the same time not desiring it to come about. In *R.* v. *Moloney* Lord Bridge gave an illustration of the distinction [the example of the man boarding a plane bound for Manchester to escape pursuit.] ...

In *R.* v. *Hancock* the House decided that the *R.* v. *Moloney* guidelines require a reference to probability. Lord Scarman said, at p. 473:

> "They also require an explanation that the greater the probability of a consequence the more likely it is that the consequence was foreseen and that if that consequence was foreseen the greater the probability is that that consequence was also intended."

When determining whether the defendant had the necessary intent, it may therefore be helpful for a jury to ask themselves two questions. (1) How probable was the consequence which resulted from the defendant's voluntary act? (2) Did he foresee that consequence?

If he did not appreciate that death or serious harm was likely to result from his act, he cannot have intended to bring it about. If he did, but thought that the risk to which he was exposing the person killed was only slight, then it may be easy for the jury to conclude that he did not intend to bring about that result. On the other hand, if the jury are satisfied that at the material time the defendant recognised that death or serious harm would be virtually certain (barring some unforeseen intervention) to result from his voluntary act, then that is a fact from which they may find it easy to infer that he intended to kill or do serious bodily harm, even though he may not have had any desire to achieve that result.

As Lord Bridge of Harwich said in *R.* v. *Moloney*: "the probability of the consequence taken to have been foreseen must be little short of overwhelming before it will suffice to establish the necessary intent." At p. 926 he uses the expression "moral certainty"; he said, at p. 929 "will lead to a certain consequence unless something unexpected supervenes to prevent it."

Where the charge is murder and in the rare cases where the simple direction is not enough, the jury should be directed that they are not entitled to infer the necessary intention, unless they feel sure that death or serious bodily harm was a virtual certainty (barring some unforeseen intervention) as a result of the defendant's actions and that the defendant appreciated that such was the case.

Where a man realises that it is for all practical purposes inevitable that his actions will result in death or serious harm, the inference may be irresistible that he intended that result, however little he may have desired or wished it to happen. The decision is one for the jury to be reached upon a consideration of all the evidence.

Appeal allowed.
Conviction quashed.
Conviction of manslaughter substituted.

Question

Lord Lane C.J. stated that "if the jury are satisfied that at the material time the defendant recognised that death or serious harm would be virtually certain ... to result from his voluntary act, then that is a fact from which they may find it easy to infer that he intended to kill or do serious bodily harm, even though he may not have had any desire to achieve that result." What should a jury infer if the defendant recognised death or serious bodily harm as being a probable, or even highly probable, result of his act?

Note

In *Walker and Hayles* (1990) 90 Cr.App.R. 226, which involved charges of attempted murder, the trial judge directed the jury that they may infer an intent to kill if the defendants knew that there was a very high degree of probability of death. The Court of Appeal, upholding the convictions, stated that it would have been better to use the words "virtual certainty" but went on to state that they did not believe there was any real difference between the two phrases. This is questionable and, in light of Lord Lane C.J.'s extra-judicial comments, judges should use the phrase "virtual certainty." Lord Lane C.J. made his comments in the House of Lords' debate on the *Report of the Select Committee of the House of Lords on Murder and Life Imprisonment* (H.L. Deb., Vol. 512, col. 480). He stated:

"It is right to say that the decision in *Nedrick* ... endeavoured to provide a satisfactory definition of the word 'intention'. ... It is equally true to say ... that in *Nedrick* the court was obliged to phrase matters as it did because of earlier decisions in your Lordships' House by which it was bound. We had to tread gingerly indeed in order not to tread upon your Lordships' toes. As a result *Nedrick* was not as clear as it should have been. However, I agree respectfully with the conclusions of the committee that 'intention' should be defined in the terms set out in paragraph 195 of the report on page 50. [The Committee adopted clause 18(b) of the Law Commission draft Criminal Code which states that 'a person acts intentionally with respect to ... a result when he acts either in order to bring it about or being aware that it will occur in the ordinary course of events.'] That seems to express clearly what in *Nedrick* we failed properly to explain."

This seems to go much further than the Court of Appeal sought to go in *Nedrick* as it defines "intention" rather than providing a test from which a jury may *infer* intention. Lord Lane C.J.'s extra-judicial pronouncement appears to accept that intention covers cases (a), (b) and (c) in the scenario, *ante*, pp. 71 and 73.

In the extracts which follow J. C. Smith suggests improvements which could be made to the Draft Criminal Code definition of intention.

J. C. Smith, "A Note on 'Intention' " [1990] Crim. L.R. 85

Possible defects in the definition

There are three respects in which the definition, so far as it relates to results, may be thought to be defective.

(i) It is intended to apply only to a person whose purpose is to cause the result in question or who, though that is not his purpose, knows that he is going to cause that result. He is not merely taking a risk of causing that result. He is going to cause it and he knows it. But because nothing is certain in human affairs successive draftsmen and courts have felt obliged to qualify the second part of the definition—he has *no substantial doubt* that the result will happen, he knows that it is *almost* certain, or *virtually* certain, or *morally* certain, to happen, or that it will happen *in the ordinary course of events*. There is a danger that any of these qualifications will be so interpreted as to blurr the distinction between intention and recklessness. . . .

This was not what the Law Commission meant as their report makes clear.

> "We have adopted the phrase 'in the ordinary course of events' to ensure that 'intention' covers the case of a person who knows that the achievement of his purpose will necessarily cause the result in question in the absence of some wholly improbable supervening event."

The first issue is whether we really need any of these qualifications to the actor's awareness that the result will happen.

(ii) The definition fails to make clear that it should be necessary to show only that the defendant knew that the consequence would happen (or was virtually certain, etc., to happen) if he succeeded in achieving his purpose; and that it is immaterial that he is far from certain that he will achieve that purpose. That this was the intention of the Law Commission appears from the passage quoted above. It also accords with the judgment of Lord Lane C.J. in *Nedrick*. But the definition in the code does not make it plain. Everyone, surely, now knows the bomb-in-the-plane case and everyone seems to agree that the bomber should be taken to intend to kill the crew although his purpose is only to destroy the cargo and not to kill anyone. Suppose, however, that the defendant knows that this type of bomb has a 50 per cent failure rate. It may be argued that the defendant does not, under the Code definition, intend the death of the crew because he is not virtually certain, etc., that they will die—he is not aware that it will happen "in the ordinary course of events," because there is a 50 per cent. chance that it will not happen at all.

(iii) The definition leaves open the possibility that a person may be held to have intended a result that it was his purpose to avoid. He knows that it will happen in the ordinary course of events—it is a virtual certainty but not an absolute certainty and his whole purpose is to avoid it. It does not make good sense to say that he intended that result. This situation is unlikely to arise in other than exceptional and desperate circumstances of which examples are given later; but that is not a good reason for not providing for it.

A Canadian solution

The Canadian Law Reform Commission has proposed a solution which avoids all these problems. The Commissioners have found the difficulties associated with the word "intent" to be so great that they have decided to drop it altogether in the latest version of their proposed re-codification of Canadian Criminal Law. Their Code utilises three "culpability requirements"—what the Law Commission's Draft Code calls "fault elements"—namely, purpose, recklessness and negligence. Clause 2(4) provides:

(a) General Requirements as to Level of Culpability. Unless otherwise provided:

(i) where the definition of a crime requires purpose, no one is liable unless as concerns its elements he acts

   (A) purposely as to the conduct specified by the definition,

   (B) purposely as to the consequences, if any, so specified, and

   (C) knowingly or recklessly as to the circumstances, if any, so specified; . . .

But the Commissioners did not feel able simply to leave the word "purposely" to be interpreted in the sense which a court or jury might consider to be its natural meaning. The clause goes on to provide a definition:

(i) A person acts purposely as to conduct if he means to engage in such conduct, and, in the case of an omission, if he also knows the circumstances giving rise to the duty to act or is reckless as to their existence.

(ii) A person acts purposely as to a consequence if he acts in order to effect:

   (A) that consequence; or

   (B) another consequence which he knows involves that consequence.

Clearly the mere change in terminology did not enable the Canadians to escape from the problem which has for so long dogged English attempts to codify. It simply transferred the problem from the definition of intention to the definition of purpose. Here then is another attempt to solve it. There are two aspects of it which are of special interest.

(i) There is nothing here about knowing that it is "virtually certain," etc., to involve that consequence. The defendant has to "know." Nothing less will do. Is this going to cause difficulty with the stock examples? Clearly the Canadian Commissioners think not. They give the well-worn bomb-in-the-plane case as an illustration of the operation of the clause. My friend, Brian Hogan, quotes the *Guinness Book of Records* to show that, very occasionally, people have fallen out of planes from great heights and survived; but is it remotely likely that the planter of the bomb will have in mind the possibility that, if the aircraft is destroyed in mid-Atlantic, as he intends, the crew might escape? Surely any jury would find, and would be right to find, that he knew that, if the bomb went off as he intended, they would be killed. Near miracles and fantastic possibilities of this kind do not enter into the ordinary person's calculations. . . .

Even where the chances of the result being avoided are significantly greater, it may be right to say that the defendant knew the result (which has occurred) would occur (if he achieved his objective). Lord Bridge's boarder of the Manchester plane (not because he wants to go to Manchester but because he wants to escape his pursuers) "knows" that he is going to Manchester even if planes are occasionally diverted to Luton unless (most unlikely) this possibility is present to his mind. He thinks, "Even Manchester is better than being caught—I'll go to Manchester."

So it is arguable that the more robust approach of the Canadian Commissioners is right and that we have nothing to lose by abandoning the technical qualification which is so very hard to express without blurring the distinction between intention and recklessness. But there are arguments against it. What of the case where the defendant gives evidence and says that he *did* contemplate the remote possibility, *e.g.* he, a devotee of the *Guinness Book of Records*, was aware of the remote chance that the crew of the doomed aircraft might escape and indeed hoped that they would? It would seem that the judge, under the Canadian proposal, must direct that jury that, if they thought the defendant might be speaking the truth, they must acquit him of an offence requiring proof of intention. Under clause 18 of the Draft Code, this is not so. The judge would tell the jury that, even if the defendant was speaking the truth, it was still open to them to find that he knew that, *in the ordinary course of events*, the crew would be killed; and the jury would be likely to convict. It seems wrong that a person who contemplated nothing more than a fantastic possibility should, on that account, be treated more leniently than one who did not. Though the simplicity of the Canadian proposal is very attractive, on balance, it seems better that we should, in this respect, stand by the Clause 18 definition. . . .

A result which will occur if the actor's purpose is achieved

(ii) The second aspect of the Canadian definition, however, is a different matter. It is completely free from the real deficiency of the English draft Code definition described above; and it can be attained without abandoning "in the ordinary course of events." The plane bomber purposely causes the death of the crew even where he knows that the bomb has a 50 per cent. failure rate because it is his purpose to blow up the plane in mid-Atlantic and he knows that doing so involves, in the ordinary course of events, killing the crew.

A result which it is the actor's purpose to avoid cannot be intended

A further advantage of this aspect of the Canadian definition is that it would make clear that a result which it is the actor's purpose to avoid cannot be intended. And (a result particularly attractive to the writer) it would knock on the head some hypothetical cases of a singularly unrealistic character which have plagued discussion in the Law Commission and elsewhere for years. They are espoused by Lord Goff in his speech in the debate on the Select Committee Report. As put by his Lordship they seem, with respect, scarcely relevant because they are cases where the result is foreseen as merely highly probable or "likely," not cases where the actor knows that the result will occur in the ordinary course of events. But let us assume, as others have when putting the same examples, that the actor knew that the result was a virtual certainty, something that would happen in the ordinary course of events. Lord Goff said:

> "A house is on fire. A father is trapped in the attic floor with his two little girls. He comes to the conclusion that unless they jump they will all be burned alive. But he also realises that if they jump they are all likely to suffer serious personal harm. The children are too frightened to jump and so in an attempt to save their lives he throws one out of the window to the crowd waiting below and jumps with the other one in his arms. All are seriously injured, and the little girl he threw out of the window dies of her injuries. On the Select Committee's proposal that unfortunate man would be a murderer. That is because he was aware that 'in the ordinary course of events' the little girl would suffer serious injury and therefore by the proposed definition he is taken to have intended to cause serious personal harm to her. He was also of course

aware that his act might cause her death. He is therefore guilty of the murder of his own little girl when he was actually trying to save her life."

One answer, and perhaps the best answer, to this might be that men who throw little girls out of attics to their deaths ought to be convicted of murder unless there is some very good reason why not; and the reason why this is not murder is that the necessity of the occasion justifies or excuses the father's conduct. Unfortunately, Lord Goff's predecessors have failed to recognise a defence of necessity and even the recently developed "duress of circumstances," like duress by threats, apparently has no application to a charge of murder. If, however, we adopt the Canadian approach there is no need to resort to defences. It appears that the father's purpose is to save his child from death or injury and if he achieves his purpose—one of the crowd catches the child—the child will not suffer death or serious, or any, injury. It does not matter how remote he believes the chances of success to be, as long as he believes there is some chance. Even if he believes that it is virtually certain that the child will be seriously injured, he does not intend serious injury if his purpose is to avoid that almost inevitable result. Unlike the bomb-in-the-plane case, he has no other purpose than to save the child.

An alternative interpretation of the example is that the father's purpose is only to save the child's life—it is not his purpose to save her from serious bodily harm because he knows that is inevitable. One cannot have a purpose of avoiding what one knows to be inevitable. Even if one of the crowd catches her she will be seriously injured. In that case, it must be conceded that he does intend to cause serious bodily harm; but it would be a very remarkable court which would hold that it is not justifiable to cause serious bodily harm to someone if that is the only way to save his life. Take the case of a miner who is trapped by his arm in a roof fall and is unconscious. There being no other way of getting him out before a further roof fall kills him, a doctor amputates his arm. To cut off a perfectly healthy arm looks like a plain case of causing grievous bodily harm; and there is absolutely no doubt that it is intentional. But who could doubt that it is justifiable or excusable? If the father in Lord Goff's example intends to cause serious bodily harm as the only way of saving the child's life, he is equally justified or excused. . . .

Need we abandon the term "intentionally"?

These effects could be achieved without following the Canadian example insofar as it abandons the traditional terms, "intentionally" and "with intent." There seems to be no particular virtue in substituting "purposely" for "intentionally" when it then becomes necessary to put the same gloss on "purposely." "Purposely" is not a word which gives rise to problems of construction and, arguably, is better left undefined to be used, when required, in its ordinary meaning.

A suggested redraft

The definition might therefore be redrafted on the following lines;

"A person acts intentionally with respect to—
    (a) . . .
    (b) a result when—
        (i) it is his purpose to cause that result; or

(ii) his purpose is to cause some other result and he knows that, if he succeeds, his act will, in the ordinary course of events, cause that result."

ii. Motive and Intention

Note

A problem with declaring that *intention* is an ordinary word is that in ordinary speech it may be used loosely to mean something else, such as *motive*.

Williams, T.C.L., p. 75

"In ordinary speech, 'intention' and 'motive' are often convertible terms. For the lawyer, the word 'motive' generally refers to some further intent which forms no part of the legal rule.

If we say that a man shot and killed his aunt with the motive of benefiting under her will, the immediate intent, which makes the act murder, is the intention or desire to kill, while the further intent or motive, which forms no part of the definition of the crime of murder, is the intention or desire to benefit under the will. Other motives are the desire to obtain the satisfaction of revenge, or to get rid of a rival, or to promote a political object. (Such motives may also be expressed in abstract terms: 'he killed her from a motive of greed/revenge/jealousy.' Motive in this sense is irrelevant to responsibility (guilt or innocence), though it may be relevant to proof, or to the quantum of punishment. The prosecution may prove a motive for the crime if it helps them to establish their case, as a matter of circumstantial evidence; but they are not legally bound to prove motive, because a 'motiveless' crime is still a crime. Conversely, the defendant may adduce evidence of his good motive in order to reduce his punishment, perhaps to vanishing-point.

Exceptionally, the term 'motive' is used in a sense relevant to responsibility in the crime of libel. Also, crimes of ulterior intent require two intents, one lying behind the other, and the second may be called motive. The crime of burglary is committed where a person enters a building or part of a building by way of trespass with intent to commit one of certain crimes therein. There is an intentional entry, with the ulterior intent of committing a crime in the house; this ulterior intent is the motive of the entry, and is sometimes referred to as such, yet here it forms part of the legal definition."

Chandler v. Director of Public Prosecutions
[1964] A.C. 763
House of Lords

C. and other appellants were members of a group seeking to further the aims of the Campaign for Nuclear Disarmament. They planned to sit on Wethersfield airfield and so prevent aircraft from taking off. They made their intentions clear but they were prevented from entering the airfield. They were charged and convicted of an offence under section 1 of the Official Secrets Act 1911, which makes it a felony 'If any person for any purpose prejudicial to the safety or interests of the state—(*a*) approaches

... any prohibited place. ... ' Wethersfield airfield was a prohibited place. The appellants claimed that their campaign was in the interests of the state and that they had no guilty intent. The Court of Criminal Appeal rejected the appeal. On further appeal:—

LORD RADCLIFFE: ... All controversies about motives or intentions or purposes are apt to become involved through confusion of the meaning of the different terms and it is perhaps not difficult to show by analysis that the ideas conveyed by these respective words merge into each other without a clear line of differentiation. Nevertheless, a distinction between motive and purpose, for instance, is familiar enough in ordinary discussion and there are branches of law in which the drawing of such a distinction is unavoidable. The Act of Parliament in this case has introduced the idea of a purpose as a determining element in the identification of the offence charged and lawyers, therefore, whose function it is to attribute meanings to words and observe relevant distinctions between different words, cannot escape from this duty merely by saying that "purpose" is a word which has no sharply defined content. They must do the best they can to find what its content is in the context of this Act.

For my part I cannot say that I see any great difficulty in doing so here. I do not think that the ultimate aims of the appellants in bringing about this demonstration of obstruction constituted a purpose at all within the meaning of the Act. I think that those aims constituted their motive, the reason why they wanted the demonstration, but they did not qualify the purpose for which they approached or sought to enter the airfield. Taking this view, I do not think that the distinction between immediate purposes and long-term purposes is the most satisfactory one that can be made. If the word "purpose" is retained at all to describe both object and motive, I think that direct and indirect purposes best describe the distinction which should be placed before a jury, since those adjectives are less likely to confuse the issue. In the result, I am of opinion that if a person's direct purpose in approaching or entering is to cause obstruction or interference, and such obstruction or interference is found to be of prejudice to the defence dispositions of the state, an offence is thereby committed, and his indirect purposes or his motives in bringing about the obstruction or interference do not alter the nature or content of his offence.

It is important to note that the case we are dealing with is one in which the appellants intended to bring about obstruction of the airfield for the sake of having an obstruction. Nothing short of an obstruction would have suited their purpose. That was the kind of demonstration that they desired and it was their intention to use the obstruction as an instrument for furthering their general campaign in favour of nuclear disarmament. I do not regard such a case, in which obstruction is directly intended, as comparable with hypothetical cases put to us in argument in which obstruction, though intended, is only an indirect purpose of entry upon a prohibited place. Is a man guilty of an offence, it was asked, if he rushes onto an airfield intending to stop an airplane taking off because he knows that a time-bomb has been concealed on board? I should say that he is not, and for the reason that his direct purpose is not to bring about an obstruction but to prevent a disaster, the obstruction that he causes being merely a means of securing that end.

The other question involved in this appeal is as to the evidence admitted or rejected by the trial judge. ... The question seems to me to come down to this: When a man has avowed that his purpose in approaching an airfield forming part of the country's defence system was to obstruct its operational activity, what, if any, evidence is admissible on the issue as to the prejudicial nature of his purpose? In my opinion the correct answer is, virtually none. This answer is not surprising if certain considerations that lie behind the protection of official secrets are borne in mind. The defence of the state from external enemies is a matter of real concern, in time of peace as in days of war. The disposition, armament and direction of the defence forces of the state are matters decided upon by the Crown and are within its jurisdiction as the executive power of the state. So are treaties and alliances with other states for mutual defence. An airfield maintained for the service of the Royal Air Force or of the air force of one of Her Majesty's allies is an instrument of defence, as are the airplanes operating from the airfield and their armament.

It follows, I think, that if a man is shown to the satisfaction of the jury to have approached an airfield with the direct purpose of obstructing its operational use, a verdict of guilty must result, provided that they are also satisfied that the airfield belongs to Her Majesty and was at the relevant date part of the defence system maintained by the Crown for the protection of the realm.

Appeal dismissed.

R. v. Hicklin
(1868) 11 Cox 19
Court of Queen's Bench

The defendant was charged with having in his possession a number of copies of an obscene book. The magistrates found this proved and ordered their destruction. On appeal to the Recorder the order was quashed on the ground that the books were not kept by the defendant for gain nor to prejudice good morals but to expose the errors of the Church of Rome. The prosecutor appealed.

COCKBURN C.J.: It seems to me, the effect of this work is mischievous, and against the law; and is not to be justified because the immediate object of the party is not to deprave the public mind, but it may be to destroy and extirpate Roman Catholicism. I think the old, sound and honest maxim that "you shall not do evil that good may come," is applicable in law as well as in morals; and here we have a certain and positive evil produced for the purpose of effecting an uncertain, remote and very doubtful good. I think, therefore, the case for the order is made out, and although I quite concur in thinking that the motive of the parties who published this work, however mistaken, was an honest one, yet I cannot suppose but what they had that intention which constitutes the criminality of the act—at any rate that they knew perfectly well that this work must have the tendency which in point of law makes it an obscene publication, namely, the tendency to corrupt the minds and morals of those into whose hands it might come. The mischief of it, I think, cannot be exaggerated, but it is not upon that I take my stand in the judgment I pronounce. I am of opinion, as the learned Recorder has found, that this is an obscene publication; I take it where a man published a work manifestly obscene, he must be taken to have had the intention which is implied from that act, and that as soon as you have an illegal act thus established, *quoad* the intention, and *quoad* the act itself, it does not lie in the mouth of the man who does it to say, "Well, I was breaking the law, but I was breaking it for some wholesome and salutary purpose." The law does not allow that. You must abide by the law, and if you accomplish your object, you must do it in a legal manner, or let it alone. You must not do it in a manner which is illegal. I think, therefore, that the Recorder's judgment must be reversed, and the conviction must be allowed to stand.

Judgment accordingly

cf. R. v. *Bourne (post,* p. 570).

Wasik, "Mens Rea, Motive, and the Problem of 'Dishonesty' in the Law of Theft" [1979] Crim.L.R. 543

" ... Austin described motive as the 'spring of action.' (Lectures on Jurisprudence (4th edn. 1879) at p. 165). He then proceeded to distinguish motive from intention, the central requirement of *mens rea,* by declaring simply: 'The intention is the aim of the act, of which the motive is the spring.' This analysis has been accepted into the criminal law. So, where X steals Y's property, X's intention is said to be to take that property unlawfully, and his motive might be, for example, greed. Motive is thus used to mean an emotion prompting an act. When used in this sense, motive must always precede intention in time. As Kenny has remarked: 'One cannot have an intention for a motive, but one can have a motive for an intention.' (Action, Emotion and Will (1963) at p. 87). Kenny then goes on to suggest that motive can thus be regarded as 'backward-looking' and intention as 'forward-looking.' It has proved necessary, however, to designate this kind of motive as 'motive *in esse'* or 'motive proper,' as the law has recognised the existence of a second function of motive in human conduct. Salmond was one of the first to point out this second meaning, where motive means 'a part of intention: Intentions are divisible into immediate intentions and ulterior intentions. The former relate to the unlawful act itself, the latter to the object for the sake of which the act is done.' So, where X, motivated by greed, steals Y's property, his reasons for perpetrating the theft have also been referred to as motive. The 'motive in prospect' is, however, 'forward-looking' rather than 'backward-looking.'

 ... [L]awyers have largely ignored the additional complexities of motive. Motive is declared emphatically, and almost *de rigueur,* to be irrelevant to criminal responsibility though it is conceded that it may be crucial in determining a man's sentence. It is true that some writers have ventured to suggest that motive is really a part of intention, or a species of intent, but many others have been anxious to refute such suggestions. A more common modern approach is to argue that if 'motive' were always confined to its first meaning of 'motive *in esse,*' and 'motive in prospect' were invariably known as 'ulterior intent,' then motive and intention would, by definition be mutually exclusive. On one level this is an attractive proposal, because it seems to reinforce the distinction between the concepts of *mens rea* and motive. Making such a distinction certainly tends towards jurisprudential tidiness, but it cannot conceal the impression that the division may sometimes be an unrealistic one. This modern 'semantic' approach brings with it the concession that in some cases 'motive in prospect' *is* relevant to criminal responsibility. Thus, in the case of burglary, for example, an intentional entry is required, together with an 'ulterior intent' of committing a certain kind of crime within the premises. Yet once it is conceded that 'motive in prospect' can in some cases be relevant to responsibility, it is arguable that 'motive *in esse'* must also become relevant, since the two varieties of motive are undoubtedly closely linked. Indeed, Bentham argued that there was *always* such a link:

'Motive refers necessarily to action. It is a pleasure, pain, or other event that prompts an action. Motive, then, in one sense of the word, must be previous to such event. But for a man to be governed by a motive, he must in every case look beyond that event which is called his action; he must look to the consequences of it: and it is only in this way that the idea of pleasure, of pain, or of any other event, can give birth to it.'

Making verbal distinctions between the two varieties of motive, or between motive and intention, though useful for analysis in many cases, should not be allowed to conceal the links which exist between them. A philosopher who has subjected the terms to protracted analysis has reached this conclusion, (Kenny, *op. cit.*, pp. 86–93):

'Motives and intentions are clearly connected, and it is not easy to make any sharp distinction between them . . . a report of an intention fills in in detail part of a pattern which a report of motive sketches out in general.'

In the vast majority of cases where the defence has raised the issue of the accused's motive as being relevant to his responsibility, the judiciary have re-emphasised the traditional irrelevance of motive; but in some more recent cases the judges, in seeking to implement an increasingly subjectively—orientated criminal law, have found such distinctions more difficult to make, [The author referred to *Chandler* v. *D.P.P. (ante)*]. . . .

Even if the importance of retaining independent standards in the law is agreed upon, the argument that all matters of motive should thereby be excluded in the determination of criminal responsibility overstates the size of the potential problem. It is part of my contention that in a significant number of cases motive is already taken into account, and that in such cases the motives do not threaten to undermine the law. Perhaps it is inevitable that a system of criminal law which embodies independent standards whilst also seeking to base liability upon subjective fault akin to moral responsibility, will tend to take a rather inconsistent line on the relevance of the accused's motive for committing the criminal act. It is suggested here that this inconsistency is illustrated in English law by the repeated articulation of the general exclusionary rule, while at the same time motive really *is* admitted as relevant to responsibility in a significant, and increasing, number of cases.

Where, for example, an excuse in law does not operate by negativing a positive element in an offence, *mens rea* or *actus reus*, the efficacy of the excuse often turns upon something which appears to be part of the accused's motive for committing the criminal offence. Motives of fear and self-preservation are surely of fundamental importance in the cases of duress and self-defence, and those of anger and fear are crucial in the case of provocation. 'Good motive' is taken into account in homicide by way of partial excuse under the diminished responsibility rules. . . . [O]ne of the most significant examples [is] the issue of dishonesty in theft and related offences.

Liability for theft requires that the prosecution prove beyond reasonable doubt that the accused acted dishonestly when he appropriated property belonging to another with the intention of permanently depriving the other party of the property. It seems indisputable that 'dishonesty' (or 'honesty') is a very different kind of concept than, say, intention. While intention can meaningfully be described as a 'mental element,' 'honesty' rather reflects a code of social conduct which is ethically based, the main tenets of which are claimed to be widely shared in a civilised society.

. . . The element of dishonesty provides the accused with an opportunity to account for his conduct in a fuller and more meaningful way than if the offence was phrased purely in terms of *mens rea*.

'Dishonesty' thus gives the accused a chance to explain 'why' the alleged offence occurred instead of just 'how' it occurred (*i.e.* for certain reasons rather than intentionally or recklessly), and this appears to admit explanations involving the accused's motive for committing the act charged."

iii. Knowledge

Law Com. No. 177

"8.10 *'Knowingly': knowledge and 'wilful blindness'*. . . .
[T]he state of mind which is to be assimilated to 'actual knowledge' for the purposes of criminal liability is that of so-called 'wilful blindness'. English criminal law has commonly treated a person as knowing something if, being pretty sure that it is so, he deliberately avoids making an examination or asking questions that might confirm the fact—he avoids taking advantage of an available means of 'actual knowledge'. It is this state of mind which, we believe, has to be captured by a short form of words. Clause 18(a) therefore treats a person as acting 'knowingly' with respect to a circumstance 'not only when he is aware that it exists or will exist, but also when he avoids taking steps that might confirm his belief that it exists or will exist.' "

Note

Statute may require knowledge expressly by use of that word or one of its variants. But even where an express requirement of knowledge is not included in the statute, the courts have frequently implied such a requirement: see, *e.g. Sweet* v. *Parsley* (*post*, p. 190). In *Roper* v. *Taylor's Central Garages* [1951] 2 T.L.R. 284, Devlin J. stated that "knowingly" only says expressly what is normally implied. He went on to explain that there are different degrees of knowledge:

"There are, I think, three degrees of knowledge which it may be relevant to consider in cases of this kind. The first is actual knowledge, which the justices may find because they infer it from the nature of the act done, for no man can prove the state of another man's mind; and they may find it even if the defendant gives evidence to the contrary. They may say, 'We do not believe him; we think that this was his state of mind.' They may feel that the evidence falls short of that, if they do they have then to consider what might be described as knowledge of the second degree; whether the defendant was, as it has been called, shutting his eyes to an obvious means of knowledge. Various expressions have been used to describe that state of mind. I do not think it necessary to look further, certainly not in cases of this type, than the phrase which Lord Hewart C.J. used in a case under this section, *Evans* v. *Dell* (1937) 53 T.L.R. 310, where he said (at p. 313): ' . . . the respondent deliberately refrained from making inquiries, the results of which he might not care to have.'
The third kind of knowledge is what is generally known in law as constructive knowledge: it is what is encompassed by the words 'ought to have known' in the phrase 'knew or ought to have known.' It does not mean actual knowledge at all; it means that the defendant had in effect the means of knowledge. When, therefore, the case of the prosecution is that the defendant failed to make what they think were reasonable inquiries it

is, I think, incumbent on them to make it plain which of the two things they are saying. There is a vast distinction between a state of mind which consists of deliberately refraining from making inquiries the result of which the person does not care to have, and a state of mind which is merely neglecting to make such inquiries as a reasonable and prudent person would make. If that distinction is kept well in mind I think that justices will have less difficulty than this case appears to show they have had in determining what is the true position. The case of shutting the eyes is actual knowledge in the eyes of the law: the case of merely neglecting to make inquiries is not knowledge at all—it comes within the legal conception of constructive knowledge, a conception which, generally speaking, has no place in the criminal law."

Where knowledge is required a court may be satisfied that wilful blindness suffices. In *Westminster City Council* v. *Croyalgrange Ltd.* [1986] 2 All E.R. 353, 359, Lord Bridge stated:

"it is always open to the tribunal of fact, when knowledge on the part of a defendant is required to be proved, to base a finding of knowledge on evidence that the defendant had deliberately shut his eyes to the obvious or refrained from inquiry because he suspected the truth but did not want to have his suspicion confirmed."

How precise must a person's knowledge be if he is to be liable for knowingly committing a specified offence? See the case which follows.

R. v. Taaffe
[1984] A.C. 539
House of Lords

On his arraignment on a charge of having been knowingly concerned in the fraudulent evasion of the prohibition on the importation of cannabis resin, contrary to section 170(2) of the Customs and Excise Management Act 1979 and the Misuse of Drugs Act 1971, T pleaded not guilty. No evidence having been called, the recorder was asked to rule on the question whether T's version of events, if accepted by the jury, would entitle him to be acquitted. T's version was: (i) that he had been enlisted by a third party in Holland to import a substance from that country into England in fraudulent evasion of the prohibition on its importation and had so imported it; (ii) the substance had in fact been cannabis, importation of which was prohibited by the 1971 Act; (iii) T had mistakenly believed the substance to be currency; (iv) currency was not subject to any such prohibition; (v) T believed that it was. The recorder ruled that, even on T's version of events, he would be obliged to direct the jury to convict. Thereupon T pleaded guilty and was sentenced. T appealed and the Court of Appeal quashed his conviction. The Crown appealed.

LORD SCARMAN delivered the following opinion with which the remainder of their Lordships agreed: My Lords, the certified question in this appeal by the Crown from the decision of the Court of Appeal quashing the respondent's conviction in the Crown Court at Gravesend, neatly summarises the assumed facts upon which the learned recorder ruled that,

even if they were proved to the satisfaction of a jury, the respondent
would not be entitled to be acquitted. The question is in these terms:

> "When a defendant is charged with an offence, contrary to section
> 170(2) of the Customs and Excise Management Act 1979, of being
> knowingly concerned in the fraudulent evasion of the prohibition on the
> importation of a controlled drug—Does the defendant commit the
> offence where he: (a) imports prohibited drugs into the United
> Kingdom; (b) intends fraudulently to evade a prohibition on importa-
> tion; but (c) mistakenly believes the goods to be money and not drugs;
> and (d) mistakenly believes that money is the subject of a prohibition
> against importation?"

In effect, the learned recorder answered the question in the affirmative and
the Court of Appeal in the negative. ...

Lord Lane C.J. [in the Court of Appeal] construed the section under
which the respondent was charged as creating not an offence of absolute
liability but an offence of which an essential ingredient is a guilty mind. To
be "knowingly concerned" meant, in his judgment, knowledge not only of
the existence of a smuggling operation but also that the substance being
smuggled into the country was one the importation of which was
prohibited by statute. The respondent thought he was concerned in a
smuggling operation but believed that the substance was currency. The
importation of currency is not subject to any prohibition. Lord Lane C.J.
concluded, at p. 631:

> "[The respondent] is to be judged against the facts that he believed
> them to be. Had this indeed been currency and not cannabis, no offence
> would have been committed."

Lord Lane C.J. went on to ask this question:

> "Does it make any difference that the [respondent] thought wrongly
> that by clandestinely importing currency he was committing an
> offence?"

The Crown submitted that it does. The court rejected the submission: the
respondent's mistake of law could not convert the importation of currency
into a criminal offence: and importing currency is what it had to be
assumed that the respondent believed he was doing.

My Lords, I find the reasoning of the Lord Chief Justice compelling. I
agree with his construction of section 170(2) of the Act of 1979: and the
principle that a man must be judged upon the facts as he believes them to
be is an accepted principle of the criminal law when the state of a man's
mind and his knowledge are ingredients of the offence with which he is
charged.

Appeal dismissed

Question

Could T have been convicted of attempt to evade the prohibition
on importation contrary to section 170(2) of the 1979 Act? (See
Chapter 7, *infra*.)

Note

Statute prohibits the importation of many different substances
and the penalties available vary depending upon the substance
illegally imported. This raises the question whether D believing he

is importing prohibited goods the penalty for which is light, may be convicted of, and sentenced for, importing a prohibited substance the penalty for which is heavy? In *Ellis, Street and Smith* (1986) 84 Cr.App.R. 235, the appellants were convicted of being knowingly concerned in the fraudulent evasion of the prohibition on importation of a controlled drug, namely cannabis, contrary to section 170(2) of the Customs and Excise Management Act 1979. Cannabis is a Class B drug and the maximum penalty for its importation is fourteen years imprisonment. The appellants actually believed that they were importing pornographic materials which carries a maximum penalty of two years. The Court of Appeal upheld their convictions following the decision in *Hennessy* (1979) 68 Cr.App.R. 419 (approved in *Shivpuri* [1987] A.C. 1, H.L.) that all that the accused had to know was that he was importing prohibited goods; he need not know their nature. Thus if D believes he is importing prohibited pornography or prohibited birds eggs in a sealed container when, in fact, it contains heroin, he will be guilty of the offence of importing a Class A drug which carries a maximum sentence of life imprisonment even though, had he known the true facts, he would never have considered doing so.

Questions

1. Is D truly knowingly concerned in the fraudulent evasion of the prohibition on the importation of a controlled drug where he knows he is engaging in a smuggling operation but is mistaken as to the substance being smuggled? Why should he not be judged according to the facts as he believed them to be and be convicted of attempting to commit the offence he believed he was committing?

2. Is knowledge previously acquired but subsequently forgotten sufficient to support a conviction? See the case which follows.

R. v. Russell
(1984) 81 Cr.App.R. 315
Court of Appeal

Police officers stopped D's car and found a cosh under the driver's seat. D was convicted of possessing an offensive weapon in a public place. His defence had been that he had forgotten that he had put the cosh there. D appealed arguing that the trial judge had failed to direct the jury that it was for the prosecution to prove that D had the cosh with him "knowingly."

JUPP J.: We were referred to the case of *Cugullere* (1961) 45 Cr.App.R. 108; [1961] 1 W.L.R. 858, brought under the same section of the Prevention of Crime Act 1953, in which the Court of Criminal Appeal said, at the bottom of p. 110 and p. 860 respectively: "This court is clearly of the opinion that the words 'has with him in any public place' must mean 'knowingly has with him in any public place'. If some innocent person has a cosh slipped into his pocket by an escaping rogue, he would not be guilty of having it with him within the meaning of the section, because he would be quite innocent of any knowledge that it had been put into his pocket. In the judgment of this court, the section cannot apply in circumstances such as those. It is, therefore, extremely important in any case under this section for the judge to give a careful direction to the jury on the issue of possession. The first thing the jury have to be satisfied about, and it is always a question for the jury, is whether the accused person knowingly had with him the alleged offensive weapon." ...

The appellant's defence in the present case is not that, having had a cosh slipped under his driving seat by some third party, he was innocent of any knowledge that it had been put there. It is that he himself put the cosh under the driving seat, but until the police found and showed it him, he had forgotten all about it. Whether or not the jury would have accepted it, this defence should have been properly left to the jury, but it was not.

It was submitted on behalf of the Crown in this Court that there is a distinction between "not knowing" and "having forgotten". The appellant, it is said, always knew how he came to put the cosh under the driving seat, although he only recalled it when the police confronted him with the cosh, and asked him to explain it.

In our judgment, the Court in *Cugullere*, in saying that the words of the statute must be construed as "knowingly had with him", were not merely dealing with the situation where a defendant has an offensive weapon put within his reach by a stranger without his knowing it. They were applying the general principle of criminal responsibility which makes it incumbent on the prosecution to prove full *mens rea*. The well-known observations of Lord Reid in *Sweet* v. *Parsley* (1969) 53 Cr.App.R. 221, 225, [1970] A.C. 132, are relevant here: "It is firmly established by a host of authorities that *mens rea* is an essential ingredient of every offence unless some reason can be found for holding that that is not necessary. It is also firmly established that the fact that other sections of the Act expressly require *mens rea*, for example because they contain the word 'knowingly', is not in itself sufficient to justify a decision that a section which is silent as to *mens rea* creates an absolute offence. In the absence of a clear indication in the Act that an offence is intended to be an absolute offence, it is necessary to go outside the Act and examine all relevant circumstances in order to establish that this must have been the intention of Parliament. I say 'must have been', because it is a universal principle that if a penal provision is reasonably capable of two interpretations, that interpretation which is most favourable to the accused must be adopted".

It would in our judgment be wrong to hold that a man knowingly has a weapon with him if his forgetfulness of its existence or presence in his car is so complete as to amount to ignorance that it is there at all. This is not a defence which juries would in the ordinary way be very likely to accept, but if it is raised it should be left to them for their decision.

Appeal allowed.
Conviction quashed.

iv. Recklessness

Note

Most crimes may be committed *intentionally* or *recklessly*. As recklessness provides the baseline for liability in most offences it is important that the term be clearly defined. However, as with *intention, recklessness* has thrown up definitional problems in the last fifteen years or so. The word currently is used in two senses when once it appeared to have a single meaning in the context of the criminal law. The word *reckless* (and its variants) has only been used in statutes in recent years, *e.g.* the Criminal Damage Act 1971. Formerly the word *maliciously* was used. This was defined as meaning *intention* or *recklessness*.

In C.L.G.P. Glanville Williams defined recklessness to mean *advertent negligence* as opposed to *inadvertent negligence*.

Williams, *C.L.G.P.* section 24

"Negligence is of two kinds, being either advertent negligence (commonly called recklessness) or inadvertent negligence. Both advertent and inadvertent negligence may be found either as to surrounding circumstances, or as to consequences. Here, we are concerned with advertent negligence (recklessness) in relation to consequences. . . .

Recklessness as to consequence occurs when the actor does not desire the consequence, but foresees the possibility and consciously takes the risk. In inadvertent negligence, on the other hand, there is no such foresight. . . .

Convenience requires a narrow use of the term 'negligence' to signify inadvertent negligence unless the context concludes this meaning. Recklessness can thus be contrasted with negligence, though in a more general sense both are species of the same genus.

If the actor foresaw the probability of the consequence he is regarded as reckless, even though he fervently desired and hoped for the exact opposite of the consequence, and even though he did his best (short of abandoning his main project) to avoid it. Judges in speaking of recklessness frequently insert words to the effect that the defendant 'did not care whether he caused damage or not,' but the better view is that this is irrelevant. Recklessness is any determination to pursue conduct with knowledge of the risks involved though without a desire that they should eventuate. . . .

Although this meaning of recklessness is now generally accepted, three factors imperil its stability. The first results from the etymology of the word in the English language. A man who is reckless is literally a man who does not reck, that is to say one who does not care; on this line of reasoning, reckless and careless become synonyms. This would matter little if 'careless' kept its primary meaning of one who does not care, but in fact 'careless' has come to be applied to persons who may care very much about the harmful result of their acts but are constitutionally incapable of preventing those results. It is only too easy for this widened meaning of 'careless' to infect the word 'reckless.'

The etymological similarity of 'reckless' and 'careless' is the more unfortunate because of a second factor, the constant pressure to extend the reach of the criminal law on account of the supposed policy of the individual case. Judges sometimes wish to punish a particular defendant who is thought to have been guilty of improper conduct, without remembering an even more imperative requirement of public policy: that the technical terms of the law should retain unequivocal meanings. To allow 'reckless' and 'careless' to become interchangeable would leave us without adequate means to differentiate two concepts.

The third inflationary factor results from another linguistic association, namely in the formulas commonly used to instruct juries. The need for a formula arises from the difficulty of proving recklessness. If the issue is whether the defendant was reckless as to a given consequence, the question is whether he foresaw the possibility of that consequence; but he will probably deny that he foresaw it, and it is impossible to look directly into his mind to know whether he is speaking the truth. Usually the question will have to be solved by examining the defendant's conduct and his opportunities of knowledge. Yet conduct is by no means so certain a guide to the issue of recklessness as it is to that of intention. When a man bends himself to secure a result, he will often leave evidence of telltale pieces of behaviour which are inexplicable except on the assumption that he intended the result. But recklessness may be a mere passing realisation, instantly dismissed, which leaves no mark upon conduct. Also, a man is capable of self-deception: he may decide that an unpleasant result is not likely because he does not want it to be likely.

On the issue of recklessness, these considerations may be put before the jury. There is no objection to instructing the jury to consider whether the defendant *must* have foreseen the consequence, but it is fatally easy to confuse this with the question whether the defendant *ought* as a reasonable man to have foreseen it. The latter question presupposes an objective test of the reasonable man, and the accused person's actual foresight is immaterial. The former question is directed exclusively to the accused's actual foresight, and the test of what a reasonable man would have foreseen is merely a step in reasoning. For example, it may be shown that the accused is mentally subnormal, or that on the occasion in question he was drunk, or suffering from some fear, anger, or other excitement which deprived him of the ability to look circumspectly to the probable outcome of his conduct. These facts would not, according to the usual view, be relevant to an issue of inadvertent negligence, if that were before the court; but they are very relevant to the issue of recklessness. They may lead the tribunal to decide that the accused did not foresee the consequence, even though a person somewhat differently situated would have foreseen it. In short, a judgment of inadvertent negligence rests merely on a comparison between the conduct of the accused and that of a reasonable man, while a judgment of recklessness uses the concept of the reasonable man only as a guide to what went on in the accused's mind, and only so long as it can plausibly be assumed that the accused's mind accorded with the normal at the time of his act.

It must be confessed that, defined in this way, recklessness is not a concept that is likely to secure many convictions, if the law is properly administered. Recklessness as a form of *mens rea* is some enlargement upon the requirement of intention, but not a considerable one. This, at least, is true for recklessness as to the consequence of conduct. There is, however, another application of the concept of recklessness, namely as to the existence of present facts, *i.e.* the circumstances surrounding conduct. A person is said to be reckless as to a surrounding circumstance if he is aware of the possibility that such a circumstance exists and does an act regardless of it."

Question

Williams spoke of three factors which could imperil the stability of the meaning of recklessness; to what extent do the cases which follow establish the prophetic quality of Williams' comments?

Note

The courts originally gave recklessness a *subjective* meaning.

R. v. Cunningham
[1957] 2 Q.B. 396
Court of Criminal Appeal

C stole a gas meter from the cellar of a house and in doing so fractured a gas pipe. Gas escaped, percolated through the cellar wall to the adjoining house, and entered a bedroom with the result that W, when she was asleep, inhaled a considerable quantity of the gas. C was convicted of unlawfully and maliciously causing W to take a noxious thing, so as thereby to endanger her life contrary to section 23 of the Offences Against the Person Act 1861. The judge directed the jury that "maliciously" meant "wickedly"—doing "something which he has no business to do and perfectly well knows it."

BYRNE J. read the judgment of the court: The act of the appellant was clearly unlawful and therefore the real question for the jury was whether it was also malicious within the meaning of section 23 of the Offences Against the Person Act 1861.

Before this court Mr. Brodie has taken three points, all dependent upon the construction of that section. Section 23 provides: "Whosoever shall unlawfully and maliciously administer to or cause to be administered to or taken by any other person any poison or other destructive or noxious thing, so as thereby to endanger the life of such person, or so as thereby to inflict upon such person any grievous bodily harm, shall be guilty of felony. ...."

Mr. Brodie argued, first, that mens rea of some kind is necessary. Secondly that the nature of the mens rea required is that the appellant must intend to do the particular kind of harm that was done, or, alternatively, that he must foresee that that harm may occur yet nevertheless continue recklessly to do the act. Thirdly, that the judge misdirected the jury as to the meaning of the word "maliciously." He cited the following cases: *R. v. Pembliton* [*post*, p. 175], *R. v. Latimer* [*post*, p. 176] and *R. v. Faulkner* (1877) 13 Cox C.C. 550. In reply, Mr Snowden, on behalf of the Crown, cited *R. v. Martin* [*post*, p. 176].

We have considered those cases, and we have also considered, in the light of those cases, the following principle which was propounded by the late Professor C. S. Kenny in the first edition of his Outlines of Criminal Law published in 1902 and repeated in 1952: "In any statutory definition of crime, malice must be taken not in the old vague sense of wickedness in general but as requiring either (1) An actual intention to do the particular kind of harm that in fact was done; or (2) recklessness as to whether such harm should occur or not (*i.e.* the accused has foreseen that the particular kind of harm might be done and yet has gone on to take the risk of it). It is neither limited to nor does it indeed require any ill will towards the person injured." The same principle is repeated by Mr. Turner in his 10th edition of Russell on Crime at p. 1592.

We think that this is an accurate statement of the law. It derives some support from the judgments of Lord Coleridge C.J. and Blackburn J. in *Pembliton's* case (1874) L.R. 2 C.C.R. 119. In our opinion the word "maliciously" in a statutory crime postulates foresight of consequence. ...

With the utmost respect to the learned judge, we think it is incorrect to say that the word "malicious" in a statutory offence merely means wicked.

We think the judge was, in effect, telling the jury that if they were satisfied that the appellant had acted wickedly—and he had clearly acted wickedly in stealing the gas meter and its contents—they ought to find that he had acted maliciously in causing the gas to be taken by Mrs. Wade so as thereby to endanger her life.

In our view it should have been left to the jury to decide whether, even if the appellant did not intend the injury to Mrs. Wade, he foresaw that the removal of the gas meter might cause injury to someone but nevertheless removed it. We are unable to say that a reasonable jury, properly directed as to the meaning of the word "maliciously" in the context of section 23, would without doubt have convicted.

In these circumstances this court has no alternative but to allow the appeal and quash the conviction.

Appeal allowed

Notes

1. For further consideration of "maliciously" see Chapter 9 on Non-Fatal Offences Against the Person.

2. The Law Commission, in Working Paper No. 31, *Codification of the Criminal Law, General Principles: The Mental Element in Crime* (1970) and in its Report, *The Mental Element in Crime* (Law Com. No. 89), attributed a subjective meaning to *recklessness*. The Criminal Damage Act 1971 resulted from the work of the Law Commission (Law Com. No. 29, *Criminal Law Report on Offences of Damage to Property*). The Act sought to revise and simplify the law in relation to offences of damage to property. The term *reckless* as used in section 1 of the Act was construed by the Court of Appeal to mean *subjective recklessness*; the clearest statement of principle was given by Geoffrey Lane L.J. in *R. v. Stephenson* [1979] Q.B. 695. D, who suffered from schizophrenia, crept into a hollow in a large haystack and lit a fire to keep warm. The stack caught fire resulting in £3,500 of damage. Medical evidence was given that D might not have had the same ability to foresee or appreciate risks as the mentally normal person. The trial judge directed the jury that they could find D guilty if satisfied that he had closed his mind to the obvious fact of risk from his act and that schizophrenia might be a reason which made a person close his mind to the obvious fact of risk. In effect he was directing the jury to convict if the risk of damage would have been obvious to a reasonable person. The Court of Appeal quashed the conviction, Geoffrey Lane L.J. stating:

"A man is reckless when he carries out the deliberate act appreciating that there is a risk that damage to property may result from his act. It is however not the taking of every risk which could properly be classed as reckless. The risk must be one which it is in all the circumstances unreasonable for him to take.

Proof of the requisite knowledge in the mind of the defendant will in most cases present little difficulty. The fact that the risk of some damage would have been obvious to anyone in his right mind in the position of the defendant is not conclusive proof of the defendant's knowledge, but it may well be and in many cases doubtless will be a matter which will drive the jury to the conclusion that the defendant himself must have appreciated the risk. The fact that he may have been in a temper at the time would not normally deprive him of knowledge or foresight of the risk. If he had the necessary knowledge or foresight and his bad temper merely caused him to disregard it or put it to the back of his mind not caring whether the risk materialised, or if it merely deprived him of the self-control necessary to prevent him from taking the risk of which he was aware, then his bad temper will not avail him. ... We wish to make it clear that the test remains subjective, that the knowledge or appreciation or risk of some damage must have entered the defendant's mind even though he may have suppressed it or driven it out."

Note

In 1981 the House of Lords had cause to consider the definition of *recklessness* as used in the Criminal Damage Act 1971. A reversal of the position enunciated in *Stephenson* was the outcome.

R. v. Caldwell
[1982] A.C. 341
House of Lords

In pursuit of a grievance which he thought he had against the proprietor of a hotel, the respondent set fire to the hotel. There were 10 guests living there at the time. The fire was discovered before any serious damage occurred. The appeal was mainly concerned with his defence of intoxication, as to which see *post*, p. 257, but the House took the opportunity to consider the meaning of recklessness in the Criminal Damage Act 1971.

LORD DIPLOCK: ... [The respondent] was indicted at the Central Criminal Court on two counts of arson under section 1(1) and (2) respectively, of the Criminal Damage Act 1971. That section reads as follows:

"1.—(1) A person who without lawful excuse destroys or damages any property belonging to another intending to destroy or damage any such property or being reckless as to whether any such property would be destroyed or damaged shall be guilty of an offence.
    (2) A person who without lawful excuse destroys or damages any property, whether belonging to himself or another. ...
        (*a*)   intending to destroy or damage any property or being reckless as to whether any property would be destroyed or damaged; and
        (*b*)   intending by the destruction or damage to endanger the life of another or being reckless as to whether the life of another would be thereby endangered;
shall be guilty of an offence.
    (3) An offence committed under this section by destroying or damaging property by fire shall be charged as arson."

Count 1 contained the charge of the more serious offence under section 1(2) which requires intent to endanger the life of another or recklessness as to whether the life of another would be endangered. To this count the respondent pleaded not guilty. ...
Count 2 contained the lesser offence under section 1(1) to which the respondent pleaded guilty.

The recorder directed the jury that self-induced drunkenness was not a defence to count 1, and the jury convicted him on this count. ... [u]nder section 1(2)(*b*) there are two alternative states of mind as respects endangering the life of another. ... One is intention that a particular thing should happen in consequence of the *actus reus*, viz., that the life of another person (should be endangered, (this was not relied on by the Crown in the instant case). The other is recklessness as to whether that particular thing should happen or not. The same dichotomy of *mentes reae*, intention and recklessness, is to be found throughout the section; in subsection (1) and paragraph (*a*) of subsection (2) as well as in paragraph (*b*); and "reckless" as descriptive of a state of mind must be given the same meaning in each of them.

My Lords, the Criminal Damage Act 1971 replaced almost in their entirety the many and detailed provisions of the Malicious Damage Act 1861. Its purpose, as stated in its long title was to *revise* the law of England and Wales as to offences of damage to property. As the brevity of the Act suggests, it must have been hoped that it would also simplify the law.

In the Act of 1861, the word consistently used to describe the *mens rea* that was a necessary element in the multifarious offences that the Act created was "maliciously"—a technical expression, not readily intelligible to juries, which became the subject of considerable judicial exegesis. This culminated in a judgment of the Court of Criminal Appeal in *R.* v. *Cunningham*, (*ante*, p. 109) which approved, as an accurate statement of the law, what had been said by Professor Kenny in his *Outlines of Criminal Law* (1st Edn., 1902):

> "In any statutory definition of a crime, 'malice' must be taken ... as requiring either (1) an actual intention to do the particular *kind* of harm that in fact was done; or (2) recklessness as to whether such harm should occur or not (*i.e.* the accused has foreseen that the particular kind of harm might be done and yet has gone on to take the risk of it)."

My Lords, in this passage Professor Kenny was engaged in defining for the benefit of students the meaning of "malice" as a term of art in criminal law. To do so he used ordinary English words in their popular meaning. Among the words he used was "recklessness," the noun derived from the adjective "reckless," of which the popular or dictionary meaning is: careless, regardless, or heedless, of the possible harmful consequences of one's acts. It presupposes that if thought were given to the matter by the doer before the act was done, it would have been apparent to him that there was a real risk of its having the relevant harmful consequences; but, granted this, recklessness covers a whole range of states of mind from failing to give any thought at all to whether or not there is any risk of those harmful consequences, to recognising the existence of the risk and nevertheless deciding to ignore it. Conscious of this imprecision in the popular meaning of recklessness as descriptive of a state of mind, Professor Kenny, in the passage quoted, was, as it seems to me, at pains to indicate by the words in brackets the particular species within the genus reckless states of mind, that constituted "malice" in criminal law. This parenthetical restriction on the natural meaning of recklessness was necessary to an explanation of the meaning of the adverb "maliciously" when used as a term of art in the description of an offence under the Malicious Damage Act 1861 (which was the matter in point in *R.* v. *Cunningham*); but it was not directed to and consequently has no bearing on the meaning of the adjective "reckless" in section 1 of the Criminal Damage Act 1971. To use it for that purpose can, in my view, only be misleading.

My Lords, the restricted meaning that the Court of Appeal in *R.* v. *Cunningham* had placed on the adverb "maliciously" in the Malicious Damage Act 1861 in cases where the prosecution did not rely upon an actual intention of the accused to cause the damage that was in fact done called for a meticulous analysis by the jury of the thoughts that passed through the mind of the accused at or before the time he did the act that caused the damage, in order to see on which side of a narrow dividing line they fell. If it had crossed his mind that there was a risk that someone's property might be damaged but, because his mind was affected by rage or excitement or confused by drink, he did not appreciate the seriousness of the risk or trusted that good luck would prevent its happening, this state of mind would amount to malice in the restricted meaning placed upon that term by the Court of Appeal; whereas if, for any of these reasons, he did not even trouble to give his mind to the question whether there was any risk of damaging the property, this state of mind would not suffice to make him guilty of an offence under the Malicious Damage Act 1861.

Neither state of mind seems to me to be less blameworthy than the other; but if the difference between the two constituted the distinction between what does and what does not in legal theory amount to a guilty state of mind for the purposes of a statutory offence of damage to property, it would not be a practicable distinction for use in a trial by jury. The only person who knows what the accused's mental processes were is the accused himself—and probably not even he can recall them accurately when the rage or excitement under which he acted had passed, or he has sobered up if he were under the influence of drink at the relevant time. If the accused gives evidence that because of his rage, excitement or drunkenness the risk of particular harmful consequences of his acts simply did not occur to him, a jury would find it hard to be satisfied beyond reasonable doubt that his true mental process was not that, but was the slightly different mental process required if one applies the restricted meaning of "being reckless as to whether" something would happen, adopted by the Court of Appeal in *R.* v. *Cunningham*

My Lords, I can see no reason why Parliament when it decided to revise the law as to offences of damage to property should go out of its way to perpetuate fine and impracticable distinctions such as these, between one mental state and another. One would think that the sooner they were got rid of, the better.

When cases under section 1(1) of the new Act, in which the prosecution's case was based upon the accused having been "reckless as to whether ... property would be destroyed or damaged," first came before the Court of Appeal, the question as to the meaning of the expression "reckless" in the context of that subsection appears to have been treated as soluble simply by posing and answering what had by then, unfortunately, become an obsessive question among English lawyers. Is the test of recklessness "subjective" or "objective"? The first two reported cases, in both of which judgments were given off the cuff, are first *R.* v. *Briggs* [1977] 1 W.L.R. 605, *R.* v. *Parker (Daryl)* [1977] 1 W.L.R. 600. Both classified the test of recklessness as "subjective." This led the court in *Briggs* to say: "A man is reckless in the sense required when he carries out a deliberate act knowing that there is some risk of damage resulting from that act but nevertheless continues in the performance of that act." This leaves over the question whether the risk of damage may not be so slight that even the most prudent of men would feel justified in taking it, but it excludes that kind of recklessness that consists of acting without giving any thought at all to whether or not there is any risk of harmful consequences of one's act; even though the risk is great and would be

obvious if any thought were given to the matter by the doer of the act.
Parker, however, opened the door a chink by adding as an alternative to
the actual knowledge of the accused that there is some risk of damage
resulting from his act and his going on to take it, a mental state described
as "closing his mind to the obvious fact" that there is such a risk.

R. v. *Stephenson* (*ante*, p. 110), the first case in which there was full
argument, though only on one side, and a reserved judgment, slammed
the door again upon any less restricted interpretation of "reckless" as to
whether particular consequences will occur than that originally approved
in *Briggs*. ... The court ... made the assumption that although Parliament
in replacing the Act of 1861 by the Act of 1971 had discarded the word
"maliciously" as descriptive of the *mens rea* of the offences of which the
actus reus is damaging property, in favour of the more explicit phrase
"intending to destroy or damage any such property or being reckless as to
whether any such property would be destroyed," it nevertheless intended
the words to be interpreted in precisely the same sense as that in which
the single adverb "maliciously" had been construed by Professor Kenny in
the passage that received the subsequent approval of the Court of Appeal
in R. v. *Cunningham*.

My Lords, I see no warrant for making any such assumption in an Act
whose declared purpose is to revise the then existing law as to offences of
damage to property, not to perpetuate it. "Reckless" as used in the new
statutory definition of the *mens rea* of these offences is an ordinary English
word. It had not by 1971 become a term of legal art with some more
limited esoteric meaning than that which it bore in ordinary speech—a
meaning which surely includes not only deciding to ignore a risk of
harmful consequences resulting from one's acts that one has recognised as
existing, but also failing to give any thought to whether or not there is any
such risk in circumstances where, if any thought were given to the matter,
it would be obvious that there was.

If one is attaching labels, the latter state of mind is neither more nor less
"subjective" than the first. But the label solves nothing. It is a statement of
the obvious; *mens rea* is, by definition, a state of mind of the accused
himself at the time he did the physical act that constitutes the *actus reus* of
the offence; it cannot be the mental state of some non-existent,
hypothetical person.

Nevertheless, to decide whether someone has been "reckless" whether
harmful consequences of a particular kind will result from his act, as
distinguished from his actually intending such harmful consequences to
follow, does call for some consideration of how the mind of the ordinary
prudent individual would have reacted to a similar situation. If there were
nothing in the circumstances that ought to have drawn the attention of an
ordinary prudent individual to the possibility of that kind of harmful
consequence, the accused would not be described as "reckless" in the
natural meaning of that word for failing to address his mind to the
possibility; nor, if the risk of the harmful consequences was so slight that
the ordinary prudent individual upon due consideration of the risk would
not be deterred from treating it as negligible, could the accused be
described as "reckless" in its ordinary sense if, having considered the risk,
he decided to ignore it. (In this connection the gravity of the possible
harmful consequences would be an important factor. To endanger life
must be one of the most grave). So to this extent, even if one ascribes to
"reckless" only the restricted meaning, adopted by the Court of Appeal in
Stephenson and *Briggs*, of foreseeing that a particular kind of harm might
happen and yet going on to take the risk of it, it involves a test that would
be described in part as "objective" in current legal jargon. Questions of

criminal liability are seldom solved by simply asking whether the test is subjective or objective.

In my opinion, a person charged with an offence under section 1(1) of the Criminal Damage Act 1971 is "reckless as to whether or not any property would be destroyed or damaged" if (1) he does an act which in fact creates an obvious risk that property will be destroyed or damaged and (2) when he does the act he either has not given any thought to the possibility of there being any such risk or has recognised that there was some risk involved and has nonetheless gone on to do it. That would be a proper direction to the jury; cases in the Court of Appeal which held otherwise should be regarded as overruled.

Where the charge is under section 1(2) the question of the state of mind of the accused must be approached in stages, corresponding to paragraphs (a) and (b). The jury must be satisfied that what the accused did amounted to an offence under section 1(1), either because he actually intended to destroy or damage the property or because he was reckless (in the sense that I have described) as to whether it might be destroyed or damaged. Only if they are so satisfied must the jury go on to consider whether the accused also either actually intended that the destruction or damage of the property should endanger someone's life or was reckless (in a similar sense) as to whether a human life might be endangered. ...

LORDS KEITH OF KINKEL and ROSKILL agreed with LORD DIPLOCK].

LORD EDMUND-DAVIES, (with whom LORD WILBERFORCE agreed): ... The words "intention" and "recklessness" have increasingly displaced in statutory crimes the word "maliciously" which has frequently given rise to difficulty in interpretation. [His Lordship then cited the passage from *Cunningham*, quoted by Lord Diplock, *supra*].

My Lords, my noble and learned friend, Lord Diplock, somewhat dismissively describes Professor Kenny as having been "engaged in defining for the benefit of students the meaning of 'malice' as a term of art in criminal law" ... I have to say that I am in respectful, but profound, disagreement. The law in action compiles its own dictionary. In time, what was originally the common coinage of speech acquires a different value in the pocket of the lawyer than when in the layman's purse. Professor Kenny used lawyers' words in lawyers' sense to express his distillation of an important part of the established law relating to *mens rea*, and he did so in a manner accurate not only in respect of the law as it stood in 1902 but also as it has been applied in countless cases ever since, both in the United Kingdom and in other countries where the common law prevails; see, for example in Western Australia, *Lederer* v. *Hutchins* [1961] W.A.R. 99, and, in the United States of America, Jethro Brown's "General Principles of Criminal Law," 2nd Edition, 1960, 115. And it is well known that the Criminal Damage Act 1971 was in the main the work of the Law Commission, who, in their Working Paper No. 31 (1970) defined recklessness by saying:

> "A person is reckless if, (a) by knowing that there is a risk that an event may result from his conduct or that a circumstance may exist, he takes that risk, and (b) it is unreasonable for him to take it, having regard to the degree and nature of the risk which he knows to be present."

It was surely with this contemporaneous definition and the much respected decision of *Cunningham* in mind that the draftsman proceeded to his task of drafting the Criminal Damage Act 1971.

It has therefore to be said that, unlike negligence, which has to be judged objectively, recklessness involves foresight of consequences, combined with an objective judgment of the reasonableness of the risk taken. And recklessness *in vacuo* is an incomprehensible notion. It *must* relate to foresight of risk of the particular kind relevant to the charge preferred, which, for the purpose of section 1(2), is the risk of endangering life and nothing other than that.

So if a defendant says of a particular risk, "It never crossed my mind," a jury could not on those words alone properly convict him of recklessness simply because they considered that the risk *ought* to have crossed his mind, though his words might well lead to a finding of negligence. But a defendant's admission that he "closed his mind" to a particular risk could prove fatal, for "A person cannot, in any intelligible meaning of the words, 'close his mind to a risk' unless he first realises that there is a risk; and if he realises that there is a risk, that is the end of the matter." (Glanville Williams, Textbook of Criminal Law, p. 79).

In the absence of exculpatory factors, the defendant's state of mind is therefore all-important where recklessness is an element in the offence charged, and section 8 of the Criminal Justice Act 1967 has laid down that:

"A court or jury, in determining whether a person has committed an offence,—
(a) shall not be bound in law to infer that he intended *or foresaw* a result of his actions by reason only of its being a natural and probable consequence of those actions; but
(b) shall decide whether he did intend *or foresee* that result by reference to all the evidence, drawing such inferences from the evidence as appear proper in the circumstances."

My Lords, it is unnecessary to examine at length the proposition that ascertainment of the state of mind known as "recklessness" is a *subjective* exercise, for the task was expansively performed by Geoffrey Lane L.J. (as he then was) in *Stephenson* (*ante*, p. 110).

[The House dismissed the appeal on the grounds that self-induced intoxication was not a defence to section 2(1) where the charge was based on recklessness, see *post*, p. 257].

Appeal dismissed

Questions

1. Do you agree with Lord Diplock that to ask a jury to distinguish between a defendant who foresaw a risk and one who ought to have foreseen a risk calls for "meticulous analysis"? Is this analysis any more meticulous than that required of a jury in any other case where it is required to decide on the defendant's state of mind?

2. Are the distinctions between *subjective* and *objective* recklessness as "fine and impracticable" as Lord Diplock suggests?

3. Do you agree with Lord Diplock that the term *recklessness* had not by 1971 become a legal term of art or was Lord Edmund-Davies correct when he stated that the law acquires its own dictionary?

4. If "reckless" is an "ordinary English word" (Lord Diplock) is it not strange that the majority in *Caldwell* "prevails not only over the weighty dissent of Lords Wilberforce and Edmund-Davies but also over the substantial body of judicial opinion in the cases of *Briggs*,

Stephenson and other cases in the Court of Appeal and Divisional Court." (Smith [1981] Crim.L.R. 393)? One possible answer to this question would be that "even 'ordinary' words (and especially abstract words) are variously understood—everyone may 'know what they mean' but, without knowing it, use them with different meanings." (Griew, "Consistency, Communication and Codification: Reflections on Two Mens Rea Words" in Glazebrook, pp. 57, 58.)

5. Lord Diplock framed his "objective" test of recklessness to catch individuals who might plead that because of rage, excitement or drunkenness they did not appreciate the risk of damaging property; if the accused pleads that he did not appreciate the risk for some other reason, does this mean that he must be found not guilty? (see *Elliot* v. *C.*, *infra*) *For example*, D. is a 14-year-old girl baby-sitting for neighbours. Feeling cold she decides to light the coal fire. The coal is damp and will not light. She finds paraffin in the garden shed and pours this over the coal. She ignites this thereby causing a conflagration which causes considerable damage to the house. D. has never before lit a coal fire being used to central heating. If the risk of damage was *obvious*, would D. be guilty of arson? If the fire put at risk the children sleeping upstairs, would D. be guilty of recklessly damaging property being reckless whether life was endangered?

Note

In *R.* v. *Lawrence* [1982] A.C. 510, decided at the same time as *Caldwell*, the House of Lords considered the meaning of "recklessly" in the context of causing death by reckless driving. (The offences of reckless driving and causing death by reckless driving have since been replaced by section 1 of the Road Traffic Act 1991 with the offences of dangerous driving and causing death by dangerous driving.) Their Lordships decided that the *Caldwell* test of recklessness should be applied to reckless driving. Lord Diplock stated:

"Recklessness on the part of the doer of an act does presuppose that there is something in the circumstances that would have drawn the attention of an ordinary prudent individual to the possibility that his act was capable of causing the kind of serious harmful consequences that the section which creates the offence was intended to prevent, and that the risk of those harmful consequences occurring was not so slight that an ordinary prudent individual would feel justified in treating them as negligible. It is only when this is so that the doer of the act is acting "recklessly" if before doing the act, he either fails to give any thought to the possibility of there being any such risk or, having recognised that there was such risk, he nevertheless goes on to do it."

Question

In *Reid* [1992] 1 All E.R. 673, Lord Keith of Kinkel stated (at p. 674): "Absence of something from a person's mind is as much part of his state of mind as its presence. Inadvertence to risk is no less a subjective state of mind than is disregard of a recognised risk. If there is nothing to go upon apart from what actually happened, the natural inference is that the [accused's] state of mind was one or other of those described by Lord Diplock. It would, however, be quite impossible for any juryman to say which it was, and in particular for him to be satisfied beyond reasonable doubt that it was the first state of mind rather than the second. So logically, if only the first state of mind constituted the relevant mens rea, it would be impossible ever to get a conviction."

Lord Keith was dealing with reckless driving and the "first" state of mind he referred to was advertence to a risk while the "second" was inadvertence. If Lord Keith is correct, is he suggesting that all convictions in cases where only the *"Cunningham"* test for recklessness suffices are unsafe or unsatisfactory?

Notes

1. There is a lacuna in the *Caldwell/Lawrence* recklessness test, namely the situation where, although it is proved there was an obvious risk, the defendant gave thought to the matter and wrongly concluded that there was no risk or that the risk was negligible in the sense that it was one which a reasonable and prudent person might take.

In *Chief Constable of Avon and Somerset Constabulary* v. *Shimmen* (1986) 84 Cr.App.R. 7, D sought to rely on this lacuna in his defence to a charge of criminal damage. D was a self-defence aficionado who sought to demonstrate his skill to his friends by kicking at and narrowly missing a shop window. In fact D broke the window. D stated in his defence that he believed "he had eliminated as much risk as possible by missing by two inches instead of two millimetres." His submission essentially was that he recognised the risk but thought he had minimized it so that no damage would result. The Divisional Court concluded that D was reckless as he recognised the risk and did not take adequate precautions to eliminate it.

It is arguable that a person cannot be considered reckless where he believes he has taken adequate precautions to eliminate a risk as his state of mind then is one of believing that, because of his precautions, there is no risk; the Divisional Court did not deal specifically with this issue. However, if a person believes he has minimized the risk rather than eliminated it (which would appear to have been Shimmen's belief) and there is no social utility in the act to be performed (as was the case here) then there is no justification for running such a risk, *i.e.* the reasonable and prudent person would not take such a risk. J. C. Smith states in his *Commentary* to the above case [1986] Crim.L.R. 802:

"Taking even the slightest risk with the property of another can be justified only if there is some acceptable reason for taking the risk. This is, of course, an objective question to be answered by the judge and jury or magistrates. It may fairly be assumed that no one would regard as reasonable the taking of any risk of destruction of a valuable shop window in order to demonstrate to a few friends the actor's skill in self-defence."

2. Another question left undecided by *Caldwell* and *Lawrence* was whether a defendant would be found guilty where the risk was not obvious to him (by reason of age, lack of experience, or lack of understanding) even though such a risk would have been obvious to the reasonably prudent individual. The answer came in the following case.

Elliot v. C. (a minor)
[1983] 1 W.L.R. 939
Queen's Bench Division

C, a 14-year-old schoolgirl, in a remedial class at school, who had been out all night without sleep, entered a garden shed. She found white spirit which she poured on the carpet in the shed and ignited it. The shed was destroyed by the fire. The justices found C not guilty of destroying the shed and contents contrary to section 1(1) of the Criminal Damage Act 1971. The justices concluded that because of her age, limited understanding, lack of experience of white spirit and exhaustion, the risk of destroying the shed would not have been obvious to her or been appreciated by her if she had given thought to the matter. The prosecution appealed.

GLIDEWELL J.: ... [T]he magistrates accepted that they were bound to follow the "model direction" of Lord Diplock which I have read. It was, however, argued before them, and again before us by counsel for the respondent ... that when, in the first part of his test, Lord Diplock referred to "an act which in fact creates an obvious risk that property will be destroyed or damaged," he meant a risk which was obvious to the particular defendant. This argument was accepted by the magistrates. ...

Before us, counsel for the appellant has argued forcefully that the magistrates were wrong to adopt that interpretation of the decision in *Caldwell*. He submits that the phrase "creates an obvious risk" means that the risk is one which must have been obvious to a reasonably prudent man, not necessarily to the particular defendant if he or she had given thought to it. It follows, says counsel, that if the risk is one which would have been obvious to a reasonably prudent person, once it has also been proved that the particular defendant gave no thought to the possibility of there being such a risk, it is not a defence that because of limited intelligence or exhaustion she would not have appreciated the risk even if she had thought about it.

It is right to say, as counsel for the appellant pointed out to us, that there are passages in the speech of Lord Diplock in *Caldwell* which suggest that his Lordship was indeed using the phrase "creates an obvious risk" as meaning, "creates a risk which was obvious to the particular defendant." Thus, his Lordship said ([1981] 1 All E.R. 961 at 964, [1982] A.C. 341 at 351):

"Among the words [Professor Kenny] used was 'recklessness,' the noun derived from the adjective 'reckless,' of which the popular or dictionary meaning is 'careless, regardless, or heedless of the possible harmful consequences of one's acts.' It presupposes that, if thought were given to the matter by the doer before the act was done, it would have been apparent to him that there was a real risk of its having the relevant harmful consequences. ... "

Speaking of another earlier decision of the Court of Appeal, in *R.* v. *Briggs* [1977] 1 All E.R. 475, [1977] 1 W.L.R. 605, he said ([1981] 1 All E.R. 961 at 965, [1982] A.C. 341 at 353): " ... even though the risk is great and would be obvious if any thought were given to the matter by the doer of the act."

He said ([1981] 1 All E.R. 961 at 967, [1982] A.C. 341 at 355):

"So, in the instant case, the fact that the respondent was unaware of the risk of endangering the lives of residents in the hotel owing to his self-induced intoxication would be no defence if that risk would have been obvious to him had he been sober."

The last passage was based on the earlier decision of the House of Lords in *R.* v. *Majewski* (*post*, p. 246), a decision relating to the effect of self-induced intoxication on intent. But, quite apart from the *Majewski* test, the decision of the majority in *Caldwell* that intoxication, even if it resulted in the defendant not thinking at all whether there was a risk that property or life would be endangered, nevertheless did not take him out of the state of mind properly described as "reckless" is only consistent in my view with their Lordships meaning by the phrase "creates an obvious risk" creates a risk obvious to the reasonably prudent person.

That the submission of counsel for the appellant is correct is to my mind, however, put beyond a peradventure by two later decisions of the House of Lords.

[His Lordship cited the discussion of "reckless" by Lord Diplock in *Lawrence* (*supra*, p. 117) and *Miller* (*supra*, p. 26).]

In the light of these last two authorities, we are in my judgment bound to hold that the word reckless in section 1 of the Criminal Damage Act 1971 has the meaning ascribed to it by counsel for the appellant. It is only fair to the magistrates in the present case to say that it seems that they were not referred to the decision in *R.* v. *Lawrence*, and *R.* v. *Miller* had not, when they reached their decision, been heard by the House of Lords. ...

ROBERT GOFF L.J.: I agree with the conclusion reached by Glidewell J. but I do so simply because I believe myself constrained to do so by authority. I feel moreover that I would be lacking in candour if I were to conceal my unhappiness about the conclusion which I feel compelled to reach. ...

[His Lordship quoted Lord Diplock's model direction in *Caldwell* and continued.] Now, if that test is applied literally in the present case, the conclusion appears inevitable that, on the facts found by the magistrates, the respondent was reckless whether the shed and contents would be destroyed; because first she did an act which created an obvious risk that the property would be destroyed, and second she had not given any thought to the possibility of there being any such risk.

Yet, if I next pause ... and ask myself the question: would I, having regard only to the ordinary meaning of the word, consider this girl to have been, on the facts found, *reckless* whether the shed and contents would be destroyed, my answer would, I confess, be in the negative. This is not a case where there was a deliberate disregard of a known risk of damage or injury of a certain type or degree; nor is it a case where there was mindless indifference to a risk of such damage or injury, as is expressed in common speech in the context of motoring offences (though not, I think, of arson) as "blazing on regardless"; nor is it even a case where failure to give thought to the possibility of the risk was due to some blameworthy cause, such as intoxication. This is a case where it appears that the only basis on which the accused might be held to have been reckless would be if the appropriate test to be applied was purely objective: a test which might in some circumstances be thought justifiable in relation to certain conduct (*e.g.* reckless driving), particularly where the word "reckless" is used simply to characterise the relevant conduct. But such a test does not appear at first sight to be appropriate to a crime such as that under consideration in the present case, especially as recklessness in that crime has to be related to a particular consequence. I therefore next ask myself the question whether I can, consistently with the doctrine of precedent, sensibly interpreted, legitimately construe or qualify the principle stated by Lord Diplock in *Caldwell* so as to accommodate what I conceive to be the appropriate result on the facts of the present case, bearing in mind that those facts are very different from the facts under consideration by the House of Lords in *Caldwell*, where the defendant had set fire to a hotel when in a state of intoxication.

Here again, it would be unrealistic if I were to disguise the fact that I am well aware that the statement of principle by Lord Diplock in *Caldwell* has been the subject of comment, much of it critical, in articles written by jurists; and that I have studied certain of these articles with interest. I find it striking that the justices, in reaching their conclusion in the present case, have done so (no doubt in response to an argument advanced on the respondent's behalf) by imposing on Lord Diplock's statement of principle a qualification similar to one considered by Professor Glanville Williams in his article "Recklessness Redefined" (1981) 40 C.L.J. 252 at 270–271. This is that a defendant should only be regarded as having acted recklessly by virtue of his failure to give any thought to an obvious risk that property would be destroyed or damaged, where such risk would have been obvious *to him* if he had given any thought to the matter. However, having studied Lord Diplock's speech, I do not think it would be consistent with his reasoning to impose any such qualification. I say that not only because this qualification does not appear in terms in his conclusion which I have already quoted, but also because, when considering earlier in his speech Professor Kenny's definition of recklessness (which he rejected as being too narrow), Lord Diplock expressly adverted to the fact that that definition presupposed that "if thought were given to the matter by the doer before the act was done, it would have been apparent *to him* that there was a real risk of its having the relevant harmful consequences ... " (see [1981] 1 All E.R. 961 at 964. [1982] A.C. 341 at 351; my emphasis). It seems to me that, having expressly considered that element in Professor Kenny's test, and having (as I think) plainly decided to omit it from his own formulation of the concept of recklessness, it would not now be legitimate for an inferior court, in a case under this particular subsection, to impose a qualification which had so been rejected by Lord Diplock himself. It follows that for that reason alone I do not feel able to uphold the reasoning of the magistrates in the present case. But I wish to add that, for my part, I doubt whether this qualification can be justified in any event. Where there is no thought of the consequences, any further inquiry necessary for the purposes of establishing guilt should prima facie be directed to the question why such thought was not given, rather than to the purely hypothetical question of what the particular person would have appreciated had he directed his mind to the matter.

Appeal allowed

Questions

1. In *Caldwell* Lord Diplock was concerned to define recklessness in such a way as to ensure that a defendant could not secure an acquittal by pleading that because of his intoxication he failed to recognise an obvious risk. Is it conceivable that C, in the above case, falls within the same category of blameworthiness as the intoxicated Caldwell?

2. Will C's conviction serve as a deterrent to other mentally retarded people? In favour of the judgment in *Caldwell* it can, at least, be argued that Caldwell could choose whether or not to get himself drunk; do people such as C have any choice with regard to their mental deficiencies?

3. If no sympathy was to be shown to the accused who was incapable of foreseeing risks obvious to the ordinary prudent man, would it be possible to improve the accused's chances of acquittal by at least accrediting to the ordinary prudent man the age and such of the accused's characteristics as would affect his appreciation of the risk? The answer was provided in the following case.

R. v. Stephen Malcolm R.
(1984) 79 Cr.App.R. 334
Court of Appeal

The appellant, when aged 15, committed a series of burglaries. He and his accomplices, believing that a woman and her daughter had informed on them to the police, threw three petrol bombs at the woman's house near the daughter's bedroom, causing loud bangs and sheets of flame. The appellant claimed that he intended only to frighten and that he did not realise that if a petrol bomb had gone through the daughter's window it might have killed her. He was convicted of arson contrary to section 1(2)(*b*) of the Criminal Damage Act 1971.

ACKNER L.J.: ... The point of law which is raised before us is the point which [counsel for the appellant] took before Judge Abdela. It is said that the learned judge erred in law in deciding that the test of recklessness as to whether life was endangered was as follows: A person is guilty of the offence if (i) he does an act which in fact creates a risk to the ordinary prudent man, *i.e.* one of mature years and understanding, that life will be endangered; (ii) he did the act not having given thought to the possibility of such a risk; or (iii) recognising that there was some risk, he nonetheless continued the act.

The learned judge, it is urged, was wrong in law because he failed to apply the law in relation to what constitutes the "ordinary prudent man" and failed adequately to consider *D.P.P.* v. *Camplin* (*post*, p. 517). He should have found that the ordinary prudent man is synonymous with the reasonable man and therefore the jury should have had regard to the particular situation of the appellant, namely his age, and any other characteristics which would affect his appreciation of the risk.

This arson, it is accepted by [counsel for the appellant] was serious. For the ordinary prudent adult there was plainly an obvious risk of endangering the life of another. Thus the sole question which this appeal raises is whether the learned judge was wrong in the ruling which he gave. ... [Counsel for the appellant] submits that the same approach as in *D.P.P.* v. *Camplin* (*supra*) applies where recklessness is the issue before the jury.

[His Lordship discussed *Camplin*; considered *Caldwell*, *Lawrence* and *Miller* before dealing at length with *Elliot* v. *C.* (*ante*, p. 119).]

In the face of [these authorities, counsel for the appellant] sought to induce us to adopt a *via media*. He said he accepted it would be wrong to ask the question whether the defendant himself was aware of the risk, but it would be right to inquire whether a person of the age of the defendant and with his characteristics which might be relevant to his ability to foresee the risk, would have appreciated it. He drew our attention in particular to the submission made by the prosecution before the justices in *Elliott's* case "that in relation to the defendant aged 14 years, the proper approach was whether such risk would have been obvious to a normal 14 year old child." Therefore he said he was not seeking to relate the test to the particular defendant, but merely, so to speak, to a class of which he is a member. This, he says, provides him with the same logical basis of approach to the reasonable man or the reasonably prudent person as *D.P.P.* v. *Camplin* (*supra*) had suggested. We do not think that that *via media* was for one moment in the mind of Lord Diplock. The opportunity so to ingraft this important modification on the principle which he had enunciated had arisen in the subsequent cases and would have been just the sort of point (if it was a valid one) which we would have expected the House of Lords to have desired to have dealt with, thus clearing up the position, when they had the opportunity to do so when considering whether or not to give leave in *Elliott's* case (*supra*). If they had desired to say, for instance, that the age of the defendant was a factor to which particular regard must be had in applying the test, then *Elliott* was just the sort of case to do that, excising, if appropriate, any reference to any other ephemeral characteristics such as exhaustion from which the girl was said to be suffering. But they did not take that opportunity. We do not think that we should seek by this subtlety to avoid applying principles which we also have difficulty in accepting. We respectfully share the regrets voiced by Robert Goff L.J. that in essence "recklessness" has now been construed synonymously with "carelessness."

We therefore dismiss the appeal against conviction. Although we would have preferred that the judge should have at least been entitled in law to have left to the jury the question, would a boy of the defendant's age have appreciated that to have thrown petrol bombs very close to the windows of this dwelling house was a danger to the life of the occupants of that house, we have little doubt that on the facts of this case the answer would have been clearly in the affirmative. ...

Appeal dismissed

Note

Elliot v. *C.*, *Stephen (Malcom R.)* and *Bell* [1984] 3 All E.R. 842 (where D.'s inability to foresee risks due to schizophrenia was held to be irrelevant) establish that an accused is to be judged against the standard of the ordinary reasonable person even though this is a standard which he may be constitutionally incapable of attaining. If the reasonable prudent person is not invested with any of the

accused's characteristics for the purposes of deciding on recklessness, might s/he nevertheless have the benefit of hindsight or
expert knowledge? This question arose in the following case.

R. v. Sangha
[1988] 2 All E.R. 385
Court of Appeal

D set fire to furniture in a flat. There was no risk of the lives of the
occupants being endangered as they were not present. Unknown to D
there was also no danger to occupants of adjacent flats because of the
special construction of the building. D was charged with the offence of
damaging property being reckless whether the life of another would be
thereby endangered, contrary to section 1(2)(b) of the Criminal Damage
Act 1971. It was argued that D could not have been reckless whether life
was endangered if there was, in fact, no risk to life. D was convicted
and appealed.

TUCKER J.: It is clear that in the present case the relevant time is the time
when the two armchairs were set alight. That is the point at which the
ordinary prudent man would recognise that some risk of danger to life
would be created.

There may of course be cases of arson where the lives not only of the
occupants would be endangered, but also of those who might come to
their rescue, or of firemen who might have to put out the blaze. But in the
present case counsel for the Crown did not stress that aspect.

In our judgment, when consideration is given whether an act of setting
fire to something creates an obvious and serious risk of damaging property
and thereby endangering the life of another, the test to be applied is this:
is it proved that an ordinary prudent bystander would have perceived an
obvious risk that property would be damaged and that life would thereby
be endangered? The ordinary prudent bystander is not deemed to be
invested with expert knowledge relating to the construction of the
property, nor to have the benefit of hindsight. The time at which his
perception is material is the time when the fire is started.

Section 1(2) of the 1971 Act uses the word "would" in the context of
recklessness whether property would be destroyed or damaged, and
whether the life of another would be thereby endangered. We interpret
this word "would" as going to the expectations of the normal prudent
bystander.

Applying this test to the facts of the case before us, it is clear that in
setting fire to these armchairs as the jury found the appellant did, he
created a risk which was obvious and serious that property would be
damaged and that the life of another would thereby be engandered. The
fact that there were special features here which prevented the risk from
materialising is irrelevant.

Appeal dismissed

Note

The test of recklessness established by *Caldwell* and *Lawrence* is
therefore quite clearly objective (although Lord Diplock may have
disliked the use of such a label). But to which offences does the
objective test of recklessness apply?

Rape

After its decision in *Pigg* [1982] 1 W.L.R. 762, in which the Court of Appeal held, *obiter*, that the *Caldwell* and *Lawrence* test of recklessness applied with regard to the issue of consent, the Court subsequently changed its stance in *R. v. Satnam S. and Kewal S.* (1984) 78 Cr.App.R. 149 (see *post*, p. 641) where Bristow J. held that Lord Diplock's test of recklessness did not apply to section 1(1) of the Sexual Offences (Amendment) Act 1976 stating—

"*Caldwell* [and] *Lawrence* ... were concerned with recklessness in a different context and under a different statute.

The word 'reckless' in relation to rape involves a different concept to its use in relation to malicious damage or, indeed, in relation to offences against the person. In the latter cases the foreseeability, or possible foreseeability, is as to the consequences of the criminal act. In the case of rape the foreseeability is as to the state of mind of the victim."

Question

Is the distinction drawn between recklessness as to consequences and recklessness as to circumstances a valid one?

Statutory Offences which may be committed recklessly

In *Seymour* [1983] 2 A.C. 493, H.L., (*post*, p. 559) a case of "motor manslaughter," Lord Roskill stated:

"[I]t would be quite wrong to give the adjective 'reckless' or the adverb 'recklessly' a different meaning according to whether the statutory or the common law offence [causing death by reckless driving or reckless manslaughter, respectively] were charged. 'Reckless' should today be given the same meaning in relation to all offences which involve 'recklessness' as one of the elements unless Parliament has otherwise ordained."

This dictum was *obiter* going much further than was required for decision of the case before the House, although the case did conclude that the *Caldwell* test applies to the common law offence of reckless manslaughter.

The offences of common assault, assault occasioning actual bodily harm and indecent assault are statutory offences (see the Criminal Justice Act 1988, s.39 and *D.P.P. v. Taylor and Little* [1992] 1 All E.R. 299, the Offences Against the Person Act 1861, s.47, and the Sexual Offences Act 1956, ss.14 and 15, respectively) but assault is defined at common law. Assault may be committed recklessly (see *Venna* [1976] Q.B. 421, *post*, p. 586). In *Kimber* [1983] 1 W.L.R. 1118, a case involving indecent assault, the Court of Appeal adopted a subjective test of recklessness without making any reference to *Caldwell*. The dictum of Lord Roskill in *Seymour*, however, gave rise to a short period of confusion in relation to other offences involving assault. In *D.P.P. v. K. (A Minor)* [1990] 1 W.L.R. 1067, the Divisional Court held that the *Caldwell* test applied on a charge of assault occasioning actual bodily harm. In *R.*

v. *Spratt* [1990] 1 W.L.R. 1073, the Court of Appeal declared that *D.P.P.* v. *K.* was wrongly decided, McCowan L.J. going on to state:

"The words 'unless Parliament has otherwise ordained' may well have been intended to refer not only to modern Acts of Parliament which use the word 'recklessly' but also to the 1861 Act, where the word 'maliciously' is used. However, the history of the interpretation of the 1861 Act shows that, whether or not the word 'maliciously' appears in the section in question, the courts have consistently held that the mens rea of every type of offence against the person covers both actual intent and recklessness, in the sense of taking the risk of harm ensuing with foresight that it might happen. (See *R.* v. *Ward* (1872) L.R. 1 C.C.R. 356, *R.* v. *Bradshaw* (1878) 14 Cox C.C. 83, *R.* v. *Cunningham* [1957] 2 All E.R. 412, [1957] 2 Q.B. 396 and *R.* v. *Venna* [1975] 3 All E.R. 788, [1976] Q.B. 421.) Hence, according to judicial interpretation of the 1861 Act, these are all instances where Parliament 'has otherwise ordained'.

The sentence "Reckless" should today be given the same meaning in relation to all offences which involve "recklessness" as one of the elements unless Parliament has otherwise ordained' seems to us to be obiter. In any event we cannot believe that by the use of those words their Lordships intended to cast any doubt either on the decision in *R.* v. *Cunningham* or, more importantly for present purposes, on the decision in *R.* v. *Venna*, which was approved by the House of Lords in both *D.P.P.* v. *Majewski* and *R.* v. *Caldwell*.

Finally, counsel for the Crown argues that while *R.* v. *Venna* says that *Cunningham* recklessness will amount to guilt under s.47, it does not say that nothing else will do. In other words, it is now possible to add on failure to give thought to the possibility of risk as also qualifying for guilt. We do not accept that interpretation of the decision in *R.* v. *Venna*. Moreover, we are not attracted by what would be the consequence of accepting the argument of counsel for the Crown, namely that responsibility for the offence of assault occasioning actual bodily harm (in respect of which Parliament used neither the word 'maliciously' nor 'recklessly') would be wider than for the offence of unlawful wounding (in respect of which Parliament used the word 'maliciously').

Accordingly, we consider ourselves bound by *R.* v. *Venna*."

Statutory Offences which may be Committed 'Maliciously'

In *Cunningham* (*ante*, p. 109) *maliciously* was construed to mean *intentionally* or *recklessly*, using the latter term in its subjective sense. Did *Caldwell* effect any change in this area? In *W.* (*A Minor*) v. *Dolbey* [1983] Crim.L.R. 681, the Divisional Court held that *Caldwell* did not apply to offences where the mens rea was expressed by the term "maliciously" and that the definition of this term in *Cunningham* still stood. The House of Lords considered this issue in two appeals which were heard together, *R.* v. *Savage*, *R.* v. *Parmenter* [1991] 4 All E.R. 698. Lord Ackner stated:

"III *In order to establish an offence under s.20 of the 1861 Act, must the prosecution prove that the defendant actually foresaw that his act would cause harm, or is it sufficient to prove that he ought so to have foreseen?*

Although your Lordships' attention has been invited to a plethora of decided cases, the issue is a narrow one. Is the decision of the Court of

Criminal Appeal in *R.* v. *Cunningham* [1957] 2 All E.R. 412, [1957] 2 Q.B. 396 still good law, subject only to a gloss placed upon it by the Court of Appeal, Criminal Division in *R.* v. *Mowatt* [1967] 3 All E.R. 47, [1968] 1 Q.B. 421, or does the later decision of your Lordships' House in *R.* v. *Caldwell* [1981] 1 All E.R. 961, [1982] A.C. 341 provide the answer to this question? . . .

R. v. *Caldwell*

Mr. Sedley Q.C. [counsel for the respondent Parmenter] has not invited your Lordships to reconsider the majority decision of your Lordships' House. He chose a much less ambitious task. He submits that *R.* v. *Cunningham* cannot be bad law, since it is inconceivable that your Lordships' House, in its majority judgment, would have steered such a careful path around it. Your Lordships, having power to overrule it, would, so he submits, have felt obliged to do so in order to avoid creating a false double standard of 'recklessness'. He further submits that it is significant that Lord Diplock, whose speech represented the views of the majority of your Lordships, nowhere suggests that his own judgment in *R.* v. *Mowatt* [1967] 3 All E.R. 47, [1968] 1 Q.B. 421, which clarified or modified *R.* v. *Cunningham*, was of doubtful validity. . . . "

[His Lordship examined the decisions in *Caldwell, Lawrence* and *Seymour* and continued.]

"Before returning to the submission made by Mr. Sedley, to which I have referred above, I think it is now convenient to go back in time to the decisions of the Court of Appeal in *R.* v. *Mowatt* [1967] 3 All E.R. 47, [1968] 1 Q.B. 421, to which reference has already been made. The facts of that case were simple. On 30 September 1966 in the early hours of the morning the defendant and a companion stopped a third man in the street and asked him whether there was a pub anywhere nearby. The defendant's companion then snatched a £5 note from the third man's breast-pocket and ran off. The third man chased him without success and returned to the defendant, grasping him by the lapels and demanding to know where his companion had gone. The defendant then struck the third man, knocking him down. Two police officers saw the defendant sit astride the third man and strike him repeated blows in the face, pull him to his feet and strike him again, knocking him down and rendering him almost unconscious. The defendant admitted inflicting the first blow but claimed it was self-defence. He was tried on an indictment which included a count for wounding with intent to do grievous bodily harm contrary to s.18 of the Offences Against the Person Act 1861. In summing up on this count the trial judge told the jury they were entitled to return a verdict of unlawful wounding under s.20 of the Act. However in his summing up, while explaining the meaning of the word 'unlawfully' so far as it was relevant to the defence of self-defence, he gave no direction as to the meaning of 'maliciously'.

The importance of this case is that the Court of Appeal considered *R.* v. *Cunningham* and, although modifying or explaining an important feature of that decision, in no way queried its validity. The judgment of the Court of Appeal, to which I have already made references, was, as previously stated, given by Diplock L.J., as he then was. It is of course one of Mr. Sedley's points that, although *R.* v. *Mowatt* was not referred to in *R.* v. *Caldwell*, it was most unlikely that its existence was overlooked, particularly by Lord Diplock. Diplock L.J. observed that 'unlawfully and maliciously' was a fashionable phrase of parliamentary draftsmen in 1861 (see [1967] 3 All E.R. 47 at 49, [1968] 1 Q.B. 421 at 425). It ran as a theme, with minor variations, through the Malicious Damage Act 1861, and the Offences Against the Person Act 1861. He then referred to the 'very special' facts in R. v. *Cunningham* and observed:

'No doubt on these facts the jury should have been instructed that they must be satisfied before convicting the accused *that he was aware* that physical harm to some human being was a possible consequence of his unlawful act in wrenching off the gas meter. In the words of the court " 'maliciously' in a statutory crime postulates foresight of consequence" (see [1957] 2 All E.R. 412 at 414, [1957] 2 Q.B. 396 at 399), and on this proposition we do not wish to cast any doubt.' (My emphasis.)

Subsequently, he added ([1967] 3 All E.R. 47 at 50, [1968] 1 Q.B. 421 at 426):

'In the offence under s.20 and in the alternative verdict which may be given on a charge under s.18—for neither of which is any specific intent required—the word "maliciously" does import on the part of the person who unlawfully inflicts the wound or other grievous bodily harm an *awareness* that his act may have the consequence of causing some physical harm to some other person. That is what is meant by "the particular kind of harm" in the citation from PROFESSOR KENNY'S OUTLINES OF CRIMINAL LAW (18th edn, 1962, para. 158a, p. 202). It is quite unnecessary that the *accused* should have foreseen that his unlawful act might cause physical harm of the gravity described in the section, i.e., a wound or serious physical injury. It is enough that *he* should have foreseen that some physical harm to some person, albeit of a minor character, might result.' (My emphasis.)

Mr. Sedley submitted that in R. v. *Caldwell* your Lordships' House could have followed either of two possible paths to its conclusion as to the meaning of 'recklessly' in the 1971 Act. These were: (a) to hold that R. v. *Cunningham* (and R. v. *Mowatt*) were wrongly decided and to introduce a single test, wherever recklessness was an issue; or (b) to accept that R. v. *Cunningham* (subject to the R. v. *Mowatt* 'gloss' to which no reference was made) correctly states the law in relation to the Offences Against the Persons Act 1861, because the word 'maliciously' in that statute was a term of legal art which imported into the concept of recklessness a special restricted meaning, thus distinguishing it from 'reckless' or 'recklessly' in modern 'revising' statutes then before the House, where those words bore their then popular or dictionary meaning.

I agree with Mr. Sedley that manifestly it was the latter course which the House followed. Therefore in order to establish an offence under s.20 the prosecution must prove either that the defendant intended or that he actually foresaw that his act would cause harm."

v. Wilfulness

Arrowsmith v. Jenkins
[1963] 2 Q.B. 561
Divisional Court

The defendant addressed a public meeting on the highway and was convicted on an information alleging wilful obstruction of the highway, by standing on it and causing others to congregate.

LORD PARKER C.J.: The sole question here is whether the defendant has contravened section 121(1) of the Highways Act 1959. That section provides: "If a person, without lawful authority or excuse, in any way wilfully obstructs the free passage along a highway he shall be guilty of an offence and shall be liable in respect thereof to a fine not exceeding forty shillings."

I am quite satisfied that section 121(1) of the Act of 1959, on its true construction, is providing that if a person, without lawful authority or excuse, intentionally as opposed to accidentally, that is, by an exercise of his or her free will, does something or omits to do something which will cause an obstruction or the continuance of an obstruction, he or she is guilty of an offence. Mr. Wigoder, for the defendant, has sought to argue that if a person—and I think that this is how he puts it—acts in the genuine belief that he or she has lawful authority to do what he or she is doing then, if an obstruction results, he or she cannot be said to have wilfully obstructed the free passage along a highway.

Quite frankly, I do not fully understand that submission. It is difficult, certainly, to apply in the present case. I imagine that it can be put in this way: that there must be some *mens rea* in the sense that a person will only be guilty if he knowingly does a wrongful act. I am quite satisfied that that consideration cannot possibly be imported into the words "wilfully obstructs" in section 121(1) of the Act of 1959. If anybody, by an exercise of free will, does something which causes an obstruction, then an offence is committed. There is no doubt that the defendant did that in the present case.

Appeal dismissed

Cf. *Eaton* v. *Cobb* [1950] 1 All E.R. 1016.

Lewis v. Cox
[1985] Q.B. 509
Queen's Bench Division

The defendant's friend was arrested for being drunk and disorderly and placed in the back of a police vehicle. The defendant opened the rear door of the vehicle to ask his friend where he was being taken but a police constable closed the door warning him that he would be arrested for obstruction if he opened it again. When the constable returned to the driver's seat of the vehicle the defendant opened the door once more, whereupon the constable arrested him for obstructing him. The defendant was charged with wilfully obstructing a police constable in the execution of his duty, contrary to section 51(3) of the Police Act 1964. The justices acquitted the defendant and the prosecution appealed.

WEBSTER J.: ... The justices found as a fact that the opening of the rear door of the van by the defendant was not aimed at the police, and that he did not intend to obstruct the police.

It was accepted by counsel on behalf of the defendant that the arrest of Marsh was lawful, and that the defendant's conduct in opening the door on the second occasion in fact obstructed the police because it prevented the prosecutor from driving the police vehicle away, which he would have done had the defendant not opened the door. The contention before the justices, which was substantially the same as the contention made on his behalf before this court, was that the defendant did not wilfully obstruct the police because his actions were not aimed at the police. The expression "aimed at the police" is an expression taken from the judgment of Griffiths L.J. in *Hills* v. *Ellis* [1983] Q.B. 680, 685, to which I will refer more fully later in this judgment.

The justices considered that the principle laid down by the decision in that case was that a person is guilty of wilful obstruction of a police constable in the execution of his duty if he deliberately does some act which is aimed at the police and if that act, viewed objectively, obstructs the police. They concluded that on the evidence before them the defendant had done no deliberate aggressive act which was aimed at the police, but that his sole aim was to ask Marsh where he was to be taken and that, as the actions of the defendant were not aimed at the police, the justices were of the opinion that they could not convict him of the offence, and they accordingly dismissed the charge against him.

The question which they ask for the opinion of this court is whether the principles applied by them were those laid down in *Hills* v. *Ellis*; they also ask whether, given the evidence in the case, the decision to dismiss the charge was perverse and unreasonable. For the moment I will consider only the first of those two questions.

For my part, I approach this question, in the first place, by disregarding any decision as to the meaning of the words "wilful" or "wilfully" in any context other than that of the section in question. This is because whereas, for instance, this court has held in *Arrowsmith* v. *Jenkins* (*ante*, p. 128) that the wilful obstruction of a highway, contrary to section 121 of the Highways Act 1959, does not import *mens rea* in the sense that a person will only be guilty of that offence if he knowingly did a wrongful act, there is a line of authority, to which I will turn, that the word "wilfully" in the context of section 51(3) of the Police Act 1964 connotes an element of *mens rea*. I find it necessary to consider this line of authority, although not every case in it, in some detail because it cannot, in my view, confidently be asserted that the test, whether the actions of the defendant are "aimed at the police," is the definitive and authoritative test.

It can, however, in my view be confidently stated, as I have already mentioned, that the word "wilfully" imports an element of *mens rea*. In *Betts* v. *Stevens* [1910] 1 K.B. 1 ... Darling J., dealing with the question of intention, said, at p. 8: "The gist of the offence to my mind lies in the intention with which the thing is done."

In *Willmott* v. *Atack* [1977] Q.B. 498 ... Croom-Johnson J., who gave the first judgment, said, at pp. 504–505:

> "When one looks at the whole context of section 51, dealing as it does with assaults upon constables in subsection (1) and concluding in subsection (3) with resistance and wilful obstruction in the execution of the duty, I am of the view that the interpretation of this subsection for which the defendant contends is the right one. It fits the words 'wilfully obstructs' in the context of the subsection, and in my view there must be something in the nature of a criminal intent of the kind which means that it is done with the idea of some form of hostility to the police with the intention of seeing that what is done is to obstruct, and that it is not enough merely to show that he intended to do what he did and that it did in fact have the result of the police being obstructed."

May J. agreed ...
Lord Widgery C.J. .... [also] agreed. ...

In *Moore* v. *Green* [1983] 1 All E.R. 663, ... McCullough J. said at p. 665:

> "I do not understand the reference to 'hostility' to indicate a separate element of the offence. I understand the word to bear the same meaning

as the phrase which Croom-Johnson J. used immediately afterwards, namely 'the intention of seeing that what is done is to obstruct' ... "

Griffiths L.J. agreed with the judgment of McCullough J.

Finally, on this aspect of the matter, I return to *Hills* v. *Ellis*. ...

Griffiths L.J. cited the same passage from the judgment of Croom-Johnson J. in *Willmott* v. *Atack* and continued, at p. 685:

"The defendant's counsel argues from that passage that as the motive here was merely to correct an officer's error, it cannot be said that he, the defendant, was acting with any hostility towards the police. But in my view, the phrase 'hostility to the police' in that passage means no more than that the actions of the defendant are aimed at the police. There can be no doubt here that his action in grabbing the officer's arm was aimed at that officer. It was an attempt to get that officer to desist from the arrest that he was making. In my view, this is as clear a case as we can have of obstructing a police officer in the course of his duty, and the justices came to the right decision."

McCullough J. agreed with the judgment of Griffiths L.J., and added, at p. 686:

"I am uncertain what Croom-Johnson J. had in mind when he used the word 'hostility' ... Hostility suggests emotion and motive, but motive and emotion are alike irrelevant in criminal law. What matters is intention, that is, what state of affairs the defendant intended to bring about. What motive he had while so intending is irrelevant. What is meant by 'an intention to obstruct?' I would construe 'wilfully obstructs' as doing deliberate actions with the intention of bringing about a state of affairs which, objectively regarded, amount to an obstruction as that phrase was explained by Lord Parker C.J. in *Rice* v. *Connolly* [1966] 2 Q.B. 414, 419B, that is, making it more difficult for the police to carry out their duty. The fact that the defendant might not himself have called that state of affairs an obstruction is, to my mind, immaterial. That is not to say that it is enough to do deliberate actions which, in fact, obstruct; there must be an intention that those actions should result in the further state of affairs to which I have been referring."

Lord Parker C.J. on the same page of his judgment in *Rice* v. *Connolly* said that "wilful" in the context of this section "not only in my judgment means 'intentional' but something which is done without lawful excuse;" and his explanation of "wilfully obstructs" as being something which makes it more difficult for the police to carry out their duties was taken by him from the judgment of Lord Goddard C.J. in *Hinchliffe* v. *Sheldon* [1955] 1 W.L.R. 1207, where Lord Goddard C.J. said, at p. 1210; "Obstructing, for the present purpose, means making it more difficult for the police to carry out their duties."

For my part I conclude that, although it may not be unhelpful in certain cases to consider whether the actions of a defendant were aimed at the police, the simple facts which the court has to find are whether the defendant's conduct in fact prevented the police from carrying out their duty, or made it more difficult for them to do so, and whether the defendant intended that conduct to prevent the police from carrying out their duty or to make it more difficult to do so.

In the present case the test which the justices applied was whether the defendant had deliberately done some act which was aimed at the police, they found that his actions were not aimed at the police and they accordingly dismissed the charge. In my view, for the reasons which I have given, the justices did not ask themselves the right question for the purposes of the present case, or the whole of the right question.

I turn, therefore, to the second question which they ask, which is whether, given the evidence in the case, the decision to dismiss the charge was perverse and unreasonable. . . .

For my part I conclude . . . that if the justices had directed themselves properly in the way in which I have set out they must, on the evidence, have decided that the defendant, when he opened the door on the second occasion, intended to make it more difficult for the police to carry out their duties, even though that was not his predominate intention, and they ought, therefore, to have convicted him of the charge against him.

My answer to the second part of the question, therefore, is that given the evidence in the case, the justices' decision to dismiss the charge was perverse and unreasonable, and I would accordingly allow this appeal and remit the case to the justices with a direction to them to convict.

KERR L.J.: I agree with Webster J.'s analysis of the authorities. The *actus reus* is the doing of an act which has the effect of making it impossible or more difficult for the police to carry out their duty. The word "wilfully" clearly imports an additional requirement of *mens rea*. The act must not only have been done deliberately, but with the knowledge and intention that it will have this obstructive effect. But in the absence of a lawful excuse, the defendant's purpose or reason for doing the act is irrelevant, whether this be directly hostile to, or "aimed at," the police, or whether he has some other purpose or reason.

Appeal allowed.
Case remitted with direction to convict.

Questions

1. Is the word "wilfully" in section 121(1) of the Highways Act 1959 (now s.137(1) of the Highways Act 1980) redundant? *cf. Lewis* v. *Dickinson* [1976] Crim.L.R. 442.

2. How does the interpretation of "wilfully" in *Arrowsmith* v. *Jenkins* differ from that in *Lewis* v. *Cox*?

Note

The courts have also struggled in their search for an appropriate interpretation of "wilful" in the context of "wilful neglect" under the Children and Young Persons Act 1933.

R. v. Sheppard
[1980] 3 All E.R. 899
House of Lords

The youngest child of Mr. and Mrs. S. died at the age of 16 months from malnutrition and hypothermia. Three appointments to see a paediatrician had been made by the Health Visitor but the appellants had failed to attend. They were convicted of causing cruelty by wilful neglect under section 1 of the Children and Young Persons Act 1933. The Court of Appeal felt bound by authority to uphold the direction of the trial judge that no element of foresight of harm was necessary for the offence, but granted leave to appeal to the House of Lords.

LORD DIPLOCK: ... In the light of the trial judge's instructions given to the jury as to the law applicable to the offence charged, it can safely be inferred from the verdicts of guilty that the jury found (1) that injury to Martin's health had in fact been caused by the failure of each of the parents to have him examined by a doctor in the period prior to his death and (2) that any reasonable parents, *i.e.* parents endowed with ordinary intelligence and not indifferent to the welfare of their child, would have recognised from the manifest symptoms of serious illness in Martin during that period that a failure to have him examined by a doctor might well result in unnecessary suffering or injury to his health ...

Their real defence, if it were capable of amounting to a defence in law, was that they did not realise that the child was ill enough to need a doctor; they had observed his loss of appetite and failure to keep down his food, but had genuinely thought that this was due to some passing minor upset to which babies are prone, from which they recover naturally without medical aid and which medical treatment can do nothing to alleviate or to hasten recovery.

We do not know whether the jury would have thought that this explanation of the parents' failure to have Martin examined by a doctor might be true. In his instructions the judge had told the jury that to constitute the statutory offence with which the parents were charged it was unnecessary for the Crown to prove that at the time when it was alleged the parents should have had the child seen by a doctor either they in fact knew that their failure to do so involved a risk of causing him unnecessary suffering or injury to health or they did not care whether this was so or not. ...

The Court of Appeal, regarding themselves as bound by the same line of authority, felt compelled to dismiss the parents' appeal ... but certified as the point of law of general public importance involved in their decision to dismiss the appeal:

"What is the proper direction to be given to a jury on a charge of wilful neglect of a child under s.1 of the Children and Young Persons Act 1933 as to what constitutes the necessary mens rea of the offence?"

The relevant provisions of section 1 are in the following terms:

"(1) If any person who has attained the age of sixteen years and has the custody, charge, or care of any child or young person under that age, wilfully assaults, ill-treats, neglects, abandons, or exposes him, or causes or procures him to be assaulted, ill-treated, neglected, abandoned, or exposed, in a manner likely to cause him unnecessary suffering or injury to health (including injury to or loss of sight, or hearing, or limb, or organ of the body, and any mental derangement), that person shall be guilty of a misdemeanour, and shall be liable—(a) on conviction on indictment, to a fine, or alternatively, or in addition thereto, to imprisonment for any term not exceeding two years. ...

(2) For the purposes of this section—(a) a parent or other person legally liable to maintain a child or young person shall be deemed to have neglected him in a manner likely to cause injury to his health if he has failed to provide adequate food, clothing, medical aid or lodging for him, or if, having been unable otherwise to provide such food, clothing, medical aid or lodging, he has failed to take steps to procure it to be provided under enactments applicable in that behalf. ... "

... My Lords, the language in which the relevant provisions of the 1933 Act are drafted consists of ordinary words in common use in the English language. If I were to approach the question of their construction untrammelled (as the House is) by authority I should have little hesitation in saying that where the charge is one of wilfully neglecting to provide a child with adequate medical aid, which in appropriate cases will include precautionary medical examination, the prosecution must prove (1) that the child did in fact need medical aid at the time at which the parent is charged with having failed to provide it and (2) either that the parent was aware at that time that the child's health might be at risk if it were not provided with medical aid or that the parent's unawareness of this fact was due to his not caring whether the child's health were at risk or not.

In view of the previous authorities, however, which reach a different conclusion, it becomes necessary to analyse more closely the wording and structure of sections 1(1) and (2)(*a*). ...

The presence of the adverb "wilfully" qualifying all five verbs, "assaults, ill-treats, neglects, abandons, or exposes," makes it clear that any offence under section 1 requires *mens rea*, a state of mind on the part of the offender directed to the particular act or failure to act that constitutes the *actus reus* and warrants the description "wilful." The other four adverbs refer to positive acts, "neglect" refers to failure to act, and the judicial explanation of the state of mind denoted by the statutory expression "wilfully" in relation to the doing of a positive act is not necessarily wholly apt in relation to a failure to act at all. The instant case is in the latter category, so I will confine myself to considering what is meant by wilfully neglecting a child in a manner likely to cause him unnecessary suffering or injury to health. ...

The *actus reus* of the offence with which the accused were charged in the instant case does not involve construing the verb "neglect" for the offence fell within the deeming provision; and the only question as respects the *actus reus* was: did the parents fail to provide for Martin in the period before his death medical aid that was in fact adequate in view of his actual state of health at the relevant time? This, as it seems to me, is a pure question of objective fact to be determined in the light of what has become known *by the date of the trial* to have been the child's actual state of health at the relevant time. It does not depend on whether a reasonably careful parent, with knowledge of those facts only which such a parent might reasonably be expected to observe for himself, would have thought it prudent to have recourse to medical aid. ... If failure to use the hypothetical powers of observation, ratiocination and foresight of consequences [of the reasonable man] is to constitute an ingredient of a criminal offence it must surely form part not of the *actus reus* but of the *mens rea*.

It does not, however, seem to me that the concept of the reasonable parent ... has any part to play in the *mens rea* of an offence in which the description of the *mens rea* is contained in the single adverb "wilfully." In the context of doing a child a positive act (assault, ill-treat, abandon or expose) that is likely to have specified consequences (to cause him unnecessary suffering or injury to health), "wilfully," which must describe the state of mind of the actual doer of the act, may be capable of bearing the narrow meaning that the wilfulness required extends only to the doing of the physical act itself which in fact results in the consequences described, even though the doer thought that it would not and would not have acted as he did had he foreseen a risk that those consequences might follow. Although this is a possible meaning of "wilfully," it is not the natural meaning even in relation to positive acts defined by reference to the consequences to which they are likely to give rise; and, in the context of the section, if this is all the adverb "wilfully" meant it would be otiose. Section 1(1) would have the same effect if it were omitted; for even in absolute offences (unless vicarious liability is involved) the physical act relied on as constituting the offence must be wilful in the limited sense, for which the synonym in the field of criminal liability that has now become the common term of legal art is "voluntary."

So much for "wilfully" in the context of a positive act. To "neglect" a child is to omit to act, to fail to provide adequately for . . . its physical needs. . . . For reasons already given the use of the verb "neglect" cannot, in my view, of itself import into the criminal law the civil law concept of negligence. The *actus reus* in a case of wilful neglect is simply a failure, for whatever reason, to provide the child whenever it in fact needs medical aid with the medical aid it needs. Such a failure as it seems to me could not be properly described as "wilful" unless the parent *either* (1) had directed his mind to the question whether there was some risk (though it might fall far short of a probability) that the child's health might suffer unless he were examined by a doctor and provided with such curative treatment as the examination might reveal as necessary, and had made a conscious decision, for whatever reason, to refrain from arranging for such medical examination, *or* (2) had so refrained because he did not care whether the child might be in need of medical treatment or not.

As regards the second state of mind, this imports the concept of recklessness which is a common concept in *mens rea* in criminal law. It is not to be confused with negligence in the civil law of tort (see *Andrews* v. *Director of Public Prosecutions* [1937] A.C. 576 at 582–583). In speaking of the first state of mind I have referred to the parent's knowledge of the existence of some risk of injury to health rather than of probability. The section speaks of an act or omission that is "likely" to cause unnecessary suffering or injury to health. The word is imprecise. It is capable of covering a whole range of possibilities from "it's on the cards" to "it's more probable than not"; but, having regard to the parent's lack of skill in diagnosis and to the very serious consequences which may result from failure to provide a child with timely medical attention, it should in my view be understood as excluding only what would fail to be described as highly unlikely.

I turn now to the authorities. [His Lordship referred to *R.* v. *Downes* (1875) 1 Q.B.D. 25].

To the judgment of Lord Russell C.J. in *R.* v. *Senior* [1899] 1 Q.B. 283, may be ascribed the origin of the construction of section 1(1) of the Children and Young Persons Act 1933 that has since been followed. . . .

Lord Russell C.J. . . . said ([1899] 1 Q.B. 283 at 290–291):

" 'Wilfully' means that the act is done deliberately and intentionally, not by accident or inadvertence, but so that the mind of the person who does the act goes with it. Neglect is the want of reasonable care—that is, the omission of such steps as a reasonable parent would take, such as are usually taken in the ordinary experience of mankind. . . . "

Lord Russell C.J.'s brief explanation of the meaning of "wilfully" is confined to positive physical acts. In relation to these he equiparates wilful acts with acts that would now be described as "voluntary." I do not myself think that this was right even in relation to positive physical acts of which the statutory definition included the characteristic that they were likely to have certain consequences; but its meaning in relation to positive acts is clear. I find its meaning obscure, however, in relation to a failure to do a physical act where the failure is not deliberate or intentional in the sense that consideration had been given whether or not to do it and a conscious choice made not to do it. To speak of the mind going with the act is inappropriate to omissions, but the contrast drawn between "deliberately and intentionally" and "by inadvertence" is at least susceptible of the meaning that if the accused has not addressed his mind to the question whether or not to do the physical act he is accused of omitting to do his failure to do the act is not to be treated as "wilful."

R. v. Senior, however, appears to have been treated as having decided that if the child did in fact need medical treatment it did not matter whether the accused parent actually knew or ought to have known that medical treatment was needed; he was nonetheless guilty of the offence of wilfully neglecting the child if all that he knew was that the child had not been seen by a doctor. This appears from the judgment of the Court of Appeal in R. v. Lowe [1973] Q.B. 702 at 707. So R. v. Senior has been regarded as deciding that the offence under section 1(1) of the 1933 Act is an absolute offence.

My Lords, I have already said why I do not think that R. v. Senior did so decide,. . . .

[W]hat your Lordships are faced with is a consistent practice of the courts, extending over many years without any reported exceptions, of treating R. v. Senior as if it were a binding authority for the proposition that the statutory offence of wilfully neglecting a child by failing to provide him with adequate medical aid is an absolute offence.

In many fields of law I should hesitate long before recommending this House to overturn a long-standing judicial acceptance of a particular meaning for a statutory provision. Communis error facit lex is often a good maxim in promoting legal certainty in matters in which people arrange their affairs in reliance on the accepted meaning of a law. But three reasons persuade me not to apply the maxim in the instant case. The climate of both parliamentary and judicial opinion has been growing less favourable to the recognition of absolute offences over the last few decades, a trend to which section 1 of the Homicide Act 1957 and section 8 of the Criminal Justice Act 1967 bear witness in the case of Parliament, and in the case of the judiciary is illustrated by the speeches in this House in Sweet v. Parsley (post, p. 190). Secondly, the Court of Appeal in the instant case has expressed its own feeling of unease about the present state of the authorities by which it regards itself as bound and has granted leave to appeal in order that those authorities may be reviewed by your Lordship's House. Thirdly, and most importantly, the common error, as I believe it to have been, has operated to the disadvantage of the accused and to correct it will spare from criminal conviction those only who are free from any moral guilt.

To give to section 1(1) of the 1933 Act the meaning which I suggest it bears would not encourage parents to neglect their children nor would it reduce the deterrent to child neglect provided by the section. It would afford no defence to parents who do not bother to observe their children's health or, having done so, do not care whether their children are receiving the medical examination and treatment that they need or not; it would involve the acquittal of those parents only who through ignorance or lack of intelligence are genuinely unaware that their child's health may be at risk if it is not examined by a doctor to see if it needs medical treatment. And, in view of the abhorrence which magistrates and juries feel for cruelty to helpless children, I have every confidence that they would not readily be hoodwinked by false claims by parents that it did not occur to them that an evidently sick child might need medical care.

In the instant case it seems likely that on the evidence the jury, if given the direction which I have suggested as correct, would have convicted one or both of the accused; but I do not think it possible to say with certainty that they would. It follows that in my opinion these appeals must be allowed and that the certified question should be answered: "The proper direction to be given to a jury on a charge of wilful neglect of a child under s.1 of the Children and Young Persons Act 1933 by failing to provide adequate medical aid is that the jury must be satisfied (1) that the child did in fact need medical aid at the time at which the parent is charged with failing to provide it (the *actus reus*) and (2) either that the parent was aware at that time that the child's health might be at risk if it was not provided with medical aid or that the parent's unawareness of this fact was due to his not caring whether his child's health was at risk or not (the *mens rea*).

[LORD KEITH and LORD EDMUND-DAVIES delivered opinions in which they agreed with LORD DIPLOCK; LORD SCARMAN and LORD FRASER delivered dissenting opinions].

Questions

1. Do you agree with Lord Diplock that, if the word "wilfully" were given a narrow meaning extending only to the doing of the positive act, and not its consequences, it would be otiose in section 1(1)? Is a parent who admonishes a child with a slap committing a voluntary act? Is it therefore a "wilful" assault? Or is it not an assault at all because it is "lawful"?

2. If the parent in question 1 is not committing an assault because parents are allowed to use reasonable disciplinary measures, is Lord Diplock right to assert it is only in the *"mens rea"* of an offence that the reasonable man concept will be found?

3. Both Lord Fraser and Lord Scarman believed that the deterrent effect of the offence would be reduced if the prosecution had to prove foresight of the consequences of neglect. Can this hypothesis be tested?

vi. Proposals for Reform

In the Draft Criminal Code Bill the Law Commission uses the term *fault element* in preference to the common law phrase *mens rea*. Clause 6 defines *fault element* as follows—

"fault element" means any element of an offence consisting—
(a) of a state of mind with which a person acts; or
(b) of a failure to comply with a standard of conduct; or
(c) partly of such a state of mind and partly of such a failure;
and "fault," "degree of fault", and related expressions, shall be construed accordingly;

In paras. 8.1 and 8.2 of the *Commentary on Draft Criminal Code Bill* (Law Com. No. 177) the Law Commission state—

"8.1 *Meaning of 'fault'*. The sense in which the word 'fault' is used in the Code is indicated by the definition of 'fault element' in clause 6. 'Fault element' means—

'any element of an offence consisting
(a) of a state of mind with which a person acts; or
(b) of a failure to comply with a standard of conduct; or

(c)   partly of such a state of mind and partly of such a failure.'

The 'fault' required for an offence will depend upon the definition of the offence (and that definition may prescribe more than one 'fault element'). A 'state of mind' may be required: e.g. 'knowledge' that a circumstance exists, or the 'intention' to cause a result. A 'failure to comply with a standard of conduct' may suffice: e.g. a failure to take reasonable care to know of relevant circumstances or to avoid some result. Or a fault element may be complex, involving both a state of mind and a failure to comply with a standard: e.g. 'recklessness' (being aware of a risk and unreasonably taking it: see clause 18(c)) or 'dishonesty' (which involves consideration of the actor's state of mind and an assessment of his conduct—of which that state of mind is a part—in relation to prevailing standards).

8.2 A person does not necessarily commit an offence if with any fault required he does the act specified for it; he may be able to rely on a defence which renders his conduct entirely blameless. The word 'fault' is therefore not ideal. But its use as a rough translation of the traditional Latin phrase *'mens rea'* is perfectly familiar; and the neutral expression 'mental element' will not do, because it does not embrace non-compliance with standards as well as states of mind."

Clause 18 defines the fault terms. The purpose of this clause is two-fold—

Para. 8.4

8.4 *Towards certainty and consistency.* This clause gives effect to two main features of the policy declared in our Mental Element Report [(1978), Law Com. No. 89]:

(i)   to encourage consistency in the language of the criminal law, by providing a standard vocabulary of key fault terms; and

(ii) to promote certainty as to the meaning of that language. The absence of agreement about the meanings of commonly-used terms has been a particular source of difficulty.

Draft Criminal Code Bill, Clause18

"**Fault terms**

18. For the purposes of this Act and of any offence other than a pre-Code offence as defined in section 6 (to which section 2(3) applies) a person acts—

(a)   'knowingly' with respect to a circumstance not only when he is aware that it exists or will exist, but also when he avoids taking steps that might confirm his belief that it exists or will exist;

(b)   'intentionally' with respect to—

(i)   a circumstance when he hopes or knows that it exists or will exist;

(ii) a result when he acts either in order to bring it about or being aware that it will occur in the ordinary course of events;

(c) 'recklessly' with respect to—
  (i) a circumstance when he is aware of a risk that it exists or will exist;
  (ii) a result when he is aware of a risk that it will occur;
  and it is, in the circumstances known to him, unreasonable to take the risk;

and these and related words (such as 'knowledge', 'intention', 'recklessness') shall be construed accordingly unless the context otherwise requires."

Appendix B of the Code Report provides the following illustrations of the operation of the fault terms in Clause 18.

"Knowingly

18(i) D is handed a packet by E. The packet contains heroin. D chooses not to open the packet and therefore does not see what it contains. If D believes it to contain heroin, he is 'knowingly' in possession of heroin.

Intentionally

18(ii) D plants a bomb on an aeroplane with the purpose of destroying the aeroplane in flight and recovering the sum for which the cargo is insured. It is not D's purpose to kill the crew but he is aware that their deaths will occur in the ordinary course of events. D 'intends' to cause death and will be guilty of murder if the crew are killed by the explosion.

Recklessly

18(iii) D tries unsuccessfully to have sexual intercourse with P, who does not consent. If D is aware that P may not be consenting, he acts 'recklessly' (since it is clearly unreasonable to take the risk of non-consent) and is guilty of attempted rape. (Under cl. 49(2) recklessness with respect to a circumstance (such as consent) suffices for an attempt where it suffices for the offence attempted. Recklessness includes an element of awareness and therefore suffices for the offence of rape under cl. 89).

18(iv) D, without justification or excuse, throws a brick at O, who is standing not far from a window belonging to P. D realises that the brick may break the window (or damage some other property belonging to another). He is guilty of recklessly destroying or damaging the window if the brick breaks it.

18(v) D, shooting at a bird on his estate, injured P, a poacher who was crouching in the undergrowth. D knew that poachers sometimes operated in this part of the estate and was aware that there was a risk of such injury. Whether D caused personal harm recklessly depends on whether it was reasonable for him to take the risk. That is the question for the court or jury to decide, having regard to all the circumstances that were known to D."

Draft Criminal Code Bill, Clause 19

"Degrees of fault

19.—(1) An allegation in an indictment or information of knowledge or intention includes an allegation of recklessness.

(2) A requirement of recklessness is satisfied by knowledge or intention.

(3) This section does not apply to pre-Code offences as defined in section 6 (to which section 2(3) applies)."

Illustration

"19   D is indicted for intentionally causing serious personal harm to P. He may be convicted of recklessly causing serious personal harm or recklessly causing personal harm to P (see cl. 8(1)(b)); the allegation of recklessness being included in that of intention, these offences are 'included offences' in relation to the offence charged." ·

Draft Criminal Code Bill, Clause 20

"**General requirement of fault**

20.—(1) Every offence requires a fault element of recklessness with respect to each of its elements other than fault elements, unless otherwise provided.

(2) Subsection 1 does not apply to pre-Code offences as defined in section 6 (to which section 2(3) applies)."

Illustrations

"20(i)   Under clause 147 a person commits burglary if he enters a building as a trespasser intending to steal in the building. Nothing is said as to any fault required in respect of the fact that the entrant is a trespasser. The offence is committed only if the entrant knows that, or is reckless whether, he is trespassing.

20(ii)   An offence of causing polluting matter to enter a watercourse is enacted after the Code comes into force. In the absence of provision to the contrary the offence requires (a) an intention to cause the matter to enter the watercourse or recklessness whether it will do so, and (b) knowledge that the matter is a pollutant or recklessness whether it is."

3. MISTAKE

Notes

An area of the law that has been in an unsatisfactory state for some time is that of mistake. What effect does a mistake have on the liability of a defendant where his mistake relates to an element of the *actus reus* of the offence with which he is charged?

There are many mistakes which a defendant may make, some of which may be relevant to his ultimate liability. A mistake may be such as to negate the *mens rea* of the defendant in respect of a circumstance of the offence (*i.e.* an *actus reus* element). However, if *mens rea* is not required in respect of a particular circumstance, a mistake thereto may be of no relevance. A mistake may also be made with regard to circumstances which justify or excuse the commission of an offence such as pleas of self-defence or duress.

A question which has taxed judicial minds over the last century is whether a mistake must be a reasonable one before it serves to relieve a defendant of liability. Unfortunately the judicial answers to this question have differed, lacking consistency and coherent exposition of principle.

There are two basic categories into which mistakes may be grouped: *relevant* mistakes and *irrelevant* mistakes. Most uncertainty and inconsistency has arisen in respect of the first category.

i. Relevant Mistakes

A mistake is *relevant* where it relates to either a definitional element of the offence (*i.e.* an *actus reus* element) or a possible justificatory or excusatory claim (more generally referred to as defences). At one time, if a mistake was to operate to negate liability, it had to be a reasonable one. The House of Lords in *D.P.P.* v. *Morgan* (*infra*) opened the way for mistakes which were simply honest, although unreasonable, to operate to negate liability in certain circumstances. The effect of this decision, and the offspring it has generated, is that the category of relevant mistakes must now be divided into two sub-categories: mistakes which relate to definitional matters and those which relate to non-definitional matters.

(1) *Mistake as to a definitional element of the offence*

(a) **Mistake negating *mens rea*:**

Where an offence requires intention or recklessness on the part of the defendant, may he be convicted if he makes a mistake as to one of the required circumstances of the offence, *i.e.* the definitional facts? In other words, does the *mens rea* requirement apply only to the doing of the act or does it also apply to the surrounding circumstances? Several cases established that where the word "wilfully" was used to define the *mens rea* requirement, a mistake as to the surrounding circumstances would act to negate the defendant's *mens rea* (see *Eaton* v. *Cobb* [1950] 1 All E.R. 1016; *Wilson* v. *Inyang* [1951] 2 K.B. 799; *Bullock* v. *Turnbull* [1952] 2 Lloyd's Rep. 303; *Wilmott* v. *Atack* [1977] Q.B. 498; *Ostler* v. *Elliott* [1980] Crim.L.R. 584; but *cf. Cotterill* v. *Penn* [1936] 1 K.B. 53).

Would the same result ensue where a statute required intention or recklessness?

James L.J., giving judgment in *R.* v. *Smith (David)* [1974] Q.B. 354, said of section 1(1) of the Criminal Damage Act 1971:

> "Construing the language of [the] section we have no doubt that the *actus reus* is 'destroying or damaging any property belonging to another.' It is not possible to exclude the words 'belonging to another' which describe the 'property.' Applying the ordinary principles of *mens rea*, the intention and recklessness and the absence of lawful excuse required to constitute the offence have reference to property belonging to another. It follows that, in our judgment, no offence is committed under this section if a person destroys or causes damage to property belonging to another if he does so in the honest though mistaken belief that the property is his own, and provided that the belief is honestly held it is irrelevant to consider whether or not it is a justifiable belief."

Shortly after the decision in *Smith* the House of Lords was faced
with the issue of which parts of the definition of an offence (all or
some) are qualified by the requirement of a mental element, and
whether a mistake as to such part must be *reasonable* if it is to affect
the defendant's liability.

D.P.P. v. Morgan
[1976] A.C. 182
House of Lords

The appellant invited three friends to have intercourse with his wife
telling them that her signs of resistance were not to be interpreted as
lack of consent: she enjoyed it better that way. In fact she was not
consenting but they thought she was. The friends were charged with
rape, the appellant with aiding and abetting. They appealed against the
direction of the trial judge that their belief in her consent must be
reasonable.

LORD CROSS OF CHELSEA: . . . The question of law which is raised by the
appeal is whether the judge was right in telling the jury that, if they came
to the conclusion that Mrs. Morgan had not consented to the intercourse
in question but that the defendants believed or may have believed that she
was consenting to it, they must nevertheless find the defendants guilty of
rape if they were satisfied that they had no reasonable grounds for so
believing. . . .
    The Sexual Offences Act 1956 which provides by section 1(1) that it is an
offence "for a man to rape a woman" contains no definition of the word
"rape." No one suggests that rape is an "absolute" offence to the
commission of which the state of mind of the defendant with regard to the
woman's consent is wholly irrelevant. The point in dispute is as to the
quality of belief which entitles the defendant to be acquitted and as to the
"evidential" burden of proof with regard to it. ⌐.
    Finally, I must refer to an alternative submission, made by counsel for
the appellant—namely, that in *R.* v. *Tolson, post,* p. 159, the court was
wrong in saying that to afford a defence to a charge of bigamy the
mistaken belief of the defendant had to be based on reasonable grounds. It
is, of course true that the question whether a mistaken belief honestly held
but based on no reasonable grounds would have afforded a defence was
not argued in that case. . . . But *R.* v. *Tolson* was decided over 80 years
ago. It is accepted as a leading authority in the law of bigamy not only in
this country (see *R.* v. *King* [1964] 1 Q.B. 285 and *R.* v. *Gould* [1968] 2 Q.B.
65) but also in Australia (see *Thomas* v. *The King* (1937) 59 C.L.R. 279).
Moreover, the phrase "an honest and reasonable belief entertained by the
accused of the existence of facts, which, if true, would make the act
charged against him innocent" (23 Q.B.D. 168, 181) has been adopted on
several occasions as a definition of *mens rea* generally applicable to cases
where the offence is not an absolute one but the words defining it do not
expressly or impliedly indicate that some particular *mens rea* is required to
establish it: see *Bank of New South Wales* v. *Piper* [1897] A.C. 383; by Lord
Reid in *R.* v. *Warner* [1969] 2 A.C. 256, 268 and by Lord Diplock in *Sweet* v.
Parsley [1970] A.C. 132, 164, 165. Counsel did not refer us to any case in
which the propriety of the inclusion of the element of "reasonableness"
has been doubted; and its inclusion was, in fact, approved in *R.* v. *King*
[1964] 1 Q.B. 285 and by Lord Diplock in *Sweet* v. *Parsley.* So, even if I had
been myself inclined to think that the inclusion of the element of

reasonableness was wrong, I would not have thought it right for us to call it in question in this case. In fact, however, I can see no objection to the inclusion of the element of reasonableness in what I may call a *"Tolson"* case. If the words defining an offence provide either expressly or impliedly that a man is not to be guilty of it if he believes something to be true, then he cannot be found guilty if the jury think that he may have believed it to be true, however inadequate were his reasons for doing so. But, if the definition of the offence is on the face of it "absolute" and the defendant is seeking to escape his prima facie liability by defence of mistaken belief, I can see no hardship to him in requiring the mistake—if it is to afford him a defence—to be based on reasonable grounds. As Lord Diplock said in *Sweet* v. *Parsley* [1970] A.C. 132 (*post*, p. 190) there is nothing unreasonable in the law requiring a citizen to take reasonable care to ascertain the facts relevant to his avoiding doing a prohibited act. To have intercourse with a woman who is not your wife is, even today, not generally considered to be a course of conduct which the law ought positively to encourage and it can be argued with force that it is only fair to the woman and not in the least unfair to the man that he should be under a duty to take reasonable care to ascertain that she is consenting to the intercourse and be at the risk of a prosecution if he fails to take such care. So if the Sexual Offences Act 1956 had made it an offence to have intercourse with a woman who was not consenting to it, so that the defendant could only escape liability by the application of the *"Tolson"* principle, I would not have thought the law unjust.

But, as I have said, section 1 of the Act of 1956 does not say that a man who has sexual intercourse with a woman who does not consent to it commits an offence; it says that a man who rapes a woman commits an offence. Rape is not a word in the use of which lawyers have a monopoly and the first question to be answered in this case, as I see it, is whether according to the ordinary use of the English language a man can be said to have committed rape if he believed that the woman was consenting to the intercourse and would not have attempted to have it but for this belief, whatever his grounds for so believing. I do not think that he can. Rape, to my mind, imports at least indifference as to the woman's consent. I think, moreover, that in this connection the ordinary man would distinguish between rape and bigamy. To the question whether a man who goes through a ceremony of marriage with a woman believing his wife to be dead, though she is not, commits bigamy, I think that he would reply "Yes,—but I suppose that the law contains an escape clause for bigamists who are not really to blame." On the other hand, to the question whether a man, who has intercourse with a woman believing that she is consenting to it, though she is not, commits rape, I think that he would reply "No. If he was grossly careless then he may deserve to be punished but not for rape." That being my view as to the meaning of the word "rape" in ordinary parlance, I next ask myself whether the law gives it a different meaning. There is very little English authority on the point but what there is—namely, the reported directions of several common law judges in the early and middle years of the last century—accords with what I take to be the ordinary meaning of the word. The question has been canvassed in a number of recent cases in New South Wales and Victoria but there is only one of them—*R.* v. *Daly* [1968] V.R. 257—that I find of much assistance. In none of the others do the judges advert to the fact that to include an intention to have intercourse whether or not the woman consents in the definition of rape and to say that a reasonable mistake with regard to consent is an available defence to a charge of rape are two incompatible alternatives which cannot be combined in a single direction to a jury—as, incidentally, the judge combined them in one passage in his summing up in this case. In *R.* v. *Daly* the court, as well as drawing that distinction which I regard as fundamental, indicated pretty clearly that it thought—as I do—that the former approach to the problem was the right one. For these reasons, I think that the summing up contained a misdirection. ...

LORD HAILSHAM OF ST. MARYLEBONE: ... If it be true, as the learned judge says [in his summing up to the jury] "in the first place," that the prosecution have to prove that

> "each defendant intended to have sexual intercourse without her consent, not merely that he intended to have intercourse with her but that he intended to have intercourse without her consent,"

the defendant must be entitled to an acquittal if the prosecution fail to prove just that. The necessary mental ingredient will be lacking and the only possible verdict is "not guilty." If, on the other hand, as is asserted in the passage beginning "secondly," it is necessary for any belief in the woman's consent to be "a reasonable belief" before the defendant is entitled to an acquittal, it must either be because the mental ingredient in rape is not "to have intercourse and to have it without her consent" but simply "to have intercourse" subject to a special defence of "honest and reasonable belief," or alternatively to have intercourse without a reasonable belief in her consent. Counsel for the Crown argued for each of these alternatives, but in my view each is open to insuperable objections of principle. No doubt it would be possible, by statute, to devise a law by which intercourse, voluntarily entered into, was an absolute offence, subject to a "defence" or belief whether honest or honest and reasonable, of which the "evidential" burden is primarily on the defence and the "probative" burden on the prosecution. But in my opinion such is not the crime of rape as it has hitherto been understood. The prohibited act in rape is to have intercourse without the victim's consent. The minimum *mens rea* or guilty mind in most common law offences, including rape, is the intention to do the prohibited act, and that is correctly stated in the proposition stated "in the first place" of the judge's direction. In murder the situation is different, because the murder is only complete when the victim dies, and an intention to do really serious bodily harm has been held to be enough if such be the case.

The only qualification I would make to the direction of the learned judge's "in the first place" is the refinement for which ... there is both Australian and English authority, that if the intention of the accused is to have intercourse *nolens volens*, that is recklessly and not caring whether the victim be a consenting party or not, that is equivalent on ordinary principles to an intent to do the prohibited act without the consent of the victim.

The alternative version of the learned judge's direction would read that the accused must do the prohibited act with the intention of doing it without an honest and reasonable belief in the victim's consent. This in effect is the version which took up most of the time in argument, and although I find the Court of Appeal's judgment difficult to understand, I think it the version which ultimately commended itself to that court. At all events I think it the more plausible way in which to state the learned judge's "secondly." In principle, however, I find it unacceptable. I believe that "*mens rea*" means "guilty or criminal mind," and if it be the case, as seems to be accepted here, that mental element in rape is not knowledge but intent, to insist that a belief must be reasonable to excuse is to insist that either the accused is to be found guilty of intending to do that which in truth he did not intend to do, or that his state of mind, though innocent of evil intent, can convict him if it be honest but not rational. ...

I believe the law on this point to have been correctly stated by Lord Goddard C.J. in *R.* v. *Steane* [1947] K.B. 997, 1004, (*ante*, p. 75) when he said:

" ... if on the totality of the evidence there is room for more than one view as to the intent of the prisoner, the jury should be directed that it is for the prosecution to prove the intent to the jury's satisfaction, and if, on a review of the whole evidence, they either think that the intent did not exist or they are left in doubt as to the intent, the prisoner is entitled to be acquitted."

That was indeed, a case which involved a count where a specific, or, as Professor Smith has called it, an ulterior, intent was, and was required to be, charged in the indictment. But, once it be accepted that an intent of whatever description is an ingredient essential to the guilt of the accused I cannot myself see that any other direction can be logically acceptable. Otherwise a jury would in effect be told to find an intent where none existed or where none was proved to have existed. I cannot myself reconcile it with my conscience to sanction as part of the English law what I regard as logical impossibility, and, if there were any authority which, if accepted would compel me to do so, I would feel constrained to declare that it was not to be followed. However for reasons which I will give, I do not see any need in the instant case for such desperate remedies.

The beginning of wisdom in all the "*mens rea*" cases to which our attention was called is, as pointed out by Stephen J. in *R.* v. *Tolson* (*post*, p. 159), that "*mens rea*" means a number of quite different things in relation to different crimes. ... It follows from this, surely, that it is logically impermissible, as the Crown sought to do in this case, to draw a necessary inference from decisions in relation to offences where *mens rea* means one thing, and cases where it means another, and in particular from decisions on the construction of statutes, whether these be related to bigamy, abduction or the possession of drugs, and decisions in relation to common law offences. It is equally impermissible to draw direct or necessary inferences from decisions where the *mens rea* is, or includes, a state of opinion, and cases where it is limited to intention (a distinction I referred to in *R.* v. *Hyam* (*ante*, p. 78) or between cases where there is a special "defence," like self-defence or provocation and cases where the issue relates to the primary intention which the prosecution has to prove.

Once one has accepted, what seems to be abundantly clear, that the prohibited act in rape is non-consensual sexual intercourse, and that the guilty state of mind is an intention to commit it, it seems to me to follow as a matter of inexorable logic that there is no room either for a "defence" of honest belief or mistake, or of a defence of honest and reasonable belief or mistake. Either the prosecution proves that the accused had the requisite intent, or it does not. In the former case it succeeds, and in the latter it fails. Since honest belief clearly negatives intent, the reasonableness or otherwise of that belief can only be evidence for or against the view that the belief and therefore the intent was actually held, and it matters not whether, to quote Bridge J. in the passage cited above, "the definition of a crime includes no specific element beyond the prohibited act." If the mental element is primarily an intention and not a state of belief it comes within his second proposition and not his third. Any other view, as for insertion of the word "reasonable" can only have the effect of saying that a man intends something which he does not.

By contrast, the appellants invited us to overrule the bigamy cases from *R. v. Tolson* (*post*, p. 159) onwards and perhaps also *R. v. Prince*, L.R. 2 C.C.R. 154 (the abduction case) as wrongly decided at least in so far as they purport to insist that a mistaken belief must be reasonable. . . .

Although it is undoubtedly open to this House to reconsider *R. v. Tolson* and the bigamy cases, and perhaps *R. v. Prince* which may stand or fall with them, I must respectfully decline to do so in the present case. Nor is it necessary that I should. I am not prepared to assume that the statutory offences of bigamy or abduction are necessarily on all fours with rape, and before I was prepared to undermine a whole line of cases which have been accepted as law for so long, I would need argument in the context of a case expressly relating to the relevant offences. I am content to rest my view of the instant case on the crime of rape by saying that it is my opinion that the prohibited act is and always has been intercourse without consent of the victim and the mental element is and always has been the intention to commit that act, or the equivalent intention of having intercourse willy-nilly not caring whether the victim consents or no. A failure to prove this involves an acquittal because the intent, an essential ingredient, is lacking. It matters not why it is lacking if only it is not there, and in particular it matters not that the intention is lacking only because of a belief not based on reasonable grounds. I should add that I myself am inclined to view *R. v. Tolson* as a narrow decision based on the construction of a statute, which prima facie seemed to make an absolute statutory offence, with a proviso, related to the seven-year period of absence, which created a statutory defence. The judges in *R. v. Tolson* decided that this was not reasonable, and, on general jurisprudential principles, imported into the statutory offence words which created a special "defence" of honest and reasonable belief of which the "evidential" but not the probative burden lay on the defence. I do not think it is necessary to decide this conclusively in the present case. But if this is the true view there is a complete distinction between *Tolson* and the other cases based in statute and the present.

I may also add that I am not impressed with the analogy based on the decision in *Wilson v. Inyang* [1951] 2 K.B. 799, 803 which has attracted the attention of some academic authors. That clearly depends on the construction of the words "wilfully and falsely" where they are used in the relevant statute. Also, though I get some support from what I have been saying from the reasoning of the decision in *R. v. Smith (David)* (*post*, p. 864), I nevertheless regard that case as a decision on the Criminal Damage Act 1971, rather than a decision covering the whole law of criminal liability.

For the above reasons I would answer the question certified in the negative, but would apply the proviso to the Criminal Appeal Act on the ground that no miscarriage of justice has or conceivably could have occurred.

LORD FRASER OF TULLYBELTON: . . . Most offences, whether at common law or under statute, include some mental element, but the description of the offence normally refers only to the prohibited act, leaving the mental element to be implied. . . .

All the definitions of rape quoted to us which made any reference to the state of mind required of the rapist included a statement to the effect that: "one of the elements of the crime of rape is an intention on the part of an accused person to have intercourse without consent." I take that quotation from *R. v. Flannery and Prendergast* [1969] V.R. 31, 32, decided by the full Court in Victoria.

The argument for the Crown in support of an affirmative answer to the question in this case was not supported by any English decision on rape. It was supported by reference to English decisions in relation to other offences which are more or less analogous to rape, and to Australian decisions on rape, some of which I have already referred to. The English case upon which most reliance was placed was *R. v. Tolson (post, p. 159)*, which was concerned with bigamy, and which decided that a bona fide belief *on reasonable grounds* in the death of the husband at the time of the second marriage afforded a good defence to the indictment of bigamy. The main argument in the case was concerned with the question whether a mistaken belief could be a defence to a charge of bigamy at all, and comparatively little attention was given to the subsidiary point of whether the belief had to be based upon reasonable grounds. The case seems to me therefore of only limited assistance for the present purpose. We were invited to overrule *Tolson* but, as it has stood for over 80 years, and has been followed in many later cases, I would not favour that course. But in my opinion the case is distinguishable from the present. Bigamy was a statutory offence under the Offences Against the Person Act 1861, section 57. So far as appears from the words of the section, bigamy was an absolute offence, except for one defence set out in a proviso, and it is clear that the mental element in bigamy is quite different from that in rape. In particular, bigamy does not involve any intention except that intention to go through a marriage ceremony, unlike rape in which I have already considered the mental element. So, if a defendant charged with bigamy believes that his spouse is dead, his belief does not involve the absence of any intent which forms an essential ingredient in the offence, and it is thus not comparable to the belief of a defendant charged with rape that the woman consents. The difficulty of arguing by analogy from one offence to another is strikingly illustrated by reference to the case of *R. v. Prince* (1875) 13 Cox C.C. 138. That case dealt with abduction of a girl under the age of 16, an offence created by section 55 of the Act of 1861. Bramwell B., with whom five other judges concurred, held that a mistaken and reasonable belief by the defendant that the abducted girl was aged 16 or more was no excuse, because abduction of a young girl was immoral as well as illegal, although a mistaken and reasonable belief by the defendant that he had the consent of the girl's father would have been an excuse. If such differences can exist about mistaken beliefs of different facts in one offence, it is surely dangerous to argue from one offence to another. No doubt a rapist, who mistakenly believes that the woman is consenting to intercourse, must be behaving immorally, by committing fornication or adultery. But those forms of immoral conduct are not intended to be struck at by the law against rape; indeed, they are not now considered appropriate to be visited with penalties of the criminal law at all. There seems to be no reason why they should affect the consequences of the mistaken belief.

I feel more difficulty about the Australian, and especially the Victorian, rapes cases. I have already referred to their definition of the crime of rape as including an intention to have intercourse against the consent of the woman. Notwithstanding that, certain of them contain judicial dicta that a mistaken belief by the accused that the woman was consenting was no defence unless based upon reasonable grounds (see *R. v. Burles* [1947] V.L.R. 392, 402), but in none of these cases did the precise point with which we are now concerned arise for decision. In some of them the court accepted that *mens rea* would be excluded by the mistaken belief only if it was based on reasonable grounds. But they did so either because authorities which they considered binding on them "constrained" them to do so (*R.* v. *Sperotto and Salvietti* (1970) 71 S.R. (N.S.W.) 334, 339), or by reference to particular authorities without separate consideration of the point (*R.* v. *Flannery and Prendergast* [1969] V.R. 31, 34). Accordingly, these cases do not contribute any additional argument tending to resolve the logical difficulty to which I have referred in considering the learned judge's direction in this case, and which seems to me insuperable. The authority referred to in *Flannery* was *R.* v. *Warner* [1969] 2 A.C. 256 where Lord Reid at p. 276C quoted with approval the following words from *Bank of New South Wales* v. *Piper* [1897] A.C. 383:

> "the absence of mens rea consists of an *honest and reasonable* belief entertained by the accused of the existence of fact which if true, would make the act charged against him innocent." (My italics).

Later in his speech Lord Reid said, at p. 280C:

> "Mens rea or its absence is a subjective test, and any attempt to substitute an objective test for serious crime has been successfully resisted."

With the greatest respect I cannot see how it could be a subjective test, if the absence of *mens rea* includes the essentially objective element of being reasonable.

For these reasons, I am of the opinion that there is no authority which compels me to answer the question in this case in what I would regard as an illogical way. I would therefore answer the question in the negative—that is in favour of the accused. But, for the reasons stated by my noble and learned friend, Lord Hailsham of St. Marylebone and Lord Edmund-Davies, I would apply the proviso to the Criminal Appeal Act 1968, section 2(1), and I would refuse the appeal.

[Lord Simon of Glaisdale and Lord Edmund-Davies dissented.]

Appeal dismissed

Note

Although the decision in *D.P.P.* v. *Morgan* was on the whole welcomed by legal academics it was widely denounced in the Press. As a result a Committee, chaired by Heilbron J., was set up to consider the implications of the case. The Committee's Report (Cmnd. 6352 (1976)) accepted the decision as consistent with the subjective approach to the mental element in crime, but recommended that the offence of rape be statutorily defined. This was implemented in the Sexual Offences (Amendment) Act 1976.

Three different academic reactions are discernible. There are those who welcomed the decision but wished it had gone further; those who felt it achieved the right balance and those who remained unconvinced that it was right to exclude reasonableness. The extracts below illustrate each of these points of view.

Smith and Hogan, Criminal Law (7th ed.), pp. 217–218

"One unfortunate aspect of the discussion of the bigamy cases in *Morgan* is that it suggests a very strict approach to the problem of the implication of *mens rea* into statutory offences. ... These *dicta* ... suggest that, where a statute uses no words expressly importing *mens rea*, the mental element which the court will require the prosecution to prove will be minimal—to go through a ceremony of marriage, to have sexual intercourse etc., and that it will then be for the accused to introduce evidence sufficient to raise a doubt whether he did not, on reasonable grounds, have a belief inconsistent with some material element in the *actus reus*."

Rupert Cross, "Centenary Reflections on Prince's Case" (1975) 91 L.Q.R. 540 at 551

"I have made suggestions which may, I fear, antagonise, for opposite reasons, two bodies of opinion to which I am accustomed to pay respect. The first is the opinion of a number of academic lawyers who are, if the expression can be permitted, 'in total bondage to the subjectivist bug'; the second is the opinion of that section of the press which, if the expression can be permitted, is 'dedicated to the vindication of outrages.'

There are academics who think that mistake of fact should always be a defence however unreasonable it may be; but, to say the least, I have toyed with the view that there are situations in which the law may properly require that the mistake should be a reasonable one. One such situation is that in which the mistake is pleaded as a total excuse for a deliberate resort to violence. Surely it is arguable that gross failure to exercise a reasonable judgment in these circumstances should be punished, so long as it is never forgotten that 'detached reflection cannot be demanded in the presence of an uplifted knife.' Another situation in which the law may properly require that a mistake of fact should be reasonable is perhaps that of intercourse with girls beneath the age of 16. The object of the legislation on this subject is to protect young girls against themselves. If their consent to the intercourse is immaterial, why should their statements with regard to their age provide an over-credulous accused with a defence. The requirement of reasonableness may at least do a little to insure that men do not jump to conclusions they desire to reach.

I can understand why the decision in *Morgan* came as a shock to those who rightly consider it to be one of the functions of the criminal law to vindicate the outrage of rape, although it is probably true to say that the case is exceptional. The number of situations in which a jury could entertain no reasonable doubt concerning the prosecutrix's evidence of protest and resistance and, at the same time, give any credence to the accused's assertion that he nonetheless believed her to be consenting to intercourse must be small. ... [O]ne reason why the maximum punishment for rape is life imprisonment is that the common man considers rapists to be very wicked people. Someone who believes, albeit without reasonable cause, that the woman is consenting may well be stupid and insentive, but he is not wicked in the sense in which the rapist is wicked."

C. Wells, "Swatting the Subjectivist Bug" [1982] Crim.L.R. 209 at 212–213

"Are objective standards necessarily inconsistent with individual guilt or culpability? An interesting feature discernible in the acclaim accorded to the decision in *Morgan* v. *D.P.P.* is the lack of sympathy for Morgan as a defendant and its limited potential in future cases. It is often pointed out that the decision is not a rapists' charter since few defendants would be able to convince a jury that they *actually* believed the woman was not consenting. But is the defendant who does so believe without culpability? The definition of rape requires that the woman was not consenting. If there is sufficient evidence to satisfy a jury that consent was absent, can it not be argued that this is sufficient to distinguish, in terms of culpability, the mistaken defendant from those men who have never had sexual intercourse with a woman who was not consenting? If the defendant is so out of touch with the reality of the situation, is there not a suggestion that he should take more care to ensure that his sexual partner is willing? Social protection might be better served by the punishment of a defendant who failed to acquaint himself with this (seemingly) elementary fact. But would the pillar of personal guilt be demolished in the process? Is a system of criminal law only 'just' if it confines itself to punishing those who 'feel' culpable? 'The state of the actor's mind or conscience is a factual claim. Guilt, fault and culpability are normative judgments, based on an evaluation of the actor's conduct and state of mind' (Fletcher: at p. 509). Fletcher goes on to suggest that an alternative method of assessing culpability would combine both objective and subjective elements.

> 'The assessment of attribution and accountability obviously requires the application of standards to the particular situation of the actor ... the standard has a variety of forms, but it always recurs to the same normative question: could the actor have been fairly expected to avoid the act of wrongdoing? Did he or she have a fair opportunity to perceive the risk, to avoid the mistake, to resist the external pressure ... ?' (at p. 510)

It could be argued that, although the mistaken 'rapist' is culpable, he is not as culpable as the deliberate rapist and that his crime should not be rape but some lesser offence such as 'negligent sexual invasion.' "

Fletcher, Rethinking Criminal Law, p. 703

"There are some cases in which any mistake is sufficient to preclude liability, others in which the mistake prevails only if free from fault. An adequate method would help us classify cases into these two groups. Yet [in *D.P.P.* v. *Morgan*] both Lord Cross' reliance on ordinary language and Lord Hailsham's reliance on textbook definitions prove to be little more than tools for rationalising the result in this case, and it is not even clear that the rationalization favours the right result. ...

If we can determine the elements of the definition, then the claim is that the required intent encompasses these and only these elements. But how do we determine whether non-consent is part of the definition of rape? The definition, it will be recalled, is the minimal set of elements necessary to incriminate the actor. Consider the following scale of elements arranged in order of ascending incrimination:

1. touching
2. sexual contact
3. forcible sexual contact
4. non-consensual, forcible sexual contact

It is difficult to argue that touching *per se* is incriminating. ... Sexual contact is obviously different. Intimate touching of the genitals is hardly routine; the touching requires a good reason. The reason, or the justification, might be the consent of the person touched or it might be the necessity of performing an operation in an emergency situation. This seems to me to be sufficient to regard the definition of rape as sexual penetration, with consent functioning as a ground for regarding the sexual act as a shared expression of love rather than as an invasion of bodily integrity.

The case in *Morgan* is even clearer, for the penetration was forcible. It is conceivable that a woman would enjoy being taken by force and that her consent would justify the forcible penetration. But it would be implausible to treat non-consent as well as force as necessary conditions for rendering the sexual act suspect. There seems to be little doubt that under the circumstances of *Morgan*, the consent of the woman should have functioned as a justification. And if that is the case, it is wrong to regard the intent required for rape as encompassing a belief in non-consent. If the perpetrators were mistaken about the supposed justification for forcible intercourse, their wrongful act might well be excused. But if the focus is on excusing their conduct, it is appropriate to require—in this case as in *Tolson* and *Sweet*—that their mistake be free from fault. If they were personally culpable in believing Morgan's lies about his wife, they could hardly claim their acts were blameless and therefore properly excused.

One might be tempted to think that the actual decision in *Morgan*, holding that any mistake about consent bars liability, expresses the mores of the new sexual morality. The stigma of fornication has softened; therefore one should have to show more in order to make out a case that sexual acts are socially unacceptable. It seems to follow that what makes rape wrong is non-consent, and therefore non-consent should be included in the definition of the offence. This argument is seductive, but ... changing attitudes towards chastity hardly diminish the evil of rape. Indeed one can well argue the opposite view.

The more seriously one takes the sexual autonomy of adult men and women, the more incriminating an act of forcible intercourse of the type prosecuted in *Morgan*. Further, if consensual sexual acts are socially acceptable, it does not follow that non-consent is a necessary component of the definition and therefore encompassed in the required intent."

See also Sellers, "Mens Rea and the Judicial Approach to Bad Excuses" (1978) 41 M.L.R. 245, and Richard S. Tur (1981) 1 Ox.J.Leg. Stud. 432 where he discusses a decision of the Canadian Supreme Court, *R.* v. *Pappajohn* (1980) 111 D.L.R. 1 that the jury need not be directed on honest mistake unless there is some external evidence (such as Morgan's advice to his friends about his wife's "simulated resistance") to support it.

Question

Rupert Cross is prepared to countenance a requirement of reasonableness where "mistake is pleaded as a total excuse for a deliberate resort to violence." Would this not include rape?

Note

Whilst *Morgan* dealt with the issue of mistakes in relation to the offence of rape, the question which remained to be answered was whether the principle enunciated therein also applied to honest but unreasonable mistakes in respect of definitional elements in other offences. At first, in *Phekoo* [1981] 1 W.L.R. 1117, the Court of Appeal held that *Morgan* was confined to the offence of rape and mistakes as to definitional elements in other offences had to be based on reasonable grounds if they were to operate to negate liability.

D. Cowley, "The Retreat from Morgan" [1982] Crim.L.R. 198 at 206–208

"What is particularly remarkable about the apparent eagerness to retreat from *Morgan* is the lack of any really convincing judicial justification for requiring reasonableness in mistake cases. . . .

One theory suggests that whether the objective test of mistake applies depends upon where in respect of the relevant issue the evidential burden lies, and that where an evidential burden lies on the accused to show that he believed in facts inconsistent with the offence, 'a bald assertion of belief for which the accused can indicate no reasonable ground is evidence of insufficient substance to raise any issue requiring the jury's consideration.' (*per* Lord Simon in *Morgan* at 367). It is respectfully submitted that this theory is unsound and that there is no connection between the incidence of the evidential burden and the question whether the mistake must be reasonable, the main reason being that an evidential burden on the defendant merely requires him to give some *reasonable evidence of belief* as opposed to *evidence of reasonable belief*. It may well be the case that his assertion of belief is not 'bald' but is fully corroborated by independent evidence leading the jury to accept that the unreasonable belief was in fact held and, in such circumstances, the defendant will have discharged the burden cast upon him.

An alternative reason for requiring the belief to be reasonable put forward by Lord Simon is the fact that the victim must be 'vindicated' by punishing, *e.g.* an assailant who has made an unreasonable mistake: 'The policy of the law in this regard could well derive from its concern to hold a fair balance between the victim and the accused. It would hardly seem just to fob off a victim of a savage assault with such comfort as he could derive from knowing that his injury was caused by a belief, however absurd, that he was about to attack the accused.' One cannot but agree with Professor Williams' opinion ((1975) N.L.J. 968, 969) that this is not only a somewhat old-fashioned view of the criminal law but also fails to explain who is vindicated when a bigamist is punished. The lawful spouse, in particular, may not care a jot about the bigamy.

Perhaps the current judicial insistence on there being reasonable grounds for mistaken belief can, rather, be put down to a simple lack of confidence in the jury as the final arbiter of fact. If so, such judicial mistrust is very reminiscent of the somewhat misconceived and blinkered popular reaction to the decision in *Morgan*. What was apparently overlooked by those whose passions were aroused by *Morgan's* effect on the law of rape, and those whose railing against the case implied a serious lack of faith in the tribunal of fact in criminal cases, was not the total lack of gullibility of that particular jury who decided that the defendants' tale as to Mrs Morgan's consent to their intercourse with her was 'a pack of lies,' but also the ultimate result of the case—the dismissal of the defendants' appeals against conviction. There is little evidence there to support the often heard claim that a requirement of mere honest belief facilitates bogus defences, and before seeking to impose any kind of restriction upon the freedom of the jury to determine issues of fact the judiciary might reflect upon the oft-quoted words of Dixon J. that ' . . . a lack of confidence in the ability of a tribunal correctly to estimate evidence of states of mind and the like can never be sufficient ground for excluding from inquiry the most fundamental element in a rational and humane criminal code.' (*Thomas* v. *R.* (1937) 59 C.L.R. 279 at 309)."

Note

In the case below the Court of Appeal considered whether the *Morgan* principles applied where the appellant was charged with indecent assault.

R. v. Kimber
[1983] 1 W.L.R. 1118
Court of Appeal

LAWTON L.J. read the following judgment of the court: The appeal raises these points. First, can a defendant charged with an indecent assault on a woman raise the defence that he believed she had consented to what he did? The trial judge, Mr. Recorder Smyth Q.C. ruled that he could not. Secondly, if he could, did the jury have to consider merely whether his belief was honestly held or, if it was, did they have to go on to consider whether it was based on reasonable grounds? Another way of putting these points is to ask whether the principles upon which the House of Lords decided *R.* v. *Morgan* [1976] A.C. 182 should be applied to a charge of indecent assault on a woman. ...

The burden of proving lack of consent rests upon the prosecution. ... The consequence is that the prosecution has to prove that the defendant intended to lay hands on his victim without her consent. If he did not intend to do this, he is entitled to be found not guilty; and if he did not so intend because he believed she was consenting, the prosecution will have failed to prove the charge. It is the defendant's belief, not the grounds on which it was based, which goes to negative the intent.

In analysing the issue in this way we have followed what was said by the majority in *R.* v. *Morgan* [1976] A.C. 182: see Lord Hailsham of St. Marylebone at p. 214F-H and Lord Fraser of Tullybelton at p. 237E-G. If, as we adjudge, the prohibited act in indecent assault is the use of personal violence to a woman without her consent, then the guilty state of mind is the intent to do it without her consent. Then, as in rape at common law, the inexorable logic, to which Lord Hailsham referred in *R.* v. *Morgan*, takes over and there is no room either for a "defence" of honest belief or mistake, or of a "defence" of honest and reasonable belief or mistake: [1976] A.C. 182, 214F-H.

The decision in *R.* v. *Morgan*, probably because of its sordid facts and the improbability of the defence raised, caused unease amongst lawyers and some members of the public. Parliament reacted by passing the Sexual Offences (Amendment) Act 1976. The courts from time to time have shown a propensity to distinguish other offences from the common law concept of rape so as to avoid having to follow the reasoning in *R.* v. *Morgan*. This has been described by one academic writer as "The Retreat from *Morgan*" (see, *ante*, p. 142). Since each case must be decided after careful analysis as to what constituted a prohibited act and what is the nature of the *mens rea*, if any, which has to be proved, a detailed consideration of these cases would be *obiter* for the purposes of this judgment. In these circumstances we do not intend to adjudge whether these cases were correctly decided or to attempt to distinguish them from this case. The application of the *Morgan* principle to offences other than indecent assault on a woman will have to be considered when such offences come before the courts. We do, however, think it necessary to consider two of them because of what was said in the judgments. The first is a decision of the Divisional Court in *Albert* v. *Lavin* [1982] A.C. 546. The offence charged was assaulting a police officer in the execution of his duty, contrary to section 51 of the Police Act 1964. The defendant in his defence contended, *inter alia*, that he had not believed the police officer to be such and in consequence had resisted arrest. His counsel analysed the offence in the same way as we have done and referred to the reasoning in *Morgan*. Hodgson J., delivering the leading judgment, rejected this argument and in doing so said, at pp. 561–562:

> "But in my judgment Mr. Walker's ingenious argument fails at an earlier stage. It does not seem to me that the element of unlawfulness can properly be regarded as part of the definitional elements of the offence. In defining a criminal offence the word 'unlawful' is surely tautologous and can add nothing to its essential ingredients ... And no matter how strange it may seem that a defendant charged with assault can escape conviction if he shows that he mistakenly but unreasonably thought his victim was consenting but not if he was in the same state of mind as to whether his victim had a right to detain him, that in my judgment is the law."

We have found difficulty in agreeing with this reasoning, even though the judge seems to be accepting that belief in consent does entitle a defendant to an acquittal on a charge of assault. We cannot accept that the word "unlawful" when used in a definition of an offence is to be regarded as "tautologous." In our judgment the word "unlawful" does import an essential element into the offence. If it were not there social life would be unbearable, because every touching would amount to a battery unless there was an evidential basis for a defence. This case was considered by the House of Lords. The appeal was dismissed, but their Lordships declined to deal with the issue of belief.

In *R.* v. *Phekoo* [1981] 1 W.L.R. 1117 ... [Hollings J., refering to *Morgan* stated] "It seems to us clear that this decision was confined and intended to be confined to the offence of rape." We do not accept that this was the intention of their Lordships in *Morgan's* case. Lord Hailsham of St. Marylebone started his speech by saying that the issue as to belief was a question of great academic importance in the theory of English criminal law.

In our judgment the recorder should have directed the jury that the prosecution had to make them sure that the appellant never had believed that [the woman] was consenting. As he did not do so, the jury never considered an important aspect of his defence.

[Lawton J., however, concluded that no reasonable jury, properly directed, would have accepted the appellant's account and that he was, at least, reckless as to whether the woman was consenting. Accordingly, there had been no miscarriage of justice.]

Appeal dismissed

(b) Mistake as to a justificatory claim

Where a defendant has, *prima facie*, committed the offence charged, having brought about the *actus reus* with the requisite *mens rea*, will a claim of justification serve to negate his liability where it is based upon a mistaken belief. For example, if D intentionally wounds X in the mistaken belief that X is about to attack him, will his plea of self-defence succeed to negate his liability where it is an honestly held belief or must the belief also be a reasonable one?

In *Albert* v. *Lavin* [1982] A.C. 546, the Divisional Court held that a mistaken belief on the part of the defendant that his act was justified on the basis of self-defence, had to be based on reasonable grounds. Is a claim of justification something separate from the definitional elements of an offence? If so there might be some reason in principle for requiring such mistakes to be reasonable. Alternatively, is the absence of a justificatory claim part of the definitional elements of the offence? If so, does *Morgan* apply or is it to be confined to rape and kindred offences. Glanville Williams has been a strong proponent of the second view.

Williams, T.C.L. p. 138

"No other rule of the substantive criminal law distinguishes between the definitional and defence elements of a crime, and it is a distinction that it is impossible to draw satisfactorily. A rule creating a *defence* merely supplies additional details of the scope of the *offence*. To regard the offence as subsisting independently of its limitations and qualifications is unrealistic. The defence is a negative condition of the offence, and is therefore an integral part of it. What we regard as part of the offence and what as part of a defence depends only on traditional habits of thought or accidents of legal drafting; it should have no bearing on the important question of criminal liability. For example, it is purely a matter of convenient drafting whether a statute says, on the one hand, that damaging the property of another without his consent is a crime, or, on the other hand, that damaging the property of another is a crime but that his consent is a defence. In fact we regard the non-consent of the owner as a definitional element, but there is no particular reason why this should be so, and the question of guilt or innocence should not depend on it. (see 2 Leg.Stud. 233)"

This view was echoed in the Court of Appeal in the following case.

R. v. Williams (Gladstone)
(1984) 78 Cr.App.R. 276
Court of Appeal

Mason saw a youth rob a woman. He chased and caught him but the youth broke free. The appellant then witnessed Mason catch the youth again and knock him to the ground. Mason told the appellant that he was a police officer (which was untrue) and that he was arresting the youth for mugging a woman. The appellant asked to see his warrant card. When Mason failed to produce one, a struggle ensued, during which the appellant punched Mason in the face. He was charged with assault occasioning actual bodily harm. He claimed that he honestly believed that the youth was being unlawfully assaulted by Mason and that he was trying to rescue him. As Mason was acting lawfully, the appellant had made a mistake. The jury were directed that his mistake would be relevant if it was honest and based on reasonable grounds. He was convicted and appealed on the ground that the judge had misdirected the jury.

LORD LANE C.J. gave the judgment of the court: "Assault" ... is an act by which the defendant, intentionally or recklessly, applies unlawful force to the complainant. There are circumstances in which force may be applied to another lawfully. Taking a few examples: first, where the victim consents, as in lawful sports, the application of force to another will, generally speaking, not be unlawful. Secondly, where the defendant is acting in self-defence: the exercise of any necessary and reasonable force to protect himself from unlawful violence is not unlawful. Thirdly, by virtue of section 3 of the Criminal Law Act 1967, a person may use such force as is reasonable in the circumstances in the prevention of crime or in effecting or assisting in the lawful arrest of an offender or suspected offender or persons unlawfully at large. In each of those cases the defendant will be guilty if the jury are sure that first of all he applied force to the person of another, and secondly that he had the necessary mental element to constitute guilt.

The mental element necessary to constitute guilt is the intent to apply unlawful force to the victim. We do not believe that the mental element can be substantiated by simply showing an intent to apply force and no more.

What then is the situation if the defendant is labouring under a mistake of fact as to the circumstances? What if he believes, but believes mistakenly, that the victim is consenting, or that it is necessary to defend himself, or that a crime is being committed which he intends to prevent? He must then be judged against the mistaken facts as he believes them to be. If judged against those facts or circumstances the prosecution fail to establish his guilt, then he is entitled to be acquitted.

The next question is, does it make any difference if the mistake of the defendant was one which, viewed objectively by a reasonable onlooker, was an unreasonable mistake? ...

It is upon this point that the large volume of historical precedent ... is concerned. But in our judgment the answer is provided by the judgment of this Court in *Kimber* (*ante*, p. 153) by which ... we are bound ...

We respectfully agree with what Lawton L.J. said [in *Kimber*] with regard both to the way in which the defence should have been put and also with regard to his remarks as to the nature of the defence. The reasonableness or unreasonableness of the defendant's belief is material to the question of whether the belief was held by the defendant at all. If the belief was in fact held, its unreasonableness, so far as guilt or innocence is concerned, is neither here nor there. It is irrelevant. Were it otherwise, the defendant would be convicted because he was negligent in failing to recognise that the victim was not consenting or that a crime was not being committed and so on. In other words the jury should be directed first of all that the prosecution have the burden or duty of proving the unlawfulness of the defendant's actions; secondly, if the defendant may have been labouring under a mistake as to the facts, he must be judged according to his mistaken view of the facts; thirdly, that is so whether the mistake was, on an objective view, a reasonable mistake or not.

In a case of self-defence, where self-defence or the prevention of crime is concerned, if the jury came to the conclusion that the defendant believed, or may have believed, that he was being attacked or that a crime was being committed, and that force was necessary to protect himself or to prevent the crime, then the prosecution have not proved their case. If however the defendant's alleged belief was mistaken and if the mistake was an unreasonable one, that may be a powerful reason for coming to the conclusion that the belief was not honestly held and should be rejected.

Even if the jury come to the conclusion that the mistake was an unreasonable one, if the defendant may genuinely have been labouring under it, he is entitled to rely upon it.

We have read the recommendations of the Criminal Law Revision Committee, Part IX, paragraph 72(a), in which the following passage appears: "The common law defence of self-defence should be replaced by a statutory defence providing that a person may use such force as is reasonable in the circumstances as he believes them to be in the defence of himself or any other person." In the view of this Court that represents the law as expressed in *D.P.P.* v. *Morgan* and in *Kimber* and we do not think that the decision of the Divisional Court in *Albert* v. *Lavin* from which we have cited can be supported.

Appeal allowed
Conviction quashed

Williams was considered in *R.* v. *O'Grady* [1987] 3 W.L.R. 321, C.A. (*post*, p. 270). The Judicial Committee of the Privy Council reviewed the whole area in the following case.

Beckford v. R.
[1988] A.C. 130
Privy Council

At the appellant's trial for murder the judge directed the jury that if the appellant had a *reasonable* belief that his life was in danger or that he was in danger of serious bodily injury he was entitled to be acquitted on the grounds of self-defence.

LORD GRIFFITHS: ... It is accepted by the prosecution that there is no difference on the law of self-defence between the law of Jamaica and the English common law and it therefore falls to be decided whether it was correctly decided by the Court of Appeal in *R.* v. *Williams* (*ante*, p. 155) that the defence of self-defence depends upon what the accused "honestly" believed the circumstances to be and not upon the reasonableness of that belief—what the Court of Appeal in Jamaica referred to as the "honest belief" and "reasonable belief" schools of thought.

There can be no doubt that prior to the decision of the House of Lords in *R.* v. *Morgan* (*ante*, p. 142) the whole weight of authority supported the view that it was an essential element of self-defence not only that the accused believed that he was being attacked or in imminent danger of being attacked but also that such belief was based on reasonable grounds.

The question then is whether the present Lord Chief Justice, Lord Lane, in *R.* v. *Williams*, was right to depart from the law as declared by his predecessors in the light of the decision of the House of Lords in *R.* v. *Morgan*. *R.* v. *Morgan* was a case of rape and counsel for the Crown has submitted that the decision of the majority turned solely upon their view of the specific intention required for the commission of that crime and accordingly had no relevance to the law of self-defence. ...

In *R.* v. *Morgan* each member of the House of Lords held that the *mens rea* required to commit rape is the knowledge that the woman is not consenting or recklessness as to whether she is consenting or not. From this premise the majority held that unless the prosecution proved that the man did not believe the woman was consenting or was at least reckless as to her consent they had failed to prove the necessary *mens rea* which is an essential ingredient of the crime. . . .

In *R*. v. *Williams*, the decision in *R*. v. *Morgan* was carried a step further and in their Lordships' view to its logical conclusion. . . .

In the course of his judgment Lord Lane C.J. discussing the offence of assault said, at p. 280:

> "The mental element necessary to constitute guilt is the intent to apply unlawful force to the victim. We do not believe that the mental element can be substantiated by simply showing an intent to apply force and no more."

And later in the judgment, at p. 280, he expressly disapproved the decision of the Divisional Court in *Albert* v. *Lavin* [1982] A.C. 546 in which it was said that the word "unlawful" was tautologous and not part of the definitional element of assaulting a police officer in the course of his duty. In so doing Lord Lane C.J. was expressing the same view of *Albert* v. *Lavin* that had been previously expressed by Lawton L.J. in *R*. v. *Kimber* (*ante*, p. 153).

The common law recognises that there are many circumstances in which one person may inflict violence upon another without committing a crime, as for instance, in sporting contests, surgical operations or in the most extreme example judicial execution. The common law has always recognised as one of these circumstances the right of a person to protect himself from attack and to act in the defence of others and if necessary to inflict violence on another in so doing. If no more force is used than is reasonable to repel the attack such force is not unlawful and no crime is committed. Furthermore a man about to be attacked does not have to wait for his assailant to strike the first blow or fire the first shot; circumstances may justify a pre-emptive strike.

It is because it is an essential element of all crimes of violence that the violence or the threat of violence should be unlawful that self-defence, if raised as an issue in a criminal trial, must be disproved by the prosecution. If the prosecution fail to do so the accused is entitled to be acquitted because the prosecution will have failed to prove an essential element of the crime namely that the violence used by the accused was unlawful.

If then a genuine belief, albeit without reasonable grounds, is a defence to rape because it negatives the necessary intention, so also must a genuine belief in facts which if true would justify self-defence be a defence to a crime of personal violence because the belief negates the intent to act unlawfully. Their Lordships therefore approve . . . *R*. v. *Williams*, as correctly stating the law of self defence. . . .

Looking back, *R*. v. *Morgan* can now be seen as a landmark decision in the development of the common law returning the law to the path upon which it might have developed but for the inability of an accused to give evidence on his own behalf. . . .

There may be a fear that the abandonment of the objective standard demanded by the existence of reasonable grounds for belief will result in the success of too many spurious claims of self-defence. The English experience has not shown this to be the case. The Judicial Studies Board with the approval of the Lord Chief Justice has produced a model direction on self-defence which is now widely used by judges when summing up to juries. The direction contains the following guidance:

> "Whether the plea is self-defence or defence of another, if the defendant may have been labouring under a mistake as to the facts, he must be judged according to his mistaken belief of the facts: that is so whether the mistake was, on an objective view, a reasonable mistake or not."

Their Lordships have heard no suggestion that this form of summing up has resulted in a disquieting number of acquittals. This is hardly surprising for no jury is going to accept a man's assertion that he believed that he was about to be attacked without testing it against all the surrounding circumstances. In assisting the jury to determine whether or not the accused had a genuine belief the judge will of course direct their attention to those features of the evidence that make such a belief more or less probable. Where there are no reasonable grounds to hold a belief it will surely only be in exceptional circumstances that a jury will conclude that such a belief was or might have been held.

Their Lordships therefore conclude that the summing up in this case contained a material misdirection and ... the test to be applied for self-defence is that a person may use such force as is reasonable in the circumstances as he honestly believes them to be in the defence of himself or another.

Appeal allowed

(c) The Problem of Tolson

When the House of Lords decided *Morgan* it had the opportunity to deal with *Tolson*; it chose not to do so leaving an unsatisfactory decision which cannot be reconciled with more recent cases.

R. v. Tolson
(1889) 23 Q.B.D. 168
Court for Crown Cases Reserved

The defendant was deserted by her husband, and afterwards heard that he had been lost at sea. Five years after last seeing her husband, the defendant went through a ceremony of marriage with another man. Her husband was still alive. She was convicted of bigamy, a felony under section 57, Offences Against the Person Act 1861, which is set out in the judgment of Cave J. below. Her conviction was quashed by a majority of nine judges to five.

CAVE J.: ... At common law an honest and reasonable belief in the existence of circumstances, which, if true, would make the act for which a prisoner is indicted an innocent act has always been held to be a good defence. This doctrine is embodied in the somewhat uncouth maxim "*Actus non facit reum, nisi mens sit rea.*" Honest and reasonable mistake stands in fact on the same footing as absence of the reasoning faculty, as in infancy, or perversion of that faculty, as in lunacy. Instances of the existence of this common law doctrine will readily occur to the mind. So far as I am aware it has never been suggested that these exceptions do not equally apply in the case of statutory offences unless they are excluded expressly or by necessary implication. In *R. v. Prince* (1875) L.R. 2 C.C.R. 154, in which the principle of mistake underwent much discussion, it was not suggested by any of the judges that the exceptional honest and reasonable mistake was not applicable to all offences, whether existing at common law or created by statute. As I understand the judgments in that case the difference of opinion was as to the exact extent of the exception. ...

It is argued, however, that, assuming the general exception to be as stated, yet the language of the Act (24 & 25 Vict. c. 100, s.57), is such that that exception is necessarily excluded in this case. Now, it is undoubtedly within the competence of the legislature to enact that a man shall be branded as a felon and punished for doing an act which he honestly and reasonably believes to be lawful and right. ... But such a result seems so revolting to the moral sense that we ought to require the clearest and most indisputable evidence that such is the meaning of the Act. It is said that this inference necessarily arises from the language of the section in question, and particularly of the proviso. The section (omitting immaterial parts) is in these words. "Whosoever, being married, shall marry any other person during the life of the former husband or wife, ... shall be guilty of felony ... : provided that nothing in this section contained shall extend ... to any person marrying a second time whose husband or wife shall have been continually absent from such person for the space of seven years then last past, and shall not have been known by such person to be living within that time. ... " It is argued that the first part is expressed absolutely; but, surely, it is not contended that the language admits of no exception, and therefore that a lunatic who, under the influence of a delusion, marries again, must be convicted; and, if an exception is to be admitted where the reasoning faculty is perverted by disease, why is not an exception equally to be admitted where the reasoning faculty, although honestly and reasonably exercised, is deceived? But it is said that the proviso is inconsistent with the exception contended for; and, undoubtedly, if the proviso covers less ground or only the same ground as the exception, it follows that the legislature has expressed an intention that the exception shall not operate until after seven years from the disappearance of the first husband. But if, on the other hand, the proviso covers more ground than the general exception, surely it is no argument to say that the legislature must have intended that the more limited defence shall not operate within the seven years because it has provided that a less limited defence shall only come into operation at the expiration of those years.

What must the accused prove to bring herself within the general exception? She must prove facts from which the jury may reasonably infer that she honestly and on reasonable grounds believed her first husband to be dead before she married again. What must she prove to bring herself within the proviso? Simply that her husband has been continually absent for seven years; and, if she can do that, it will be no answer to prove that she had no reasonable grounds for believing him to be dead or that she did not honestly believe it. Unless the prosecution can prove that she knew her husband to be living within the seven years she must be acquitted. The honesty and reasonableness of her belief is no longer in issue. Even if it could be proved that she believed him to be alive all the time, as distinct from knowing him to be so, the prosecution must fail. The proviso, therefore, is far wider than the general exception; and the intention of the legislature, that a wider and more easily established defence should be open after seven years from the disappearance of the husband, is not necessarily inconsistent with the intention that a different defence, less extensive and more difficult of proof, should be open within the seven years.

STEPHEN J.: My view of the subject is based upon a particular application of the doctrine usually, though I think not happily, described by the phrase *"non est reus, nisi mens sit rea."* ... The principle involved appears to me, when fully considered, to amount to no more than this. The full definition of every crime contains expressly or by implication a proposition as to state of mind. Therefore, if the mental element of any conduct alleged to be a crime is proved to have been absent in any given case, the crime so defined is not committed; or, again, if a crime is fully defined, nothing amounts to that crime which does not satisfy the definition. Crimes are in the present day much more accurately defined by statute or otherwise than they formerly were. The mental element of most crimes is marked by one of the words "maliciously," "fraudulently," "negligently," or "knowingly," but it is the general—I might, I think, say, the invariable—practice of the legislature to leave unexpressed some of the mental elements of crime. In all cases whatever, competent age, sanity and some degree of freedom from some kinds of coercion are assumed to be essential to criminality, but I do not believe they are ever introduced into any statute by which any particular crime is defined.

The meaning of the words "malice," "negligence" and "fraud" in relation to particular crimes has been ascertained by numerous cases. Malice means one thing in relation to murder, another in relation to the Malicious Mischief Act, and a third in relation to libel, and so of fraud and negligence.

With regard to knowledge of fact, the law, perhaps, is not quite clear, but it may, I think, be maintained that in every case knowledge of fact is to some extent an element of criminality as much as competent age and sanity. To take an extreme illustration, can anyone doubt that a man who, though he might be perfectly sane, committed what would otherwise be a crime in a state of somnambulism, would be entitled to be acquitted? And why is this? Simply because he would not know what he was doing. ...

It is said, first, that the words of 24 & 25 Vict. c. 100, s.57, are absolute, and that the exceptions which that section contains are the only ones which are intended to be admitted, and this it is said is confirmed by the express proviso in the section—an indication which is thought to negative any tacit exception. It is also supposed that the case of R. v. *Prince* (1875) L.R. 2 C.C.R. 154, decided on section 55, confirms this view. I will begin by saying how far I agree with these views. First, I agree that the case turns exclusively upon the construction of section 57 of 24 & 25 Vict. c. 100. ... Of course, it would be competent to the legislature to define a crime in such a way as to make the existence of any state of mind immaterial. The question is solely whether it has actually done so in this case. ...

In the first place I will observe upon the absolute character of the section. It appears to me to resemble most of the enactments contained in the Consolidation Acts of 1861, in passing over the general mental elements of crime which are presupposed in every case. ... It will be found that either by using the words wilfully and maliciously, or by specifying some special intent as an element of particular crimes, knowledge of fact is implicitly made part of the statutory definition of most modern definitions of crime, but there are some cases in which this cannot be said. Such are section 55, on which R. v. *Prince* was decided, section 56, which punishes the stealing of "any child under the age of fourteen years," section 49, as to procuring the defilement of any "woman or girl under the age of twenty-one," in each of which the same question might arise as in R. v. *Prince*; to these I may add some of the provisions of the Criminal Law Amendment Act of 1885. Reasonable belief that a girl of sixteen or upwards is a defence to the charge of an offence under sections 5, 6 and 7, but this is not provided for as to an offence against section 4, which is meant to protect girls under thirteen.

It seems to me that as to the construction of all these sections the case of R. v. *Prince* is a direct authority. It was the case of a man who abducted a girl under sixteen, believing, on good grounds, that she was above that age. Lord Esher, then Brett J., was against the conviction. His judgment establishes at much length, and, as it appears to me, unanswerably, the principle above explained, which he states as follows: "That a mistake of facts on reasonable grounds, to the extent that, if the facts were as believed, the acts of the prisoner would make him guilty of no offence at all, is an excuse, and that such an excuse is implied in every criminal charge and every criminal enactment in England."

Lord Blackburn, with whom nine other judges agreed, and Lord Bramwell, with whom seven others agreed, do not appear to me to have dissented from this principle, speaking generally; but they held that it did not apply fully to each part of every section to which I have referred. Some of the prohibited acts they thought the legislature intended to be done at the peril of the person who did them, but not all.

The judgment delivered by Lord Blackburn proceeds upon the principle that the intention of the legislature in section 55 was "to punish the abduction unless the girl was of such an age as to make her consent an excuse."

Lord Bramwell's judgment proceeds upon this principle: "The legislature has enacted that if anyone does this wrong act he does it at the risk of her turning out to be under sixteen. This opinion gives full scope to the doctrine of the *mens rea*. If the taker believed he had her father's consent, though wrongly, he would have no *mens rea*; so if he did not know she was in anyone's possession nor in the care or charge of anyone. In those cases he would not know he was doing the act forbidden by statute."

All the judges, therefore, in *R. v. Prince* agreed on the general principle, though they all, except Lord Esher, considered that, the object of the legislature being to prevent a scandalous and wicked invasion of parental rights (whether it was to be regarded as illegal apart from the statute or not), it was to be supposed that they intended that the wrongdoer should act at his peril. . . .

The general principle is clearly in favour of the prisoner, but how does the intention of the legislature appear to have been against them? It could not be the object of Parliament to treat the marriage of widows as an act to be if possible prevented as presumably immoral. The conduct of the [woman] convicted was not in the smallest degree immoral, it was perfectly natural and legitimate. Assuming the facts to be as [she] supposed, the infliction of more than a nominal punishment on [her] would have been a scandal. Why, then, should the legislature be held to have wished to subject [her] to punishment at all . . . ?

It is argued that the proviso that a remarriage after seven years' separation shall not be punishable, operates as a tacit exclusion of all other exceptions to the penal part of the section. It appears to me that it only supplies a rule of evidence which is useful in many cases, in the absence of explicit proof of death. But it seems to me to show not that belief in the death of one married person excuses the marriage of the other only after seven years' separation, but that mere separation for that period had the effect which reasonable belief of death caused by other evidence would have at any time. It would to my mind be monstrous to say that seven years' separation should have a greater effect in excusing a bigamous marriage than positive evidence of death, sufficient for the purpose of recovering a policy of assurance or obtaining probate of a will, would have. . . .

Conviction quashed

[A reasonable belief that the first marriage had been dissolved has also been held to be a defence to bigamy: *R. v. Gould* [1968] 1 All E.R. 849.]

Edward Griew, "States of Mind, Presumptions and Inferences" in Criminal Law: Essays in Honour of J.C. Smith (ed. P. Smith, 1987) 68, 73–74

"The generalisations in *Tolson* about *mens rea* and about the effect of mistaken belief make it a leading case. But it should also have been recognised a long while ago as a misleading one. For by the middle of the present century the legal context and climate in which states of mind were discussed and investigated had undergone important relevant changes. Firstly, because a defendant could now give evidence (from 1898), the best evidence of her state of mind, short of a confession, would in most cases be available. She could explain that she did indeed make a mistake that others (more intelligent, less tired or stressed, even simply less careless) would not have made. If she did not give evidence, or if her evidence was found quite implausible, the common-sense conclusion that she knew what others would have known remained available and might be expected to be reached. But there was no need now for, in effect, a presumption, having substantive force, that she knew obvious things or made only reasonable mistakes. Secondly, the burden of proof had shifted—or its correct location was acknowledged (in 1935). All that the defendant's evidence need do was to induce the tribunal of fact to think it possible that she made the mistake she claimed to have made. Thirdly, the scholars were at last expounding a 'general part' of the criminal law, providing practitioners, for the first time, with an adequate intellectual basis for the elimination of old inconsistencies and confusions. The landmark event, of course, was the publication of Glanville Williams' treatise, *Criminal Law—The General Part*, in 1953. Yet in spite of these and other changes, and in spite of contradictions apparent on its face, *Tolson* has continued for nearly one hundred years to be cited as current authority almost without critical comment. The latest citation (contemporary with the writing of this essay in the summer of 1986) is that by the House of Lords in *Pharmaceutical Society of Great Britain* v. *Storkwain Ltd.* (*post*, p. 196). A submission that 'words appropriate to require *mens rea* in accordance with *R.* v. *Tolson*' must be read into the statutory provision under consideration in that case is still treated as being, 'in other words,' the submission that:

' ... the subsection must be read subject to the implication that a necessary element in the ... offence ... is the absence of belief, held honestly and on reasonable grounds, in the existence of facts which, if true, would make the act innocent.'

Tolson therefore stands as my exemplar of an inappropriately operating system of precedent.

When a statute creates an offence it does not recapitulate all the defences traditionally allowed by the criminal law; yet it must have been the intention of Parliament that these defences should apply. Similarly, since the requirement of *mens rea* is a traditional principle of law, for serious crimes, it is reasonable to suppose that Parliament meant it to govern the statute.

Stephen J. stated this argument in a much-quoted passage. (See, *ante*, p. 160.) It is too long to reproduce, but may be summarised. The judge begins by saying that 'the full definition of every crime contains a proposition as to a state of mind.' Then he spells this out again by saying that if the mental element is absent there is no crime; and he clearly means this proposition to apply to crimes created by statute as well as at common law, so that all alike require a mental element. There follows a series of instances showing that where a person does not know a fact required for the crime he lacks the mental element and so cannot be guilty. Finally, however, the judge confines his proposition to cases where the defendant's belief that the facts were innocent was not merely in good faith but was based on reasonable grounds. This implies that if the defendant genuinely but unreasonably believed in the existence of justifying facts he has no defence, even though in that case he lacked the mental element that is supposed to be required. The reference to reasonable grounds departs from the purely subjective element that the judge has hitherto been propounding, and introduces an objective test. There is, therefore, a basic contradiction in the judgment. . . .

Stephen J. is assuming that the mental element required for a crime is knowledge of a particular fact, which we may call A (*e.g.* 'I am still married'). The defendant's defence is that he believed that the fact present was not-A ('I am not now married'). A defence of belief in not-A is of course the same thing as denying knowledge of A. But Stephen J. says that belief in not-A is no defence unless it is reasonable. If it is unreasonable, the defendant is convicted although he believed not-A, *i.e.* although he did not know A. Yet the judge says that the defendant must know A. So he contradicts himself: QED. His judgment would make a person guilty of bigamy although the only mental element was that of intending to enter into a valid marriage—a state of mind that almost all of us possess at some time in our lives.

Although the question of reasonable belief was not before the court in *Tolson*, and although Stephen J. and some other members of the court were clearly guilty of self-contradiction, the idea started in *Tolson* was perpetuated in later bigamy cases. Time and again the judges have said that a mistake of fact, to be a defence to a charge of bigamy, must be reasonable."

Questions

1. In *Morgan* Lord Fraser said "bigamy does not involve any intention except the intention to go through a marriage ceremony"; if this is correct, wherein lies the guilty state of mind in bigamy which distinguishes a bigamist from every other person who marries?

2. Is there any justification in convicting a person of bigamy who mistakenly believes he or she is free to marry?

(2) *Mistake as to a non-definitional element i.e. as to an excusatory claim*

Peter Alldridge, "The Coherence of Defences" [1983] Crim.L.R. 665–666

"The basis of a claim of justification is that it speaks to the act, a claim of excuse to whether the actor is properly regarded as responsible for it. A claim of justification involves saying, 'I am responsible for what was done, but I am not an appropriate object for punishment because what was done, although an invasion of an interest of another which is generally protected by the criminal law, was done in circumstances which gave me a legal right to do it.' The reason for there being such a legal right is that the behaviour was such as should be encouraged (carrying out the order of the court, arresting offenders, preventing crime, some instances of necessity, consent), or at the very least legally tolerated (self-defence, other cases of consent). The claim of excuse is a different sort of claim altogether. Here D admits, 'There was an unjustified invasion of a legally protected interest.'

But s/he says, 'the normal inference from the fact that my action caused the invasion to the conclusion that I am responsible for it ought not to be drawn: some factor operates which makes that normal inference unwarranted.'

[A]n exculpatory defence must be an excuse or justification but cannot be both. The point of the claim of justification is that D was a responsible actor. Knowledge of sufficient circumstances to make the invasion of P's interest tolerable, and thus establish the right to invade it, is itself a prerequisite of that right. The point of a claim of excuse is that D was not a responsible actor. A coherent defence cannot contain elements the rationale of which is that D was a responsible actor, together with elements whose rationale is that D was not."

Fletcher, Rethinking Criminal Law, pp. 798–800, 810–812

The Theory of Excuses

"Interposing a claim of excuse concedes that there is a wrong to be excused. The claim challenges the attribution of the wrongdoing to the actor. If the excuse is valid, then, as a matter of definition, the actor is not accountable or culpable for the wrongful act. The focus of the excuse is not on the act in the abstract, but on the circumstances of the act and the actor's personal capacity to avoid either an intentional wrong or the taking of an excessive risk. Insanity and involuntary intoxication are paradigmatic excuses. Duress and necessity are regarded as excuses in some legal systems, but not in others. . . .

In a case of justified conduct, the act typically reflects well on the actor's courage or devotion to the public interest. If he disables an aggressor in order to save the life of another, his conduct speaks well for his courage; if as a police officer he disables a felon seeking to escape, his conduct testifies at least to his devotion to duty. Justifications require good reasons for violating the prohibitory norm; someone who chooses to act on these reasons is likely to deserve respect and praise rather than blame.

The distinguishing feature of excusing conditions is that they preclude an inference from the act to the actor's character. Typically, if a bank teller opens a safe and turns money over to a stranger, we can infer that he is dishonest. But if he does all this at gunpoint, we cannot infer anything one way or the other about his honesty. Typically, if a driver knowingly runs over someone lying in the roadway, we might infer something about the driver's indifference to human life. But we cannot make that inference if the choice open to the driver was going over a cliff or continuing down the incline and running over someone lying in the roadway. Similarly, if someone violates a legal prohibition under an unavoidable mistake about the legality of his conduct, we cannot infer anything about his respect for law and the rights of others. The same breakdown in the reasoning from conduct to character occurs in cases of insanity, for it is implicit in the medical conception of insanity that the actor's true character is distorted by his mental illness. . . .

The single most difficult point in the theory of excuses is the relationship between excuses and the norms that govern our conduct. The nature of a justification is that the claim is grounded in an implicit exception to the prohibitory norm. The 'right' of self-defence carves out a set of cases in which violation of the norm is permissible. When the principles of justification are rendered concrete in particular cases, the result is a precedent that other people may properly rely upon in similar cases. If a court recognises a privilege, based on necessity, to shoot a rabies-stricken dog in order to protect children in the neighbourhood, the result modifies the norm against the destruction of property. If deadly force is adjudged permissible against a threatened rape, the norm against homicide is *pro tanto* contracted. In similar cases arising in the future, similarly situated actors may rely on these recognised privileges in planning their conduct. The only requirement for claiming the precedent is the general legal rule that the new case may not be significantly different in its relevant facts.

Excuses bear a totally different relationship to prohibitory norms. They do not constitute exceptions or modifications of the norm, but rather a judgment in the particular case that an individual cannot be fairly held accountable for violating the norm. This fundamental difference means that cases acknowledging that conduct in a particular situation is excused do not generate precedents that other people may rely on in the future. This is obvious in cases of mistake of law, for the judgment of the court serves to advise the public of the rule in question, and therefore in the future there is even less excuse for ignorance of the particular law. ...

Excuses have this peculiar quality, for they occupy a hiatus between two concepts of law. Law in the narrow sense consists solely of the norms prohibiting conduct and laying down the criteria of justification. Law in the broad sense encompasses the total set of criteria that affects the outcomes of particular case. In the ring between these two circles of law, one finds the criteria of excuses as well as other conditions—such as criteria of immunity and the statute of limitations—that affect the outcome of particular cases."

(See further, Glanville Williams, "The Theory of Excuses" [1982] *Crim.L.R.* 732.)

R. v. Graham
(1981) 74 Cr.App.R. 235
Court of Appeal

LORD LANE C.J.: [I]n general, if a mistake is to excuse what would otherwise be criminal, the mistake must be a reasonable one. ...

The correct approach [is] (1) Was the defendant, or may he have been, impelled to act as he did because, as a result of what he reasonably believed [X] had said or done, he had good cause to fear that if he did not so act [X] would kill him or (if this is to be added) cause him serious physical injury? (2) If so, have the prosecution made the jury sure that a sober person of reasonable firmness, sharing the characteristics of the defendant, would not have responded to whatever he reasonably believed [X] said or did by taking part in the killing?

Note

Lord Lane C.J.'s dicta were approved by the House of Lords in *R. v. Howe and Bannister* [1987] 2 W.L.R. 568. In neither case was mistake an issue, so what was said was strictly *obiter*.

Questions

1. Is there any basis in principle why a mistake in respect of an excusatory claim must be based on reasonable grounds when a mistake in respect of a justificatory claim need not be?

2. Is it possible to reconcile Lord Lane's statement in *Williams*, that a defendant must be judged on the basis of the facts as he believed them to be, with his pronouncement in *Graham*?

Proposals for Reform

Draft Criminal Code Bill

"Proof or disproof of states of mind

14. A court or jury, in determining whether a person had, or may have had, a particular state of mind, shall have regard to all the evidence including, where appropriate, the presence or absence of reasonable grounds for having that state of mind.

Ignorance or mistake of law

21. Ignorance or mistake as to a matter of law does not affect liability to conviction of an offence except—

(a)   where so provided; or
(b)   where it negatives a fault element of the offence."

In para. 8.32 of the *Commentary on Draft Criminal Code Bill* (Law Com. No. 177) the Law Commission state—

"8.32 *Ignorance or mistake negativing a fault element.* 'Ignorance of the law is no defence' is a popular aphorism with a good deal of power to mislead. It therefore seems worthwhile to state, in paragraph (b), the truth that a mistake as to the law, equally with one as to fact, can be the reason why a person is not at fault in the way prescribed for an offence."

Appendix B of the Code Report provides the following illustrations—

21(i)   D, removing property from a flat at the end of his tenancy, intentionally damages a fixture. It is a landlord's fixture but D thinks that it belongs to himself. He is not guilty of intentionally damaging property belonging to the landlord.

21(ii)   It is an offence for a person to act as auditor of a company at a time when he knows that he is disqualified from appointment to that office. D, a director of X Ltd., does not know that a director of a company is disqualified from appointment as its auditor. He acts as auditor of X Ltd. He is not guilty of the offence."

Defences

Draft Criminal Code Bill

"Belief in circumstance affording a defence

41.—(1) Unless otherwise provided, a person who acts in the belief that a circumstance exists has any defence that he would have if the circumstance existed.

(2) Subsection (1) does not apply in respect of a defence specially provided for a pre-Code offence as defined in section 6 (to which section 2(3) applies).

(3) Any requirement as to proof or disproof of a defence applies to proof or disproof of a belief mentioned in subsection (1)."

In paras. 12.6–12.8 of the *Commentary on Draft Criminal Code Bill* (Law Com. No. 177) the Law Commission state—

"12.6 *A statutory presumption*. If knowledge of a particular circumstance is an element of an offence, a belief that that circumstance does not exist means that the offence is not committed. Subsection (1) provides a presumption in favour of a corresponding rule for defences, namely, that a person who acts in the belief that a circumstance exists has any defence that he would have if it existed. The Code thus gives general effect to the *prima facie* principles that a person is to be judged, for purposes of criminal liability, on the facts as he believed them to be. This is the tendency, though not the universal effect, of recent judicial developments in the field of defences. It is desirable that the Code should provide consistently for offences and defences, leaving it to Parliament in particular contexts, if it thinks fit, to exclude the application of this subsection or to limit a defence of belief in the existence of an 'exempting circumstance' to a case of a belief based on reasonable grounds. Where a defendant relies on this subsection, the absence of reasonable grounds for the belief he claims to have held is, of course, relevant in determining whether he did hold it.

12.7 *Mistake as to one element of a defence*. A defence may have two or more elements, each of which is, in the language of the Code, an 'exempting circumstance', and a person's mistaken belief may be as to the existence of one such circumstance. Subsection (1) places him in the position that he would be in if his belief were true. For example, a person may be guilty of manslaughter rather than murder if he kills under provocation—that is, if something done or said causes him to lose his self-control (clauses 55(a) and 58). If he mistakenly believes that just such a thing has been done or said, the supposed provocation is treated as actual provocation, and other elements of this special defence to murder (the alleged loss of self-control and the question whether the provocation was sufficient ground for the loss of self-control) are then considered on that basis.

12.8 *Voluntary intoxication*. Subsection (1) has to be read subject to clause 22 (1)(b) and (3). A person who was voluntarily intoxicated is credited, in the case of an offence requiring a fault element of recklessness, with the understanding of the relevant matter that he would have had if he had been sober. Similarly, in the case of an offence requiring a fault element of failure to comply with a standard of care, or requiring no fault, a person who was voluntarily intoxicated is treated as not having believed that an exempting circumstance existed if a reasonable sober person would not have done so."

Note

If the Draft Criminal Code Bill was to be enacted the fine distinctions between definitional elements and excusatory claims (outlined *supra*) would no longer exist; a defendant would be judged on the facts as he believed them to be whether or not there were reasonable grounds for that belief.

ii. Irrelevant Mistakes

(1) Mistake and Strict Liability
(2) Ignorance of the Law
(3) Transferred Malice

Mistakes can only be relevant in crimes which require proof of some mental element. As the preceding sections indicate, the courts, in allocating mistake to one category or another, are making decisions as to what that mental element is and to what parts of the *actus reus* it is to apply. The rules deduced from the cases can be stated without reference to mistake as such. Thus of bigamy it can be said that proof of intention is necessary for the act of getting married while as to the circumstances of being married only negligence is needed. Where an offence is interpreted as not even requiring negligence as to an element of the *actus reus* it is said to be an offence of strict liability. *Prince*, below, illustrates how the creation of such an offence renders the mistake of no legal consequence.

The converse of the opening statement of the above paragraph is not true: mistakes are sometimes irrelevant in *mens rea* crimes. Ignorance of the law is often no defence. In these cases, as in *Prince*, the mistake is *rendered* irrelevant by the law even though, had things been as the defendant supposed, there would have been no offence. However, in cases of transferred malice, the mistake is legally irrelevant because it is immaterial to D.'s culpability whether the victim is the intended one or someone else.

(1) *Mistake and strict liability*

R. v. Prince (1875) L.R. 2 C.C.R. 154: Section 55 of the Offences Against the Person Act 1861 provides that it is an offence "unlawfully [to] take ... any unmarried girl, being under the age of 16 years, out of the possession and against the will of her father. ... " Prince was convicted under this section despite having reasonable grounds to believe the girl concerned was over 16. The following passage is from the judgment of Blackburn J. in which nine other judges concurred (at L.R. 2 C.C.R. 154, 170): "The question ... is reduced to this, whether the words in s.55 [*supra*], are to be read as if they were 'being under the age of sixteen, and he knowing she was under that age.' No such words are contained in the statute, nor is there the word 'maliciously,' 'knowingly,' or any other word used that can be said to involve a similar meaning." See also *R. v. McPherson* [1980] Crim.L.R. 654.

R. v. Miller [1975] 1 W.L.R. 1222: The offence of driving a motor vehicle on a road while disqualified under section 99(6) of the Road Traffic Act 1972 (now s.103 of the Road Traffic Act 1988) was held to have been committed despite the defendant's belief that he was driving on a private road. James L.J., p. 1226: "[W]e have reached the clear conclusion that section 99 ... provides an offence which is proved once the prosecution establish the facts which were not disputed in the present case, namely, that there was driving by a person who was at that time disqualified ...

and that it is not relevant for a defendant to raise the question of his state of mind in order to show ... a mistaken belief as to the nature of the place where the driving was taking place."

R. v. *Howells* [1977] 2 W.L.R. 716: It is an offence under section 1 of the Firearms Act 1968 to possess a revolver without a firearm certificate. Under section 58(2) this does not apply to antique firearms, "purchased ... or possessed as a curiosity or ornament." D thought he possessed an antique; in fact it was a modern reproduction. His appeal against conviction was dismissed by the Court of Appeal, Brown L.J., p. 725: "This court has reached the decision that s.1 should be construed strictly ... to allow a defence of honest and reasonable belief that the firearm was an antique and therefore excluded would be likely to defeat the clear intention of the Act."

L. H. Leigh, *Strict and Vicarious Liability* (1982), pp. 58–61

" ... Lord Diplock in *Sweet* v. *Parsley* suggested that a general due diligence defence might be possible at common law. [S]uch a defence [exists] in Australia and Canada. It is appropriate at this juncture to examine its antecedents and extent, before considering the question upon what basis it might be introduced into English law.

The Australian formulation derives from *Proudman* v. *Dayman* (1943) 67 C.L.R. 536). The charge was that the accused permitted a person, not being the holder of a licence for the time being in force, to drive a motor vehicle on a public road. The question arose whether the accused could raise a defence of honest and reasonable mistake to the charge. Although on the facts there was no basis for such a defence, Dixon J. held that reasonable mistake might be raised as a defence to a charge of a strict liability offence. The reasoning adopted by His Honour was that a holding that the prosecution need not prove intention or recklessness to procure a conviction does not imply that fault has no part in the case. His Honour thus states:

'It is one thing to deny that a necessary ingredient of the offence is positive knowledge of the fact that the driver holds no subsisting licence. It is another to say that an honest belief founded on reasonable grounds that he is licensed cannot exculpate a person who permits him to drive. As a general rule an honest and reasonable belief in a state of facts which, if they existed, would make the defendant's act innocent affords an excuse for doing what would otherwise be an offence.' (at 540)

From this it followed that, save in an exceptional case where liability is truly intended to be absolute, the accused might defend himself by showing that he exercised due diligence to comply with the law. The affinity of this thought to those English cases which insisted that an absence of *mens rea* words simply shifted the burden of proof is plain.

The result of this approach is to create three categories of statutory offences: those in which the prosecution must prove full *mens rea*: those in which it need not prove *mens rea* but the accused may raise as a defence to a charge that he or she exercised all due diligence: and those in which liability is absolute. In this latter case, the legislature must make it clear that absolute liability is intended.

It is impossible to indicate what view English courts will ultimately take of the place of fault as a common law principle. In *Sweet* v. *Parsley* Lords

Reid, Pearce and Diplock intimated that the question of due diligence defences may not be entirely foreclosed by authority. In *R.* v. *Warner*, Lord Guest had thought that the half-way house represented by the Australian cases was blocked by the decision in *Woolmington* v. *D.P.P.* that the Crown must prove, beyond a reasonable doubt, all the elements of the case. In *Sweet* v. *Parsley*, Lord Diplock intimates that this point may need to be reconsidered: *Woolmington*, his Lordship states, is no bar to the use of honest and reasonable mistake as a solvent of strict liability cases since it only decides that where there is evidence of a defence, a jury must consider it and acquit the accused unless they are sure that the accused did not hold a particular belief, or there are no reasonable grounds for it.

Dicta in *Morgan* also suggest that a common law no fault defence is possible, but they are very confused. The *ratio* of the case is that in rape, an honest mistake as to the existence of the elements of the offence is a defence. The House of Lords was, however, obliged to explain away a series of cases on bigamy which held that a mistake had both to be honest and reasonable to afford a defence. Lord Cross drew a distinction between offences which require *mens rea* and those which do not. Some *mens rea* offences specify the mental element required for the offence: in respect of them, mistake need only be honest. Other *mens rea* offences do not specify any mental element: in their case, mistake must be both honest and reasonable. Where no *mens rea* is required at all, mistake will not excuse the defendant. On this view, a mistake defence would only be available where a court was prepared to construe an offence which is silent as to the mental element, as involving *mens rea*. Why there should be a difference between two classes of *mens rea* offences is obscure. Lord Hailsham took a different view of the bigamy cases. He treated the leading case, *Tolson*, as a narrow decision based on the construction of a statute which *prima facie* appeared to create an absolute offence subject to a statutory defence related to a seven year period of absence. His Lordship suggests this explanation:

> 'The judges ... decided that this was not reasonable, and, on general jurisprudential principles, imported into the statutory offence words which created a special "defence" of honest and reasonable belief of which the "evidential," but not the probative burden lay on the defence.'

If Lord Hailsham's suggestion were adopted, there would be no reason why honest and reasonable mistake, or a showing by the accused that he used due diligence to comply with the law, should not afford a defence to crimes of strict liability generally, subject always to the power of Parliament to legislate so as to exclude it. If the general jurisprudential principle referred to (whatever it may be) can be invoked to prevent injustice in one case, there seems no reason why it could not be invoked in another. No doubt a tendency to do so would be most marked where a penalty of imprisonment was available and sometimes imposed for the offence, or where the stigma attaching to conviction for that offence was very considerable. Where the usual penalty was a fine, an inference that no such defence was intended might well be drawn, as it might where an adequate statutory scheme of defences was already provided. But all these are possibilities latent in *dicta* in leading cases; no court has sought to build upon them. It cannot be said with certainty therefore, whether the courts will continue to recognise defences based upon particular statutory words, or whether they will take the further step of creating a general due diligence defence which would be displaced only where a particular scheme made it clear that no such defence was intended."

Question

Would the defence of honest and reasonable belief stated by Dixon J. in *Proudman* v. *Dayman* have availed the defendants in *Prince, Miller* and *Howells, supra*, if it had existed in English common law?

(2) *Ignorance of the law*

R. v. *Smith, post*, p. 864 and *R.* v. *Gould* [1968] 1 All E.R. 849 indicate that mistake of civil law can preclude a person from having the requisite mental element for a particular offence.

Secretary of State for Trade and Industry v. Hart
[1982] 1 All E.R. 817
Queen's Bench Division

Hart acted as the auditor of two companies although as a director of each company he was disqualified from so doing by virtue of section 161(2) of the Companies Act 1948. He was charged with acting as an auditor of a company knowing that he was disqualified for appointment as auditor, contrary to s.161(2) of the 1948 Act and section 13(5) and (6) of the Companies Act 1976. Hart submitted that as he did not know of the statutory provisions disqualifying him, he could not be guilty. The magistrate dismissed the case because of Hart's ignorance of the law and the Secretary of State appealed.

WOOLF J.: . . . The fact that Mr. Hart, during the relevant period, had acted as auditor of those companies, at a time when he was disqualified as alleged in the information, was not in dispute before the stipendiary magistrate. The only matter that was in issue was whether or not Mr. Hart had the necessary *mens rea* to constitute the offences which were alleged. . . .

In subs. (2) [of section 161] it is stated:

"None of the following persons shall be qualified for appointment as auditor of a company—(*a*) an officer or servant of the company; (*b*) a person who is a partner of or in the employment of an officer or servant of the company; (*c*) a body corporate."

The term "officer" is defined in s.455 of that Act as including a director, manager or secretary. So clearly, because of the provisions of subs. (2), although Mr. Hart had been authorised to act as an auditor, he was not qualified to hold the appointment in a company in respect of which he was a director or secretary. . . .
Subsection (5) [of section 13 of the 1976 Act] provides:

"No person shall act as auditor of a company at a time when he knows that he is disqualified for appointment to that office; and if an auditor of a company to his knowledge becomes so disqualified during his term of office he shall thereupon vacate his office and give notice in writing to the company that he has vacated it by reason of such disqualification."

Subsection (5) therefore creates the disqualification which arises as a result of persons holding particular offices. . . .

Subsection (6) of s.13 of the 1976 Act widens the categories of persons who could be guilty of a criminal offence in relation to this matter. It provides:

"Any person who acts as auditor in contravention of subsection (5) above or fails without reasonable excuse to give notice of vacating his office as required by that subsection shall be guilty of an offence and liable on conviction on indictment to a fine and on summary conviction to a fine not exceeding £40 for every day during which the contravention continues."

It is subss. (5) and (6) of s.13 of the 1976 Act that this court is primarily concerned with in answering the question posed by this appeal. Counsel on behalf of the Secretary of State argues that when subss. (5) and (6) are read together the position is one where a person is guilty of an offence under those provisions if he knows the facts or circumstances which cause him to be disqualified but nonetheless acts as an auditor. He contends that it is not necessary for a person charged with an offence under those subsections also to know as a matter of law he is disqualified. He submits that it is sufficient if he knows the facts and circumstances, because like anyone else a person acting as an auditor should be aware of the provisions of the law which deal with the disqualification for an appointment to the office of auditor.

This is, however, as I have already pointed out, a criminal offence which is created by s.13(5) and (6). In my view it is at least equally consistent with the ordinary meaning of the words which are used in those subsections, that their effect is that a person is not guilty of an offence and is not disqualified from acting as an auditor unless he in fact knows not only the relevant facts but also that in consequence of the facts he is disqualified by the law for appointment to the office. The words in their ordinary interpretation are wholly consistent with a view of the subsections which means that a person in the position of Mr. Hart must be aware of the statutory restrictions which exist against his holding the appointment. . . .

[T]he wording we have to consider, introduced by s.13 of the Companies Act 1976, clearly requires some form of *mens rea*, and clearly requires it expressly. . . . Counsel for the Secretary of State concedes that the offence here created is not an absolute offence. . . . However, he wishes to introduce a limited form of knowledge as being necessary. In my view it would be wrong to introduce such a limitation, bearing in mind the express words here are open to the interpretation which I have indicated. Because it is wrong, and would be an undesirable limitation on the normal principles of statutory construction in relation to a criminal offence, to qualify what is required as *mens rea*, it is my view that the stipendiary magistrate in this case came to the right decision.

ORMROD L.J.: [After referring to subsections (5) and (6) of section 13 of the 1976 Act] (T)he offence, as was correctly set out in the information, is that Mr. Hart acted as an auditor of a company at a time when he knew that he was disqualified for that appointment. And interpreting the language quite simply, it seems to me to indicate that Mr. Hart is not guilty of a criminal offence unless he knew that he was disqualified.

If that means that he is entitled to rely on ignorance of the law as a defence, in contrast to the usual practice and the usual rule, the answer is that the section gives him that right. . . .

Appeal dismissed

Question

Would the result have been different if Mr. Hart's submission had been that while he knew he was disqualified under the Companies Acts from acting as an auditor, he did not know that this constituted a criminal offence?

Note

Compare the outcome in *Hart* with *Grant* v. *Borg* [1982] 1 W.L.R. 638, where the accused (a non-patrial with limited leave to remain in the United Kingdom) was charged with knowingly remaining beyond the time limited by the leave, contrary to section 24(1)(*b*)(i) of the Immigration Act 1971. On the issue whether a mistake, as to whether "leave to remain" had expired, was relevant, Lord Bridge stated:

> "The principle that ignorance of the law is no defence in crime is so fundamental that to construe the word 'knowingly' in a criminal statute as requiring not merely knowledge of the facts material to the offender's guilt, but also knowledge of the relevant law, would be revolutionary and, to my mind, wholly unacceptable."

Ignorance of the law in the sense of not realising that a particular act is prohibited is rarely a defence. People are presumed to know the law. Two justifications have been advanced for this constructive knowledge:

Oliver Wendell Holmes, *The Common Law* (1881), p. 48:
"[T]o admit the excuse at all would be to encourage ignorance ... and justice to the individual is rightly outweighed by the larger interests on the other side of the scales."

Hall, p. 382:
"If that plea [mistake of law] were valid, the consequence would be: wherever a defendant in a criminal case thought the law was thus and so, he is to be treated as though the law were thus and so, i.e. *the law actually is thus and so*. But such a doctrine would contradict the essential requisites of a legal system. ... " (italics in original).

Hall's view seems logically attractive but does any defence of mistake, whether of fact or law, alter either factual reality or the law itself? In any case, this view fails to recognise that ignorance of the law does sometimes affect culpability. When an offence is confined to a particular class of prohibited persons and the means of discovering who is in that class are obscure, ignorance may be excused: Lord Evershed in *Lim Chin Aik* v. *The Queen*, *post*, p. 187, [1963] A.C. 160, 171: "[T]he maxim [ignorance of the law is no excuse] cannot apply to such a case as the present where it appears that there is ... no provision ... for the publication in any form of an order of the kind made in the present case or any other provision designed to enable a man by appropriate inquiry to find out what 'the law' is." The United States' Supreme Court has allowed a defence of ignorance to an offence of "failing to register as a convicted person": *Lambert* v. *California* 355 U.S. 225 (1957). The court drew a distinction between crimes of commission, where ignorance could never be a defence, and crimes of omission, where it may be, unless the failure to act is under circumstances which should alert the doer to the consequences of such failure. Mr. Justice Douglas said, at p. 232: "Were it otherwise, the evil would be as great as it is when the law is written in print too fine to read, or in language foreign to the community." Can this be reconciled with Holmes's statement above? See, generally, A. J. Ashworth, "Excusable Mistake of Law" [1974] Crim.L.R. 652.

(3) *Transferred malice*

R. v. Pembliton
(1874) L.R. 2 C.C.R. 119
Court for Crown Cases Reserved

The defendant was a member of a group who were fighting outside the public-house called The Grand Turk. He picked up a large stone and threw it at those with whom he had been fighting. The stone passed over their heads and broke a window of the public-house. The defendant was indicted for "unlawfully and maliciously" committing damage under the Malicious Damage Act 1861, s.51. The jury found that he had intended to strike the persons at whom he aimed the stone and that he did not intend to break the window.

LORD COLERIDGE C.J.: I am of the opinion that the evidence does not support the conviction. The indictment is under [section 51, Malicious Damage Act 1861] which deals with malicious injuries to property, and the section expressly says that the act is to be unlawful and malicious. There is also the fifty-eighth section, which makes it immaterial whether the offence has been committed from malice against the owner of the property or otherwise, that is, from malice against someone not the owner of the property. In both these sections it seems to me that what is intended by the statute is a wilful doing of an intentional act. Without saying that if the case had been left to them in a different way the conviction could not have been supported, if, on these facts, the jury had come to the conclusion that the prisoner was reckless of the consequence of his act, and might reasonably have expected that it would result in breaking the window, it is sufficient to say that the jury have expressly found the contrary. . . .

BLACKBURN J.: We have not now to consider what would be malice aforethought to bring a given case within the common law definition of murder; here the statute says that the act must be unlawful and malicious, and malice may be defined to be "where any person wilfully does an act injurious to another without lawful excuse." Can this man be considered, on the case submitted to us, as having wilfully broken a pane of glass? The jury might perhaps have found on this evidence that the act was malicious, because they might have found that the prisoner knew that the natural consequence of his act would be to break the glass, and although that was not his wish, yet that he was reckless whether he did it or not;

but the jury have not so found, and I think it is impossible to say in this case that the prisoner has maliciously done an act which he did not intend to do.

Conviction quashed

R. v. Latimer
(1886) 17 Q.B.D. 359
Court for Crown Cases Reserved

L., who was quarrelling with C. in a public-house aimed a blow at C. with his belt. The belt glanced off C. and severely injured R. In answer to questions by the recorder the jury found that the striking of R. was purely accidental and not such a consequence of the blow as the prisoner ought to have expected to follow. They also found that the blow was unlawful and malicious. L. was found guilty of unlawful and malicious wounding.

LORD COLERIDGE C.J.: We are of opinion that this conviction must be sustained. It is common knowledge that a man who has an unlawful and malicious intent against another, and, in attempting to carry it out, injures a third person, is guilty of what the law deems malice against the person injured, because the offender is doing an unlawful act, and has that which the judges call general malice, and that is enough. ... So, but for *R. v. Pembliton (supra)*, there would not have been the slightest difficulty. Does that case make any difference? I think not, and, on consideration, that it was quite rightly decided. But it is clearly distinguishable, because the indictment in *R. v. Pembliton* was on the Act making unlawful and malicious injury to property a statutory offence punishable in a certain way, and the jury expressly negatived, the facts expressly negatived, any intention to do injury to property, and the court held that under the Act making it an offence to injure any property there must be an intent to injure property. *R. v. Pembliton*, therefore, does not govern the present case, and on no other ground is there anything to be said for the prisoner.

Conviction affirmed

(See also *R. v. Mitchell* [1983] 2 W.L.R. 938.)

R. v. Martin
(1881) 8 Q.B.D. 54
Court for Crown Cases Reserved

Shortly before the end of a theatrical performance the defendant, with the intention of causing terror in the minds of persons leaving the theatre, put out the lights on a staircase which a large number would descend. He also put an iron bar across a doorway with the intention of obstructing the exit. As a result several persons were injured. He was charged with unlawfully and maliciously inflicting grievous bodily harm and was convicted. The jury found these intentions in reply to questions put to them.

LORD COLERIDGE C.J.: I am unable to entertain any doubt as to the propriety of this conviction. The prisoner was indicted under [section 20 of the Offences Against the Person Act 1861], which enacts that "whosoever shall unlawfully and maliciously wound, or inflict any grievous bodily harm upon any other person, either with or without any weapon or instrument, shall be guilty of misdemeanour, etc." [He then stated the facts.]

Upon these facts the prisoner was convicted, and the jury found all that was necessary to sustain the conviction. The prisoner must be taken to have intended the natural consequences of that which he did. He acted "unlawfully and maliciously," not that he had any personal malice against the particular individuals injured, but in the sense of doing an unlawful act calculated to injure, and by which others were in fact injured. Just as in the case of a man who unlawfully fires a gun among a crowd, it is murder if one of the crowd is thereby killed. The prisoner was most properly convicted.

STEPHEN J.: I am entirely of the same opinion, but I wish to add that the recorder seems to have put the case too favourably for the prisoner, for he put it to the jury to consider whether the prisoner did the act "as a mere piece of foolish mischief." Now, it seems to me, that if the prisoner did that which he did as a piece of foolish mischief unlawfully and without excuse, he did it "wilfully," that is "maliciously," within the meaning of the statute. I think it important to notice this as the word "malicious" is capable of being misunderstood. Lord Blackburn (then Mr. Justice Blackburn) in the cases of *R.* v. *Ward* (1872) L.R. 1 C.C.R. 356 at p. 360 and *R.* v. *Pembliton*, above, lays it down that a man acts "maliciously" when he wilfully and without lawful excuse does that which he knows will injure another.

Conviction affirmed

Questions

1. The defendant in *Martin*, above, had no mental element in relation to any particular person. Was the decision in *Latimer*, *supra*, decided in a similar vein?

2. Has the time come to move away from notions of "transferred malice" and to recognise that the problem to which it relates is soluble by the straightforward application of the principles of *actus reus* and *mens rea* without the need for recourse to this artificial doctrine? See the article which follows.

I. H. E. Patient, "Transferred Malice—A Misleading Misnomer" (1990) 54 J.C.L. 116–124

"Assume that X aims a shot at A, intending to kill A. The shot misses the intended victim, but hits and kills B instead. There are two ways of looking at this situation.

The first approach is based on the notion that one must distinguish between a 'killing of victim A' and a 'killing of victim B'. As to A, the intended killing did not succeed. Hence, there might be a charge of attempted murder. As to B, there was no intention to kill 'B', hence no murder of B. However, a lesser form of homicide, namely manslaughter, might be given, either in the form of constructive manslaughter (the unlawful act need not be directed against the eventual victim) or in the form of reckless killing (if B stood close to A there would be at least an obvious risk that B might be hit).

Alternatively, one might ignore the particular identity of the victim. The *actus reus* of homicide is not the 'killing of A' or the 'killing of B', but in

more general terms the 'killing of a human being'. Accordingly, the
required intention is that of 'killing a human being'. On that basis, X, in
our example, has committed a murder of B, for he killed a human being
(namely B) and he did so with the required intention of killing a human
being (namely A). This second, more streamlined, solution is capable of
avoiding certain practical difficulties, especially of proof, and moreover
represents, it is submitted, the more correct approach in principle,
provided it is clearly seen as resting on the application of the general
principles of *actus reus* and *mens rea*. Unfortunately, it is often rationalised
in a different manner, namely as an instance of so called 'transferred
malice'. In other words, the case is seen as one where the intention to kill
victim A is 'transferred' to victim B. Such a view must be based on the
assumption that the *mens rea* for murder is the killing (or causing of
grievous bodily harm) to a particular victim, namely, in our case, an
'intention to kill A' as opposed to an 'intention to kill B', so that the
required intention can then be 'transferred' from one victim to the other.
This kind of thinking seems to be, consciously or otherwise, influenced by
a preoccupation with the form of the indictment, where, of course, the
particular victim is referred to. Now that the principles of *actus reus* and
mens rea have become more clearly established, not least as the direct and
indirect result of increasing codification, such a misleading way of thinking
must be challenged, in order to curb the creation of avoidable difficulties.
Significantly, one of the early leading cases, *R.* v. *Latimer* [*ante*, p. 176],
which is often relied upon as an authority for the notion of transferred
malice, in fact rejects that concept and adopts the approach described
above of simply applying the principles of *actus reus* and *mens rea*. The
facts of the case were these: the prisoner, X, aimed a blow at A with his
belt. The belt bounded off and struck B, who stood close by, and caused
wounds to her (B's) face. X was convicted under section 20 of the Offences
Against the Person Act 1861. An appeal was taken on the ground that X
could not be guilty of injuring B, as he did not intend to injure her.

   This argument could only be conceived on the implied assumption that
the offence in question was the wounding of a particular victim, namely B,
as opposed to the wounding of another victim, A. The court made short
shrift of this idea. The *actus reus* of the offence in section 20 is the inflicting
of grievous bodily harm upon *any other person* and the prisoner had the
necessary *general malice*. It was, therefore, not a question of establishing an
intention to injure a particular victim, which would then be 'transferred' to
another victim. Rather, the accused had the necessary 'general' *mens rea* of
intending to inflict grievous bodily harm upon any (other) person.
Whether that person was A or B, was irrelevant.

   Now let us assume that X hurls a stone at A, intending to injure him,
but that the stone misses A and instead breaks a window in front of which
A has been standing. X is charged with causing criminal damage to the
window. The *actus reus* of the offence is the destroying of the property
belonging to another. The necessary *mens rea* would be the intention to
destroy such property or recklessness as to such destruction. In the
situation above, there is clearly no intention to destroy the window. A
conviction will turn on whether there is at least recklessness, which on the
facts is not unlikely. In such a situation the idea of marrying the *actus reus*
of causing damage to property, to the *mens rea* of intending to injure a
person, seems absurd and would not occur to someone who simply
applies the principles of *actus reus* and *mens rea* and who has never thought
in terms of 'transferring' elements of a charge. The facts and reasoning
outlined above are in essence those of *R.* v. *Pembliton* [*ante*, p. 175], a
decision under the then Malicious Damage Act 1861. The court quashed

the conviction for malicious damage which had been based on a finding by the jury that the accused had thrown the stone 'intending to strike [people] but not to break the window'. The court thus rejected an attempt to borrow (or transfer) an 'intention to injure' as *mens rea* for a completely different offence, namely the 'damaging of property.' A conviction might have been upheld, had the jury found that there was at least recklessness *as to the window, i.e.* had the prisoner thrown the stone 'knowing that there was a window near which it might probably hit'.

To summarise the argument so far: In the cases under discussion, the original plan misfires in that a target, other than that envisaged, is affected. ... Whether there is liability concerning the substituted target, turns solely on whether the necessary *mens rea* relating to the *actus reus* in question, is given. There is no transfer of any kind involved. If the *actus reus* is described as the 'wounding of any other person' (s.20 Offences Against the Person Act 1861), then an intention to wound another person constitutes the required *mens rea*, irrespective of whether the intention relates to a person called 'A' or 'B'. To use the terminology of the new Draft Criminal Code Bill, A, as much as B, is 'capable of being the victim of the offence', since he is capable of coming under the description 'any other person'. Hence, if X, intending to wound A, wounds B by mistake, X can be guilty of wounding B. He wounds another person and he intends to do so. Both *actus reus* and *mens rea* of the relevant offence are given. Anyone who sees this as involving a transfer, can do so only on the basis of a distorted, artificially narrowed view of *mens rea*. He must assume that section 20 requires an 'intention to wound B' as opposed to an 'intention to wound A', so that, B having actually been injured in place of A, the intention relating to A can be 'transferred' to B. That, as has been explained above, is *not* the approach in the relevant cases. By way of contrast, let it be assumed that B, the substitute-victim in our example, is a police constable and that X is charged with assaulting a constable in the execution of his duty under section 51(1) of the Police Act 1964. X's intention to assault a non-policeman, A, cannot—it is submitted—constitute the necessary *mens rea* for the charge. For the *actus reus* in section 51 requires not 'any person', but 'a constable' and A, not being a constable, is in the words of clause 24 of the Draft Code, not capable of being the victim of the offence in section 51. Thus, it is entirely a matter of testing the *mens rea* against the wording of the relevant *actus reus*. To see this as a situation where a 'transfer from one victim to another is impossible' would be inappropriate and distorting. The victim of the offence in section 51 cannot be A in the first place.

Occasionally, an offence requires a specific intent directed against a particular victim. An example is section 24 of the Offences Against the Person Act 1861, which speaks of maliciously administering a poison or other noxious thing to any person with intent to annoy *such* (not 'any') person. Assume that X intends to annoy A by making him ill. To this end he mixes an emetic into a drink which he expects A to consume. Things do not go according to plan. B drinks from the glass intended for A and becomes violently ill. Is X liable under section 24 for the harm done to B? At first glance it looks as though the only possible basis for such liability must be a transfer of X's specific intent directed against A, to B. However, it should not be forgotten that, apart from a specific intent, the offence also requires first of all basic *mens rea* namely intention or recklessness (as is made over-abundantly clear by the term 'maliciously'). Hence, in order to establish X's liability, it must be shown that he intended to administer a noxious substance to *any* person or was reckless as to the doing thereof. Only then, over and above such basic *mens rea*, do the prosecution have to establish the specific intent, namely the intention to annoy *such* person. In our hypothetical case X administers a noxious substance to a(ny) person, namely B, intending to administer that substance to a(ny) person, namely A, with, furthermore, the intention of annoying *such* person, *i.e.* A. Thus, even in these cases, where a statute stipulates a specific intent relating to a particular victim, liability concerning the substitute-target is not based on any notions of transfer. . . .

In conclusion then, there have been in the Criminal Law two inconsistent rationalisations of the assumption of liability concerning a substitute-victim (or substitute-subject-matter). In times when the form of the indictment had to be of paramount importance, the temptation was to think in terms of an intention relating to a particular named victim (or object), which intention would then be 'transferred' to the substitute-target. In more recent times the *actus reus* of an offence is defined with greater precision, so that it becomes simply a matter of testing the *mens rea* in the light of the wording of the relevant *actus reus*. Thus, the *mens rea* either relates to a victim or subject-matter as described in the *actus reus*, or it does not. Or, in the words of the Draft Code, it either relates 'to a person or thing capable of being the victim or subject-matter of the offence' or it does not. There is, on this basis, nothing that could be transferred. Unfortunately, clause 24 of the Draft Criminal Code Bill appears to combine both these inconsistent approaches. Whether a 'person or thing is capable of being the victim or subject-matter of the offence' can only be tested against the definition of the relevant offence and it thus, it is submitted, embodies the correct *actus reus/mens rea* approach. However, the unfortunate reference in the margin of the clause to 'transferred' fault, together with any notions of transference, should be jettisoned. Otherwise this is likely to preserve an outdated approach which, lacking in precision, is capable of creating incidental difficulties."

Proposals for reform

Draft Criminal Code Bill

"Transferred fault and defences

24.—(1) In determining whether a person is guilty of an offence, his intention to cause, or his recklessness whether he causes, a result in relation to a person or thing capable of being the victim or subject-matter of the offence shall be treated as an intention to cause or, as the case may be, recklessness whether he causes that result in relation to any other person or thing affected by his conduct.

(2) Any defence on which a person might have relied on a charge of an offence in relation to a person or thing within his contemplation is open to him on a charge of the same offence in relation to a person or thing not within his contemplation."

Commentary on Draft Criminal Code Bill, Law Com. No. 177

"Clause 24: Transferred fault and defences

8.56 Subsection (1) restates the doctrine known as 'transferred intent' and subsection (2) provides a corresponding rule as to 'transferred' defences.

8.57 *Transferred fault.* A general statement on transferred fault has the following practical justifications:

(i) Where a person intends to affect one person or thing (X) and actually affects another (Y), he may be charged with an offence of attempt in relation to X; or it may be possible to satisfy a court or jury, without resort to the doctrine, that he was reckless with respect to Y. But an attempt charge may be impossible (where it is not known until trial that the defendant claims to have had X and not Y in contemplation); or inappropriate (as not describing the harm done adequately for labelling or sentencing purposes). Moreover, recklessness with respect to Y may be insufficient to establish the offence or incapable of being proved. The rule stated by this subsection overcomes these difficulties.

(ii) The drafting of particular offences is simplified. This may be seen by comparing section 1 of the Criminal Damage Act 1971 with its Code equivalent in clause 180, which is written with the present subsection in mind.

8.58 *Transfer 'only within the same crime'.* If an offence can be committed only in respect of a particular class of person or thing, the actor's intention or recklessness, to be 'transferred', must relate to such a person or thing—that is, in the words of the subsection, to 'a person or thing capable of being the victim or subject-matter of the offence'. If, on the other hand, the person or thing actually affected is not so capable, the external elements of the offence are not made out and the question of transferring the actor's fault does not arise.

8.59 *Wording of offences and charges.* The subsection treats an intention to affect X as an intention to affect Y (who is actually affected). So where an offence requires an affecting of a person with intention to affect *him* (as opposed to 'any person'), there can still be a conviction; and a charge of an offence committed against Y with the intention of affecting Y can be proved by evidence of an intention to affect X. Case law on these points is not consistent; but the results achieved by the subsection are convenient and are in keeping with the best authority.

8.60 *Mistake as to victim.* Clause 24(1) is so worded as to deal also with the case of an irrelevant mistake about the identity of the victim or subject-matter of an offence. The argument, 'I thought Y was X; I intended to hit X; therefore I did not intend to hit Y', hardly needs a statutory answer; but this provision incidentally provides one.

8.61 *Transferred defences.* Subsection (2), providing for the transfer of defences, will be useful for the avoidance of doubt. It enables a person who affects an uncontemplated victim to rely on a defence that would have been available to him if he had affected the person or thing he had in contemplation."

Illustrations in Appendix B

"24(i)   D does an act by which he intends to injure O. He misses O but injures P, whom he does not intend to injure or have in mind as likely to be injured. He is guilty of intentionally causing personal harm to another. He may be convicted of this offence on an indictment or information alleging an intention to cause personal harm to P.

24(ii)   D wishes to injure O. He aims a blow at P, believing him to be O. He is guilty of attempting to cause personal harm to P. If he hits and injures P, he is guilty of intentionally causing personal harm to P.

24(iii) D, under provocation, aims a shot at O with intent to kill him. The shot misses O and kills P. D may raise the plea of provocation under clause 58."

4. STRICT LIABILITY

i. The Evolution of Strict Liability

"Justice," the British Section of the International Commission of Jurists, has estimated that, of the 7,200 separate offences listed in Stone's Justices' Manual for 1975, over half did not require proof of a mental element. (Justice, *Breaking the Rules* (1980)).

Sayre, "Public Welfare Offences" (1933) 33 Col.L.R. 55

"The growth of a distinct group of offences punishable without regard to any mental element dates from about the middle of the nineteenth century. Before this, convictions for crime without proof of a *mens rea* are to be found only occasionally, chiefly among the nuisance cases. In the early days newspaper proprietors might also be punished ... for libel without proof of *mens rea*, for in libel prosecutions actual criminal knowledge on the part of the owners or publishers of newspapers would often be a matter so difficult to ascertain as to make proof well-nigh impossible. Yet to treat as criminal newspaper owners who were altogether innocent of any criminal intent seemed so harsh and unjust a doctrine and so out of accord with established legal principles that in 1836 an act of Parliament was passed to make this no longer possible [Lord Campbell's Act: s.7 allowed a newspaper proprietor to escape liability by proving that the publication was made 'without his authority, consent or knowledge.'] But apart from exceptional isolated cases criminal liability depended upon proof of a criminal intent. ...

The decisions permitting convictions of light police offences without proof of a guilty mind came just at the time when the demands of an increasingly complex social order required additional regulation of an administrative character unrelated to questions of personal guilt; the movement also synchronised with the trend of the day away from nineteenth century individualism toward a new sense of the importance of collective interests. The result was almost inevitable. The doctrine first evolved in the adulterated food and liquor cases came to be recognised as a special class of offence for which no *mens rea* was required. ... The interesting fact that the same development took place in both England and the United States at about the same time strongly indicates that the movement has been not merely an historical accident but the result of the changing social conditions and beliefs of the day. ...

The problem is how to draw the line between those offences which do and those which do not require *mens rea*. Clearly, it will not depend on whether the crime happens to be a common law or statutory offence. ... Some courts have suggested that the line depends upon the distinction between *mala in se* and *mala prohibita*; and this seems to depend essentially upon whether or not the offence is inherently immoral. But this also is ... unsound. ... Many offences which are held not to require proof of *mens rea* are highly immoral; and many requiring it are not inherently immoral at all. ...

Neither can the dividing line be drawn according to the gravity or the lightness of the offence. Petty larceny is a much lighter and less dangerous offence than selling narcotics or poisoned food, yet the former requires *mens rea* and the latter not. . . .

How then can one determine practically which offences do and which do not require *mens rea*, when the statute creating the offence is . . . silent?. . . . [T]wo cardinal principles stand out upon which the determination must turn.

The first relates to the character of the offence. All criminal enactments in a sense serve the double purpose of singling out wrongdoers for the purpose of punishment or correction and of regulating the social order. But often the importance of the one far outweighs the other. . . .

The second criterion depends upon the possible penalty. If this be serious . . . the individual interest of the defendant weighs too heavily to allow conviction without proof of a guilty mind. . . . Crimes punishable with prison sentences, therefore, ordinarily require proof of a guilty intent."

ii. The Present Uncertainty

Williams, T.C.L., p. 934

"In general, the authorities on strict liability are so conflicting that it is impossible to abstract any coherent principle on when this form of liability arises and when it does not."

However, it is possible to detect trends. It can be said that up to 1969 and the case of *Sweet* v. *Parsley* (*post*, p. 190), the stricter approach exemplified in *Prince* (*ante*, p. 169), requiring close attention to the actual statutory words, generally prevailed over the more liberal attitude implicit in *Tolson* (*ante*, p. 159). But consistency was, and still is, lacking.

Cundy v. Le Cocq
(1884) 13 Q.B.D. 207
Queen's Bench Division

C., a licensed victualler, sold liquor to a person who was drunk. C. was unaware of the drunkenness, but he was nevertheless convicted of unlawfully selling liquor to a drunken person, contrary to section 13 of the Licensing Act 1872. C. appealed to the Divisional Court.

STEPHEN J.: I am of opinion that this conviction should be affirmed. Our answer to the question put to us turns upon this, whether the words of the section under which this conviction took place, taken in connection with the general scheme of the Act, should be read as constituting an offence only where the licensed person knows or has means of knowing that the person served with intoxicating liquor is drunk, or whether the offence is complete where no such knowledge is shown. I am of opinion that the words of the section amount to an absolute prohibition of the sale of liquor to a drunken person, and that the existence of a bona fide mistake as to the condition of the person served is not an answer to the charge, but is a matter only for mitigation of the penalties that may be imposed. I am led to that conclusion both by the general scope of the Act, which is for the repression of drunkenness, and from a comparison of the

various sections under the head "offences against public order." Some of
these contain the word "knowingly," as for instance section 14, which
deals with keeping a disorderly house, and section 16, which deals with
the penalty for harbouring a constable. Knowledge in these and other
cases is an element in the offence; but the clause we are considering says
nothing about the knowledge of the state of the person served. I believe
the reason for making this prohibition absolute was that there must be a
great temptation to a publican to sell liquor without regard to the sobriety
of the customer, and it was thought right to put upon the publican the
responsibility of determining whether his customer is sober. Against this
view we have had quoted the maxim that in every criminal offence there
must be a guilty mind; but I do not think that maxim has so wide an
application as it is sometimes considered to have. In old time, and as
applicable to the common law or to earlier statutes, the maxim may have
been of general application; but a difference has arisen owing to the
greater precision of modern statutes. It is impossible now, as illustrated by
the cases of *R. v. Prince* (ante, p. 169), and *R. v. Bishop* (1880) 5 Q.B.D. 259,
to apply the maxim generally to all statutes, and the substance of all the
reported cases is that it is necessary to look at the object of each Act that is
under consideration to see whether and how far knowledge is of the
essence of the offence created. Here, as I have already pointed out, the
object of this part of the Act is to prevent the sale of intoxicating liquor to
drunken persons, and it is perfectly natural to carry that out by throwing
on the publican the responsibility of determining whether the person
supplied comes within that category.

I think, therefore, the conviction was right and must be affirmed.

Conviction affirmed

Sherras v. De Rutzen
[1895] 1 Q.B. 918
Queen's Bench Division

S, a licensed victualler, was convicted under section 16(2) of the
Licensing Act 1872, for having unlawfully supplied liquor to a police
constable on duty without having the authority of a superior officer of
such constable for so doing. S reasonably believed that the constable
was off duty. He appealed to quarter sessions and thence to the
Divisional Court.

DAY J.: I am clearly of opinion that this conviction ought to be quashed.
This police constable comes into the appellant's house without his armlet,
and with every appearance of being off duty. The house was in the
immediate neighbourhood of the police-station, and the appellant believed,
and he had very natural grounds for believing, that the constable was off
duty. In that belief he accordingly served him with liquor. As a matter of
fact, the constable was on duty—but does that fact make the innocent act
of the appellant an offence? I do not think it does. He had no intention to
do a wrongful act; he acted in the bona fide belief that the constable was
off duty. It seems to me that the contention that he committed an offence
is utterly erroneous. An argument has been based on the appearance of
the word "knowingly" in subsection (1) of section 16, and its omission in
subsection (2). In my opinion the only effect of this is to shift the burden
of proof. In cases under subsection (1) it is for the prosecution to prove the
knowledge, while in cases under subsection (2) the defendant has to prove
that he did not know. That is the only inference I draw from the insertion

of the word "knowingly" in the one subsection and its omission in the other.

It appears to me that it would be straining the law to say that this publican, acting as he did in the bona fide belief that the constable was off duty, and having reasonable grounds for that belief, was nevertheless guilty of an offence against the section for which he was liable both to a penalty and to have his licence indorsed.

WRIGHT J.: I am of the same opinion. There are many cases on the subject, and it is not very easy to reconcile them. There is a presumption that *mens rea*, an evil intention, or a knowledge of the wrongfulness of the act, is an essential ingredient in every offence; but that presumption is liable to be displaced either by the words of the statute creating the offence or by the subject-matter with which it deals, and both must be considered: *Nichols* v. *Hall* (1873) L.R. 8 C.P. 322. One of the most remarkable exceptions was in the case of bigamy. It was held by all the judges, on the statute 1 Jac. 1, c. 11, that a man was rightly convicted of bigamy who had married after an invalid Scotch divorce, which had been obtained in good faith, and the validity of which he had no reason to doubt: *Lolly's Case* (1812) R. & R. 237. Another exception, apparently grounded on the language of a statute, is *Prince's Case* (1875) L.R. 2 C.C.R. 154, where it was held by 15 judges against one that a man was guilty of abduction of a girl under 16, although he believed, in good faith and on reasonable grounds, that she was over that age. Apart from isolated and extreme cases of this kind, the principal classes of exceptions may perhaps be reduced to three. One is a class of acts which, in the language of Lush J. in *Davies* v. *Harvey* (1874) L.R. 9 Q.B. 433, are not criminal in any real sense, but are acts which in the public interest are prohibited under a penalty. ... Another class comprehends some, and perhaps all, public nuisances. ... Lastly, there are many cases in which, although the proceeding is criminal in form, it is really only a summary mode of enforcing a civil right. ... But, except in such cases as these, there must in general be guilty knowledge on the part of the defendant, or of someone whom he has put in his place to act for him, generally, or in the particular matter, in order to constitute an offence. It is plain that if guilty knowledge is not necessary, no care on the part of the publican could save him from a conviction under section 16, subsection (2), since it would be as easy for the constable to deny that he was on duty when asked, or to produce a forged permission from his superior officer, as to remove his armlet before entering the public-house. I am, therefore, of opinion that this conviction ought to be quashed.

Conviction quashed

Question

Do the two cases above represent a conflict of authority, as Glanville Williams suggests (C.L.G.P., p. 223)? Or can a rationale be found in the distinction between the risk of serving a drunk, and that of serving a constable on duty? See the case below.

Reynolds v. G. H. Austin & Sons Ltd.
[1951] 2 K.B. 135
King's Bench Division

A women's guild organised an outing and arranged with a company, who carried on the business of operating motor-coaches, to convey in a motor-coach a party at a fixed price per person. The organiser of the outing caused to be exhibited in a shop an advertisement giving particulars of the trip which stated "Few tickets left. Apply within." The company had no knowledge and no reasonable means of discovering that any such advertisement had been made. The outing took place and the company, who held no road service licence covering the journey in question, were charged with having used the motor-coach in contravention of section 72 of the Act of 1930 on the ground that by the condition of section 25, subsection (1)(*b*), of the Act of 1934, such journey "must be made without previous advertisement to the public of the arrangements therefor." The information was dismissed and the prosecutor appealed.

DEVLIN J.: . . . The main weight of the case for the prosecutor rests on the contention that this statute belongs to a class in which *mens rea* should be dispensed with. There is no doubt that some of the provisions of the Road Traffic Acts do fall within that class: see, for example, *Griffiths* v. *Studebakers Ltd.* [1924] 1 K.B. 102. It may seem, on the face of it, hard that a man should be fined, and, indeed, made subject to imprisonment, for an offence which he did not know that he was committing. But there is no doubt that the legislature has for certain purposes found that hard measure to be necessary in the public interest. The moral justification behind such laws is admirably expressed in a sentence by Dean Roscoe Pound in his book *The Spirit of the Common Law*, at p. 52: see *The Law Quarterly Review*, Vol. 64, p. 176. "Such statutes," he says, "are not meant to punish the vicious will but to put pressure upon the thoughtless and inefficient to do their whole duty in the interest of public health or safety or morals." Thus a man may be made responsible for the acts of his servants, or even for defects in his business arrangements, because it can be fairly said that by such sanctions citizens are induced to keep themselves and their organisations up to the mark. Although, in one sense, the citizen is being punished for the sins of others, it can be said that, if he had been more alert to see that the law was observed, the sin might not have been committed. But if a man is punished because of an act done by another, whom he cannot reasonably be expected to influence or control, the law is engaged, not in punishing thoughtlessness or inefficiency, and thereby promoting the welfare of the community, but in pouncing on the most convenient victim. Without the authority of express words, I am not willing to conclude that Parliament can intend what would seem to the ordinary man (as plainly it seemed to the justices in this case) to be the useless and unjust infliction of a penalty. . . .

I think it a safe general principle to follow (I state it negatively, since that is sufficient for the purposes of this case), that where the punishment of an individual will not promote the observance of the law either by that individual or by others whose conduct he may reasonably be expected to influence then, in the absence of clear and express words, such punishment is not intended.

There is another way in which the matter may be tested. In the case of statutes which apparently dispense with *mens rea*, it is sometimes said that it is the doing of an act which is absolutely prohibited that itself supplies the *mens rea*. In many such cases it is impossible to do the prohibited act without being conscious of it; and though in such cases there may be no moral guilt if the accused does not know that he was doing wrong, this is an excuse which the law cannot permit. In other cases it is possible, by taking heed, to avoid the doing of the prohibited act. In *Cundy* v. *Le Cocq*, (*ante*, p. 183), in which the decision turned partly on the wording of the

Act, it was also said that the object of the Act was to put upon the publican the responsibility of determining for himself whether a person supplied with drink was sober or not, and so conceivably to punish him for an error of judgment. But in the present case, as I have pointed out, not only are there no means of knowledge open to the accused but there are no data available to him on which he could arrive at any determination whether the law was likely to be broken or not. Even after the event it would need a judicial inquiry, covering the past activites of the organiser and each of the passengers, before it could be determined whether it had been broken. An express carriage is not a type of vehicle which can be identified by observation. No driver on one of these expeditions could answer the question whether or not he was driving an express carriage. In truth, an express carriage is an abstract conception. A vehicle may begin as an ordinary vehicle and become an express carriage in the course of its journey if a passenger insists on dismounting. It is a creature of statute; and a creature which, in its habits of appearing and disappearing (and, (I suspect, of leaving a grin behind it at the legal complications which its behaviour may cause), has many of the attributes of the Cheshire cat. In these circumstances, it would be going further than any decided case has yet gone, and further than I am willing to go without the clearest authority, to construe the statute as imposing an absolute prohibition.

Appeal dismissed

Lim Chin Aik v. The Queen
[1963] A.C. 160
Privy Council

The appellant was charged with and convicted of contravening section 6(2) of the Immigration Ordinance 1952 of the State of Singapore by remaining in Singapore (after having entered) when he had been prohibited from entering by an order made by the Minister under section 9. At the trial there was no evidence from which it could properly be inferred that the order had in fact come to the notice or attention of the appellant. He appealed, ultimately to the Privy Council.

LORD EVERSHED: That proof of the existence of a guilty intent is an essential ingredient of a crime at common law is not at all in doubt. The problem is of the extent to which the same rule is applicable in the case of offences created and defined by statute or statutory instrument. ...

Mr. Gratiaen founded his argument upon the formulation of the problem contained in the judgment of Wright J. in *Sherras's* case (*ante*, p. 184). The language of that learned and experienced judge was as follows: "There is a presumption that *mens rea*, or evil intention or knowledge of the wrongfulness of the act, is an essential ingredient in every offence, but that presumption is liable to be displaced either by the words of the statute creating the offence or by the subject-matter with which it deals, and both must be considered." ...

Their Lordships accept as correct the formulation cited from the judgment of Wright J. They are fortified in that view by the fact that such formulation was expressly accepted by Lord du Parcq in delivering the judgment of the Board in the case in 1947 of *Srinivas Mall Bairoliya* v. *King-Emperor* (1947) I.L.R. 26 Pat. 460, a case which unfortunately has not found its way into the Law Reports. ... Lord du Parcq, after citing with approval the judgment already quoted of Lord Wright J., also adopted the language of Lord Goddard C.J. in the case of *Brend* v. *Wood* (1946) 62 T.L.R. 462, D.C.: "It is in my opinion of the utmost importance for the protection of the liberty of the subject that a court should always bear in mind that unless a statute either clearly or by necessary implication rules out *mens rea* as a constituent part of a crime a defendant should not be found guilty of an offence against the criminal law unless he has got a guilty mind."

The adoption of these formulations of principle does not, however, dispose of the matter. ... The difficulty remains of their application. What should be the proper inferences to be drawn from the language of the statute or statutory instrument under review—in this case of sections 6 and 9 of the Immigration Ordinance? More difficult, perhaps, still what are the inferences to be drawn in a given case from the "subject-matter with which [the statute or statutory instrument] deals"?

Where the subject-matter of the statute is the regulation for the public welfare of a particular activity—statutes regulating the sale of food and drink are to be found among the earliest examples—it can be and frequently has been inferred that the legislature intended that such activities should be carried out under conditions of strict liability. The presumption is that the statute or statutory instrument can be effectively enforced only if those in charge of the relevant activities are made responsible for seeing that they are complied with. When such a presumption is to be inferred, it displaces the ordinary presumptions of *mens rea.* ...

But it is not enough in their Lordships' opinion merely to label the statute as one dealing with a grave social evil and from that to infer that strict liability was intended. It is pertinent also to inquire whether putting the defendant under strict liability will assist in the enforcement of the regulations. That means that there must be something he can do, directly or indirectly, by supervision or inspection, by improvement of his business methods or by exhorting those whom he may be expected to influence or control, which will promote the observance of the regulations. Unless this is so, there is no reason in penalising him, and it cannot be inferred that the legislature imposed strict liability merely in order to find a luckless victim. This principle has been expressed and applied in *Reynolds* v. *G. H. Austin & Sons Ltd.* (*ante*, p. 185) and *James & Son Ltd.* v. *Smee* [1955] 1 Q.B. 78. Their Lordships prefer it to the alternative view that strict liability follows simply from the nature of the subject-matter and that persons whose conduct is beyond any sort of criticism can be dealt with by the imposition of a nominal penalty. This latter view can perhaps be supported to some extent by the dicta of Kennedy L.J. in *Hobbs* v. *Winchester Corporation*, and of Donovan J. in *R.* v. *St. Margaret's Trust Ltd.* [1958] 1 W.L.R. 522. But though a nominal penalty may be appropriate in an individual case where exceptional lenience is called for, their Lordships cannot, with respect, suppose that it is envisaged by the legislature as a way of dealing with offenders generally. Where it can be shown that the imposition of strict liability would result in the prosecution and conviction of a class of persons whose conduct could not in any way affect the observance of the law, their Lordships consider that, even where the statute is dealing with a grave social evil, strict liability is not likely to be intended.

Their Lordships apply these general observations to the Ordinance in the present case. The subject-matter, the control of immigration, is not one in which the presumption of strict liability has generally been made. Nevertheless, if the courts of Singapore were of the view that unrestricted immigration is a social evil which it is the object of the Ordinance to control most rigorously, their Lordships would hesitate to disagree. That is a matter peculiarly within the cognisance of the local courts. But Mr Le Quesne was unable to point to anything that the appellant could possibly have done so as to ensure that he complied with the regulations. It was not, for example, suggested that it would be practicable for him to make continuous inquiry to see whether an order had been made against him. Clearly one of the objects of the Ordinance is the expulsion of prohibited persons from Singapore, but there is nothing that a man can do about it if, before the commission of the offence, there is no practical or sensible way in which he can ascertain whether he is a prohibited person or not.

Mr. Le Quesne, therefore, relied chiefly on the text of the Ordinance and their Lordships return, accordingly, to the language of the two material sections. It is to be observed that the Board is here concerned with one who is said (within the terms of section 6(3) to have "contravened" the subsection by "remaining" in Singapore (after having entered) when he had been "prohibited" from entering by an "order" made by the Minister containing such prohibition. It seems to their Lordships that, where a man is said to have contravened an order or an order of prohibition, the common sense of the language presumes that he was aware of the order before he can be said to have contravened it. Their Lordships realise that this statement is something of an over-simplification when applied to the present case; for the "contravention" alleged is of the unlawful act, prescribed by subsection (2) of the section, of remaining in Singapore after the date of the order of prohibition. Nonetheless it is their Lordships' view that, applying the test of ordinary sense to the language used, the notion of contravention here alleged is more consistent with the assumption that the person charged had knowledge of the order than the converse. But such a conclusion is in their Lordships' view much reinforced by the use of the word "remains" in its context. It is to be observed that if the respondent is right a man could lawfully enter Singapore and could thereafter lawfully remain in Singapore until the moment when an order of prohibition against his entering was made; that then, instanter, his purely passive conduct in remaining—that is, the mere continuance, quite unchanged, of his previous behaviour, hitherto perfectly lawful—would become criminal. These considerations bring their Lordships clearly to the conclusion that the sense of the language here in question requires for the commission of a crime thereunder *mens rea* as a constituent of such crime; or at least there is nothing in the language used which suffices to exclude the ordinary presumption. Their Lordships do not forget the emphasis placed by Mr. Le Quesne on the fact that the word "knowingly" or the phrases "without reasonable cause" or "without reasonable excuse" are found in various sections of the Ordinance (as amended) but find no place in the section now under consideration—see, for example, sections 16(4), 18(4), 19(2), 29, 31(2) and 56(d) and (e) of the Ordinance. In their Lordships' view the absence of such a word or phrase in the relevant section is not sufficient in the present case to prevail against the conclusion which the language as a whole suggests. In the first place, it is to be noted that to have inserted such words as "knowingly" or "without lawful excuse" in the relevant part of section 6(3) of the Act would in any case not have been sensible. Further, in all the various instances where the word or phrase is used in the other sections of the Ordinance before-mentioned the use is with reference to the doing of some specific act or the failure to do some specific act as distinct from the mere passive continuance of behaviour theretofore perfectly lawful. Finally, their Lordships are mindful that in the *Sherras* case itself the fact that the word "knowingly" was not found in the subsection under consideration by the court but was found in another subsection of the same section was not there regarded as sufficient to displace the ordinary rule.

Appeal allowed

Sweet v. Parsley
[1970] A.C. 133
House of Lords

Miss Sweet, a teacher, let rooms in a farmhouse to students. She did not reside in the farmhouse but retained one room for her own use for occasional overnight stays when she visited to collect the rent and check the property. After the police had searched the premises, finding evidence that cannabis had been smoked there, Miss Sweet was convicted by magistrates of being concerned in the management of premises which were used for the purpose of smoking cannabis, contrary to section 5(*b*) of the Dangerous Drugs Act 1965. The magistrates found that Miss Sweet did not exercise any control over her tenants and that she had no knowledge that the house was being used for the purpose of smoking cannabis. Her appeal to the Divisional Court was dismissed and she appealed to the House of Lords.

LORD REID: A Divisional Court dismissed her appeal, holding that she had been concerned in the management of those premises. The reasons given for holding that she was managing the property were that she was in a position to choose her tenants: that she could put them under as long or as short a tenancy as she desired and that she could make it a term of any letting that smoking of cannabis was not to take place. All these reasons would apply to every occupier who lets out parts of his house or takes in lodgers or paying guests. But this was held to be an absolute offence following the earlier decision in *Yeandel* v. *Fisher* [1966] 1 Q.B. 440.

How has it come about that the Divisional Court has felt bound to reach such an obviously unjust result? It has in effect held that it was carrying out the will of Parliament because Parliament has chosen to make this an absolute offence. And, of course, if Parliament has so chosen the courts must carry out its will, and they cannot be blamed for any unjust consequences. But has Parliament so chosen?

I dealt with this matter at some length in *Warner* v. *Metropolitan Police Commissioner* [1969] 2 A.C. 256. On reconsideration I see no reason to alter anything which I there said. But I think that some amplification is necessary. Our first duty is to consider the words of the Act: if they show a clear intention to create an absolute offence that is an end of the matter. But such cases are very rare. Sometimes the words of the section which creates a particular offence make it clear that *mens rea* is required in one form or another. Such cases are quite frequent. But in a very large number of cases there is no clear indication either way. In such cases there has for centuries been a presumption that Parliament did not intend to make criminals of persons who were in no way blameworthy in what they did. That means that whenever a section is silent as to *mens rea* there is a presumption that, in order to give effect to the will of Parliament, we must read in words appropriate to require *mens rea*. ... [I]t is firmly established by a host of authorities that *mens rea* is an essential ingredient of every offence unless some reason can be found for holding that that is not necessary.

It is also firmly established that the fact that other sections of the Act expressly require *mens rea*, for example because they contain the word "knowingly," is not in itself sufficient to justify a decision that a section which is silent as to *mens rea* creates an absolute offence. In the absence of a clear indication in the Act that an offence is intended to be an absolute offence, it is necessary to go outside the Act and examine all relevant circumstances in order to establish that this must have been the intention of Parliament. I say "must have been" because it is a universal principle that if a penal provision is reasonably capable of two interpretations, that interpretation which is most favourable to the accused must be adopted.

What, then, are the circumstances which it is proper to take into account? In the well-known case of *Sherras* v. *De Rutzen* (*ante*, p. 184), Wright J. only mentioned the subject-matter with which the Act deals. But he was there dealing with something which was one of a class of acts which "are not criminal in any real sense, but are acts which in the public interest are prohibited under a penalty." It does not in the least follow that when one is dealing with a truly criminal act it is sufficient merely to have regard to the subject-matter of the enactment. One must put oneself in the position of a legislator. It has long been the practice to recognise absolute offences in this class of quasi-criminal acts, and one can safely assume that, when Parliament is passing new legislation dealing with this class of offences, its silence as to *mens rea* means that the old practice is to apply. But when one comes to acts of a truly criminal character, it appears to me that there are at least two other factors which any reasonable legislator would have in mind. In the first place a stigma still attaches to any person convicted of a truly criminal offence, and the more serious or more disgraceful the offence the greater the stigma. So he would have to consider whether, in a case of this gravity, the public interest really requires that an innocent person should be prevented from providing his innocence in order that fewer guilty men may escape. And equally important is the fact that fortunately the Press in this country are vigilant to expose injustice and every manifestly unjust conviction made known to the public tends to injure the body politic by undermining public confidence in the justice of the law and of its administration. But I regret to observe that, in some recent cases where serious offences have been held to be absolute offences, the court has taken into account no more than the wording of the Act and the character and seriousness of the mischief which constitutes the offence.

The choice would be much more difficult if there were no other way open than either *mens rea* in the full sense or an absolute offence; for there are many kinds of case where putting on the prosecutor the full burden of proving *mens rea* creates great difficulties and may lead to many unjust acquittals. But there are at least two other possibilities. Parliament has not infrequently transferred the onus as regards *mens rea* to the accused, so that, once the necessary facts are proved, he must convince the jury that on balance of probabilities he is innocent of any criminal intention. I find it a little surprising that more use has not been made of this method: but one of the bad effects of the decision of this House in *Woolmington* v. *D.P.P.* [1935] A.C. 462, may have been to discourage its use. The other method would be in effect to substitute in appropriate classes of cases gross negligence for *mens rea* in the full sense as the mental element necessary to constitute the crime. It would often be much easier to infer that Parliament must have meant that gross negligence should be the necessary mental element than to infer that Parliament intended to create an absolute offence. A variant of this would be to accept the view of Cave J. in *R.* v. *Tolson* (*ante*, p. 159). This appears to have been done in Australia where authority appears to support what Dixon J. said in *Proudman* v. *Dayman* (1941) 67 C.L.R. 536, 540: "As a general rule an honest and reasonable belief in a state of facts which, if they existed, would make the defendant's act innocent affords an excuse for doing what would otherwise be an offence." It may be that none of these methods is wholly satisfactory but at least the public scandal of convicting on a serious charge persons who are in no way blameworthy would be avoided.

If this section means what the Divisional Court have held that it means, then hundreds of thousands of people who sublet part of the premises or take in lodgers or are concerned in the management of residential premises or institutions are daily incurring a risk of being convicted of a serious offence in circumstances where they are in no way to blame. For the greatest vigilance cannot prevent tenants, lodgers or inmates or guests whom they bring in from smoking cannabis cigarettes in their own rooms. It was suggested in argument that this appellant brought this conviction on herself because it is found as a fact that when the police searched the premises there were people there of the "beatnik fraternity." But surely it would be going a very long way to say that persons managing premises of any kind ought to safeguard themselves by refusing accommodation to all who are of slovenly or exotic appearance, or who bring in guests of that kind. And unfortunately drug taking is by no means confined to those of unusual appearance.

Speaking from a rather long experience of membership of both Houses, I assert with confidence that no Parliament within my recollection would have agreed to make an offence of this kind an absolute offence if the matter had been fully explained to it. So, if the court ought only to hold an offence to be an absolute offence where it appears that that must have been the intention of Parliament, offences of this kind are very far removed from those which it is proper to hold to be absolute offences.

I must now turn to the question what is the true meaning of section 5 of the 1965 Act ... is the "purpose" the purpose of the smoker or the purpose of the management? ... It is clear that the purpose is the purpose of the management ... So if the purpose is the purpose of the management, the question whether the offence ... is absolute can hardly arise.

I would allow the appeal and quash the appellant's conviction.

LORD MORRIS OF BORTH-Y-GEST: My Lords, it has frequently been affirmed and should unhesitatingly be recognised that it is a cardinal principle of our law that *mens rea*, an evil intention or a knowledge of the wrongfulness of the act, is in all ordinary cases an essential ingredient of guilt of a criminal offence. It follows from this that there will not be guilt of an offence created by the statute unless there is *mens rea* or unless Parliament has by the statute enacted that guilt may be established in cases where there is no *mens rea*. ...

But as Parliament is supreme it is open to Parliament to legislate in such a way that an offence may be created of which someone may be found guilty though *mens rea* is lacking. ... But I would again quote with appreciation (as I did in *Warner's* case [1969] 2 A.C. 256) the words of Lord Goddard C.J., in *Brend* v. *Wood* (1946) L.T. 306, 307, when he said: "It is of the utmost importance for the protection of the liberty of the subject that a court should always bear in mind that, unless a statute, either clearly or by necessary implication, rules out *mens rea* as a constituent part of a crime, the court should not find a man guilty of an offence against the criminal law unless he has a guilty mind." ...

The inquiry must be made, therefore, whether Parliament has used words which expressly enact or impliedly involve that an absolute offence is created. Though sometimes help in construction is derived from noting the presence or the absence of the word "knowingly," no conclusive test can be laid down as a guide in finding the fair, reasonable and commonsense meaning of language. But in considering whether Parliament has decided to displace what is a general and somewhat fundamental rule it would not be reasonable lightly to impute to Parliament an intention to create an offence in such a way that someone could be convicted of it who by all reasonable and sensible standards is without fault. ... [Lord Morris allowed the appeal, concluding that knowledge on the part of the accused of the particular purpose for which the premises were being used, had to be proved to support a conviction.]

LORD PEARCE: My Lords, the prosecution contend that any person who is concerned in the management of premises where cannabis is in fact smoked even once, is liable, though he had no knowledge and no guilty mind. This is, they argue, a practical act intended to prevent a practical evil. Only by convicting some innocents along with the guilty can sufficient pressure be put upon those who make their living by being concerned in the management of premises. Only thus can they be made alert to prevent cannabis being smoked there. And if the prosecution have to prove knowledge or *mens rea*, many prosecutions will fail and many of the guilty will escape. I find that argument wholly unacceptable.

... [O]ne must remember that normally *mens rea* is still an ingredient of any offence. Before the court will dispense with the necessity for *mens rea* it has to be satisfied that Parliament so intended. The mere absence of the word "knowingly" is not enough. But the nature of the crime, the punishment, the absence of social obloquy, the particular mischief and the field of activity in which it occurs, and the wording of the particular section and its context, may show that Parliament intended that the act should be prevented by punishment regardless of intent or knowledge.

Viewing the matter on these principles, it is not possible to accept the prosecution's contention. ... It is one thing to make a man absolutely responsible for his own acts and even vicariously liable for his servants if he engaged in a certain type of activity. But it is quite another matter to make him liable for persons over whom he has no control. ... I see no real, useful object achieved by such hardship to the innocent. And so wide a possibility of injustice to the innocent could not be justified by any benefit achieved in the determent and punishment of the guilty. If, therefore, the words creating the offence are as wide in their application as the prosecution contend, Parliament cannot have intended an offence to which absence of knowledge or *mens rea* is no defence. ...

LORD DIPLOCK: The expression "absolute offence" ... is an imprecise phrase currently used to describe an act for which the doer is subject to criminal sanctions even though when he did it he had no *mens rea*, ...

[O]nly too frequently the actual words used by Parliament to define the prohibited conduct are in themselves descriptive only of a physical act and bear no connotation as to any particular state of mind on the part of the person who does the act. Nevertheless, the mere fact that Parliament has made the conduct a criminal offence gives rise to *some* implication about the mental element of the conduct proscribed. ...

[T]he importance of the actual decision of the nine judges who constituted the majority in *R.* v. *Tolson* (*ante*, p. 159) which concerned a charge of bigamy under section 57 of the Offences Against the Person Act 1861, was that it laid down as a general principle of construction of any enactment, which creates a criminal offence, that, even where the words used to describe the prohibited conduct would not in any other context connote the necessity for any particular mental element, they are nevertheless to be read as subject to the implication that a necessary element in the offence is the absence of a belief, held honestly and upon reasonable grounds, in the existence of facts which, if true, would make the act innocent. As was said by the Privy Council in *Bank of New South Wales* v. *Piper* [1897] A.C. 383, 389, 390, the absence of *mens rea* really consists in such a belief by the accused.

This implication stems from the principle that it is contrary to a rational and civilised criminal code, such as Parliament must be presumed to have intended, to penalise one who has performed his duty as a citizen to ascertain what acts are prohibited by law (*ignorantia juris non excusat*) and has taken all proper care to inform himself of any facts which would make his conduct lawful.

Where penal provisions are of general application to the conduct of ordinary citizens in the course of their everyday life the presumption is that the standard of care required of them in informing themselves of facts which would make their conduct unlawful, is that of the familiar common law duty of care. But where the subject-matter of a statute is the regulation of a particular activity involving potential danger to public health, safety or morals in which citizens have a choice as to whether they participate or not, the court may feel driven to infer an intention of Parliament to impose by penal sanctions a higher duty of care on those who choose to participate and to place upon them an obligation to take whatever measures may be necessary to prevent the prohibited act, without regard to those considerations of cost or business practicability which play a part in the determination of what would be required of them in order to fulfil the ordinary common law duty of care. But such an inference is not lightly to be drawn, nor is there any room for it unless there is something that the person on whom the obligation is imposed can do directly or indirectly, by supervision or inspection, by improvement of his business methods or by exhorting those whom he may be expected to influence or control, which will promote the observance of the obligation [see *Lim Chin Aik* v. *R.*, *ante*, p. 187].

The numerous decisions in the English courts since *R.* v. *Tolson* in which this later inference has been drawn rightly or, as I think, often wrongly, are not easy to reconcile with others where the court has failed to draw the inference, nor are they always limited to penal provisions designed to regulate the conduct of persons who choose to participate in a particular activity as distinct from those of general application to the conduct of ordinary citizens in the course of their everyday life. It may well be that had the significance of *R.* v. *Tolson* been appreciated here, as it was in the High Court of Australia, our courts, too, would have been less ready to infer an intention of Parliament to create offences for which honest and reasonable mistake was no excuse.

Its importance as a guide to the construction of penal provisions in statutes of general application was recognised by Dixon J. in *Maher* v. *Musson* (1934) 52 C.L.R. 100, 104, and by the majority of the High Court of Australia in *Thomas* v. *The King* (1937) 59 C.L.R. 279. It is now regularly adopted in Australia as a general principle of construction of statutory provisions of this kind.

By contrast, in England the principle laid down in *R.* v. *Tolson* has been overlooked until recently (see *R.* v. *Gould* [1968] 2 Q.B. 65) partly because the *ratio decidendi* was misunderstood by the Court of Criminal Appeal in *R.* v. *Wheat and Stocks* [1921] 2 K.B. 119 and partly, I suspect, because the reference in *R.* v. *Tolson* to the mistaken belief as being a "defence" to the charge of bigamy was thought to run counter to the decision of your Lordships' House in *Woolmington* v. *D.P.P.* [1935] A.C. 462. That expression might have to be expanded in the light of what was said in *Woolmington's* case, though I doubt whether a jury would find the expansion much more informative than describing the existence of the mistaken belief as a defence to which they should give effect unless they felt sure either that the accused did not honestly hold it or, if he did, that he had no reasonable grounds for doing so.

Woolmington's case affirmed the principle that the onus lies upon the prosecution in a criminal trial to prove all the elements of the offence with which the accused is charged. It does not purport to lay down how that onus can be discharged as respects any particular elements of the offence. This, under our system of criminal procedure, is left to the common sense of the jury. *Woolmington's* case did not decide anything so irrational as that the prosecution must call evidence to prove the absence of any mistaken belief by the accused in the existence of facts which, if true, would make the act innocent, any more than it decided that the prosecution must call evidence to prove the absence of any claim of right in a charge of larceny. The jury is entitled to presume that the accused acted with knowledge of the facts, unless there is some evidence to the contrary originating from the accused who alone can know on what belief he acted and on what ground the belief, if mistaken, was held. What *Woolmington's* case did decide is that where there is any such evidence the jury after considering it and also any relevant evidence called by the prosecution on the issue of the existence of the alleged mistaken belief should acquit the accused unless they feel sure that he did not hold the belief or that there were no reasonable grounds upon which he could have done so.

This, as I understand it, is the approach of Dixon J. to the onus of proof of honest and reasonable mistaken belief as he expressed it in *Proudman* v. *Dayman* (1941) 67 C.L.R. 536, 541. Unlike the position where a statute expressly places the onus of proving lack of guilty knowledge on the accused, the accused does not have to prove the existence of mistaken belief on the balance of probabilities; he has to raise a reasonable doubt as to its non-existence.

It has been objected that the requirement laid down in *R.* v. *Tolson* (*ante*, p. 159) and the *Bank of New South Wales* v. *Piper* [1897] A.C. 383 that the mistaken belief should be based on reasonable grounds introduces an objective mental element into *mens rea*. This may be so, but there is nothing novel in this. The test of the mental element of provocation which distinguishes manslaughter from murder has always been at common law and now is by statute the objective one of the way in which a reasonable man would react to provocation. There is nothing unreasonable in requiring a citizen to take reasonable care to ascertain the facts relevant to his avoiding doing a prohibited act.

[His Lordship concluded that the "purpose" which had to be proved was that of the person concerned in the management of the premises. Since the appellant had no knowledge of the use being made of the premises, his Lordship held the appeal should be allowed.]

Appeal allowed

[The Misuse of Drugs Act 1971 incorporated "knowingly" in this offence.]

Note

Although *Sweet* v. *Parsley* represented a distinct change in judicial attitude, it is difficult to assess its effect. What is involved in the field of so-called "regulatory offences" is a vast number of diverse statutory provisions which are not easily accommodated under the umbrella of general principle. How, in any case, is the distinction to be drawn between the "quasi" and the "truly" criminal act? In *Alphacell* v. *Woodward* [1972] A.C. 824, the House of Lords upheld a conviction under section 2(1)(*a*) of the Rivers (Prevention of Pollution) Act 1951 ("causing" polluted matter to enter a river) although there was proof neither of knowledge nor negligence. A second or subsequent conviction under this section carries with it the possibility of a sentence of imprisonment. The case illustrates the tension between the principle of confining criminal liability to "quasi" criminal offences and the principle of protecting the public from potentially dangerous activities. Lord Salmon, at p. 848: "Section 2(1)(*a*) ... is undoubtedly a penal section. [The appellants contend] that it follows that if it is capable of two or more meanings then the meaning most favourable to the subject should be adopted. ... I do not agree. It is of the utmost public importance that our rivers should not be polluted. The risk of pollution, particularly from the vast and increasing number of riparian industries is very great." Individuals who engage in potentially dangerous pastimes, such as the possession of firearms, may also find themselves subject to the rigours of strict liability: *R.* v. *Howells* [1977] 2 W.L.R. 716 (*ante*, p. 170).

The tension referred to above was evident in a recent House of Lords case.

Pharmaceutical Society of Great Britain v. Storkwain Ltd.
[1986] 2 All E.R. 635
House of Lords

The respondents brought informations against the appellants alleging they were guilty of offences under section 58(2)(*a*) and section 67(2) of the Medicines Act 1968, having sold on prescription medicines to customers who had presented prescriptions which proved to be forgeries. The appellants believed in good faith and on reasonable grounds that the prescriptions were valid. The magistrates dismissed the informations. The Divisional Court allowed the appeal of the respondents. The appellants appealed to the House of Lords.

LORD GOFF OF CHIEVELEY: My Lords, this appeal is concerned with a question of construction of section 58 of the Medicines Act 1968. ... The Divisional Court certified the following point of law as being of general public importance:

"Whether the prosecution have to prove mens rea where an information is laid under Section 58(2)(*a*) of the Medicines Act 1968 where the allegation is that the supply of 'prescription only' drugs was made by the [defendant] in accordance with a forged prescription and without fault on [his] part."

... For the appellants, counsel submitted [*inter alia*] that there must, in accordance with the well-recognised presumption, be read into section 58(2)(*a*) words appropriate to require *mens rea* in accordance with *R.* v. *Tolson* (*ante*, p. 159); in other words, to adopt the language of Lord Diplock in *Sweet* v. *Parsley* [1970] A.C. 132 at 163, the subsection must be read subject to the implication that a necessary element in the prohibition (and hence in the offence created by the subsection together with section 67(2) of the 1968 Act) is the absence of belief, held honestly and on reasonable grounds, in the existence of facts which, if true, would make the act innocent. ...

I am unable to accept counsel's submission, for the simple reason that it is, in my opinion, clear from the 1968 Act that Parliament must have intended that the presumption of *mens rea* should be inapplicable to section 58(2)(*a*). First of all, it appears from the 1968 Act that, where Parliament wished to recognise that *mens rea* should be an ingredient of an offence created by the Act, it has expressly so provided. Thus, taking first of all offences created under provisions of Pt. II of the 1968 Act, express requirements of *mens rea* are to be found both in section 45(2) and section 46(1), (2) and (3) of the Act. More particularly, in relation to offences created by Pt. III and Pts. V and VI of the 1968 Act, section 121 makes detailed provision for a requirement of *mens rea* in respect of certain specified sections of the act, including sections 63 to 65 (which are contained in Pt. III), but significantly not section 58, nor indeed sections 52 and 53. ... It is very difficult to avoid the conclusion that, by omitting section 58 from those sections to which section 121 is expressly made applicable, Parliament intended that there should be no implication of a requirement of *mens rea* in section 58(2)(*a*). This view is fortified by subss. (4) and (5) of section 58 itself. Subsection (4)(*a*) provides that any order made by the appropriate ministers for the purposes of section 58 may provide that section 58(2)(*a*) or (*b*), or both, shall have effect subject to such exemptions as may be specified in the order. From this subsection alone it follows that the ministers, if they think it right, can provide for exemption where there is no *mens rea* on the part of the accused. Subsection (5) provides that any exemption conferred by an order in accordance with subsection (4)(*a*) may be conferred subject to such conditions or limitations as may be specified in the order. From this it follows that, if the ministers, acting under subs. (4), were to confer an exemption relating to sales where the vendor lacked the requisite *mens rea*, they may nevertheless circumscribe their exemption with conditions and limitations which render the exemption far narrower than the implication for which counsel for the appellants contends should be read into the statute itself. I find this to be very difficult to reconcile with the proposed implication.

It comes as no surprise to me, therefore, to discover that the relevant order in force at that time, the Medicines (Prescriptions Only) Order 1980, is drawn entirely in conformity with the construction of the statute which I favour. ...

For these reasons, which are substantially the same as those which are set out in the judgments of Farquharson and Tudor Price JJ. in the Divisional Court, I am unable to accept the submissions advanced on behalf of the appellants. I gratefully adopt as my own the following passage from the judgment of Farquharson J. ([1985] 3 All E.R. 4 at 10):

" ... it is perfectly obvious that pharmacists are in a position to put illicit drugs and perhaps other medicines on the market. Happily this rarely happens but it does from time to time. It can therefore be readily understood that Parliament would find it necessary to impose a heavier liability on those who are in such a position, and make them more strictly accountable for any breaches of the Act."

I would therefore answer the certified question in the negative, and dismiss the appeal with costs.

Certified question answered in negative. Appeal dismissed

Note

The courts are vigilant to protect public safety. Where this consideration is weighty the courts may find that it displaces the presumption of *mens rea*. This will be the result particularly where the courts consider that the imposition of strict liability will encourage greater vigilance on the part of those regulated by the statute: see the case *infra*.

Gammon (Hong Kong) Ltd. and Others v. Attorney General of Hong Kong
[1984] 2 All E.R. 503
Privy Council

The appellants were respectively the registered contractor, the project manager and the site agent for building works on a site in Hong Kong. Part of a temporary lateral support system collapsed. The company was charged with a material deviation from an approved plan in contravention of subsection (2A)(*b*) of section 40 of the Hong Kong Building Ordinance (revised edn. 1981), and with carrying out works in a manner likely to cause risk of injury or damage in contravention of sub-section (2B)(*b*). The project manager and the site engineer were charged under sub-section (2B)(*b*), respectively, with carrying out works, and permitting them to be carried on in a manner likely to cause risk of injury or damage.

LORD SCARMAN delivered the judgment of the Board: ...

i. The general law
    ... The question in the appeal is whether the ordinance, correctly interpreted, provides a sound reason for holding that the offences created by subss. (2A)(*b*) and (2B)(*b*) of section 40 of the ordinance are offences of strict liability. ...
    In their Lordships' opinion, the law relevant to this appeal may be stated in the following propositions: (1) there is a presumption of law that *mens rea* is required before a person can be held guilty of a criminal offence; (2) the presumption is particularly strong where the offence is "truly criminal" in character; (3) the presumption applies to statutory offences, and can be displaced only if this is clearly or by necessary implication the effect of the statute; (4) the only situation in which the presumption can be displaced is where the statute is concerned with an issue of social concern; public safety is such an issue; (5) even where a statute is concerned with such an issue, the presumption of *mens rea* stands unless it can also be shown that the creation of strict liability will be effective to promote the objects of the statute by encouraging greater vigilance to prevent the commission of the prohibited act.

ii. The ordinance
    Their Lordships turn to consider the purpose and subject matter of the ordinance. Its overall purpose is clearly to regulate the planning, design and construction of the building works to which it relates in the interests of safety. It covers a field of activity where there is, especially in Hong

Kong, a potential danger to public safety. And the activity which the ordinance is intended to regulate is one in which citizens have a choice whether they participate or not. Part IV (section 40) of the ordinance makes it very clear that the legislature intended that criminal sanctions for contraventions of the ordinance should be a feature of its enforcement. But it is not to be supposed that the legislature intended that any of the offences created by the ordinance should be offences of strict liability unless it is plain, from a consideration of the subject-matter of the ordinance and of the wording of the particular provision creating the offence, that an object of the ordinance, *e.g.* the promotion of greater vigilance by those having responsibility under the ordinance, would be served by the imposition of strict liability.

The appellants submit that there is no necessity for strict liability in respect of any of the offences charged. Their first submission is that strict liability would not promote greater vigilance. If the persons charged had no knowledge of an essential fact, what could they have done to avoid its occurrence? Their second submission is more comprehensive. They submit that strict liability in respect of any offence created by the ordinance would run counter to the structure and character of the ordinance. The ordinance, it is submitted, relies not on criminal liability but on the elaborate and stringent provisions for the registration of persons qualified to ensure that its requirements are met.

So far as the first submission is concerned, their Lordships are satisfied that strict liability would help to promote greater vigilance in the matters covered by the two offenders with which this appeal is concerned (the material deviation under subs. (2A)(*b*) and the risk of injury or damage under subs. (2B)(*b*). The second submission is more formidable. Their Lordships, however, reject it also. Their Lordships agree with the view expressed by the Court of Appeal as to the purpose and subject-matter of the ordinance. The Court of Appeal saw no injustice in the imposition of heavy penalties for offences under the ordinance "whether resulting from intentional infringement of the law, negligence or incompetence." They made this powerful comment:

"Any large scale building operation will almost inevitably produce circumstances in which a departure from the generally accepted standards (whether of work or materials) will be likely to cause danger. Indeed, the extent of the danger and of the damage which may be done will frequently be enormous. It therefore behoves the incompetent to stay away and the competent to conduct themselves with proper care. A building contractor who delegates his legal responsibilities to an agent can fairly be held liable if he appoints an agent who is incompetent or careless: he should regulate his business in such a way as to avoid, on the one hand, the appointment of incompetent agents and, on the other, the consequences of any carelessness by a competent agent. Only if he is made responsible for seeing that the statutory standards are maintained can the purpose of the legislature be attained and in such a case as this the presumption of strict liability displaces the ordinary presumption of mens rea: see *Lim Chin Aik* v. *R.* (*ante*, p. 187)."

Important as are the provisions of the ordinance for the registration, disqualification and discipline of persons qualified, authorised and registered to perform the duties and obligations required by the ordinance, the legislature by enacting Pt. IV (section 40) of the ordinance clearly took the view that criminal liability and punishment were needed as a deterrent against slipshod or incompetent supervision, control or execution of building works. The imposition of strict liability for some offences clearly would emphasise to those concerned the need for high standards of care in the supervision and execution of work. The view that their Lordships have reached, after the thorough review of the ordinance and history ... is that, where the ordinance provides for an offence in terms which are silent or ambiguous as to the need for full *mens rea* covering all its essential ingredients, the wording of the particular provision must be carefully examined against the background and in the context of the ordinance to determine whether it is necessary to interpret the silence or resolve the ambiguity in favour of *mens rea* or of strict liability.

Put in positive terms, the conclusion of the Board is that it is consistent with the purpose of the ordinance in its regulation of the works to which it applies that at least some of the criminal offences which it creates should be of strict liability. It is a statute the subject matter of which may properly be described as—

> "the regulation of a particular activity involving potential danger to public health [and] safety ... in which citizens have a choice whether they participate or not ... "

(See [1970] A.C. 132 at 163 *per* Lord Diplock.)

> Whether, therefore, a particular provision of the statute creates an offence of full *mens rea* or of strict liability must depend on the true meaning of the words of the particular provision construed with reference to its subject-matter and to the question whether strict liability in respect of all or any of the essential ingredients of the offence would promote the object of the provision. ...

iii. Subsections (2A) and (2B)

Their Lordships now turn to consider the two subsections in detail and separately; for it does not follow that, if one subsection should create an offence of strict liability, the other must also do so. But first a few observations on certain features common to both.

The first common feature is that both subsections have a characteristic of which Lord Reid spoke in *Sweet* v. *Parsley* [1970] A.C. 132 at 149. The specific provisions subsections (2A)(*b*) and (2B)() belong to that:

> "multitude of criminal enactments where the words of the Act simply make it an offence to do certain things but where everyone agrees that there cannot be a conviction without proof of mens rea in some form."

Each provision clearly requires a degree of *mens rea*, but each is silent whether it is required in respect of all the facts which together constitute the offence created. The issue here is, therefore, a narrow one. Does subs. (2A)(*b*) require knowledge of the materiality of the deviation? Does subs. (2B)(*b*) require knowledge of the likelihood of risk of injury or damage?

The second common feature is that each provision appears in a section which creates many other offences, the wording of some, though not all, of which clearly requires full *mens rea*.

A third common feature is that the maximum penalties for the offences which they create are heavy: a fine of $250,000 and imprisonment for three years. There is no doubt that the penalty indicates the seriousness with which the legislature viewed the offences.

The first of these features raises the determinative question in the appeal. Their Lordships will, therefore, consider it later in respect of each subsection.

The second feature, in their Lordships' opinion, proves nothing. One would expect a wide range of very different offences in a statute which establishes a comprehensive system of supervision and control over a great range of complicated works in diverse circumstances. And it can be said with equal force that a feature of section 40 is that in many cases where *mens rea* is required it expressly says so, and that, where a defence of reasonable excuse or lack of knowledge is to be available, it makes express provision to that end; examples may be seen in subss. (1B), (10), (2A)(c), (2C), (6), (7) and (7A).

The severity of the maximum penalties is a more formidable point. But it has to be considered in the light of the ordinance read as a whole. For reasons which their Lordships have already developed, there is nothing inconsistent with the purpose of the ordinance in imposing severe penalties for offences of strict liability. The legislature could reasonably have intended severity to be a significant deterrent, bearing in mind the risks to public safety arising from some contraventions of the ordinance. Their Lordships agree with the view on this point of the Court of Appeal. It must be crucially important that those who participate in or bear responsibility for the carrying out of works in a manner which complies with the requirements of the ordinance should know that severe penalties await them in the event of any contravention or non-compliance with the ordinance by themselves or by anyone over whom they are required to exercise supervision or control.

Subsection (2A)

... The wording of paragraph (b) clearly requires knowledge of the approved plan and of the fact of deviation. But in their Lordships' view it would be of little use in promoting public safety if it also required proof of knowledge of the materiality of the deviation. As it was put on behalf of the Attorney-General, if the offence requires knowledge of the materiality of the deviation to be proved, the defendant is virtually judge in his own cause. The object of the provision is to assist in preventing material deviations from occurring. If a building owner, an authorised person or a registered person is unaware of the materiality of the deviation which he authorises (and knowledge of the deviation is necessary), he plainly ought to be. He is made liable to criminal penalties because of the threat to public safety arising from material deviations from plans occurring within the sphere of his responsibility. The effectiveness of the ordinance would be seriously weakened if it were open to such a person to plead ignorance of what was material. In the words already quoted of the Court of Appeal, " ... it behoves the incompetent to stay away and the competent to conduct themselves with proper care."

Subsection (2B)

The construction of subsection (2B)(b) is more difficult, but their Lordships are satisfied that it imposes strict liability for substantially the same reasons as those which have led them to this conclusion in respect of subsection (2A)(b). The offence created clearly requires a degree of *mens rea*. A person cannot carry out works or authorise or permit them to be carried out in a certain manner unless he knows the manner which he is employing, authorising or permitting. ...

Their Lordships find some support for their view that subsection (2B)(b) is an offence of strict liability in the wording of the offence created by subsection (2B)(a). The wording of paragraph (a) points to strict liability, once injury or damage has in fact been caused. Anyone who has carried out, authorised or permitted work to be carried out in a manner which has in fact caused injury or damage is caught.

Conclusion
For these reasons their Lordships conclude that to the extent indicated the offences charged against the appellants are of strict liability.

Appeal dismissed; case remitted to magistrate

Note

In 1978, in the case below, the Canadian Supreme Court produced a three-fold classification of crimes.

R. v. City of Sault Ste Marie
(1978) 85 D.L.R. (3d) 161
Supreme Court of Canada

The City of Sault Ste Marie entered into an agreement with C. Co. Ltd. to dispose of all the city's refuse. As a direct result of the methods of disposal used by the company, the Root River and Cannon Creek became polluted. The company was convicted under section 32(1) of the Ontario Water Resources Act. The question arose whether the City should also be convicted under section 32(1) which provided: '[E]very municipality or person that discharges or deposits, or causes or permits the discharge ... of any material ... into any water ... that may impair the quality of water, is guilty of an offence."

DICKSON J. FOR THE COURT: In the present appeal the Court is concerned with offences variously referred to as "statutory," "public welfare," "regulatory," "absolute liability," or "strict responsibility," which are not criminal in any real sense, but are prohibited in the public interest. Although enforced as penal laws through the utilization of the machinery of the criminal law, the offences are in substance of a civil nature and might well be regarded as a branch of administrative law to which traditional principles of criminal law have but limited application. They relate to such everyday matters as traffic infractions, sales of impure food, violations of liquor laws, and the like. In this appeal we are concerned with pollution.

The mens rea point
The distinction between the true criminal offence and the public welfare offence is one of prime importance. Where the offence is criminal, the Crown must establish a mental element, namely that the accused who committed the prohibited act did so intentionally or recklessly, with knowledge of the facts constituting the offence, or with wilful blindness toward them. Mere negligence is excluded from the concept of the mental element required for conviction. Within the context of a criminal prosecution a person who fails to make such inquiries as a reasonable and prudent person would make, or who fails to know facts he should have known, is innocent in the eyes of the law.

In sharp contrast, "absolute liability" entails conviction on proof merely that the defendant committed the prohibited act constituting the *actus reus* of the offence. There is no relevant mental element. It is no defence that the accused was entirely without fault. He may be morally innocent in every sense, yet be branded as a malefactor and punished as such.

Public welfare offences obviously lie in a field of conflicting values. It is essential for society to maintain, through effective enforcement, high standards of public health and safety. Potential victims of those who carry on latently pernicious activities have a strong claim to consideration. On the other hand, there is a generally held revulsion against punishment of the morally innocent.

Public welfare offences evolved in mid-19th century Britain (*R.* v. *Woodrow* (1846) 15 M. & W. 404, and *R.* v. *Stephens* (1866) L.R. 1 Q.B. 702) as a means of doing away with the requirement of *mens rea* for petty police offences. The concept was a judicial creation, founded on expediency. That concept is now firmly embedded in the concrete of Anglo-American and Canadian jurisprudence, its importance heightened by the ever-increasing complexities of modern society.

Various arguments are advanced in justification of absolute liability in public welfare offences. Two predominate. Firstly, it is argued that the protection of social interests requires a high standard of care and attention on the part of those who follow certain pursuits and such persons are more likely to be stimulated to maintain those standards if they know that ignorance or mistake will not excuse them. The removal of any possible loophole acts, it is said, as an incentive to take precautionary measures beyond what would otherwise be taken, in order that mistakes and mishaps be avoided. The second main argument is one based on administrative efficiency. Having regard to both the difficulty of proving mental culpability and the number of petty cases which daily come before the Courts, proof of fault is just too great a burden in time and money to place upon the prosecution. To require proof of each person's individual intent would allow almost every violator to escape. This, together with the glut of work entailed in proving *mens rea* in every case would clutter the docket and impede adequate enforcement as virtually to nullify the regulatory statutes. In short, absolute liability, it is contended, is the most efficient and effective way of ensuring compliance with minor regulatory legislation and the social ends to be achieved are of such importance as to override the unfortunate by-product of punishing those who may be free of moral turpitude. In further justification, it is urged that slight penalties are usually imposed and that conviction for breach of a public welfare offence does not carry the stigma associated with conviction for a criminal offence.

Arguments of greater force are advanced against absolute liability. The most telling is that it violates fundamental principles of penal liability. It also rests upon assumptions which have not been, and cannot be, empirically established. There is no evidence that a higher standard of care results from absolute liability. If a person is already taking every reasonable precautionary measure, is he likely to take additional measures, knowing that however much care he takes, it will not serve as a defence in the event of breach? If he has exercised care and skill, will conviction have a deterrent effect upon him or others? Will the injustice of conviction lead to cynicism and disrespect for the law, on his part and on the part of others? These are among the questions asked. The argument that no stigma attaches does not withstand analysis, for the accused will have suffered loss of time, legal costs, exposure to the processes of the criminal law at trial and, however one may downplay it, the opprobrium of conviction. It is not sufficient to say that the public interest is engaged and, therefore, liability may be imposed without fault. In serious crimes, the public interest is involved and *mens rea* must be proven. The administrative argument has little force. In sentencing, evidence of due diligence is admissible and therefore the evidence might just as well be heard when considering guilt. . . .

Public welfare offences involve a shift of emphasis from the protection of individual interests to the protection of public and social interests. The unfortunate tendency in many past cases has been to see the choice as between two stark alternatives: (i) full *mens rea*; or (ii) absolute liability. In respect of public welfare offences (within which category pollution offences fall) where full *mens rea* is not required, absolute liability has often been imposed. English jurisprudence has consistently maintained this dichotomy: see "Criminal Law, Evidence and Procedure," 11 Hals., 4th ed., pp. 20–22, paragraph 18. There has, however, been an attempt in Australia, in many Canadian Courts, and, indeed in England, to seek a middle position, fulfilling the goals of public welfare offences while still not punishing the entirely blameless. There is an increasing and impressive stream of authority which holds that where an offence does not require full *mens rea*, it is nevertheless a good defence for the defendant to prove that he was not negligent. . . .

The case which gave the lead in this branch of the law is the Australian case of *Proudman* v. *Dayman* (1941) 67 C.L.R. 536. . . .

In the House of Lords case of *Sweet* v. *Parsley* (*ante*, p. 190), Lord Reid noted the difficulty presented by the simplistic choice between *mens rea* in the full sense and an absolute offence. He looked approvingly at attempts to find a middle ground. Lord Pearce, in the same case, referred to the "sensible half-way house" which he thought the Courts should take in some so-called absolute offences. The difficulty, as Lord Pearce saw it, lay in the opinion of Viscount Sankey, L.C. in *Woolmington* v. *D.P.P.* [1935] A.C. 462, if the full width of that opinion were maintained. Lord Diplock, however, took a different and, in my opinion, a preferable view, [1970] A.C. 132 at p. 164:

> *Woolmington's* case did not decide anything so irrational as that the prosecution must call evidence to prove the absence of any mistaken belief by the accused in the existence of facts which, if true, would make the act innocent, any more than it decided that the prosecution must call evidence to prove the absence of any claim of right in a charge of larceny. The jury is entitled to presume that the accused acted with knowledge of the facts, unless there is some evidence to the contrary originating from the accused who alone can know on what belief he acted and on what ground the belief, if mistaken, was held.

In *Woolmington's* case the question was whether the trial judge was correct in directing the jury that the accused was required to prove his innocence. Viscount Sankey L.C., referred to the strength of the presumption of innocence in a criminal case and then made the statement, universally accepted in this country, that there is no burden on the prisoner to prove his innocence; it is sufficient for him to raise a doubt as to his guilt. . . . There is nothing in *Woolmington's* case, as I comprehend it, which stands in the way of adoption, in respect of regulatory offences, of a defence of due care, with burden of proof resting on the accused to establish the defence on the balance of probabilities. . . .

It may be suggested that the introduction of a defence based on due diligence and the shifting of the burden of proof might be better implemented by legislative act. In answer, it should be recalled that the concept of absolute liability and the creation of a jural category of public welfare offences are both the product of the judiciary and not of the Legislature. The development to date of this defence, in the numerous decisions I have referred to, of Courts in this country as well as in Australia and New Zealand, has also been the work of Judges. The present case offers the opportunity of consolidating and clarifying the doctrine.

The correct approach, in my opinion, is to relieve the Crown of the burden of proving *mens rea*, having regard to *Pierce Fisheries* [1970] 12

D.L.R. (3d) 1591, and to the virtual impossibility in most regulatory cases of proving wrongful intention. In a normal case, the accused alone will have knowledge of what he has done to avoid the breach and it is not improper to expect him to come forward with the evidence of due diligence. This is particularly so when it is alleged, for example, that pollution was caused by the activities of a large and complex corporation. Equally, there is nothing wrong with rejecting absolute liability and admitting the defence of reasonable care.

In this doctrine it is not up to the prosecution to prove negligence. Instead, it is open to the defendant to prove that all due care has been taken. This burden falls upon the defendant as he is the only one who will generally have the means of proof. This would seem unfair as the alternative is absolute liability which denies an accused any defence whatsoever. While the prosecution must prove beyond a reasonable doubt that the defendant committed the prohibited act, the defendant must only establish on the balance of probabilities that he has a defence of reasonable care.

I conclude, for the reasons which I have sought to express, that there are compelling grounds for the recognition of three categories of offences rather than the traditional two:

1. Offences in which *mens rea*, consisting of some positive state of mind such as intent, knowledge, or recklessness, must be proved by the prosecution either as an inference from the nature of the act committed, or by additional evidence.

2. Offences in which there is no necessity for the prosecution to prove the existence of *mens rea*; the doing of the prohibited act *prima facie* imports the offence, leaving it open to the accused to avoid liability by proving that he took all reasonable care. This involves consideration of what a reasonable man would have done in the circumstances. The defence will be available if the accused reasonably believed in a mistaken set of facts which, if true, would render the act or omission innocent, or if he took all reasonable steps to avoid the particular event. These offences may properly be called offences of strict liability. Mr. Justice Estey so referred to them in *Hickey* [1976] 68 D.L.R. (3d) 88.

3. Offences of absolute liability where it is not open to the accused to exculpate himself by showing that he was free of fault.

Offences which are criminal in the true sense fall in the first category. Public welfare offences would, *prima facie*, be in the second category. They are not subject to the presumption of full *mens rea*. An offence of this type would fall in the first category only if such words as "wilfully," "with intent," "knowingly," or "intentionally" are contained in the statutory provision creating the offence. On the other hand, the principle that punishment should in general not be inflicted on those without fault applies. Offences of absolute liability would be those in respect of which the Legislature had made it clear that guilt would follow proof merely of the proscribed act. The over-all regulatory pattern adopted by the Legislature, the subject-matter of the legislation, the importance of the penalty, and the precision of the language used will be primary considerations in determining whether the offence falls into the third category.

The Divisional Court of Ontario concluded that s.32(1) created a *mens rea* offence.

The words "cause" and "permit" fit much better into an offence of strict liability than either full *mens rea* or absolute liability. Since section 32(1) creates a public welfare offence, without a clear indication that liability is absolute, and without any words such as "knowingly" or "wilfully" expressly to import *mens rea*, application of the criteria which I have outlined above undoubtedly places the offence in the category of strict liability.

Appeals dismissed and a new trial ordered

[This classification has not proved to be free of difficulty. See *Strasser* v. *Roberge* (1980) 103 D.L.R. (3d) 193.]

Note

Unlike the High Court of Australia and the Supreme Court of Canada, English courts have not developed a general due diligence (or "no-negligence") defence to offences of strict liability, although Lord Diplock did suggest in *Sweet* v. *Parsley* that it might be possible at common law. However, Parliament often does provide for a due diligence defence; see, *e.g.* Offices, Shops and Railway Premises Act 1963, s.67; Trade Descriptions Act 1968, s.24(3). A refinement of the due diligence defence in many statutes is the imposition of the requirement that the accused, not only prove due diligence, but that he also prove that the contravention was due to the act or default of a third party: see, *e.g.* Food Safety Act 1990, s.21(2), Medicines Act 1968, s.121. Some statutes merely require disclosure of the identity of the third party alleged to be responsible for the contravention: see, *e.g.* Consumer Safety Act 1978, s.2(6).

Leigh in *Strict and Vicarious Liability* (1982), states:

"The justification for absolute liability, rather than strict liability subject to a due diligence defence, cannot, surely, be that absolute liability conduces to greater care in a way that strict liability does not. The problem rather is that in some areas the burden of proving that an accused did not exercise due diligence, would be well-nigh impossible for the prosecution to discharge. Enforcement would, if such a defence were provided, become too difficult, and great harm would result from contravention. Hence the individual is virtually made an insurer of his conduct, subject perhaps to very narrowly expressed defences of the sort outlined above. Problems of pollution have certainly been viewed in these terms. Legislation dealing with poisons is stricter still. An employer whose employee sells or supplies poisons in contravention of the Poisons Rules cannot defend himself by showing that the employee acted contrary to orders, and any material fact known to the employee is deemed to be known to the employer. (Poisons Act 1972, s.8(2)(*a*) and (*b*)). Again, the employer is made an insurer of his enterprise."

iii. Critique

It is evident from the cases in the preceding section that a number of justifications are advanced for the imposition of strict liability. In *Sault Ste Marie* (*supra*) the two predominant arguments were seen as improved standards of prevention (*i.e.* the public will be better protected from the inherent risks in certain activities), and greater administrative efficiency (*i.e.* that efficacious enforcement is only possible where there is no burden on the prosecution to prove a mental element). On their own both these arguments could be used to favour the abolition of *mens rea* in all crimes. (See Wootton, *infra*).

Two further glosses are thus added. On the one hand it is suggested that strict liability does not eliminate fault as a basis of liability but that the fault element is determined at an earlier stage of the criminal process. Such an argument can lead to different conclusions. (See Paulus, Thomas and Smith, below.) On the other hand, it is said that, since these offences are not "true" crimes, the concept of *mens rea* is not required to prevent the injustice of punishing the "morally" innocent. This approach leads to difficulties in deciding whether it is the nature of the prohibited activity or the fact that no mental element is required which renders these "quasi" crimes. A vicious circle may arise in which strict liability is imposed to protect the public from the risks inherent in certain activities, while that protection is undermined by sentencing lightly defendants who, by virtue of the use of discretionary enforcement policies, have at the very least been negligent. (See Walker, *infra*). At a different level of analysis, it can be questioned whether either strict liability or negligence acts as an incentive to greater safety precautions (Hutchinson, *infra*).

Ingeborg Paulus, "Strict Liability: Its Place in Public Welfare Offences" (1978) 20 Crim.L.Q. 445:

"Theoretical legal reasoning repeatedly stresses that strict liability ... is unjust and holds persons liable for offences for which they are morally blameless. Yet empirical researchers assessing the law in action are not alarmed about strict liability offences and their enforcement. ... [W]henever studies have been made investigating the workings of strict liability, the persons involved in the administration of public welfare offences, especially those concerning food and drug laws, have stressed that strict liability generally does not penalise offenders who are not also clearly guilty. ... [T]he personnel in charge of enforcement rarely prosecute unless they find an element of fault or *mens rea* present in the offence. But the *availability* of strict liability prosecutions greatly facilitates their work."

[The studies referred to are: Smith and Pearson, "The Value of Strict Liability" [1969] Crim.L.R. 5; W. G. Carson, "Some Sociological Aspects of Strict Liability and the Enforcement of Factory Legislation" (1970) 33 M.L.R. 396; F. J. Remington, *et al.*, "Liability Without Fault Criminal Statutes" [1965] Wis.L.R. 625. To these can be added: Law Commission, Pub. Working Paper No. 30, Strict Liability and the Enforcement of the Factories Act 1961 (1970) and Law Reform Commission of Canada, "Studies in Strict Liability" (Ottawa, 1974).]

D. A. Thomas, "Form and Function in Criminal Law" in Glazebrook, p. 30:

"The effect of imposing strict liability is not necessarily to eliminate fault as a requirement of liability, but to delegate to the enforcer both the responsibility of deciding what kind of fault will in general justify a prosecution (with the certainty of conviction) and the right to determine whether in the circumstances of the particular case that degree of fault is present. The main objections to the concept of strict liability are thus procedural rather than substantive, and the questions to be addressed to the proponent of a statute creating an offence of strict liability are: 'Why is it not possible to incorporate into the definition of the offence the nature of the fault which is likely in practice to be required as a condition precedent to prosecution, and why is it not possible for the existence of this fault to be determined in accordance with the normal processes of the law?' At the very least, there can be no justification for enacting an offence of strict liability which is not balanced by a provision allowing the question whether fault existed or not to be raised in the trial as an affirmative defence, and any offence of strict liability where the gravity of the offence would be enhanced by the offender's knowledge of the relevant circumstances should be the lowest step in a hierarchy of offences including similar offences requiring proof of knowledge or intent."

J. C. Smith [1966] Crim.L.R. 505, commenting on *Lockyer* v. *Gibb* [1967] 2 Q.B. 243, a case on possession of drugs where the defendant did not know that what she possessed *was* a drug:

"The interpretation of statutes so as to create offences of strict liability in fact creates difficulties of sentencing which have not been faced up to by the courts. Take a case in which the accused is tried on indictment. The judge tells the jury to convict if they are satisfied that (i) D knew he was in possession of the thing, and (ii) the thing is a dangerous drug. They convict. If these are the only facts proved against D it would be quite scandalous to do other than give him an absolute discharge. If D ought to have known the thing was a drug, then he is in some degree blameworthy; if he in fact knew it was a drug, he is more blameworthy. But the jury need not consider these questions. How does the judge know on what basis he should sentence? He is discouraged from asking the jury the question at all. The judge presumably makes up his own mind. His view of the facts may differ completely from that of the jury—if they have a view. Thus what is really the fundamental issue of fact in the case is withdrawn from the jury and decided by the judge alone. The position in the case of a magistrates' court is a little easier because the magistrates at least know on what facts the conviction is based; but it is unsatisfactory that they may come to the sentencing stage without having considered whether the accused bears any moral responsibility whatever for the 'offence' which has been committed. This question must be considered before a sentence can be imposed. Presumably it is dealt with in the informal way in which other findings of fact relating only to sentence are handled. But this is hardly satisfactory, when it is really the most fundamental issue of fact in the case which is being considered. On what basis was the fine of £10 in the present case imposed? The magistrate must have thought that the defendant was in some degree blameworthy or he would presumably have granted an absolute discharge. Yet he was evidently not satisfied beyond reasonable doubt that the defendant knew that the substance was a dangerous drug. Did he then fine her because she ought to have known? Or was he satisfied with a lower degree of proof (she probably knew)?"

Nigel Walker, Crime and Punishment in Britain (1965), p. 33:

"The number of people killed or injured in road accidents each year is more than ten times the numbers involved in all the forms of assault recorded in the Criminal Statistics. Many of these casualties were due to the victim's own negligence or disobedience of rules; but even if we allow for this by halving the figures, it is clear that anti-social use of vehicles is a much more important source of death, bereavement, physical suffering and disablement than any intentional forms of violence. Yet the penal system treats motoring offences far less seriously than crimes of violence or even of dishonesty. Inadvertence is the excuse offered by most people accused of illegal parking, speeding or disobeying traffic signals, and that partly because this defence is so hard to disprove, partly in the hope of making the negligent driver less negligent, the law has been drafted so that even negligent transgressions are offences. This encourages the impression that *most* such transgressions are merely negligent, although it is very doubtful whether this is so."

Allan C. Hutchinson, Note on Sault Ste Marie (1979), 17 Osgoode Hall Law Journal 415, 429 (fn. 78):

"An application of the presently favoured 'economic perspective,' as represented by Richard A. Posner and other members of the so-called Chicago School, to the problem offers some interesting insights into the relative efficiency of strict liability and negligence as methods of combating the type of harm and safeguarding the interests that public welfare offences are intended to protect. According to such an analysis, where the primary object of an offence is accident prevention, as is the case with public welfare offences, there is little to choose between strict liability and negligence. Whichever basis of liability is employed, the standard of care taken by the potential injurer is likely to be influenced almost exclusively by the result of balancing the cost of precautions against the predicted cost of the penalty. If the preventive costs are lower, then precautions will be taken whether the offence is one of negligence or strict liability. But if the penalty is lower, then neither negligence nor strict liability is likely to encourage the taking of precautions. Therefore, the choice of liability standards has no effect on the level of safety achieved. Moreover, it is possible, yet surprising to many, that, if either basis of liability is to bring about some long term effect, the imposition of strict liability is more likely than negligence to result in an improvement in accident prevention. As regards negligence, liability is usually determined on the existing state of sophistication of the technology of accident prevention and, as such, presents little or no incentive to advance such knowledge by investing in its research and development. On the other hand, strict liability may engender greater safety, as there is more of an incentive to encourage and engage in the research into and the development of precautionary measures:

> 'If [for example, a railroad company] were liable for all accidents . . . , it would compare the liability that it could not avoid by means of existing safety precautions without the feasibility of developing new precautions that would reduce that liability. If safety research and development seemed likely to reduce accident costs by more than the cost of research and development, the [company] would undertake it. . . . (Posner, *The Economic Analysis of Law* (2d ed. Boston: Little, Brown, 1977) at 138).'

Such an approach is overly simplistic. The validity of the argument is contingent on two dubious assumptions: that penalties will remain minimal and unrealistic, and that the intangible costs (*i.e.* loss of reputation in the community, political embarrassment, unsettling of shareholders) will be negligible. Moreover, it fails to take into account the possible and positive gains that are available if the polluter shows himself to be a morally and socially responsible member of the community. There is much more to law and life than the cold and relentless logic of economic reasoning."

iv. Proposals for Reform

See clause 20 Draft Criminal Code Bill (*ante*, p. 140).

In contrast to the general trend one commentator has ardently advocated the increase in crimes of strict liability:

Baroness Wootton, Crime and The Criminal Law (2nd ed., 1981), pp. 46–48

"If, however, the primary function of the courts is conceived as the prevention of forbidden acts, there is little cause to be disturbed by the multiplication of offences of strict liability. If the law says that certain things are not to be done, it is illogical to confine this prohibition to occasions on which they are done from malice aforethought: for at least the material consequences of an action, and the reasons for prohibiting it, are the same whether it is the result of sinister malicious plotting, of negligence or of sheer accident. A man is equally dead and his relatives equally bereaved whether he was stabbed or run over by a drunken motorist or by an incompetent one; and the inconvenience caused by the loss of your bicycle is unaffected by the question whether or not the youth who removed it had the intention of putting it back, if in fact he had not done so at the time of his arrest. It is true, of course, as Professor Hart has argued, that the material consequences of an action by no means exhaust its effects. 'If one person hits another, the person struck does not think of the other as *just* a cause of pain to him. ... If the blow was light but deliberate, it has a significance for the person struck quite different from an accidental much heavier blow.' To ignore this difference, he argues, is to outrage 'distinctions which not only underlie morality, but pervade the whole of our social life.' That these distinctions are widely appreciated and keenly felt no one would deny. Often perhaps they derive their force from a purely punitive or retributive attitude; but alternatively they may be held to be relevant to an assessment of the social damage that results from a criminal act. Just as a heavy blow does more damage than a light one, so also perhaps does a blow which involves psychological injury do more damage than one in which the hurt is purely physical.

The conclusion to which this argument leads is, I think, not that the presence or absence of the guilty mind is unimportant, but that *mens rea* has, so to speak—and this is the crux of the matter—*got into the wrong place*. Traditionally, the requirement of the guilty mind is written into the actual definition of a crime. No guilty intention, no crime, is the rule. Obviously this makes sense if the law's concern is with wickedness: where there is no guilty intention, there can be no wickedness. But it is equally obvious, on the other hand, that an action does not become innocuous merely because whoever performed it meant no harm. If the object of the criminal law is to prevent the occurrence of socially damaging actions, it would be absurd to turn a blind eye to those which were due to carelessness, negligence or even accident. The question of motivation is *in the first instance* irrelevant.

But only in the first instance. At a later stage, that is to say, after what is now known as conviction, the presence or absence of guilty intention is all-important for its effect on the appropriate measures to be taken to prevent a recurrence of the forbidden act. The prevention of accidental deaths presents different problems from those involved in the prevention of wilful murders. The results of the actions of the careless, the mistaken, the wicked and the merely unfortunate may be indistinguishable from one another, but each case calls for a different treatment. Tradition, however, is very strong, and the notion that these differences are relevant only after the fact has been established that the accused committed the forbidden act seems still to be deeply abhorrent to the legal mind. Thus Lord Devlin, discussing the possibility that judges might have taken the line that all 'unintentional' criminals might be dealt with simply by the imposition of a nominal penalty, regards this as the 'negation of law.' 'It would,' [Devlin, Lord, *Samples of Law Making* (OUP, 1962) p. 73] he says, 'confuse the function of mercy which the judge is dispensing when imposing the penalty with the function of justice. It would have been to deny to the citizen due process of law because it would have been to say to him, in effect: "Although we cannot think that Parliament intended you to be punished in this case because you have really done nothing wrong, come to us, ask for mercy, and we shall grant mercy". .... In all criminal matters the citizen is entitled to the protection of the law ... and the mitigation of penalty should not be adopted as the prime method of dealing with accidental offenders.'

Within its own implied terms of reference the logic is unexceptionable. If the purpose of the law is to dispense punishment tempered with mercy, then to use mercy as a consolation for unjust punishment is certainly to give a stone for bread. But these are not the implied terms of reference of strict liability. In the case of offences of strict liability the presumption is not that those who have committed forbidden actions must be punished, but that appropriate steps must be taken to prevent the occurrence of such actions.''

J. C. Smith, "Responsibility in Criminal Law," in Barbara Wootton, Essays in Her Honour (1986) eds., Bean and Whynes. 141 at 153

"This brings me to what I regard as the major difficulty in Lady Wootton's theory. It is essentially a practical one. The only question for the court of trial is to be 'Did he do it?' Whether he did it intentionally, recklessly, negligently, or by sheer accident is irrelevant. In any event the person who did it is to be passed on to the 'sentencer' who will consider what should be done to ensure that he does not do it again. Now if the court of trial has to disregard the question of fault, so too surely do the police and the prosecuting authority (or whatever takes its place). If we allow the police or prosecutor to decide to proceed or not on the basis of whether or not the defendant was at fault, we do indirectly what we will not permit to be done directly. We allow the crucial decision which is now made formally and openly on proper evidence in court to be made informally, privately, and on whatever evidence the prosecutor, in his wisdom, or lack of it, considers relevant. The logic of the system requires the prosecution of *all* cases because even if the forbidden result has resulted from 'sheer accident,' the sentencer is under a duty to consider whether there is anything to be done to ensure that the 'offender' does not have such accidents again. Everyone who causes injury to another person, everyone who damages another's property, could, and should, be brought to court. Every buyer or seller of goods who makes an innocent misrepresentation, every bona-fide purchaser of goods in fact stolen, the surgeon whose patient dies on the operating table, the Good Samaritan who innocently gives help to a person escaping after committing an arrestable offence—all these have brought about the harm which it is the object of the law to prevent; so they should be subject to process of law so as to ensure that they do not cause the harm again. The business of the courts would be enormously multiplied. And to what purpose? What is to be done with all those who (like Ball and Mrs Tolson) have behaved reasonably and have had the misfortune to cause the forbidden result by sheer accident—except to tell them to continue to behave reasonably?

It is reasonably safe to assume that what would in fact happen is that, however illogically, the fault test would be applied at the police or prosecution stage. This would be prompted, not only by the natural sense of justice of those operating the system, but also by their realization of the futility of invoking legal process against one who has behaved entirely reasonably.

A further practical difficulty is that the system would put enormous discretion into the hands of the sentencer. He would apparently have the same power in law over one who caused death accidentally as over a murderer. It is difficult to believe that such a large discretion would be tolerable. It would dilute, if not destroy, the criminal law as a moral force and that at a time when the decline of religious belief has, as Lady Wootton herself says, created a dangerous vacuum. The shift from punishment to prevention may be intended to remove the moral basis of the law; but if, as some believe, one of the major reasons why people do not commit crimes is the sense of guilt which attaches to them, should not the aim be to enhance the sense of guilt rather than otherwise? To remove the element of fault is to empty the law of moral content. If murder were, in law, no different from accidental death, should we be so inhibited from committing murder as most of us are?"

The Model Penal Code

"S.1.04(1) An offence defined by this Code or by any other statute of this State, for which a sentence of [death or of] imprisonment is authorised, constitutes a crime. Crimes are classified as felonies, misdemeanours or petty misdemeanours.

(5) An offence defined by this Code or by any other statute of this State constitutes a violation if it is so designated in this Code or in the law defining the offence or if no other sentence than a fine, or fine and forfeiture or other civil penalty is authorised upon conviction or if it is defined by a statute other than this Code which now provides that the offense shall not constitute a crime. A violation does not constitute a crime and conviction of a violation shall not give rise to any disability or legal disadvantage based on conviction of a criminal offence.

S.2.05(1) The requirements of culpability prescribed by Sections 2.01 and 2.02 [of which the minimum is negligence] do not apply to:

(a) offences which constitute violations, unless the requirement involved is included in the definition of the offence or the Court determines that its application is consistent with effective enforcement of the law defining the offence; or

(b) offences defined by statutes other than the Code, insofar as a legislative purpose to impose absolute liability for such offences or with respect to any material element thereof plainly appears."

Justice, Breaking the Rules, 1980

[In recommending a similar division between "crimes" and "contraventions" in this country, *Justice* envisages the following:]

"Section 4.12 In practice, the sort of procedure we have in mind would work something like this:—

(a) whenever the public authority charged with responsibility for the relevant sector of public conduct obtained evidence amounting to a *prima facie* case of a contravention, it would notify the alleged contravenor by letter and invite his explanation;

(b) failing a satisfactory explanation within a fixed time, the authority would impose a prescribed penalty, and notify the contravenor what his options are;

(c) those options would be either to comply with the penalty imposed (*e.g.* to pay a fine) or, if he challenged the imposition of the penalty, to give notice of his objection (on a form supplied to him) to his local Magistrates' Court;

(d) if such a notice is given, the burden would be on the authority to satisfy the Magistrates' Court, by sworn evidence and beyond reasonable doubt, that the alleged contravenor had committed the contravention complained of."

Question

The Law Commission proposal in clause 20(1) would create a presumption in favour of *mens rea* which Parliament could rebut. The M.P.C. and "Justice" propose that "offences" of strict liability should be separately classified. Would either of these proposals tend to increase the incidence of strict liability? Is either approach preferable?

CHAPTER 4

MENTAL INCAPACITY

	PAGE		PAGE
1. Insanity	215	4. Intoxication	246
i. Disease of the Mind	219	i. Specific and Basic Intent	246
ii. The Nature and Quality of		ii. Becoming Intoxicated with	
the Act	223	Intent—the "Dutch Courage"	
iii. Uncontrollable Impulse	226	Problem	265
2. Automatism	226	iii. Intoxication and Defences	268
3. Proposals for Reform	237	iv. Proposals for Reform	273

Notes

1. In this chapter defences which relate to the defendant's mental capacity will be considered. Duress, necessity and self-defence are dealt with in Chapter 5. Provocation and diminished responsibility, because they are only available in murder, are dealt with in Chapter 8.

2. In a criminal trial the defendant's mental state at three separate points in time may be relevant:

(i) the time when the *actus reus* was committed;
(ii) the time when the defendant is called to plead to the charge against him;
(iii) the time when the court comes to consider the appropriate sentence where the defendant has been convicted.

In this book (i) will be considered. On (ii) see J. Sprack, *Emmins on Criminal Procedure* (1992), pp. 94–95; on (iii) see H. Wasik, *Emmins on Sentencing* (1993).

3. With regard to (i) there are three ways in which the issue of the defendant's mental state may be raised;

(a) on a plea of insanity;
(b) a plea that the *actus reus* was committed while the defendant was in a state of automatism; and
(c) on a plea of diminished responsibility where the charge is murder (see Chap. 8).

4. The section which follows is concerned with the law's treatment of insanity which provides a complete defence to a charge where the defendant was insane at the time the *actus reus* of the offence was committed. Previously the defence carried with it the consequence that the defendant would be ordered by the court to be admitted to a mental hospital under section 37 of the Mental Health Act 1983 subject to restriction without limit of time under section 41. The defendant would be detained until the Home Secretary or a Mental Health Tribunal ordered his release on being satisfied that detention was no longer necessary for the protection

of the public. This automatic committal to a mental hospital for an indeterminate period was one of the deterrents against pleading insanity as a defence. Some defendants preferred to plead guilty and cast themselves upon the mercy of the judge sentencing them rather than rely on a defence which was technically available to them. The Criminal Procedure (Insanity and Unfitness to Plead) Act 1991 has changed this. Section 3 substitutes a new section 5 of the Criminal Procedure (Insanity) Act 1964 providing the judge with discretion in the disposal he chooses. The substituted section 5 provides—

"**5.**—(1) This section applies where—

(a) a special verdict is returned that the accused is not guilty by reason of insanity; or

(b) findings are recorded that the accused is under a disability and that he did the act or made the omission charged against him.

(2) Subject to subsection (3) below, the court shall either—

(a) make an order that the accused be admitted, in accordance with the provisions of Schedule 1 to the Criminal Procedure (Insanity and Unfitness to Plead) Act 1991, to such hospital as may be specified by the Secretary of State; or

(b) where they have the power to do so by virtue of section 5 of that Act, make in respect of the accused such one of the following orders as they think most suitable in all the circumstances of the case, namely—

    (i) a guardianship order within the meaning of the Mental Health Act 1983;

    (ii) a supervision and treatment order within the meaning of Schedule 2 to the said Act of 1991; and

    (iii) an order for his absolute discharge.

(3) Paragraph (b) of subsection (2) above shall not apply where the offence to which the special verdict or findings relate is an offence the sentence for which is fixed by law."

This provision may discourage defendants from pleading guilty where the defence of insanity might be available to them, although they will still be stigmatised by being labelled "insane". The 1991 Act also did not address the problem of the legal definition of insanity which is grossly outdated and fails to recognise developments in medical knowledge.

1. INSANITY

M'Naghten's Case
(1843) 10 Cl. & F. 200; 8 E.R. 718

M'Naghten was indicted for murder and acquitted on the ground of insanity. In consequence debates took place in the House of Lords, and it was decided to take the opinion of the judges as to the nature and extent of the unsoundness of mind which would excuse the commission of a felony of this sort. Five questions were put to the judges in the terms set out in the following extract from their opinions.

TINDAL C.J.: (Delivering the opinion of all the judges except Maule J.): The first question proposed by your Lordships is this: "What is the law respecting alleged crimes committed by persons afflicted with insane delusion in respect of one or more particular subjects or persons: as, for instance, where at the time of the commission of the alleged crime the accused knew he was acting contrary to law, but did the act complained of with a view, under the influence of insane delusion, of redressing or revenging some supposed grievance or injury, or of producing some supposed public benefit?"

In answer to which question, assuming that your Lordships' inquiries are confined to those persons who labour under such partial delusions only, and are not in other respects insane, we are of opinion that, notwithstanding the party accused did the act complained of with a view, under the influence of insane delusion, of redressing or revenging some supposed grievance or injury, or of producing some public benefit, he is nevertheless punishable according to the nature of the crime committed, if he knew at the time of committing such crime that he was acting contrary to law; by which expression we understand your Lordships to mean the law of the land.

Your Lordships are pleased to inquire of us, secondly, "What are the proper questions to be submitted to the jury, where a person alleged to be afflicted with insane delusion respecting one or more particular subjects or persons, is charged with the commission of a crime (murder, for example), and insanity is set up as a defence?" And, thirdly, "In what terms ought the question to be left to the jury as to the prisoner's state of mind at the time when the act was committed?" And as these two questions appear to us to be more conveniently answered together, we have to submit our opinion to be, that the jurors ought to be told in all cases that every man is to be presumed to be sane, and to possess a sufficient degree of reason to be responsible for his crimes, until the contrary be proved to their satisfaction; and that to establish a defence on the ground of insanity, it must be clearly proved that, at the time of the committing of the act, the party accused was labouring under such a defect of reason, from disease of the mind, as not to know the nature and quality of the act he was doing; or, if he did know it, that he did not know he was doing what was wrong. The mode of putting the latter part of the question to the jury on these occasions has generally been, whether the accused at the time of doing the act knew the difference between right and wrong: which mode, though rarely, if ever, leading to any mistake with the jury, is not, as we conceive, so accurate when put generally and in the abstract, as when put with reference to the party's knowledge of right and wrong in respect of the very act with which he is charged. If the question were to be put as to the knowledge of the accused solely and exclusively with reference to the law of the land, it might tend to confound the jury, by inducing them to believe that an actual knowledge of the law of the land was essential in order to lead to a conviction: whereas the law is administered upon the principle that everyone must be taken conclusively to know it, without proof that he does know it. If the accused was conscious that the act was one which he ought not to do, and if that act was at the same time contrary to the law of the land, he is punishable: and the usual course therefore has been to leave the question to the jury, whether the party accused had a sufficient degree of reason to know that he was doing an act that was wrong: and this course we think is correct, accompanied with such observations and explanations as the circumstances of each particular case may require.

The fourth question which your Lordships have proposed to us is this: "If a person under an insane delusion as to existing facts, commits an offence in consequence thereof, is he thereby excused?" To which question the answer must, of course, depend on the nature of the delusion: but, making the same assumption as we did before, namely, that he labours under such partial delusion only, and is not in other respects insane, we think he must be considered in the same situation as to responsibility as if the facts with respect to which the delusion exists were real. For example, if under the influence of his delusion he supposes another man to be in the act of attempting to take away his life, and he kills that man, as he supposes, in self-defence, he would be exempt from punishment. If this delusion was that the deceased had inflicted a serious injury to his character and fortune, and he killed him in revenge for such supposed injury, he would be liable to punishment.

The question lastly proposed by your Lordships is: "Can a medical man conversant with the disease of insanity, who never saw the prisoner previously to the trial, but who was present during the whole trial and the examination of all the witnesses, be asked his opinion as to the state of the prisoner's mind at the time of the commission of the alleged crime, or his opinion whether the prisoner was conscious at the time of doing the act that he was acting contrary to law, or whether he was labouring under any and what delusion at the time?" In answer thereto, we state to your Lordships, that we think the medical man, under the circumstances supposed, cannot in strictness be asked his opinion in the terms above stated, because each of those questions involves the determination of the truth of the facts deposed to, which it is for the jury to decide, and the questions are not mere questions upon a matter of science, in which such evidence is admissible. But where facts are admitted or not disputed, and the question becomes substantially one of science only, it may be convenient to allow the question to be put in that general form, though the same cannot be insisted on as a matter of right.

Question

Do you agree with Glanville Williams that "the three M'Naghten questions are principally concerned with *mens rea*" (T.C.L., p. 644)?

C. Wells "Whither Insanity?" [1983] Crim.L.R. 787–788 & 793–794

"Insanity, along with the related defences of automatism and intoxication, raises very clearly the social protection role of the criminal law. The recent cases of *Bailey* [*infra.* p. 234] and *Sullivan* [*infra.* p. 220] illustrate this point. At one level they merely confirm the status quo—epilepsy is a 'disease of the mind,' diabetes is not. At another, they give an insight into the difficulty of pursuing the dual models of individual responsibility and social protection. In neither case is there any attempt to locate the argument within a theoretical context. And yet unless there is more clarity as to whether insanity is treated as a condition, like infancy, barring the jurisdiction of the court, or as an excuse for the particular act, the operation of the defence and its effect on other defences such as automatism and intoxication will continue to confound ... "

Very few defendants choose to avail themselves of the insanity defence. Although nominally an acquittal, the special verdict of 'not guilty by reason of insanity' is little less than 'a direction to punish but not to punish criminally.' ... The choice therefore for mentally disordered defendants is that between conviction (and the possibility at least of a determinate sentence) and a rather double-edged acquittal. Some defendants may be able to argue that they were in a state of automatism and thus add the possibility of a full acquittal. Because this represents a more attractive choice it is not surprising that it is in this sort of case that the courts have most often been asked to draw a line between the sane and the insane. But not infrequently the decision can also become entwined with the intoxication defence. The possibility of conceptual confusion on a large scale is thus opened—from insanity as a precluding or excusing condition through automatism on the basis of the 'no act' plea to the qualification of that plea by the doctrine of self-induced automatism. The issue then becomes one of whether to apply the rationale of the intoxication defence to the automaton whose condition is self-induced other than through drink or drugs. This may seem a long way from insanity. The paradigm mad person and the paradigm drunk may have little in common but appeal cases rarely deal with the unitary paradigm. *Bailey* (the case of the diabetic) is no exception. Considered with *Sullivan* (the epilepsy case), it confronts the problematic issue of when automatism should be treated as insanity. *Bailey* also raises the important, related, question of the limitations on automatism as a defence when it is self induced. . . .

> 'It has for centuries been recognised that if a person was, at the time of his unlawful act, mentally so disordered that it would be unreasonable to impute guilt to him, he ought not to be held liable for conviction and punishment.'

This type of 'reason is since reason long has been' argument was employed also by the Butler Committee and is of course a somewhat inadequate starting point for an inquiry into insanity, particularly in view of changing ideas about criminal responsibility. And, as with much discussion in this area, it skates over the dual effect of the insanity verdict, concentrating only on the absolvent quality and ignoring its concomitant of indefinite detention.

One view prevalent in the English literature is that insanity excuses because it negatives the mental element in crime. There are two problems with this. Unless *mens rea* is here being given the wider normative meaning of 'the state of mind stigmatised as wrongful by the criminal law,' it is not easy to see that insanity does necessarily negative *mens rea*. It only does so if *mens rea* consists of a subjective mental element. Where it is an objective form of recklessness or negligence, or where there is a crime of strict liability, then the argument that insanity excuses because it precludes *mens rea* breaks down. And if one took the wider normative view of *mens rea*, then the argument would be somewhat tautologous; it would amount to saying that an insane person is not responsible because the stigmatised wrongful state of mind includes only the sane.

The other problem with the *mens rea* view of insanity is that it is an implicit acknowledgement that the insanity defence is about disposal rather than responsibility. A sane person who lacks *mens rea* is normally acquitted. If insanity is a 'defence' because it amounts to lack of *mens rea*, then it is otiose.

Thus an exploration of insanity and responsibility has either to go beyond *mens rea*, or, if a normative view is taken, it has to justify the exclusion of the insane.''

Note

M'Naghten places the burden of proof on the defendant. It was held in R. v. *Sodeman* [1936] 2 All E.R. 1138 that this requires proof on a balance of probability. Both the Criminal Law Revision

Committee (11th Report, Cmnd. 4991 (1972), s.1.40) and the Butler Committee on Mentally Abnormal Offenders (Cmnd. 6244 (1975), s.18.39) recommended that this burden should be on the prosecution. In the Draft Criminal Code, Clause 35, either the defence or prosecution may prove mental disorder on a balance of probabilities. See *Bratty, post,* p. 227, for an explanation of the working of the burden of proof where insanity is run with other defences.

i. Disease of the Mind

R. v. Kemp
[1957] 1 Q.B. 399
Bristol Assizes

The defendant was charged with causing grievous bodily harm to his wife. He suffered from arteriosclerosis which had not given rise to general mental trouble but caused temporary loss of consciousness during which state the attack was made. He did not plead insanity.

DEVLIN J.: In this case it is conceded that everything [in the third and fourth answers in *M'Naghten's Case*] applies here, except for "disease of the mind. . . . " The law is not concerned with the brain but with the mind, in the sense that "mind" is ordinarily used, the mental faculties of reason, memory and understanding. If one read for "disease of the mind" "disease of the brain," it would follow that in many cases pleas of insanity would not be established because it could not be proved that the brain had been affected in any way, either by degeneration of the cells or in any other way. In my judgment the condition of the brain is irrelevant and so is the question of whether the condition of the mind is curable or incurable, transitory or permanent. There is no warranty for introducing those considerations into the definition in the M'Naghten Rules. Temporary insanity is sufficient to satisfy them. It does not matter whether it is incurable and permanent or not.

I think that the approach of Mr. Lee (for the Crown) to the definition in the Rules is the right one. He points out the order of the words "a defect of reason, from disease of the mind." The primary thing that has to be looked for is the defect of reason. "Disease of the mind" is there for some purpose, obviously, but the prime thing is to determine what is admitted here, namely, whether or not there is a defect of reason. In my judgment, the words "from disease of the mind" are not to be construed as if they were put in for the purpose of distinguishing between diseases which have a mental origin and diseases which have a physical origin, a distinction which in 1843 was probably little considered. They were put in for the purpose of limiting the effect of the words "defect of reason." A defect of reason is by itself enough to make the act irrational and therefore normally to exclude responsibility in law. But the Rule was not intended to apply to defects of reason caused simply by brutish stupidity without rational power. It was not intended that the defence should plead "although with a healthy mind he nevertheless had been brought up in such a way that he had never learned to exercise his reason, and therefore he is suffering from a defect of reason." The words ensure that unless the defect is due to a diseased mind and not simply to an untrained one there is insanity within the meaning of the Rule.

Hardening of the arteries is a disease which is shown on the evidence to be capable of affecting the mind in such a way as to cause a defect, temporarily or permanently, of its reasoning, understanding and so on, and so as is my judgment a disease of the mind which comes within the meaning of the Rules.

Verdict: Guilty but insane

R. v. Sullivan
[1984] A.C. 156
House of Lords

The appellant was charged with inflicting grievous bodily harm on P. At his trial he admitted the act but asserted by way of defence that he had done so while in an epileptic seizure. The trial judge ruled that this amounted to a defence of insanity rather than a defence of automatism. The appellant then changed his plea to guilty of assault occasioning actual bodily harm and was convicted of that offence. He appealed against the conviction but the Court of Appeal upheld the judge's ruling and dismissed the appeal. He appealed to the House of Lords.

LORD DIPLOCK: The evidence as to the pathology of a seizure due to psychomotor epilepsy can be sufficiently stated for the purposes of this appeal by saying that after the first stage, the prodram, which precedes the fit itself, there is a second stage, the ictus, lasting a few seconds, during which there are electrical discharges into the temporal lobes of the brain of the sufferer. The effect of these discharges is to cause him in the post-ictal stage to make movements which he is not conscious that he is making, including, and this was a characteristic of previous seizures which Mr. Sullivan had suffered, automatic movements of resistance to anyone trying to come to his aid. These movements of resistance might, though in practice they very rarely would, involve violence . . .
[His lordship reviewed the M'Naghten rules and *Bratty*, p. 227 *infra* and continued.] In the instant case, as in *Bratty*, the only evidential foundation that was laid for any finding by the jury that Mr. Sullivan was acting unconsciously and involuntarily when he was kicking Mr. Payne, was that when he did so he was in the post-ictal stage of a seizure of psychomotor epilepsy. The evidential foundation in the case of Bratty, that he was suffering from psychomotor epilepsy at the time he did the act with which he was charged, was very weak and was rejected by the jury; the evidence in Mr. Sullivan's case, that he was so suffering when he was kicking Mr. Payne, was very strong and would almost inevitably be accepted by a properly directed jury. It would be the duty of the judge to direct the jury that if they did accept that evidence the law required them to bring in a special verdict and none other. The governing statutory provision is to be found in section 2 of the Trial of Lunatics Act 1883. This says "the jury *shall* return a special verdict . . . "
My Lords, I can deal briefly with the various grounds on which it has been submitted that the instant case can be distinguished from what constituted the ratio decidendi in *Bratty* v. *Attorney-General for Northern Ireland* [1963] A.C. 386, and that it falls outside the ambit of the M'Naghten Rules.
First, it is submitted the medical evidence in the instant case shows that psychomotor epilepsy is not a disease of the mind, whereas in *Bratty* it was accepted by all the doctors that it was. The only evidential basis for this submission is that Dr. Fenwick said that in medical terms to constitute

a "disease of the mind" or "mental illness," which he appeared to regard as interchangeable descriptions, a disorder of brain functions (which undoubtedly occurs during a seizure in psychomotor epilepsy) must be prolonged for a period of time usually more than a day; while Dr. Taylor would have it that the disorder must continue for a minimum of a month to qualify for the description "a disease of the mind."

The nomenclature adopted by the medical profession may change from time to time; Bratty was tried in 1961. But the meaning of the expression "disease of the mind" as the cause of "a defect of reason" remains unchanged for the purposes of the application of the M'Naghten Rules. I agree with what was said by Devlin J. in *R. v. Kemp* (*ante*, p. 219), that "mind" in the M'Naghten Rules is used in the ordinary sense of the mental faculties of reason, memory and understanding. If the effect of a disease is to impair these faculties so severely as to have either of the consequences referred to in the latter part of the rules, it matters not whether the aetiology of the impairment is organic, as in epilepsy, or functional, or whether the impairment itself is permanent or is transient and intermittent, provided that it subsisted at the time of commission of the act. The purpose of the legislation relating to the defence of insanity, ever since its origin in 1800, has been to protect society against recurrence of the dangerous conduct. The duration of a temporary suspension of the mental faculties of reason, memory and understanding, particularly if, as in Mr. Sullivan's case, it is recurrent, cannot on any rational ground be relevant to the application by the courts of the M'Naghten Rules, though it may be relevant to the course adopted by the Secretary of State, to whom the responsibility for how the defendant is to be dealt with passes after the return of the special verdict of "not guilty by reason of insanity."

To avoid misunderstanding I ought perhaps to add that in expressing my agreement with what was said by Devlin J. in *Kemp*, where the disease that caused the temporary and intermittent impairment of the mental faculties was arteriosclerosis, I do not regard that learned judge as excluding the possibility of non-insane automatism (for which the proper verdict would be a verdict of "not guilty") in cases where temporary impairment (not being self-induced by consuming drink or drugs) results from some external physical factor such as a blow on the head causing concussion or the administration of an anaesthetic for therapeutic purposes. I mention this because in *R. v. Quick* [1973] Q.B. 910, Lawton L.J. appears to have regarded the ruling in *Kemp* as going as far as this. If it had done, it would have been inconsistent with the speeches in this House in *Bratty*, (*post*, p. 227) where *Kemp* was alluded to without disapproval by Viscount Kilmuir L.C. at p. 403, and received the express approval of Lord Denning, at p. 411. The instant case, however, does not in my view afford an appropriate occasion for exploring possible causes of non-insane automatism.

The only other submission in support of Mr. Sullivan's appeal which I think is necessary to mention is that, because the expert evidence was to the effect that Mr. Sullivan's acts in kicking Mr. Payne were unconscious and thus "involuntary" in the legal sense of that term, his state of mind was not one dealt with by the M'Naghten Rules at all, since it was not covered by the phrase "as not to know the nature and quality of the act he was doing." Quite apart from being contrary to all three speeches in this House in *Bratty v. A.-G. for Northern Ireland* this submission appears to me, with all respect to counsel, to be quite unarguable. Dr. Fenwick himself accepted it as an accurate description of Mr. Sullivan's mental state in the post-ictal stage of a seizure. The audience to whom the phrase in the M'Naghten Rules was addressed consisted of peers of the realm in the

1840's when certain orotundity of diction had not yet fallen out of fashion. Addressed to an audience of jurors in the 1980's it might more aptly be expressed as "He did not know what he was doing."

My Lords, it is natural to feel reluctant to attach the label of insanity to a sufferer from psychomotor epilepsy of the kind to which Mr. Sullivan was subject, even though the expression in the context of a special verdict of "not guilty by reason of insanity" is a technical one which includes a purely temporary and intermittent suspension of the mental faculties of reason, memory and understanding resulting from the occurrence of an epileptic fit. But the label is contained in the current statute, it has appeared in this statute's predecessors ever since 1800. It does not lie within the power of the courts to alter it. Only Parliament can do that. It has done so twice; it could do so once again.

Sympathise though I do with Mr. Sullivan, I see no other course open to your Lordships than to dismiss this appeal.

[The other Law Lords agreed with Lord Diplock's speech.]

Appeal dismissed.

Questions

1. If, as Lord Diplock stated, the purpose of the M'Naghten Rules is "to protect society against the recurrence of the dangerous conduct," was this purpose furthered by the procedure followed in *Sullivan* when the guilty plea was accepted? (see E. Lederman "Non-Insane and Insane Automatism: Reducing the Significance of a Problematic Distinction" (1985) 34 I.C.L.Q. 819)

2. Did Sullivan's conviction serve any other purpose such as deterring other epileptics from injuring others while in an epileptic seizure?

3. Does the distinction between external physical factors and internal organic or functional factors provide a sound basis for identifying those who are dangerous and from whom society needs to be protected?

4. Do, and if so should, the M'Naghten Rules apply to defendants who suffer from retarded development, *i.e.* is mental deficiency a disease of the mind?

Note

In *Bratty* v. *Attorney-General for Northern Ireland* [1963] A.C. 386 (*post*, p. 227) Lord Denning stated, at p. 412:

> "It seems to me that any mental disorder which has manifested itself in violence and is prone to recur is a disease of the mind. At any rate it is the sort of disease for which a person should be detained in hospital rather than be given an unqualified acquittal."

This dictum was not approved in *Sullivan* which focused on the cause of the defect of reason rather than the consequences flowing from it. In *Burgess* [1991] 2 W.L.R. 1206, the accused sought to plead automatism due to sleep walking on a charge of wounding with intent to do grievous bodily harm contrary to section 18 of the Offences Against the Person Act 1861. The trial judge ruled that this was a plea of insanity. The appellant appealed against the finding of the jury that he was not guilty by reason of insanity. The Court of Appeal expressed its approval of Lord Denning's "definition" of "disease of the mind". Lord Lane C.J. adding this qualification (at p. 1212):

"It seems to us that if there is a danger of recurrence that may be an added reason for categorising the condition as a disease of the mind. On the other hand, the absence of the danger of recurrence is not a reason for saying that it cannot be a disease of the mind."

This revival of Lord Denning's dictum is hardly helpful (nor was it necessary for deciding the appeal). Firstly, mental disorders may manifest themselves in other ways which do not involve violence, for example, pyromania or kleptomania; if these conditions are due to an internal cause they will be labelled diseases of the mind. In *Hennessy* [1989] 1 W.L.R. 287, D, whilst in a hyperglycaemic episode due to failure to take insulin which he claimed was due to stress, anxiety and depression, took a motor vehicle without authority and drove whilst disqualified. The offences were not violent but the Court of Appeal held that D's plea was one of insanity as diabetes being an internal factor amounted to a disease of the mind. Stress, anxiety and depression, while they may be caused by external factors, were not themselves external factors. Secondly, there are conditions which manifest themselves in violence which do not fall within the definition of disease of the mind approved in *Sullivan* as the case of *Quick* (*post*, p. 230) discloses.

ii. The Nature and Quality of the Act

Note

The basis of the M'Naghten Rules is "defect of reason" (not emotion or will) and the result of the defect of reason must be that the accused either did not know what he was doing or did not know that what he was doing was wrong.

R. v. Codere
(1916) 12 Cr.App.R. 21
Court of Criminal Appeal

The appellant had been convicted of murder. Insanity was the only defence raised at the trial. Under section 5(4) of the Criminal Appeal Act 1907, the Court of Criminal Appeal have power to quash the sentence and order the appellant to be detained as insane.

LORD READING C.J.: . . . Mr. Foote (on behalf of Codere) has addressed an argument to us based on *M'Naghten's Case*, which is the classic authority on the subject, which in substance resolved itself into this, that we must assume that when the law says that the question is whether the accused was labouring under such a defect of reason, from disease of the mind, as not to know the nature and quality of the act he was doing, we must read "nature" to have reference to the physical act, and "quality" to refer to the morality of the act, and that therefore the jury should be asked if he knew he was doing wrong. The argument advanced is that the judge ought to tell the jury that "quality" means, "Did the accused person know that the act was immoral?" and when one stops and asks the meaning of "immoral" we get to the first of the difficulties which faced Mr. Foote.

It is said that "quality" is to be regarded as characterising the moral, as contrasted with the physical, aspect of the deed. The court cannot agree with that view of the meaning of the words "nature and quality." The court is of opinion that in using the language "nature and quality" the judges were only dealing with the physical character of the act, and were not intending to distinguish between the physical and moral aspects of the act. That is the law as it has been laid down by judges in many directions to juries, and as the court understands it to be at the present time.

We then come to the second branch of the test, namely, if he knew the physical nature of the act did he know that he was doing wrong? Mr. Foote has argued that it is not enough that he knew the act was contrary to law and punishable by law, and that, even if he did know that ... yet the jury ought to have been told that they must find a special verdict (of guilty but insane) ... unless they came to the conclusion that he knew that the act was morally wrong. The question of the distinction between morally and legally wrong opens wide doors. In a case of this kind, namely, killing, it does not seem debatable that the appellant could have thought that the act was not morally wrong, judged by the ordinary standards, when the act is punishable by law, and is known by him to be punishable by law. It was suggested at one time in the course of argument that the question should be judged by the standard of the accused, but it is obvious that this proposition is wholly untenable, and would tend to excuse crimes without number, and to weaken the law to an alarming degree. It is conceded now that the standard to be applied is whether according to the ordinary standard adopted by reasonable men the act was right or wrong. ... Once it is clear that the appellant knew that the act was wrong in law, then he was doing an act which he was conscious he ought not to do, and as it was against the law, it was punishable by law; assuming, therefore, that he knew the nature and quality of the act, he was guilty of murder, and was properly convicted.

The difficulty no doubt arises over the words "conscious that the act was one which he ought not to do," but, looking at all the answers in *M'Naghten's Case*, it seems that if it is punisable by law it is an act which he ought not to do, and that is the meaning in which the phrase is used in that case. There may be minor cases before a court of summary jurisdiction where that view may be open to doubt, but in cases such as these the true view is what we have just said.

Application dismissed

Question

Under an insane delusion that his wife is possessed by evil, D. decides to kill her and does so. Does his delusion relate to the nature and quality of his act entitling him to plead insanity?

R. v. Windle
[1952] 2 Q.B. 826
Court of Criminal Appeal

The appellant gave his wife a fatal dose of aspirin. He admitted that he had done so, and said he supposed he would hang for it. The appellant's only defence was that of insanity. At the trial, Devlin J. ruled that there was no evidence to go to the jury on the defence of insanity.

LORD GODDARD C.J.: The point we have to decide in this case can be put into a very small compass. We are asked to review what are generally known as the M'Naghten Rules, and possibly to make new law. ... The argument before us has really been on what is the meaning of the word "wrong". ... Mr. Shawcross (for Windle) ... suggested that the word "wrong" as it was used in the M'Naghten Rules, did not mean contrary to law but has some kind of qualified meaning, such as morally wrong, and that if a person was in such a state of mind through a defect of reason that, although he knew that what he was doing was wrong in law, he thought that it was beneficial or kind or praiseworthy, that would excuse him.

Courts of law can only distinguish between that which is in accordance with law and that which is contrary to law. There are many acts which, to use an expression which is to be found in some of the old cases, are contrary to the law of God and man. For instance, in the Decalogue will be found the laws "Thou shalt not kill" and "Thou shalt not steal." Those acts are contrary to the law of man and also to the law of God. If the seventh commandment is taken, "Thou shalt not commit adultery," although that is contrary to the law of God, so far as the criminal law is concerned it is not contrary to the law of man. That does not mean that the law encourages adultery; I only say that it is not a criminal offence. The law cannot embark on the question, and it would be an unfortunate thing if it were left to juries to consider whether some particular act was morally right or wrong. The test must be whether it is contrary to law. ...

In the opinion of the court there is no doubt that in the M'Naghten Rules "wrong" means contrary to law and not "wrong" according to the opinion of one man or of a number of people on the question of whether a particular act might or might not be justified. In the present case, it could not be challenged that the appellant knew that what he was doing was contrary to law, and that he realised what punishment the law provided for murder.

Appeal dismissed

Questions

1. Consider the questions raised by these last two cases. Is what is legally wrong always morally wrong? In *Codere* the judge was prepared to conceive of a negative answer only in minor crimes dealt with by courts of summary jurisdiction.

2. Would D be entitled to rely on the insanity defence if he believed his act was morally wrong although because of a disease of the mind he failed to appreciate that it was contrary to law? (Compare the approach of the High Court of Australia in *Stapleton v. R.* (1952) 86 C.L.R. 358 with *Windle*.)

3. *Codere* approves the test "the ordinary standard adopted by reasonable men," *Windle* indicates that the test is "whether it is contrary to law." Does this alter the law? Was the creation of a new test essential for the decision in *Windle*?

4. If the test is one of insanity is an objective test of any sort appropriate? Consider the passage in *Codere* which indicates that a subjective standard would "weaken the law to an alarming degree."

iii. Uncontrollable Impulse

Notes

1. Will an individual be able to rely on the insanity defence where he appreciates the nature and quality of his conduct and knows that it is contrary to the law but, because of a defect of reason due to a disease of the mind, is unable to prevent himself from acting as he did? When the defence of uncontrollable impulse was raised in *Sodeman* v. *R.* [1936] 2 All E.R. 1138, the Privy Council (at. p. 1140), rejected the proposition "that the rules in *M'Naghten's* Case are no longer to be treated as an exhaustive statement of the law with regard to insanity, and that there is to be engrafted upon those rules another rule that where a man knows that he is doing what is wrong, nonetheless he may be held to be insane if he is caused to do the act by an irresistible impulse produced by disease."

This was further explained in *Attorney-General for South Australia* v. *Brown* [1960] A.C. 432 where, in an appeal to the Privy Council, Lord Tucker said (at p. 449) "At various times in the past attempts have been made to temper the supposed harshness or unscientific nature of the M'Naghten Rules. These attempts were supported by the high authority of Sir James Fitz-James Stephen, but in the end the Rules remain in full force and their harshness has in this country been to some extent alleviated by the recent legislative enactment affording the defence of diminished responsibility. . . .

"Their Lordships must not, of course, be understood to suggest that in a case where evidence has been given (and it is difficult to imagine a case where such evidence would be other than medical evidence) that irresistible impulse is a symptom of the particular disease of the mind from which a prisoner is said to be suffering and as to its effect on his ability to know the nature and quality of his act or that his act is wrong it would not be the duty of the judge to deal with the matter in the same way as any other relevant evidence given at the trial."

For the way in which "irresistible impulse" has been treated in the defence of diminished responsibility, see *R.* v. *Byrne, post*, p. 530.

2. The "defect of reason" must arise "from a disease of the mind." The question may arise whether a person's state of automatism (where clearly reason is not only defective but completely absent) arises from a disease of the mind. These cases are dealt with in the next section. A similar problem can be seen in the section on intoxication, *post*, p. 246.

2. AUTOMATISM

Note

The defence of automatism arises initially as one form of denial that the prosecution has proved that the *actus reus* was voluntary (see *ante*, p. 14). But acquittal will not necessarily follow. If the origin of the automatic state is a disease of the mind, a finding of insanity will result. *Kemp, Bratty, Quick* and *Bailey, infra* illustrate the problems facing the courts in this borderland between the two defences. Where the origin is self-induced intoxication, the defendant is subject to the limitations of that defence: see *Majewski, post*, p. 246. Even where the defendant's state is attributable to neither of those factors a person who is at fault in losing the capacity for voluntary control of his or her actions cannot rely on this defence: *Quick* and *Bailey, infra*. This imports a similar notion to that which qualifies intoxication as a denial of *mens rea*: self-induced incapacity may be culpable.

Thus it is only in extremely confined circumstances that the defence can be successfully raised. See Williams, T.C.L., 662–666 for a description of the common causes of automatism.

Bratty v. A.-G. for Northern Ireland
[1963] A.C 386
House of Lords

The appellant strangled a girl. He said in a statement to the police that when he was with her he had "a terrible feeling" and "a sort of blackness" came over him. At the trial there was medical evidence that he might have been suffering from psychomotor epilepsy. To a charge of murder he raised three defences: automatism, lack of intent for murder, and insanity. The judge refused to leave the first two to the jury, and they rejected the plea of insanity. This was affirmed by the Court of Criminal Appeal in Northern Ireland. He appealed to the House of Lords.

VISCOUNT KILMUIR AND LORD MORRIS OF BORTH-Y-GEST delivered speeches dismissing the appeal with which LORDS TUCKER and HODSON agreed.

LORD DENNING: My Lords, in the case of *Woolmington* v. *D.P.P.* A.C. 462, 482, Viscount Sankey L.C. said that "when dealing with a murder case the Crown must prove (a) death 'as a result of a voluntary act of the accused,' and (b) malice of 'the accused.' " The requirement that it should be a voluntary act is essential, not only in a murder case, but also in every criminal case. No act is punishable if it is done involuntarily: and an involuntary act in this context—some people nowadays prefer to speak of it as "automatism"—means an act which is done by the muscles without any control by the mind, such as a spasm, a reflex action or a convulsion; or an act done by a person who is not conscious of what he is doing, such as an act done whilst suffering from concussion or whilst sleep-walking. . . .

The term "involuntary act" is, however, capable of wider connotations: and to prevent confusion it is to be observed that in the criminal law an act is not to be regarded as an involuntary act simply because the doer does not remember it. When a man is charged with dangerous driving, it is no defence to him to say "I don't know what happened. I cannot remember a 'thing,' " see *Hill* v. *Baxter* [1958] 1 Q.B. 277. Loss of memory afterwards is never a defence in itself, so long as he was conscious at the time . . . see *Russell* v. *H.M. Advocate* 1946 S.C.(J.) 37; *R.* v. *Podola* [1960] 1 Q.B. 325. Nor is an act to be regarded as an involuntary act simply because the doer could not control his impulse to do it. When a man is charged with murder, and it appears that he knew what he was doing, but he could not resist it, then his assertion "I couldn't help myself" is no defence in itself, see *A.-G. for South Australia* v. *Brown* (1960) A.C. 432: though it may go towards a defence of diminished responsibility, in places where that defence is available, see *R.* v. *Byrne*, [*post*, p. 530]: but it does not render his act involuntary so as to entitle him to an unqualified acquittal. Nor is an act to be regarded as an involuntary act simply because it is unintentional or its consequences are unforeseen. When a man is charged with dangerous driving, it is no defence for him to say, however truly, "I did not mean to drive dangerously. ... " But even though it is absolutely prohibited, nevertheless he has a defence if he can show that it was an involuntary act in the sense that he was unconscious at the time and did not know what he was doing. ...

Another thing to be observed is that it is not every involuntary act which leads to a complete acquittal. Take first an involuntary act which proceeds from a state of drunkenness. If the drunken man is so drunk that he does not know what he is doing, he has a defence to any charge, such as murder or wounding with intent, in which a specific intent is essential, but he is still liable to be convicted of manslaughter or unlawful wounding for which no specific intent is necessary, see *Beard* [1920] A.C. 479.

Again, if the involuntary act proceeds from a disease of the mind, it gives rise to a defence of insanity, but not to a defence of automatism. Suppose a crime is committed by a man in a state of automatism or clouded consciousness due to a recurrent disease of the mind. Such an act is no doubt involuntary, but it does not give rise to an unqualified acquittal, for that would mean that he would be let at large to do it again. The only proper verdict is one which ensures that the person who suffers from the disease is kept secure in a hospital so as not to be a danger to himself or others. That is a verdict of guilty but insane.

Once you exclude all the cases I have mentioned, it is apparent that the category of involuntary acts is very limited. ...

My Lords, I think that Devlin J. was quite right in *Kemp's* case in putting the question of insanity to the jury, even though it had not been raised by the defence. When it is asserted that the accused did an involuntary act in a state of automatism, the defence necessarily puts in issue the state of mind of the accused man: and thereupon it is open to the prosecution to show what his true state of mind was. The old notion that only the defence can raise a defence of insanity is now gone. The prosecution are entitled to raise it and it is their duty to do so rather than allow a dangerous person to be at large. ...

Upon the other point discussed by Devlin J., namely, what is a "disease of the mind" within the M'Naghten Rules, I would agree with him that this is a question for the judge. The major mental diseases, which the doctors call psychoses, such as schizophrenia, are clearly diseases of the mind. But in *Charlson* [1955] 1 W.L.R. 317, ... , Barry J. seems to have assumed that other diseases such as epilepsy or cerebral tumour are not diseases of the mind, even when they are such as to manifest themselves in violence. I do not agree with this. It seems to me that any mental disorder which has manifested itself in violence and is prone to recur is a disease of the mind. At any rate it is the sort of disease for which a person should be detained in hospital rather than be given an unqualified acquittal. ...

In the present case the defence raised both automatism and insanity. And herein lies the difficulty because of the burden of proof. If the accused says he did not know what he was doing, then, so far as the defence of automatism is concerned, the Crown must prove that the act was a voluntary act, see *Woolmington's* case. But so far as the defence of insanity is concerned, the defence must prove that the act was an involuntary act due to disease of the mind, see *M'Naghten's* case [*ante*, p. 215].

... I think that the difficulty is to be resolved by remembering that, whilst the *ultimate* burden rests on the Crown of proving every element essential in the crime, nevertheless in order to prove that the act was a voluntary act, the Crown is entitled to rely on the *presumption* that every man has sufficient mental capacity to be responsible for his crimes: and that if the defence wish to displace that presumption they must give some evidence from which the contrary may reasonably be inferred. Thus a drunken man is presumed to have the capacity to form the specific intent necessary to constitute the crime, unless evidence is given from which it can reasonably be inferred that he was incapable of forming it. ...

The presumption of mental capacity of which I have spoken is a provisional presumption only. It does not put the legal burden on the defence in the same way as the presumption of sanity does. It leaves the legal burden on the prosecution, but nevertheless, until it is displaced, it enables the prosecution to discharge the ultimate burden of proving that the act was voluntary. Not because the presumption is evidence itself, but because it takes the place of evidence. In order to displace the presumption of mental capacity, the defence must give sufficient evidence from which it may reasonably be inferred that the act was involuntary. The evidence of the man himself will rarely be sufficient unless it is supported by medical evidence which points to the cause of the mental incapacity. ...

When the only cause that is assigned for an involuntary act is drunkenness, then it is only necessary to leave drunkenness to the jury, with the consequential directions, and not to leave automatism at all. When the only cause that is assigned for it is a disease of the mind, then it is only necessary to leave insanity to the jury, and not automatism. When the cause assigned is concussion or sleep-walking, there should be some evidence from which it can reasonably be inferred before it should be left to the jury. ...

Once a proper foundation is thus laid for automatism, the matter becomes at large and must be left to the jury. As the case proceeds, the evidence may weigh first to one side and then to the other: and so the burden may appear to shift to and fro. But at the end of the day the legal burden comes into play and requires that the jury should be satisfied beyond reasonable doubt that an act was a voluntary act.

I am clearly of opinion that, if the act of George Bratty was an involuntary act, as the defence suggested, the evidence attributed it solely to a disease of the mind and the only defence open was the defence of insanity. There was no evidence of automatism apart from insanity. There was, therefore, no need for the judge to put it to the jury. And when the jury rejected the defence of insanity, they rejected the only defence disclosed by the evidence. ...

I would, therefore, dismiss the appeal.

Appeal dismissed

Question

Lord Denning stated that "any mental disorder which has manifested itself in violence and is prone to recur is a disease of the mind." By this did Lord Denning mean that a disease of the mind was a mental disorder which was prone to recur and manifest itself again in a violent way; or, did he simply mean that it was a mental disorder which had in the past manifested itself in violence and which disorder was prone to recur? See next case.

R. v. Quick and Paddison
[1973] Q.B. 910
Court of Appeal

The appellant, who was a diabetic, was a psychiatric nurse. He was charged with assaulting a patient at the hospital where he worked. He said he could not remember the incident but that on the day it occurred he had taken his prescribed insulin, a small breakfast, some whisky, a quarter of a bottle of rum, and had no lunch. Medical evidence showed he was suffering at the time from hypoglycaemia, a deficiency of blood sugar after an injection of insulin. The appellant changed his plea to guilty after the judge rejected his defence of automatism on the grounds that the only defence open to him was insanity.

LAWTON L.J., for the court: In its broadest aspects these appeals raise the question what is meant by the phrase "a defect of reason from disease of the mind" within the meaning of the M'Naghten Rules. More particularly the question is whether a person who commits a criminal act whilst under the effects of hypoglycaemia can raise a defence of automatism, as the appellants submitted was possible, or whether such a person must rely on a defence of insanity if he wishes to relieve himself of responsibility for his acts, as Bridge J. ruled. . . .

Our examination of such authorities as there are must start with *Bratty v. A.-G. for Northern Ireland, supra,* because the judge ruled as he did in reliance on that case. The House of Lords . . . accepted that automatism as distinct from insanity could be a defence if there was a proper foundation in the evidence for it. In this case, if Quick's alleged condition could have been caused by hypoglycaemia Bridge J.'s ruling was right. The question remains, however, whether a mental condition arising from hypoglycaemia does amount to a disease of the mind. All their Lordships based their speeches on the basis that such medical evidence as there was pointed to Bratty suffering from a "defect of reason from disease of the mind" and nothing else. Lord Denning discussed in general terms what constitutes a disease of the mind [His Lordship then quoted the passage on "disease of the mind," *supra*].

If this opinion is right and there are no restricting qualifications which ought to be applied to it, Quick was setting up a defence of insanity. He may have been at the material time in a condition of mental disorder manifesting itself in violence. Such manifestations had occurred before and might recur. The difficulty arises as soon as the question is asked whether he should be detained in a mental hospital? No mental hospital would admit a diabetic merely because he had a low blood sugar reaction; and common sense is affronted by the prospect of a diabetic being sent to such a hospital when in most cases the disordered mental condition can be rectified quickly by pushing a lump of sugar or a teaspoonful of glucose into the patient's mouth.

The "affront to common sense" argument, however, has its own inherent weakness, as counsel for the Crown pointed out. If an accused is shown to have done a criminal act whilst suffering from a "defect of reason from disease of the mind," it matters not "whether the disease is curable or incurable ... temporary or permanent" (see *R.* v. *Kemp* [*ante* p. 219], *per* Devlin J.). If the condition is temporary, the Secretary of State may have a difficult problem of disposal; but what happens to those found not guilty by reason of insanity is not a matter for the courts.

In *R.* v. *Kemp*, where the violent act was alleged to have been done during a period of unconsciousness arising from arteriosclerosis, counsel for the accused submitted that his client had done what he had during a period of mental confusion arising from a physical, not a mental disease. Devlin J. rejected this argument saying:

> "It does not matter, for the purposes of the law, whether the defect of reasoning is due to a degeneration of the brain or to some other form of mental derangement. That may be a matter of importance medically, but it is of no importance to the law, which merely has to consider the state of mind in which the accused is, not how he got there."

Applied without qualification of any kind, Devlin J.'s statement of the law would have some surprising consequences. Take the not uncommon case of the rugby player who gets a kick on the head early in the game and plays on to the end in a state of automatism. If, whilst he was in that state, he assaulted the referee it is difficult to envisage any court adjudging that he was not guilty by reason of insanity. Another type of case which could occur is that of the dental patient who kicks out whilst coming round from an anaesthetic. The law would be in a defective state if a patient accused of assaulting a dental nurse by kicking her whilst regaining consciousness could only excuse himself by raising the defence of insanity.

In *Hill* v. *Baxter* [1958] 1 Q.B. 277, the problem before the Divisional Court was whether the accused had put forward sufficient evidence on a charge of dangerous driving to justify the justices adjudging that he should be acquitted, there having been no dispute that at the time when his car collided with another one he was at the driving wheel. At the trial the accused had contended that he became unconscious as a result of being overcome by an unidentified illness. The court (Lord Goddard C.J., Devlin and Pearson JJ.) allowed an appeal by the prosecution against the verdict of acquittal. In the course of examining the evidence which had been put forward by the accused the judges made some comments of a general nature. Lord Goddard C.J. referred to some observations of Humphreys J. in *Kay* v. *Butterworth* (1945) 173 L.T. 191 which seemed to indicate that a man who became unconscious whilst driving due to the onset of a sudden illness should not be made liable at criminal law and went on as follows, at 282,

> "I agree that there may be cases when the circumstances are such that the accused could not really be said to be driving at all. Suppose he had a stroke or an epileptic fit, both instances of what may properly be called Acts of God; he might well be in the driver's seat even with his hands on the wheel but in such a state of unconsciousness that he could not be said to be driving. ... In this case, however, I am content to say that the evidence falls far short of what would justify a court holding that this man was in some automatous state."

Lord Goddard C.J. did not equate unconsciousness due to a sudden illness, which must entail the malfunctioning of the mental process of the sufferer, with disease of the mind, and in our judgment no one outside the court of law would. Devlin J. in his judgment at 285 accepted that some temporary loss of consciousness arising *accidentally* (the italics are ours) did not call for a verdict based on insanity. It is not clear what he meant by "accidentally." The context suggests that he may have meant "unexpectedly" as can happen with some kind of virus infections. He went on as follows:

> "If, however, disease is present the same thing may happen again and therefore since 1800 the law has provided that persons acquitted on this ground should be subject to restraint."

If this be right anyone suffering from a tooth abscess who knows from past experience that he reacts violently to anaesthetics because of some constitutional bodily disorder which can be attributed to disease might have to go on suffering or take the risk of being found insane unless he could find a dentist who would take the risk of being kicked by a recovering patient. It seems to us that the law should not give the words "defect of reason from disease of the mind" a meaning which would be regarded with incredulity outside the court.

The last of the English authorities is *Watmore* v. *Jenkins* [1962] 2 Q.B. 572. ... In the course of the argument in that case counsel for the accused is reported as having submitted, on the basis of how Lord Murray had directed the jury in *H.M. Advocate* v. *Ritchie* 1926 J.C. 45:

> "Automatism is a defence to a charge of dangerous driving provided that a person takes reasonable steps to prevent himself from acting involuntarily in a manner dangerous to the public. It must be caused by some factor which he could not reasonably foresee and not by a self-induced incapacity. ... "

Subject to the problem of whether the conduct said to have been done in a state of automatism was caused by a disease of the mind, we agree with this submission. In this case, had the jury been left to decide whether the appellant Quick at the material time was insane, or in a state of automatism or just drunk, they probably would not have any difficulty in making up their minds.

[His Lordship then referred to some Commonwealth cases].

. . .

In this quagmire of law seldom entered nowadays save by those in desperate need of some kind of defence, *Bratty* v. *A.-G. for Northern Ireland, supra,* provides the only firm ground. Is there any discernible path? We think there is—judges should follow in a common sense way their sense of fairness. This seems to have been the approach of the New Zealand Court of Appeal in *R.* v. *Cottle* [1958] N.Z.L.R. 999, and of Sholl J. in *R.* v. *Carter* [1959] V.R. 105. In our judgment no help can be obtained by speculating (because that is what we would have to do) as to what the judges who answered the House of Lords' questions in 1843 meant by disease of the mind, still less what Sir Matthew Hale meant in the second half of the 17th century [(1682) Vol. J, Ch. IV.] A quick backward look at the state of medicine in 1843 will suffice to show how unreal it would be to apply the concepts of that age to the present time. Dr. Simpson had not yet started his experiments with chloroform, the future Lord Lister was only 16 and laudanum was used and prescribed like aspirins are today. Our task has been to decide what the law means now by the words "disease of the mind." In our judgment the fundamental concept is of a malfunctioning of the mind caused by disease. A malfunctioning of the mind of transitory effect caused by the application to the body of some external factor such as violence, drugs including anaesthetics, alcohol and hypnotic influences cannot fairly be said to be due to disease. Such malfunctioning, unlike that caused by a defect of reason from disease of the mind, will not always relieve an accused from criminal responsibility. A self-induced incapacity will not excuse—see *R.* v. *Lipman,* [1970] 1 Q.B.

152, nor will one which could have been reasonably foreseen as a result of either doing, or omitting to do something, as, for example, taking alcohol against medical advice after using certain prescribed drugs, or failing to have regular meals whilst taking insulin. From time to time difficult borderline cases are likely to arise. When they do, the test suggested by the New Zealand Court of Appeal in *R.* v. *Cottle* is likely to give the correct result, *viz.* can this mental condition be fairly regarded as amounting to or producing a defect of reason from disease of the mind?

In this case Quick's alleged mental condition, if it ever existed, was not caused by his diabetes but by his use of insulin prescribed by his doctor. Such malfunctioning of the mind as there was, was caused by an external factor and not by a bodily disorder in the nature of a disease which disturbed the working of his mind. It follows in our judgment that Quick was entitled to have his defence of automatism left to the jury and that Bridge J.'s ruling as to the effect of the medical evidence called by him was wrong. Had the defence of automatism been left to the jury, a number of questions of fact would have to be answered. If he was in a confused mental condition, was it due to a hypoglycaemic episode or to too much alcohol? If the former, to what extent had he brought about his condition by not following his doctor's instructions about taking regular meals? Did he know that he was getting into a hypoglycaemic episode? If Yes, why did he not use the antidote of eating a lump of sugar as he had been advised to do? On the evidence which was before the jury Quick might have had difficulty in answering these questions in a manner which would have relieved him of responsibility for his acts. We cannot say, however, with the requisite degree of confidence, that the jury would have convicted him. It follows that this conviction must be quashed on the ground that the verdict was unsatisfactory.

Appeal allowed

Questions

1. Lawton L.J. stated that the law should not give the words "defect of reason from disease of the mind" a meaning which would be regarded with incredulity outside the court. Is it arguable that the distinction between automatism arising from intrinsic causes and that arising from extrinsic causes, itself affronts common sense in that, implicit in the distinction is the conclusion that diabetes is a disease of the mind?

2. Quick's hypoglycaemic condition arose from taking insulin, drinking alcohol and not eating sufficient food. The opposite condition, hyperglycaemia (excess blood-sugar) arises where insulin is missing from the blood; this condition can have similar effects to hypoglycaemia. If Quick had committed the assault in a hyperglycaemic episode, what would have been the result under the principles expounded by the Court of Appeal? (See *Hennessy, ante,* p. 223.)

3. What would be the position of D, an epileptic, who fails to take drugs which completely suppress epileptic seizures, and who, in the course of a seizure, thrashes violently injuring V.? Would it make any difference if D. knew that such failure could lead to seizures and violence on his part? (See *Bailey, post,* p. 234.)

4. If the criterion for sane automatism is that it is due to an extrinsic cause, how would the courts react to an automatic act due

to the effects of a disease caused by a bacterial or viral infection? For example, D. suffering from bacterial meningitis and in a convulsive fit, hits V. On a charge of causing grievous bodily harm D. pleads automatism; would he succeed? E, who is suffering from arteriosclerosis, falls into an autonomic state and hits X. On a charge of causing grievous bodily harm E pleads automatism; would he succeed? If the outcome in each case differs, can this be justified on any logical and substantive basis?

Self-induced automatism

Note

If non-insane automatism leads to a complete acquittal based on the doctrine of voluntariness, will this principle lead to the same outcome where it can be shown that the autonomic state was self-induced?

In *Quick* Lawton L.J. stated:

"A self-induced incapacity will not excuse ... nor will one which could have been reasonably foreseen as a result of either doing, or omitting to do something, as, for example, taking alcohol against medical advice after using certain prescribed drugs, or failing to have regular meals while taking insulin."

On the basis of this dictum Quick's autonomic state appears to have been self-induced by not eating or taking a lump of sugar when the first signs of hypoglycaemia manifested themselves. However, his conviction was quashed as his defence of automatism had not been left to the jury. The effect of *Quick*, however, appeared categorically to rule out the defence of automatism where it was self-induced.

R. v. Bailey
[1983] 1 W.L.R. 760
Court of Appeal

The appellant was charged with wounding with intent and with an alternative count of unlawful wounding contrary to sections 18 and 20 respectively of the Offences Against the Person Act 1861. His defence was automatism caused by hypoglycaemia which was due to his failure to take sufficient food after taking insulin, although he had taken some sugar and water. He claimed, accordingly, that he lacked the specific intent required for the purpose of s.18 and the basic intent required for the purpose of s.20. The judge directed the jury that as the appellant's incapacity was self-induced he could not plead automatism. The appellant was convicted of causing grievous bodily harm with intent, contrary to s.18. He appealed.

GRIFFITHS L.J.: ... But in [*Quick*] [t]he Court of Appeal held that [the ruling upon which the present trial judge had based his direction] was wrong and that the malfunctioning caused by the hypoglycaemia was not a disease of the mind and that the appellant was entitled to have his defence considered by the jury. Lawton L.J. said, at p. 922:

"Such malfunctioning, unlike that caused by a defect of reason from disease of the mind, will not always relieve an accused from criminal responsibility. A self-induced incapacity will not excuse (see *R.* v. *Lipman* [1970] 1 Q.B. 152), nor will one which could have been reasonably foreseen as a result of either doing, or omitting to do something, as, for example, taking alcohol against medical advice after using certain prescribed drugs, or failing to have regular meals while taking insulin. From time to time difficult border line cases are likely to arise. When they do, the test suggested by the New Zealand Court of Appeal in *R.* v. *Cottle* [1958] N.Z.L.R. 999, 1011 is likely to give the correct result, *viz.*, can this mental condition be fairly regarded as amounting to or producing a defect of reason from disease of the mind?"

But in that case, the offence, assault occasioning actual bodily harm, was an offence of basic intent. No specific intent was required. It is now quite clear that even if the incapacity of mind is self-induced by the voluntary taking of drugs or alcohol, the specific intent to kill or cause grievous bodily harm may be negatived: see *R.* v. *Majewski* [1977] A.C. 443, (*post*, p. 246). This being so, as it is conceded on behalf of the Crown, the direction to which we have referred cannot be correct so far as the offence under section 18 is concerned.

But it is also submitted that the direction is wrong or at least in too broad and general terms, so far as the section 20 offence is concerned. If ... *Quick* correctly represents the law, then the direction given by the recorder was correct so far as the second count was concerned even though the appellant may have had no appreciation of the consequences of his failure to take food and even though such failure may not have been due to deliberate abstention but because of his generally distressed condition. In our judgment the passage from Lawton L.J.'s judgment was obiter and we are free to re-examine it.

Automatism resulting from intoxication as a result of a voluntary ingestion of alcohol or dangerous drugs does not negative the mens rea necessary for crimes of basic intent, because the conduct of the accused is reckless and recklessness is enough to constitute the necessary mens rea in assault cases where no specific intent forms part of the charge: see *R.* v. *Majewski* [1977] A.C. 443, 476 in the speech of Lord Elwyn Jones L.C. and in the speech of Lord Edmund-Davies where he said, at p. 496, quoting from *Stroud, Mens Rea* (1914), p. 115:

"The law therefore establishes a conclusive presumption against the admission of proof of intoxication for the purpose of disproving mens rea in ordinary crimes. Where this presumption applies, it does not make 'drunkenness itself' a crime, but the drunkenness is itself an integral part of the crime, as forming, together with the other unlawful conduct charged against the defendant, a complex act of criminal recklessness."

The same considerations apply where the state of automatism is induced by the voluntary taking of dangerous drugs: see *R.* v. *Lipman* [1970] Q.B. 152 where a conviction for manslaughter was upheld, the appellant having taken L.S.D. and killed his mistress in the course of an hallucinatory trip. It was submitted on behalf of the Crown that a similar rule should be applied as a matter of public policy to all cases of self-induced automatism. But it seems to us that there may be material distinctions between a man who consumes alcohol or takes dangerous drugs and one who fails to take sufficient food after insulin to avert hypoglycaemia.

It is common knowledge that those who take alcohol to excess or certain sorts of drugs may become aggressive or do dangerous or unpredictable things, they may be able to foresee the risks of causing harm to others but nevertheless persist in their conduct. But the same cannot be said without more of a man who fails to take food after an insulin injection. If he does appreciate the risk that such a failure may lead to aggressive, unpredictable and uncontrollable conduct and he nevertheless deliberately runs the risk or otherwise disregards it, this will amount to recklessness. But we certainly do not think that it is common knowledge, even among diabetics, that such is a consequence of a failure to take food and there is no evidence that it was known to this appellant. Doubtless he knew that if he failed to take his insulin or proper food after it, he might lose consciousness, but as such he would only be a danger to himself unless he put himself in charge of some machine such as a motor car, which required his continued conscious control.

In our judgment, self-induced automatism, other than that due to intoxication from alcohol or drugs, may provide a defence to crimes of basic intent. The question in each case will be whether the prosecution have proved the necessary element of recklessness. In cases of assault, if the accused knows that his actions or inaction are likely to make him aggressive, unpredictable or uncontrolled with the result that he may cause some injury to others and he persists in the action or takes no remedial action when he knows it is required, it will be open to the jury to find that he was reckless.

Turning again to *R. v. Quick* and the passage we have quoted, we think that notwithstanding the unqualified terms in which the proposition is stated, it is possible that the court may not have intended to lay down such an absolute rule. In the following paragraph Lawton L.J. considers a number of questions, which are not necessarily exhaustive, which the jury might have wanted to consider if the issue had been left to them. One such question was whether the accused knew that he was getting into a hypoglycaemic episode and if so why he did not use the antidote of taking sugar which he had been advised to do. These questions suggest that even if the hypoglycaemia was induced by some action or inaction by the accused his defence will not necessarily fail.

In the present case the recorder never invited the jury to consider what the appellant's knowledge or appreciation was of what would happen if he failed to take food after his insulin or whether he realised that he might become aggressive. Nor were they asked to consider why the appellant had omitted to take food in time. They were given no direction on the elements of recklessness. Accordingly, in our judgment there was also a misdirection in relation to the second count in the indictment of unlawful wounding.

But we have to consider whether, notwithstanding these misdirections, there has been any miscarriage of justice and whether the jury properly directed could have failed to come to the same conclusion. As Lawton L.J. said in *Quick's* case at p. 922, referring to the defence of automatism, it is a "quagmire of law seldom entered nowadays save by those in desperate need of some kind of a defence. . . . " This case is no exception. We think it very doubtful whether the appellant laid a sufficient basis for the defence to be considered by the jury at all. But even if he did we are in no doubt that the jury properly directed must have rejected it. Although an episode of sudden transient loss of consciousness or awareness was theoretically possible it was quite inconsistent with the graphic description that the appellant gave to the police both orally and in his written statement. There was abundant evidence that he had armed himself with the iron bar and gone to Mr. Harrison's house for the purpose of attacking him because he wanted to teach him a lesson and because he was in the way.

Moreover the doctor's evidence to which we have referred showed it was extremely unlikely that such an episode could follow some five minutes after taking sugar and water. For these reasons we are satisfied that no miscarriage of justice occurred and the appeal will be dismissed.

Appeal dismissed

Questions

1. A drunkard has no defence to a crime of basic intent (see pp. 246–265 *infra*). As a result of *Bailey* an automaton who has brought about his own state of automatism may have a defence. Is this difference one which can be justified on grounds of policy or principle?

2. The court in *Bailey* did not presume recklessness because of the absence of common knowledge amongst diabetics that failure to take food after insulin might result in aggressive behaviour. How might a court come to such a conclusion? What would happen if directions on prescriptions of insulin were to include such a warning?

3. Bailey was charged with an offence for which the test for recklessness was the *Cunningham* one. What ought the result to have been if his offence had been one to which the *Caldwell* recklessness test applied? See *Hardie, post*, p. 260.

4. Schiffer, in *Mental Disorder and the Criminal Trial Process* (1978), gives examples of statistical studies which show that "(1) violent behaviour of any sort is unusual in epileptic automatisms; (2) the vast majority of epileptics have never experienced fugue state automatism; and (3) amongst those who do . . . it is a relatively rare occurrence." (p. 93). In light of the fact that a person in hypoglycaemic coma though unconscious may still perform normal functions, as if a robot, is it tenable to conclude (as a reading of *Bailey* and *Sullivan* would seem to dictate) that epileptics represent a greater danger to the public than diabetics? If not, is the distinction between external and internal organic causes, a fatuous one?

5. Schiffer (at p. 100) states that hypoglycaemic coma may be caused by overproduction of insulin by the pancreas. How would the courts have treated Bailey if his automatism had resulted from this cause?

3. PROPOSALS FOR REFORM

Draft Criminal Code Bill, Clause 33

"Automatism and physical incapacity

33.—(1) A person is not guilty of an offence if—

(a) he acts in a state of automatism, that is, his act—
    (i) is a reflex, spasm or convulsion; or

(ii) occurs while he is in a condition (whether of sleep, unconsciousness, impaired consciousness or otherwise) depriving him of effective control of the act; and

(b) the act or condition is the result neither of anything done or omitted with the fault required for the offence nor of voluntary intoxication.

(2) A person is not guilty of an offence by virtue of an omission to act if—

(a) he is physically incapable of acting in the way required; and
(b) his being so incapable is the result neither of anything done or omitted with the fault required for the offence nor of voluntary intoxication."

In paras. 11.2–11.5 of the *Commentary on Draft Criminal Bill* (Law Com. No. 177) the Law Commission state—

"11.2 *Limited function of subsection (1)*. The main function of clause 3(1) is to protect a person who acts in a state of automatism from conviction of an offence of strict liability. It is conceded that he does 'the act' specified for the offence; but the clause declares him not guilty. One charged with an offence requiring fault in the form of failure to comply with a standard of conduct may also have to rely on the clause. On the other hand, a state of automatism will negative a fault requirement of intention or knowledge or (normally) recklessness; so a person charged with an offence of violence against another, or of criminal damage, committed when he was in a condition of impaired consciousness, does not rely on this clause for his acquittal but on the absence of the fault element of the offence.

11.3 *Conditions within the subsection*. Subsection (1)(a) refers to acts of two kinds:

(i) an act over which the person concerned, although conscious, has no control: the 'reflex, spasm or convulsion'. Such an act would rarely, if ever, be the subject of a prosecution.
(ii) an act over which the person concerned does not have effective control because of a 'condition' of "sleep, unconsciousness, impaired consciousness or otherwise". We believe that the references to 'impaired consciousness' and to deprivation of 'effective' control are justified both on principle and by some of the leading cases. The governing principle should be that a person is not guilty of an offence if, without relevant fault on his part, he cannot choose to act otherwise than as he does. The acts of the defendants in several cases have been treated as automatous although it is far from clear, and even unlikely, that they were entirely unconscious when they did the acts and although it cannot confidently be said that they exercised no control, in any sense of that phrase, over their relevant movements. . . .

11.5 *Prior fault*. Subsection (1)(b) excepts from the protection of the subsection cases in which the state of automatism itself is the result of relevant fault on the part of the person affected or of voluntary intoxication. A person charged with an offence that may be committed by negligence can be convicted if his state of automatism was the result of his own negligent conduct. Under clause 22(1)(a) a person who was unaware of a risk by reason of voluntary intoxication is credited, when charged with an offence of recklessness, with the awareness that he would have had if sober; and clause 33(1)(b) ensures that he cannot escape liability for the offence by a plea of automatism. Paragraph (b) is intended to produce the same results as the common law.''

Appendix B of the Code Report provides the following illustrations of the operation of clause 33.

Clause 33(1)	33(i)	D, driving a car, has a sudden "black-out", as a result of which the car mounts the kerb and comes to rest against a wall. D is not guilty of driving without due care and attention.
Clause 33(1)(b)	33(ii)	D, driving a car, feels himself becoming drowsy. He continues driving and in due course falls asleep at the wheel. He is guilty of driving without due care and attention both before and after falling asleep.
	33(iii)	D is charged with recklessly causing personal harm to P when in a condition of impaired consciousness caused by alcohol, drugs or medicine. He cannot rely on his "state of automatism" if he was "voluntarily intoxicated".
clause 33 (2)	33(iv)	As in example 33(1). The car also passes a red traffic light. D is not guilty of failing to comply with a traffic sign.
	33(v)	D is involved in a traffic accident which he is under a duty to report to the police within twenty four hours. He is seriously injured in the accident and spends more than a day in intensive care. He is not guilty of the offence of failing to report the accident.

Draft Criminal Code Bill, Clauses 34–40

''**34.** In this Act—

'mental disorder' means—

(a) severe mental illness; or
(b) a state of arrested or incomplete development of mind; or
(c) a state of automatism (not resulting only from intoxication) which is a feature of a disorder, whether organic or functional and whether continuing or recurring, that may cause a ~~similar~~ state on another occasion;

'return a mental disorder verdict' means—

(a) in relation to trial on indictment, return a ~~verdict that the~~ defendant is not guilty on evidence of mental ~~disorder~~
(b) in relation to summary trial, dismiss the inform~~ation on evidence of~~ mental disorder;

'severe mental illness' means a mental illness whi~~ch has one or more of~~ the following characteristics—

(a) lasting impairment of intellectual functions shown by failure of memory, orientation, comprehension and learning capacity;
(b) lasting alteration of mood of such degree as to give rise to delusional appraisal of the defendant's situation, his past or his future, or that of others, or lack of any appraisal;
(c) delusional beliefs, persecutory, jealous or grandiose;
(d) abnormal perceptions associated with delusional misinterpretation of events;
(e) thinking so disordered as to prevent reasonable appraisal of the defendant's situation or reasonable communication with others;

'severe mental handicap' means a state of arrested or incomplete development of mind which includes severe impairment of intelligence and social functioning.

35.—(1) A mental disorder verdict shall be returned if the defendant is proved to have committed an offence but it is proved on the balance of probabilities (whether by the prosecution or by the defendant) that he was at the time suffering from severe mental illness or severe mental handicap.

(2) Subsection (1) does not apply if the court or jury is satisfied beyond reasonable doubt that the offence was not attributable to the severe mental illness or severe mental handicap.

(3) A court or jury shall not, for the purposes of a verdict under subsection (1), find that the defendant was suffering from severe mental illness or severe mental handicap unless two medical practitioners approved for the purposes of section 12 of the Mental Health Act 1983 as having special experience in the diagnosis or treatment of mental disorder have given evidence that he was so suffering.

(4) Subsection (1), so far as it relates to severe mental handicap, does not apply to an offence under section 106(1), 107 or 108 (sexual relations with the mentally handicapped).

36. A mental disorder verdict shall be returned if—

(a) the defendant is acquitted of an offence only because, by reason of evidence of mental disorder or a combination of mental disorder and intoxication, it is found that he acted or may have acted in a state of automatism, or without the fault required for the offence, or believing that an exempting circumstance existed; and
(b) it is proved on the balance of probabilities (whether by the prosecution or by the defendant) that he was suffering from mental disorder at the time of the act.

37. A defendant may plead 'not guilty by reason of mental disorder'; and

(a) if the court directs that the plea be entered the direction shall have the same effect as a mental disorder verdict; and
(b) if the court does not so direct the defendant shall be treated as having pleaded not guilty.

38.—(1) Whether evidence is evidence of mental disorder or automatism is a question of law.

(2) The prosecution shall not adduce evidence of mental disorder, or contend that a mental disorder verdict should be returned, unless the defendant has given or adduced evidence that he acted without the fault required for the offence, or believing that an exempting circumstance or in a state of automatism, or (on a charge of murder) when from mental abnormality as defined in section 57(2).

(3) The court may give directions as to the stage of the proceedings at which the prosecution may adduce evidence of mental disorder.

39. Schedule 2 has effect with respect to the orders that may be made upon the return of a mental disorder verdict, to the conditions governing the making of those orders, to the effects of those orders and to related matters.

40. A defendant shall not, when a mental disorder verdict is returned in respect of an offence and while that verdict subsists, be found guilty of any other offence of which, but for this section, he might on the same occasion be found guilty—

(a)   on the indictment, count or information to which the verdict relates; or

(b)   on any other indictment, count or information founded on the same facts."

In paras. 11.9–11.28 of the *Commentary on Draft Criminal Bill* (Law Com. No. 177) the Law Commission state—

"Code provisions on mental disorder

11.9 *Butler Committee.* The Butler Committee [in *Report of the Committee on Mentally Abnormal Offenders* (1975) Cmnd. 6244] proposed substantial reform of the law and procedure relating to the effect of mental disorder on criminal liability and the disposal of persons acquitted because of mental disorder. The necessity of incorporating in the projected Criminal Code an appropriate provision to replace the outdated 'insanity' defence was one justification given by the Committee for its review of the subject. We ourselves are persuaded that implementation of the Committee's proposals would greatly improve this area of the law. We have, however, found it necessary to suggest some important modifications of those proposals. Clauses 34 to 40 therefore aim to give effect to the policy of the Butler Committee as modified by us in ways that will be explained in the following paragraphs.

11.10 *The present 'insanity defence'.* Before considering the structure of the proposed law, it will be convenient to refer to that of the present law. The *M'Naghten Rules*, together with statutory provisions, produce a 'special verdict' ('not guilty by reason of insanity') . . . in two kinds of case.

(i)   The first case is that where it is proved (rebutting the so-called 'presumption of sanity') that, because of 'a defect of reason, from disease of the mind', the defendant did not 'know the nature and quality of the act he was doing'. If the defendant 'did not know what he was doing', he must have lacked any fault required for the offence charged; so, in modern terms at least, this first element in the *M'Naghten Rules* has the appearance of a rule, not about guilt, but about burden of proof and disposal. The defendant should in any case be acquitted, but he must prove that he should be; and his acquittal is to be treated as the occasion for his detention as a matter of social defence.

(ii)   The second case is that where, because of 'a defect of reason, from disease of the mind', the defendant 'did not know he was doing what was wrong.' This is a case, then, in which the Rules afford a defence properly so called: a person who would otherwise be guilty is not guilty 'by reason of insanity'. But, once again, social defence requires his detention in hospital.

11.11 *Structure of the proposed provisions.* Clauses 35 and 36, following the structure proposed by the Butler Committee, are similarly concerned with two kinds of case, in each of which there is to be a verdict of acquittal in special form ('not guilty on evidence of mental disorder'). On the return of a mental disorder verdict the court would have flexible disposal powers. ...

(a) *Clause 35(1).* In one case all the elements of the offence are proved but severe mental disorder operates as a true defence. This is equivalent to case (ii) above.

(b) *Clause 36.* In the other case an acquittal is inevitable because the prosecution has failed to prove that the defendant acted with the required fault (or to disprove his defence of automatism or mistake); but the reason for that failure is evidence of mental disorder, and it is proved that the defendant was indeed suffering from mental disorder at the time of the act. This differs from case (i) above in casting no burden on the defendant of proving his innocence. ... "

"Clause 34: Mental disorder: definitions

11.13 *'Mental disorder'; 'severe mental illness'; 'severe mental handicap'.* These terms are considered below, in the context of the provisions in which they are crucial. The Butler scheme renounces the outdated terms 'insanity' and 'disease of the mind'. ...

Clause 35: Case of mental disorder verdict: defence of severe disorder

11.15 Subsection (1) provides that even though he has done the act specified for the offence with the fault required, a defendant is entitled to an acquittal, in the form of a mental disorder verdict, if he was suffering from severe mental illness or severe mental handicap at the time. This implements the Butler Committee's conception with some modifications.

11.16 *Attributability of offence to disorder: a rebuttable presumption.* One aspect of the Committee's recommendation has proved controversial. The Committee acknowledged that—

'it is theoretically possible for a person to be suffering from a severe mental disorder which has in a causal sense nothing to do with the act or omission for which he is being tried';

but they found it 'very difficult to imagine a case in which one could be sure of the absence of any such connection'. They therefore proposed, in effect, an irrebuttable presumption that there was a sufficient connection between the severe disorder and the offence. This proposal is understandable in view of the limitation of the defence to a narrow range of very serious disorders; and its adoption would certainly simplify the tasks of psychiatric witnesses and the court. Some people, however, take the view that it would be wrong in principle that a person should escape conviction if, although severely mentally ill, he has committed a rational crime which was uninfluenced by his illness and for which he ought to be liable to be punished. They believe that the prosecution should be allowed to persuade the jury (if it can) that the offence was not attributable to the disorder. We agree. Subsection (2) provides accordingly. We believe that it must improve the acceptability of the Butler Committee's generally admirable scheme as the basis of legislation.

11.17 *'Severe mental illness'* is defined in clause 34 in the terms proposed by the Butler Committee. Severe mental illness, for the purpose of this exemption from criminal liability, ought in the Committee's view, to be closely defined and restricted to serious cases of psychosis (as that term is currently understood). The Committee recommended, as the preferable mode of definition, the identification of 'the abnormal mental phenomena which occur in the various mental illnesses and which when present would be regarded by common consent as being evidence of severity'. We believe that this symptomatic mode of definition has much to commend it. The psychiatric expert will give evidence in terms of strict 'factual tests', rather than of abstractions (such as 'disease of the mind' or 'severe mental illness' itself) or diagnostic labels. The method allocates appropriate functions to the law itself (in laying down the test of criminal responsibility), to the expert (in advising whether the test is satisfied) and to the tribunal of fact (in judging, by reference to the whole of the case, whether that advice is soundly given). . . .

11.19 *'Severe mental handicap'* is defined in clause 34. The expression used by the Butler Committee was 'severe subnormality', which was defined in the Mental Health Act 1959, section 4, in terms apt for the Committee's purpose. But the expression 'severe mental impairment' has since replaced 'severe subnormality' in mental health legislation (the latter term having fallen out of favour). 'Severe mental impairment' has the following meaning:

'a state of arrested or incomplete development of mind which includes severe impairment of intelligence and social functioning and is associated with abnormally aggressive or seriously irresponsible conduct on the part of the person concerned'.

This definition is not a happy one for present purposes; exemption from criminal liability on the ground of severe mental handicap ought not to be limited to a case where the handicap is associated with aggressive or irresponsible conduct. We therefore propose that the expression 'severe mental handicap' be used, with the same definition as 'severe mental impairment' down to the word 'functioning'. This will give effect to the Butler Committee's intentions and has the approval of our Royal College advisers.

11.20 *Burden of proof.* Subsection (1) permits proof of severe disorder by either prosecution or defendant. Normally it will be for the defendant to prove it, as his defence to the charge. This is as proposed by the Butler Committee. But there may be a case in which the defendant adduces evidence of mental disorder on an issue of fault or automatism and the prosecution responds with evidence of severe disorder and in such a case it may be the prosecution evidence (or a combination of prosecution and defence evidence) which results in a mental disorder verdict under clause 35(1). . . .

Clause 36: Case for mental disorder verdict: evidence of disorder

11.23 *Broad effect of the clause.* Evidence of mental disorder may be the reason why the court or jury is at least doubtful whether the defendant acted with the fault required for the offence. The Butler Committee recommended that, although in such a case there must be an acquittal, this acquittal should be in the qualified form 'not guilty on evidence of mental disorder' where it is proved that the defendant was in fact suffering from mental disorder at the time of his act. Clause 36 gives effect to this recommendation, significantly modified by the adoption of a narrower meaning of 'mental disorder' than that proposed by the Committee.

11.24 *Cases covered by the clause.* The clause adapts the Committee's proposal to the conceptual structure of the Code. First, it provides that the mental disorder verdict is not to be returned unless evidence of mental disorder is the only reason for an acquittal. The provision must not affect a case in which the defendant is entitled to an acquittal on some additional ground having nothing to do with mental disorder. Secondly, it refers not only to absence of fault but also (a) to automatism and (b) to a belief in a circumstance of defence. (a) Automatism is mentioned because the acquittal of one who acted in a state of automatism is not grounded only in absence of 'fault' (see clause 33). (b) A person may commit an act of violence because of a deluded belief that he is under attack and must defend himself. Within the scheme of the Code—which draws a distinction between elements of offences (including fault elements) and defences—such a person would not, when relying on his delusion, be denying 'the fault for the offence'. His mentally disordered belief must therefore be separately mentioned in the paragraph. ...

11.26 *'Mental disorder': the Butler Committee's proposal.* The Butler Committee proposed to adopt in principle the Mental Health Act definition of 'mental disorder'—namely, 'mental illness, arrested or incomplete development of mind, psychopathic disorder and any other disorder or disability of mind'—subject only to the exclusion of 'transient states not related to other forms of mental disorder and arising solely as a consequence of (a) the administration, maladministration or non-administration of alcohol, drugs or other substances or (b) physical injury.'

11.27 We are surprised that such an extremely wide definition, designed for the very different purposes of the Mental Health Act, should have been thought suitable as the basis of a qualified acquittal, subject only to the exclusion of certain 'transient states not related to other forms of mental disorder'. If this proposal were followed, the result might be to subject too many acquitted persons to a possibly stigmatising or distressing verdict and to inappropriate control through the courts' disposal powers. The cases attracting a mental disorder verdict under this clause should, we think, be strictly limited. We therefore exclude 'mental illness' (not being 'severe') and 'any other disorder or disability of mind' from our definition. We also exclude 'psychopathic disorder' as being, we believe, irrelevant to the existence of 'fault' in the technical sense.

11.28 *'Mental disorder': the proposed definition.* We define 'mental disorder' in clause 34 to include (only):

(a) 'severe mental illness' (as defined in the same section): the defendant who lacked fault, or believed in the existence of an exempting circumstance, because of a psychotic distortion of perception or understanding, will receive a mental disorder verdict and be amenable to the court's powers of restraint.

(b) 'arrested or incomplete development of mind': this category from the Mental Health Act definition of 'mental disorder' survives our amendment of the Butler Committee's proposal. We must, however, express a doubt as to whether it should do so. Some persons against whom fault cannot be proved might receive mental disorder verdicts, and become subject to the protective powers of the criminal courts, although under the present law they would receive unqualified acquittals. It may be thought more appropriate to leave any acquitted persons within this category who represent a danger to themselves or others to be dealt with under Part II of the Mental Health Act 1983.

(c) (in effect) pathological automatism that is liable to recur: it would not, we think, be acceptable to propose that the courts should lose all control over a person acquitted because of what is now termed 'insane automatism'. Paragraph (c) of our definition requires the 'state of automatism' (see clause 33(1)) to be 'a feature of a disorder ... that may cause a similar state on another occasion'. This qualification confines the mental disorder verdict to those possibly warranting some form of control that the court can impose. It may nevertheless be felt by some that the paragraph includes too much. The Butler Committee wished, in particular, to protect from a mental disorder verdict a diabetic who causes a harm in a state of confusion after failing to take his insulin. We do not think, however, that there is a satisfactory way of distinguishing between the different conditions that may cause repeated episodes of disorder; nor do we think it necessary to do so. There is not, so far as we can see, a satisfactory basis for distinguishing between (say) a brain tumour or cerebral arteriosclerosis on the one hand and diabetes or epilepsy on the other. If any of these conditions causes a state of automatism in which the sufferer commits what would otherwise be an offence of violence, his acquittal should be 'on evidence of mental disorder'. Whether a diabetic so affected has failed to seek treatment, or forgotten to take his insulin, or decided not to do so, may affect the court's decision whether to order his discharge or to take some other course. What is objectionable in the present law is the offensive label of 'insanity' and the fact that the court is obliged to order the hospitalisation of the acquitted person, in effect as a restricted patient. With the elimination of these features under the Butler Committee's scheme, the verdict should not seem preposterous in the way that its present counterpart does."

Appendix B of the Code Report provides the following illustrations of the operation of clause 35 and 36.

"35   D intentionally sets fire to P's house when suffering from a mental illness having one or more of the severe features listed in clause 34. On a charge of arson he is entitled to a mental disorder verdict unless the jury is satisfied beyond reasonable doubt that the offence was not attributable to the illness.

36(i)   D is charged with intentionally causing serious personal harm to P. He was unaware of his violent act. It occurred when he was in a state of

...aired consciousness during an epileptic episode of a kind to which ... is prone. The impairment of consciousness was a feature of a ...disorder that may cause a similar state on another occasion. A mental disorder verdict must be returned. The court has power to make any of a number of orders or to discharge D (cl. 39 and Sched. 2).

(ii)   The same charge as in example 36(i). A similar explanation of the attack is given. The medical evidence leads the court or jury to think that the explanation may be true; D must therefore be acquitted. But they are not satisfied (on the whole of the medical evidence, including any adduced by the prosecution) that it is in fact true; so there will not be a mental disorder verdict, mental disorder not having been proved.

36(iii)   The same charge as in example 36(i). There is evidence that D, who suffers from diabetes, had taken insulin on medical advice. This had caused a fall in his blood-sugar level which deprived him of control or awareness of his movements. If D is acquitted, a mental disorder verdict is not appropriate. His 'disorder of mind' was caused by the insulin, an 'intoxicant' (see cl. 25(6)(a)). It was therefore a case of 'intoxication' and not of 'mental disorder' (cl. 34)."

4. INTOXICATION

Note

A person may become intoxicated through the consumption of drink or drugs. Whatever the cause of the intoxication, the law treats the intoxicated offender the same. Intoxication is not *per se* a defence; rather, a defendant who relies on intoxication is saying that because of his intoxication he did not have the necessary *mens rea* for the offence. Thus, if D, although intoxicated (whether voluntarily or involuntarily) has formed the necessary intent for the crime he will be guilty (see *Sheehan* [1975] 1 W.L.R. 739 and *Davies* [1983] Crim.L.R. 741). If D's intoxication leaves him incapable of forming the *mens rea* for the offence with which he is charged, or if he claims that he did not form the *mens rea* for the offence because he was intoxicated, he will not necessarily be acquitted; the outcome will hinge on whether the offence is one of specific or basic intent.

i. Specific and Basic Intent

D.P.P. v. Majewski
[1976] 2 W.L.R. 623
House of Lords

M appealed against convictions of assault occasioning actual bodily harm and assault of a police constable in the execution of his duty on the ground that he was too intoxicated, through a combination of drugs and alcohol, to form the appropriate *mens rea*. M was a drug addict who, over the previous two days, had consumed a large quantity of amphetamines and barbiturates before spending an evening drinking at the pub where the offences were committed. M admitted that he had sometimes "gone paranoid" but this was the first time he had "completely blacked out." Medical evidence was given that such a state of "pathological intoxication" was uncommon and that automatism due to the ingestion of alcohol together with either amphetamines or barbiturates was unlikely; it was more likely for a person intoxicated in this way to know what he was doing at the time but to suffer an "amnesic patch" later.

LORD ELWYN-JONES L.C.: ...

The Court of Appeal dismissed the appeal against conviction but granted leave to appeal to your Lordships' House certifying that the following point of law of general public importance was involved:

"Whether a defendant may properly be convicted of assault notwithstanding that, by reason of his self-induced intoxication, he did not intend to do the act alleged to constitute the assault. ... "

[T]he crux of the case for the Crown was that, illogical as the outcome may be said to be, the judges have evolved for the purpose of protecting the community a substantive rule of law that, in crimes of basic intent as distinct from crimes of specific intent, self-induced intoxication provides no defence and is irrelevant to offences of basic intent, such as assault.

The case of counsel for the appellant was that there was no such substantive rule of law and that if there was, it did violence to logic and ethics and to fundamental principles of the criminal law which had been evolved to determine when and where criminal responsibility should arise. His main propositions were as follows: (i) No man is guilty of a crime (save in relation to offences of strict liability) unless he has a guilty mind. (ii) A man who, though not insane, commits what would in ordinary circumstances be a crime when he is in such a mental state (whether it is called "automatism" or "pathological intoxication" or anything else) that he does not know what he is doing, lacks a guilty mind and is not criminally culpable for his actions. (iii) This is so whether the charge involves a specific (or "ulterior") intent or one involving only a general (or "basic") intent. (iv) The same principle applies whether the automatism was the result of causes beyond the control of the accused or was self-induced by the voluntary taking of drugs or drink. (v) Assaults being crimes involving a guilty mind, a man who in a state of automatism unlawfully assaults another must be regarded as free from blame and be entitled to acquittal. (vi) It is logically and ethically indefensible to convict such a man of assault; it also contravenes s.8 of the Criminal Justice Act 1967. (vii) There was accordingly a fatal misdirection.

A great deal of the argument in the hearing of the appeal turned on the application to the established facts of what Cave J. in *R.* v. *Tolson* [*ante*, p. 159] called "the somewhat uncouth maxim 'actus non facit reum, nisi mens sit rea. ... ' "

[His Lordship quoted from Stephen J.'s judgment in *Tolson, ante*, p. 159, and from Lord Simon's speech in *Morgan, ante*, p. 142, on the meaning of "basic intent"].

If a man consciously and deliberately takes alcohol and drugs not on medical prescription, but in order to escape from reality, to go "on a trip," to become hallucinated, whatever the description may be, and thereby disables himself from taking the care he might otherwise take and as a result by his subsequent actions causes injury to another—does our criminal law enable him to say that because he did not know what he was doing he lacked both intention and recklessness and accordingly is entitled to an acquittal?

Originally the common law would not and did not recognise self-induced intoxication as an excuse. Lawton L.J. spoke of the "merciful relaxation" to that rule which was introduced by the judges during the 19th century, and he added:

"Although there was much reforming zeal and activity in the 19th century Parliament never once considered whether self-induced intoxication should be a defence generally to a criminal charge. It would have been a strange result if the merciful relaxation of a strict rule of law had ended, without any Parliamentary intervention, by whittling it away to such an extent that the more drunk a man became, provided he stopped short of making himself insane, the better chance he had of acquittal. ... The common law rule still applied but there were exceptions to it which Lord Birkenhead L.C., *D.P.P.* v. *Beard* [1920] A.C. 479, tried to define by reference to specific intent."

There are, however, decisions of eminent judges in a number of Commonwealth cases in Australia and New Zealand (but generally not in Canada nor in the United States), as well as impressive academic comment in this country, to which we have been referred supporting the view that it is illogical and inconsistent with legal principle to treat a person who of his own choice and volition has taken drugs and drink, even though he thereby creates a state in which he is not conscious of what he is doing, any differently from a person suffering from the various medical conditions like epilepsy or diabetic coma and who is regarded by the law as free from fault. However, our courts have for a very long time regarded in quite another light the state of self-induced intoxication. The authority which for the last half century has been relied on in this context has been the speech of Lord Birkenhead L.C. in *D.P.P.* v. *Beard*, at 494:

"Under the law of England as it prevailed until early in the nineteenth century voluntary drunkenness was never an excuse for criminal misconduct; and indeed the classic authorities broadly assert that voluntary drunkenness must be considered rather an aggravation than a defence. This view was in terms based upon the principle that a man who by his own voluntary act debauches and destroys his will power, shall be no better situated in regard to criminal acts than a sober man."

Lord Birkenhead L.C. made an historical survey of the way the common law from the 16th century on dealt with the effect of self-induced intoxication on criminal responsibility. This indicates how, from 1819 on, the judges began to mitigate the severity of the attitude of the common law in such cases as murder and serious violent crime when the penalties of death or transportation applied or where there was likely to be sympathy for the accused, as in attempted suicide. Lord Birkenhead L.C., at 499, concluded that (except in cases where insanity was pleaded) the decisions he cited—

"establish that where a specific intent is an essential element in the offence, evidence of a state of drunkenness rendering the accused incapable of forming such an intent should be taken into consideration in order to determine whether he had in fact formed the intent necessary to constitute the particular crime. If he was so drunk that he was incapable of forming the intent required he could not be convicted of a crime which was committed only if the intent was proved. ... In a charge of murder based upon intention to kill or to do grievous bodily harm, if the jury are satisfied that the accused was, by reason of his drunken condition, incapable of forming the intent to kill or to do grievous bodily harm ... he cannot be convicted of murder. But nevertheless unlawful homicide has been committed by the accused, and consequently he is guilty of unlawful homicide without malice aforethought, and that is manslaughter: *per* Stephen J. in *Doherty's Case* (1887) 16 Cox C.C. 306, 307. [He concluded the passage:] the law is plain beyond all question that in cases falling short of insanity a condition of drunkenness at the time of committing an offence causing death can only, when it is available at all, have the effect of reducing the crime from murder to manslaughter."

From this it seemed clear—and this is the interpretation which the judges have placed on the decision during the ensuing half-century—that it is only in the limited class of cases requiring proof of specific intent that drunkenness can exculpate. Otherwise in no case can it exempt completely from criminal liability.

Unhappily what Lord Birkenhead L.C. described as "plain beyond question" becomes less plain in the later passage in his speech at 504, on which counsel for the appellant not unnaturally placed great emphasis. It reads:

"I do not think that the proposition of law deduced from these earlier cases is an exceptional rule applicable only to cases in which it is necessary to prove a specific intent in order to constitute the graver crime—*e.g.*, wounding with intent to do grievous bodily harm or with intent to kill. It is true that in such cases the specific intent must be proved to constitute the particular crime, but this is, on ultimate analysis, only in accordance with the ordinary law applicable to crime, for, speaking generally (and apart from certain special offences), a person cannot be convicted of a crime unless the mens was rea. Drunkenness, rendering a person incapable of the intent, would be an answer, as it is for example in a charge of attempted suicide."

Why then would it not be an answer in a charge of manslaughter, contrary to the earlier pronouncement? In my view these passages are not easy to reconcile, but I do not dissent from the reconciliation suggested by my noble and learned friend Lord Russell of Killowen. Commenting on the passage in 1920 shortly after it was delivered, however, Stroud wrote, (1920) 36 L.Q.R. at 270:

"The whole of these observations ... suggest an extension of the defence of drunkenness far beyond the limits which have hitherto been assigned to it. The suggestion, put shortly, is that drunkenness may be available as a defence, upon any criminal charge, whenever it can be shown to have affected *mens rea*. Not only is there no authority for the suggestion; there is abundant authority, both ancient and modern, to the contrary."

It has to be said that it is on the latter footing that the judges have applied the law before and since *Beard's* case and have taken the view that self-induced intoxication, however gross and even if it has produced a condition akin to automatism, cannot excuse crimes of basic intent such as the charges of assault which have given rise to the present appeal.

[His Lordship quoted Lord Denning in *Gallagher, post*, p. 265, and in *Bratty, ante*, p. 227].

In no case has the general principle of English law as described by Lord Denning in *Gallagher's* case and exposed again in *Bratty's* case been overruled in this House and the question now to be determined is whether it should be.

I do not for my part regard that general principle as either unethical or contrary to the principles of natural justice. If a man of his own volition takes a substance which causes him to cast off the restraints of reason and conscience, no wrong is done to him by holding him answerable criminally for any injury he may do while in that condition. His course of conduct in reducing himself by drugs and drink to that condition in my view supplies the evidence of mens rea, of guilty mind certainly sufficient for crimes of basic intent. It is a reckless course of conduct and recklessness is enough to constitute the necessary mens rea in assault cases: see *R*. v. *Venna* [*post*, p. 586], *per* James L.J. The drunkenness is itself an intrinsic, an integral part of the crime, the other part being the evidence of the unlawful use of force against the victim. Together they add up to criminal recklessness. On this I adopt the conclusion of Stroud that:

"It would be contrary to all principle and authority to suppose that drunkenness [and what is true of drunkenness is equally true of intoxication by drugs] can be a defence for crime in general on the ground that 'a person cannot be convicted of a crime unless the *mens* was *rea*.' By allowing himself to get drunk and thereby putting himself in such a condition as to be no longer amenable to the law's commands, a man shows such regardlessness as amounts to *mens rea* for the purpose of all ordinary crimes."

This approach is in line with the American Model Code, s.2.08(2),

"When recklessness establishes an element of the offence, if the actor, due to self-induced intoxication, is unaware of a risk of which he would have been aware had be been sober, such unawareness is immaterial."

Acceptance generally of intoxication as a defence (as distinct from the exceptional cases where some additional mental element above that of ordinary mens rea has to be proved) would in my view undermine the criminal law and I do not think that it is enough to say, as did counsel for the appellant, that we can rely on the good sense of the jury or of magistrates to ensure that the guilty are convicted. It may well be that Parliament will at some future time consider, as I think it should, the recommendation in the Butler Committee Report on Mentally Abnormal Offenders that a new offence of "dangerous intoxication" should be created [*post*, p. 273]. But in the meantime it would be irresponsible to abandon the common law rule, as "mercifully relaxed," which the courts have followed for a century and a half. ...

The final question that arises is whether s.8 of the Criminal Justice Act 1967 has had the result of abrogating or qualifying the common law rule. That section emanated from the consideration the Law Commission gave to the decision of the House in *D.P.P.* v. *Smith* [1961] A.C. 290. Its purpose and effect was to alter the law of evidence about the presumption of intention to produce the reasonable and probable consequences of one's acts. It was not intended to change the common law rule. In referring to "all the evidence" it meant all the *relevant* evidence. But if there is a substantive rule of law that in crimes of basic intent, the factor of intoxication is irrelevant (and such I hold to be the substantive law), evidence with regard to it is quite irrelevant. Section 8 does not abrogate the substantive rule and it cannot properly be said that the continued application of that rule contravenes the section. For these reasons, my conclusion is that the certified question should be answered Yes, that there was no misdirection in this case and that the appeal should be dismissed.

My noble and learned friends and I think it may be helpful if we give the following indication of the general lines on which in our view the jury should be directed as to the effect on the criminal responsibility of the accused of drink or drugs or both, whenever death or physical injury to another person results from something done by the accused for which there is no legal justification and the offence with which the accused is charged is manslaughter or assault at common law or the statutory offence of unlawful wounding under s.20, or of assault occasioning actual bodily harm under s.47 of the Offences Against the Person Act 1861.

In the case of these offences it is no excuse in law that, because of drink or drugs which the accused himself had taken knowingly and willingly, he had deprived himself of the ability to exercise self-control, to realise the possible consequences of what he was doing or even to be conscious that he was doing it. As in the instant case, the jury may be properly instructed that they "can ignore the subject of drink or drugs as being in any way a defence to" charges of this character.

[LORD DIPLOCK agreed with the speech of Lord Elwyn-Jones and with Lord Russell's explanation of *Beard*.]

LORD SIMON also agreed but added "by way of marginal comment": ... a considerable difficulty in this branch of the law arises from the terminology which has been used. ... [I]t is desirable that the terms used should be defined, unambiguous and used consistently.

There is an immediate difficulty. Fundamental to the criminal law is the concept of mens rea. But, first, this phrase is taken from a legal maxim phrased in highly elliptical Latin. Secondly, apart from the quite exceptional case of one type of treason, there is no such thing as a "guilty mind." The criminal law prohibits certain defined conduct (actus reus). But it goes on to say that a person who perpetrates such conduct is not criminally responsible, in general, unless such conduct is accompanied by a wrongful state of mind which is expressed or implied in the definition of the offence (mens rea). This wrongful state of mind can vary greatly with the various offences contained in the criminal code, as is shown by the quotations by my noble and learned friend, Lord Elwyn-Jones L.C., from the judgment of Stephen J. in *R. v. Tolson*. Mens rea is therefore on ultimate analysis the state of mind stigmatised as wrongful by the criminal law which, when compounded with the relevant prohibited conduct, constitutes a particular offence. There is no juristic reason why mental incapacity (short of *M'Naghten* insanity) brought about by self-induced intoxication, to realise what one is doing or its probable consequences should not be such a state of mind stigmatised as wrongful by the criminal law; and there is every practical reason why it should be.

But, in order to understand this branch of the law in general and *D.P.P. v. Beard* in particular, it is desirable to have further tools of analysis. A term that appears frequently in discussion of this aspect of the law and crucially in *Beard* is "specific intent." Smith and Hogan, Criminal Law, 3rd edn., 1973, 47 justly criticise this term as potentially ambiguous, since it has been used in three different senses. The first sense is that particular state of mind which, when compounded with prohibited conduct, constitutes a particular offence. This is an unnecessary and misleading usage; and, since "specific intent" has been frequently and usefully employed in other senses, should merely be abandoned. A second sense in which "specific intent" has been used is what in *D.P.P. v. Morgan* [ante, p. 142] I called "ulterior intent," having taken the term from Smith and Hogan. I needed that particular concept for the analysis on which I ventured in *D.P.P. v. Morgan*; unfortunately, my argument failed to command the assent of the majority of the appellate committee, or, on further appeal, some academic commentators and the Advisory Group on the Law of Rape (1975) Cmnd. 6352. But I would not wish it to be thought that I consider "ulterior intent" as I defined it in *Morgan* as interchangeable with "specific intent" as that term was used by Stephen, for example, in his Digest, by Lord Birkenhead L.C. in *Beard* or by Lord Denning and others in commenting on *Beard*. "Ulterior intent," which I can here summarily describe as a state of mind contemplating consequences beyond those defined in the actus reus, is merely one type of "specific intent" as that term was used by Lord Birkenhead L.C., etc. "Ulterior intent" does not accurately describe the state of mind in the crime of doing an act likely to assist the enemy (*R. v. Steane* [1947] K.B. 997, *ante*, p. 75) or causing grievous bodily harm with intent to do some grievous bodily harm (Offences Against the Person Act 1861, s.18, as amended by the Criminal Law Act 1967) or even murder. None of these requires by its definition contemplation of consequences extending beyond the actus reus.

I still have the temerity to think that the concept of "crime of basic intent" is a useful tool of analysis; and I explained what I meant by it in the passage in *Morgan* generously cited by my noble and learned friend, Lord Elwyn-Jones L.C. It stands significantly in contrast with "crime of specific intent" as that term was used by Stephen's Digest and by Lord Birkenhead L.C. in *Beard*. The best description of "specific intent" in this sense that I know is contained in the judgment of Fauteux J. in *R. v. George* (1960) 128 Can.Crim. Cas. 289, 301:

> "In considering the question of *mens rea*, a distinction is to be made between (i) intention as applied to acts considered in relation to their purposes and (ii) intention as applied to acts apart from their purposes. A general intent attending the commission of an act is, in some cases, the only intent required to constitute the crime while, in others, there must be, in addition to that general intent, a specific intent attending the purpose for the commission of the act."

In short, where the crime is one of "specific intent" the prosecution must in general prove that the purpose for the commission of the act extends to the intent expressed or implied in the definition of the crime. ...

As I have ventured to suggest, there is nothing unreasonable or illogical in the law holding that a mind rendered self-inducedly insensible (short of *M'Naghten* insanity), through drink or drugs, to the nature of a prohibited act or to its probable consequences is as wrongful a mind as one which consciously contemplates the prohibited act and foresees its probable consequences (or is reckless whether they ensue). The latter is all that is required by way of mens rea in a crime of basic intent. But a crime of specific intent requires something more than contemplation of the prohibited act and foresight of its probable consequences. The mens rea in a crime of specific intent requires proof of a purposive element. This purposive element either exists or not; it cannot be supplied by saying that the impairment of mental powers by self-induced intoxication is its equivalent, for it is not. So that the 19th century development of the law as to the effect of self-induced intoxication on criminal responsibility is juristically entirely acceptable; and it need be a matter of no surprise that Stephen stated it without demur or question.

LORD SALMON: ... [A]n assault committed accidentally is not a criminal offence. A man may, *e.g*, thoughtlessly throw out his hand to stop a taxi, or open the door of his car and accidentally hit a passer-by and perhaps unhappily cause him quite serious bodily harm. In such circumstances, the man who caused the injury would be liable civilly for damages but clearly he would have committed no crime.

There are many cases in which injuries are caused by pure accident. I have already given examples of such cases: to these could be added injuries inflicted during an epileptic fit, or whilst sleep-walking, and in many other ways. No one, I think, would suggest that any such case could give rise to criminal liability.

It is argued on behalf of the appellant that a man who makes a vicious assault may at the material time have been so intoxicated by drink or drugs that he no more knew what he was doing than did any of the persons in the examples I have given and that therefore he too cannot be found guilty of a criminal offence.

To my mind there is a very real distinction between such a case and the examples I have given. A man who by voluntarily taking drink and drugs gets himself into an aggressive state in which he does not know what he is doing and then makes a vicious assault can hardly say with any plausibility that what he did was a pure accident which should render him immune from any criminal liability. Yet this in effect is precisely what counsel for the appellant contends that the learned judge should have told the jury.

A number of distinguished academic writers support this contention on the ground of logic. As I understand it, the argument runs like this. Intention, whether special or basic (or whatever fancy name you choose to give it), is still intention. If voluntary intoxication by drink or drugs can, as it admittedly can, negative the special or specific intention necessary for the commission of crimes such as murder and theft, how can you justify in strict logic the view that it cannot negative a basic intention, *e.g.* the intention to commit offences such as assault and unlawful wounding? The answer is that in strict logic this view cannot be justified. But this is the view that has been adopted by the common law of England, which is founded on common sense and experience rather than strict logic. There is no case in the 19th century when the courts were relaxing the harshness of the law in relation to the effect of drunkenness on criminal liability in which the courts ever went so far as to suggest that drunkenness, short of drunkenness producing insanity, could ever exculpate a man from any offence other than one which required some special or specific intent to be proved.

[His Lordship then discussed *Beard*.]

As I have already indicated, I accept that there is a degree of illogicality in the rule that intoxication may excuse or expunge one type of intention and not another. This illogicality is, however, acceptable to me because the benevolent part of the rule removes undue harshness without imperilling safety and the stricter part of the rule works without imperilling justice. It would be just as ridiculous to remove the benevolent part of the rule (which no one suggests) as it would be to adopt the alternative of removing the stricter part of the rule for the sake of preserving absolute logic. Absolute logic in human affairs is an uncertain guide and a very dangerous master. The law is primarily concerned with human affairs. I believe that the main object of our legal system is to preserve individual liberty. One important aspect of individual liberty is protection against physical violence. . . .

If, as I think, this long-standing rule was salutary years ago when it related almost exclusively to drunkenness, and hallucinatory drugs were comparatively unknown, how much more salutary is it today when such drugs are increasingly becoming a public menace? My Lords, I am satisfied that this rule accords with justice, ethics, and common sense. . . . I agree with my noble and learned friend, Lord Elwyn-Jones L.C., that, for the reasons he gives, s.8 of the Criminal Justice Act 1967 does not touch the point raised in this appeal, and I also agree that direction along the lines laid down by my noble and learned friend Lord Elwyn-Jones L.C., should be given by trial judges to juries in the kind of cases to which my noble and learned friend refers.

My Lords, for these reasons, I would dismiss the appeal.

[LORD EDMUND-DAVIES delivered a speech in favour of dismissing the appeal].

LORD RUSSELL OF KILLOWEN: There are two aspects of *Beard's* case [1920] A.C. 479, which have given rise to misunderstanding as to what was there said. One misunderstanding is that a passage in the speech of Lord Birkenhead L.C. is inconsistent with and indeed contradictory of the main tenor thereof. The other is that it lays down or assumes that rape is a crime of specific intent.

[His Lordship cited the passage from p. 504 of *Beard* quoted by Lord Elwyn-Jones, *ante*, p. 248].

... In my opinion this passage is not to be taken as stating in effect the opposite of the whole previous tenor of the speech in the course of denying the applicability of the statement in *R. v. Meade* [1909] 1 K.B. 895. The clue to the cited passage appears to me to be in the words "in order to constitute the graver crime." In my opinion the passage cited does no more than to say that special intent cases are not restricted to those crimes in which the absence of a special intent leaves available a lesser crime embodying no special intent, but embrace all cases of special intent even though no alternative lesser criminal charge is available. And the example given of attempted suicide is just such a case.

The second aspect of *Beard* to which I have referred relates to two passages. The first is:

"My Lords, drunkenness in this case could be no defence unless it could be established that Beard at the time of committing the rape was so drunk that he was incapable of forming the intent to commit it, which was not in fact, and manifestly, having regard to the evidence, could not be contended. For in the present case the death resulted from two acts or from a succession of acts, the rape and the act of violence causing suffocation. These acts cannot be regarded separately and independently of each other. The capacity of the mind of the prisoner to form the felonious intent which murder involves is in other words to be explored in relation to the ravishment; and not in relation merely to the violent act which gave effect to the ravishment."

The second is: "There was certainly no evidence that he was too drunk to form the intent of committing rape."

In my opinion these passages do not indicate an opinion that rape is a crime of special intent. All that is meant is that conscious rape is required to supply "the felonious intent which murder involves." For the crime of murder special or particular intent is always required for the necessary malice aforethought. This may be intent to kill or intent to cause grievous bodily harm: or in a case such as *Beard* of constructive malice, this required the special intent *consciously to commit* the violent felony of rape in the course and furtherance of which the act of violence causing death took place. *Beard* therefore, in my opinion does not suggest that rape is a crime of special or particular intent.

I too would dismiss this appeal.

Appeal dismissed

[It should be pointed out that felony-murder, with which Beard was concerned, was abolished by the Homicide Act 1957].

Questions

1. Lord Elwyn-Jones states that self-induced intoxication is "a reckless course of conduct" and that "recklessness is enough to constitute the necessary *mens rea* in assault cases." In what sense(s) is the word "reckless" being used in these two statements?

2. Although Lord Simon agreed with Lord Elwyn-Jones he also said "*Mens rea* is . . . the state of mind stigmatised as wrongful by the criminal law. . . . There is no juristic reason why mental incapacity . . . brought about by self-induced intoxication, to realise what one is doing . . . should not be such a state of mind stigmatised as wrongful." Is this compatible with describing such intoxication as "reckless?"

3. Lord Salmon and Lord Edmund-Davies admitted that the decision was illogical. Do you agree? See Dashwood: "Logic and the Lords in Majewski" [1977] Crim.L.R. 532 and 591, and Sellers: "*Mens Rea* and the Judicial Approach to Bad Excuses" (1978) 41 M.L.R. 245.

4. Barlow in "Drug Intoxication and the Principle of *Capacitas Rationalis*" (1984) 100 L.Q.R. 639, at 646 states:

"Given that self induced intoxication creates a risk that harmful conduct of some diverse kind may result, it would almost always be forensically impossible to demonstrate that a specific risk was known and ignored, at the point before the drug was used. Can it really be said that the accused in *D.P.P.* v. *Majewski* soberly foresaw on Sunday morning before he began intoxicating himself with amphetamines, barbiturates and alcohol that he might consequently commit an assault on Monday evening? The most he could have foreseen at that point was that intoxication might create a wide range of risks to other people or their property. That he might become irrational and might be reduced to a socially dangerous entity. That is not the essence of criminal recklessness."

Do you agree?

Note

It is clear from *Garlick* [1981] Crim.L.R. 178 that when intoxication is raised as a defence to a crime of specific intent the question in issue is not whether the defendant was incapable of forming the intent but whether, even if still capable, he or she did form that intent.

Williams, Textbook of Criminal Law, pp. 471–73

"The rule in *Majewski* depends on the assumption that an intelligible distinction can be made between specific and basic intent. But the law lords in that and other cases, while unanimous that there is such a distinction, and while agreeing on some of its applications, have failed to agree on a definition of the two intents. What can be said is that the definition that best fits the actual decisions, and the one representing the dominant judicial opinion, is the one we had before for what we then preferred to call 'ulterior intent.' A specific intent is an intent going beyond the intent to do the act in question. The bodily movement is willed or intentional, and it is done with some further intent specified in the offence. In murder (the judges appear to suppose), it is an act done with intent to cause death; in the crime of wounding or causing g.b.h. with intent, an act done with intent to cause g.b.h.; in burglary, trespass with certain unlawful intents, and so on.

The courts have not stated clearly how they conceive the intent as specific. Perhaps in the case of causing g.b.h. with intent to cause g.b.h. they do not realise that the words 'with intent' are used in a somewhat unusual sense, or it does not suit their purpose to advert to this. The phrase 'with intent' in the definition of a crime normally refers to an ulterior intent (*e.g.* in the crime of assault with intent to rob, or wounding with intent to resist arrest), but in the crime of causing g.b.h. with intent to cause g.b.h. no such ulterior intent is required. Causing g.b.h. with intent to cause it merely means intentionally causing g.b.h.

Another possible explanation depends on the fact pointed out before, that while some verbs have consequences wrapped into them, some have not. When we talk of killing (or wounding) a person, we may conceptualise or verbalise the event in either of two ways. We may take killing (or wounding) to mean doing an act (striking, etc.) that causes death (or a wound), where the act and its consequence are treated as two separate events; or we may have a composite notion of 'doing an act of killing' (or 'an act of wounding'), where the result is included in the notion of the act. The choice is only a question of words, but it is a choice with legal implications under the rule in *Majewski*. Traditionally, murder is thought of as a 'killing,' and that is how it is legally described. But, the judges' scheme being to have a rule that will let the drunkard off the graver charge only, they decide to think of murder for this particular purpose as 'an act done with intent to cause death (and succeeding in that purpose)' rather than as a self-contained act of 'intentional killing.' Similarly, they regard an intentional wounding as 'doing an act with intent to cause a wound' rather than an act of 'intentional wounding.' This is one of many examples that could be given of judges making a meaningless distinction of language yield legal results.

It is not even true that murder is necessarily an intentional killing. Intentionally causing grievous bodily harm without intent to kill is murder if death results. Besides, if one can turn a crime into one of specific intent by saying that achieving a result by doing an act with intent to achieve it involves a specific intent, then I commit a crime of specific intent when I move my fist with intent to bring it into painful contact with your nose, and succeed in doing so, or when I put your car in motion as a result of having done something (started the engine, etc.) with that purpose; yet neither of these crimes (assault, and taking a conveyance) involves a specific intent in law. Reasoning based on the idea of specific intent is phoney.

Further, the distinction accords only roughly with a social or moral classification of crimes. There is no social difference between stealing someone else's watch and deliberately smashing someone else's watch, but the first (theft) is regarded as a crime of specific intent while the second (criminal damage) is a crime of basic intent.

Another anomaly emerges when one compares criminal damage with wounding with intent. 'Wounding with intent' under O.A.P.A. s.18 in most cases merely means intentionally wounding, and it is precisely analogous to intentionally damaging property. Now if a drunkard on the rampage swings an iron bar at a window and smashes it, the jury (or magistrates) can (subject to what is to be said later) convict him under the rule in *Majewski* of intentionally damaging the window, the jury being instructed to disregard his intoxication when the offence is one of basic intent, as this offence is. But if he had wounded a man by doing essentially the same thing, his intoxication would have been taken into account on a charge under section 18 to help show that he did not intend to wound anyone, the crime under section 18 being one of specific intent.

There is no relevant difference between the two cases on the facts. The man broke the window, or he caused the window to be broken; he wounded the victim, or he caused the victim to be wounded. Why should the court's choice of words be such as to make the first crime one of basic intent and the second crime one of specific intent?

Do not think that what I am saying will be of the slightest use to you in legal practice. The judges will resolutely close their minds to any argument based on ordinary legal, linguistic or logical reasoning in this area of policy. It is not even profitable to cite the explicit language of an Act of Parliament. The decision in *Majewski* is a classical illustration of the truth that no authority can compel judges to arrive at a decision to which they are strongly averse. When counsel for Majewski used a logical argument in the House of Lords criticising the doctrine of specific intent, he was informed that 'the common law of England is founded on common sense and experience rather than strict logic.' Their lordships therefore approved the dichotomy of criminal intent notwithstanding that they had reached no agreement between themselves on its basis, and notwithstanding that no definition of the two intents explains the purported applications of the distinction made by the courts and approved in *Majewski*. So ours not to reason why; we must just respectfully receive the twin lists of crimes of specific and basic intent as handed down to us."

Note

Section 1(2) of the Criminal Damage Act 1971 provides:

"A person who without lawful excuse destroys or damages any property, whether belonging to himself or another. . . .
(a) intending to destroy or damage any property or being reckless as to whether any property should be destroyed or damaged; and
(b) intending by the destruction or damage to endanger the life of another or being reckless as to whether the life of another would be thereby endangered;
shall be guilty of an offence."

In *R.* v. *Caldwell* (*infra*), the House of Lords held that whether this is a crime of specific or basic intent depends on the basis of the charge.

R. v. Caldwell
[1981] 2 All E.R. 961
House of Lords

The facts appear, *ante*, p. 111.

The certified question was as follows: "Whether evidence of self-induced intoxication can be relevant to the following questions—(a)

Whether the defendant intended to endanger the life of another; and (b)
Whether the defendant was reckless as to whether the life of another
would be endangered, within the meaning of section 1(2)(b) of the
Criminal Damage Act 1971."

LORD DIPLOCK: As respects the charge under section 1(2) the prosecution
did not rely upon an actual intent of the respondent to endanger the lives
of the residents but relied upon his having been reckless whether the lives
of any of them would be endangered. His act of setting fire to it was one
which the jury were entitled to think created an obvious risk that the lives
of the residents would be endangered; and the only defence with which
your Lordships are concerned is that the respondent had made himself so
drunk as to render him oblivious of that risk.

If the only mental state capable of constituting the necessary *mens rea* for
an offence under section 1(2) were that expressed in the words "intending
by the destruction or damage to endanger the life of another," it would
have been necessary to consider whether the offence was to be classified
as one of "specific" intent for the purposes of the rule of law which this
House affirmed and applied in *R. v. Majewski*, and this it plainly is. But
this is not, in my view, a relevant inquiry where "being reckless as to
whether the life of another would be thereby endangered" is an alternative
mental state that is capable of constituting the necessary *mens rea* of the
offence with which he is charged.

The speech of the Lord Chancellor in *Majewski* with which Lord Simon
of Glaisdale, Lord Kilbrandon and I agreed, is authority that self-induced
intoxication is no defence to a crime in which recklessness is enough to
constitute the necessary *mens rea.* . . .

Reducing oneself by drink or drugs to a condition in which the restraints
of reason and conscience are cast off was held to be a reckless course of
conduct and an integral part of the crime. The Lord Chancellor accepted as
correctly stating English law the provision in section 208 of the American
Model Penal Code:

> "When recklessness establishes an element of the offence, if the actor,
> due to self-induced intoxication, is unaware of a risk of which he would
> have been aware had he been sober, such unawareness is immaterial."

So, in the instant case, the fact that the respondent was unaware of the
risk of endangering the lives of residents in the hotel owing to his self-
induced intoxication, would be no defence if that risk would have been
obvious to him had he been sober.

. . . [T]he Court of Appeal in the instant case regarded the case as
turning upon whether the offence under section 1(2) was one of "specific"
intent or "basic" intent. Following a recent decision of the Court of Appeal
by which they were bound, *R. v. Orpin* (1980) 70 Cr.App.R. 306, they held
that the offence under section 1(2) was one of "specific" intent in contrast
to the offence under section 1(1) which was of basic intent. This would be
right if the only *mens rea* capable of constituting the offence were an actual
intention to endanger the life of another. For the reasons I have given,
however, classification into offences of "specific" and "basic" intent is
irrelevant where being reckless as to whether a particular harmful
consequence will result from one's act is a sufficient alternative *mens rea*. I
would give the following answers to the certified questions:

(a) If the charge of an offence under section 1(2) of the Criminal
    Damage Act 1971 is framed so as to charge the defendant only with
    "*intending* by the destruction or damage" [of the property] "to

endanger the life of another," evidence of self-induced intoxication can be relevant to his defence.

(b) If the charge is, or includes, a reference to his "being reckless as to whether the life of another would thereby be endangered," evidence of self-induced intoxication is not relevant.

LORDS KEITH of KINKEL and ROSKILL agreed with this statement of the law. LORD WILBERFORCE agreed with LORD EDMUND-DAVIES.

LORD EDMUND-DAVIES: [T]he view expressed by my noble and learned friend Lord Diplock "that the speech of the Lord Chancellor in *Majewski* is authority that self-induced intoxication is no defence to a crime in which recklessness is enough to constitute the necessary *mens rea*" . . . is a view which, with respect, I do not share. In common with all noble and learned Lords hearing that appeal, Lord Elwyn-Jones L.C. adopted the well-established (though not universally favoured) distinction between basic and specific intents. *Majewski* related solely to charges of assault, undoubtedly an offence of basic intent, and the Lord Chancellor made it clear that his observations were confined to offences of that nature. . . . My respectful view is that *Majewski* accordingly supplies no support for the proposition that, in relation to crimes of specific intent (such as section 1(2)(b) of the 1971 Act) incapacity to appreciate the degree and nature of the risk created by his action which is attributable to the defendant's self-intoxication is an irrelevance. The Lord Chancellor was dealing simply with crimes of basic intent, and in my judgment it was strictly within that framework that he adopted the view expressed in the American Penal Code [s.2.08] and recklessness as an element in crimes of specific intent was, I am convinced, never within his contemplation.

For the foregoing reasons, the Court of Appeal were in my judgment right in quashing the conviction under section 1(2)(b) and substituting a finding of guilty of arson contrary to section 1(1) and (3) of the 1971 Act.

. . . [I]t was recently predicted that, "There can hardly be any doubt that *all* crimes of recklessness except murder will now be held to be crimes of basic intent within *Majewski*." (Glanville Williams, "Textbook of Criminal Law," 1978, p. 431). That prophecy has been promptly fulfilled by the majority of your Lordships, for, with the progressive displacement of "maliciously" by "intentionally or recklessly" in statutory crimes, that will surely be the effect of the majority decision in this appeal. That I regret, for the consequence is that, however grave the crime charged, if recklessness can constitute its *mens rea* the fact that it was committed in drink can afford no defence. It is a very long time since we had so harsh a law in this country. Having revealed in *Majewski* (pp. 495B–497C) my personal conviction that, on grounds of public policy, a plea of drunkenness cannot exculpate crimes of basic intent and so exercise unlimited sway in the criminal law, I am nevertheless unable to concur that your Lordships' decision should now become the law of the land. For, as Eveleigh L.J. said in *Orpin* (*supra*, at p. 312):

" . . . there is nothing inconsistent in treating intoxication as irrelevant when considering the liability of a person who has willed himself to do that which the law forbids (for example, to do something which wounds another), and yet to make it relevant when a further mental state is postulated as an aggravating circumstance making the offence even more serious."

By way of postscript I would add that the majority view demonstrates yet again the folly of totally ignoring the recommendations of the Butler

Committee (Report on Mentally Abnormal Offenders. Cmnd. 6244, 1975, paras. 18, 53–58).

Appeal dismissed

Note

See *post*, p. 273 for the Butler Committee recommendations.

Question

If D is charged with an offence of basic intent and pleads intoxication in defence, he will be found guilty on the basis that becoming voluntarily intoxicated raises an irrebuttable presumption of recklessness. If the offence is one requiring *Cunningham* recklessness, can it be said that *actus reus* and *mens rea* coincide? What is the act to which D's reckless state of mind relates? What if D did not appreciate the risk of intoxication and its possible results when he consumed the particular drug? (See *Hardie infra*.)

R. v. Hardie
[1985] 1 W.L.R. 64
Court of Appeal

When the relationship with the woman with whom he had been living broke down, the appellant became upset and took several Valium tablets belonging to the woman. He was unaware of the effect the tablets might have. Several hours later he started a fire in the bedroom of the flat while the woman and her daughter were in the sitting room. He was charged with damaging property with intent to endanger life or being reckless whether life would be endangered contrary to s.1(2) of the Criminal Damage Act 1971. He argued in his defence that the effect of the Valium had been to prevent him having *mens rea*. The judge directed the jury that this could not provide a defence as he had voluntarily self-administered the drug. He appealed on grounds of misdirection.

PARKER L.J.: ... It is clear from *R. v. Caldwell* [1982] A.C. 341 that self-induced intoxication can be a defence where the charge is only one of specific intention. It is equally clear that it cannot be a defence where, as here, the charge included recklessness. Hence, if there was self-intoxication in this case the judge's direction was correct. The problem is whether, assuming that the effect of the Valium was to deprive the appellant of any appreciation of what he was doing it should properly be regarded as self-induced intoxication and thus no answer. ...

R. v. Majewski was a case of drunkenness resulting from alcoholic consumption by the accused whilst under the influence of non-medically prescribed drugs. *R. v. Caldwell* was a case of plain drunkenness. There can be no doubt that the same rule applies both to self-intoxication by alcohol and intoxication by hallucinatory drugs, but this is because the effects of both are well-known and there is therefore an element of recklessness in the self-administration of the drug. *R. v. Lipman* [1970] 1 Q.B. 152 is an example of such a case.

"Intoxication" or similar symptoms may, however, arise in other circumstances. In *R. v. Bailey* (*ante*, p. 234) this court had to consider a case where a diabetic had failed to take sufficient food after taking a normal dose of insulin and struck the victim over the head with an iron bar. The judge directed the jury that the defence of automatism, *i.e.* that the mind did not go with the act, was not available because the incapacity was self-induced. It was held that this was wrong on two grounds (a) because on the basis of *R. v. Majewski* it was clearly available to the offence embodying specific intent and (b) because although self-induced by the omission to take food it was also available to negative the other offence which was of basic intent only.

[Having referred to the judgment of Griffiths L.J., *ante*, p. 234, his Lordship continued]

In the present instance the defence was that the Valium was taken for the purpose of calming the nerves only, that it was old stock and that the appellant was told it would do him no harm. There was no evidence that it was known to the appellant or even generally known that the taking of Valium in the quantity taken would be liable to render a person aggressive or incapable of appreciating risks to others or have other side effects such that its self-administration would itself have an element of recklessness. It is true that Valium is a drug and it is true that it was taken deliberately and not taken on medical prescription, but the drug is, in our view, wholly different in kind from drugs which are liable to cause unpredictability or aggressiveness. It may well be that the taking of a sedative or soporific drug will, in certain circumstances, be no answer, for example in a case of reckless driving, but if the effect of a drug is merely soporific or sedative the taking of it, even in some excessive quantity, cannot in the ordinary way raise a *conclusive* presumption against the admission of proof of intoxication for the purpose of disproving mens rea in ordinary crimes, such as would be the case with alcoholic intoxication or incapacity or automatism resulting from the self-administration of dangerous drugs.

In the present case the jury should not, in our judgment, have been directed to disregard any incapacity which resulted or might have resulted from the taking of Valium. They should have been directed that if they came to the conclusion that, as a result of the Valium, the appellant was, at the time, unable to appreciate the risks to property and persons from his actions they should then consider whether the taking of the Valium was itself reckless. We are unable to say what would have been the appropriate direction with regard to the elements of recklessness in this case for we have not seen all the relevant evidence, nor are we able to suggest a model direction, for circumstances will vary infinitely and model directions can sometimes lead to more rather than less confusion. It is sufficient to say that the direction that the effects of Valium were necessarily irrelevant was wrong.

Appeal allowed

Questions

1. Is it possible to reconcile *Hardie* with *Caldwell* and *Elliott* v. *C.* [1983] 1 W.L.R. 939 (*ante*, p. 119)? For example, D is mentally retarded. He finds some Valium tablets in the medicine cabinet and consumes them rendering himself intoxicated. In this state he sets fire to property. He is charged with criminal damage and in his defence it is argued that D did not realise that Valium could render him intoxicated and incapable of appreciating risks. The prosecution argue that as D is generally incapable of appreciating risks, *Elliott* v. *C.* should be followed rather than *Hardie*. How might this issue be decided.

2. In determining whether the self-administration of a drug such as Valium "would itself have an element of recklessness," is it the *Cunningham* or *Caldwell* test of recklessness which is applicable? (*Cf. Bailey, ante,* p. 234.)

3. To which drugs does the *Majewski* rule apply and which fall under the *Hardie* exception?

Note

In R. v. *O'Connor* (1979–80) 29 A.L.R. 449, the High Court of Australia departed from *Majewski*, holding by a four-to-three majority that self-induced intoxication could be a defence to any crime. The court held that evidence that the defendant acted involuntarily or unintentionally as a result of intoxication might properly be considered by a jury in deciding whether the prosecution had proved beyond reasonable doubt that the defendant acted voluntarily and intended to commit the offence. If there is a reasonable doubt whether the defendant acted voluntarily and intentionally, he should be acquitted.

N. L. A. Barlow, "Drug Intoxication and the Principle of Capacitas Rationalis" (1984) 100 L.Q.R. 639, 646–652

"As both *Majewski* and *O'Connor* demonstrate, the preoccupation of the courts and other contributors to this question, one of the most seriously disputed issues in modern criminal law, is with the contemporaneous presence of the *mens rea* and the *actus reus* elements in the intoxicated act of the accused. In my submission this is a misdirected focus. There is a principle of greater relevance and weight to the question of responsibility for harm caused during intoxication than the *actus reus* and *mens rea* principles. This is the principle embodied in the fundamental responsibility requirement of rational capacity. The presumption that an accused has sufficient rational capacity to understand the meaning of his action is the first postulate of the criminal law. It must be considered in all criminal proceedings before consideration of any other principle of responsibility, including *mens rea* and *actus reus*, may properly begin. What precisely then is the principle of *capacitas rationalis* and what are the legal and factual differences between it and the *mens rea* and *actus reus* principles.

The principle of *capacitas rationalis* embodies the free-will-retributive idea that man is a rational being with the capacity to understand his actions intelligently and control them accordingly. Both in theory and in practice its positive effect is to operate as a pre-condition to punishment; as a standard, a criterion, for determining eligibility for and immunity from punishment. Before a man may be punished, he must have had the capacity to understand the criminal import of his conduct. Thus an enquiry into the mental capacity of an accused person if concluded in his favour has the effect of putting him beyond the court's, retributively based, powers to punish—although not beyond its utilitarian based powers to detain and treat without denunciation on social defence grounds.

Like all other properly so-called presumptions, the presumption of capacity may be rebutted. . . .

[T]he principle of rational capacity, of *capacitas rationalis*, should for the purpose of criminal law analysis . . . be positively regarded as an essential element of criminal guilt, of prior importance to the two other fundamental responsibility requirements, all three of which, *capacitas rationalis, actus reus,* and *mens rea,* must ultimately be established by the Crown. . . .

[I]n what circumstances is the presumption rebutted and the accused person found to have 'acted,' using that word in a causal sense of motor function only, without rational capacity? The two most obvious and traditionally recognised exceptions are those factual situations embraced by the defences of infancy and insanity. In infancy cases the child's mind has not yet matured sufficiently to enable us to say with confidence (whether we be psychiatrists or parents) that he or she understood the criminal nature of the wrong. The capacity for rational judgment is not yet properly developed. With insanity cases the irrationality is caused not by immaturity but by certain complex psychological or physiological forces which have caused a radical breakdown in the agent's rational powers (which may have fully matured) particularly in the essential human interaction between the senses and the brain. Neither the pleas of infancy or insanity are defences rooted in the concepts of *actus reus* or *mens rea.* Both in law and science they are distinct. Capacity concerns the power to exercise rational judgment. The capacity defences of insanity and infancy imply the absence of this power. If a person is unable to exercise control over his physical actions, as where he is blown by the wind into another person, his absence of motor control, his causal impotence, his lack of *actus reus,* requires his acquittal in respect of any subsequent charge, say, of assault. The concept of *mens rea* is concerned not with rational nor causal power but with the power of perception, of relevant knowledge. Because our sensory perceptions are defective or inefficient does not mean that the power of rational judgment is absent. . . .

A person who mistakes a human being for a deer and shoots to kill it will not be acquitted because of a temporary loss of rational power. He will be acquitted of murder because of a mistake in perception. Similarly we do not equate the infant's incapacity to rationally understand the reality of the external world with a temporary misinterpretation of that reality akin to a mistake of the sort embraced by the *mens rea* principle. The infant's perceptive powers may be acute, as is often the case with children, and yet the child's rational capacity, particularly the power to evaluate the moral quality of actions, may still be far from mature. So neither the defence of infancy nor insanity are based on the absence of *mens rea* or have anything to do with *actus reus.* They are, rather, based on the absence of rational capacity.

Like the incapacities of insanity and infancy the state of intoxication also involves the absence of rational power. . . .

[I]nsanity and involuntary intoxication have identical legal as well as identical psychological significance. Unlike a *mens rea* instance of mistake or ignorance of fact, which may involve a temporary, though not irrational, error of perception, a loss of rational capacity may involve a complete loss of mental powers during the agent's distraction from reality. At the very least it involves an inability to comprehend the full moral significance and hence criminal import of conduct. Either one of these characteristics are common to the conditions of insanity, infancy and intoxication. Neither is common to any of the mental states excused under the *mens rea* principle. It is for this reason that the legal significance of harms caused during intoxication must be assessed under the principle of rational capacity and not the *mens rea* and contemporaneity principle as has been erroneously assumed by so many modern jurists.

To recapitulate then, because intoxication, a condition of irrationality, raises an issue of *capacitas rationalis* of the power to appreciate the distinction between right and wrong, the *mens rea* and *actus reus* principles which respectively concern issues of cognition and causalty are irrelevant. We do not in fact even reach the stage where they might be considered. So the current debate, raging throughout the courtrooms and campuses of the common law world and reaching its zenith in the judgments in and literature on *D.P.P.* v. *Majewski* and *R.* v. *O'Connor* over whether the logic of the contemporaneity principle is in intoxication cases sacrificed at the expense of a 'public policy' inspired concept of recklessness as in *Majewski*, or is upheld on the basis that there must be a concurrence of *actus reus* harm and *mens rea* intention as in *O'Connor*, is misconceived and cannot assist in the assessment of responsibility for punishment of crimes caused during intoxication. In seeking to discover the reasons for such punishment we must forget all about the contemporaneity principle and instead focus our attention entirely upon the issue of rational capacity. . . .

[W]hy [do] we excuse irrational conduct arising out of infancy and insanity and punish that arising out of voluntary intoxication as laid down in *Majewski*. We need some independent positive justification for this seemingly inconsistent result.

I propose to provide this by demonstrating that the punishment of harms caused during intoxication is a necessary consequence of the presumption of rational capacity. That our reasons for this are first of all logical rather than utilitarian and arise essentially out of the meaning and purpose of the presumption of capacity because the factual distinction between natural and artificial irrationality logically calls for different moral and therefore legal assessment.

The presumption of *capacitas rationalis* is a retributivist assessment of the intellectual nature of man. It refers only to his innate characteristics. In his natural state man is endowed with the potential for rational capacity, a potential which he fully realises upon majority and which he will maintain unless it is radically broken down by other innate organic or psychological forces beyond his personal control. Even when a man elects the irrationality that goes with extreme intoxication his capacity for rational control is still latently there and will reassert itself when intoxication departs. The duration of intoxication irrationality may be fairly precisely determined in that sobriety and hence rationality will inevitably return once the human metabolism has consumed the drug, or at least exhausted it of its psychotropic properties. The same cannot be said of any naturally caused irrationality such as infancy or insanity. So the presumption of *capacitas rationalis* is a dictate of physiological fact; a description of rationality in its natural human state. In its essential meaning the presumption does not contemplate the extension of the protection (from punishment) arising upon its rebuttal to artificial instances of irrationality.

The presumption of *capacitas rationalis* functions as a forensic device to implement certain retributive propositions about punishment, specifically the notion that man is naturally endowed with rationality. It must be considered in the context of a theory which imputes the individual with moral as well as causal responsibility for those of his actions which he may naturally elect and direct. The presumption is falsified if we attempt to accommodate within the same meaning both the proposition that man is inherently rational and that man is rational by choice. The two statements describe two factually distinct, indeed opposed, conditions which by virtue of their contradiction, call for different, logically for contrary, moral and legal assessment. If we prescribe in our retributive model of law that those instances of irrationality caused by innate, organically uncontrollable, forces are not morally punishable, as we do *via* the defences of infancy and insanity, we are bound in consistency, by virtue of our very identification of the cause of the irrationality as determinative of the issue of responsibility, to regard those instances of irrationality caused by artificial forces in a contrary light. In short we are logically bound to punish.

It follows that *Majewski* and *O'Connor* preoccupied as they are with the search for a contemporaneous *mens rea* and *actus reus* in an intoxicated and irrational mind cannot assist in the determination of responsibility for crimes caused during self induced irrationality. This is the case whether the intoxication is moderate and merely impairs *mens rea* cognition or extreme and impairs *actus reus* capacity for causal control, resulting in automatism. Majewski was therefore correctly convicted but for the wrong reasons. O'Connor was incorrectly acquitted. Both accuseds freely discarded their presumed rationality. The logic and purpose of the *capacitas rationalis* principle which excuses only involuntary irrationality dictate that both accused should have been convicted and the circumstance of intoxication considered only as a mitigation factor on sentence. The recognition of the requirement of *capacitas rationalis* as the first essential element of criminal guilt prior even to *actus reus* and *mens rea* elements, and its logical application in cases of self induced irrationality, provide the theoretical basis for responsibility and punishment for crimes caused during voluntary intoxication."

Questions

1. Would Barlow convict of a specific intent crime an intoxicated D if he had "freely discarded his presumed rationality?"
2. What difference is there between Barlow's reason for punishing D—"free discarding of presumed rationality"—and Lord Simon's—"a mind rendered self-inducedly insensible . . . is as wrongful a mind as one which consciously contemplates the prohibited act and foresees its probable consequences . . . "?

ii. Becoming Intoxicated "With Intent"—the "Dutch Courage" Problem

If D drinks to give himself "Dutch courage" to commit an offence, may he rely on his intoxication in defence to support a plea that when he committed the offence he was so drunk that he either did not form or was incapable of forming the necessary intent? See next case.

Attorney-General for Northern Ireland v. Gallagher
[1963] A.C. 349
House of Lords

The respondent was convicted of the murder of his wife. The defence was that of insanity under the M'Naghten Rules or, in the alternative, that at the time of the commission of the crime the respondent was by reason of drink incapable of forming the intent required in murder and was therefore guilty only of manslaughter. The respondent had indicated an intention to kill his wife before taking the alcohol. The Court of Criminal Appeal in Northern Ireland allowed an appeal on the ground that the judge in his summing-up directed the jury to apply the tests laid down in the M'Naghten Rules to the time when alcohol was taken and not to the time when the actual murder was committed.

LORD DENNING: My Lords, this case differs from all others in the books in that the accused man, whilst sane and sober, before he took to the drink, had already made up his mind to kill his wife. This seems to me to be far worse—and far more deserving of condemnation—than the case of a man who, before getting drunk has no intention to kill, but afterwards in his cups, whilst drunk, kills another by an act which he would not dream of doing when sober. Yet by the law of England in this latter case his drunkenness is no defence even though it has distorted his reason and his will-power. So why should it be a defence in the present case? And is it made any better by saying that the man is a psychopath?

The answer to the question is, I think, that the case falls to be decided by the general principle of English law that, subject to very limited exceptions, drunkenness is no defence to a criminal charge, nor is a defect of reason produced by drunkenness. This principle was stated by Sir Matthew Hale in his *Pleas of the Crown*, I, p. 32, in words which I would repeat here. "This vice" (drunkenness) "doth deprive men of the use of reason, and puts many men into a perfect, but temporary, phrenzy. . . . By the laws of England such a person shall have no privilege by this voluntary contracted madness, but shall have the same judgment as if he were in his right senses."

The general principle can be illustrated by looking at the various ways in which drunkenness may produce a defect of reason:

(a) It may impair a man's powers of perception so that he may not be able to foresee or measure the consequences of his actions as he would if he were sober. Nevertheless he is not allowed to set up his self-induced want of perception as a defence. Even if he did not himself appreciate that what he was doing was dangerous, nevertheless, if a reasonable man in his place, who was not befuddled with drink, would have appreciated it, he is guilty: see *R. v. Meade* [1909] 1 K.B. 895, as explained in *D.P.P.* v. *Beard* [1920] A.C. 479.

(b) It may impair a man's power to judge between right or wrong, so that he may do a thing when drunk which he would not dream of doing while sober. He does not realise he is doing wrong. Nevertheless he is not allowed to set up his self-induced want of moral sense as a defence. In *Beard's* case Lord Birkenhead L.C. distinctly ruled that it was not a defence for a drunken man to say he did not know he was doing wrong.

(c) It may impair a man's power of self-control so that he may more readily give way to provocation than if he were sober. Nevertheless he is not allowed to set up his self-induced want of control as a defence. The acts of provocation are to be assessed, not according to their effect on him personally, but according to the effect they would have on a reasonable man in his place. The law on this point was previously in doubt (see the cases considered in *Beard's* case), but it has since been resolved by *R. v. McCarthy* [1954] 2 Q.B. 105, *Bedder* v. *D.P.P.* [1954] 1 W.L.R. 1119 and section 3 of the Homicide Act 1957.

The general principle which I have enunciated is subject to two exceptions:

1. If a man is charged with an offence in which a specific intention is essential (as in murder, though not in manslaughter), then evidence of drunkenness, which renders him incapable of forming that intention, is an answer: see *Beard's* case. This degree of drunkenness is reached when the man is rendered so stupid by drink that he does not know what he is doing (see *R. v. Moore* (1852) 3 C. & K. 153), as where, at a christening, a drunken nurse put the baby behind a large fire, taking it for a log of wood (*Gentleman's Magazine*, 1748, p. 570); and where a drunken man thought his friend (lying in his bed) was a theatrical dummy placed there and

stabbed him to death (*The Times*, January 13, 1951). In each of those cases it would not be murder. But it would be manslaughter.

2. If a man by drinking brings on a distinct disease of the mind such as delirium tremens, so that he is temporarily insane within the M'Naghten Rules, that is to say, he does not at the time know what he is doing or that it is wrong, then he has a defence on the ground of insanity: see *R.* v. *Davis* (1881) 14 Cox 563 and *Beard's* case.

Does the present case come within the general principle or the exceptions to it? It certainly does not come within the first exception. This man was not incapable of forming an intent to kill. Quite the contrary. He knew full well what he was doing. He formed an intent to kill, he carried out his intention and he remembered afterwards what he had done. And the jury, properly directed on the point, have found as much, for they found him guilty of murder. Then does the case come within the second exception? It does not, to my mind, for the simple reason that he was not suffering from a disease of the mind brought on by drink. He was suffering from a different disease altogether. As the Lord Chief Justice observed in his summing-up: "If this man was suffering from a disease of the mind, it wasn't of a kind that is produced by drink."

So we have here a case of the first impression. The man is a psychopath. That is, he has a disease of the mind which is not produced by drink. But it is quiescent. And whilst it is quiescent he forms an intention to kill his wife. He knows it is wrong but still he means to kill her. Then he gets himself so drunk that he has an explosive outburst and kills his wife. At that moment he knows what he is doing but he does not know it is wrong. So in that respect—in not knowing it is wrong—he has a defect of reason at the moment of killing. If that defect of reason is due to the drink, it is no defence in law. But if it is due to the disease of the mind, it gives rise to a defence of insanity. No one can say, however, whether it is due to the drink or to the disease. It may well be due to both in combination. What guidance does the law give in this difficulty? That is, as I see it, the question of general public importance which is involved in this case.

My Lords, I think the law on this point should take a clear stand. If a man, whilst sane and sober, forms an intention to kill and makes preparation for it, knowing it is a wrong thing to do, and then gets himself drunk so as to give himself Dutch courage to do the killing, and whilst drunk carries out his intention, he cannot rely on this self-induced drunkenness as a defence to a charge of murder, nor even as reducing it to manslaughter. He cannot say that he got himself into such a stupid state that he was incapable of an intent to kill. So also when he is a psychopath, he cannot by drinking rely on his self-induced defect of reason as a defence of insanity. The wickedness of his mind before he got drunk is enough to condemn him, coupled with the act which he intended to do and did do. A psychopath who goes out intending to kill knowing it is wrong, and does kill, cannot escape the consequences by making himself drunk before doing it. That is, I believe, the direction which the Lord Chief Justice gave to the jury and which the Court of Criminal Appeal found to be wrong. I think it was right and for this reason I would allow the appeal.

I would agree, of course, that if before the killing he had discarded his intention to kill or reversed it—and then got drunk—it would be a different matter. But when he forms the intention to kill and without interruption proceeds to get drunk and carry out his intention, then his drunkenness is no defence and nonetheless so because it is dressed up as a defence of insanity. There was no evidence in this case of any interruption and there was no need for the Lord Chief Justice to mention it to the jury.

I need hardly say, of course, that I have here only considered the law of Northern Ireland. In England a psychopath such as this man might now be in a position to raise a defence of diminished responsibility under section 2 of the Homicide Act 1957. ...

Appeal allowed

iii. Intoxication and Defences

Jaggard v. Dickinson
[1980] 3 All E.R. 716
Queen's Bench Division

The appellant went to a house late one night. She was drunk. She thought it was a house belonging to a friend. She believed, correctly, that her friend would not object to her breaking in. It was the wrong house. She appealed against a conviction under section 1(1) of the Criminal Damage Act 1971, on the ground that, despite her intoxication, she was entitled to rely on the defence of lawful excuse under s.5(2) and (3) of the Act (*post.* p. 860).

MUSTILL J.: ... It is convenient to refer to the exculpatory provisions of s.5(2) as if they created a defence while recognising that the burden of disproving the facts referred to by the subsection remains on the prosecution. The magistrates held that the appellant was not entitled to rely on s.5(2) since the belief relied on was brought about by a state of self-induced intoxication.

In support of the conviction counsel for the respondent advanced an argument which may be summarised as follows (i) Where an offence is one of "basic intent," in contrast to one of "specific intent," the fact that the accused was in a state of self-induced intoxication at the time when he did the acts constituting the actus reus does not prevent him from possessing the mens rea necessary to constitute the offence: see *D.P.P.* v. *Morgan* [*ante*, p. 142] *D.P.P.* v. *Majewski* [*ante*, p. 246]. (ii) Section 1(1) of the 1971 Act creates an offence of basic intent: see *R.* v. *Stephenson* [1979] Q.B. 695. (iii) Section 5(3) has no bearing on the present issue. It does not create a separate defence, but is no more than a partial definition of the expression "without lawful excuse" in s.1(1). The absence of lawful excuse forms an element in the means rea: see *R.* v. *Smith* [*post*, p. 864]. Accordingly, since drunkenness does not negative mens rea in crimes of basic intent, it cannot be relied on as part of a defence based on s.5(2).

Whilst this is an attractive submission, we consider it to be unsound, for the following reasons. In the first place, the argument transfers the distinction between offences of specific and of basic intent to a context in which it has no place. The distinction is material where the defendant relies on his own drunkenness as a ground for denying that he had the degree of intention or recklessness required in order to constitute the offence. Here, by contrast, the appellant does not rely on her drunkenness to displace an inference of intent or recklessness; indeed she does not rely on it at all. Her defence is founded on the state of belief called for by s.5(2). True, the fact of the appellant's intoxication was relevant to the defence under s.5(2) for it helped to explain what would otherwise have been inexplicable, and hence lent colour to her evidence about the state of her belief. This is not the same as using drunkenness to rebut an inference of intention or recklessness. Belief, like intention or recklessness, is a state of mind; but they are not the same states of mind.

Can it nevertheless be said that, even if the context is different, the principles established by *Majewski* ought to be applied to this new situation? If the basis of the decision in *Majewski* had been that drunkenness does not prevent a person from having an intent or being reckless, then there would be grounds for saying that it should equally be left out of account when deciding on his state of belief. But this is not in our view what *Majewski* decided. The House of Lords did not conclude that intoxication was irrelevant to the fact of the defendant's state of mind, but rather that, whatever might have been his actual state of mind, he should for reason of policy be precluded from relying on any alteration in that state brought about by self-induced intoxication. The same considerations of policy apply to the intent or recklessness which is the mens rea of the offence created by s.1(1) and that offence is accordingly regarded as one of basic intent (see *R. v. Stephenson*). It is indeed essential that this should be so, for drink so often plays a part in offences of criminal damage, and to admit drunkenness as a potential means of escaping liability would provide much too ready a means of avoiding conviction. But these considerations do not apply to a case where Parliament has specifically required the court to consider the defendant's actual state of belief, not the state of belief which ought to have existed. This seems to us to show that the court is required by s.5(3) to focus on the existence of the belief, not its intellectual soundness; and a belief can be just as much honestly held if it is induced by intoxication as if it stems from stupidity, forgetfulness or inattention.

It was, however, urged that we could not properly read s.5(2) in isolation from s.1(1), which forms the context of the words "without lawful excuse" partially defined by s.5(2). Once the words are put in context, so it is maintained, it can be seen that the law must treat drunkenness in the same way in relation to lawful excuse (and hence belief) as it does to intention and recklessness, for they are all part of the mens rea of the offence. To fragment the mens rea, so as to treat one part of it as affected by drunkenness in one way and the remainder as affected in a different way, would make the law impossibly complicated to enforce.

If it had been necessary to decide whether, for all purposes, the mens rea of an offence under s.1(1) extends as far as an intent (or recklessness) as to the existence of a lawful excuse, I should have wished to consider the observations of James L.J., delivering the judgment of the Court of Appeal in *R. v. Smith* [*post*, p. 864]. I do not however find it necessary to reach a conclusion on this matter and will only say that I am not at present convinced that, when these observations are read in the context of the judgment as a whole, they have the meaning which the respondent has sought to put on them. In my view, however, the answer to the argument lies in the fact that any distinctions which have to be drawn as to the relevance of drunkenness to the two subsections arises from the scheme of the 1971 Act itself. No doubt the mens rea is in general indivisible, with no distinction being possible as regards the effect of drunkenness. But Parliament has specifically isolated one subjective element, in the shape of honest belief, and has given it separate treatment and its own special gloss in s.5(3). This being so, there is nothing objectionable in giving it special treatment as regards drunkenness, in accordance with the natural meaning of its words.

In these circumstances, I would hold that the magistrates were in error when they decided that the defence furnished to the appellant by s.5(2) was lost because she was drunk at the time. I would therefore allow the appeal.

Appeal allowed
Conviction quashed

Question

1. Is there any reason in principle or policy why a drunken defendant who believes that property belonging to P is his own and damages it, should be convicted whereas a drunken D who destroys P's property believing it belongs to Q and that Q would consent, will be acquitted because his drunken belief is covered by s.5(2)?

Note

In *Young* [1984] 1 W.L.R. 654, the appellant was charged with possessing a controlled drug with intent to supply. His defence, based on s.28(3) of the Misuse of Drugs Act 1971, was that because of intoxication he "neither believed nor suspected nor had reason to suspect that the substance ... in question was a controlled drug." The Courts-Martial Appeal Court accepted that where there is an exculpatory statutory defence of honest belief, self-induced intoxication is a factor which must be considered in the context of a subjective consideration of the individual state of mind. However, with regard to the phrase *"nor had reason to suspect"* in s.28(3) the court held that this was not a matter which was entirely personal and individual calling for subjective consideration; rather it involved the concept of objective rationality to which self-induced intoxication is irrelevant.

R. v. O'Grady
[1987] Q.B. 995
Court of Appeal

A was convicted of manslaughter having been charged with murder. A and V, a friend, had been drinking heavily and spent the night at A's flat. During the night they fought. A claimed that he had been attacked by V while asleep and that he had fought to subdue him, stating to the police, "If I had not hit him I would be dead myself." The judge directed the jury that if, due to his intoxication, A mistakenly thought he was under attack, he would be entitled to defend himself but he was not entitled to go beyond what was reasonable because of his mind being affected by drink. A appealed on the grounds that (1) the judge was wrong to limit the reference to mistake as to the existence of an attack; he should have included the possibility of mistake as to the severity of an attack, and (2) the judge in effect divorced the reasonableness of A's reaction from his state of mind at the time.

LORD LANE C.J.: ... As to the first two grounds, these require an examination of the law as to intoxication in relation to mistake. ...

As McCullough J., when granting leave, pointed out helpfully in his observations for the benefit of the court:

"Given that a man who *mistakenly* believes he is under attack is entitled to use reasonable force to defend himself, it would seem to follow that, if he *is* under attack and mistakenly believes the attack to be more serious than it is, he is entitled to use reasonable force to defend himself against an attack of the severity he believed it to have. If one allows a mistaken belief induced by drink to bring this principle into operation, an act of gross negligence (viewed objectively) may become lawful even though it results in the death of the innocent victim. The drunken man would be guilty of neither murder nor manslaughter."

How should the jury be invited to approach the problem? One starts with the decision of this court in *R. v. Williams (Gladstone)* (1983) 78 Cr.App.R. 276 [*ante*, p. 155], namely, that where the defendant might have been labouring under a mistake as to the facts he must be judged according to that mistaken view, whether the mistake was reasonable or not. It is then for the jury to decide whether the defendant's reaction to the threat, real or imaginary, was a reasonable one. The court was not in that case considering what the situation might be where the mistake was due to voluntary intoxication by alcohol or some other drug.

We have come to the conclusion that where the jury are satisfied that the defendant was mistaken in his belief that any force or the force which he in fact used was necessary to defend himself and are further satisfied that the mistake was caused by voluntarily induced intoxication, the defence must fail. We do not consider that any distinction should be drawn on this aspect of the matter between offences involving what is called specific intent, such as murder, and offences of so called basic intent, such as manslaughter. Quite apart from the problem of directing a jury in a case such as the present where manslaughter is an alternative verdict to murder, the question of mistake can and ought to be considered separately from the question of intent. A sober man who mistakenly believes he is in danger of immediate death at the hands of an attacker is entitled to be acquitted of both murder and manslaughter if his reaction in killing his supposed assailant was a reasonable one. What his intent may have been seems to us to be irrelevant to the problem of self-defence or no. Secondly, we respectfully adopt the reasoning of McCullough J. already set out.

This brings us to the question of public order. There are two competing interests. On the one hand the interest of the defendant who has only acted according to what he believed to be necessary to protect himself, and on the other hand that of the public in general and the victim in particular who, probably through no fault of his own, has been injured or perhaps killed because of the defendant's drunken mistake. Reason recoils from the conclusion that in such circumstances a defendant is entitled to leave the Court without a stain on his character.

We find support for that view in the decision of the House of Lords in *R. v. Majewski* [1977] A.C. 443, and in particular in the speeches of Lord Simon of Glaisdale and Lord Edmund-Davies. We cite a passage from the speech of Lord Simon of Glaisdale, at p. 476:

"(1) One of the prime purposes of the criminal law, with its penal sanctions, is the protection from certain proscribed conduct of persons who are pursuing their lawful lives. Unprovoked violence has, from time immemorial, been a significant part of such proscribed conduct. To accede to the argument on behalf of the appellant would leave the citizen legally unprotected from unprovoked violence where such violence was the consequence of drink or drugs having obliterated the capacity of the perpetrator to know what he was doing or what were its consequences. (2) Though the problem of violent conduct by intoxicated persons is not new to society, it has been rendered more acute and menacing by the more widespread use of hallucinatory drugs. For example, in R. v. *Lipman* [1970] 1 Q.B. 152, the accused committed his act of mortal violence under the hallucination (induced by drugs) that he was wrestling with serpents. He was convicted of manslaughter. But, on the logic of the appellant's argument, he was innocent of any crime."

Lord Edmund-Davies said, at p. 492:

"The criticism by the academics of the law presently administered in this country is of a two-fold nature: (1) It is illogical and therefore inconsistent with legal principle to treat a person who of his own volition has taken drink or drugs any differently from a man suffering from some bodily or mental disorder of the kind earlier mentioned or whose beverage had, without his connivance, been 'laced' with intoxicants; (2) it is unethical to convict a man of a crime requiring a guilty state of mind when ex hypothesi, he lacked it."

Lord Edmund-Davies then demonstrated the fallacy of those criticisms.

Finally we draw attention to the decision of this court in R. v. *Lipman* [1970] 1 Q.B. 152 itself. The defence in that case was put on the grounds that the defendant, because of the hallucinatory drug which he had taken, had not formed the necessary intent to found a conviction for murder, thus resulting in his conviction for manslaughter. If the appellant's contentions here are correct, Lipman could successfully have escaped conviction altogether by raising the issue that he believed he was defending himself legitimately from an attack by serpents. It is significant that no one seems to have considered that possibility. . . .

We have therefore come to the conclusion that a defendant is not entitled to rely, so far as self-defence is concerned, upon a mistake of fact which has been induced by voluntary intoxication. . . .

Appeal dismissed

Questions

1. Under the rule in *Majewski*, D can only use evidence of voluntary intoxication to establish lack of *mens rea* if the offence is one of "specific intent," but D may be convicted of an offence of basic intent. This promotes the policy of protecting the public from those who, by becoming intoxicated, render themselves a danger to society. As *O'Grady* had been convicted of the basic intent offence of manslaughter, was there any need for the court to abandon the *Majewski* rule in relation to a defence of self-defence? Would the court have promoted the policy of protecting the public against the intoxicated offender by applying the *Majewski* rule and upholding *O'Grady's* conviction?

2. In *Gladstone Williams* (*ante*, p. 155), in respect of assault, Lord Lane C.J. stated that "the mental element necessary to constitute guilt is the intent to apply unlawful force to the victim. We do not believe that the mental element can be substantiated by simply showing an intent to apply force and no more." In *Beckford* v. *R.* [1987] 3 W.L.R. 611 Lord Griffiths stated that "it is an essential element of all crimes of violence that the violence or threat of violence should be unlawful." If this reasoning is followed, is it not

the case that a drunken defendant who pleads self-defence is saying that, by reason of his mistake, he did not intend to use unlawful violence but rather he believed he was justified in using force in self-defence? If so, should not *Majewski* be applied thereby providing for acquittal where the offence is one of specific intent but, if it is one of basic intent, recklessness in becoming intoxicated might be substituted for recklessness in respect of using unlawful violence?

3. In *Gladstone Williams* the Court of Appeal, under Lord Lane C.J., adopted the recommendations of the Criminal Law Revision Committee on self-defence in its 14th Report, declaring that they represented the existing law. Is it not surprising that in the present case, where the law was unclear, the Court of Appeal, again under Lord Lane C.J., ignored the C.L.R.C.'s further recommendations (14th Report, Cmnd. 7844, para. 277) which stated that the defence of self-defence should be available for offences of specific intent where the mistake was wholly or partly induced by drink or drugs, but not for offences of basic intent?

4. If the situation in *O'Grady* arises now will the defendant be convicted of murder or manslaughter?

Note

In *O'Connor* [1991] Crim. L.R. 135, the Court of Appeal treated the *obiter* decision in *O'Grady* as binding on them. D, who was drunk, was arguing with V in a public house. In the course of the argument D head-butted V about three times as a result of which V died. D was convicted of murder having argued in his defence that he believed he was acting in self-defence. The Court of Appeal held that the trial judge was correct to conclude that intoxication was irrelevant on the question whether D believed he was acting in self-defence. The conviction for murder was quashed, however, as the trial judge had not directed the jury to take account of D's intoxication when considering whether he had formed the specific intent to cause grievous bodily harm. The decision in *O'Connor* highlights the illogicality of the decision in *O'Grady*; the jury must ignore D's intoxication when considering whether he believed he was acting in self-defence but they must take it into account in deciding whether he intended to kill or cause grievous bodily harm. It will be surprising if juries are not left confused by such a direction.

iv. Proposals for Reform

Report of the Committee on Mentally Abnormal Offenders (the Butler Committee) 1975, Cmnd. 6244

"Offences Committed while Intoxicated
19. We suggest measures to deal with people who become violent when voluntarily intoxicated. We propose that it should be an offence for a person while voluntarily intoxicated to do an act (or make an omission) that would amount to a dangerous offence if it were done or made with

the requisite state of mind for such offence. The offence would not be charged in the first instance but the jury would be directed to find on this offence in the event of intoxication being successfully raised as a defence to the offence originally charged. We define 'dangerous' and 'voluntary intoxication' for this purpose. We suggest penalties for the new offence. (§§ 18.51–18.59).

[18.55. A dangerous offence for this purpose should be defined as one involving injury to the person (actual bodily harm) or death or consisting of a sexual attack on another, or involving the destruction of or causing damage to property so as to endanger life. A dangerous offence is to be regarded as charged if the jury can convict of it under the indictment.

18.56. 'Voluntary intoxication' would be defined to mean intoxication resulting from the intentional taking of drink or a drug knowing that it is capable in sufficient quantity of having an intoxicating effect; provided that intoxication is not voluntary if it results in part from a fact unknown to the defendant that increases his sensitivity to the drink or drug. The concluding words would provide a defence to a person who suffers from hypoglycaemia, for example, who does not know that in that condition the ingestion of a small amount of alcohol can produce a state of altered consciousness, as well as to a person who has been prescribed a drug on medical grounds without warning of the effect it may produce. We do not think it necessary to define intoxication, drink or drug, because this offence would be a fall-back offence, relevant only when the defendant has been acquitted on another charge by reason of evidence of intoxication.

18.57. These provisions would mean that the offence would be one of strict liability (not requiring proof of a mental element or other fault) in respect of the objectionable behaviour, but would require the fault element of becoming voluntarily intoxicated. A mistaken belief in a circumstance of excuse (such as that the victim was about to attack so that the force was necessary by way of defence, or that the victim consented) would not be a defence unless a sober person might have made the same mistake.]"

Draft Criminal Code Bill

Intoxication

"**22.**—(1) Where an offence requires a fault element of recklessness (however described), a person who was voluntarily intoxicated shall be treated—

(a) as having been aware of any risk of which he would have been aware had he been sober;

(b) as not having believed in the existence of an exempting circumstance (where the existence of such a belief is in issue) if he would not have so believed had he been sober.

(2) Where an offence requires a fault element of failure to comply with a standard of care, or requires no fault, a person who was voluntarily intoxicated shall be treated as not having believed in the existence of an exempting circumstance (where the existence of such a belief is an issue) if a reasonable sober person would not have so believed.

(3) Where the definition of a fault element or of a defence refers, or requires reference, to the state of mind or conduct to be expected of a reasonable person, such person shall be understood to be one who is not intoxicated.

(4) Subsection (1) does not apply—

(a) to murder (to which section 55 applies); or

(b) to the case (to which section 36 applies) where a person's unawareness or belief arises from a combination of mental disorder and voluntary intoxication.

(5)—

(a) 'Intoxicant' means alcohol or any other thing which, when taken into the body, may impair awareness or control.

(b) 'Voluntary intoxication' means the intoxication of a person by an intoxicant which he takes, otherwise than properly for a medicinal purpose, knowing that it is or may be an intoxicant.

(c) For the purposes of this section, a person 'takes' an intoxicant if he permits it to be administered to him.

(6) An intoxicant, although taken for a medicinal purpose, is not properly so taken if—

(a) (i) it is not taken on medical advice; or

(ii) it is taken on medical advice but the taker fails then or thereafter to comply with any condition forming part of the advice; and

(b) the taker is aware that the taking, or the failure, as the case may be may result in his doing an act capable of constituting an offence of the kind in question;

and accordingly intoxication from such taking or failure is voluntary intoxication.

(7) Intoxication shall be taken to have been voluntary unless evidence is given, in the sense stated in section 13(2), that it was involuntary."

Illustrations

"Clause 22(1)(a)

22(i) D, who is voluntarily intoxicated, tries unsuccessfully to have sexual intercourse with P, who does not consent. D is treated as having been aware of the risk of P's non-consent if he would have been aware of the risk had he been sober. He may therefore be convicted of attempted rape. (Compare example 18(iii).)

If D succeeds in having intercourse with P believing, wrongly, that she is consenting, he will be treated as not having held that belief if he would not have held it had he been sober (cl. 88), and accordingly he may be convicted of rape.

22(ii) D is charged with intentionally causing serious personal harm to P. He testifies that he was drunk and that he intended to break a window but was not aware of any risk that he might cause personal harm to any person. If it is found that this story may reasonably be true he must be acquitted of the offence charged; but, if he would have been aware of a risk of causing personal harm to a person had he been sober, he may be convicted of recklessly causing personal harm to P.

Clause 22(1)(b)

22(iii) D is charged with intentionally causing serious personal harm to P. D mistakenly believed that P was making a murderous attack on him and that there was no other way in which he could save his life. He was voluntarily intoxicated and would not have made the mistake had he been sober. For the purposes of the defence under clause 44, he can rely on his belief in relation to the offence specifically charged but not in relation to the included offence of recklessly causing serious personal harm.

22(iv)   D is charged with recklessly damaging property belonging to P. D, who was voluntarily intoxicated, damaged the property intentionally, believing that it belonged to his friend, E, who would not have objected to his doing so. If he had been sober, he would have realised that the property in question was not E's. He will be treated as if he knew that the property did not belong to E and will not be able to rely on the defence in clause 184.

Clause 22(4)(b)

22(v)   D is charged with intentionally causing serious personal harm to P. D, who suffers from brain damage, drank alcohol and then attacked P. He claims that he did not know what he was doing and the medical evidence is that his lack of awareness was due to the combined effect of the brain damage and the alcohol. If D may not have known what he was doing he must be acquitted and if, on the balance of probabilities, the medical evidence is correct, a mental disorder verdict should be returned (cl. 36).

Clause 22(5)(b) and (6)

22(vi)   D, a diabetic, having taken insulin in accordance with his doctor's instructions, omits to take food as directed. He knows from experience that this may result in his behaving in an aggressive and uncontrollable way. He loses consciousness due to hypoglycaemia and, while unconscious, strikes P. The insulin is not taken 'properly for a medicinal purpose' and D is voluntarily intoxicated. If he is charged with recklessly causing personal harm, he may not rely on clause 33 (automatism and physical incapacity) and is to be treated as having struck the blow, being aware that it might cause personal harm.

22(vii)   As in example 22(vi), except that D, though aware that failure to take food may result in loss of conciousness, is not aware that it may cause him to do any act. If charged with recklessly causing personal harm, he is regarded as having been involuntarily intoxicated and may rely on clause 33 and on clause 22(1). He could not do so if charged with careless driving, because of his awareness that failure to take food might result in unconsciousness and loss of control of a motor vehicle if he drove one."

Commentary on Draft Criminal Code Bill, Law Com. No. 177

"Clause 22: Intoxication

8.33 This clause provides for the effect of intoxication upon the liability of a person who causes the external elements of an offence. It aims to reproduce the present law on this topic with modifications recommended by the Criminal Law Revision Committee (*Fourteenth Report: Offences Against the Person* (1980), Cmnd. 7844, Part VI.). It is a somewhat complex clause because it restates relatively complex law. We have kept it as simple as possible by omitting aspects of the corresponding clause in the Code team's Bill that we regarded as strictly speaking redundant (as we explain below). The provision of a simpler clause on intoxication could only result from a major law reform exercise. That was not in question as an aspect of the present project. But, like the majority of the Criminal Law Revision

Committee, we are not in any case persuaded that the law as stated in clause 22 would be seriously unsatisfactory.

8.34 *Involuntary intoxication; offences requiring intention, knowledge, etc.* The legal position in relation to situations not referred to by clause 22 is to be deduced from the rest of the Code, read with the enactment creating the offence charged. Thus, the clause has nothing to say about evidence of *involuntary* intoxication, which is accordingly to be treated like any other evidence tending to show that the defendant lacked the fault required for the offence charged. If the evidence shows no more that that the defendant more readily gave way to passion or temptation than he would have done if he had been sober, it may be a mitigating factor but it will not be a defence. Again, when the offence charged requires proof of intention, knowledge or belief, evidence of *voluntary* intoxication is to be treated like any other evidence tending to show that the defendant lacked the state of mind in question. This is presently the position in relation to any offence classified as an offence of 'specific intent'. And once again, with such an offence as with any other, intoxication will have no bearing on liability to conviction if it merely affected the defendant's emotional reaction or reduced his inhibitions. There is no need for express provision on these matters.

8.35 *Offences of recklessness.* So far as proof of the fault element of an offence is concerned, the law at present has a special rule for the effect of voluntary intoxication where the offence charged is one of so-called 'basic intent'. We agree with the view of the Criminal Law Revision Committee that this should be replaced by a rule, modelled upon the corresponding provision of the American Law Institute's Model Penal Code, relating to any offence requiring a fault element of recklessness. Subsection (1)(a) provides that a person who was voluntarily intoxicated is to be treated, for the purposes of such an offence, as having been aware of any risk of which he would have been aware had he been sober. Subsection (1) applies to an offence requiring recklessness 'however described'. So, for example, if any offences requiring 'malice' survive the enactment of the Code, they will be governed by the subsection since 'maliciously' is satisfied by proof of recklessness, as defined in clause 18(c); and the same will be true of any offences enacted after the Code which employ the concept of recklessness but use different terminology to describe it.

8.36 Subsection (1) applies to an offence requiring a fault element of recklessness even where it also requires, expressly or by implication, an element of intention or knowledge. So, for example, any charge of rape no doubt implies an allegation of an intention to have sexual intercourse; but paragraph (a) nonetheless applies to an alleged 'fault element of recklessness' constituted by the defendant's having been aware that the woman was not consenting to the intercourse.

8.37 A defendant who was intoxicated may, however, deny that he intended to do any act at all, having no control over, or awareness of, his movements. Charged with recklessly causing serious personal harm by beating a woman, he says that because of his drugged condition he was unconscious. Clause 33 (1)(b) makes it clear that he cannot rely on his condition as a 'state of automatism' if it arose from voluntary intoxication. He is to be treated as having beaten the woman, being aware of any risk of causing harm of which he would have been aware had he been sober.

8.38 *Belief in exempting circumstances.* Just as a person may, because of intoxication, lack the state of mind required for an offence, so he may have the state of mind required for a defence—as when, being drunk, he mistakenly believes that P is making a murderous attack on him and retaliates, as he supposes, in self-defence. As with the fault elements of offences, we believe that it is unnecessary to refer in this clause to the relevant effect of involuntary intoxication. Evidence of involuntary intoxication will, without special provision, be treated like any other evidence tending to show that the defendant held any belief or had any other state of mind which is an element of a defence.

8.39 Where intoxication is voluntary, its effect depends on the fault element of the offence charged. Subsection (1)(b) follows the recommendation of the Criminal Law Revision Committee:

' ... in offences in which recklessness constitutes an element of the offence, if the defendant because of a mistake due to voluntary intoxication holds a belief which, if held by a sober man, would be a defence to the charge but which the defendant would not have held had he been sober, the mistaken belief should be immaterial.'

8.40 A slightly stricter rule must apply to offences not requiring a fault element of recklessness. Subsection (2) therefore provides that, where the offence charged involves a fault element of failure to comply with a standard of care, or requires no fault, the defendant is to be treated as not having believed in the existence of an exempting circumstance if a reasonable sober person would not have so believed.

8.41 In *Jaggard* v. *Dickinson* [1981] Q.B. 527 the defendant was allowed to rely on a drunken belief that she was damaging property belonging to a person who would consent to her doing so. The effect of subsection (1)(b) is to reverse this decision. This is justified, not only on the ground that it follows from the Committee's recommendations, but also because that decision creates an anomalous distinction (between mistake as to the non-existence of an element of an offence and mistake as to the existence of a circumstance affording a defence) which it would be wrong to perpetuate in the Code.

8.42 *Mistake and offences requiring intention.* The same anomaly would be introduced if the Code were to adopt a dictum of the Court of Appeal in *O'Grady* [1987] Q.B. 995 at 999, to the effect that a defendant, on a charge of an offence of 'specific intent' equally with one of 'basic intent', would not be able to rely upon evidence of an intoxicated mistaken belief in an occasion for self-defence. The court was concerned that one who kills because of a drunken mistake should not be 'entitled to leave the court without a stain on his character'. But a conviction of manslaughter will of course be available (and similarly, in a case of serious personal harm, a conviction of an offence of recklessly causing such harm); and it would, we believe, be unthinkable to convict of murder a person who thought, for whatever reason, that he was acting to save his life and who would have been acting reasonably if he had been right. Moreover, the Code should if possible provide consistently for all defences; it would not be appropriate to try to devise a special rule for self-defence alone, or generally for the use of force in public or private defence (clause 44) or in defence of property (clause 185). In all the circumstances we are satisfied that the dictum referred to must be ignored in framing the present clause. The result is consistent with the view of the Criminal Law Revision Committee on this topic.

8.43 *Intoxication and reasonableness.* It would seem obvious that, when the law prescribes a standard of reasonable behaviour, this must relate to the standard to be expected of a sober person. But the fact that the point has been argued in the Court of Appeal in two modern cases (*Woods* (1981) 74 Cr. App. R. 312; *Young* [1984] 1 W.L.R. 654) suggests the desirability of including in the Code the principle that those cases establish, to avoid the matter being reopened. The principle is stated in subsection (3). In *Young* the Court of Appeal thought that, in determining whether a person 'has reason to suspect', it is 'an unnecessary gloss to introduce the concept of the reasonable man'. It is, however, impossible to state a principle concerning intoxication or sobriety without a reference to a person. It does not necessarily follow that the judge need refer to such a person in directing the jury, though it may sometimes be convenient to do so."

CHAPTER 5

DEFENCES

	PAGE		PAGE
1. Defences in General	280	i. Scope of the Defences	331
2. Duress	281	ii. The Issues of Imminence and Pre-emptive Strike	339
i. An Imminent Threat of Death or Serious Injury	282	iii. Is there a Duty to Retreat?	342
ii. The Test for Duress	284	iv. Unknown Circumstances of Justification	345
iii. Voluntary Association with Criminal Organisation	287	v. To Which Offences do the Defences Apply?	346
iv. Duress and Murder	292	vi. Reasonable Force	347
3. Necessity	314	vii. Mistake	350
i. A Defence of Necessity	314	viii. Excessive Force	350
ii. Duress of Circumstances	319	5. Proposals for Reform	353
iii. Necessity, Duress of Circumstances and Homicide	321	i. General Principals	353
iv. A Common Law Defence of Necessity	324	ii. Duress	355
4. Self-Defence and Kindred Defences	330	iii. Necessity	358
		iv. Self-Defence and Kindred Defences	360

1. DEFENCES IN GENERAL

A. T. H. Smith, "On Actus Reus and Mens Rea" in Reshaping the Criminal Law (ed. Glazebrook), p. 97

"When speaking colloquially lawyers are inclined to call any reason advanced by a defendant in support of an acquittal a 'defence.' These include such explanations as alibi, infancy, mistake, accident, and insanity. When they use the term more precisely, they point out that automatism—for example—is not really a defence at all, but a denial that the prosecution has proved part of its case: the prosecution has failed to show that the defendant acted with *mens rea*. It has now been accepted by no less a body than the House of Lords that, where the definition of any particular crime includes intention or recklessness, any mistake that has the effect of preventing the formation of these states of mind must exculpate, whether it be a reasonable mistake or not. This is so because mistake prevents the formation of the particular *mens rea* which must be established as part of the prosecution case. Duress, necessity, self-defence, and infancy, on the other hand, are said to be properly described as 'defences,' because they do not negative either traditional *mens rea* or *actus reus*, but operate in some way independently. . . .

It is possible to make a distinction between defences which are justificatory in character, and those which are excuses. It has not found much favour in Anglo-American jurisprudence, partly no doubt because of Stephen's emphatic assertion that it 'involves no legal consequences,' a reproach guaranteed to deprive it of any significance it might otherwise have enjoyed. Briefly stated, the distinction is that we excuse the actor because he is not sufficiently culpable or at fault, whereas we justify an act because we regard it as the most appropriate course of action in the circumstances, even though it may result in harm that would, in the absence of the justification, amount to a crime. It does not follow that, because the distinction between the two is not formally taken in our law that it is altogether without significance, particularly where the law is in a state of flux. The reasons why, and the circumstances in which, we are prepared to excuse may be altogether different from the corresponding reasons for justification. We admit excuses as 'an expression of compassion for one of our kind caught in a maelstrom of circumstances.' A plea of justification, by contrast, is founded upon the law's preference, in social and policy terms, for one course of action rather than another.

Where a defendant successfully pleads a defence such as prevention of crime or self-defence, he argues that what he did was not unlawful, and he is able to point to a specific rule—in the one case of statutory origin, and in the other, in common law—to substantiate his plea. It may be, however, that a plea of justification has not crystallised into one of these specific defences, but is of a more nebulous sort.

For example, although it appears that there is no general defence of necessity in that there is no rule to which a defendant can appeal to justify his having chosen to bring about a proscribed harm, there is nevertheless a principle infiltrating the legal system, given efficacy through a variety of legal inlets, that where a person is placed by force of circumstance in the position of having to choose between two evils, his act is justified if he chooses the lesser one. In that somewhat fitful sense, necessity operates as a 'defence.' Some would say that a person who commits a *prima facie* unlawful act as a result of necessity is not blameworthy or at fault and hence lacks *mens rea*. But it does not necessarily follow that we exculpate him for that reason. An alternative explanation is that where the act done is the lesser of two evils, it is justified or lawful—that there was no *actus reus* notwithstanding that the conduct falls literally within the terms of the definition of the offence.

Analysis of crime in terms of *actus reus* and *mens rea*, and the mechanical application of statutes, tend to obscure the principles of harm and illegality on which criminal liability is based. Unless these principles find expression either in the definition of the crime itself (*e.g.* by the inclusion of 'unlawfully') or in some express exculpatory rule, it seems that our legal system is incapable of giving effect to them. Whereas the judges are adept at interpreting legislation in such a way as to introduce traditional *mens rea*, if necessary by reading words into the statutes, they will only infrequently allow considerations of principle to override the plain words of a statute. Only by providing in a code for a defence of necessity, therefore, is it possible to ensure that this principle is preserved in a form in which it will invariably prevail."

See also G. Williams, "The Theory of Excuses" [1982] Crim.L.R. 732.

2. DURESS

Wasik, "Duress and Criminal Responsibility" [1977] Crim.L.R. 453

"There seems to be general agreement among lawyers that criminal responsibility should follow when an individual chooses to perform an act proscribed by the criminal law, when he has both the capacity and a fair opportunity or chance to adjust his behaviour to conform with the law. It follows that no individual should be held responsible if he had no opportunity to choose an alternative to breaking the law. As the philosophers put it: there should be no ascription of responsibility to the accused unless 'he could have acted otherwise.' Much attention has been paid to this requirement by philosophers but lawyers, by contrast, have not shown a great deal of interest. Perhaps the main reason for this is the practical rarity of such problems. It is much more common for an accused to plead mistake or lack of intention as an excuse than to plead that he had no choice but to act as he did. Cases in which the defence of duress is raised are probably the most frequent of this small group. ...

A comparison has sometimes been made between the defence of duress and that of automatism. The suggestion is that in duress, the accused claims that there was no act by *him*; in automatism the accused claims that there was no *act* by him. Both defences are then seen as containing what may in loose terminology be called 'an involuntary act' on the part of the accused. But this is misleading, as the element of voluntariness is quite different in the two excuses. Where the defence of automatism succeeds, the accused has had no opportunity at all to exercise choice with regard to the performing of the act, and thus he cannot be held responsible for it. ... By contrast, in duress, there is an issue of choice. If a man is threatened with physical injury unless he assists in a criminal enterprise, he has the choice (albeit a difficult one) of assisting in the crime or facing the consequences. The question here is whether the accused had a fair opportunity to make the choice."

i. An imminent threat of death or serious injury

R. v. Hudson and Taylor
[1971] 2 Q.B. 202
Court of Appeal

H. and T. who were aged 17 and 19 respectively, were charged with perjury in a case in which they were witnesses to an unlawful wounding incident. They admitted that they had given false evidence but raised the defence of duress. This took the form of threats before the trial that unless they did so they would be "cut up." The recorder directed the jury that the defence was not available since the threat was not immediate. On appeal the Crown contended that the plea should have failed on the additional ground that they should have sought police protection before the trial.

LORD WIDGERY C.J.: ... it is clearly established that duress provides a defence in all offences including perjury (except possibly treason or murder as a principal) if the will of the accused has been overborne by threats of death or serious personal injury so that the commission of the alleged offence was no longer the voluntary act of the accused. This appeal raises two main questions: first, as to the nature of the necessary threat and, in particular, whether it must be "present and immediate"; secondly, as to the extent to which a right to plead duress may be lost if the accused has failed to take steps to remove the threat as, for example, by seeking police protection.

It is essential to the defence of duress that the threat shall be effective at the moment when the crime is committed. The threat must be a "present" threat in the sense that it is effective to neutralise the will of the accused at that time. Hence an accused who joins a rebellion under the compulsion of threats cannot plead duress if he remains with the rebels after the threats have lost their effect and his own will has had a chance to re-assert itself (*McCrowther's Case* (1746) Fost. 13; and *A.-G. v. Whelan* [1934] I.R. 518).

Similarly a threat of future violence may be so remote as to be insufficient to overpower the will at the moment when the offence was committed, or the accused may have elected to commit the offence in order to rid himself of a threat hanging over him and not because he was driven to act by immediate and unavoidable pressure. In none of these cases is the defence of duress available because a person cannot justify the commission of a crime merely to secure his own peace of mind.

When, however, there is no opportunity for delaying tactics, and the person threatened must make up his mind whether he is to commit the criminal act or not, the existence at that moment of threats sufficient to destroy his will ought to provide him with a defence even though the threatened injury may not follow instantly, but after an interval. This principle is illustrated by *Subramaniam* v. *Public Prosecutor* [1956] 1 W.L.R. 965, when the appellant was charged in Malaya with unlawful possession of ammunition and was held by the Privy Council to have a defence of duress, fit to go to the jury, on his plea that he had been compelled by terrorists to accept the ammunition and feared for his safety if the terrorists returned.

In the present case the threats of Farrell were likely to be no less compelling, because their execution could not be effected in the court room, if they could be carried out in the streets of Salford the same night. Insofar, therefore, as the recorder ruled as a matter of law that the threats were not sufficiently present and immediate to support the defence of duress we think that he was in error. He should have left the jury to decide whether the threats had overborne the will of the appellants at the time when they gave the false evidence.

Counsel for the Crown, however, contends that the recorder's ruling can be supported on another ground, namely, that the appellants should have taken steps to neutralise the threats by seeking police protection either when they came to court to give evidence, or beforehand. He submits on grounds of public policy that the accused should not be able to plead duress if he had the opportunity to ask for protection from the police before committing the offence and failed to do so. The argument does not distinguish cases in which the police would be able to provide effective protection, from those when they would not, and it would, in effect, restrict the defence of duress to cases where the person threatened had been kept in custody by the maker of the threats, or where the time interval between the making of the threats and the commission of the offence had made recourse to the police impossible. We recognise the need to keep the defence of duress within reasonable bounds but cannot accept so severe a restriction on it. The duty, of the person threatened, to take steps to remove the threat does not seem to have arisen in an English case but in full review of the defence of duress in the Supreme Court of Victoria (*R.* v. *Hurley*, *R.* v. *Murray* [1967] V.R. 526), a condition of raising the defence was said to be that the accused "had no means, with safety to himself, of preventing the execution of the threat."

In the opinion of this court it is always open to the Crown to prove that the accused failed to avail himself of some opportunity which was reasonably open to him to render the threat ineffective, and that on this being established the threat in question can no longer be relied on by the defence. In deciding whether such an opportunity was reasonably open to the accused the jury should have regard to his age and circumstances, and to any risks to him which may be involved in the course of action relied on.

In our judgment the defence of duress should have been left to the jury in the present case, as should any issue raised by the Crown and arising out of the appellants' failure to seek police protection. The appeals will, therefore, be allowed and the convictions quashed.

Appeals allowed

Notes

In *R. v. Valderrama-Vega* [1985] Crim.L.R. 220 C.A., the appellant was charged with the importation of prohibited drugs from Colombia. He pleaded duress on the basis that a Mafia-type organisation had threatened injury or death to himself and his family. In addition he said that he needed money as he was under severe financial pressure and he had also been threatened with disclosure of his homosexuality. The Court of Appeal held that it was wrong to direct the jury that duress was a defence only where the defendant acted "*solely* as the result of threats of death or serious injury to himself or his family." Rather these threats must be a *sine qua non* of the defendant's decision to commit the offence although he may have had other motives.

Most of the cases have involved threats to kill or injure the accused. Will threats to kill or injure others be sufficient to found the defence of duress? In *R. v Ortiz* (1986) 83 Cr.App.R. 173, the Court of Appeal assumed that a threat to injure the accused's wife or family could do so. This is confirmed by *Martin* [1989] 1 All E.R. 652 (*post*, p. 320). In *R. v Hurley* [1967] V.R. 526, the Supreme Court of Victoria held that threats to kill or seriously injure the accused's common law wife could amount to duress. In *Conway* [1989] Q.B. 290 (*post*, p. 319) a threat to the passenger in the accused's car was sufficient. It has still to be determined whether a threat to a complete stranger would suffice to found the defence.

ii. The test for duress

R. v. Graham
[1982] 1 W.L.R. 294
Court of Appeal

G, a practising homosexual, lived with his wife (W) and K, another homosexual. G took Valium for an anxiety state and this made him susceptible to bullying. K was a violent man. One night K attacked W with a knife but G intervened. Next day W left home; K and G remained drinking heavily and G took more Valium than was prescribed. K suggested killing W and at K's suggestion G telephoned her luring her back to the flat. When she arrived K put a flex round her neck and told G to take hold of the other end of the flex and pull it on. He did so, he claimed, only because he was afraid of K. He was convicted of murder, the Crown having conceded that duress could be raised as a defence. G appealed on the ground that the judge had misdirected the jury.

LORD LANE C.J.: The prosecution at the trial conceded that, on those facts, it was open to the defence to raise the issue of duress. In other words, they were not prepared to take the point that the defence of duress is not available to a principal in the first degree to murder. Consequently, the interesting question raised by the decisions in *D.P.P. for Northern Ireland* v. *Lynch* [1975] A.C. 653 (*post*, p. 292) and *Abbott* v. *The Queen* [1977] A.C. 755 (*post*, p. 295) was not argued before us. We do not have to decide it. We pause only to observe that the jury would no doubt have been puzzled to learn that whether the appellant was to be convicted of murder or acquitted altogether might depend on whether the plug came off the end of the percolator flex when he began to pull it. . . .

The direction which the judge gave to the jury required them to ask themselves two questions. First, a subjective question which the judge formulated:

"Was this man at the time of the killing taking part . . . because he feared for his own life (or) personal safety as a result of the words or the conduct . . . on the part of King, either personally experienced by him, or genuinely believed in by him . . . "

Neither side in the present appeal has taken issue with the judge on this question. We feel, however, that, for purposes of completeness, we should say that the direction appropriate in this particular case should have been in these words: "Was this man at the time of the killing taking part because he held a well-grounded fear of death (or serious physical injury) as a result of the words or conduct on the part of King?" The bracketed words may be too favourable to the defendant. The point was not argued before us.

The judge then went on to direct the jury that if the answer to that first question was "yes," or "he may have been," the jury should then go on to consider a second question importing an objective test of reasonableness. This is the issue which arises in this appeal. Mr. Kennedy for the appellant contends that no second question arises at all; the test is purely subjective. He argues that if the appellant's will was in fact overborne by threats of the requisite cogency, he is entitled to be acquitted and no question arises as to whether a reasonable man, with or without his characteristics, would have acted similarly.

Mr. Sherrard, for the Crown, on the other hand, submits that such dicta as can be found on the point are in favour of a second test; this time an objective test. He argues that public policy requires this and draws an analogy with provocation. He submits that while the judge was right to pose a second question, he formulated it too favourably to the appellant. The question was put to the jury in the following terms:

"Taking into account all the circumstances of the case, including the age, sex, sexual propensities and other characteristics personal to the defendant, including his state of mind and the amount of drink or drugs he had taken, was it reasonable for the defendant to behave in the way he did, that is to take part in the murder of his wife . . . as a result of the fear . . . present at the time in his mind. . . . The test of reasonableness in this context is: would the defendant's behaviour in all the particular circumstances to which I have just referred reflect the degree of self-control and firmness of purpose (which) everyone is entitled to expect that his fellow citizens would exercise in society as it is today."

If the references to drink and drugs had been omitted, the judge's phraseology would have been in line with the direction given in cases of provocation: see *R.* v. *Camplin* [1978] A.C. 705 (*post*, p. 517) and *R.* v. *Newell* (1980) 71 Cr.App.R. 331 (*post*, p. 522). By using those words the judge introduced, says Mr. Sherrard, transitory factors and self-induced factors peculiar to the appellant and having no place in an objective test.

There is no direct binding authority on the questions whether the test is solely subjective or, if objective, how it is to be formulated. The point did not arise for decision in *Lynch's* case [1975] A.C. 653 but Lord Wilberforce, at p. 683, cited, with apparent approval, "as a statement of principle" a passage from the judgment of Rumpff J. in *S. v. Goliath*, 1972 (3) S.A. 1, 25 (Translation, p. 480), which included the following words:

"it seems to me to be irrational ... to exclude compulsion as a complete defence to murder if the threatened party was under such a strong duress that a reasonable person would not have acted otherwise under the same duress."

A little later Lord Wilberforce went on, at pp. 684–685:

"The judges have always assumed responsibility for deciding questions of principle relating to criminal liability and guilt, and particularly for setting the standards by which the law expects normal men to act. In all such matters as capacity, sanity, drunkenness, coercion, necessity, provocation, self-defence, the common law, through the judges, accepts and sets the standards of right thinking men of normal firmness and humanity at a level at which people can accept and respect."

Lord Morris of Borth-y-Gest, at p. 670, referred to "the standards of honest and reasonable men" of which the law should take account.

Lord Edmund-Davies, at p. 711, referred, with apparent approval, to a passage from the judgment of Murnaghan J. in *A.-G. v. Whelan* [1934] I.R. 518, 526, as follows:

"threats of immediate death or serious personal violence so great as to overbear the ordinary power of human resistance should be accepted as a justification for acts which would otherwise be criminal."

Lord Simon of Glaisdale mentioned subjectivity, on p. 696, but only in relation to belief in the existence of the threat, not in regard to the defendant's conduct in reaction to the threat. ...

[Having considered *Archbold Criminal Pleading & Practice* (40th ed, 1979), Smith & Hogan, *Criminal Law* (4th ed., 1978) and the Law Commission *Report on Defences of General Application* (1977) (Law Com. No. 83), para. 2.28, his lordship continued.]

As a matter of public policy, it seems to us essential to limit the defence of duress by means of an objective criterion formulated in terms of reasonableness. Consistency of approach in defences to criminal liability is obviously desirable. Provocation and duress are analogous. In provocation the words or actions of one person break the self-control of another. In duress the words or actions of one person break the will of another. The law requires a defendant to have the self-control reasonably to be expected of the ordinary citizen in his situation. It should likewise require him to have the steadfastness reasonably to be expected of the ordinary citizen in his situation. So too with self-defence, in which the law permits the use of no more force than is reasonable in the circumstances. And, in general, if a mistake is to excuse what would otherwise be criminal, the mistake must be a reasonable one.

It follows that we accept Mr. Sherrard's submission that the direction in this case was too favourable to the appellant. The Crown having conceded that the issue of duress was open to the appellant and was raised on the evidence, the correct approach on the facts of this case would have been as follows. (1) Was the defendant, or may he have been, impelled to act as he did because, as a result of what he reasonably believed King had said or done, he had good cause to fear that if he did not so act King would kill him or (if this is to be added) cause him serious physical injury? (2) If so, have the prosecution made the jury sure that a sober person of reasonable firmness, sharing the characteristics of the defendant, would not have responded to whatever he reasonably believed King said or did by taking part in the killing? The fact that a defendant's will to resist has been eroded by the voluntary consumption of drink or drugs or both is not relevant to this test.

We doubt whether the Crown were right to concede that the question of duress ever arose on the facts of this case. The words and deeds of King relied on by the defence were far short of those needed to raise a threat of the requisite gravity. However, the Crown having made the concession, the judge was right to pose the second objective question to the jury. His only error lay in putting it too favourably to the appellant.

The appeal is dismissed.

Appeal dismissed.

Question

Lord Lane stated that "[c]onsistency of approach in defences to criminal liability is obviously desirable." Has Lord Lane been consistent in his approach with regard to the issue of mistake in respect of the facts upon which a defence is based? (See *R.* v. *Gladstone Williams, post*, p. 155).

Note

Lord Lane's formulation of the test for duress was approved by the House of Lords in *R.* v. *Howe, ante*, p. 296.

iii. Voluntary association with criminal organisation

R. v. Sharp
[1987] 1 Q.B. 833
Court of Appeal

A was convicted of manslaughter and pleaded guilty to robbery and attempted robbery. He had joined a gang of robbers which carried out a series of armed robberies of sub-post offices. This series culminated in the offence which resulted in the death of the sub-postmaster who was shot by H. A was tried on a count charging murder and submitted that he had acted under duress as he had only taken part in the last robbery because a gun had been pointed at his head by H who threatened to blow it off if he did not participate. The trial judge rejected this submission and A appealed.

LORD LANE C.J.: ... [E]verything in this appeal depends upon whether the judge was correct or not in ruling that a defendant who has voluntarily joined a gang such as this cannot subsequently rely upon the defence of duress.

So we turn to examine the situation which lies behind Mr. Mylne's submission to the judge, and again the submissions to this court, namely, that the common law knows no such exception to the defence of duress. ... [H]e submits that it is not for this court, or indeed any other court, to

usurp the function of Parliament and to introduce into the common law a
rule which, in his submission, has previously been held to form part of it.

No one could question that if a person can avoid the effects of duress by
escaping from the threats, without damage to himself, he must do so. In
other words if there is a moment at which he is able to escape, so to
speak, from the gun being held at his head by Hussey, or the equivalent
of Hussey, he must do so. It seems to us to be part of the same argument,
or at least to be so close to the same argument as to be practically
indistinguishable from it, to say that a man must not voluntarily put
himself in a position where he is likely to be subjected to such compulsion.

... But we are fortified in the view ... that this is part of the common
law and always has been, by certain matters which appear in the speeches
of their Lordships in *D.P.P. for Northern Ireland* v. *Lynch* [1975] A.C. 653
(*post*, p. 292). Although *Lynch's* case has been the subject of certain adverse
comment since the date of those speeches, nevertheless the passages to
which we wish to refer have not, as far as we know, been the subject of
criticism.

First of all in the speech of Lord Morris of Borth-y-Gest appears this
passage, at p. 668:

> "Where duress is in issue many questions may arise such as whether
> threats are serious and compelling or whether (as on the facts of the
> present case may specially call for consideration) a person the subject of
> duress could reasonably have extricated himself or could have sought
> protection or had what has been called a 'safe avenue of escape.' Other
> questions may arise such as whether a person is only under duress as a
> result of being in voluntary association with those whom he knew
> would require some course of action. In the present case, as duress was
> not left to the jury, we naturally do not know what they thought of it at
> all."

A little later Lord Morris of Borth-y-Gest again said, at p. 670:

> "In posing the case where someone is 'really' threatened I use the word
> 'really' in order to emphasise that duress must never be allowed to be
> the easy answer of those who can devise no other explanation of their
> conduct nor of those who readily could have avoided the dominance of
> threats nor of those who allow themselves to be at the disposal and
> under the sway of some gangster-tyrant. Where duress becomes an
> issue courts and juries will surely consider the facts with care and
> discernment."

Here, of course, I interpolate, Hussey was the archetypal gangster-tyrant.

I turn from Lord Morris of Borth-y-Gest to the speech of Lord
Wilberforce, at p. 679:

> "It is clear that a possible case of duress, on the facts, could have been
> made. I say 'a possible case' because there were a number of matters
> which the jury would have had to consider if this defence had been left
> to them. Among these would have been whether Meehan, though
> uttering no express threats of death or serious injury, impliedly did so
> in such a way as to put the appellant in fear of death or serious injury;
> whether, if so, the threats continued to operate throughout the
> enterprise; whether the appellant had voluntarily exposed himself to a
> situation in which threats might be used against him if he did not
> participate in a criminal enterprise (the appellant denied that he had
> done so); whether the appellant had taken every opportunity open to
> him to escape from the situation of duress. In order to test the validity

of the judge's decision to exclude this defence, we must assume on this appeal that these matters would have been decided in favour of the appellant."

Finally, so far as the passages in favour of the contention which we are supporting are concerned, in the speech of Lord Simon of Glaisdale appears this passage, at p. 687:

"I spoke of the social evils which might be attendant on the recognition of a general defence of duress. Would it not enable a gang leader of notorious violence to confer on his organisation by terrorism immunity from the criminal law? Every member of his gang might well be able to say with truth, 'It was as much as my life was worth to disobey.' Was this not in essence the plea of the appellant? We do not, in general, allow a superior officer to confer such immunity on his subordinates by any defence of obedience to orders: why should we allow it to terrorists? Nor would it seem to be sufficient to stipulate that no one can plead duress as a defence who had put himself into a position in which duress could be exercised on himself."

We draw assistance from the fact that common law jurisdictions as well as Commonwealth jurisdictions throughout the world have adopted this rule almost unanimously (although the wording in their various statutes differs the one from the other), which is an indication to us that this may well have been, and indeed was, throughout a principle of the common law.

The matter was stated clearly by Winneke C.J. of the State of Victoria in *R.* v. *Hurley and Murray* [1967] V.R. 526, ...

... [A] person who without threat of death or serious violence voluntarily makes himself a party to a criminal enterprise cannot excuse his criminal conduct in participating in that enterprise by showing that after he had embraced the cause he was subjected to threats of violence at the hands of the other parties to ensure that he did not resile from the bargain he had voluntarily entered into."

That was the precise description of what happened in this case between the appellant and Hussey.

Then Winneke C.J. went on to cite from the Criminal Codes of Queensland, Western Australia and Tasmania, each of which contained a provision to that very effect. He cited the first Criminal Code from Canada. He cited the New Zealand codification of the criminal law, and he cited also the well-known American textbook, *Perkins on Criminal Law* (1957), where the following passage appears, at p. 843:

"If D for example is compelled under threat of death to provide a getaway car for robbers, or to assist them in some other way, he is not guilty of robbery. ... He cannot be a perpetrator of a robbery of which he is innocent. This is not comparable in any way to the claim that one who willingly joins in the robbery was compelled during the perpetration to do something against his will. Such a claim will be rejected because the situation was the result of extreme culpability on his part."

Two American decisions are cited there by name.

We are therefore, in the light of that persuasive authority and the indications in their Lordships' speeches in *D.P.P. for Northern Ireland* v. *Lynch* [1975] A.C. 653 of the opinion that the judge, Kenneth Jones J., was correct in the decision which he reached.

We are further fortified in that view by the judgment of Lord Lowry C.J. of Northern Ireland, in *R.* v. *Fitzpatrick* [1977] N.I. 20. Let me read the brief headnote once again in order to indicate the nature of the decision. It runs as follows:

"If a person by joining an illegal organisation or a similar group of men with criminal objectives and coercive methods, voluntarily exposes and submits himself to illegal compulsion, he cannot rely on the duress to which he has voluntarily exposed himself as an excuse either in respect of the crimes he commits against his will or in respect of his continued but unwilling association with those capable of exercising upon him the duress which he calls in aid."

Turning to the body of the judgment, there are just three passages which we would like to cite to indicate the way in which the judgment of Lord Lowry C.J. went. The first reads, at p. 22:

"the judge held that, having joined the I.R.A. and voluntarily exposed himself to the risk of compulsion by the I.R.A. to commit crimes on its behalf, the appellant was not entitled to rely on the defence of duress exercised by that organisation. In so holding the learned trial judge cited the well known passage from Stephen's *History of the Criminal Law of England*, vol. 2, p. 108, which was referred to by Lord Edmund-Davies in *R.* v. *Lynch* [1975] N.I. 35, 112: 'If a man chooses to expose and still more if he chooses to submit himself to illegal compulsion, it may not operate even in mitigation of punishment. It would surely be monstrous to mitigate the punishment of a murderer on the ground that he was a member of a secret society by which he would have been assassinated if he had not committed murder.' "

The second passage reads, at p. 23:

"Counsel on both sides have informed us that the point is devoid of judicial authority and we have not found anything to suggest the contrary. Therefore we have to decide, in the absence of judicial decisions, what is the common law. Assistance may be sought from the opinions of textwriters, judicial dicta and the reports of Commissions and legal committees, and from analogies with legal systems which share our common law heritage, with a view to considering matters of general principle and arriving at the answer. Mr. Curran drew to our attention the penal codes of Canada, New Zealand and the State of Queensland and we have also considered among others the penal codes of Western Australia and the State of New York as well as the draft code of 1879 prepared by the Royal Commission of which Mr. Justice Stephen was a member and the American Model Penal Code. All these codes and draft codes contain various provisions withholding from members of unlawful organisations the right to rely on a defence of duress."

Then Lord Lowry C.J. cites two extracts from the various codes and authorities which he indicates in précis in the passage which I have read. There is no need for us to go into that and there is no need for us to cite further from Lord Lowry C.J., except for one passage, where he said, at p. 26:

"We consider that the widespread adoption of such limiting provisions with regard to duress shows that the framers of the codes and drafts which we have mentioned considered that this exclusory doctrine was already part of the common law and the Law Commission's recommendation indicates the view of a distinguished body of jurists, (whose recommendations are in general favourable to duress as a defence), that participation in unlawful associations or conspiracies should disqualify the accused from relying on it."

In other words, in our judgment, where a person has voluntarily, and with knowledge of its nature, joined a criminal organisation or gang which he knew might bring pressure on him to commit an offence and was an active member when he was put under such pressure, he cannot avail himself of the defence of duress. Mr. Mylne concedes that such a ruling is the end of his appeal. The appeal is therefore dismissed.

Appeal dismissed.

Question

Would the joining of a criminal organisation or gang automatically disentitle a defendant from raising duress as a defence or must the organisation or gang be one which he knew used violence to enforce its discipline? See next case.

R. v. Shepherd
(1988) 86 Cr.App.R. 47
Court of Appeal

A was a member of a gang of shoplifters. At his trial on a charge of burglary, he raised the defence of duress claiming he had played a willing part in a previous offence but, when he expressed a desire to give up, had been threatened by P with violence to himself and his family. (While awaiting trial A had been assaulted by P, for which offence P had been given a prison sentence.) The trial judge withdrew the defence of duress from the jury because of A's original voluntary participation in the criminal organisation. A appealed.

MUSTILL L.J.: At the conclusion of the argument we had arrived at the following opinion:
(1) Although it is not easy to rationalise the existence of duress as a defence rather than a ground of mitigation, it must in some way be founded on a concession to human frailty in cases where the defendant has been faced with a choice between two evils.
(2) The exception which exists where the defendant has voluntarily allied himself with the person who exercises the duress must be founded on the assumption that, just as he cannot complain if he had the opportunity to escape the duress and failed to take it, equally no concession to frailty is required if the risk of duress is freely undertaken.
(3) Thus, in some instances it will follow inevitably that the defendant has no excuse: for example, if he has joined a group of people dedicated to violence as a political end, or one which is overtly ready to use violence for other criminal ends. Members of so called paramilitary illegal groups, or gangs of armed robbers, must be taken to anticipate what may happen to them if their nerve fails, and cannot be heard to complain if violence is indeed threatened.
(4) Other cases will be difficult. There is no need for recourse to extravagant examples. Common sense must recognise that there are certain kinds of criminal enterprises the joining of which, in the absence of any knowledge of propensity to violence on the part of one member, would not lead another to suspect that a decision to think better of the whole

affair might lead him into serious trouble. The logic which appears to underlie the law of duress would suggest that if trouble did unexpectedly materialise, and if it put the defendant into a dilemma in which a reasonable man might have chosen to act as he did, the concession to human frailty should not be denied to him.

Having arrived at these conclusions on the argument addressed to us, it appeared to us plain there had been a question which should properly have been put to the jury and that the appeal must accordingly be allowed. We intimated that this would be so, whilst taking the opportunity to put our reasons in writing.

Naturally a proper scepticism would have been in order when the defence came to be examined at the trial, for there were many aspects on which the appellant could have been pressed. In particular, his prior knowledge of P would require investigation. At the same time the trial would not have been a foregone conclusion, since the concerted shoplifting enterprise did not involve violence to the victim either in anticipation or in the way it was actually put into effect. The members of the jury have had to ask themselves whether the appellant could be said to have taken the risk of P's violence simply by joining a shoplifting gang of which he was a member. Of course even if they were prepared to give the appellant the benefit of the doubt in this respect, an acquittal would be far from inevitable. The jury would have then to consider the nature and timing of the threats, and the nature and persistence of the offences, in order to decide whether the defendant was entitled to be exonerated. It may well be that, in the light of the evidence as it emerged, convictions would have followed. But the question was never put to the test. The issues were never investigated. The jury were left with no choice but to convict.

In these circumstances we saw no alternative but to hold that the convictions could not stand.

Appeal allowed
Conviction quashed

iv. Duress and murder

The question whether duress is available as a defence to a charge of murder has come before the House of Lords or Privy Council on three occasions. The case which follows was the first occasion.

D.P.P. v. Lynch
[1975] A.C. 653
House of Lords

The appellant was the driver of a car which contained members of the IRA in Northern Ireland on an expedition in which they shot and killed a police officer. He said that he was not a member of the IRA and was convinced that he would be shot if he did not obey the leader of the group. The trial judge held that the defence of duress was not available to an aider and abettor of murder. The Court of Criminal Appeal in Northern Ireland dismissed his appeal.

LORD MORRIS OF BORTH-Y-GEST: ... The issue in the present case is therefore whether there is any reason why the defence of duress, which in respect of a variety of offences has been recognised as a possible defence, may not also be a possible defence on a charge of being a principal in the second degree to murder. I would confine my decision to that issue. It may be that the law must deny such a defence to an actual killer, and that the law will not be irrational if it does so.

Though it is not possible for the law always to be worked out on coldly logical lines there may be manifest factual differences and contrasts between the situation of aider and abettor to a killing and that of the actual killer. Let two situations be supposed. In each let it be supposed that there is a real and effective threat of death. In one a person is required under such duress to drive a car to a place or to carry a gun to a place with knowledge that at such place it is planned that X is to be killed by those who are imposing their will. In the other situation let it be supposed that a person under such duress is told that he himself must there and then kill X. In either situation there is a terrible agonising choice of evils. In the former to save his life the person drives the car or carries the gun. He may cling to the hope that perhaps X will not be found at the place or that there will be a change of intention before the purpose is carried out or that in some unforeseen way the dire event of a killing will be averted. The final and fatal moment of decision has not arrived. He saves his own life at a time when the loss of another life is not a certainty. In the second (if indeed it is a situation likely to arise) the person is told that to save his life he himself must personally there and then take an innocent life. It is for him to pull the trigger or otherwise personally to do the act of killing. There, I think, before allowing duress as a defence it may be that the law will have to call a halt. May there still be force in what long ago was said by Hale?

"Again, if a man be desperately assaulted, and in peril of death, and cannot otherwise escape, unless to satisfy his assailant's fury he will kill an innocent person then present, the fear and actual force will not acquit him of the crime and punishment of murder, if he commit the fact; for he ought rather to die himself, than kill an innocent."

(see *Hale's Pleas of the Crown*, vol. 1, p. 51). Those words have over long periods of time influenced both thought and writing but I think that their application may have been unduly extended when it is assumed that they were intended to cover all cases of accessories and aiders and abettors. . . .

It is most undesirable that, in the administration of our criminal law, cases should arise in which, if there is a prosecution leading to a conviction, a just conclusion will only be attained by an exercise thereafter of the prerogative of granting a pardon. I would regret it, therefore, if upon an application of legal principles such cases could arise. Such principles and such approach as will prevent them from arising would seem to me to be more soundly based. . . .

LORD WILBERFORCE: What reason then can there be for excepting murder? One may say—as some authorities do (*cf. A.-G.* v. *Whelan* [1934] I.R. 518, 526 *per* Murnaghan J., *R.* v. *Hurley and Murray* [1967] V.R. 526, 543 *per* Smith J.) that murder is the most heinous of crimes: so it may be, and in some circumstances, a defence of duress in relation to it should be correspondingly hard to establish. Indeed, to justify the deliberate killing by one's own hand of another human being may be something that no pressure or threat even to one's own life which can be imagined can justify—no such case ever seems to have reached the courts. But if one accepts the test of heinousness, this does not, in my opinion, involve that all cases of what is murder in law must be treated in the same way.

Heinousness is a word of degree, and that there are lesser degrees of heinousness, even of involvement in homicide, seems beyond doubt. An accessory before the fact, or an aider or abettor, may (not necessarily must) bear a less degree of guilt than the actual killer: and even if the rule of exclusion is absolute, or nearly so in relation to the latter, it need not be so in lesser cases. Nobody would dispute that the greater the degree of heinousness of the crime, the greater and less resistible must be the degree of pressure, if pressure is to excuse. Questions of this kind where it is necessary to weigh the pressures acting upon a man against the gravity of the act he commits are common enough in the criminal law, for example with regard to provocation and self-defence: their difficulty is not a reason for a total rejection of the defence. To say that the defence may be admitted in relation to some degrees of murder, but that its admission in cases of direct killing by a first degree principal is likely to be attended by such great difficulty as almost to justify a ruling that the defence is not available, is not illogical. It simply involves the recognition that by sufficiently adding to the degrees, one may approach an absolute position.

So I find no convincing reason, on principle, why, if a defence of duress in the criminal law exists at all, it should be absolutely excluded in murder charges whatever the nature of the charge; hard to establish, yes, in case of direct killing so hard that perhaps it will never be proved: but in other cases to be judged, strictly indeed, on the totality of facts. Exclusion, if not arbitrary, must be based either on authority or policy. I shall deal with each. . . .

The broad question remains how this House, clearly not bound by any precedent, should now state the law with regard to this defence in relation to the facts of the present case. I have no doubt that it is open to us, on normal judicial principles, to hold the defence admissible. We are here in the domain of the common law: our task is to fit what we can see as principle and authority to the facts before us, and it is no obstacle that these facts are new. The judges have always assumed responsibility for deciding questions of principle relating to criminal liability and guilt, and particularly for setting the standards by which the law expects normal men to act. In all such matters as capacity, sanity, drunkenness, coercion, necessity, provocation, self-defence, the common law, through the judges, accepts and sets the standards of right-thinking men of normal firmness and humanity at a level which people can accept and respect. The House is not inventing a new defence: on the contrary, it would not discharge its judicial duty if it failed to define the law's attitude to this particular defence in particular circumstances. I would decide that the defence is in law admissible in a case of aiding and abetting murder, and so in the present case. I would leave cases of direct killing by a principal in the first degree to be dealt with as they arise.

It is said that such persons as the appellant can always be safeguarded by action of the executive which can order an imprisoned person to be released. I firmly reject any such argument. A law, which requires innocent victims of terrorist threats to be tried for murder and convicted as murderers, is an unjust law even if the executive, resisting political pressures, may decide, after all, and within the permissible limits of the prerogative to release them. Moreover, if the defence is excluded in law, much of the evidence which would prove the duress would be inadmissible at the trial, not brought out in court, and not tested by cross-examination. The validity of the defence is far better judged by a jury, after proper direction and a fair trial, than by executive officials; and if it is said that to allow the defence will be to encourage fictitious claims of pressure I have enough confidence in our legal system to believe that the process of law is a better safeguard against this than inquiry by a government department.

LORD EDMUND-DAVIES agreed that duress was a defence to a principal in the second degree to murder and also indicated that he might accept the defence as being available for the principal offender. LORD SIMON and LORD KILBRANDON dissented.

Appeal allowed
Retrial Ordered

Abbott v. The Queen
[1977] A.C. 755
Privy Council

The appellant claimed the defence of duress on a charge of murder as a principal in the first degree. By a majority of three to two the Privy Council held that the defence was not available to a principal.

LORD SALMON delivered the majority judgment of their Lordships:
Whilst their Lordships feel bound to accept the decision of the House of Lords in *Lynch's* case they find themselves constrained to say that had they considered (which they do not) that that decision is an authority which requires the extension of the doctrine to cover cases like the present they would not have accepted it. ...
Counsel for the appellant has argued that the law now presupposes a degree of heroism of which the ordinary man is incapable and which therefore should not be expected of him and that modern conditions and concepts of humanity have rendered obsolete the rule that the actual killer cannot rely on duress as a defence. Their Lordships do not agree. In the trials of those responsible for wartime atrocities such as mass killings of men, women or children, inhuman experiments on human beings, often resulting in death, and like crimes, it was invariably argued for the defence that these atrocities should be excused on the ground that they resulted from superior orders and duress: if the accused had refused to do these dreadful things, they would have been shot and therefore they should be acquitted and allowed to go free. This argument has always been universally rejected. Their Lordships would be sorry indeed to see it accepted by the common law of England.

LORD WILBERFORCE and LORD EDMUND-DAVIES dissenting:
The starting point in this appeal must be the decision of the House of Lords in *D.P.P. for Northern Ireland* v. *Lynch* [*supra*] which decision was not available to the trial judge in this case or to the Court of Appeal. This established that on a murder charge the defence of duress is open to a person accused as a principal in the second degree. Not only has the actual decision in *Lynch* to be respected but also its implications, for it was based upon a consideration in some depth of topics scarcely adverted to by their Lordships in the present appeal. The question that immediately arises is whether any acceptable distinction can invariably be drawn between a principal in the first degree to murder and one in the second degree, with the result that the latter may in certain circumstances be absolved by his plea of duress, while the former may never even advance such a plea.
The simple fact is that *no* acceptable basis of distinction has even now been advanced. In *Lynch* Lord Simon of Glaisdale and Lord Kilbrandon

who dissented, adverted to the absence of any valid distinction as a ground for holding that duress should be available to *neither*. ...

Lynch having been decided as it was, the most striking feature of the present appeal is the lack of any indication, in the judgment of the majority *why* a flat declaration that in no circumstances whatsoever may the actual killer be absolved by a plea of duress makes for sounder law and better ethics. In truth, the contrary is the case. For example D attempts to kill P but, though injuring him, fails. When charged with attempted murder he may plead duress (*R.* v. *Fagan* (unreported), September 20, 1974, and several times referred to in *Lynch*). Later P dies and D is charged with his murder; if the majority of their Lordships are right, he now has no such plea available. Again, no one can doubt that our law would today allow duress to be pleaded in answer to a charge, under section 18 of the Offences Against the Person Act 1861, of wounding with intent. Yet, here again, should the victim die after the conclusion of the first trial, the accused when faced with a murder charge would be bereft of any such defence. It is not the mere lack of logic that troubles one. It is when one stops to consider why duress is *ever* permitted as a defence even to charges of great gravity that the lack of any moral reason justifying its *automatic* exclusion in such cases as the present becomes so baffling and so important.

The majority have deemed it right to resurrect in the present appeal objections to the admissibility of a plea of duress which, if accepted, would leave *Lynch* with only vestigial authority, even though the decisions resulted from their demolition. One example of this is the alleged ease with which bogus pleas of duress can be advanced, and the so-called "charter for terrorists, gang leaders and kidnappers" originally raised by Lord Simon of Glaisdale in *D.P.P. for Northern Ireland* v. *Lynch* just as though the pleas of duress had merely to be raised for an acquittal automatically to follow. But the realistic view is that, the more dreadful the circumstances of the killing, the heavier the evidential burden of an accused advancing such a plea, and the stronger and more irresistible the duress needed before it could be regarded as affording any defence. ...

Appeal dismissed

The issue was finally settled in the following case:

R. v. Howe and Others
[1987] 1 A.C. 417
House of Lords

H and B, with C and M, participated in the assault and then killing of two victims. On the first occasion H and B were principals in the second degree. On the second occasion they jointly strangled the victim. On a third occasion the intended victim escaped. At their trial on two counts of murder and one of conspiracy to murder they pleaded duress claiming that they had feared for their own lives if they had not done as M directed. The judge left the defence of duress to the jury in respect of the first murder and the conspiracy charge but not in respect of the second murder. The appellants were convicted on all three counts.

LORD HAILSHAM OF MARYLEBONE L.C.: [The first of the three questions certified by the Court of Appeal is as follows:] "(1) Is duress available as a defence to a person charged with murder as a principal in the first degree (the actual killer)?" ... In my opinion, this must be decided on principle and authority, and the answer must in the end demand a reconsideration of the two authorities of *D.P.P. for Northern Ireland* v. *Lynch* and *Abbott* v. *The Queen*. . . .

The present case, in my opinion, affords an ideal and never to be repeated opportunity to consider as we were invited expressly to do by the respondent, the whole question afresh, if necessary, by applying the *Practice Statement (Judicial Precedent)* [1966] 1 W.L.R. 1234 to the decision in *Lynch*.

I therefore consider the matter first from the point of view of authority. On this I can only say that at the time when *Lynch* was decided on the balance of weight in an unbroken tradition of authority dating back to Hale and Blackstone seems to have been accepted to have been that duress was not available to a defendant accused of murder. I quote only from Hale and Blackstone. Thus *Hale's Pleas of the Crown* (1736), vol. 1, p. 51:

> "if a man be desperately assaulted, and in peril of death, and cannot otherwise escape, unless to satisfy his assailant's fury he will kill an innocent person then present, the fear and actual force will not acquit him of the crime and punishment of murder, if he commit the fact; for he ought rather to die himself, than kill an innocent: . . . "

Blackstone, Commentaries on the Laws of England (1857 ed.), vol. 4, p. 28 was to the same effect. He wrote that a man under duress: "ought rather to die himself than escape by the murder of an innocent." . . .

Before I leave the question of reported authority I must refer to . . . *R.* v. *Dudley and Stephens* (*post*, p. 321). That is generally and, in my view correctly, regarded as an authority on the availability of the supposed defence of necessity rather than duress. But I must say frankly that, if we were to allow this appeal, we should, I think, also have to say that *Dudley and Stephens* was bad law. There is, of course, an obvious distinction between duress and necessity as potential defences; duress arises from the wrongful threats of violence of another human being and necessity arises from any other objective dangers threatening the accused. This, however, is, in my view a distinction without a relevant difference, since on this view duress is only that species of the genus of necessity which is caused by wrongful threats. I cannot see that there is any way in which a person of ordinary fortitude can be excused from the one type of pressure on his will rather than the other. . . .

I do not think that the decision in *Lynch* can be justified on authority and that, exercising to the extent necessary, the freedom given to us by the *Practice Statement (Judicial Precedent)* which counsel for the respondent urged us to apply, I consider that the right course in the instant appeal is to restore the law to the condition in which it was almost universally thought to be prior to *Lynch*. It may well be that that law was to a certain extent unclear and to some extent gave rise to anomaly. But these anomalies I believe to be due to a number of factors extraneous to the present appeal and to the intrinsic nature of duress. The first is the mandatory nature of the sentence in murder. The second resides in the fact that murder being a "result" crime, only being complete if the victim dies within the traditional period of a year and a day and that, in consequence, a different crime may be charged according to whether or not the victim actually succumbs during the prescribed period. The third lies in the fact . . . that, as matters stand, the *mens rea* in murder consists not simply in an intention to kill, but may include an intent to commit grievous bodily harm. It has always been possible for Parliament to clear up this branch of the law (or indeed to define more closely the nature and extent of the availability of duress as a defence). But Parliament has conspiciously, and perhaps deliberately, declined to do so. In the meantime, I must say that the attempt made in *Lynch* to clear up this situation by judicial legislation has proved to be an excessive and perhaps improvident use of the undoubted power of the courts to create new law by creating precedents in individual cases.

This brings me back to the question of principle. I begin by affirming that, while there can never be a direct correspondence between law and morality, an attempt to divorce the two entirely is and has always proved to be, doomed to failure, and, in the present case, the overriding objects of the criminal law must be to protect innocent lives and to set a standard of conduct which ordinary men and women are expected to observe if they are to avoid criminal responsibility. . . .

In general, I must say that I do not at all accept in relation to the defence of murder it is either good morals, good policy or good law to suggest, as did the majority in *Lynch* and the minority in *Abbott* that the ordinary man of reasonable fortitude is not to be supposed to be capable of heroism if he is asked to take an innocent life rather than sacrifice his own. Doubtless in actual practice many will succumb to temptation, as they did in *Dudley and Stephens*. But many will not, and I do not believe that as a "concession to human frailty" the former should be exempt from liability to criminal sanctions if they do. I have known in my own lifetime of too many acts of heroism by ordinary human beings of no more than ordinary fortitude to regard a law as either "just or humane" which withdraws the protection of the criminal law from the innocent victim and casts the cloak of its protection upon the coward and the poltroon in the name of a "concession to human frailty."

I must not, however, underestimate the force of the arguments on the other side, advanced as they have been with such force and such persuasiveness by some of the most eminent legal minds, judicial and academic, in the country.

First, amongst these is, perhaps, the argument from logic and consistency. A long line of cases, it is said, carefully researched and closely analysed, established duress as an available defence in a wide range of crimes, some at least, like wounding with intent to commit grievous bodily harm, carrying the heaviest penalties commensurate with their gravity. To cap this, it is pointed out that at least in theory, a defendant accused of this crime under section 18 of the Offences Against the Person Act 1861, but acquitted on the grounds of duress, will still be liable to a charge of murder if the victim dies within the traditional period of one year and a day. I am not, perhaps, persuaded of this last point as much as I should. It is not simply an anomaly based on the defence of duress. It is a product of the peculiar *mens rea* allowed on a charge of murder which is not confined to an intent to kill. More persuasive, perhaps, is the point based on the availability of the defence of duress on a charge of attempted murder, where the actual intent to kill is an essential prerequisite. It may be that we must meet this casus omissus in your Lordships' House when we come to it. It may require reconsideration of the availability of the defence in that case too.

I would, however, prefer to meet the case of alleged inconsistency head on. Consistency and logic, though inherently desirable, are not always prime characteristics of a penal code based like the common law on custom and precedent. Law so based is not an exact science. All the same, I feel I am required to give some answer to the question posed. If duress is available as a defence to some crimes of the most grave why, it may legitimately be asked, stop at murder, whether as accessory or principal and whether in the second or the first degree? But surely I am entitled to believe that some degree of proportionality between the threat and the offence must, at least to some extent, be a preprequisite of the defence under existing law. Few would resist threats to the life of a loved one if the alternative were driving across the red lights or in excess of 70 m.p.h. on the motorway. But ... it would take rather more than the threat of a slap on the wrist or even moderate pain or injury to discharge the evidential burden even in the case of a fairly serious assault. In such a case the "concession to human frailty" is no more than to say that in such circumstances a reasonable man of average courage is entitled to embrace as a matter of choice the alternative which a reasonable man would regard as the lesser of two evils. Other considerations necessarily arise where the choice is between the threat of death or *a fortiori* of serious injury and deliberately taking an innocent life. In such a case a reasonable man might reflect that one innocent human life is at least as valuable as his own or that of his loved one. In such a case a man cannot claim that he is choosing the lesser of two evils. Instead he is embracing the cognate but morally disreputable principle that the end justifies the means.

I am not so shocked as some of the judicial opinions have been at the need, if this be the conclusion, to invoke the availability of administrative as distinct from purely judicial remedies for the hardships which might otherwise occur in the most agonising cases. Even in *Dudley and Stephens* in 1884 when the death penalty was mandatory and frequently inflicted, the prerogative was used to reduce a sentence of death by hanging to one of six months in prison. In murder cases the available mechanisms are today both more flexible and more sophisticated. The trial judge may make no minimum recommendation. He will always report to the Home Secretary, as he did in the present case of Clarkson and Burke. The Parole Board will always consider a case of this kind with a High Court judge brought into consultation. In the background is always the prerogative and, it may not unreasonably be suggested, that is exactly what the prerogative is for. If the law seems to bear harshly in its operation in the case of a mandatory sentence on any particular offender there has never been a period of time when there were more effective means of mitigating its effect than at the present day. It may well be thought that the loss of a clear right to a defence justifying or excusing the deliberate taking of an innocent life in order to emphasise to all the sanctity of a human life is not an excessive price to pay in the light of these mechanisms. Murder, as every practitioner of the law knows, though often described as one of the utmost heinousness, is not in fact necessarily so, but consists in a whole bundle of offences of vastly differing degrees of culpability, ranging from brutal, cynical and repeated offences like the so called Moors murders to the almost venial, if objectively immoral, "mercy killing" of a beloved partner. ...

During the course of argument it was suggested that there was available to the House some sort of half way house between allowing these appeals and dismissing them. The argument ran that we might treat duress in murder as analogous to provocation, or perhaps diminished responsibility, and say that, in indictments for murder, duress might reduce the crime to one of manslaughter. I find myself quite unable to accept this. The cases show that duress, if available and made out, entitles the accused to a clean acquittal, without, it has been said, the "stigma" of a conviction. Whatever other merits it may have, at least the suggestion makes nonsense of any pretence of logic or consistency in the criminal law. It is also contrary to principle. Unlike the doctrine of provocation, which is based on emotional loss of control, the defence of duress, as I have already shown, is put forward as a "concession to human frailty" whereby a conscious decision, it may be coolly undertaken, to sacrifice an innocent human life is made as an evil lesser than a wrong which might otherwise be suffered by the accused or his loved ones at the hands of a wrong doer. The defence of diminished responsibility (which might well, had it then been available to *Dudley and Stephens*, have prevailed there) is statutory in England though customary in Scotland, the law of its origin. But in England at least it has a conceptual basis defined in the Homicide Act 1957 which is totally distinct from that of duress if duress be properly analysed and understood. Provocation (unique to murder and not extending even to "section 18" offences) is a concession to human frailty due to the extent that even a reasonable man may, under sufficient provocation temporarily lose his self control towards the person who has provoked him enough. Duress, as I have already pointed out, is a concession to human frailty in that it allows a reasonable man to make a conscious choice between the reality of the immediate threat and what he may reasonably regard as the lesser of two evils. Diminished responsibility as defined in the Homicide Act 1957 depends on abnormality of mind impairing mental responsibility. It may overlap duress or even necessity. But it is not what we are discussing in the instant appeal.

LORD GRIFFITHS: . . . For centuries it was accepted that English criminal law did not allow duress as a defence to murder. . . . [I]n *R. v. Dudley and Stephens*, the defence of necessity was denied to the men who had killed the cabin boy and eaten him in order that they might survive albeit only Stephens was the actual killer. The reasoning that underlies that decision is the same as that which denies duress as a defence to murder. It is based upon the special sanctity that the law attaches to human life and which denies to a man the right to take an innocent life even at the price of his own or another's life.

There are surprisingly few reported decisions on duress but it cannot be gainsaid that the defence has been extended, particularly since the second war, to a number of crimes. I think myself it would have been better had this development not taken place and that duress had been regarded as a factor to be taken into account in mitigation as Stephen suggested in his *History of the Criminal Law of England* (1883) vol. 2, p. 108. However, as Lord Morris of Borth-y-Gest said in *D.P.P. for Northern Ireland v. Lynch* [1975] A.C. 653, 670, it is too late to adopt that view. And the question now is whether that development should be carried a step further and applied to a murderer who is the actual killer, and if the answer to this question is no, whether there is any basis upon which it can be right to draw a distinction between a murderer who did the actual killing and a murderer who played a different part in the design to bring about the death of the victim. . . .

[A]re there any present circumstances that should impel your Lordships to alter the law that has stood for so long and to extend the defence of duress to the actual killer? My Lords, I can think of none. It appears to me that all present indications point in the opposite direction. We face a rising tide of violence and terrorism against which the law must stand firm recognising that its highest duty is to protect the freedom and lives of those that live under it. The sanctity of human life lies at the root of this ideal and I would do nothing to undermine it, be it ever so slight.

On this question your Lordships should, I believe, accord great weight to the opinion of the Lord Chief Justice who by virtue of his office and duties is in far closer touch with the practical application of the criminal law and better able to evaluate the consequence of a change in the law than those of us who sit in this House. This is what Lord Lane C.J. had to say in his judgment in this case [1986] Q.B. 626, 641:

"It is true that to allow the defence to the aider and abettor but not to the killer may lead to illogicality, as was pointed out by this court in *R. v. Graham (ante, p. 284)*, where the question in issue in the instant case was not argued, but that is not to say that any illogicality should be cured by making duress available to the actual killer rather by removing it from the aider and abettor. Assuming that a change in the law is desirable or necessary, we may perhaps be permitted to express a view. The whole matter was dealt with in extenso by Lord Salmon in his speech in *Abbott v. The Queen* to which reference has already been made. He dealt there with the authorities. It is unnecessary for us in the circumstances to repeat the citations which he there makes. It would, moreover, be impertinent for us to try to restate in different terms the contents of that speech with which we respectfully agree. Either the law should be left as it is or the defence of duress should be denied to anyone charged with murder, whether as a principal in the first degree or otherwise. It seems to us that it would be a highly dangerous relaxation in the law to allow a person who has deliberately killed, maybe a number of innocent people, to escape conviction and punishment altogether because of a fear that his own life or those of his family might be in danger if he did not; particularly so when the defence of duress is so easy to raise and may be so difficult for the prosecution to disprove beyond reasonable doubt, the facts of necessity being as a rule known only to the defendant himself. That is not to say that duress may not be taken into account in other ways, for example by the parole board. Even if, contrary to our views, it were otherwise desirable to extend the defence of duress to the actual killer, this is surely not the moment to make any such change, when acts of terrorism are commonplace and opportunities for mass murder have never been more readily to hand."

My Lords, in my view we should accept the advice of Lord Lane C.J. and the judges who sat with him, and decline to extend the defence to the actual killer. If the defence is not available to the killer what justification can there be for extending it to others who have played their part in the murder. I can, of course, see that as a matter of commonsense one participant in a murder may be considered less morally at fault than another. The youth who hero-worships the gangleader and acts as lookout man whilst the gang enter a jeweller's shop and kill the owner in order to steal is an obvious example. In the eyes of the law they are all guilty of murder, but justice will be served by requiring those who did the killing to serve a longer period in prison before being released on licence than the youth who acted as lookout. However, it is not difficult to give examples where moral fault may be thought to attach to a participant in murder who was not the actual killer; I have already mentioned the example of a contract killing, when the murder would never have taken place if a contract had not been placed to take the life of the victim. Another example would be an intelligent man goading a weakminded individual into a killing he would not otherwise commit.

It is therefore neither rational nor fair to make the defence dependent upon whether the accused is the actual killer or took some other part in the murder. I have toyed with the idea that it might be possible to leave it to the discretion of the trial judge to decide whether the defence should be available to one who was not the killer, but I have rejected this as introducing too great a degree of uncertainty into the availability of the defence. I am not troubled by some of the extreme examples cited in favour of allowing the defence to those who are not the killer such as a woman motorist being highjacked and forced to act as getaway driver, or a pedestrian being forced to give misleading information to the police to protect robbery and murder in a shop. The short, practical answer is that it is inconceivable that such persons would be prosecuted; they would be called as the principal witnesses for the prosecution.

As I can find no fair and certain basis upon which to differentiate between participants to a murder and as I am firmly convinced that the law should not be extended to the killer, I would depart from the decision of this House in *D.P.P. for Northern Ireland* v. *Lynch* and declare the law to be that duress is not available as a defence to a charge of murder, or to attempted murder. I add attempted murder because it is to be remembered that the prosecution have to prove an even more evil intent to convict of attempted murder than in actual murder. Attempted murder requires proof of an intent to kill, whereas in murder it is sufficient to prove an intent to cause really serious injury.

It cannot be right to allow the defence to one who may be more intent upon taking a life than the murderer. This leaves, of course, the anomaly that duress is available for the offence of wounding with intent but not to murder if the victim dies subsequently. But this flows from the special regard that the law has for human life, it may not be logical but it is real and has to be accepted.

I do not think that your Lordships should adopt the compromise solution of declaring that duress reduces murder to manslaughter. Where the defence of duress is available it is a complete excuse. This solution would put the law back to lines upon which Stephen suggested it should develop by regarding duress as a form of mitigation. English law has rejected this solution and it would be yet another anomaly to introduce it for the crime of murder alone. I would have been more tempted to go down this road if the death penalty had remained for murder. But the sentence for murder although mandatory and expressed as imprisonment for life, is in fact an indefinite sentence, which is kept constantly under review by the parole board and the Home Secretary with the assistance of the Lord Chief Justice and the trial judge. I have confidence that through this machinery the respective culpability of those involved in a murder case can be fairly weighed and reflected in the time they are required to serve in custody.

LORD MACKAY OF CLASHFERN: ... The first question ... that arises in this appeal is whether any distinction can be made between this case and the *Lynch* case. ... While ... *Lynch* was decided by reasoning which does not extend to the present case, the question remains whether there is a potential distinction between this case and that of *Lynch* by which to determine whether or not the defence of duress should be available. ...

I have not been able to find any writer of authority that is able to give rational support for the view that the distinction between principals in the first degree and those in the second degree is relevant to determine whether or not duress should be available in a particular case of murder. Whatever may have divided Lord Wilberforce and Lord Edmund-Davies on the one hand, from Lord Simon of Glaisdale and Lord Kilbrandon on the other, it is apparent that all agree that this is not a distinction which should receive practical effect in the law.

I have not found any satisfactory formulation of a distinction which would be sufficiently precise to be given practical effect in law and at the same time differentiate between levels of culpability so as to produce a satisfactory demarcation between those accused of murder, who should be entitled to resort to the defence of duress and those who were not.

The House is therefore, in my opinion, faced with the unenviable decision of either departing altogether from the doctrine that duress is not available in murder or of departing from the decision of this House in *Lynch*. While a variety of minor attacks on the reasoning of the majority were mounted by counsel for the Crown in the present case, I do not find any of these sufficiently important to merit departing from *Lynch* on these grounds. I do, however, consider that having regard to the balance of authority on the question of duress as a defence to murder prior to *Lynch*, for this House now to allow the defence of duress generally in response to a charge of murder would be to effect an important and substantial change in the law. In my opinion too, it would involve a departure from the decision in the famous case of *R. v. Dudley and Stephens*. The justification for allowing a defence of duress to a charge of murder is that a defendant should be excused who killed as the only way of avoiding death himself or preventing the death of some close relation such as his own well-loved child. This essentially was the dilemma which Dudley and Stephens faced and in denying their defence the court refused to allow this consideration to be used in a defence to murder. If that refusal was right in the case of Dudley and Stephens it cannot be wrong in the present appeals. Although the result of recognising the defence advanced in that case would be that no crime was committed and in the case with which we are concerned that a murder was committed and a particular individual was not guilty of it (subject to the consideration of the second certified question) that does not distinguish the two cases from the point of view now being considered.

To change the law in the manner suggested by counsel for the appellants in the present case would, in my opinion, introduce uncertainty over a field of considerable importance.

So far I have referred to the defence of duress as if it were a precisely defined concept but it is apparent from the decisions that it is not so and I cannot do better in this connection than to refer to what Lord Simon of Glaisdale said on this point in *Lynch* [1975] A.C. 653, 686:

"Before turning to examine these considerations, it is convenient to have a working definition of duress—even though it is actually an extremely vague and elusive juristic concept. I take it for present purposes to denote such [well grounded] fear, produced by threats, of death or grievous bodily harm [or unjustified imprisonment] if a certain act is not done, or overbears the actor's wish to perform the act, and is effective, at the time of the act, in constraining him to perform it. I am quite uncertain whether the words which I have put in square brackets should be included in any such definition. It is arguable that the test should be purely subjective, and that it is contrary to principle to require the fear to be a reasonable one. Moreover, I have assumed, on the basis of *R. v. Hudson* [1971] 2 Q.B. 202 that threat of future injury may suffice, although *Stephen's Digest of the Criminal Law* art. 10 is to the contrary. Then the law leaves it also quite uncertain whether the fear induced by threats must be of death or grievous bodily harm, or whether threatened loss of liberty suffices: cases of duress in the law of contract suggest that duress may extend to fear of unjustified imprisonment; but the criminal law returns no clear answer. It also leaves entirely unanswered whether, to constitute such a general criminal defence, the threat must be of harm to the person required to perform the act, or extends to the immediate family of the actor (and how immediate?), or to any person. Such questions are not academic, in these days when hostages are so frequently seized."

To say that a defence in respect of which so many questions remain unsettled should be introduced in respect of the whole field of murder is not to promote certainty in the law. . . .

In my opinion, we would not be justified in the present state of the law in introducing for the first time into our law the concept of duress acting to reduce the charge to one of manslaughter even if there were grounds on which it might be right to do so. On that aspect of the matter the Law Commission took the view that where the defence of duress had been made out it would be unjust to stigmatise the person accused with a conviction and there is clearly much force in that view. . . . It seems to me plain that the reason that it was for so long stated by writers of authority that the defence of duress was not available in a charge of murder was because of the supreme importance that the law afforded to the protection of human life and that it seemed repugnant that the law should recognise in any individual in any circumstances, however extreme, the right to choose that one innocent person should be killed rather than another. In my opinion, that is the question which we still must face. Is it right that the law should confer this right in any circumstances, however extreme? While I recognise fully the force of the reasoning which persuaded the majority of this House in *Lynch* to reach the decision to which they came in relation to a person not the actual killer, it does not address directly this question in relation to the actual killer. I am not persuaded that there is good reason to alter the answer which Hale gave to this question. No development of the law or progress in legal thinking which have taken place since his day have, to my mind, demonstrated a reason to change this fundamental answer. In the circumstances which I have narrated of a report to Parliament from the Law Commission concerned *inter alia* with this very question it would seem particularly inappropriate to make such a change now. For these reasons, in my opinion, the first certified question should be answered in the negative.

It follows that, in my opinion, the House should decline to follow the decision in *Lynch*. . . . Up to the present time, the courts have been declining to allow an actual killer to plead the defence of duress while allowing it to a person charged with murder who was not the actual killer as is illustrated in the circumstances of these appeals. Lord Lane C.J. in *R. v. Graham*, illustrated how technical and puzzling in practice the distinction could be. In my opinion, it would not be right to allow this state of affairs to continue. I recognise that this decision leaves certain apparent anomalies in the law but I regard these as consequences of the fact that murder is a result related to crime with a mandatory penalty. Consequently no distinction is made in penalty between the various levels of culpability. Differentiation in treatment once sentence has been pronounced depends upon action by the Crown advised by the executive government although that may be affected by a recommendation which the court is empowered to make. Where a person has taken a minor part in a wounding with intent and is dealt with on that basis he may receive a very short sentence. If sufficiently soon after that conviction the victim dies, on the same facts with the addition of the victim's death caused by the wounding he may be sentenced to life imprisonment. This is simply one illustration of the fact that very different results may follow from a set of facts together with the death of a victim from what would follow the same facts if the victim lived.

[Lord Bridge of Harwich and Lord Brandon of Oakbrook made speeches dismissing the appeal.]

Appeals dismissed

Questions

1. Lord Hailsham, knowing of many acts of heroism by ordinary people, concluded that a law which protected the "coward and the poltroon" could not be regarded as either "just or humane." Is there a general duty in the criminal law to be a hero? Against what standard is a defendant usually judged? (See self-defence, *post*, p. 330, provocation, *post*, p. 513, and *Miller*, *ante*, p. 26.) Does Lord Hailsham provide any clear refutation of the statement by Wechsler and Michael in "A rationale of the law of homicide" (1937) 37 Col.L.R. 738, that "when a third person's life is also at stake even the path of heroism is obscure"?

2. Lord Griffiths stated "I would do nothing to undermine [the sanctity of human life], be it ever so slight." Does the criminal law unequivocally protect this ideal? (See self-defence, mistake and provocation.)

3. Lord Griffiths supported the view of Lord Lane C.J. in the Court of Appeal that the defence should not be afforded to a murderer as the "defence of duress is so easy to raise and may be so difficult for the prosecution to disprove." If this is the case, does not the same criticism apply to all defences? Is Lord Griffiths' view reconcilable with Lord Hailsham's view that "juries have been commendably robust" in rejecting the defence where appropriate (which they did in the case before their Lordships)? Bearing in mind their Lordships' approval of Lord Lane's statement of the test for duress in *Graham*, whereby the defendant will be judged against the standard of the "sober person of reasonable firmness sharing the defendant's characteristics," is it any more likely that the unmeritorious defendant would succeed on a defence of duress where the charge is one of murder as opposed to theft or wounding or any other offence?

4. Lords Hailsham and MacKay placed considerable emphasis on the precedent of *Dudley and Stephens*, *post*, p. 321, in dictating the result of the instant appeals. Is it true, as Lord Hailsham asserted, that that case has met with "very wide acceptance"? Is the defence of necessity wholly analogous to duress? Is necessity based on excuse or justification? Is it available for all offences (except murder)?

5. Lords Hailsham, Griffiths and MacKay placed considerable emphasis on the writers of the past (all of whom could be traced back to Hale) who stated that duress was not available as a defence to a charge of murder. Was this approach to be commended in light of the counsel of Lords Wilberforce and Edmund-Davies in *Abbott* at 771, where they stated:

"Great stress has been laid by the majority of their Lordships upon the apparent unanimity with which great writers of the past have rejected duress as a defence, but, on any view, they have to be read with circumspection in these days, for the criminal courts have long accepted duress as an available defence to a large number of crimes from which those same writers withheld it."?

6. Lord Bridge stated that it is "by legislation alone ... that the scope of the defence of duress can be defined with the degree of precision which, if it is to be available in murder at all, must surely be of critical importance." Lord MacKay also believed the defence was too uncertain for it to be extended to cover an actual killer. As duress is a common law defence (like self-defence and provocation) how did it develop in the first place? If duress is uncertain, is it not also uncertain in relation to other offences? What role do their Lordships envisage for judges if it is not to develop and clarify the common law? Is it arguable, as Milgate states in "Duress and the criminal law: another about turn by the House of Lords" (1988) 47 C.L.J. 61, that *Howe* is "a major piece of judicial legislation, based on an apparently cursory examination of principle and policy"?

7. Lord MacKay, having rejected the idea that, in relation to a murder charge, duress should operate like the defence of provocation and reduce the charge to one of manslaughter, sought to support his view by quoting from Law Com. No. 83 that "where the defence of duress had been made out it would be unjust to stigmatise the person accused with a conviction." Is Lord MacKay's reasoning convincing in light of the decision in *Howe* and the proposals of the Law Commission (see *post*, p. 355)?

8. Lords Hailsham and Griffiths expressed the view that the issue of duress in murder would best be dealt with by the Executive through the agency of the Parole Board or Royal Pardon. Do you agree in light of Lord Wilberforce's judgment in *Lynch*, *ante*, p. 293?

9. Lord Griffiths was of the opinion that duress should not be available on a charge of attempted murder. Would duress also need to be removed as a potential defence to charges under section 18 of the Offences Against the Person Act 1861? What would happen if, after an acquittal following a defence of duress on a charge under section 18, the victim died within a year and a day?

Note

The decision in *Howe* left unresolved the question whether duress was a defence to attempted murder. This question arose for decision in the following case.

R. v. Gotts

[1992] 2 W.L.R. 284

House of Lords

A, aged sixteen, was threatened with death by his father unless he killed his mother who had fled the matrimonial home. A followed his mother and stabbed her in the street but was restrained by bystanders so that, although she sustained serious injuries, she did not die. A pleaded duress on a charge of attempted murder. The trial judge ruled that duress was not available on a charge of attempted murder whereupon A pleaded guilty and an order of three years probation was made against him. The Court of Appeal dismissed A's appeal against his conviction.

LORD JAUNCEY OF TULLICHETTLE (with whom Lords Templeman and Browne-Wilkinson agreed):

[His Lordship, having referred to *Hale's Pleas of the Crown* (1736), Blackstone, *Commentaries on the Laws of England* (1776), Stephen, *History of the Criminal Law of England* (1883) and Kenny, *Outlines of Criminal Law* (13th ed., 1929) concluded:]

My Lords, there is nothing in the writings to which I have referred which leads me to conclude that at common law duress is or is not a defence to attempted murder. In arriving at this conclusion or lack of it I am fortified by the fact that Lord Lane C.J. [1991] 1 Q.B. 660, 667 came to a similar view where he said:

"In these circumstances we are not constrained by a common law rule or by authority from considering whether the defence of duress does or does not extend to the offence of attempted murder." . . .

[His Lordship referred to *Lynch*, *Abbott* and *Howe* and concluded that these cases did not decide the question whether duress is available on a charge of attempted murder.]

As the question is still open for decision by your Lordships it becomes a matter of policy how it should be answered. It is interesting to note that there is no uniformity of practice in other common law countries. The industry of Mr. Miskin who appeared with Mr. Farrer disclosed that in Queensland, Tasmania, Western Australia, New Zealand and Canada duress is not available as a defence to attempted murder but that it is available in almost all of the states of the United States of America. The reason why duress has for so long been stated not to be available as a defence to a murder charge is that the law regards the sanctity of human life and the protection thereof as of paramount importance. Does that reason apply to attempted murder as well as to murder? As Lord Griffiths pointed out in [*Howe*, at p. 445] an attempt to kill must be proved in the case of attempted murder but not necessarily in the case of murder. Is there logic in affording the defence to one who intends to kill but fails and denying it to one who mistakenly kills intending only to injure? If I may give two examples:

(1a) A stabs B in the chest intending to kill him and leaves him for dead. By good luck B is found whilst still alive and rushed to hospital where surgical skill saves his life.

(1b) C stabs D intending only to injure him and inflicts a near identical wound. Unfortunately D is not found until it is too late to save his life.

I see no justification or logic or morality for affording a defence of duress to A who intended to kill when it is denied to C who did not so intend.

(2a) E plants in a passenger aircraft a bomb timed to go off in midflight. Owing to bungling it explodes while the aircraft is still on the ground with the result that some 200 passengers suffer physical and mental injuries of which many are permanently disabling, but no one is killed.

(2b) F plants a bomb in a light aircraft intending to injure the pilot before it takes off but in fact it goes off in mid-air killing the pilot who is the sole occupant of the airplane.

It would in my view be both offensive to common sense and decency that E if he established duress should be acquitted and walk free without a stain on his character notwithstanding the appalling results which he has achieved, whereas F who never intended to kill should, if convicted in the absence of the defence, be sentenced to life imprisonment as a murderer.

It is of course true that withholding the defence in any circumstances will create some anomalies but I would agree with Lord Griffiths (*Reg.* v. *Howe* [1987] A.C. 417, 444A) that nothing should be done to undermine in any way the highest duty of the law to protect the freedom and lives of those that live under it. I can therefore see no justification in logic, morality or law in affording to an attempted murderer the defence which is withheld from a murderer. The intent required of an attempted murderer is more evil than that required of a murderer and the line which divides the two offences is seldom, if ever, of the deliberate making of the criminal. A man shooting to kill but missing a vital organ by a hair's breadth can justify his action no more than can the man who hits that organ. It is pure chance that the attempted murderer is not a murderer and I entirely agree with what Lord Lane C.J. [1991] 1 Q.B. 660, 667 said: that the fact that the attempt failed to kill should not make any difference.

For the foregoing reasons I have no doubt that the Court of Appeal reached the correct conclusion and that the appeal should be dismissed.

LORD LOWRY (with whom Lord Keith of Kinkel agreed): ... The basic proposition for the appellant is that at common law duress has always been a defence for those charged with every crime except murder, most forms of treason and possibly (for a short time) robbery and that to add attempted murder to the exceptions would not be justified. The trial judge, whose words I have cited earlier, may seem to have adopted the first part of this proposition but not the second. The answer by the Crown I suggest, has to be that attempted murder *is* at common law an exception to the general rule and was an exception at the time when the appellant tried to kill his mother. ...

The foundation of the Crown's agrument is that, accepting the sanctity of human life as the basis for denying the defence of duress in murder, both logic and morality demand that that defence must be withheld from one who tried (albeit unsuccessfully), and therefore *intended*, to kill, when one considers that in murder the defence is withheld not only from the deliberate killer but also from the killer who intended only to inflict very serious injury and from all principals in the second degree, whatever their mens rea. But the logic and, to some extent, also the morality of this proposition are open to attack, as follows:

1. Treason, too, is an excluded offence and it does not invariably involve killing or attempting or conspiring to kill. It is the ultimate crime against the state (a man-made, as distinct from a divinely ordained, offence).

2. The principle that a person ought to die himself rather than kill an innocent is attractive but does not touch the case in which the killer did not intend to cause death, nor does it touch a principal in the second degree either, if he merely intended the victim to suffer serious personal injury.

3. There is much authority to show that duress can be relevant which involves a threat not to the killer, but to others, in particular his wife and children, which fundamentally alters the moral problem: see *R.* v. *Brown and Morley* (1968) S.A.S.R. 467, 498, *per* Bray C.J.; *R.* v. *Hurley and Murray*

[1967] V.R. 526; *Abbott* v. *The Queen* [1977] A.C. 755, 767A and 769F, *per* Lord Salmon; *R.* v. *Howe* [1987] A.C. 417, 433, *per* Lord Hailsham of St. Marylebone L.C., and at p. 453, *per* Lord Mackay of Clashfern, and also various statutory codes and the Law Commission's draft Bill on A Criminal Code for England and Wales (vol. 1, App. A) (1989) (Law Com. No. 177), the combined effect of which is to show that threats to harm others can be a basis for the defence of duress.

My Lords, I suggest that the only thing which can reconcile the anomalies that have been a prolific source of comment is the stark fact of death. Murder is a result related crime, as Lord Hailsham of St. Marylebone L.C. and Lord Mackay of Clashfern both observed in *R.* v. *Howe*, at pp. 430 and 457. Thus, to exclude treason and murder relates the doctrine of duress to serious results (admittedly an unsuccessful *attempt* to subvert the government can itself be treason), namely, danger to the state or a crime committed with guilty intent and resulting in, but not necessarily aimed at, loss of life, and does not specially relate that doctrine to a scale of moral turpitude. It is founded on practical considerations and not on a moral value judgment: the recourse to moral values was found in Hale's explanation (*Pleas of the Crown*, vol. 1, p. 51), which related only to murder (and certainly not to robbery) and which, even in relation to murder, did not serve to justify the law's attitude, since it did not cover the guilty causation of death while intending merely to injure.

Blackstone's explanation that crimes created by the laws of society are in relation to duress distinguished from natural offences, so declared by the law of God (*Commentaries on the Laws of England*, 2nd. ed., vol. 4, p. 30), equally fails to satisfy, since treason is typically a crime created by the laws of society for its own protection and because the explanation does not contemplate a mere intent to injure.

I sympathise with the proposition that attempted murder should be recognised as an exempted crime. But from the point of view of deterrence this idea holds no special attraction. If one makes the somewhat artificial assumption (without which the principle of deterrence has no meaning) that a potential offender will know when the defence of duress is not available, one then has to realise that, whatever the law may be about *attempted* murder, one who sets out to kill under threat will be guilty of murder if he succeeds. Therefore the deterrent is in theory operative already. The moral position, too, is clouded, because *Director of Public Prosecutions for Northern Ireland* v. *Lynch* [1975] A.C. 653, in this respect alone affirming the majority opinion of the Court of Criminal Appeal in Northern Ireland, affirmed that the offender, even when acting under duress, intends to commit the crime (of murder, not attempted murder). But his guilty intent is of a special kind: "coactus voluit," as the Latin phrase has it. Thus the denial of the duress defence, based on moral principles, is not straightforward. It may not be just a case of the law saying: "Although you did not succeed, you intended to kill. Therefore you cannot rely on duress." The law might equally well say: "As with other offenders who allege duress, your guilty intent was caused by threats. Therefore, since the intended victim did not die, you, like other offenders, can rely on those threats as a defence. If the victim had died in circumstances amounting to murder or if treason had been the crime, it would of course have been different." This emphasises the point that murder is a result-related crime.

The choice is between the two views propounded by Lord Lane C.J. [1991] 1 Q.B. 660, 664F–G and 667B: (1) *if* the common law recognised that murder and treason were the only excepted crimes, then we are bound to accept that as the law, whether it seems a desirable conclusion or not; the fact that there is no binding decision on the point does not weaken a rule of the common law which has stood the test of time; or (2) we are not constrained by a common law rule or by authority from considering whether the defence of duress does or does not extend to the offence of attempted murder.

I consider that the view to be preferred is that which is contained in the first of these propositions and that to adopt the second would result in an unjustified judicial change in the law. It is only with diffidence that I would express an opinion on the criminal law which conflicts with that of such highly respected authorities as the present Lord Chief Justice and my noble and learned friend, Lord Griffiths, but on this occasion I feel obliged to do so. I proceed to give my reasons for this conclusion.

Both judges and textwriters have pointed out that the law on the subject is vague and uncertain. ... There have, moreover, been few cases in which the doctrine of duress has been directly in issue either with regard to the offences in relation to which it may provide a defence or as to the kind of threatening conduct which may constitute duress. There has, for all that, been considerable discussion and debate. In such an atmosphere it is easy for the discussion to focus on what the law ought to be rather than on what it is, and that is an unsatisfactory basis for the exercise of criminal jurisdiction. But, in my opinion, this vagueness ought not to encourage innovation which makes a departure from the received wisdom even if that wisdom is imperfect. This is particularly true if the innovation is retrospective in effect, to the prejudice of an accused person.

Hale's philosophical explanation of withholding the duress defence (*Pleas of the Crown*, vol. 1, p. 51) is not a good starting-point for putting attempted murder in the category of murder and treason or for saying that it is in that category already. The intention of the offender is evil, but when the attempt has failed the sentence is variable, although someone who kills through compassion or who kills intending only to injure receives a fixed sentence (until recently a capital sentence). That a man who did not mean to kill can be found guilty of murder and will receive a mandatory life sentence is arguably a blot on our legal system but that is the law and this fact sets murder apart. ...

To withhold in respect of *every* crime the defence of duress, leaving it to the court (or, in relation to fixed penalty crimes, the executive) to take mitigating circumstances into account, seems logical. But to withhold that defence only from a selected list of serious crimes (some of which incur variable penalties) is questionable from a sentencing point of view, as indeed the sentence in the present case shows. The defence is withheld on the ground that the crime is so odious that it must not be palliated; and yet, if circumstances are allowed to mitigate the punishment, the principle on which the defence of duress is withheld has been defeated.

The fact that the sentence for attempted murder is at large is, with respect to those who think otherwise, no justification for withholding the defence of duress. Quite the reverse, because it is the theoretical inexcusability of murder and treason which causes those crimes (the fixed penalty for which can be mitigated only by the executive) to be deprived of the duress defence. ...

Having referred in the Court of Appeal's judgment [1991] 1 Q.B. 660 to the wise observations of Lord Griffiths in *R. v. Howe* [1987] A.C. 417 on the undesirability of making available the defence of duress to any person who has deliberately killed, Lord Lane C.J. said [1991] 1 Q.B. 660, 667: "It seems to us that if those considerations are well founded, the fact that the attempt failed to kill *should* not make any difference." (Emphasis supplied.) But in my submission everything except the turpitude of attempted murder points away from saying that that offence is already at common law outside the ambit of the duress defence. And I further suggest that actual wickedness is not shown to be a dominant factor in the calculation compared with the result.

As I have said, your Lordships are concerned to say what the law is and not what it ought to be. So far from clearing the way for judges to declare that attempted murder is an excepted crime, the uncertainty and vagueness surrounding duress ought to induce caution before deciding to reject the received wisdom on the subject. What we can be clear about is that the common law regards duress as *generally available* but not available in cases of murder and treason, and the statutory codes treat duress as generally available except as expressly mentioned. Your Lordships will have noted what was said by members of this House when comparing the functions of Parliament and the judges in *R.* v. *Howe*, and I would invite your Lordships' attention to two further statements on the subject. In *Abbot* v. *The Queen* [1977] A.C. 755. Lord Salmon said, at p. 767:

> "Judges have no power to create new criminal offences; nor in their Lordships' opinion, for the reasons already stated, have they the power to invent a new defence to murder which is entirely contrary to fundamental legal doctrine accepted for hundreds of years without question. If a policy change of such a fundamental nature were to be made it could, in their Lordships view, be made only by Parliament. Whilst their Lordships strongly uphold the right and indeed the duty of the judges to adapt and develop the principles of the common law in an orderly fashion they are equally opposed to any usurpation by the courts of the functions of Parliament."

And in *R.* v. *Howe* [1987] A.C. 417 Lord Mackay, speaking of what I may perhaps call judicial legislation, said, at pp. 449–450:

> "In approaching this matter, I look for guidance to Lord Reid's approach to the question of this House making a change in the prevailing view of the law in *Myers* v. *Director of Public Prosecutions* [1965] A.C. 1001, 1021–1022, where he said: 'I have never taken a narrow view of the functions of this House as an appellate tribunal. The common law must be developed to meet changing economic conditions and habits of thought, and I would not be deterred by expressions of opinion in this House in old cases. But there are limits to what we can or should do. If we are to extend the law it must be by the development and application of fundamental principles. We cannot introduce arbitrary conditions or limitations: that must be left to legislation. And if we do in effect change the law, we ought in my opinion only to do that in cases where our decision will produce some finality or certainty.' "

Lord Reid was speaking in a different context (about hearsay evidence), but I suggest that the principles espoused in both of the passages which I have cited are appropriate to the present case. It could be said that what your Lordships have recently done with regard to marital rape (*R.* v. *R.* [1991] 3 W.L.R. 767) was in a modern context to "adapt and develop the principles of the common law," in the words of Lord Salmon. But, with regard to attempted murder and duress, it does not seem to me that any question of adaptation or development can arise. In these circumstances I respectfully cannot subscribe to the view that it would not be harmful to declare that attempted murder is an excepted crime and thereby possibly deprive the appellant of a defence which was available at the time of his offence. By parity of reasoning I do not think it is satisfactory to say, "Let us declare this crime to be excepted, and Parliament can undo our work if it sees fit" if there is a substantial risk (and for my part I think it is much more) that we shall be anticipating Parliament instead of allowing Parliament to make a policy decision after reasoned debate.

My Lords, what I have just said reminds me that this question was presented by the Crown to your Lordships as a question of policy and that *R.* v. *Howe* [1987] A.C. 417 was cited as an example of a policy decision. But in fact no example could be more misleading. The appellants in that case pressed your Lordships to accept the lead of the minority in *Abbott* v. *The Queen* [1977] A.C. 755 and to *make* a policy decision by coming into line with what is now acknowledged to be the erroneous decision of this House in *R.* v. *Lynch* [1975] A.C. 653 and your Lordships refused to do so *both* because the common law said that duress was not available in relation to murder *and* because the policy of the law was served by adhering to that position. What Lord Lane C.J. said in the Court of Appeal, at p. 664F, is the complete answer to an appeal to policy: if the common law recognised that murder and treason were the only excepted crimes, then we are bound to accept that as the law, whether it seems a desirable conclusion or not.

If the common law has had a policy towards duress heretofore, it seems to have been to go by the result and not primarily by the intent and, if a change of policy is needed with regard to criminal liability, it must be made prospectively by Parliament and not retrospectively by a court.

I am not influenced in favour of the appellant by the supposed illogicality of distinguishing between attempted murder on the one hand and conspiracy and incitement to murder on the other and I agree on this point with the view of Lord Lane C.J.: short of murder itself, attempted murder is a special crime. But I am not swayed in favour of the Crown by the various examples of the anomalies which are said to result from holding that the duress defence applies to attempted murder. As Lord Lane C.J. said, at p. 668B, it would be possible to suggest anomalies wherever the line is drawn. The real logic would be to grant or withhold the duress defence universally.

Attempted murder, however heinous we consider it, was a misdemeanour. Until 1861 someone who shot and missed could suffer no more than two years' imprisonment and I submit that, when attempted murder became a felony, that crime, like many other serious felonies, continued to have available the defence of duress.

My Lords, having considered all the arguments on either side, I am of the opinion that your Lordships *are* constrained by a common law rule (though not by judicial authority) from holding that the defence of duress does not apply to attempted murder. Accordingly, I would allow the appeal, quash the conviction and set aside the probation order but, in the special circumstances of this case, I would not propose that a new trial be ordered.

Appeal dismissed

Questions

1. Was the decision of the majority one of principle or policy?
2. J. Raz in "The rule of law and its virtue" (1977) 93 *L.Q.R.* 195, 198–199 states:

"*All laws should be prospective, open and clear.* One cannot be guided by a retroactive law. It does not exist at the time of action ... The law must be open and adequately publicised. If it is to guide people they must be able to find out what it is. For the same reason its meaning must be clear. An ambiguous, vague, obscure or imprecise law is likely to mislead or confuse at least some of those who desire to be guided by it."

Were these principles observed by the majority in *Gotts*? If someone seeking to know the law in advance of action inquired whether duress is a defence to the offences of wounding with intent contrary to section 18 of the Offences Against the Person Act 1861, or incitement to kill or conspiracy to murder, would it be possible to provide a clear answer?

3. Lord Keith of Kinkel stated at pp. 285–286:

"The principal argument against allowing the defence of duress to a charge of attempted murder appears to be what is said to be the illogicality of denying the defence to one who has killed while intending only to wound with intent to inflict grievous bodily harm, while admitting it in the case of one who has intended to kill but chanced to fail to do so. considering that the intent is more evil in the latter case than in the former, so it is claimed, the person who has intended to kill but failed should not be treated more leniently. But I find it difficult to accept that a person acting under duress had a truly evil intent. He does not actually desire the death of the victim. In the case of a man who is compelled by threats against his wife and children to drive a vehicle loaded with explosives into a checkpoint, the object being to kill those manning it, but that object having fortunately failed, the driver is likely to be as relieved at the outcome as anyone else. It would be hard to condemn him as having had an evil intent. The logical solution may be to withhold the defence in the case of all crimes, leaving the circumstances of the duress to be taken into account in mitigation. But that solution is not open to the court in the present state of the law. It could only be brought about by Parliament."

Is it likely that the argument in future may move to the meaning of intent with an accused charged with attempted murder who seeks to plead duress relying on authorities such as *Steane* [1947] K.B. 997 (*ante*, p. 75) and *Gillick* v. *West Norfolk and Wisbech Area Health Authority* [1986] A.C. 112 (*post*, p. 316)? See the extract from his commentary on *Howe* by J.C. Smith which follows.

J. C. Smith, Commentary [1987] Crim.L.R. 483–484

" . . . *Duress and intent* Lord Hailsham agreed with the opinions of Lords Kilbrandon and Edmund-Davies in *Lynch* that duress does not negative intention. Where the defence of duress is allowed, this is notwithstanding the fact that the defendant intended to commit the crime. It is submitted that this is right—but it is surely inconsistent with *Steane* [1947] K.B. 997, recently accepted as rightly decided by the House in *Moloney* [1985] A.C. 905. Steane, of course, knew that he was doing an act of assistance to the enemy war effort but was held not to intend to assist the enemy because his purpose was to avert the threat of the concentration camp to himself and his family. If that negatived intention, so surely does a purpose of saving one's own life. The present case suggests that *Steane* would have been more properly acquitted on the ground that he acted with intent to assist the enemy under duress. Unfortunately, however, it is likely to continue to bedevil discussion of the meaning of intention.

There is a similar problem with *Gillick's* case [1986] A.C. 112 and the matter of the *mens rea* of an aider and abettor of crime. The reason why a doctor who gives contraceptive advice to a girl under the age of 16 is not guilty of aiding and abetting the commission of an offence under section 6 of the Sexual Offences Act 1956 is nowhere clearly spelt out in the speeches of the majority, but one view for which there is considerable support is that he lacks the necessary intent. But if it is said that the hypothetical doctor, doing an act which he knows will promote, encourage or facilitate the commission of an offence, is not guilty because his real intention is to protect the girl, how can it be said that a person intends to aid and abet murder when his real object is to save himself or others from death? If that object does not negative intention to aid and abet, surely, *a fortiori*, the object of protecting the girl cannot do so."

3. NECESSITY

i. A defence of necessity?

Note

Criminal lawyers have for a considerable time debated the question whether a general defence of necessity exists in English law. Duress by threats relates to the situation where a person commits an offence to avoid a greater evil of death or serious injury to himself or another threatened by a third party. The defence operates to excuse him from criminal liability. Necessity relates to the situation where a person commits an offence to avoid a greater evil to himself or another which would ensue from the circumstances in which he or that other are placed. It was thought that if the defence of necessity existed it operated as a justification rendering the accused's conduct lawful. The dicta in the cases both as to the existence of the defence and its operation as either an excuse or justification are scant and contradictory.

Early writers on English law such as Bracton, Coke and Hale all quoted maxims which conceded that necessity might justify conduct which would otherwise be unlawful. In *Moore* v. *Hussey* (1609) Hob 96, Hobart J. stated "All laws admit certain cases of just excuse, when they are offended in the letter, and where the offender is under necessity, either of compulsion or inconvenience." The examples of necessity these writers supplied were pulling down a house to prevent a fire spreading, a prisoner escaping from a burning jail although statute made prison-breach a felony, jettisoning cargo to save a vessel in a storm (see *Mouse's Cases*) (1620) 12 Co. Rep. 63). *Obiter dicta* in twentieth century cases have been inconclusive. In *Buckoke* v. *G.L.C.* [1971] Ch. 655, 668 Lord Denning stated:

"During the argument I raised the question: Might not the driver of a fire engine be able to raise the defence of necessity? I put this illustration: A driver of a fire engine with ladders approaches the traffic lights. He sees 200 yards down the road a blazing house with a man at an upstairs window in extreme peril. The road is clear in all directions. At that moment the lights turn red. Is the driver to wait for 60 seconds, or more, for the lights to turn green? If the driver waits for that time, the man's life will be lost. I suggested to both counsel that the driver might be excused in crossing the lights to save the man. He might have the defence of necessity. Both counsel denied it. They would not allow him any defence in law. The circumstances went to mitigation, they said, and did not take away his guilt. If counsel are correct—and I accept that they are—nevertheless such a man should not be prosecuted. He should be congratulated."

[The particular question in this case is of academic interest only since drivers of fire engines, police cars and ambulances are now allowed in emergencies to regard red traffic lights as warnings to give way (Traffic Signs Regulations and General Directions, S.I. 1975 No. 1536 reg. 34(1)(b)). They are also permitted to exceed speed limits (Road Traffic Regulation Act 1967, s.79).]

Similarly in *London Borough of Southwark* v. *Williams* [1971] 2 All E.R. 175, 179 Lord Denning stated:

"[I]f hunger were once allowed to be an excuse for stealing, it would open a way through which all kinds of disorder and lawlessness would pass. So here. If homelessness were once admitted as a defence to trespass, no one's house could be safe. Necessity would open a door which no man could shut. It would not only be those in extreme need who would enter. There would be others who would imagine that they were in need, or would invent a need, so as to gain entry. Each man would say his need was greater than the next man's. The plea would be an excuse for all sorts of wrongdoing. So the courts must, for the sake of law and order, take a firm stand. They must refuse to admit the pleas of necessity to the hungry and the homeless; and trust that their distress will be relieved by the charitable and the good."

Edmund Davies L.J. considered that there was a defence of necessity but it would not avail the squatters in the instant case as the defence was dependent on there being "an urgent situation of imminent peril."

In several traffic cases there are *obiter dicta* to the effect that there is a defence of necessity. In *Johnson* v. *Phillips* [1976] 1 W.L.R. 65, a motorist was instructed by a police officer to reverse the wrong way down a narrow one-way street in order to allow ambulances access to injured persons further up the street. On his refusal he was charged with wilful obstruction of a constable in the execution of his duty. Wien J., p. 69:

"The precise question that has to be answered in the instant case may be put thus: has a constable in purported exercise of his power to control traffic on a public road the right under common law to disobey a traffic regulation such as going the wrong way along a one-way street? If he himself has that right then it follows that he can oblige others to comply with his instructions to disobey such a regulation. If, for example, a bomb had been planted in The Windsor public house and the exit from Cannon Street had in some way been blocked, could he lawfully reverse a police vehicle and oblige any other motorist then present in the road to reverse his own vehicle? The answer is yes, provided that in the execution of his duty he was acting to protect life or property: see *Hoffman* v. *Thomas* [1974] 1 W.L.R. 374, 379. ... In the judgment of this court a constable would be entitled, and indeed under a duty, to give such instruction if it were reasonably necessary for the protection of life or property."

In *Woods* v. *Richards* [1977] R.T.R. 201, Eveleigh J. stated—

"In so far as the defence of necessity is relied on ... [t]here is no evidence at all in this case of the nature of the emergency to which the defendant [a police officer] was being summoned. As the defence of necessity to the extent that it exists must depend on the degree of emergency or the alternative danger to be averted, it is quite impossible in the present case to express the view that the defence was open to the defendant."

This view suggests that had there been evidence of the nature of the emergency the defence could have been considered by weighing that emergency against the manner in which the defendant drove his car which had given rise to the charge of careless driving. See also *R.* v. *O'Toole* (1971) Cr.App.R. 206.

More recently cases involving driving offences have given rise to the recognition of the defence of duress of circumstances (see *post*, pp. 319–320).

In several other cases the decisions appear to have been based on necessity although that term was not used. In *R.* v. *Bourne, post*, p. 570, a surgeon in a London hospital performed an abortion on a 14-year-old rape victim. He was charged with *unlawfully* using an instrument with intent to procure a miscarriage, contrary to section 58 of the Offences Against the Person Act 1861, Macnaghten J., in directing the jury, defined the word "unlawfully" to mean an act "not done in good faith for the purpose only of preserving the life of the mother." As necessity is a defence of justification, and justification renders lawful an act which would otherwise be unlawful, was Macnaghten J. impliedly directing the jury on necessity? (See Lord Edmund-Davies in *Southwark London Borough Council* v. *Williams* [1971] Ch. 734, at 746.)

In *Gillick* v. *West Norfolk A.H.A.* [1986] A.C. 112, the House of Lords stated that where a doctor prescribed contraceptives for a girl under 16, he would not be guilty of aiding, abetting, counselling or procuring the offence of unlawful sexual intercourse committed by her with a man provided certain circumstances pertained. These were detailed by Lord Scarman as follows—

"Clearly a doctor who gives a girl contraceptive advice or treatment not because in his clinical judgment the treatment is medically indicated for the maintenance or restoration of her health but with the intention of facilitating her having unlawful sexual intercourse may well be guilty of a criminal offence. It would depend, as my noble and learned friend, Lord Fraser of Tullybelton, observes, upon the doctor's intention—a conclusion hardly to be wondered at in the field of the criminal law. ... He may prescribe only if she has the capacity to consent or if exceptional circumstances exist which justify him in exercising his clinical judgment without parental consent. The adjective 'clinical' emphasises that it must be a medical judgment based upon what he honestly believes to be necessary for the physical, mental, and emotional health of his patient. The bona fide exercise by a doctor of his clinical judgment must be a complete negation of the guilty mind which is an essential ingredient of the criminal offence of aiding and abetting the commission of unlawful sexual intercourse."

Question

If a doctor knows that contraceptives will encourage an underage girl to engage in sexual intercourse but he prescribes them to protect her physically, emotionally and mentally from the trauma of unwanted pregnancy or even abortion, how can his motive in prescribing the contraceptives negate his guilty mind? Is this not in reality a defence of necessity providing a justification for the doctor's act which otherwise would be criminal?

In the case which follows necessity was given recognition by the House of Lords.

In Re F. (Mental Patient: Sterilisation)
[1990] 2 A.C. 1
House of Lords

(For the facts of this case see *post*, p. 587.)

LORD GOFF OF CHIEVELEY: That there exists in the common law a principle of necessity which may justify action which would otherwise be unlawful is not in doubt. But historically the principle has been seen to be restricted to two groups of cases, which have been called cases of public necessity and cases of private necessity. The former occurred in the Great Fire of London in 1666. The latter cases occurred when a man interfered with another man's property in the public interest—for example (in the days before we could dial 999 for the fire brigade) the destruction of another man's house to prevent the spread of a catastrophic fire, as indeed occurred when a man interfered with another's property to save his own person or property from imminent danger—for example, when he entered upon his neighbour's land without his consent, in order to prevent the spread of fire onto his own land.

There is, however, a third group of cases, which is also properly described as founded upon the principle of necessity and which is more pertinent to the resolution of the problem in the present case. These cases are concerned with action taken as a matter of necessity to assist another person without his consent. To give a simple example, a man who seizes another and forcibly drags him from the path of an oncoming vehicle, thereby saving him from injury or even death, commits no wrong. But there are many emanations of this principle, to be found scattered through the books. These are concerned not only with the preservation of the life or health of the assisted person, but also with the preservation of his property (sometimes an animal, sometimes an ordinary chattel) and even with certain conduct on his behalf in the administration of his affairs. Where there is a pre-existing relationship between the parties, the intervenor is usually said to act as an agent of necessity on behalf of the principal in whose interests he acts, and his action can often, with not too much artificiality, be referred to the pre-existing relationship between them. Whether the intervenor may be entitled either to reimbursement or to remuneration raises separate questions which are not relevant in the present case.

We are concerned here with action taken to preserve the life, health or well-being of another who is unable to consent to it. Such action is sometimes said to be justified as arising from an emergency; in *Prosser and Keeton, Handbook on Torts*, 5th ed. (1984), p. 117, the action is said to be privileged by the emergency. Doubtless, in the case of a person of sound mind, there will ordinarily have to be an emergency before such action taken without consent can be lawful; for otherwise there would be an opportunity to communicate with the assisted person and to seek his consent. But this is not always so; and indeed the historical origins of the principle of necessity do not point to emergency as such as providing the criterion of lawful intervention without consent. The old Roman doctrine of negotiorum gestio presupposed not so much an emergency as a prolonged absence of the dominus from home as justifying intervention by the gestor to administer his affairs. The most ancient group of cases in the common law, concerned with action taken by the master of a ship in distant parts in the interests of the shipowner, likewise found its origin in the difficulty of communication with the owner over a prolonged period of time—a difficulty overcome today by modern means of communication. In those cases, it was said that there had to be an emergency before the master could act as agent of necessity; though the emergency could well be of some duration. But when a person is rendered incapable of communication either permanently or over a considerable period of time (through illness or accident or mental disorder), it would be an unusual use of language to describe the case as one of "permanent emergency"—if indeed such a state of affairs can properly be said to exist. In truth, the relevance of an emergency is that it may give rise to a necessity to act in the interests of the assisted person, without first obtaining his consent. Emergency is however not the criterion or even a pre-requisite; it is simply a frequent origin of the necessity which impels intervention. The principle is one of necessity, not of emergency.

We can derive some guidance as to the nature of the principle of necessity from the cases on agency of necessity in mercantile law. When reading those cases, however, we have to bear in mind that it was there considered that (since there was a pre-existing relationship between the parties) there was a duty on the part of the agent to act on his principal's behalf in an emergency. From these cases it appears that the principle of necessity connotes that circumstances have arisen in which there is a necessity for the agent to act on his principal's behalf at a time when it is in practice not possible for him to obtain his principal's instructions so to do. In such cases, it has been said that the agent must act bona fide in the interests of his principal: see *Prager* v. *Blatspiel Stamp & Heacock Ltd.* [1924] 1 K.B. 566, 572 *per* McCardie J. A broader statement of the principle is to be found in the advice of the Privy Council delivered by Sir Montague Smith in *Australasian Steam Navigation Co.* v. *Morse* (1872) L.R. 4 P.C. 222, 230, in which he said.

> "when by the force of circumstances a man has the duty cast upon him of taking some action for another, and under that obligation, adopts the course which, to the judgment of a wise and prudent man, is apparently the best for the interest of the persons for whom he acts in a given emergency, it may properly be said of the course so taken, that it was, in a mercantile sense, necessary to take it."

In a sense, these statements overlap. But from them can be derived the basic requirements, applicable in these cases of necessity, that, to fall within the principle, not only (1) must there be a necessity to act when it is not practicable to communicate with the assisted person, but also (2) the action taken must be such as a reasonable person would in all the circumstances take, acting in the best interests of the assisted person.

(For further extracts from Lord Goff's speech see *post*, pp. 589–595.)

Questions

1. Did Lord Goff recognise necessity as an excuse or justification?
2. The three categories of situation which give rise to a defence of necessity are quite narrow; would the doctors in *Bourne* or *Gillick* be able to bring themselves within any of these categories if charged with a criminal offence?

ii. Duress of circumstances

Note

The categories of situation giving rise to a defence of necessity are very narrow. In recent years, however, the defence of duress has been widened to cover an imminent threat of death or serious injury arising from the circumstances in which the accused finds himself. The cases have all involved driving offences where the accused has driven recklessly (see *Willer* (1986) 83 Cr.App.R. 225; *Conway* [1988] 3 All E.R. 1025) or has driven whilst disqualified from driving (see *Martin* [1989] 1 All E.R. 652) or has driven with excess alcohol (see *D.P.P.* v. *Bell* [1992] Crim.L.R. 176) in order to avoid a threat of death or serious injury to himself or a third party. In cases of duress by threats the party issuing the threats dictates the criminal offence the accused must commit to avoid the threatened harm; in the cases of duress of circumstances which have arisen the accused has chosen to commit a particular crime to avoid the threatened harm but the defence does not appear to be limited to such situations (see *Martin, post*, p. 320). In *Conway* Woolf L.J. explained the rationale of the defence in the following terms (at p. 1029):

> "As the learned editors point out in Smith and Hogan *Criminal Law* (6th edn. 1988) p 225, to admit a defence of 'duress of circumstances' is a logical consequence of the existence of the defence of duress as that term is ordinarily understood, ie 'do this or else'. This approach does no more than recognise that duress is an example of necessity. Whether 'duress of circumstances' is called 'duress' or 'necessity' does not matter. What is important is that, whatever it is called, it is subject to the same limitations as the 'do this or else' species of duress. As Lord Hailsham LC said in his speech in R. v. *Howe* [1987] 1 All ER 771 at 777, [1987] AC 417 at 429:
> 'There is, of course, an obvious distinction between duress and necessity as potential defences: duress arises from the wrongful threats or violence of another human being and necessity arises from any other objective dangers threatening the accused. This, however, is, in my view a distinction without a relevant difference, since on this view

duress is only that species of the genus of necessity which is caused by wrongful threats. I cannot see that there is any way in which a person of ordinary fortitude can be excused from the one type of pressure on his will rather than the other."

In *Martin* Simon Brown J. sought to summarise the principles relating to duress of circumstances (at pp. 653–654):

"The principles may be summarised thus: first, English law does, in extreme circumstances, recognise a defence of necessity. Most commonly this defence arises as duress, that is pressure on the accused's will from the wrongful threats or violence of another. Equally however it can arise from other objective dangers threatening the accused or others. Arising thus it is conveniently called 'duress of circumstances'.

Second, the defence is available only if, from an objective standpoint, the accused can be said to be acting reasonably and proportionately in order to avoid a threat of death or serious injury.

Third, assuming the defence to be open to the accused on his account of the facts, the issue should be left to the jury, who should be directed to determine these two questions: first, was the accused, or may he have been, impelled to act as he did because as a result of what he reasonably believed to be the situation he had good cause to fear that otherwise death or serious physical injury would result; second, if so, would a sober person of reasonable firmness, sharing the characteristics of the accused, have responded to that situation by acting as the accused acted? If the answer to both those questions was Yes, then the jury would acquit; the defence of necessity would have been established.

That the defence is available in cases of reckless driving is established by *R.* v. *Conway* itself and indeed by an earlier decision of the court in *R.* v. *Willer* (1986) 83 Cr App R 225. *R.* v. *Conway* is authority also for the proposition that the scope of the defence is no wider for reckless driving than for other serious offences. As was pointed out in the judgment, 'reckless driving can kill' (see [1988] 3 All ER 1025 at 1029, [1988] 3 WLR 1238 at 1244).

We see no material distinction between offences of reckless driving and driving whilst disqualified so far as the application and scope of this defence is concerned. Equally we can see no distinction in principle between various threats of death; it matters not whether the risk of death is by murder or by suicide or indeed by accident. One can illustrate the latter by considering a disqualified driver being driven by his wife, she suffering a heart attack in remote countryside and he needing instantly to get her to hospital."

Questions

1. When Lord Hailsham stated that "duress is only that species of genus of necessity which is caused by wrongful threats" was he correct and is this statement reconcilable with Lord Goff's speech in *Re F.*, *i.e.* can a genus which is a justification give birth to a species which is an excuse?

2. Will the existence of the defence of duress of circumstances assist or obstruct the future development of a general defence of necessity based on the concept of balancing of harms? (*Cf.* American Model Penal Code, s.3.02, *post*, p. 324.)

3. D, driving his car approaches a traffic light which changes to red. Further along the road he sees a child fall into a river. D drives on both ignoring the traffic light and breaking the speed limit to effect a rescue of the child. On being tried for both driving offences could D plead in his defence either necessity or duress of circumstances (*cf.* Lord Denning in *Buckoke* and *Conway* and *Martin*)?

iii. Necessity, duress of circumstances and homicide

Duress by threats is no defence to a charge of murder (see *Howe*, *ante*, p. 296) and the same applies to duress of circumstances (see Woolf L.J. in *Conway*, *ante*, p. 319). Is there a residual defence of necessity to a charge of homicide?

R. v. Dudley and Stephens
(1884) 14 Q.B.D. 273
Queen's Bench Division

D and S and a boy were cast away from a ship on the high seas and drifted for 20 days in an open boat. They had hardly any food or water during that time, and fearing they would all die soon unless they obtained some sustenance D and S killed the boy, who was likely to die first anyway, and ate his flesh. Four days later they were rescued, and were subsequently indicted for the boy's murder. The jury found the facts of the case in a special verdict and the case was adjourned for argument before five judges.

LORD COLERIDGE C.J.: ... Now it is admitted that the deliberate killing of this unoffending and unresisting boy was clearly murder, unless the killing can be justified by some well-recognised excuse admitted by the law. It is further admitted that there was in this case no such excuse, unless the killing was justified by what has been called "necessity." But the temptation to the act which existed here was not what the law has ever called necessity. Nor is this to be regretted. Though law and morality are not the same, and many things may be immoral which are not necessarily illegal, yet the absolute divorce of law from morality would be of fatal consequence; and such divorce would follow if the temptation to murder in this case were to be held by law an absolute defence of it. It is not so. To preserve one's life is generally speaking a duty, but it may be the plainest and the highest duty to sacrifice it. War is full of instances in which it is a man's duty not to live, but to die. The duty, in case of shipwreck, of a captain to his crew, of the crew to the passengers, of soldiers to women and children, as in the noble case of the *Birkenhead*; these duties impose on man the moral necessity, not of the preservation, but of the sacrifice of their lives for others, from which in no country, least of all, it is to be hoped, in England, will men shrink, as indeed, they have not shrunk. It is not correct, therefore, to say that there is any absolute or unqualified necessity to preserve one's life. "*Necesse est ut eam, non ut vivam,*" is a saying of a Roman officer quoted by Lord Bacon himself with high eulogy in the very chapter on necessity to which so much reference has been made. It would be a very easy and cheap display of common-place learning to quote from Greek and Latin authors, from Horace, from Juvenal, from Cicero, from Euripides, passage after passage, in which the duty of dying for others has been laid down in glowing and emphatic language as resulting from the principles of heathen ethics; it is enough in a Christian country to remind ourselves of the Great Example whom we profess to follow. It is not needful to point out the lawful danger of admitting the principle which has been contended for. Who is to be the judge of this sort of necessity? By what measure is the comparative value of lives to be measured? Is it to be strength or intellect, or what? It is plain that the principle leaves to him who is to profit by it to determine the necessity which will justify him in deliberately taking another's life to save his own. In this case the weakest, the youngest, the most unresisting, was chosen. Was it more necessary to kill him than one of the grown men? The answer must be "No." ...

It must not be supposed that in refusing to admit temptation to be an excuse for crime it is forgotten how terrible the temptation was; how awful the suffering; how hard in such trials to keep the judgment straight and the conduct pure. We are often compelled to set up standards we cannot reach ourselves, and to lay down rules which we could not ourselves satisfy. But a man has no right to declare temptation to be an excuse, though he might himself have yielded to it, nor allow compassion for the criminal to change or weaken in any manner the legal definition of the crime. It is therefore our duty to declare that the prisoners' act in this case was wilful murder, that the facts as stated in the verdict are no legal justification of the homicide; and to say that in our unanimous opinion the prisoners are upon this special verdict guilty of murder.

Sentence of death
Commuted later to six months' imprisonment

Question

Consider and compare the following examples often found in textbooks:

A shipwrecked sailor, clinging to a plank which will only support the weight of one man, prevents another from grasping the plank, so that that other dies by drowning.

The man on the plank is pushed off by the swimmer, who takes his place, leaving him to drown.

The lower of two roped rock-climbers slips and falls. The upper is not strong enough to hold him and to save himself from a certain fall, cuts the lower man free, so that he falls to his death.

X, Y and Z are stranded at the foot of a cliff with the tide coming in. A rope ladder is lowered to them which X starts to ascend but fearing heights he stops and clings to it petrified refusing to move up or down. Y, fearing that he and Z will drown, tells Z, who is immediately below X on the ladder, to pull X off. Z does so and X falls to the rocks below where he dies from drowning while Y and Z climb to safety.

Note

In *U.S.* v. *Holmes* (1842) 25 Fed.Cas. 360, the accused was convicted of the manslaughter of 16 passengers whom he had thrown out of an overcrowded lifeboat. The judge would it seems have allowed a defence of necessity if the choice had been made by the drawing of lots.

The extracts below illustrate the moral and philosophical challenge which necessity as a defence to homicide presents.

Cross "Murder under Duress" (1978) 28 U.T.L.J. 369, at 377

"Speaking of the hypothetical case of the two shipwrecked mariners struggling for a plank only large enough for one, [Kant] said: 'A penal law applying to such a situation could never have the effect intended, for the threat of an evil that is still uncertain (being condemned to death by a judge) cannot outweigh the fear of an evil that is certain (being drowned). Hence we must judge that, although an act of self-preservation through violence is not inculpable, it is still unpunishable.' ...

[I]n the context, I find myself wholly unable to distinguish this defence from that of duress, and I feel bound to say that the English Law Commission has achieved the apotheosis of absurdity by recommending that our proposed criminal code should provide for a defence of duress while excluding any general defence of necessity. Surely Lord Simon of Glaisdale was speaking in unanswerable terms when he said in the course of his dissenting speech in *Lynch* (*ante*, p. 292) 'It would be a travesty of justice and an invitation to anarchy to declare that an innocent life may be taken with impunity if the threat to one's own life is from a terrorist but not when from a natural disaster like ship- or plane-wreck.' "

Kenny, Freewill and Responsibility (1978, Routledge & Kegan Paul), pp. 36–38

"In everyday language people are often said to be compelled to do things when no actual force is used but the actions are performed to avert the threat of violent action or imminent disaster. These are cases where it will be natural for the agent to say that he 'had no choice' ... but in fact the action is a voluntary one, arising out of a choice between evils. When the choice ... is posed as a result of the wrongful threats of another, lawyers speak of 'duress'; when it arises through the operation of natural causes, they prefer to speak of 'necessity.' ... To me the decision [in *Dudley & Stephens*] seems ethically sound. ... The principle that one should never intentionally take innocent life would be contested by supporters of euthanasia. ... The decision in *Dudley and Stephens* can be justified by the narrower principle that one should not take innocent life in order to save one's own life. This principle seems to me, as it did to Lord Coleridge in 1884, to be correct: it seems likely to reduce the overall number of innocent deaths. Certainly I would rather be in an open boat with companions who accepted the principle than in company with lawyers who accepted necessity as a defence to murder."

Williams, C.L.G.P., §237

" ... Where it is merely a case of life for life, the doctrine of necessity must generally be silent, because the two lives must be accounted equal in the eye of the law and there is nothing to choose between them. Necessity cannot justify in such circumstances; but they may go so strongly in alleviation that the accused is discharged without punishment (where this is possible) or pardoned. The technical conviction merely records that in the eye of the law the act was wrongful. The necessary and reasonable consequence of this view is that resistance to the act on the part of the victim is lawful.

It seems that the position is different where the killing results in a net saving of life. Here it seems that the killing should be regarded as not merely excusing from punishment but as legally justifying. We need a general rule, and one allowing necessity as a defence to homicide where the minority are killed to preserve the majority is on the whole more satisfactory than the opposite.

A strong instance of this kind of justification is the action of a ship's captain in a wreck. He can determine who are to enter the first lifeboat; he can forbid overcrowding; and it makes no difference that the passengers who are not allowed to enter the lifeboat will inevitably perish with the ship. The captain, in choosing who are to live, is not guilty of killing those who remain. He would not be so guilty even though he kept some of the passengers back from the boat at revolver-point. ... "

A. L. I., Model Penal Code, section 3.02

"Conduct which the actor believes necessary to avoid a harm or evil to himself or another is justifiable provided that (1) the harm or evil sought to be avoided by such conduct is greater than that sought to be prevented by the law defining the offence charged. ..."

See also Gross, *A Theory of Criminal Justice* (Oxford, 1979), pp. 26, 27.

iv. A common law defence of necessity?

Note

The Supreme Court of Canada has recognised a common law defence of necessity: *Morgantaler* v. *The Queen* (1975) 53 D.L.R. (3d) 161. In *Perka et al.* v. *The Queen, infra,* the Supreme Court developed the defence on the basis of excuse.

Perka et al. v. The Queen
(1984) 13 D.L.R. (4th) 1
Supreme Court of Canada

The accused were charged with importing and possessing narcotics for the purpose of trafficking as a result of their arrest in Canadian waters in possession of a large quantity of marijuana. They raised the defence of necessity, alleging the cargo was destined for Alaska but that they were forced to make for the Canadian shore in order to make temporary repairs because of problems with the vessel which were aggravated by deteriorating weather. The ship ran aground and the captain, fearing that the vessel was going to capsize, ordered the crew to off-load the cargo. The jury acquitted. An appeal by the Crown to the British Columbian Court of Appeal was allowed and a new trial ordered on the ground that the trial judge had erred in refusing to permit the Crown to adduce certain rebuttal evidence concerning the defence of necessity. On appeal by the accused to the Supreme Court of Canada, the Crown also contended that the trial judge had erred in leaving the defence of necessity to the jury.

DICKSON J.:

(b) *The Conceptual Foundation of the Defence*

In *Morgentaler* v. *The Queen* (1975) 53 D.L.R. (3d) 16, I characterised necessity as an "ill-defined and elusive concept." Despite the apparently growing consensus as to the existence of a defence of necessity that statement is equally true today.

This is no doubt in part because, though apparently laying down a single rule as to criminal liability, the "defence" of necessity in fact is capable of embracing two different and distinct notions. As Mr. Justice Macdonald observed succinctly but accurately in *R.* v. *Salvador et al.* (1981) 59 C.C.C. (2d) 521, at p. 542: "Generally speaking, the defence of necessity covers all cases where non-compliance with law is excused by an emergency or justified by the pursuit of some greater good."

Working Paper 29 of the Law Reform Commission of Canada, *Criminal Law The General Part: Liability and Defences* (1982), p. 93, makes this same point in somewhat more detail:

> "The rationale of necessity, however, is clear. Essentially it involves two factors. One is the avoidance of greater harm or the pursuit of some greater good, the other is the difficulty of compliance with law in emergencies. From these two factors emerge two different but related principles. The first is a utilitarian principle to the effect that, within certain limits, it is justifiable in an emergency to break the letter of the law if breaking the law will avoid a greater harm than obeying it. The second is a humanitarian principle to the effect that, again within limits, it is excusable in an emergency to break the law if compliance would impose an intolerable burden on the accused."

Despite any superficial similarities, these two principles are in fact quite distinct and many of the confusions and the difficulties in the cases (and, with respect, in academic discussions) arise from a failure to distinguish between them.

Criminal theory recognises a distinction between "justifications" and "excuses." A "justification" challenges the wrongfulness of an action which technically constitutes a crime. The police officer who shoots the hostage-taker, the innocent object of an assault who uses force to defend himself against his assailant, the good Samaritan who commandeers a car and breaks the speed laws to rush an accident victim to the hospital, these are all actors whose actions we consider *rightful*, not wrongful. For such actions people are often praised, as motivated by some great or noble object. The concept of punishment often seems incompatible with the social approval bestowed on the doer.

In contrast, an "excuse" concedes the wrongfulness of the action but asserts that the circumstances under which it was done are such that it ought not to be attributed to the actor. The perpetrator who is incapable, owing to a disease of the mind, of appreciating the nature and consequences of his acts, the person who labours under a mistake of fact, the drunkard, the sleepwalker: these are all actors of whose "criminal" actions we disapprove intensely, but whom, in appropriate circumstances, our law will not punish.

Packer, *The Limits of the Criminal Sanction* (1968), expresses the distinction thus at p. 113:

> " ... conduct that we choose not to treat as criminal is 'justifiable' if our reason for treating it as noncriminal is predominantly that it is conduct

that we applaud, or at least do not actively seek to discourage: conduct is 'excusable' if we deplore it but for some extrinsic reason conclude that it is not politic to punish it."

It will be seen that the two different approaches to the "defence" of necessity from Blackstone forward correspond, the one to a justification, the other to an excuse. . . . [T]he criminal law recognises and our *Criminal Code* codifies a number of specific categories of justification and excuse. The remainder, those instances that conform to the general principle but do not fall within any specific category such as self-defence on the one hand or insanity on the other, purportedly fall within the "residual defence" of necessity.

As a "justification" this residual defence can be related to Blackstone's concept of a "choice of evils." It would exculpate actors whose conduct could reasonably have been viewed as "necessary" in order to prevent a greater evil than that resulting from the violation of the law. As articulated, especially in some of the American cases, it involves a utilitarian balancing of the benefits of obeying the law as opposed to disobeying it, and when the balance is clearly in favour of disobeying, exculpates an actor who contravenes a criminal statute. This is the "greater good" formulation of the necessity defence: in some circumstances, it is alleged, the values of society, indeed of the criminal law itself, are better promoted by disobeying a given statute than by observing it.

With regard to this conceptualization of a residual defence of necessity, I retain the scepticism I expressed in *Morgentaler*, *supra*, at p. 497 C.C.C., p. 209 D.L.R., p. 678 S.C.R. It is still my opinion that, "[n]o system of positive law can recognise any principle which would entitle a person to violate the law because on his view the law conflicted with some higher social value." The *Criminal Code* has specified a number of identifiable situations in which an actor is justified in committing what would otherwise be a criminal offence. To go beyond that and hold that ostensibly illegal acts can be validated on the basis of their expediency, would import an undue subjectivity into the criminal law. It would invite the courts to second-guess the Legislature and to assess the relative merits of social policies underlying criminal prohibitions. Neither is a role which fits well with the judicial function. Such a doctrine could well become the last resort of scoundrels and, in the words of Edmund Davies L.J. in *Southwark London Borough Council* v. *Williams et al.*, [1971] Ch. 734 [at p. 746], it could "very easily become simply a task for anarchy."

Conceptualised as an "excuse," however, the residual defence of necessity is, in my view, much less open to criticism. It rests on a realistic assessment of human weakness, recognising that a liberal and humane criminal law cannot hold people to the strict obedience of laws in emergency situations where normal human instincts, whether of self-preservation or of altruism, overwhelmingly impel disobedience. The objectivity of the criminal law is preserved; such acts are still wrongful, but in the circumstances they are excusable. Praise is indeed not bestowed, but pardon is, when one does a wrongful act under pressure, which, in the words of Aristotle in *The Nicomachean Ethics* (translator Rees, p. 49), "overstrains human nature and which no one could withstand."

George Fletcher, *Rethinking Criminal Law*, describes this view of necessity as "compulsion of circumstance" which description points to the conceptual link between necessity as an excuse and the familiar criminal law requirement that in order to engage criminal liability, the actions constituting the *actus reus* of an offence must be voluntary. Literally, this voluntariness requirement simply refers to the need that the prohibited physical acts must have been under the conscious control of the actor. Without such control, there is, for purposes of the criminal law, no act. The excuse of necessity does not go to voluntariness in this sense. The lost Alpinist who, on the point of freezing to death, breaks open an isolated mountain cabin is not literally behaving in an involuntary fashion. He has control over his actions to the extent of being physically capable of abstaining from the act. Realistically, however, his act is not a "voluntary" one. His "choice" to break the law is no true choice at all; it is remorselessly compelled by normal human instincts. This sort of involuntariness if often described as "moral or normative involuntariness." Its place in criminal theory is described by Fletcher at pp. 804–5 as follows:

> "The notion of voluntariness adds a valuable dimension to the theory of excuses. That conduct is involuntary—even in the normative sense— explains why it cannot fairly be punished. Indeed, H. L. A. Hart builds his theory of excuses on the principle that the distribution of punishment should be reserved for those who voluntarily break the law. Of the arguments he advances for this principle of justice, the most explicit is that it is preferable to live in a society where we have the maximum opportunity to choose whether we shall become the subject of criminal liability. In addition Hart intimates that it is ideologically desirable for the government to treat its citizens as self-actuating, choosing agents. This principle of respect for individual autonomy is implicitly confirmed whenever those who lack an adequate choice are excused for their offences."

I agree with this formulation of the *rationale* for excuses in the criminal law. In my view, this *rationale* extends beyond specific codified excuses and embraces the residual excuse known as the defence of necessity. At the heart of this defence is the perceived injustice of punishing violations of the law in circumstances in which the person had no other viable or reasonable choice available; the act was wrong but it is excused because it was realistically unavoidable.

Punishment of such acts, as Fletcher notes at p. 813, can be seen as purposeless as well as unjust:

> " ... involuntary conduct cannot be deterred and therefore it is pointless and wasteful to punish involuntary actors. This theory ... of pointless punishment, carries considerable weight in current Anglo-American legal thought."

Relating necessity to the principle that the law ought not to punish involuntary acts leads to a conceptualisation of the defence that integrates it into the normal rules for criminal liability rather than constituting it as a *sui generis* exception and threatening to engulf large portions of the criminal law. Such a conceptualisation accords with our traditional legal, moral and philosophic views as to what sorts of acts and what sorts of actors ought to be punished. In this formulation it is a defence which I do not hesitate to acknowledge and would not hesitate to apply to relevant facts capable of satisfying its necessary prerequisites.

(c) *Limitations on the Defence*
In *Morgentaler* v. *The Queen*, ... I was of the view that any defence of necessity was restricted to instances of non-compliance "in urgent situations of clear and imminent peril when compliance with the law is demonstrably impossible." In my opinion, this restriction focuses directly on the "involuntariness" of the purportedly necessitous behaviour by

providing a number of tests for determining whether the wrongful act was truly the only realistic reaction open to the actor or whether he was in fact making what in fairness could be called a choice. If he was making a choice, then the wrongful act cannot have been involuntary in the relevant sense.

The requirement that the situation be urgent and the peril be imminent, tests whether it was indeed unavoidable for the actor to act at all. ...

At a minimum the situation must be so emergent and the peril must be so pressing that normal human instincts cry out for action and make a counsel of patience unreasonable.

The requirement that compliance with the law be "demonstrably impossible" takes this assessment one step further. Given that the accused had to act, could he nevertheless realistically have acted to avoid the peril or prevent the harm, without breaking the law? *Was there a legal way out*? I think this is what Bracton means when he lists "necessity" as a defence providing the wrongful act was not "avoidable." The question to be asked is whether the agent had any real choice: could he have done otherwise? If there is a reasonable legal alternative to disobeying the law, then the decision to disobey becomes a voluntary one, impelled by some consideration beyond the dictates of "necessity" and human instincts. The importance of this requirement that there be no reasonable legal alternative cannot be overstressed.

Even if the requirements for urgency and "no legal way out" are met, there is clearly a further consideration. There must be some way of assuring proportionality. No rational criminal justice system, no matter how humane or liberal, could excuse the infliction of a greater harm to allow the actor to avert a lesser evil. In such circumstances we expect the individual to bear the harm and refrain from acting illegally. If he cannot control himself we will not excuse him. ...

I would therefore add to the preceding requirements a stipulation of proportionality expressible, as it was in *Morgentaler*, by the proviso that the harm inflicted must be less than the harm sought to be avoided.

(d) *Illegality or contributory fault*

The Crown submits that there is an additional limitation on the availability of the defence of necessity. Citing *Salvador, supra*, it argues that because the appellants were committing a crime when their necessitous circumstances arose, they should be denied the defence of necessity as a matter of law. ...

I have considerable doubt as to the cogency of such a limitation. If the conduct in which an accused was engaging at the time the peril arose was illegal, then it should clearly be punished, but I fail to see the relevance of its illegal character to the question of whether the accused's subsequent conduct in dealing with this emergent peril ought to be excused on the basis of necessity. At most the illegality—or if one adopts Jones J.A.'s approach, the immorality—of the preceding conduct will colour the subsequent conduct in response to the emergency as also wrongful. But that wrongfulness is never in any doubt. Necessity goes to *excuse* conduct, not to *justify* it. Where it is found to apply it carries with it no implicit vindication of the deed to which it attaches. That cannot be over-emphasised. Where the defence of necessity to succeed in the present case, it would not in any way amount to a vindication of importing controlled substances nor to a critique of the law prohibiting such importation. It would also have nothing to say about the comparative social utility of breaking the law against importing as compared to obeying the law. The question, as I have said, is never whether what the accused has done is wrongful. It is always and by definition, wrongful. The question is whether what he has done is voluntary. Except in the limited sense I intend to discuss below, I do not see the relevance of the legality or even the morality of what the accused was doing at the time the emergency arose to this question of the voluntariness of the subsequent conduct.

In *Salvador*, Jones J.A., cited sources in support of his view that illegal conduct should act as a bar to the necessity defence. These sources do not support that view but do support a closely related notion—that if the accused's own "fault" (including negligence or recklessness) is responsible for the events giving rise to the necessity, he may not rely on the necessity defence.

In my view, the better approach to the relationship of fault to the availability of necessity as a defence is based once again on the question of whether the actions sought to be excused were truly "involuntary." If the necessitous situation was clearly foreseeable to a reasonable observer, if the actor contemplated or ought to have contemplated that his actions would likely give rise to an emergency requiring the breaking of the law, then I doubt whether what confronted the accused was in the relevant sense an emergency. His response was in that sense not "involuntary." "Contributory fault" of this nature, but only of this nature, is a relevant consideration to the availability of the defence. ...

If the accused's "fault" consists of actions whose clear consequences were in the situation that actually ensued, then he was not "really" confronted with an emergency which compelled him to commit the unlawful act he now seeks to have excused. In such situations the defence is unavailable. Mere negligence, however, or the simple fact that he was engaged in illegal or immoral conduct when the emergency arose will not disentitle an individual to rely on the defence of necessity. ...

(f) Preliminary conclusions as to the defence of necessity

It is now possible to summarise a number of conclusions as to the defence of necessity in terms of its nature, basis and limitations:

(1) the defence of necessity could be conceptualised as either a justification or an excuse;

(2) it should be recognised in Canada as an excuse, operating by virtue of s.7(3) of the *Criminal Code*;

(3) necessity as an excuse implies no vindication of the deeds of the actor;

(4) the criterion is the moral involuntariness of the wrongful action;

(5) this involuntariness is measured on the basis of society's expectation of appropriate and normal resistance to pressure;

(6) negligence or involvement in criminal or immoral activity does not disentitle the actor to the excuse of necessity;

(7) actions or circumstances which indicate that the wrongful deed was not truly involuntary do disentitle;

(8) the existence of a reasonable legal alternative similarly disentitles; to be involuntary the act must be inevitable, unavoidable and afford no reasonable opportunity for an alternative course of action that does not involve a breach of the law;

(9) the defence only applies in circumstances of imminent risk where the action was taken to avoid a direct and immediate peril;

(10) where the accused places before the court sufficient evidence to raise the issue, the onus is on the Crown to meet it beyond a reasonable doubt.

Appeals dismissed

Questions

1. Does the theory of excuses provide a more sound and coherent conceptual foundation for the defence of necessity than the theory of justification? See Miriam Gur-Ayre "Should the criminal law distinguish between necessity as a justification and necessity as an excuse?" (1986) 102 L.Q.R. 71.

2. Wilson J. in *Perka et al.* stated that "the nature of an excuse is to personalise the plea so that, while justification looks to the rightness of the act, excuse speaks to the compassion of the court for the actor." Do you agree?

3. In deciding whether there was necessity, the questions a jury might consider were expressed by Dickson J. as follows: "[g]iven that the accused had to act, could he nevertheless realistically have acted to avoid the peril or prevent the harm, without breaking the law? *Was there a legal way out?*" How might a jury answer these questions on the facts of *Perka et al.*?

4. SELF-DEFENCE AND KINDRED DEFENCES

Note

This section covers those situations where force is used by a defendant to protect himself, or his property, or others or to prevent crime. Pleas based on these grounds are not strictly "defences" in the sense that duress is a defence; a successful plea means that the accused's conduct was justified and thus lawful. However the term defence will be used as it appears in the cases and textbooks.

G. Williams "The theory of excuses" [1982] Crim.L.R. 732 at 739

"At any rate, for present English law private defence is clearly a matter of justification, not merely of according mercy to a defender. (Lord MacDermott C.J. referred to it as a 'plea of justification' in *Devlin* v. *Armstrong* [1971] N.I. 13). If the choice is between injury to an aggressor and injury to a defender, it is better that the injury be suffered by the aggressor, for two reasons. First, it is the aggressor who is the prime cause of the mischief. Secondly, a rule allowing defensive action tends to inhibit aggression, or at least to restrain its continuance, as a rule forbidding defensive action would tend to promote it. It follows that if a person acts against a wrongdoer in the actual necessity of private defence, no one who assists him should be guilty as bringing about a wrongful act, whatever may have been the reason why he lent his assistance."

Winn L.J. stated in *R.* v. *Wheeler* [1967] W.L.R. 1531, at p. 1533:

" . . . wherever there has been a killing, or indeed the infliction of violence not proving fatal, in circumstances where the defendant puts forward a justification such as self-defence, such as provocation, such as resistance to a violent felony, it is very important and indeed quite essential that the jury should understand, and that the matter should be so put before them that there is no danger of their failing to understand, that none of those issues of justification are properly to be regarded as defences: unfortunately there is sometimes a regrettable habit of referring to them as, for example, the defence of self-defence. In particular, where a judge does slip into the error or quasi error of referring to such explanations as defences, it is particularly important that he should use language which suffices to make it clear to the jury that they are not defences in respect of which any onus rests upon the accused, but are matters which the prosecution must disprove as an essential part of the prosecution case before a verdict of guilty is justified."

(Reiterated in *R.* v. *Abraham* [1973] 1 W.L.R. 1270.)

i. Scope of the defences

(a) *Self-defence*

R. v. Scully
(1824) C. & P. 319; 171 E.R. 1213
Gloucester Assizes

The defendant was set to watch his master's premises. He saw a man on the garden wall and hailed him. This man said to another, "Tom, why don't you fire?" The defendant hailed the man on the wall again and he said, "Shoot and be d—d," whereupon he shot at the man on the wall, aiming at his legs. He missed and shot the deceased whom he had not seen. The defendant was charged with manslaughter.

GARROW B.: Any person set by his master to watch a garden or yard, is not at all justified in shooting at or injuring in any way persons who may come into those premises, even in the night: and if he saw them go into his master's hen roost, he would still not be justified in shooting them. He ought first to go and see if he could not take measures for their apprehension. But here the life of the prisoner was threatened and if he considered his life in actual danger, he was justified in shooting the deceased as he had done; but, if not considering his own life in danger, he rashly shot that man, who was only a trespasser, he would be guilty of manslaughter.

Verdict: Not guilty

(b) *Defence of others*

R. v. Rose
(1884) 15 Cox 540
Oxford Assizes

The defendant was a weakly young man of 22; his father was a powerful man. Recently the father had been drinking excessively and whilst intoxicated he was of the opinion that his wife had been unfaithful to him. He had threatened her life and she was so frightened that she had frequently hidden everything in the house that could be used as a weapon. On the night in question the family had retired to separate bedrooms when the father had started abusing and arguing with his wife, threatening to murder her. He rushed from his room, seized his wife, and forced her up against the balusters in such a way as to give the impression that he was cutting her throat. The daughter and the mother shouted "murder," whereupon the defendant ran from his room. He is said to have fired a gun to frighten his father—no trace of his shot was found, and then he fired again, hitting his father in the eye and killing him. On arrest he said, "Father was murdering mother. I shot on one side to frighten him: he would not leave her, so I shot him." He was charged with murder.

LOPES J.: Homicide is excusable if a person takes away the life of another in defending himself, if the fatal blow which takes away life is necessary for his preservation. The law says not only in self-defence such as I have described may homicide be excusable, but also it may be excusable if the fatal blow inflicted was necessary for the preservation of life. In the case of parent and child, if the parent had reason to believe that the life of a child is in imminent danger by reason of an assault by another person, and that the only possible, fair and reasonable means of saving the child's life is by doing something which will cause the death of that person, the law excuses that act. It is the same of a child with regard to a parent; it is the same in the case of husband and wife. Therefore, I propose to lay the law before you in this form: If you think, having regard to the evidence, and drawing fair and proper inferences from it, that the prisoner at the Bar acted without vindictive feeling towards his father when he fired the shot, if you think that at the time he fired that shot he honestly believed, and had reasonable grounds for the belief, that his mother's life was in imminent peril, and that the fatal shot which he fired was absolutely necessary for the preservation of her life, then he ought to be excused, and the law will excuse him, from the consequences of the homicide. If, however, on the other hand, you cannot come to this conclusion, if you think, and think without reasonable doubt, that it is not a fair inference to be drawn from the evidence, but are clearly of opinion that he acted vindictively, and had not such a belief as I have described to you, or had not reasonable grounds for such a belief, then you must find him guilty of murder.

Verdict: Not guilty

R. v. Duffy
[1967] 1 Q.B. 63
Court of Criminal Appeal

The appellant's sister was fighting. It was the appellant's case that she went to rescue her sister and that this was justifiable as self-defence. They were both convicted of unlawful wounding.

EDMUND-DAVIES J.: ... defending counsel throughout relied upon the plea that the appellant was acting in self-defence, a plea which he submitted extended to the action of the appellant in seeking to rescue her sister. It is established that such a defence is not restricted to the person attacked. It has been said to extend to "the principal civil and natural relations." Hale's Pleas of the Crown, Vol. 1, p. 484, gives as instances master and servant, parent and child, and husband and wife who, if they even kill an assailant in the necessary defence of each other, are excused, the act of the relative assisting being considered the same as the act of the party himself.

But no reported case goes outside the relations indicated, although the editor of Kenny's Outlines of Criminal Law, 18th ed. (1962), p. 198, says that " ... perhaps the courts will now take a still more general view of this duty of the strong to protect the weak." Be that as it may, the judge seems to have found himself limited by the fact that no reported decision extended self-defence to a case where, as here, a sister went to the rescue of a sister, and the direction given to the jury as far as this appellant is concerned was this: "So far as I can see, members of the jury, in this case, the defence of self-defence is not open to Lilian Duffy. There is no suggestion whatever that she personally was attacked and it is my direction to you to approach this case on the footing that it is no defence for Lilian Duffy to say she was going to the assistance of her sister. ... "

The source of error in this case, as it appears to this court is, as we have said, that everyone, including counsel at the trial and again before us, seems to have overlooked that in reality and in law the case of Lilian Duffy was not trammelled by any technical limitations on the application of the plea of self-defence, and this court is not here concerned to consider what those limitations are. Quite apart from any special relations between the person attacked and his rescuer, there is a general liberty even as between strangers to prevent a felony. That is not to say, of course, that a newcomer may lawfully join in a fight just for the sake of fighting. Such conduct is wholly different in law from that of a person who in circumstances of necessity intervenes with the sole object of restoring the peace by rescuing a person being attacked. That, credible or otherwise, was the basic defence advanced by the appellant. She herself tied no lawyer's label to her tale. It is true that the judge said: "I need only remind you again that it is Lilian Duffy's case that she was going to the rescue of her sister and that was why she hit Akbar with a bottle, she could not get him off her sister." But his earlier directions had indicated that such a case afforded no defence in law. We think that this was a misdirection. The necessity for intervening at all and the reasonableness or otherwise of the manner of intervention were matters for the jury. It should have been left to them to say whether, in view of the appellant's proved conduct, such a defence could possibly be true, they being directed that the intervener is permitted to do only what is necessary and reasonable in all the circumstances for the purpose of rescue. ...

Appeal allowed

See also *Devlin* v. *Armstrong, post*, p. 336.

(c) *Defence of property*

R. v. Hussey
(1924) 18 Cr.App.R. 160
Court of Criminal Appeal

The appellant given an invalid notice to quit his rooms by his landlady, refused to do so. The landlady with two friends, armed with a hammer, a spanner, a poker and a chisel, tried to break down the door to the appellant's room which he had barricaded. A panel of the door was broken and the appellant fired through the hole wounding the friends of the landlady. He was charged with unlawfully wounding them and convicted. He appealed on the ground that the distinction between self-defence and defence of one's house had not been drawn to the attention of the jury.

LORD HEWART C.J.: No sufficient notice had been given to the appellant to quit his room, and therefore he was in the position of a man who was defending his house. In Archbold's Criminal Pleading, Evidence and Practice, 26th ed., p. 887, it appears that: "In defence of a man's house, the owner or his family may kill a trespasser who would forcibly dispossess him of it, in the same manner as he might, by law, kill in self-defence a man who attacks him personally; with the distinction, however, that in defending his home he need not retreat, as in other cases of self-defence, for that would be giving up his house to his adversary." [See now 40th ed., § 2472.] That is still the law, but not one word was said about that distinction in the summing-up, which proceeded on the foundation that the defence was the ordinary one of self-defence. The jury, by their verdict, negatived felonious intent, and with a proper direction they might have come to a different conclusion. The appeal must therefore be allowed.

Conviction quashed

Note

The landlady in *Hussey*, above, would now be committing an offence under the Protection from Eviction Act 1977, s.1, and under the Criminal Law Act 1977, s.6. Had the case arisen today, Hussey could have relied on the defence of prevention of crime.

(d) *Prevention of crime*

Criminal Law Act 1967, section 3

"(1) A person may use such force as is reasonable in the circumstances in the prevention of crime, or in effecting or assisting in the lawful arrest of offenders or suspected offenders or of persons unlawfully at large.

(2) Subsection (1) above shall replace the rules of common law on the question when force used for a purpose mentioned in the subsection is justified by that purpose."

Question

Did section 3(1) supersede the common law defences of self-defence, defence of others and defence of property?

Ashworth, "Self-Defence and The Right to Life" (1975) C.L.J. 282, 284

"Does the English criminal law on self-defence consist of a number of rules and exceptions laid down at common law, or is it governed by a general standard of 'reasonableness' laid down by statute? At first blush it seems extraordinary that such an elementary point should remain in doubt, not least because the statute in question (the Criminal Law Act 1967) has been in force for several years. Professors Smith and Hogan state, in their influential work [Criminal Law, now 6th ed. (1988) p. 243], that the common law rules no longer represent English law; the practice of the courts suggest otherwise. What are, or were, those rules? The two principal requirements are that the force should have been necessary for self-defence and reasonable in the circumstances. The requirement of necessity supports two separate limitations. The first is that it should have been necessary to use force rather than employing non-violent means of self-protection. From this limitation derives the so-called 'duty to retreat': when an individual's purpose in a threatening situation is to save himself from injury or death, it cannot be necessary for him to inflict harm on an assailant if there is a safe avenue of withdrawal open to him. To this duty there have always been certain exceptions. A second limitation is that the amount of force should have been no more than necessary for the purpose of self-defence. Courts have occasionally merged this with the requirement of reasonableness, which demands a sense of proportion between the harm inflicted and the harm thereby prevented, but the two requirements are theoretically distinct.

What are the grounds for arguing that the common law has been overruled by section 3 of the Criminal Law Act 1967? The section enacts that 'a person may use such force as is reasonable in the circumstances in the prevention of crime,' and that this provision 'shall replace the rules of the common law' on the justifiability of force used in the prevention of crime. Smith and Hogan argue that 'self-defence and defence of others invariably arise out of an attempt to commit a crime by the assailant and thus consist in the use of force to prevent the commission of the crime.' It therefore follows that cases of self-defence should be decided according to the general test of reasonableness laid down by section 3, and that all the old common law authorities should be regarded as repealed. Now, even on the assumption that the conflation of the two grounds of justification would be logical and desirable, there are good reasons why it is unacceptable as an analysis of English law. In the first place, section 3 was not intended to alter the law on self-defence. Furthermore, the courts continue to deal with cases by reference to the common law. Indeed in not one of the appellate decisions reported since 1967 has there been even a passing reference to section 3 as relevant to self- defence."

CLRC, *14th Report, Offences Against the Person*, § 281: "Section 3 applies to most cases of self-defence . . . however, in a few cases the attacker may not be committing a crime because, for example, he is a child under 10 years old, insane, in a state of automatism, or under a material mistake of fact."

Question

D, a nurse in a mental hospital, is attacked by X a patient wielding a meat cleaver. X had escaped from a secure ward for the violently insane. D knowing this nevertheless defends himself with a crutch. He hits X over the head fracturing his skull. If self-defence has been swallowed up by section 3 of the Criminal Law Act 1967, could D plead prevention of crime on a charge under section 20 Offences Against the Person Act 1861 of unlawfully and maliciously inflicting grievous bodily harm?

Notes

1. Smith and Hogan, p. 257, suggest that although section 3 has swallowed up self-defence, in point of policy D. in the above situation should have a defence. What would this defence be? Would it be the common law defence of self-defence?!

2. The case *infra* is interesting as it raises not only the issue of the relationship between the common law and section 3 of the Criminal Law Act 1967 (or its Northern Irish equivalent), but also other issues such as the imminence of the threat and defence of

others. (This case must be read in light of *R. v. Gladstone Williams, ante,* p. 155).

Devlin v. Armstrong
[1971] N.I. 13
Court of Appeal for Northern Ireland

The case arose out of serious disturbances in Londonderry in August 1969. The appellant exhorted a crowd of people, who had been stoning the police, to build barricades and to fight the police with petrol bombs. Her grounds of appeal against four convictions of riotous behaviour and incitement to riotous behaviour were that she reasonably believed that the police were about to act unlawfully in assaulting people and damaging property and so her behaviour was justified.

LORD MACDERMOTT L.C.J.: with whom Curran and McKeigh L.JJ. agreed, after describing the events in some detail:

The findings of the case indicate that the state of disorder which I have described involved a violent and aggressive resistance to constitutional authority, and if the relevant facts and considerations ended with the tale of events already told, the inescapable conclusion would be that the appellant and those associated with her opposing the police by the means described were participants in a riot and guilty of riotous behaviour.

As I have stated, the answer to this, as advanced on behalf of the appellant, is one of justification. She did what she did, it was submitted, because she believed honestly and reasonably that the police were about to assault people and damage property in the Bogside. The learned resident magistrate did not accept the factual basis of this submission, but that finding has become entwined with one respecting the admissibility of certain evidence which the appellant sought to adduce in support of this plea and I shall, therefore, assume for present purposes that in fact, the appellant did honestly and reasonably believe that the police were about to behave unlawfully in the manner mentioned. Thus arises what I have called the principal issue. Does this plea of justification afford a defence to the charges? At this point I do not need to distinguish between the offences of inciting to riotous behaviour and behaving riotously. If this defence meets one of these offences it must, in the circumstances, meet the other.

The conclusion I have reached on this issue is against the appellant. In my opinion the submission under discussion fails as an answer to any of the charges. Since there is a dearth of authority on the point and various principles have been invoked on one side and the other, I shall enumerate the reasons which, separately and in conjunction, have led me to this view.

1. At any rate one common purpose of the rioters and the appellant was, beyond any question, to keep the police from entering or establishing themselves in the Bogside and to achieve this by force. The appellant's contention that the honesty and reasonableness of her apprehensions (as I have assumed them to be for the sake of the argument) robbed her actions of the *mens rea* necessary to constitute the offences charged must, to my mind, fail once the nature of this common purpose has been demonstrated. If it were conceded that her apprehensions supplied a motive for her actions and incitements, that in itself would fall well short of neutralising her intentions as manifested by the manner of her participation.

2. Reliance was also placed upon the doctrine of self-defence. The general nature of this doctrine may be taken as described in Russell on Crime, 12th ed. (1964) vol. I, p. 680, thus:

"The use of force is lawful for the necessary defence of self or others or of property; but the justification is limited by the necessity of the occasion, and the use of unnecessary force is an assault."

The plea of self-defence may afford a defence where the party raising it uses force, not merely to counter an actual attack, but to ward off or prevent an attack which he has honestly and reasonably anticipated. In that case, however, the anticipated attack must be imminent: see *R.* v. *Chisam* (1963) 47 Cr.App.R. 130, 134, and the excerpt from Lord Normand's judgment in *Owens* v. *H.M. Advocate*, 1946 S.C. (J) 119, which is there quoted and which runs:

"In our opinion self-defence is made out when it is established to the satisfaction of the jury that the panel believed that he was in imminent danger and that he held that belief on reasonable grounds. Grounds for such belief may exist though they are founded on a genuine mistake of fact."

That there was a distinction between the right of self-defence and the right to prevent a felony appears from *R.* v. *Duffy*, (*ante*, p. 332), but the latter right has gone with the abolition of the distinctions between felony and misdemeanour and its place is now taken in this jurisdiction by section 3 of the Criminal Law Act (Northern Ireland), 1967, subsection (1) which says:

"a person may use such force as is reasonable in the circumstances in the prevention of crime. ... "

However reasonable and convinced the appellant's apprehensions may have been, I find it impossible to hold that the danger she anticipated was sufficiently specific or imminent to justify the actions she took as measures of self-defence. The police were then in the throes of containing a riot in the course of their duty, and her interventions at that juncture were far too aggressive and premature to rank as justifiable effort to prevent the prospective danger of the police getting out of hand and acting unlawfully which, as I have assumed, she anticipated.

3. Where force is used either in exercise of the right of self-defence or, under section 3 of the Act of 1967, in the prevention of crime, it must be reasonable in the circumstances. This consideration alone seems to me fatal to the appellant's plea of justification. Whatever her fears and however genuine they may have been, to organise and encourage the throwing of petrol bombs was, I would hold, an utterly unwarranted and unlawful reaction. The night of August 12 had demonstrated the capacity of these lethal weapons to injure and destroy and nothing that had happened or was likely to happen could excuse the appellant in facilitating and encouraging their use.

4. The plea of justification, whether based on the doctrine of self-defence or the statutory right to prevent crime, appears to me to place a further difficulty when the offence sought to be justified is that of inciting others to riotous behaviour. While there was evidence of a general fear of the police amongst people of the Bogside, there is nothing in the findings or facts of the case to show that those who were exhorted by the appellant to riot were actuated by any honest and reasonable apprehension of unlawful violence on the part of the police such as she is assumed to have had. Her

incitements were, therefore, directed to encouraging others to do what for them was prima facie unlawful. It cannot be taken for granted that those she addressed were opposing the police or what she says were her reasons, and this all the more as the rioting had started in opposition to the parade and before the police had entered the Bogside. In my opinion the plea of self-defence cannot be availed of where what is sought to be justified is an incitement to unjustifiable crime. I know of no authority to the contrary, and on this ground as well I would hold that the plea fails.

5. As I understood his argument Sir Dingle Foot at one stage sought, in the alternative, to broaden the appellant's plea of justification by putting it on the basis of a collective right of self-defence arising out of some collective necessity. He frankly admitted that there was no clear authority of such a concept, but drew our attention to a passage from the judgment of Lord Mansfield in *R. v. Stratton and Ors.* (1779) 21 St.Tr. 1045 at 1224, which is mentioned by Mr. Justice Stephen in his *History of the Criminal Law* (1883), vol. ii, 109, in relation to the plea of compulsion by necessity. In that case the accused, who were charged for deposing Lord Pigot from the Government of Madras, defended themselves on the ground that Lord Pigot's argument had been such that it was necessary for them to do so in the interests of the Madras Presidency. After speaking of cases of natural necessity, such as self-defence, Lord Mansfield continued:

"As to civil necessity, none can happen in corporations, societies, and bodies of men deriving their authority under the Crown and therefore subordinate; no case ever did exist in government to which they can apply, they have a superior at hand, and therefore I cannot be warranted to put to you any case of civil necessity that justifies illegal acts, because the case not existing, nor being supposed to exist, there is not authority in the law books nor any adjudged case upon it. Imagination may suggest, you may suggest so extraordinary a case as would justify a man by force overturning a magistrate and beginning a new government all by force, I mean in India, where there is no superior nigh them to apply to; in England it cannot happen; but in India you may suppose a possible case, but in that case it must be imminent, extreme, necessity; there must be no other remedy to apply to for redress; it must be very imminent, it must be very extreme, and in the whole they do, they must appear clearly to do with a view of preserving the society and themselves—with a view of preserving the whole."

On this aspect Sir Dingle pressed his suit with a delicate circumspection, leaving it to the court to apply such part of Lord Mansfield's words as might be considered appropriate. I need only say that I can find nothing in the passage quoted to justify the actions of the appellant or the rioters whom she incited. It is one thing to act for the best in some case of extreme necessity, where the forces of law and order are absent or have ceased to act in that capacity. It is quite another to fight against and seek to expel a lawfully constituted constabulary while acting as such in the execution of its proper functions.

6. The ambit of the doctrine of self-defence may be wider than it once was, but when considered apart from the statutory right to which I have referred, some special nexus or relationship between the party relying on the doctrine to justify what he did in aid of another, and that other, would still appear to be necessary. Without attempting to define that factor, I cannot accept, on the material available, that it existed as between the appellant and the people of the Bogside. There is nothing to suggest that she belonged to or had property or a home in that district, and her status

as a Member of Parliament would not, of itself, afford her protection by supplying a special relationship. It would seem as though she came in as a visitor and made common cause with the rioters, but I cannot regard that as an adequate relationship on which to found a defence of justification by way of self-defence.

7. Finally, the outbreak of rioting on August 12 and 13 imposed a duty on more than the constabulary. The private citizen has authority in law to help in the suppression of riots, and it is his common law duty to assist the constabulary to this end: see Russell on Crime, 12th ed. (1964), pp. 270 *et seq.*, and, in particular, the *Bristol Riots* case (1832) 3 St.Tr. (N.S.) 1 at 4 and 5, and *R. v. Pinney* (1832) 3 St.Tr. (N.S.) 11. That obligation, which rested upon the appellant as well as others, made it impossible, in my opinion, for her to find any legal justification for her conduct in aiding and encouraging the rioters as she undoubtedly did.

Appeals dismissed

R. v. McInnes [1971] 1 W.L.R. 1600, Edmund-Davies L.J. at p. 1610: "Section 3(1) of the Criminal Law Act 1967 provides that "A person may use such force as is reasonable in the circumstances in the prevention of crime ... " and in our judgment the degree of force permissible in self-defence is similarly limited."

ii. The Issues of Imminence and the Pre-Emptive Strike

See *Devlin v. Armstrong, ante,* p. 336.

Attorney-General's Reference (No. 2 of 1983)
[1984] Q.B. 456
Court of Appeal

The defendant's shop in Toxteth had been attacked and damaged by rioters. Fearing further attacks he made some petrol bombs which he intended to use purely as a last resort to repulse raiders from his shop. He was charged with an offence under section 4 of the Explosive Substances Act 1883, namely, of having made an explosive substance in such circumstances as to give rise to a reasonable suspicion that he had not made it for a lawful object. He pleaded that his lawful object was self-defence and the jury acquitted. The Attorney-General referred for the court's opinion the question whether the defence of self-defence was available to a defendant charged with an offence under section 4 of the 1883 Act.

LORD LANE C.J.: ... Counsel for the Crown argued at trial that self-defence did not provide a valid defence to the respondent on this charge because such a plea is available only to justify actual violence by a defendant. Mr. Hill contends that it does not exist as a justification for preliminary and premeditated acts anticipatory of an act of violence by the defendant in the absence of any express statutory provision therefor. ...

Mr. Hill submits that to allow a man to justify in advance his own act of violence for which he has prepared runs wholly contrary to the principle and thinking behind legitimate self-defence and legitimate defence of property. Both are defences which the law allows to actual violence by a defendant, and both are based on the principle that a man may be justified in extremis in taking spontaneous steps to defend himself, others of his family and his property against actual or mistakenly perceived violent attack. It was argued that if a plea of self-defence is allowed to section 4 of the Act of 1883 the effect would be that a man could write his own immunity for unlawful acts done in preparation for violence to be used by him in the future. Rather than that, goes on the argument, in these circumstances a man should protect himself by calling on the police or by barricading his premises or by guarding them alone or with others, but not with petrol bombs. . . .

[In *R. v. Fegan* [1972] N.I. 80 Lord MacDermott C.J. said, at p. 87:]

"Possession of a firearm for the purpose of protecting the possessor or his wife or family from acts of violence, *may* be possession for a lawful object. But the lawfulness of such a purpose cannot be founded on a mere fancy, or on some aggressive motive. The threatened danger must be reasonably and genuinely anticipated, must appear reasonably imminent, and must be of a nature which could not reasonably be met by more pacific means. A lawful object in this particular field therefore falls within a strictly limited category and cannot be such as to justify going beyond what the law may allow in meeting the situation of danger which the possessor of the firearm reasonably and genuinely apprehends."

. . . In our judgment, approaching *a priori* the words "lawful object" it might well seem open to a defendant to say, "My lawful object is self-defence." The respondent in this case said that his intentions were to use the petrol bombs purely to protect his premises should any rioters come to his shop. It was accordingly open to the jury to find that the respondent has made them for the reasonable protection of himself and his property against this danger. The fact that in manufacturing and storing the petrol bombs the respondent committed offences under the Act of 1875 did not necessarily involve that when he made them his object in doing so was not lawful. The means by which he sought to fulfil that object were unlawful, but the fact that he could never without committing offences reach the point where he used them in self-defence did not render his object in making them for that purpose unlawful. The object or purpose or end for which the petrol bombs were made was not itself rendered unlawful by the fact that it could not be fulfilled except by unlawful means. The fact that the commission of other offences was unavoidable did not result in any of them becoming one of the respondent's objects. . . .

In the judge's summing up the threatened danger was assumed, as was the respondent's anticipation of it. Also assumed, no doubt upon the basis of the evidence led, was the imminence of the danger. What the judge upon the facts of the case before him left to the jury was the reasonableness of the means adopted for the repulsion of raiders. . . .

In our judgment a defendant is not left in the paradoxical position of being able to justify acts carried out in self-defence but not acts immediately preparatory to it. There is no warrant for the submission on behalf of the Attorney-General that acts of self-defence will only avail a defendant when they they have been done spontaneously. There is no question of a person in danger of attack "writing his own immunity" for violent future acts of his. He is not confined for his remedy to calling in the police or boarding up his premises.

He may still arm himself for his own protection, if the exigency arises, although in so doing he may commit other offences. That he may be guilty of other offences will avoid the risk of anarchy contemplated by the reference. It is also to be noted that although a person may "make" a petrol bomb with a lawful object, nevertheless if he remains in possession of it after the threat has passed which made his object lawful, it may cease to be so. It will only be very rarely that circumstances will exist where the manufacture or possession of petrol bombs can be for a lawful object.

For these reasons the point of law referred by Her Majesty's Attorney-General for the consideration of this court is answered by saying: the defence of lawful object is available to a defendant against whom a charge under section 4 of the Act of 1883 has been preferred, if he can satisfy the jury on balance of probabilities that his object was to protect himself or his family against imminent apprehended attack and to do so by means which he believed were no more than reasonably necessary to meet the force used by the attackers.

Opinion accordingly

J. C. Smith, Commentary [1984] Crim.L.R. 290

"If the respondent intended to use the bombs only in circumstances in which it would have been lawful to do so, then it seems to follow inevitably that he had them in his possession 'for a lawful object,' and so was not guilty of the offence under the Explosives Substances Act 1883. In determining whether the object was lawful, the court was looking forward to the contemplated actual use of the weapons, so it was not really necessary to decide whether the preparatory acts were lawful or not. So regarded, the decision is a narrow one; and indeed, it seems to have accepted that the respondent was committing an offence of manufacturing and storing explosives without a licence, contrary to the Explosives Act 1875. Nor does any doubt seem to have been cast on *Evans* v. *Wright* [1964] Crim.L.R. 466 and the other cases under the Prevention of Crime Act 1953 which hold that there is no lawful authority or reasonable excuse for carrying an offensive weapon in a public place for purposes of self-defence, unless there is 'an imminent particular threat affecting the particular circumstances in which the weapon was carried': *Evans* v. *Hughes* [1972] 3 All E.R. 412 at 415. A person who intends to use an offensive weapon only in reasonable defence has it 'for a lawful object'; yet it seems to be accepted that, unless there is an 'imminent' threat, he commits an offence under the 1953 Act. A taxi-driver might be justified in using the two feet of rubberhose with a piece of metal inserted in the end which he carries for the purposes of self-defence, when he is the victim of a violent attack; but he was committing an offence, at least until the moment when the attack was imminent, by having the article with him in a public place: *Grieve* v. *Macleod* 1967, S.L.T. 70.

The reasons of policy for such an approach are obvious. The court does not want to create a situation in which the manufacture and carrying of weapons will proliferate. The court says, however, that in their judgment, a defendant was not left in the paradoxical position of being able to justify acts carried out in self-defence but not acts immediately preparatory to it; but the justification is somewhat illusory if, as the court also says, he might at the same time commit other offences.

Self-defence is a defence at common law. It applies not only to common law offences but also to statutory offences, although the statutory definition gives no hint of the existence of any such defence—see, for example, sections 18 and 20 of the Offences Against the Person Act 1861. If the common law defence applies to these offences, why not to other offences such as those under the Explosive Substances Act 1875? If I am being shot at by a dangerous criminal and I pick up the revolver which has been dropped by a wounded policeman and fire it in self-defence, am I really guilty of an offence under the Firearms Act 1968, s.1, of being in possession of firearms without holding a firearm certificate? It seems strange that the circumstances might justify me in killing my assailant with the revolver and yet not justify me in being in possession of it. If self-defence is justifiable, it surely ought to be a defence to all crimes. If it is not justifiable, it is a defence to none.

Because the only question in the present case was whether the respondent was in possession for a 'lawful object,' the question whether the preliminary acts were justifiable did not really arise; but the better view seems to be that at least those acts which are immediately preparatory to the use of reasonable force in self-defence are justifiable to the same extent as the actual use of force."

Question

In the bank robbery example, if Professor Smith was charged with an offence under section 1 of the Firearms Act 1968, could he now plead duress of circumstances?

Note

In *Beckford* v. *The Queen* [1988] 1 A.C. 130 P.C., Lord Griffiths stated at p. 144:

"The common law recognises that there are many circumstances in which one person may inflict violence upon another without committing a crime, as for instance, in sporting contests, surgical operations or in the most extreme example judicial execution. The common law has always recognised as one of these circumstances the right of a person to protect himself from attack and to act in the defence of others and if necessary to inflict violence on another in so doing. If no more force is used than is reasonable to repel the attack such force is not unlawful and no crime is committed. Furthermore a man about to be attacked does not have to wait for his assailant to strike the first blow or fire the first shot; circumstances may justify a pre-emptive strike.

It is because it is an essential element of all crimes of violence that the violence or the threat of violence should be unlawful that self-defence, if raised as an issue in a criminal trial, must be disproved by the prosecution. If the prosecution fail to do so the accused is entitled to be acquitted because the prosecution will have failed to prove an essential element of the crime namely that the violence used by the accused was unlawful."

iii. Is there a Duty to Retreat?

R. v. Bird
[1985] 1 W.L.R. 816
Court of Appeal

The appellant was charged with unlawful wounding having lunged at a young man with a glass in her hand, injuring him. She claimed that he had slapped and pushed her so that her back was to the wall and that she acted in self-defence without realising until later that she had been holding the glass in her hand. She was convicted.

LORD LANE C.J.: ... The relevant passages in the summing up are these—first, towards the beginning of the direction to the jury:

"You cannot wrap up an attack in the cloak of self-defence and it is necessary that a person claiming to exercise a right of self-defence should demonstrate by her action that she does not want to fight. At one time it was thought that in order to demonstrate that, that the person seeking to raise a question of self-defence had to retreat. That is not so any longer at all, but there is an obligation to see whether the person claiming to exercise the right of self-defence should have demonstrated that she does not want to fight at all."

Towards the end of the summing up the judge used these words:

"You will have to consider whether in the circumstances of this case self-defence has any application at all. Does it look to you that this lady, who was behaving in this fashion, had demonstrated that she did not want to fight and if she had demonstrated that she did not want to fight, was the use of the glass with a hard blow which broke it, reasonable in the circumstances? All these are matters for you and not for me."

Those words were taken very largely from a decision of this court in *R. v. Julien* [1969] 1 W.L.R. 839. That was an ex tempore judgment by Widgery L.J. to which I was a party as was Karminski L.J. The passage from which the words are taken reads, at p. 842:

"The third point taken by Mr. McHale is that the deputy chairman was wrong in directing the jury that before the appellant could use force in self-defence he was required to retreat. The submission here is that the obligation to retreat before using force in self-defence is an obligation which only arises in homicide cases. As the court understands it, it is submitted that if the injury results in death then the accused cannot set up self-defence except on the basis that he had retreated before he resorted to violence. On the other hand, it is said that where the injury does not result in death (as in the present case) the obligation to retreat does not arise.

The sturdy submission is made that an Englishman is not bound to run away when threatened, but can stand his ground and defend himself where he is. In support of this submission no authority is quoted, save that Mr. McHale has been at considerable length and diligence to look at the text books on the subject, and has demonstrated to us that the text books in the main do not say that preliminary retreat is a necessary prerequisite to the use of force in self-defence. Equally, it must be said that the text books do not state the contrary either; and it is, of course, well known to us all that for very many years it has been common form for judges directing juries where the issue of self-defence is raised in any case (be it a homicide case or not) to say that the duty to retreat arises.

It is not, as we understand it, the law that a person threatened must take to his heels and run in the dramatic way suggested by Mr. McHale, but what is necessary is that he should demonstrate by his actions that he does not want to fight. He must demonstrate that he is prepared to temporise and disengage and perhaps to make some physical withdrawal: and that that is necessary as a feature of the justification of self-defence is true, in our opinion, whether the charge is a homicide charge or something less serious. Accordingly, we reject Mr. McHale's third submission."

That decision was to some extent followed later in *R.* v. *McInnes* [1971] 1 W.L.R. 1600. The judgment of the court was delivered by Edmund-Davies L.J., and the passage in question reads, at p. 1607:

"The first criticism of the judge's treatment of self-defence is that he misdirected the jury in relation to the question of whether an attacked person must do all he reasonably can to retreat before he turns upon his attacker. The direction given was in these terms: 'In our law if two men fight and one of them after a while endeavours to avoid any further struggle and retreats as far as he can, and then when he can go no further turns and kills his assailant to avoid being killed himself, that homicide is excusable, but notice that to show that homicide arising from a fight was committed in self-defence it must be shown that the party killing had retreated as far as he could, or as far as the fierceness of the assault would permit him.'

One does not have to seek far for the source of this direction. It was clearly quoted from *Archbold Criminal Pleading Evidence & Practice*, 37th ed. (1969), p. 780, para. 2495, which is in turn based upon a passage in *Hale's Pleas of the Crown* (1800) vol. 1, pp. 481, 483. In our judgment, the direction was expressed in too flexible terms and might, in certain circumstances, be regarded as significantly misleading. We prefer the view expressed by the full court of Australia that a failure to retreat is only an *element* in the consideration upon which the reasonableness of an accused's conduct is to be judged (see *Palmer* v. *The Queen* [1971] 2 W.L.R. 831, 840) or, as it is put in *Smith and Hogan Criminal Law*, 2nd ed. (1969), p. 231: ' . . . simply a factor to be taken into account in deciding whether it was necessary to use force, and whether the force used was reasonable.''

Had the judgment stopped there, there would have been no difficulty. But it continues by citing the passage from the judgment in *R.* v. *Julien* which we have already read.

The court in *R.* v. *Julien* was anxious to make it clear that there was no duty, despite earlier authorities to the contrary, actually to turn round or walk away from the scene. But reading the words which were used in that judgment, it now seems to us that they placed too great an obligation upon a defendant in circumstances such as those in the instant case, an obligation which is not reflected in the speeches in *Palmer* v. *The Queen* [1971] A.C. 814.

The matter is dealt with accurately and helpfully in *Smith and Hogan Criminal Law*, 5th ed. (1983), p. 327:

"There were formerly technical rules about the duty to retreat before using force, or at least fatal force. This is now simply a factor to be taken into account in deciding whether it was necessary to use force, and whether the force was reasonable. If the only reasonable course is to retreat, then it would appear that to stand and fight must be to use unreasonable force. There is, however, no rule of law that a person attacked is bound to run away if he can; but it has been said that—' . . . what is necessary is that he should demonstrate by his actions that he does not want to fight. He must demonstrate that he is prepared to temporise and disengage and perhaps to make some physical withdrawal.' [*R.* v. *Julien* [1969] 1 W.L.R. 839, 842]. It is submitted that it goes too far to say that action of this kind is *necessary*. It is scarcely consistent with the rule that it is permissible to use force, not merely to counter an actual attack, but to ward off an attack honestly and reasonably believed to be imminent. A demonstration by [the defendant] at the time that he did not want to fight is, no doubt, the best evidence that he was acting reasonably and in good faith in self-defence; but it is no more than that. A person may in some circumstances so act without temporising, disengaging or withdrawing; and he should have a good defence."

We respectfully agree with that passage. If the defendant is proved to have been attacking or retaliating or revenging himself, then he was not truly acting in self-defence. Evidence that the defendant tried to retreat or tried to call off the fight may be a cast-iron method of casting doubt on the suggestion that he was the attacker or retaliator or the person trying to revenge himself. But it is not by any means the only method of doing that.

It seems to us therefore that in this case the judge—we hasten to add through no fault of his own—by using the word "necessary" as we did in the passages in the summing up to which we have referred, put too high an obligation upon the appellant.

Appeal allowed
Conviction quashed

iv. Unknown circumstances of justification

If circumstances actually exist which would justify the use of force against V, must D know of or believe in the existence of these circumstances if he is to plead self-defence or prevention of crime or lawful arrest in respect of a charge arising from his use of force? This problem of "unknown circumstances of justification" arose in *Dadson* (1850) 4 Cox C.C. 358. D, a constable, was on duty watching a copse from which wood had been stolen. V emerged from the copse carrying wood which had been stolen. He ran away when D called to him and D shot him so that he could arrest him. D was convicted of shooting at V with intent to cause him grievous bodily harm. D had sought to raise the justification that he was shooting to arrest an escaping felon. Stealing wood was only a felony where the thief had two previous convictions for that offence. In fact V had several such convictions and thus was a felon but D did not know this. D's conviction was upheld as he was not justified in shooting V as the fact that V was committing a felony was not known to him at the time.

When the Criminal Law Act 1967 was passed it was argued by some that sections 2 and 3 had the effect of reversing *Dadson*. (The Police and Criminal Evidence Act 1984, s.24(4) replaced s.2.) It was argued that if a person actually had committed an arrestable offence an arrest of him would be lawful even though the arresting officer did not know nor suspect on reasonable grounds that he had committed that offence. The Law Commission in its reports on *Codification of the Criminal Law* (Law Com. Nos. 143 and 177) recommended that an accused should be able to rely on unknown circumstances of justification in any case where the use of force was necessary and reasonable (*contra*, see Hogan, "The *Dadson* principle" [1989] Crim.L.R. 679). In *Chapman* (1988) 89 Cr.App.R. 190, the Divisional Court effectively reaffirmed *Dadson* pointing out that if a person is unaware of circumstances justifying an arrest he cannot perform a lawful arrest as he will not be able to comply with section 28(3) of the Police and Criminal Evidence Act 1984 which requires that he inform the suspect of the grounds for the arrest. If an arrest is unlawful it follows that any force used to effect it is likewise unlawful.

Question

D, looking out from his bedroom, spies the head and shoulders of V, his life-long sworn enemy, protruding above a wall 50 metres away. D takes aim with his rifle and shoots V. wounding him. Unknown to D, V was about to depress a plunger wired to an explosive charge below where D was standing which, if it had exploded, would have killed D. D is charged with wounding with intent to do grievous bodily harm contrary to section 18 of the Offences Against the Person Act 1861. Will D succeed on a plea of self-defence or prevention of crime? See Draft Criminal Code, clause 44, *post*, p. 360.

v. To Which Offences do the Defences Apply?

R. v. Renouf
[1986] 1 W.L.R. 522
Court of Appeal

The appellant was charged with reckless driving. He had driven his car in pursuit of another vehicle, the occupants of which had assaulted him and damaged his car, he forced the vehicle off the road and rammed it. He was convicted after the trial judge directed that s.3(1) of the Criminal Law Act 1967 was incapable of affording a defence to the charge of reckless driving. He appealed.

LAWTON L.J.: ... The evidence relating to edging the Volvo off the road was what the prosecution alleged amounted to the reckless driving as charged. It did create an obvious and serious risk of causing physical harm to the occupants of the Volvo and of damage to it. On the evidence this was the only risk upon which the allegation of recklessness could be based. There was no risk to oncoming traffic; and nothing more than a tenuous suggestion that there might have been a risk to any traffic there may have been (and there was none) on a side road nearby. ...

This case has to be considered in the light of the evidence which was said to have amounted to reckless driving. This evidence had two facets: one was what the prosecution alleged to be the acts of recklessness; and the other was that these same acts amounted to the use of reasonable force for the purpose of assisting in the lawful arrest of offenders. In our judgment it is only when evidence has these two facets that section 3(1) of the Criminal Law Act 1967 can apply. This being so, the occasions for relying on that section will be rare, certainly not when the reckless acts were antecedent to the use of force. In our judgment the alleged presence of these two facets in the appellant's evidence concerning why he did the acts which the prosecution said were reckless was capable of providing him with a defence. It is no answer for the prosecution to submit, as Mr. Clark did, that the wording of sections 1 and 2 of the Road Traffic Act 1972 shuts out any possibility of such a defence because they contained no words such as "lawful excuse." Nor does section 20 of the Offences

Against the Persons Act 1861; but section 3(1) had been used to provide a defence to charges under that section.

The only other point which calls for consideration is whether what the appellant said he did amounted to the use of "force." That word is one of ordinary usage in English and does not require judicial interpretation. In that usage a jury might consider that the appellant had forced the Volvo off the road on to the grass verge. The trial judge used the word "force" in this sense in the course of his summing up.

In our judgment, on the unusual evidence in case, the judge should have left to the jury the appellant's defence based on section 3(1) of the Act of 1967. They might have accepted it because they found the appellant not guilty of causing criminal damage to the Volvo when he rammed it in order to stop it moving. They could only have done so because of his defence of "lawful excuse."

Appeal allowed

vi. Reasonable Force

R. v. Shannon
(1980) 71 Cr.App.Rep. 192
Court of Appeal

The appellant was charged with murder by stabbing while being attacked. He worked for the same firm as the deceased and there had been some history of friction between them. It was alleged that he stabbed in revenge, punishment, retaliation or pure aggression. His defence was self-defence and absence of intent to cause grievous bodily harm. After being directed on the intent of murder, the jury were asked to consider the issue of self-defence: "Did the defendant use more force than necessary in the circumstances?" The jury returned a verdict of guilty of manslaughter. He appealed against conviction.

ORMROD L.J., for the court: Mr. Fox Andrews, Q.C. for the appellant has criticised the learned judge's summing up on the basis of the well-known passage in the speech of Lord Morris of Borth-y-Gest giving the advice of the Privy Council in *Palmer* v. *R.* [1971] A.C. 814, 831, 832, *post*, p. 350. He submits that the learned judge overlooked one important sentence in that advice, which reads thus: "If a jury thought that in a moment of unexpected anguish a person attacked had only done what he honestly and instinctively thought was necessary, that would be most potent evidence that only reasonable defensive action had been taken."

This proposition is, as it were, a bridge between what is sometimes referred to as "the objective test," that is what is reasonable judged from the viewpoint of an outsider looking at a situation quite dispassionately, and "the subjective test," that is the viewpoint of the accused himself with the intellectual capabilities of which he may in fact be possessed and with all the emotional strains and stresses to which at the moment he may be subjected.

The learned judge dealt fully with the relevant evidence and the law, and finally left this question to the jury: "Has the prosecution satisfied you that Mr. Shannon used more force than was reasonable in the circumstances?, because that goes solely to the question: Did he lawfully kill Mr. Meredith?" This summarises the burden of his direction to the jury. Mr. Fox Andrews argues that the judge ought to have invited the jury to consider whether the appellant, at the moment of stabbing, "honestly and instinctively thought that this action was necessary" to his defence and to have told them that if they thought that that was right and provided an adequate reason for the stabbing, it could be strong evidence that only reasonable defensive action had been taken.

Mr. Fox Andrews in effect urged that the learned judge had concentrated so much on the state of the appellant's mind in relation to the intent necessary to establish the charge of murder that he had, unwittingly, obscured this subjective element in self-defence. . . .

The learned judge, in the course of his summing up, used verbatim several extracts from Lord Morris's statement of the law in *Palmer* v. *R.* (*supra*), but throughout the summing up, and at the end he left the jury with the bald question, "Are you satisfied that the appellant used more force than was necessary in the circumstances?" without Lord Morris's qualification that if they came to the conclusion that the appellant honestly thought, without having to weigh things to a nicety, that what he did was necessary to defend himself, they should regard that as "most potent evidence" that it was actually reasonably necessary. In other words, if the jury came to the conclusion that the stabbing was the act of a desperate man in extreme difficulties, with his assailant dragging him down by the hair, they should consider very carefully before concluding that the stabbing was an offensive and not a defensive act, albeit it went beyond what an onlooker would regard as reasonably necessary. . . .

In the judgment of this Court the evidence of the appellant, if accepted by the jury, raised the questions (a) whether the stabbing was in fact the act of a desperate man trying to defend himself and to force his assailant to let go of his hair and (b) whether, although not reasonably necessary by an objective standard, nonetheless, to use Lord Morris's words, the appellant honestly and instinctively thought that it was; in which case his honest belief would be "most potent evidence" that he had only taken defensive action; in other words, in the circumstances the stabbing was essentially defensive in character. The case for the prosecution, on the other hand, if accepted by the jury, was a perfect illustration of a man going over to the offensive and stabbing by way of revenge, punishment, retaliation or pure aggression.

The learned judge touched on this aspect of the matter when he was directing the jury on the issue of intent in relation to a charge of murder. At the end of the summing up he said this: "If you think that he lashed out because he lost his temper, having been treated in this painful, humiliating, frightening way, then you may think—it is a matter for you—that because he lost his temper in those circumstances he gave little or no thought to what might be the consequences of lashing out and in those circumstances he did not form the intent suggested. This is the matter which you must consider, clearly. The more a man loses his temper, the less likely he may be to consider what are likely to be the consequences of his acts even though when he is in a balanced state of mind he realises that if you lash out with scissors and it lands and you do it with force then it is going to do a lot of personal injury." But on the issue of self-defence he, effectively, excluded the state of the accused's mind. In other words, by leaving that issue to the jury on the bald basis of "Did the appellant use more force than was necessary in the cir- cumstances?" the learned judge may have precluded the jury from considering the real issue, which, to paraphrase Lord Morris in *Palmer* v. *R.* was "was this stabbing within the conception of necessary self-defence judged by the standards of common sense, bearing in mind the position of the appellant at the moment of the stabbing, or was it a case of angry retaliation or pure aggression on his part."

It is, we think, significant that in relation to intent, that is applying the test of what was in the accused's mind, the jury concluded that it was not murder but only manslaughter on the basis of no intent to cause really serious bodily harm, but seem to have excluded the appellant's state of mind in considering self-defence.

In those circumstances the Court came to the conclusion, not without considerable hesitation and anxiety, that the verdict of manslaughter was unsafe and unsatisfactory and ought to be quashed, which was done on April 15, 1980.

Appeal allowed
Conviction quashed

Att.-Gen. for Northern Ireland's Reference
[1977] A.C. 105
House of Lords

The reference was based on a case in which a soldier was charged with murder after shooting at the deceased in the mistaken belief that he was a member of the I.R.A., a proscribed organisation.

LORD DIPLOCK: To kill or wound another person is *prima facie* unlawful. There may be circumstances, however, which render the act of shooting and any killing which results from it lawful; and an honest and reasonable belief by the accused in the existence of facts which if true would have rendered his act lawful is a defence to any charge based on the shooting. So for the purposes of the present reference one must ignore the fact that the deceased was an entirely innocent person and must deal with the case as if he were a member of the Provisional I.R.A. and a potentially dangerous terrorist, as the accused honestly and reasonably believed him to be. . . .

What amount of force is "reasonable in the circumstances" for the purpose of preventing crime is, in my view, always a question for the jury in a jury trial, never a "point of law" for the judge.

The form in which the jury would have to ask themselves the question in a trial for an offence against the person in which this defence was raised by the accused, would be: Are we satisfied that no reasonable man a) with knowledge of such facts as were known to the accused or reasonably believed by him to exist b) in the circumstances and time available to him for reflection c) could be of the opinion that the prevention of the risk of harm to which others might be exposed if the suspect were allowed to escape justified exposing the suspect to the risk of harm to him that might result from the kind of force that the accused contemplated using?

To answer this the jury would have first to decide what were the facts that did exist and were known to the accused to do so and what were mistakenly believed by the accused to be facts. In respect of the latter the jury would have had to decide whether any reasonable man on the material available to the accused could have shared that belief. . . .

The jury would have also to consider how the circumstances in which the accused had to make his decision whether or not to use force and the shortness of the time available to him for reflection, might affect the judgment of a reasonable man. In the facts that are to be assumed for the purposes of the reference there is material upon which a jury might take the view that the accused had reasonable grounds for apprehension of imminent danger to himself and other members of the patrol if the deceased were allowed to get away and join armed fellow-members of the

Provisional I.R.A. who might be lurking in the neighbourhood, and that the time available to the accused to make up his mind what to do was so short that even a reasonable man could only act intuitively. This being so, the jury in approaching the final part of the question should remind themselves that the postulated balancing of risk against risk, harm against harm, by the reasonable man is not undertaken in the calm analytical atmosphere of the court-room after counsel with the benefit of hindsight have expounded at length the reasons for and against the kind of degree of force that was used by the accused; but in the brief second or two which the accused had to decide whether to shoot or not and under all the stresses to which he was exposed.

In many cases where force is used in the prevention of crime or in effecting an arrest there is a choice as to the degree of force to use. On the facts that are to be assumed for the purposes of the reference the only options open to the accused were either to let the deceased escape or to shoot at him with a service rifle. A reasonable man would know that a bullet from a self-loading rifle if it hit a human being, at any rate at the range at which the accused fired, would be likely to kill him or to injure him seriously. So in one scale of the balance the harm to which the deceased would be exposed if the accused aimed to hit him was predictable and grave and the risk of its occurrence high. In the other scale of the balance it would be open to the jury to take the view that it would not be unreasonable to assess the kind of harm to be averted by preventing the accused's escape as even graver—the killing or wounding of members of the patrol by terrorists in ambush, and the effect of this success by members of the Provisional I.R.A. in encouraging the continuance of the armed insurrection and all the misery and destruction of life and property that terrorist activity in Northern Ireland has entailed. The jury would have to consider too what was the highest degree at which a reasonable man could have assessed the likelihood that such consequence might follow the escape of the deceased if the facts had been as the accused knew or believed them reasonably to be.

Note

Part a) of the question to be left to the jury must now be read in light of *R.* v. *Gladstone Williams*. This modification has no impact on the remainder of Lord Diplock's judgment.

vii. Mistake

See *R.* v. *Gladstone Williams, ante,* p. 155, *Beckford* v. *The Queen, ante,* p. 157 and *O'Connor* [1991] Crim.L.R. 135.

viii. Excessive Force

Palmer v. The Queen
[1971] A.C. 814
Privy Council

A group of men, including the appellant went to buy ganja. The accused had a gun. A dispute arose and the men left with the ganja but without paying. A chase ensued and a man was shot. The appellant was charged with murder and claimed self-defence. He was convicted of murder and appealed.

LORD MORRIS OF BORTH-Y-GEST: . . . On behalf of the appellant it was contended that if where self-defence is an issue in a case of homicide a jury came to the conclusion that an accused person was intending to defend himself then an intention to kill or to cause grievous bodily harm would be negatived: so it was contended that if in such a case the jury came to the conclusion that excessive force had been used the correct verdict would be one of manslaughter: hence it was argued that in every case where self-defence is left to a jury they must be directed that there are the three possible verdicts, viz. guilty of murder, guilty of manslaughter, and not guilty. But in many cases where someone is intending to defend himself he will have had an intention to cause serious bodily injury or even to kill, and if the prosecution satisfy the jury that he had one of these intentions in circumstances in which or at a time when there was no justification or excuse for having it—then the prosecution will have shown that the question of self-defence is eliminated. All other issues which on the facts may arise will be unaffected.

An issue of self-defence may of course arise in a range and variety of cases and circumstances where no death has resulted. The tests as to its rejection or its validity will be just the same as in a case where death has resulted. In its simplest form the question that arises is the question: Was the defendant acting in necessary self-defence? If the prosecution satisfy the jury that he was not then all other possible issues remain.

. . . In their Lordships' view the defence of self-defence is one which can be and will be readily understood by any jury. It is a straightforward conception. It involves no abstruse legal thought. It requires no set words by way of explanation. No formula need be employed in reference to it. Only common sense is needed for its understanding. It is both good law and good sense that a man who is attacked may defend himself. It is both good law and good sense that he may do, but may only do what is reasonably necessary. But everything will depend upon the particular facts and circumstances. Of these a jury can decide. It may in some cases be only sensible and clearly possible to take some simple avoiding action. Some attacks may be serious and dangerous. Others may not be. If there is some relatively minor attack it would not be common sense to permit some action of retaliation which was wholly out of proportion to the necessities of the situation. If an attack is serious so that it puts someone in immediate peril then immediate defensive action may be necessary. If the moment is one of crisis for someone in imminent danger he may have to avert the danger by some instant reaction. If the attack is all over and no sort of peril remains then the employment of force may be by way of revenge or punishment or by way of paying off an old score or may be pure aggression. There may no longer be any link with a necessity of defence. Of all these matters the good sense of a jury will be the arbiter. There are no prescribed words which must be employed in or adopted in a summing up. All that is needed is a clear exposition, in relation to the particular facts of the case, of the conception of necessary self-defence. If there has been no attack then clearly there will have been no need for defence. If there has been attack so that defence is reasonably necessary it will be recognised that a person defending himself cannot weigh to a nicety the exact measure of his necessary defensive action. If a jury thought that in a moment of unexpected anguish a person attacked had only done what he honestly and instinctively thought was necessary that would be most potent evidence that only reasonable defensive action had been taken. A jury will be told that the defence of self-defence, where the evidence makes its raising possible, will only fail if the prosecution show beyond doubt that what the accused did was not by way of self-defence.

But their Lordships consider, in agreement with the approach in the *De Freitas* case (1960) 2 W.I.R. 523, that if the prosecution have shown that what was done was not done in self-defence then that issue is eliminated from the case. If the jury consider that an accused acted in self-defence or if the jury are in doubt as to this then they will acquit. The defence of self-defence either succeeds so as to result in an acquittal or it is disproved in which case as a defence it is rejected. In a homicide case the circumstances may be such that it will become an issue as to whether there was provocation so that the verdict might be one of manslaughter. Any other possible issues will remain. If in any case the view is possible that the intent necessary to constitute the crime of murder was lacking then that matter would be left to the jury.

Appeal dismissed

Question

Does it follow that because the defendant honestly believed that the force which he used was necessary, a jury will always find that the degree of force which he used was reasonably necessary?

Note

Palmer was followed by the Court of Appeal in *McInnes* [1971] 1 W.L.R. 1600. In the *Attorney-General for Northern Ireland's Reference* (No. 1 of 1975) [1977] A.C. 105, Lord Dilhorne said that where death results from the use of excessive force in prevention of crime or in effecting an arrest, and the accused intended to kill or do grievous bodily harm, he would be guilty of murder and not manslaughter.

In the case of *R. v. MacKay* [1957] V.R. 560, the Supreme Court of Victoria recognised a qualified defence to murder based on the excessive use of force in circumstances where some force would have been lawful. A killing in such circumstances would result in a manslaughter verdict. This defence was confirmed by the High Court of Australia in *R. v. Howe* (1958) 100 C.L.R. 448 and again in *Viro v. The Queen* (1978) 141 C.L.R. 88. In *Palmer* the Privy Council considered these authorities but decided not to follow them. However, in *Zecevic v. D.P.P.* (1987) 61 A.L.J.R. 375, by a majority of five to two, the High Court of Australia abolished the defence. The majority were motivated by a desire firstly, to simplify the defence of self-defence to make it more readily understandable by juries; secondly, to make for consistency between homicide and other crimes; and thirdly, to bring Australian common law into line with *Palmer*, English common law and the law of the Code States of Australia. Prior to this development there was a rising tide of support in England for the Australian qualified defence; both Smith and Hogan, *Criminal Law* (7th ed. 1992, at p. 261) and Glanville Williams, *Textbook of Criminal Law* (2nd ed., 1983, at pp. 546–547) are in favour of the importation of the defence into the English common law, while the C.L.R.C. (Fourteenth Report, Cmnd. 7844, para. 288) and the Law Commission (Law Com. No. 177, Draft Criminal Code Bill, clause 59) recommended the introduction of a defence similar to the Australian qualified defence.

For further discussion of this development see David Lanham, "Death of a qualified defence?" (1988) 104 L.Q.R. 239.

5. PROPOSALS FOR REFORM

i. General Principles

Draft Criminal Code

"Acts justified or excused by law

45.—(1) A person does not commit an offence by doing an act which is justified or excused by—

(a) any enactment; or
(b) any 'enforceable Community right' as defined in section 2(1) of the European Communities Act 1972; or
(c) any rule of the common law continuing to apply to virtue of section 4(4)."

Commentary on Draft Criminal Code Bill, Law Com. No. 177

"12.2 *Defence not specified in the Code*. As the Code team explained in their Report, it is impossible to specify in the code all those circumstances which amount to defences because they justify or excuse the doing of acts that would otherwise be offences. For, first, the full statement of some defences would involve reducing doctrines of the civil law to statutory forms for the purpose of their application in criminal cases, a task which it would not be appropriate for us to undertake even if it were in principle desirable that it should be done. Secondly, the exact specification or application, or even the existence, of some defences cannot be stated with confidence in the present state of the law. Such defences, of which necessity is the most obvious example, must be left to develop at common law. The Code can state a limited number of general defences that are well-developed (see clauses 41, 42 and 44) or capable of being closely defined (see clause 43). Having done so, it cannot do more than make clear that that is not an exhaustive statement of defences and that other circumstances of justification and excuse continue to apply. We are persuaded by the team's arguments and, with the exception of the clause mentioned in the following paragraph, we have in general adopted their proposals as to the appropriate contents of this part of the Code.

12.4 *Acts justified or excused by law*. The Code team's clause 49 forms the basis of our own clause 45(c). The paragraph may be said to have two functions. On the one hand, as already said, it preserves known defences not specified in the Code. Examples are given in the commentary on clause 45, below. On the other hand, it will permit the development of existing defences and even the emergence of defences not at present known to the law. Common law principles of justification and excuse are not static. They are developed by the judges as occasion arises and attitudes change. The history of duress by threats in recent years is a striking example of the development of a known defence. Our comment on clause 43 refers to recent cases revealing the existence of an analogous defence of duress of circumstances. Clause 45(c), or rather clause 4(4) to which it refers, preserves the power of the courts to determine the existence, extent and application of any justification or excuse provided by the common law.

12.5 *'Unlawfully' and 'without lawful excuse' not employed in the Code.* Parliament has sometimes qualified the statement of offences with the words 'unlawfully' or 'without lawful excuse'. There has been no consistency in this usage, however, and the use of such words does not seem to have been necessary for the purpose of importing general defences. The Code provisions on general defences, including clause 45(c), ensure that they are unnecessary in the statement of offences in Part II."

Draft Criminal Code Bill

"Belief in circumstance affording a defence

41.—(1) Unless otherwise provided, a person who acts in the belief that a circumstance exists has any defence that he would have if the circumstance existed.

(2) Subsection (1) does not apply in respect of a defence specially provided for a pre-Code offence as defined in section 6 (to which section 2(3) applies).

(3) Any requirement as to proof or disproof of a defence applies to proof or disproof of a belief mentioned in subsection (1)."

Commentary on Draft Criminal Code Bill, Law Com. No. 177

"12.6 *A statutory presumption.* If knowledge of a particular circumstance is an element of an offence, a belief that that circumstance does not exist means that the offence is not committed. Subsection (1) provides a presumption in favour of a corresponding rule for defences, namely, that a person who acts in the belief that a circumstance exists has any defence that he would have if it existed. The Code thus gives general effect to the *prima facie* principle that a person is to be judged, for purposes of criminal liability, on the facts as he believed them to be. This is the tendency, though not the universal effect, of recent judicial developments in the field of defences. It is desirable that the Code should provide consistently for offences and defences, leaving it to Parliament in particular contexts, if it thinks fit, to exclude the application of this subsection or to limit a defence of belief in the existence of an 'exempting circumstance' to a case of a belief based on reasonable grounds. Where a defendant relies on this subsection, the absence of reasonable grounds for the belief he claims to have held is, of course, relevant in determining he did hold it.

12.7 *Mistake as to one element of a defence.* A defence may have two or more elements, each of which is, in the language of the Code, an 'exempting circumstance', and a person's mistaken belief may be as to the existence of one such circumstance. Subsection (1) places him in the position that he would be in if his belief were true. For example, a person may be guilty of manslaughter rather than murder if he kills under provocation—that is, if something done or said causes him to lose his self-control (clauses 55(a) and 58). If he mistakenly believes that just such a thing has been done or said, the supposed provocation is treated as actual provocation, and other elements of this special defence to murder (the alleged loss of self-control and the question whether the provocation was sufficient ground for the loss of self-control) are then considered on that basis.

12.8 *Voluntary intoxication*. Subsection (1) has to be read subject to clause 22(1)(b) and (3). A person who was voluntarily intoxicated is credited, in the case of an offence requiring a fault element of recklessness, with the understanding of the relevant matter that he would have had if he had been sober. Similarly, in the case of an offence requiring a fault element of failure to comply with a standard of care, or requiring no fault, a person who was voluntarily intoxicated is treated as not having believed that an exempting circumstance existed if a reasonable sober person would not have done so.

12.9 *Application of the clause*. Subsection (2) ensures that subsection (1) does not affect the law relating to 'pre-Code offences'—those created by or under pre-Code legislation. Whether a principle equivalent to that stated by subsection (1) applies in relation to a defence specially proved for a pre-Code offence will depend on the application and interpretation of the relevant legislation as though the Code has not been enacted (clause 2(3)) or on any relevant rule of the common law (clauses 4(5), 45(c)).

12.10 *Burden of proof*. Subsection (3) puts the burden of proof in relation to a belief in a defence where it lies in relation to the defence itself."

ii. Duress

Draft Criminal Code Bill

"Duress by threats

42.—(1) A person is not guilty of an offence [to which this section applies] when he does an act under duress by threats.

[(2) This section applies to any offence other than murder or attempt to murder.]

(3) A person does an act under duress by threats if—

(a) he does it because he knows or believes—
  (i) that a threat has been made to cause death or serious personal harm to himself or another if the act is not done; and
  (ii) that the threat will be carried out immediately if he does not do the act or, if not immediately, before he or that other can obtain official protection; and
  (iii) that there is no other way of preventing the threat being carried out; and
(b) the threat is one which in all the circumstances (including any of his personal circumstances that affect its gravity) he cannot reasonably be expected to resist.

(4) It is immaterial that the person doing the act believes, or that it is the case, that any official protection available in the circumstances will or may be ineffective.

(5) Subsection (1) does not apply to a person who has knowingly and without reasonable excuse exposed himself to the risk of such a threat.

(6) A wife has no defence (except under this section) by virtue of having done an act under the coercion of her husband."

Illustrations

Clause 42(1)–(3)

42(i) "D takes part in a terrorist attack on a public house. He does so because E, the leader of the terrorist group, has told him that he (D) will be 'severely punished' if he does not. D knows E's reputation for extreme violence and believes that E is threatening serious injury to himself or a member of his family. He does not believe that he has time to put himself under police protection before he must take part in the attack or suffer his 'punishment'. If clause 42(5) does not apply (see example 42(iv)), whether D has the defence of duress in respect of offences to which he is a party depends on a question to be answered by the jury: could D reasonably be expected to resist the threat as he understood it? The jury must have regard to all the circumstances, some of which would be: (a) the nature of the offences; (b) the part played by D; (c) D's age and any other personal characteristics affecting the gravity of the threat; (d) current attitudes to what may properly be expected of citizens facing threats from terrorists.

42(ii) As in example 42(i), except that E communicates no threat to D. D is falsely told by F, and believes, that E will 'severely punish' him if he does not take part in the raid. The result is the same as if the threat were actually made—that is, the same as in example 42(i).

Clause 42(1)–(4)

42(iii) As in example 42(i), except that D realises that he has time to put himself under police protection. He believes, however, that the police cannot effectively protect him and his family from E. This belief, even if justified, is immaterial. The defence of duress is not available to D.

Clause 42(1)–(5)

42(iv) As in example 42(i), except that D is himself a member of the terrorist group. When he joined he knew that the group sometimes violently punished its members for disobedience. If he had no reasonable excuse for joining the group (see example 42(v)), the defence of duress is not available to him.

42(v) As in example 42(iv). D is a police officer. He joined the group in that capacity, posing as a committed terrorist. If this constituted a 'reasonable excuse' for joining the group, the defence of duress may be available to him. If it is, the jury may wish to take the fact that he is a police officer into account in deciding whether he could reasonably have been expected to resist the threat."

Commentary on Draft Criminal Code Bill, Law Com. No. 177

"Clause 42: Duress by threats

12.11 This clause provides a defence of duress by threats similar to that available at common law. We draw attention below to certain proposed departures from the common law position. The subject is one upon which we made recommendations, with a draft Bill, in 1977 [*Report on Defences of*

General Application (1977), Law Com. No. 83]. The present clause benefits, in its content, from the further consideration which we have been able to give to the subject in the light of the Code team's work and of recent consultation, and, in method, from clause 1 of our earlier draft Bill as modified in clause 47 of the Code team's Bill.

12.12 *Nomenclature.* We call the defence 'duress by threats' to distinguish it from the related defence of duress of circumstances which we propose in clause 43. Subsection (1) makes available the phrase 'acting under duress by threats' for use elsewhere.

12.13 *Availability of the defence.* In our earlier Report we recommended that duress should be a defence to all crimes. This was noticed by members of the House of Lords in *Howe*, [*ante*, p. 296], where, however, it was held that duress is not a defence to murder. Lord Bridge of Harwich expressed the view that if duress is to be made a defence to murder 'the proper means to effect such a reform is by legislation such as that proposed by the Law Commission." It is only by legislation, Lord Bridge observed, 'that the scope of the defence of duress can be defined with the degree of precision which, if it is to be available in murder at all, must surely be of critical importance.' The topic is, of course, a controversial one; and the decision in *Howe* has itself proved controversial. In the circumstances we have thought it right that our draft clause should reflect that decision by providing (in subsection (2)) that the defence does not apply to murder or attempt to murder. Exceptionally, we place this aspect of the clause within square brackets, as an indication that our recommendation on the point has not been abandoned.

12.14 *Elements of the defence: (a) what the actor must know or believe.* Subsection (3) sets out the circumstances in which a person does an act under duress by threats. The first requirement is that he must know of, or believe in the existence of, a threat to himself or another if he does not do the act. Paragraph (a) lays down three conditions:

   (i)   The threat, following the prevailing judicial review and that of most modern codes, must be one of death or serious personal harm to himself or another.
   (ii) The threat must be, or he must believe that it is, one that will be carried out immediately or before he or the other can obtain official protection. In this connection subsection (4) provides that it is immaterial that, in fact or as he believes, any available official protection will or may be ineffective. This gives effect to our earlier proposal which, although questioned by the Code team, was strongly supported on consultation by the South-Eastern Circuit (Southwark) Scrutiny Group.
   (iii) There must be, or he must believe that there is, no other way of preventing the threat being carried out.

12.15 *'Knows or believes'.* The emphasis in subsection (3)(a) on the actor's knowledge or belief reflects the fact that a defence of duress depends essentially upon a state of mind. In this respect the clause somewhat departs from the prevailing judicial view, according to which a person's belief in the existence of a threat must be 'reasonably' held if it is to found the defence. This requirement would, we believe, be inconsistent with the tendency of judicial developments in other contexts. It would also be at odds with the general policy of the Code, in keeping with those developments, of assigning the reasonableness of a person's asserted belief to the domain of evidence.

12.16 *Elements of the defence: (b) actor cannot be expected to resist threat.* The threat must be one which the actor cannot reasonably be expected to resist; and the circumstances to be considered for this purpose include his personal circumstances as they affect the gravity of the threat. This follows our earlier recommendation of a test of what can reasonably be expected 'of the defendant in question. ... Threats directed against a weak, immature of disabled person may well be much more compelling than the same threats directed against a normal healthy person'. This was quoted by the Court of Appeal in *Graham*, where the resistance to be expected was held to be that of 'a sober person of reasonable firmness', though one 'sharing the characteristics of the defendant'. A person's 'firmness', however, is itself one of his characteristics that may affect the gravity of the threat to him; and we are not convinced that personal characteristics can be separated in the way that the *Graham* test appears to contemplate. The test stated in subsection (3)(b) therefore departs in one respect from that of the Court of Appeal.

12.17 *Voluntary exposure to duress.* Subsection (5) provides that the defence is not available to a person who has voluntarily and without reasonable excuse exposed himself to the risk of a relevant threat—as, for example, by joining a criminal group which he knows may threaten with violence a member who is reluctant to commit offences in its service. This is the effect of recent case law and is consistent with our own earlier recommendation on the point.

12.18 *Marital coercion.* Subsection (6) abolishes this common law defence."

iii. Necessity

Note

There is no defence of necessity in the Draft Criminal Code Bill. If it exists at common law as a defence clause 45 will permit its continued development.

Draft Criminal Code Bill

"Duress of circumstances

43.—(1) A person is not guilty of an offence [to which this section applies] when he does an act under duress of circumstances.

(2) A person does an act under duress of circumstances if—

(a) he does it because he knows or believes that it is immediately necessary to avoid death or serious personal harm to himself or another; and

(b) the danger that he knows or believes to exist is such that in all the circumstances (including any of his personal characteristics that effect [*sic*] its gravity) he cannot reasonably be expected to act otherwise.

(3) This section—

[(a) applies to any offence other than murder or attempt to murder;]
(b) does not apply—
- (i) to a person who uses force for any of the purposes referred to in section 44(1) or 185; or
- (ii) to a person who acts in the knowledge or belief that a threat of a kind described in section 42(3)(a)(i) has been made; or
- (iii) to a person who has knowingly and without reasonable excuse exposed himself to the danger."

Illustrations

"Clause 43(1) and (2)

43(i) It is an offence to drive a motor vehicle on a road with a proportion of alcohol in the blood in excess of a prescribed limit. 'Driving' for this purpose includes steering. The proportion of alcohol in D's blood is above the limit. Having gone to sleep in the passenger seat of E's car, he wakes to find himself alone in the car, which is running out of control down a steep hill towards children playing on the street. D, to avoid serious injury to himself or the children, steers the car into a wall, damaging the car. The defence of duress of circumstances may be available to him on a charge of the driving offence or of damaging property. It is a question for the tribunal of fact whether he could reasonably have been expected to act otherwise than as he did.

43(ii) D's child, P, is a passenger in D's car. P is taken ill. D exceeds the speed limit in order to get P to hospital as quickly as possible. If D believed that it was immediately necessary to drive at that speed in order to save P from death or serious harm, and if in the circumstances he could not reasonably have been expected to do otherwise, he is not guilty of the speeding offence."

Commentary on Draft Criminal Code Bill, Law Com. No. 177

"Clause 43: Duress of circumstances

12.20 *Analogy with duress by threats.* Clause 43 adopts with minor amendments a clause which the Code team included in their Bill under the title 'defence of necessity'. It provides a defence to one who acts in order to avoid an imminent danger of death or serious personal harm to himself or another if in the circumstances he cannot reasonably be expected to act otherwise. The defence is modelled, so far as appropriate, on the defence of duress by threats. The Code team, who observed that the kind of situation covered by their clause is sometimes called 'duress of circumstances', were critical of our failure, in the Report on Defences of General Application, to recognise the force of the analogy with duress by threats. We are now persuaded that, as the team put it, '[t]he impact of some situations of imminent peril upon persons affected by them is hardly different in kind from that of threats such as give rise to the defence of duress' [Law Com. No. 143, para. 13.25]; and we are satisfied that the proposed defence should be provided by the Code.

12.21 *Authority.* We are fortified in this conclusion by the fact the Court of Appeal has twice recently, in the context of the offence of reckless driving, recognised a defence of this kind—though without having occasion to consider all its details or to give it general application. In

Conway [*ante*, p. 319], the later of the two cases, the defence was said to be conveniently called 'duress of circumstances'. We agreed. It is appropriate thus to emphasise the analogy with the case of threats.

12.22 *Elements of defence.* Subsection (2) states the elements of the defence. Like duress by threats, it is limited to cases where death or serious personal harm is threatened. The danger must be imminent. Like duress by threats, the defence is limited 'by means of an objective criterion formulated in terms of reasonableness'; but once again the standard, of conduct required is that applicable to one having the actor's personal characteristics so far as they affect the gravity of the danger.

12.23 *Application of defence.* Subsection (3) excludes murder and attempt to murder from the scope of the defence (but in square brackets, as with clause 42(2)) (para. (a)); avoids any inconvenient overlap between this and certain other defences (para. (b)(i) and (ii)); and sustains the analogy with duress by threats by excluding the case where the actor has knowingly and without reasonable excuse exposed himself to the danger (para. (b)(iii))."

iv. Self-defence and Kindred defences

Draft Criminal Code Bill

"Use of force in public or private defence

44.—(1) A person does not commit an offence by using such force as, in the circumstances which exist or which he believes to exist, is immediately necessary and reasonable—

- (a) to prevent or terminate crime, or to effect or assist in the lawful arrest of an offender or suspected offender or of a person unlawfully at large;
- (b) to prevent or terminate a breach of the peace;
- (c) to protect himself or another from unlawful force or unlawful personal harm;
- (d) to prevent or terminate the unlawful detention of himself or another;
- (e) to protect property (whether belonging to himself or another) from unlawful appropriation, destruction or damage; or
- (f) to prevent or terminate a trespass to his person or property.

(2) In this section, except where the context otherwise requires, 'force' includes, in addition to force against a person—

- (a) force against property;
- (b) a threat of force against person or property; and
- (c) the detention of a person without the use of force.

(3) For the purposes of this section, an act is 'unlawful' although a person charged with an offence in respect of it would be acquitted on the ground only that—

- (a) he was under ten years of age; or
- (b) he lacked the fault required for the offence or believed that an exempting circumstance existed; or

(c)　he acted in pursuance of a reasonable suspicion; or

(d)　he acted under duress, whether by threats or of circumstances; or

(e)　he was in a state of automatism or suffering from severe mental illness or severe mental handicap.

(4) Notwithstanding subsection (1), a person who believes circumstances to exist which would justify or excuse the use of force under that subsection has no defence if—

(a)　he knows that the force is used against a constable or a person assisting a constable; and

(b)　the constable is acting in the execution of his duty,

unless he believes the force to be immediately necessary to prevent personal harm to himself or another.

(5) A person does not commit an offence by doing an act immediately preparatory to the use of such force as is referred to in subsection (1).

(6) Subsection (1) does not apply where a person causes unlawful conduct or an unlawful state of affairs with a view to using force to resist or terminate it; but subsection (1) may apply although the occasion for the use of force arises only because he does anything he may lawfully do, knowing that such an occasion may arise.

(7) The fact that a person had an opportunity to retreat before using force shall be taken into account, in conjunction with other relevant evidence, in determining whether the use of force was immediately necessary and reasonable.

(8) A threat of force may be reasonable although the use of the force would not be.

(9) This section is without prejudice to the generality of section 185 (criminal damage: protection of person or property) or any other defence."

Illustrations

"Clause 44(1)(a)

44(i)　D shoots P who is about to attack him with a knife. If this action is necessary and reasonable to prevent P from killing or causing serious personal harm to D, D commits no offence. (It would be immaterial that D was unaware that P was armed with a knife, or was about to attack.)

44(ii)　D shoots P whom he believes to be about to attack him with a knife. If this action would have been necessary and reasonable to prevent P killing, or causing serious personal harm to D, had D's belief been true, D commits no offence, even if P was unarmed, or was not in fact about to attack.

Clause 44(3)(a)

44(iii)　D, a shopkeeper, sees P, whom he knows to be under the age of 10, take a watch from the counter and run off with it. D seizes P and takes the watch from him by force. If it is necessary to use force to prevent P from appropriating the watch and the force used is reasonable, D commits no offence.

Clause 44(3)(b)

44(iv)　D's tenant, P, is about to destroy certain fixtures in the leased premises. P wrongly believes that the fixtures belong to him. Although P lacks the fault for the offence of causing damage to property belonging to another, D may use reasonable and necessary force to protect his property.

44(v)   Wrongly believing that D is about to attack him, P makes what he
        believes to be a counter-attack on D. If P is using no more force than
        would be necessary and reasonable if the circumstances were as he
        believed them to be, he is not committing any offence; but D may use
        necessary and reasonable force to repel P's attack.

Clause 44(3)(c)

44(vi) P, a police officer, reasonably but wrongly believing D to be an armed,
        dangerous criminal, X, points a revolver at him. D, believing that he is
        about to be shot, strikes P and causes him serious personal harm. If in
        the light of D's belief this action is necessary and reasonable to prevent
        personal harm to D, he commits no offence, even though he knows that
        P is a police officer acting lawfully.

Clause 44(4)

44(vii) P, a constable, is arresting Q. D, who believes that P has no grounds
         for making the arrest, uses force against P to free Q. In fact P has
         reasonable grounds for suspecting that Q has committed an arrestable
         offence. D has no defence under this section to a charge of assault or
         causing personal harm.

44(viii) As in example 44(vii), but D also believes that P is about to cause Q
         personal harm. If the force used by D would have been necessary and
         reasonable to prevent the apprehended personal harm to a person
         wrongfully arrested, D commits no offence.

Clause 44(5)

44(ix) P, an armed criminal, shoots a policeman who drops his revolver. D, a
        bystander, fearing that P is about to shoot him, picks up the revolver to
        use it in self-defence. D is not guilty of being in possession of a firearm
        without a firearm certificate or of having with him an offensive weapon.

Clause 44(6)

44(x)   A gang of youths (the A group) shout taunts at a rival gang (the B
        group) until the latter attack them. D, a member of the A group, is
        attacked by P, a member of the B group, with a knife. D, who also has
        a knife, stabs P and kills or injures him. D has no defence under
        subsection (1) to a charge of murder, manslaughter or causing personal
        harm.

44(xi) Members of a political group, X, hold a lawful meeting. They know
        from experience that they are almost certain to be attacked by members
        of the rival group, Y. They are so attacked, and D, a member of the X
        group, kills or injures P, a member of the Y group. D may rely on
        subsection (1)."

Commentary on Draft Criminal Code Bill, Law Com. No. 177

"Clause 44: Use of force in public or private defence

12.24 *Function of the clause.* This clause, together with clause 185
(protection of person or property by acts causing destruction of or damage
to property), would replace existing statutory and common law principles
defining the circumstances in which a person has a defence to a charge of
committing a crime involving the use of force. The clause could be
invoked, for example, on a charge of murder or any violent offence against
the person or an offence of criminal damage to property. But the clause
states principles of the criminal law only. It does not (as section 3 of the

Criminal Law Act 1967 does) affect civil liability in any way. A person may have a defence under the section yet remain liable in damages for assault or negligence.

12.25 *Eliminating inconsistency.* The clause seeks in principle to restate existing law and does so in as much detail as the authorities reasonably permit. But the law should also be consistent and the present law relating to the use of force varies according to the circumstances in indefensible ways. For example, if a person is charged with damaging property belonging to another and his defence is that he was defending his own property, section 5(2) of the Criminal Damage Act 1971 applies and the test is whether he *believed* that what he did was reasonable; but if his defence is that he was defending his person, or that of another, the test at common law is whether what he did *was* reasonable. If he is charged with criminal damage by killing or injuring an aggressive dog, the result will vary according to whether he was defending his trousers or his leg—and he is likely to have a better chance of acquittal if it was his trousers. Clause 44 (together with clause 185) will eliminate such insupportable distinctions.

12.26 *The form of subsection (1).* Subsection (1) is stated in slightly more complex terms than might be expected. It provides that a person does not commit an offence by using such force as, 'in the circumstances which exist or which he believes to exist', is immediately necessary and reasonable to (in brief) prevent crime, effect a lawful arrest, prevent or terminate a breach of the peace, or protect person or property from unlawful acts. The reference to circumstances which the person using force *believes to exist* would ideally be omitted, leaving the case of mistaken belief to be catered for by clause 41 (belief in circumstance affording a defence). It is included, however, in order to bring out the force of the words 'circumstances *which exist*' (meaning, which actually exist, whether or not the person using force is aware of the fact). These words are themselves included because the powers of arrest without a warrant granted by the Police and Criminal Evidence Act 1984 apply where a person 'is in the act of committing', or 'is guilty of', or 'is about to commit', an arrestable offence, as well as when the arrester has reasonable grounds for suspecting one of these things to be the case. It has seemed necessary, for the sake of consistency, to apply clause 44 for all purposes, and not apply that of arrest, to the case where as a matter of fact justifying circumstances exist. For an arrester may also be preventing crime and, in doing so, protecting himself or another person from attack or some property from damage. It would be unacceptable to apply different principles to the same use of force in relation to its different purposes.

(For a contrary view see, *ante*, p. 345.)

12.29 *'Unlawful'.* Paragraphs (c), (d) and (e) of subsection (1) permit the use of force against 'unlawful' acts. An act (for example, a trespass) may be unlawful under the civil law although not criminal. Subsection (3), a somewhat technical provision, is concerned with cases in which, to avoid any uncertainty, the Code needs to declare that for the purposes of the section the behaviour of a person against whom force is used is 'unlawful' although, if it were the subject of a criminal charge, that person would be acquitted. For example, it ought to be clear, without the need to resort to what may be uncertain principles of the law of tort, that one who is attacked with a dagger by a nine-year-old or by a person suffering from severe mental illness may use reasonable and necessary force in self-defence although his attacker is immune from criminal liability (clauses 32(1) and 35(1)).

12.30 Where a person properly using force for a purpose mentioned in subsection (1)(c), (d) or (e) is unaware of the facts that would ground the acquittal of the person against whom he uses it, he will be protected by subsection (1) (without resort to subsection (3)) because of his belief in circumstances rendering the other's conduct 'unlawful' in the sense of criminal. Resort to subsection (3) is therefore necessary only when the person using force is aware of the special facts.

12.31 It is sometimes lawful to arrest and to use reasonable force against a person because he is reasonably, though perhaps quite wrongly, suspected of some wrongdoing. For example, under the Police and Criminal Evidence Act 1984, any person may arrest without a warrant anyone whom he has reasonable grounds for suspecting to be committing an arrestable offence; and, under the Criminal Law Act 1967, the arrester may use reasonable force to make the arrest. Subsection (3)(c) relates to the position in the criminal law of the wrongly (though reasonably) suspected person who resists arrest or uses force to defend himself against force reasonably used by the arrester. The effect of subsection (3)(c) is that, with one important qualification, he does not commit an offence by using reasonable force to resist that arrest. Whatever the position in the civil law (which is unaffected by the subsection) a person should not, in our opinion, be guilty of an offence merely because he resists, and uses reasonable force to resist, an arrest which is not justified by the actual facts. For the purposes of the subsection, the arrester's conduct is 'unlawful'; but neither the arrester nor the resister is guilty of any offence. The same principle applies to an innocent person's defence of his property and for the other purposes of the section.

12.32 *Exception for lawful act of constable.* Subsection (4) states the important qualification referred to in the preceding paragraph. Where the person making the arrest is a constable acting in the execution of his duty, the suspected person must submit to arrest even if he is perfectly innocent and the constable's suspicion, though reasonable, is in fact mistaken. The suspect will commit an offence if he resists arrest and further offences if he uses force, whether against the constable or a person assisting him to carry out his duty. This is so even if he believes the arrest to be unlawful, unless he also believes there is 'imminent danger of injury.' It is one thing to require the wrongly suspected person to submit to arrest. It is quite another to say that he must submit to the infliction of person harm or even death. The effect of the subsection is that he does not commit an offence by using force which he believes to be immediately necessary to prevent such harm to himself or another innocent person. This is so even in the case where he is aware of the circumstances giving rise to the policeman's reasonable suspicion, that it so say, he knows that he is resisting the lawful, though mistaken, use of force. The subsection in no way limits the present right to resist an unlawful arrest, whether by a constable or not.

12.33 *Preparatory acts.* Subsection (5) ensures that criminal liability (most obviously, under legislation prohibiting the possession of firearms or offensive weapons) will not attach to an act immediately preparatory to a use of force permitted by subsection (1).

12.34 *Self-induced occasions for the use of force.* The effect of the first part of subsection (6) is that subsection (1) provides no defence to a person who deliberately provokes the very attack against which he then defends himself. On the other hand, it is important to preserve the liberty of the citizen to go about his lawful business even if he knows that he is likely to be met by unlawful violence from others. If he does so and is attacked he may defend himself. The second part of subsection (6) so provides.

12.35 *Opportunity to retreat.* Subsection (7) restates the law, only recently clarified by the Court of Appeal in *Bird* [1985] 1 W.L.R. 816, on the significance of the defendant's having had an opportunity to retreat before using force. Although the fact that he had such an opportunity so relevant to the court's or jury's consideration of whether his use of force was immediately necessary and reasonable, it is not conclusive of the question and is simply to be taken into account together with other relevant evidence."

CHAPTER 6

DEGREES OF RESPONSIBILITY

	PAGE		PAGE
1. Accomplices	366	iv. *Mens Rea* of an Accessory	379
i. Principals and Accessories	366	v. Accessory not Convictable as	
ii. Innocent Agency	368	a Principal	402
iii. Aids Abets Counsels or Pro-		2. Vicarious Liability	408
cures	374	3. Corporations	413

1. ACCOMPLICES

i. Principals and Accessories

Notes

The actual perpetrator of a crime or part of a crime, or one who effects it through an innocent agent, is guilty of the crime as principal. One who does not perpetrate a crime but participates in it is punishable as an accessory if he aids, abets, counsels or procures the principal offender to commit the crime. See Accessories and Abettors Act 1861, section 8, in the judgment of Lord Widgery C.J. in *Att.-Gen.'s Reference (No. 1 of 1975)*, *post*, p. 374, and as to summary offences, Magistrates' Courts Act 1980, section 44. His punishment is the same as that of the principal.

The words "aid and abet, counsel and procure" may all be used together to charge a person who is alleged to have participated in a crime otherwise than as the principal or as accessory after the fact; *Re Smith* (1858) 3 H. & N. 227; *Ferguson* v. *Weaving*, *post*, p. 387. Such a person may also be charged as a principal: see *Maxwell* v. *D.P.P. for Northern Ireland*, *post*, p. 388. Indeed if two persons are present at the scene of a crime and it is not clear which committed the act and which did no more than help, it is not necessary to show which was the actual perpetrator in order to convict them both: see *Mohan* v. *R.*, *post*, p. 367. A person charged as an accessory may be convicted as a principal: see *R.* v. *Cogan & Leak*, *post*, p. 369.

The terminology has changed over the years, and several terms used in cases before 1967 are now obsolete, a fact which must be borne in mind in reading such cases. The actual perpetrator was called the first principal, or the principal in the first degree. Secondary parties were of two kinds, in felonies principals in the second degree or accessories before the fact, in misdemeanours aiders and abettors, or counsellors and procurers. The technical distinction between the two kinds of secondary party still exists but is not important (see Accessories, *infra*). It is nowadays usual to use two terms only, principal for the actual perpetrator, and accessory for any kind of secondary party.

Although principal and accessory are equally guilty, the distinction between them is still of importance because (1) the definition of a crime is almost always in terms applicable only to a principal, and the liability of an accessory follows from the terms of the Accessories and Abettors Act 1861, section 8, or Magistrates' Courts' Act 1980, section 44; (2) the *mens rea* required of an accessory is different from that of a principal and (3) not all accessories who participate with the appropriate *mens rea* are liable for the offence.

One who aids a criminal *after* the commission of a crime to avoid detection or arrest or trial is not technically a party, although the old term for such a person was accessory after the fact. He may be guilty of one of several offences against the administration of justice, of which the most prominent is assisting an offender, contrary to section 4, Criminal Law Act 1967.

Mohan v. R.
[1967] 2 A.C. 187
Privy Council

D. was quarrelling with M., when R., who was D.'s father, ran out of his house and attacked M. with a cutlass. While R. was chasing M., D. went off and returned with another cutlass. Both struck many blows at M., who collapsed and later died. He was found to be wounded in the back and in the leg. It appeared that death was caused only by the leg wound. D. and R. were convicted of murder, and appealed on the ground that, as there was no evidence of a pre-arranged plan to attack M., the Crown must show which of them struck the fatal blow.

LORD PEARSON: [The appellants' argument] will be considered on the hypothesis that the death may have been caused solely by the leg wound. The question then arises whether each of the appellants can be held responsible for the leg wound, when it may have been inflicted by the other of them. There is conflicting evidence as to which of them struck the blow on M.'s leg, the evidence for the prosecution tending to show that the appellant D. struck it and the evidence for the defence tending to show that the appellant R. struck it. There is uncertainty on that point.

Also it cannot be inferred with any certainty from the evidence that the appellants had a pre-arranged plan for their attack on M.

It is, however, clear from the evidence for the defence as well as from the evidence for the prosecution, that at the material time both the appellants were armed with cutlasses, both were attacking M., and both struck him. It is impossible on the facts of this case to contend that the fatal blow was outside the scope of the common intention. The two appellants were attacking the same man at the same time with similar weapons and with the common intention that he should suffer grievous bodily harm. Each of the appellants was present, and aiding and abetting the other of them in the wounding of M.

That is the feature which distinguishes this case from cases in which one of the accused was not present or not participating in the attack or not using any dangerous weapon, but may be held liable as a conspirator or an accessory before the fact or by virtue of a common design if it can be shown that he was party to a pre-arranged plan in pursuance of which the fatal blow was struck. In this case one of the appellants struck the fatal blow, and the other of them was present aiding and abetting him. In such cases the prosecution do not have to prove that the accused were acting in pursuance of a pre-arranged plan.

Appeals dismissed

Note

The principle in this case does not apply if it is not proved that both were involved in some capacity or other. "Where two people were jointly indicted, and the evidence did not point to one rather than the other, they both ought to be acquitted because the prosecution had not proved its case. The uncertainty could not be resolved by convicting both": *Collins & Fox* v. *Chief Constable of Merseyside* [1988] Crim.L.R. 247 (D.C.).

ii. Innocent Agency

Note

If A aids or encourages B to commit the *actus reus* of a crime, it may be that B, for some reason personal to himself, is not guilty of the crime. The question of A's liability arises. If B is "principal" and commits no crime, it would appear that there is no crime to which A can be an accessory. Sometimes the logic of that has to be accepted: see *Thornton* v. *Mitchell, infra.* In other cases, the logic is avoided by holding that A is the principal, since he used B as an innocent agent to commit what would be a crime if done by A: see *R.* v. *Cogan & Leak, infra.* In other cases, it is possible to convict A by holding that although B is not guilty, or not prosecutable, a crime was nevertheless committed by him, in which A was an accessory: see *R.* v. *Bourne, R.* v. *Austin, infra.*

Thornton v. Mitchell
[1940] 1 All E.R. 339
King's Bench Division

A bus driver reversed his bus according to the signals of his conductor, who failed to notice some persons standing behind the bus. The driver could not possibly see behind the bus and had to rely on the signals of the conductor. The persons standing behind the bus were injured. The driver was charged with careless driving, and the conductor with aiding and abetting, counselling and procuring the commission of that offence. The charge against the driver was dismissed, but the conductor was convicted. He appealed.

LORD HEWART C.J.: [The justices] say in paragraph 8: "We being of opinion that the conductor [had been very negligent] held that he was guilty of aiding, abetting, counselling and procuring the said Hollindrake to drive without due care and attention, and accordingly we inflicted a fine." In my opinion, this case is *a fortiori* on *Morris* v. *Tolman* [1923] 1 K.B. 166, to which our attention has been directed. I will read one sentence from the judgment of Avory J. at p. 171: " ... in order to convict, it would be necessary to show that the respondent was aiding and abetting the principal, but a person cannot aid another in doing something which that other has not done."

That I think is the very thing which these justices have decided that the bus conductor did. In one breath they say that the principal did nothing which he should not have done and in the next breath they hold that the bus conductor aided and abetted the driver in doing something which had not been done or in not doing something which he ought to have done. I really think that, with all respect to the ingenuity of counsel for the respondent, the case is too plain for argument.

Appeal allowed

Note

The reason why the bus conductor could not be convicted of careless driving as principal was because it was impossible to construe the word "drive" in the relevant section of the Road Traffic Act as referring to the conduct of anyone other than the immediate driver. See, Williams, *Textbook*, p. 370. There would seem to be limits beyond which the concept of agency will not stretch, *i.e.* wherever a crime needs personal action by the offender. Rape would appear to be such a crime, but see next case.

R. v. Cogan and Leak
[1976] 1 Q.B. 217
Court of Appeal

L. forced his wife to have sexual intercourse with C. C. was charged with rape and L. was charged with aiding, abetting, counselling and procuring C. to commit rape. C. was acquitted of rape on it appearing that he did not know that L.'s wife was not consenting to the intercourse. L. was convicted and appealed.

LAWTON L.J.: ... Leak's appeal against conviction was based on the proposition that he could not be found guilty of aiding and abetting Cogan to rape his wife if Cogan was acquitted of that offence as he was deemed in law to have been when his conviction was quashed: see section 2(3) of the Criminal Appeal Act 1968. Leak's counsel, Mr. Herrod, conceded however, that his proposition had some limitations. The law on this topic lacks clarity as a perusal of some of the textbooks shows: see *Smith and Hogan, Criminal Law*, 3rd ed. (1973), pp. 106–109; *Glanville Williams, Criminal Law*, 2nd ed. (1961), pp. 386–390, 406–408; *Russell on Crime*, 12th ed. (1964), vol. 1, p. 128. We do not consider it appropriate to review the law generally because, as was said by this court in *R. v. Quick* [1973] Q.B. 910, 923, when considering this kind of problem:

> "The facts of each case ... have to be considered and in particular what is alleged to have been done by way of aiding and abetting."

The only case which Mr. Herrod submitted had a direct bearing upon the problem of Leak's guilt was *Walters v. Lunt* [1951] 2 All E.R. 645. In that case the respondents had been charged, under section 33(1) of the Larceny Act 1916, with receiving from a child aged seven years, certain articles knowing them to have been stolen. In 1951, a child under eight years was deemed in law to be incapable of committing a crime: it followed that at the time the charge had not been proved. That case is very different from this because here one fact is clear—the wife had been raped. Cogan had had sexual intercourse with her without her consent. The fact that Cogan was innocent of rape because he believed that she was consenting does not affect the position that she was raped.

Her ravishment had come about because Leak had wanted it to happen and had taken action to see that it did by persuading Cogan to use his body as the instrument for the necessary physical act. In the language of the law the act of sexual intercourse without the wife's consent was the *actus reus*: it had been procured by Leak who had the appropriate *mens rea*, namely, his intention that Cogan should have sexual intercourse with her without her consent. In our judgment it is irrelevant that the man whom Leak had procured to do the physical act himself did not intend to have sexual intercourse with the wife without her consent. Leak was using him as a means to procure a criminal purpose.

Before 1861 a case such as this, pleaded as it was in the indictment, might have presented a court with problems arising from the old distinctions between principals and accessories in felony. Most of the old law was swept away by section 8 of the Accessories and Abettors Act 1861 and what remained by section 1 of the Criminal Law Act 1967. The modern law allowed Leak to be tried and punished as a principal offender. In our judgment he could have been indicted as a principal offender. It would have been no defence for him to submit that if Cogan was an "innocent" agent, he was necessarily in the old terminology of the law a principal in the first degree, which was a legal impossibility as a man cannot rape his own wife during cohabitation. The law no longer concerns itself with niceties of degrees in participation in crime; but even if it did Leak would still be guilty. The reason a man cannot by his own physical act rape his wife during cohabitation is because the law presumes consent from the marriage ceremony: see Hale, *Pleas of the Crown* (1778), vol. 1, p. 629. There is no such presumption when a man procures a drunken friend to do the physical act for him. Hale C.J. put this case in one sentence, at p. 629:

" ... tho in marriage she hath given up her body to her husband, she is not to be by him prostituted to another": see *loc. cit.*

Had Leak been indicted as a principal offender, the case against him would have been clear beyond argument. Should he be allowed to go free because he was charged with "being aider and abettor to the same offence"? If we are right in our opinion that the wife had been raped (and no one outside a court of law would say that she had not been), then the particulars of offence accurately stated what Leak had done, namely, he had procured Cogan to commit the offence. This would suffice to uphold the conviction. We would prefer, however, to uphold it on a wider basis. In our judgment convictions should not be upset because of mere technicalities of pleading in an indictment. Leak knew what the case against him was and the facts in support of that case were proved. But for the fact that the jury thought that Cogan in his intoxicated condition might have mistaken the wife's sobs and distress for expressions of her consent, no question of any kind would have arisen about the form of pleading. By his written statement Leak virtually admitted what he had done. As Judge Chapman said in *R. v. Humphreys* [1965] 3 All E.R. 689, 692:

"It would be anomalous if a person who admitted to a substantial part in the perpetration of a misdemeanour as aider and abettor could not be convicted on his own admission merely because the person alleged to have been aided and abetted was not or could not be convicted."

In the circumstances of this case it would be more than anomalous: it would be an affront to justice and to the common sense of ordinary folk. It was for these reasons that we dismissed the appeal against conviction. . . .

Appeal against conviction dismissed

Note

At the date of this case, a husband could not ordinarily be guilty of personally raping his wife. But see now *R. v. R.* [1992] A.C. 599, *post*, p. 640.

Questions

1. If the person who had forced Mrs. Leak to submit to intercourse with Cogan had been her *sister*, rather than her husband, would the result have been the same? See section 1 of the Sexual Offences (Amendment) Act 1976, *post*, p. 632.

2. In *R. v. Bourne* (1952) 36 Cr.App.R. 125, the C.C.A. upheld a conviction of a husband for aiding and abetting his wife to commit buggery with a dog, although the facts showed that the wife, who was the only possible principal, would have been able to raise the defence of duress had she been charged with committing buggery with the dog. The reason given was that a plea of duress admits the crime but prays to be excused punishment on the grounds of duress. Is the stated reason an acceptable one? See *ante*, p. 302.

3. Would the doctrine of agency have offered a better solution to the problems posed in *R. v. Bourne*?

Note

The doctrine employed in *R. v. Bourne, supra*, that although the principal actor may have a complete defence, there is nonetheless a crime, to which secondary participants can be parties, is sometimes less artificial than it was in that case. See next case.

R. v. Austin
[1981] 1 All E.R. 374
Court of Appeal

A child of three years was in the lawful custody of her mother J.K. R.K., the father, got an order from a Maryland Court awarding control of the child to him, which order was not enforceable in England. R.K. employed A and others to help him take the child by force. R.K. snatched the child from J.K. in a street in Winchester, and while A and others confused the pursuit, reached Heathrow and was able to leave the country with the child. A and others were convicted of child stealing and appealed.

WATKINS L.J.: At the close of the case for the Crown in the Crown Court at Winchester counsel for the appellants . . . made a number of concessions on behalf of the appellants. He has repeated them to this court. They are: (1) that each of these appellants aided and abetted King in taking Lara away from the possession of her mother; (2) that the child was taken by King by the use of force on the mother and the child. It was also conceded that they all knew the child was in the lawful possession of the mother, since there was no order in this country which affected her right to that at the material time and the order of the American court could not affect it in any practical way. It was also admitted that they had the intention to deprive the mother of possession of the child.

Having regard to those admissions and the background of this affair, one looks at section 56 of the 1861 [Offences Against the Person] Act which provides:

"Whosoever shall unlawfully ... by force ... take away ... any child under the age of fourteen years, with intent to deprive any parent ... of the possession of such child ... shall be liable, at the discretion of the court ... to be imprisoned: Provided, that no person who shall have claimed any right to the possession of such child, or shall be the mother or shall have claimed to be the father of an illegitimate child, shall be liable to be prosecuted by virtue hereof on account of the getting possession of such child ... "

... A parent who seeks, especially when there is no order of a court in existence affecting the ordinary common law right of possession of parents to a child, to take away that child from the other parent by force will inevitably commit the offence of child stealing under section 56, unless it be shown that at the time there was lawful excuse for the use of the force as a means of taking the child away. Accordingly, apart from the proviso, King on the known facts could have had no defence if charged with this offence.

Undoubtedly King could properly have claimed a right of possession to the child and so have gained the protection of the proviso. What would have been the effect of that? The effect would have been that, although he had committed the offence of child stealing, because he was the child's father and could claim a right to possession of the child, he would not have been prosecuted. It is submitted on the appellant's behalf that the proviso also protects a class of persons wide enough to include those who aid a person such as the father of the child in gaining possession of his child by force. They become his agents for the purpose. Many persons have from time to time the temporary possession of a child as agents of parents. Why are they not protected to the same extent as parents when regaining possession as agents of parents?

In our view the only sensible construction of the proviso allows of its protection being granted to a small class of persons only, which includes the father and the mother of the child, whether the child be legitimate or illegitimate or a guardian appointed by a testamentary document, or by an order conferring the status of guardianship, or a person to whom is granted an order conferring some form of care, control, custody or access. We can think of no other who could claim exemption from prosecution by reason of the proviso.

What of these appellants? They had no good reason for doing what they did. They had no right to assert, and no interest in, the possession of the child. They were the paid hirelings of King to aid him in the commission of a criminal offence, namely stealing a child, and with him they committed it as aiders and abettors. While King may shelter behind the proviso, there is no room there for them. Parliament in its wisdom undoubtedly decided that the mischiefs of matrimonial discord which are unhappily so widespread should not give rise to wholesale criminal prosecutions arising out of disputes about children, about who should have possession and control of them. That and that alone is the reason for the existence of the proviso to section 56. Thus, as we have said, its application is confined to the select class of persons we have endeavoured to define. ...

Appeals dismissed

Draft Criminal Code Bill

"**Parties to offences:**

25. Unless otherwise provided—

    (a) a person may be guilty of an offence as a principal or as an accessory;

    (b) defences apply to both principals and accessories.

26.—(1) A person is guilty of an offence as a principal if, with the fault required for the offence—

    (a) he does the act or acts specified for the offence; or

    (b) he does at least one such act and procures, assists or encourages any other such acts done by another; or

    (c) he procures, assists or encourages such act or acts done by another who is not himself guilty of the offences because—

        (i) he is under ten years of age; or

        (ii) he does the act or acts without the fault required for the offence; or

        (iii) he has a defence.

(2) A person guilty of an offence by virtue of the attribution to him of an element of the offence under section 29 (vicarious liability) is so guilty as a principal.

(3) Subsection (1)(c) applies notwithstanding that the definition of 20 the offence—

    (a) implies that the specified act or acts must be done by the offender personally; or

    (b) indicates that the offender must comply with a description which applies only to the other person referred to in subsection (1)(c)."

Commentary on Draft Criminal Code; Law Com. 177

"9.11. *Liability as principal or accessory*? The technical problem is whether persons acting through innocent agents are to be guilty as principals in all cases, or accessories in all cases, or as principals in some cases and as accessories in others ...

9.12. *The solution proposed* achieves, we believe, the maximum availability of clarity, simplicity and consistency. It is to treat all persons acting through innocent agents as principals (subsection (1)(c) and to make clear for the avoidance of doubt that this includes those in the troublesome exceptional cases (subsection (3)) ... "

Question

If the Code had been in force, would it have made any difference in the cases of *Thornton* v. *Mitchell, Walters* v. *Lunt* (referred to in *R.* v. *Cogan & Leak, ante*, p. 369), *R.* v. *Cogan & Leak, R.* v. *Bourne, R.* v. *Austin*?

iii. Aids, Abets, Counsels or Procures

Attorney-General's Reference (No. 1 of 1975)
[1975] Q.B. 773
Court of Appeal

The facts appear in the judgment.

LORD WIDGERY C.J.: This case comes before the court on a reference from the Attorney-General, under section 36 of the Criminal Justice Act 1972, and by his reference he asks the following question:

> "Whether an accused, who surreptitiously laced a friend's drinks with double measures of spirits when he knew that his friend would shortly be driving his car home, and in consequence his friend drove with an excessive quantity of alcohol in his body and was convicted of the offence under section 6(1) of the Road Traffic Act 1972, is entitled to a ruling of no case to answer on being later charged as an aider and abettor, counsellor and procurer, on the ground that there was no shared intention between the two, that the accused did not by accompanying him or otherwise positively encourage the friend to drive, or on any other ground."

. . . The present question has no doubt arisen because in recent years there have been a number of instances where men charged with driving their motor cars with an excess quantity of alcohol in the blood have sought to excuse their conduct by saying that their drinks were "laced," as the jargon has it; that is to say, some strong spirit was put into an otherwise innocuous drink and as a result the driver consumed more alcohol than he had either intended to consume or had the desire to consume. The relevance of all that is not that it entitles the driver to an acquittal because such driving is an absolute offence, but that it can be relied on as a special reason for not disqualifying the driver from driving. Hence no doubt the importance which has been attached in recent months to the possibility of this argument being raised in a normal charge of driving with excess alcohol.

The question requires us to say whether on the facts posed there is a case to answer and, needless to say, in the trial from which this reference is derived the judge was of the opinion that there was no case to answer and so ruled. We have to say in effect whether he is right.

The language in the section which determines whether a "secondary party," as he is sometimes called, is guilty of a criminal offence committed by another embraces the four words "aid, abet, counsel or procure." The origin of those words is to be found in section 8 of the Accessories and Abettors Act 1861, which provides:

> "Whosoever shall aid, abet, counsel or procure the commission of any misdemeanor, whether the same be a misdemeanour at common law or by virtue of any Act passed or to be passed, shall be liable to be tried, indicted and punished as a principal offender."

Thus, in the past, when the distinction was still drawn between felony and misdemeanor, it was sufficient to make a person guilty of a misdemeanour if he aided, abetted, counselled or procured the offence of another. When the difference between felonies and misdemeanors was abolished in 1967, section 1 of the Criminal Law Act 1967 in effect provided that the same test should apply to make a secondary party guilty either of treason or felony.

Of course it is the fact that in the great majority of instances where a secondary party is sought to be convicted of an offence there has been a contact between the principal offender and the secondary party. Aiding and abetting almost inevitably involves a situation in which the secondary party and the main offender are together at some stage discussing the plans which they may be making in respect of the alleged offence, and are in contact so that each knows what is passing through the mind of the other.

In the same way it seems to us that a person, who counsels the commission of a crime by another, almost inevitably comes to a moment when he is in contact with that other, when he is discussing the offence with that other and when, to use the words of the statute, he counsels the other to commit the offence.

The fact that so often the relationship between the secondary party and the principal will be such that there is a meeting of minds between them caused the trial judge in the case from which this reference is derived to think that this was really an essential feature of proving or establishing the guilt of the secondary party and, as we understand his judgment, he took the view that in the absence of some sort of meeting of minds, some sort of mental link between the secondary party and the principal, there could be no aiding, abetting or counselling of the offence within the meaning of the section.

So far as aiding, abetting and counselling is concerned we would go a long way with that conclusion. It may very well be, as I said a moment ago, difficult to think of a case of aiding, abetting or counselling when the parties have not met and have not discussed in some respects the terms of the offence which they have in mind. But we do not see why a similar principle should apply to procuring. We approach section 8 of the Act of 1861 on the basis that the words should be given their ordinary meaning, if possible. We approach the section on the basis also that if four words are employed here, "aid, abet, counsel or procure," the probability is that there is a difference between each of those four words and the other three, because, if there were no such difference, then Parliament would be wasting time in using four words where two or three would do. Thus, in deciding whether that which is assumed to be done under our reference was a criminal offence we approach the section on the footing that each word must be given its ordinary meaning.

To procure means to produce by endeavour. You procure a thing by setting out to see that it happens and taking the appropriate steps to produce that happening. We think that there are plenty of instances in which a person may be said to procure the commission of a crime by another even though there is no sort of conspiracy between the two, even though there is no attempt at agreement or discussion as to the form which the offence should take. In our judgment the offence described in this reference is such a case.

If one looks back at the facts of the reference: the accused surreptitiously laced his friend's drink. This is an important element and, although we are not going to decide today anything other than the problem posed to us, it may well be that, in similar cases where the lacing of the drink or the introduction of the extra alcohol is known to the driver quite different considerations may apply. We say that because, where the driver has no knowledge of what is happening, in most instances he would have no means of preventing the offence from being committed. If the driver is unaware of what has happened, he will not be taking precautions. He will get into his car seat, switch on the ignition and drive home, and, consequently, the conception of another procuring the commission of the offence by the driver is very much stronger where the driver is innocent of all knowledge of what is happening, as in the present case where the lacing of the drink was surreptitious.

The second thing which is important in the facts set out in our reference is that, following and in consequence of the introduction of the extra alcohol, the friend drove with an excess quantity of alcohol in his blood. Causation here is important. You cannot procure an offence unless there is a causal link between what you do and the commission of the offence, and here we are told that in consequence of the addition of this alcohol the driver, when he drove home, drove with an excess quantity of alcohol in his body.

Giving the words their ordinary meaning in English, and asking oneself whether in those circumstances the offence has been procured, we are in no doubt that the answer is that it has. It has been procured because, unknown to the driver and without his collaboration, he has been put in a position in which in fact he has committed an offence which he never would have committed otherwise. We think that there was a case to answer and that the trial judge should have directed the jury that an offence is committed if it is shown beyond reasonable doubt that the defendant knew that his friend was going to drive, and also knew that the ordinary and natural result of the additional alcohol added to the friend's drink would be to bring him above the recognised limit of 80 milligrammes per 100 millilitres of blood.

It was suggested to us that, if we held that there may be a procuring on the facts of the present case, it would be but a short step to a similar finding for the generous host, with somewhat bibulous friends, when at the end of the day his friends leave him to go to their own homes in circumstances in which they are not fit to drive and in circumstances in which an offence under the Road Traffic Act 1972 is committed. The suggestion has been made that the host may in those circumstances be guilty with his guests on the basis that he has either aided, abetted, counselled or procured the offence.

The first point to notice in regard to the generous host is that that is not a case in which the alcohol is being put surreptitiously into the glass of the driver. That is a case in which the driver knows perfectly well how much he has to drink and where to a large extent it is perfectly right and proper to leave him to make his own decision.

Furthermore, we could say that, if such a case arises, the basis on which the case will be put against the host is, we think, bound to be on the footing that he has supplied the tool with which the offence is committed. This, of course, is a reference back to such cases as those where oxy-acetylene equipment was bought by a man knowing it was to be used by another for a criminal offence: see *R. v. Bainbridge* [1960] 1 Q.B. 129. There is ample and clear authority as to the extent to which supplying the tools for the commission of an offence may amount to aiding and abetting for present purposes.

Accordingly, so far as the generous host type of case is concerned we are not concerned at the possibility that difficulties will be created, as long as it is borne in mind that in those circumstances the matter must be approached in accordance with well-known authority governing the provision of the tools for the commission of an offence, and never forgetting that the introduction of the alcohol is not there surreptitious, and that consequently the case for saying that the offence was procured by the supplier of the alcohol is very much more difficult.

Our decision on the reference is that the question posed by the Attorney-General should be answered in the negative.

Opinion accordingly

Question

How is this decision likely to affect the frequency of the "my drink was laced" plea?

Notes

1. "To procure means to produce by endeavour." If the charge is of procuring only, intention in the accused that the offence shall be committed must be shown, but if the charge is of aiding, abetting, counselling and procuring (as it usually is) recklessness (in the *Cunningham* sense—see, *ante*, p. 109 as to the commission of the offence is sufficient: see *Blakely* v. *D.P.P.* [1991] R.T.R. 405 (D.C.).

2. In *R.* v. *Calhaen* [1985] Q.B. 808 (C.A.) it was held that "counselling," unlike "procuring," needs no causal connection between the counselling and the offence.

3. It has been said that the attempt to give different meanings to the words "aids, abets, counsels, procures" is misguided and useless; see *infra*.

J. C. Smith; "Aid, abet, counsel or procure" in Reshaping the Criminal Law (1978, ed. Glazebrook), p. 122

"The formula adopted in section 8 of the Accessories and Abettors Act 1861 and other nineteenth and twentieth century statutes is the most modern in a long line from very early times. . . .

Other earlier and later statutes, however, use different formulae in which the words, 'helping,' 'maintaining,' 'commanding,' 'contriving,' 'assisting,' 'directing' and 'hiring' and others recur. . . .

Foster (Crown Law, p. 121) agreed that it is true that penal statutes must be strictly construed but said that 'it is equally true that we are not to be governed by the sound, but by the well-known, true, legal import of the words.' He reviewed the large variety of words used in various statutes to describe the activity of accessories and concluded that such words are technical expressions to be given their legal meaning.

> From these different modes of expression, all plainly descriptive of the same offence, I think one may safely conclude, that in the construction of statutes which oust clergy in the case of *Participes Criminis*, we are not to be governed by the bare sound, but by the true legal import of the words. And also, that every person who cometh within the description of these statutes, various as they are in point of expression, is in the judgment of the legislature an accessory before the fact; unless he is present at the fact, and in that case he is undoubtedly a principal.

According to this highly authoritative view, the actual words used are of no significance once it is clear that they were intended to incorporate the common law concepts of secondary participation. That these are concepts of the common law is clear. It was recognised by Coke, Hale and the subsequent writers of authority that it was not necessary for a statute to provide for the liability of secondary parties. It was sufficient for Parliament to prescribe the offence and liability for secondary participation followed by implication. Yet, for some reason, Parliament sometimes made express provision and sometimes did not. When express provision was made, there was no consistency in the terminology used: but whatever the words, the same concept of the common law applied.

What then of the words used in section 8 of the Accessories and Abettors Act 1861, and section 35 of the Magistrates' Court Act 1952? According to C. S. Greaves, the editor of the third and fourth editions of *Russell on Crime*, and the draftsman of the 1861 legislation, section 8 'is really only a declaration of the common law on the subject.' This opinion has been followed by the courts on several occasions. It is submitted that this is the right view and that as Sir Francis Adams puts it: 'Nothing is to be gained by attempting to distinguish between the meaning of different words used in this connection.' "

Notes

1. In *Ferguson* v. *Weaving* (for facts, see *post*, p. 387), the defendant, although "absent," was charged with aiding, abetting, counselling and procuring. Lord Goddard C.J.:

> "At the hearing an application was made to amend the information against the respondent by the deletion of the words 'aid and abet,' so that the information charged her only with counselling and procuring the commission of the offences. Before us it was contended on her behalf that, even if the facts on which the prosecution relied were accepted, they could only establish a case of aiding and abetting, and that there was no evidence that the respondent in any way counselled or procured the commission of the said offences. It is well known that the words 'aid and abet' are apt to describe the action of a person who is present at the time of the commission of an offence and takes some part therein. He is then described as an aider and abettor, whereas the words 'counsel and procure' are appropriate to a person who, though not present at the commission of the offence, is an accessory before the fact. That all these words may be used together to charge a person who is alleged to have participated in an offence otherwise than as a principal in the first degree was established by *Re Smith* (1858) 3 H. & N. 227. Whether, where the words 'counsel and procure' alone are used, there must be a proof of something more than would establish a case of being an accessory before the fact is not one which we feel necessary to decide in this case. ... As we are satisfied that the respondent cannot be convicted as a participant, to use a compendious expression, in the offences charged against the persons who consumed the intoxicating liquor, we give no decision on it."

2. *Smith*, "*Aid, Abet, Counsel or Procure*," *supra*, p. 377: It is submitted that the true position is as follows. The distinction between "aiding and abetting" and "counselling and procuring," like that between principal and accessory, depends on one consideration only, namely whether the defendant was present (again in the large sense in which the common law understood that term) or absent. Notwithstanding the ordinary meaning of the words, the distinction does not turn in any way on the nature of the acts done by the defendant. Any act which would amount to "aiding and abetting" if done while present at the crime would amount to "counselling and procuring" if done while absent. Any act which would amount to "counselling and procuring" when done in the absence of the principal would amount to "aiding and

abetting" if done while present at the crime. ... If it is right to regard the words "aid and abet" as indicative of the liability of a person present and the words "counsel and procure" as indicative of the liability of a person absent, it is obvious that these are highly technical terms. It is inconsistent so to treat the words in one context and yet to regard them as words of ordinary meaning in another.

3. Until 1987, there was one case where a party's liability turned on whether he was present or absent. One who was *absent* could not be convicted of a greater crime than the principal: *R. v. Richards* [1974] Q.B. 776. However this case was overruled by the House of Lords in *R. v. Howe* [1987] A.C. 417, *ante,* p. 296.

iv. Mens Rea of an Accessory

Note

The accessory must have knowingly supplied help or encouragement to the principal: see *R. v. Clarkson, infra.* It is sufficient if he knew that the principal was likely to commit the crime; he need not have desired him to do so: see *N.C.B. v. Gamble, infra.* He must have known of the circumstances which made the principal's act criminal, even in the case of a strict liability offence: see *Ferguson* v. *Weaving, infra.* He need not have foreseen the precise circumstances, *e.g.* time and place of commission, provided that the crime which happened was within his contemplation: see *Maxwell* v. *D.P.P. for Northern Ireland, infra.* It follows that if the principal went beyond what the accessory contemplated, that might serve to excuse the accessory: see *R. v. Slack, infra.*

(a) Help or encouragement knowingly supplied

R. v. Clarkson
[1971] 1 W.L.R. 1402
Court-Martial Appeal Court

The accused were charged with aiding and abetting three offences of rape. The evidence was that the accused, who had been drinking heavily, heard a disturbance in a room. They went in and stood watching whilst a woman was raped. They gave neither physical assistance nor verbal encouragement. They were convicted and appealed.

MEGAW L.J.: ... Let it be accepted, and there was evidence to justify this assumption, that the presence of those two defendants in the room where the offence was taking place was not accidental in any sense and that it was not by chance, unconnected with the crime, that they were there. Let it be accepted that they entered the room when the crime was committed because of what they had heard, which indicated that a woman was being raped, and they remained there.

R. v. Coney (1882) 8 Q.B.D. 534, decided that non-accidental presence at the scene of the crime is not conclusive of aiding and abetting. The jury has to be told by the judge, or in this case the court-martial has to be told by the judge advocate, in clear terms what it is that has to be proved before they can convict of aiding and abetting; what it is of which the jury or the court-martial, as the case may be, must be sure as matters of inference before they can convict of aiding and abetting in such a case where the evidence adduced by the prosecution is limited to non-accidental presence.

What has to be proved is stated in R. v. *Coney* by Hawkins J. in a well-known passage in his judgment, at p. 557:

> "In my opinion, to constitute an aider and abettor some active steps must be taken by word, or action, with the intent to instigate the principal, or principals. Encouragement does not of necessity amount to aiding and abetting, it may be intentional or unintentional, a man may unwittingly encourage another in fact by his presence, by misinterpreted words, or gestures, or by his silence, or non-interference or he may encourage intentionally by expressions, or gestures, or actions intended to signify approval. In the latter case he aids and abets, in the former he does not. It is no criminal offence to stand by, a mere passive spectator of a crime, even of a murder. Non-interference to prevent a crime is not itself a crime. But the fact that a person was voluntarily and purposely present witnessing the commission of a crime, and offered no opposition to it, though he might reasonably be expected to prevent and had the power so to do, or at least to express his dissent, might under some circumstances, afford cogent evidence upon which a jury would be justified in finding that he wilfully encouraged and so aided and abetted. But it would be purely a question for the jury whether he did so or not."

It is not enough, then, that the presence of the accused has, in fact, given encouragement. It must be proved that the accused intended to give encouragement; that he *wilfully* encouraged. In a case such as the present, more than in many other cases where aiding and abetting is alleged, it was essential that that element should be stressed; for there was here at least the possibility that a drunken man with his self-discipline loosened by drink, being aware that a woman was being raped, might be attracted to the scene and might stay on the scene in the capacity of what is known as a voyeur; and, while his presence and the presence of others might in fact encourage the rapers or discourage the victim, he, himself, enjoying the scene or at least standing by assenting, might not intend that his presence should offer encouragement to rapers and would-be rapers or discouragement to the victim; he might not realise that he was giving encouragement; so that, while encouragement there might be, it would not be a case in which, to use the words of Hawkins J., the accused person "wilfully encouraged."

A further point is emphasised in passages in the judgment of the Court of Criminal Appeal in *R.* v. *Allan* [1965] 1 Q.B. 130, 135, 138. That was a case concerned with participation in an affray. The court said, at p. 135:

> "in effect, it amounts to this: that the judge thereby directed the jury that they were duty bound to convict an accused who was proved to have been present and witnessing an affray if it was also proved that he nursed an intention to join in if help was needed by the side he favoured and this notwithstanding that he did nothing by words or deeds to evince his intention and outwardly played the role of a purely passive spectator. It was said that, if that direction is right, where A and B behave themselves to all outward appearances in an exactly similar manner, but it be proved that A had the intention to participate if needs

be, whereas B had no such intention, then A must be convicted of being a principal in the second degree to the affray, whereas B should be acquitted. To do that, it is objected, would be to convict A on his thoughts, even though they found no reflection in his actions."

The other passage in the judgment is at p. 138:

"In our judgment, before a jury can properly convict an accused person of being a principal in the second degree to an affray, they must be convinced by the evidence that, at the very least, he by some means or other encouraged the participants. To hold otherwise would be, in effect, as the appellants' counsel rightly expressed it, to convict a man on his thoughts, unaccompanied by any physical act other than the fact of his mere presence."

From that it follows that mere intention is not in itself enough. There must be an intention to encourage; and there must also be encouragement in fact, in cases such as the present case.

So we come to what was said by the judge advocate. First there was the guidance which he gave to the court after the submissions had been made at the close of the prosecution's case. The relevance of that to the matters which the court now has to decide has already been mentioned. There is a passage in that guidance in which the judge advocate said:

"You have been told correctly the position as regards an aider and abettor, and that is all that the accused is charged with in these three charges. To be an aider and abettor, a person need not take any active steps in the commission of a crime, but he must be in a position to render assistance or encouragement by actual or constructive presence, and he must share a common intention with them that the crime should be committed. An illustration is that of a jeweller's shop. One man will throw a brick through the window and somebody else will snatch the valuables inside. It might be said that they were the people who actually committed the offence itself, but on such an occasion there will be somebody standing by with a motor car to enable the others to make their getaway. Probably someone is on the corner to make sure there is no policeman about to arrive on the scene. One or two others may be present to thrust out a leg and trip up anybody who may interfere or get in the way, if necessary, of those who will go in pursuit. They are sharing a common intention that the offence should be committed and they are aiders and abettors. Other people may be standing by, but the mere fact that a person watches and just stands by without sharing the common purpose of the others, is not guilty of aiding and abetting."

The judge advocate draws the analogy which is commonly drawn where direction is given of two persons jointly indicted, for example, of committing burglary. One actually enters the house and the other stands outside to keep watch. That analogy, in the view of this court, is misleading in relation to what was involved in the present case. For it presupposes a prior meeting of minds between the persons concerned as to the crime to be committed. The man who stands outside and does not go in is guilty of burglary; but it cannot in such a case properly be said that he has taken no active step in the commission of the offence. He has gone to the place where he is, and he has conducted himself as he does, as a part of the joint plan which, in its totality, is intended to procure commission of the crime.

In the view of this court the echo of that false analogy unfortunately continued throughout when the judge advocate came to sum up the matter to the court-martial. . . . This court has come to the conclusion that the court might have misunderstood the relevant principles that ought to be applied. It might have been left under the impression that it could find these two defendants guilty on the basis of their continuing, non-accidental presence, even though it was not sure that the necessary inferences to be drawn from the evidence included (i) an intention to encourage and (ii) actual encouragement. While we have no doubt that those inferences could properly have been drawn in respect of each defendant on each count, so that verdicts of guilty could properly have been returned, we cannot say that the court-martial, properly directed, would necessarily have drawn those inferences. Accordingly the convictions of the defendants Clarkson and Carroll must be quashed.

Appeals allowed

Questions

1. If A is able to control B's behaviour, and does not do so, with the result, expected by A, that B commits a crime, what is the significance, on a charge of aiding, abetting, counselling or procuring B's crime, of A's failure?

2. Ought it to make any difference whether A's power to control B is a legal one or merely a physical or psychological one? See *Cassady* v. *Morris* [1975] Crim.L.R. 398; *Du Cros* v. *Lambourne* [1907] 1 K.B. 40; *R.* v. *Harris* [1964] Crim.L.R. 54.

3. A's wife B tells him that she is going to kill herself and their infant children. A protests but does nothing to stop B, who throws her children into a river and jumps in herself, so that they are all drowned. Has A aided, abetted, counselled or procured (i) the murder of the children, (ii) the suicide of B? See Suicide Act 1961, s.2(1), p. 575 (*cf. R.* v. *Russell* [1933] V.L.R. 59).

(b) Knowledge enough

National Coal Board v. Gamble
[1959] 1 Q.B. 11
Queen's Bench Division

The National Coal Board had an instalment contract with the Central Electricity Authority for a supply of coal to be delivered at a colliery into lorries sent by a carrier on behalf of the authority. In pursuance of this contract W. Ltd., a carrier, sent a lorry in the charge of its servant M. into the colliery. The method of loading was for a lorry-driver to place his lorry under the Board's hopper and tell the hopper operator to stop when the driver thought he had enough coal on his lorry. The lorry was then driven to the colliery weighbridge which was in the charge of H., a servant of the Board. H., after weighing the lorry and its load, would give the driver a ticket showing the weight of coal loaded, which ticket operated as a delivery note, so that the sale of the load of coal was then complete and the property in the coal passed from the Board to the purchaser.

M. went through this procedure, but when H. weighed his lorry and load he discovered that they together exceeded the maximum permitted weight for a vehicle being driven on a road. H. drew M.'s attention to this fact, and there was also a large notice at the door of the weighbridge office warning drivers that the Board was not responsible for the use of any vehicle on a road which was loaded beyond its authorised capacity. On being asked by H. if he intended to take this load (which he could easily have offloaded) M. said that he would risk it. H. then handed M. the weighbridge ticket and M. drove the overloaded lorry out of the colliery onto a road, thereby committing an offence against the Motor Vehicles (Construction and Use) Regulations 1955.

The Board were charged with and convicted of aiding, abetting, counselling and procuring the carrier W. Ltd. to commit the offence under the Regulations. The Board appealed.

DEVLIN J.: A person who supplies the instrument for a crime or anything essential to its commission aids in the commission of it; and if he does so knowingly and with intent to aid, he abets it as well and is therefore guilty of aiding and abetting. I use the word "supplies" to comprehend giving, lending, selling or any other transfer of the right of property. In a sense a man who gives up to a criminal a weapon which the latter has a right to demand from him aids in the commission of the crime as much as if he sold or lent the article. But this has never been held to be aiding in law: see *R.* v. *Lomas* (1913) 110 L.T. 239; and *R.* v. *Bullock* [1955] 1 W.L.R. 1. The reason, I think, is that in the former case there is in law a positive act and in the latter only a negative one. In the transfer of property there must be either a physical delivery or a positive act of assent to a taking. But a man who hands over to another his own property on demand, although he may physically be performing a positive act, in law is only refraining from detinue. Thus in law the former act is one of assistance voluntarily given and the latter is only a failure to prevent the commission of the crime by means of forcible detention, which would not even be justified except in the case of felony. Another way of putting the point is to say that aiding and abetting is a crime that requires proof of *mens rea*, that is to say, of intention to aid as well as of knowledge of the circumstances, and proof of the intent involves proof of a positive act of assistance voluntarily done.

These considerations make it necessary to determine at what point the property in the coal passed from the Board and what the Board's state of knowledge was at that time. If the property had passed before the Board knew of the proposed crime, there was nothing they could legally do to prevent the driver of the lorry from taking the overloaded lorry out onto the road. If it had not, then they sold the coal with knowledge that an offence was going to be committed. (His Lordship repeated the facts as found in the case).

In these circumstances, the property in the coal passed on delivery to the carrier in accordance with Rule 5 of section 18 of the Sale of Goods Act, 1893. If the delivery was complete after loading and before weighing, the Board has not until after delivery any knowledge that an offence had been committed. But where weighing is necessary for the purpose of the contract, as, for example, in order to ascertain the price of an instalment, the property does not pass until the weight has been agreed. In *Simmons* v. *Swift* (1826) 5 B. & C. 857, the parties agreed to buy and sell "the bark stacked at Redbrook at £9.5s. per ton." It was held that the property did not pass until the bark had been weighed and the price ascertained. Bayley J. said that the concurrence of the seller was necessary and he might insist on keeping possession until the bark had been weighed.

It was contended on behalf of the Board that H. had no option after weighing but to issue a ticket for the amount then in the lorry. I think this contention is unsound. In the circumstances of this case the loading must be taken as subject to adjustment; otherwise, if the contract were for a limited amount, the seller might make an over-delivery or an under-delivery which could not thereafter be rectified and the carrier might be contractually compelled to carry away a load in excess of that legally permitted. I think that delivery of the coal was not completed until after the ascertained weight had been assented to and some act was done signifying assent and passing the property. The property passed when H. asked M. whether he intended to take the load and M. said he would risk it and when mutual assent was, as it were, sealed by the delivery and acceptance of the weighbridge ticket. He could, therefore, after he knew of the overload, have refused to transfer the property in the coals.

This is the conclusion to which the justices came. Mr. Thompson submits on behalf of the Board that it does not justify a verdict of guilty of aiding and abetting. He submits, first, that even if knowledge of the illegal purpose had been acquired before delivery began, it would not be sufficient for the verdict; and secondly, that if he is wrong about that, the knowledge was acquired too late and the Board was not guilty of aiding and abetting simply because H. failed to stop the process of delivery after it had been initiated.

On his first point Mr. Thomas submits that the furnishing of an article essential to the crime with knowledge of the use to which it is to be put does not of itself constitute aiding and abetting; there must be proved in addition a purpose or motive of the defendant to further the crime or encourage the criminal. Otherwise, he submits, there is no *mens rea*.

I have already said that in my judgment there must be proof of an intent to aid. I would agree that proof that the article was knowingly supplied is not conclusive evidence of intent to aid. R. v. *Fretwell* (1862) L. & C. 161, is authority for that. R. v. *Steane* [1947] K.B. 997, in which the defendant was charged with having acted during the war with intent to assist the enemy contrary to the Defence Regulations then in force, makes the same point. But prima facie—R. v. *Steane* makes this clear also—a man is presumed to intend the natural and probable consequences of his acts, and the consequence of supplying essential material is that assistance is given to the criminal. It is always open to the defendant, as in R. v. *Steane*, to give evidence of his real intention. But in this case the defence called no evidence. The prima facie presumption is therefore enough to justify the verdict, unless it is the law that some other mental element besides intent is necessary to the offence.

This is what Mr. Thompson argues, and he describes the additional element as the purpose or motive of encouraging the crime. No doubt evidence of an interest in the crime or of an express purpose to assist it will greatly strengthen the case of the prosecution. But an indifference to the result of the crime does not of itself negative abetting. If one man deliberately sells to another a gun to be used for murdering a third, he may be indifferent about whether the third man lives or dies and interested only in the cash profit to be made out of the sale, but he can still be an aider and abettor. To hold otherwise would be to negative the rule that *mens rea* is a matter of intent only and does not depend on desire or motive.

The authorities, I think, support this conclusion, though none has been cited to us in which the point has been specifically argued and decided. . . .

The same principle has been applied in civil cases where the seller has sued upon a contract for the supply of goods which he knew were to be used for an illegal purpose. In some of the authorities there is a suggestion that he could recover on the contract unless it appeared that in addition to knowledge of the purpose he had an interest in the venture and looked for payment to the proceeds of the crime. But in *Pearce* v. *Brooks* (1866) L.R. 1 Ex. 213, Pollock C.B. stated the law as follows:

"I have always considered it as settled law that any person who contributes to the performance of an illegal act by supplying a thing with the knowledge that it is going to be used for that purpose, cannot recover the price of the thing so supplied. If, to create that incapacity, it was ever considered necessary that the price should be bargained or expected to be paid out of the fruits of the illegal act (which I do not stop to examine), that proposition has been overruled by the cases I have referred to, and has now ceased to be law."

The case chiefly relied on by Mr. Thompson was *R.* v. *Coney* (1882) 8 Q.B.D. 534. In that case the defendants were charged with aiding and abetting an illegal prize fight at which they had been present. The judgments all refer to "encouragement," but it would be wrong to conclude from that that proof of encouragement is necessary to every form of aiding and abetting. Presence on the scene of the crime without encouragement or assistance is no aid to the criminal; the supply of essential material is. Moreover, the decision makes it clear that encouragement can be inferred from mere presence. Cave J., who gave the leading judgment, said of the summing-up: "It may mean either that mere presence unexplained is evidence of encouragement, and so of guilt, or that mere presence unexplained is conclusive proof of encouragement, and so of guilt. If the former is the correct meaning I concur in the law so laid down; if the latter, I am unable to do so." This dictum seems to me to support the view I have expressed. If voluntary presence is prima facie evidence of encouragement and therefore of aiding and abetting, it appears to me to be *a fortiori* that the intentional supply of an essential article must be prima facie evidence of aiding and abetting.

As to Mr. Thompson's alternative point, I have already expressed the view that the facts show an act of assent made by H. after knowledge of the proposed illegality and without which the property would not have passed. If some positive act to complete delivery is committed after knowledge of the illegality, the position in law must, I think, be just the same as if the knowledge had been obtained before the delivery had been begun. Of course, it is quite likely that H. was confused about the legal position and thought that he was not entitled to withhold the weighbridge ticket. There is no *mens rea* if the defendant is shown to have a genuine belief in the existence of circumstances which, if true, would negative an intention to aid; see *Wilson* v. *Inyang* [1951] 2 K.B. 799; but this argument, which might have been the most cogent available to the defence, cannot now be relied upon, because H. was not called to give evidence about what he thought or believed.

Appeal dismissed

Notes

1. Lord Goddard C.J. delivered a concurring judgment. Slade J. dissented on the ground that the alleged aider must have assisted or encouraged the principal offender. "It is not sufficient that the alleged abettor should be proved to have done some act, or to have made some omission, without which the principal offender would not have committed the offence; nor is it sufficient that such act or

omission had the effect of facilitating the commission of the offence or that it in fact operated on the mind of the principal offender so as to decide him to commit it. The prosecution must prove that the act or omission upon which they rely as constituting the alleged aiding and abetting was done or made with a view to assisting or encouraging the principal offender to commit the offence or, in other words, with the motive of endorsing the commission of the offence." His Lordship considered that the facts found by the magistrates did not support the inference that H. meant to encourage M. in any way.

2. Devlin J.'s discussion becomes heavily involved with the civil law of sale, the passing of property, and the ability of a seller to sue on a contract tainted by illegality. It seems inappropriate for the criminal law to be entangled with the civil law this way. Perhaps Slade J.'s solution, requiring a positive motive of endorsing the commission of the offence, is too lax, at any rate where a *serious* crime is *substantially* facilitated by the accessory's act. But in other cases, the law perhaps ought to excuse an "indifferent" provider of assistance (*i.e.* one who knows that a crime may be committed but does not wish it to happen). In *Gillick* v. *West Norfolk & Wisbech A.H.A.* [1986] A.C. 112, the question arose whether a doctor who provided contraceptives to a girl under 16 years of age, knowing that that would facilitate her having sexual intercourse with a man, would necessarily be an accessory to the man's offence if that intercourse took place. Lord Scarman (at p. 190) thought that if the provision was a bona fide exercise of his clinical judgment "it must be a complete negation of the guilty mind which is an essential ingredient of the criminal offence of aiding and abetting the commission of unlawful sexual inter-course." Lord Bridge (at p. 194) agreed with the trial judge that the doctor would not be guilty either because the provision was not directly assisting the offence, or because the doctor's knowledge of the circumstances of the proposed offence was not sufficiently specific. (On specificity of knowledge, see, *post*, p. 388.)

Questions

Would it be practicable for the law to excuse some "indifferent" helpers because:

(a) the principal offence is trivial?
(b) the aid supplied is trivial and could easily be got from others?
(c) the aid supplied was in the normal course of a legitimate business?
(d) the accessory makes known his disapproval of the offence? (*cf.* Draft Criminal Code, Clause 27(6)(b), *post*, p. 408.)
(e) the accessory was merely "refraining from detinue" (see Devlin J., *ante*, p. 383)? On this note *Garrett* v. *Arthur Churchill (Glass) Ltd.* [1969] 2 All E.R. 1141 (D.C.). The question was whether A was knowingly concerned in the export of a valuable goblet without an export licence. A was

holding the goblet as agent for B, who was in America. A told B that the export needed a licence; but B said that his agency was terminated and ordered him to hand over the goblet to a courier at Heathrow. A did so and the courier took the goblet out of the country. It was held that "albeit there was a legal duty in ordinary circumstances to hand over the goblet once the agency was determined, I do not think that an action would lie for breach of that duty, if the handing over would constitute the offence of being knowingly concerned in its exportation": *per* Lord Parker C.J., at p. 1145.

Ferguson v. Weaving
[1951] 1 K.B. 814
King's Bench Division

Section 4 of the Licensing Act, 1921, made it an offence for any person, except during the permitted hours, to consume on licensed premises any intoxicating liquor. In a large public-house managed by W, customers were found consuming liquor outside permitted hours and were convicted of an offence under the section. There was no evidence that W knew that the liquor was being consumed, which had been supplied by waiters employed by her who had neglected to collect the glasses in time. A charge against W of counselling and procuring the customers' offence was dismissed and the prosecutor appealed.

LORD GODDARD C.J.: There can be no doubt that this court has more than once laid it down in clear terms that before a person can be convicted of aiding and abetting the commission of an offence, he must at least know the essential matters which constitute the offence. ... The magistrate in this case has acquitted the licensee of any knowledge of the matters which constituted the principal offence, but it is said that the cases established that the knowledge of her servants must be imputed to her. ... We now turn to [these] cases. ... It is unnecessary to go through them all because the principle which applies was laid down, not for the first time, in *Linnett* v. *Metropolitan Police Commissioner* [1946] K.B. 290. All the cases on the subject were quoted, and, in giving judgment, I said: "The principle underlying these decisions does not depend upon the legal relationship existing between master and servant or between principal and agent; it depends on the fact that the person who is responsible in law, as, for example, a licensee under the licensing Acts, has chosen to delegate his duties, powers and authority to another."

We will assume for the purpose of this case that the licensee had delegated to the waiters the conduct and management of the concert room, and if the Act had made it an offence for a licensee knowingly to permit liquor to be consumed after hours, then the fact that she had delegated management and control of the concert room to the waiters would have made their knowledge her knowledge. In this case there is no substantive offence in the licensee at all. The substantive offence is committed only by the customers. She can aid and abet the customers if she knows that the customers are committing the offence, but we are not prepared to hold that knowledge can be imputed to her so as to make her not a principal offender, but an aider and abettor. So to hold would be to establish a new principle in criminal law and one for which there is no authority. If

Parliament had desired to make a licensee guilty of an offence by allowing persons to consume liquor after hours it would have been perfectly easy so to provide in the section. But a doctrine of criminal law that a licensee who has knowledge of the facts is liable as a principal in the second degree is no reason for holding that if she herself has no knowledge of the facts but that someone in her employ and to whom she may have entrusted the management of the room did know them, this makes her an aider and abettor. As no duty is imposed on her by the section to prevent the consumption of liquor after hours there was no duty in this respect that she could delegate to her employees. While it may be that the waiters could have been prosecuted for aiding and abetting the consumers, as to which we need express no opinion, we are clearly of opinion that the licensee could not be. To hold to the contrary would, in our opinion, be an unwarranted extension of the doctrine of vicarious responsibility in criminal law."

Appeal dismissed

Notes

1. For vicarious liability, see, *post*, p. 408.
2. *Callow* v. *Tillstone* (1900) 83 L.T. 411 (Q.B.D.). A, a veterinary surgeon, negligently examined a carcase and certified it as fit for human consumption, when it was not, as A ought to have known. B, a butcher, was convicted of exposing for sale meat unfit for human consumption. *Held*, A was not guilty of aiding and abetting B's offence.

Question

A's intentional act has facilitated the commission by B of the offence of driving over the blood/alcohol limit.

     (i)   He knows (intends) that B shall drive, but is merely reckless as to whether he is over the limit;

    (ii) He knows that B is over the limit, but is merely reckless as to whether he will drive while in that state.

Is there a relevant difference between these two cases? See *Carter* v. *Richardson* [1974] R.T.R. 314 as to (i), and *Blakely* v. *D.P.P.* [1991] R.T.R. 405 as to (ii); and see, *post*, p. 433 as to recklessness as to circumstance in attempts.

(c) Scope of the Common Design

Maxwell v. D.P.P. for Northern Ireland
[1978] 1 W.L.R. 1350
House of Lords

The facts are set out in the speech of Lord Hailsham.

LORD HAILSHAM OF ST. MARYLEBONE: My Lords, in my opinion this appeal should be dismissed. The applicant was the owner and driver of the guide car in what subsequently turned out to be a terrorist attack by members of the criminal and illegal organisation known as the Ulster Volunteer Force

(UVF) on a public house owned by a Roman Catholic licensee at 40, Grange Road, Toomebridge and known as the Crosskeys Inn. The attack was carried out on the night of January 3, 1976 by the occupants of a Cortina car and took the form of throwing a pipe bomb containing about five pounds of explosive into the hallway of the public house. The attack failed because the son of the proprietor had the presence of mind to pull out the burning fuse and detonator and throw it outside the premises where the detonator exploded either because the fuse had reached the detonator or on contact with the ground.

The appellant was tried on October 13, 1976, on an indictment containing four counts to two of which he pleaded guilty. This appeal is concerned with the remaining two counts (numbered 1 and 2) on which he was convicted at the Belfast City Commission by MacDermott J. sitting without a jury. ...

It will be seen that, in the above counts, the accused was charged, as the general law permits, as a principal, but the real case against him was that, as the driver of the guide car, he was what used to be known as an accessory before the fact. Although no complaint is made about the form of the counts I agree with the view expressed by my noble and learned friend Viscount Dilhorne of the desirability in these cases of aiding, abetting, counselling or procuring, of drawing the particulars of offence in such a way as to disclose with greater clarity the real nature of the case that the accused has to answer.

The only substantial matter to be discussed in the appeal is the degree of knowledge required before an accused can be found guilty of aiding, abetting, counselling, or procuring. To what extent must the accused be proved to have particular knowledge of the crime in contemplation at the time of his participation and which was ultimately committed by its principal perpetrators? For myself I am content for this purpose to adopt the words of Lord Parker C.J. in *R*. v. *Bainbridge* [1960] 1 Q.B. 129 when, after saying that it is not easy to lay down a precise form of words which will cover every case, he observed at p. 134 " ... there must not be merely suspicion but knowledge that a crime of the type in question was intended ... " and the words of Lord Goddard C.J. in *Johnson* v. *Youden* [1950] 1 K.B. 544, 546, endorsed by this House in *Churchill* v. *Walton* [1967] 2 A.C. 224, 236 that "Before a person can be convicted of aiding and abetting the commission of an offence he must at least know the essential matters which constitute that offence." The only question in debate in the present appeal is whether the degree of knowledge possessed by the appellant was of the "essential matters constituting" the offence in fact committed, or, to put what in the context of the instant case is exactly the same question in another form, whether the appellant knew that the offence in which he participated was "a crime of the type" described in the charge.

For that purpose I turn to two passages in the findings of fact of the learned judge. The first is as follows: "In my judgment, the facts of this case make it clear to me that the accused knew the men in the Cortina car were going to attack the Inn and had the means of attacking the Inn with them in their car. The accused may not, as he says, have known what form the attack was going to take, but in my judgment he knew the means of the attack, be they bomb, bullet or incendiary device, were present in that car."

In the second passage MacDermott J. said: "In my judgment, the accused knew that he was participating in an attack on the Inn. He performed an important role in the execution of that attack. He knew that the attack was one which would involve the use of means which would result in danger to life or damage to property. In such circumstances, where an admitted terrorist participates actively in a terrorist attack, having knowledge of the type of attack intended, if not of the weapon chosen by his colleagues, he can in my view be properly charged with possession of the weapon with which it is intended that life should be endangered or premises seriously damaged."

The learned judge also found *inter alia* that the word "job" (as used in the appellant's statements) is "synonymous with military action which raises, having regard to the proven activities of the UVF, the irresistible inference [that] the attack would be one of violence in which people would be endangered or premises seriously damaged."

There was no dispute that there was ample evidence to support all these findings and it follows that the only question is whether the passages contain some self-misdirection in point of law. As to this I agree with the opinion of Sir Robert Lowry C.J. (in the Court of Criminal Appeal for Northern Ireland) when he said [1978] 1 W.L.R. 1363, 1375: "The facts found here show that the appellant, as a member of an organisation which habitually perpetrates sectarian acts of violence with firearms and explosives, must, as soon as he was briefed for his role, have contemplated the bombing of the Crosskeys Inn as not the only possibility but one of the most obvious possibilities among the jobs which the principals were likely to be undertaking and in the commission of which he was intentionally assisting. He was therefore in just the same situation, so far as guilty knowledge is concerned, as a man who had been given a list of jobs and told that one of them would be carried out."

The only argument attacking this passage of any substance directed to your Lordships on the part of the appellant was to the effect that since at the time of the commission of the offence there was no generalised offence of terrorism as such the state of ignorance which must be assumed in favour of the accused as to the precise weapon (*e.g.* bomb, bullets, or incendiary device) or type of violence to be employed in the concerted "job" contemplated was such as to make him ignorant of some or all of the "essential ingredients" of the two offences charged in the particulars of offence in which a "pipe bomb" is specified, and one at least of which, had it been committed, would or at least might have been laid under a separate penal provision.

I regard this point as frankly unarguable. I would consider that bullet, bomb, or incendiary device, indeed most if not all types of terrorist violence, would all constitute offences of the same "type" within the meaning of *R. v. Bainbridge* and that so far as *mens rea* is concerned "the essential ingredients" of all and each of the offences within the other authorities I have cited were each and all contained within the guilty knowledge of the appellant at the time of his participation. The fact that, in the event, the offence committed by the principals crystallised into one rather than the other of the possible alternatives within his contemplation only means that in the event he was accessory to that specific offence rather than one of the others which in the event was not the offence committed. Obviously there must be limits to the meaning of the expression "type of offence" and a minimum significance attached to the expression "essential ingredients" in this type of doctrine, but it is clear that if an alleged accessory is perfectly well aware that he is participating in one of a limited number of serious crimes and one of these is in fact committed he is liable under the general law at least as one who aids, abets, counsels or procures that crime even if he is not actually a principal. Otherwise I can see no end to the number of unmeritorious arguments which the ingenuity of defendants could adduce. This disposes of the present appeal, which seems to me to be as lacking in serious plausibility as it is wholly devoid of substantial merits. ...

LORD SCARMAN: My Lords, I also would dismiss this appeal. The question it raises is as to the degree of knowledge required by law for the attachment of criminal responsibility to one who assists another (or others) to commit or attempt crime.

In *Johnson* v. *Youden* [1950] 1 K.B. 544 the Divisional Court held that before a person can be convicted of aiding and abetting the commission of an offence he must at least know the essential matters which constitute the offence. He does not have to know that the facts constitute an offence: for ignorance of the law is no defence. In *R.* v. *Bainbridge* the Court of Criminal Appeal (for England and Wales) held that it was not necessary that the accused should know the particular crime intended or committed by those whom he assisted, and upheld a direction in which the judge had made it clear that it was enough if the accused knew the type of crime intended.

Counsel for the appellant submits that, if *R.* v. *Bainbridge* is to be followed, there is no evidence in the present case that the appellant knew the particular type of crime intended, *i.e.* doing an act with intent to cause an explosion of the nature likely to endanger life or cause serious injury to property. Counsel is really submitting that, if his client's conviction be upheld on either of the two counts with which his appeal is concerned (count 1, doing an act with intent to cause an explosion, and count 2, possession of an explosive substance with intent), your Lordships will be extending the law beyond the decision in *R.* v. *Bainbridge* and that, even if that decision be good law, such extension is unjustifiable.

I think *R.* v. *Bainbridge* was correctly decided. But I agree with counsel for the appellant that in the instant case the Court of Criminal Appeal in Northern Ireland has gone further than the Court of Criminal Appeal for England and Wales found it necessary to go in *R.* v. *Bainbridge*. It is not possible in the present case to declare that it is proved, beyond reasonable doubt, that the appellant knew a bomb attack upon the Inn was intended by those whom he was assisting. It is not established, therefore, that he knew the particular type of crime intended. The Court, however, refused to limit criminal responsibility by reference to knowledge by the accused of the type or class of crime intended by those whom he assisted. Instead, the Court has formulated a principle which avoids the uncertainties and ambiguities of classification. The guilt of an accessory springs, according to the Court's formulation, "from the fact that he contemplates the commission of one (or more) of a number of crimes by the principal and he intentionally lends his assistance in order that such a crime will be committed": *per* Sir Robert Lowry C.J. "The relevant crime," the Lord Chief Justice continues, "must be within the contemplation of the accomplice, and only exceptionally would evidence be found to support the allegation that the accomplice had given the principal a completely blank cheque."

The principle thus formulated has great merit. It directs attention to the state of mind of the accused—not what he ought to have in contemplation, but what he did have: it avoids definition and classification while ensuring that a man will not be convicted of aiding and abetting any offence his principal may commit, but only one which is within his contemplation. He may have in contemplation only one offence, or several: and the several which he contemplates he may see as alternatives. An accessory who leaves it to his principal to choose is liable, provided always the choice is made from the range of offences from which the accessory contemplates the choice will be made. Although the court's formulation of the principle goes further than in the earlier cases, it is a sound development of the law and in no way inconsistent with them. I accept it as good judge-made law in a field where there is no statute to offer guidance.

Upon the facts as found by the trial judge (there was no jury because of the Northern Ireland (Emergency Provisions) Act 1973), the appellant knew he was guiding a party of men to the Crosskeys Inn on a UVF military-style "job," *i.e.* an attack by bomb, incendiary or bullet on persons or property. He did not know the particular type of offence intended, but he must have appreciated that it was very likely that those whom he was assisting intended a bomb attack on the inn.

If the appellant contemplated, as he clearly did, a bomb attack as likely, he must also have contemplated the possibility that the men in the car, which he was leading to the Inn, had an explosive substance with them. Though he did not know whether they had it with them or not, he must have believed it very likely that they did. In the particular circumstances of this case, the inference that the two offences of possessing the explosive and using it with intent to cause injury or damage were within the appellant's contemplation is fully justified upon the evidence. The appellant was rightly convicted, and I would dismiss his appeal.

Appeal dismissed

(d) Acts beyond the Common Design

R. v. Saunders and Archer
(1573) 2 Plowden 473; 75 E.R. 706
Warwick Assizes

John Saunders had a wife whom he intended to kill, in order that he might marry another woman with whom he was in love, and he opened his design to ... Alexander Archer, and desired his assistance and advice in the execution of it, who advised him to put an end to her life by poison. With this intent the said Archer bought the poison, *viz.* arsenick and roseacre, and delivered it to the said John Saunders to give to his wife, who accordingly gave it to her, being sick, in a roasted apple, and she eat a small part of it, and gave the rest to ... Eleanor Saunders, an infant, about three years of age, who was the daughter of her and the said John Saunders her husband. And the said John Saunders seeing it, blamed his wife for it, and said that apples were not good for such infants; to which his wife replied that they were better for such infants than for herself: and the daughter eat the poisoned apple, and the said John Saunders, her father, saw her eat it, and did not offer to take it from her lest he should be suspected, and afterwards the wife recovered, and the daughter died of the said poison.

Whether or not this was murder in John Saunders, the father, was somewhat doubted, for he had no intent to poison his daughter, nor had he any malice against her, but on the contrary he had a great affection for her, and he did not give her the poison, but his wife ignorantly gave it her, and although he might have taken it from the daughter, and so have preserved her life, yet the not taking it from her did not make it a felony, for it was all one whether he had been present or absent, as to this point, inasmuch as he had no malice against the daughter, nor any inclination to do her any harm. But at last the said justices, upon consideration of the matter, and with the assent of Saunders, Chief Baron, who had the examination of the said John Saunders before, and who had signified his opinion to the said justices ... were of opinion that the said offence was murder in the said John Saunders. And the reason thereof ... was because the said John Saunders gave the poison with the intent to kill a person, and in the giving of it he intended that death should follow. And when death followed from his act, although it happened in another person than her whose death he directly meditated, yet it shall be murder in him, for he was the original cause of the death.

But the most difficult point in this case, and upon which the justices conceived greater doubt than upon the offence of the principal, was, whether or no Archer should be adjudged accessory to the murder. For the offence which Archer committed was the aid and advice which he gave to Saunders, and that was only to kill his wife, and no other, for there was no parol communication between them concerning the daughter, and although by the consequences which followed from the giving of the poison by Saunders the principal, it so happened that the daughter was killed, yet Archer did not precisely procure her death, nor advise him to kill her, and therefore whether or no he should be accessory to this murder which happened by a thing consequential to the first act, seemed to them to be doubtful. ... Upon conference before had with the justices of both Benches, they were agreed that they ought not to give judgment against the said Alexander Archer, because they took the law to be that he could not be adjudged accessory to the said offence of murder, for that he did not assent that the daughter should be poisoned, but only that the wife should be poisoned, which assent cannot be drawn further than he gave it, for the poisoning of the daughter is a distinct thing from that to which he was privy, and therefore he shall not be adjudged accessory to it. ...

Question

If Saunders had been absent when his wife gave the poisoned apple to their daughter, he would still have been guilty, as the cases on transferred malice show, in particular, *R. v. Latimer, ante,* p. 176. Moreover, Archer would now become liable as a party to the murder.

Why does the law treat Archer differently depending upon whether Saunders, who is guilty in any event, knew or did not know of the giving of the apple to his child?

R. v. Slack
[1989] 3 All E.R. 90
Court of Appeal

S and B were burgling the flat of an old lady. S passed B a knife "to threaten the old lady with if she starts screaming." While S was out of the room, B cut her throat. S was convicted of murder and appealed.

LORD LANE C.J.: The appellant's case put forward by counsel was simply that, although he was undoubtedly jointly guilty of robbery, he was in no way party to the murder.

Counsel for the appellant submits that the judge misdirected the jury as to the mental element which the prosecution must prove before the secondary participant in a joint enterprise can be convicted of murder, the actual killing having been done by the primary party. ...

Accordingly it is the written directions on murder which we must examine to see whether they accord with the law. They ran as follows:

"1. Did the Accused intend to kill or cause grievous bodily harm to Mrs Crowder in the sense that he agreed with Buick that in the course of their joint enterprise Mrs Crowder should either be killed e.g., so that she could not give evidence against them or should be caused grievous bodily harm e.g. so that she could not prevent them robbing her and did she die as a result of such conduct by Buick? If so, Accused is guilty of murder. 2. Did the Accused contemplate and foresee that Buick *might* kill or cause grievous bodily harm to Mrs Crowder as part of their joint enterprise and did she die as a result of such conduct by Buick? If so it is open to you to find that he so intended and that he is guilty of murder." (The judge's emphasis.)

It is to the second question that objection is taken, on the ground that it wrongly equates foresight and contemplation with intent. The directions, submits counsel for the appellant, should have been to this effect: assuming that Buick murdered Mrs Crowder, has it been proved to the requisite extent that (a) at the time of the killing Buick and the appellant were taking part in a joint enterprise and (b) the appellant intended that Mrs Crowder be killed or caused really serious harm should the necessity arise?

Some confusion has arisen as to the proper direction to be given to a jury in these circumstances. That seems to be partly due to some of the observations of the Judicial Committee of the Privy Council in *Chan Wing-siu* v. *R.* [1985] A.C. 168. There three assailants armed with knives burst into the flat of a prostitute, intent it seems on robbery. One of them murdered the prostitute's husband. It could scarcely be doubted that there was a joint agreement to kill or inflict serious injury if necessary. The trial judge's direction in that case, so far as it is relevant, was as follows:

"You may convict ... of murder if you come to the conclusion ... that the accused contemplated that either of his companions might use a knife to cause bodily injury on one ... of the occupants. ... "

In upholding the conviction Sir Robin Cooke, in the course of delivering the judgment of the Board, said (at p. 175):

"The case must depend rather on the wider principle whereby a secondary party is criminally liable for acts by the primary offender of a type which the former foresees but does not necessarily intend. That there is such a principle is not in doubt. It turns on contemplation or, putting the same idea in other words, authorisation, which may be express but is more usually implied. It meets the case of a crime foreseen as a possible incident of the common unlawful enterprise. The criminal culpability lies in participating in the venture with that foresight."

Their Lordships expressly adopted the principle enunciated by the five-judge court in *R.* v. *Anderson and Morris* [1966] 2 Q.B. 110 at 118–110, where Lord Parker CJ, delivering the judgment of the court, said:

" ... where two persons embark on a joint enterprise ... that includes liability for unusual consequences if they arise from the execution of the agreed joint enterprise but (and this is the crux of the matter) ... if one of the adventurers goes beyond what has been tacitly agreed as part of the common enterprise, his co-adventurer is not liable for the consequences of that unauthorised act. Finally ... it is for the jury in every case to decide whether what was done was part of the joint enterprise, or went beyond it and was in fact an act unauthorised by that joint enterprise."

The Judicial Committee seems primarily to have been concerned with the problem posed by a conditional agreement, e.g. "We do not want to kill or seriously injure, but if necessary we will."

Chan Wing-siu v. *R.* was considered and approved by this court in *R.* v. *Ward* (1986) 85 Cr.App.R. 71. The appellant's submissions in that case were that the decisions of the House of Lords in *R.* v. *Moloney* [1985] A.C. 905 (*ante*, p. 81) and *R.* v. *Hancock* [1986] A.C. 455 (*ante*, p. 86) had the effect of completely altering the law relating to joint enterprise and that no man can be convicted of murder unless it is specifically decided against him that he had a murderous intent, and since intent had to be read against the decisions in *R.* v. *Moloney* and *R.* v. *Hancock* the jury ought to be directed on the basis of those cases.

This court in *R.* v. *Ward* reiterated the passage from *R.* v. *Anderson and Morris* cited above and went on to hold that *R.* v. *Moloney* and *R.* v. *Hancock* had had no effect on the well-known and well-established principles of joint enterprise.

As counsel for the appellant rightly points out, difficulties have arisen from the decision of another division of this court in *R.* v. *Barr* (1986) 88 Cr.App.R. 362 [which did not follow the decision in *R.* v. *Ward*.]

. . . What the court in that case did was, first, unwittingly to overlook the full effect of the earlier judgment in *R.* v. *Ward* and, second, to regard the necessary intent to be proved in the case of A, the principal party, as the same as that to be proved in the case of B, the secondary party. A must be proved to have intended to kill or do serious harm at the time he killed. B may not be present at the killing; he may be a distance away, for example, waiting in the getaway car; he may be in another part of the house; he may not know that A has killed; he may have hoped (and probably did) that A would not kill or do serious injury. If, however, as part of their joint plan it was understood between them expressly or tacitly that if necessary one of them would kill or do serious harm as part of their common enterprise, then B is guilty of murder.

As appears from the cases we have cited, the direction may be in a variety of different forms. Provided that it is made clear to the jury that for B to be guilty he must be proved to have lent himself to a criminal enterprise involving the infliction, if necessary, of serious harm or death or to have had an express or tacit understanding with A that such harm or death should, if necessary, be inflicted, the precise form of words in which the jury are directed is not important. As Sir Robin Cooke observed in *Chan Wing-siu* v. *R.* [1985] A.C. 168 at 179:

> "No one formula is exclusively preferable; indeed it may be advantageous in a summing up to use more than one. For the question is not one of semantics."

. . . In our judgment the second question posed by the judge in the instant case in his written directions to the jury was in accordance with the principles we have endeavoured to express. The question made it clear to the jury that the appellant must have at least tacitly agreed that, if necessary, serious harm should be done to Mrs Crowder, or that he lent himself to the infliction of such harm. There was ample evidence before the jury on which they could come to the conclusion that the prosecution had satisfied them so as to feel sure on these matters so far as the appellant was concerned.

The appeal is accordingly dismissed.

Appeal dismissed

Note

Some doubt having arisen as to whether tacit agreement and lending oneself to the infliction of harm [see last paragraph, above] were alternatives in that either would suffice for conviction, Lord Lane in *R.* v. *Hyde* [1990] 3 All E.R. 892, 896, took the opportunity to clarify matters:

"It has been pointed out by Professor Smith, in his commentary on *R.* v. *Wakely* [1990] Crim.L.R. 119 at 120–121, that in the judgments in *R.* v. *Slack* and also in *R.* v. *Wakely* itself, to both of which I was a party, insuffficient attention was paid by the court to the distinction between on the one hand tacit agreement by B that A should use violence, and on the other hand a realisation by B that A, the principal party, may use violence despite B's refusal to authorise or agree to its use. Indeed in *R.* v. *Wakely* we went so far as to say:

'The suggestion that a mere foresight of the real or definite possibility of violence being used is sufficient to constitute the mental element of murder is prima facie, academically speaking at least, not sufficient.'

On reconsideration, that passage is not in accordance with the principles set out by Sir Robin Cooke which we were endeavouring to follow and was wrong, or at least misleading. If B realises (without agreeing to such conduct being used) that A may kill or intentionally inflict serious injury, but nevertheless continues to participate with A in the venture, that will amount to a sufficient mental element for B to be guilty of murder if A, with the requisite intent, kills in the course of the venture. As Professor Smith points out, B has in those circumstances lent himself to the enterprise and by so doing he has given assistance and encouragement to A in carrying out an enterprise which B realises may involve murder."

Note

In *Chan Wing-Sui* v. *R.*, the Privy Council had also to consider the question of what degree of likelihood of the principal crime being committed must the defendant contemplate before it can be said that the crime was within his contemplation.

SIR ROBIN COOKE: " . . . The matter has been examined by appellate courts in Australia and New Zealand. In *Johns* v. *The Queen* (1980) 143 C.L.R. 108 the High Court of Australia rejected an argument that at common law an accessory before the fact is not liable for the crime, although contemplated by him as an act which might be done in the course of the venture, unless it was more probable than not that the criminal act charged would take place. Stephen J. in his judgment at p. 122 and Mason, Murphy and Wilson JJ. in a joint judgment, at pp. 130–131, approved the following statement by Street C.J. in the Supreme Court of New South Wales:

'an accessory before the fact bears, as does a principal in the second degree, a criminal liability for an act which was within the contempla-tion of both himself and the principal in the first degree as an act which might be done in the course of carrying out the primary criminal intention—an act contemplated as a possible incident of the originally planned particular venture.'

The joint judgment added that such an act is one which falls within the parties' own purpose and design precisely because it is within their contemplation and is foreseen as a possible incident of the execution of their planned enterprise. Stephen J., at p. 119, taking a phrase from *Howard on Criminal Law*, 3rd ed. (1967), p. 276, spoke of contemplation by the parties of a 'substantial risk' that the killing would occur. The same phrase was used by the High Court in a case of extraordinary facts, *Miller* v. *The Queen* (1980) 55 A.L.J.R. 23. There approval was given to a direction to the effect that the accused was guilty of murder if the common plan included the possible murder of girls, so that the parties to the plan contemplated as a substantial risk the murder of any girl who was picked up, even though it was not contemplated that murder would occur in the course of every drive.

Those two Australian authorities were cited to, and strongly influenced, the Hong Kong Court of Appeal in the present case. In *R.* v. *Gush* [1980] 2 N.Z.L.R. 92, delivering a judgment of the New Zealand Court of Appeal, Richmond P. applied the approach in *Johns* v. *The Queen*, when interpreting a provision in section 66(2) of the Crimes Act 1961 making a person liable as a party 'if the commission of that offence was known to be a probable consequence of the prosecution of the common purpose.' After discussing the range of meanings which 'probable' may bear, he said, at p. 95, that the statutory objects would be largely frustrated if in this provision the word was treated as meaning more probable than not. Instead the court in *R.* v. *Gush* preferred the interpretation that, in the particular context, 'probable' denoted an event that could well happen.

In agreement with the courts in Hong Kong, Australia and New Zealand, their Lordships regard as wholly unacceptable any argument that would propose, as any part of the criteria of the guilt of an accomplice, whether on considering in advance the possibility of a crime of the kind in the event actually committed by his co-adventurers he thought that it was more than an even risk. ... What public policy requires was rightly identified in the submissions for the Crown. Where a man lends himself to a criminal enterprise knowing that potentially murderous weapons are to be carried, and in the event they are in fact used by his partner with an intent sufficient for murder, he should not escape the consequences by reliance upon a nuance of prior assessment, only too likely to have been optimistic.

On the other hand, if it was not even contemplated by the particular accused that serious bodily harm would be intentionally inflicted, he is not a party to murder. ...

In some cases in this field it is enough to direct the jury by adapting to the circumstances the simple formula common in a number of jurisdictions. For instance, did the particular accused contemplate that in carrying out a common unlawful purpose one of his partners in the enterprise might use a knife or a loaded gun with the intention of causing really serious bodily harm?

The present was such a case. It was not necessary for the trial judge to say more on the subject than he did. ...

... [But] where there is an evidential foundation for a remoteness issue, it may be necessary for the judge to give the jury more help. Although a risk of a killing or serious bodily harm has crossed the mind of a party to an unlawful enterprise, it is right to allow for a class of case in which the risk was so remote as not to make that party guilty of a murder or intentional causing of grievous bodily harm committed by a co-adventurer in the circumstances that in the event confronted the latter. But if the party accused knew that lethal weapons, such as a knife or a loaded gun, were to be carried on a criminal expedition, the defence should succeed only very rarely.

In cases where an issue of remoteness does arise it is for the jury (or other tribunal of fact) to decide whether the risk *as recognised by the accused* was sufficient to make him a party to the crime committed by the principal. Various formulae have been suggested—including a substantial risk, a real risk, a risk that something might well happen. No one formula is exclusive preferable; indeed it may be advantageous in a summing up to use more than one. For the question is not one of semantics. What has to be brought home to the jury is that occasionally a risk may have occurred to an accused's mind—fleetingly or even causing him some deliberation—but may genuinely have been dismissed by him as altogether negligible. If they think there is a reasonable possibility that the case is in that class, taking the risk should not make that accused a party to such a crime of intention as murder or wounding with intent to cause grievous bodily harm. The judge is entitled to warn the jury to be cautious before reaching that conclusion; but the law can do no more by way of definition; it can only be for the jury to determine any issue of that kind on the facts of the particular case."

Questions

1. Is it the result of *Chan Wing-Siu* that, where the principal's crime is one of intent, the accessory's mental state is satisfied by something less than intention? *Cf.* Draft Criminal Code, clause 27(1) *post*, p. 407.

2. Are there crimes where the *mens rea* needed of an accessory is greater than that needed of the principal? See *Ferguson* v. *Weaving*, *ante*, p. 387.

3. A and B agree to rob a post office and to cosh any person who resists.

(*a*) B coshes someone who resists. Can A escape by proving that he had taken part in many post-office raids and it was never necessary to cosh anyone because no-one ever resisted?

(*b*) B recognises an old enemy in the queue of unresisting customers and coshes him to pay off old scores. Is A an accessory to this attack?

4. A and B agree to rob a post office, carrying coshes in order to intimidate any persons on the scene. A positively forbids B from hitting anyone, but he knows from previous experience that B is excitable while on a raid, and that it is possible that he will lose his self-control and hit someone. B does hit a witness V on the head with his cosh and kills him. Is A guilty of the murder of V?

(e) Withdrawal

R. v. Becerra
(1975) 62 Cr.App.R. 212
Court of Appeal

B. broke into a house with C. and G., intending to steal. B. gave a knife to C. to use if necessary on anyone interrupting them. The tenant of the upstairs flat L. came down to investigate the noise. B. said, "There's a bloke coming. Let's go," jumped out of the window and ran away. C.

stabbed L. with the knife, killing him. At his trial for murder, B. contended that he had withdrawn from the joint adventure before the attack on L. The jury were directed that his words and departure through the window were insufficient to constitute a withdrawal. B. was convicted, and sought leave to appeal.

ROSKILL L.J.: Mr. Owen [for the appellant] says that in that passage which I have just read, the learned judge in effect, though perhaps not in so many words, withdrew the defence of "withdrawal" from the jury, because the learned judge was saying to the jury that the only evidence of Becerra's suggested "withdrawal" was the remark, if it were made, "Come on let's go," coupled with the fact of course that Becerra then went out through the window and ran away and that that could not in those circumstances amount to "withdrawal" and therefore was not available as a defence, even if they decided the issue of common design against Becerra. It is upon that passage in the summing-up that Mr. Owen has principally focused his criticism.

It is necessary, before dealing with that argument in more detail, to say a word or two about the relevant law. It is a curious fact, considering the number of times in which this point arises where two or more people are charged with criminal offences, particularly murder or manslaughter, how relatively little authority there is in this country upon the point. But the principle is undoubtedly of long standing.

Perhaps it is best first stated in *R.* v. *Saunders and Archer* (*ante*, p. 392), in a note by *Plowden*, p. 476, thus: " . . . for if I command one to kill J.S. and before the Fact done I go to him and tell him that I have repented, and expressly charge him not to kill J.S. and he afterwards kills him, there I shall not be Accessory to this Murder, because I have countermanded my first Command, which in all Reason shall discharge me, for the malicious Mind of the Accessory ought to continue to do ill until the Time of the Act done, or else he shall not be charged; but if he had killed J.S. before the Time of my Discharge or Countermand given, I should have been Accessory to the Death, notwithstanding my private Repentance."

The next case to which I may usefully refer is some 250 years later, but over 150 years ago: *R.* v. *Edmeads and Others* (1828) 3 C. & P. 390, where there is a ruling of Vaughan B. at a trial at Berkshire Assizes, upon an indictment charging Edmeads and others with unlawfully shooting at game keepers. At the end of his ruling the learned Baron said on the question of common intent, at p. 392, "that is rather a question for the jury; but still, on this evidence, it is quite clear what the common purpose was. They all draw up in lines, and point their guns at the game-keepers, and they are all giving their countenance and assistance to the one of them who actually fires the gun. If it could be shewn that either of them separated himself from the rest, and showed distinctly that he would have no hand in what they were doing, the objection would have much weight in it."

I can go forward over 100 years. Mr. Owen (to whose juniors we are indebted for their research into the relevant Canadian and United States cases) referred us to several Canadian cases, to only one of which is it necessary to refer in detail, a decision of the Court of Appeal of British Columbia in *R.* v. *Whitehouse* (alias *Savage*) (1941) 1 W.W.R. 112. I need not read the headnote. The Court of Appeal held that the trial judge concerned in that case, which was one of murder, had been guilty of misdirection in his direction to the jury on this question of "withdrawal." The matter is, if I may most respectfully say so, so well put in the leading judgment of Sloan J.A., that I read the whole of the passage at pp. 115

and 116: "Can it be said on the facts of this case that a mere change of mental intention and a quitting of the scene of the crime just immediately prior to the striking of the fatal blow will absolve those who participate in the commission of the crime by overt acts up to that moment from all the consequences of its accomplishment by the one who strikes in ignorance of his companions' change of heart? I think not. After a crime has been committed and before a prior abandonment of the common enterprise may be found by a jury there must be, in my view, in the absence of exceptional circumstances, something more than a mere mental change of intention and physical change of place by those associates who wish to dissociate themselves from the consequences attendant upon their willing assistance up to the moment of the actual commission of that crime. I would not attempt to define too closely what must be done in criminal matters involving participation in a common unlawful purpose to break the chain of causation and responsibility. That must depend upon the circumstances of each case but it seems to me that one essential element ought to be established in a case of this kind: Where practicable and reasonable there must be timely communication of the intention of abandon the common purpose from those who wish to dissociate themselves from the contemplated crime to those who desire to continue in it. What is 'timely communication' must be determined by the facts of each case but where practicable and reasonable it ought to be such communication, verbal or otherwise, that will serve unequivocal notice upon the other party to the common unlawful cause that if he proceeds upon it he does so without the further aid and assistance of those who withdraw. The unlawful purpose of him who continues alone is then his own and not one in common with those who are no longer parties to it nor liable to its full and final consequences." The learned judge then went on to cite a passage from 1 Hale's *Pleas of the Crown* 618 and the passage from *R. v. Saunders and Archer* to which I have already referred.

In the view of each member of this Court, that passage, if we may respectfully say so, could not be improved upon and we venture to adopt it in its entirety as a correct statement of the law which is to be applied in this case.

The last case, an English one, is *R. v. Croft* [1944] 1 K.B. 295, a well known case of a suicide pact where, under the old law, the survivor of a suicide pact was charged with and convicted of murder. It was sought to argue that he had withdrawn from the pact in time to avoid liability (as the law then was) for conviction for murder.

The Court of Criminal Appeal, comprising Lawrence J. (as he then was), Lewis and Wrottesley JJ. dismissed the appeal and upheld the direction given by Humphreys J. to the jury at the trial. Towards the end of the judgment Lawrence J. said (pp. 297 and 298): " ... counsel for the appellant complains—although I do not understand that the point had ever been taken in the court below—that the summing-up does not contain any reference to the possibility of the agreement to commit suicide having been determined or countermanded. It is true that the learned judge does not deal expressly with that matter except in a passage where he says: 'Even if you accept his statement in the witness-box that the vital and second shot was fired when he had gone through the window, he would still be guilty of murder if she was then committing suicide as the result of an agreement which they had mutually arrived at that that should be fate of both of them, and it is no answer for him that he altered his mind after she was dead and did not commit suicide himself.' ... The authorities, such as they are, show in our opinion, that where a person has acted as an accessory before the fact, he must give express and actual countermand or revocation of the advising, counselling, procuring, or abetting which he had given before."

It seems to us that those authorities make plain what the law is which has to be applied in the present case.

We therefore turn back to consider the direction which the learned judge gave in the present case to the jury and what was the suggested evidence that Becerra had withdrawn from the common agreement. The suggested evidence is the use by Becerra of the words "Come on let's go," coupled, as I said a few moments ago, with his act in going out through the window. The evidence, as the judge pointed out, was that Cooper never heard that nor did the third man. But let it be supposed that that was said and the jury took the view that it was said.

On the facts of this case, in the circumstances then prevailing, the knife having already been used and being contemplated for further use when it was handed over by Becerra to Cooper for the purpose of avoiding (if necessary) by violent means the hazards of identification, if Becerra wanted to withdraw at that stage, he would have to "countermand," to use the word that is used in some of the cases or "repent" to use another word so used, in some manner vastly different and vastly more effective than merely to say "Come on, let's go" and go out through the window.

It is not necessary, on this application, to decide whether the point of time had arrived at which the only way in which he could effectively withdraw, so as to free himself from joint responsibility for any act Cooper thereafter did in furtherance of the common design, would be physically to intervene so as to stop Cooper attacking Lewis, as the judge suggested, by interposing his own body between them or somehow getting in between them or whether some other action might suffice. That does not rise for decision here. Nor is it necessary to decide whether or not the learned judge was right or wrong, on the facts of this case, in that passage which appears at the bottom of p. 206, which Mr. Owen criticised: "and at least take all reasonable steps to prevent the commission of the crime which he had agreed the others should commit." It is enough for the purposes of deciding this application to say that under the law of this country as it stands, and on the facts (taking them at their highest in favour of Becerra), that which was urged as amounting to withdrawal from the common design was not capable of amounting to such withdrawal. Accordingly Becerra remains responsible, in the eyes of the law, for everything that Cooper did and continued to do after Becerra's disappearance through the window as much as if he had done them himself.

Application refused

Notes

"A declared intent to withdraw from a conspiracy to dynamite a building is not enough, if the fuse has been set; he must step on the fuse," *per* McDermott J. in *Eldredge* v. *U.S.*, 62F. 2nd 449 (1932). That leaves the question of what will be enough if it *is* timely. Roskill L.J. appears to indicate that at some stage a point of time will be reached where only physical prevention of the crime, or at least all reasonable steps to prevent it, will exculpate the accessory, leaving open the question of what will suffice before that point of time is reached.

R. v. *Grundy* [1977] Crim.L.R. 543 (C.A.): Six weeks before a burglary, A gave information to the burglars about the premises to be attacked, the habits of the owner and other matters. For two weeks before the burglary, "he had been trying to stop them breaking in" [although it does not appear that he warned the householder or the police]. *Held,* his defence of withdrawal should have been left to the jury.

R. v. Whitefield (1983) 79 Cr.App.R. 36 (C.A.); W. told G. that the occupant of the flat next to his was away; he agreed to break in with G. by way of his own flat's balcony and to divide the spoils. Later he told G. he would take no part, but on the night in question, he heard G. breaking in via the coal chute, and took no steps to stop him. "In this case there was ... evidence ... that he had served unequivocal notice on G. that if he proceeded with the burglary he would do so without the aid or assistance of the appellant. In his ruling the judge stated that such notice was not enough, and that in failing to communicate with the police or take any other steps to prevent the burglary he remained "liable in law for what happened, for everything that was done that night." In the judgment of the court, in making that statement the judge fell into an error of law" (at p. 40).

Questions

1. What ought to be the law's objectives in this area? To encourage repentance, or to encourage efforts to undo the harm done by the initial encouragement?
2. If the latter, is it likely that "unequivocal notice to the principal that if he goes on it will be without the aid or assistance of the accessory" will often be a significant undoing of the harm done by the initial encouragement?
3. If in *Whitefield*, the telling of G. that the flat was unoccupied without any promise of assistance in the actual break-in would be enough to implicate W., why should the making and later withdrawal of the promise make any difference to his liability?
4. Whichever object is to be preferred, need notice to the principal be insisted on if steps are taken to frustrate the enterprise?
5. Ought the requirements for withdrawal to be different if the accessory has supplied the principal with the means for committing the crime? Might it have made a difference in *Becerra* if B. had not supplied C. with the knife?

Notes

See Lanham, *Accomplices and Withdrawal* (1981) 97 L.Q.R. 575, and compare Draft Criminal Code, clause 27(8), *post,* p. 408.

v. Accessory Not Convictable as a Principal

Sayce v. Coupe
[1953] 1 Q.B. 1
Queen's Bench Division

C. was charged with aiding, abetting, counselling and procuring a person unknown to sell tobacco otherwise than as a licensed retailer of tobacco contrary to section 13 of the Tobacco Act 1842 as amended. It appeared that C. had purchased the tobacco from a person who was not a licensed retailer. The magistrates dismissed the charge, and the prosecutor appealed.

LORD GODDARD C.J.: [Counsel for the accused] has argued that because the statute does not make it an offence to buy, but only makes it an offence to sell, we ought to hold that the offence of aiding and abetting the sale ought not to be preferred or could not be preferred. It is obvious that it can be preferred. The statute does not make it an offence to buy, but obviously, on ordinary general principles of criminal law, if in such case a person knows the circumstances and knows, therefore, that an offence is being committed and takes part in, or facilitates the commission of the offence, he is guilty as a principal in the second degree, for it is impossible to say that a person who buys does not aid and abet the sale.

Appeal allowed

R. v. Tyrrell
[1894] 1 Q.B. 710
Court for Crown Cases Reserved

Tyrrell, a girl aged between 13 and 16, was convicted of aiding and abetting one Ford to commit the misdemeanour of having unlawful carnal knowledge of her, which was an offence under Criminal Law Amendment Act 1885, s.5. (See now, Sexual Offences Act 1956, s.6.)

Counsel for the accused: Under [the Offences Against the Person Act 1861], section 58, a woman is not indictable for administering poison or other noxious thing to herself with intent to procure abortion, unless she is with child when she does so; but she is liable to conviction and punishment if, with the same intent, she administers poison, etc. to another woman, though the other be not with child. . . . *R. v. Whitchurch* (1890) 24 Q.B.D. 420 . . . therefore has no application here. It is impossible that the legislature, in passing the Criminal Law Amendment Act 1885, can have intended that the women and girls for whose protection it was passed should be liable to prosecution and punishment under it. Part I, in which section 5 comes, is headed "Protection of Women and Girls." A girl under 16 is treated as of so immature a mind as not to be capable of consenting. The Act assumes that she has no *mens rea*, and she cannot, therefore, be treated as capable of aiding and abetting. If a girl is liable to be convicted of aiding and abetting an offence under section 5 she is also liable to conviction for aiding and abetting the felony made punishable by section 4, and she would then be liable to be sentenced to penal servitude for life, because an accessory before the fact to a felony may be punished as a principal. The result would be to render the Act inoperative, because girls would not come forward to give evidence. The Criminal Law Amendment Act, 1885, s.5, created no new offence, and for 600 years it has never been suggested that such an offence as that charged against the defendant could be committed at common law.

LORD COLDERIDGE C.J.: The Criminal Law Amendment Act, 1885, was passed for the purpose of protecting women and girls against themselves. At the time it was passed there was a discussion as to what point should be fixed as the age of consent. That discussion ended in a compromise, and the age of consent was fixed at 16. With the object of protecting women and girls against themselves the Act of Parliament has made illicit connection with a girl under that age unlawful; if a man wishes to have such illicit connection he must wait until the girl is 16, otherwise he breaks the law; but it is impossible to say that the Act, which is absolutely silent about aiding and abetting or soliciting or inciting, can have intended that the girls for whose protection it was passed should be punishable under it for the offences committed upon themselves. I am of opinion that this conviction ought to be quashed.

MATHEW J.: I am of the same opinion. I do not see how it would be possible to obtain convictions under the statute if the contention for the Crown were adopted, because nearly every section which deals with offences in respect of women and girls would create an offence in the woman or girl. Such a result cannot have been intended by the legislature. There is no trace in the statute of any intention to treat the woman or girl as criminal.

Conviction quashed

R. v. Whitehouse
[1977] Q.B. 868
Court of Appeal

W. pleaded guilty to a charge of inciting his 15-year-old daughter to commit incest with him. On appeal against sentence, the Court of Appeal gave him leave to appeal against conviction on the view that he may have pleaded guilty to an offence which was unknown to the law.

SCARMAN L.J.: ... We can turn now to consider whether the indictment disclosed an offence known to the law. The count standing by itself does disclose such an offence because the count merely alleges incitement to commit incest. But when one goes on to the particulars one sees that the defendant is charged with inciting his daughter, a girl aged 15, to commit incest with him. The Crown recognises that there are difficulties in the drafting of the indictment. The Crown recognises that under section 11 of the Sexual Offences Act 1956 a girl aged 15 cannot commit incest. The relevant subsection is (1) and I read it:

"It is an offence for a woman of the age of 16 or over to permit a man whom she knows to be her ... father ... to have sexual intercourse with her by her consent."

It is of course accepted by the Crown that at common law the crime of incitement consists of inciting another person to commit a crime. When one looks at this indictment in the light of the particulars of the offence pleaded, one sees that it is charging the defendant with inciting a girl to commit a crime which in fact by statute she is incapable of committing. If therefore the girl was incapable of committing the crime alleged, how can the defendant be guilty of the common law crime of incitement? The Crown accepts the logic of that position and does not seek in this court to rely on section 11 of the Act of 1956 or to suggest that this man could be guilty of inciting his daughter to commit incest, to use the old phrase, as a principal in the first degree. But the Crown says that it is open to them upon this indictment to submit that it covers the offence of inciting the girl to aid and abet the man to commit the crime of incest upon her. Section 10

of the Act of 1956 makes it an offence for a man to have sexual intercourse
with a woman whom he knows to be his daughter, and the Crown says
that upon this indictment it is possible to say that the defendant has
committed an offence known to the law the offence being that of inciting
his daughter under the age of 16 to aid and abet him to have sexual
intercourse with her.

... We are prepared to assume, for the purposes of this appeal, that the
indictment can be cured, and accordingly we now read the indictment as
an indictment charging this man with the offence of inciting a girl of 15 to
aid and abet him to commit incest with her.

Is there such an offence known to the law? The difficulty arises from
two features of the law to which I have already referred. First, at common
law the crime of incitement consists of inciting another person to commit a
crime. This was laid down in *R. v. Higgins* (1801) 2 East 5 many years ago
and is well described in the very beginning of Chapter 10 of Smith and
Hogan, *Criminal Law*, 3rd ed. (1973), p. 172. The authors cite a passage
from *S. v. Nkosiyana* 1966 (4) S.A. 655, 658, which includes this sentence:
"An inciter is one who reaches and seeks to influence the mind of another
to the commission of a crime." The second difficult feature of the law is
section 11 of the Act of 1956 to which I have already referred. A woman
under the age of 16 cannot commit the crime of incest. But, says the
Crown, a man can commit incest, and so they go on to make their
submission that a girl of 15 can aid and abet him to do so.

There is no doubt of the general principle, namely, that a person,
provided always he or she is of the age of criminal responsibility, can be
guilty of aiding or abetting a crime even though it be a crime which he or
she cannot commit as a principal in the first degree. There are two famous
illustrations in the books of this principle. A woman can aid and abet a
rape so as herself to be guilty of rape, and a boy at an age where he is
presumed impotent can nevertheless aid and abet a rape. The cases, which
are very well known, are first in time *R. v. Eldershaw* (1828) 3 C. & P. 396.
In that case Vaughan B., in the course of a six line judgment, the brevity
of which I wish I could emulate, says "This boy being under 14, he
cannot, by law, be found guilty of a rape, except as a principal in the
second degree." So much for the boy.

The position in regard to a woman is stated by Bowen L.J. in one-line-
and-a-half in *R. v. Ram* (1893) 17 Cox C.C. 609, where two prisoners, a Mr.
and Mrs. Ram, were indicted jointly for rape upon Annie Edkins of the
age of 13. It was submitted that the woman could not be indicted for rape.
Bowen L.J. declined to quash the indictment for rape as against the female
prisoner.

Those cases clearly establish, and have been regarded for a very long
time as establishing, the general principle to which I have referred.

But what if the person alleged to be aiding and abetting the crime is
herself the victim of the crime? This poses the short question with which
this appeal is concerned. Before we consider it we would comment that, if
indeed it be the law that this girl aged 15 can be guilty of incest as the
aider and abettor of a man who is seeking to have intercourse with her,
then one has the strange situation that, although she cannot be guilty of
the crime of incest under the section which formulates the conditions
under which a woman may be found guilty of that crime, yet through this
doctrine of aiding and abetting she can be guilty of the offence when it is
committed by a man. That is an odd conclusion, but not necessarily to be
rejected because of its oddity.

The important matters in our judgment are these. First this girl, aged 15,
belongs to a class which is protected, but not punished, by sections 10 and

11 of the Sexual Offences Act 1956, and secondly the girl is alleged to be the victim of this notional crime. The whole question has an air of artificiality because nobody is suggesting either that the father has committed incest with her or that she has aided and abetted him to commit incest upon her. What is suggested is that the father has committed the crime of incitement because by his words and conduct he has incited her to do that which, of course, she never has done.

The question in our judgment is determined by authority. It is, strictly speaking, persuasive authority only because it deals with a different Act of Parliament, but it is a decision by a strong court which has declared a principle which is as applicable to the statutory provision with which we are concerned as to that with which that case was concerned. The case is *R.* v. *Tyrrell*, [*ante*, p. 403]. [After reciting the facts and quoting the judgment of Coleridge L.C.J.]. In our judgment it is impossible, as a matter of principle, to distinguish *R.* v. *Tyrrell* from the present case. Clearly the relevant provisions of the Sexual Offences Act 1956 are intended to protect women and girls. Most certainly, section 11 is intended to protect girls under the age of 16 from criminal liability, and the Act as a whole exists, in so far as it deals with women and girls exposed to sexual threat, to protect them. The very fact that girls under the age of 16 are protected from criminal liability for what would otherwise be incest demonstrates that this girl who is said to have been the subject of incitement was being incited to do something which, if she did it, could not be a crime by her.

One can only avoid that conclusion if one can pray in aid the doctrine of aiding and abetting and apply it to a crime committed by a man under section 10. But *R.* v. *Tyrrell* makes it clear that to do that would be to impose criminal liability upon persons whom Parliament has intended should be protected, not punished.

We have therefore come to the conclusion, with regret, that the indictment does not disclose an offence known to the law because it cannot be a crime on the part of this girl aged 15 to have sexual intercourse with her father, though it is of course a crime, and a very serious crime, on the part of the father. There is here incitement to a course of conduct, but that course of conduct cannot be treated as a crime by the girl. Plainly a gap or lacuna in the protection of girls under the age of 16 is exposed by this decision. It is regrettable indeed that a man who importunes his daughter under the age of 16 to have sexual intercourse with him but does not go beyond incitement cannot be found guilty of a crime. ... It may be that the legislature will consider it desirable to stop that gap. But in our judgment, applying the principles of the common law relating to the crime of incitement, and taking note of the decision of *R.* v. *Tyrrell* in relation to legislation similar to the Sexual Offences Act 1956, we have to declare the existence of the lacuna to which I have referred. There was incitement; but it was not incitement to crime. The girl's notional crime—because she never did commit it—is unknown to the law and therefore there can be no offence by him, the inciter. ...

Appeal against conviction allowed

Notes

1. Section 54 of the Criminal Law Act 1977 now makes it an offence for a man or boy to incite to have sexual intercourse with him a girl under the age of 16 whom he knows to be his granddaughter, daughter, sister or half-sister.

2. The rationale of *Tyrrell* and *Whitehouse* appears to be that the statute never meant to include under-age girls, because it was passed for their protection. (It may be doubted if that was the reason for section 10 of the Sexual Offences Act 1956, which says nothing about the age of the woman concerned. A more convincing reason is that section 11 makes an under-age girl unconvictable as principal, leading to the conclusion that she is not to be liable as an accessory either.) Other reasons apart from the protection principle could in appropriate cases be advanced for concluding that a statute was not intended to cover particular classes of people, *e.g.* that in penalising the unlicenced sale of tobacco, Parliament must have had both parties to the sale in mind, and the fact that it did not penalise the seller is an indication that it did not want him to be punished. However English law appears, on this question, to take no account of any reason other than the protection principle, see *Sayce* v. *Coupe, ante,* p. 402.

3. It was proposed to generalise this reason for implied exclusion of accessorial liability by providing that "a person does not become an accessory to an offence if the offence is so defined that his conduct in it is inevitably incidental to its commission and such conduct is not expressly penalised" (Law Com. W.P. 43, 1972 Proposition 8). This would cover such cases as *Sayce* v. *Coupe,* and form a better reason for excluding young girls in sexual cases. See, generally, Hogan, "Victims as Parties to Crime" [1962] Crim.L.R. 683. However, the Codemakers concluded that the reaction of consulted parties to the W.P. 43 proposal was unfavourable, see Law Com. No. 143, and the Draft Criminal Code therefore rests entirely on the "victim" rule of exclusion, see Clause 27(7), *infra.*

4. On the law as it is at present, apart from the rule of statutory exclusion involved in *R.* v. *Tyrrell* and *R.* v. *Whitehouse,* and the rule that a victim cannot be guilty of conspiracy (see Section 2(1) Criminal Law Act 1977, *post,* p. 460, there is no *general* rule that a victim cannot be a party to an offence. For example if A allows B to inflict bodily harm on him without what the law regards as a good reason, he will be an accessory to that crime: see *post,* p. 595. But where consent is a defence to the crime, the "victim's" participation may mean that no crime has been committed.

Draft Criminal Code

Accessories

"**27.**—(1) A person is guilty of an offence as an accessory if—

(a) he intentionally procures, assists or encourages the act which constitutes or results in the commission of the offence by the principal; and

(b) he knows of, or (where recklessness suffices in the case of the principal) is reckless with respect to, any circumstance that is an element of the offence; and

(c) he intends that the principal shall act, or is aware that he is or may be acting, or that he may act, with the fault (if any) required for the offence.

(2) In determining whether a person is guilty of an offence as an accessory it is immaterial that the principal is unaware of that person's act of procurement or assistance.

(3) Assistance or encouragement includes assistance or encouragement arising from a failure by a person to take reasonable steps to exercise any authority or to discharge any duty he has to control the relevant acts of the principal in order to prevent the commission of the offence.

(4) Subject to subsection (5), a person may be guilty of an offence as an accessory although he does not foresee, or is not aware of, a circumstance of the offence which is not an element of it (for example, the identity of the victim or the time or place of its commission, where this is not an element of the offence).

(5) Notwithstanding section 24(1) (transferred fault), where a person's act of procurement, assistance or encouragement is done with a view to the commission of an offence only in respect of a specified person or thing, he is not guilty as an accessory to an offence intentionally committed by the principal in respect of some other person or thing.

(6) A person is not guilty of an offence as an accessory by reason of anything he does—

(a)   with the purpose of preventing the commission of the offence; or
(b)   with the purpose of avoiding or limiting any harmful consequences of the offence and without the purpose of furthering its commission; or
(c)   because he believes that he is under an obligation to do it and without the purpose of furthering the commission of the offence.

(7) Where the purpose of an enactment creating an offence is the protection of a class of persons no member of that class who is a victim of such an offence can be guilty of that offence as an accessory.

(8) A person who has encouraged the commission of an offence is not guilty as an accessory if before its commission—

(a)   he countermanded his encouragement with a view to preventing its commission; or
(b)   he took all reasonable steps to prevent its commission."

2. VICARIOUS LIABILITY

R. v. Huggins (1730) 2 Strange 869: H., the Warden of the Fleet prison was charged with aiding and abetting B, a turnkey, in the murder of A, a prisoner who was so neglected by B that he died. The jury found a special verdict and the case was argued before all the judges. "It is a point not to be disputed but that in criminal cases the principal is not answerable for the act of the deputy, as he is in civil cases; they must each answer for their own acts and stand or fall by their own behaviour. All the authors that treat of criminal proceedings, proceed on the foundation of this distinction; that to affect the superior by the act of the deputy, there must be the command of the deputy, which is not found in this case. The duress in this case consisted in the first taking him against his consent, and putting him in that room, and the keeping him there so long without necessaries, which was the occasion of his death. Now none of these circumstances are found as against the prisoner. The jury does not say he directed his being put into the room; that he knew how long he had been there, that he was without the necessaries in the indictment, or was ever kept there after the time the prisoner saw him, which was fifteen days before his death. ... " Judgment: Not Guilty.

Mousell Bros. v. *London and North Western Ry.* [1917] 2 K.B. 836, 845 (C.A.):

ATKIN J.: "I think that the authorities cited ... make it plain that while prima facie a principal is not to be made criminally responsible for the acts of his servants, yet the legislature may prohibit an act or enforce a duty in such words as to make the prohibition or the duty absolute; in which case the principal is liable if the act is in fact done by his servants. To ascertain whether a particular Act of Parliament has that effect or not regard must be had to the object of the statute, the words used, the nature of the duty laid down, the person upon whom it is imposed, the person by whom it would in ordinary circumstances be performed, and the person upon whom the penalty is imposed."

Notes

1. Discovering the Parliamentary intention involves first asking whether strict liability was intended (on this, see *ante*, p. 190) because on the whole if *mens rea* is required for a conviction, a guiltless master cannot be convicted (although *Mousell's* case is itself an exception, the offence being "giving a false account with intent to avoid tolls," which was held to import vicarious liability). If the statute contains such words as "knowingly," "maliciously," "fraudulently," the master is not usually fixed with the knowledge malice or fraud of his servant. And if the offence consists of "permitting," "suffering" or "allowing" something to happen, a master does not do so merely because his servant permits, suffers or allows: see *James & Son* v. *Smee* [1955] 1 Q.B. 78. All this is however, subject to the doctrine of delegation, as to which see *Vane* v. *Yiannopoulos, infra.*

2. Even if the offence is one of strict liability, much depends on the key verb used in the statute to describe the conduct prohibited: some activities by a servant can be attributed to the master with more plausibility than others. "Using" is apt for vicarious liability, so if a servant uses a vehicle on his master's business, the master will often be held to be using it: see *James & Son* v. *Smee* [1955] 1 Q.B. 78; *John Henshall (Quarries) Ltd.* v. *Harvey* [1965] 2 Q.B. 233. Compare "driving"—only the actual driver can be said to be doing this: *cf. Thornton* v. *Mitchell, ante,* p. 368.

Williams, Criminal Law: The General Part, section 96, p. 281 (citations omitted)

" ... It seems we are now to witness the compiling of a new 'judicial dictionary' which will distinguish between those verbs in respect of which the servant's conduct can be regarded as the master's, and those in which it cannot. We must take it as settled by authority that a sale or use or (perhaps) presentation of a play by a servant, if within the general scope of his authority (though forbidden in the precise circumstances), is a sale or use or presentation by the master. On the other hand, it has been held that a representation made by the servant in the course of selling is not a representation by the master. A servant's 'ill-treating' of an animal cannot be attributed to his master. A receiving by a servant does not make his

master guilty of 'receiving' stolen goods. So also a giving of credit by a
servant is not a giving of credit by the master, and a demand for an illegal
premium by a servant is not a demand by the master. Although the point
has not been expressly decided, it seems that a master could not be
convicted of an offence of 'driving' a vehicle through his servant, for in
law it is only the actual driver who drives. Yet it has been held that a bus
company 'carries' its passenger and is apparently responsible for an
offence in relation to carriage committed by the conductor. ...

To make the law more difficult still, the same verb may possibly be
construed to create vicarious responsibility in a 'public welfare offence' but
not in one of the traditional crimes. Thus when a servant is in *de facto*
possession of a thing on behalf of his master, the possession may be
attributed to the master for the purpose of a public welfare offence, and
yet not attributed to him for the purpose of the crime of receiving stolen
goods. This way of reconciling the authorities may lead to the somewhat
surprising conclusion that the presentation of an unlicensed stage play is a
'public welfare offence.' Again, the context of the verb may modify its
meaning: for example, the word 'use' may be restricted by the purport of
the section to persons of a particular class."

Notes

1. Where vicarious responsibility is held to exist, it is not, in the
absence of some express provision in the statute, any defence to
show that the act of the servant was in defiance of the master's
instructions: *Coppen* v. *Moore (No. 2)* [1898] 2 Q.B. 306 (D.C.)

2. Except when the master is a company and the servant a
director (as to which see *post*, p. 413), whether or not the offence is
one where vicarious liability is held to be intended, it seems that in
no case will a master be primarily or vicariously liable for *aiding and
abetting* an offence, without personal knowledge of the essential
matters constituting the offence. On such a charge, the knowledge
of the servant is not imputed to the master (see *Ferguson* v.
Weaving, ante, p. 387. *N.C.B.* v. *Gamble, ante,* p. 382 is not an
authority to the contrary because there the master invited the court
to identify him with the servant whose acts and knowledge
constituted the aiding and abetting: see [1959] 1 Q.B. 26.

Draft Criminal Code

"**Vicarious liability**

29.—(1) Subject to subsection (3), an element of an offence (other than a
fault element) may be attributed to a person by reason of an act done by
another only if that other is—

(a)   specified in the definition of the offence as a person whose act may
       be so attributed; or
(b)   acting within the scope of his employment or authority and the
       definition of the offence specifies the element in terms which apply
       to both persons.

(2) Subject to subsection (3), a fault element of an offence may be
attributed to a person by reason of the fault of another only if the terms of
the enactment creating the offence so provide.

(3) This section does not affect the application in relation to any pre-Code offence (as defined in section 6) of any existing rule whereby a person who has delegated to another the management of premises or of a business or activity may, in consequence of the acts and fault of the other, have the elements of the offence attributed to him."

Commentary on Draft Criminal Code: Law Com. 177

"9.49 *Independent contractors.* The reference in paragraph (b) to a person's 'acting within the scope of his authority' extends, of course, to a case in which the person who does the prohibited act is acting for the defendant not as an employee but as an independent contractor. The clause does not distinguish between the person who 'uses' the defendant's vehicle as his employee and the person who 'uses' the defendant's vehicle on a single occasion because the defendant has asked him to do so, whether or not for payment. This does not mean that a person will necessarily be liable for the act of his independent contractor even where the offence employs a verb like 'uses'. The matter remains one for judicial interpretation. It is one thing to hold that a person carrying on a business of supplying milk or heavy building materials 'uses' a vehicle if he employs an independent contractor to supply those things in the contractor's vehicle. It would be quite another thing to hold that a householder 'uses' the removal van owned by the firm of removers whom he engages to carry his furniture to a new residence."

Question

Do you agree that, in the matter of "using" an independent contractor's van, there is a distinction between a person in the business of supplying building materials and a person moving furniture to a new residence?

Note

Under the present law, if the offence involved is not one of strict liability a master without knowledge of what is being done is normally not vicariously liable. To this rule, the doctrine of delegation forms an exception. See *infra.*

Vane v. Yiannopoullos
[1965] A.C. 486
House of Lords

By section 22(1) of the Licensing Act 1961: "If—(a) the holder of a justices' on-licence knowingly sells or supplies intoxicating liquor to persons to whom he is not permitted by the conditions of the licence to sell or supply it ... he shall be guilty of an offence."

The licensee of a restaurant had been granted a justices' on-licence subject to the condition that intoxicating liquor was to be sold only to persons ordering meals. He employed a waitress, whom he had instructed to serve drinks only to customers ordering meals, but on one occasion, whilst he was on another floor of the restaurant, the waitress served drinks to two youths who did not order a meal. The licensee did not know of that sale. He was charged with knowingly selling intoxicating liquor on the premises to persons to whom he was not permitted to sell, contrary to section 22(1)(*a*) of the Act. The magistrate dismissed the information and the prosecutor appealed, ultimately to the House of Lords.

LORD EVERSHED (after reviewing many cases cited by the appellant): But the effect of these numerous cases appears to my mind to be that (subject to the exception which follows) where the scope and purpose of the relevant Act is the maintenance of proper and accepted standards of public order in licensed premises or other comparable establishments, there arises under the legislation what Channell J. [in *Emary* v. *Nolloth* [1903] 2 K.B. 264] called a "quasi-criminal offence" which renders the licensee or proprietor criminally liable for the acts of his servants, though there may be no *mens rea* on his part. On the other hand, where the relevant regulation imports the word "knowingly" as a condition of liability on the part of the licensee or proprietor the result will be different. "Knowledge," that is *mens rea* in a real sense, on the part of the licensee or proprietor should normally be established as a fact if he is to be held liable under the statute. To this second proposition it appears, however, that, for better or worse, it should now be accepted that something further may be added—namely, that in the absence of proof of actual knowledge, nevertheless the licensee or proprietor may be held liable if he be shown, in the language of the judgments to which I have referred, in a real sense, effectively to have "delegated" his proprietary or managerial functions. If it be asked what is meant by delegation, it may be said ... that the expression will cover cases where the licensee or proprietor has handed over all the effective management of his premises, where he in truth connives at or wilfully closes his eyes to what in fact is being done. But I prefer to attempt nothing further in the way of definition applicable to any of the classes of case which have arisen; for I venture, for my part, to think that in the light of the numerous authorities the answer to any given case will generally depend upon the common sense of the jury or magistrate concerned, in light of what I believe can now be fairly and sensibly derived from the effect of the numerous cases referred to in the argument, to some of which I have alluded. On the one hand, where there is absent from the statutory prohibition the word "knowingly" applied to the licensee, I think that it should now be accepted that he may yet be held, and properly held, liable for breaches of the conditions of the licence committed by his servants in conscious disregard of those conditions, in spite of his own innocence, where a contrary view would, in the language of Viscount Reading C.J. [in *Mousell Brothers, Ltd.* v. *London and North Western Railway Co.* [1917] 2 K.B. 836], be regarded as fairly likely to stultify what, upon its fair construction, was the purpose of the legislation. On the other hand, where statutory liability on the licensee's part is qualified by the word "knowingly" (or some similarly clear term) then actual knowledge—that is, *mens rea*—is prima facie required. But I also think, in the light of the cases which have come before the Divisional Court during the present century, that it is right and sensible to hold that, even in the absence of that knowledge on the licensee's part, he may yet fairly and sensibly be held liable where he has in truth and reality "delegated" his powers, functions and responsibilities in the sense indicated in the examples which I have cited from the authorities. I do not attempt any further definition. As I have said, I think the result in any given case will depend upon the common sense of the jury or magistrate in light of what I think to be the effect of the numerous decisions.

So far, however, as the present case is concerned, I feel no doubt that the decision of the Divisional Court was right. There was clearly no "knowledge" in the strict sense proved against the licensee: I agree also with the Lord Chief Justice that there was no sufficient evidence of such "delegation" on his part of his powers, duties and responsibilities to render him liable on that ground. I would therefore without hesitation dismiss the appeal.

Appeal dismissed

Note

The delegation principle is to be abolished for Code and post-Code offences: Clause 29(2), *ante*, p. 410; but pre-existing cases where it has been held to apply are not to be affected: Clause 29(3).

3. CORPORATIONS

Notes

1. By Interpretation Act 1978, section 5, schedule 1, in every Act, unless the contrary intention appears, "person" includes a body of persons corporate or unincorporate.

2. A corporation is *vicariously* liable to exactly the same extent as a natural person: see last section. However a corporation is also directly liable for acts performed by some natural persons who are identified with it.

Tesco Supermarkets Ltd. v. Nattrass
[1972] A.C. 153
House of Lords

T.S. Ltd. was charged with an offence under the Trade Descriptions Act 1968. It sought to raise a defence under section 24(1) on the grounds that the commission of the offence was due to the act or default of another person, namely the manager of the store at which it was committed, and it exercised all due diligence to avoid the commission of the offence. The magistrates found that the company had set up a proper system, so it had exercised all due diligence; but the manager, who had failed to carry out his part under the system, was not "another person." The company, on conviction, appealed to the Divisional Court which held that the manager was "another person" but the company had not exercised all due diligence. The company appealed to the House of Lords.

LORD REID: My Lords, the appellants own a large number of supermarkets in which they sell a wide variety of goods. The goods are put out for sale on shelves or stands, each article being marked with the price at which it is offered for sale. The customer selects the articles he wants, takes them to the cashier, and pays the price. From time to time the appellants, apparently by way of advertisement, sell "flash packs" at prices lower than the normal price. In September 1969 they were selling Radiant washing powder in this way. The normal price was 3s. 11d. but these packs were marked and sold at 2s. 11d. Posters were displayed in the shops drawing attention to this reduction in price.

These prices were displayed in the appellants' shop at Northwich on September 26. Mr. Coane, an old age pensioner, saw this and went to buy a pack. He could only find packs marked 3s. 11d. He took one to the cashier who told him that there were none in stock for sale at 2s. 11d. He paid 3s. 11d. and complained to an inspector of weights and measures. This resulted in a prosecution under the Trade Descriptions Act 1968 and the appellants were fined £25 and costs.

Section 11(2) provides:

> "If any person offering to supply any goods gives, by whatever means, any indication likely to be taken as an indication that the goods are being offered at a price less than that at which they are in fact being offered he shall, subject to the provisions of this Act, be guilty of an offence."

It is not disputed that that section applies to this case. The appellants relied on section 24(1) which provides:

> "In any proceedings for an offence under this Act it shall, subject to subsection (2) of this section, be a defence for the person charged to prove—(*a*) that the commission of the offence was due to a mistake or reliance on information supplied to him or to the act or default of another person, an accident or some other cause beyond his control; and (*b*) that he took all reasonable precautions and exercised all due diligence to avoid the commission of such an offence by himself or any person under his control."

The relevant facts as found by the magistrates were that on the previous evening a shop assistant, Miss Rogers, whose duty it was to put out fresh stock found that there were no more of the specially marked packs in stock. There were a number of packs marked with the ordinary price so she put them out. She ought to have told the shop manager, Mr. Clement, about this, but she failed to do so. Mr. Clement was responsible for seeing that the proper packs were on sale, but he failed to see to this although he marked his daily return "all special offers O.K." The magistrates found that if he had known about this he would either have removed the poster advertising the reduced price or given instructions that only 2s. 11d. was to be charged for the packs marked 3s. 11d.

Section 24(2) requires notice to be given to the prosecutor if the accused is blaming another person and such notice was duly given naming Mr. Clement.

In order to avoid conviction the appellants had to prove facts sufficient to satisfy both parts of section 24(1) of the Act of 1968. The magistrates held that they

> "had exercised all due diligence in devising a proper system for the operation of the said store and by securing so far as was reasonably practicable that it was fully implemented and thus had fulfilled the requirements of section 24(1)(*b*)."

But they convicted the appellants because in their view the requirements of section 24(1)(*a*) had not been fulfilled: they held that Clement was not "another person" within the meaning of that provision.

The Divisional Court held that the magistrates were wrong in holding that Clement was not "another person." The respondent did not challenge this finding of the Divisional Court so I need say no more about it than that I think that on this matter the Divisional Court was plainly right. But that court sustained the conviction on the ground that the magistrates had applied the wrong test in deciding that the requirements of section 24(1)(*b*) had been fulfilled. In effect that court held that the words "he took all reasonable precautions ... " do not mean what they say: "he" does not mean the accused, it means the accused and all his servants who were acting in a managerial or supervisory capacity. I think that earlier authorities virtually compelled the Divisional Court to reach this strange construction. So the real question in this appeal is whether these earlier authorities were rightly decided. ...

In my judgment the main object of these provisions must have been to distinguish between those who are in some degree blameworthy and those who are not, and to enable the latter to escape from conviction if they can show that they were in no way to blame. I find it almost impossible to suppose that Parliament or any reasonable body of men would as a matter of policy think it right to make employers criminally liable for the acts of some of their servants but not for those of others and I find it incredible that a draftsman, aware of that intention, would fail to insert any words to express it. But in several cases the courts, for reasons which it is not easy to discover, have given a restricted meaning to such provisions. It has been held that such provisions afford a defence if the master proves that the servant at fault was the person who himself did the prohibited act, but that they afford no defence if the servant at fault was one who failed in his duty of supervision to see that his subordinates did not commit the prohibited act. Why Parliament should have thought to have intended this distinction or how as a matter of construction these provisions can reasonably be held to have that meaning is not apparent.

In some of these cases the employer charged with the offence was a limited company. But in others the employer was an individual and still it was held that he, though personally entirely blameless, could not rely on these provisions if the fault which led to the commission of the offence was the fault of a servant in failing to carry out his duty to instruct or supervise his subordinates.

Where a limited company is the employer difficult questions do arise in a wide variety of circumstances in deciding which of its officers or servants is to be identified with the company so that his guilt is the guilt of the company.

I must start by considering the nature of the personality which by a fiction the law attributes to a corporation. A living person has a mind which can have knowledge or intention or be negligent and he has hands to carry out his intentions. A corporation has none of these: it must act through living persons, though not always one or the same person. Then the person who acts is not speaking or acting for the company. He is acting as the company and his mind which directs his acts is the mind of the company. There is no question of the company being vicariously liable. He is not acting as a servant, representative, agent or delegate. He is an embodiment of the company or, one could say, he hears and speaks through the persona of the company, within his appropriate sphere, and his mind is the mind of the company. If it is a guilty mind then that guilt is the guilt of the company. It must be a question of law whether, once the facts have been ascertained, a person in doing particular things is to be regarded as the company or merely as the company's servant or agent. In that case any liability of the company can only be a statutory or vicarious liability.

In *Lennard's Carrying Co. Ltd.* v. *Asiatic Petroleum Co. Ltd.* [1915] A.C. 705 the question was whether damage had occurred without the "actual fault or privity" of the owner of a ship. The owners were a company. The fault was that of the registered managing owner who managed the ship on behalf of the owners and it was held that the company could not dissociate itself from him so as to say that there was no actual fault or privity on the part of the company. Viscount Haldane L.C. said, at pp. 713, 714:

"For if Mr. Lennard was the directing mind of the company, then his action must, unless a corporation is not to be liable at all, have been an action which was the action of the company itself within the meaning of section 502. . . . It must be upon the true construction of that section in such a case as the present one that the fault or privity is the fault or privity of somebody who is not merely a servant or agent for whom the company is liable upon the footing respondeat superior, but somebody for whom the company is liable because his action is the very action of the company itself."

Reference is frequently made to the judgment of Denning L.J. in *H. L. Bolton (Engineering) Co. Ltd.* v. *T. J. Graham & Sons Ltd.* [1957] 1 Q.B. 159. He said, at p. 172:

"A company may in many ways be likened to a human body. It has a brain and nerve centre which controls what it does. It also has hands which hold the tools and act in accordance with directions from the centre. Some of the people in the company are mere servants and agents who are nothing more than hands to do the work and cannot be said to represent the mind or will. Others are directors and managers who represent the directing mind and will of the company, and control what it does. The state of mind of these managers is the state of mind of the company and is treated by the law as such."

In that case the directors of the company only met once a year: they left the management of the business to others, and it was the intention of those managers which was imputed to the company. I think that was right. There have been attempts to apply Lord Denning's words to all servants of a company whose work is brain work, or who exercise some managerial discretion under the direction of superior officers of the company. I do not think that Lord Denning intended to refer to them. He only referred to those who "represent the directing mind and will of the company, and control what it does."

I think that is right for this reason. Normally the board of directors, the managing director and perhaps other superior officers of a company carry out the functions of management and speak and act as the company. Their subordinates do not. They carry out orders from above and it can make no difference that they are given some measure of discretion. But the board of directors may delegate some part of their functions of management giving to their delegate full discretion to act independently of instructions from them. I see no difficulty in holding that they have thereby put such a delegate in their place so that within the scope of the delegation he can act as the company. It may not always be easy to draw the line but there are cases in which the line must be drawn. *Lennard's* case was one of them.

In some cases the phrase alter ego has been used. I think it is misleading. When dealing with a company the word alter is I think misleading. The person who speaks and acts as the company is not alter. He is identified with the company. And when dealing with an individual no other individual can be his alter ego. The other individual can be a servant, agent, delegate or representative but I know of neither principle nor authority which warrants the confusion (in the literal or original sense) of two separate individuals. . . .

In the next two cases a company was accused and it was held liable for the fault of a superior officer. In *D.P.P.* v. *Kent and Sussex Contractors Ltd.* [1944] K.B. 146 he was the transport manager. In *R.* v. *I.C.R. Haulage Ltd.* [1944] K.B. 551 it was held that a company can be guilty of common law conspiracy. The act of the managing director was held to be the act of the company. I think that a passage in the judgment is too widely stated, at p. 559:

"Where in any particular case there is evidence to go to a jury that the criminal act of an agent, including his state of mind, intention, knowledge or belief is the act of the company, and, in cases where the presiding judge so rules, whether the jury are satisfied that it has been proved, must depend on the nature of the charge, the relative position of the officer or agent, and the other relevant facts and circumstances of the case."

... I think that the true view is that the judge must direct the jury that if they find certain facts proved then as a matter of law they must find that the criminal act of the officer, servant or agent including his state of mind, intention, knowledge or belief is the act of the company. I have already dealt with the considerations to be applied in deciding when such a person can and when he cannot be identified with the company. I do not see how the nature of the charge can make any difference. If the guilty man was in law identifiable with the company then whether his offence was serious or venial his act was the act of the company but if he was not so identifiable then no act of his, serious or otherwise, as the act of the company itself.

In *John Henshall (Quarries) Ltd.* v. *Harvey* [1965] 2 Q.B. 233 a company was held not criminally responsible for the negligence of a servant in charge of a weighbridge. In *Magna Plant* v. *Mitchell* (unreported) April 27, 1966, the fault was that of a depot engineer and again the company was held not criminally responsible. I think these decisions were right. In the *Magna Plant* case Lord Parker C.J. said:

" ... knowledge of a servant cannot be imputed to the company unless he is a servant for whose actions the company are criminally responsible, and as the cases show, that only arises in the case of a company where one is considering the acts of responsible officers forming the brain, or in the case of an individual, a person to whom delegation in the true sense of the delegation of management has been passed."

I agree with what he said with regard to a company. But delegation by an individual is another matter. It has been recognised in licensing cases but that is in my view anomalous (see *Vane* v. *Yiannopoullos, ante*, p. 411).
...

What good purpose could be served by making an employer criminally responsible for the misdeeds of some of his servants but not for those of others? It is sometimes argued—it was argued in the present case—that making an employer criminally responsible, even when he has done all that he could to prevent an offence, affords some additional protection to the public because this will induce him to do more. But if he has done all he can how can he do more? I think that what lies behind this argument is a suspicion that magistrates too readily accept evidence that an employer has done all he can to prevent offences. But if magistrates were to accept as sufficient a paper scheme and perfunctory efforts to enforce it they would not be doing their duty—that would not be "due diligence" on the part of the employer.

Then it is said that this would involve discrimination in favour of a large employer like the appellants against a small shopkeeper. But that is not so. Mr. Clement was the "opposite number" of the small shopkeeper and he was liable to prosecution in this case. The purpose of this Act must have been to penalise those at fault, not those who were in no way to blame.

The Divisional Court decided this case on a theory of delegation. In that they were following some earlier authorities. But they gave far too wide a meaning to delegation. I have said that a board of directors can delegate part of their functions of management so as to make their delegate an embodiment of the company within the sphere of the delegation. But here the board never delegated any part of their functions. They set up a chain of command through regional and district supervisors, but they remained in control. The shop managers had to obey their general directions and also take orders from their superiors. The acts or omissions of shop managers were not acts of the company itself.

In my judgment the appellants established the statutory defence. I would therefore allow this appeal.

[Lord Morris of Borth-y-Gest, Viscount Dilhorne, Lord Pearson and Lord Diplock delivered speeches agreeing that the appeal should be allowed.]

Appeal allowed

Note

The state of mind of the controlling officers is *not* the state of mind of the company where those officers are accused of committing a crime against the company: see *R. v. Gomez, post,* p. 663. See also Draft Criminal Code, clause 30(6), *post,* p. 422.

Question

1. Statute makes it an offence for a manufacturer of widgets to sell any widgets in the making of which blotto has been used. (The statute contains no provisions corresponding to section 20, 23, and 24 of Trade Descriptions Act.) Widgets Ltd. is a manufacturer of widgets. Alan is managing and sales director of Widgets Ltd., Bob is the director in charge of production, and Carl is a salesman employed by the company. A quantity of widgets is sold to one of the company's customers. The sale was arranged by Carl who, unlike Alan, knew that Bob had used blotto in their manufacture. Consider the criminal liability of all concerned.

Note

The distinction between superior servants who are identified with the corporation and lower servants who are not, poses problems for a prosecution of a corporation for a *mens rea* offence, *e.g.* manslaughter, where there is no vicarious liability and the culpable attitudes are found only among individual servants who are not identified with the corporation. A corporation can be indicted for manslaughter, but it is unlikely that it will be convicted.

S. Field and N. Jorg: Corporate Liability and Manslaughter: should we be going Dutch? [1991] Crim. L.R. 157.

"This bifurcation of the corporate structure limits the potential effectiveness of legal controls in several ways. First, Wells has recently pointed out that one effect of this identification doctrine is that the more diffuse the company structure, the more it devolves power to semi-autonomous managers, the easier it will be to avoid liability. (Manslaughter and Corporate Crime (1989) 138 N.L.J. 931.) This is of particular importance given the increasing tendency of many organisations specifically to decentralise *safety* services. It is clearly in the interest of shrewd and unscrupulous management to do so. Braithwaite's study (Corporate Crime in the Pharmaceutical Industry (1984) 102) of the pharmaceutical industry pointed out the way that companies sought to abrogate responsibility for the quality of their safety research by using contract laboratories, where the effects of fierce competition over price on the standard of safety checks could be said to be responsibility of the laboratory itself. If corporations perceive themselves to be a risk of prosecution for corporate manslaughter, an analogous process of decentralisation *within* the corporation might be developed to evade liability.

Secondly, the limits of criminal liability constructed by the identification doctrine do not reflect properly the limits of the moral responsibility of the corporation itself. This cannot be limited to responsibility for the acts of high-ranking officials such as company directors. Priorities in hierarchical organisations like corporations are set predominantly from above. It is these priorities that determine the social context within which a corporation's shop-floor workers and the like make decisions about working practices. A climate of safety or unsafety may permeate the entire organisation but be created at the highest level. Thus, if criminal law is to reflect this moral responsibility, in appropriate cases legal responsibility ought to extend to acts done by the 'hands' of the corporation. . . .

Of course, there are those who have argued that the very idea of corporations being morally responsible is nonsensical. Only the individual human being can be said to have moral personality and to be morally responsible for his/her acts. But we would argue (following French) (*Collective and Corporate Responsibility* (1984)) that the policies, standing orders, regulations and institutionalised practices of corporations are evidence of corporate aims, intentions and knowledge that are not reducible to the aims, intentions and knowledge of individuals within the corporation. Such regulations and standing orders are authoritative, not because any particular individual devised them, but because they have emerged from a decision-making process recognised as authoritative with the corporation. These regulations and standing orders are also evidence of corporate capacity to differentiate right from wrong and act accordingly, to think ethically in terms of the consequences of corporate actions for others and to give reasoned explanations to the outside world. There is a strong argument for seeing such capacities for reasoning, understanding and control of conduct as the essence of moral personality and the basis of moral responsibility. . . .

The problem with the identification doctrine is that the dichotomy it creates (between the acts of high-ranking officials and shop-floor workers) fails to acknowledge the indissoluble connections between individuals in collective enterprises like the corporation. This is a specific manifestation of broader difficulties in understanding human actions in terms of the acts of atomistic individuals. The cultural theorist, Raymond Williams (*The Long Revolution* (1965), Chapter 3) stressed that, in the understanding of human action, it is the complex web of relationships into which each person enters that should be the focus of analysis, rather than the abstractions of 'individual' or 'society'. Each individual is shaped by his/her contracts with a vast range of social institutions and groupings, themselves shaped by interactions with a further range of such units. Each of these 'organisations' is precisely an embodiment of relationships both within and outside itself: 'there is no real point at which we can break off this process, to isolate an independent substance.' This is palpably true of the process of work within corporations. But if the focus of analysis has to be the necessary connections and relations between people inside and outside such organisations, to sever layers of the organisations is to render analysis and thus proper judgment impossible. If for instance, a fence is removed from a machine by an individual shop floor worker, we must look to the relations within the corporation and its wider relations with other organisations, to the relationships between the shop floor and supervisory staff, between supervisory staff and management, between management and competing enterprises and state institutions. These interdependencies are often clearly visible, as we will show in our discussion of recent disasters. It may be that the extent to which criminal law can accommodate such interrelationships is limited, given its fundamental premises. A legal process which requires the charging and sanctioning of individual legal personalities inevitably limits enquiry. However, the criteria for liability ought at least to show some sensitivity to the broader context.

The problems of the identification doctrine are exacerbated in England and Wales by the rejection of aggregation of fault. It was submitted in *R.* v. *H.M.Coroner for East Kent, ex.p. Spooner* (1989) 88 Cr. App. R. 10 (D.C.) that it was not necessary to find someone identified with the corporation who was individually liable in order to make that corporation liable. It was argued that it was possible or ought to be possible to aggregate together the fault of several of the directing minds so that various acts of minor negligence or recklessness could be seen *in toto* as involving more serious fault on the part of the corporation itself. Bingham L.J. responded to this argument:

> 'I do not think the aggregation argument assists the applicants. A case against a personal defendant cannot be fortified by evidence against another defendant. The case against a corporation can only be made by evidence properly addressed to showing guilt on the part of the corporation as such.' (at p. 16)

But this is a circular argument. The *issue* is whether the *mens rea* of the corporation can be established by aggregating the fault of those who embody the corporation. The last sentence merely begs the question: what represents 'proper' evidence in this context? The aggregation argument is thus rejected without serious argument. Mr. Justice Turner was equally dismissive in the P. & O. trial, saying that the aggregation argument ran 'directly counter to all the cases that have recently been decided in the House of Lords.' *R.* v. *Stanley* Central Criminal Court, Oct. 19, 1990. Given the lack of clear authoritative argument on the subject, it is unfortunate that he did not choose to identify these precedents.

Elsewhere, courts have taken a different view. In *United States* v. *Bank of New England* 821 F. 2nd. 844 (1987) the Court of Appeal of the First Federal Circuit said:

> '[a] collective knowledge instruction is entirely appropriate in the context of corporate criminal liability. Corporations compartmentalize knowledge, subdividing the elements of specific duties and operations into smaller components. The aggregate of those components constitutes the corporation's knowledge of a particular operation.'

The practical effects of rejecting the doctrine can be quickly illustrated. A key indication of the seriousness with which a corporation treats safety is the development of clearly delineated responsibilities for the scrutiny and revision of safety procedures. One of the many factors leading to both the Zeebrugge and the King's Cross disasters was the failure to identify properly the respective areas of responsibility of particular individuals and groups within the overall corporate structure. There was uncertainty as to whether any director was solely responsible for safety within the the then Townsend Thoresen shipping company, despite a Department of Transport recommendation that an individual ashore be given responsibility of monitoring 'technical and safety aspects.' In general, directors did not have specific areas of responsibility. Furthermore, the Sheen Report found Company Standing Orders delineating safety responsibilities on ship to be ambiguous and incomplete. Yet no individual had particular responsibility for ensuring they were properly drafted. The Fennell Report into the King's Cross fire also identified confusion as to responsibility for passenger safety as a key cause of the disaster. London Regional Transport thought they had delegated this responsibility to its operating companies (London Underground Ltd. and London Buses). But London Underground felt it had assumed responsibility only for the safe operation of the underground *system* rather than its physical structures.

This failure to delineate responsibilities will always cause problems if fault cannot be aggregated. If responsibility for the proactive development of safety monitoring is not vested in any particular group or individual, it becomes harder to say of any particular 'directing mind' that his/her failure to consider such matters represents a *culpable* failure by that individual. If one cannot say this, without aggregation of fault, the corporation itself cannot be found culpable. Collective responsibility becomes lost in the crevices between the responsibilities of individuals. This was a key factor in enabling P. & O. to avoid criminal responsibility. Mr. Justice Turner stressed, in directing the acquittals, that individual senior members of management had not got to know about most previous 'open-door incidents.' But this is exactly what one would expect if no individual was clearly given the responsibility to monitor safety. Even when managers received suggestions from Masters that indicator lights be fitted in the Bridge, no individual was given a responsibility to establish whether existing procedures were always effective (*i.e.* reliance on subordinates to close the bow doors.) If anyone [had] done so, previous 'open-door' incidents known to some Masters would surely have been discovered. Mr. Justice Turner concluded that, from a position of ignorance of these incidents, the prudent individual would not have perceived the risk of injury as 'obvious and serious.' This was fatal to the prosecution's claim of reckless manslaughter. But the real issue, why nobody knew the key information, could not be raised.

The problems of Anglo-Welsh law in this area seem to be generated by a failure to develop criteria for the judging of collective processes. The identification doctrine severs the necessary connections between individuals within such processes and the rejection of aggregation leads to an inappropriately individualist approach. ... "

Note

See Draft Criminal Code: Clause 30(2), *infra*.

Draft Criminal Code

"Corporations

30.—(1) A corporation may be guilty of an offence not involving a fault element by reason of—

    (a) an act done by its employee or agent, as provided by section 29; or

(b) an omission, state of affairs or occurrence that is an element of the offence.

(2) A corporation may be guilty—

(a) as a principal, of an offence involving a fault element; or
(b) as an accessory, of any offence,

only if one of its controlling officers, acting within the scope of his office and with the fault required, is concerned in the offence.

(3)—

(a) 'Controlling officer' of a corporation means a person participating in the control of the corporation in the capacity of a director, manager, secretary or other similar officer (whether or not he was, or was validly, appointed to any such office).
(b) In this subsection 'director', in relation to a corporation established by or under any enactment for the purpose of carrying on under national ownership any industry or part of an industry or undertaking, being a corporation whose affairs are managed by the members thereof, means a member of the corporation.
(c) Whether a person acting in a particular capacity is a controlling officer is a question of law.

(4) A controlling officer is concerned in an offence if he does, procures, assists, encourages or fails to prevent the acts specified for the offence.

(5) For the purposes of subsection (4), a controlling officer fails to prevent an act when he fails to take steps that he might take—

(a) to ensure that the act is not done; or
(b) where the offence may be constituted by an omission to do an act or by a state of affairs or occurrence, to ensure that the omission is not made or to prevent or end the state of affairs or occurrence.

(6) A controlling officer does not act 'within the scope of his office' if he acts with the intention of doing harm or of concealing harm done by him or another to the corporation.

(7) A corporation cannot be guilty of an offence that is not punishable with a fine or other pecuniary penalty.

(8) A corporation has a defence consisting of or including—

(a) a state of mind only if—
    (i) all controlling officers who are concerned in the offence; or
    (ii) where no controlling officer is so concerned, all other employees or agents who are so concerned,
    have that state of mind;
(b) the absence of a state of mind only if no controlling officer with responsibility for the subject-matter of the offence has that state of mind;
(c) compliance with a standard of conduct required of the corporation itself only if it is complied with by the controlling officers with responsibility for the subject-matter of the offence.

Liability of Officers of Corporation

31.—(1) Where a corporation is guilty of an offence, other than a pre-Code offence as defined in section 6 (to which section 2(3) applies), a controlling officer of the corporation who is not apart from this section guilty of the offence is guilty of it as an accessory if—

(a) knowing that or being reckless whether the offence is being or will be committed, he intentionally fails to take steps that he might take to prevent its commission; or

(b) the offence does not involve a fault element and its commission is attributable to any neglect on his part.

(2) Subsection (1) applies to a member of a corporation managed by its members as it applies to a controlling officer."

CHAPTER 7

INCHOATE OFFENCES

	PAGE		PAGE
1. Attempts	424	3. Incitement	473
i. Mental Element	426		
ii. *Actus Reus*	437	4. Impossibility in Relation to In-	
2. Conspiracy	451	choate Offences	478
i. Statutory Conspiracies	451	i. Attempt	478
ii. Common Law Conspiracies	462	ii. Conspiracy	490
iii. Jurisdiction	467	iii. Incitement	491

Note

Intending to commit an offence is not itself an offence, but one who sets out to commit an offence may commit one of the inchoate crimes of attempt, conspiracy or incitement. They were common law crimes and incitement still is, but attempt is now defined and punished in the Criminal Attempts Act 1981, and conspiracy in Part I of the Criminal Law Act 1977, as amended by the Criminal Attempts Act 1981.

1. ATTEMPTS

Criminal Attempts Act 1981, Sections 1, 4(5), 6(1)

"Section 1: (1) If, with intent to commit an offence to which this section applies, a person does an act which is more than merely preparatory to the commission of the offence, he is guilty of attempting to commit the offence.

(2) A person may be guilty of attempting to commit an offence to which this section applies even though the facts are such that the commission of the offence is impossible.

(3) In any case where—

(a) apart from this subsection a person's intention would not be regarded as having amounted to an intent to commit an offence; but

(b) if the facts of the case had been as he believed them to be, his intention would be so regarded,

then, for the purposes of subsection (1) above, he shall be regarded as having had an intent to commit that offence.

(4) This section applies to any offence which, if it were completed, would be triable in England and Wales as an indictable offence, other than—

(a) conspiracy (at common law or under section 1 of the Criminal Law Act 1977 or any other enactment);

(b) aiding, abetting, counselling, procuring or suborning the commission of an offence;

(c) offences under section 4(1) (assisting offenders) or 5 (1) (accepting or agreeing to accept consideration for not disclosing information about an arrestable offence) of the Criminal Law Act 1967.

Section 4: (3) Where, in proceedings against a person for an offence under section 1 above, there is evidence sufficient in law to support a finding that he did an act falling within subsection (1) of that section, the question whether or not his act fell within that subsection is a question of fact."

Section 6: (1) The offence of attempt at common law and any offence at common law of procuring materials for crime are hereby abolished for all purposes not relating to acts done before the commencement of this Act.

Notes

1. Section 1 applies to indictable offences only. An attempt to commit a summary offence is only an offence if the statute creating the offence specifically makes it so. In deciding whether such an attempt has been committed, a court will work to the same definition as for an attempt to commit an indictable offence: see section 3(4) (5).

2. In the common law of attempt existing before August 1981, there was much uncertainty surrounding the definition of the *actus reus*, especially in cases where the crime attempted was, for one reason or another, impossible to commit. Some uncertainty also attached to the *mens rea*. The difficulties are outlined in Law Com. No. 102: Attempt, and Impossibility in Relation to Attempt, Conspiracy and Incitement 1980. The Law Commission's proposals for dealing with those difficulties were reproduced, although not exactly, in the Act. The common law of Attempt was abolished: Section 6(1), *supra*. However this did not at first prevent the Courts from referring to many of the pre-Act authorities. For proposals in the Draft Criminal Code, see *infra*, p. 450.

3. The Law Commission, after deciding that the three separate inchoate offences should be retained, and that a general law of attempt (rather than a redefinition of every crime to make it wide enough to catch preparatory as well as completed conduct) was still needed (paras. 2.4–2.6), considered whether the concept of *attempt* should be retained.

Law Com. No. 102

"§ 2.7 The final preliminary question is, assuming that an inchoate offence is needed in the field presently covered by the law of attempt, whether that concept should be retained or whether some other concept should be substituted for it. We have already pointed out that the main justification for the retention of inchoate offences is the need to permit the law to impose criminal sanctions in certain cases where a crime has been contemplated but not in fact committed. It is, however, a fundamental principle of our law that it should not seek to penalise the mere intention to commit a crime. As the Working Party said (1973) W.P. 50, § 65—

'The mere intention in a serious case constitutes a social danger, but provided that it remains no more than intention, no intervention is justifiable. It is only when some act is done which sufficiently manifests the existence of the social danger present in the intent that authority should intervene. It is necessary to strike a balance in this context between individual freedom and the countervailing interest of the community.'

In some cases, as the Working Party pointed out, the problem of balancing social and individual interests—

'has been met by the adoption of a technique other than the law of attempt, for example, by the creation of offences of procurement, possession, threats and going equipped. Provisions of this kind, however, relate only to specific crimes and particular types of attempt in relation to these crimes. They do not purport to offer more than a partial remedy. There are in a few instances specific attempts in statutes creating the substantive offence, relating for the most part to sexual offences, but this is not the practice in more recent codifying Acts. Within a limited sphere (for example, official secrets) another solution has been found by going back a stage further than the earliest stage at which the present law of attempt seeks to operate and providing that acts "preparatory to" the commission of substantive offences shall in themselves constitute offences. Generally, however, English law has hitherto not travelled back this far in the chain of causation unless the preparatory act itself constitutes a substantive offence, as where forgery is committed as a preliminary step in an ultimate intended offence of deception.'

§ 2.8 Another relevant consideration is that, if it is accepted that some kind of inchoate offence is needed to penalise conduct at present dealt with by the law of attempt, it is worth retaining that name for the offence. Not only is the word 'attempt' one which is in everyday use, but it may cogently be argued that the conduct which the law should aim to penalise is, broadly speaking, that which the layman would regard as 'attempting' to commit an offence. This desirable coincidence of social policy and ordinary language could not survive a drastic expansion of the meaning of "attempt" to encompass all preparatory acts.

§ 2.9 ... We therefore conclude that the Working Party were correct in their view that the concept of attempt should be retained in preference to any possible alternative."

Note

In the Law Commission's view, punishable preparatory acts should be limited to those which a layman would describe as trying to commit an offence. This philosophy, embodied in the use of the ordinary word "attempt" as the name for the offence, confines the ambit of the law more narrowly than some might think desirable from the point of view of public protection. See, as to the *mens rea*, Note, p. 432, and as to *actus reus*, Williams, *infra*, p. 448.

i. Mental Element

R. v. MOHAN
[1976] Q.B. 1
Court of Appeal

M. drove his car straight at a policeman, who managed to jump out of the way. M. was convicted of attempting by wanton driving to cause bodily harm to the policeman. The jury were directed that it was sufficient for the prosecution to prove that he was reckless as to whether bodily harm would be caused by his driving. M. appealed.

JAMES L.J., for the Court: Mr. Bueno's argument for the Crown was that the judge was right in his direction that the Crown did not have to prove, in relation to count 2, any intention in the mind of the defendant. His argument was that where the attempt charged is an attempt to commit a crime which itself involves a specific state of mind, then to prove the attempt the Crown must prove that the accused had that specific state of mind, but where the attempt relates to a crime which does not involve a specific state of mind, the offence of attempt is proved by evidence that the accused committed an act or acts proximate to the commission of the complete offence and which unequivocally point to the completed offence being the result of the act or acts committed. Thus to prove a charge of attempting to cause grievous bodily harm with intent there must be proof that the accused intended to cause grievous bodily harm at the time of the act relied on as the attempt. But, because the offence of causing bodily harm by wanton or furious driving, prescribed by section 35 of the Offences against the Person Act 1861, does not require proof of any intention or other state of mind of the accused, proof of attempt to commit that crime does not involve proof of the accused's state of mind, but only that he drove wantonly and that the wanton driving was proximate to, and pointed unequivocally to, bodily harm being caused thereby.

The attraction of this argument is that it presents a situation in relation to attempts to commit a crime which is simple and logical, for it requires in proof of the attempt no greater burden in respect of mens rea than is required in proof of the completed offence. The argument in its extreme form is that an attempt to commit a crime of strict liability is itself a strict liability offence. It is argued that the contrary view involves the proposition that the offence of attempt includes mens rea when the offence which is attempted does not and in that respect the attempt takes on a graver aspect than, and requires an additional burden of proof beyond that which relates to, the completed offence.

Mr. Glass, for the defendant, does not shrink from this anomalous situation. His argument was expressed in words which he cited from *Smith and Hogan, Criminal Law*, 3rd ed. (1973), p. 191.

"Whenever the definition of the crime requires that some consequence be brought about by (the defendant's) conduct, it must be proved, on a charge of attempting to commit that crime, that (the defendant) intended that consequence; and this is so even if, on a charge of committing the complete crime, recklessness as to that consequence—or even some lesser degree of mens rea—would suffice."

That, Mr. Glass argued, is an accurate statement of the law.

In support of his argument he cited the words of Lord Goddard C.J. in *R. v. Whybrow* (1951) 35 Cr.App.R. 141, 146:

"Therefore, if one person attacks another, inflicting a wound in such a way that an ordinary, reasonable person must know that at least grievous bodily harm will result, and death results, there is the malice aforethought sufficient to support the charge of murder. But, if the charge is one of attempted murder, the intent becomes the principal ingredient of the crime. It may be said that the law, which is not always logical, is somewhat illogical in saying that, if one attacks a person intending to do grievous bodily harm and death results, that is murder, but that if one attacks a person and only intended to do grievous bodily harm, and death does not result, it is not attempted murder, but wounding with intent to do grievous bodily harm. It is not really illogical because, in that particular case, the intent is the essence of the crime while, where the death of another is caused, the necessity is to prove malice aforethought, which is supplied in law by proving intent to do grievous bodily harm."

[After citations from *R. v. Hyam* [1975] A.C. 55, *ante*, p. 78.]

We do not find in the speeches of their Lordships in *R. v. Hyam* anything which binds us to hold that mens rea in the offence to attempt is proved by establishing beyond reasonable doubt that the accused knew or correctly foresaw that the consequences of his act unless interrupted would "as a high degree of probability," or would be "likely" to, be the commission of the complete offence. Nor do we find authority in that case for the proposition that a reckless state of mind is sufficient to constitute the mens rea in the offence of attempt.

Prior to the enactment of section 8 of the Criminal Justice Act 1967, the standard test in English law of a man's state of mind in the commission of an act was the forseeable or natural consequence of the act. Therefore it could be said that when a person applied his mind to the consequences that did happen and foresaw that they would probably happen he intended them to happen, whether he wanted them to happen or not. So knowledge of the foreseeable consequence could be said to be a form of "intent." Section 8 reads:

"A court or jury, in determining whether a person has committed an offence, (*a*) shall not be bound in law to infer that he intended or foresaw a result of his actions by reason only of its being a natural and probable consequence of those actions; but (*b*) shall decide whether he did intend or foresee that result by reference to all the evidence, drawing such inferences from the evidence as appear proper in the circumstances."

Thus, upon the question whether or not the accused had the necessary intent in relation to a charge of attempt, evidence tending to establish directly, or by inference, that the accused knew or foresaw that the likely consequence, and, even more so, the highly probable consequence, of his act—unless interrupted—would be the commission of the completed offence, is relevant material for the consideration of the jury. In our judgment, evidence of knowledge of likely consequences, or from which knowledge of likely consequences can be inferred, is evidence by which intent may be established but it is not, in relation to the offence of attempt, to be equated with intent. If the jury find such knowledge established they may and, using common sense, they probably will find intent proved, but it is not the case that they must do so.

An attempt to commit a crime is itself an offence. Often it is a grave offence. Often it is as morally culpable as the completed offence which is attempted but not in fact committed. Nevertheless it falls within the class of conduct which is preparatory to the commission of a crime and is one step removed from the offence which is attempted. The court must not strain to bring within the offence of attempt conduct which does not fall within the well-established bounds of the offence. On the contrary, the court must safeguard against extension of those bounds save by the authority of Parliament. The bounds are presently set requiring proof of specific intent, a decision to bring about, in so far as it lies within the accused's power, the commission of the offence which it is alleged the accused attempted to commit, no matter whether the accused desired that consequence of his act or not.

In the present case the final direction was bad in law.

Appeal allowed

Notes

1. *Narrow meaning of Intention*: In rejecting foresight of probable consequences as "intention" in respect of Attempts, the Court distinguished *Hyam* v. *D.P.P.*, a murder case which laid down that such foresight generally is intention. But see now *R.* v. *Moloney*, *ante*, p. 81, which differs from *Hyam* v. *D.P.P.* on this.

2. *Intention as to Context*: According to James L.J., attempt requires specific intent, "a decision to bring about, in so far as it lies in the accused's power, the commission of the offence which it is alleged the accused attempted to commit." The Law Commission, adopting this dictum, paraphrased it as "an intent to commit the crime attempted," and accordingly section 1, Criminal Attempts Act 1981 uses that expression. However, the phrase is ambiguous, because if an offence requires intention for the *result* of D.'s conduct but is satisfied by recklessness as to the context in which the conduct takes place (*e.g.* rape, obtaining by deception), it can be questioned whether D. "intends to commit the offence," if he is intentional as to the result but only reckless as to context. But see next case.

R v. Khan and Others
[1990] 2 All E.R. 783
Court of Appeal

Six men were charged with rape and attempted rape of a 16-year-old girl. It appeared that some of them had not succeeded in having intercourse with her. The appellants were convicted of attempted rape. On appeal:–

RUSSELL L.J., for the Court: These appeals raise the short but important point of whether the offence of attempted rape is committed when the defendant is reckless as to the woman's consent to sexual intercourse. The appellants submit that no such offence is known to the law ...

The judge dealt with [the question of consent in] the offence of rape as follows:

"It must first be proved in this case that [the complainant] did not in fact consent. If she did or if in your view she may have done in relation to any of the defendants, you may acquit them without considering the position further. If, however, you decide that she did not in fact consent, the next question is: did the defendant in question know that she was not consenting? If you are unsure about that, go on to ask whether he was reckless as to whether the girl was consenting or not, and reckless in this context could be simply defined ... as the state of mind of the particular defendant that he could not care less either way whether she consented or not. If you are sure that was his state of mind, then he was behaving recklessly and he would be guilty of the offence ... "

No complaint is made about this direction. The judge then turned to the charges of attempted rape and said:

" . . . As in the case of rape, the principles relevant to consent apply in exactly the same way as in attempted rape. I do not suppose you need me to go through it again. Apply the same principles as to rape."

It is the last three sentences that counsel for the appellants submit amount to a material misdirection, for it is argued that recklessness as a state of mind on the part of the offender has no place in the offence of attempted rape.

We remind ourselves first of the statutory definition of rape to be found in s. 1(1) of the Sexual Offences (Amendment) Act 1976:

"For the purposes of section 1 of the Sexual Offences Act 1956 (which relates to rape) a man commits rape if—(a) he has unlawful sexual intercourse with a woman who at the time of the intercourse does not consent to it; and (b) at that time he knows that she does not consent to the intercourse or he is reckless as to whether she consents to it . . . "

Section 1(1) of the Criminal Attempts Act 1981 created a new statutory offence as follows:

"If, with intent to commit an offence to which this section applied, a person does an act which is more than preparatory to the commission of the offence, he is guilty of attempting to commit the offence."

This section applies to rape.

The impact of the words of s. 1 of the 1981 Act and in particular the words "with intent to commit an offence" has been the subject matter of much debate amongst distinguished academic writers. We were referred to and we have read and considered an article by Professor Glanville Williams entitled "The Problem of Reckless Attempts" [1983] Crim.L.R. 365. The argument there advanced is that recklessness can exist within the concept of attempt and support is derived from *R.* v. *Pigg* [1982] 2 All ER 591, [1982] 1 WLR 762, albeit that authority was concerned with the law prior to the 1981 Act. The approach also receives approval from Smith and Hogan *Criminal Law* (6th edn, 1988) pp. 287–289.

Contrary views, however, have been expressed by Professor Griew and Mr Richard Buxton QC, who have both contended that the words "with intent to commit an offence" involve an intent as to every element constituting the crime.

Finally, we have had regard to the observations of Mustill LJ giving the judgment of the Court of Appeal, Criminal Division in *R.* v. *Millard and Vernon* [1987] Crim.L.R. 393. That was a case involving a charge of attempting to damage property the particulars of offence reading:

"Gary Mann Millard and Michael Elliot Vernon, on 11th May 1985, without lawful excuse, attempted to damage a wooden wall at the Leeds Road Football Stand belonging to Huddersfield Town Association Football Club, intending to damage the said wall or being reckless as to whether the said wall would be damaged."

Mustill LJ said (and we read from the transcript):

"The appellants' case is simple. They submit that in ordinary speech the essence of an attempt is a desire to bring about a particular result, coupled with steps towards that end. The essence of recklessness is either indifference to a known risk or (in some circumstances) failure to advert to an obvious risk. The two states of mind cannot co-exist. Section 1(1) of the Criminal Attempts Act 1981 expressly demands that a person shall have an intent to commit an offence if he is to be guilty of an attempt to commit that offence. The word 'intent' may, it is true, have a specialised meaning in some contexts. But even if this can properly be attributed to the word where it is used in s. 1(1) there is no warrant for reading it as embracing recklessness, nor for reading into it whatever lesser degree of mens rea will suffice for the particular substantive offence in question. For an attempt nothing but conscious volition will do. Accordingly, that part of the particulars of offence which referred to recklessness was meaningless, and the parts of the direction which involved a definition of recklessness, and an implied invitation to convict if the jury found the appellants to have acted recklessly, were misleading. There was thus, so it was contended, a risk that the jury convicted on the wrong basis and the verdict cannot safely be allowed to stand. At the conclusion of the argument it appeared to us that this argument was logically sound and that it was borne out by the authorities cited to us, especially *R.* v. *Whybrow* (1951) 35 Cr.App.R. 141, *Cunliffe* v. *Goodman* [1950] 1 All E.R. 720 at 724, [1950] 2 K.B. 237 at 253 and *R.* v. *Mohan* (*ante*, p. 426), and that it was not inconsistent with anything in *Hyam* v. *D.P.P.* [1974] 2 All E.R. 41, [1975] A.C. 55. Our attention had, however, been drawn to a difference of opinion between commentators about the relationship between the mens rea in an attempt and the ingredients of the substantive offence, and we therefore reserved judgment so as to consider whether the question was not perhaps more difficult than it seemed. In the event we have come to the conclusion that there does exist a problem in this field, and that it is by no means easy to solve, but also that it need not be solved for the purpose of deciding the present appeal. In our judgment two different situations must be distinguished. The first exists where the substantive offence consists simply of the act which constitutes the actus reus (which for present purposes we shall call the 'result') coupled with some element of volition, which may or may not amount to a full intent. Here the only question is whether the 'intent' to bring about the result called for by s. 1(1) is to be watered down to such a degree, if any, as to make it correspond with the mens rea of the substantive offence. The second situation is more complicated. It exists where the substantive offence does not consist of one result and one mens rea, but rather involves not only the underlying intention to produce the result, but another state of mind directed to some circumstance or act which the prosecution must also establish in addition to proving the result. The problem may be illustrated by reference to the offence of attempted rape. As regards the substantive offence the 'result' takes the shape of sexual intercourse with a woman. But the offence is not established without proof of an additional circumstance (namely that the woman did not consent), and a state of mind relative to that circumstance (namely that the defendant knew she did not consent, or was reckless as to whether she consented). When one turns to the offence of attempted rape, one thing is obvious, that the result, namely the act of sexual intercourse, must be intended in the full sense. Also obvious is the fact that proof of an intention to have intercourse with a woman, together with an act towards that end, is not enough: the offence must involve proof of something about the woman's consent, and something about the defendant's state of mind in relation to that consent. The problem is to decide precisely what that something is. Must the prosecution prove not only that the defendant intended the act, but also that he intended it to be non-consensual? Or should the jury be directed to consider two different states of mind, intent as to the act and recklessness as to the circumstances? Here the commentators differ: contrast Smith and Hogan *Criminal Law* (5th edn, 1983) p. 255 ff. with a note on the Act by Professor Griew in *Current Law Statutes 1981*."

We must now grapple with the very problem that Mustill LJ identifies in the last paragraph of the passage cited.

In our judgment an acceptable analysis of the offence of rape is as follows: (1) the intention of the offender is to have sexual intercourse with a woman: (2) the offence is committed if, but only if, the circumstances are that (a) the woman does not consent *and* (b) the defendant knows that she is not consenting or is reckless as to whether she consents.

Precisely the same analysis can be made of the offence of attempted rape: (1) the intention of the offender is to have sexual intercourse with a woman: (2) the offence is committed if, but only if, the circumstances are that (a) the woman does not consent *and* (b) the defendant knows that she is not consenting or is reckless as to whether she consents.

The only difference between the two offences is that in rape sexual intercourse takes place whereas in attempted rape it does not, although there has to be some act which is more than preparatory to sexual intercourse. Considered in that way, the intent of the defendant is precisely the same in rape and in attempted rape and the mens rea is identical, namely an intention to have intercourse plus a knowledge of or recklessness as to the woman's absence of consent. No question of attempting to achieve a reckless state of mind arises; the attempt relates to the physical activity; the mental state of the defendant is the same. A man does not recklessly have sexual intercourse, nor does he recklessly attempt it. Recklessness in rape and attempted rape arises not in relation to the physical act of the accused but only in his state of mind when engaged in the activity of having or attempting to have sexual intercourse.

If this is the true analysis, as we believe it is, the attempt does not require any different intention on the part of the accused from that for the full offence of rape. We believe this to be a desirable result which in the instant case did not require the jury to be burdened with different directions as to the accused's state of mind, dependent on whether the individual achieved or failed to achieve sexual intercourse.

We recognise, of course, that our reasoning cannot apply to all offences and all attempts. Where, for example as in causing death by reckless driving or reckless arson, no state of mind other than recklessness is involved in the offence, there can be no attempt to commit it.

In our judgment, however, the words "with intent to commit an offence" to be found in s.1 of the 1981 Act mean, when applied to rape, "with intent to have sexual intercourse with a woman in circumstances where she does not consent and the defendant knows or could not care less about her absence of consent." The only "intent", giving that word its natural and ordinary meaning, of the rapist is to have sexual intercourse. He commits the offence because of the circumstances in which he manifests that intent, i.e. when the woman is not consenting and he either knows it or could not care less about the absence of consent.

Accordingly, we take the view that in relation to the four appellants the judge was right to give the directions that he did when inviting the jury to consider the charges of attempted rape.

Appeals against conviction dismissed

Notes

The choice of the ordinary word "attempt" as the name for this inchoate crime has implications for the mental element required. That word, with its common synonym "try," is pregnant with intuitive judgments about whether any particular set of facts does or does not constitute the preparatory crime we are discussing. If A tries to have sexual intercourse with a woman when he does not know and could not care less whether she is consenting, that may be "felt" to be an attempt to rape her. But if A tries to do something which he knows will risk damage to B's property, he is not, in common parlance, trying to damage B's property, and his conduct does not "feel" like attempted criminal damage (and that is so despite the fact that if he succeeded in doing what he *was* trying to do and B's property was damaged, he would be guilty of criminal damage, since the crime is satisfied by recklessness as to the damage).

The ambiguity of the expression in section 1, Criminal Attempts Act 1981 "with intent to commit an offence." led the first draft of the Criminal Code (Cl. 53(1)) to provide that in relation to attempt, intention of committing the offence "means an intention in respect of all the elements of the offence." This would require knowledge or hope that the woman was not consenting before there could be attempted rape. But a case decided at common law, *Pigg* (1976), had already held that recklessness as to consent was sufficient for attempted rape. This, and further reflection on the matter, led the Law Commission to propose in the Second Draft of the Code (Cl. 49), that an intention to commit an offence is an intention in respect of all the elements of the offence other than fault elements, *except that recklessness with respect to a circumstance suffices, where it suffices for the offence itself.* (Emphasis supplied). Since in the offence of rape, recklessness as to consent suffices, so it should in attempted rape. In their commentary (para. 13.45), the Law Commission say:

> "A major implication of the proposed rule is that it erects a distinction between 'circumstances' and other elements of the substantive offence attempted. This distinction may occasionally be difficult to apply. We are prepared to tolerate the difficulty because in the mainstream cases where the rule is likely to operate, namely rape and obtaining by deception, the rule appears to work well. The distinction between act (sexual intercourse) and circumstances (non-consent), or between result (obtaining) and circumstances (the falsity of the representation) is plain on the face of the definition of the offences."

Nevertheless, the distinction between circumstantial and other elements of the offence attempted is not always plain on the face of that offence's definition, and the difficulties will sometimes have to be faced. The circumstances can be defined as the context in which the action is done, but this does not advance matters much. In one sense, the action can be described as the physical movement of the actor, with everything else in the situation relegated to context. For example, the situation is that A fires a gun towards B's window. It can be said that what A does is to crook his index finger, which happens to be round the trigger of a gun, which happens to be loaded, and happens to be pointing in the direction of a window which happens to belong to B. A more meaningful description of what A does would be fuller and would include some of the context in which A crooks his finger, as "A pulls the trigger", or "A fires the gun," or "A fires the gun at a window," or "A fires the gun at B's window." If B's window is damaged as a result, and A is charged with criminal damage, to be convicted he must be shown to have *mens rea* with regard to all the elements in the situation, but according to the definition of the offence, he need not intend or know all of them; it is sufficient if he is reckless as to the causing of the damage, *i.e.* if he is reckless as to the gun being loaded and as to its being pointed at the window. If A misses the window and is charged with attempting to damage property, must he be shown to *know* that the gun is loaded and is pointed in the general direction of the window? Not if these factors are properly described as "circumstantial," because the full offence is satisfied by recklessness as to them. But it cannot sensibly or intuitively be described as an attempt to damage a window if A pulls the trigger not knowing but suspecting that the gun is loaded, and not appreciating (however culpably) that the gun is pointing at the window. These factors must be intended or known before we would say that A is trying to damage the window.

On the other hand, if A attempts to have intercourse with a non-consenting B, not knowing that she does not consent, but not caring at all whether she does or not, we feel that that is an attempted rape. The factor of absence of consent, unlike *e.g.* the factor of endangerment of the window, can truly be described as circumstantial in that recklessness as to that factor is sufficient for an attempt. Identifying factors in the full offence which the actor is charged with attempting which are purely circumstantial and which do not therefore require to be intended by him, requires us to isolate precisely the action and result (as opposed to context) required by the full offence. There have been various suggestions as to how this may be done, (see Duff, *The Circumstances of an Attempt* [1991] C.L.J.100); however that author concludes that all of them, including his own, are highly complex, involving over-subtle argumentation. He proposes instead a simpler test which does not rely on a distinction between the pure circumstances and the other aspects of an offence.

Duff, The Circumstances of an Attempt [1991] C.L.J.100, 112

"The simpler test is this. Would the agent necessarily commit the relevant complete offence if she succeeded in doing what she is trying to do? Alternatively, is she trying to do something which would constitute the commission of that complete offence if she succeeded in doing it? If the answer is 'Yes', she is guilty of attempting to commit that offence.

We first ask what the agent is trying to do, insofar as that relates to some aspect of the *actus reus* of the complete offence. We then ask whether, given the facts as they actually exist, and her state of mind insofar as that is relevant to the complete offence, she would commit the complete offence if she succeeded in doing what she is trying to do; whether, that is, she would bring about its complete *actus reus* with the requisite *mens rea*.

A man tries to have sexual intercourse with a woman, realising that she might not consent to it; and in fact she does not consent. Given the existence of that fact, and his recklessness as to it, he would commit rape if he succeeded in having intercourse with her; so he is guilty of attempted rape.

I try to persuade a client to buy a picture which I assure her is a genuine Picasso. Though I hope it is genuine, I realise that it might well not be; and it is in fact a fake. I am trying to obtain her money by inducing her to believe that it is a Picasso. Since my statement that it is a Picasso is in fact false, and I am reckless as to its falsity, I will commit the offence of obtaining property by deception if I succeed in doing what I am trying to do. I am therefore guilty of attempting to commit that offence if I fail to persuade her to buy the picture.

A man tries to persuade a girl to go away with him for a weekend in Paris. She is in fact under sixteen, unmarried, and in the legal possession of a parent who does not consent to the trip; if the trip went ahead, it would amount to taking the girl out of the possession of her parent against his will. If he has the *mens rea* needed for the complete offence as to the facts that the girl is under sixteen, unmarried, and in the possession of a parent who does not consent to the trip, he is guilty of attempted abduction: for he would commit the complete offence if he succeeded in doing what he is trying to do—in taking her away for the weekend.

A woman tries to persuade a boy to go to her flat. He is in fact under sixteen, and in taking him to her flat she would be removing him from the lawful control of someone having lawful control of him. She is guilty of attempted child abduction unless she can claim some lawful authority or excuse, or show that she believed him to be over sixteen: for she is trying to do something (to take him to her flat) which would, given the facts as they actually exist, constitute the commission of that offence if she succeeded in doing it. Since the 'removal from lawful control' which the complete offence involves is not a *consequence* of her taking him to her flat, but is rather what that action would itself amount to in that context, she need only intend and try to take him to her flat; she need not also intend 'to remove him from someone's lawful control' (which would require the hope or belief that there is someone who has lawful control of him).

If a man tries to have sexual intercourse with a woman who is in fact a mental defective, he is guilty of an attempt unless 'he does not know and has no reason to suspect her to be a defective'. For if he succeeds in doing what he is trying to do (to have intercourse with this woman) he will, given that she is a mental defective and that he knows or has reason to suspect that she is, commit the complete offence. If a man tries to have sexual intercourse with a girl who is in fact fifteen he is guilty of an attempt unless he is under twenty-four, has not previously been charged with a like offence and reasonably believes her to be at least sixteen. For if he succeeds in doing what he is trying to do (having intercourse with this girl) he will, given that she is fifteen and that he cannot offer this statutory defence, commit the complete offence.

The last two examples show that this test fits most happily with the view that attempts should require, not necessarily recklessness, but whatever *mens rea* is required for the complete offence as to the aspects of the offence for which they do not require intention. I think this is the right view to take: for if we can properly convict the defendant of the complete offence if he succeeds in doing what he is trying to do, it is hard to see why we should not convict him of an attempt to commit the offence if he fails. If we think that we should not convict of an attempt a man of thirty who reasonably but mistakenly believes his intended sexual partner to be over sixteen, we should surely also think it wrong to convict him of the complete offence if he succeeds in having intercourse with her.

In the cases discussed so far, this test requires just the same *mens rea* for an attempt as for the complete offence: but this is not always so. I fire at a target, realising that my shot might miss the target and hit a bystander. I am guilty of wounding if my shot does hit and wound her, but I am not guilty of attempted wounding if it does not: for in succeeding in doing what I am trying to do (to hit the target) I would not commit the complete offence; attempted wounding thus requires an intention to wound. I am guilty of attempted criminal damage if I try to damage something which I realise might be, and which actually is, another's property: for if I succeeded in damaging it I would, given that it is another's property and I am reckless as to that fact, commit the complete offence. But if, without intending to cause damage, I do what I realise might damage what I know to be another's property, I am not guilty of attempted criminal damage if no damage is caused: since what I am trying to do does not now include damaging anything, in succeeding in doing what I am trying to do I would not commit the complete offence. . . .

But suppose I try to light a bonfire, which will in fact damage my neighbour's trees if I succeed in lighting it. It might be argued that, by the test offered here, I am guilty of attempted criminal damage if I am reckless as to the risk of causing such damage: for it is a fact that I will commit the complete offence (of recklessly damaging another's property) if I succeed in doing what I am trying to do. Thus by this test attempted criminal damage need not involve an intention to damage anything: it is enough that I try to do something which would in fact cause damage to another's property if I succeeded in doing it, and am reckless as to whether such damage will be caused.

If this argument is right, it constitutes a serious objection to the test I have suggested; it would show that by this test attempts need not involve intention as to any aspect of the *actus reus* of the complete offence. But it actually misinterprets the test. In this example, the claim that I will commit the complete offence if I succeed in doing what I am trying to do rests on a *prediction* of what *else* will happen if I succeed: the prediction that, if I succeed in lighting the fire, this will have the further consequence of damage to my neighbour's property. But no such predictions of the further consequences of my successful actions were needed in the other cases I have discussed. In those cases the claim that the agent would commit the complete offence if she succeeded in doing what she was trying to do was the claim that, given the facts which already obtained at the time of her action, success in doing what she was trying to do would itself *constitute* the commission of the complete offence; no prediction of what else would happen if she succeeded was needed. The test asks whether the agent will *necessarily* commit the complete offence if she succeeds; or whether what she is trying to do would *constitute* the commission of the complete offence. These questions do not require a contingent prediction of what would happen if she succeeded: they ask what would be involved in the very fact of her success, given the actual context in which she is acting."

Question

Suppose it is an offence to use or attempt to use a motor vehicle which does not comply with the regulations as to, *inter alia*, effective brakes. The offence is strict as to non-compliance with the regulation, *i.e.* no mental state of any kind is required as to that circumstance. A was stopped as he was about to drive off in a borrowed car which had defective brakes, although he did not know and had no means of knowing that fact. Can A be convicted of attempting to use a motor vehicle which does not comply with the regulations?

ii. Actus Reus

Note

There may be many stages between the formulation of an intention to commit a crime and the actual commission of it. At some stage after formulation of intention and before actual commission, the point will be reached at which the actor can be said to have attempted it and so be guilty of the crime of attempt. The common law never succeeded in what is probably an impossible task, namely, formulating a general test which would, on being applied to any set of facts, infallibly indicate whether the crucial point had been reached. About the only two propositions which could be taken as settled were (1) that not all things done on the way to commission of an intended crime were attempts at it (some early steps were regarded as too remote), and (2) that if the accused had done the last act which he knew was needed for full commission, it was an attempt by him.

Various tests were suggested in the cases or in writings, such as the first step on the road to full commission, the final step before full commission (sometimes qualified by the view that even a final step was not enough if the accused could still withdraw from full commission); the doing of an act which unequivocally showed what crime was intended; the taking of a substantial step towards commission of the offence. (For a review of these theories, see Law Com. 102 §§ 2.22 2.37.) None of them yielded satisfactory results across the whole band of possible cases. The only general test consistently quoted in the authorities was that formulated in *R.* v. *Eagleton* (1855) 6 Cox C.C. 559, 571 by Parke B.: "The mere intention to commit a misdemeanour is not criminal. Some act is required and we do not think that all acts towards committing a misdemeanour are indictable. Acts remotely leading towards the commission of the offence are not to be considered as attempts to commit it, but acts immediately connected with it are ... " This was usually called the proximity test. Proximity was accepted by the House of Lords in *D.P.P.* v. *Stonehouse* (1978) A.C. 55 as the true test, although there was little agreement on how to define the concept more exactly, and of course without more exact definition the test is so vague as to be of but limited use.

Law Com. No. 102

(Footnotes as in the original)

3. Recommendations as to the actus reus

"§ 2.45 In the light of the case law, the opinions of writers and the various approaches to the *actus reus* already described, we must make it clear that in our view there is no magic formula which can now be produced to define precisely what constitutes an attempt. ... Of the various approaches, only the 'proximity' test has produced results which may be thought broadly acceptable. Its disadvantages are that hitherto it has not worked well in some cases, and that it is imprecise. It shares the latter disadvantage with all other approaches but its flexibility does enable difficult cases to be reconsidered and their authority questioned. Further, where cases are so dependent on what are sometimes fine differences of degree, we think it is eminently appropriate for the question whether the conduct in a particular case amounts to an attempt to be left to the jury. This suggests that a relatively similar definition based on the 'proximity' approach is the best which can be hoped for.

(a) *Content of the Actus Reus*

§ 2.46 The first element in a statutory test of proximity should be the drawing of the distinction between acts of preparation and acts which are sufficiently proximate to the offence. This is a truism repeated in many cases including the most recent. It is nonetheless useful because it recognises that certain forms of conduct, in almost all circumstances which can be envisaged, do not amount to an attempt. Possession of implements for the purpose of committing an offence is an obvious example which, as we have noted, is at present dealt with by other means. Reconnoitring the place contemplated for the commission of the intended offence is another example of conduct which it is difficult to regard as more than an act of preparation: it would not ordinarily be called an attempt.

§ 2.47 The definition of sufficient proximity must be wide enough to cover two varieties of cases; first, those in which a person has taken all the steps towards the commission of a crime which he believes to be necessary as far as he is concerned for that crime to result, [27] such as firing a gun at another and missing. Normally such cases cause no difficulty. Secondly, however, the definition must cover those instances where a person has to take some further step to complete the crime, assuming that there is evidence of the necessary mental element on his part to commit it; for example, when the defendant has raised the gun to take aim at another but has not yet squeezed the trigger. We have reached the conclusion that, in regard to these cases, it is undesirable to recommend anything more complex than a rationalisation of the present law.

§ 2.48 In choosing the words to be used to describe this rationalisation of the present law, we have had to bear in mind that they will be the subject of consideration and interpretation by the courts. For this reason we have rejected a number of terms which have already been used with some frequency in reported cases, such as acts which are 'proximate to,' or 'closely connected' or 'immediately connected' with the offence attempted. The literal meaning of 'proximate' is 'nearest, next before or after (in place, order, time, connection of thought, causation, etc.).' Thus, were this term part of a statutory description of the *actus reus* of attempt, it would clearly be capable of being interpreted to exclude all but the 'final act'; this would not be in accordance with the policy outlined above. The term 'immediately connected' is in our view inappropriate for the same reason. And acts which may be 'closely connected' in the sense that they have advanced a considerable way towards the completed offence may nonetheless bear no qualitative resemblance to the acts required for completion. For example, it is arguable that what the appellant in *R.* v.

---

[27] This is on the assumption that he is the actual perpetrator; if his part in the commission is a minor one, none of his acts may get beyond the state of preparation: see *D.P.P.* v. *Stonehouse* [1978] A.C. 55, 86, *per* Lord Edmund-Davies.

Robinson (*post*, p. 441) had done had no close qualitative connection with that remainder to be done—making a claim on the insurance company—even though in terms of quantity his conduct as a whole had advanced far towards his objective. This potential ambiguity therefore precludes use of that term.

§ 2.49 The foregoing considerations lead us to *recommend* as the most appropriate form of words to define the *actus reus* of attempt *any act which goes so far towards the commission of the offence attempted as to be more than an act of mere preparation.*

(b) *Issues of Law and Fact*
§ 2.50 The final element of the offence of attempt which requires consideration in the present context is the respective functions of the judge and jury. We have noted that the 'substantial step' approach would require the judge to direct the jury as a matter of law as to whether particular conduct, if proved, constitutes a substantial step. (§ 2.30) ... Since then, the majority in *D.P.P.* v. *Stonehouse* has, as we have noted, approved the decision in *R.* v. *Cook* in which Lord Parker C.J. stated that, 'while in every case it is for the judge to rule whether there is any evidence capable of constituting an attempt, it is always for the jury to say whether they accept it as amounting to an attempt. That involves ... a careful direction in every case on the general principle with regard to what acts constitute attempts': (1963) 48 Cr.App.R. 98, 102. We agree with this view: as factual situations may be infinitely varied and the issue of whether an accused's conduct has passed beyond mere preparation to commit an offence may depend upon all the surrounding circumstances, it is appropriate to leave the final issue to be decided as a question of fact, although 'the judge may sum up in such a way as to make it plain that he considers that the accused is guilty and should be convicted.' *D.P.P.* v. *Stonehouse* [1978] A.C. 55, 80, *per* Lord Salmon. Furthermore, this division of function between judge and jury is in accord with the principle that it is for the judge to tell the jury what the law is, but for the jury to say whether on the facts the accused has been brought within the provisions of the offence with which he has been charged. If the conduct is such that in law it cannot constitute more than an act of preparation the judge must direct the jury to acquit ... ".

Dennis, "The Elements of Attempt" [1980] Crim.L.R. 758, 768

"These proposals give rise to a number of misgivings.
1. *Imprecision.* Even given the premise that precise definition is impossible, the Law Commission's test is more open-textured than any of the common law tests which it replaces. The form of words chosen does very little more than indicate that some acts do constitute attempts ('more than preparatory') and some acts do not ('preparatory'). The descriptive words '[an act] which goes so far towards the commission of the offence' do not constitute a qualitative distinction between these two categories: they merely indicate that a scale of conduct is in contemplation, and that at some point along it a line is drawn to fix the threshold of liability.
What the Law Commission have done then is to take a principle—that in order to preserve a balance between the interests of the individual and those of society not all acts towards the commission of an offence should be punishable—and erect it into a rule to be applied by the tribunal to resolve individual cases, but without giving it any further content. How is this principle/rule to be applied?

One radical answer would have been to take the current fashion to extremes, and to turn the whole issue over to the jury, asking them to construe the word 'preparatory' as an ordinary word of the English language. All they would then need to do would be to decide whether the defendant's acts went beyond their understanding of that term. It appears, however, that the Law Commission do not wish to go as far as this. The judge is to retain control in the first instance of the limits of preparation. 'If the conduct is such that *in law it cannot constitute more than an act of preparation* the judge must direct the jury to acquit.' (Emphasis supplied). To this extent then the application of the test is a matter of law, but no guidance is given in the draft Bill on how this question of law should be determined. We may assume that a judge will decide, for example, that evidence of 'reconnoitring the place intended for the commission of the offence' is evidence of an act of preparation only, but on what basis is he to reach the conclusion? Certainly he will be in some difficulty if he turns to the pre-existing common law because the Law Commission have cogently criticised all the common law theories and endeavoured to replace them with the codified offence.

2. *Role of the Jury.* Pursuing this theme, how are the jury to apply the test if the evidence passes the judge? (We may assume that [section 4(3)] does have the effect of requiring the issue of whether D's conduct fell within [section 1(1)] to be left to the jury, although it does not actually say so). They are still being given a very large issue to decide, and it is submitted that the 'question of fact' represents a considerable extension of that term. It normally refers to the finding of primary facts (did D practise a deception?), evaluation of primary facts against a fixed standard (was the force used by D reasonable?), and, more controversially, the determination of statutory words where they are used as ordinary words of the English language (was D dishonest?). In this case the jury are *not* being asked to decide the meaning of the word attempt, or any other word, as a matter of ordinary language. Rather they are being asked expressly to determine whether D's act fell within a subsection of a criminal statute. Putting the matter in these terms connotes a question of interpretation and classification, and it is submitted that it is simply leaving too much to the jury to ask them to perform the task with such an imprecise criterion.

The practical risks involved are those of perverse verdicts and inconsistent verdicts. Perverse verdicts of acquittal may occur where the law is, or should be, clear that a sufficient act of attempt has taken place, as where D has committed the last act he intended to commit. The Law Commission anticipate this objection and argue that the risk can be obviated by clarity in identifying the contested issue and by commenting on the evidence, if necessary in strong terms. Fair enough, but there is still no guidance on how the contested issue could be clarified in a direction, and what benefit is gained by leaving the question open if the answer is clear?

Inconsistent verdicts are a much more serious danger. The Law Commission commented at the beginning of this section of the Report that 'in the absence of any definition of the conduct required for an attempt, there would be little assistance which a judge could give in directing the jury, and this could lead to unacceptable discrepancies and very marked inconsistencies in jury verdicts in similar cases. (§ 2.19) It has been argued that the test in [section] 1(1) does not take the definition of attempt very much further. In the absence of any statutory guidance on how the test is to be interpreted, there is a real risk that different juries may adopt different criteria to deal with essentially similar material facts. Suppose that the facts of *Robinson* (*infra*) and of *Comer* v. *Bloomfield* (*infra*) recur. The judge leaves the issue to the jury in both cases, realising that the Law Commission wished the boundaries of 'preparation' to be altered so that the conduct in these cases was at least capable of amounting to an attempt. Jury A convict on the facts of *Robinson*, arguing that this was an elaborate deception showing firmness of purpose, and that it was not necessary that the deception should have come to the notice of the intended victim of the fraud. Jury B acquit on the facts of *Comer* v. *Bloomfield* arguing that the accused had not actually made a claim for the loss of his vehicle and that his enquiry about it was not an act showing clear unlawful purpose. If this example is not far fetched, the result brings the law into disrepute, since the accused in case B had clearly gone further than the accused in case A."

Notes

R. v. *Robinson* and *Comer* v. *Bloomfield* were criticised by the Law Commission as cases where the result, to the man in the street, appears to be contrary to common sense (§ 2.39). Nevertheless, in this scene-setting type of case, the dangers of inconsistent verdicts may have receded, in that the Court of Appeal seems to take the view, contrary to that of the Law Commission, that such cases are not capable of being attempts in law.

R. v. *Robinson* [1915] 2 K.B. 342. D, a jeweller, insured his stock against theft and contrived to be found tied up, with his safe empty. He told the policeman who found him that he had been the victim of a burglary. Later he confessed that his object was to make a false claim on his insurers. He did not submit any claim. *Held* (C.A.) no attempt at obtaining money by false pretences, the acts done being too remote.

Comer v. *Bloomfield* (1970) 55 Cr.App.R. 305. D drove his vehicle into the depths of a wood and reported it stolen. He enquired of insurers whether a claim would lie for its loss, but did not make a claim. *Held* (Div.Ct.), no attempt to obtain money by deception. See also R. v. *Ilyas* (1983) 78 Cr.App.R. 17, which was decided after the Criminal Attempts Act had been passed but on facts which required to be judged at common law. The facts were on all fours with those in *Comer* v. *Bloomfield* and the result was the same.

R. v. *Widdowson* (1985) 82 Cr.App.R. 314. D, wishing to obtain a van on hire-purchase terms but knowing that he would not be accepted as credit-worthy, filled in a credit enquiries form in the name of another person. *Held* (C.A.) not an attempt to obtain services (the hire-purchase of a van) by deception.

"Assuming that the finance company had responded favourably to proposal, it still remained for the appellant to seek a hire purchase deal from them. To our minds it is that step which would constitute an attempt to obtain the services relied upon in this case. If one asks whether this appellant had carried out every step which it was necessary for him to perform to achieve the consequences alleged to have been attempted, the answer must be that he did not.

Equally, it seems to us, this appellant's acts cannot be described as immediately rather than merely remotely connected with the specific offence alleged to have been attempted. Thus whichever of the tests described in *Ilyas* is applied, what the appellant did cannot reasonably be described as more than merely preparatory."

R. v. Gullefer
(1986) [1990] 3 All E.R. 882
Court of Appeal

The appellant was convicted of attempted theft. During a race at a greyhound racing stadium the appellant had climbed on to the track in front of the dogs and in an attempt to distract them had waved his arms. His efforts were only marginally successful and the stewards decided it was unnecessary to declare "no race." Had they done so the bookmakers would have had to repay the amount of his stake to any punter, but would not have been liable to pay any winnings to those punters who would have been successful had the race been valid. The appellant told the police he had attempted to stop the race because the dog on which he had staked £18 was losing. He had hoped for a "no race" declaration and the recovery of his stake. The appellant's main ground of appeal was that the acts proved to have been carried out by the appellant were not "sufficiently proximate to the completed offence of theft to be capable of comprising an attempt to commit theft."

LORD LANE C.J. for the Court: The main burden of counsel's submission to us has been the third ground of appeal, namely that the acts proved to have been carried out by the appellant were not "sufficiently proximate to the completed offence of theft to be capable of comprising an attempt to commit theft."

We have been referred to a number of decisions, many of them of respectable antiquity, which show, if nothing else, the difficulties which abound in this branch of the criminal law. The present law is, however, now enshrined in the words of the Criminal Attempts Act 1981. Section 1(1) provides:

"If, with intent to commit an offence to which this section applies, a person does an act which is more than merely preparatory to the commission of the offence, he is guilty of attempting to commit the offence."

Section 4(3) provides:

"Where, in proceedings against a person for an offence under section 1 above, there is evidence sufficient in law to support a finding that he did an act falling within subsection (1) of that section, the question whether or not his act fell within that subsection is a question of fact."

Thus the judge's task is to decide whether there is evidence on which a jury could reasonably come to the conclusion that the defendant had gone beyond the realm of mere preparation and had embarked on the actual commission of the offence. If not, he must withdraw the case from the jury. If there is such evidence, it is then for the jury to decide whether the defendant did in fact go beyond mere preparation. That is the way in which the judge approached this case. He ruled that there was sufficient evidence. Counsel for the appellant submits that he was wrong in so ruling.

The first task of the court is to apply the words of the 1981 Act to the facts of the case. Was the appellant still in the stage of preparation to commit the substantive offence, or was there a basis of fact which would entitle the jury to say that he had embarked on the theft itself? Might it properly be said that when he jumped on to the track he was trying to steal £18 from the bookmaker?

Our view is that it could not properly be said that at that stage he was in the process of committing theft. What he was doing was jumping onto the track in an effort to distract the dogs, which in its turn, he hoped, would have the effect of forcing the stewards to declare "no race", which would in its turn give him the opportunity to go back to the bookmaker and demand the £18 he had staked. In our view there was insufficient evidence for it to be said that he had, when he jumped onto the track, gone beyond mere preparation.

So far at least as the present case is concerned, we do not think that it is necessary to examine the authorities which preceded the 1981 Act, save to say that the sections we have already quoted in this judgment seem to be a blend of various decisions, some of which were not easy to reconcile with others.

However, in deference to the arguments of counsel, we venture to make the following observations. Since the passing of the 1981 Act, a division of this court in *R. v. Ilyas* (1983) 78 Cr.App.R. 17 has helpfully collated the authorities. As appears from the judgment in that case, there seem to have been two lines of authority. The first was exemplified by the decision in *R. v. Eagleton* (1855) Dears CC 515. That was a case where the defendant was alleged to have attempted to obtain money from the guardians of a parish by falsely pretending to the relieving officer that he had delivered loaves of bread of the proper weight to the outdoor poor when in fact the loaves were deficient in weight.

Parke B, delivering the judgment of the court of nine judges, said (Dears CC 515 at 538):

> "Acts remotely leading towards the commission of the offence are not to be considered as attempts to commit it, but acts immediately connected with it are, and if, in this case, after the credit with the relieving officer for the fraudulent overcharge, any *further step* on the part of the defendant had been necessary to obtain payment, as the making out a further account or producing the vouchers to the Board, we should have thought that the obtaining credit in account with the relieving officer would not have been sufficiently proximate to the obtaining the money. But, on the statement in this case, no other act on the part of the defendant would have been required. It was the last act, *depending on himself*, towards the payment of the money, and therefore it ought to be considered as an attempt." (Parke B's emphasis.)

Lord Diplock in *D.P.P. v. Stonehouse* [1978] A.C. 55 at 68, having cited part of that passage from *R. v. Eagleton* added: 'In other words the offender must have crossed the Rubicon and burnt his boats.'

The other line of authority is based on a passage in *Stephen's Digest of the Criminal Law* (5th edn, 1894) art 50:

> "An attempt to commit a crime is an act done with intent to commit that crime, and forming part of a series of acts which would constitute its actual commission if it were not interrupted."

As Lord Edmund-Davies points out in *DPP v. Stonehouse* at 85–86, that definition has been repeatedly cited with judicial approval: see Byrne J in *Hope v. Brown*, [1954] 1 W.L.R. 250 at 253 and Lord Parker CJ in *Davey v. Lee*, [1968] 1 Q.B. 366 at 370. However, as Lord Parker CJ in the latter case points out, *Stephen's* definition falls short of defining the exact point of time at which the series of acts can be said to begin.

It seems to us that the words of the 1981 Act seek to steer a midway course. They do not provide, as they might have done, that the *R. v. Eagleton* test is to be followed, or that, as Lord Diplock suggested, the defendant must have reached a point from which it was impossible for him to retreat before the actus reus of an attempt is proved. On the other hand the words give perhaps as clear a guidance as is possible in the circumstances on the point of time at which *Stephen's* "series of acts" begins. It begins when the merely preparatory acts come to an end and the defendant embarks on the crime proper. When that is will depend of course on the facts in any particular case. ...

Appeal allowed: Conviction quashed

R. v. Jones
[1990] 3 All E.R. 886
Court of Appeal

Jones was convicted of attempted murder in the circumstances outlined in the judgment. He appealed on the ground that the correct test of an attempt was whether the defendant had committed the last act prior to the full offence being committed.

TAYLOR L.J. for the Court: The appellant, a married man, started an affair with a woman named Lynn Gresley in 1985. She lived with him in Australia during 1986. In September 1987, back in England, she began a relationship with the victim, Michael Foreman. She continued, however to see the appellant, to whom she was still very attached. In November 1987 she decided to break off the relationship with the appellant, but he continued to write to her, begging her to come back to him.

On 12 January 1988 the appellant applied for a shotgun certificate, and three days later bought two guns in company with two companions. He bought two more guns a few days later on his own. On 23 January he shortened the barrel of one of them and test fired it twice the following day.

The appellant told a colleague at work that he would be away on Tuesday, 26 January. On 24 January he phoned Lynn Gresley in a distraught state. The next day he apologised, but she again refused his invitation to resume their relationship. The appellant then told his wife that he had packed a bag as he was going to Spain to do some work on their chalet. On 26 January he left home dressed normally for work, saying that he would telephone his wife whether he was leaving for Spain that evening.

That same morning, the victim, Michael Foreman, took his daughter to school by car as usual. After the child left the car, the appellant appeared, opened the door and jumped into the rear seat. He was wearing overalls, a crash helmet with the visor down, and was carrying a bag. He and the victim had never previously met. He introduced himself, said he wanted to sort things out and asked the victim to drive on. When they stopped on a grass verge, the appellant handed over a letter he had received from Lynn. Whilst the victim read it, the appellant took the sawn-off shotgun from the bag. It was loaded. He pointed it at the victim at a range of some ten to twelve inches. He said. "You are not going to like this" or similar words. The victim grabbed the end of the gun and pushed it sideways and upwards. There was a struggle during which the victim managed to throw the gun out of the window. As he tried to get out, he felt a cord over his head pulling him back. He managed to break free and run away, taking the gun with him. From a nearby garage he telephoned the police.

Meanwhile, the appellant drove off in the victim's car. He was arrested jogging away from it carrying his holdall. He said that he had done nothing and only wanted to kill himself. His bag contained a hatchet, some cartridges and a length of cord. He also had a sharp kitchen knife which he threw away. In the appellant's car parked near the school was £stg1,500 together with a quantity of French and Spanish money. The evidence showed that the safety catch of the shotgun had been in the on position. The victim was unclear whether the appellant's finger was ever on the trigger. When interviewed, the appellant declined to make any comment.

At the end of the prosecution case, after the above facts had been given in evidence, a submission was made to the judge that the charge of attempted murder should be withdrawn from the jury. It was argued that since the appellant would have had to perform at least three more acts before the full offence could have been completed, i.e. remove the safety catch, put his finger on the trigger and pull it, the evidence was insufficient to support the charge. The[re] was a discussion as to the proper construction of s.1(1) of the Criminal Attempts Act 1981. After hearing full argument, the judge ruled against the submission and allowed the case to proceed on count 1. Thereafter, the appellant gave evidence. In the result, the jury convicted him unanimously of attempted murder. It follows that they found that he intended to kill the victim.

The sole ground of appeal is that the judge erred in law in his construction of s.1(1) and ought to have withdrawn the case. ...

Counsel for the appellant puts forward three broad propositions. First, he says that for about a century, two different tests as to the actus reus of attempt have been inconsistently applied by the courts. ...

[After quoting from Parke B.'s judgment in *R.* v. *Eagleton* (1855) Dears C.C. 515]: Accordingly, the test deriving from *R.* v. *Eagleton* was said to be the "last act" test. It was adopted in a number of cases, e.g. *R.* v. *Robinson* [1915] 2 K.B. 342. In *D.P.P.* v. *Stonehouse*, [1978] A.C. 55 at 68 Lord Diplock referred to *R.* v. *Eagleton* as the locus classicus, adopted some of the words of Parke B and summarised them in the graphic phrase: "In other words the offender must have crossed the Rubicon and burnt his boats."

The other test referred to by counsel for the appellant derives from *Stephen's Digest of the Criminal Law* (5th edn. 1894) art. 50, where it was stated thus:

> "An attempt to commit a crime is an act done with intent to commit that crime, and forming part of a series of acts which would constitute its actual commission if it were not interrupted."

Lord Edmund-Davies noted in *D.P.P.* v. *Stonehouse* that *Stephen's* definition has been repeatedly cited with approval. He referred to its adoption in *Hope* v. *Brown* [1954] 1 All E.R. 330 at 332, and *Davey* v. *Lee* [1968] 1 Q.B. 366. It was also applied in *R.* v. *Linneker* [1906] 22 K.B. 99, where *R.* v. *Eagleton* was not cited.

In some cases, including three since the 1981 Act, both tests have been considered, and the court has found it unnecessary to decide between them, holding that the result in those cases would have been the same, whichever applied (see *R.* v. *Ilyas* (1983) 78 Cr.App.R. 17, *R.* v. *Widdowson* (1986) 82 Cr.App.R. 314 and *R.* v. *Boyle* (1986) 84 Cr.App.R. 270).

The second proposition of counsel for the appellant is that s 1(1) of the 1981 Act has not resolved the question which is the appropriate test.

Third, he submits that the test deriving from *R.* v. *Eagleton* should be adopted.

This amounts to an invitation to construe the statutory words by reference to previous conflicting case law. We believe this to be misconceived. The 1981 Act is a codifying statute. It amends and sets out completely the law relating to attempts and conspiracies. In those circumstances the correct approach is to look first at the natural meaning of the statutory words, not to turn back to earlier case law and seek to fit some previous test to the words of the section. In *Bank of England* v. *Vagliano Bros* [1891] A.C. 107 at 144–145, Lord Herschell, referring to a codifying Act, said:

> "I think the proper course is in the first instance to examine the language of the statute and to ask what is its natural meaning, uninfluenced by any considerations derived from the previous state of the law, and not to start with inquiring how the law previously stood, and then, assuming that it was probably intended to leave it unaltered, to see if the words of the enactment will bear an interpretation in conformity with this view. If a statute, intended to embody in a code a particular branch of the law, is to be treated in this fashion, it appears to me that its utility will be almost entirely destroyed, and the very object with which it was enacted will be frustrated. The purpose of such a statute surely was that on any point specifically dealt with by it, the law should be ascertained by interpreting the language used instead of, as before, by roaming over a vast number of authorities in order to discover what the law was. ... I am of course far from asserting that resort may never he had to the previous state of the law for the purpose of aiding in the construction of the provisions of the code. If, for example, a provision be of doubtful import, such resort would be perfectly legitimate."

This approach was adopted by Lord Lane CJ presiding over this court in *R.* v. *Gullefer* ...

[After quoting the last paragraph reproduced, *ante*, p. 444 of Lord Lane's judgment]. We respectfully adopt those words. We do not accept counsel's contention that s. 1(1) of the 1981 Act in effect embodies the "last act" test derived from *R.* v. *Eagleton*. Had Parliament intended to adopt that test, a quite different form of words could and would have been used.

It is of interest to note that the 1981 Act followed a report from the Law Commission on *Attempt, and Impossibility in Relation to Attempt, Conspiracy and Incitement* (Law. Com. no. 102). [His lordship quoted paras. 2.47, 2.48, *ante* p. 438].

Clearly, the draftsman of s. 1(1) must be taken to have been aware of the two lines of earlier authority and of the Law Commission's report. The words "an act which is more than merely preparatory to the commission of the offence "would be inapt if they were intended to mean" the last act which lay in his power towards the commission of the offence."

Looking at the plain natural meaning of s. 1(1) in the way indicated by Lord Lane CJ, the question for the judge in the present case was whether there was evidence from which a reasonable jury, properly directed, could conclude that the appellant had done acts which were more than merely preparatory. Clearly his actions in obtaining the gun, in shortening it, in loading it, in putting on his disguise and in going to the school could only be regarded as preparatory acts. But, in our judgment, once he had got into the car, taken out the loaded gun and pointed it at the victim with the intention of killing him, there was sufficient evidence for the consideration of the jury on the charge of attempted murder. It was a matter for them to decide whether they were sure that those acts were more than merely preparatory. In our judgment, therefore, the judge was right to allow the case to go to the jury, and the appeal against conviction must be dismissed.

Appeal against conviction dismissed

R. v. Campbell [1991] Crim. L.R. 268 (C.A.): C appealed against a conviction of attempted robbery. Police had information leading them to believe that an attempt might be made to rob a sub-post office, and watched the premises. On the day in question, C was seen lurking in the vicinity. He rode a motor cycle along the road and walked around. He wore a crash helmet and gloves. He was seen to put on sunglasses and then put his right hand into a pocket which seemed to contain something heavy. He stopped about 30 yards from the post office and took off his sunglasses. He looked around before turning away. Half an hour later he walked back towards the post office. He was arrested in front of the post office. He was searched and an imitation gun, sunglasses and a threatening note were found on him. He admitted that he had been reconnoitring the post office and had intended using the note to frighten the person behind the counter. The trial judge rejected a submission of no case to answer. *Held*, quashing his conviction, the judge should not have made any reference to the previous law; moreover, since several acts remained to be done by C and he had not even gained the place where he would be in a position to carry out the offence, the judge should have withdrawn the case from the jury.

K.J.M. Smith: Proximity in Attempt: Lord Lane's Midway Course [1991] Crim.L.R. 576, 577.

" ... Lord Lane C.J. saw pre Act case law as amply illustrating the 'difficulties which abound in this branch of the criminal law,' but that the 'present law is ... now enshrined in the Criminal Attempts Act ... ' Are we then to take it that references to pre-Act decisions should never cross the lips of counsel in future attempt cases? Well not quite, for a few paragraphs later Lord Lane qualifies his earlier comment by noting: 'So far as the *present* case is concerned, we do not think it is necessary to examine the authorities which preceded the Act of 1981'; the implication being that in some (unspecified) situations admission of common law authorities would be permissible for some (unspecified) purposes. There is little doubt that the subsequent Court of Appeal judgment in *Jones* construed *Gullefer's* relegation of pre-Act cases in this modified sense: 'the correct approach is to look *first* at the natural meaning of the statutory words.' And seeking to reinforce this construction, the Court of Appeal cited an extract from Lord Herschell's speech on statutory interpretation from *Bank of England* v. *Vagliano Brothers* which accepted that resort to the 'previous state of the law [to interpret] a provision ... of doubtful import ... would be perfectly legitimate.'

It, therefore, seems that pre-Act authorities may still be enlisted in *some* circumstances to assist a court in settling what acts may be 'more than merely preparatory.' However, no direct clues are offered by the Court of Appeal in *Gullefer* or *Jones* as to when such earlier case law may be prayed in aid, and to what effect. Yet, if anything is of 'doubtful import,' surely the unforthcoming formula set out in the 1981 Act takes a lot of beating: doubt on the proximity question lurks in relation to almost any activity falling short of the unsuccessful defendant's 'last act.' "

Note

Section 4(3) leaves the judges with no power to say what does amount to an attempt (it is declared to be a question of fact), but with a power to say what does *not* amount to an attempt. The cases extracted in this section appear to show that they still hold that the scene-setting case exemplified by *R.* v. *Robinson* (which the Law Commission thought ought to be capable of being found to be an attempt), is not an attempt. The same can be said about going to the place where the offence was intended to happen, equipped to commit it, but not actually pointing the gun at the intended victim. From the point of view of public protection, the definition of attempt may be thought to be drawn too narrowly.

Williams: Wrong Turnings in the Law of Attempt [1991] Crim.L.R. 417, 419.

"The root problem with the law is that it looks at the facts retrospectively: backwards from the moment when the crime was intended to be committed, instead of forwards from the time when the defendant started to make his criminal intention a reality. Counting backwards, the court in *Jones* was prepared to hold that pointing the loaded gun with intention to murder was an attempt, even though the safety catch was perhaps still on and the defendant perhaps did not have his finger on the trigger. The court would probably have gone further, if the occasion had demanded, to the extent of holding that an attempt was committed when the defendant started to pull the gun out; there was a decision to this effect. But the court did not think that lying in wait for the victim with the loaded gun at the school gate was an attempt. Why not?

Presumably because in ordinary language there would not at that point be what is called an attempt to kill. Granting this opinion for the sake of argument, why should the law be in thrall to the ordinary meaning of the word 'attempt'? This is the name of the offence, but the whole law of an offence is not necessarily contained in its name. The ordinary meaning of murder is intentional killing; but unintentionally causing a person's death by doing something with intent to cause him serious injury is another instance of murder in law. Entering someone's house with the sole intent of raping the lady of the house would not normally be called burglary, but it is burglary in law. Crimes can be applied beyond their paradigm cases.

The other possible reason for holding that lying in wait was not an attempt is that a person who lies in wait for his victim may not distinctively signify a criminal intention. But this reason did not apply to Jones: he was waiting where his victim was expected to come, and he was in disguise, armed with a gun, and carrying foreign exchange in readiness for flight abroad. Anyway, the courts have abandoned the idea that an attempt must be unequivocally referable to the crime intended.

Perhaps lying in wait would not be held to go beyond mere preparation, if the point were argued. But go further back still. What about Jones's acts in buying the shotgun, shortening the barrel, loading it, and disguising himself? The particular question can be settled by bringing a charge under the Firearms Act, but there is a more general question relating to acquiring the tools or other materials of crime (materials that may be ambiguous in themselves, like a carving knife).

Before the Criminal Attempts Act the traditional attitude towards attempts was apparently relaxed in one respect. Acquiring materials for certain crimes, though an act of preparation, was held to be either an attempt or a special common-law offence. But the Act (Section 6(1), *ante*, p. 425) is retrogressive on this. The commission was minded to continue the common-law notion of attempt in full purity, so the Act expressly abolishes these special offences. And the commission of 1989, which produced the Draft Code, though different in composition from the commission of 1981 evidently decided to pursue the same course.

To effect a real reform of this part of the law we need to get away from retrospective reasoning and substitute prospective reasoning. In other words, we need express legislation adopting a 'substantial step' definition of an attempt. Such a reform was embodied in the Model Penal Code of the American Law Institute, which has been widely accepted in legislation in the United States. Section 5.01, after stating the 'substantial step' test in subsection (1), works it out in businesslike detail in subsection (2) (here slightly shortened).

'(1) Conduct shall not be held to constitute a substantial step . . . unless it is strongly corroborative of the actor's criminal purpose . . . '

Pausing there, this obviously means that the conduct must be strongly corroborative not merely of the defendant's criminal inclinations but of his formed purpose of commit this particular crime. Remote preparations, such as enquiries to establish the possibility of committing a particular crime, should be ruled out under this test.

'(2) The following, if strongly corroborative of the actor's criminal purpose, shall not be held insufficient as a matter of law: (*a*) lying in wait, searching for or following the contemplated victim of the crime; (*b*) enticing or seeking to entice the contemplated victim of the crime to go to the place contemplated for its commission; (*c*) reconnoitering the place contemplated for the commission of the crime; (*d*) unlawful entry of a structure, vehicle or enclosure in which it is contemplated that the crime will be committed; (*e*) possession of materials to be employed in the commission of the crime, which are specially designed for such unlawful use or which can serve no lawful purpose of the actor under the circumstances; (*g*) soliciting an innocent agent to engage in conduct constituting an element of the crime.'

This list beautifully clarifies nearly all the matters that have been litigated in England, most of which we have either failed to settle or settled in an impolitic way. (I would add to it: '(*h*) deceiving any person for the purpose of committing the crime,' and (*i*) 'preparing a deception for the purpose of any crime involving deception or fraud' (both of which Robinson did).

The Working Party . . . recommended the adoption of a 'substantial step' test in the future code, but the commission rejected it. . . . The following were the reasons that guided the commission, as they eventually surfaced in Law Com. No. 102, together with the answers I would like to make.

(1) It was feared that the substantial step text would widen the law of attempt too much (para. 2.32). Certainly it would widen the law, but no example is given of how it would widen it too much. Perhaps the commission had in mind the serious doubts that were felt about the old 'sus' legislation (now repealed), but the following points may be made. (*a*) The 'sus' legislation enabled evidence to be given of the defendant's previous convictions; this is not proposed for charges of attempt. (*b*) The provision in the Model Penal Code requires proof of an act that is 'strongly corroborative of the actor's criminal purpose.' This should be enough to keep the law of attempt within bounds. (It may be noticed that the

requirement is missing from the Draft Code's provision on articles acquired for the purpose of criminal damage, with which the commission appears to be content). (c) If desired, the items about reconnoitring and unlawful entry could be omitted from the list of examples in the M.P.C. provision, though I think this would be a mistake. (d) All the acts listed in the M.P.C. provision would be overt acts from which a conspiracy could be deduced if they were committed by two people together; why should the fact of numbers make any difference to criminal liability? (The commission proposed no reduction in the scope of conspiracy.)

(2) The commission acknowledged that at one time the proximity rule appeared to be working unsatisfactorily, and it mentioned *Robinson* as such an unsatisfactory case, where 'the result reached would, to the man in the street, appear to be contrary to common sense' (para. 2.39). But the commission offered its opinion that 'the position has changed to some extent since the Working Party reported' (para. 2.33). How the commission thought it had changed, we are not told.

(3) The substantial step test had been criticised because it was incapable of further description or elucidation (para. 2.33). Replies: first, this is not true of the substantial step test: the M.P.C. gave the test a large measure of clarification by means of examples. Secondly, the commission's objection is impressively true of its own test of an act 'going beyond mere preparation,' which is to be left without any statutory examples. The commission of 1989 included examples of attempts in its Report on the Code, but in selecting them it carefully refrained from shedding any glimmer of light on what goes and what does not go beyond mere preparation, in doubtful cases. Thus it seems that the commission was not interested in further describing or elucidating its own test. (In any case, the commission did not intend its examples to be part of the enacted code.)

(4) Of all the commission's anaemic objections, the feeblest was its idea that if the substantial step test were adopted, the offence could no longer properly be called an attempt. As I have already said, this problem has not prevented the extension of crimes like murder and burglary beyond the scope popularly understood from their names. Anyway, I would not grant the objection. I do not think it an abuse of language to say that Kenneth Jones started his attempt as soon as he set out with his firearm, his disguise and his Spanish money, or even when he acquired the firearm and his disguise with the firm purpose of using it in the offence; nor would there be any linguistic objection to saying that an attempt was committed by various rogues who have got off charges on the proximity issue, such as Robinson ... "

Draft Criminal Code, Clause 49

"Attempt to commit an offence

(1) A person who, intending to commit an indictable offence, does an act that is more than merely preparatory to the commission of the offence is guilty of attempt to commit the offence.

(2) For the purposes of subsection (1), an intention to commit an offence is an intention with respect to all the elements of the offence other than fault elements, except that recklessness with respect to a circumstance suffices where it suffices for the offence itself.

(3) 'Act' in this section includes an omission only where the offence intended is capable of being committed by an omission.

(4) Where there is evidence to support a finding that an act was more than merely preparatory to the commission of the offence intended, the

question whether that act was more than merely preparatory is a question of fact.

(5) Subject to section 52(1), this section applies to any offence which, if it were completed, would be triable in England and Wales as an indictable offence, other than an offence under section 4(1) (assisting offenders) or 5(1) (accepting or agreeing to accept consideration for not disclosing information about an arrestable offence) of the Criminal Law Act 1967.

(6) It is not an offence under this section, or under any enactment referred to in section 51, to attempt to procure, assist or encourage as an accessory the commission of an offence by another; but—

(a) a person may be guilty as an accessory to an attempt by another to commit an offence; and

(b) this subsection does not preclude a charge of attempt to incite (under section 47 or any other enactment), or of attempt to conspire (under section 48 or any other enactment), to commit an offence."

2. CONSPIRACY

D.P.P. v. *Nock* [1978] A.C. 977: "Lord Tucker [in *B.O.T.* v. *Owen* (*post*, p. 467)] by stressing the 'auxiliary' nature of the crime of conspiracy, and by explaining its justification as being to prevent the commission of substantive offence, has placed the crime firmly in the same class and category as attempts to commit a crime. Both are criminal because they are steps towards the commission of a substantive offence. The distinction between the two is that whereas a 'proximate' act is that which constitutes the crime of attempt, agreement is the necessary ingredient in conspiracy. The importance of the distinction is that agreement may, and usually will, occur well before the first step which can be said to be an attempt. The law of conspiracy thus makes possible an earlier intervention by the law to prevent the commission of the substantive offence."; *per* Lord Scarman.

Note

Conspiracy was a common law offence, consisting of "the agreement of two or more to do an unlawful act, or to do a lawful act by unlawful means": *per* Willes J. in *Mulcahy* v. *R.* (1868) L.R. 3 H.L. 306. "Unlawful" in this context covered all crimes, even summary offences, some torts, fraud, the corruption of public morals and the outraging of public decency. The aim of the Law Commission (Law Com. No. 76, § 1.111) is to confine conspiracy to agreements to commit crimes. This aim is partially achieved by sections 1 and 5 of the Criminal Law Act 1977 (see *infra*). However, pending a comprehensive review of offences of fraud and of the law relating to obscenity and indecency, conspiracies to defraud, and to corrupt public morals or outrage public decency, are preserved.

i. Statutory Conspiracies

Criminal Law Act 1977, section 1

"Section 1: *The offence of conspiracy* (1) Subject to the following provisions of this Part of this Act, if a person agrees with any other person or persons that a course of conduct shall be pursued which, if the agreement is carried out in accordance with their intentions, either—

(*a*)   will necessarily amount to or involve the commission of any offence or offences by one or more of the parties to the agreement, or

(*b*)   would do so but for the existence of facts which render the commission of the offence or any of the offences impossible,

he is guilty of conspiracy to commit the offence or offences in question. [Substituted by section 5(1) Criminal Attempts Act 1981].

(2) Where liability for any offence may be incurred without knowledge on the party of the person committing it of any particular fact or circumstance necessary for the commission of the offence, a person shall nevertheless not be guilty of conspiracy to commit that offence by virtue of subsection (1) above unless he and at least one other party to the agreement intend or know that that fact or circumstance shall or will exist at the time when the conduct constituting the offence is to take place.

(3) Where in pursuance of any agreement the acts in question in relation to any offence are to be done in contemplation or furtherance of a trade dispute (within the meaning of the Trade Union and Labour Relations Act 1974) that offence shall be disregarded for the purposes of subsection (1) above provided that it is a summary offence which is not punishable with imprisonment.

(4) In this Part of this Act 'offence' means an offence triable in England and Wales, except that it includes murder notwithstanding that the murder in question would not be so triable if committed in accordance with the intentions of the parties to the agreement."

(a) *Agreement*

Note

Since the forbidden "act" in conspiracy is agreement, and agreement is a mental process, it is more difficult than with most crimes to separate out *mens rea* and *actus reus*.

The agreement must be that a course of conduct will be pursued which, if the agreement is carried out in accordance with their intentions, will necessarily amount to or involve the commission of an offence by one or more parties to the agreement. (Questions of impossibility will be discussed later.) There is no requirement that any conspirator should take any steps towards carrying out the agreement.

Inherent in the kind of agreement required is that D must intend that the agreement be carried out and the projected crime committed by one or more of the conspirators; but the statutory definition does not require D to intend himself to play any part in carrying out the agreement. This was the position at common law, and the Law Commission (Law Com. 76, para. 1.38) drafted section 1(1) to ensure that that position should continue. However this intention was frustrated by the next case.

R. v. Anderson
[1986] A.C. 27
House of Lords

D and A, in custody in relation to entirely unconnected offences, spent one night in the same cell. D, who was expecting to be released soon, agreed with A to participate in a scheme to secure A's escape from prison. D was to meet A's brother and another man and supply diamond wire, which they would then smuggle in to A. D was also to do further acts to facilitate the escape. He was to be paid £20,000 for his assistance. He received £2,000 on account from A's brother, but was injured in a road accident before anything further happened. He did not supply the wire, and took no further part in the scheme. D admitted that he had intended to supply the wire on payment of another £10,000 on account, but said he would then have gone abroad and taken no further part in the plan, which he believed was doomed to failure. His submission that he lacked the mental element for conspiracy to effect an escape, in that he did not intend or expect the plan to be carried into effect, was rejected by the judge and by the Court of Appeal, which also held that, even if he was not a principal in conspiracy he could be convicted of aiding abetting counselling and procuring the conspiracy of the other two men (see 80 Cr.App.R. 64, 77). On appeal to the House of Lords on both of these questions:

LORD BRIDGE OF HARWICH: The Act of 1977, subject to exceptions not presently material, abolished the offence of conspiracy at common law. It follows that the elements of the new statutory offence of conspiracy must be ascertained purely by interpretation of the language of section 1(1) of the Act of 1977. For purposes of analysis it is perhaps convenient to isolate the three clauses each of which must be taken as indicating an essential ingredient of the offence as follows: (1) "if a person agrees with any other person or persons that a course of conduct shall be pursued" (2) "which will necessarily amount to or involve the commission of any offence or offences by one or more of the parties to the agreement" (3) "if the agreement is carried out in accordance with their intentions."

Clause (1) presents, as it seems to me, no difficulty. It means exactly what it says and what it says is crystal clear. To be convicted, the party charged must have agreed with one or more others that "a course of conduct shall be pursued." What is important is to resist the temptation to introduce into this simple concept ideas derived from the civil law of contract. Any number of persons may agree that a course of conduct shall be pursued without undertaking any contractual liability. The agreed course of conduct may be a simple or an elaborate one and may involve the participation of two or any larger number of persons who may have agreed to play a variety of roles in the course of conduct agreed.

Again, clause (2) could hardly use simpler language. Here what is important to note is that it is not necessary that more than one of the participants in the agreed course of conduct shall commit a substantive offence. It is, of course, necessary that any party to the agreement shall have assented to play his part in the agreed course of conduct, however innocent in itself, knowing that the part to be played by one or more of the others will amount to or involve the commission of an offence.

It is only clause (3) which presents any possible ambiguity. The heart of the submission for the appellant is that in order to be convicted of conspiracy to commit a given offence the language of clause (3) requires that the party charged should not only have agreed that a course of conduct shall be pursued which will necessarily amount to or involve the commission of that offence by himself or one or more other parties to the agreement, but must also be proved himself to have intended that that offence should be committed. Thus, it is submitted here that the appellant's case that he never intended that Andaloussi should be enabled to escape from prison raised an issue to be left to the jury, who should have been directed to convict him only if satisfied that he did so intend. I do not find it altogether easy to understand why the draftsman of this provision chose to use the phrase "in accordance with their intentions." But I suspect the answer may be that this seemed a desirable alternative to the phrase "in accordance with its terms" or any similar expression, because it is a matter of common experience in the criminal courts that the "terms" of a criminal conspiracy are hardly ever susceptible of proof. The evidence from which a jury may infer a criminal conspiracy is almost invariably to be found in the conduct of the parties. This was so at common law and remains so under the statute. If the evidence in a given case justifies the inference of an agreement that a course of conduct should be pursued, it is a not inappropriate formulation of the test of the criminality of the inferred agreement to ask whether the further inference can be drawn that a crime would necessarily have been committed if the agreed course of conduct had been pursued in accordance with the *several* intentions of the parties. Whether that is an accurate analysis or not, I am clearly driven by consideration of the diversity of roles which parties may agree to play in criminal conspiracies to reject any construction of the statutory language which would require the prosecution to prove an intention on the part of each conspirator that the criminal offence or offences which will necessarily be committed by one or more of the conspirators if the agreed course of conduct is fully carried out should in fact be committed. A simple example will illustrate the absurdity to which this construction would lead. The proprietor of a car hire firm agrees for a substantial payment to make available a hire car to a gang for use in a robbery and to make false entries in his books relating to the hiring to which he can point if the number of the car is traced back to him in connection with the robbery. Being fully aware of the circumstances of the robbery in which the car is proposed to be used he is plainly a party to the conspiracy to rob. Making his car available for use in the robbery is as much a part of the relevant agreed course of conduct as the robbery itself. Yet, once he has been paid, it will be a matter of complete indifference to him whether the robbery is in fact committed or not. In these days of highly organised crime the most serious statutory conspiracies will frequently involve an elaborate and complex agreed course of conduct in which many will consent to play necessary but subordinate roles, not involving them in any direct participation in the commission of the offence or offences at the centre of the conspiracy. Parliament cannot have intended that such parties should escape conviction of conspiracy on the basis that it cannot be proved against them that they intended that the relevant offence or offences should be committed.

There remains the important question whether a person who has agreed that a course of conduct will be pursued which, if pursued as agreed, will necessarily amount to or involve the commission of an offence is guilty of statutory conspiracy irrespective of his intention, and, if not, what is the *mens rea* of the offence. I have no hesitation in answering the first part of the question in the negative. There may be many situations in which perfectly respectable citizens, more particularly those concerned with law enforcement, may enter into agreements that a course of conduct shall be pursued which will involve commission of a crime without the least intention of playing any part in furtherance of the ostensibly agreed criminal objective, but rather with the purpose of exposing and frustrating the criminal purpose of the other parties to the agreement. To say this is in no way to encourage schemes by which police act, directly or through the agency of informers, as agents provocateurs for the purpose of entrapment. That is conduct of which the courts have always strongly disapproved. But it may sometimes happen, as most of us with experience in criminal trials well know, that a criminal enterprise is well advanced in the course of preparation when it comes to the notice either of the police or of some honest citizen in such circumstance that the only prospect of exposing and frustrating the criminal is that some innocent person should play the part of an intending collaborator in the course of criminal conduct proposed to be pursued. The *mens rea* implicit in the offence of statutory conspiracy must clearly be such as to recognise the innocence of such a person, notwithstanding that he will, in literal terms, be obliged to agree that a course of conduct be pursued involving the commission of an offence.

I have said already, but I repeat to emphasise its importance, that an essential ingredient in the crime of conspiring to commit a specific offence or offences under section 1(1) of the Act of 1977 is that the accused should agree that a course of conduct be pursued which he knows must involve the commission by one or more of the parties to the agreement of that offence or those offences. But, beyond the mere fact of agreement, the necessary *mens rea* of the crime is, in my opinion, established if, and only if, it is shown that the accused, when he entered into the agreement, intended to play some part in the agreed course of conduct in furtherance of the criminal purpose which the agreed course of conduct was intended to achieve. Nothing less will suffice; nothing more is required.

Applying this test to the facts which, for the purposes of the appeal, we must assume, the appellant, in agreeing that a course of conduct be pursued that would, if successful, necessarily involve the offence of effecting Andaloussi's escape from lawful custody, clearly intended, by providing diamond wire to be smuggled into the prison, to play a part in the agreed course of conduct in furtherance of that criminal objective. Neither the fact that he intended to play no further part in attempting to effect the escape, nor that he believed the escape to be impossible, would, if the jury had supposed they might be true, have afforded him any defence.

In the result, I would answer the first part of the certified question in the affirmative and dismiss the appeal. Your Lordships did not find it necessary to hear argument directed to the second part of the certified question and it must, therefore, be left unanswered.

Lords Scarman, Diplock, Keith and Brightman agreed.

Appeal dismissed

Notes

1. " ... An essential ingredient in the crime of conspiring to commit a specific offence ... is that the accused shall agree that a course of conduct be pursued which he knows must involve the commission by one or more parties to the agreement of that offence. ... But, beyond the mere fact of agreement, the necessary *mens rea* of the crime ... is established if, and only if, it is shown that the accused, when he entered into the agreement, intended to play some part in the agreed course of conduct in furtherance of the criminal purpose which the agreed course of conduct was intended to achieve. Nothing less will suffice, nothing more is required."

This dictum was considered and "explained" by the Court of Appeal in *R.* v. *Siracusa* (1989) 90 Cr.App.R. 340. There was a large and complicated agreement to import various prohibited drugs at various times. The parties were charged with conspiracy to contravene section 170(2)(b) Customs and Excise Management Act 1979, which prohibits the import of various classes of drugs with various penalties attached. In *R.* v *Shivpuri* [1987] A.C.1 (*post*, p. 485), the House of Lords held that for this offence the *mens rea* required was an intention to import any prohibited drug, not necessarily one of the class actually imported. In the course of dismissing the appeals in the present case, O'Connor L.J. said:

"[The dictum above quoted] must be read in the context of that case. We think it obvious that Lord Bridge cannot have been intending that the organiser of a crime who recruited others to carry it out would not himself be guilty of conspiracy unless it could be proved that he intended to play some active part himself thereafter. ... Participation in a conspiracy is infinitely variable; it can be active or passive. If the majority shareholder and director of a company consents to the company being used for drug smuggling carried out in the company's name by a fellow director and minority shareholder, he is guilty of conspiracy. Consent, that is the agreement or adherence to the agreement, can be inferred if it is proved that he knew what was going on and the intention to participate in the furtherance of the criminal purpose is also established by his failure to stop the unlawful activity.

... The *mens rea* sufficient to support the commission of a substantive offence will not necessarily be sufficient to support a charge of conspiracy to commit that offence. An intent to cause grievous bodily harm is sufficient to support a charge of murder, but it is not sufficient to support a charge of conspiracy to murder, or of attempt to murder. We have come to the conclusion that if the prosecution charge a conspiracy to contravene section 170(2) of the Customs and Excise Management Act by the importation of heroin, then the prosecution must prove that the agreed course of conduct was the importation of heroin. This is because the essence of the crime of conspiracy is the agreement and, in simple terms, you do not prove an agreement to import heroin by proving an agreement to import cannabis."

2. The defendant must know that what is projected is a crime, otherwise it cannot be said that he agreed to a course of conduct involving the commission of a crime. This is the position even if the *offence* can be committed without full knowledge of a fact or circumstance which makes the conduct criminal. Section 1(2) Criminal Law Act 1977, *ante*, p. 452, provides that in such a case, to be guilty of *conspiring* to commit the offence, D and at least one other party must intend or know that that fact or circumstance shall or will exist at the time when the conduct constituting the offence is to take place, Thus: it is an offence to use in a vehicle fuel on which the appropriate duty has not been paid; to convict D of this offence it is not necessary to show that he knew that the duty had not been paid. But if D is charged with conspiracy to use in a vehicle fuel on which duty has not been paid, it must be shown that he and at least one other party knew that the duty had not been paid. (Compare the similar rule in aiding and abetting, *ante*, p. 387.) It is the offence of rape to have intercourse with a non-consenting woman being reckless as to whether she is

consenting or not. D agrees with C to have intercourse with a woman, who in fact is non-consenting; D does not know this, but could not care less whether she will consent or not. To convict D of conspiracy to rape, it must be shown that both he *and* C knew she would not consent. (Compare *R.* v. *Khan* and the different rule on attempt, *ante*, p. 429.)

3. But, according to Lord Bridge in *Anderson*, it is not necessary that D should intend that the crime should be carried out; it is sufficient if he knows that another party to the agreement intends to commit it.

Question

The brother of A and B had been murdered, apparently on the orders of P, a dangerous criminal. A and B agreed to meet near P's house on June 14, when they knew that P would be away, and reconnoitre a place to ambush him; on June 16 they would return, lie in wait for P and kill him. At the time of the agreement, each privately thought that the enterprise was too dangerous, and resolved not to be present on the 16th. In order not to appear too fainthearted, each intended to be present on the 14th and assist in fixing a place of ambush, but each intended to arrange some pressing business to keep him away on the day of the attack, which each expected the other to carry out alone. Are they guilty of conspiracy to murder?

(b) *The scope of the agreement*

The defendant must have agreed "that a course of conduct will be pursued which will necessarily amount to or involve the commission of any offence or offences by one or more of the parties to the agreement if the agreement is carried out in accordance with their intentions," section 1(1) of the Criminal Law Act 1977, *ante* p. 451.

Notes

1. Conduct ... "which will necessarily amount to or involve" an offence.

Law Com. 76. Draft Bill, Clause 1. Explanatory Note 3

"Subsection 1 requires that the parties must agree on a course of conduct which if carried out will *necessarily* amount to an offence; so, for example, an agreement to beat up a nightwatchman will be a conspiracy to cause grievous bodily harm and not conspiracy to murder, notwithstanding that, if the agreement were carried out and the watchman died, there would be an offence of murder."

2. "if the agreement is carried out"
The agreement need not be to the effect that the course of conduct must necessarily be carried out; only to the effect that, if it is carried out, it will necessarily involve a crime. The fact that the

agreement will only be carried out if some condition precedent, *e.g.* it is safe, necessary, expedient, etc., is satisfied, is nothing to the point.

In *R.* v. *Jackson* [1985] Crim.L.R. 442. A and B agreed that if C, then on trial for burglary, was convicted they would do acts likely to pervert the course of justice. It was held that this was a conspiracy to pervert the course of justice. Planning was taking place for a contingency and if that contingency occurred the conspiracy would necessarily involve the commission of an offence. "Necessarily" is not to be held to mean that there must inevitably be the carrying out of the offence; it means, if the agreement is carried out in accordance with the plan, there must be the commission of the offence referred to in the conspiracy count.

In *R.* v. *Reed* [1982] Crim.L.R. 819, 820. Donaldson L.J. considered two examples: "In the first A and B agree to drive from London to Edinburgh in a time which can be achieved without exceeding the speed limits, but only if the traffic they encounter is exceptionally light. Their agreement will not necessarily involve the commission of any offence, even if it is carried out in accordance with their intentions, and they do arrive from London to Edinburgh within the agreed time. Accordingly the agreement does not constitute the offence of statutory conspiracy or indeed of any offence. In the second example, A and B agree to rob a bank, if when they arrive at the bank it seems safe to do so. Their agreement will necessarily involve the commission of the offence of robbery if it is carried out in accordance with their intentions. Accordingly they are guilty of the statutory offence of conspiracy."

Question

Can it be said that in the first example, A and B agreed to exceed the speed limit if it proved necessary in order to arrive at Edinburgh on time? If it can, what distinction is there between the two examples, or between the first example and the facts in *R.* v. *Reed*? Compare the "true object of the agreement" test said to be involved in cases of conspiracies with a foreign element in *Att.-Gen.'s Reference No. 1 of 1982, post,* p. 470.

(c) *Parties*

Notes

1. *At least two conspirators.* It takes two to agree, so if A is adjudged not to have agreed with B, it would appear to follow that B has not agreed with A. From this it was thought to be a rule that if A were acquitted of conspiracy with B, a conviction of B for conspiracy with A (if there were no other conspirators involved) could not possibly stand. This alleged rule was abolished by the House of Lords in *D.P.P.* v. *Shannon* [1975] A.C. 717, where the following passage from *R.* v. *Andrews-Weatherfoil Ltd.* [1972] 1 W.L.R. 118, 125 was approved.

"As long as it is possible for persons concerned in a single offence to be tried separately, it is inevitable that the verdicts returned by the two juries will on occasion appear to be inconsistent with one another. Such a result may be due to differences in the evidence presented at the two trials or simply to the different views which the juries separately take of the witnesses. ... When inconsistent verdicts are returned by the same jury, the position is usually more simple. If the inconsistency shows that the single jury was confused, or self contradictory, its conclusions are unsatisfactory or unsafe and neither verdict is reliable. Very often, however, an apparent inconsistency reflects no more than the jury's strict adherence to the judge's direction that they must consider each case separately and that evidence against one may not be admissible against the other: for example, where there is a signed confession. So too, where the verdicts are returned by different juries the inconsistency does not, of itself, indicate that the jury which returned the verdict was confused or misled or reached an incorrect conclusion on the evidence before it. The verdict 'not guilty' includes 'not proven'."

The decision in *D.P.P.* v. *Shannon* was confirmed by Criminal Law Act 1977:

Criminal Law Act 1977

"Section 5:(8) The fact that the person or persons who, so far as appears from the indictment on which any person has been convicted of conspiracy, were the only other parties to the agreement on which his conviction was based have been acquitted of conspiracy by reference to that agreement (whether after being tried with the person convicted or separately) shall not be a ground for quashing his conviction unless under all the circumstances of the case his conviction is inconsistent with the acquittal of the other person or persons in question.

(9) Any rule of law or practice inconsistent with the provisions of subsection (8) above is hereby abolished."

2. *Effect of exempt parties* If A is charged with conspiring with B to commit a crime, and it appears that B would incur no liability for the crime if it were consummated, two questions arise.

The first question is, does B's exemption in respect of the contemplated crime mean that he cannot be convicted of *conspiring* to commit the crime?

If B has some personal exemption which prevents him from being convicted as first principal of the contemplated crime, then, as seen (*ante*, p. 402) this does not always prevent him from being convicted as a secondary party to that crime. There is no reason why he should not be guilty of conspiracy to commit a crime to which he could be a secondary party. But if B could not be guilty either as a principal or as a secondary party, he ought not to be convicted of conspiring to commit the crime. The policy of the law which excluded B from liability as a party to the crime ought, to be consistent, to exclude him from liability for conspiracy to commit the crime. The Law Commission so recommended (see Law Com. No. 76, § 1.56), disapproving of the only authority in favour of liability: *R.* v. *Whitchurch* (1890) 24 Q.B.D. 420. However the provision giving effect to this recommendation was not adopted by Parliament, as was noted by the Court of Appeal in *R.* v. *Burns* (1984) 79 Cr.App.R. 173, 179. This was in the course of upholding the conviction of a father of a child conspiring with others to steal it from the mother, although by the terms of section 56 of the Offences Against the Person Act 1861 (*ante*, p. 372) he could not have been prosecuted for child-stealing.

"Accordingly one considers the question of conspiracy and exempt persons on such authority as exists in respect of this little used branch of the criminal law. There is a paucity of it. We find none that leads us to say that it is in any way wrong or unjust for a person who is exempt, in the sense that James Burns was, from prosecution for the substantive offence to be proceeded against for the crime of conspiracy. The dangers of permitting a father of children to collect a posse of men and suddenly to launch a seige of the home of his erstwhile wife, to break in and then snatch away sleeping children are surely self-evident. The criminal law does not in our view permit that sort of conduct. When a father who is exempt under section 56 behaves in that way, it is, in our judgment, not only lawful but right and just that the prosecution should be free to bring a charge of conspiracy against him."

On the question of when personal exemption from liability as a principal entails exemption from accessorial liability, see *ante*, p. 407.

The second question is, does B's exemption from liability for the crime contemplated mean that A is not guilty of conspiracy with him? If B's "exemption" is because he did not know that the crime was to be committed, then the whole agreement between A and B did not involve the commission of the crime, and it must follow that A has not agreed in the terms required by section 1. (See *ante*, p. 451). As to other exemptions, the Law Commission concluded that A should never be guilty of conspiracy with B if B had a personal exemption in respect of the agreed-on crime (§ 1.57). This also was not acted on, and the strictly limited answers to both questions are contained in section 2.

Criminal Law Act 1977, section 2

"Section 2—(1) A person shall not by virtue of section 1 above be guilty of conspiracy to commit any offence if he is an intended victim of that offence.

(2) A person shall not by virtue of section 1 above be guilty of conspiracy to commit any offence or offences if the only other person or persons with whom he agrees are (both initially and at all times during the currency of the agreement) persons of any one or more of the following descriptions, that is to say—

(*a*)   his spouse;
(*b*)   a person under the age of criminal responsibility; and
(*c*)   an intended victim of that offence or of each of those offences."

Note

Code Proposals: (1) On the question of B's personal exemption in respect of the contemplated crime protecting him from conviction of *conspiracy* to commit it, the draft Code continues the principle expressed in section 2(1), but instead of "intended victim," (which was thought to be too wide), substitutes the notion of "protected person," *i.e.* one who is not only an intended victim, but also belongs to a class of persons which the enactment of the crime was intended to protect.

(2) On the question of A's liability when his "co-conspirator" B is his spouse or a child under the age of criminal responsibility or the intended victim, the Law Commission has changed its mind: see Commentary on Code, paras. 13.28–13.32). It now disapproves of the rule that spouses cannot conspire with each other, and as to children under age and intended victims, A is to be liable for conspiracy with them just as though they were "normal" persons: see Clause 48(8), *infra*.

Questions

Which of the following persons (a) are under the Criminal Law Act 1977, and (b) would be under the Draft Criminal Code if it were enacted, guilty of conspiracy?

1. A, a foreman, agrees with B, an operative, that B will operate a dangerous machine in a factory without a guard as required by regulations. This is an offence under the regulations. B is injured as a result.

2. C persuades D, a child of 9 years of age, to walk out of a shop with goods for which C has not paid and does not intend to pay. Does it make any difference whether D knows or does not know that he is doing anything wrong?

Draft Criminal Code, Clause 48

"(1) A person is guilty of conspiracy to commit an offence or offences if—

(a) he agrees with another or others that an act or acts shall be done which, if done, will involve the commission of the offence or offences by one or more of the parties to the agreement; and
(b) he and at least one other party to the agreement intend that the offence or offences shall be committed.

(2) For the purposes of subsection (1) an intention that an offence shall be committed is an intention with respect to all the elements of the offence (other than fault elements), except that recklessness with respect to a circumstance suffices where it suffices for the offence itself.

(3) Subject to section 52, 'offence' in this section means any offence triable in England and Wales; and

(a) it extends to an offence of murder which would not be so triable; but
(b) it does not include a summary offence, not punishable with imprisonment, constituted by an act or acts agreed to be done in contemplation of a trade dispute.

(4) Where the purpose of an enactment creating an offence is the protection of a class of persons, no member of that class who is the intended victim of such an offence can be guilty of conspiracy to commit that offence.

(5) A conspiracy continues until the agreed act or acts is or are done, or until all or all save one of the parties to the agreement have abandoned the intention that such act or acts shall be done.

(6) A person may become a party to a continuing conspiracy by joining the agreement constituting the offence.

(7) It is not offence under this section, or under any enactment referred to in section 51, to agree to procure, assist or encourage as an accessory the commission of an offence by a person who is not a party to such an agreement; but—

- (a) a person may be guilty as an accessory to a conspiracy by others; and
- (b) this subsection does not preclude a charge of conspiracy to incite (under section 47 or any other enactment) to commit an offence.

(8) A person may be convicted of conspiracy to commit an offence although—

- (a) no other person has been or is charged with such conspiracy;
- (b) the identity of any other party to the agreement is unknown;
- (c) any other party appearing from the indictment to have been a party to the agreement has been or is acquitted of such conspiracy, unless in all the circumstances his conviction is inconsistent with the acquittal of the other; or
- (d) the only other party to the agreement cannot be convicted of such conspiracy (for example, because he was acting under duress by threats (section 42), or he was a child under ten years of age (section 32(1)) or he is immune from prosecution)."

ii. Common Law Conspiracies

Criminal Law Act 1977

"Section 5: *Abolitions, savings, transitional provisions, consequential amendments and repeals.* (1) Subject to the following provisions of this section, the offence of conspiracy at common law is hereby abolished.

(2) Subsection (1) above shall not affect the offence of conspiracy at common law so far as relates to conspiracy to defraud. [As amended by Criminal Justice Act 1987, section 12, below].

(3) Subsection (1) above shall not affect the offence of conspiracy at common law if and in so far as it may be committed by entering into an agreement to engage in conduct which—

- (a) tends to corrupt public morals or outrages public decency, but
- (b) would not amount to or involve the commission of an offence if carried out by a single person otherwise than in pursuance of an agreement.

(7) Incitement to commit the offence of conspiracy (whether the conspiracy incited would be the offence at common law or under section 1 above or any other enactment) shall cease to be offences. [As amended by Criminal Attempts Act 1981, section 10.]"

Criminal Justice Act 1987

"Section 12: *Charges of and penalty for conspiracy to defraud.* (1) If—

- (a) a person agrees with any other person or persons that a course of conduct shall be pursued; and

(b) that course of conduct will necessarily amount to or involve the commission of any offence or offences by one or more of the parties to the agreement if the agreement is carried out in accordance with their intentions,

the fact that it will do so shall not preclude a charge of conspiracy to defraud being brought against any of them in respect of the agreement.

(2) In section 5(2) of the Criminal Law Act 1977, the words from 'and' to the end are hereby repealed.

(3) A person guilty of conspiracy to defraud is liable on conviction on indictment to imprisonment for a term not exceeding 10 years or a fine or both."

(a) *Conspiracy to defraud*

Scott v. Metropolitan Police Commissioner
[1975] A.C. 819
House of Lords

S. agreed with employees of cinema owners temporarily to abstract, without permission of the owners, films, without the knowledge or consent of the copyright owners, for the purpose of making infringing copies and distributing them on a commercial basis. He was convicted of conspiracy to defraud the copyright owners, and appealed.

VISCOUNT DILHORNE: The Court of Appeal certified that a point of law of general public importance was involved in the decision to dismiss the appeal against conviction on count one, namely,

"Whether on a charge of conspiracy to defraud, the Crown must establish an agreement to deprive the owners of their property by deception; or whether it is sufficient to prove an agreement to prejudice the rights of another or others without lawful justification and in circumstances of dishonesty."

Before the House Mr. Blom-Cooper put forward three contentions, his main one being that which he advanced unsuccessfully before the Court of Appeal and Judge Hines that there could not be a conspiracy to defraud without deceit. ...

Mr. Blom-Cooper's main submission was based on the well known dicta of Buckley J. in *In re London and Globe Finance Corporation Ltd.* [1903] 1 Ch. 728, 732:

"To deceive is, I apprehend, to induce a man to believe that a thing is true which is false, and which the person practising the deceit knows or believes to be false. To defraud is to deprive by deceit: it is by deceit to induce a man to act to his injury. More tersely it may be put, that to deceive is by falsehood to induce a state of mind; to defraud is by deceit to induce a course of action."

Mr. Blom-Cooper, while not submitting that an intent to defraud necessarily includes an intention to deceive, nevertheless submitted that a man could not be defrauded unless he was deceived. Buckley J.'s definition was, he said, exhaustive and as the conspiracy charged in count one did not involve any deceit of the companies and persons who owned the copyright and the distribution rights of the films which had been copied, the conviction on that count could not, he submitted, stand.

In a great many and it may be the vast majority of fraud cases the fraud has been perpetrated by deceit and in many cases Buckley J.'s dicta have been quoted in charges to juries. It does not, however, follow that it is an exhaustive definition of what is meant by "defraud." Buckley J. had to decide when a prima facie case had been shown "of doing some or one of the acts" mentioned in sections 83 and 84 of the Larceny Act 1861 "with intent to deceive or defraud." He did not have to make or to have to attempt to make an exhaustive definition of what was meant by "defraud."

Stephen, History of the Criminal Law of England (1883), vol. 2, contains the following passage, at p. 121:

> "Fraud—There has always been a great reluctance amongst lawyers to attempt to define fraud, and this is not unnatural when we consider the number of different kinds of conduct to which the word is applied in connection with different branches of it. I shall not attempt to construct a definition which will meet every case which might be suggested, but there is little danger in saying that whenever the words 'fraud' or 'intent to defraud' or 'fraudulently' occur in the definition of a crime two elements at least are essential to the commission of the crime: namely, first, deceit or an intention to deceive or in some cases mere secrecy; and, secondly, either actual injury or possible injury or an intent to expose some person either to actual injury or to a risk of possible injury by means of that deceit or secrecy."

Stephen thus recognises that a fraud may be perpetrated without deceit by secrecy and that an intend to defraud need not necessarily involve an intent to deceive. In vol. 3 of his *History* at p. 121 he says that:

> "Offences relating to property fall into two principal classes, namely, fraudulent offences which consist in its misappropriation, and mischievous offences which consist in its destruction or injury. Theft is the typical fraudulent offence, ... "

The definition of the common law offence of simple larceny had as one of its elements the fraudulent taking and carrying away (see *Hawkins' Pleas of the Crown*, 6th ed. (1777), Book I, p. 134; *East's Pleas of the Crown*, vol. II (1803), pl. 553). "Fraudulently" is used in the definition of larceny by a bailee in section 3 of the Larceny Act 1861 (24 & 25 Vict. c. 96) and in the definition of larceny in section 3 of the Larceny Act 1916. Theft always involves dishonesty. Deceit is not an ingredient of theft. These citations suffice to show that conduct to be fraudulent need not be deceitful.

The Criminal Law Revision Committee in their Eighth Report on "Theft and Related Offences" (1966)(Cmnd. 2977) in paragraph 33 expressed the view that the important element of larceny, embezzlement and fraudulent conversion was "undoubtedly the dishonest appropriation of another person's property"; in paragraph 35 that the words "dishonestly appropriates" meant the same as "fraudulently converts to his own use or benefit, or the use or benefit of any other person," and in paragraph 39 that "dishonestly" seemed to them a better word than "fraudulently."

Parliament endorsed these views in the Theft Act 1968, which by section 1(1) defined theft as the dishonest appropriation of property belonging to another with the intention of permanently depriving the other of it. Section 17 of that Act replaces section 82 and 83 of the Larceny Act 1861 and the Falsification of Accounts Act 1875. The offences created by those sections and by that Act made it necessary to prove that there had been an "intent to defraud." Section 17 of the Theft Act 1968 substitutes the words "dishonestly with a view to gain for himself or another or with intent to cause loss to another" for the words "intent to defraud."

If "fraudulently" in relation to larceny meant "dishonestly" and "intent to defraud" in relation to falsification of accounts is equivalent to the words now contained in section 17 of the Theft Act 1968 which I have quoted, it would indeed be odd if "defraud" in the phrase "conspiracy to defraud" has a different meaning and means only a conspiracy which is to be carried out by deceit.

In the course of the argument many cases were cited. It is not necessary to refer to all of them. Many were cases in which the conspiracy alleged was to defraud by deceit. Those cases do not establish that there can only be a conspiracy to defraud if deceit is involved and there are a number of cases where that was not the case.

[After citing various cases] Indeed, in none of these cases was it suggested that the conviction was bad on the ground that the conspiracy to defraud did not involve deceit of the person intended to be defrauded. If that had been a valid ground for quashing the conviction it is, I think, inconceivable that the point would not have been taken, if not by counsel, by the court. . . .

In the course of delivering the judgment of the Court of Appeal in R. v. *Sinclair* [1968] 1 W.L.R. 1246, where the defendants had been convicted of conspiracy to cheat and defraud a company, its shareholders and creditors by fraudulently using its assets for purposes other than those of the company and by fraudulently concealing such use, James J. said at p. 1250:

"To cheat and defraud is to act with deliberate dishonesty to the prejudice of another person's proprietary right."

Again, one finds in this case no support for the view that in order to defraud a person that person must be deceived.

One must not confuse the object of a conspiracy with the means by which it is intended to be carried out. In the light of the cases to which I have referred, I have come to the conclusion that Mr. Blom-Cooper's main contention must be rejected. I have not the temerity to attempt an exhaustive definition of the meaning of "defraud." As I have said, words take colour from the context in which they are used, but the words "fraudulently" and "defraud" must ordinarily have a very similar meaning. If as I think, and as the Criminal Law Revision Committee appears to have thought, "fraudulently" means "dishonestly," then "to defraud" ordinarily means, in my opinion, to deprive a person dishonestly of something which is his or of something to which he is or would or might but for the perpetration of the fraud be entitled. . . .

In this case the accused bribed servants of the cinema owners to secure possession of films in order to copy them and in order to enable them to let the copies out on hire. By so doing Mr. Blom-Cooper conceded they inflicted more than nominal damage to the goodwill of the owners of the copyright and distribution rights of the films. By so doing they secured for themselves profits which but for their actions might have been secured by those owners just as in R. v. *Button* (1848) 3 Cox C.C. 229, the defendants obtained profits which might have been secured by their employer. In the circumstances it is, I think, clear that they inflicted pecuniary loss on those owners.

Reverting to the questions certified by the Court of Appeal, the answer to the first question is in my opinion in the negative. I am not very happy about the way in which the second question is phrased although the word "prejudice" has been not infrequently used in this connection. If by "prejudice" is meant "injure," then I think that an agreement by two or more by dishonesty to deprive a person of something which is his or to which he is or would be or might be entitled and an agreement by two or more by dishonesty to injure some proprietory right of his, suffices to constitute the offence of conspiracy to defraud.

In my opinion this appeal should be dismissed.

Appeal dismissed

Notes

1. Just as deceit is not necessary for a conspiracy to defraud, neither is an intent (in the sense of purpose) that the victim shall suffer injury in some proprietory right. In *Wai Yu-Tsang* v. *R.* [1991] 4 All E.R. 664, the following direction by a trial judge was approved by the Privy Council, when upholding a conviction of conspiracy to defraud:

> "It is fraud if it is proved that there was the dishonest taking of a risk which there was no right to take, which – to [D's] knowledge at least – would cause detriment or prejudice to another, detriment or prejudice to the economic or proprietary rights of another. That detriment or prejudice to somebody else is very often incidental to the purpose of the fraudsman himself. The prime object of the fraudsmen is usually to gain some economic advantage for themselves, any detriment or prejudice to somebody else is often secondary to that objective, but nonetheless is a contemplated or predictable outcome of what they do. If the interests of some other person – the economic or proprietary interests of some other person are imperilled, that is sufficient to constitute fraud even though no loss is actually suffered and even though the fraudsman himself did not desire to bring about any loss."

2. In *R.* v. *Ayres* [1984] A.C. 447, 455, Lord Bridge, dealing with section 5 as it existed before amendment by section 12 of the Criminal Justice Act 1987 said "According to the true construction of the Act, an offence which amounts to a common law conspiracy to defraud must be charged as such and not as a statutory conspiracy under section 1. Conversely a section 1 conspiracy cannot be charged as a common law conspiracy to defraud." The extreme width of conspiracy to defraud as defined in *Scott* v. *M.P.C.* covering agreements to commit crimes, *e.g.* theft or obtaining by deception, meant that these agreements must be charged as conspiracies to defraud, and not as conspiracies to steal, or obtain by deception. It was therefore held that the effect of section 5 was to cut down conspiracy to defraud to agreements which, if carried into effect, would *not* necessarily involve the commission of any substantive criminal offence by any of the conspirators: *R.* v. *Ayres*, at p. 459. The effect of section 12 of the Criminal Justice Act 1987, *ante*, p. 462, is to restore the offence of conspiracy to defraud to what it was held to be in *Scott* v. *M.P.C.* An agreement, *e.g.* to steal, is therefore both a statutory and a common law conspiracy and may be charged as either.

3. The problem remains as to whether conspiracy to defraud could be abolished without leaving unacceptable gaps in the law.

The Law Commission, returning to the matter in 1987, reached a provisional view that it could be, but that there would be lost significant procedural and practical advantages of being able to charge the offence, particularly in large scale fraud cases: W.P. 104.

4. An agreement to deceive a public official into breaching his duty is a conspriacy to defraud: *D.P.P.* v. *Withers* [1975] A.C. 842.

(b) *Conspiracies to corrupt public morals or outrage public decency*

Note

Agreements to do these things are certainly criminal conspiracies. They were common law conspiracies before the 1977 Act: see *Knuller* v. *D.P.P.* [1973] A.C. 435. According to section 5(3), *ante,* p. 462, an agreement to do either of them is still a common law conspiracy if and insofar as corrupting public morals or outraging public decency is a crime in its own right (*i.e.* a crime if done by one person without any agreement with someone else). They probably are offences in their own right, and thus agreements to commit them are statutory conspiracies to commit those crimes. But it is thought to be open to the House of Lords to hold that they do not exist as offences, in which case agreements to do them would remain as common law conspiracies.

iii. Jurisdiction

Note

Conspiracies are nowadays often international in character. Since "all crime is local" and "The jurisdiction over the crime belongs to the country where the crime is committed ... ": *per* Lord Haldane L.C. in *MacLeod* v. *Att.-Gen. for New South Wales* [1891] A.C. 455, 458, and since the essence of conspiracy is the agreement, it might be thought that the only question on jurisdiction is whether the agreement was made in this country. However this is not so. For the purposes of discussion, "international" conspiracies may be divided into two classes: (a) Agreement here to do acts abroad and (b) Agreement abroad to do acts here.

(a) *Agreement here to do acts abroad*

Board of Trade v. Owen
[1957] A.C. 602
House of Lords

O and others conspired in England to produce false documents in Germany in order to obtain from the Government of the Federal Republic licences to export goods from Germany. Their convictions of conspiracy were quashed by the Court of Criminal Appeal, and the Crown appealed to the House of Lords

LORD TUCKER: ... The question then remains whether the fact that the evidence disclosed a conspiracy here to make false representations in Germany and obtain a licence there renders the conspiracy one which cannot be made the subject of a criminal prosecution, and if the answer is that it is not indictable here, is that because it was not a conspiracy to commit a crime, or are all conspiracies to do acts abroad, whether criminal or only unlawful, outside the purview of the criminal courts of this country?

If such conspiracies are punishable in the criminal courts of England, it is, in any case, remarkable that in the long history of the English criminal law no case has been found in which anyone has ever been convicted of such an offence. ...

It is the law on this subject which your Lordships are now asked to expound in relation to agreements to commit crimes or other unlawful acts out of the jurisdiction in a country where criminal conspiracy is according to the evidence given at the trial, unknown to its own law. The gist of the offence being the agreement, whether or not the object is attained, it may be asked why should it not be indictable if the object is situate abroad. I think the answer to this is that it is necessary to recognize the offence to aid in the preservation of the Queen's peace and the maintenance of law and order within the realm with which, generally speaking, the criminal law is alone concerned. ...

[After quoting from Holdsworth, *History of English Law*, Vol. V, p. 203]. Accepting the above as the historical basis of the crime of conspiracy, it seems to me that the whole object of making such agreements punishable is to prevent the commission of the substantive offence before it has even reached the stage of an attempt, and that it is all part and parcel of the preservation of the Queen's peace within the realm. I cannot, therefore, accept the view that the locality of the acts to be done and of the object to be attained are matters irrelevant to the criminality of the agreement.

Returning to the present case, the trial judge, in his summing up, directed the jury as follows: 'You have in particular to accept it from me, and this is what the argument was all about during one of the occasions when you were out, that if two people conspire in this country to do something unlawful by the law of this country, for example, commit a fraud, or utter forged documents, then it is an offence even if they agree to commit their fraud or their uttering of forged documents abroad." After verdict and sentence and in granting a certificate of appeal, Donovan J. explained in detail his reasons for giving this direction. He said: "I regard it as unlawful in English law to defraud a foreign subject in such a way that the foreign subject could sue the tortfeasor in this country—which I think Z.A.K. could have done, and could still do in the present case." I think, however, his decision was really based on broader grounds, as shown by the passage which immediately follows: "Then remembering that it is the agreement which constitutes the crime, whether the unlawful object is effected or not, I cannot on principle see how the conspiracy constituted by such an agreement becomes untriable here simply because the crime or tort has been committed abroad. Logic does not compel such a conclusion. Considerations of the public weal do not compel it either. It would be of no benefit to this country if it became the sanctuary for conspirators, provided only that they concluded their unlawful plots abroad. Anomalies there may be, of course, but they exist whatever the true conclusion." In the above passage I have no doubt that the learned judge in using the words "simply because the crime or tort has been committed abroad" meant "simply because the crime or tort is to be committed abroad."

These observations have great force and it was on this foundation that the Attorney-General based his case before your Lordships. The Court of Criminal Appeal, after considering the authorities and pointing out that by statute certain acts are crimes punishable in England wherever committed, *e.g.,* murder, bigamy, offences against the Foreign Enlistment Act, the Official Secrets Act and the Merchant Shipping Act, proceeded: "In our opinion the true rule is that a conspiracy to commit a crime abroad is not indictable in this country unless the contemplated crime is one for which an indictment would lie here. That does not mean that there must always be found a statutory provision declaring that the crime is punishable here because if persons do acts abroad for the purpose of defrauding someone in this country, they are indictable here and accordingly a conspiracy to do such an act would be indictable. For instance, if two persons agreed here to stage a sham burglary abroad in order to collect insurances from English underwriters the conspiracy would be indictable here though the overt act was to be done abroad, because if the plot was carried out the obtaining or attempting to obtain the insurance money would be clearly indictable. In the present case the plot, though formed here, was carried out in Germany and assuming, as we have, that Z.A.K. were defrauded and not only deceived, the persons defrauded were Germans in Germany. In our opinion no offence was committed in Germany for which the appellants could have been indicted in England and consequently in our opinion the conspiracy is not indictable." . . .

The Attorney-General based his case principally on the contention that, the essence of the crime being the agreement, it is immaterial where it is intended to be carried out or on whom the crime or fraud is to be perpetrated. It is, he said, unnecessary to allege in the count the locality of the scene of the designed operations, while it is necessary to state the locality of the agreement to give jurisdiction to the court of trial. But, alternatively, while saying he was not concerned to show in what particular category of conspiracy the present case came, he submitted that, being a conspiracy to defraud, it came within the class of conspiracies to do acts which are mala in se and, as such, clearly criminal in their nature, irrespective of locality. He contended that acts which were criminal at common law, such as murder and theft, although subsequently made statutory offences, were to be regarded as crimes, even if, for procedural or other reasons, they were not punishable here. And in this category he sought to include "frauds." . . .

My Lords, this argument is an attractive one and it accords to some extent with the views expressed by Wright J. in the passages already cited from his Law of Criminal Conspiracies and Agreements, where he refers more than once to acts which "ought to be" regarded as "crimes" although they may not in fact be punishable and suggests this as the test for determining whether a particular conspiracy should be regarded as criminal. But it is significant that he also considered the task of classifying the acts which would determine the criminality of conspiracy was one for the legislature.

Ideas as to what acts are mala in se vary widely in different periods of time and in different parts of the civilized world. This classification is none the less one which may still be of assistance in certain spheres of the law, but the criminal law requires the maximum degree of definition and so uncertain a test as this seems to me ill-suited for the determination of the limits of criminality in the field of conspiracy. . . .

My Lords, I share the views of R. S. Wright J. and Stephen J. that the task of determining what conspiracies, if any, in this already indeterminate field are to be triable and punishable in this country when the acts planned would not themselves have been indictable here if carried out abroad is not one which is suitable for your Lordships sitting in your judicial capacity. In this connexion I would make further reference to Sir William Holdsworth. At p. 277 of volume III he wrote: "Moreover, at all periods of our history it has been far more difficult to extend the criminal law by a process of judicial decision than any other branch of the law. There has always been a wholesome dread of enlarging its boundaries by anything short of an Act of the legislature." No one has ever been convicted of such a conspiracy, and if it is in the public interest that such conspiracies should be triable and punishable here, it is, I think, for the legislature so to determine. The comity of nations can hardly require the acceptance of the Crown's contentions in the present case, having regard to the non-recognition of conspiracy as a crime in Germany. Moreover, in the field of criminal law the comity of nations can best be served by treaties of extradition.

I have reached the conclusion that the decision of the Court of Criminal Appeal that a conspiracy to commit a crime abroad is not indictable in this country unless the contemplated crime is one for which an indictment would lie here is correct, and from what I have already said it necessarily follows that a conspiracy of the nature of that charged in count 3 as proved in evidence—which, in my view, was a conspiracy to attain a lawful object by unlawful means, rather than to commit a crime—is not triable in this country, since the unlawful means and the ultimate object were both outside the jurisdiction. In so deciding I would, however, reserve for future consideration the question whether a conspiracy in this country which is wholly to be carried out abroad may not be indictable here on proof that its performance would produce a public mischief in this country or injury a person here by causing him damage abroad.

My Lords, for these reasons I would dismiss this appeal.

Appeal dismissed

Notes

1. As to statutory conspiracies, section 1(4) Criminal Law Act 1977, *ante*, p. 452, follows the law laid down in this case.

2. The point reserved by Lord Tucker in the last paragraph of his speech was considered by *Att.-Gen's Reference (No. 1 of 1982)* [1983] Q.B. 751 (C.A.), where it was held that unintended side-effects of performance abroad on the economic interests of a resident here did not make a conspiracy indictable here if it would not otherwise be indictable.

(b) *Agreement abroad to do acts here*

The Criminal Law Act 1977 makes no specific reference to this, but see next case.

R. v. Sansom
(1990) 92 Cr.App.R. 115
Court of Appeal

S and others were convicted of conspiracy to evade the prohibition on the import of cannabis. The appeal was dealt with on the footing that they had agreed while abroad to import into Belgium from Morocco half a ton of cannabis resin. The consignment was to be shipped from

Morocco in the vessel Lady Rose and trans-shipped in international waters from the Lady Rose into the fishing boat Danny Boy, on which it would be taken into Belgium. One of the conspirators chartered the Danny Boy in England and sailed it out to meet the Lady Rose. It was contended that on these facts the Court had no jurisdiction to try the appellants for conspiracy.

TAYLOR L.J.: ... A submission was made to the learned judge, and has been repeated on appeal, on behalf of Sansom and Williams that the court had no jurisdiction to try the count of conspiracy. The agreement was alleged to have been made abroad and it was contended that to constitute a triable offence in England there would have to be proven some unlawful act in England in pursuance of the conspiracy. If, as the defence alleged, the Danny Boy was arrested outside territorial waters, no such unlawful act could be proved. The learned judge rejected the submission, basing his decision on *D.P.P.* v. *Doot* [1973] A.C.807. In that case the House of Lords held that a conspiracy entered into abroad could be prosecuted in England if the parties acted in England in concert and in pursuance of the agreement. Viscount Dilhorne, at p. 825C said:

"Proof of acts done by the accused in this country may suffice to prove that there was at the time of those acts a conspiracy in existence in this country to which they were parties and, if that is proved, then the charge of conspiracy is within the jurisdiction of the English courts, even though the initial agreement was made outside the jurisdiction."

Lord Pearson said, p. 827E:

"On principle, apart from authority, I think (and it would seem the Court of Appeal also thought) that a conspiracy to commit in England an offence against English law ought to be triable in England if it has been wholly or partly performed in England. In such a case the conspiracy has been carried on in England with the consent and authority of all the conspirators. It is not necessary that they should all be present in England. One of them, acting on his own behalf and as agent for the others, has been performing their agreement, with their consent and authority, in England. In such a case the conspiracy has been committed by all of them in England."

Lord Salmon said, at p. 833F:

"Suppose a case in which evidence existed of a conspiracy hatched abroad by ... drug pedlars to smuggle large quantities of dangerous drugs on to some stretch of the English coast. Suppose the conspirators came to England for the purpose of carrying out the crime and were detected by the police reconnoitring the place where they proposed to commit it, but doing nothing which by itself would be illegal, it would surely be absurd if the police could not arrest them then and there but had to take the risk of waiting and hoping to be able to catch them as they were actually committing or attempting to commit the crime. Yet that is precisely what the police would have to do if a conspiracy entered into abroad to commit a crime here were not in the circumstances postulated recognised by our law as a criminal offence which our courts had any jurisdiction to try."

At p. 835B–C Lord Salmon went further. There he said:

"It is, unfortunately, by no means unlikely that cases may arise in the future in which there will be conclusive evidence of persons having conspired abroad to commit serious crimes in England and then having done acts here in furtherance of the conspiracy and in preparation for the commission of those crimes yet none of these acts will in itself be unlawful. Although such a case would be very different from the present, if the reasoning upon which I have based this opinion is sound it follows that such persons could properly be arrested and tried for conspiracy in our courts."

That view was supported by the learned authors of *Smith and Hogan on Criminal Law*, 6th ed. (1988), p. 269. They say:

"Whether such a conspiracy is indictable if the parties take no steps in England to implement it has not been decided. It is submitted that the better view is that any of the parties entering the jurisdiction during the continuance of the agreement should be indictable at common law."

In *Somchai Liangsiriprasert* v. *The Government of the United States of America and Another* [1990] 3 W.L.R. 606, the Privy Council on July 2, 1990 upheld that view. The case concerned a conspiracy to import heroin to the United States from Thailand, the proceeds to be collected in Hong Kong. Lord Griffiths, giving the advice of the Board, stated that in general English criminal law is local in its effect and does not concern itself with crimes abroad. There are exceptions. At p. 614, *post*, he said:

"There has as yet however been no decision in which it has been held that a conspiracy entered into abroad to commit a crime in England is a common law crime triable in English courts in the absence of any overt act pursuant to the conspiracy taking place in England. There are however a number of *dicta* in judgments and academic commentaries suggesting that it should be so."

Lord Griffiths then reviewed the authorities and, at p. 620, he continued:

"But why should an overt act be necessary to found jurisdiction? In the case of conspiracy in England the crime is complete once the agreement is made and no further overt act needs be proved as an ingredient of the crime. The only purpose of looking for an overt act in England in the case of a conspiracy entered into abroad can be to establish the link between the conspiracy and England or possibly to show the conspiracy is continuing. But if this can be established by other evidence, for example the taping of conversations between the conspirators showing a firm agreement to commit the crime at some future date, it defeats the preventative purpose of the crime of conspiracy to have to wait until some overt act is performed in pursuance of the conspiracy.

Unfortunately in this century crime has ceased to be largely local in origin and effect. Crime is now established on an international scale and the common law must face this new reality. Their Lordships can find nothing in precedent, comity or good sense that should inhibit the common law from regarding as justiciable in England inchoate crimes committed abroad which are intended to result in the commission of criminal offences in England. Accordingly a conspiracy entered into in Thailand with the intention of committing the criminal offence of trafficking in drugs in Hong Kong is justiciable in Hong Kong even if no overt act pursuant to the conspiracy has yet occurred in Hong Kong."

Although not binding on this Court, the decision of the Privy Council has of course very strong persuasive force especially when coupled with the earlier *dicta* in *D.P.P.* v. *Doot*. It was argued that *Somchai* referred only to the common law. The present conspiracy was charged as contrary to the Criminal Law Act 1977 which does not in terms deal with extra-territorial conspiracies. We reject that argument for three reasons. First, it cannot have been the intention of Parliament in enacting the 1977 Act to alter the common law rules as to extra-territorial conspiracies without specific words. Secondly, since conspiracies to defraud are not within the scope of the 1977 Act, the appellants' argument would produce the absurdity that the *Somchai* principle would apply to them but not to other conspiracies. Finally, we consider that the Privy Council, knowing that most conspiracies in English law are now covered by the 1977 Act, would specifically have indicated that the important principle they were enunciating in regard to conspiracy only applied to the restricted categories of common law conspiracy now surviving, had that been intended. In our judgment the principle propounded in *Somchai* by Lord Griffiths should now be regarded as the law of England on this point. In the present case there was clear evidence that one of the alleged conspirators, Wilkins, had acted in England in pursuance of the alleged conspiracy which was still subsisting by commissioning the Danny Boy and sailing in her to collect the cannabis from the Lady Rose. Accordingly, the trial judge (dealing with the point before the decision in *Somchai*) reached the correct conclusion in accordance with that decision, but was in any event right even had the law been restricted to the statements in *D.P.P.* v. *Doot* (*supra*). This ground of appeal therefore fails.

Sansom's Appeal allowed on other grounds

Note

The Law Commission (in Law Com. 180 (1989) Jurisdiction over Offences of Fraud and Dishonesty with a Foreign Element) propose to make listed offences (*i.e.* most offences under Theft Acts 1968 and 1978 and Forgery & Counterfeiting Act 1981) triable here if any part of the offence took place in England or Wales (Cl. 2, Draft Bill). Moreover, every party to a conspiracy (i) to commit a listed offence which would be triable here, or (ii) to defraud in England or Wales, should be triable here, wherever the conspiracy is formed and whether or not anything is done in England or Wales to further the conspiracy (Cl. 3b). Every party to (i) a conspiracy to perform abroad what, if performed in England or Wales, would constitute a listed offence or (ii) a conspiracy to defraud outside England or Wales should be triable here if at least one conspirator (through his own or his agent's acts) became a party to it in England or Wales, or if he (or his agent) did anything here in relation to the formation of the conspiracy or in pursuance of it (Cl. 5).

3. INCITEMENT

Notes

1. Counselling a crime which is not committed does not make the counsellor an aider and abettor in the counselled crime: *R.* v. *Gregory* (1867) L.R. 1 C.C.R. 77; but the counsellor is guilty of the offence of incitement. "But it is argued, that a mere intent to commit evil is not indictable, without an act done; but is there not

an act done, when it is charged that the defendant solicited another to commit a felony? The solicitation is an act": *per* Lord Kenyon C.J. in *R.* v. *Higgins* (1801) 2 East 5.

2. The solicitation is an act by the incitor: but no act at all is required from the incitee. "It matters not that no steps have been taken towards the commission of the attempt or of the substantive offence. It matters not, in other words, whether the incitement had any effect at all. It is merely the incitement or the attempting to incite which constitutes the offence": *per* Lord Widgery C.J. in *R.* v. *Assistant Recorder of Kingston-upon-Hill* [1969] 2 Q.B. 58.

3. If the solicitation reaches the mind of the incitee, it is the full offence of incitement even if the solicitation has no effect on that mind, *e.g.* if the incitee is completely unmoved, or has already decided to commit the crime anyway. Attempting to incite occurs where the solicitation (*e.g.* in a letter) does not reach the mind of the incitee: see *R.* v. *Ransford* (1874) 13 Cox 9.

4. An incitement made by A to B to commit a crime necessarily involved inciting B to conspire with A, an attempt by A to conspire with B, and an attempt by A to counsel or procure an offence by B. These three offences, being redundant, have been abolished: see section 5(7) Criminal Law Act 1977; section 1(4) Criminal Attempts Act 1981, *ante*, p. 424. However it has been held that incitement to incite is still an offence known to the law, *e.g.* where A incites B to incite C to kill V: *R.* v. *Sirat* (1985) 83 Cr.App.R. 41; *R.* v. *Evans* [1986] Crim.L.R. 470. And see Draft Criminal Code, Clause 47(5), *post*, p. 478.

(a) *Actus Reus*

Notes

1. The incitement, which may be addressed to the world in general, may consist in persuasion (*i.e.* urging), or threats or pressure.

R. v. *Most* (1881) 7 Q.B.D. 244 (C.C.C.R.): M published in London an article in a newspaper urging readers in foreign countries to assassinate their Heads of State. *Held*, incitement to murder under section 4 of the Offences Against the Person Act 1861.

Race Relations Board v. *Applin* [1973] Q.B. 815, 825 (C.A.): A. sent a circular to W's neighbours, complaining about W's taking coloured foster children. His object was to get W to take white foster children only. The question was whether this was an incitement of W to do an unlawful act under the Race Relations Act 1968. Lord Denning M.R.: "[It was suggested] that to 'incite' means to urge or spur on by advice, encouragement or persuasion, and not otherwise, I do not think the word is so limited, at any rate in the present context. A person may 'incite' another to do an act by threatening or by pressure, as well as by persuasion." A had therefore incited W.

Invicta Plastics v. *Clare* [1976] R.T.R. 251 (Div. Ct.): I.P. advertised for sale a device which was not illegal to own, but was illegal to operate without a licence, which was unlikely to be given. The device, when operated by a car driver, gave him warning when a police radar trap was set. *Held*, approving Lord Denning's remarks in *Applin's* case (above), I.P. incited readers of the advertisement to commit an offence under the Wireless Telegraphy Act 1949.

2. The incitement must be to do an act which, if done by the incitee, would be a crime by him. In *R.* v. *Whitehead* [1977] Q.B. 868 (see *ante*, p. 404) A urged B to commit incest, which B was legally not able to commit as either a principal or an accessory. *Held*, A was not guilty of common law incitement.

3. The fact that B does not know that what he is being urged to do would be a crime by him means that A is not guilty of incitement, although he may be guilty of attempting to commit a crime through an innocent agent. (See *ante*, p. 368.)

Question

A urges B to drink V's wine. A knows that V does not and would not consent to this, and thinks that B has similar knowledge. In fact B thinks that V consents to his drinking the wine. Is A guilty of inciting B to steal V's wine?

R. v. Curr
[1968] 2 Q.B. 944
Court of Appeal

Curr lent money and in return took as security family allowance vouchers which the borrower signed for him. He got another woman to cash these vouchers for him at a Post Office. He was charged with (*inter alia*) soliciting this woman to commit a summary offence under section 9(*b*) of the Family Allowances Act 1945 (see *infra*). Curr appealed against his conviction at quarter sessions.

FENTON ATKINSON J.: The facts shortly were these, that he was in fact a trafficker in family allowance books. His method was to approach some married woman who had a large family of children and lend her money on the security of her family allowance book. A woman would borrow from him, let us say, £6, and would sign three of the vouchers in her family allowance book to the value of, let us say £9, and hand over the book to him as security. He then had a team of women agents whom he sent out to cash the vouchers, and he would pocket the proceeds in repayment of the loans and thereafter return the books. ... He agreed quite frankly that he knew he was not legally entitled to receive these payments, and that it could be risky. ...

Count 3 was of soliciting the commission of a summary offence contrary to section 9(b) of the Act of 1945. ... Mr. Kershaw (for Curr) took a preliminary point on that count that incitement to commit a summary offence is not in fact an indictable offence, and he referred to some old authorities which might lend some countenance to that view. But it appears to this court that Parliament in the Magistrates' Courts Act, 1952, in paragraph 20 of Schedule I, has in fact recognised incitement of this kind as an indictable offence, and it is not necessary, therefore, to go further into that matter, all the more because Mr. Kershaw's main point is this, that the offence the commission of which the defendant is said to have solicited is not an absolute statutory offence, but it is one requiring knowledge on the part of the female agent that she is doing something unlawful in receiving the allowance.

Section 9 is headed "Penalty for obtaining or receiving payment wrongfully," and provides:

> "If any person— ... (b) obtains or receives any such sum as on account of an allowance, either as in that person's own right or as on behalf of another, knowing that it was not properly payable, or not properly receivable by him or her; that person shall be liable on summary conviction to imprisonment for a term not exceeding three months or to a fine not exceeding fifty pounds ... "

Mr. Kershaw's argument was that if the woman agent in fact has no guilty knowledge, knowing perhaps nothing of the assignment, or supposing that the defendant was merely collecting for the use and benefit of the woman concerned, then she would be an innocent agent, and by using her services in that way the defendant would be committing the summary offence himself, but would not be inciting her to receive money knowing that it was not receivable by her. He contends that it was essential to prove, to support this charge, that the woman agent in question ... knew the allowances were not properly receivable by her. [Counsel for the Crown's] answer to that submission was that the woman agent must be presumed to know the law, and if she knew the law, she must have known, he contends, that the allowance was not receivable by her. ...

The argument is that in no other circumstances [than those set out in the book, *e.g.* during illness] may an agent lawfully collect for the use and benefit of the book holder. ...

In our view the prosecution argument here gives no effect to the word "knowing" in section 9(b), and in our view the defendant could only be guilty on count 3 if the woman solicited, that is, the woman agent sent to collect the allowance, knew that the action she was asked to carry out amounted to an offence. ... But the assistant recorder never [dealt] with the question of the knowledge of the woman agents, and in the whole of the summing-up dealing with this matter he proceeded on the assumption that either guilty knowledge in the woman agent was irrelevant, or, alternatively, that any woman agent must be taken to have known that she was committing an offence under section 9(b).

Appeal allowed

(b) Mens Rea

The incitor must intend the incitee to do an act which would be a crime by him.

Questions

In *Curr*, above, the court said: "In our view the defendant could only be guilty [of incitement] if the woman solicited ... knew that the action she was asked to carry out amounted to an offence." Since it is never necessary for the incited person to intend to commit the offence, is not the Court stating the wrong test? Should it not be, did Curr know that the act required of the women would be an offence by her? Would the result of the case have been different if it had fallen to be decided under the definition of incitement contained in the Draft Criminal Code, *infra*?

Law Com. 177: Commentary on Draft Criminal Code

"Para. 13.9 ... The essence of incitement ... is the incitor's state of mind in relation to the state of mind of the incitee. It is undoubtedly sufficient if the incitor intends that the incitee shall act with the fault required for the substantive offence. ... It should also be sufficient if the incitee believes that the person incited, if he acts at all, will do so with the fault required. For example, if D seeks to persuade E to have sexual intercourse with Mrs. D, D believing that E knows that Mrs. D does not consent to it, there seems to be a clear case of incitement to rape. It should not be necessary to prove that it was D's intention that E should have that knowledge. Whenever the fault required for the substantive offence includes knowledge or recklessness as to circumstances (such as absence of consent), it is likely to be more appropriate for the purposes of the indictment to refer to the incitor's belief that such knowledge or recklessness exists rather than his intention that it should."

Questions

A wishes to frighten V. by putting his property at risk of being damaged, but does not wish to cause actual damage. A seeks to persuade B to do an act which will certainly damage V.'s property. Neither A nor B knows of this certainty, but A knows that the act will cause a risk of damage.

(a) B does not and cannot know of the risk. Is this incitement by A to cause criminal damage? Does it make any difference whether A knows or believes in B's lack of knowledge or recklessness?

(b) B knows of the risk. Is this incitement to cause criminal damage, if A knows that B knows? Is this incitement if A does not know but believes that B might know of the risk?

See discussion of recklessness in Attempts, *ante*, p. 433.

Draft Criminal Code

"**47.**—(1) A person is guilty of incitement to commit an offence or offences if—

(a) he incites another to do or cause to be done an act or acts which, if done, will involve the commission of the offence or offences by the other; and

(b) he intends or believes that he other, if he acts as incited, shall or will do so with the fault required for the offence or offences.

(2) Subject to section 52(1), 'offence' in this section means any offence triable in England and Wales.

(3) Where the purpose of an enactment creating an offence is the protection of a class of persons, no member of that class who is the intended victim of such an offence can be guilty of incitement to commit that offence.

(4) A person may be convicted of incitement to commit an offence although the identity of the person incited is unknown.

(5) It is not an offence under this section, or under any enactment referred to in section 51, to incite another to procure, assist or encourage as an accessory the commission of an offence by a third person; but—

(a)   a person may be guilty as an accessory to the incitement by another of a third person to commit an offence; and

(b)   this subsection does not preclude a charge of incitement to incite (under this section or any other enactment), or of incitement to conspire (under section 48 or any other enactment), or of incitement to attempt (under section 49 or any other enactment), to commit an offence."

4. IMPOSSIBILITY IN RELATION TO INCHOATE OFFENCES

Note

This section deals with the position where what D attempts to do, or incites another to do, or conspires with another to do, is in some respects impossible. The question is, should that mean that D is not guilty as charged, even if all the other elements of attempt, incitement or conspiracy are present? It is evident that the answer, whatever it is, should not differ depending upon which inchoate offence is involved. The Draft Criminal Code, Clause 50(1) proposes, "A person may be guilty of incitement conspiracy or attempt to commit an offence, although the commission of the offence is impossible, if it would be possible in the circumstances which he believes or hopes exist or will exist at the relevent time." This does not reflect the present law, which has different answers for the various inchoate offences. This is because (1) the leading case, *Haughton* v. *Smith, infra,* set out the law on impossible attempts in a way which was widely regarded as unsatisfactory; (2) it was subsequently decided that that unsatisfactory law applied to the other inchoate offences also; but (3) statutory attempts to rectify the position apply only to attempts and statutory conspiracy. Common law conspiracy and incitement thus continue to be governed by the principles enunciated in *Haughton* v. *Smith.*

i. Attempt

Note

No one attempts to do that which he knows to be impossible (the same can be said of inciting and conspiring). Anyone who appears to do so is therefore making a mistake of some sort. The kinds of mistake possibly involved are three.

1. He mistakes the criminal law, and assumes that it prohibits what he is aiming at. Since the criminal law is not interested in his projected conduct, it follows that it will not punish him for achieving what he desires; *a fortiori* if he merely goes some way towards achieving it. The fact that he believes he is defying the law can make no difference. There has never been any liability where this kind of mistake is involved, and that is still the position. An example would be where D., knowing he has English lace, and

thinking the law prohibits the import of English lace without payment of duty, attempts to avoid the payment of duty on his lace.

2. Where, because of mistake about the facts, D. believes that the factual result he wishes is possible of attainment, *e.g.* D. tries to kill someone with a dose of poison which is too small to kill, or tries to shoot someone out of the range of his gun, or tries to break into a safe which is too strong for the tools he uses. In these cases of "inadequate means," there may be an attempt, but the House of Lords in *Haughton* v. *Smith, infra* denied that it could be an attempt if what D. attempted was absolutely impossible, as where the subject matter did not exist or did not exist in the form he imagined, *e.g.* where D. attempted to take money from a pocket or purse which contained no money, or where D. attempted to deceive a person who knew the truth and could not be deceived.

3. Where because of a mistake about the facts, D. believes that the factual result he wishes is criminal, *e.g.* D. wishes to smuggle in French lace, on which he knows that duty is payable, but the lace in his possession is in fact English lace, on which no duty is payable; or D. wishes to handle stolen goods, but the goods involved in his plan are not stolen. There was controversy about this class of mistake, and this handling non-stolen goods problem received different answers in cases from Commonwealth and American jurisdictions. This particular problem was involved in *Haughton* v. *Smith*, and the House decided that that particular mistake, and all mistakes in this class, prevented D.'s conduct from being an attempt.

Haughton v. Smith
[1975] A.C. 746
House of Lords

A van load of stolen meat was intercepted by the police, and allowed to continue its journey with two policemen concealed inside. S later did acts amounting to handling the meat. On the view that the goods' restoration to lawful custody meant that they were no longer stolen (see *post*, p. 809), S was not charged with handling stolen goods, but with attempting to handle stolen goods contrary to section 22, Theft Act 1968 (see *post*, p. 803). He was convicted, his appeal was allowed by the Court of Appeal, and the prosecution further appealed.

LORD HAILSHAM OF ST. MARYLEBONE, L.C.: I was at first inclined to think that section 22 of the Theft Act 1968 was drafted in such a way as to permit the construction that to be stolen for the purpose of section 22(1) it was sufficient that the goods had been stolen without continuing to be stolen at the time of the handling, provided, of course, that the accused believed them at the time of the handling to be stolen. I thought that the expression "believed" in the subsection aided the view that it could cover a state of facts where the defendant believed the goods to be stolen when they were not in fact still stolen at that moment of time. But, on consideration, I am sure that this would be a false construction, and that the expression "believed" was inserted to guard against acquittals which had taken place under the former Larceny Act when it was necessary to prove knowledge that the goods were stolen and belief was not enough. If I were not already certain that this was the true meaning of section 22(1), the provisions of section 24, and, in particular, section 24(3), would, I think, clinch the matter. In my view, it is plain that, in order to constitute the offence of handling, the goods specified in the particulars of offence must not only be believed to be stolen, but actually continue to be stolen goods at the moment of handling. Once this is accepted as the true construction of the section, I do not think that it is possible to convert a completed act of handling, which is not itself criminal because it was not the handling of stolen goods, into a criminal act by the simple device of alleging that it was an attempt to handle stolen goods on the ground that at the time of handling the accused falsely believed them still to be stolen. In my opinion, this would be for the courts to manufacture a new criminal offence not authorised by the legislature.

This would be enough to decide the result of this appeal, but both counsel invited us to take a wider view of our obligations, and, since the question was discussed by the Court of Appeal in general terms and since I believe that the result of our decision is to overrule a number of decided cases, at least to some extent, I feel bound to accede to this invitation. The question certified by the Court of Appeal was:

> "If stolen goods are returned to lawful custody and thus cease to be stolen by virtue of section 24(3) of the Theft Act 1968 can a person who subsequently dishonestly handles goods believing them to be stolen be guilty of the offence of attempting to handle stolen goods?"

I have already given a negative answer to this question, but the range of the discussion before us demands a wider consideration of the principles involved. . . .

I note that in the New Zealand case of *R.* v. *Donnelly* [1970] N.Z.L.R. 980, which, except in so far as it relates to the construction of the relevant New Zealand statutes, is very much on all fours with this, Turner J., adopts a six-fold classification. He says, at p. 990:

> "He who sets out to commit a crime may in the event fall short of the complete commission of that crime for any one of a number of reasons. *First*, he may, of course, simply change his mind before committing any act sufficiently overt to amount to an attempt. *Second*, he may change his mind, but too late to deny that he had got so far as an attempt. *Third*, he may be prevented by some outside agency from doing some act necessary to complete commission of the crime—as when a police offer interrupts him while he is endeavouring to force the window open, but before he has broken into the premises. *Fourth*, he may suffer no such outside interference, but may fail to complete the commission of the crime through ineptitude, inefficiency or insufficient means. The jemmy which he has brought with him may not be strong enough to force the window open. *Fifth*, he may find that what he is proposing to do is after all impossible—not because of insufficiency of means, but because it is for some reason physically not possible, whatever means be adopted. He who walks into a room intending to steal, say a specific diamond ring, and finds that the ring is no longer there, but has been removed by the owner to the bank, is thus prevented from committing the crime which he intended, and which, but for the supervening physical impossibility imposed by events he would have committed. *Sixth*, he may without interruption efficiently do every act which he set out to do, but may be saved from criminal liability by the fact that what

he has done, contrary to his own belief at the time, does not after all amount in law to a crime."

On the whole, though I hope it will never be subjected to too much analysis, as it is merely a convenient exposition and illustration of classes of case which can arise, I find this classification more satisfactory than Lord Widgery's dual classification. Applying the three principles derived from my primary definitions, I would seek to obtain the following results. (1) In the first case no criminal attempt is committed. At the relevant time there was no *mens rea* since there had been a change of intention, and the only overt acts relied on would be preparatory and not immediately connected with the completed offence. (2) In the second case there is both *mens rea* and an act connected immediately with the offence. An example would be an attempted rape where the intended victim was criminally assaulted, but the attacker desisted at the stage immediately before he had achieved penetration. It follows that there is a criminal attempt. (3) The third case is more difficult because, as a matter of fact and degree, it will depend to some extent on the stage at which the interruption takes place, and the precise offence the attempt to commit which is the subject of the charge. In general, however, a criminal attempt is committed, assuming that the proximity test is passed. (4) In the fourth case there is ample authority for the proposition that, assuming the proximity test is passed, a criminal attempt is committed. But here casuistry is possible. Examples were given in argument of shots at an intended victim which fail because he is just out of range, or because, as in the case of the well known popular novel, *The Day of the Jackal*, the intended victim moves at the critical moment, or when a dose of poison insufficient to kill is administered with intent to murder. In all these cases the attempt is clearly criminal. (5) The fifth case is more complicated. It is clear that an attempt to obtain money by a false pretence which is not in fact believed, is criminal notwithstanding that the consequences intended were not achieved: see *R. v. Hensler* (1870) 11 Cox C.C. 570. The same would be true of an attempted murder when the victim did not actually die for whatever reason. But I do not regard these as true, or at least not as typical, examples of the fifth class. They belong rather to the fourth, since the criminal had done all that he intended to do, and all that was necessary to complete the crime was an act or event wholly outside his control. *R. v. M'Pherson* (1857) Dears. & B. 197 where the conviction was quashed, may be regarded as simply a case where a man was charged with one thing and convicted of another. But both the facts and the reasoning of the judges are much closer to the example postulated by Turner J. in *R. v. Donnelly* as typical of the fifth class, though Turner J.'s own opinion to the effect that the attempt is criminal depends on the terms of the New Zealand statute and has no application to English law. In *R. v. M'Pherson* the reasoning of the English judges on English law was to the contrary. Cockburn C.J. said, at p. 201:

"Here the prisoner had the *intention* to steal before he went into the house; but when he got there the goods specified in the indictment were not there; how then could he *attempt* to steal those goods? There can be no attempt *asportare* unless there is something *asportare*."

Bramwell B., anticipating the decisions in *R. v. Collins* (1864) 9 Cox C.C. 497, said, at p. 201:

"The argument that a man putting his hand into an empty pocket might be convicted of attempting to steal, appeared to me at first plausible; but

suppose a man, believing a block of wood to be a man who was his
deadly enemy, struck it a blow intending to murder, could he be
convicted of attempting to murder the man he took it to be?"

And, in giving judgment, Cockburn C.J. said, at p. 202:

"The word attempt clearly conveys with it the idea, that if the attempt
had succeeded the offence charged would have been committed, and
therefore the prisoner might have been convicted if the things
mentioned in the indictment or any of them had been there; but
attempting to commit a felony is clearly distinguishable from intending
to commit it. An attempt must be to do that which, if successful, would
amount to the felony charged; but here the attempt never could have
succeeded, as the things which the indictment charges the prisoner with
stealing had already been removed—stolen by somebody else."

And Bramwell B. was equally emphatic.

Clearly Cockburn C.J. and Bramwell B. were of the view that Turner J.'s
example of his fifth class of inchoate act was not a criminal attempt. *R. v.
M'Pherson*, was followed in *R. v. Collins*, by a court which also included
Cockburn C.J. and Bramwell B. and was the identical case postulated by
Bramwell B. in the earlier case of a man putting his hand into an empty
pocket. . . .

It was not long, however, before the decision in *R. v. Collins* was
challenged by Lord Coleridge C.J. in *R. v. Brown* (1889) 24 Q.B.D. 357, 359
as "no longer law," but without giving reasons and in *R. v. Ring* (1892) 17
Cox C.C. 491, 492 (an early "mugging" case on the Metropolitan Railway)
with even greater emphasis and even fewer reasons. Since then *R. v.
Collins* has generally been held to be bad law. On this I express no
concluded opinion, but in general I regard the reasoning in *R. v. M'Pherson*
and *R. v. Collins* as sound and in general I would consider that "attempts"
in Turner J.'s fifth class of case are not indictable in English law, and I
consider that the purported overruling of *R. v. Collins* needs further
consideration. In addition to the reported cases, we postulated in
argument a number of real and imaginary instances of this class. In *The
Empty Room*, Sherlock Holmes' enemy, Colonel Maron, was induced to fire
at a wax image of the detective silhouetted in the window, though Holmes
prudently rejected Inspector Lestrade's advice to prefer a charge of
attempted murder and so the matter was never tested; in *R. v. White* [1910]
2 K.B. 124, a man who put a small quantity of cyanide in a wine glass, too
small to kill, was held guilty of attempted murder. This was an example of
the fourth of Turner J.'s cases and therefore criminal. But quaere, what
would have been the position if the glass administered had contained pure
water, even though the accused believed falsely that it contained cyanide?
We discussed the situation when a would-be murderer attempts to
assassinate a corpse, or a bolster in a bed, believing it to be the living body
of his enemy, or when he fires into an empty room believing that it
contained an intended victim; and we had our attention drawn to an
American case where the accused fired at a peephole in a roof believed to
be in use by a watching policeman who was in fact a few yards away. In
most of these cases, a statutory offence of some kind (*e.g.* discharging a
firearm with intent to endanger life) would be committed in English law,
but in general I would think that a charge of an attempt to commit the
common law offence of murder would not lie since, if the contemplated
sequence of actions had been completed (as in some of the supposed
instances they were) no substantive offence could have been committed of
the type corresponding to the charge of attempt supposed to be laid. I get

some support for this view from the summing up of Rowlatt J. in *R.* v. *Osborn* (1919) 84 J.P. 63. But I prefer to rest on the principle above stated, since *Osborn* was couched in more popular language than is appropriate to what has become a somewhat theoretical discussion. At the end of the day there must be a question of fact for the jury. The judge may direct them what facts, if established, could constitute an attempt, or would be evidence of an attempt. The jury alone can decide whether there was an attempt.

(6) Turner J.'s sixth class of case was where a man efficiently does "without interruption every act which he set out to do, but may be saved from criminal liability by the fact that what he has done, contrary to his own belief at the time, does not after all amount to a crime." This is really equivalent to Lord Widgery's second class. I have already explained that I consider that the present appeal fails on the proper construction of section 22 of the Theft Act 1968. But I think that this is a special example of a wider principle, and I agree with Turner J.'s conclusion about it.

> "Suppose a man takes away an umbrella from a stand with intent to steal it, believing it not to be his own, but it turns out to be his own, could he be convicted of attempting to steal?"

In *R.* v. *Villensky* [1892] 2 Q.B. 597 Lord Coleridge C.J. in circumstances not unlike the present, following *R.* v. *Dolan* (1855) Dears.C.C. 436, held that prisoners could [not] be indicted under the old law for receiving stolen goods, and made no reference to the possibility of a conviction for attempt.

In *R.* v. *Williams* [1893] 1 Q.B. 320, 321, the same Lord Chief Justice said that a boy below the age at which he could be properly indicted for rape could not be convicted on the same facts for an attempt. I do not agree with the contrary opinion of Hawkins J. in the same case, even though it was possibly supported by the rest of the court. The same reasoning would apply to a case of unlawful carnal knowledge (*cf. R.* v. *Waite* [1892] 2 Q.B. 600), whether, as there, it was the male who was by reason of age incapable in law of committing the offence, or the female who was in law incapable by reason of her age of having it committed against her, and it would not, in my view, matter in the latter case that the male falsely believed her to be under age. Support for his view is to be found in *D.P.P.* v. *Head* [1959] A.C. 83, which was a charge of a completed offence in relation to a mental defective, but counsel for the respondent made considerable play with the argument *a silentio* to be derived from the fact that no one suggested the possibility of a conviction for an attempt. In my view, it is a general principle that Turner J.'s sixth class of attempts are not criminal, not because the acts are not proximate or because the intention is absent, but because the second of the three propositions I derive from the two judicial definitions I cited above is not satisfied. The acts are not part of a series "which would constitute the actual commission of the offence if it were not interrupted." In this event the often discussed question whether the legal impossibility derives from a mistake of fact or law on the part of the accused is hardly relevant.

This discussion enables me to deal with the cases cited in the judgment of the Court of Appeal. Like Lord Widgery C.J., I disagree with the decision in *People* v. *Rojas* (1961) 10 Cal.Rptr. 465 and prefer the decisions in *R.* v. *Donnelly* [1970] N.Z.L.R. 980 and *People* v. *Jaffe* (1960) 185 N.Y. 496 (overruling the decisions in the lower courts, *cf.* (1906) 98 N.Y.S. 406). I agree with the decision in *R.* v. *Percy Dalton (London) Ltd.* (1984) 33 Cr.App.R. 102, and particularly with the quotation from Birkett J. cited by Lord Widgery C.J. in the present case, where he said, at p. 110:

"Steps on the way to the commission of what would be a crime, if the acts were completed, may amount to attempts to commit that crime, to which, unless interrupted, they would have led; but steps on the way to the doing of something, which is thereafter done, and which is no crime, cannot be regarded as attempts to commit a crime."

I would add to the last sentence a rider to the effect that equally steps on the way to do something which is thereafter *not* completed, but which if done would not constitute a crime cannot be indicted as attempts to commit that crime. It is, of course, true that, at least in theory, some villains will escape by this route. But in most cases they can properly be charged with something else—statutory offences like breaking and entering with intent etc., or loitering with intent etc., using an instrument with intent etc., discharging or possessing a firearm with intent etc., or as here, common law offences like conspiring to commit the same offence as that the attempt to commit which is charged, or even committing a substantive offence of a different kind, as here, stealing or attempting to steal.

Lord Reid, Lord Morris and Viscount Dilhorne delivered speeches for dismissing the appeal; Lord Salmon agreed with Lord Hailsham.

Appeal dismissed

Notes

1. The Law Commission criticised the ratio of *Haughton* v. *Smith*.

Law. Com. No. 102

§ 2.96: "We think it would be generally accepted that if a man possesses the appropriate *mens rea* and commits acts which are sufficiently proximate to the *actus reus* of a criminal offence, he is guilty of attempting to commit that offence. Where, with that intention, he commits acts which, if the facts were as he believed them to be, would have amounted to the *actus reus* of the full crime or would have been sufficiently proximate to amount to an attempt, we cannot see why this failure to appreciate the true facts should, in principle, relieve him of liability for the attempt. We stress that this solution to the problem does not punish people simply for their intentions. The necessity for proof of proximate acts remains."

2. As to the differences between "inadequate means" and absolute impossibility, one of its criticisms centred on the very fine distinctions it required the Court to draw.

Law. Com. No. 102

§ 2.64 "In *R.* v. *Farrance* (1977) 67 Cr.App.R. 136, the defendant had been convicted of attempting to drive when he had a blood alcohol concentration above the prescribed limit contrary to section 6(1) of the Road Traffic Act 1972. The facts were that the clutch of his car had burnt out, so that although the defendant could operate the engine he could not drive the car. The Court of Appeal upheld the conviction on the grounds that a burnt out clutch was only an impediment to the commission of a crime, similar to the inadequate burglar's tool or the would-be poisoner's insufficient dose. It is not clear what the court's answer would have been if the car had had no petrol or if its transmission had completely seized up."

3. The Commission's proposals for rectifying the position were amended during the passage of the Act, and eventually emerged as section 1(2) and (3), *ante,* p. 424. In *Anderton* v. *Ryan* [1985] A.C. 560, the House of Lords held that the statutory wording had not affected the *ratio* of *Haughton* v. *Smith,* which was still of authority. However the House speedily reconsidered this position. See *infra.*

R. v. Shivpuri
[1987] A.C. 1.
House of Lords

The facts appear in the speech of Lord Bridge.

LORD BRIDGE OF HARWICH. My Lords, on February 23, 1984 the appellant was convicted at the Crown Court at Reading of two attempts to commit offences. The offences attempted were being knowingly concerned in dealing with (count 1) and in harbouring (count 2) a class A controlled drug, namely diamorphine, with intent to evade the prohibition of importation imposed by section 3(1) of the Misuse of Drugs Act 1971, contrary to section 170(1)(*b*) of the Customs and Excise Management Act 1979. On November 5, 1984, the Court of Appeal, Criminal Division dismissed his appeals against conviction but certified that a point of law of general public importance was involved in the decision and granted leave to appeal to your Lordships' House. The certified question granted on November 13, 1984 reads:

"Does a person commit an offence under Section 1, Criminal Attempts Act, 1981, where, if the facts were as at that person believed them to be, the full offence would have been committed by him, but where on the true facts the offence which that person set out to commit was in law impossible, *e.g.* because the substance imported and believed to be heroin was not heroin but a harmless substance?"

The facts plainly to be inferred from the evidence, interpreted in the light of the jury's guilty verdicts, may be shortly summarised. The appellant, on a visit to India, was approached by a man named Desai, who offered to pay him £1,000 if, on his return to England, he would receive a suitcase which a courier would deliver to him containing packages of drugs which the appellant was then to distribute according to instructions he would receive. The suitcase was duly delivered to him in Cambridge. On November 30, 1982, acting on instructions, the appellant went on to Southall station to deliver a package of drugs to a third party. Outside the station he and the man he had met by appointment were arrested. A package containing a powdered substance was found in the appellant's shoulder bag. At the appellant's flat in Cambridge, he produced to customs officers the suitcase from which the lining had been ripped out and the remaining packages of the same powdered substance. In answer to questions by customs officers and in a long written statement the appellant made what amounted to a full confession of having played his part, as described, as recipient and distributor of illegally imported drugs. The appellant believed the drugs to be either heroin or cannabis. In due course the powdered substance in the several packages was scientifically analysed and found not to be a controlled drug but snuff or some similar harmless vegetable matter. . . .

The certified question depends on the true construction of the Criminal Attempts Act 1981. The Act marked an important new departure since, by section 6, it abolished the offence of attempt at common law and substituted a new statutory code governing attempts to commit criminal offences. It was considered by your Lordships' House last year in *Anderton* v. *Ryan* after the decision in the Court of Appeal which is the subject of the present appeal. That might seem an appropriate starting point from which to examine the issues arising in this appeal. But your Lordships have been invited to exercise the power under the 1966 Practice Statement to depart from the reasoning in that decision if it proves necessary to do so in order to affirm the convictions appealed against in the instant case. I was not only a party to the decision in *Anderton* v. *Ryan*, I was also the author of one of the two opinions approved by the majority which must be taken to express the House's ratio. That seems to me to afford a sound reason why, on being invited to examine the language of the statute in its application to the facts of this appeal, I should initially seek to put out of the mind what I said in *Anderton* v. *Ryan*. Accordingly, I propose to approach the issue in the first place as an exercise in statutory construction, applying the language of the Act to the facts of the case, as if the matter were *res integra*. If this leads me to the conclusion that the appellant was not guilty of any attempt to commit a relevant offence, that will be the end of the matter. But, if this initial exercise inclines me to reach a contrary conclusion, it will then be necessary to consider whether the precedent set by *Anderton* v. *Ryan* bars that conclusion or whether it can be surmounted either on the ground that the earlier decision is distinguishable or that it would be appropriate to depart from it under the 1966 Practice Statement.

(After reading section 1, *ante*, p. 424). Applying this language to the facts of the case, the first question to be asked is whether the appellant intended to commit the offences of being knowingly concerned in dealing with and harbouring drugs of class A or class B with intent to evade the prohibition on their importation. Translated into more homely language the question may be rephrased, without in any way altering the legal significance, in the following terms: did the appellant intend to receive and store (harbour) and in due course pass on to third parties (deal with) packages of heroin or cannabis which he knew had been smuggled into England from India? The answer is plainly Yes, he did. Next, did he, in relation to each offence, do an act which was more than merely preparatory to the commission of the offence? The act relied on in relation to harbouring was the receipt and retention of the packages found in the lining of the suitcase. The act relied on in relation to dealing was the meeting at Southall station with the intended recipient of one of the packages. In each case the act was clearly more than preparatory to the commission of the *intended* offence; it was not and could not be more than merely preparatory to the commission of the *actual* offence, because the facts were such that the commission of the actual offence was impossible. Here then is the nub of the matter. Does the "act which is more than merely preparatory to the commission of the offence" in section 1(1) of the 1981 Act (the *actus reus* of the statutory offence of attempt) require any more than an act which is more than merely preparatory to the commission of the offence which the defendant intended to commit? Section 1(2) must surely indicate a negative answer; if it were otherwise, whenever the facts were such that the commission of the actual offence was impossible, it would be impossible to prove an act more than merely preparatory to the commission of that offence and subsections (1) and (2) would contradict each other.

This very simple, perhaps over-simple, analysis leads me to the provisional conclusion that the appellant was rightly convicted of the two offences of attempt with which he was charged. But can this conclusion stand with *Anderton* v. *Ryan*? The appellant in that case was charged with an attempt to handle stolen goods. She bought a video recorder believing it to be stolen. On the facts as they were to be assumed it was not stolen. By a majority the House decided that she was entitled to be acquitted. I have re-examined the case with care. If I could extract from the speech of Lord Roskill or from my own speech a clear and coherent principle distinguishing those cases of attempting the impossible which amount to offences under the statute from those which do not, I should have to consider carefully on which side of the line the instant case fell. But I have to confess that I can find no such principle.

Running through Lord Roskill's speech and my own in *Anderton* v. *Ryan* is the concept of "objectively innocent" acts which, in my speech certainly, are contrasted with "guilty acts." A few citations will make this clear. Lord Roskill said [1985] A.C. 560 at 580):

"My Lords, it has been strenuously and ably argued for the respondent that these provisions involve that a defendant is liable to conviction for an attempt even where his actions are innocent but he erroneously believes facts which, if true, would make those actions criminal, and further, that he is liable to such conviction whether or not in the event his intended course of action is completed."

He proceeded to reject the argument. I referred to the appellant's purchase of the video recorder and said [1985] A.C. 560 at 582): "Objectively considered, therefore, her purchase of the recorder was a perfectly proper commercial transaction."

A further passage from my speech stated [1985] A.C. 560 at 582–583):

"The question may be stated in abstract terms as follows. Does s.1 of the 1981 Act create a new offence of attempt where a person embarks on and completes a course of conduct, which is objectively innocent, solely on the ground that the person mistakenly believes facts which, if true, would make the course of conduct a complete crime? If the question may be answered affirmatively it requires convictions in a number of surprising cases: the classic case, put by Bramwell B. in *R.* v. *Collins* (1864) 9 Cox C.C. 497 at 498, of the man who takes away his own umbrella from a stand, believing it not to be his own and with intent to steal it; the case of the man who has consensual intercourse with a girl over 16 believing her to be under that age; the case of the art dealer who sells a picture which he represents to be and which is in fact a genuine Picasso, but which the dealer mistakenly believes to be a fake. The common feature of all these cases, including that under appeal, is that the mind alone is guilty, the act is innocent."

I then contrasted the case of the man who attempts to pick the empty pocket, saying [1985] A.C. 560 at 583):

"Putting the hand in the pocket is the guilty act, the intent to steal is the guilty mind, the offence is appropriately dealt with as an attempt, and the impossibility of committing the full offence for want of anything in the pocket to steal is declared by [subs. (2)] to be no obstacle to conviction."

If we fell into error, it is clear that our concern was to avoid convictions in situations which most people, as a matter of common sense, would not regard as involving criminality. In this connection it is to be regretted that we did not take due note of para. 2.97 of the Law Commission Report, Criminal Law: Attempt and Impossibility in Relation to Attempt, Conspiracy and Incitement (1980) (Law Com. No. 102) which preceded the enactment of the 1981 Act, which reads:

> "If it is right in principle that an attempt should be chargeable even though the crime which it is sought to commit could not possibly be committed, we do not think that we should be deterred by the consideration that such a change in our law would also cover some extreme and exceptional cases in which a prosecution would be theoretically possible. An example would be where a person is offered goods at such a low price that he believes that they are stolen, when in fact they are not; if he actually purchases them, upon the principles which we have discussed he would be liable for an attempt to handle stolen goods. Another case which has been much debated is that raised in argument by Bramwell B. in *R.* v. *Collins.* If A takes his own umbrella, mistaking it for one belonging to B and intending to steal B's umbrella, is he guilty of attempted theft? Again, on the principles which we have discussed he would in theory be guilty, but in neither case would it be realistic to suppose that a complaint would be made or that a prosecution would ensue."

The prosecution in *Anderton* v. *Ryan* itself falsified the Commission's prognosis in one of the "extreme and exceptional cases." It nevertheless probably holds good for other such cases, particularly that of the young man having sexual intercourse with a girl over 16, mistakenly believing her to be under that age, by which both Lord Roskill and I were much troubled.

However that may be, the distinction between acts which are "objectively innocent" and those which are not is an essential element in the reasoning in *Anderton* v. *Ryan* and the decision, unless it can be supported on some other ground, must stand or fall by the validity of this distinction. I am satisfied on further consideration that the concept of "objective innocence" is incapable of sensible application in relation to the law of criminal attempts. The reason for this is that any attempt to commit an offence which involves "an act which is more than merely preparatory to the commission of the offence" but which for any reason fails, so that in the event no offence is committed, must *ex hypothesi*, from the point of view of the criminal law, be "objectively innocent." What turns what would otherwise, from the point of view of the criminal law, be an innocent act into a crime is the intent of the actor to commit an offence. I say "from the point of view of the criminal law" because the law of tort must surely here be quite irrelevant. A puts his hand into B's pocket. Whether or not there is anything in the pocket capable of being stolen, if A intends to steal his act is a criminal attempt; if he does not so intend his act is innocent. A plunges a knife into a bolster in a bed. To avoid the complication of an offence of criminal damage, assume it to be A's bolster. If A believes the bolster to be his enemy B and intends to kill him, his act is an attempt to murder B; if he knows the bolster is only a bolster, his act is innocent. These considerations lead me to the conclusion that the distinction sought to be drawn in *Anderton* v. *Ryan* between innocent and guilty acts considered "objectively" and independently of the state of mind of the actor cannot be sensibly maintained.

Another conceivable ground of distinction which was to some extent canvassed in argument, both in *Anderton* v. *Ryan* and in the instant case, though no trace of it appears in the speeches in *Anderton* v. *Ryan*, is a distinction which would make guilt or innocence of the crime of attempt in a case of mistaken belief dependent on what, for want of a better phrase, I will call the defendant's dominant intention. Accordingly to the theory necessary to sustain this distinction, the appellant's dominant intention in *Anderton* v. *Ryan* was to buy a cheap video recorder; her belief that it was stolen was merely incidental. Likewise in the hypothetical case of attempted unlawful sexual intercourse, the young man's dominant intention was to have intercourse with the particular girl; his mistaken belief that she was under 16 was merely incidental. By contrast, in the instant case the appellant's dominant intention was to receive and distribute illegally imported heroin or cannabis.

While I see the superficial attraction of this suggested ground of distinction, I also see formidable practical difficulties in its application. By what test is a jury to be told that a defendant's dominant intention is to be recognised and distinguished from his incidental but mistaken belief? But there is perhaps a more formidable theoretical difficulty. If this ground of distinction is relied on to support the acquittal of the appellant in *Anderton* v. *Ryan*, it can only do so on the basis that her mistaken belief that the video recorder was stolen played no significant part in her decision to buy it and therefore she may be acquitted of the intent to handle stolen goods. But this line of reasoning runs into head-on collision with section 1(3) of the 1981 Act. The theory produces a situation where, apart from the subsection, her intention would not be regarded as having amounted to any intent to commit an offence. Section 1(3)(*b*) then requires one to ask whether, if the video recorder had in fact been stolen, her intention would have been regarded as an intent to handle stolen goods. The answer must clearly be Yes, it would. If she had bought the video recorder knowing it to be stolen, when in fact it was, it would have availed her nothing to say that her dominant intention was to buy a video recorder because it was cheap and that her knowledge that it was stolen was merely incidental. This seems to me fatal to the dominant intention theory.

I am thus led to the conclusion that there is no valid ground on which *Anderton* v. *Ryan* can be distinguished. I have made clear my own conviction, which as a party to the decision (and craving the indulgence of my noble and learned friends who agreed in it) I am the readier to express, that the decision was wrong. What then is to be done? If the case is indistinguishable, the application of the strict doctrine of precedent would require that the present appeal be allowed. Is it permissible to depart from precedent under the 1966 Practice Statement *Note* notwithstanding the especial need for certainty in the criminal law? The following considerations lead me to answer the question affirmatively. Firstly, I am undeterred by the consideration that the decision in *Anderton* v. *Ryan* was so recent. The 1966 Practice Statement is an effective abandonment of our pretention to infallibility. If a serious error embodied in a decision of this House has distorted the law, the sooner it is corrected the better. Secondly, I cannot see how, in the very nature of the case, anyone could have acted in reliance on the law as propounded in *Anderton* v. *Ryan* in the belief that he was acting innocently and now find that, after all, he is to be held to have committed a criminal offence. Thirdly, to hold the House bound to follow *Anderton* v. *Ryan* because it cannot be distinguished and to allow the appeal in this case would, it seems to me, be tantamount to a declaration that the 1981 Act left the law of criminal attempts unchanged following the decision in *Haughton* v. *Smith*. Finally, if, contrary to my present view, there is a valid ground on which it would be proper to distinguish cases similar to that considered in *Anderton* v.

Ryan, my present opinion on that point would not foreclose that the option of making such a distinction in some future case. . . .

I would answer the certified question in the affirmative and dismiss the appeal.

Appeal dismissed

Note

Although the whole House agreed with Lord Bridge's speech overruling *Anderton* v. *Ryan* (and therefore that Mrs. Ryan was guilty of attempted handling), Lord Hailsham, with Lord Elwyn-Jones and Lord Mackay, also held that *Anderton* v. *Ryan* was distinguishable on the ground that the sole intent of Shivpuri was to evade the prohibition on the import of drugs, whereas "the only intention of Mrs. Ryan was to buy a particular video cassette recorder at a knock-down price and the fact that she believed it to be stolen formed no part of that intention" (*per* Lord Hailsham, at p. 337).

It is misleading to describe her intention to buy this particular recorder at a low price as "her only intention," and to say that the fact that she believed it to be stolen was "no part of that intention." A crime is committed intentionally if the forbidden result is *desired* and the circumstances making it forbidden are *known* to the actor. (See Chap. 3.) If the recorder had been stolen, her intention to buy that object knowing it to be stolen would be an intention to handle stolen goods. Section 1(3) provides that, since that would be her intention on the facts as she thinks them to be, it is her intention on the facts as they are.

But in any event section 1(3) is redundant. Intention is a state of mind which does not depend on the facts as they are. Otherwise, as has been pointed out by J. C. Smith [1986] Crim.L.R. 540, as often as the facts change, the defendant's intention will change even though he is unaware of the changes in the facts. His intention cannot be affected by situational changes of which he is unaware. If D. intends to handle goods, which are, as he knows, stolen, he intends to handle stolen goods, and it cannot be said that that *intention* is no longer there if, unknown to him, they have ceased to exist as stolen goods.

On the difficulties involved in Lord Hailsham's suggested distinction, see J. C. Smith [1986] Crim.L.R. 539–541.

ii. Conspiracy

Note

In *D.P.P.* v. *Nock* [1978] A.C. 979, the defendants agreed to extract cocaine from a substance which, unknown to them, contained none. It was held by the House of Lords that "logic and justice seem to require that the question as to the effect of the impossibility of the substantive offence should be answered in the same way, whether the crime charged be conspiracy or attempt" (*per* Lord Scarman, at p. 997). The principles of *Haughton* v. *Smith*, *ante*, p. 479, therefore applied and since the result agreed on by the defendants—extraction of cocaine—was absolutely impossible, their agreement was not punishable.

So far as concerns statutory conspiracies, section 1(1) of the Criminal Law Act 1977 (*ante*, p. 452) includes in the definition of conspiracy an agreement which would amount to or involve the commission of an offence but for the existence of facts which render the commission of the offence impossible. However common law conspiracies are unaffected by the section, and are still governed by *D.P.P.* v. *Nock* and, presumably, the principles laid down in *Haughton* v. *Smith*.

iii. Incitement

R. v. Fitzmaurice
[1983] Q.B. 1083
Court of Appeal

X asked A to find someone to rob a woman on a certain day while walking between her place of work and a bank by snatching wages from her. A agreed and recruited B, C & D to do the job. Unknown to any of them, the proposed robbery of the woman was a complete fiction, invented by X. His plan was to obtain a reward by telling the police of a raid on a security van calling at the bank at the time of B, C & D's planned raid. B, C & D were arrested by the police under the impression that they were lying in wait for the security van. A was convicted of inciting B, C & D to commit robbery by robbing a woman at Bow. He appealed on the ground, *inter alia*, that he could not be guilty of inciting B, C & D to commit a crime which could not be committed.

NEILL J., delivering the judgment of the Court: Incitement is one of three inchoate offences, incitement, conspiracy and attempt. Mr. Cocks argued that there was no logical basis for treating the three offences differently when considering their application in circumstances where the complete offence would be impossible to commit, and that therefore the court should apply the principles laid down by the House of Lords in the case of attempts in *Haughton* v. *Smith* and in the case of conspiracy in *D.P.P.* v. *Nock*.

Mr. Cocks pointed to the fact that though the law as laid down by the House of Lords in those two cases had been altered by statute by section 1(2) and section 5(1) of the Criminal Attempts Act 1981, there had been no change in the law relating to the offence of incitement. Accordingly, he said, the common law rules as to impossibility should be applied.

It is to be observed that the omission of the crime of incitement from the Criminal Attempts Act 1981 followed the recommendations of the Law Commission in their report (1980) Law Com. No. 102 and was in accordance with the draft Bill set out in appendix A to that report. The Law Commission explained the omission of incitement from the draft Bill on the basis that in their view the House of Lords in *D.P.P.* v. *Nock* was prepared to distinguish the law relating to incitement from that relating to attempts: see paragraphs 4.2 to 4.4. We have had to give careful attention to these paragraphs in the Law Commission's Report. We have also had to consider with care the passage in the speech of Lord Scarman in *D.P.P.* v.

Nock [1978] A.C. 979 which appears to have formed the basis for the decision by the Law Commission to exclude incitement from their recommendations for change and from their draft Bill. In *D.P.P.* v. *Nock* Lord Scarman made reference to two cases which had been cited to their Lordships. He said, at p. 999:

"Our attention was also drawn in two cases, upon which it may be helpful to comment very briefly. In *R.* v. *McDonough* (1962) 47 Cr.App.R. 37 the Court of Criminal Appeal held that an incitement to receive stolen goods was complete on the making of the incitement even though there were no stolen goods—perhaps even, no goods at all. In *Haggard* v. *Mason* [1976] 1 W.L.R. 186 the Divisional Court held that the offence of offering to supply a controlled drug was committed, even though the drug in fact supplied was not a controlled drug. Neither of these cases infringes the principle of *Haughton* v. *Smith*: for in each case, as Lord Widgery C.J. pointed out in *Haggard* v. *Mason* (p. 189), the offence was complete. In *McDonough,* (1962) 47 Cr.App.R. 37 the *actus reus* was the making of the incitement and in *Haggard's* case it was the making of the offer."

We have come to the conclusion that, on analysis, this passage in Lord Scarman's speech does not support the proposition that cases of incitement are to be treated quite differently at common law from cases of attempt or conspiracy.

The decision in *Haggard* v. *Mason* related to the statutory offence of offering to supply a controlled drug and, as Lord Scarman pointed out, the *actus reus* which the prosecution had to prove was the making of the offer. The explanation of *McDonough's* case, as it seems to us, is that though there may have been no stolen goods or no goods at all which were available to be received at the time of the incitement, the offence of incitement to receive stolen goods could nevertheless be proved because it was not impossible that at the relevant time in the future the necessary goods would be there.

In our view, therefore, the right approach in a case of incitement is the same as that which was underlined by Lord Scarman in *D.P.P.* v. *Nock* when he considered the offence of conspiracy. In every case it is necessary to analyse the evidence with care to decide the precise offence which the defendant is alleged to have incited. Lord Scarman said, at p. 995:

"The indictment makes plain that the Crown is alleging in this case a conspiracy to commit a crime: and no one has suggested that the particulars fail to disclose an offence known to the law. But the appellants submit, and it is not disputed by the Crown, that the agreement as proved was narrower in scope than the conspiracy charged. When the case was before the Court of Appeal, counsel on both sides agreed that the evidence went to prove that the appellants agreed together to obtain cocaine by separating it from the other substance or substances contained in a powder which they had obtained from one of their co-defendants, a Mr. Mitchell. They believed that the powder was a mixture of cocaine and lignocaine, and that they would be able to produce cocaine from it. In fact the powder was lignocaine hydrochloride, an anaesthetic used in dentistry, which contains no cocaine at all. It is impossible to produce, by separation of otherwise, cocaine from lignocaine. . . .

"The trial judge in his direction to the jury, and the Court of Appeal in their judgment dismissing the two appeals, treated this impossibility as an irrelevance. In their view the agreement was what mattered: and there was plain evidence of an agreement to produce cocaine, even though unknown to the two conspirators it could not be done. Neither the trial judge nor the Court of Appeal thought it necessary to carry their analysis of the agreement further. The trial judge described it simply as an agreement to produce cocaine. The Court of Appeal thought it enough that the prosecution had proved 'an agreement to do an act which was forbidden by section 4 of the Misuse of Drugs Act 1971.' Both descriptions are accurate, as far as they go. But neither contains any reference to the limited nature of the agreement proved: it was an agreement upon a specific course of conduct with the object of producing cocaine, and limited to that course of conduct. Since it could not result in the production of cocaine, the two appellants by pursuing it could not commit the statutory offence of producing a controlled drug.''

In our view these words suggest the correct approach at common law to any inchoate offence. It is necessary in every case to decide on the evidence what was the course of conduct which was (as the case may be) incited or agreed or attempted. In some cases the evidence may establish that the persuasion by the inciter was in quite general terms whereas the subsequent agreement of the conspirators was directed to a specific crime and a specific target. In such cases where the committal of the specific offence is shown to be impossible it may be quite logical for the inciter to be convicted even though the alleged conspirators (if not caught by section 5 of the Criminal Attempts Act 1981) may be acquitted. On the other hand, if B and C agree to kill D and A, standing beside B and C, though not intending to take any active part whatever in the crime, encourages them to do so, we can see no satisfactory reason, if it turns out later that D was already dead, why A should be convicted of incitement to murder whereas B and C at common law would be entitled to an acquittal on a charge of conspiracy. The crucial question is to establish on the evidence the course of conduct which the alleged inciter was encouraging.

We return to the facts of the instant case. Mr. Cocks submitted that the "crime" which Bonham and the two Browns were being encouraged to commit was a mere charade. The appellant's father was not planning a real robbery at all and therefore the appellant could not be found guilty of inciting the three men to commit it. In our judgment, however, the answer to Mr. Cocks's argument is to be found in the facts which the prosecution proved against the appellant. As was made clear by Mr. Purnell on behalf of the Crown, the case against the appellant was based on the steps he took to recruit Bonham. At the stage the appellant believed that there was to be a wage snatch and he was encouraging Bonham to take part in it. As Mr. Purnell put it, "The appellant thought he was recruiting for a robbery not for a charade." It is to be remembered that the particulars of offence in the indictment included the words "by robbing a woman at Bow." By no stretch of the imagination was that an impossible offence to carry out and it was that offence which the appellant was inciting Bonham to commit.

For these reasons, therefore, we are satisfied that the appellant was rightly convicted. The appeal is dismissed.

Appeal dismissed.

Questions

1. "The appellant (A) thought he was recruiting for a robbery not a charade." Could X have been convicted of inciting A to commit robbery by robbing a woman at Bow?

2. A incites B to handle goods which they both think are stolen. In fact they have already been recaptured by the police, and are no longer stolen goods. Is A guilty of inciting B to handle stolen goods?

CHAPTER 8

HOMICIDE

	PAGE		PAGE
1. The *Actus Reus* of Homicide	495	i. Unlawful Act Manslaughter	546
2. Murder	497	ii. Reckless Manslaughter	557
i. The Penalty for Murder	497	5. Other Unlawful Homicides	568
ii. The Mental Element in Murder	497	i. Infanticide	568
		ii. Child Destruction	568
iii. Proposals for Reform	505	iii. Abortion	568
3. Special Defences	513	iv. Suicide	575
i. Provocation	513	v. Causing Death by Driving	576
ii. Diminished Responsibility	528	6. Reform of the Law of Homicide	577
4. Involuntary Manslaughter	545		

Note

The true homicides are murder, manslaughter, infanticide, and causing death by driving (as to the latter see *post*, pp. 576–577). Suicide was an offence until the Suicide Act 1961; some aspects of the crime still remain. Child destruction is a near-homicide which is always dealt with as a homicide. Abortion, similarly, approximates to homicide and is best dealt with in this section.

1. THE ACTUS REUS OF HOMICIDE

Note

The common element in homicides is the *actus reus*, expressed by Coke as follows:

"Unlawfully killing a reasonable person who is in being and under the King's Peace, the death following within a year and a day": Coke, 3 Inst. 47.

In relation to the meaning of the word "unlawfully" see *R. v. Williams, ante*, p. 155 and *Beckford* v. *R., ante*, p. 157.

The principal problem in determining the *actus reus* in homicide is that of causation. This is a general problem, basic to criminal liability, although the majority of cases concern homicide. These have been discussed above (see p. 33). Peculiar to homicide, however, is the year and a day rule.

R. v. Dyson
[1908] 2 K.B. 454
Court of Criminal Appeal

The appellant was indicted for the manslaughter of his child. The evidence was that in November 1906 he beat the child into unconsciousness and its skull was fractured. For this offence he received a sentence of four months' imprisonment in the magistrates' court. In December 1907 the appellant again beat the child and severely bruised its face and head. In February 1908 the child developed traumatic meningitis and died in March 1908. By this time the marks of the injuries inflicted in December 1907 had disappeared. The medical evidence was that the fractured skull was the main cause of death but that the later acts of violence would accelerate the death. The defence contended that the fracture was the sole cause of death. The appellant was found guilty and appealed against conviction.

LORD ALVERSTONE C.J.: The jury convicted the prisoner, who appeals against that conviction upon the ground that the judge misdirected the jury in that he left it to them to find the prisoner guilty if they considered the death to have been caused by the injuries inflicted in 1906.

That was clearly not a proper direction, for, whatever one may think of the merits of such a rule of law, it is undoubtedly the law of the land that no person can be convicted of manslaughter where the death does not occur within a year and a day after the injury was inflicted, for in that event it must be attributed to some other cause. ... The proper question to have been submitted to the jury was whether the prisoner accelerated the child's death by the injuries which he inflicted in December 1907.

Conviction quashed

Note

See also *R.* v. *Coroner for Inner West London, ex p. De Luca* [1989] 3 All E.R. 414.

Questions

1. Is this rule of remoteness necessary? The Criminal Law Revision Committee's 14th Report on Offences Against the Person (Cmnd. 7844, 1980) suggested that "it would be wrong for a person to remain almost indefinitely at risk for prosecution for murder. A line has to be drawn somewhere and in our opinion the present law operates satisfactorily" (section 39).

2. Should there be a legal definition of death? See *R.* v. *Malcherek, ante,* p. 46; Williams, T.C.L. pp. 279–285, and C.L.R.C., 14th Report, § 37.

3. What is a life in being? See next case.

R. v. Poulton
(1832) 5 C. & P. 330; 172 E.R. 997
Central Criminal Court

The defendant had given birth to a child. Its body was found with a ligature round its neck. Three medical witnesses called for the prosecution all said that although the child had breathed they could not tell whether the child had been completely born, as breathing can take place during birth. The defendant was charged with murder.

LITTLEDALE J.: With respect to birth the being born must mean that the whole body is brought into the world: and it is not sufficient that the child respires in the progress of the birth. Whether the child was born alive depends mainly upon the evidence of the medical man. None of them say that the child was born alive; they only say that it had breathed. . . .

Not guilty of murder

Note

The period 1830–40 saw many cases on this point reported by Carrington and Payne, *e.g. R. v. Brain* (1834) 6 C. & P. 349, *R. v. Crutchley* (1837) 7 C. & P. 814 and *R. v. Reeves* (1839) 9 C. & P. 25, which last case added the point that the umbilical cord need not be severed for there to be a life in being. This legal test is not apparently in accord with medical opinion where the emphasis is on breathing; see Stanley B. Atkinson, "Life, Birth and Live Birth" (1904) 20 L.Q.R. 134, 141 *et seq.* As long as the child has "lived" it does not matter that the injuries causing its death occurred while it was still in the womb: *R. v. West* (1848) 2 Car. & Kir. 784. See also child destruction and abortion, *post*, p. 568.

2. MURDER

i. The Penalty for Murder

Note

"The punishment for murder in the old days was a mandatory death sentence; now, by a quirk of language, it was to be a mandatory life sentence" (Williams, T.C.L., p. 247). Capital punishment for murder was abolished by the Murder (Abolition of the Death Penalty) Act 1965 which replaced the unhappy compromise of partial abolition established by the Homicide Act 1957.

The unusual feature of the penalty for murder is that it is mandatory. The judge has no discretion other than to recommend that the convicted person be detained in prison for a specified minimum term of years (1965 Act, s.1(2)). The *Report of the Select Committee of the House of Lords on Murder and Life Imprisonment* (H.L. Paper 78–1, 1989), para. 118, recommended that the mandatory sentence for murder should be abolished. The mandatory sentence, whether death or life, has been a crucial factor in the shaping of the law of homicide, insanity and diminished responsibility. Any discussion of reform of the law of homicide is forced to take account of this. See *post*, p. 505.

ii. The Mental Element in Murder

R. Goff, "The Mental Element in the Crime of Murder" (1988) 104 L.Q.R. 30, 33

"I must emphasise that murder is a crime at common law; and that the definition of the mental element is therefore a common law, and not a statutory, definition. ... The mental element in the crime of murder used to be called 'malice aforethought.' This is, of course, thoroughly misleading; since neither premeditation nor malice towards the victim were necessary. Furthermore, there were three kinds of malice aforethought; express malice, implied malice, and constructive malice. Express malice was simple; that existed where the defendant actually intended to kill his victim. Implied malice existed when he intended to cause 'grievous bodily harm' to his victim and, by so doing, killed him. Constructive malice existed in two circumstances: first, when the defendant killed his victim in the course of, or in furtherance of, committing a felony (as a serious crime was then called); and second, when the defendant killed his victim in the course of, or for the purpose of, resisting an officer of justice, or resisting or avoiding or preventing a lawful arrest, or effecting or assisting an escape or rescue from legal custody. However, we need spend little time on constructive malice, because in English law this category of murder was abolished by section 1 of the Homicide Act 1957."

Homicide Act 1957, section 1

"(1) Where a person kills another in the course or furtherance of some other offence, the killing shall not amount to murder unless done with the same malice aforethought (express or implied) as is required for a killing to amount to murder when not done in the course or furtherance of another offence.

(2) For the purposes of the foregoing subsection, a killing done in the course or for the purpose of resisting an officer of justice or of resisting or avoiding or preventing a lawful arrest, or of affecting or assisting an escape or rescue from legal custody, shall be treated as a killing in the course or furtherance of an offence."

R. v. Vickers
[1957] 2 Q.B. 664
Court of Criminal Appeal

The appellant broke into a shop intending to steal. He was seen by the occupant of the living quarters above, an elderly woman of 72. He struck her many blows and kicked her in the face. She died as a result. The appellant was convicted of capital murder.

LORD GODDARD C.J.: ... The point that has been raised on the appellant's behalf turns entirely on section 1(1) of the Homicide Act, 1957, which came into force this year.

The marginal note to that section (s.1(1)), which, of course, is not part of the section but may be looked at as some indication of its purpose, is: "Abolition of 'constructive malice.' "

"Constructive malice" is an expression which I do not think will be found in any particular decision, but it is to be found in the textbooks, and is something different from implied malice. The expression "constructive malice" is generally used where a person causes death during the course of carrying out a felony which involves violence—that always amounted to murder. There may be many cases in which a man is not intending to cause death, as, for instance, where he gives a mere push and a person falls and strikes his head or falls down the stairs and breaks his neck, and although the push would never have been considered in the ordinary way as an act which would be likely to cause death, yet if it was done in the course of carrying out a felony it would amount to murder. Another illustration of "constructive malice" would be if a man raped a woman, and she died in the course of the struggle. The fact that he may only have used a moderate or even small degree of violence in the struggle would have been no defence to a charge of murder, because if he caused death, he did so during the commission of the felony of rape. Another instance of constructive malice which was always held sufficient to amount to murder was if a police officer was killed in the execution of his duty. If a person was resisting arrest before the Act of 1957 and caused the death of a police officer, although he might only have used a little violence on the officer he was guilty of murder. Murder is, of course, killing with malice aforethought, but "malice aforethought" is a term of art. It has always been defined in English law as, either an express intention to kill, as could be inferred when a person, having uttered threats against another, produced a lethal weapon and used it on a victim, or implied, where, by a voluntary act, the accused intended to cause grievous bodily harm to the victim and the victim died as the result. If a person does an act which amounts to the infliction of grievous bodily harm he cannot say that he only intended to cause a certain degree of harm. It is called *malum in se* in the old cases and he must take the consequences. If he intends to inflict grievous bodily harm and that person dies, that has always been held in English law, and was at the time this Act was passed, sufficient to imply the malice aforethought which is a necessary constituent of murder.

It will be observed that the section preserves implied malice as well as express malice, and the words "Where a person kills another in the course or furtherance of some other offence" cannot, in our opinion, be referred to the infliction of the grievous bodily harm if the case which is made against the accused is that he killed a person by having assaulted the person with intent to do grievous bodily harm, and from the bodily harm he inflicted that person dies. The "furtherance of some other offence" must refer to the offence he was committing or endeavouring to commit other than the killing, otherwise there would be no sense in it. It was always the English law, as I have said, that if death was caused by a person in the course of committing a felony involving violence that was murder. Therefore, in the present case it is perfectly clear that the words "Where a person kills another in the course or furtherance of some other offence" must be attributed to the burglary he was committing. The killing was in the course or furtherance of that burglary. He killed that person in the course of the burglary because he realised that the victim recognised him and he therefore inflicted grievous bodily harm on her, perhaps only intending to render her unconscious, but he did intend to inflict grievous bodily harm by the blows he inflicted upon her and by kicking her in the face, of which there was evidence. The section goes on: "the killing shall not amount to murder unless done with the same malice aforethought (express or implied) as is required for a killing to amount to murder when not done in the course or furtherance of another offence." It would seem clear, therefore, that the legislature is providing that where one has a killing committed in the course or furtherance of another offence, that other offence must be ignored. What have to be considered are the circumstances of the killing, and if the killing would amount to murder by reason of the express or implied malice, then that person is guilty of capital murder. It is not enough to say he killed in the course of the felony unless the killing is done in a manner which would amount to murder ignoring the commission of felony. It seems to the court, therefore, that in the present case, a burglar attacked a householder to prevent recognition. The householder died as the result of blows inflicted upon her—blows or kicks or both—and if this section had not been passed there could be no doubt that the appellant would have been guilty of murder. He is guilty of murder because he has killed a person with the necessary malice aforethought being implied from the fact that he intended to do grievous bodily harm. . . .

The court desires to say quite firmly that in considering the construction of section 1(1) it is impossible to say that the doing of grievous bodily harm is the other offence which is referred to in the first line and a half of the section. One has to show, independently of the fact that the accused is committing another offence, that the act which caused the death was done with malice aforethought as implied by law. The existence of express or implied malice is expressly preserved by the Act and, in our opinion, a perfectly proper direction was given by Hinchcliffe J. to the jury, and accordingly this appeal fails and is dismissed.

Appeal dismissed

Director of Public Prosecutions v. Smith
[1961] A.C. 290
House of Lords

The appellant was driving a car containing some stolen property when a policeman told him to draw into the kerb. Instead he accelerated and the constable clung on to the side of the car. The car followed an erratic course and the policeman fell in front of another car and was killed. The appellant drove on for 200 yards, dumped the stolen property, and then returned. He was charged with capital murder. The judge directed the jury to consider whether the appellant intended to cause the officer grievous bodily harm. He was convicted but the Court of Criminal Appeal quashed the conviction for capital murder and substituted one for manslaughter. The Crown appealed to the House of Lords, which restored the conviction for capital murder.

VISCOUNT KILMUIR L.C.: . . . The last criticism of the summing-up which was raised before your Lordships was in regard to the meaning which the learned judge directed the jury was to be given to the words "grievous bodily harm." The passages of which complaint is made are the following: "When one speaks of an intent to inflict grievous bodily harm upon a person, the expression grievous bodily harm does not mean for that purpose some harm which is permanent or even dangerous. It simply means some harm which is sufficient seriously to interfere with the victim's health or comfort."

"In murder the killer intends to kill, or to inflict some harm which will seriously interfere for a time with health or comfort."

"If the accused intended to do the officer some harm which would seriously interfere at least for a time with his health and comfort, and thus perhaps enable the accused to make good his escape for the time being at least that would be murder too."

The direction in these passages was clearly based on the well-known direction of Willes J. in *R. v. Ashman* (1858) 1 F. & F. 88 and on the words used by Graham B. in *R. v. Cox* (1818) R. & R. 362 (C.C.R.). Indeed, this is a direction which is commonly given by judges in trials for the statutory offence under section 18 of the Offences Against the Person Act 1861, and has on occasions been given in murder trials: *cf. R. v. Vickers (ante,* p. 498).

My Lords, I confess that whether one is considering the crime of murder or the statutory offence, I can find no warrant for giving the words "grievous bodily harm" a meaning other than that which the words convey in their ordinary and natural meaning. "Bodily harm" needs no explanation, and "grievous" means no more and no less than "really serious". ...

It was, however, contended before your lordships on behalf of the respondent, that the words ought to be given a more restricted meaning in considering the intent necessary to establish malice in a murder case. It was said that the intent must be to do an act "obviously dangerous to life" or "likely to kill." It is true that in many of the cases the likelihood of death resulting has been incorporated into the definition of grievous bodily harm, but this was done, no doubt, merely to emphasise that the bodily harm must be really serious, and it is unnecessary, and I would add inadvisable, to add anything to the expression "grievous bodily harm" in its ordinary and natural meaning.

To return to the summing-up in the present case, it is true that in the two passages cited the learned judge referred to "grievous bodily harm" in the terms used by Willes J. in *R.* v. *Ashman*, but in no less than four further passages, and in particular in the vital direction given just before the jury retired he referred to "serious hurt" or "serious harm." Read as a whole, it is, I think, clear that there was no misdirection. Further, on the facts of this case it is quite impossible to say that the harm which the respondent must be taken to have contemplated could be anything but of a very serious nature coming well within the term of "grievous bodily harm."

Before leaving this appeal I should refer to a further contention which was but faintly adumbrated, namely, that section 1(1) of the Homicide Act 1957, had abolished malice constituted by a proved intention to do grievous bodily harm, and that, accordingly, *R.* v. *Vickers* (*ante*, p. 498), which held the contrary, was wrongly decided. As to this it is sufficient to say that in my opinion the Act does not in any way abolish such malice. The words in parenthesis in section 1(1) of the Act and a reference to section 5(2) make this clear beyond doubt.

Appeal allowed

Note

In *R.* v. *Hyam* [1975] A.C. 55, *ante*, p. 78, the issue whether intention to cause grievous bodily harm constituted malice aforethought, was left in doubt as Lords Diplock and Kilbrandon held that it was not sufficient *mens rea* for murder. Lord Diplock stated:

"[T]he now familiar expression 'grievous bodily harm' appears to owe its place in the development of the English law of homicide to its use in 1803 in Lord Ellenborough's Act (43 Geo. 3, c. 58), which made it a felony to shoot at, stab or cut any other person 'with intent ... to murder, ... maim, disfigure, or disable, ... or ... do some other grievous bodily harm ... ' [section 1]. ... For my part, I am satisfied that the decision of this House in *D.P.P.* v. *Smith* was wrong in so far as it rejected the submission that in order to amount to the crime of murder the offender, if he did not intend to kill, must have intended or foreseen as a likely consequence of his act that human life would be endangered. ... I think the reason why this House fell into error was because it failed to appreciate that the concept of 'intention to do grievous bodily harm' only became relevant to the common law of murder as a result of the passing of Lord Ellenborough's Act in 1803 and the application to the new felony thereby created of the then current common law doctrine of constructive malice. This led this House to approach the problem as one of the proper construction of the words 'grievous bodily harm' which because, though *only* because, of the doctrine of constructive malice had over the past 100 years become part of the standard definition of *mens rea* in murder, as well as part of the statutory definition of *mens rea* in the statutory felony of causing grievous bodily harm with intent to cause grievous bodily harm. I do not question that in the statutory offence 'grievous bodily harm' bears the meaning ascribed to it by this House in *D.P.P.* v. *Smith* but the actual problem which confronted this House in *D.P.P.* v. *Smith* and the Court of Criminal Appeal in *R.* v. *Vickers* was a much more complex one. . . . "

Lord Hailsham and Viscount Dilhorne expressly approved *Vickers*. Viscount Dilhorne stated:

"I now turn to the second contention advanced on behalf of the appellant. This has two facets: first, that the reference to the intent to cause grievous bodily harm has been based on the law that killing in the course or furtherance of a felony is murder, and that when the Homicide Act 1957 was enacted abolishing constructive malice it meant that it no longer sufficed to establish intent to do grievous bodily harm; and, secondly, that, if intent to do grievous bodily harm still made a killing murder, it must be intent to do grievous bodily harm of such a character that life was likely to be endangered.

Committing grievous bodily harm was for many, many years, and until all felonies were abolished, a felony. Consequently so long as the doctrine of constructive malice was part of the law of England, to secure a conviction for murder it was only necessary to prove that the death resulted from an act committed in the course of or in furtherance of the commission of grievous bodily harm. But when one looks at the cases and the old textbooks, one does not find any indication that proof of intent to do grievous bodily harm was an ingredient of murder only on account of the doctrine of constructive malice. Indeed, one finds the contrary. . . .

This was recognised in the report of the Royal Commission on Capital Punishment (1953) (Cmnd. 8932). Their five propositions stated in paragraph 76 which were, so the report said, generally accepted to be properly included in the category of murder, were

' . . . all cases where the accused either *intended* to cause death or grievous bodily harm or *knew* that his act was likely to cause death or grievous bodily harm.'

The Royal Commission went on to recommend the abolition of constructive malice, and in paragraph 123 suggested a clause for inclusion in a Bill to bring that about.

Section 1 of the Homicide Act 1957 is in all material respects similar to the clause proposed. It would, indeed, be odd if the Royal Commission by recommending the abolition of constructive malice had in fact proposed the abolition of intent to do grievous bodily harm as an ingredient of murder when the commission had not intended and did not recommend that. Parliament may, of course, do more by an Act than it intends but if, as in my opinion was the case, intent to do grievous bodily harm was entirely distinct from constructive malice, then the conclusion that

Parliament did so by the Homicide Act 1957 must be rejected. In my opinion, *R.* v. *Vickers* was rightly decided and this House was right in saying that that was so in *D.P.P.* v. *Smith.*

I now turn to the second facet of the appellant's contention, namely, that the words 'grievous bodily harm' are to be interpreted as meaning harm of such a character as is likely to endanger life. . . .

Our task is to say what, in our opinion, the law is, not what it should be. In the light of what I have said, in my opinion, the words 'grievous bodily harm' must, as Viscount Kilmuir said [in *D.P.P.* v. *Smith*] be given their ordinary and natural meaning and not have the gloss put on them for which the appellant contends. . . .

To change the law to substitute 'bodily injury known to the offender to be likely to cause death' for 'grievous bodily harm' is a task that should . . . be left to Parliament if it thinks such a change expedient. . . . I share the view of the majority of the Royal Commission that such a change would not lead to any great difference in the day-to-day administration of the law."

Note

Lord Cross was not prepared to decide on the issue as it had not been fully argued before the House.

The matter was finally resolved in the following case:

R. v. Cunningham
[1981] 2 All E.R. 863
House of Lords

The appellant suspected (wrongly) that the victim was associating with the woman he planned to marry. The victim died from blows struck by the appellant with a chair. He appealed against his conviction for murder on the grounds that to tell the jury that intending really serious harm was sufficient for murder was a misdirection. The Court of Appeal dismissed his appeal but certified that a point of law of general public importance was involved.

LORD HAILSHAM OF ST. MARYLEBONE L.C.: with whom Lords Wilberforce, Simon of Glaisdale and Bridge of Harwich agreed; . . . The real nerve of Lord Diplock's argument [in *R.* v. *Hyam*], however, does, as it seems to me, depend on the importance to be attached to the passing in 1803 of Lord Ellenborough's Act (43 Geo. 3 c. 58) by which, for the first time, wounding with the intent to inflict grievous bodily harm became a felony. This, Lord Diplock believes, rendered it possible to apply the doctrine of "felony murder" as defined in Stephen's category (c), abolished in 1957, to all cases of felonious wounding, where death actually ensued from the wound. The abolition of "felony murder" in 1957 was thus seen to enable the judiciary to pursue the mental element in murder behind the curtain imposed on it by the combined effect of the statutory crime of felonious wounding and the doctrine of constructive malice, and so to arrive at a position in which the mental element could be redefined in terms either of an intention to kill, or an intention actually to endanger human life, to correspond with the recommendations of the Fourth Report of Her Majesty's Commissioners on Criminal Law (March 8, 1839).

It seems to me, however, that this highly ingenious argument meets with two insuperable difficulties. I accept that it appears to be established that the actual phrase "grievous bodily harm," if not an actual coinage by Lord Ellenborough's Act, can never be found to have appeared in print before it, though it has subsequently become current coin, and has passed into the general legal jargon of statute law, and the cases decided thereon. But counsel, having diligently carried us through the institutional writers on homicide, starting with Coke, and ending with East, with several citations from the meagre reports available, only succeeded in persuading me at least that, even prior to Lord Ellenborough's Act of 1803, and without the precise label "grievous bodily harm," the authors and the courts had consistently treated as murder, and therefore unclergiable, any killing with intent to do serious harm, however described, to which the label "grievous bodily harm," as defined by Viscount Kilmuir L.C. in *D.P.P.* v. *Smith* [1961] A.C. 290 at 334 reversing the "murder by pinprick" doctrine arising from *R.* v. *Ashman* (1858) 1 F. & F. 88, could properly have been applied. . . . There is a second difficulty in the way of treating Lord Ellenborough's Act as providing the kind of historical watershed demanded by Lord Diplock's speech and contended for in the instant appeal by the appellant's counsel. This consists in the fact that, though the nineteenth century judges might in theory have employed the felony-murder rule to apply to cases where death ensued in the course of a felonious wounding, they do not appear to have done so in fact. No case was cited where they did so. On the contrary, there appears to be no historical discontinuity between criminal jurisprudence before and after 1803. Stephen never so treated the matter (either in his text, or except in the last few lines, in his Note XIV). It was not so treated in the Australian case of *La Fontaine* v. *R.* (1976) 136 C.L.R. 62 (after *Hyam*, but in a jurisdiction in which the constructive malice rule still applied). . . .

Counsel for the appellant used one further ground, not found in Lord Diplock's opinion, for supporting the minority view in *Hyam*. This was the difficulty which, as he suggested, a jury would find in deciding what amounted to an intention to inflict "grievous bodily harm" or "really serious bodily harm" as formulated in *Smith*. I do not find this argument convincing. For much more than a hundred years juries have constantly been required to arrive at the answer to precisely this question in cases falling short of murder (*e.g.* the s.18 cases). I cannot see that the fact that death ensues should render the identical question particularly anomalous, or its answer, though admittedly more important, any more difficult. Nor am I persuaded that a reformulation of murder so as to confine the *mens rea* to an intention to endanger life instead of an intention to do really serious bodily harm would either improve the clarity of the law or facilitate the task of juries in finding the facts. On the contrary, in cases where death has ensued as the result of the infliction of really serious injuries I can see endless opportunity for fruitless and interminable discussion of the question whether the accused intended to endanger life and thus expose the victim to a probable danger of death, or whether he simply intended to inflict really serious injury. . . . In my opinion, *Vickers* was a correct statement of the law as it was after amendment by the Homicide Act 1957, and in *Smith* and *Hyam* your Lordships were right to indorse *Vickers*. . . .

LORD EDMUND-DAVIES: The minority dissents of Lord Diplock and Lord Kilbrandon, in *Hyam*, above, were based on their conclusions that the law as to intent in murder had been incorrectly stated by this House in *Smith* and that exposure of the error should lead to a quashing of Hyam's conviction for murder. In the present case, on the other hand, your Lordships have unanimously concluded and now reiterate that the law as to murderous intent was correctly stated in *R.* v. *Vickers*. Even so, is now the time and is this House the place to reveal and declare (so as to "avoid injustice") what ought to be the law and, in the light of that revelation, here and now to recant from its former adoption of *Vickers*?

My lords, I would give a negative answer to the question. I say this despite the fact that, after much veering of thought over a period of years, the view I presently favour is that there should be no conviction for murder unless an intent to kill is established, the wide range of punishment for manslaughter being fully adequate to deal with all less heinous forms of homicide. I find it passing strange that a person can be convicted of murder if death results from, say, his intentional breaking of another's arm, an action which, while undoubtedly involving the infliction of "really serious harm" and, as such, calling for severe punishment, would in most cases be unlikely to kill. And yet, for the lesser offence of attempted murder, nothing less than an intent to kill will suffice. But I recognise the force of the contrary view that the outcome of intentionally inflicting serious harm can be so unpredictable that anyone prepared to act so wickedly has little ground for complaint if, where death results, he is convicted and punished as severely as one who intended to kill.

So there are forceful arguments both ways. And they are arguments of the greatest public consequence, particularly in these turbulent days when, as Lord Hailsham L.C. has vividly reminded us, violent crimes have become commonplace. Resolution of that conflict cannot, in my judgment, be a matter for your Lordships' House alone. It is a task for none other than Parliament, as the constitutional organ best fitted to weigh the relevant and opposing factors. Its solution has already been attempted extra-judicially on many occasions, but with no real success. My Lords, we can do none other than wait to see what will emerge when the task is undertaken by the legislature, as I believe it should be when the time is opportune. . . .

Appeal dismissed

iii. Proposals for reform

D. A. Thomas, "Form and Function in Criminal Law" in Reshaping the Criminal Law (ed. Glazebrook), pp. 21, 25

"No better example can be found of the failure of all those concerned with development of the criminal law—including Parliament and the appellate judiciary as well as the advisory bodies—to see the substantive law in a functional context than the history of the definition of murder from 1960 to the present day. With few exceptions, discussions of the propriety of the objective test of intention and the proper scope of the offence have proceeded on the same lines for 18 years with only a passing reference to the fact that what was being decided by establishing a definition had utterly changed. In 1960 the questions in issue in *D.P.P.* v. *Smith* were hanging matters, and Smith was sentenced to death on his original conviction. The Law Commission's Report on Imputed Criminal Intent, which was the first attempt to clarify the implications of the case and propose amending legislation, followed the abolition of the death penalty for murder. The statute which implemented part of the Law Commission's proposals also created the Parole Board. As a result of these two developments the definition of the offence of murder was no longer concerned with the scope of liability to the death penalty, and had become a means of establishing the respective roles of judge and Parole Board in determining the period of time to be served by a person convicted of homicide and (incidentally) the manner in which that decision was to be made. This fundamental change in the nature of what was actually being decided had little obvious impact on the thinking of the House of Lords when the matter was reconsidered in 1974 [*R.* v. *Hyam, ante,* p. 78], six years after the new system of dealing with murderers had been established. With the exception of Lord Kilbrandon who (with respect) drew the wrong conclusions, their Lordships did not relate their arguments to the realities of the processes of determining the disposal of those convicted of murder and manslaughter. The problem of defining murder was essentially a formal question, to be considered and decided in terms which would have been equally relevant 100 years ago.

The results of maintaining a separation between the development of the substantive criminal law on the one hand and procedure and penal policy on the other is a system of dealing with homicide and grave personal violence which makes no sense at all in functional terms. A man strikes another with a broken glass in a public-house fight in circumstances which would normally lead to a sentence of three or four years' imprisonment for causing grievous bodily harm with intent; fortuitously the victim dies from his injuries, and unless either the prosecution or the jury will relax the law the assailant is convicted of murder and subject to a mandatory sentence of life imprisonment. In another case the defendant makes a determined attempt to kill his victim, using carefully contrived means based on thoughtful preparations; despite his best endeavours his plans miscarry and he is convicted of attempted murder: his sentence is absolutely within the discretion of the sentencing judge. Two men act in concert in the murder of a third. The first is convicted of murder and receives the mandatory sentence of life imprisonment. The second tenders evidence of psychopathic disorder and secures a reduction in his guilt to manslaughter by reason of diminished responsibility: the judge exercises his discretion to sentence him to life imprisonment. Some years pass: the first, having paid his debt (or at least made a down-payment on it) to society, is released by the Home Secretary on the recommendation of the Parole Board. His co-defendant, having established to the satisfaction of the jury—possibly in the face of prosecution evidence to the contrary—that he is suffering from psychopathic disorder—remains in custody, denied parole on the grounds that he is too dangerous to be released. What is counsel's duty in such a case? Should he advise his client to plead guilty as a sane murderer, in the hope of achieving parole within a decade, or aim for an immediate forensic victory which his client may in the long term find to be of the pyrrhic variety? A provision originally intended to mitigate the severity of the law by reducing the scope of liability to the death penalty has, in the context of changes in penal practice, become potentially a trap, at least for the accused person whose defence is based on a condition which is likely to continue and justify precautionary custody.

Other examples abound. The present definition of murder (whatever its precise terms may be) is clearly not a satisfactory basis for selecting offenders for a unique variety of sentencing procedure. In so far as the mandatory life sentence is justified by the special problems of estimating the chances of future violence by those who have killed once, the existence of special defences such as diminished responsibility and provocation, introduced in earlier times for different purposes, undermines the logic of the sentence by excepting from its scope just those offenders who are most likely to prove dangerous for the future. If the justification for the mandatory life sentence is the unique gravity of the offence and the need to emphasise the particular abhorrence of society for the murderer, that justification is at least diluted by the extension of the definition of murder to include the fortuitous killer. The extension of the definition of murder by the felony-murder rule and the recognition of an intention to inflict grievous bodily harm as a sufficient mental state for conviction may have made some sense in the days when the offence was capital, as directing the supposedly unique deterrent effect of the death sentence at the potential offender who was prepared to risk the use of grave violence to achieve his objects. Now that justification has gone, the effect of the extension of the definition of murder beyond intentional killing weakens whatever morally educative force the mandatory life sentence possesses.

A reconstruction of the law of homicide must begin with a decision on the nature of the sentencing structure which is to be attached to the offences concerned. It would clearly be absurd to design a series of definitions on the assumption that a mandatory sentence in some form will continue to exist for murder, and then enact those definitions against the background of a discretionary sentence. The present shape of the law of murder is the product of the process of reducing the scope of the death penalty; a new approach must start with sentencing structure and proceed to establish the graduations and degrees of liability necessary to the rational operation of that structure."

Report of the Advisory Council on the Penal System, "Sentences of Imprisonment" Home Office, 1978

"Section 224 Although murder has been traditionally and distinctively considered the most serious crime, it is not a homogeneous offence but a crime of considerable variety. It ranges from deliberate cold-blooded killing in pursuit of purely selfish ends to what is commonly referred to as "mercy killing." Instead of automatically applying a single sentence to such an offence, we believe that sentences for murder should reflect this variety with correspondingly variable terms of imprisonment or, in the exceptional case, even with a non-custodial penalty. This is primarily because we do not think that anyone should, without the most specific justification, be subjected to the disadvantages which we see in indeterminate sentencing (see paragraph 226). It is also because we cannot believe that the problems of predicting future behaviour at the time of conviction are inherently more difficult in a murder case than in any other case where there is a measure of instability, or that judges are any less able to make predictions or to assess degrees of culpability in murder cases than in any others. But it is also because efforts to alleviate the harshness of the mandatory penalty have led to complications in legal proceedings for which we believe there can be no proper justification.

Section 225 The efforts at alleviation to which we refer are, first of all, the two special defences of provocation and diminished responsibility which, if successful, reduce the conviction to manslaughter. Although a conviction for manslaughter may be considered less of a stigma than a conviction for murder, to the offender the important difference often is that the lesser conviction avoids the mandatory penalty. The jurisprudence that has developed out of this defence demonstrates the conceptual difficulties of seeking to mitigate a penal consequence via the substantive law. Provocation may be a factor in any crime; it can and does properly affect the sentence passed on the offender, but only in this one case does it reduce the finding of guilt to a lesser offence. Similarly, the legal concept which enables the defence of diminished responsibility, under section 2 of the Homicide Act 1957, to reduce the crime of murder to manslaughter, creates difficulties. If the mental incapacity is not sufficient to negative the requisite mental element for murder, there are problems in describing the offence as any other crime. If judges had discretion in sentencing, the issues of provocation and diminished responsibility could be considered in their proper place, as mitigating factors in the sentencing process."

Report of the Select Committee of the House of Lords on Murder and Life Imprisonment (H.L. Paper 78–1, Session 1988–89), para. 118

"Opinion of the Committee
118. The Committee agree with the majority of their witnesses that the mandatory life sentence for murder should be abolished. Among the considerations which carried most weight with the Committee was the weight of judicial opinion in England and Wales. The Lord Chief Justice and 12 out of 19 judges of the High Court and the Court of Appeal were in favour of a discretionary sentence. The Committee also note that the great majority of judges who took part in the vote in the House of Lords in 1965 were in favour of the discretionary sentence."

Note

The Law Commission Draft Criminal Code Bill incorporates, with a few modifications, the recommendations of the Criminal Law Revision Committee, Fourteenth Report, *Offences Against the Person*, Cmnd. 7844 (1980). On the question of the *mens rea* of murder the arguments have centred on whether a state of mind other than an intent to kill should suffice and if so what this should be.

Criminal Law Revision Committee, 14th Report, Offences Against the Person, Cmnd. 7844 (1980), paras. 19–31

"Principles
19. It is the mental element in murder which distinguishes it from involuntary manslaughter. If, as we recommend in paragraph 15, murder is to continue to be a crime distinct from manslaughter, we need to define the mental element which will distinguish the gravest from the less grave homicides. We recognise that a mental element defined in terms of the defendant's intention (or, in certain circumstances, recklessness) with respect to the consequences of his act is an imperfect instrument with which to achieve this distinction. Many other factors affect the gravity of the offence. The defendant's motive may be of the greatest significance. An intentional killing done out of compassion may be much less reprehensible than a merely reckless killing committed in the course of a robbery. It is, however, not practicable to provide in the definition of an offence for the wide variety of motives which may induce men to act. It is equally impracticable to take into account other surrounding circumstances which may make the killing more or less heinous. The most that a definition can achieve is that the generality of cases falling within the definition of the graver offence will be more heinous than the generality of cases falling within the definition of the less grave offence. One of the principal reasons for preserving murder as a separate offence is the stigma that attaches to it and the deterrent effect which that stigma may have. It is important that the definition of murder should, so far as possible, ensure that those convicted of murder will be deserving of the stigma. Too wide a law of murder would not only be unjust but would also tend to diminish the stigma to which we (and most of those who commented on our Working Paper) attach value.

Liability where there is no recklessness as to death

20. In our opinion the mental element of murder is too broadly stated in *Hyam*. . . .

[The C.L.R.C. rejected the proposition that it is murder if a person kills by doing an act knowing that serious bodily harm is a [highly] probable result of the act.]

21. . . . [I]t is wrong in principle that a person should be liable to be convicted of murder who neither intended nor was reckless as to the most important element in the offence, namely death. The consequence of that is that an intention to cause serious bodily harm if standing alone should cease to be a sufficient mental element for murder.

22. It is sometimes argued that a person who intends to cause serious bodily harm *must* realise that there is a risk of causing death; but this is not necessarily so. The more serious the injury intended, the more likely it is that the jury will be satisfied that the defendant knew that his act might kill. In principle we do not consider that anything less than the intention to kill should in future suffice for murder (see paragraph 23 below), but we do indeed propose that, additionally, one who intends serious injury foreseeing a risk of death should be guilty of murder (paragraph 28 below). Thus, the escaping robber who has shot at and killed a pursuing police officer would be likely to be convicted of murder even though he claimed that he only intended to stop his victim from continuing the pursuit. A jury would probably be satisfied that the robber knew that his act might kill; but there are many types of bodily harm which might be considered serious where no one would expect that death might occur. There is no legal definition of "serious bodily harm" and we do not propose one; but it may be supposed that a jury might find that to break a man's arm would be to cause him serious injury. No doubt a person intentionally inflicting such an injury would deserve severe punishment; but it would seem quite inappropriate to convict him of murder if his victim dies because of some unusual physiological condition he has.

Should all reckless killings be murder?

23. We considered whether to propose a definition of murder in terms of intentional or reckless killing, but it seemed to us such a wide offence that it could not be called murder. It would include many killings that are now manslaughter and would not be generally thought to be murder. Under *Hyam* a person is not guilty of murder unless he foresees a [high] probability of death (or serious injury), whereas a person may be reckless (in the sense in which both the Law Commission and this Committee use the term) if he foresees any possibility of causing death where the risk he is taking is an unreasonable one. A builder who uses a method of construction which he knows might, in some circumstances, be dangerous to life, might be guilty of an unlawful homicide if a fatal accident results; but it would be wrong to hold him guilty of the same offence as the deliberate killer and for him to be subject to a mandatory sentence of life imprisonment. 'We recognise that a very grave result may follow from taking a risk thought to be merely a slight one, for example where thieves cut railway signalling cable and cause a derailment with much loss of life. Such conduct could be severely punished under our proposals, as under the existing law; but it would not generally be regarded as murder and we do not think it should be the same offence in law as those killings which everyone would instantly recognise as murder.'

Should killing with a high degree of recklessness be murder?

24. If reckless conduct causing death is not enough to make a man guilty of murder, why should there not be a conviction for that offence if the defendant knows that there is a high probability or even a mere probability or a serious risk that death will be caused? ... What is a high probability? or a mere probability? Or a serious risk? Some may think that there is a probability if death is more likely than not to result—the 3 to 2 odds on chance—and that there is a high probability if the odds are shorter (but how much shorter?). Others may think that there is a probability when the odds are much longer. Should a man who kills another while playing an adaptation of 'Russian roulette' be guilty of murder if he knows there is a bullet in one of the six chambers of the revolver? Or in two, three, four or five chambers? It has been suggested that, since the outcome of death is so serious, knowledge of a statistically small risk of causing death could be held to be knowledge of probability and even high probability. We do not accept that suggestion, but the fact that it can be made confirms our opinion as to the unsatisfactory nature of the formula.

25. We appreciate that it is difficult to draw the line between what we recommend should be the meaning of intention and the high probability test mentioned in *Hyam*. To confine intention to wanting a particular result to happen would be too rigid. ...

Should killing ever be murder when death is not intended?

28. We think that murder should be extended beyond intentional killing in one respect. There is one category of reckless killing where we believe there would be general agreement that the stigma of murder is well merited. That is where the killer intended unlawfully to cause serious bodily injury and knew that there was a risk of causing death. The intention to cause serious bodily injury puts this killing into a different class from that of a person who is merely reckless, even gravely reckless. The offender has shot, stabbed or otherwise seriously injured the victim, and the circumstances are so grave that the jury can find that he must have realised that there was a risk of causing death. For example, he has shot at a pursuer when he is escaping after a robbery, intending only to disable the pursuer but appreciating that there was a risk of wounding him mortally. The line between this and an intentional killing is so fine that both cases are justifiably classified as murder, as they are in the present law. To classify this particular type of risk-taking as murder does not involve the danger of escalation to cases of recklessness in general, since it is tied specifically to circumstances in which the defendant intended to inflict serious injury. ...

30. In view of the strong public feeling about terrorism, we think it right to reiterate that we recognise that our proposals would not bring within the law of murder some forms of terrorist killing, for example, by those who plant bombs designed to damage property and cause fear (rather than to take life) and therefore timed to explode when it is unlikely that anyone will be around. Such persons may not think it probable that their acts will cause death or serious injury to anyone (and may not therefore be guilty of murder under the existing law). Nor, *a fortiori*, would they have the intent required for murder under our proposals above. Yet they must clearly appreciate that there is some risk that their acts will cause death. It is equally plain that the risk is one which it is unreasonable to take, and that to take it therefore constitutes recklessness in the sense in which we propose that term should be used in the law relating to offences against the person. Under our proposals such conduct would constitute manslaughter, punishable by a maximum penalty of life imprisonment,

and would merit and no doubt receive either a life sentence or a long determinate sentence, but on balance we do not think that it should form part of the law of murder. ...

Recommendations

31. We therefore conclude that it should be murder:

(a) if a person, with intent to kill, causes death and
(b) if a person causes death by an unlawful act intended to cause serious injury and known to him to involve a risk of causing death (paragraphs 19–29).

In addition, if Parliament favours a [further] provision ... we recommend that it should be on the following lines: that it should be murder if a person causes death by an unlawful act intended to cause fear (of death or serious injury) and known to the defendant to involve a risk of causing death."

Draft Criminal Code Bill

"Murder

54.—(1) A person is guilty of murder if he causes the death of another—

(a) intending to cause death; or
(b) intending to cause serious personal harm and being aware that he may cause death,

unless section 56, 58, 59, 62 or 64 applies.

Commentary on Draft Criminal Code Bill, Law Com. No. 177

14.6 The proposals modify the present law in two respects. (i) An intention to cause serious personal harm is at present a sufficient fault for murder. Under the clause, this will not be so unless the defendant is also aware that he may cause death. (ii) At present, the defendant's awareness that it is 'virtually certain' that his conduct will cause death or serious personal harm is only evidence that he intended such a result. Under the Code, the state of mind will be intention. The judge will direct the jury that, if the defendant was aware that, in the ordinary course of events, his act would cause death or serious personal harm, he intended death or serious personal harm."

Report of the Select Committee of the House of Lords on Murder and Life Imprisonment (H.L. Paper 78–1, Session 1988–89), paras. 66–71

"66. The Committee consider that the time has come when the law of murder in England and Wales should be defined, as the great majority of crimes already are, by statute. The Committee believe, however, that it is impossible to produce a statutory definition which will infallibly include all the most heinous killings. They agree with the proposition of the CLRC that:

'the most a definition can achieve is that the generality of cases falling within the definition of the graver offence will be more heinous than the generality of cases falling within the less grave offence'.

67. The Committee's proposed definition of the crime of murder reflects their opinion that there are two respects in which it would not be appropriate simply to codify the existing common law.

68. First, the Committee agree with those witnesses who argue that a person who intends only to cause serious personal harm and does not foresee even the possibility of death should not be liable to conviction of murder if death happens to result from his act. A person is not generally liable to conviction of a serious crime where the prohibited result was not only unintended but also unforeseen. This seems to the Committee to be a good rule of moral responsibility which should certainly apply to the most serious crime of all, murder. While the law continues to have two categories of homicide, unforeseen but unlawful killings are properly left to the law of manslaughter.

69. Second, the Committee agree with the opinion of the Law Commission that, for the reasons given by the Commission, it is desirable to clarify the meaning of 'intention' as stated in the recent cases. The Commission wrote (p. 120):

> 'The concept of a state of mind that falls short of 'desire or motive' that the result be caused but is something more than foresight that the result is a virtual certainty is difficult for the ordinary person to grasp. The practical effect of *Nedrick* [*ante*, p. 90] seems to be to leave to the jury to characterise the defendant's foresight of the virtual certainty of result as 'intention', or not, as they think right in all the circumstances of the case. We believe that, in appropriate cases, the jury will be better assisted if they are told exactly what the concept of intention embraces as a matter of law, which will be the effect of adopting the definition proposed by the Commission."

70. Professor Glanville Williams put the same point cogently in a paper submitted to the Committee:

> 'An intelligent jury may be fogged at being told that they can infer x, when they are not told what x is (but only what it is not)' (Appendix 7, p. 121).

On the other hand, the Lord Chief Justice stated in evidence to the Committee:

> 'If, of course the jury come to the conclusion that [the accused] realised that it was almost certain that somebody would be killed, that *is* murder' (Lord Lane's emphasis).

A direction to that effect would leave the jury in no doubt about the question they must answer.

71. The Committee therefore recommend that murder should be defined on the lines proposed by the Law Commission in their draft Criminal Code, clause 54(1):

'A person is guilty of murder if he causes the death of another—

(a) intending to cause death; or
(b) intending to cause serious personal harm and being aware that he may cause death ... '

and that, for the purposes of the law of murder, 'intention' should be defined on the lines proposed in clause 18(b) of the draft Criminal Code:

> 'A person acts 'intentionally' with respect to ... a result when he acts either in order to bring it about or being aware that it will occur in the ordinary course of events.' "

Note

A killing which would otherwise amount to murder will be reduced to manslaughter if the defendant was provoked or suffered from diminished reponsibility.

3. SPECIAL DEFENCES

i. Provocation

Homicide Act 1957, section 3

"Where on a charge of murder there is evidence on which the jury can find that the person charged was provoked (whether by things done or by things said or by both together) to lose his self control, the question whether the provocation was enough to make a reasonable man do as he did shall be left to be determined by the jury; and in determining that question the jury shall take into account everything both done and said according to the effect which, in their opinion, it would have on a reasonable man."

Notes

1. Although provocation is usually raised by the defence the onus of proof, that the situation was not one of provocation, lies on the prosecution and this must be made clear to the jury, *R.* v. *Cascoe* [1970] 2 All E.R. 833.

2. Section 3 creates a test which leaves two questions for the jury to consider: (a) whether the defendant was provoked to lose his self-control (the *subjective* question), and (b) whether a reasonable man would have been provoked to lose his self-control and do as the defendant did (the *objective* question). The subjective question remains the same as it did at common law where the leading authority was *Duffy* [1949] 1 All E.R. 932n, where the Court of Appeal approved the summing up of Devlin J. who stated:

"Provocation is some act or series of acts done by the dead man to the accused which would cause in any reasonable person and actually causes in the accused, a sudden and temporary loss of self-control, rendering the accused so subject to passion as to make him for the moment not master of his mind."

Later in his summing up he stated:

"Indeed, circumstances which induce a desire for revenge are inconsistent with provocation, since the conscious formulation of a desire for revenge means that a person has had time to think, to reflect, and that would negative a sudden temporary loss of self-control, which is of the essence of provocation."

These dicta were approved subsequently in *R.* v. *Ibrams and Gregory* (1981) 74 Cr.App.R. 154, where the Court of Appeal upheld the trial judge's decision to withdraw the issue of provocation from the jury where the facts revealed that the attack on the deceased took place five days after the last incident of provocation had occurred. It is crucial to a defence of provocation that the accused should suffer a sudden and temporary loss of self-control (see *Thornton* [1992] 1 All E.R. 306). This need not be immediate upon the last act of provocation but "the longer the delay and the stronger the evidence of deliberation on the part of the defendant, the more likely it will be that the prosecution will negative provocation" (*Ahluwalia* [1993] Crim.L.R. 63). But while the loss of self-control must be sudden, there is no requirement that the provocation be sudden. It may have continued over a long period and the jury are bound to take into account everything done and said according to the effect which, in their opinion, it would have on a reasonable man (see *Thornton* and *Pearson* [1992] Crim.L.R. 193).

3. While Devlin J. in *Duffy* spoke of an "act or series of acts done by the dead man to the accused," it is clear from section 3 that it is not a requirement of the defence that the victim direct the provocative acts at the accused; the provocation may arise from acts done to third parties. In *Pearson* M. and W. killed their violent and tyrranical father. M. had been subjected to violence and abuse for eight years while W. was away from home. W. returned home to protect M. from further violence becoming, himself, the target for violence. It was held by the Court of Appeal that the whole history of violence against M. was relevant to W.'s defence of provocation.

4. In the following case the court was concerned with what could amount to provocation.

R. v. Doughty
(1986) 83 Cr.App.R. 319
Court of Appeal

The appellant was charged with the murder of his 17-day old son. He raised the defence of provocation based on the baby's persistent crying and restlessness. The judge refused to leave this defence to the jury and the appellant was convicted of murder.

STOCKER L.J., after outlining the facts, referred to the judge's direction to the jury:

"In my judgment the perfectly natural episodes or events of crying and restlessness by a 17 day old baby does not constitute evidence of provocation in relation to the first subjective question. Put another way, the crying and restlessness of a 17 day old baby cannot be utilised as being provocative to enable the defendant to raise the defence of provocation. Though provocation can be constituted by conduct or words which are not unlawful, provocation cannot be founded, in my judgment, on the perfectly natural episodes or events arising in the life of a 17 day old baby. It is notorious that every baby born cries, that every baby can at times be burdensome. It is notorious that a baby of 17 days is incapable of sustaining his own life, that he is defenceless and harmless. These notorious facts are common to every baby who is only days old. I think that the episodes or events in the life of the baby of 17 days old could not have been in the mind of Parliament when section 3 became the law. The words of section 3, I quote: 'Whether by things done or words said or by both together'—are not, in my judgment, apposite to embrace the perfectly ordinary, certain, and natural episodes or events in the life of a 17 day old baby. Further, common law directions cannot be construed as including these natural and certain episodes that occur in the life of every baby of days old. Finally, I think civilised society dictates that the natural episodes occurring in the life of a baby only days old have to be endured and cannot be utilised as the foundation of subjective provocation to enable his killer to escape a conviction for murder."

It is not necessary to read the remaining few lines of that direction.

Before turning to the arguments that have been put before this court, it seems to us appropriate to cite the precise terms of section 3 of the Homicide Act 1957 . . . : (See *ante*, p. 513).

Mr. Price submitted that on the proper construction of that section, the judge was bound to leave to the jury the question of provocation, particularly in the light of the admission made by Mr. Klevan for the Crown that there was a causal connection between the crying of the baby and the appellant's response. Mr. Price submitted that this was a classic case for leaving the issue to the jury and he referred us to the case of the *D.P.P.* v. *Camplin* (*ante*, p. 517). The facts need not be recited. It was a case in which there was an appeal against the direction that a judge gave on the topic of provocation. Lord Diplock said this at [1978] A.C. 716:

"My Lords, this section was intended to mitigate in some degree the harshness of the common law of provocation as it had been developed by recent decisions in this House. It recognises and retains the dual test: the provocation must not only have caused the accused to lose his self-control but must also be such as might cause a reasonable man to react to it as the accused did. Nevertheless it brings about two important changes in the law. The first is: it abolishes all previous rules of law as to what can or cannot amount to provocation and in particular the rule of law that, save in the two exceptional cases I have mentioned, words unaccompanied by violence could not do so. Secondly it makes it clear that if there was any evidence that the accused himself at the time of the act which caused the death in fact lost his self-control in consequence of some provocation however slight it might appear to the judge, he was bound to leave to the jury the question, which is one of opinion not of law: whether a reasonable man might have reacted to that provocation as the accused did."

Mr. Price also referred us to Professor Glanville Williams' *Textbook on Criminal Law*, 2nd ed., 1983, at p. 534. Professor Williams wrote this: "The Homicide Act, in allowing insults as provocation, inevitably alters the position, because an insult uttered in private is neither a crime nor even a tort. Section 3 contains no restriction to unlawful acts, and the courts seem to be ready to allow any provocative conduct to be taken into consideration, even though that conduct was itself provoked by the defendant. Consequently, there is no longer any reason why the defence should not be available (if the jury uphold it) to the jilted lover who kills the object of his affections or her new lover, or the man who kills a constantly crying baby. Even the rule about lawful blows seems to survive only as a consideration that the jury can take into account when applying the test of reasonableness."

Mr. Klevan for the Crown reiterated before us that there was no doubt that there was a causal link between the crying and the response, but submitted that not everything should be allowed to be considered as evidence upon which provocation could be founded, and that such acts should be limited to cases where there is some element of wrongfulness, however slight and referred to the further examples considered by Professor Glanville Williams on the page to which reference has just been made. He submitted that the learned judge's direction was correct and that public policy required that the cries of a baby even if persistent should not found a plea of provocation.

With respect to the learned judge, we are unable to accept those arguments. We appreciate the reasons which the learned judge gave for reaching the conclusion that he did, but we are unable to construe section 3 in such a light. The first sentence of section 3 reads: "Where on a charge of murder there is evidence on which the jury can find that the person charged was provoked ... to lose his self-control." There is no doubt, and it is not in dispute, that there was here evidence upon which the appellant was—I use the word loosely—"provoked" to lose his self-control. Part of that evidence has been cited earlier in this judgment.

The reasoning which the learned judge gave, understandable though it was, involves, in our view, adding in to section 3 words which are not there, presumably by way of restriction. It is accepted by Mr. Klevan that there was evidence which linked causally the crying of the baby with the response of the appellant. Accordingly, in our view, it seems inevitable that that being so the section is mandatory and requires the learned judge to leave the issue of the objective test to the jury.

Mr. Klevan also referred us to what might, in shorthand, be called the "floodgates proposition," that if the learned judge's direction was wrong it opens up the possibility that in any case in which there is a battered baby allegation and the baby dies, the argument based on provocation may be raised. We feel that even if that submission was right it could not be allowed to dissuade us from putting a construction on section 3 which, in our view, its wording plainly constrains. We also feel that reliance can be placed upon the common sense of juries upon whom the task of deciding the issue is imposed by section 3 and that that common sense will ensure that only in cases where the facts fully justified it would their verdict be likely to be that they would hold that a defendant's act in killing a crying child would be the response of a reasonable man within the section. That matter is, in our view, imposed by Parliament upon the jury, not upon a judge, and the common sense of juries can be relied upon not to bring in perverse verdicts where the facts do not justify the conclusion.

In our view, therefore, though fully understanding his reasons, we are of the view that the learned judge was wrong in not leaving the issue of provocation to the jury.

> *Appeal allowed in part.*
> *Conviction for murder quashed.*
> *Conviction of manslaughter substituted.*
> *Sentence varied.*

Note

In *Davies* [1975] Q.B. 691, the Court of Appeal accepted that provocation may emanate from some person other than the victim.

Question

D returns to his new car parked in a meter bay to discover that someone has driven into it smashing one of the headlights. He is so angry at this that he flares up into a rage and when a traffic warden commences to peruse the meter which is registering "Excess Charge" he hits him with a bottle of wine causing the traffic warden an injury from which he dies. The trial judge refuses to leave provocation to the jury. D appeals. How might the Court of Appeal decide this issue?

(b) *The objective question*

In the following case the House of Lords examined the changes from the common law which section 3 had introduced in relation to the subjective question and also decided upon the characteristics to be attributed to the reasonable man under the objective question.

R. v. Camplin
[1978] A.C. 705
House of Lords

The facts appear in the speech of Lord Diplock, below, in which Lords Fraser of Tullybelton and Scarman concurred.

LORD DIPLOCK: The respondent, Camplin, who was 15 years of age, killed a middle-aged Pakistani, Mohammed Lal Khan, by splitting his skull with a chapati pan, a heavy kitchen utensil like a rimless frying pan. At the time, the two of them were alone together in Khan's flat. At Camplin's trial for murder before Boreham J. his only defence was that of provocation so as to reduce the offence to manslaughter. According to the story that he told in the witness box but which differed materially from that which he had told the police, Khan had buggered him in spite of his resistance and had then laughed at him. Whereupon Camplin had lost his self-control and attacked Khan fatally with the chapati pan.

In his address to the jury on the defence of provocation Mr. Baker, who was counsel for Camplin, had suggested to them that when they addressed their minds to the question whether the provocation relied on was enough to make a reasonable man do as Camplin had done, what they ought to consider was not the reaction of a reasonable adult but the reaction of a reasonable boy of Camplin's age. The judge thought that this was wrong in law. So in his summing-up he took pains to instruct the jury that they must consider whether:

" ... the provocation was sufficient to make a reasonable man in like circumstances act as the defendant did. Not a reasonable boy, as Mr. Baker would have it, or a reasonable lad; it is an objective test—a reasonable man."

The jury found Camplin guilty of murder. On appeal the Court of Appeal (Criminal Division) allowed the appeal and substituted a conviction for manslaughter upon the ground that the passage I have cited from the summing-up was a misdirection. The court held that

" ... the proper direction to the jury is to invite the jury to consider whether the provocation was enough to have made a reasonable person of the same age as the defendant in the same circumstances do as he did."

The point of law of general public importance involved in the case has been certified as being:

"Whether on the prosecution for murder of a boy of 15, where the issue
of provocation arises, the jury should be directed to consider the
question under section 3 of the Homicide Act 1957 whether the
provocation was enough to make a reasonable man do as he did by
reference to a 'reasonable adult' or by reference to a 'reasonable boy of
15.' "

My Lords, the doctrine of provocation in crimes of homicide has always
represented an anomaly in English law. In crimes of violence which result
in injury short of death, the fact that the act of violence was committed
under provocation which had caused the accused to lose his self-control
does not affect the nature of the offence of which he is guilty. It is merely
a matter to be taken into consideration in determining the penalty which it
is appropriate to impose. Whereas in homicide provocation effects a
change in the offence itself from murder for which the penalty is fixed by
law (formerly death and now imprisonment for life) to the lesser offence of
manslaughter for which the penalty is in the discretion of the judge.

The doctrine of provocation has a long history of evolution at common
law. Such changes as there had been were entirely the consequence of
judicial decision until Parliament first intervened by passing the Act of
1957. Section 3 deals specifically with provocation and alters the law as it
had been expounded in the cases, including three that had been decided
comparatively recently in this House, viz., *Mancini* v. *D.P.P.* [*post*, p. 524];
Holmes v. *D.P.P.* [1946] A.C. 588 and *Bedder* v. *D.P.P.* [1954] 1 W.L.R.
1119. One of the questions of this appeal is to what extent propositions as
to the law of provocation that are laid down in those cases and in
particular in *Bedder* ought to be treated as being of undiminished authority
despite the passing of the Act. ...

[W]ith two exceptions actual violence offered by the deceased to the
accused remained the badge of provocation right up to the passing of the
Act of 1957. The two exceptions were the discovery by a husband of his
wife in the act of committing adultery and the discovery of a father of
someone committing sodomy on his son; but these apart, insulting words
or gestures unaccompanied by physical attack did not in law amount to
provocation.

The "reasonable man" was a comparatively late arrival in the law of
provocation. As the law of negligence emerged in the first half of the 19th
century he became the anthropomorphic embodiment of the standard of
care required by the law. It would appear that Keating J. in *R.* v. *Welsh*
(1869) 11 Cox C.C. 336 was the first to make use of the reasonable man as
the embodiment of the standard of self-control required by the criminal
law of persons exposed to provocation; and not merely as a criterion by
which to check the credibility of a claim to have been provoked to lose his
self-control made by an accused who at that time was not permitted to
give evidence himself. This had not been so previously and did not at once
become the orthodox view. In his *Digest of the Criminal Law* published in
1877 and his *History of the Criminal Law of England* published in 1883 Sir
James Fitzjames Stephen makes no reference to the reasonable man as
providing a standard of self-control by which to decide the question
whether the facts relied upon as provocation are sufficient to reduce the
subsequent killing to manslaughter. He classifies and defines the kind of
conduct of the deceased that alone are capable in law of amounting to
provocation; and appears to treat the questions for the jury as being
limited to (1) whether the evidence establishes conduct by the deceased
that falls within one of the defined classes; and, if so, (2) whether the
accused was thereby actually deprived of his self-control.

The reasonable man referred to by Keating J. was not then a term of legal art nor has he since become one in criminal law. . . . At least from as early as 1914 (see *R.* v. *Lesbini* [1914] 3 K.B. 1116) the test of whether the defence of provocation is entitled to succeed has been a dual one; the conduct of the deceased to the accused must be such as (1) might cause in any reasonable or ordinary person and (2) actually causes in the accused a sudden and temporary loss of self-control as the result of which he commits the unlawful act that kills the deceased. But until the Act of 1957 was passed there was a condition precedent which had to be satisfied before any question of applying this dual test could arise. The conduct of the deceased had to be of such a kind as was incapable in law of constituting provocation; and whether it was or not was a question for the judge, not for the jury. This House so held in *Mancini* v. *D.P.P.* [*post*, p. 524], where it also laid down a rule of law that the mode of resentment, as for instance the weapon used in the act that caused the death, must bear a reasonable relation to the kind of violence that constituted the provocation.

It is unnecessary for the purposes of the present appeal to spend time on a detailed account of what conduct was or was not capable in law of giving rise to a defence of provocation immediately before the passing of the Act of 1957. It had remained much the same as when Stephen was writing in the last quarter of the nineteenth century. What, however, is important to note is that this House in *Holmes* v. *D.P.P.* [1946] A.C. 588 had recently confirmed that words alone, save perhaps in circumstances of a most extreme and exceptional nature, were incapable in law of constituting provocation.

My Lords, this was the state of law when *Bedder* v. *D.P.P.* [1954] 1 W.L.R. 1119 fell to be considered by this House. The accused had killed a prostitute. He was sexually impotent. According to his evidence he had tried to have sexual intercourse with her and failed. She taunted him with his failure and tried to get away from his grasp. In the course of her attempts to do so she slapped him in the face, punched him in the stomach and kicked him in the groin; whereupon he took a knife out of his pocket and stabbed her twice and caused her death. The struggle which led to her death thus started because the deceased taunted the accused with his physical infirmity; but in the state of the law as it then was taunts unaccompanied by any physical violence did not constitute provocation. The taunts were followed by violence on the part of the deceased in the course of her attempt to get away from the accused, and it may be that this subsequent violence would have a greater effect upon the self-control of an impotent man already enraged by the taunts than it would have had upon a person conscious of possessing normal physical attributes. So there might have been some justification for the judge to instruct the jury to ignore the fact that the accused was impotent when they were considering whether the deceased's conduct amounted to such provocation as would cause a reasonable or ordinary person to lose his self-control. This indeed appears to have been the ground on which the Court of Criminal Appeal had approved the summing up when they said, at p. 1121:

> "no distinction is to be made in the case of a person who, though it may not be a matter of temperament, is physically impotent, is conscious of that impotence, *and therefore mentally liable to be more excited unduly* if he is 'twitted' or attacked on the subject of that particular infirmity."

This statement, for which I have myself supplied the emphasis, was approved by Lord Simonds L.C. speaking on behalf of all the members of this House who sat on the appeal; but he also went on to lay down the broader proposition, at p. 1123, that

"It would be plainly illogical not to recognise an unusually excitable or pugnacious temperament in the accused as a matter to be taken into account but yet to recognise for that purpose some unusual physical characteristic, be it impotence or another."

... [Section 3 of the 1957 Act] was intended to mitigate in some degree the harshness of the common law of provocation as it had been developed by recent decisions in this House. It recognises and retains the dual test: the provocation must not only have caused the accused to lose his self-control but must also be such as might cause a reasonable man to react to it as the accused did. Nevertheless it brings about two important changes in the law. The first is: it abolishes all previous rules of law as to what can or cannot amount to provocation and in particular the rule of law that, save in the two exceptional cases I have mentioned, words unaccompanied by violence could not do so. Secondly it makes it clear that if there was any evidence that the accused himself at the time of the act which caused the death in fact lost his self-control in consequence of some provocation however slight it might appear to the judge, he was bound to leave to the jury the question, which is one of opinion not of law: whether a reasonable man might have reacted to that provocation as the accused did.

I agree with my noble and learned friend Lord Simon of Glaisdale that since this question is one for the opinion of the jury the evidence of witnesses as to how they think a reasonable man would react to the provocation is not admissible.

The public policy that underlay the adoption of the "reasonable man" test in the common law doctrine of provocation was to reduce the incidence of fatal violence by preventing a person relying upon his own exceptional pugnacity or excitability as an excuse for loss of self-control. The rationale of the test may not be easy to reconcile in logic with more universal propositions as to the mental element in crime. Nevertheless it has been preserved by the Act of 1957 but falls to be applied now in the context of a law of provocation that is significantly different from what it was before the Act was passed.

Although it is now for the jury to apply the "reasonable man" test, it still remains for the judge to direct them what, in the new context of the section, is the meaning of this apparently inapt expression, since powers of ratiocination bear no obvious relationship to powers of self-control. Apart from this the judge is entitled, if he thinks it helpful, to suggest considerations which may influence the jury in forming their own opinion as to whether the test is satisfied; but he should make it clear that these are not instructions which they are required to follow; it is for them and no one else to decide what weight, if any, ought to be given to them.

As I have already pointed out, for the purposes of the law of provocation the "reasonable man" has never been confined to the adult male. It means an ordinary person of either sex, not exceptionally excitable or pugnacious, but possessed of such powers of self-control as everyone is entitled to expect that his fellow citizens will exercise in society as it is today. A crucial factor in the defence of provocation from earliest times has been the relationship between the gravity of provocation and the way in which the accused retaliated, both being judged by the social standards of the day. When Hale was writing in the seventeenth century, pulling a man's nose was thought to justify retaliation with a sword; when *Mancini* v. *D.P.P.* [*post*, p. 524] was decided by this House, a blow with a fist would not justify retaliation with a deadly weapon. But so long as words unaccompanied by violence could not in law amount to provocation the relevant proportionality between provocation and retaliation was primarily one of degrees of violence. Words spoken to the accused before the violence started were not normally to be included in the proportion sum. But now that the law has been changed so as to permit of words being treated as provocation even though unaccompanied by any other acts, the gravity of verbal provocation may well depend upon the particular characteristics or circumstances of the person to whom a taunt or insult is addressed. To taunt a person because of his race, his physical infirmities or some shameful incident in his past may well be considered by the jury to be more offensive to the person addressed, however equable his temperament, if the facts on which the taunt is founded are true than it would be if they were not. It would stultify much of the mitigation of the previous harshness of the common law in ruling out verbal provocation as capable of reducing murder to manslaughter if the jury could not take into consideration all those factors which in their opinion would affect the gravity of taunts or insults when applied to the person to whom they are addressed. So to this extent at any rate the unqualified proposition accepted by this House in *Bedder* v. *D.P.P.* [1954] 1 W.L.R. 1119 that for the purposes of the "reasonable man" test any unusual physical characteristics of the accused must be ignored requires revision as a result of the passing of the Act of 1957.

That he was only 15 years of age at the time of the killing is the relevant characteristic of the accused in the instant case. It is a characteristic which may have its effects on temperament as well as physique. If the jury think that the same power of self-control is not to be expected in an ordinary, average or normal boy of 15 as in an older person, are they to treat the lesser powers of self-control possessed by an ordinary, average or normal boy of 15 as the standard of self-control with which the conduct of the accused is to be compared?

It may be conceded that in strict logic there is a transition between treating age as a characteristic that may be taken into account in assessing the gravity of the provocation addressed to the accused and treating it as a characteristic to be taken into account in determining what is the degree of self-control to be expected of the ordinary person with whom the accused's conduct is to be compared. But to require old heads upon young shoulders is inconsistent with the law's compassion to human infirmity to which Sir Michael Foster ascribed the doctrine of provocation more than two centuries ago. The distinction as to the purposes for which it is legitimate to take the age of the accused into account involves considerations of too great nicety to warrant a place in deciding a matter of opinion, which is no longer one to be decided by a judge trained in logical reasoning but is to be decided by a jury drawing on their experiences of how ordinary human behings behave in real life. ...

In my view *Bedder*, like *Mancini* v. *D.P.P.* [*post*, p. 524], and *Holmes* v. *D.P.P.* [1946] A.C. 588, ought no longer to be treated as an authority on the law of provocation.

In my opinion a proper direction to a jury on the question left to their exclusive determination by section 3 of the Act of 1957 would be on the following lines. The judge should state what the question is using the very terms of the section. He should then explain to them that the reasonable man referred to in the question is a person having the power of self-control to be expected of an ordinary person of the sex and age of the accused, but in other respects sharing such of the accused's characteristics as they think would affect the gravity of the provocation to him; and that the question is not merely whether such a person would in like circumstances be provoked to lose his self-control but also whether he would react to the provocation as the accused did.

I accordingly agree with the Court of Appeal that the judge ought not to have instructed the jury to pay no account to the age of the accused even though they themselves might be of opinion that the degree of self-control to be expected in a boy of that age was less than in an adult. So to direct them was to impose a fetter on the right and duty of the jury which the Act accords to them to act upon their own opinion on the matter.

I would dismiss this appeal.

Appeal dismissed

Note

The main impact of *Camplin* is on the notional "reasonable person." Lord Diplock's suggested direction to the jury contains two kinds of characteristics which the "reasonable person" might acquire: universal qualities, such as age or sex, and personal idiosyncracies, for example impotence. It is already clear that some "personal" characteristics will be ignored—hot-temperedness, for example. In *Newell*, below, the Court of Appeal suggests a restricted role for those personal characteristics which can be included, *i.e.* that they will only be relevant where the provocation was directed at them.

R. v. Newell
(1980) 71 Cr.App.R. 331
Court of Appeal

The appellant as a chronic alcoholic who battered a friend to death. He claimed that he was provoked by disparaging remarks about his former cohabitee made by the victim. The trial judge told the jury that they had to assume that the remarks were made to a sober man, and to ask themselves whether any of them would have so reacted.

LORD LANE L.C.J.: ... Mr. Ashe Lincoln [counsel for the appellant] submits that the learned judge should have directed the jury in these terms: "Do you consider that the accused, being emotionally depressed and upset, as he was, and in the physical condition of a chronic alcoholic, was reasonably provoked by the words used and reacted in a way in which he might reasonably be expected to have reacted, on the basis that he had had a very large amount to drink, and had had a suicidal overdose of drugs four days previously, and that he was in a state of toxic confusion."

It seems to us that to acertain the meaning of the speeches in *D.P.P.* v. *Camplin* (above) it is necessary to consider the meaning of the word "characteristics" as used in those speeches. To do so we find it helpful to refer, as we were invited to do by Mr. Crespi, to *McGregor* [1962] N.Z.L.R. 1069, referred to by Lord Simon of Glaisdale. First, we would read the material parts of section 169 of the New Zealand Crimes Act 1961: "(1) Culpable homicide that would otherwise be murder may be reduced to manslaughter if the person who caused the death did so under provocation. (2) Anything done or said may be provocation if—(*a*) In the circumstances of the case it was sufficient to deprive a person having the power of self-control of an ordinary person, but otherwise having the characteristics of the offender, of the power of self-control; and (*b*) It did in fact deprive the offender of the power of self-control and thereby induced him to commit the act of homicide. (3) Whether there is any evidence of provocation is a question of law. (4) Whether, if there is evidence of provocation, the provocation was sufficient as aforesaid, and whether it did in fact deprive the offender of the power of self-control and thereby induced him to commit the act of homicide, are questions of fact."

In *McGregor* (*supra*) the judgment of the court was delivered by North J., and contains the following passage which appears to us to be entirely apt to the situation in the instant case:

"The Legislature has given us no guide as to what limitations might be imposed, but perforce there must be adopted a construction which will ensure regard being had to the characteristics of the offender without wholly extinguishing the ordinary man. The offender must be presumed to possess in general the power of self-control of the ordinary man, save in so far as his power of self-control is weakened because of some particular characteristic possessed by him. It is not every trait or disposition of the offender that can be invoked to modify the concept of the ordinary man. The characteristic must be something definite and of sufficient significance to make the offender a different person from the ordinary run of mankind, and have also a sufficient degree of permanence to warrant its being regarded as something constituting part of the individual's character or personality. A disposition to be unduly suspicious or to lose one's temper readily will not suffice, nor will a temporary or transitory state of mind such as a mood of depression, excitability or irascibility. These matters are either not of sufficient significance or not of sufficient permanency to be regarded as 'characteristics' which would enable the offender to be distinguished from the ordinary man. The 'unusually excitable or pugnacious individual' spoken of in *Lesbini* [1941] 3 K.B. 1116 is no more entitled to special consideration under the new section than he was when that case was decided. Still less can a self-induced transitory state be relied upon, as where it arises from the consumption of liquor. The word 'characteristics' in the context of this section is wide enough to apply not only to physical qualities but also to mental qualities and such more indeterminate attributes as colour, race and creed. It is to be emphasised that of whatever nature the characteristic may be, it must be such that it can fairly be said that the offender is thereby marked off or distinguished from the ordinary man of the community. Moreover, it is to be equally emphasised that there must be some real connection between the nature of the provocation and the particular characteristic of the offender by which it is sought to modify the ordinary man test. The words or conduct must have been exclusively or particularly provocative to the individual because, and only because, of the characteristic. In short, there must be some direct connection between the provocative words or conduct and the characteristic sought to be invoked as warranting some departure from the ordinary man test. Such a connection may be seen readily enough where the offender possesses some unusual physical peculiarity. Though he might in all other respects be an ordinary man, provocative words alluding for example to some infirmity or deformity from which he was suffering might well bring about a loss of self-control. So too, if the colour, race or creed of the offender be relied on as constituting a characteristic, it is to be repeated that the provocative words or conduct must be related to the particular characteristic relied upon. Thus, it would not be sufficient, for instance, for the offender to claim merely that he belongs to an excitable race, or that members of his nationality are accustomed to resort readily to the use of some lethal weapon. Here again, the provocative act or words require to be directed at the particular characteristic before it can be relied upon. Special difficulties, however, arise when it becomes necessary to consider what purely mental peculiarities may be allowed as characteristics.

In our opinion it is not enough to constitute a characteristic that the offender should merely in some general way be mentally deficient or weak-minded. To allow this to be said would, as we have earlier indicated, deny any real operation to the reference made in the section to the ordinary man, and it would, moreover, go far towards the admission of a defence of diminished responsibility without any statutory authority in this country to sanction it. There must be something more, such as provocative words or acts directed to a particular phobia from which the offender suffers. Beyond that, we do not think it is advisable that we should attempt to go."

That passage, and the reasoning therein contained, seem to us to be impeccable. It is not only expressed in plain, easily comprehended language; it represents also, we think, the law of this country as well as that of New Zealand. In the present case the only matter which could remotely be described as a characteristic was the appellant's condition of chronic alcoholism. Assuming that that was truly a characteristic (and we expressly make no determination as to that), nevertheless it had nothing to do with the words by which it is said that he was provoked. There was no connection between the derogatory reference to the appellant's girl friend and the suggestion of a possible homosexual act and his chronic alcoholism. It had nothing at all to do with the words by which it is said that he was provoked.

If the test set out in *McGregor* (*supra*) is applied, the learned judge in the instant case was right in not inviting the jury to take chronic alcoholism into account on the question of provocation.

The other matters advanced by Mr. Ashe Lincoln as being characteristics which the jury should have been invited to consider, in examining what a reasonable man might or would have done, are not characteristics at all. The appellant's drunkenness, or lack of sobriety, his having taken an overdose of drugs and written a suicide note a few days previously, his grief at the defection of his girl friend, and so on, are none of them matters which can properly be described as characteristics. They were truly transitory in nature, in the light of the words and reasoning of North J., in *McGregor's* case (*supra*) . . . .

Appeal dismissed

(c) *The reasonable relationship factor*

Note

In *Mancini* v. *D.P.P.* [1942] A.C. 1, the House of Lords held that a judge could decline to leave the defence of provocation to the jury where the "mode of resentment" did not "bear a reasonable relationship to the provocation." The issue arose in the following case whether this rule of reasonable relationship still applied in light of section 3 of the Homicide Act 1957.

R. v. Brown
[1972] 2 Q.B. 229
Court of Appeal

TALBOT J.: ... What [counsel for the appellant] complains of, and the court is greatly indebted to him for the clarity of his argument, is that the judge misdirected the jury on what has been called the "reasonable relationship" rule, that is, that the mode of retaliation must bear a reasonable relationship to the provocation if the offence is to be reduced to manslaughter. There is also the question as to what effect section 3 of the Homicide Act 1957 has upon this rule. It is necessary therefore to examine this rule in some detail. The starting point so far as this court is concerned is *Mancini* v. *D.P.P.* [1942] A.C. 1. In the speech of Viscount Simon L.C. there is the well-known passage, at p. 9:

"It is of particular importance (a) to consider whether a sufficient interval has elapsed since the provocation to allow a reasonable man time to cool, and (b) to take into account the instrument with which the homicide was effected, for to retort, in the heat of passion induced by provocation, by a simple blow, is a very different thing from making use of a deadly instrument like a concealed dagger. In short, the mode of resentment must bear a reasonable relationship to the provocation if the offence is to be reduced to manslaughter."

One of the points argued before us was whether this was a statement of legal principle or whether it was intended as a guide to one of the considerations which a jury has to take into account on the element of provocation, namely, whether a reasonable man would have lost his self-control and acted as the accused did. It seems to this court that this was not a statement of legal principle and it is noted that this also is the view of the editor of *Russell on Crime*, 12th ed. (1964), expressed at p. 548. ... It was also considered in *Phillips* v. *The Queen* [1969] 2 A.C. 130. In that case the Privy Council considered the effect of an enactment, the Offences Against the Person (Amendment) Law (Jamaica), No. 43 of 1958, which contains a provision identical with section 3 of the Homicide Act 1957. Lord Diplock said, at p. 137:

"In their Lordships' view the only changes in the common law doctrine of provocation which were effected by section 3c of the Offences Against the Person (Amendment) Law (Jamaica), No. 43 of 1958 were (1) to abolish the common law rule that words unaccompanied by acts could not amount to provocation and (2) to leave exclusively to the jury the function of deciding whether or not a reasonable man would have reacted to the provocation in the way in which the defendant did. These two changes are interrelated. ... In their Lordships' view section 3c of Law No. 43 of 1958, in referring to the question to be left to be determined by the jury as being 'whether the provocation was enough to make a reasonable man do as he [sc. the person charged] did' explicitly recognises that what the jury have to consider, once they have reached the conclusion that the person charged was in fact provoked to lose his self-control is not merely whether in their opinion the provocation would have made a reasonable man lose his self-control but whether, having lost his self-control, he would have retaliated in the same way as the person charged in fact did."

Dealing with the words of Viscount Simon L.C. in *Mancini's* case, Lord Diplock said, at p. 138:

"Since the passing of the legislation, it may be prudent to avoid the use of the precise words of Viscount Simon in *Mancini* v. *D.P.P.* 'the mode of resentment must bear a reasonable relationship to the provocation' unless they are used in a context which makes it clear to the jury that this is not a rule of law which they are bound to follow, but merely a consideration which may or may not commend itself to them. But their Lordships would repeat, it is the effect of the summing-up as a whole that matters and not any stated verbal formula used in the course of it."

To this we would add that in our opinion Parliament, when using simple and straightforward language in section 3, was endeavouring to lay down the precise test which the jury should apply.

In the view of this court, when considering whether the provocation was enough to make a reasonable man do as the accused did it is relevant for a jury to compare the words or acts or both of these things which are put forward as provocation with the nature of the act committed by the accused. It may be for instance that a jury might find that the accused's act was so disproportionate to the provocation alleged that no reasonable man would have so acted. We think therefore that a jury should be instructed to consider the relationship of the accused's acts to the provocation when asking themselves the question "Was it enough to make a reasonable man do as he did?" We feel that Lord Diplock's warning should be followed and that it would be better not to use the precise words of Viscount Simon unless it is made quite clear that it is not a rule of law which the jury have to follow.

Note

In *Phillips* v. *R.* [1969] 2 A.C. 130, the Privy Council rejected the submission that there were not degrees of loss of self-control. Counsel had argued that once it was conceded that the defendant had lost his self-control and that a reasonable man may have done so, any consideration of the issue of reasonable relationship between the provocation and the reaction was superfluous as "there is no intermediate stage between icy detachment and going berserk." The Privy Council stated (at p. 137):

"This premise, unless the argument is purely semantic, must be based upon human experience and is, in their Lordships view, false. The average man reacts to provocation according to its degree with angry words, with a blow of the hand, possibly, if the provocation is gross and there is a dangerous weapon to hand, with that weapon."

For a contrary view see Brett, "The Physiology of Provocation," [1970] Crim.L.R. 634.

(d) *Self-induced provocation*

R. v. Johnson
[1989] 1 W.L.R. 740
Court of Appeal

The appellant and the deceased were drinking at a night club. The deceased's female companion taunted the appellant who then made threats of violence to her and thereafter to the deceased himself. The appellant made to leave the club but was followed by the deceased who poured beer over him. The deceased removed his jacket and pinned the appellant against a wall whereupon the deceased's female companion attacked him by punching his head and pulling his hair. The appellant drew a knife and lunged at the deceased stabbing him once in the chest. The appellant claimed he feared being "glassed" and had acted in self-defence. The judge ruled that the provocation was self-induced and refused to direct the jury on this issue. The appellant was convicted of murder and appealed.

WATKINS L.J.: (After referring to section 3 of the Homicide Act 1957, his Lordship continued.)

In *R.* v. *Camplin* [1978] A.C. 705, 716, Lord Diplock said that this section:

"makes it clear that if there was any evidence that the accused himself at the time of the act which caused the death in fact lost his self-control in consequence of some provocation however slight it might appear to the judge, he was bound to leave to the jury the question ... whether a reasonable man might have reacted to that provocation as the accused did." ...

[The] evidence may not have been powerfully suggestive of provocation. But it was, in our view, rather more than tenuous. It is easily conceivable, we think that the jury, if directed on the issue, would have come to the conclusion that the appellant was so provoked as to reduce murder to manslaughter. Therefore, subject only to the question of self-induced provocation referred to by the judge, in our judgment this defence should have been left to the jury.

There was undoubtedly evidence to suggest that, if the appellant had lost his self-control, it was his own behaviour which caused others to react towards him in the way we have described.

We were referred to the decision of the Privy Council in *Edwards* v. *The Queen* [1973] A.C. 648. In that case the trial judge had directed the jury, at p. 658:

"In my view the defence of provocation cannot be of any avail to the accused in this case ... it ill befits the accused in this case, having gone there with the deliberate purpose of blackmailing this man—you may well think it ill befits him to say out of his own mouth that he was provoked by any attack. In my view the defence of provocation is not one which you need consider in this case."

The full court in Hong Kong held that this direction was erroneous. The Privy Council agreed with the full court. On the particular facts of the case Lord Pearson, giving the judgment of the Board, said, at p. 658:

"On principle it seems reasonable to say that—(1) a blackmailer cannot rely on the predictable results of his own blackmailing conduct as constituting provocation ... and the predictable results may include a considerable degree of hostile reaction by the person sought to be blackmailed ... (2) but if the hostile reaction by the person sought to be blackmailed goes to extreme lengths it might constitute sufficient provocation even for the blackmailer; (3) there would in many cases be a question of degree to be decided by the jury."

Those words cannot, we think, be understood to mean, as was suggested to us, that provocation which is "self-induced" ceases to be provocation for the purposes of section 3.

The relevant statutory provision being considered by the Privy Council was in similar terms to section 3. In view of the express wording of section 3, as interpreted in *R.* v. *Camplin* [1978] A.C. 705 which was decided after *Edwards* v. *The Queen* [1973] A.C. 648, we find it impossible to accept that the mere fact that a defendant caused a reaction in others, which in turn led him to lose his self-control, should result in the issue of provocation being kept outside a jury's consideration. Section 3 clearly provides that the question is whether things done or said or both provoked the defendant to lose his self-control. If there is any evidence that it may have done, the issue must be left to the jury. The jury would then have to consider all the circumstances of the incident, including all the relevant behaviour of the defendant, in deciding (a) whether he was in fact provoked and (b) whether the provocation was enough to make a reasonable man do what the defendant did.

Accordingly, whether or not there were elements in the appellant's conduct which justified the conclusion that he had started the trouble and induced others, including the deceased, to react in the way they did, we are firmly of the view that the defence of provocation should have been left to the jury.

Verdict of murder set aside.
Conviction of manslaughter substituted.

ii. Diminished Responsibility

Homicide Act 1957, section 2

"(1) Where a person kills or is a party to the killing of another, he shall not be convicted of murder if he was suffering from such abnormality of mind (whether arising from a condition of arrested or retarded development of mind or any inherent causes or induced by disease or injury) as substantially impaired his mental responsibility for his acts and omissions in doing or being a party to the killing.

(2) On a charge of murder, it shall be for the defence to prove that the person charged is by virtue of this section not liable to be convicted of murder.

(3) A person who but for this section would be liable, whether as principal or as accessory, to be convicted of murder shall be liable instead to be convicted of manslaughter."

Criminal Procedure (Insanity) Act 1964, section 6

"Where on a trial for murder the accused contends

(a) that at the time of the alleged offence he was insane so as not to be responsible according to law for his actions; or
(b) that at the time he was suffering from such abnormality of mind as is specified in subsection (1) of section (2) of the Homicide Act 1957 (diminished responsibility)

the court shall allow the prosecution to adduce or elicit evidence tending to prove the other of those contentions, and may give directions as to the stage of the proceedings at which the prosecution may adduce such evidence."

Note

As with insanity, the onus of proof which the defence have to discharge is on a balance of probabilities: *R. v. Dunbar* [1958] 1 Q.B. 1. This partial defence has largely replaced insanity as a defence to murder. In 1989, for example, there was a successful plea of diminished responsibility in 69 cases, as opposed to one finding of not guilty by reason of insanity, and in 1990 the figures were 47 and one. (See Appendix 9 of the Butler Report (Cmnd. 6244, 1975) for a table comparing the number of insanity pleas before and after 1957.)

The limitations of the insanity defence have already been discussed, *ante*, p. 215. Williams, T.C.L. 686, says of section 2 both that it "has had highly beneficial results" and that it contains "as embarrassing a formula for a scientifically-minded witness as could be devised." The success of the formula lies in the fact that it uses neither exclusively "legal" nor exclusively "medical" concepts. "Abnormality of mind" is imprecise and has been given wide interpretation by the courts, see *Byrne*, below. "Mental responsibility," as the Butler report comments, is "either a concept of law or a concept of morality; it is not a clinical fact relating to the defendant. . . . [Y]et psychiatrists commonly testify to impaired 'mental responsibility' under section 2." (section 19.5).

S. Dell, "Diminished Responsibility Reconsidered" [1982] Crim.L.R. 809, 813–814

"[T]here was disagreement between doctors on the issue of diminished responsibility in no more than 13 per cent. of the cases in which the defence was raised. In about half of the cases where there was disagreement, it arose because one of the doctors considered that there was no abnormality of mind. In the other half, there was agreement as to the presence of some mental abnormality, but disagreement as to whether it substantially impaired the offender's mental responsibility.

These two types of disgreement raise different issues. The presence or absence of mental abnormality is a technical psychiatric question, and one on which doctors as experts could on occasion be expected to disagree. In the main their disagreements occurred in relation to the milder cases of mental illness and personality disorder, where there was room for debate on the question of where normality ceases and abnormality begins.

The second area of disagreement—whether mental responsibility was or was not impaired—raises different issues. The Butler Committee pointed out that mental responsibility in the context of section 2 is not a clinical matter on which doctors have expertise, but a legal or a moral question. Glanville Williams has persuasively argued that it cannot sensibly be regarded as a legal question: it is really a moral one. But although the presence or absence of mental responsibility is not a medical matter, doctors grapple with it: and in half the cases where they disagreed with each other on the issue of diminished responsibility, it was on the moral and not the psychiatric aspects of the case that they disagreed. For example, in one case an offender was seen by the prison medical officer and an independent psychiatrist, both of whom found him suffering from an abnormality of mind which they described in virtually identical terms: hysterical psychopathy associated with impulsive and manipulative behaviour. But the independent psychiatrist's report went on to say 'I see no indication to raise a consideration of diminished responsibility,' whilst the prison medical officer wrote 'I would be prepared to say that his responsibility was substantially diminished.' Neither doctor cited in his report any reason for the view he took, and in the event neither was required to give evidence on the matter, as a plea of guilty to diminished responsibility manslaughter was accepted.

There were other cases where the doctors agreed on the presence of mental abnormality, and then disagreed not as to whether there was impairment of mental responsibility, but as to whether it was substantial. For example, a brain-damaged psychopath who killed in the course of a robbery was regarded by the defence as being of substantially diminished reponsibility, while the prison medical officer held that his responsibility was diminished 'to a certain extent ... but this does not amount to a substantial degree of impairment.' Again, the bases of judgments of this kind were not given in the medical reports, and it is not easy to see what they might have been. For, as the Butler Committee pointed out: 'the idea that ability to conform to the law can be measured is particularly puzzling, and doctors have no special qualifications or expertise which fits them to undertake so puzzling a task. That they are nevertheless prepared to undertake it, and that judges (in Butler's view 'surprisingly') are prepared to let them do so, demonstrates the determination of both professions to gloss over the difficulties in section 2 in the interests of making it work."

Note

This Heath Robinson approach to reducing murder to manslaughter is perhaps best explained by the fact that section 2 has two, not always compatible, functions. On the one hand, it is "a device for ... untying the hands of the judge in murder cases" (Butler Report, section 19.8), while on the other it allows for a display of public sympathy for the domestic, one-off murderer. Problems arise when the sympathy is absent, but the defendant is clearly mentally abnormal within the section. Diminished responsibility is a question of fact but if the jury is perverse in the face of fact and medical evidence, the Court of Appeal will upset the verdict: *R.* v. *Matheson* [1958] 1 W.L.R. 474, and *Walton* v. *R.*, *post*, p. 535. Difficulties have also arisen where the court, with the prosecution's consent, agrees to accept the defence plea of diminished responsibility. See *R.* v. *Vinagre*, *post*, p. 537 and the discussion following it.

R. v. Byrne
[1960] 2 Q.B. 396
Court of Criminal Appeal

The appellant admitted murder but raised the defence of diminished responsibility. The defence failed and he appealed against the verdict of misdirection in the summing-up.

LORD PARKER C.J.: The appellant was convicted of murder before Stable J. at Birmingham Assizes and sentenced to imprisonment for life. The victim was a young woman whom he strangled in the Y.W.C.A. hostel, and after her death he committed horrifying mutilations upon her dead body. The facts as to the killing were not disputed, and were admitted in a long statement made by the accused. The only defence was that in killing his victim the accused was suffering from diminished responsibility as defined by section 2 of the Homicide Act 1957, and was, accordingly, guilty not of murder but of manslaughter.

Three medical witnesses were called by the defence, the senior medical officer at Birmingham Prison and two specialists in psychological medicine. Their uncontradicted evidence was that the accused was a sexual psychopath, that he suffered from abnormality of mind, as indeed was abundantly clear from the other evidence in the case, and that such abnormality of mind arose from a condition of arrested or retarded development of mind or inherent causes. The nature of the abnormality of mind of a sexual psychopath, according to the medical evidence, is that he suffers from violent perverted sexual desires which he finds it difficult or impossible to control. Save when under the influence of his perverted sexual desires he may be normal. All three doctors were of opinion that the killing was done under the influence of his perverted sexual desires, and although all three were of opinion that he was not insane in the technical sense of insanity laid down in the M'Naghten Rules it was their view that his sexual psychopathy could properly be described as partial insanity.

In his summing-up the judge, after summarising the medical evidence, gave to the jury a direction of law on the correctness of which this appeal turns. He told the jury that if on the evidence they came to the conclusion that the facts could be fairly summarised as follows:

"(1) from an early age he has been subject to these perverted violent desires, and in some cases has indulged his desires; (2) the impulse or urge of these desires is stronger than the normal impulse or urge of sex to such an extent that the subject finds it very difficult or perhaps impossible in some cases to resist putting the desire into practice; (3) the act of killing this girl was done under such an impulse or urge; and (4) that setting aside these sexual addictions and practices this man was normal in every other respect"; those facts with nothing more would not bring a case within the section, and do not constitute subh abnormality of mind as substantially to impair a man's mental responsibility for his acts. "In other words," he went on, "mental affliction is one thing. The section is there to protect them. The section is not there to give protection where there is nothing else than what is vicious and depraved."

Taken by themselves these words are unobjectionable, but it is contended on behalf of the appellant that the direction taken as a whole involves a misconstruction of the section, and had the effect of withdrawing from the jury an issue of fact which it was peculiarly their province to decide.

Section 2 of the Homicide Act 1957, is dealing with the crime of murder in which there are at common law two essential elements: (1) the physical act of killing another person, and (2) the state of mind of the person who kills or is a party to the killing, namely, his intention to kill or to cause grievous bodily harm. Subsection (1) of section 2 does not deal with the first element. It modified the existing law as respects the second element, that is, the state of mind of the person who kills or is a party to the killing.

Before the passing of the Homicide Act 1957, a person who killed or was party to a killing could escape liability for murder—as for any other crime requiring *mens rea*—if he showed that at the time of the killing he was insane within the meaning of the M'Naghten Rules, that is, "that he was labouring under such a defence of reason from disease of the mind as not to know the nature and quality of the act that he was doing, or if he did know it that he did not know that he was doing wrong." If established, this defence negatives *mens rea* and the accused was and still is entitled to a special verdict of "guilty of the act but insane" at the time of doing the act, which is an acquittal of any crime. The test is a rigid one: it relates solely to a person's intellectual ability to appreciate: (a) the physical act that he is doing, and (b) whether it is wrong. If he has such intellectual ability, his power to control his physical acts by exercise of his will is irrelevant.

The ability of the accused to control his physical acts by exercise of his will was relevant before the passing of the Homicide Act 1957, in one case only—that of provocation. Loss of self-control on the part of the accused so as to make him for the moment not master of his mind had the effect of reducing murder to manslaughter if: (i) it was induced by an act or series of acts done by the deceased to the accused, and (ii) such act or series of acts would have induced a reasonable man to lose his self-control and act in the same manner as the accused acted. (See *R*. v. *Duffy* [1949] 1 All E.R. 932n. (C.C.A.)).

Whether loss of self-control induced by provocation negatived the ordinary presumption that a man intends the natural ordinary consequences of his physical acts so that, in such a case, the prosecution had failed to prove the essential mental element in murder (namely, that the accused intended to kill or to inflict grievous bodily harm) is academic for the purposes of our consideration. What is relevant is that loss of self-control has always been recognised as capable of reducing murder to manslaughter, but that the criterion has always been the degree of self-control which would be exercised by a reasonable man, that is to say, a man with a normal mind.

It is against that background of the existing law that section 2(1) of the Homicide Act 1957, falls to be construed. To satisfy the requirements of the subsection the accused must show: (a) that he was suffering from an abnormality of mind, and (b) that such abnormality of mind (i) arose from a condition of arrested or retarded development of mind or any inherent causes or was induced by disease or injury and (ii) was such as substantially impaired his mental responsibility for his acts in doing or being a party to the killing.

"Abnormality of mind," which has to be contrasted with the time-honoured expression in the M'Naghten Rules "defect of reason," means a state of mind so different from that of ordinary human beings that the reasonable man would term it abnormal. It appears to us to be wide enough to cover the mind's activities in all its aspects, not only the perception of physical acts and matters, and the ability to form a rational judgment as to whether an act is right or wrong, but also the ability to exercise will-power to control physical acts in accordance with that rational judgment. The expression "mental responsibility for his acts" points to a consideration of the extent to which the accused's mind is answerable for his physical acts which must include a consideration of the extent of his ability to exercise will-power to control his physical acts.

Whether the accused was at the time of the killing suffering from any "abnormality of mind" in the broad sense which we have indicated above is a question for the jury. On this question medical evidence is no doubt of importance, but the jury are entitled to take into consideration all the evidence, including the acts or statements of the accused and his demeanour. They are not bound to accept the medical evidence if there is other material before them which, in their good judgment, conflicts with it and outweighs it.

The aetiology of the abnormality of mind (namely, whether it arose from a condition of arrested or retarded development or any inherent causes, or was induced by disease or injury) does, however, seem to be a matter determined on expert evidence.

Assuming that the jury are satisfied on the balance of probabilities that the accused was suffering from "abnormality of mind" from one of the causes specified in the parenthesis of the subsection, the crucial question nevertheless arises: was the abnormality such as substantially impaired his mental responsibility for his acts in doing or being a party to the killing? This is a question of degree and essentially one for the jury. Medical evidence is, of course, relevant, but the question involves a decision not merely as to whether there was some impairment of the mental responsibility of the accused but whether such impairment can properly be called "substantial," a matter upon which juries may quite legitimately differ from doctors.

Furthermore, in a case where the abnormality of mind is one which affects the accused's self-control the step between "he did not resist his impulse" and "he could not resist his impulse" is, as the evidence in this case shows, one which is incapable of scientific proof. *A fortiori* there is no scientific measurement of the degree of difficulty which an abnormal person finds in controlling his impulses. These problems which in the present state of medical knowledge are scientifically insoluble, the jury can only approach in a broad common sense way. This court has repeatedly approved directions to the jury which have followed directions given in Scots cases where the doctrine of diminished responsibility forms part of the common law. We need not repeat them. They are quoted in *R. v. Spriggs* [1958] 1 Q.B. 270. They indicate that such abnormality as "substantially impairs his mental responsibility" involves a mental state which in popular language (not that of the M'Naghten Rules) a jury would regard as amounting to partial insanity or being on the borderline of insanity.

It appears to us that the judge's direction to the jury that the defence under section 2 of the Act was not available even though they found the facts set out in Nos. 2 and 3 of the judge's summary, amounted to a direction that difficulty or even inability of an accused person to exercise will power to control his physical acts could not amount to such abnormality of mind as substantially impairs his mental responsibility. For the reasons which we have already expressed we think that this construction of the Act is wrong. Inability to exercise will power to control physical acts, provided that it is due to abnormality of mind from one of the causes specified in the parenthesis in the subsection is, in our view, sufficient to entitle the accused to the benefit of the section; difficulty in controlling his physical acts depending on the degree of difficulty, may be. It is for the jury to decide on the whole of the evidence whether such inability or difficulty has, not as a matter of scientific certainty but on the balance of probabilities, been established, and in the case of difficulty whether the difficulty is so great as to amount in their view to a substantial impairment of the accused's mental responsibility for his acts. The direction in the present case thus withdrew from the jury the essential determination of fact which it was their province to decide.

As already indicated, the medical evidence as to the appellant's ability to control his physical acts at the time of the killing was all one way. The evidence of the revolting circumstances of the killing and the subsequent mutilations as of the previous sexual history of the appellant pointed, we think plainly, to the conclusion that the accused was what would be described in ordinary language as on the borderline of insanity or partially insane. Properly directed, we do not think that the jury could have come to any other conclusion than that the defence under section 2 of the Homicide Act was made out.

The appeal will be allowed and a verdict of manslaughter substituted for the verdict of murder. The only possible sentence having regard to the tendencies of the accused is imprisonment for life. The sentence will, accordingly, not be disturbed.

Appeal allowed

Note

The review of Scots cases by Lord Goddard in R. v. *Spriggs*, referred to above, is as follows (see [1958] 1 Q.B. 274):

"I had in mind *H.M. Advocate* v. *Braithwaite*, 1945 S.C. (J.) 55, where Lord Cooper, Lord Justice-Clerk, gave this charge to the jury with regard to diminished responsibility: 'Now I have got to give you the most accurate instruction I can on this delicate question. The Solicitor-General read to you a passage from the charge of the Lord Justice-Clerk in the case of *Savage*, 123 S.C. (J.) 49, and I am going to read a sentence or two again, because it seems to me to give as explicit and clear a statement of the sort of thing which you have to look for as I can find. He says: 'It is very difficult to put it in a phrase'—and I respectfully agree—'but it has been put in this way; that there must be aberration or weakness of mind; that there must be some form of mental unsoundness; that there must be a state of mind which is bordering on, though not amounting to, insanity; that there must be a mind so affected that responsibility is diminished from full responsibility to partial responsibility—in other words, the prisoner in question must be only partially accountable for his actions.' And then he adds: 'And I think one can see running through the cases that there is implied ... that there must be some form of mental disease.' The matter has been put in different words by other judges. I notice in a later case (*Muir* v. *H.M. Advocate*, 1933 S.C. (J.) 46, 49) that the condition was referred to for short as "partial insanity"; and that this was explained as meaning 'that weakness or great peculiarity of mind which the law has recognised as possibly differentiating a case of murder from one of culpable homicide.' And, finally, to give you one last test, the question as put by the late Lord Clyde in the same case, quoting from a charge to a jury by Lord Moncrieff, was stated thus: 'Was he, owing to his mental state, of such inferior responsibility that his act should have attributed to it the quality not of murder but of culpable homicide?' You will see, ladies and gentlemen, the stress that has been laid in all these formulations upon weakness of intellect, aberration of mind, mental unsoundness, partial insanity, great peculiarity of mind, and the like.' "

Questions

1. In the third question, namely, whether "the abnormality was such as substantially impaired the defendant's mental responsibility for his acts in doing or being a party to the killing?", is the jury being asked to consider the defendant's capacity to comprehend and conform to the standards laid down by the law or are they being asked to consider whether, in light of his abnormality he is morally culpable? In other words, is the issue for the jury one of capacity of liability? See Griew, "The Future of Diminished Responsibility" [1987] Crim.L.R. 75.

2. Can it be argued that in *Byrne*, Lord Parker is suggesting that medical evidence is conclusive on "abnormality of mind" but not on whether that resulted in "substantial impairment"? Do the cases below provide any elucidation? See M. D. Cohen, "Medical Evidence and Diminished Responsibility" [1981] N.L.J. 667.

Walton v. The Queen
(1978) 66 Cr.App.R. 25
Privy Council

The appellant was driving home with his girlfriend and her mother when he stopped the car. His girlfriend thought he was "acting funny" and flagged down another car. The appellant shot and killed a passenger in a car which stopped. His defence to murder was diminished responsibility (which, in the Barbadian legislation, was identical with section 2 of the 1957 Act). He called two psychiatrists and a psychologist in his support. The Crown led no medical evidence. There was no evidence of any history of mental disorder. The jury convicted him of murder. The conviction was upheld by the Court of Appeal of Barbados. On appeal to the Privy Council.

LORD KEITH OF KINKEL delivered the judgment of the Board: ... It was argued by Mr. Murray, for the appellant, that in the light of the uncontradicted medical evidence to the effect that the appellant suffered from an abnormality of mind which substantially impaired his mental responsibility for his acts, the jury was bound to accept that the defence of diminished responsibility had been established, and that the trial judge should have so directed them. Mr. Murray relied upon *R. v. Matheson* [1958] 1 W.L.R. 474 and *R. v. Bailey* (1978) 66 Cr.App.Rep. 31n. In the first of these cases the accused, who had a long recorded history of conduct indicative of mental abnormality, had killed a 15-year-old boy under peculiarly revolting circumstances. Three medical witnesses testified at the trial that they were satisfied that the accused's mind was so abnormal as substantially to impair his mental responsibility, giving their reasons for that view, and no medical evidence was led in rebuttal. The jury returned a verdict of guilty of murder. The Court of Criminal Appeal quashed that verdict and substituted one of manslaughter. Lord Goddard C.J., delivering the judgment of the Court, having referred to the medical evidence, said (at p. 478): "What then were the facts or circumstances which would justify a jury in coming to a conclusion contrary to the unchallenged evidence of these gentlemen? While it has often been emphasised, and we would repeat, that the decision in these cases, as in those in which insanity is pleaded, is for the jury and not for doctors, the verdict must be founded on evidence. If there are facts which would entitle a jury to reject or differ from the opinions of the medical men, this Court would not, and indeed could not, disturb their verdict, but if the doctor's evidence is unchallenged and there is no other on this issue, a verdict contrary to their opinion would not be 'a true verdict in accordance with the evidence.'" After considering other circumstances of the case Lord Goddard continued, at p. 479: "If then there is unchallenged evidence that there is abnormality of mind and consequent substantial impairment of mental responsibility and no facts or circumstances appear that can displace or throw doubt on that evidence, it seems to the Court that we are bound to say that a verdict of murder is unsupported by the evidence."

In *R. v. Bailey* the appellant, who was just 17 years of age at the time, had met a girl aged 16 years and with no apparent motive had battered her to death with an iron bar. In support of a defence of diminished responsibility the evidence of three medical witnesses was led, including a senior prison medical officer. All expressed the opinion that the appellant suffered from epilepsy, which substantially impaired his mental responsibility. The prison medical officer thought it highly probable that the appellant was at the time of the killing in an epileptic upset or fit. The Court of Criminal Appeal substituted a verdict of manslaughter for the jury's verdict of murder. Lord Parker C.J., delivering the judgment of the Court, said (p. 32): "This Court has said on many occasions that of course juries are not bound by what the medical witnesses say, but at the same time they must act on evidence, and if there is nothing before them, no facts and no circumstances shown before them which throw doubt on the medical evidence, then that is all that they are left with, and the jury, in those circumstances, must accept it."

These cases make clear that upon an issue of diminished responsibility the jury are entitled and indeed bound to consider not only the medical evidence but the evidence upon the whole facts and circumstances of the case. These include the nature of the killing, the conduct of the accused before, at the time of and after it and any history of mental abnormality. It being recognised that the jury on occasions may properly refuse to accept medical evidence, it follows that they must be entitled to consider the quality and weight of that evidence. As was pointed out by Lord Parker C.J. in *R. v. Byrne* [*ante*, p. 530], what the jury are essentially seeking to ascertain is whether at the time of the killing the accused was suffering from a state of mind bordering on but not amounting to insanity. That task is to be approached in a broad common sense way.

In the present case their Lordships are of opinion that, in so far as they can judge of the medical evidence from the trial judge's notes, the jury were entitled to regard it as not entirely convincing. Dr. Patricia Bannister, whose evidence was subjected to quite lengthy cross-examination, expressed an opinion as to the appellant's state of mind which in terms satisfied the statutory definition. The particular mental abnormality which she identified was that of an extremely immature personality. Mr. Browne, the clinical psychologist, found the appellant to be of average intellectual ability with good observational ability and clear thinking. He supported Dr. Patricia Bannister's evidence by describing the appellant as having an inadequate personality enhanced by emotional immaturity and a low tolerance level. The evidence of Dr. Lawrence Bannister was merely to the effect that he treated the appellant for depression, with disappointing results. It is plain that the quality and weight of this medical evidence fell a long way short of that in *Matheson's* case and in *Bailey's* case. The jury also had before them evidence about the conduct of the appellant before, during and after killing, including that of a number of conflicting statements about it made by him to the police and to Dr. Patricia Bannister. They may well have thought there was nothing in that evidence indicative of a man whose mental state bordered on insanity. There was also the appellant's unsworn statement regarding his having suffered in the past from severe headache, blackouts, sleeplessness and lack of memory, supported to some extent by Miss Watson, but no objective evidence of any history of mental disorder. In both these aspects the case is in marked contradistinction to *Matheson's* case.

Having carefully considered the relevant evidence, their Lordships have come to be of opinion that in all the circumstances the jury were entitled not to accept as conclusive the expression of opinion by Dr. Patricia

Bannister that the appellant's mental condition satisfied the statutory definition of diminished responsibility, and to conclude, as they did, that the defence had not on balance of probabilities been established.

Their Lordships will therefore humbly advise Her Majesty that the appeal should be dismissed.

Appeal dismissed

R. v. Vinagre
(1979) 69 Cr.App.R. 104
Court of Appeal

The appellant, who suspected his wife of infidelity, stabbed her to death. His plea of diminished responsibility was accepted by the trial judge who sentenced him to life imprisonment. It was against this that he appealed. The Court of Appeal considered the wider issue of when such a plea should be accepted.

LAWTON L.J.: ... In this case there were medical examinations of the accused by psychiatrists. Two medical reports were produced. We find them rather unusual documents, because the substance of them was this, that the appellant at the material time was suffering from a mental condition which was described in picturesque, if inaccurate, language as the "Othello syndrome," which was defined as being "morbid jealousy for which there was no cause." ...

Such medical evidence as was before the Court came from the Crown. In those circumstances there was not much point in the defence producing any other psychiatric evidence. Indeed there was a danger that they might have produced a hard-headed psychiatrist who would not have had much use for the Othello syndrome.

As a result, when the case came before the trial judge, Mr. Baker, on behalf of the accused, was able to tender the plea to manslaughter on the grounds of diminished responsibility on the basis that that was what the Crown themselves were saying. The learned judge, as I have already stated, accepted the plea.

We wish to call attention to the history of the acceptance of pleas on grounds of diminished responsibility. After the passing of the Homicide Act 1957, the question arose as to whether Courts could accept pleas to manslaughter on grounds of diminished responsibility. The Court of Criminal Appeal decided in *R. v. Matheson* [1958] 1 W.L.R. 474, that that was not to be done. After that decision until 1962 in all cases of this kind the verdict of the jury had to be taken. The wording of the Homicide Act 1957 indicates that that may well have been the intention of Parliament, because the burden of proving diminished responsibility was upon the defendant. Between 1957 and 1962 there were distressing cases in which a distraught woman (or sometimes a man but usually a distraught woman) had to sit in the dock listening to hours of evidence of what she had done when she was in a state of mental imbalance. Some judges thought that that was wrong. As a result in 1962 the judges decided that pleas of manslaughter on grounds of diminished responsibility could be accepted.

Thompson J. and I were both judges at the time and we are sure that it was never intended that pleas should be accepted on flimsy grounds. As Scarman L.J. pointed out two or three years ago in *R. v. Ford* (1976) (*unrep.*) cases are tried by the Courts and not by psychiatrists. It seems to us that pleas to manslaughter on the grounds of diminished responsibility should only be accepted when there is clear evidence of mental imbalance.

We do not consider that in this case there was clear evidence of mental imbalance. There was clear evidence of a killing by a jealous husband which, until modern times, no one would have thought was anything else but murder.

Be that as it may, Park J. did accept the plea and he listened to the submissions by Mr. Baker on behalf of the appellant as to how the case should be disposed of. ...

Having been told by the psychiatrist that he was satisfied that there would be no recurrence, Mr. Baker so informed the learned judge, who was somewhat sceptical about this and in the course of sentencing the appellant he said: "I am told that you are in no danger; you are no longer any danger to the public but for my part, I am not able to say when you will be fit to resume your place in society." ...

The way things happened has put this Court in a difficulty because if this man is suffering from the Othello syndrome, he may suffer from it again. In other words he is in a state of mental imbalance which may at some future date make him a danger to the public. On the other hand there was some assertion before Park J. that, whatever he may have been suffering from at the time when he killed his wife, he was not likely to suffer from it in the future. That was left unresolved, the judge taking a different view to that which was being urged upon him by Mr. Baker.

We feel that we have no alternative but to approach this case on the basis that Mr. Baker's instructions were correct. In those circumstances the appellant at the time of the trial, and certainly today, is not suffering from the kind of mental imbalance which would justify keeping him in custody until such time as the Home Secretary and the parole board think that it is safe to release him. Accordingly we quash the sentence of life imprisonment and substitute for it a sentence of seven years' imprisonment. To that extent the appeal against sentence is allowed.

Appeal allowed
Sentence varied

Notes

1. In *R. v. Cox* [1968] 1 W.L.R. 308, at 310, Winn L.J. for the Court of Appeal "[F]rom the very outset of the trial it was quite clear ... that the medical evidence available ... showed perfectly plainly that [the plea of diminished responsibility] was a plea which it would have been proper to accept. ... The Court desires to say yet again ... that there are cases where, on an indictment for murder, it is perfectly proper, where the medical evidence is plainly to this effect, to treat the case as one of substantially diminished responsibility and accept, if it be tendered, a plea to manslaughter on that ground, and avoid a trial for murder."

2. Both the Butler Committee on Abnormal Offenders (Cmnd. 6244, 1975, § 19.19) and the Criminal Law Revision Committee (14th Report, Offences Against the Person, (Cmnd. 7844, 1980, §§ 95, 96)) recommend that, in clear cases, it should be possible to avoid indicting for murder at all so that the period between committal and trial is not spent under the shadow of an unrealistic charge.

3. Susanne Dell, "Diminished Responsibility Reconsidered" [1982] Crim.L.R. 809, at 812, gives statistics which show that in 80 per cent. of cases in which diminished responsibility is raised as a

defence, the plea is accepted and in only 20 per cent. of cases did the issue go before a jury.

4. The abnormality of the mind must result from arrested or retarded development, or any inherent causes or be induced by disease or injury. In *Vinagre*, above, jealousy, or "Othello syndrome," was accepted as a disease for these purposes. Mercy killings have also resulted in diminished responsibility pleas being successful as in *Price, The Times*, December 22, 1971, where a father placed his severely handicapped son in a river and watched him float away. Pre-menstrual syndrome and post-natal depression have also been accepted as diseases for the purposes of the test (see *Reynolds, The Times*, April 23, 1988 and S. Edwards, "Mad, bad or pre-menstrual?" (1988) 138 N.L.J. 456).

5. However, *Vinagre*, above, and the trial of *Peter Sutcliffe*, the "Yorkshire Ripper" (at the Old Bailey, April-May 1981, *The Times*, May 23, 1981) illustrate the difficulties of, on the one hand, pursuing a humane procedure to protect the mentally disordered and, on the other, striving to preserve the public interest in murderers being convicted as such. Sutcliffe tendered pleas of diminished responsibility to 13 charges of murder. The psychiatric reports were unanimous in suggesting that Sutcliffe was a paranoid schizophrenic. The judge, however, deemed it to be in the public interest that a jury should determine this matter and the trial proceeded. The jury returned convictions for murder. The case highlights, if nothing else, the extent to which murder and manslaughter are divided not by the niceties of legal definitions but by public gut reaction. Mercy killers or women suffering from pre-menstrual syndrome or post-natal depression perhaps evoke more sympathy than a paranoid schizophrenic. And this raises the question of the proper roles of prosecution, judge and jury. Who is to be the arbiter of the place which any particular homicide is to take on the scale of heinousness?

Intoxication and diminished responsibility

Note

The problem of discovering the cause of a defendant's abnormality of mind may be complicated by his or her ingestion of alcohol or other drugs.

R. v. Tandy
[1989] 1 W.L.R. 350
Court of Appeal

The appellant, an alcoholic, having drunk nine-tenths of a bottle of vodka strangled her 11-year-old daughter. On her plea of diminished responsibility the judge directed the jury that, if they concluded she had voluntarily taken her first drink of the day, she could not claim that the resultant abnormality of mind was due to the disease of alcoholism. The appellant was convicted of murder and appealed.

WATKINS L.J.: ... There were three principal areas of conflict between the medical witnesses called at the trial on behalf of the appellant and the medical witness called by the Crown. The first was whether alcoholism is or is not a disease. ... The second area of conflict between the doctors was whether the appellant's drinking on the Wednesday was voluntary or involuntary. ... The third area of conflict in the medical evidence was on the question whether, if the appellant had not taken drink that day, she would have strangled her daughter. ...

The ground of appeal is that there was material misdirection of the jury in regard to the defence of diminished responsibility. The relevant passages in the summing up are where the judge said:

"The choice [of the appellant whether to drink or not to drink on Wednesday 5 March 1986] may not have been easy but ... if it was there at all it is fatal to this defence, because the law simply will not allow a drug user, whether the drug be alcohol or any other, to shelter behind the toxic effects of the drug which he or she need not have used."

And where he stated earlier:

"If she had taken no drink on 5 March 1986, or if you were satisfied that Dr. Wood is right in saying that judgment and emotional response would have been grossly impaired even if no drink had been taken, then the answer would be easy, but clearly she did take drink on 5 March and if she did that as a matter of choice, she cannot say in law or in common sense that the abnormality of mind which resulted was induced by disease."

Mr. Stewart, the appellant's counsel, submits that these are misdirections, because (1) the medical evidence had been unanimous that there might be compulsion to drink at least after the first drink of the day; that it was the cumulative effect of the consumption of 90 per cent. of the bottle of vodka which caused her to be in the state of intoxication she was in at the time of the killing; by his directions the judge removed the question of compulsion after the taking of the first drink from the jury's consideration; (2) the directions removed from the jury's consideration Dr. Wood's evidence that the alcoholism alone produced an abnormal state of mind which substantially impaired her mental responsibility for her acts; (3) the directions removed from the jury the issue which this court in *R*. v. *Fenton* (1975) 61 Cr.App.R. 261, 263 recognised could arise when an accused person provides such a craving for drink as to produce in itself an abnormality of mind. Lord Widgery C.J.'s actual words were:

"cases may arise hereafter where the accused proves such a craving for drink or drugs as to produce in itself an abnormality of mind; but that is not proved in this case. The appellant did not give evidence and we do not see how self-induced intoxication can of itself produce an abnormality of mind due to inherent causes." ...

The defence of diminished responsibility was derived from the law of Scotland, in which one of the colloquial names for the defence was "partial insanity." Normal human beings frequently drink to excess and when drunk do not suffer from abnormality of mind, within the meaning of that phrase in section 2(1) of the Act of 1957.

Whether an accused person was at the time of the act which results in the victim's death suffering from any abnormality of mind is a question for the jury; and, as the court stated in *R*. v. *Byrne*, although medical evidence is important on this question, the jury are not bound to accept medical evidence if there is other material before them from which in their judgment a different conclusion may be drawn.

The Court of Appeal in *R.* v. *Gittens* [1984] Q.B. 698 said that it was a misdirection to invite the jury to decide whether it was inherent causes on the one hand or drink and pills on the other hand which were the main factor in causing the appellant in that case to act as he did. The correct direction in that case was to tell the jury that they had to decide whether the abnormality arising from the inherent causes substantially impaired the appellant's responsibility for his actions. Lord Lane C.J. said, at p. 703:

"Where alcohol or drugs are factors to be considered . . . the best approach is that . . . approved by this court in *R.* v. *Fenton*, 61 Cr.App.R. 261. . . . The jury should be directed to disregard what, in their view, the effect of the alcohol or drugs upon the defendant was, since abnormality of mind induced by alcohol or drugs is not (generally speaking) due to inherent cases. . . . Then the jury should consider whether the combined effect of the other matters which do fall within the section amounted to such abnormality of mind as substantially impaired the defendant's mental responsibility. . . . "

In the summing up and in the document headed "Questions for the jury," the judge set out the three matters which the defence had to establish on the balance of probability for the defence of diminished responsibility to succeed. No criticism of that part of the summing up or that part of the "Questions for the jury" has been made nor could it have been.

So in this case it was for the appellant to show (1) that she was suffering from an abnormality of mind at the time of the act of strangulation; (2) that that abnormality of mind was induced by disease, namely, the disease of alcoholism; and (3) that the abnormality of mind induced by the disease of alcoholism was such as substantially impaired her mental responsibility for her act of strangling her daughter.

The principles involved in seeking answers to these questions are, in our view, as follows. The appellant would not establish the second element of the defence unless the evidence showed that the abnormality of mind at the time of the killing was due to the fact that she was a chronic alcoholic. If the alcoholism has reached the level at which her brain had been injured by the repeated insult from intoxicants so that there was gross impairment of her judgment and emotional responses, then the defence of diminished responsibility was available to her, provided that she satisfied the jury that the third element of the defence existed. Further, if the appellant were able to establish that the alcoholism had reached the level where although the brain had not been damaged to the extent just stated, the appellant's drinking had become involuntary, that is to say she was no longer able to resist the impulse to drink, then the defence of diminished responsibility would be available to her, subject to her establishing the first and third elements, because if her drinking was involuntary, then her abnormality of mind at the time of the act of strangulation was induced by her condition of alcoholism.

On the other hand, if the appellant had simply not resisted an impulse to drink and it was the drink taken on the Wednesday which brought about the impairment of judgment and emotional response, then the defence of diminished responsibility was not available to the appellant.

In our judgment the direction which the judge gave the jury accurately reflected these principles. There was evidence on which the jury, directed as they were, could reach their verdict. The appellant had chosen to drink vodka on the Wednesday rather than her customary drink of Cinzano. Her evidence was that she might not have had a drink at all on the Tuesday. She certainly did not tell the jury that she must have taken drink on the Tuesday or Wednesday because she could not help herself. She had been able to stop drinking at 6.30 p.m. on the Wednesday evening although her supply of vodka was not exhausted. Thus her own evidence indicated that she was able to exercise some control even after she had taken the first drink, contrary to the view of the doctors. There was the evidence of Dr. Lawson that the appellant would have had the ability on that Wednesday to abstain from taking the first drink of the day.

Mr. Smith, who appeared for the Crown, pointed out in his submissions that the abnormality of mind described by Dr. Wood and Dr. Milne was of grossly impaired judgment and emotional responses and it did not include an irresistible craving for alcohol.

The three matters on which the appellant relies in the perfected grounds of appeal for saying that there was a misdirection can be dealt with shortly. As to the first, in our judgment the judge was correct in telling the jury that if the taking of the first drink was not involuntary, then the whole of the drinking on the Wednesday was not involuntary. Further, as we have pointed out, the appellant's own evidence indicated that she still had control over her drinking on that Wednesday after she had taken the first drink.

As to the second, the jury were told correctly that the abnormality of mind with which they were concerned was the abnormality of mind at the time of the act of strangulation and as a matter of fact by that time on that Wednesday the appellant had drunk 90 per cent. of a bottle of vodka.

On the third point, we conclude that for a craving for drink or drugs in itself to produce an abnormality of mind within the meaning of section 2(1) of the Act of 1957, the craving must be such as to render the accused's use of drink or drugs involuntary. Therefore, in our judgment the judge correctly defined how great the craving for drink had to be before it would in itself produce an abnormality of mind. In any event, it was not the evidence of the doctors called on behalf of the appellant that her abnormality of mind included, let alone consisted solely, of a craving for alcohol.

For those reasons we find that there was no material misdirection of the jury and we dismiss this appeal.

Appeal dismissed.

Reform

Notes

1. The Butler Committee on Mentally Abnormal Offenders (Cmnd. 6244) put forward two reform proposals. The first, preferred solution, recommended that the mandatory life sentence for murder be abolished leaving the judge with a discretion in passing sentence. As a result, the diminished responsibility defence could be abolished. The Committee stated at paragraph 19.5 of the Report:

"19.5 The wording of section 2, as the Judges readily conceded, is open to criticism from several aspects. 'Abnormality of mind' is an extremely imprecise phrase, even as limited by the parentheses and defined by the Court of Appeal (see the foregoing paragraph). 'Mental responsibility,' a phrase not to be found elsewhere in any statute, has created difficulty both for doctors and for jurors. It is either a concept of law or a concept of morality; it is not a clinical fact relating to the defendant. 'Legal responsibility' means liability to conviction (and success in a defence of diminished responsibility does not save the defendant from conviction of manslaughter); 'moral responsibility' means liability to moral censure (but moral questions do not normally enter into the definition of a crime). It seems odd that psychiatrists should be asked and agree to testify as to legal or moral responsibility. It is even more surprising that courts are prepared to hear that testimony. Yet psychiatrists commonly testify to impaired 'mental responsibility' under section 2. Several medical witnesses pointed out to us that the difficulty is made worse by the use of the word 'substantial.' The idea that ability to conform to the law can be measured is particularly puzzling. (See the discussion in paragraph 18.16). Despite the difficulties of the section in relation to psychiatry the medical profession is humane and the evidence is often stretched, as a number of witnesses remarked. Not only psychopathic personality but reactive depressions and dissociated states have been testified to be due to 'inherent causes' within the section."

If this solution was rejected, the second solution the Committee proposed involved amendment of section 2. The amended defence would not impose a burden of proof on the defendant, and in addition, would allow the prosecution, with the consent of the defence, to indict the defendant for manslaughter where there was evidence that the defence of diminished responsibility could be established. The amended section would provide as follows:

"Where a person kills or is party to the killing of another, he shall not be convicted of murder if there is medical or other evidence that he was suffering from a form of mental disorder as defined in section 4 of the Mental Health Act 1959 and if, in the opinion of the jury, the mental disorder was such as to be an extenuating circumstance which ought to reduce the offence to manslaughter."

2. According to section 1(2) of the Mental Health Act 1983, "mental disorder" means "mental illness, arrested or incomplete development of mind, psychopathic disorder and any other disorder or disability of mind and 'mentally disordered' shall be construed accordingly."

Criminal Law Revision Committee, 14th Report, "Offences Against the Person," Cmnd. 7844 (1980), paras. 91–93

"Diminished responsibility was introduced into English law as a defence to murder by section 2 of the Homicide Act 1957. . . . The wording of section 2 has created problems for doctors, judges and juries. Psychiatrists are sometimes expected by lawyers to testify in terms that go outside their professional competence. They are required to testify whether the defendant's abnormality of mind substantially impaired his mental responsibility. The section refers to mental responsibility, which is a legal concept not a medical one; and the jury have to consider as a question of fact whether the abnormality of mind, which is a medical concept, has substantially impaired the defendant's mental responsibility. Some jurors probably have difficulty in understanding these concepts. It is the duty of judges to explain the meaning of section 2 to juries: it is not enough for them to read out the section (*Terry* [1961] 2 Q.B. 314).

There can be no doubt that the wording of section 2 of the Homicide Act 1957 is unsatisfactory. We agree that the ... rewording [suggested by the Butler Committee] ... provides a more easily recognisable diagnostic framework for doctors giving evidence, and the task of judges would be made easier. However, when we considered the rewording we had two reservations. First, we are concerned about the requirement that the defendant, when he killed, must be suffering 'from a form of mental disorder as defined in section 4 of the Mental Health Act 1959 ... '. The Butler Committee were of opinion that this rewording would not materially alter the practical effect of the section. Initially, however, we felt some doubt about whether the rewording might be to some extent restrictive and leave outside the revised definition some offenders who are now regarded by the courts as falling within section 2. The kind of case we had in mind was the depressed father who kills a severely handicapped subnormal child or a morbidly jealous person who kills his or her spouse. In our experience such defendants are not necessarily suffering from a mental disorder of such a kind as to justify the making of a hospital order and are commonly dealt with by the courts, following the section 2 verdict, under the ordinary sentencing provisions applicable to manslaughter, for example, by a relatively short custodial sentence or a conditional discharge or probation order. Because of our doubts, this matter was further considered by the medical advisers to the Department of Health and Social Security, who have advised that the proposed rewording would not exclude the kind of cases we had in mind. Having looked at the matter again, we are satisfied that this view is right having regard to the wide terms in which the definition of mental disorder in section 4 of the Mental Health Act 1959 is drafted. We now accept that the types of mental disturbance we had in mind would be within the definition of mental disorder in section 4 of the Act of 1959, and therefore within the rewording proposed by the Butler Committee for section 2 of the Homicide Act 1957, notwithstanding that they fall outside the criteria of section 60 of the Act of 1959 and are not such as to justify the making of a hospital order.

Our other reservation with regard to the Butler Committee's rewording of the section is that we think that in one respect it may be too lax. The new definition recommended provides that a defendant shall not be convicted of murder if there is evidence that he was suffering from a mental disorder 'and if, in the opinion of the jury, the mental disorder was such as to be an extenuating circumstance which ought to reduce the offence to manslaughter.' We appreciate that the concluding words are intended to leave it to the jury to assess whether in all the circumstances the mental disorder is such as ought to reduce the offence to manslaughter, and we agree that any Bill dealing with diminished responsibility should make it clear that the function of the jury extends to this issue as well as to the question whether some degree of mental disorder is present. However, if this formula were implemented a judge would have to direct a jury to consider, first, whether the defendant was suffering from a mental disorder as defined by section 4, secondly, if he was, whether the mental disorder was an extenuating circumstance and, thirdly, whether that extenuating circumstance was such that it ought to reduce the offence from murder to manslaughter. On that final question the judge would have to give some guidance to the jury as to what extenuating circumstances ought to reduce the offence, and in practice that means that the mental disorder has to be substantial enough to reduce the offence to manslaughter. We consider that the definition should be tightened up so as to include that ingredient upon which the jury will have to be directed, which will give to the jury the necessary guidance. A form of wording which in our opinion tightens up the latter part of the proposed definition and which we favour is ' ... the mental disorder was such as to be substantial enough reason to reduce the offence to manslaughter.' But two other ways of dealing with the laxity in the Butler Committee formula are:

> (ii) ' ... the mental disorder was of such a degree as to be a substantial reason to reduce murder to manslaughter' or
> (iii) ' ... the defendant was suffering from mental disorder to such a degree that he ought not to be held responsible for murder and that in consequence the offence ought to be reduced to manslaughter.'

We have been informed that of our suggested wordings the medical advisers to the Department of Health and Social Security, prefer the first, as we do, since (notwithstanding that similar words are used in section 60 of the Mental Health Act 1959) they consider that phrases like 'such a degree as' in the second and third form of the suggested rewording might present difficulties to doctors as it is not possible to measure degrees of mental disorder. There could therefore be no assurance of comparability between opinions given by different doctors in different cases, which would add to the difficulties of the medical witness."

Note

The Draft Criminal Code Bill adopts in clause 56 the recommendations of the C.L.R.C. with one alteration; the term "mental abnormality" is preferred to "mental disorder" as the latter term is used in clause 36 for the purpose of mental disorder verdicts. (For clause 56 see *infra*, p. 578).

4. INVOLUNTARY MANSLAUGHTER

Notes

1. Manslaughter which has been reduced from murder because of provocation or diminished responsibility (often called "voluntary" manslaughter) has been dealt with in the preceding section. "Involuntary" manslaughter, with which this section is concerned, is a generic term comprising those homicides which occupy "the shifting sands between the uncertain ... definition of murder and the unsettled boundaries of excusable or accidental death." (Hogan, "The Killing Ground: 1964–73" [1974] Crim.L.R. 387, 391).

2. "Involuntary" manslaughter can be divided into manslaughter by unlawful act and reckless manslaughter (in many older cases the term "gross negligence manslaughter" was used). The same case will often give rise to a consideration of both: see *R. v. Goodfellow*, *infra*. In *R. v. Larkin* (1944) 29 Cr.App.R. 18, a case where the jury's verdict of manslaughter could have been based on a finding of provocation or of unlawful act, the Court of Criminal Appeal

deprecated the practice of asking the foreman to explain the basis of the jury's verdict. Humphreys J., for the court, at p. 27:

"As we in this country think, trial by jury is the best method yet devised for dealing with serious criminal cases, and the jury is the best possible tribunal to decide whether a man is guilty and, if he is guilty, of what he is guilty, subject to the direction in law of the judge; but no one has ever suggested that a jury is composed of persons who are likely to be able to give at a moment's notice a logical explanation of how and why they arrive at their verdict. That was what Oliver, J., was inviting the jury to do in this case, and, as has been already observed, inviting the foreman to do so, and accepting from the foreman something with which, perhaps, the other eleven did not agree. The unhappy result was that the foreman, no doubt thoroughly confused, gave two totally inconsistent answers. That incident cannot, in our opinion, be of any importance whatever from the point of view of this appeal against conviction. It was something which happened after the trial was over, so far as the jury were concerned, and if it has any effect at all, it must be an effect upon the sentence. But it must be understood that this court deprecates questions being put to a jury upon the meaning of the verdict which they have returned. If the verdict appears to be inconsistent, proper questions may be put by a judge to invite the jury to explain what they mean, but where a verdict has been returned which is perfectly plain and unambiguous, it is most undesirable that the jury should be asked any further questions about it at all."

The tables *infra*, pp. 548–549, indicate the frequency with which homicides initially charged as murder result in convictions for manslaughter. About 80 per cent. of homicide suspects are ultimately convicted. Of those convicted for the years 1980–1990, 39 per cent. were convicted of murder, 18 per cent. of manslaughter by reason of diminished responsibility, 42 per cent. of manslaughter as a result of provocation, an unlawful and dangerous act or recklessness and one per cent of infanticide.

i. Unlawful Act Manslaughter

(a) *The act causing death must be unlawful*

R. v. Franklin
(1883) 15 Cox 163
Sussex Assizes

The defendant was indicted with manslaughter. He took a box from another man's stall on West Pier, Brighton, and threw it into the sea. The box hit and killed a man who was swimming. The prosecution argued that the question of the defendant's negligence was immaterial, since it was manslaughter where death ensued in consequence of any wrongful act.

FIELD J.: I am of opinion that the case must go to the jury upon the broad ground of negligence and not upon the narrow ground proposed by the learned counsel, because it seems to me—and I may say that in this view my brother Mathew agrees—that the mere fact of a civil wrong committed by one person against another ought not to be used as an incident which is a necessary step in a criminal case. I have a great abhorrence of constructive crime. . . .

Verdict: Guilty

Note

Counsel in this case had relied upon R. v. *Fenton* (1830) 1 Lew. 179, in which Tindal C.J. had formulated this proposition:

"If death ensues as the consequence of a wrongful act, an act which the party who commits it can neither justify nor excuse, it is not accidental death, but manslaughter. If the wrongful act was done under circumstances which show an attempt to kill, or do any serious injury in the particular case, or any general malice, the offence becomes that of murder. In the present instance the act was one of mere wantonness and sport, but still the act was wrongful, it was a trespass. The only question therefore is whether the death of the party is to be fairly and reasonably considered as a consequence of such wrongful act; if it followed from such wrongful act as an effect from a cause, the offence is manslaughter; if it is altogether unconnected with it, it is an accidental death."

Field J. rejected this harsh rule that a civil wrong could constitute the unlawful act for the purposes of manslaughter. This left undecided what constituted such an unlawful act.

R. v. Church
[1966] 1 Q.B. 59
Court of Criminal Appeal

The appellant was mocked by a woman and fought with her knocking her unconscious. He failed to revive her and in a panic, thinking she was dead, threw her into the river where she drowned. The appellant was acquitted of murder but convicted of manslaughter. He appealed on the ground of a misdirection as to manslaughter.

EDMUND-DAVIES J.: Two passages in the summing-up are here material [to manslaughter by an unlawful act causing death]. They are these: (1) "If by an unlawful act of violence done deliberately to the person of another, that other is killed, the killing is manslaughter even though the accused never intended either death or grievous bodily harm to result. If this woman was alive, as she was, when he threw her into the river, what he did was the deliberate act of throwing a living body into the river. That is an unlawful killing and it does not matter whether he believed she was dead or not, and that is my direction to you," and (2) "I would suggest to you, though it is of course for you to approach your task as you think fit, that a convenient way of approaching it would be to say: What do we think about this defence that he honestly believed the woman to be dead? If you think that is true, why then, as I have told you, your proper verdict would be one of manslaughter, not murder."

Such a direction is not lacking in authority: see, for example, *Shoukatallie* v. *The Queen* [1962] A.C. 81 and Dr. Glanville Williams' Criminal Law (1961), 2nd ed., p. 173. Nevertheless, in the judgment of this court it was a

Criminal Statistics, England and Wales (Cm. 1935, 1990)

Table 4.7(a) Suspects indicted for homicide by outcome of proceedings[1]

England and Wales — Number of persons

Indictment and outcome	1980	1981	1982	1983	1984	1985	1986	1987	1988	1989	1990
Indictment:											
Murder	429	454	441	418	465	498[7]	546	566	553[7]	520	330
Manslaughter	101	82	81[6]	98	112	83[7]	105	105	69	66	29
Infanticide	7	7	4	7	2	7	3	1	7	–	1
Total[2]	537	543	526	523	579	588	654	672	629	586	360[8]
Outcome:											
Not convicted of homicide[3]											
Not tried—count to remain on file[4]	4	1	3	4	–	–	4	–	–	–	–
	3	2	1	–	3	2	2	2	–	5	–
Found unfit to plead											
Found not guilty by reason of insanity	1	–	–	2	1	1	1	–	–	1	1
Convicted of lesser offence	38[5]	28	15	32	34	33	52	55	36	49	21
Acquitted on all counts	68[5]	64	65	68	90	90[5]	89	97	92	89	65
Total	114	95	84	106	128	126	148	154	128	144	87
Total convicted of homicide	423	448	442	417	451	462	506	518	501	442	273

Table 4.7(b) Suspects convicted of homicide[1] by type of homicide

England and Wales

Number of persons

Year initially recorded	Total indicated for homicide	Convicted of homicide				
		Total	Murder	Section 2 Manslaughter	Other Manslaughter	Infanticide
1980	537	423	140	88	186	9
1981	543	443	167	87	187	7
1982	526	442	161	102	173	6
1983	523	417	153	80	174	10
1984	579	451	171	77	201	2
1985	584	462	173	74	207	8
1986	654	506	208	81	214	3
1987	672	518	222	77	218	1
1988	628	501	198	71	224	8
1989	586	442	204	69	168	1
1990	360[8]	273	116	47	107	3

(1) As at 1 September 1991; figures are subject to revision as cases are dealt with by the police and by the courts, or as further information becomes available.

(2) Including suspects of offences no longer recorded as homicide. Table S2.1(A) of the supplementary tables 1990 shows figures of persons indicated for homicide and the number of these found guilty or acquitted which may be different from those shown here because this table shows the year in which the offence was recorded, whereas Table S2.1(A) shows the year in which the trial was concluded. Table S2.1(A) is on a principal offence basis and thus shows a person indicated for homicide but convicted of some other offence under the other offence; also, the results of appeals against conviction have been taken into account here but not in Table S2.1(A).

(3) The offences for which these persons were indicated may nevertheless remain currently recorded as homicide.

(4) This usually implies that the suspect has been dealt with for some other less serious offence.

(5) Including 3 persons committed for trial on a voluntary bill of indictment.

(6) Including 1 person committed for trial on a voluntary bill of indictment.

(7) Including 2 persons committed for trial on a voluntary bill of indictment.

(8) In addition there were 292 suspects for whom court proceedings were not completed by 1 September 1991.

misdirection. It amounted to tell the jury that, whenever any unlawful act is committed in relation to a human being which resulted in death there must be, at least, a conviction for manslaughter. This might at one time have been regarded as good law. ... But it appears to this court that the passage of years has achieved a transformation in this branch of the law and, even in relation to manslaughter, a degree of *mens rea* has become recognised as essential. To define it is a difficult task, and in *Andrews* v. *D.P.P.* [1937] A.C. 576, Lord Atkin spoke of the "element of 'unlawfulness' which is the elusive factor." Stressing that we are here leaving entirely out of account those ingredients of homicide which might justify a verdict of manslaughter on the grounds of (a) criminal negligence, or (b) provocation, or (c) diminished responsibility, the conclusion of this court is that an unlawful act causing the death of another cannot, simply because it is an unlawful act, render a manslaughter verdict inevitable. For such a verdict inexorably to follow, the unlawful act must be such as all sober and reasonable people would inevitably recognise must subject the other person to, at least, the risk of some harm resulting therefrom, albeit not serious harm. See, for example, *R.* v. *Franklin*, [*ante*, p. 529]; *R.* v. *Senior* [1899] 1 Q.B. 283; *R.* v. *Larkin* [1943] 1 K.B. 174 in the judgment of the court delivered by Humphrey J.; *R.* v. *Buck & Buck* (1960) 44 Cr.App.R. 213, and *R.* v. *Hall* (1961) 45 Cr.App.R. 366.

If such be the test, as we adjudge it to be, then it follows that in our view it was a misdirection to tell the jury *simpliciter* that is mattered nothing for manslaughter whether or not the appellant believed Mrs. Nott to be dead when he threw her in the river. But, quite apart from our decision that the direction on criminal negligence was an adequate one in the circumstances, such a misdirection does not, in our judgment, involve that the conviction for manslaughter must or should be quashed.

Appeal dismissed

Notes

1. In *Andrews* v. *D.P.P.* [1937] A.C. 576, Lord Atkin stated:

"There is an obvious difference in the law of manslaughter between doing an unlawful act and doing a lawful act with a degree of carelessness which the legislature makes criminal. If it were otherwise a man who killed another while driving without due care and attention would *ex necessitate* commit manslaughter."

Thus a manslaughter verdict cannot be based on an act which is unlawful simply because it has been performed negligently; it must be unlawful for some other reason, namely that the defendant had the *mens rea* required for the offence which constituted the unlawful act.

2. The following case makes it clear that *mens rea* for the unlawful act must be established subjectively.

R. v. Lamb
[1967] 2 Q.B. 981
Court of Appeal

The appellant, in fun, pointed a revolver at a friend. He knew that there were two bullets in the chambers, but neither was opposite the barrel.

He pulled the trigger and because of the action of the cylinder, which rotated before firing, a bullet was fired and the friend killed. He did not appreciate that the cylinder rotated automatically. The appellant was convicted of manslaughter and appealed against this.

SACHS J.: ... [I]n the course of his summing-up, the trial judge no doubt founded himself on the part of the judgment of Edmund-Davies J. in *R.* v. *Church* when he says: "The unlawful act must be such as all sober and reasonable people would inevitably recognise must subject the other person to, at least, the risk of some harm resulting therefrom, albeit not serious harm."

Unfortunately, however, he fell into error as to the meaning of the word "unlawful" in that passage and pressed upon the jury a definition with which experienced counsel for the Crown had disagreed during the trial and which he found himself unable to support on the appeal. The trial judge took the view that the pointing of the revolver and the pulling of the trigger was something which could of itself be unlawful even if there was no attempt to alarm or intent to injure. This view is exemplified in a passage in his judgment which will be cited later.

It was no doubt on that basis that he had before commencing his summing-up stated that he was not going "to involve the jury in any consideration of the niceties of the question whether or not the action of the "accused did constitute or did not constitute an assault"; and thus he did not refer to the defence of accident or the need for the prosecution to disprove accident before coming to a conclusion that the act was unlawful.

Mr. Mathew [for the Crown], however, had at all times put forward the correct view that for the act to be unlawful it must constitute at least what he then termed "a technical assault." In this court moreover he rightly conceded that there was no evidence to go to the jury of any assault of any kind. Nor did he feel able to submit that the acts of the defendant were on any other ground unlawful in the criminal sense of that word. Indeed no such submission could in law be made: if, for instance, the pulling of the trigger had had no effect because the striking mechanism or the ammunition had been defective no offence would have been committed by by defendant.

Another way of putting it is that *mens rea*, being now an essential ingredient in manslaughter (compare *Andrews* v. *D.P.P.* and *R.* v. *Church*), that could not in the present case be established in relation to the first ground except by proving that element of intent without which there can be no assault.

It is perhaps as well to mention that when using the phrase "unlawful in the criminal sense of that word" the court has in mind that it is long settled that it is not in point to consider whether an act is unlawful merely from the angle of civil liabilities. That was first made in the "Brighton Pier" case (*R.* v. *Franklin*). ...

Appeal allowed

Note

A problem decision in this area, however, is that of *Cato* [1976] 1 W.L.R. 110 (*ante*, p. 34) where the Court of Appeal suggested that the unlawful act need not itself be a crime. Lord Widgery stated, at p. 118:

"Strangely enough, . . . although the possession or supply of heroin is an offence, it is not an offence to take it, and although supplying it is an offence, it is not an offence to administer it. . . .

Of course if the conviction on count 2 remains (that is the charge under section 23 of the Offences Against the Person Act 1861 of administering a noxious thing), then that in itself would be an unlawful act. . . .

But . . . had it not been possible to rely on [that] charge, . . . we think there would have been an unlawful act there, and we think the unlawful act would be described as injecting the deceased Farmer with a mixture of heroin and water which at the time of the injection and for the purposes of the injection the accused had unlawfully taken into his possession."

The suggestion that D could be convicted even if the section 23 count was excised from the indictment is *obiter* and appears to be wrong. Possession of heroin is an offence but D's possession of it did not cause the victim's death. This view is confirmed by the fact that in *Dalby* (1982) 74 Cr.App.R. 348, the Court of Appeal expressed the opinion that even the act of supplying a controlled drug to the victim was not an act which *caused* direct harm. The Court affirmed the view that the unlawful act itself must be one which subjects the victim to the risk of some harm; in the instant case it was the victim's own use of the drug in a form and quantity which was dangerous which caused the harm.

(b) *The unlawful act must be dangerous*

Church made it clear that there must be an unlawful act and that it must be dangerous. Two issues left unresolved were (i) whether "harm" was limited to physical harm, and (ii) whether the accused had to be aware that his act was dangerous.

In *Dawson* (1985) 81 Cr.App.R. 150, the Court of Appeal resolved the first issue declaring that there must be a risk of physical harm, rather than emotional disturbance, arising from the unlawful act. Watkins L.J. went on to state (at p. 157) that the requirement of proving harm could be satisfied where "the unlawful act so shocks the victim as to cause him physical injury," for example, a heart attack.

The second issue was addressed in the cases which follow.

D.P.P. v. Newbury
[1977] A.C. 500
House of Lords

The appellants, two 15-year-old boys, pushed into the path of an oncoming train a piece of paving stone which some workmen had left on the parapet of a railway bridge. The stone killed the guard of the train. They were convicted of manslaughter and their appeal was dismissed by the Court of Appeal which nevertheless certified the following point of law: "Can a defendant be properly convicted of manslaughter, when his mind is not affected by drink or drugs, if he did not foresee that his act might cause harm to another?"

LORD SALMON, Lords Diplock, Simon of Glaisdale and Kilbrandon agreeing: ... The learned trial judge did not direct the jury that they should acquit the appellants unless they were satisfied beyond a reasonable doubt that the appellants had foreseen that they might cause harm to someone by pushing the piece of paving stone off the parapet into the path of the approaching train. In my view the learned trial judge was quite right not to give such a direction to the jury. The direction which he gave is completely in accordance with established law, which, possibly with one exception to which I shall presently refer, has never been challenged. In *R. v. Larkin* (1944) 29 Cr.App.R. 18, Humphreys J. said, at p. 23:

> "Where the act which a person is engaged in performing is unlawful, then if at the same time it is a dangerous act, that is, an act which is likely to injure another person, and quite inadvertently the doer of the act causes death of that other person by that act then he is guilty of manslaughter."

I agree entirely with Lawton L.J. that that is an admirably clear statement of the law which has been applied many times. It makes it plain (a) that an accused is guilty of manslaughter if it is proved that he intentionally did an act which was unlawful and dangerous and that that act inadvertently caused death and (b) that it is necessary to prove that the accused knew that the act was unlawful or dangerous. This is one of the reasons why cases of manslaughter vary so infinitely in their gravity. They may amount to little more than pure inadvertence and sometimes to little less than murder.

I am sure that in *R. v. Church* [*ante*, p. 547] Edmund-Davies J. in giving the judgment of the court, did not intend to differ from or qualify anything which had been said in *R. v. Larkin*. Indeed he was restating the principle laid down in that case by illustrating the sense in which the word "dangerous" should be understood. Edmund-Davies J. said at p. 70:

> "For such a verdict" (guilty of manslaughter) "inexorably to follow, the unlawful act must be such as all sober and reasonable people would inevitably recognise must subject the other person to, at least, the risk of some harm resulting therefrom, albeit not serious harm."

The test is still the objective test. In judging whether the act was dangerous the test is not did the accused recognise that it was dangerous but would all sober and reasonable people recognise its danger.

Mr. Esyr Lewis in his very able argument did not and indeed could not contend that the appellants' act which I have described was lawful but he did maintain that the law stated in *Larkin's* case had undergone a change as a result of a passage in the judgment of Lord Denning M.R. in *Gray v. Barr* [1971] 2 Q.B. 554, 568 which reads as follows:

> "In manslaughter of every kind there must be a guilty mind. Without it, the accused must be acquitted [see *R. v. Lamb, supra*]. In the category of manslaughter relating to an unlawful act, the accused must do a dangerous act with the intention of frightening or harming someone, or with the realisation that it is likely to frighten or harm someone, and nevertheless he goes on and does it, regardless of the consequences. If his act does thereafter, in unbroken sequence, cause the death of another, he is guilty of manslaughter."

I do not think that Lord Denning M.R was attempting to revolutionise the law relating to manslaughter if his judgment is read in the context of the tragic circumstances of the case. ...

R. v. *Lamb* was referred to by Lord Denning M.R. for the proposition that in manslaughter there must always be a guilty mind. This is true of every crime except those of absolute liability. The guilty mind usually depends on the intention of the accused. Some crimes require what is sometimes called a specific intention, for example murder, which is killing with intent to inflict grievous bodily harm. Other crimes need only what is called a basic intention, which is an intention to do the acts which constitute the crime. Manslaughter is such a crime: see *R.* v. *Larkin* and *R.* v. *Church. R.* v. *Lamb* is certainly no authority to the contrary. . . .

Lawton L.J. had observed that in manslaughter cases, some judges are now directing juries not in accordance with the law as correctly laid down in *R.* v. *Larkin* and *R.* v. *Church* but in accordance with the observations of Lord Denning M.R. in *Gray* v. *Barr* taken in their literal sense. For the reasons I have already given they should cease to do so.

My Lords, I dismiss the appeal.

R. v. Dawson
(1985) 81 Cr.App.R. 150
Court of Appeal

D and E robbed V.'s filling station wearing masks and armed with a pickaxe handle and replica gun. Shortly afterwards V, who had a serious heart condition, died of a heart attack. D and E were convicted of manslaughter and appealed.

WATKINS L.J.: . . .

We look finally at the direction, "That is to say all reasonable people who knew the facts that you know." What the jury knew included, of course, the undisputed fact that the deceased had a very bad heart which at any moment could have ceased to function. It may be the judge did not intend that this fact should be included in the phrase "the facts that you know." If that was so, it is regrettable that he did not make it clear. By saying as he did, it is argued "including the fact that the gun was a replica" and so on, the jury must have taken him to be telling them that all facts known to them, including the heart condition, should be taken into account in performing what is undoubtedly an objective test. We think there was a grave danger of that.

This test can only be undertaken upon the basis of the knowledge gained by a sober and reasonable man as though he were present at the scene of and watched the unlawful act being performed and who knows that, as in the present case, an unloaded replica gun was in use, but that the victim may have thought it was a loaded gun in working order. In other words, he has the same knowledge as the man attempting to rob and no more. It was never suggested that any of these appellants knew that their victim had a bad heart. They knew nothing about him.

A jury must be informed by the judge when trying the offence of manslaughter what facts they may and those which they may not use for the purpose of performing the test in the second element of this offence. The judge's direction here, unlike the bulk of an admirable summing-up, lacked that necessary precision and in the form it was given may, in our view, have given the jury an erroneous impression of what knowledge they could ascribe to the sober and reasonable man.

For these reasons we see no alternative to quashing the convictions for manslaughter as unsafe and unsatisfactory. The appeal against the convictions for manslaughter is therefore allowed.

R. v. Watson
[1989] 1 W.L.R. 684
Court of Appeal

D and E broke a window and entered the house of Mr. Moyler who, unknown to D and E, was aged 87, lived alone and suffered from a serious heart condition. D and E were disturbed by Mr. Moyler and abused him verbally and left without stealing anything. Mr. Moyler died 90 minutes later. D and E were convicted of manslaughter and appealed contending, *inter alia*, that the sober and reasonable bystander should only be ascribed the knowledge which they had at the moment they entered the house.

LORD LANE C.J.: . . .
The first point taken on behalf of the appellant is this. When one is deciding whether the sober and reasonable person (the bystander) would realise the risk of some harm resulting to the victim, how much knowledge of the circumstances does one attribute to the bystander? The appellant contends that the unlawful act here was the burgulary as charged in the indictment.

The charge was laid under section 9(1)(*a*) of the Theft Act 1968, the allegation being that the appellant had entered the building as a trespasser with intent to commit theft. Since that offence is committed at the first moment of entry, the bystander's knowledge is confined to that of the defendant at that moment. In the instant case there was no evidence that the appellant, at the moment of entry, knew the age or physical condition of Mr. Moyler or even that he lived there alone.

The judge clearly took the view that the jury were entitled to ascribe to the bystander the knowledge which the appellant gained during the whole of his stay in the house and so directed them. Was this a misdirection? In our judgment it was not. The unlawful act in the present circumstances comprised the whole of the burglarious intrusion and did not come to an end upon the appellant's foot crossing the threshold or windowsill. That being so, the appellant (and therefore the bystander) during the course of the unlawful act must have become aware of Mr. Moyler's frailty and approximate age, and the judge's directions were accordingly correct. We are supported in this view by the fact that no one at the trial seems to have thought otherwise.

Note

The sober and reasonable bystander will also be aware of the background to the unlawful act (which includes preparatory acts done by the accused) as this sets the act in context for the purpose of determining its objective dangerousness. In *Ball* Crim.L.R. 730, D loaded a shotgun with two cartridges taken from his pocket which contained both live and blank cartridges. He fired the gun at V killing her. Appealing against his conviction of manslaughter, D argued that the objective assessment of the danger of his act should be based on his mistaken belief that he was firing a blank cartridge and not on the actual fact that he was firing a live cartridge. Dismissing the appeal Lord Lane C.J. stated:

"[Once it is] established . . . that the act was both unlawful and that he intended to commit the assaults, the question whether the act is a dangerous one is to be judged not by the appellant's appreciation but by that of the sober and reasonable man, and it is impossible to impute into his appreciation the mistaken belief of the appellant that what he was doing was not dangerous because he thought he had a blank cartridge in the chamber. At that stage the appellant's intention, foresight or knowledge is irrelevant."

Question

Consider D's liability for manslaughter where he fires a blank cartridge and V dies (i) as a result of diving for cover and fracturing her skull on a rock, (ii) as a result of a heart attack, V having no history of heart disease, and (iii) as a result of a cut sustained in diving for cover, V (unknown to D) being a haemophiliac.

(c) *Must the unlawful act be "directed at" the victim?*

R. v. Goodfellow
(1986) 83 Cr.App.R. 23
Court of Appeal

The appellant, who lived in a council house, wished to be rehoused. He set fire to his house while his wife, three children and another woman were in the house. The appellant, using a ladder, rescued two of his children, but the other child, his wife and the other woman all died as the fire spread more rapidly than had been anticipated. The appellant was convicted of manslaughter and appealed.

LORD LANE C.J.: . . . It seems to us that this was a case which was capable of falling within either or both types of manslaughter. On the *Lawrence* aspect [*i.e.* manslaughter by a reckless act], *post*, p. 557, the jury might well have been satisfied that the appellant was acting in such a manner as to create an obvious and serious risk of causing physical injury to some person, and secondly that he, having recognised that there was some risk involved, had nevertheless gone on to take it.

This was equally, in our view, a case for the "unlawful and dangerous act" direction. Where the defendant does an unlawful act of such a kind as all sober and reasonable people would inevitably recognise must subject another person to, at least, the risk of some harm resulting therefrom, albeit not serious harm and causes death thereby, he is guilty of manslaughter: *Church* (*ante*, p. 547).

Lord Salmon in *D.P.P.* v. *Newbury* (*ante*, p. 552) approved a dictum of Humphreys J. in *Larkin* [1943] 1 All E.R. 217, 219: "Where the act which a person is engaged in performing is unlawful, then if at the same time it is a dangerous act, that is, an act which is likely to injure another person, and quite inadvertently he causes the death of that other person by that act, then he is guilty of manslaughter." Their Lordships in that case (*Newbury*) expressly disapproved of a passage in the judgment of Lord Denning M.R. in the civil case of *Gray* v. *Barr* [1971] 2 All E.R. 949, 956, in which he asserted that the unlawful act must be done by the defendant with the intention of frightening or harming someone or with the realisation that it is likely to frighten or harm someone. That decision of the House of Lords is, of course, binding upon us.

It is submitted by Mr. Stewart on behalf of the appellant that this was not a case of "unlawful act" manslaughter, because the actions of the appellant were not directed at the victim. The authority for that proposition is said to be *Dalby* (1982) 74 Cr.App.R. 348.

In that case the appellant, a drug addict, supplied a class A drug which he had lawfully obtained to a friend, also an addict. Each injected himself intravenously. After the appellant had left, the friend administered to himself two further injections, the nature of which was unknown. When the appellant returned he was unable to wake up his friend. When medical help eventually arrived, the friend was found to be dead. The appellant was convicted of manslaughter either on the unlawful and dangerous act basis, or alternatively on the basis that he was grossly negligent in not calling an ambulance at an earlier stage.

It was held that since the act of supplying the scheduled drug was not an act which caused direct harm and since the unlawful act of supply of the dangerous drug by Dalby *per se* did not constitute the *actus reus* of the offence of manslaughter, the conviction had to be quashed. Waller L.J., at p. 352, said: " . . . where the charge of manslaughter is based on an unlawful and dangerous act, it must be an act directed at the victim and likely to cause immediate injury, however slight."

However we do not think that he was suggesting that there must be an intention on the part of the defendant to harm or frighten or a realisation that his acts were likely to harm or frighten. Indeed it would have been contrary to the dicta of Lord Salmon in *D.P.P.* v. *Newbury* (*supra*) if he was. What he was, we believe, intending to say was that there must be no fresh intervening cause between the act and the death. Indeed at p. 351 he said this: " . . . the supply of drugs would itself have caused no harm unless the deceased had subsequently used the drugs in a form and quantity which was dangerous." . . .

The questions which the jury have to decide on the charge of manslaughter of this nature are: (1) Was the act intentional? (2) Was it unlawful? (3) Was it an act which any reasonable person would realise was bound to subject some other human being to the risk of physical harm, albeit not necessarily serious harm? (4) Was that act the cause of death?

Whatever indications the judge may have given earlier as to his intentions, he did in fact direct the jury on this type of manslaughter in the passage which we have already quoted. It is true that he went further and added observations which were more appropriate to the *Lawrence* type of manslaughter. If anything, those passages resulted in a direction which was more favourable to the appellant than if they had been omitted.

Appeal dismissed

ii. Reckless Manslaughter

Note

The second basis upon which a person may be found guilty of involuntary manslaughter is that of recklessness. This area, however, has been blighted for many years by judicial imprecision in the use of terms. For many years the terms recklessness and gross negligence were used, sometimes interchangeably, to support convictions for manslaughter.

In *R.* v. *Bateman* (1925) 19 Cr.App.R. 8, Lord Hewart C.J. stated the test as follows:

"[I]n order to establish criminal liability the facts must be such that, in the opinion of the jury, the negligence of the accused went beyond a mere matter of compensation between subjects and showed such disregard for the life and safety of others as to amount to a crime against the state and conduct deserving punishment."

This passage is circular in its reasoning, leaving it to the jury to determine when the negligence displayed by the defendant becomes sufficiently gross to attract criminal liability.

In *Andrews* v. *D.P.P.* [1937] A.C. 576, Lord Atkin approved of *Bateman* stating:

"The substance of the judgment is most valuable, and in my opinion is correct. . . . The principle to be observed is that cases of manslaughter in driving motor cars are but instances of a general rule applicable to all charges of homicide by negligence. Simple lack of care such as will constitute civil liability is not enough: for purposes of the criminal law there are degrees of negligence: and a very high degree of negligence is required to be proved before the felony is established. Probably of all the epithets that can be applied 'reckless' most nearly covers the case. It is difficult to visualise a case of death caused by reckless driving in the connotation of that term in ordinary speech which would not justify a conviction for manslaughter: but it is probably not all-embracing, for 'reckless' suggests an indifference to risk whereas the accused may have appreciated the risk, and intended to avoid it, and yet shown in the means adopted to avoid the risk such a degree of negligence as would justify a conviction."

In *Lamb* (*ante*, p. 550) Sachs J. shed a remarkable degree of confusion on the area conflating negligence with recklessness and alternating between a subjective test and an objective test. He stated:

"When the gravamen of a charge is criminal negligence—often referred to as recklessness—of an accused, the jury have to consider among other matters the state of his mind, and that includes the question of whether or not he thought that that which he was doing was safe. In the present case it would, of course, have been fully open to a jury, if properly directed, to find the defendant guilty because they considered his view as to there being no danger was formed in a criminally negligent way. But he was entitled to a direction that the jury should take into account the fact that he had undisputably formed that view and that there was expert evidence as to this being an understandable view."

The above cases suggested that in gross negligence manslaughter the risk of harm must have been of death (or at the very least grievous bodily harm) ensuing for a conviction to follow.

A conviction for manslaughter could also follow where the defendant had been subjectively reckless as to death or some bodily harm resulting from his conduct (see *R.* v. *Pike* [1961] Crim.L.R. 114 and *Gray* v. *Barr* [1971] 2 All E.R. 949). In *Stone* v. *Dobinson* [1977] Q.B. 354, subjective recklessness as to health and welfare was found to be sufficient to support a manslaughter verdict.

The status of the above decisions is doubtful in light of the cases which follow.

R. v. Seymour
[1983] 2 A.C. 493
House of Lords

S, when driving his lorry, was involved in a slight collision with a car driven by B, a woman with whom he lived and with whom he had recently quarrelled. S drove his lorry again against the car intending to shunt it out of his way and in so doing, B who had got out of her car, was crushed between the car and the lorry. B suffered severe injuries from which she later died. S was indicted and convicted of manslaughter.

LORD ROSKILL: [After stating the facts] My Lords in recent years and indeed since the enactment of section 8 of the Road Traffic Act 1956 when the statutory offence of causing death by reckless or dangerous driving was first created, charges of "motor manslaughter" have been comparatively rare. It is common knowledge that the statutory offence was created carrying a maximum penalty of five years' imprisonment because of the extreme reluctance of juries to convict motorists of manslaughter. After 1956 when the statutory offence was created, the practice in England and Wales was to charge the offence of causing death by dangerous driving only and not by reckless driving.

The subsequent legislative history of this offence has recently been twice discussed in your Lordships' House, first in the speech of my noble and learned friend Lord Diplock in *R.* v. *Lawrence* (*ante*, p. 117) and secondly in my speech in *R.* v. *Governor of Holloway Prison, Ex p. Jennings* [1983] 1 A.C. 624 and requires no further repetition. Suffice it to say that by reason of the enactment of section 50 of the Criminal Law Act 1977, the former provisions of section 8 of the Act of 1956, which by 1977 had become section 1(1) of the Road Traffic Act 1972, were replaced by a new section 1 which provided that "a person who causes the death of another person by driving a motor vehicle on a road recklessly shall be guilty of an offence."

This enactment in due course gave rise to two questions. First, what was the meaning of the word "reckless" in this new section? Or, to put the same point in other words, what was the proper direction for the trial judge to give to a jury as to the test to be applied in determining whether or not a person charged under this section was guilty of the offence charged? Secondly, and in particular having regard to the speech of Lord Atkin in *Andrews* v. *D.P.P.* [1937] A.C. 576, 584, did the common law offence of manslaughter by reckless driving of a motor vehicle survive the enactment of section 50 of the Act of 1977, for if it did so survive there would be two offences, one at common law and the other by statute which, since the ingredients of each were indistinguishable, would be co-extensive, though one carried the maximum penalty of imprisonment for life, and the other of five years' imprisonment only.

The meaning of the words "reckless" and "recklessly" came before your Lordships' House in two cases, *R. v. Caldwell (ante,* p. 111) and in *R. v. Lawrence (ante,* p. 117) ...

As to the second question, there had been, as Watkins L.J. said in giving the judgment of the Court of Appeal (Criminal Division) in the present case, a body of opinion which thought that the common law offence of manslaughter by the reckless driving of a motor vehicle must be taken to have been impliedly repealed by section 50 of the Act of 1977, or possibly earlier. That view was taken by the Divisional Court in *Jennings* [1982] 1 W.L.R. 949. But your Lordships' House in that case unanimously held otherwise. The argument founded on implied repeal was rejected for the reasons given in my speech [1983] 1 A.C. 624, 639–644 which I will not repeat. But I added at p. 644, "No doubt the prosecuting authorities today would only prosecute for manslaughter in the case of death caused by the reckless driving of a motor vehicle on a road in a very grave case."

My Lords, *Jennings* was decided on July 29, 1982, over a year after Mrs. Burrows death and some six months after the appellant's trial at Northampton Crown Court. This trial also preceded the hearing of *Jennings* in the Divisional Court. As already stated, the appellant was charged only with manslaughter, no doubt because of the view which the prosecuting authorities took of the gravity of the case. Your Lordships were told that a plea of guilty to the statutory offence, had that also been charged, was proffered but was rejected by learned counsel for the Crown. I agree with the view of the Court of Appeal that this was an entirely proper course for counsel for the Crown to have adopted. The jury was, of course, unaware of this fact.

After the close of the evidence, Mr. Michael Connell Q.C., for the appellant, invited the learned judge not to give the jury what I will call for brevity the *"Lawrence* direction" *simpliciter,* arguing that that direction was applicable only where the statutory offence was charged. He submitted that where the common law offence of manslaughter was charged, the jury should be directed that the Crown must further prove that the appellant recognised that some risk was involved and had nonetheless proceeded to take that risk.

The learned judge rejected the submission and gave the *"Lawrence* direction" subject only to the omission of any reference to the "obvious and serious risk ... of doing substantial damage to property": see *R. v. Lawrence* [1982] A.C. 510, 526. In my view, he was entirely right not to refer to damage to property, a reference to which was irrelevant in this case and might well have confused the jury. His admirably clear direction not only properly reflected the decision of this House in *Lawrence* but also Lord Atkin's speech in *Andrews* [1937] A.C. 576. I quote the relevant passages:

"The second question you have to decide; was the driving that caused those injuries reckless? If so, then it is manslaughter. If you are not satisfied that it was reckless, then the verdict is not guilty. To amount to reckless driving mere negligence is not enough. His conduct must go beyond the question of compensation between citizens and amount to, in your view, criminal conduct requiring punishment. You have to be satisfied upon the question of recklessness that he drove in such a manner as to create an obvious and serious risk of causing physical harm to some other person who might happen to be using the road at the time. ... Once you are satisfied that the matter of his driving was such as to create an obvious and serious risk of causing physical harm to a person using the road at the time, you also have to be satisfied that driving in that manner he did so without having given any thought to the possibility of there being any such risk, or alternatively, having recognised that there was some risk involved, nonetheless went on to take it; in other words, he was reckless. He reckoned not of the consequences.

"In determining the quality of his driving, you apply the standards of the ordinary reasonable motorist. You, of course, take into account all the evidence including his explanation. ... "

As already stated, the appellant was convicted. He appealed and his appeal to the Court of Appeal was dismissed. By the date of the appeal, *Jennings* had been decided in your Lordships' House. The reasons given for the dismissal of his appeal were in substance, that since your Lordships' House had held that the ingredients of the common law and statutory offences were identical, the *Lawrence* decision, which was appropriate when the statutory offence was charged, must be equally appropriate when the common law offence of manslaughter was charged. The Court of Appeal (Criminal Division) granted the appellant a certificate in the following terms:

"Where manslaughter is charged and the circumstances of the offence are that the victim was killed as a result of the reckless driving of the defendant on a public highway; should the trial judge give the jury the direction suggested in *R. v. Lawrence* in its entirety; or should the direction be that only a recognition by the defendant that some risk was involved and he had nonetheless gone on to take it would be sufficient to establish the commission of the offence?" ...

My Lords, I would accept the submission of Mr. Hamilton for the Crown that once it is shown that the two offences co-exist it would be quite wrong to give the adjective "reckless" or the adverb "recklessly" a different meaning according to whether the statutory or the common law offence is charged. "Reckless" should today be given the same meaning in relation to all offences which involve "recklessness" as one of the elements unless Parliament has otherwise ordained. That this has been so in the past is shown by the respective decisions of the Court of Criminal Appeal and the Court of Appeal (Criminal Division) in *R. v. Church* [1968] 1 Q.B. 59, 68, and *R. v. Lowe* [1973] Q.B. 702, 708, to neither of which was the attention of this House drawn in either *R. v. Caldwell* or *Lawrence*. This was also clearly the view taken by the Court of Appeal (Criminal Division) in *R. v. Pigg* [1982] 1 W.L.R. 762: see especially the judgment of Lord Lane C.J. at pp. 770–772, with all the reasoning in which I respectfully agree.

In truth, [counsel for the appellant's] argument is an attempt to overcome an anomaly resulting from the amendment of the law in 1977, an amendment made not for the purpose of effecting a reform of substantive law but, as my noble and learned friend, Lord Diplock pointed out in his speech in *Lawrence* [1982] A.C. 510, 524, in connection with the re-distribution of criminal business between the Crown Courts and magistrates' courts. The very difficulty which Mr. Connell encountered in trying to distinguish between a defendant who gave no thought to a risk to which he was indifferent and who even if he had thought of that risk would have acted in precisely the same way and a defendant who gave no thought to a risk because it never crossed his mind that the risk existed, is eloquent of the need to prescribe a simple and single meaning of the adjective "reckless" and the adverb "recklessly" throughout the criminal law unless Parliament has otherwise ordained in a particular case. That simple and single meaning should be the ordinary meaning of those words as stated in this House in *Caldwell* and in *Lawrence*.

Parliament must however be taken to have intended that "motor manslaughter" should be a more grave offence than the statutory offence. While the former still carries a maximum penalty of imprisonment for life, Parliament has thought fit to limit the maximum penalty for the statutory offence to five years' imprisonment, the sentence in fact passed by the learned trial judge upon the appellant upon his conviction for manslaughter. This difference recognises that there are degrees of turpitude which will vary according to the gravity of the risk created by the manner of a defendant's driving. In these circumstances your Lordships may think that in future it will only be very rarely that it will be appropriate to charge "motor manslaughter": that is where, as in the instant case, the risk of death from a defendant's driving was very high. ...

In England and Wales it is for the prosecution and not for the court to decide what charge or charges should be made against a particular defendant. The prosecution is entitled to consider all the circumstances of the case before so deciding. In the instant case the prosecution properly charged manslaughter and manslaughter alone. In doing so the prosecution took the risk that a jury might have refused to convict the appellant of that crime though on the evidence it is difficult to see how any reasonable jury could have acquitted him of that offence. But had he been acquitted he would have gone unpunished even though the jury might have convicted him of the statutory offence had that been charged.

In my opinon that consideration cannot justify the joinder of both charges in a single indictment. In future if in any case in England and Wales any such joinder should occur I think it must behove the trial judge to require the prosecution to elect upon which of the two counts in the indictment they wish to proceed and not to allow the trial to proceed upon both counts. This may result in a different practice prevailing in England and Wales from that which has prevailed in Scotland, a part of the United Kingdom over which no criminal jurisdiction is exercised by this House. But since it is clear that the substantive law is the same in both countries, differences in practice may be thought to be not of great importance.

I would therefore answer the certified question as follows: "Where manslaughter is charged and the circumstances are that the victim was killed as a result of the reckless driving of the defendant on a public highway, the trial judge should give the jury the direction suggested in *R. v. Lawrence* but it is appropriate also to point out that in order to constitute the offence of manslaughter the risk of death being caused by the manner of the defendant's driving must be very high."

I would dismiss this appeal.

Appeal Dismissed

Questions

1. Is the decision in *Seymour* consistent with *Lawrence* (*ante*, p. 117) which required the conduct to be accompanied by "an obvious and serious risk of causing physical injury to some other person" whereas Lord Roskill stated that "in order to constitute the offence of manslaughter the risk of death being caused by the manner of the defendant's driving must be very high"? If these statements do not amount to the same thing, what is the risk which must exist (see *Goodfellow, supra*, (1986) 83 Cr.App.R. 23 and *Kong Cheuk Kwan v. R., infra*, p. 563).

2. What does Lord Fraser of Tullybelton mean when he states (in the course of his speech, which is not here reproduced) that

"although the legal ingredients of the two offences [of manslaughter and causing death by reckless driving] are the same, the degree of recklessness required for the conviction of the statutory offence is less than that required for conviction of the common law crime"? Does he mean that manslaughter requires a high risk of death while causing death by reckless driving requires only an obvious risk of causing injury? If so, are the legal ingredients of the offences the same?

3. Would it be manslaughter where death resulted from an act done in circumstances where there was an obvious and serious risk of substantially damaging property? See the following case.

Note

The offence of causing death by reckless driving has been replaced by that of "causing death by dangerous driving, section 1 of the Road Traffic Act 1991.

Kong Cheuk Kwan v. R.
(1985) 82 Cr.App.R. 18
Privy Council

The appellant was the captain of a hydrofoil which collided with another hydrofoil in perfect weather conditions. There was resultant loss of life and the appellant was convicted of manslaughter. The captain and deck officer of the other vessel were acquitted of manslaughter.

LORD ROSKILL read the opinion of the Board: ... [T]he learned judge ... was encouraged by counsel to adopt and did adopt as the basis for his direction a long passage which first made its appearance in paragraph 20.49 of the Second Supplement to *Archbold's Criminal Pleading Evidence and Practice* (1982) 41st Ed. and which purports to reflect the decisions of the House of Lords in *Caldwell* and *Lawrence*. ...

Their Lordships find it necessary to set out the text of the direction in full. The relevant part appears as one very long single sentence in the transcript but that very long single sentence requires to be broken down for the purpose of analysis:

"The direction I give you, which I have had typed because I think this is not a trial involving test of memories so I am going to give you a copy of this before you retire, but I will read (it) out, this is the direction on the question of manslaughter by negligence. That is that the defendant and, of course, each of them considered separately, is guilty of manslaughter if the Crown have proved beyond reasonable doubt, firstly, that at the time he caused the deceased's death and, of course, you must be satisfied that each of the accused did cause the deceased's death, there was something in the circumstances which would have drawn the attention of an ordinary prudent individual and in this case you would consider the ordinary prudent deck officer or helmsman in the position of the defendant, to the possibility that his conduct was capable of causing some injury albeit not necessarily serious to the deceased including injury to health, which does not apply here, and that the risk was not so slight that an ordinary prudent individual would feel justified in treating it as negligible and that, secondly, before the act or omission which caused the deceased's death, the defendant either failed to give any thought to the possibility of there being any such risk or having recognised that there was such a risk he, nevertheless, went on to take the risk, or was guilty of such a high degree of negligence in the means that he adopted to avoid the risk as to go beyond a mere matter of compensation between subjects and showed in your opinion, such disregard for the life and safety of others as to amount to a crime against the State and conduct deserving punishment." ...

With profound respect this direction cannot be supported. There is (as in the paragraph in the Supplements to *Archbold*) confusion between (1) causing death by an illegal act of violence, (2) what was said in *R.* v. *Caldwell* (3) what was said in *R.* v. *Lawrence* and (4) what had half a century previously been said by the Court of Criminal Appeal in *Bateman* (1925) 19 Cr.App.R. 8.

The Court of Appeal was obviously critical of this passage but in a careful judgment felt in the light of all the authorities able to conclude that other later passages in the summing up, including repeated references to "gross negligence" put the matter sufficiently right. It is to be observed that from beginning to end of the summing-up neither the word "reckless" nor the word "recklessness" ever appears. ...

Though *Caldwell* and *Lawrence* are referred to in the preface to the 41st edition as "extraordinary decisions" (a view which the editor is of course at liberty to express in his preface if he so wishes) they are understandably not referred to in the original text of paragraph 20.49 though there is a passing reference to them in the final sentence of paragraph 20.49. No doubt it was this omission which necessitated the addition of paragraph (7) in the Second Supplement. But the view, whether correct or not, that the two decisions are "extraordinary" cannot justify complete misrepresentation as to their effect in a text book of great authority widely used in England and Wales and elsewhere as in Hong Kong where the relevant criminal law is the same.

It thus becomes necessary for their Lordships to restate the current position though in so doing they are largely repeating what was said in those two decisions which have themselves since been applied in two further decisions in the House of Lords, *Government of United States* v. *Jennings* [1983] 1 A.C. 624 and *Seymour* (1983) 77 Cr.App.R. 215; [1983] 2 A.C. 493. In *Caldwell* [1982] A.C. 341 the House was concerned with and only with the meaning of the word "reckless" in the statutory context of section 1 of the Criminal Damage Act 1971. Any relationship between "recklessness" in arson cases and "recklessness" in cases of causing death by reckless driving or of motor manslaughter was not there under consideration. The crucial passage is in the speech of Lord Diplock with which the other members of the majority of the House agreed and appears at p. 354. Their Lordships think it right to quote this passage in full:

"Nevertheless, to decide whether someone has been 'reckless' as to whether harmful consequences of a particular kind will result from this act, as distinguished from his actually intending such harmful consequences to follow, does call for some consideration of how the mind of the ordinary prudent individual would have reacted to a similar situation. If there were nothing in the circumstances that ought to have drawn the attention of an ordinary prudent individual to the possibility of that kind of harmful consequence, the accused would not be described as 'reckless' in the natural meaning of that word for failing to address his mind to the possibility; nor, if the risk of the harmful consequences was so slight that the ordinary prudent individual upon due consideration of the risk would not be deterred from treating it as negligible, could the accused be described as 'reckless' in its ordinary sense if, having considered the risk, he decided to ignore it. (In this connection the gravity of the possible harmful consequences would be an important factor. To endanger life must be one of the most grave.) ... In my opinion a person charged with an offence under section 1(1) of the Criminal Damage Act 1971 is 'reckless as to whether any such property would be destroyed or damaged' if (1) he does an act which in fact creates an obvious risk that property would be destroyed or damaged and (2) when he does the act he either has not given any thought to the possibility of there being any such risk or has recognised that there was some risk involved and has nonetheless gone on to do it. That would be a proper direction to the jury: cases in the Court of Appeal which held otherwise should be regarded as overruled."

Lord Diplock was in that passage thus stating (in part) a negative proposition. He was dealing with the factual situation where there was nothing to alert the ordinary prudent individual to the possibility of harmful consequences or where the possibility was so slight that the individual could properly treat the risk as negligible. Such conduct was not "reckless" within the ordinary meaning of that ordinary English word.

Their Lordships now move to *Lawrence* [1982] A.C. 510. There the House was dealing with death caused by reckless driving. The House unanimously accepted the view of the majority in *R. v. Caldwell* as to the meaning of "reckless" and of "recklessness." It applied that ruling to the statutory offence of causing death by reckless driving and suggested a model direction in such cases.

Lord Diplock, on this occasion speaking for all the noble and learned Lords then present, said, after quoting from his speech in *Lawrence*, (at p. 526):

"In my view, an appropriate instruction to the jury on what is meant by driving recklessly would be that they must be satisfied of two things: first, that the defendant was in fact driving the vehicle in such a manner as to create an obvious and serious risk of causing physical injury to some other person who might happen to be using the road or of doing substantial damage to property; and second, that in driving in that manner the defendant did so without having given any thought to the possibility of there being any such risk or, having recognised that there was some risk involved, had nonetheless gone on to take it. It is for the jury to decide whether the risk created by the manner in which the vehicle was being driven was both obvious and serious and, in deciding this, they may apply the standard of the ordinary prudent motorist as represented by themselves."

Their Lordships emphasise that in this passage Lord Diplock was speaking of an obvious and serious risk of causing physical injury created by the defendant. He was not there concerned to deal with cases where the conduct complained of was a defendant's reaction or lack of reaction to such a risk created by another person.

Finally in *Seymour* the House of Lords held that the appropriate direction in motor manslaughter cases was the same as had been suggested in *Lawrence* in cases where only the statutory offence had been charged. Their Lordships think it right to add that the word added at the end of the answer to the certified question regarding the very high degree of the risk of death were added not to alter the pre-existing law as to manslaughter by recklessness but only to point to those cases in which it still might be thought appropriate to charge the common law rather than the statutory offence.

It is plain that, as often happens in English criminal and civil law, the law applicable to involuntary manslaughter has developed on a case by case basis and indeed has developed rapidly in recent years since the offence of causing death by reckless driving appeared in section 50 of the Criminal Law Act 1977.

Their Lordships are of the view that the present state of the relevant law in England and Wales and thus in Hong Kong is clear. The model direction suggested in *Lawrence* and held in *Seymour* equally applicable to cases of motor manslaughter requires first, proof that the vehicle was in fact being driven in such a manner as to create an obvious and serious risk of causing physical injury to another and second, that the defendant so drove either without having given any thought to the possibility of there being such a risk or having recognised that there was such a risk nevertheless took it. Once that direction is given, it is for the jury to decide whether or not on their view of the evidence the relevant charge has been proved.

In principle their Lordships see no reason why a comparable direction should not have been given in the present case as regards that part of the case which concerned the alleged navigation of the *Flying Goldfinch* by Kong and indeed as regards the alleged navigation of the *Flying Flamingo* by the other two defendants. Did their respective acts of navigation create an obvious and serious risk of causing physical damage to some other ship and thus to other persons who might have been travelling in the area of the collision at the material time? If so did any of the defendants by their respective acts of navigation so navigate either without having given any thought to the possibility of that risk or, while recognising that the risk existed, take that risk?

Unfortunately this direction was not given. The direction given and its source in *Archbold*, 41st ed., Second Supplement, in the passage which reads "his conduct was capable of causing some injury albeit not necessarily serious to the deceased ... and that the risk was not so slight that an ordinary prudent individual would feel justified in treating it as negligible" has been taken from Lord Diplock's negative proposition. This has then been turned round and the proposition treated as an affirmative statement of the relevant risk. With all respect, that cannot be justified and in their Lordships' view vitiates the direction. The first part of the second limb purports to repeat in part the model direction in *Lawrence* (*supra*) but unhappily that direction is vitiated by the reference back to the statement of the nature of this risk to which their Lordships have already referred. The second part of the second limb appears to be a throwback to *Bateman* [1925] 19 Cr.App.R. 8. Though Lord Atkin in his speech in *Andrews* v. *D.P.P.* [1937] A.C. 576 did not disapprove of what was there said, he clearly thought, (at p. 583), that it was better to use the word "reckless" rather than to add to the word "negligence" various possible vituperative epithets. Their Lordships respectfully agree. Indeed they further respectfully agree with the comment made by Watkins L.J. in delivering the judgment of the Court of Appeal (Criminal Division) in *Seymour* (1983) 76 Cr.App.R. 211, 216:

"We have to say that the law as it stands compels us to reject Mr. Connell's persuasive submissions and to hold that the judge's directions were correct, although we are of the view that it is no longer necessary or helpful to make reference to compensation and negligence. The *Lawrence* direction on recklessness is comprehensive and of general application to all offences, including manslaughter involving the driving of motor vehicles recklessly and should be given to juries without in any way being diluted. Whether a driver at the material time was conscious of the risk he was running or gave no thought to its existence, is a matter which affects punishment for which purposes the judge will have to decide, if he can, giving the benefit of doubt to the convicted person, in which state of mind that person had driven at the material time."

Appeal allowed
Conviction quashed

Questions

1. Would a person be guilty of manslaughter where he gives thought to the possibility of death resulting from his act but wrongly and unreasonably concludes that the risk does not exist? Would such a person have been guilty under the gross negligence test? Would Lamb be guilty of manslaughter under the *Seymour* test? (See *Lamb, ante*, p. 550, where the Court of Appeal thought that, given a proper direction on gross negligence, he could have been convicted of manslaughter.)

2. In explaining *Seymour* Lord Roskill stated:

"Their Lordships think it right to add that the word[s] added at the end of the answer to the certified question regarding the very high degree of the risk of death were added not to alter the pre-existing law as to manslaughter by recklessness, but only to point to those cases in which it still might be thought appropriate to charge the common law rather than the statutory offence."

If an obvious risk of death is not an essential element of reckless manslaughter, what is the harm, the risk of which must be obvious, which is required for a verdict of manslaughter to follow?

3. In *Kong Cheuk Kwan* Lord Roskill referred to the risk of causing physical damage in his suggested direction only because such damage in the circumstances necessarily would create an obvious risk of serious injury to other persons. Would it be manslaughter where the risk of substantial damage to property was obvious but the presence of people in the vicinity was not reasonably foreseeable? Brabyn in "A Sequel to *Seymour*, Made in Hong Kong: The Privy Council decision of *Kong Cheuk Kwan* v. *R*." [1987] Crim.L.R. 84, n. 41, presents the following problem:

"Suppose D was a worker on C's farm. C was away for the day and no other people lived or worked on the farm. D drove C's tractor around the farm in a manner which created an obvious and serious risk of substantial damage to property, *i.e.* to the tractor but, since there was no reason to suppose anyone else was in the vicinity, no obvious risk of injury to another. D lost control of the tractor which ran into a large ditch, unhappily crushing and killing a tramp who happened to be sleeping there. Tramps were not a common feature of the neighbourhood."

5. OTHER UNLAWFUL HOMICIDES

i. Infanticide

Infanticide Act 1938, section 1

"(1) Where a woman by any wilful act or omission causes the death of her child being a child under the age of twelve months, but at the time of the act or omission the balance of her mind was disturbed by reason of her not having fully recovered from the effect of giving birth to the child or by reason of the effect of lactation consequent upon the birth of the child, then, notwithstanding that the circumstances were such that but for this Act the offence would have amounted to murder, she shall be guilty of felony, to wit of infanticide, and may for such offence be dealt with and punished as if she had been guilty of the offence of manslaughter of the child."

Note

Less than half-a-dozen women are convicted of this offence per year and a custodial sentence is rare.

ii. Child Destruction

Infant Life (Preservation) Act 1929, section 1

"(1) Subject as hereinafter in this subsection provided, any person who, with intent to destroy the life of a child capable of being born alive, by any wilful act causes a child to die before it has an existence independent of its mother, shall be guilty of felony, to wit, of child destruction, and shall be liable on conviction thereon to imprisonment for life: Provided that no person shall be found guilty of an offence under this section unless it is proved that the act which caused the death of the child was not done in good faith for the purpose only of preserving the life of the mother.

"(2) For the purposes of this Act, evidence that a woman had at any material time been pregnant for a period of twenty-eight weeks or more shall be prima facie proof that she was at that time pregnant of a child capable of being born alive."

Note

Neither this offence nor abortion below, are true homicides, see *ante*, p. 495. For a discussion of the proviso to subsection (1), see Abortion, particularly the case of *R. v. Bourne*, below.

iii. Abortion

Offences Against the Person Act 1861, section 58

"Every woman being with child, who, with intent to procure her own miscarriage, shall unlawfully administer to herself any poison or other noxious thing, or shall unlawfully use any instrument or other means whatsoever with the like intent, and whosoever, with intent to procure the miscarriage of any woman, whether she be or be not with child, shall unlawfully administer to her or cause to be taken by her any poison or other noxious thing, or shall unlawfully use any instrument or other means whatsoever with the like intent, shall be guilty of felony, and being convicted thereof shall be liable to [imprisonment] for life."

Notes

Complications follow when the woman is not pregnant but does what would otherwise fall within the section. Note the cases of *Whitchurch* (1890) 24 Q.B.D. 42 and *Sockett* (1908) 24 T.L.R. 893 on conspiracy and aiding and abetting respectively, the combined effect of which is to destroy the duality of the offences in section 58. The woman who is not pregnant commits no wrong if she attempts to procure her own miscarriage unaided. If she has help, the helper is guilty under the second part of the section, they are both guilty of conspiracy and the woman herself is guilty of aiding and abetting the helper.

Various acts of preparation are made specifically criminal under the following section:

Offences Against the Person Act 1861, section 59

"Whosoever shall unlawfully supply or procure any poison or other noxious thing, or any instrument or thing whatsoever, knowing that the same is intended to be unlawfully used or employed with intent to procure the miscarriage of any woman, whether she be or not be with child, shall be guilty of a misdemeanour, and being convicted thereof shall be liable to [imprisonment] not exceeding five years."

The number of convictions for illegally procuring an abortion has greatly diminished since the Abortion Act 1967 which allows for lawful medical termination.

Abortion Act 1967, as amended by section 37 of the Human Fertilisation and Embryology Act 1990

1. *Medical termination of pregnancy*
"(1) Subject to the provisions of this section, a person shall not be guilty of an offence under the law relating to abortion when a pregnancy is terminated by a registered medical practitioner if two registered medical practitioners are of the opinion, formed in good faith—

 (a) that the pregnancy has not exceeded its twenty-fourth week and that the continuance of the pregnancy would involve risk, greater than if the pregnancy were terminated, or injury to the physical or mental health of the pregnant woman or any existing children of her family; or
 (b) that the termination is necessary to prevent grave permanent injury to the physical or mental health of the pregnant woman; or
 (c) that the continuance of the pregnancy would involve risk to the life of the pregnant woman, greater than if the pregnancy were terminated; or
 (d) that there is a substantial risk that if the child were born it would suffer from such physical or mental abnormalities as to be seriously handicapped. . . .

(3) Except as provided by subsection (4) of this section, any treatment for the termination of pregnancy must be carried out in a hospital vested in the Secretary of State for the purpose of his functions under the National Health Service Act 1977 or the National Health Service (Scotland) Act 1978, or in a place for the time being approved for the purposes of this section by the Secretary of State.

(4) Subsection (3) of this section, and so much of subsection (1) as relates to the opinion of two registered medical practitioners, shall not apply to the termination of a pregnancy by a registered practitioner in a case where he is of the opinion, formed in good faith, that the termination is immediately necessary to save the life or to prevent grave permanent injury to the physical or mental health of the pregnant woman."

The 1967 Act was in some senses merely a declaration and clarification of the interpretation given by at least one Old Bailey judge to section 58: see the case below.

R. v. Bourne
[1939] 1 K.B. 687
Central Criminal Court

The accused performed an operation on a girl of 14 who was pregnant as a result of a rape. The pregnancy was terminated with the consent of the girl's parents. The accused claimed that to continue the pregnancy would have caused serious injury to the girl.

MACNAGHTEN J. in summing up the case to the jury said: . . . A man of the highest skill, openly, in one of our great hospitals, performs the operation. Whether it was legal or illegal you will have to determine, but he performs the operation as an act of charity, without fee or reward, and unquestionably believing that he was doing the right thing, and that he ought, in the performance of his duty as a member of a profession devoted to the alleviation of human suffering, to do it. That is the case that you have to try today. . . .

The defendant is charged with an offence against section 58 of the Offences Against the Person Act, 1861. . . . But, as in the case of homicide, so also in the case where an unborn child is killed, there may be justification for the act.

Nine years ago Parliament passed an Act called the Infant Life (Preservation) Act, 1929. Section 1, subsection 1 . . . provides for the case where a child is killed by a wilful act at the time when it is being delivered in the ordinary course of nature; but in my view the proviso that it is necessary for the Crown to prove that the act was not done in good faith for the purpose only of preserving the life of the mother is in accordance with what has always been the common law of England with regard to the killing of an unborn child. No such proviso is in fact set out in section 58 of the Offences Against the Person Act, 1861; but the words of that section are that any person who "unlawfully" uses an instrument with intent to procure miscarriage shall be guilty of felony. In my opinion the word "unlawfully" is not, in that section, a meaningless word. I think it imports the meaning expressed by the proviso in section 1, subsection 1, of the Infant Life (Preservation) Act 1929, and that section 58 of the Offences Against the Person Act, 1861, must be read as if the words making it an offence to use an instrument with intent to procure a miscarriage were qualified by a similar proviso.

In this case, therefore, my direction to you in law is this—that the burden rests on the Crown to satisfy you beyond reasonable doubt that the defendant did not procure the miscarriage of the girl in good faith for the purpose only of preserving her life. If the Crown fails to satisfy you of that, the defendant is entitled by the law of this land to a verdict of acquittal. If, on the other hand, you are satisfied that what the defendant did was not done by him in good faith for the purpose only of preserving the life of the girl, it is your duty to find him guilty. It is said, and I think said rightly, that this is a case of great importance to the public and, more especially, to the medical profession; but you will observe that it has nothing to do with the ordinary case of procuring abortion. ... In those cases the operation is performed by a person of no skill, with no medical qualifications, and there is no pretence that it is done for the preservation of the mother's life. Cases of that sort are in no way affected by the consideration of the question which is put before you today.

What then is the meaning to be given to the words "for the purpose of preserving the life of the mother." There has been much discussion in this case as to the difference between danger to life and danger to health. It may be that you are more fortunate than I am, but I confess that I have found it difficult to understand what the discussion really meant, since life depends upon health, and it may be that health is so gravely impaired that death results. ... Mr. Oliver [for the accused] wanted you to give what he called a wide and liberal meaning to the words "for the purpose of preserving the life of the mother." I should prefer the word "reasonable" to the words "wide and liberal." I think you should take a reasonable view of those words.

It is not contended that those words mean merely for the purposes of saving the mother from instant death. There are cases, we are told, where it is reasonably certain that a pregnant woman will not be able to deliver the child which is in her womb and survive. In such a case where the doctor anticipates, basing his opinion upon the experience of the profession, that the child cannot be delivered without the death of the mother, it is obvious that the sooner the operation is performed the better. The law does not require the doctor to wait until the unfortunate woman is in peril of immediate death. In such a case he is not only entitled, but it is his duty to perform the operation with a view to saving her life.

Here let me diverge for one moment to touch upon a matter that has been mentioned to you, the various views which are held with regard to this operation. Apparently there is a great difference of opinion even in the medical profession itself. Some there may be, for all I know, who hold the view that the fact that a woman desires the operation performed is a sufficient justification for it. Well, that is not the law: the desire of a woman to be relieved of her pregnancy is no justification at all for performing the operation. On the other hand there are people who, from what are said to be religious reasons, object to the operation being performed under any circumstances. That is not the law either. On the contrary, a person who holds such an opinion ought not to be an obstetrical surgeon, for if a case arose where the life of the woman could be saved by performing the operation and the doctor refused to perform it because of his religious opinions and the woman died, he would be in grave peril of being brought before this court on a charge of manslaughter by negligence. He would have no better defence than a person who, again for some religious reason, refused to call in a doctor to attend his sick child, where a doctor could have been called in and the life of the child could have been saved. If the father, for a so-called religious reason, refused to call in a doctor, he is also answerable to the criminal law for the death of his child. I mention these two extreme views merely to show that the law lies between them. It permits the termination of pregnancy for the purpose of preserving the life of the mother.

As I have said, I think those words ought to be construed in a reasonable sense, and, if the doctor is of opinion, on reasonable grounds and with adequate knowledge, that the probable consequences of the continuance of the pregnancy will be to make the woman a physical or mental wreck, the jury are quite entitled to take the view that the doctor who, under those circumstances and in that honest belief, operates, is operating for the purpose of preserving the life of the mother. ...

Verdict: Not guilty

Note

The lawfulness of the role of nurses in the conduct of abortions was considered by the House of Lords.

Royal College of Nursing of the United Kingdom v. Department of Health and Social Security
[1981] 1 All E.R. 545
House of Lords

Medical induction has largely replaced the surgical method of terminating pregnancies of over three months. The procedure is in two stages, the second of which is carried out by nurses. The Department issued a circular to the nursing profession stating that no offence was committed by nurses who participated in this stage provided that the person who decided on the termination, initiated it and remained responsible for its overall conduct and control, was a doctor. The Royal College sought a declaration that the advice on the circular was wrong and that nurses would be contravening section 58 of the 1861 Act.

LORD DIPLOCK: The Abortion Act 1967 which it falls to this House to construe is described in its long title as "An Act to amend and clarify the law relating to termination of pregnancy by registered medical practitioners." The legalisation of abortion, at any rate in circumstances in which the termination of the pregnancy is not essential in order to save the mother's life, is a subject on which strong moral and religious convictions are held; and these convictions straddle the normal party political lines. That, no doubt, is why the Act, which incorporates a "conscience clause" that I shall be quoting later, started its Parliamentary life as a private member's Bill and, maybe for that reason, it lacks that style and consistency of draftsmanship both internal to the Act itself and in relation to other statutes which one would expect to find in legislation that had its origin in the office of Parliamentary counsel.

Whatever may be the technical imperfections of its draftsmanship, however, its purpose in my view becomes clear if one starts by considering what was the state of the law relating to abortion before the passing of the Act, what was the mischief that required amendment, and in what respects was the existing law unclear.

In England the law "relating to abortion" which it was the purpose of the Act to amend and clarify, is defined in s 6 of the Act itself as meaning "sections 58 and 59 of the Offences Against the Person Act 1861." [*ante*, pp. 568–569].

... It had long been generally accepted that abortion was lawful where it was necessary to save the pregnant woman's life; but what circumstances, if any, short of this, legitimised termination of a pregnancy does not appear to have attracted judicial notice until, in 1938, the matter was put to a sagaciously selected test by Mr Aleck Bourne, a well-known obstetrical surgeon at St Mary's Hospital, London. ...

The summing-up by Macnaghten J. in *R. v. Bourne* resulted in an acquittal. So the correctness of his statement of the law did not undergo examination by any higher authority. It still remained in 1967 the only judicial pronouncement on the subject.

... Such then was the unsatisfactory and uncertain state of the law that the Abortion Act 1967 was intended to amend and clarify. What the Act sets out to do is to provide an exhaustive statement of the circumstances in which treatment for the termination of a pregnancy may be carried out lawfully. That the statement, which is contained in s.1, is intended to be exhaustive appears from s.5(2):

> "For the purposes of the law relating to abortion, anything done with intent to procure the miscarriage of a woman is unlawfully done unless authorised by section 1 of this Act."

This sets aside the interpretation placed by Macnaghten J. in *R. v. Bourne* on the word 'unlawfully" in ss.58 and 59 of the Offences Against the Person Act 1861.

The "conscience clause" which I have already mentioned is also worth citing before coming to the crucial provisons of s.1. It is s.4(1) and so far as is relevant for the present purposes it reads:

> " ... no person shall be under any duty, whether by contract or by any statutory or other legal requirement, to participate in any treatment authorised by this Act to which he has a conscientious objection ... "

... I have spoken of the requirements of the Act as to the way in which "treatment for the termination of the pregnancy" is to be carried out rather than using the word "termination" or "terminated" by itself, for the draftsman appears to use the longer and the shorter expressions indiscriminately, as is shown by a comparison between subsections (1) and (3) of section 1, and by the reference in the conscience clause to "treatment authorised by this Act." Furthermore, if "termination" or "terminated" meant only the event of miscarriage and not the whole treatment undertaken with that object in mind, lack of success, which apparently occurs in 1 per cent. to 2 per cent. of cases, would make all who had taken part in the unsuccessful treatment guilty of an offence under section 58 or section 59 of the Offences Against the Person Act 1861. This cannot have been the intention of Parliament.

The requirement of the Act as to the way in which the treatment is to be carried out, which in my view throws most light on the second aspect of its policy and the true construction of the phrase in sub-section (1) of section 1 which lies at the root of the dispute between the parties to this appeal, is the requirement in subsection (3) that, except in cases of dire emergency, the treatment must be carried out in a national health service hospital (or private clinic specifically approved for that purpose by the minister). It is in my view evident that, in providing that treatment for termination of pregnancies should take place in ordinary hospitals Parliament contemplated that (conscientious objections apart) like other hospital treatment, it would be undertaken as a team effort in which, acting on the instructions of the doctor in charge of the treatment, junior doctors, nurses, paramedical and other members of the hospital staff would each do things forming part of the whole treatment which it would be in accordance with accepted medical practice to entrust to a member of the staff possessed of their respective qualifications and experience.

Subsection (1) although it is expressed to apply only "when a pregnancy is terminated by a registered medical practitioner" ... also appears to contemplate treatment that is in the nature of a team effort and to extend its protection to all those who play a part in it. The exoneration from guilt is not confined to the registered medical practitioner by whom a pregnancy is terminated, it extends to any person who takes part in the treatment for its termination.

What limitation on this exoneration is imposed by the qualifying phrase, "when a pregnancy is terminated by a registered medical practitioner"? In my opinion, in the context of the Act, what it requires is that a registered medical practitioner, whom I will refer to as a doctor, should accept responsibility for all stages of the treatment for the termination of the pregnancy. The particular method to be used should be decided by the doctor in charge of the treatment for termination of the pregnancy; he should carry out any physical acts, forming part of the treatment, that in accordance with accepted medical practice are done only by qualified medical practitioners, and should give specific instructions as to the carrying out of such parts of the treatment as in accordance with accepted medical practice are carried out by nurses or other members of the hospital staff without medical qualifications. To each of them, the doctor, or his substitute, should be available to be consulted or called on for assistance from beginning to end of the treatment. In other words, the doctor need not do everything with his own hands; the requirements of the subsection are satisfied when the treatment for termination of a pregnancy is one prescribed by a registered medical practitioner carried out in accordance with his directions and of which a registered medical practitioner remains in charge throughout.

My noble and learned friend Lord Wilberforce has described the successive steps taken in the treatment for termination of pregnancies in the third trimester by medical induction; and the parts played by registered medical practitioners and nurses respectively in the carrying out of the treatment. This treatment satisfies the interpretation that I have placed on the requirements of section 1 of the Act. I would accordingly allow the appeal and restore the declaration made by Woolf J.

LORDS KEITH OF KINKEL and ROSKILL delivered concurring speeches, LORDS WILBERFORCE and EDMUND-DAVIES dissented.

Appeal allowed

Question

Lord Diplock states in *Royal College of Nursing of the United Kingdom* v. *Department of Health and Social Security* that section 5(2) of the Abortion Act 1967 makes it clear that section 1 provides an "exhaustive statement of the circumstances in which the treatment for the termination of a pregnancy may be carried out lawfully." Does this mean that the operation of common law defences is excluded? Consider the following situation: D is a final year medical student. He and his wife, V, are trapped in an isolated cottage by a blizzard and are unable to make contact with the outside world. V is pregnant and develops complications. D honestly believes (and subsequent examination by registered medical practitioners confirms his belief to have been correct) that it is immediately necessary to terminate the pregnancy to save V's life. He is charged with an offence under section 58 of the Offences Against the Person Act 1861 and seeks to plead duress of circumstances. Would D succeed?

iv. Suicide

Suicide Act 1961

Section 1: "The rule of law whereby it is a crime for a person to commit suicide is hereby abrogated."

Section 2: "(1) A person who aids, abets, counsels or procures the suicide of another, or an attempt by another to commit suicide, shall be liable on conviction on indictment to imprisonment for a term not exceeding fourteen years.

(2) If on the trial of an indictment for murder or manslaughter it is proved that the accused aided, abetted, counselled or procured the suicide of the person in question, the jury may find him guilty of that offence."

Homicide Act 1957, section 4

"(1) It shall be manslaughter, and shall not be murder, for a person acting in pursuance of a suicide pact between him and another to kill the other or be a party to the other killing himself or being killed by a third person. ...

(3) For the purposes of this section 'suicide pact' means a common agreement between two or more persons having for its object the death of all of them, whether or not each is to take his own life, but nothing done by a person who enters into a suicide pact shall be treated as done by him in pursuance of the pact unless it is done while he has the settled intention of dying in pursuance of the pact."

Notes

Any doubt as to whether it is an offence to *attempt* to aid, or abet suicide was settled in *R. v. McShane* (1977) 66 Cr.App.R. 97 in which Orr L.J. said, at p. 102:

> "[E]very attempt to commit an offence is an offence at common law whether the crime attempted is one by statute or at common law. ... It follows in our judgment that the appellant was properly charged under count 1 with an offence of attempting to aid or abet, counsel or procure the suicide of Mrs. Mott and none the less so because the crime defined in section 2(1) of the Suicide Act 1961 is itself of the nature of an attempt."

An area surrounded not only by legal doubt but also by difficult, and ultimately insoluble, questions of moral philosophy is that of euthanasia. A person who kills another at the other's request will be liable for murder since consent is no defence. This is mitigated where the killing is in pursuance of a suicide pact (section 4 of the Homicide Act 1957, above), and, possibly, where a doctor administers drugs, which alleviate pain but shorten life. At the trial of Dr. Adams in 1957 Devlin J. (as he then was) said that the administration of drugs to relieve pain would not amount to legal causation. This is a grey, untested, area maintained by the turning of a blind eye by prosecuting authorities. See D. Brahams "A Visit to the USA" (1988) 38 N.L.J. 383.

As far as aiding and abetting suicide is concerned the decision to prosecute rests solely with the Director of Public Prosecutions whose consent is required for any proceedings (section 2(4) of the Suicide Act 1961). "Exit," a society campaigning for voluntary euthanasia, published a booklet giving details of methods of committing suicide.

In *Attorney-General* v. *Able and Others* [1984] 1 Q.B. 795, the Attorney-General sought a declaration that "in specified cir- cumstance" distribution of the guide was an offence under section 2(1) of the Suicide Act 1961. In response the Society sought a declaration that supply of the booklet was lawful. Wolf J. refused to grant either declaration. He held that supply could be an offence where done with the necessary intent but without proof of the necessary intent it could not be said in advance that any particular supply would be an offence. See Smith "Assisting in Suicide—The Attorney-General and the Voluntary Euthanasia Society" [1983] Crim.L.R. 579.

See generally Williams, *The Sanctity of Life and the Criminal Law*, Chap. 8; Williams, "Euthanasia" 41 *Medico Legal Journal* 14; Kennedy, "The Legal Effect of Requests by the Terminally Ill and Aged not to receive further Treatment from Doctors" [1976] Crim.L.R. 21; C.L.R.C. 14th Report, sections 126–129.

v. Causing death by driving

Road Traffic Act 1991, sections 1 and 3

"1. Offences of dangerous driving

For sections 1 and 2 of the Road Traffic Act 1988 there shall be substituted—
1. 'Causing death by dangerous driving.
A person who causes death of another person by driving a mechanically propelled vehicle dangerously on a road or other public place is guilty of an offence.
2. Dangerous driving.
A person who drives a mechanically propelled vehicle dangerously on a road or other public place is guilty of an offence.
2A. Meaning of dangerous driving.
(1) For the purposes of sections 1 and 2 above a person is to be regarded as driving dangerously if (and, subject to subsection (2) below, only if)—
(a) the way he drives falls far below what would be expected of a competent and careful driver, and
(b) it would be obvious to a competent and careful driver that driving in that way would be dangerous.
(2) A person is also to be regarded as driving dangerously for the purposes of sections 1 and 2 above if it would be obvious to a competent

and careful driver that driving the vehicle in its current state would be dangerous.

(3) In subsections (1) and (2) above 'dangerous' refers to danger either of injury to any person or of serious damage to property; and in determining for the purposes of those subsections what would be expected of, or obvious to, a competent and careful driver in a particular case, regard shall be had not only to the circumstances of which he could be expected to be aware but also to any circumstances shown to have been within the knowledge of the accused.

(4) In determining for the purposes of subsection (2) above the state of a vehicle, regard may be had to anything attached to or carried on or in it and to the manner in which it is attached or carried.'

3. Causing death by careless driving when under influence of drink or drugs.

Before section 4 of the Road Traffic Act 1988 there shall be inserted—

3A. 'Causing death by careless driving when under influence of drink or drugs.

(1) If a person causes the death of another person by driving a mechanically propelled vehicle on a road or other public place without due care and attention, or without reasonable consideration for other persons using the road or place, and—

(a) he is, at the time when he is driving, unfit to drive through drink or drugs, or
(b) he has consumed so much alcohol that the proportion of it in his breath, blood or urine at that time exceeds the prescribed limit, or
(c) he is, within 18 hours after that time, required to provide a specimen in pursuance of section 7 of this Act, but without reasonable excuse fails to provide it.

he is guilty of an offence.

(2) For the purposes of this section a person shall be taken to be unfit to drive at any time when his ability to drive properly is impaired.

(3) Subsection (1)(b) and (c) above shall not apply in relation to a person driving a mechanically propelled vehicle other than a motor vehicle.' "

6. REFORM OF THE LAW OF HOMICIDE

The Draft Criminal Code Bill adopts, with a few modifications, the reforms proposed by the C.L.R.C. in their 14th Report (Cmnd. 7844).

Draft Criminal Code Bill

Murder

For clause 54 see *ante*, p. 511.

"Manslaughter

55. A person is guilty of manslaughter if—

(a) he is not guilty of murder by reason only of the fact that a defence provided by section 56 (diminished responsibility), 58 (provocation) or 59 (use of excessive force) applies; or

(b)   he is not guilty of murder by reason only of the fact that, because of voluntary intoxication, he is not aware that death may be caused or believes that an exempting circumstance exists; or

(c)   he causes the death of another—

(i)   intending to cause serious personal harm; or

(ii)   being reckless whether death or serious personal harm will be caused.

Diminished responsibility

56.—(1) A person who, but for this section, would be guilty of murder is not guilty of murder if, at the time of his act, he is suffering from such mental abnormality as is a substantial enough reason to reduce his offence to manslaughter.

(2) In this section 'mental abnormality' means mental illness, arrested or incomplete development of mind, psychopathic disorder, and any other disorder or disability of mind, except intoxication.

(3) Where a person suffering from mental abnormality is also intoxicated, this section applies only where it would apply if he were not intoxicated.

Evidence of mental abnormality

57.—(1) Whether evidence is evidence of mental abnormality is a question of law.

(2) Where on a charge of murder or attempted murder the defendant has given or adduced evidence of mental disorder, severe mental handicap or automatism, the prosecution may adduce evidence of mental abnormality; but the court may give directions as to the stage of the proceedings at which it may do so.

(3) Where a person is charged with murder (or attempted murder) the prosecution may, with his consent, adduce evidence of mental abnormality at the committal proceedings, whereupon the magistrates' court may commit him for trial for manslaughter (or attempted manslaughter).

(4) Where the defendant has been committed for trial for murder (or attempted murder) the prosecution may, with the consent of the defendant, serve notice in accordance with Rules of Court of evidence of mental abnormality and indict him for manslaughter (or attempted manslaughter).

Provocation

58. A person who, but for this section, would be guilty of murder is not guilty of murder if—

(a)   he acts when provoked (whether by things done or by things said or by both and whether by the deceased person or by another) to lose his self-control; and

(b)   the provocation is, in all the circumstances (including any of his personal characteristics that affect its gravity), sufficient ground for the loss of self-control.

Use of excessive force

59. A person who, but for this section, would be guilty of murder is not guilty of murder if, at the time of his act, he believes the use of the force which causes death to be necessary and reasonable to effect a purpose referred to in section 44 (use of force in public or private defence), but the force exceeds that which is necessary and reasonable in the circumstances which exist or (where there is a difference) in those which he believes to exist.

Jurisdiction over murder and manslaughter

60. A person is guilty of murder or manslaughter (where section 54 or 55 applies) if—

(a) he causes a fatal injury to another to occur within the ordinary limits of criminal jurisdiction, whether his act is done within or outside and whether the death occurs within or outside those limits;

(b) he causes the death of another anywhere in the world by an act done within the ordinary limits of criminal jurisdiction; or

(c) being a British citizen, he causes the death of another anywhere in the world by an act done anywhere in the world.

Attempted manslaughter

61. A person who attempts to cause the death of another, where section 56, 58 or 59 would apply if death were caused, is not guilty of attempted murder but is guilty of attempted manslaughter.

Suicide pack killing

62.—(1) A person who, but for this section, would be guilty of murder is not guilty of murder but is guilty of suicide pact killing if his act is done in pursuance of a suicide pact between himself and the person killed.

(2) 'Suicide pact' means an agreement between two or more persons having for its object the death of all of them, whether or not each is to take his own life, but nothing done by a person who enters into a suicide pact shall be treated as done by him in pursuance of the pact unless it is done while he has the settled intention of dying in pursuance of the pact.

(3) A person acting in pursuance of a suicide pact between himself and another is not guilty of attempted murder but is guilty of attempted suicide pact killing if he attempts to cause the death of the other.

Complicity in suicide

63. A person is guilty of an offence if he procures, assists or encourages suicide or attempted suicide committed by another.

Infanticide

64.—(1) A woman who, but for this section, would be guilty of murder or manslaughter of her child is not guilty of murder or manslaughter, but is guilty of infanticide, if her act is done when the child is under the age of twelve months and when the balance of her mind is disturbed by reason of the effect of giving birth or of circumstances consequent upon the birth.

(2) A woman who in the circumstances specified in subsection (1) attempts to cause the death of her child is not guilty of attempted murder but is guilty of attempted infanticide.

(3) A woman may be convicted of infanticide (or attempted infanticide) although the jury is uncertain whether the child had been born or whether it had an existence independent of her when its death occurred (or, in the case of an attempt, when the act was done).

Threats to kill or cause serious personal harm

65. A person is guilty of an offence if he makes to another a threat to cause the death of, or serious personal harm to, that other or a third person, intending that other to believe that it will be carried out.

Abortion

66. A person is guilty of an offence if he intentionally causes the miscarriage of a woman otherwise than in accordance with the provisions of the Abortion Act 1967.

Self-abortion

67.—(1) A pregnant woman is guilty of an offence if she intentionally causes her own miscarriage otherwise than in accordance with the provisions of the Abortion Act 1967.

(2) Notwithstanding section 50 (impossibility) a woman who is not pregnant cannot be guilty of an attempt to commit an offence under this Act.

Supplying article for abortion

68. A person is guilty of an offence if he supplies or procures any article or substance knowing that it is to be used with the intention of causing the miscarriage of a woman otherwise than in accordance with the provisions of the Abortion Act 1967, whether the woman is pregnant or not.

Child destruction

69.—(1) A person is guilty of child destruction if he intentionally causes the death of a child capable of being born alive before the child has an existence independent of his mother, unless the act which causes death is done in good faith for the purpose only of preserving the life of the mother.

(2) The fact that a woman had at any material time been pregnant for twenty-eight weeks or more is *prima facie* proof that she was at that time pregnant of a child capable of being born alive.

(3) A person who is found not guilty of murder or manslaughter (or attempted murder or manslaughter) of a child by reason only of the fact that the jury is uncertain whether the child had been born or whether he had an existence independent of his mother when his death occurred (or, in the case of an attempt, when the act was done) shall be convicted of child destruction (or attempted child destruction)."

CHAPTER 9

NON-FATAL OFFENCES AGAINST THE PERSON

	PAGE		PAGE
1. Assault and Battery	581	i. Malicious Wounding	622
i. *Actus Reus*	582	ii. Wounding with Intent	629
ii. *Mens Rea*	586	4. Sexual Offences	632
iii. Justifications	587	i. Rape	632
2. Assault Occasioning Actual Bodily Harm	622	ii. Other Offences Involving Sexual Intercourse	644
3. Malicious Wounding and Wounding with Intent	622	iii. Indecent Assault	647

1. ASSAULT AND BATTERY

Criminal Justice Act 1988, section 39

"Common assault and battery shall be summary offences and a person guilty of either of them shall be liable to a fine not exceeding level 5 on the standard scale,[1] to imprisonment for a term not exceeding six months, or to both."

Notes

1. Section 40 of the same Act nevertheless provides that an indictment may include a count for common assault or battery if it is founded on the same facts or evidence as a count charging an indictable offence or is part of a series of offences of the same or similar character as an indictable offence which is also charged.

If such a count is not included, there can be no conviction of common assault or battery: *R.* v. *Mearns* [1991] 1 Q.B. 82 (C.A.).

2. Assault and battery are separate statutory crimes: *R.* v. *Taylor*, *R.* v. *Little* [1992] 1 All E.R. 708 (C.A.). An indictment charging assault and battery is bad for duplicity, *i.e.* as charging more than one crime.

3. Although there are many statutory crimes, in the Offences Against the Person Act 1861 and elsewhere, which are based on the concepts of assault and battery, there is no statutory definition of those concepts, the meaning of which must be sought in case

---

[1] Section 37 of the Criminal Justice Act 1982 established a standard scale of fines for summary offences. The amounts in the scale are revised from time to time to take account of the decline in the value of money. They are currently as follows:

Level 1	£200
2	£500
3	£1000
4	£2500
5	£5000

law, including civil cases, since both assault and battery are also torts. In the past there has been a practice, in statutes and in judgments, to use the term "assault" as comprehending also a battery (see *Fagan* v. *M.P.C.*, below). The Draft Criminal Law Act (*post*, p. 632) continues the practice. Now that it is clear that they are two separate crimes which must not be rolled up in one charge, the need for a new terminology is urgent.

i. Actus Reus

Fagan v. Metropolitan Police Commissioner
[1969] 1 Q.B. 439
Divisional Court

Fagan was told by a police officer to park his car at a particular spot. He drove his car on to the policeman's foot. He refused for some time to reverse off. Fagan was convicted by the magistrates of assaulting a police officer in the execution of his duty. On appeal he maintained that the initial driving on the foot was not an assault, because unintentional; nor was the refusal to drive off because this was not an act.

JAMES J. (with whom Lord Parker C.J. agreed): In our judgment the question arising, which has been argued on general principles, falls to be decided on the facts of the particular case. An assault is any act which intentionally—or possibly recklessly—causes another person to apprehend immediate and unlawful personal violence. Although "assault" is an independent crime and is to be treated as such, for practical purposes today "assault" is generally synonymous with the term "battery" and is a term used to mean the actual intended use of unlawful force to another person without his consent. On the facts of the present case the "assault" alleged involved a "battery." Where an assault involves a battery, it matters not, in our judgment, whether the battery is inflicted directly by the body of the offender or through the medium of some weapon or instrument controlled by the action of the offender. An assault may be committed by the laying of a hand upon another, and the action does not cease to be an assault if it is a stick held in the hand and not the hand itself which is laid on the person of the victim. So for our part we see no difference in principle between the action of stepping on to a person's toe and maintaining that position and the action of driving a car on to a person's foot and sitting in the car whilst its position on the foot is maintained.

To constitute the offence of assault some intentional act must have been performed: a mere omission to act cannot amount to an assault. Without going into the question whether words alone can constitute an assault, it is clear that the words spoken by the appellant could not alone amount to an assault: they can only shed a light on the appellant's action. For our part we think the crucial question is whether in this case the act of the appellant can be said to be complete and spent at the moment of time when the car wheel came to rest on the foot or whether his act is to be regarded as a continuing act operating until the wheel was removed. In our judgment a distinction is to be drawn between acts which are complete—though results may continue to flow—and those acts which are continuing. Once the act is complete it cannot thereafter be said to be a threat to inflict unlawful force upon the victim. If the act, as distinct from the results thereof, is a continuing act there is a continuing threat to inflict unlawful force. If the assault involves a battery and that battery continues there is a continuing act of assault.

For an assault to be committed both the elements of *actus reus* and *mens rea* must be present at the same time. The *"actus reus"* is the action causing the effect on the victim's mind (see the observations of Parke B. in *R.* v. *St. George post*, p. 585). The *"mens rea"* is the intention to cause that effect. It is not necessary that *mens rea* should be present at the inception of the *actus reus*; it can be superimposed upon an existing act. On the other hand the subsequent inception of *mens rea* cannot convert an act which has been completed without *mens rea* into an assault.

In our judgment the Willesden magistrates and quarter sessions were right in law. On the facts found the action of the appellant may have been initially unintentional, but the time came when knowing that the wheel was on the officer's foot the appellant (1) remained seated in the car so that his body through the medium of the car was in contact with the officer, (2) switched off the ignition of the car, (3) maintained the wheel of the car on the foot and (4) used words indicating the intention of keeping the wheel in that position. For our part we cannot regard such conduct as mere omission or inactivity.

There was a act constituting battery which at its inception was not criminal because there was no element of intention but which became criminal from the moment the intention was formed to produce the apprehension which was flowing from the continuing act. The fallacy of the appellant's argument is that it seeks to equate the facts of this case with such a case as where a motorist has accidentally run over a person and, that action having been completed, fails to assist the victim with the intent that the victim should suffer.

We would dismiss this appeal.

BRIDGE J.: I fully agree with my Lords as to the relevant principles to be applied. No mere omission to act can amount to an assault. Both the elements of *actus reus* and *mens rea* must be present at the same time, but the one may be superimposed on the other. It is in the application of these principles to the highly unusual facts of this case that I have, with regret, reached a different conclusion from the majority of the court. I have no sympathy at all for the appellant, who behaved disgracefully. But I have been unable to find any way of regarding the facts which satisfies me that they amounted to the crime of assault. This has not been for the want of trying. But at every attempt I have encountered the inescapable question: after the wheel of the appellant's car had accidentally come to rest on the constable's foot, what was it that the appellant did which constituted the act of assault? However the question is approached, the answer I feel obliged to give is: precisely nothing. The car rested on the foot by its own weight and remained stationary by its own inertia. The appellant's fault was that he omitted to manipulate the controls to set it in motion again.

Neither the fact that the appellant remained in the driver's seat nor that he switched off the ignition seem to me to be of any relevance. The constable's plight would have been no better, but might well have been worse, if the appellant had alighted from the car leaving the ignition switched on. Similarly I can get no help from the suggested analogies. If one man accidentally treads on another's toe or touches him with a stick, but deliberately maintains pressure with foot or stick after the victim protests, there is clearly an assault. But there is no true parallel between such cases and the present case. It is not, to my mind, a legitimate use of language to speak of the appellant "holding" or "maintaining" the car wheel on the constable's foot. The expression which corresponds to the reality is that used by the justices in the case stated. They say quite rightly, that he "allowed" the wheel to remain.

With a reluctantly dissenting voice I would allow this appeal and quash the appellant's conviction.

Appeal dismissed

Question

Would the reasoning in *R. v. Miller, ante,* p. 26, provide a more satisfactory way of upholding Fagan's conviction? And see Draft Criminal Code, Clause 23, *ante,* p. 32.

Fairclough v. Whipp
(1951) 35 Cr.App.R. 138
Divisional Court

The respondent invited a girl of nine to touch his exposed person. She did so and the respondent was charged with indecent assault on the girl. The justices dismissed the case and the prosecutor appealed.

LORD GODDARD C.J.: An assault can be committed without there being battery, for instance, by a threatening gesture or a threat to use violence made against a person, but I do not know of any authority that says that, where one person invites another person to touch him, that can amount to an assault. The question of consent or non-consent arises only if this is something which, without consent, would be an assault on the latter. If that which was done to the child would have been an assault if done against her will, it would also be an assault if it was done with her consent and is of an indecent nature, because she cannot consent to an indecent assault. But before we come to the question of whether there was an indecent assault we must consider whether there was an assault, and I cannot hold that an invitation to somebody to touch the invitor can amount to an assault on the invitee.

Appeal dismissed

Note

By the Indecency with Children Act 1960, the facts of this case would now disclose a crime under that Act, but that does not affect the general point about assaults.

Tuberville v. Savage
(1669) 1 Mod.Rep. 3
Court of King's Bench

Action of assault, battery and wounding. The evidence to prove a provocation was, that the plaintiff put his hand upon his sword and said, "If it were not assize-time, I would not take such language from you."—The question was, if that were an assault?—The court agreed that it was not; for the declaration of the plaintiff was, that he would not assault him, the judges being in town; and the intention as well as the act makes an assault. Therefore if one strike another upon the hand, or arm, or breast in discourse, it is no assault; but if one, intending to assault, strike at another and miss him, this is an assault; so if he hold up his hand against another in a threatening manner and say nothing, it is an assault.

Judgment for the plaintiff

Glanville Williams: "Assault and Words" [1957] Crim.L.R. 219, 220

"The rule in *Tuberville* v. *Savage*, that words may negative or end an assault, was misapplied in *Blake* v. *Barnard* (1840) 9 C. & P. 626, where the facts given in evidence were that D presented a pistol at P and said: 'If you are not quiet I will blow your brains out.' According to the report (which may not be accurate), Lord Abinger, in summing up, directed the jury that 'if the defendant, at the time he presented [the pistol] added words showing that it was not his intention to shoot the plaintiff, that would be no assault.' Although literally unimpeachable, this direction was totally inadequate having regard to the evidence that the jury had to consider. There was a great difference between the words used in *Tuberville* v. *Savage* and those used in the case at bar. In the former case, the declaration of the desire to kill was made subject to an extraneous condition ('If it were not assize-time'), which was known to the other party not to be fulfilled. The unfulfilled condition therefore nullified the threat. But in the present case, the threat was conditional upon the way the plaintiff thereafter behaved; in order to avoid being killed he had to keep quiet, and his conduct was therefore constrained by the threat. The plaintiff, in other words, was subject to the fear that if he spoke he would be shot. It is submitted that in these circumstances the presentation of the pistol was an assault. Otherwise, indeed, the highwayman who says 'Your money or your life,' at the same time presenting a weapon, would not be guilty of assault at common law—a proposition which it is impossible to believe."

R. v. St. George
(1840) 9 C. & P. 483; 173 E.R. 921
Shrewsbury Assizes

St. George was charged under statute with attempting to discharge loaded arms at the prosecutor. He had quarrelled with Durant and in a fight he took out a pistol, pointed it and tried to cock it. Although his finger was on the trigger he was prevented from drawing it. The question arose whether, if the full offence were not proved, the prisoner would be convicted of an assault, being an ingredient of the full offence.

LUDLOW, SERJT.: I submit that the prisoner cannot be convicted of an assault, unless the jury are satisfied that the pistol was loaded.

PARKE B.: It seems to me that it is an assault to point a weapon at a person though not loaded, but so near, that if loaded, it might do injury. I think the offence of pointing a loaded gun at another does involve an assault, unless it is done secretly; and I think that the presenting a fire-arm, which has the appearance of being loaded, as near that it might produce injury if it was loaded, and went off, is an assault. ... My idea is, that it is an assault to present a pistol at all, whether loaded or not. If you threw the powder out of the pan, or took the percussion cap off, and said to the party, "This is an empty pistol," then that would be no assault; for then the party must see that it was not possible that he should be injured; but if a person presents a pistol which has the appearance of being loaded and puts the party into fear and alarm, that is what it is the object of the law to prevent.

Verdict: Guilty of an assault

ii. Mens Rea

R. v. Venna
[1975] 3 All E.R. 788
Court of Appeal

D was involved in a struggle with police officers who were attempting to arrest him. He fell to the ground and then proceeded to lash out wildly with his legs. In so doing he kicked the hand of one of the police officers, fracturing a bone. His story was that he was kicking out in an attempt to get up off the ground. D was convicted of assault occasioning actual bodily harm, after the judge had directed the jury that they could find D guilty if they found that he had lashed out with his feet "reckless as to who was there, not caring one iota as to whether he kicked anybody." He appealed.

JAMES L.J. (reading the judgment of the court): ... In *Fagan* v. *M.P.C.* (*ante*, p. 582), it was said: "An assault is any act which intentionally or possibly recklessly causes another person to apprehend immediate and unlawful personal violence." In *Fagan* it was not necessary to decide the question whether proof of recklessness is sufficient to establish the *mens rea* ingredient of assault. That question falls for decision in the present case. ...

On the evidence of the appellant himself, one would have thought that the inescapable inference was that the appellant intended to make physical contact with whoever might try to restrain him. Be that as it may, in the light of the direction given, the verdict may have been arrived at on the basis of "recklessness." Counsel for the appellant cited *Ackroyd* v. *Barett* (1894) T.L.R. 115 in support of his argument that recklessness, which falls short of intention, is not enough to support a charge of battery, and argued that, there being no authority to the contrary, it is now too late to extend the law by a decision of the courts and that any extension must be by the decision of Parliament. Counsel for the appellant sought support from the distinction between the offences which are assaults and offences which by statute include the element contained in the word "maliciously," *e.g.* unlawful and malicious wounding contrary to section 20 of the Offences Against the Person Act, 1861, in which recklessness will suffice to support the charge: see *R.* v. *Cunningham* (*ante*, p. 109). Insofar as the editors of textbooks commit themselves to an opinion on this branch of the law, they are favourable to the view that recklessness is or should logically be sufficient to support the charge of assault or battery: see Glanville Williams [*Criminal Law*, 2nd ed., p. 65]; Kenny [*Outlines of Criminal Law*, 19th ed., p. 218]; Russell [*Russell on Crime*, 12th ed., vol. 1, p. 656] and Smith and Hogan [*Criminal Law*, 3rd ed., pp. 284, 286].

We think that the decision in *Ackroyd* v. *Barett* is explicable on the basis that the facts of the case did not support a finding of recklessness. The case was not argued for both sides *R.* v. *Bradshaw* (1878) 14 Cox 83, can be read as supporting the view that unlawful physical force applied recklessly constitutes a criminal assault. In our view the element of *mens rea* in the offence of battery is satisfied by proof that the defendant intentionally or recklessly applied force to the person of another. If it were otherwise, the strange consequence would be that an offence of unlawful wounding contrary to section 20 of the Offences Against the Person Act 1861 could be established by proof that the defendant wounded the victim either intentionally or recklessly, but if the victim's skin was not broken and the offence was therefore laid as an assault occasioning actual bodily harm contrary to section 47 of the 1861 Act, it would be necessary to prove that the physical force was intentionally applied.

We see no reason in logic or in law why a person who recklessly applies physical force to the person of another should be outside the criminal law of assault. In many cases the dividing line between intention and recklessness is barely distinguishable. This is such a case. In our judgment the direction was right in law; this ground of appeal fails ...

Appeal dismissed

Note

Although the *mens rea* of common assault and battery is not dealt with directly in *Savage, post*, p. 625, the implication of the latter decision is that the recklessness sufficient for these offences is *Cunningham* recklessness, and *R. v. Caldwell, ante*, p. 111, is not in point.

iii. Justifications

Note

There are particular justifications for the application of force or threats of force, *e.g.* cases of self-defence, prevention of crime, which were dealt with *ante*, p. 330. Physical contact which is generally acceptable in the ordinary conduct of social life (*e.g.* jostlings in crowds) may also be justified: see *Collins* v. *Wilcock*, referred to in *In Re F.*, below. Necessity, insofar as it is involved in Duress of Circumstances, *ante*, p. 319, does not excuse the application of force to an innocent person who is not being lawfully arrested; but necessity to preserve the life or health or well-being of the person to whom the force is applied may be a justification: see next case. Consent may *sometimes* justify: see *post*, p. 595.

(a) *Necessity*

In Re F. (Mental Patient: Sterilisation)
[1990] 2 A.C. 1
House of Lords

F., a 36-year-old mentally handicapped woman with a mental age of a small child, resided as a voluntary patient in a mental hospital. She formed a sexual relationship with a male patient. The hospital staff considered that F. would be unable to cope with the effects of pregnancy and giving birth. Since other forms of contraception were unsuitable, and it was thought undesirable to curtail F.'s freedom of movement in order to prevent sexual activity, it was felt to be in F.'s best interests for her to be sterilised. F.'s mother concurred and sought a declaration that sterilisation would not be an unlawful act by reason only of the absence of F.'s consent. The declaration was granted, and upheld by the Court of Appeal. On further appeal by the Official Solicitor:—

LORD BRANDON OF OAKBROOK: Part IV of the Mental Health Act 1983 contains provisions, which it is not necessary to detail, imposing restrictions or conditions on the giving to mentally disorded persons of certain kinds of treatment for their mental disorder. The Act, however, does not contain any provisions relating to the giving of treatment to patients for any conditions other than their mental disorder. The result is that the lawfulness of giving any treatment of the latter kind depends not on statute but the common law.

At common law a doctor cannot lawfully operate on adult patients of sound mind, or give them any other treatment involving the application of physical force however small ("other treatment"), without their consent. If a doctor were to operate on such patients, or give them other treatment, without their consent, he would commit the actionable tort of trespass to the person. There are, however, cases where adult patients cannot give or refuse their consent to an operation or other treatment. One case is where, as a result of an accident or otherwise, an adult patient is unconscious and an operation or other treatment cannot be safely delayed until he or she recovers consciousness. Another case is where a patient, though adult, cannot by reason of mental disability understand the nature or purpose of an operation or other treatment. The common law would be seriously defective if it failed to provide a solution to the problem created by such inability to consent. In my opinion, however, the common law does not so fail. In my opinion, the solution to the problem which the common law provides is that a doctor can lawfully operate on, or give other treatment to, adult patients who are incapable, for one reason or another, of consenting to his doing so, provided that the operation or other treatment concerned is in the best interests of such patients. The operation or other treatment will be in their best interests if, but only if, it is carried out in order either to save their lives, or to ensure improvement or prevent deterioration in their physical or mental health.

Different views have been put forward with regard to the principle which makes it lawful for a doctor to operate on or give other treatment to adult patients without their consent in the two cases to which I have referred above. The Court of Appeal in the present case regarded the matter as depending on the public interest. I would not disagree with that as a broad proposition, but I think that it is helpful to consider the principle in accordance with which the public interest leads to this result. In my opinion, the principle is that, when persons lack the capacity, for whatever reason, to take decisions about the performance of operations on them, or the giving of other medical treatment to them, it is necessary that some other person or persons, with appropriate qualifications, should take such decisions for them. Otherwise they would be deprived of medical care which they need and to which they are entitled.

In many cases, however, it will not only be lawful for doctors, on the ground of necessity, to operate on or give other medical treatment to adult patients disabled from giving their consent; it will also be their common law duty to do so.

In the case of adult patients made unconscious by an accident or otherwise, they will normally be received into the casualty department of a hospital, which thereby undertakes the care of them. It will then be the duty of the doctors at that hospital to use their best endeavours to do, by way of either an operation or other treatment, that which is in the best interests of such patients.

In the case of adult patients suffering from mental disability, they will normally, in accordance with the scheme of the Mental Health Act 1983, be either in the care of guardians, who will refer them to doctors for medical treatment, or of doctors at mental hospitals in which the patients either reside voluntarily or are detained compulsorily. It will then again be the duty of the doctors concerned to use their best endeavours to do, by way of either an operation or other treatment, that which is in the best interests of such patients.

The application of the principle which I have described means that the lawfulness of a doctor operating on, or giving other treatment to, an adult patient disabled from giving consent, will depend not on any approval or sanction of a court, but on the question whether the operation or other treatment is in the best interests of the patient concerned. That is, from a practical point of view, just as well, for, if every operation to be performed, or other treatment to be given, required the approval or sanction of the court, the whole process of medical care for such patients would grind to a halt.

That is not the end of the matter, however, for there remains a further question to be considered. That question is whether, in the case of an operation for the sterilisation of an adult woman of child-bearing age, who is mentally disabled from giving or refusing her consent to it, although involvement of the court is not strictly necessary as a matter of law, it is nevertheless highly desirable as a matter of good practice. In considering that question, it is necessary to have regard to the special features of such an operation. These features are: first, the operation will in most cases be irreversible; secondly, by reason of the general irreversibility of the operation, the almost certain result of it will be to deprive the woman concerned of what is widely, and as I think rightly, regarded as one of the fundamental rights of a woman, namely, the right to bear children; thirdly, the deprivation of that right gives rise to moral and emotional considerations to which many people attach great importance; fourthly, if the question whether the operation is in the best interests of the woman is left to be decided without the involvement of the court, there may be a greater risk of it being decided wrongly, or at least of it being thought to have been decided wrongly; fifthly, if there is no involvement of the court, there is a risk of the operation being carried out for improper reasons or with improper motives; and, sixthly, involvement of the court in the decision to operate, if that is the decision reached, should serve to protect the doctor or doctors who perform the operation, and any others who may be concerned it it, from subsequent adverse criticisms or claims.

Having regard to all these matters, I am clearly of the opinion that, although in the case of an operation of the kind under discussion involvement of the court is not strictly necessary as a matter of law, it is nevertheless highly desirable as a matter of good practice ...

LORD GOFF OF CHIEVELEY: My Lords, the question in this case is concerned with the lawfulness of a proposed operation of sterilisation upon the plaintiff F., a woman of 36 years of age, who by reason of her mental incapacity is disabled from giving her consent to the operation. It is well established that, as a general rule, the performance of a medical operation upon a person without his or her consent is unlawful, as constituting both the crime of battery and the tort of trespass to the person. Furthermore, before Scott Baker J. and the Court of Appeal, it was common ground between the parties that there was no power in the court to give consent on behalf of F. to the proposed operation of sterilisation, or to dispense with the need for such consent. This was because it was common ground that the parens patriae jurisdiction in respect of persons suffering from mental incapacity, formerly vested in the courts by Royal Warrant under the Sign Manual, had ceased to be so vested by revocation of the last warrant on 1 November 1960; and further that there was no statutory provision which could be invoked in its place. Before your Lordships, having regard to the importance of the matter, both those propositions were nevertheless subjected to close scrutiny. ... However, with the assistance of counsel, I for my part have become satisfied that the concessions made below on these points were rightly made. ...

It follows that, as was recognised in the courts below, if the operation upon F. is to be justified, it can only be justified on the applicable principles of common law. The argument of counsel revealed the startling fact that there is no English authority on the question whether as a matter of common law (and if so in what circumstances) medical treatment can lawfully be given to a person who is disabled by mental incapacity from consenting to it. Indeed, the matter goes further; for a comparable problem can arise in relation to persons of sound mind who are, for example, rendered unconscious in an accident or rendered speechless by a catastrophic stroke. All such persons may require medical treatment and, in some cases, surgical operations. All may require nursing care. In the case of mentally disordered persons, they may require care of a more basic kind—dressing, feeding, and so on—to assist them in their daily life, as well as routine treatment by doctors and dentists. It follows that, in my opinion, it is not possible to consider in isolation the lawfulness of the proposed operation of sterilisation in the present case. It is necessary first to ascertain the applicable common law principles and then to consider the question of sterilisation against the background of those principles.

Mr. Munby, for the Official Solicitor, advanced the extreme argument that, in the absence of a parens patriae or statutory jurisdiction, no such treatment or care of the kind I have described can lawfully be given to a mentally disordered person who is unable to consent to it. This is indeed a startling proposition, which must also exclude treatment or care to persons rendered unconscious or unable to speak by accident or illness. For centuries, treatment and care must have been given to such persons, without any suggestion that it was unlawful to do so. I find it very difficult to believe that the common law is so deficient as to be incapable of providing for so obvious a need. Even so, it is necessary to examine the point as a matter of principle.

I start with the fundamental principle, now long established, that every person's body is inviolate. As to this, I do not wish to depart from what I myself said in the judgment of the Divisional Court in *Collins* v. *Wilcock* [1984] 1 W.L.R. 1172, and in particular from the statement, at p. 1177, that the effect of this principle is that everybody is protected not only against physical injury but against any form of physical molestation.

Of course, as a general rule physical interference with another person's body is lawful if he consents to it; though in certain limited circumstances the public interest may require that his consent is not capable of rendering the act lawful. There are also specific cases where physical interference without consent may not be unlawful—chastisement of children, lawful arrest, self-defence, the prevention of crime, and so on. As I pointed out in *Collins* v. *Wilcock*, a broader exception has been created to allow for the exigencies of everyday life—jostling in a street or some other crowded place, social contact at parties, and such like. This exception has been said to be founded on implied consent, since those who go about in public places, or go to parties, may be taken to have impliedly consented to bodily contact of this kind. Today this rationalisation can be regarded as artificial; and in particular, it is difficult to impute consent to those who, by reason of their youth or mental disorder, are unable to give their consent. For this reason, I consider it more appropriate to regard such cases as falling within a general exception embracing all physical contact which is generally acceptable in the ordinary conduct of everyday life.

In the old days it used to be said, for a touching of another's person to amount to a battery, it had to be a touching "in anger" (see *Cole* v. *Turner* (1794) 6 Mod. 149, *per* Holt C.J.); and it has recently been said that the touching must be "hostile" to have that effect (see *Wilson* v. *Pringle* [1987] Q.B. 237, 253). I respectfully doubt whether that is correct. A prank that gets out of hand; an over-friendly slap on the back; surgical treatment by a surgeon who mistakenly thinks that the patient has consented to it—all these things may transcend the bounds of lawfulness, without being characterised as hostile. Indeed the suggested qualification is difficult to reconcile with the principle that any touching of another's body is, in the absence of lawful excuse, capable of amounting to a battery and a trespass. Furthermore, in the case of medical treatment, we have to bear well in mind the libertarian principle of self-determination which, to adopt the words of Cardozo J. (in *Schloendorff* v. *Society of New York Hospital* (1914) 105 N.E. 92, 93) recognises that:

> "Every human being of adult years and sound mind has a right to determine what shall be done with his own body; and a surgeon who performs an operation without his patient's consent commits an assault . . . "

This principle has been reiterated in more recent years by Lord Reid in *S.* v. *McC. (orse. S.) and M. (D.S. intervener); W.* v. *W.* [1972] A.C. 24, 43.

It is against this background that I turn to consider the question whether, and if so when, medical treatment or care of a mentally disordered person who is, by reason of his incapacity, incapable of giving his consent, can be regarded as lawful. As it recognised in Cardozo J.'s statement of principle, and elsewhere (see e.g. *Sidaway* v. *Board of Governors of the Bethlem Royal Hospital and the Maudsley Hospital* [1985] A.C. 871, 882, *per* Lord Scarman), some relaxation of the law is required to accommodate persons of unsound mind. In *Wilson* v. *Pringle*, the Court of Appeal considered that treatment or care of such persons may be regarded as lawful, as falling within the exception relating to physical contact which is generally acceptable in the ordinary conduct of everyday life. Again, I am with respect unable to agree. That exception is concerned with the ordinary events of everyday life—jostling in public places and such like—and affects all persons, whether or not they are capable of giving their consent. Medical treatment—even treatment for minor ailments—does not fall within that category of events. The general rule is that consent is necessary to render such treatment lawful. If such treatment administered without consent is not to be unlawful, it has to be justified on some other principle.

Upon what principle can medical treatment be justified when given without consent? We are searching for a principle upon which, in limited circumstances, recognition may be given to a need, in the interests of the patient, that treatment should be given to him in circumstances where he is (temporarily or permanently) disabled from consenting to it. It is this criterion of a need which points to the principle of necessity as providing justification.

[After surveying the principle of necessity (see, *ante*, p. 317]

On this statement of principle, I wish to observe that officious intervention cannot be justified by the principle of necessity. So intervention cannot be justified when another more appropriate person is available and willing to act: nor can it be justified when it is contrary to the known wishes of the assisted person, to the extent that he is capable of rationally forming such a wish. As a general rule, if the above criteria are fulfilled, interference with the assisted person's person or property (as the case may be) will not be unlawful. Take the example of a railway accident, in which injured passengers are trapped in the wreckage. It is this principle which may render lawful the actions of other citizens—railway staff, passengers or outsiders—who rush to give aid and comfort to the victims: the surgeon who amputates the limb of an unconscious passenger to free him from the wreckage; the ambulance man who conveys him to hospital; the doctors and nurses who treat him and care for him while he is still unconscious. Take the example of an elderly person who suffers a stroke which renders him incapable of speech or movement. It is by virtue of this principle that the doctor who treats him, the nurse who cares for him, even the relative or friend or neighbour who comes in to look after him, will commit no wrong when he or she touches his body.

The two examples I have given illustrate, in the one case, an emergency, and in the other, a permanent or semi-permanent state of affairs. Another example of the latter kind is that of a mentally disordered person who is disabled from giving consent. I can see no good reason why the principle of necessity should not be applicable in his case as it is in the case of the victim of a stroke. Furthermore, in the case of a mentally disordered person, as in the case of a stroke victim, the permanent state of affairs calls for a wider range of care than may be requisite in an emergency which arises from accidental injury. When the state of affairs is permanent, or semi-permanent, action properly taken to preserve the life, health or well-being of the assisted person may well transcend such measures as surgical operation or substantial medical treatment and may extend to include such humdrum matters as routine medical or dental treatment, even simple care such as dressing and undressing and putting to bed.

The distinction I have drawn between cases of emergency, and cases where the state of affairs is (more or less) permanent, is relevant in another respect. We are here concerned with medical treatment, and I limit myself to cases of that kind. Where, for example, a surgeon performs an operation without his consent on a patient temporarily rendered unconscious in an accident, he should do no more than is reasonably required, in the best interests of the patient, before he recovers consciousness. I can see no practical difficulty arising from this requirement, which derives from the fact that the patient is expected before long to regain consciousness and can then be consulted about longer term measures. The point has however arisen in a more acute form where a surgeon, in the course of an operation, discovers some other condition which, in his opinion, requires operative treatment for which he has not received the patient's consent. In what circumstances he should operate forthwith, and in what circumstances he should postpone the further treatment until he has received the patient's consent, is a difficult matter which has troubled the Canadian Courts (see *Marshall* v. *Curry* (1933) 3 D.L.R. 260, and *Murray* v. *McMurchy* (1949) 2 D.L.R. 442), but which it is not necessary for your Lordships to consider in the present case.

But where the state of affairs is permanent or semi-permanent, as may be so in the case of a mentally disordered person, there is no point in waiting to obtain the patient's consent. The need to care for him is obvious: and the doctor must then act in the best interests of his patient, just as if he had received his patient's consent so to do. Were this not so, much useful treatment and care could, in theory at least, be denied to the unfortunate. It follows that, on this point, I am unable to accept the view expressed by Neill L.J. in the Court of Appeal, that the treatment must be shown to have been necessary. Moreover, in such a case, as my noble and learned friend Lord Brandon of Oakbrook has pointed out, a doctor who has assumed responsibility for the care of a patient may not only be treated as having the patient's consent to act, but may also be under a duty so to act. . . .

In these circumstances, it is natural to treat the deemed authority and the duty as interrelated. But I feel bound to express my opinion that, in principle, the lawfulness of the doctor's action is, at least in its origin, to be found in the principle of necessity. This can perhaps be seen most clearly in cases where there is no continuing relationship between doctor and patient. The "doctor in the house" who volunteers to assist a lady in the audience who, overcome by the drama or by the heat in the theatre, has fainted away, is impelled to act by no greater duty than that imposed by his own Hippocratic oath. Furthermore, intervention can be justified in the case of a non-professional, as well as a professional, man or woman who has no pre-existing relationship with the assisted person—as in the case of a stranger who rushes to assist an injured man after an accident. In my opinion, it is the necessity itself which provides the justification for the intervention.

I have said that the doctor has to act in the best interests of the assisted person. In the case of routine treatment of mentally disordered persons, there should be little difficulty in applying this principle. In the case of more serious treatment, I recognise that its application may create problems for the medical profession; however, in making decisions about treatment, the doctor must act in accordance with a responsible and competent body of relevant professional opinion, on the principles set down in *Bolam* v. *Friern Hospital Management Committee* [1957] 1 W.L.R. 582. No doubt, in practice, a decision may involve others besides the doctor. It must surely be good practice to consult relatives and others who are concerned with the care of the patient. Sometimes, of course, consultation with a specialist or specialists will be required; and in others, especially where the decision involves more than a purely medical opinion, an inter-disciplinary team will in practice participate in the decision. It is very difficult, and would be unwise, for a court to do more than to stress that, for those who are involved in these important and sometimes difficult decisions, the overriding consideration is that they should act in the best interests of the person who suffers from the misfortune of being prevented by incapacity from deciding for himself what should be done to his own body, in his own best interests.

In the present case, your Lordships have to consider whether the foregoing principles apply in the case of a proposed operation of sterilisation upon an adult woman of unsound mind, or whether sterilisation is (perhaps with one or two other cases) to be placed in a separate category to which special principles apply. Again, Mr. Munby assisted your Lordships by deploying the argument that, in the absence of any parens patriae jurisdiction, sterilisation of an adult woman of unsound mind, who by reason of her mental incapacity is unable to consent, can never be lawful. He founded his submission upon a right of reproductive autonomy or right to control one's own reproduction, which necessarily involves the right not to be sterilised involuntarily; upon the fact that sterilisation involves irreversible interference with the patient's most important organs; upon the fact that it involves interference with organs which are functioning normally; upon the fact that sterilisation is a topic upon which medical views are often not unanimous; and upon the undesirability, in the case of a mentally disordered patient, of imposing a "rational" solution upon an incompetent patient. Having considered these submissions with care, I am of the opinion that neither singly nor as a whole do they justify the conclusion for which Mr. Munby contended. Even so, while accepting that the principles which I have stated are applicable in the case of sterilisation, the matters relied upon by Mr. Munby provide powerful support for the conclusion that the application of those principles in such a case calls for special care. There are other reasons which support that conclusion. It appears, for example, from reported cases in the United States that there is a fear that those responsible for mental patients might (perhaps unwittingly) seek to have them sterilised as a matter of administrative convenience. Furthermore, the English case of *In re D. (A Minor) (Wardship: Sterilisation)* [1976] Fam. 185 provides a vivid illustration of the fact that a highly qualified medical practitioner, supported by a caring mother, may consider it right to sterilise a mentally retarded girl in circumstances which prove, on examination, not to require such an operation in the best interests of the girl. Matters such as these, coupled with the fundamental nature of the patient's organs with which it is proposed irreversibly to interfere, have prompted courts in the United States and in Australia to pronounce that, in the case of a person lacking the capacity to consent, such an operation should only be permitted with the consent of the court. Such decisions have of course been made by courts which have vested in them the parens patriae jurisdiction, and so have power, in the exercise of such jurisdiction, to impose such a condition. They are not directly applicable in this country, where that jurisdiction has been revoked. . . .

Although the parens patriae jurisdiction in the case of adults of unsound mind is no longer vested in courts in this country, the approach adopted by the courts in the United States and in Australia provides, in my opinion, strong support for the view that, as a matter of practice, the operation of sterilisation should not be performed on an adult person who lacks the capacity to consent to it without first obtaining the opinion of the court that the operation is, in the circumstances, in the best interests of the person concerned, by seeking a declaration that the operation is lawful. (I shall return later in this speech to the appropriateness of the declaratory remedy in cases such as these.) In my opinion, that guidance should be sought in order to obtain an independent, objective and authoritative view on the lawfulness of the procedure in the particular circumstances of the relevant case, after a hearing at which it can be ensured that there is independent representation on behalf of the person upon whom it is proposed to perform the operation. This approach is consistent with the opinion expressed by Lord Templeman in *In re B. (A Minor) (Wardship: Sterilisation)* [1988] A.C. 199, 205–206, that, in the case of a girl who is still a minor, sterilisation should not be performed upon her unless she has first been made a ward of court and the court has, in the exercise of its wardship jurisdiction, given its authority to such a step. He said:

> "No one has suggested a more satisfactory tribunal or a more satisfactory method of reaching a decision which vitally concerns an individual but also involves principles of law, ethics and medical practice."

I recognise that the requirement of a hearing before a court is regarded by some as capable of deterring certain medical practitioners from advocating the procedure of sterilisation; but I trust and hope that it may come to be understood that court procedures of this kind, conducted sensitively and humanely by judges of the Family Division, so far as possible and where appropriate in the privacy of chambers, are not to be feared by responsible practitioners.

Lords Bridge of Harwich, Griffiths and Jauncey of Tullichettle agreed with Lords Brandon and Goff

Appeal dismissed

Note

The application of force or threats of force may sometimes be justified by the consent of the victim. Where it is so justified, neither common assault nor any statutory crime which involves assault is committed. However, sometimes the statute expressly provides that consent is no defence. Moreover, the common law does not recognise consent as a defence to some assaults, on the footing that "no one can license a crime." This doctrine, and the question of what is consent, need separate treatment.

(b) *When consent may justify*

R. v. Brown
(1993) Official Transcript
House of Lords

The appellants belonged to a group of sado-masochistic homosexuals who over a 10-year period from 1978 willingly participated in the commission of acts of violence against each other, including genital torture, for the sexual pleasure which it engendered in the giving and receiving of pain. The passive partner or victim in each case consented to the acts being committed and suffered no permanent injury. The activities took place in private at a number of different locations, including rooms equipped as torture chambers at the homes of three of the appellants. Video cameras were used to record the activities and the resulting tapes were then copied and distributed amongst members of the group. The tapes were not sold or used other than for the delectation of members of the group. The appellants were charged with assault occasioning actual bodily harm, contrary to s. 47 of the Offences Against the Person Act 1861, and unlawful wounding, contrary to s. 20 of that Act. The prosecution case was based very largely on the contents of the video tapes. At their trial, following a ruling by the trial judge that it was unnecessary for the prosecution to prove that the victim did not consent to the infliction of bodily harm or wounding upon him, the appellants pleaded guilty. Their appeal against conviction was dismissed by the Court of Appeal, which certified the following point of law of general public importance:— "Where A wounds or assaults B occasioning him actual bodily harm in the course of a sado-masochistic encounter, does the prosecution have to prove lack of consent on the part of B before they can establish A's guilt under s. 20 and s. 47 of the 1861 Offences Against the Person Act?" On further appeal:—

LORD TEMPLEMAN: ... In the present case each of the appellants intentionally inflicted violence upon another (to whom I refer as "the victim") with the consent of the victim and thereby occasioned actual bodily harm or in some cases wounding or grievous bodily harm. Each appellant was therefore guilty of an offence under s. 47 or s. 20 of the Act of 1861 unless the consent of the victim was effective to prevent the commission of the offence or effective to constitute a defence to the charge.

In some circumstances violence is not punishable under the criminal law. When no actual bodily harm is caused, the consent of the person affected precludes him from complaining. There can be no conviction for the summary offence of common assault if the victim has consented to the assault. Even when violence is intentionally inflicted and results in actual bodily harm, wounding or serious bodily harm the accused is entitled to be acquitted if the injury was a foreseeable incident of a lawful activity in which the person injured was participating. Surgery involves intentional violence resulting in actual or sometimes serious bodily harm but surgery is a lawful activity. Other activities carried on with consent by or on behalf of the injured person have been accepted as lawful notwithstanding that they involve actual bodily harm or may cause serious bodily harm. Ritual circumcision, tattooing, ear-piercing and violent sports including boxing are lawful activities.

In earlier days some other forms of violence were lawful and when they ceased to be lawful they were tolerated until well into the 19th century. Duelling and fighting were at first lawful and then tolerated provided the protagonists were voluntary participants. But where the result of these activities was the maiming of one of the participants, the defence of consent never availed the aggressor; see *Hawkins Pleas of the Crown* (1824), 8th ed., Chapter 15. A maim was bodily harm whereby a man was deprived of the use of any member of his body which he needed to use in order to fight but a bodily injury was not a maim merely because it was a disfigurement. The act of maim was unlawful because the King was deprived of the services of an able-bodied citizen for the defence of the realm. Violence which maimed was unlawful despite consent to the activity which produced the maiming. In these days there is no difference between maiming on the one hand and wounding or causing grievous bodily harm on the other hand except with regard to sentence.

When duelling became unlawful, juries remained unwilling to convict but the judges insisted that persons guilty of causing death or bodily injury should be convicted despite the consent of the victim.

Similarly, in the old days, fighting was lawful provided the protagonists consented because it was thought that fighting inculcated bravery and skill and physical fitness. The brutality of knuckle fighting however caused the courts to declare that such fights were unlawful even if the protagonists consented. Rightly or wrongly the courts accepted that boxing is a lawful activity.

In *R.* v. *Coney* (1882) 8 Q.B.D. 534, the court held that a prize-fight in public was unlawful. Cave J. said, at p. 539:

"The true view is, I think, that a blow struck in anger, or which is likely or is intended to do corporal hurt, is an assault, but that a blow struck in sport, and not likely nor intended to cause bodily harm, is not an assault, and that an assault being a breach of the peace and unlawful, the consent of the person struck is immaterial."

Stephen J. said, at p. 549.

"When one person is indicted for inflicting personal injury upon another, the consent of the person who sustains the injury is no defence to the person who inflicts the injury, if the injury is of such a nature, or is inflicted under such circumstances, that its infliction is injurious to the public as well as to the person injured. But the injuries given and received in prize-fights are injurious to the public, both because it is against the public interest that the lives and the health of the combatants should be endangered by blows, and because prize-fights are disorderly exhibitions, mischievous on many obvious grounds. Therefore the consent of the parties to the blows which they mutually receive does not prevent those blows from being assaults . . . In cases where life and limb are exposed to no serious danger in the common course of things, I think that consent is a defence to a charge of assault, even when considerable force is used, as, for instance, in cases of wrestling, single-stick, sparring with gloves, football and the like; but in all cases the question whether consent does or does not take from the application of force to another its illegal character, is a question of degree depending upon circumstances."

Hawkins J. said, at p. 553:

". . . whatever may be the effect of a consent in a suit between party and party, it is not in the power of any man to give an effectual consent to that which amounts to, or has a direct tendency to create, a breach of the peace; so as to bar a criminal prosecution. In other words, though a man may by consent debar himself from his right to maintain a civil action, he cannot thereby defeat proceedings instituted by the Crown in the interest of the public for the maintenance of good order; . . . He may compromise his own civil rights, but he cannot compromise the public interests."

Lord Coleridge C.J. said, at p. 567:

". . . I conceive it to be established, beyond the power of any argument however ingenious to raise a doubt, that as the combatants in a duel cannot give consent to one another to take away life, so neither can the combatants in a prize-fight give consent to one another to commit that which the law has repeatedly held to be a breach of the peace. An individual cannot by such consent destroy the right of the Crown to protect the public and keep the peace."

The conclusion is that a prize-fight being unlawful, actual bodily harm or serious bodily harm inflicted in the course of a prize-fight is unlawful notwithstanding the consent of the protagonists.

In *R. v. Donovan* [1934] 2 K.B. 498 the appellant in private beat a girl of seventeen for purposes of sexual gratification, it was said with her consent. Swift J. said, at p. 507 that:

"It is an unlawful act to beat another person with such a degree of violence that the infliction of bodily harm is a probable consequence, and when such an act is proved, consent is immaterial."

In *Att.-Gen.'s Reference (No. 6 of 1980)* [1981] Q.B. 715 where two men quarrelled and fought with bare fists Lord Lane, C.J., delivering the judgment of the Court of Appeal said, at p. 719:

". . . It is not in the public interest that people should try to cause, or should cause, each other bodily harm for no good reason. Minor struggles are another matter. So, in our judgment, it is immaterial whether the act occurs in private or in public; it is an assault if actual bodily harm is intended and/or caused. This means that most fights will be unlawful regardless of consent. Nothing which we have said is intended to cast doubt upon the accepted legality of properly conducted games and sports, lawful chastisement or correction, reasonable surgical interference, dangerous exhibitions, etc. These apparent exceptions can

be justified as involving the exercise of a legal right, in the case of
chastisement or correction, or as needed in the public interest, in the
other cases."

Duelling and fighting are both unlawful and the consent of the
protagonists affords no defence to charges of causing actual bodily harm,
wounding or grievous bodily harm in the course of an unlawful activity.

The appellants and their victims in the present case were engaged in
consensual homosexual activities. The attitude of the public towards
homosexual practices changed in the second half of this century. Change
in public attitudes led to a change in the law.

The Wolfenden Report (Report of the Committee on Homosexual
Offences and Prostitution (1957) (Cmnd. 247)) declared that the function of
the criminal law in relation to homosexual behaviour "is to preserve public
order and decency, to protect the citizen from what is offensive or
injurious, and to provide sufficient safeguards against exploitation and
corruption of others, particularly those who are especially vulnerable
because they are young, weak in body or mind, inexperienced, or in a
state of special, physical, official or economic dependence"; paragraph 13
of chapter 2.

In response to the Wolfenden Report and consistently with its
recommendations, Parliament enacted s. 1 of the Sexual Offences Act 1967
which provided, inter alia, as follows:

"(1) Notwithstanding any statutory or common law provision, ... a
homosexual act in private shall not be an offence provided that the
parties consent thereto and have attained the age of 21 years." ...

By the Act of 1967, Parliament recognised and accepted the practice of
homosexuality. Subject to exceptions not here relevant, sexual activities
conducted in private between not more than two consenting adults of the
same sex or different sexes are now lawful. Homosexual activities
performed in circumstances which do not fall within s. 1(1) of the Act of
1967 remain unlawful. Subject to the respect for private life embodied in
the Act of 1967. Parliament has retained criminal sanctions against the
practice, dissemination and encouragement of homosexual activities.

My Lords, the authorities dealing with the intentional infliction of bodily
harm do not establish that consent is a defence to a charge under the Act
of 1861. They establish that the courts have accepted that consent is a
defence to the infliction of bodily harm in the course of some lawful
activities. The question is whether the defence should be extended to the
infliction of bodily harm in the course of sado-masochistic encounters. The
Wolfenden Committee did not make any recommendations about sado-
masochism and Parliament did not deal with violence in 1967. The Act of
1967 is of no assistance for present purposes because the present problem
was not under consideration.

The question whether the defence of consent should be extended to the
consequences of sado-masochistic encounters can only be decided by
consideration of policy and public interest. Parliament can call on the
advice of doctors, psychiatrists, criminologists, sociologists and other
experts and can also sound and take into account public opinion. But the
question must at this stage be decided by this House in its judicial capacity
in order to determine whether the convictions of the appellants should be
upheld or quashed.

Counsel for some of the appellants argued that the defence of consent
should be extended to the offence of occasioning actual bodily harm under
s. 47 of the Act of 1861 but should not be available to charges of serious

wounding and the infliction of serious bodily harm under s. 20. I do not consider that this solution is practicable. Sado-masochistic participants have no way of foretelling the degree of bodily harm which will result from their encounters. The differences between actual bodily harm and serious bodily harm cannot be satisfactorily applied by a jury in order to determine acquittal or conviction.

Counsel for the appellants argued that consent should provide a defence to charges under both s. 20 and 47 because, it was said, every person has a right to deal with his body as he pleases. I do not consider that this slogan provides a sufficient guide to the policy decision which must now be made. It is an offence for a person to abuse his own body and mind by taking drugs. Although the law is often broken, the criminal law restrains a practice which is regarded as dangerous and injurious to individuals and which if allowed and extended is harmful to society generally. In any event the appellants in this case did not mutilate their own bodies. They inflicted bodily harm on willing victims. Suicide is no longer an offence but a person who assists another to commit suicide is guilty of murder or manslaughter.

The assertion was made on behalf of the appellants that the sexual appetites of sadists and masochists can only be satisfied by the infliction of bodily harm and that the law should not punish the consensual achievement of sexual satisfaction. There was no evidence to support the assertion that sado-masochist activities are essential to the happiness of the appellants or any other participants but the argument would be acceptable if sado-masochism were only concerned with sex, as the appellants contend. In my opinion sado-masochism is not only concerned with sex. Sado-masochism is also concerned with violence. The evidence discloses that the practices of the appellants were unpredictably dangerous and degrading to body and mind and were developed with increasing barbarity and taught to persons whose consents were dubious or worthless.

A sadist draws pleasure from inflicting or watching cruelty. A masochist derives pleasure from his own pain or humiliation. The appellants are middle-aged men. The victims were youths some of whom were introduced to sado-masochism before they attained the age of 21. In his judgment in the Court of Appeal, Lord Lane C.J. said that two members of the group of which the appellants formed part, namely one Cadman and the appellant Laskey:

"... were responsible in part for the corruption of a youth K ... It is some comfort at least to be told, as we were, that K has now it seems settled into a normal heterosexual relationship. Cadman had befriended K when the boy was 15 years old. He met him in a cafeteria and, so he says, found out that the boy was interested in homosexual activities. He introduced and encouraged K in "bondage affairs". He was interested in viewing and recording on videotape K and other teenage boys in homosexual scenes ... One cannot overlook the danger that the gravity of the assaults and injuries in this type of case may escalate to even more unacceptable heights."

The evidence disclosed that drink and drugs were employed to obtain consent and increase enthusiasm. The victim was usually manacled so that the sadist could enjoy the thrill of power and the victim could enjoy the thrill of helplessness. The victim had no control over the harm which the sadist, also stimulated by drink and drugs might inflict. In one case a victim was branded twice on the thigh and there was some doubt as to whether he consented to or protested against the second branding. The dangers involved in administering violence must have been appreciated by the appellants because, so it was said by their counsel, each victim was given a code word which he could pronounce when excessive harm or pain was caused. The efficiency of this precaution, when taken, depends on the circumstances and on the personalities involved. No one can feel the pain of another. The charges against the appellants were based on genital torture and violence to the buttocks, anus, penis, testicles and nipples. The victims were degraded and humiliated, sometimes beaten, sometimes wounded with instruments and sometimes branded. Bloodletting and the smearing of human blood produced excitement. There were obvious dangers of serious personal injury and blood infection. Prosecuting counsel informed the trial judge against the protests of defence counsel, that although the appellants had not contracted AIDS, two members of the group had died from AIDS and one other had contracted an HIV infection although not necessarily from the practices of the group. Some activities involved excrement. The assertion that the instruments employed by the sadists were clean and sterilized could not have removed the danger of infection, and the assertion that care was taken demonstrates the possibility of infection. Cruelty to human beings was on occasions supplemented by cruelty to animals in the form of bestiality. It is fortunate that there were no permanent injuries to a victim though no one knows the extent of harm inflicted in other cases. It is not surprising that a victim does not complain to the police when the complaint would involve him in giving details of acts in which he participated. Doctors of course are subject to a code of confidentiality.

In principle there is a difference between violence which is incidental and violence which is inflicted for the indulgence of cruelty. The violence of sado-masochistic encounters involves the indulgence of cruelty by sadists and the degradation of victims. Such violence is injurious to the participants and unpredictably dangerous. I am not prepared to invent a defence of consent for sado-masochistic encounters which breed and glorify cruelty and result in offences under ss. 47 and 20 of the Act 1861.

. . . Society is entitled and bound to protect itself against a cult of violence. Pleasure derived from the infliction of pain is an evil thing. Cruelty is uncivilised. I would answer the certified question in the negative and dismiss the appeals of the appellants against conviction.

LORD JAUNCEY OF TULLICHETTLE . . . The facts giving rise to the charges came to light as a result of police investigation into other matters. It was common ground that the receivers had neither complained to the police nor suffered any permanent injury as a result of the activities of the appellants. Although the incidents giving rise to each charge were the subject of a video-recording, these recordings were made not for sale at a profit but for the benefit of those members of the "ring", if one may so describe it, who had not had the opportunity of witnessing the events in person. Your Lordships were further informed that the activities of the appellants, who are middle aged men, were conducted in secret and in a highly controlled manner, that code words were used by the receiver when he could no longer bear the pain inflicted upon him and that when fish-hooks were inserted through the penis they were sterilised first. None of the appellants however had any medical qualifications and there was, of course, no referee present such as there would be in a boxing or football match.

The basic argument propounded by all the appellants was that the receivers having in every case consented to what was inflicted upon them no offence had been committed against ss. 20 or 47 of the Offences Against the Person Act 1861. All the appellants recognised however that so broad a proposition could not stand up and that there must be some limitation upon the harm which an individual could consent to receive at the hand of another. The line between injuries to the infliction of which an individual could consent and injuries to whose infliction he could not consent must be drawn it was argued where the public interest required. Thus except in the case of regulated sports the public interest required that injuries should not be inflicted in public where they might give rise to a breach of the peace. Lady Mallalieu for Jaggard argued that injuries to which consent would be irrelevant were those which resulted in actual expense to the public by reason, for example, of the expenses of hospital or other medical treatment, or payment of some benefit. Such injuries would be likely to be serious and to be appropriate to a s. 20 charge, whereas the consensual infliction of less serious injuries would not constitute an offence. Furthermore the presence of hostility was an essential element in the offence of assault, which element was necessarily lacking where a valid consent was present. Miss Worrall for Laskey maintained that everyone had a right to consent to the infliction on himself of bodily harm not amounting to serious harm or maiming at which point public interest intervened. She further argued that having regard to the common law offence of keeping a disorderly house and to the various offences created by the Sexual Offences Acts 1956 to 1976 it was inappropriate to use the Act of 1861 for the prosecution of sexual offences because the public interest was adequately looked after by the common law offence and the later Acts. Mr. Kershen for Brown also argued that the Act of 1861 was an inappropriate weapon to use in these cases. He submitted that while deliberate infliction of injury resulting in serious bodily harm might be an offence whether or not consent was given, deliberate consensual wounding would not be an offence if it did not cause serious bodily harm. This latter proposition would appear to draw the line somewhere down the middle of s. 20. Mr. Kershen further argued that if his primary submissions were wrong this House should, having regard to the current public interest in freedom of sexual expression, lay down new rules for sado-masochistic activities. Mr. Thwaites for Carter traced the history of the offence of maiming which deprived the King of possible service, invited your Lordships to hold that *R.* v. *Donovan* and *Att.-Gen.'s Reference* (*No. 6 of 1980*), to which I shall refer later, were wrongly decided and submitted that as a matter of principle a man could lawfully consent to the infliction of any injury upon himself which fell short of maiming.

In concluding that the consent of the receivers was immaterial to the offences charged the Court of Appeal relied on three cases, namely, *R.* v. *Coney, R.* v. *Donovan* and *Att.-Gen.'s Reference* (*No. 6 of 1980*). [After extensive quotations from *R.* v. *Coney*] In *Donovan* the appellant was charged with indecent and common assault upon a girl whom he had beaten with her consent for his own sexual gratification. In delivering the judgment of the Court of Criminal Appeal Swift J., after citing the passage in the judgment of Cave J. in *Coney*, to which I have already referred, said at p. 507:

> "If an act is unlawful in the sense of being in itself a criminal act, it is plain that it cannot be rendered lawful because the person to whose detriment it is done consents to it. No person can license another to commit a crime. So far as the criminal law is concerned, therefore, where the act charged is in itself unlawful, it can never be necessary to prove absence of consent on the part of the person wronged in order to obtain the conviction of the wrongdoer. There are, however, many acts in themselves harmless and lawful which become unlawful only if they

are done without the consent of the person affected. What is, in one case, an innocent act of familiarity or affection, may, in another, be an assault, for no other reason than that, in the one case there is consent, and in the other consent is absent. As a general rule, although it is a rule to which there are well established exceptions, it is an unlawful act to beat another person with such a degree of violence that the infliction of bodily harm is a probable consequence, and when such an act is proved, consent is immaterial."

Swift J. also observed that the passage from *Stephen's Digest* which I have quoted above needed considerable qualification in 1934. He went on to consider exceptions to the general rule that an act likely or intended to cause bodily harm is an unlawful act. Such exceptions included friendly contests with cudgels, foils or wrestling which were capable of causing bodily harm, rough and undisciplined sports or play where there was no anger and no intention to cause bodily harm and reasonable chastisement by a parent or a person in loco parentis. He might also have added necessary surgery. After referring to the fact that if the appellant acted so as to cause bodily harm could not plead the gratification of his perverted desires as an excuse, Swift J. said, at p. 509:

"Always supposing, therefore, that the blows which he struck were likely or intended to do bodily harm, we are of opinion that he was doing an unlawful act, no evidence having been given of facts which would bring the case within any of the exceptions to the general rule. In our view, on the evidence given at the trial, the jury should have been directed that, if they were satisfied that the blows struck by the prisoner were likely or intended to do bodily harm to the prosecutrix, they ought to convict him, and that it was only if they were not so satisfied, that it became necessary to consider the further question whether the prosecution had negatived consent. For this purpose we think that 'bodily harm' has its ordinary meaning and includes any hurt or injury calculated to interfere with the health or comfort of the prosecutor. Such hurt or injury need not be permanent, but must, no doubt, be more than merely transient and trifling."

It is clear from the report that the girl did in fact suffer actual bodily harm.

In *Att.-Gen.'s Reference (No. 6 of 1980)* the respondent and the victim had a fistfight in a public street which resulted in actual bodily harm to the victim. The respondent was charged with assault causing actual bodily harm and was acquitted. The question referred to the Court of Appeal was (p. 717):

"Where two persons fight (otherwise than in the course of sport) in a public place can it be a defence for one of those persons to a charge of assault arising out of the fight that the other consented to fight?"

The court answered the question in the negative. Lord Lane C.J. said, at p. 718H:

"Bearing in mind the various cases and the views of the text book writers cited to us, and starting with the proposition that ordinarily an act consented to will not constitute an assault, the question is: at what point does the public interest require the court to hold otherwise?"

He later said, at p. 719C:

"The answer to this question, in our judgment, is that it is not in the public interest that people should try to cause, or should cause, each other actual bodily harm for no good reason. Minor struggles are another matter. So, in our judgment, it is immaterial whether the act occurs in private or in public; it is an assault if actual bodily harm is intended and/or caused. This means that most fights will be unlawful regardless of consent.

"Nothing which we have said is intended to cast doubt upon the accepted legality of properly conducted games and sports, lawful chastisement or correction, reasonable surgical interference, dangerous exhibitions, etc. These apparent exceptions can be justified as involving the exercise of a legal right, in the case of chastisement or correction, or as needed in the public interest, in the other cases."

Although the reasoning in these two cases differs somewhat, the conclusion from each of them is clear, namely, that the infliction of bodily harm without good reason is unlawful and that the consent of the victim is irrelevant. In the unreported case of *R.* v. *Boyea* (28 January 1992) (see [1992] Crim.L.R. 23), in which the appellant was convicted of indecent assault on a woman, Glidewell L.J. giving the judgment of the Court of Appeal (Criminal Division) said:

"The central proposition in *Donovan* is in our view consistent with the decision of the court in the *Att.-Gen.'s Reference (No. 6 of 1980)*. That proposition can be expressed as follows: an assault intended or which is likely to cause bodily harm, accompanied by indecency, is an offence irrespective of consent, provided that the injury is not 'transient or trifling'."

Glidewell L.J. went on to point out that having regard to the change in social attitude towards sexual relations "transient and trivial" must be understood in the light of conditions prevailing in 1992 rather than in 1934.

Before considering whether the above four cases were correctly decided and if so what relevance they have to these appeals, I must say a word about hostility. It was urged upon your Lordships that hostility on the part of the inflicter was an essential ingredient of assault and that this ingredient was necessarily lacking when injury was inflicted with the consent of the receiver. It followed that none of the activities in question constituted assault. The answer to this submission is to be found in the judgment of the Court of Appeal in *Wilson* v. *Pringle* [1987] Q.B. 237 where it was said, at p. 253 that hostility could not be equated with ill will or malevolence. The judgment went on to state:

"Take the example of the police officer in *Collins* v. *Wilcock* [1984] 1 W.L.R. 1172. She touched the woman deliberately, but without an intention to do more than restrain her temporarily. Nevertheless, she was acting unlawfully and in that way was acting with hostility."

If the appellant's activities in relation to the receivers were unlawful they were also hostile and a necessary ingredient of assault was present.

It was accepted by all the appellants that a line had to be drawn somewhere between those injuries to which a person could consent to infliction upon himself and those which were so serious that consent was immaterial. They all agreed that assaults occasioning actual bodily harm should be below the line but there was disagreement as to whether all offences against s. 20 of the Act of 1861 should be above the line or only those resulting in grievous bodily harm. The four English cases to which I have referred were not concerned with the distinction between the various types of assault and did not therefore have to address the problem raised in these appeals. . . .

I prefer the reasoning of Cave J. in *Coney* and of the Court of Appeal in the later three English cases which I consider to have been correctly decided. In my view the line properly falls to be drawn between assault at common law and the offence of assault occasioning actual bodily harm created by s. 47 of the Offences Against the Person Act 1861, with the result that consent of the victim is no answer to anyone charged with the latter offence or with a contravention of s. 20 unless the circumstances fall within one of the well known exceptions such as organised sporting contests and games, parental chastisement or reasonable surgery. There is nothing in ss. 20 and 47 of the Act of 1861 to suggest that consent is either an essential ingredient of the offences or a defence thereto. ...

I would therefore dispose of these appeals on the basis that the infliction of actual or more serious bodily harm is an unlawful activity to which consent is no answer. In reaching this conclusion I have not found it necessary to rely on the fact that the activities of the appellants were in any event unlawful inasmuch as they amounted to acts of gross indecency which, not having been committed in private, did not fall within s. 1(1) of the Sexual Offences Act 1967. Notwithstanding the views which I have come to, I think it right to say something about the submissions that consent to the activity of the appellants would not be injurious to the public interest.

Considerable emphasis was placed by the appellants on the well-ordered and secret manner in which their activities were conducted and upon the fact that these activities had resulted in no injuries which required medical attention. There was, it was said, no question of proselytising by the appellants. ...

Be that as it may, in considering the public interest it would be wrong to look only at the activities of the appellants alone, there being no suggestion that they and their associates are the only practitioners of homosexual sado-masochism in England and Wales. This House must therefore consider the possibility that these activities are practised by others and by others who are not so controlled or responsible as the appellants are claimed to be. Without going into details of all the rather curious activities in which the appellants engaged it would appear to be good luck rather than good judgment which has prevented serious injury from occurring. Wounds can easily become septic if not properly treated, the free flow of blood from a person who is H.I.V. positive or who has AIDS can infect another and an inflicter who is carried away by sexual excitement or by drink or drugs could very easily inflict pain and injury beyond the level to which the receiver had consented. Your Lordships have no information as to whether such situations have occurred in relation to other sado-masochistic practitioners. It was no doubt these dangers which caused Lady Mallalieu to restrict her propositions in relation to public interest to the actual rather than the potential result of the activity. In my view such a restriction is quite unjustified. When considering the public interest potential for harm is just as relevant as actual harm. As Mathew J. said in *Coney* at p. 547:

"There is however abundant authority for saying that no consent can render that innocent which is in fact dangerous."

Furthermore, the possibility of proselytisation and corruption of young men is a real danger even in the case of these appellants and the taking of video recordings of such activities suggest that secrecy may not be as strict as the appellants claimed to your Lordships. If the only purpose of the activity is the sexual gratification of one or both of the participants what then is the need of a video recording?

My Lords I have no doubt that it would not be in the public interest that deliberate infliction of actual bodily harm during the course of homosexual sado-masochistic activities should be held to be lawful. In reaching this conclusion I have regard to the information available in these appeals and [to] such inferences as may be drawn therefrom. I appreciate that there may be a great deal of information relevant to these activities which is not available to your Lordships. When Parliament passed the Sexual Offences Act 1967 which made buggery and acts of gross indecency between consenting males lawful it had available the Wolfenden Report (1957) (Cmnd. 247) which was the product of an exhaustive research into the problem. If it is to be decided that such activities as the nailing by A of B's foreskin or scrotum to a board or the insertion of hot wax into C's urethra followed by the burning of his penis with a candle or the incising of D's scrotum with a scalpel to the effusion of blood are injurious neither to B, C and D nor to the public interest then it is for Parliament with its accumulated wisdom and sources of information to declare them to be lawful.

Two further matters only require to be mentioned. There was argument as to whether consent, where available, was a necessary ingredient of the offence of assault or merely a defence. There are conflicting dicta as to its effect. In *Coney* Stephen J. referred to consent as "being no defence", whereas in *Att.-Gen.'s Reference (No. 6 of 1980)* Lord Lane C.J. referred to the onus being on the prosecution to negative consent. In *Collins* v. *Wilcock* Goff L.J. referred to consent being a defence to a battery. If it were necessary, which it is not, in this appeal to decide which argument was correct I would hold that consent was a defence to but not a necessary ingredient in assault. . . .

My Lords, I would answer the certified question in the negative and dismiss the appeals.

LORD LOWRY: . . . Everyone agrees that consent remains a complete defence to a charge of common assault and nearly everyone agrees that consent of the victim is not a defence to a charge of inflicting really serious personal injury (or "grievous bodily harm"). The disagreement concerns offences which occasion actual bodily harm: the appellants contend that the consent of the victim is a defence to one charged with such an offence, while the respondent submits that consent is not a defence. I agree with the respondent's contention for reasons which I now explain.

The 1861 Act was one of several laudable but untidy Victorian attempts to codify different areas of the law. [After criticizing the form of the Act.] It follows that the indications to be gathered from the 1861 Act are not precise. Nevertheless, I consider that it contains fairly clear signs that, with regard to the relevance of the victim's consent as a defence, assault occasioning actual bodily harm and wounding which results in actual bodily harm are not offences "below the line", to be ranked with common assault as offences in connection with which the victim's consent provides a defence, but offences "above the line", to be ranked with inflicting grievous bodily harm and the other more serious offences in connection with which the victim's consent does not provide a defence. [After reading ss. 18, 20 and 47 in their original form] I suggest that the following points should be noted:

1. Offences against s. 18 were felonies, but offences against ss. 20 and 47 were misdemeanours. Therefore s. 20 was not associated with s. 18 and separated from s. 47 by categorisation.

2. Although s. 47 appears to describe a less serious offence than s. 20, the maximum penalty was the same. Equality was maintained at five

years' imprisonment after the distinction between felony and mis-demeanour was abolished.

3. Wounding is associated in ss. 18 and 20 with the infliction of grievous bodily harm and is naturally thought of as a serious offence, but it may involve anything from a minor breaking or puncture of the skin to a near fatal injury. Thus wounding may simply occasion actual bodily harm or it may inflict grievous bodily harm. If the victim's consent is a defence to occasioning actual bodily harm, then, so far as concerns the proof of guilt, the line is drawn, as my noble and learned friend, Lord Jauncey of Tullichettle puts it, "somewhere down the middle of s. 20", which I would regard as a most unlikely solution.

4. According to the appellants' case, if an accused person charged with wounding relies on consent as a defence, the jury will have to find whether anything more than actual bodily harm was occasioned, something which is not contemplated by s. 20.

5. The distinction between common assault and all other attacks on the person is that common assault does not necessarily involve *any* significant bodily injury. It is much easier to draw the line between *no* significant injury and *some* injury than to differentiate between degrees of injury. It is also more logical, because for one person to inflict any injury on another without good reason is an evil in itself (malum in se) and contrary to public policy.

6. That consent is a defence to a charge of common assault is a common law doctrine which the 1861 Act has done nothing to change. ...

[After considering *Coney, Donovan, Att.-Gen.'s Reference*, and the judgment of the Court of Appeal in the instant case, and noting that the Court considered that the question of consent was immaterial.] If, as I, too, consider, the question of consent is immaterial, there are prima facie offences against ss. 20 and 47 and the next question is whether there is good reason to add sado-masochistic acts to the list of exceptions contemplated in *Att.-Gen.'s Reference*. In my opinion, the answer to that question is "No".

In adopting this conclusion I follow closely my noble and learned friends Lord Templeman and Lord Jauncey. What the appellants are obliged to propose is that the deliberate and painful infliction of physical injury should be exempted from the operation of statutory provisions the object of which is to prevent or punish that very thing, the reason for the proposed exemption being that both those who will inflict and those who will suffer the injury wish to satisfy a perverted and depraved sexual desire. Sado-masochistic homosexual activity cannot be regarded as conducive to the enhancement or enjoyment of family life or conducive to the welfare of society. A relaxation of the prohibitions in ss. 20 and 47 can only encourage the practice of homosexual sado-masochism and the physical cruelty that it must involve (which can scarcely be regarded as a "manly diversion") by withdrawing the legal penalty and giving the activity a judicial imprimatur. As well as all this, one cannot overlook the physical danger to those who may indulge in sado-masochism. In this connection, and also generally, it is idle for the appellants to claim that they are educated exponents of "civilised cruelty". A proposed *general* exemption is to be tested by considering the likely *general* effect. This must include the probability that some sado-masochistic activity, under the powerful influence of the sexual instinct, will get out of hand and result in serious physical damage to the participants and that some activity will involve a danger of infection such as these particular exponents do not contemplate for themselves. When considering the danger of infection, with its inevitable threat of AIDS, I am not impressed by the argument that this threat can be discounted on the ground that, as long ago as 1967, Parliament, subject to conditions, legalised buggery, now a well-known vehicle for the transmission of AIDS.

So far as I can see, the only counter-argument is that to place a restriction on sado-masochism is an unwarranted interference with the private life and activities of persons who are indulging in a lawful pursuit and are doing no harm to anyone except, possibly, themselves. This approach, which has characterised every submission put forward on behalf of the appellants, is derived from the fallacy that what is involved here is the restraint of a lawful activity as opposed [to] the refusal to relax existing prohibitions in the 1861 Act. If in the course of buggery, as authorised by the 1967 Act, one participant, either with the other participant's consent or not, deliberately causes actual bodily harm to that other, an offence against s. 47 has been committed. The 1967 Act provides no shield. The position is as simple as that, and there is *no legal right to cause actual bodily harm* in the course of sado-masochistic activity. . . .

For all these reasons I would answer "No" to the certified question and would dismiss the appeals.

LORD MUSTILL: This is a case about the criminal law of violence. In my opinion it should be a case about the criminal law of private sexual relations, if about anything at all. Right or wrong, the point is easily made. . . . If the criminality of sexual deviation is the true ground of these proceedings, one would have expected that these above all would have been the subject of attack. Yet the picture is quite different.

The conduct of the appellants and of other co-accused was treated by the prosecuting authorities in three ways. First, there were those acts which fell squarely within the legislation governing sexual offences. These are easily overlooked, because attention has properly been concentrated on the charges which remain in dispute, but for a proper understanding of the case it is essential to keep them in view Thus, four of the men pleaded guilty either as principals or as aiders and abettors to the charges of keeping a disorderly house. . . .

Laskey also pleaded guilty to two counts of publishing an obscene article. The articles in question were video-tapes of the activities which formed the subject of some of the counts laid under the Act of 1861.

The pleas of guilty to these counts, which might be regarded as dealing quite comprehensively with those aspects of Laskey's sexual conduct which impinged directly on public order attracted sentences of four years reduced on appeal to eighteen months imprisonment and three months imprisonment respectively. Other persons, not before the House, were dealt with in a similar way.

The two remaining categories of conduct comprised private acts. Some were prosecuted and are now before the House. Others, which I have mentioned, were not. If repugnance to general public sentiments of morality and propriety were the test, one would have expected proceedings in respect of the most disgusting conduct to be prosecuted with the greater vigour. Yet the opposite is the case. Why is this so? Obviously because the prosecuting authorities could find no statutory prohibition apt to cover this conduct. Whereas the sexual conduct which underlies the present appeals, although less extreme, could at least arguably be brought within ss. 20 and 47 of the 1861 Act because it involved the breaking of skin and the infliction of more than trifling hurt.

I must confess that this distribution of the charges against the appellants at once sounds a note of warning. It suggests that the involvement of the Act of 1861 was adventitious. This impression is reinforced when one considers the title of the statute under which the appellants are charged, "Offences *Against* the Person". Conduct infringing ss. 18, 20 and 47 of the Act of 1861 comes before the Crown Courts every day. Typically it involves brutality, aggression and violence, of a kind far removed from the appellants' behaviour which, however worthy of censure, involved no animosity, no aggression, no personal rancour on the part of the person inflicting the hurt towards the recipient and no protest by the recipient. In fact, quite the reverse. Of course we must give effect to the statute if its words capture what the appellants have done, but in deciding whether this is really so it is in my opinion legitimate to assume that the choice of the Offences Against the Person Act as the basis for the relevant counts in the indictment was made only because no other statute was found which could conceivably be brought to bear upon them.

In these circumstances I find it easy to share the opinion expressed by Wills J. in *R.* v. *Clarence (post,* p. 617), a case where the accused had consensual intercourse with his wife, he knowing and she ignorant that he suffered from gonorrhoea, with the result that she was infected. The case is of general importance, since the Court for Crown Cases Reserved held that there was no offence under ss. 47 and 20, since both sections required an assault, of which the wound or grievous bodily harm was the result, and that no assault was disclosed on the facts. For present purposes, however, I need only quote from the report, at p. 30:

> "... such considerations lead one to pause on the threshold, and enquire whether the enactment under consideration could really have been intended to apply to circumstances so completely removed from those which are usually understood when an assault is spoken of, or to deal with matters of any kind involving the sexual relation or act."

I too am led to pause on the threshold. Asking myself the same question, I cannot but give a negative answer. I therefore approach the appeal on the basis that the convictions on charges which seem to me so inapposite cannot be upheld unless the language of the statute or the logic of the decided cases positively so demand. Unfortunately, as the able arguments which we have heard so clearly demonstrate, the language of the statute is opaque, and the cases few and unhelpful. To these I now turn.

Throughout the argument of the appeal I was attracted by an analysis on the following lines. First, one would construct a continuous spectrum of the infliction of bodily harm, with killing at one end and a trifling touch at the other. Next, with the help of reported cases one would identify the point on this spectrum at which consent ordinarily ceases to be an answer to a prosecution for inflicting harm. This could be called "the critical level". It would soon become plain however that this analysis is too simple and that there are certain types of special situation to which the general rule does not apply. Thus, for example, surgical treatment which requires a degree of bodily invasion well on the upper side of the critical level will nevertheless be legitimate if performed in accordance with good medical practice and with the consent of the patient. Conversely, there will be cases in which even a moderate degree of harm cannot be legitimated by consent. Accordingly, the next stage in the analysis will be to identify those situations which have been identified as special by the decided cases, and to examine them to see whether the instant case either falls within one of them or is sufficiently close for an analogy to be valid. If the answer is negative, then the court will have to decide whether simply to apply the general law simply by deciding whether the bodily harm in the case under review is above or below the critical level, or to break new ground by recognising a new special situation to which the general law does not apply.

For all the intellectual neatness of this method I must recognise that it will not do, for it imposes on the reported cases and on the diversities of human life an order which they do not possess. Thus, when one comes to map out the spectrum of ordinary consensual physical harm, to which the special situations form exceptions, it is found that the task is almost impossible, since people do not ordinarily consent to the infliction of harm. In effect, either all or almost all the instances of the consensual infliction of violence are special. They have been in the past, and will continue to be in the future, the subject of special treatment by the law.

There are other objections to a general theory of consent and violence. Thus, for example, it is too simple to speak only of consent, for it comes in various sorts. Of these, four spring immediately to mind. First, there is an express agreement to the infliction of the injury which was in the event inflicted. Next, there is express agreement to the infliction of some harm, but not to that harm which in the event was actually caused. These two categories are matched by two more, in which the recipient expressly consents not to the infliction of harm, but to engagement in an activity which creates a risk of harm: again, either the harm which actually results, or to something less. These examples do not exhaust the categories, for corresponding with each are situations of frequent occurrence in practice where the consent is not express but implied. These numerous categories are not the fruit of academic over-elaboration, but are a reflection of real life. Yet they are scarcely touched on in the cases, which just do not bear the weight of any general theory violence and consent. . . .

[After considering the law on Death, Maiming, Prizefighting, "Contact" Sports, Surgery, Lawful Correction, Dangerous Pastimes, Rough Horseplay, Prostitution, and Fighting, and concluding that he would not accept that the infliction of bodily harm, and especially the private infliction of it, is invariably criminal, absent some special factor which decrees otherwise]: For these reasons, I consider that the House is free, as the Court of Appeal in the present case was not . . . free, to consider entirely afresh whether the public interest demands the interpretation of the Act of 1861 in such a way as to render criminal under s. 47 the acts done by the appellants.

[After holding that the general tenor of the decisions of the European Court on the European Convention on Human Rights clearly favoured the right of the appellants to conduct their private lives undisturbed by the criminal law]: The purpose of this long discussion has been to suggest that the decks are clear for the House to tackle completely anew the question whether the public interest requires s. 47 of the 1861 Act to be interpreted as penalising an infliction of harm which is at the level of actual bodily harm, but not grievous bodily harm; which is inflicted in private (by which I mean that it is exposed to the view only of those who have chosen to view it); which takes place not only with the consent of the recipient but with his willing and glad co-operation; which is inflicted for the gratification of sexual desire, and not in a spirit of animosity or rage; and which is not engaged in for profit.

My Lords, I have stated the issue in these terms to stress two considerations of cardinal importance. Lawyers will need no reminding of the first, but since this prosecution has been widely noticed it must be emphasised that the issue before the House is not whether the appellants' conduct is morally right, but whether it is properly charged under the Act of 1861. When proposing that the conduct is not rightly so charged I do not invite your Lordships' House to endorse it as morally acceptable. Nor do I pronounce in favour of a libertarian doctrine specifically related to sexual matters. Nor in the least do I suggest that ethical pronouncements are meaningless, that there is no difference between right and wrong, that sadism is praiseworthy, or that new opinions on sexual morality are necessarily superior to the old, or anything else of the same kind. What I do say is that these are questions of private morality; that the standards by which they fall to be judged are not those of the criminal law; and that if these standards are to be upheld the individual must enforce them upon himself according to his own moral standards, or have them enforced against him by moral pressures exerted by whatever religious or other community to whose ethical ideals he responds. The point from which I invite your Lordships to depart is simply this, that the state should interfere with the rights of an individual to live his or her life as he or she may choose no more than is necessary to ensure a proper balance between the special interests of the individual and the general interests of the individuals who together comprise the populace at large. Thus, whilst acknowledging that very many people, if asked whether the appellants' conduct was wrong, would reply "Yes, repulsively wrong", I would at the same time assert that this does not in itself mean that the prosecution of the appellants under ss. 20 and 47 of the Offences Against the Person Act 1861 is well founded.

This point leads directly to the second. As I have ventured to formulate the crucial question, it asks whether there is good reason to impress upon s. 47 an interpretation which penalises the relevant level of harm irrespective of consent: i.e. to recognise sado-masochistic activities as falling into a special category of acts, such as duelling and prize-fighting, which "the law says shall not be done." This is very important, for if the question were differently stated it might well yield a different answer. In particular, if it were to be held that as a matter of law all infliction of bodily harm above the level of common assault is incapable of being legitimated by consent, except in special circumstances, then we would have to consider whether the public interest required the recognition of private sexual activities as being in a specially exempt category. This would be an altogether more difficult question and one which I would not be prepared to answer in favour of the appellants, not because I do not have my own opinions upon it but because I regard the task as one which the courts are not suited to perform, and which should be carried out, if at all, by Parliament after a thorough review of all the medical, social, moral and political issues, such as was performed by the Wolfenden Committee. Thus, if I had begun from the same point of departure as my noble and learned friend Lord Jauncey of Tullichettle I would have arrived at a similar conclusion; but differing from him on the present state of the law, I venture to differ.

Let it be assumed however that we should embark upon this question. I ask myself, not whether as a result of the decision in this appeal, activities such as those of the appellants should *cease* to be criminal, but rather whether the Act of 1861 (a statute which I venture to repeat once again was clearly intended to penalise conduct of a quite different nature) should in this new situation be interpreted so as to *make* it criminal. Why should this step be taken? Leaving aside repugnance and moral objection, both of which are entirely natural but neither of which are in my opinion grounds upon which the court could properly create a new crime, I can visualise only the following reasons:

1. Some of the practices obviously created a risk of genito-urinary infection, and others of septicaemia. These might indeed have been grave in former times, but the risk of serious harm must surely have been greatly reduced by modern medical science.

2. The possibility that matters might get out of hand, with grave results. It has been acknowledged throughout the present proceedings that the appellants' activities were performed as a pre-arranged ritual, which at the same time enhanced their excitement and minimised the risk that the infliction of injury would go too far. Of course things might go wrong and really serious injury or death might ensue. If this happened, those responsible would be punished according to the ordinary law, in the same way as those who kill or injure in the course of more ordinary sexual activities are regularly punished. But to penalise the appellants' conduct even if the extreme consequences do not ensue, just because they might have done so would require an assessment of the degree of risk, and the balancing of this risk against the interests of individual freedom. Such a balancing is in my opinion for Parliament, not the courts; and even if your Lordships' House were to embark upon it the attempt must in my opinion fail at the outset for there is no evidence at all of the seriousness of the hazards to which sado-masochistic conduct of this kind gives rise. This is not surprising, since the impressive argument of Mr Purnell Q.C. for the respondents did not seek to persuade your Lordships' to bring the matter within the Act of 1861 on the ground of special risks, but rather to establish that the appellants are liable *under the general law* because the level of harm exceeded the critical level marking off criminal from non-criminal consensual violence which he invited your Lordships to endorse.

3. I would give the same answer to the suggestion that these activities involved a risk of accelerating the spread of auto-immune deficiency syndrome, and that they should be brought within the Act of 1861 in the interests of public health. The consequence would be strange, since what is currently the principal cause for the transmission of this scourge, namely consenting buggery between males, is now legal. Nevertheless, I would have been compelled to give this proposition the most anxious consideration if there had been any evidence to support it. But there is none, since the case for the respondent was advanced on an entirely different ground.

4. There remains an argument to which I have given much greater weight. As the evidence in the present case has shown, there is a risk that strangers (and especially young strangers) may be drawn into these activities at an early age and will then become established in them for life. This is indeed a disturbing prospect, but I have come to the conclusion that it is not a sufficient ground for declaring these activities to be criminal under the Act of 1861. The element of the corruption of youth is already catered for by the existing legislation; and if there is a gap in it which needs to be filled the remedy surely lies in the hands of Parliament, not in the application of a statute which is aimed at other forms of wrong-doing. As regards proselytisation for adult sado-masochism the argument appears to me circular. For if the activity is not itself so much against the public interest that it ought to be declared criminal under the Act of 1861 then the risk that others will be induced to join in cannot be a ground for making it criminal.

Leaving aside the logic of this answer, which seems to me impregnable, plain humanity demands that a court addressing the criminality of conduct such as that of the present should recognise and respond to the profound dismay which all members of the community share about the apparent increase of cruel and senseless crimes against the defenceless. Whilst doing so I must repeat for the last time that in the answer which I propose I do not advocate the de-criminalisation of conduct which has hitherto been a crime; nor do I rebut a submission that a new crime should be created, penalising this conduct, for Mr. Purnell has rightly not invited the House to take this course. The only question is whether these consensual private acts are offences against the existing law of violence. To this question I return a negative response.

Accordingly I would allow these appeals and quash such of the convictions as are now before the House.

LORD SLYNN OF HADLEY: ... The facts upon which the convictions under appeal were based are sufficiently and clearly set out in the judgment of Lord Lane C.J. and fortunately it is not necessary to repeat them. Nor is it necessary to refer to other facts which are mentioned in the papers before the House which can only add to one's feeling of revulsion and bewilderment that anyone (in this case men, in other cases mutatis mutandis, men and women or women) should wish to do or to have done to him or her the acts so revealed. Some of those other facts, though no less revolting to most people than the facts set out in the charges, could not possibly have constituted an assault in any of the degrees to which I have referred.

The determination of the appeal, however, does not depend on bewilderment or revulsion or whether the right approach for the House in the appeal ought to be liberal or otherwise. The sole question is whether when a charge of assault is laid under the two sections in question, consent is relevant in the sense either that the prosecution must prove a lack of consent on the part of the person to whom the act is done or that the existence of consent by such person constitutes a defence for the person charged.

If, as seems clear on previous authority, it was a general rule of the common law that any physical touching could constitute a battery, there was an exception where the person touched expressly or impliedly consented. As Goff L.J. put it in *Collins* v. *Wilcock* "Generally speaking, consent is a defence to battery." As the word "generally" suggests the exception was itself subject to exceptions. Thus in *Stephen's Digest of the Criminal Law 3rd ed. (1883)* it is stated in article 206 "Everyone has a right to consent to the infliction upon himself of bodily harm not amounting to a maim". By way of footnote it is explained that "Injuries short of maims are not criminal at common law unless they are assaults, but an assault is inconsistent with consent". Maim could not be the subject matter of consent since it rendered a man less able to fight or defend himself. (*Hawkins Pleas of the Crown*, 8th ed., Book 1, p. 107). Nor could a person consent to the infliction of death (*Stephen's Digest*, 3rd ed. article 207) or to an infliction of bodily harm in such manner as to amount to a breach of the peace (article 208). It was "uncertain to what extent any person has a right to consent to his being put in danger of death or bodily harm by the act of another" (article 209), where the example given suggests that dangerous acts rendering serious bodily harm likely were contemplated.

The law has recognised cases were consent, expressed or implied, can be a defence to what would otherwise be an assault and cases where consent cannot be a defence. The former include surgical operations, sports, the chastisement of children, jostling in a crowd, but all subject to a reasonable degree of force being used, tattooing and ear-piercing; the latter include death and maiming. None of these situations, in most cases pragmatically accepted, either covers or is analogous to the facts of the present case.

It is, however, suggested that the answer to the question certified flows from the decisions in three cases.

The first is *R.* v. *Coney*. This is a somewhat remarkable case in that not only the two participants in a prize-fight but a number of observers were convicted of a common assault. The case was said to be relevant to the present question since it was decided that consent was not a defence to common assault. It is, however, accepted in the present appeal that consent can be a defence to common assault. Moreover it is plain from the judgment as a whole that a fight of this kind, since in public, either did, or had a direct tendency to, create a breach of the peace. It drew large crowds who gambled, who might have got excited and have fought among themselves. Moreover it was plain that such fights were brutal — the fighters went out to kill or very gravely injure their opponents and they fought until one of them died or was very gravely injured. As Mathew J. put it, at p. 544:

"... the chief incentive to the wretched combatants to fight on until (as happens too often) deadly injuries have been inflicted and life endangered or sacrificed, is the presence of spectators watching with keen interest every incident of the fight."

This emphasis on the risk of a breach of the peace and the great danger to the combatants is to be found in all of the judgments in the case. (See, for example, pp. 538, 544, 546, 554, 562, 567). ...

The second case is *R. v. Donovan*. Here the, appellant, in private for his sexual gratification, caned a girl, who consented and was paid. The appeal was allowed because the question of consent was not left to the jury yet it was said that if the act done was itself unlawful, consent to act could not be a defence. This, however, was a long way from *Coney*, upon which the essential passage in the judgment was largely based, where the act was held to be unlawful in all circumstances regardless of consent. In *Donovan* there was accepted to be an issue for the jury as to whether the prosecution had proved that the girl had not consented and whether the consent was immaterial.

The third case is the *Att.-Gen.'s Reference (No. 6 of 1980)*. Here two youths fought following an argument. There was one bystander but no suggestion of public disorder as in *Coney*. If the judgment had been limited to the fact that the fight took place in public then there would clearly have been a possibility of a breach of the peace being caused; but the court laid down (p. 719C) that even consensual fighting in private constitutes an assault on the basis that consent is no defence "where people ... try to cause ... or cause each other bodily harm for no good reason."

I am not satisfied that fighting in private is to be treated always and necessarily as so much contrary to the public interest that consent cannot be a defence. In any event I think that the question of consent in regard to a fight needs special consideration. If someone is attacked and fights back he is not to be taken as consenting in any real sense. He fights to defend himself. If two people agree to fight to settle a quarrel the persons fighting may accept the risk of being hurt; they do not consent to serious hurt, on the contrary the whole object of the fight is to avoid being hurt and to hurt the opponent. It seems to me that the notion of "consent" fits ill into the situation where there is a fight. It is also very strange that a fight in private between two youths where one may, at most, get a bloody nose should be unlawful, whereas a boxing match where one heavyweight fighter seeks to knock out his opponent and possibly do him very serious damage should be lawful.

Accordingly I do not consider that any of these three cases is conclusive in resolving the present question.

These decisions are not in any event binding upon your Lordships' House and the matter has to be considered as one of principle.

Three propositions seem to me to be clear.

It is " ... inherent in the conception of assault and battery that the victim does not consent" (Glanville Williams [1962] Crim. L.R. 74, 75).

Secondly, consent must be full and free and must be as to the actual level of force used or pain inflicted. Thirdly, there exist areas where the law disregards the victim's consent even where that consent is freely and fully given. These areas may relate to the person (e.g. a child); they may relate to the place (e.g. in public); they may relate to the nature of the harm done. It is the latter which is in issue in the present case.

I accept that consent cannot be said simply to be a defence to any act which one person does to another. A line has to be drawn as to what can and as to what cannot be the subject of consent. In this regard it is relevant to recall what was said by Stephen J. in *R. v. Coney*. Even though he was referring to the position at common law, his words seem to me to be of relevance to a consideration of the statute in question.

> "In cases where life and limb are exposed to no serious danger in the common course of things, I think that consent is a defence to a charge of assault, even when considerable force is used that, as, for instance, in cases of wrestling, single-stick, sparring with gloves, football, and the like; but in all cases the question whether consent does or does not take from the application of force to another its illegal character, is a question of degree depending upon circumstances."

There are passages in the judgment of McInerney J. in the Australian case of *Pallante* v. *Stadiums Pty. Ltd.* (No. 1) [1976] V.R. 331, where a boxing match was in issue which also seem to me to be helpful.
Thus at p. 340:

> "It is easy to understand the proposition that if the harm to which consent is alleged to have been given is really grievous, as, for instance, in a case of maiming, the consent should be treated as nugatory: see, for instance, *Stephen's Digest of Criminal Law* (1926) 7th ed., Article 290. In *Cross and Jones, An Introduction to Criminal Law*, 7th ed., p. 40, it is suggested as a reason for this conclusion that the injured person is likely to become the charge of society. This may be a good enough reason but I would think it is not the primary reason. The primary reason, I would think, is that, as a general proposition, it injures society if a person is allowed to consent to the infliction on himself of such a degree of serious physical harm. . . .
>   "Grievous bodily harm is now to be understood as meaning 'really serious bodily harm'. So understood, the dictum of Stephen J. in *Coney's* case" [i.e. at p. 549, that the infliction of the blows is regarded as injurious to the public as well as to the person injured] "may, as Cross and Jones point out in the work cited at p. 40, require to be understood as meaning that a person can lawfully consent to the infliction of bodily harm upon himself provided it falls short of being grievous bodily harm."

I do not think a line can simply be drawn between "maiming" and death on the one hand and everything else on the other hand. The rationale for negating consent when maiming occurred has gone. It is, however, possible to draw the line, and the line should be drawn, between really serious injury on the one hand and less serious injuries on the other. I do not accept that it is right to take common assault as the sole category of assaults to which consent can be a defence and to deny that defence in respect of all other injuries. In the first place the range of injuries which can fall within "actual bodily harm" is wide — the description of two beatings in the present case show that one is much more substantial than the other. Further, the same is true of wounding where the test is whether the skin is broken and where it can be more or less serious. I can see no significant reason for refusing consent as a defence for the lesser of these cases of actual bodily harm and wounding.

If a line has to be drawn, as I think it must, to be workable, it cannot be allowed to fluctuate within particular charges and in the interests of legal certainty it has to be accepted that consent can be given to acts which are said to constitute actual bodily harm and wounding. Grievous bodily harm I accept to be different by analogy with and as an extension of the old cases on maiming. Accordingly, I accept that other than for cases of grievous bodily harm or death, consent can be a defence. This in no way means that the acts done are approved of or encouraged. It means no more than that the acts do not constitute as assault within the meaning of these two specific sections of the Offences Against the Person Act 1861.

None of the convictions in the present cases have been on the basis that grievous bodily harm was caused. Whether some of the acts done in these cases might have fallen within that category does not seem to me to be relevant for present purposes.

Even if the act done constitutes common assault, actual bodily harm or wounding, it remains to be established that the act was done otherwise than in public and that it was done with full consent. I do not accept the suggested test, as to whether an offence is committed, to be whether there is expense to the state in the form of medical assistance or social security payments. It seems to me better to ask whether the act was done in private or in public: is the public harmed or offended by seeing what is done or is a breach of the peace likely to be provoked? Nor do I consider that "hostility" in the sense of "aggression" is a necessary element to an assault. It is sufficient if what is done is done intentionally and against the will of the person to whom it is done. These features in themselves constitute "hostility".

in *R. v. Wollaston* (1872) 12 Cox C.C. 180 (where indecent assault was charged) Kelly C.B., with whom the rest of the Court concurred, said, at p. 181:

> "If anything is done by one being upon the person of another, to make the act an assault, it must be done without the consent and against the will of the person upon whom it is done. Mere submission is not consent, for there may be submission without consent, and while the feelings are repugnant to the act being done. Mere submission is totally different from consent. But in the present case there was actual participation by both parties in the act done, and complete mutuality."

In the present cases there is no doubt that there was consent; indeed there was more than mere consent. Astonishing though it may seem, the persons involved positively wanted, asked for, the acts to be done to them, acts which it seems from the evidence some of them also did to themselves. All the accused were old enough to know what they were doing. The acts were done in private. Neither the applicants nor anyone else complained as to what was done. The matter came to the attention of the police "coincidentally"; the police were previously unaware that the accused were involved in these practices though some of them had been involved for many years. The acts did not result in any permanent or serious injury or disability or any infection and no medical assistance was required even though there may have been some risk of infection, even injury.

There has been much argument as to whether lack of consent is a constituent of the offence which must be proved by the prosecution or whether consent is simply raised by way of defence. . . .

It has been suggested that if the act done is otherwise unlawful then consent cannot be a defence, but it can be a defence, if the act is otherwise lawful, in respect of injury which is less than really serious injury. That would produce the result in the present case that if these acts are done by two men they would be lawful by reason of s. 1 of the Sexual Offences Act 1967, even though the acts are far away from the kinds of homosexual acts which the Wolfenden Report had in mind (see paragraph 105 of the Report); in that situation, consent, it is said, would be a defence. If on the other hand three men took part, the activity would be unlawful under the Act of 1967 so that there could be no consent to the acts done. But it would also appear to mean that if these acts were done mutatis mutandis by a man and a woman, or between two men and a woman, or a man and two women, where the activity was entirely heterosexual, consent would prevent there being an offence. I do not find that this distinction produces an acceptable result.

My conclusion is thus that as the law stands, adults can consent to acts done in private which do not result in serious bodily harm, so that such acts do not constitute criminal assaults for the purposes of the Act of 1861. My conclusion is not based on the alternative argument that for the criminal law to encompass consensual acts done in private would in itself be an unlawful invasion of privacy. If these acts between consenting adults in private did constitute criminal offences undet the Act of 1861, there would clearly be an invasion of privacy. Whether that invasion would be justified and in particular whether it would be within the derogations permitted by article 8(2) of the European Convention on Human Rights, it is not necessary, on the conclusion to which I have come, to decide, despite the interesting arguments addressed to your Lordships on that question and even on the basis that English law includes a principle parallel to that set out in the European Convention on Human Rights.

Mr Kershaw Q.C. contended in a very helpful argument that the answer to the question should be on the basis (a) of existing law or (b) that a new ruling was to be given. My conclusion is on the basis of what I consider existing law to be. I do not consider that it is necessary for the House in its judicial capacity to give what is called "a new ruling" based on freedom of expression, public opinion, and the consequences of a negative ruling on those whom it is said can only get satisfaction through these acts; indeed the latter I regard as being of no or at best of little relevance to the decision in this case. Nor do I think that it is for your Lordships to make new law on the basis of the position in other states so that English law can "keep in line". All these are essentially matters, in my view, to be balanced by the legislature if it is thought necessary to consider the making criminal of sado-masochistic acts *per se*. The problems involved are carefully analysed by Dr. L.H. Leigh in "*Sado-masochism, Consent and the Reform of the Criminal Law*" (1976) 39 M.L.R. 130.

... I agree that in the end it is a matter of policy. It is a matter of policy in an area where social and moral factors are extremely important and where attitudes can change. In my opinion it is a matter of policy for the legislature to decide. If society takes the view that this kind of behaviour, even though sought after and done in private, is either so new or so extensive or so undesirable that it should be brought now for the first time within the criminal law, then it is for the legislature to decide. It is not for the courts in the interests of "paternalism", as referred to in the passage I have quoted, or in order to protect people from themselves, to introduce, into existing statutory crimes relating to offences *against* the person, concepts which do not properly fit there. If Parliament considers that the behaviour revealed here should be made specifically criminal, then the

Offences Against the Person Act 1861 or, perhaps more appropriately, the Sexual Offences Act 1967 can be amended specifically to define it. Alternatively, if it is intended that this sort of conduct should be lawful as between two persons but not between more than two persons as falling within the offence of gross indecency, then the limitation period for prosecution can be extended and the penalties increased where sado-masochistic acts are involved. That is obviously a possible course; whether it is a desirable way of changing the law is a different question.

Accordingly I consider that these appeals should be allowed and the conviction set aside.

Appeals dismissed

Questions

1. "I am not prepared to invent a defence for sado-masochistic encounters which ... result in offences under ss. 47 and 20 of the Act of 1861": Lord Templeman, *ante*, p. 600. Were the dissentient Lords prepared to invent such a defence? If, not, what is the basis of their opinions?

2. It appears that had the injuries in *R.* v. *Brown* been "merely transient or trifling," the result might have been different. A and B were making love vigorously when A, with B's consent, did something to B which was not intended to cause, but did in fact cause her bodily harm which was more than transient or trifling. Was this an assault by A? See *R.* v. *Boyea* [1992] Crim. L.R. 574 (C.A.).

(c) What is consent?

R. v. Clarence
(1888) 22 Q.B.D. 23
Court for Crown Cases Reserved

C. was charged under both section 20 and section 47 of the Offences Against the Person Act 1861. He had had intercourse with his wife when he was suffering from a venereal disease, which was communicated to her. She would not have consented to intercourse had she known of his condition. He was convicted on both counts. On a case being reserved, a majority of nine to four held that an assault was needed for both of the crimes charged and on the facts there was no assault.

STEPHEN J.: The question in this case is whether a man who knows that he has gonorrhoea, and who by having connection with his wife, who does not know it, infects her, is or is not guilty of an offence either under section 20 of 24 and 25 Vict. c. 100, or under section 47 of the same Act. Section 20 punishes everyone who "unlawfully and maliciously inflicts any grievous bodily harm upon any other person." Section 47 punishes everyone who is convicted of "an assault occasioning actual bodily harm to any person." ...

If the present conviction is right it is clear that unless some distinction can be pointed out which does not occur to me, the sections must be held to apply, not only to venereal diseases, but to infection of every kind which is in fact communicated by one person to another by any act likely to produce it. A man who knowing that he has scarlet fever or small-pox

shakes hands with a friend and so infects him may be said to fall under
section 20 or section 47 as much as the prisoner in this case. To seize a
man's hand without his consent is an assault; but no one would consent to
such a grasp if he knew that he risked small-pox by it, and if consent in all
cases is rendered void by fraud, including suppression of the truth, such a
gesture would be an assault occasioning actual bodily harm as much as the
conduct of the prisoner in this case.

Not only is there no general principle which makes the communication
of infection criminal, but such authority as exists is opposed to such a
doctrine in relation to any disease. . . .

I now come to the construction of the precise words of the statute. [His
Lordship held that section 20 required an assault (but see now *R*. v.
Wilson, post, p. 623)].

Is the case, then, within section 47, as "an assault occasioning actual
bodily harm"? The question here is whether there is an assault. It is said
there is none, because the woman consented, and to this it is replied that
fraud vitiates consent, and that the prisoner's silence was a fraud. Apart
altogether from this question, I think that the act of infection is not an
assault at all, for the reasons already given. Infection is a kind of
poisoning. It is the application of an animal poison, and poisoning as
already shewn, is not an assault. Apart, however, from this, is the man's
concealment of the fact that he was infected such a fraud as vitiated the
wife's consent to his exercise of marital rights, and converted the act of
connection into an assault? It seems to me that the proposition that fraud
vitiates consent in criminal matters is not true if taken to apply in the
fullest sense of the word, and without qualification. It is too short to be
true, as a mathematical formula is true. If we apply it in that sense to the
present case, it is difficult to say that the prisoner was not guilty of rape,
for the definition of rape is having connection with a woman without her
consent; and if fraud vitiates consent, every case in which a man infects a
woman or commits bigamy, the second wife being ignorant of the first
marriage, is also a case of rape. Many seductions would be rapes, and so
might acts of prostitution procured by fraud, as for instance by promises
not intended to be fulfilled. These illustrations appear to shew clearly that
the maxim that fraud vitiates consent is too general to be applied to these
matters as if it were absolutely true. I do not at all deny that in some cases
it applies though it is often used with reference to cases which do not fall
within it. For instance, it has nothing to do with such cases as assaults on
young children. A young child who submits to an indecent act no more
consents to it than a sleeping or unconscious woman. The child merely
submits without consenting. The only cases in which fraud indisputably
vitiates consent in these matters are cases of fraud as to the nature of the
act done. As to fraud as to the identity of the person by whom it is done
the law is not quite clear. In *R*. v. *Flattery* (1877) 2 Q.B.D. 410, in which
consent was obtained by reporting the act as a surgical operation, the
prisoner was held to be guilty of rape. In the case where consent was
obtained by the personation of a husband, there was before the passing of
the Criminal Law Amendment Act of 1885 a conflict of authority. The last
decision in England, *R*. v. *Barrow* (1868) L.R. 1 C.C.R. 158, decided that
the act was not rape, and *R*. v. *Dee* (1884) 14 L.R.Ir. 485, decided in Ireland
in 1884, decided that it was. The Criminal Law Amendment Act of 1885
"declared and enacted" that thenceforth it should be deemed to be rape,
thus favouring the view taken in *R*. v. *Dee*. I do not propose to examine in
detail the controversies connected with these cases. The judgments in the
case of *R*. v. *Dee* examine all of them minutely, and I think they justify the
observation that the only acts of fraud which so far destroy the effect of a

woman's consent as to convert a connection consented to in fact into a rape are frauds as to the nature of the act itself, or as to the identity of the person who does the act. There is abundant authority to shew that such frauds as these vitiate consent both in the case of rape and in the case of indecent assault. I should myself prefer to say that consent in such cases does not exist at all, because the act consented to is not the act done. Consent to a surgical operation or examination is not a consent to sexual connection or indecent behaviour. Consent to connection with a husband is not consent to adultery. . . .

The woman's consent here was as full and conscious as consent could be. It was not obtained by any fraud either as to the nature of the act or as to the identity of the agent. The injury done was done by a suppression of the truth. It appears to me to be an abuse of language to describe such an act as an assault. . . .

Conviction quashed

Questions

1. Ought consent to be vitiated wherever the victim would not have consented had he known the true facts? Should it be a battery if A, wrongly suspecting that he may be developing a common cold, but keeping quiet about his suspicion, kisses B, who would not have consented if she had known of his suspicion?

2. Ought the intentional or reckless communication of disease to be, not an assault, but a distinct offence of that name? See Lynch "Criminal Liability for Transmitting Disease" [1978] Crim.L.R. 612.

3. If A, infected with a venereal disease, has consensual intercourse with B without informing her of the fact, and B becomes infected, that is not an assault occasioning actual bodily harm: *R. v. Clarence*. If A does inform B and B consents anyway, is that an assault occasioning actual bodily harm? Refer to Lynch, *supra*, at p. 613.

Latter v. Braddell
Common Pleas Division
(1880) 50 L.J.K.B 166

L. was a housemaid in the service of Mrs. B. Mrs. B. was convinced that L. was pregnant, and on her denying it, Mrs. B. called a doctor and ordered L. to submit to a medical examination. He told her to undress and let him examine her. L. protested and wept but took off her clothes and submitted to an examination, which showed that she was not pregnant. L. sued Mrs. B. and the doctor for assault. The trial judge (Lindley J.) withdrew from the jury the case against Mrs. B, and the jury found in favour of the doctor. In the Common Pleas Divisional Court, Lindley J. upheld his own decision, Lopes J. dissenting.

LINDLEY J.: . . . The plaintiff's case cannot be put higher than this, namely, that, without consulting her wishes, her mistress ordered her to submit to be examined by a doctor, in order that he might ascertain whether she (the plaintiff) was in the family way, and that she (the plaintiff) complied with that order reluctantly—that is, sobbing and protesting—and because she was told she must, and she did not know what else to do. There was, however, no evidence of any force or violence, nor of any threat of force or violence, nor of any illegal act done or threatened by the mistress beyond what I have stated; nor did the plaintiff in her evidence say that she was in fear of the mistress or of the doctor, or that she was in any way overcome by fear. ... Under these circumstances I am of opinion that there was no evidence of want of consent as distinguished from reluctant obedience or submission to her mistress's orders, and that in the absence of all evidence of coercion, as distinguished from an order which the plaintiff could comply with or not as she chose, the action cannot be maintained. ...

Note

The case went to the Court of Appeal, where the judgment of Lindley J. was unanimously upheld: see (1881) 50 L.J.Q.B. 448; but note Lopes J.'s dissenting opinion in the Divisional Court.

" ... A submission to what is done, obtained through a belief that she is bound to obey her master or mistress; or a consent obtained through a fear of evil consequences to arise to herself, induced by her master's or mistress's words or conduct, is not sufficient. In neither case would the consent be voluntarily given: it would be a consent in one sense, but a consent to which the will was not a party. The plaintiff's case is stronger. She swears she did not consent. I know not what more a person in the plaintiff's position could do unless she used physical force. She is discharged without a hearing, forbidden to speak, sent to her room, examined by her mistress's doctor alone, no other female being in the room, made to take off all her clothes, and lie naked on the bed. She complains of the treatment, cries continuously, objects to the removal of each garment and swears the examination was without her consent. Could it be said, in these circumstances, that her consent was so unmistakably given that her state of mind was not a question for the jury to consider? I cannot adopt the view that the plaintiff consented because she yielded without her will having been overpowered by force or fear of violence. That, as I have said, is not, in my opinion, an accurate definition of consent in a case like this ... "

Questions

1. Do you think that Lopes J.'s view of the matter is preferable?
2. As to "consent to which the will is not a party," if the limits of this are not drawn at force or threats of force, where should they be drawn? At belief in law that one must submit? Or at a fear of "evil consequences"? How are they to be defined?

Note

See note to *R. v. Olugboja, post,* p. 640. That case has, under the supposed influence of statute, made the question of consent in rape correspond to the view taken by Lopes J.

(d) Capacity to consent

Notes

1. There is no age or degree of mental affliction which as a matter of law precludes a person from consenting to the application of force to his body. Ability to consent is a matter of

fact, depending on the capacity of the individual. In *R.* v. *D.* [1984] A.C. 778, 806, a case of kidnapping, an ingredient of which is absence of consent on the part of the person taken or carried away, Lord Brandon said:

"I see no good reason why, in relation to the kidnapping of a child, it should not in all cases be the absence of the child's consent which is material, whatever its age may be. In the case of a very young child, it would not have the understanding or the intelligence to give its consent, so that absence of consent would be a necessary inference from its age. In the case of an older child, however, it must, I think, be a question of fact for a jury whether the child concerned has sufficient understanding and intelligence to give its consent; if, but only if, the jury considers that a child has these qualities, it must then go on to consider whether it has been proved that the child did not give its consent. While the matter will always be for the jury alone to decide, I should not expect a jury to find at all frequently that a child under 14 had sufficient understanding and intelligence to give its consent."

2. As to consent to medical treatment of minors, see *Gillick* v. *West Norfolk and Wisbech Area Health Authority* [1986] A.C. 112, where Lord Scarman quoted with approval Addy J. in the Ontario High Court in *Johnston* v. *Wellesley Hospital* (1980) 17 D.L.R. (3d) 139, 144:

"But, regardless of modern trend, I can find nothing in any of the old reported cases, except where infants of tender age or young children were involved, where the Courts have found that a person under 21 years of age was legally incapable of consenting to medical treatment. If a person under 21 years were unable to consent to medical treatment, he would also be incapable of consenting to other types of bodily interference. A proposition purporting to establish that any bodily interference acquiesced in by a youth of 20 years would nevertheless constitute an assault would be absurd. If such were the case, sexual intercourse with a girl under 21 years would constitute rape. Until the minimum age of consent to sexual acts was fixed at 14 years by a statute, the Courts often held that infants were capable of consenting at a considerably earlier age than 14 years. I feel that the law on this point is well expressed in the volume on *Medical Negligence* (1957) by Lord Nathan (p. 176): 'It is suggested that the most satisfactory solution of the problem is to rule that an infant who is capable of appreciating fully the nature and consequences of a particular operation or of particular treatment can give an effective consent thereto, and in such cases the consent of the guardian is unnecessary; but that where the infant is without the capacity, any apparent consent by him or her will be a nullity, the sole right to consent being vested in the guardian.' "

3. Capacity to consent, in the case of a fully competent adult, involves a right *not* to consent to treatment, however necessary: see *Re T.* [1992] 4 All E.R. 649 (C.A.); but no minor, of any age below 18, has power by refusing consent to treatment to override a consent by someone with parental responsibility for the minor and *a fortiori* a consent by the court: *In Re J.* [1992] 4 All E.R. 614 (C.A.), *per* Donaldson M.R.

2. ASSAULT OCCASIONING ACTUAL BODILY HARM

Offences Against the Person Act 1861, section 47

Whosoever shall be convicted upon an indictment of any assault occasioning actual bodily harm shall be liable to . . . [imprisonment for five years].

Note

This section creates a separate statutory offence which ought to be charged as "contrary to section 47": *R.* v. *Harrow Justices* [1985] 3 All E.R. 185 (Q.B.D.).

R. v. Miller
[1954] 2 Q.B. 282
Winchester Assizes

M. was charged with raping his wife and with assault on her occasioning actual bodily harm.

LYNSKEY J. (after dealing with the rape count—see *post*, p. 640—and after rejecting the view that a husband was entitled to use as much force as reasonably necessary to exercise his marital rights): The result is that in the present case I am satisfied that the second count is a valid one and must be left to the jury for their decision. The point was taken that there is no evidence of bodily harm. The bodily harm alleged is said to be the result of the defendant's actions, and they were, if the jury accept the evidence, that he threw the wife down three times. There is evidence that afterwards she was in a hysterical and nervous condition, but it is submitted by counsel for the defendant that that is not "actual bodily harm." According to Archbold's *Criminal Pleading, Evidence and Practice*, 32nd ed., p. 959:

"Actual bodily harm includes any hurt or injury calculated to interfere with the health or comfort of the prosecutor . . . "

There was a time when shock was not regarded as bodily hurt, but the day has gone by when that could be said. It seems to me now that, if a person is caused hurt or injury resulting, not in any physical injury, but in an injury to the state of his mind for the time being, that is within the definition of "actual bodily harm." On that point I would leave the case to the jury.

Verdict: "Guilty" on the second count

Note

For the *mens rea* required for this offence, see *R.* v. *Savage, R.* v. *Parmenter, post*, p. 625.

3. MALICIOUS WOUNDING AND WOUNDING WITH INTENT

i. Malicious Wounding

Offences Against the Person Act 1861, section 20

"Whosoever shall unlawfully and maliciously wound or inflict any grievous bodily harm upon any other person, either with or without any weapon or instrument, shall be guilty of [an offence and liable to a maximum penalty of five years' imprisonment]."

Notes

Unlawfully: see Justifications, above.

Wound: In *C.* v. *Eisenhower* [1984] Q.B. 331 (D.C.), the victim was shot and an airgun pellet hit him near the eye. He sustained a bruise just below the eyebrow and fluid filling the front part of the eye for a time contained red blood cells. *Held* a wound is a break in the continuity of the whole skin, and an internal rupturing of the blood vessels is not a wound.

Grievous bodily harm: The Court of Criminal Appeal in *R.* v. *Metharam* [1961] 3 All E.R. 200 adopted the dictum of Viscount Kilmuir in *D.P.P.* v. *Smith, ante,* p. 501, that "bodily harm" needs no explanation and "grievous" means no more and no less than "really serious."

Inflict: in *R.* v. *Clarence, ante,* p. 617, it was held that an assault was needed for this offence: but see next case.

R. v. Wilson
[1984] A.C. 242
House of Lords

W. was charged on a single count of inflicting grievous bodily harm contrary to section 20 Offences Against the Person Act 1861. He was convicted of assault occasioning actual bodily harm. The Court of Appeal allowed his appeal on the ground that this was not permissible in terms of section 6(3) Criminal Law Act 1967, under which such an alternative conviction would only be possible if the allegations in the indictment "amounted to or included (expressly or by implication)" an allegation of the offence of which he was convicted, *i.e.* assault. The prosecution further appealed.

LORD ROSKILL (with whom Lords Fraser, Elwyn-Jones, Edmund-Davies and Brightman agreed): What, then, are the allegations expressly or impliedly included in a charge of "inflicting grievous bodily harm." Plainly that allegation must, so far as physical injuries are concerned, at least impliedly if not indeed expressly, include the infliction of "actual bodily harm" because infliction of the more serious injuries must include the infliction of the less serious injuries. But does the allegation of "inflicting" include an allegation of "assault"? The problem arises by reason of the fact that the relevant English case law has proceeded along two different paths. In one group it has, as has already been pointed out, been held that a verdict of assault was a possible alternative verdict on a charge of inflicting grievous bodily harm contrary to section 20. In the other group grievous bodily harm was said to have been inflicted without any assault having taken place, unless of course the offence of assault were to be given a much wider significance than is usually attached to it. This problem has been the subject of recent detailed analysis in the Supreme Court of Victoria in *R.* v. *Salisbury* [1976] V.R. 452. In a most valuable judgment (I most gratefully acknowledge the assistance I have derived from that judgment in preparing this speech) the full court drew attention, in relation to comparable legislation in Victoria, to the problems which arose from this divergence in the mainstream of English authority. The problem with which your Lordships' House is now faced arose in *R.* v. *Salisbury* in a different way from the present appeals. There, the appellant was convicted of an offence against the Victorian equivalent of section 20. He appealed on the ground that the trial judge had refused to leave to the jury the possibility of convicting him on that single charge of assault occasioning actual bodily harm or of common assault. The full court dismissed the appeal on the ground that at common law these latter offences were not "necessarily included" in the offence of "inflicting grievous bodily harm." The reasoning leading to this conclusion is plain ([1976] V.R. 452 at 461):

> "It may be that the somewhat different wording of section 20 of the English Act has played a part in bringing about the existence of the two lines of authority in England, but, be that as it may, we have come to the conclusion that, although the word 'inflicts' ... does not have as wide a meaning as the word 'causes' ... the word 'inflicts' does have a wider meaning than it would have if it were construed so that inflicting grievous bodily harm always involved assaulting the victim. In our opinion, grievous bodily harm may be inflicted ... either where the accused has directly and violently 'inflicted' it by assaulting the victim, or where the accused has 'inflicted' it by doing something, intentionally, which, though it is not itself a direct application of force to the body of the victim, does directly result in force being applied violently to the body of the victim, so that he suffers grievous bodily harm. Hence, the lesser misdemeanours of assault occasioning actual bodily harm and common assault ... are not necessarily included in the misdemeanour of inflicting grievous bodily harm ... "

This conclusion was reached after careful consideration of English authorities such as *R. v. Taylor* (1869) L.R. 1 C.C.R. 194, *R. v. Martin* (1881) 8 Q.B.D. 54, *R. v. Clarence* (*ante*, p. 617), *R. v. Halliday* (1889) 61 L.T. 701. My Lords, it would be idle to pretend that these cases are wholly consistent with each other, or even that, as in *R. v. Clarence*, though there was a majority in favour of quashing the conviction then in question, the judgments of those judges among the thirteen present who formed the majority are consistent with each other. Some of these cases were not argued on both sides. Others are very inadequately reported and different reports vary. Thus Stephen J., who was in the majority in *R. v. Clarence* 22 Q.B.D. 23 at 41 described the infliction of grievous bodily harm in these words:

> "The words appear to me to mean the direct causing of some grievous injury to the body itself with a weapon, as by a cut with a knife, or without a weapon, as by a blow with the fist, or by pushing a person down. Indeed, though the word 'assault' is not used in the section, I think the words imply an assault and battery of which a wound or grievous bodily harm is the manifest immediate and obvious result. This is supported by *R. v. Taylor* ... "

But Wills J., also in the majority, was clearly of the view that grievous bodily harm could be inflicted without an assault, as for example, by creating panic. On the other hand, in *R. v. Taylor*, where the accused was charged on two counts, one under each limb of section 20, the jury convicted him of common assault. Kelly C.B. said that each count was for an offence which necessarily included an assault, and a verdict of guilty of common assault was upheld. *R. v. Taylor* is not easy to reconcile with the later cases unless it is to be supported on the basis of the wounding count in the indictment. In *R. v. Martin* (1881) 8 Q.B.D. 54 (*ante*, p. 176), on the other hand, there was no reference to the issue whether the accused's conduct in creating panic among a theatre audience constituted assault. He did an unlawful act calculated to cause injury and injury was thereby caused. He was thus guilty of an offence against section 20.

My Lords, I doubt whether any useful purpose would be served by further detailed analysis of these and other cases, since to do so would only be to repeat less felicitously what has already been done by the full court of Victoria in *R. v. Salisbury*. I am content to accept, as did the full court, that there can be an infliction of grievous bodily harm contrary to section 20 without an assault being committed. . . . [His Lordship went on to hold that although the allegations in a section 20 charge do not *expressly* include a charge of assault, they *impliedly* do so, so the terms of section 6(3) Criminal Law Act 1967 were satisfied].

Appeal allowed: conviction restored

Question

As a result of this decision, is infection by disease or poison (a) an assault? or (b) sufficient for a charge under section 20?

R. v. Savage, R. v. Parmenter
[1992] A.C. 699
House of Lords

Savage intentionally threw beer at Beal, the pint glass left her hand, broke and cut Beal. She was convicted of unlawful wounding, the jury having been directed that if they were sure she deliberately threw the beer but unintentionally let go of the glass, so that Beal was wounded, they could convict of unlawful wounding. On appeal, the Court of Appeal quashed the conviction under section 20, Offences Against the Person Act 1861 but substituted a conviction under section 47. She appealed to the House of Lords.

Parmenter was convicted of inflicting grievous bodily harm, contrary to section 20, on his baby son. His rough handling caused the breaking of the child's arm and leg bones. His case was that he did not realise that his handling of the child would cause injury. The jury were directed that they could convict if they were sure that Parmenter should have foreseen some physical harm, albeit minor, not necessarily grievous bodily harm. On appeal, the Court of Appeal allowed his appeal, but declined to substitute a conviction under section 47. The Crown appealed to the House of Lords. Both appeals were heard together.

LORD ACKNER: after outlining the facts and the certified questions:—My Lords, I will now seek to deal with the issues raised in these appeals seriatim.

I. *Is a verdict of guilty of assault occasioning actual bodily harm a permissible alternative verdict on a count alleging unlawful wounding contrary to s.20 of the 1861 Act?*

[After extensive quotation from the speech of Lord Roskill in *R. v. Wilson, ante*, pp. 623–625], I respectfully agree with this reasoning and accordingly reject the submission that *R. v. Wilson* was wrongly decided. I would therefore answer the first of the certified questions in *R. v. Savage* in the affirmative. A verdict of guilty of assault occasioning actual bodily harm is a permissible alternative verdict on a count alleging unlawful wounding contrary to s.20 of the 1861 Act.

II. *Can a verdict of assault occasioning actual bodily harm be returned upon proof of an assault together with proof of the fact that actual bodily harm was occasioned by the assault, or must the prosecution also prove that the defendant intended to cause some actual bodily harm or was reckless as to whether such harm would be caused?*

Your Lordships are concerned with the mental element of a particular kind of assault, an assault "occasioning actual bodily harm". It is common ground that the mental element of assault is an intention to cause the victim to apprehend immediate and unlawful violence or recklessness whether such apprehension be caused (see *R. v. Venna ante* p. 586). It is of course common ground that Mrs. Savage committed an assault upon Miss Beal when she threw the contents of her glass of beer over her. It is also common ground that however the glass came to be broken and Miss Beal's wrist thereby cut, it was, on the finding of the jury, Mrs. Savage's handling of the glass which caused Miss Beal "actual bodily harm". Was the offence thus established or is there a further mental state that has to be established in relation to the bodily harm element of the offence? Clearly the section, by its terms, expressly imposes no such a requirement. Does it do so by necessary implication? It uses neither the word "intentionally" nor the word "maliciously". The words "occasioning actual bodily harm" are descriptive of the word "assault", by reference to a particular kind of consequence.

In neither *R. v. Savage* nor *R. v. Spratt* [1991] 2 All E.R. 210 nor in *R. v. Parmenter* was the court's attention invited to the decision of the Court of Appeal in *R. v. Roberts* (1972) 56 Cr.App.R. 95. This is perhaps explicable on the basis that this case is not referred to in the index to *Archbold's Criminal Pleading, Evidence and Practice* (43rd edn, 1988). The relevant text states (para. 20–117): "The mens rea required [for actual bodily harm] is that required for common assault', without any authority being provided for this proposition.

It is in fact *R. v. Roberts* which provides authority for this proposition. Roberts was tried on an indictment which alleged that he indecently assaulted a young woman. He was acquitted on that charge, but convicted of assault occasioning actual bodily harm to her. The girl's complaint was that while travelling in the defendant's car he sought to make advances towards her and then tried to take her coat off. This was the last straw and, although the car was travelling at some speed, she jumped out and sustained injuries. The defendant denied he had touched the girl. He had had an argument with her and in the course of that argument she suddenly opened the door and jumped out. In his direction to the jury the chairman of quarter sessions stated: "If you are satisfied that he tried to pull off her coat and as a result she jumped out of the moving car then your verdict is guilty."

It was contended on behalf of the appellant this this direction was wrong since the chairman had failed to tell the jury that they must be satisfied that the appellant foresaw that she might jump out of the car as a result of his touching her before they could convict. The court rejected that submission. The test was, said the court (at 102):

"Was it [the action of the victim which resulted in actual bodily harm] the natural result of what the alleged assailant said and did, in the sense that it was something that could reasonably have been foreseen as the consequence of what he was saying or doing? As it was put in one of the old cases, it had got to be shown to be his act, and if of course the victim does something so "daft", in the words of the appellant in this case, or so unexpected, not that this particular assailant did not actually foresee it but that no reasonable man could be expected to foresee it, then it is only in a very remote and unreal sense a consequence of his assault, it is really occasioned by a voluntary act on the part of the victim which could not reasonably be foreseen and which breaks the chain of causation between the assault and the harm or injury."

Accordingly, no fault was found in the following direction of the chairman to the jury (at 103):

"If you accept the evidence of the girl in preference to that of the man, that means that there was an assault occasioning actual bodily harm, that means that she did jump out as a direct result of what he was threatening her with, and what he was doing to her, holding her coat, telling her that he had beaten up girls who had refused his advances, and that means that through his acts he was in law and in fact responsible for the injuries which were caused to her by her decision, if it can be called that, to get away from his violence, his threats, by jumping out of the car."

Thus, once the assault was established, the only remaining question was whether the victim's conduct was the natural consequence of that assault. The words "occasioning" raised solely a question of causation, an objective question which does not involve inquiring into the accused's state of mind.

In *R. v. Spratt* [1991] 2 All ER 210 at 219, McCowan L.J. said:

"However, the history of the interpretation of the 1861 Act shows that, whether or not the word "maliciously" appears in the section in question, the courts have consistently held that the mens rea of every type of offence against the person covers both actual intent and recklessness, in the sense of taking the risk of harm ensuing with foresight that it might happen."

McCowan L.J. then quoted a number of authorities for that proposition. The first is *R. v. Ward* (1871) L.R. 1 C.C.R. 356, but that was a case where the prisoner was charged with wounding with intent (s.18) and convicted of malicious wounding (s.20); next, *R. v. Bradshaw* (1878) 14 Cox C.C. 83, but that was a case where the accused was charged with manslaughter, which has nothing to do with a s.47 case. Then *R. v. Cunningham* [1957] 2 Q.B. 396 is quoted, a case under s.23 of the Act concerned with unlawfully and maliciously administering etc. a noxious thing which endangers life. And, finally *R. v. Venna, ante*, p. 586, in which there was no issue as to whether in a s.47 case, recklessness had to extend to actual bodily harm. Thus none of the cases cited was concerned with the mental element required in s.47 cases. Nevertheless, the Court of Appeal in *R. v. Parmenter* [1991] 2 All E.R. 225 at 232, preferred the decision in *R. v. Spratt* to that of *R. v. Savage* because the former was "founded on a line of authority leading directly to the conclusion there expressed".

My Lords, in my respectful view, the Court of Appeal in *R. v. Parmenter* was wrong in preferring the decision in *R. v. Spratt*. The decision in *R. v. Roberts* was correct. The verdict of assault occasioning actual bodily harm may be returned upon proof of an assault together with proof of the fact that actual bodily harm was occasioned by the assault. The prosecution are not obliged to prove that the defendant intended to cause some actual bodily harm or was reckless as to whether such harm would be caused.

III. *In order to establish an offence under s.20 of the 1861 Act, must the prosecution prove that the defendant actually foresaw that his act would cause harm, or is it sufficient to prove that he ought so to have foreseen?*

[His Lordship concluded that the answer is that the prosecution must prove that the defendant actually foresaw that his act would cause harm. For his consideration of this question, see *ante*, p. 126]

IV. *In order to establish an offence under s.20 is it sufficient to prove that the defendant intended or foresaw the risk of some physical harm or must he intend or foresee either wounding or grievous bodily harm?*

It is convenient to set out once again the relevant part of the judgment of Diplock L.J. in *R.* v. *Mowatt*, [1968] 1 Q.B. 421 at 426. Having considered Professor Kenny's statement, which I have quoted above, he then said:

> In the offence under s.20 ... for ... which [no] specific intent is required—the word "maliciously" does import ... an awareness that his act may have the consequence of causing some physical harm to some other person. That is what is meant by the "particular kind of harm" in the citation from Professor Kenny's Outlines of Criminal Law (18th edn, 1962, para. 158a, p. 202). It is quite unnecessary that the accused should have foreseen that his unlawful act might cause physical harm of the gravity described in the section, i.e. a wound or serious physical injury. *It is enough that he should have foreseen that some physical harm to some person, albeit of a minor character, might result."* (My emphasis.)

Mr. Sedley submits that this statement of the law is wrong. He contends that, properly construed, the section requires foresight of a wounding or grievous bodily harm. He drew your Lordships' attention to criticisms of *R.* v. *Mowatt* made by Professor Glanville Williams and by Professor J. C. Smith in their textbooks and in articles or commentaries. They argue that a person should not be criminally liable for consequences of his conduct unless he foresaw a consequence falling into the same legal category as that set out in the indictment.

Such a general principle runs contrary to the decision in *R.* v. *Roberts*, which I have already stated to be, in my opinion, correct. The contention is apparently based on the proposition that, as the actus reus of a s.20 offence is the wounding or the infliction of grievous bodily harm, the mens rea must consist of foreseeing such wounding or grievous bodily harm. But there is no such hard and fast principle. To take but two examples, the actus reus of murder is the killing of the victim, but foresight of grievous bodily harm is sufficient and, indeed, such bodily harm need not be such as to be dangerous to life. Again, in the case of manslaughter death is frequently the unforeseen consequence of the violence used.

The argument that, as ss.20 and 47 have both the same penalty, this somehow supports the proposition that the foreseen consequences must coincide with the harm actually done, overlooks the oft-repeated statement that this is the irrational result of this piecemeal legislation. The Act "is a rag-bag of offences brought together from a wide variety of sources with no attempt, as the draftsman frankly acknowledged, to introduce consistency as to substance or as to form" (see Professor J. C. Smith in his commentary on *R.* v. *Parmenter* ([1991] Crim.L.R. 43)).

If s.20 was to be limited to cases where the accused does not desire but does foresee wounding or grievous bodily harm, it would have a very limited scope. The mens rea in a s.20 crime is comprised in the word "maliciously". As was pointed out by Lord Lane C.J., giving the judgment of the Court of Appeal in *R. v. Sullivan* [1981] Crim.L.R. 46, the "particular kind of harm" in the citation from Professor Kenny was directed to "harm to the person" as opposed to "harm to property". Thus it was not concerned with the degree of the harm foreseen. It is accordingly in my judgment wrong to look upon the decision in *R. v. Mowatt* as being in any way inconsistent with the decision in *R. v. Cunningham*.

My Lords, I am satisfied that the decision in *R. v. Mowatt* was correct and that it is quite unnecessary that the accused should either have intended or have foreseen that his unlawful act might cause physical harm of the gravity described in s.20, i.e. a wound or serious physical injury. It is enough that he should have foreseen that some physical harm to some person, albeit of a minor character, might result.

In the result I would dismiss the appeal in *Savage's* case but allow the appeal in *Parmenter's* case, but only to the extent of substituting, in accordance with the provisions of s.3(2) of the Criminal Appeal Act 1968, verdicts of guilty of assault occasioning actual bodily harm contrary to s.47 of the 1861 Act for the four s.20 offences of which he was convicted.

[Lords Keith of Kinkel, Brandon of Oakbrook, Jauncey of Tullichettle and Lowry agreed]

Appeal of Savage dismissed;
appeal of Parmenter allowed
in part and conviction of
assault occasioning actual
bodily harm substituted

ii. Wounding with Intent

Offences Against the Person Act 1861, section 18

"Whosoever shall unlawfully and maliciously by any means whatever wound, or cause any grievous bodily harm to any person, with intent ... to do some grievous bodily harm to any person, or with intent to resist or prevent the lawful apprehension or detainer of any person, shall be guilty of [an offence and shall be liable to imprisonment for life]"

Notes

1. The chief difference between the offences in section 18 and section 20 are: (1) in section 20 the *mens rea* resides in the word "maliciously," whereas in section 18, that word "adds nothing" to the definition, since the *mens rea* is defined expressly: *R. v. Mowatt* [1968] 1 Q.B. 421, 426; (2) the *actus reus* in section 18 includes "causing" grievous bodily harm, which is a wider word than "inflicting" in section 20, although neither word actually requires an assault: see *R. v. Wilson, ante,* p. 623.

2. In *R. v. Bryson* [1985] Crim.L.R. 669, a case in which D.'s car drove into a group of people, allegedly as a deliberate act by D., a conviction under section 18 followed a direction "that (if he was driving) foresight of probable serious harm, whether he wished it or not, amounted to an intention to cause grievous bodily harm." This was held to be wrong, although in view of the overwhelming evidence of intention, the proviso was applied to uphold the conviction.

Questions

1. What lines should the direction have taken? See *ante*, p. 126.

2. Is it a defence to a charge under section 18 that D. did not have the appropriate intention by reason of voluntary intoxication? See *ante*, p. 246.

3. Is intentional infection by disease capable of being the offence under section 18? See *ante*, p. 618.

R. v. Bentley
(1850) 4 Cox 406
Central Criminal Court

V., a P.C. in plain clothes, but accompanied by others in uniform, informed D. that he was arresting him for suspicion of highway robbery. V. had no warrant, but reasonably believed that D. was guilty. D. refused to be arrested unless told why and by what authority he was being apprehended, and resisted, injuring V. At D.'s trial for wounding with intent to resist lawful apprehension, it was objected on his behalf that it was not shown that he knew the arrest was unlawful.

TALFORD J.: If the apprehension is in point of fact lawful, we are not permitted to consider the question, whether or not he believed it to be so, because that would lead to infinite niceties of discrimination. The rule is not, that a man is always presumed to know the law, but that no man shall be excused for an unlawful act from his ignorance of the law. It was the prisoner's duty, whatever might be his consciousness of innocence, to go to the station house and hear the precise accusations against him. He is not to erect a tribunal in his own mind to decide whether he was legally arrested or not. He was taken into custody by an officer of the law, and it was his duty to obey the law.

Verdict: Guilty

Questions

What is D.'s position with respect to a charge under section 18 in the following cases?

1. V., seeking lawfully to arrest D., laid hands on him. D., believing that V. was a person attempting to rob him, punched V. on the jaw, breaking it. D. admits that his belief was unreasonable, and that the force he used was more than was reasonably necessary to defend himself, but claims he did not intend or expect to break V.'s jaw. See Chapter 5, *ante*.

2. D. pushes over V. in order to resist what they both think is a lawful arrest by V. In the fall, V. suffers a broken skull. In fact the arrest is unlawful. See Chapter 3, *ante*.

iii. Proposals for Reform

The Draft Criminal Code, building on an earlier report of the Criminal Law Revision Committee, 14th Report (1980), contains clauses reforming the law of non-fatal, non-sexual offences against the person. However, the Law Commission, taking the view that reform in this area is too urgent to await the enactment of the

Code, have published a draft Criminal Law Act, broadly following the Code proposals. The Commission offers a restatement, and a critique, of the present law as exemplified in the cases.

Law Com. Consultation Paper 122 (1992): Offences against the Person and General Principles

7.16 "A restatement of sections 18, 20 and 47

18. A person is guilty of an offence, punishable by life imprisonment, if he wounds, or causes any serious bodily harm to, another, intending either

> (i)   to cause serious bodily harm to any person or
> (ii) to resist the lawful arrest or detention of any person.

20. A person is guilty of an offence, punishable by 5 years' imprisonment, if he wounds, or inflicts serious bodily harm upon, another, either

> (i)   intending to cause some physical harm to any person or
> (ii) foreseeing that some physical harm to any person may be caused.

47. A person is guilty of an offence, punishable by 5 years' imprisonment, if he causes any hurt or injury calculated to interfere with the health or comfort of another by an act by which he intended to cause, or that he foresaw might cause either

> (i)   any person to fear immediate and unlawful violence or
> (ii) any physical contact with any person."

"7.39 The injustice and the inefficiency of the law under the 1861 Act combine to make that law an inept vehicle for conveying society's disapproval of violence, and the penalties with which violence will be met. At best, the 1861 Act contains a muddled message: that the same penalty is envisaged for causing both serious [section 20] and minor [section 47] harm: and that although the law purports to punish and control subjective fault, that fault is not linked to the damage caused, and is irrelevant to the punishment that the law provides. That law does not clearly single out those who contemplate violence as proper objects of deterrence and punishment because of the violence that they contemplate rather than the harm that they accidentally cause: nor does it distribute that punishment according to the subjective intentions, and thus the social fault, of the accused. Such a law, resting as much as it does on chance or the causing of unintended harm, does not properly convey society's message that violence is taken seriously, and will be punished according to the seriousness of the accused's conduct."

Draft Criminal Law Act

Intentional serious injury

"**4.**—(1) A person is guilty of an offence if he intentionally causes serious injury to another.

(2) A person may be guilty of an offence under subsection (1) above if either—

(a)   the act causing serious injury is done; or
(b)   the injury occurs,

in England and Wales.

(3) Section 3 [liability for omissions] applies to an offence under this section.

Reckless serious injury

"**5.**—(1) A person is guilty of an offence if he recklessly causes serious injury to another.

(2) Section 4(2) applies also to an offence under this section.

Intentional or reckless injury

6. A person is guilty of an offence if he intentionally or recklessly causes injury to another.

Assault

8.—(1) A person is guilty of assault if—

(a)   he intentionally or recklessly applies force to or causes an impact on the body of another,
      (i)   without the consent of the other; or
      (ii) where the act is likely or intended to cause injury, with or without the consent of the other; or
(b)   he intentionally or recklessly, without the consent of the other, causes the other to believe that any such force or impact is imminent.

(2) Except where the force or impact is intended or is likely to cause injury, a person does not commit an offence under this section in respect of any force or impact that is within the limits of what is acceptable as incidental to social intercourse or to life in the community."

4. SEXUAL OFFENCES

i. Rape

Sexual Offences Act 1956, section 1

"(1) It is [an offence] for a man to rape a woman.

(2) A man who induces a married woman to have sexual intercourse with him by impersonating her husband commits rape."

Sexual Offences (Amendment) Act 1976, section 1(1)

"For the purposes of section 1 of the Sexual Offences Act 1956 . . . a man commits rape if—

(a)   he has unlawful sexual intercourse with a woman who at the time of the intercourse does not consent to it; and
(b)   at that time he knows that she does not consent to the intercourse or he is reckless as to whether she consents to it;

and references to rape in other enactments ... shall be construed accordingly."

[Section 1(2) contains a declaration that one of the matters for consideration by the jury is the existence or otherwise of reasonable grounds for belief in the woman's consent; see *D.P.P.* v. *Morgan, ante,* p. 142].

Notes

1. The word "unlawful" in section 1(1)(a) above has been held to be surplusage. Marital intercourse can constitute rape: see *R.* v. *R., post,* p. 640.
2. On the question of what is consent in offences against the person generally, see *ante,* p. 617. As to rape, see next case.

R. v. Olugboja
[1982] Q.B. 320
Court of Appeal

L raped V., and then took her companion K into an adjoining room in order to rape her. L's companion O told V. that he was going to have intercourse with her and asked her to remove her trousers, which she did because she was frightened. She did not struggle or resist when O had intercourse with her. O was convicted of rape and appealed.

DUNN L.J. delivering the judgment of the court: The question of law raised by this appeal is whether to constitute the offence of rape it is necessary for the consent of the victim of sexual intercourse to be vitiated by force, the fear of force or fraud, or whether it is sufficient to prove that in fact the victim did not consent. The offence of rape was defined for the first time by statute, in 1976. [His Lordship read section 1(1) of the Sexual Offences (Amendment) Act 1976]. In this appeal it is not disputed that the appellant had sexual intercourse with Jayne. The only questions for the jury were whether she had consented, and if she had not whether the appellant knew she had not or was reckless whether she consented or not. In this appeal we are only concerned with the *actus reus* and not with the *mens rea* of the appellant. [He summarised the evidence].

The judge dealt with the question of consent in his summing up in a number of passages. He said:

"The question of consent is a question of fact for you to decide, approaching it in a commonsense way. You are concerned, are you not, with the field of human sexual behaviour and in particular in this case teenage sexual behaviour? You have to consider it in a commonsense way applying your own experience or knowledge of human nature and your knowledge of the ways of the world."

Later he said: "Sometimes a woman gives in and submits out of fear or constraint or duress." These directions were quite general in relation to both girls.

In relation to Jayne the judge said:

"You will consider her evidence very carefully and decide whether or not there were any constraints operating on her will, so that you are satisfied that in taking her trousers down, and letting him have sexual intercourse with her, she was not, in fact, consenting to it."

Then the judge said:

"Members of the jury, you are concerned with what was the reason. Was it circumstances in which she was consenting, or was it circumstances in which there was constraint operating on her mind, fear or constraint, so that in doing that, she was doing it without her consent?"

Finally the judge said:

"Let me remind you finally that the defence point out that it is not a case where the girl was struggling or screaming. Unless what was said about intercourse and then going home contained any implied threat in it, no threats were uttered, certainly no threats of force or violence, or anything of that sort. The defence say this girl removed her own trousers and that was in itself an open invitation to sex. That of course depends on why and in what circumstances she removed her trousers. Was it because she was consenting, or was it because she was giving in out of fear or constraint, so that she was removing her own trousers without consent? It is a matter for you to decide."

The appellant was convicted of rape by a majority of eleven to one and sentenced to 30 months' imprisonment.

Counsel for the appellant, in a series of very able submissions, said that these statements by the judge constituted a misdirection. She submitted that the statutory definition of rape introduced by the 1976 amendment into section 1 of the Sexual Offences Act 1956 was declaratory only, and had not changed the common law whereby the type of threat that vitiates consent is limited to threats of violence either to the victim or as in duress to some close or near relative. She relied in support of that submission on a number of cases going back to the middle of the last century, *R. v. Hallett* (1841) 9 C. & P. 748, *R. v. Day* (1841) 9 C. & P. 722, *R. v. Wright* (1866) 4 F. & F. 967, and *R. v. Mayers* (1872) 12 Cox C.C. 311 and by analogy *Latter v. Braddell* (*ante*, p. 619) where a domestic servant whose mistress had insisted that she be examined for pregnancy by a doctor was held to have no cause of action in assault because, although she was tearful and did not wish to be examined, no force or violence or threat had been used to persuade her to undergo the examination.

Counsel for the appellant also relied on two more recent cases, *R. v. Howard* [1965] 3 All E.R. 684, and *R. v. Lang* (1975) 62 Cr.App.R. 50, where it was held that sexual intercourse after submission induced by force or the threat of force was the classic example of rape. She also relied on a case decided by Winn J., reported in The Times newspaper as a news item on 19th December 1961, where the judge appears to have withdrawn from the jury a case where a police constable was charged with rape on the basis that he had threatened the victim that he would report her for an offence unless she had sexual intercourse with him, which she did. Counsel submitted that in that case there was certainly a constraint on the will of the victim but she did not submit by reason of force or the threat of force.

Counsel for the appellant accepted that submission by the victim did not necessarily involve consent, but contended that the submission must be induced because of fear of violence: see *R. v. Day* (1841) 9 C. & P. 722. She submitted that moral or economic pressure or even blackmail causing a woman to submit to sexual intercourse could never be enough to found a charge of rape. Otherwise, she said, the film producer who induced an actress to have sexual intercourse by telling her she would not get a part in his new film if she did not, or the man who induced a woman to have sexual intercourse by telling her that if she did not he would tell her fiancé that she had been a prostitute, would be guilty of rape.

She submitted that those classes of case would constitute offences under section 2 of the 1956 Act. That section provides:

"(1) It is an offence for a person to procure a woman, by threats of intimidation, to have unlawful sexual intercourse in any part of the world ... "

Although the section was first enacted in the Criminal Law Amendment Act 1885 and was probably intended to deal with a person who procured a woman to have sexual intercourse with a third party, it also applies to a man who causes a woman to have sexual intercourse with himself. Although the section is little used, counsel for the appellant said that it is apt to cover cases of threats and intimidation falling short of threats of death or violence. The maximum penalty under the section is two years' imprisonment as compared with life imprisonment for rape. It is right that the law should confine rape to the most serious cases and that lesser offences should be dealt with under section 2.

Counsel for the appellant submitted that just as the law limits the circumstances in which any person may say he has acted involuntarily [due] to duress, which involves threats of death or violence to that person or a close relative, so it is consistent that the common law has limited the circumstances in which a woman who has had sexual intercourse may say that the act was not consensual.

Counsel submitted finally that to say, as the judge did, that any constraint on Jayne's will could negative consent constituted a misdirection. The word "constraint" includes moral as well as physical pressure and moral pressure is not enough. Even to tell a girl that she would not be taken home until she had sexual intercourse, in the absence of any threat of violence expressed or implied, would not vitiate her consent.

The definition of rape imported into the 1956 Act by the 1976 amending Act makes no mention of force, fear or fraud. It simply defines rape as being unlawful sexual intercourse with a woman who at the time of the intercourse does not consent to it. The 1976 Act by its long title is described as "An Act to amend the law relating to rape." Is it a true amending Act or is it merely declaratory of the common law? To answer that question it is necessary to look at the history of the legislation.

D.P.P. v. *Morgan* [1976] A.C 182 (*ante*, p. 142) stated the law of rape as it then stood. Their Lordships were primarily concerned with the necessary mens rea of the offence. They were not concerned with, nor did they consider, the actus reus. But there is a passage in the speech of Lord Hailsham which appears to indicate that he was accepting the common law definition of rape, that is to say sexual intercourse by force, fear or fraud (see [1976] A.C. 182 at 210).

Following the decision in *Morgan* an advisory group on the law of rape was set up under Heilbron J. The group reported to the Home Secretary on 14th November 1975 (Cmnd. 6352). Like the House of Lords in *Morgan* they were principally concerned in the material part of the report with the mens rea of the offence. However in a section headed "The Crime of Rape" there appear the following paragraphs:

"18. There is no modern definition of the crime of rape and although it is an offence under section 1 of the Sexual Offences Act 1956, the statute contains no attempt at a definition. The traditional common law definition, derived from a 17th Century writer (1 Hale 627 ff. 1 East P.C. 434) and still in use, is that rape consists in having unlawful sexual intercourse with a woman without her consent, by force, fear or fraud.

"19. This definition can be misleading, since the essence of the crime consists in having sexual intercourse with a woman without her consent and it is, therefore, rape to have intercourse with a woman who is asleep or with one who unwillingly submits without a struggle.

"20. As Smith and Hogan point out in their text book on the Criminal Law (3rd Edn., 1973, p. 326): 'Earlier authorities emphasised the use of force; but it is now clear that lack of consent is the crux of the matter and this may exist though no force is used. The test is not "was the act against her will?" but "was it without her consent?" '

"21. It is, therefore, wrong to assume that the woman must show signs of injury or that she must always physically resist before there can be a conviction for rape. We have found this erroneous assumption held by some and therefore hope that our recommendations will go some way to dispel it.

"22. The *actus reus* in rape, which the prosecution must establish for a conviction consists of (a) unlawful sexual intercourse and (b) absence of the woman's consent."

Paragraph 84 of the report is in these terms:

"Finally, as rape is a crime which is still without statutory definition, the lack of which has caused certain difficulties, we think that this legislation should contain a comprehensive definition of the offence which would emphasise that lack of consent (and not violence) is the crux of the matter."

That paragraph was incorporated into a recommendation for what was described as "declaratory legislation."

In its working paper on sexual offences of October 1980, the Criminal Law Revision Committee, under the heading "Consent in Rape" stated:

"20. Until the second half of the nineteenth century, the courts seem to have had no problems about what amounted to consent. If a woman was made by the use of force to have sexual intercourse, or submitted in fear under a threat of force, she was adjudged to have been raped. She had not consented to the intercourse. This is still the law and, in our opinion, should continue to be the law. In the ordinary case of rape there has been force or the threat of force. Where sexual intercourse is procured by fraud, there is under section 3 of the Act of 1956 a special offence which we propose should continue. The judges and Parliament have intervened, in a few situations, to interpret the notion of absence of consent so as to extend the law of rape to what are basically cases of fraud. In paragraphs 21 to 25 we consider whether the law in this respect should be altered. . . .

"24. A majority of us are of the opinion that the offence of rape should not apply when a woman has knowingly consented to the defendant putting his penis into her vagina. Mistake as to his identity, whether as a husband or otherwise, or as to the purpose for which the penetration has been made should be irrelevant. Nor should the use of threats or other intimidation short of threats of force amount to rape. Most of us are of the opinion that the distinctions drawn in the cases cannot bear the weight they have been made to carry, and we doubt whether many laymen would regard the examples we have given as cases of rape. In particular, we consider that the distress which the victim of such frauds or threats may suffer is, though a serious matter, not really comparable with the fear and shock that often accompanies true rape. Most of us therefore take the view that inducing sexual intercourse by fraud or threats (other than threats of force) or other intimidation should be criminal and attract heavy penalties but should not be forms of rape.

"25. A minority of our members consider that the present is not the right time in which to narrow the law of rape. For over 100 years now the crucial question to be asked in rape cases has been not whether the act was against the woman's will but whether it was without her consent. . . .

Those paragraphs indicate that the committee were of the opinion that under the law as it now stands consent may not only be vitiated by force or threats of force but that inducing sexual intercourse by fraud or threats (other than threats of force) or other intimidation may be sufficient to negative consent and constitute rape.

We have not been persuaded by counsel for the appellant that the position at common law before 1976 was different from that stated in the report of the advisory group, but whatever it may have been we think that Parliament must have accepted the group's recommendation in para. 84 of their report and incorporated it in the 1976 Act. Accordingly in so far as the actus reus is concerned, the question now is simply: at the time of the sexual intercourse did the woman consent to it? It is not necessary for the prosecution to prove that what might otherwise appear to have been consent was in reality merely submission induced by force, fear or fraud, although one or more of these factors will no doubt be present in the majority of cases of rape.

We do not agree, as was suggested by counsel for the appellant, that once this is fully realised there will be a large increase in prosecutions for rape. Nor, on the other hand, do we agree with the submission of counsel for the Crown that it is sufficient for a trial judge merely to leave the issue of consent to a jury in a similar way to that in which the issue of dishonesty is left in trials for offences under the Theft Act 1968. In such cases it is sufficient to direct the jury that "dishonest" is an easily understood English word and it is for them to say whether a particular transaction is properly so described or not. Although "consent" is an equally common word, it covers a wide range of states of mind in the context of intercourse between a man and a woman, ranging from actual desire on the one hand to reluctant acquiescence on the other. We do not think that the issue of consent should be left to a jury without some further direction. What this should be will depend on the circumstances of each case. The jury will have been reminded of the burden and standard of proof required to establish each ingredient, including lack of consent, of the offence. They should be directed that consent, or the absence of it, is to be given its ordinary meaning and if need be, by way of example, that there is a difference between consent and submission; every consent involves a submission, but it by no means follows that a mere submission involves consent: see *R.* v. *Day* (1841) 9 C. & P. 722 at 724, per Coleridge J. In the majority of cases, where the allegation is that the intercourse was had by force or the fear of force, such a direction coupled with specific references to and comments on the evidence relevant to the absence of real consent will clearly suffice. In the less common type of case where intercourse takes place after threats not involving violence or the fear of it, as in the examples given by counsel for the appellant, to which we have referred earlier in this judgment, we think that an appropriate direction to a jury will have to be fuller. They should be directed to concentrate on the state of mind of the victim immediately before the act of sexual intercourse, having regard to all the relevant circumstances, and in particular the events leading up to the act, and her reaction to them showing their impact on her mind. Apparent acquiescence after penetration does not necessarily involve consent, which must have occurred before the act takes place. In addition to the general direction about consent which we have outlined, the jury will probably be helped in such cases by being reminded that in this context consent does comprehend the wide spectrum of states of mind to which we earlier referred, and that the dividing line in such circumstances between real consent on the one hand and mere submission on the other may not be easy to draw. Where it is to be drawn in a given case is for the jury to decide, applying their combined good sense, experience and knowledge of human nature and modern behaviour to all the relevant facts of that case.

Looked at in this way we find no misdirection by the judge in this case. We think it would have been better not to have used the word "constraint" in explaining the offence, but whenever he used it the judge linked it with the word "fear," so that in the context the word seems to us to be unexceptional.

Appeal dismissed

Notes

1. On the effect of *fraud* on consent in rape, see the authorities discussed by Stephen J. in *R. v. Clarence, ante,* p. 617, and the following extract from *Papadimitropoulos v. R.* (1957) 98 C.L.R. 249 (High Court of Australia), a case of a man securing intercourse with a woman after pretending to go through a valid ceremony of marriage with her:

"It must be noted that in considering whether an apparent consent is unreal it is the mistake or misapprehension that makes it so. It is not the fraud producing the mistake which is material so much as the mistake itself. But if the mistake or misapprehension is not produced by the fraud of the man, there is logically room for the possibility that he was unaware of the woman's mistake so that a question of his *mens rea* may arise. So in *Lambert,* Cussen J., 'It is plain that, though in these cases the question of consent or non-consent is primarily referable to the mind of the woman, if she has really a mind, yet the mind of the man is also affected by the facts which indicate want of consent or possible want of capacity to consent' [(1919) V.L.R. at 213]. For that reason it is easy to understand why the stress has been on the fraud. But that stress tends to distract the attention from the essential inquiry, namely, whether the consent is no consent because it is not directed to the nature and character of the act. The identity of the man and the character of the physical act that is done or proposed seem now clearly to be regarded as forming part of the nature and character of the act to which the woman's consent is directed. That accords with the principles governing mistake vitiating apparent manifestations of will in other chapters of the law.

In the present case the decision of the majority of the Full Court extends this conception beyond the identity of the physical act and the immediate conditions affecting its nature to an antecedent cause—the existence of a valid marriage. In the history of bigamy that has never been done. The most heartless bigamist has not been considered guilty of rape. Mock marriages are no new thing. Before the Hardwicke Marriage Act it was a fraud easily devised and readily carried out. But there is no reported instance of an indictment for rape based on the fraudulent character of the ceremony. No indictment of rape was founded on such a fraud. Rape, as a capital felony, was defined with exactness, and although there has been some extension over the centuries in the ambit of the crime, it is quite wrong to bring within its operation forms of evil conduct because they wear some analogy to aspects of the crime and deserve punishment. The judgment of the majority of the Full Court of the Supreme Court goes upon the moral differences between marital intercourse and sexual relations without marriage. The difference is indeed so radical that it is apt to draw the mind away from the real question which is carnal knowledge without consent. It may well be true that the woman in the present case never intended to consent to the latter relationship. But, as was said before, the key to such a case as the present lies in remembering that it is the penetration of the woman's body without her consent to such penetration that makes the felony. The capital felony was not directed to fraudulent conduct inducing her consent. Frauds of that kind must be punished under other heads of the criminal law or not at all; they are not rape. To say that in the present case the facts which the jury must be taken to have found amount to wicked and heartless conduct on the part of the applicant is not enough to establish that he committed rape. To say that in having intercourse with him she supposed that she was concerned in a perfectly moral act is not to say that the intercourse was without her consent. To return to the central point; rape is carnal knowledge of a woman without her consent; carnal knowledge is the physical fact of penetration; it is the consent to that which is in question; such a consent demands a perception as to what is about to take place, as to the identity of the man and the character of what he is doing. But once the consent is comprehending and actual the inducing causes cannot destroy its reality and leave the man guilty of rape ... "

2. Personation of husband was declared to be rape by Criminal Law Amendment Act 1885, and see now section 1(2) of the Sexual Offences Act 1954, *ante*, p. 632.

Question

Does the decision in *R. v. Olugboja* affect the meaning of fraud in rape?

Smith, Comment on Olugboja [1981] Crim.L.R. 718

"The observation that the jury should be, "if need be, told the difference between consent and submission," conceals a great difficulty, namely, what is the difference between consent and submission? A person submits when he or she yields, or gives in, to pressure of some kind. A woman may reluctantly submit to sexual intercourse only because the man threatens that he will break off their relationship if she does not. Such a case is very far removed from rape but it seems to be one of submission. At the other extreme, a woman may submit because the man is holding a knife at her throat. This is plainly rape. The distinction cannot, however, be justified by a distinction between consent and submission. In both cases the woman yields because a threat is made. Submission may indeed be induced by a promise. The woman gives in only because the man promises that he will marry her if she does so. No one would say that is rape if the man intends to keep the promise (and it is clearly not rape in law even if he does not) but is it not a case of submission? . . .

It is probable that the Sexual Offences (Amendment) Act 1976 has not changed the definition of rape in this respect (or, indeed, in the light of *Morgan* [1976] A.C. 182, in any other respect). The definition commonly cited before the Act was that "Rape consists in having sexual intercourse with a woman without her consent by force, fear or fraud," following Hale and East. The definition was not entirely accurate because it was clear that a man might be guilty of rape where there was no force, fear or fraud—as for example where he had intercourse with a sleeping or insensible woman. Moreover, not all fraud was enough to negative consent. Even the bigamist who induced a woman to marry him by representing that he was single was not guilty of rape and, *a fortiori*, less fundamental representations would not found a charge of rape. "Fear" also had to be given a limited meaning—the complainant's fear of losing her job or the attentions of her lover was not enough.

It is very doubtful if the bounds of the crime of rape can be satisfactorily drawn by a distinction between consent and submission. It is probably a matter of policy that certain types of threat or fraud have been considered to negative consent in law and, if so, it seems right that that policy should continue as before, notwithstanding the statutory definition of rape in the 1976 Act. To allow the jury to decide on the basis of a distinction between consent and submission would seem to be dangerously vague and judicial explanations of such an uncertain distinction would produce problems of their own."

Notes

1. In its Working Paper, § 24 (quoted by Dunn L.J. *ante*, p. 636), the C.L.R.C. thought that cases of fraud should be entirely excluded from rape; but in their final report, *Sexual Offences*, Cmnd. 9213, they changed their minds on this: § 2.24. However, to counter the imprecision which they thought had been imported into the law by *R.* v. *Olugboja*, the Committee propose that the cases where intercourse induced by fraud is rape should be expressly and exhaustively stated by statute, *viz.* fraud as to the nature of the act and impersonation of a husband or any other man: § 2.25. Similarly, statute should provide that threats, explicit or implicit, against the woman or anyone else, of immediate force, but no other threats, should be capable of initiating consent: § 2.29. Other fraud and other threats should continue to be dealt with under section 3 and section 2 of the Sexual Offences Act 1956, as to which see *post*, p. 644.

For discussion and criticism of these proposals, see Temkin, *Rape and the Legal Process* (1987) pp. 63–71. The gist of the proposals is embodied in Draft Criminal Code Bill, cl. 89(2), *post*, p. 644.

2. At common law, it was at one time impossible for a husband to be convicted of personally raping his wife. (But see *R.* v. *Cogan & Leak*, *ante*, p. 369.) More recent decisions allowed some cases where such a conviction was possible: see *R.* v. *Steele* (1977) 65 Cr.App.R. 22 (C.A.). The whole doctrine of husband's immunity was completely abolished by the House of Lords in *R.* v. *R.* [1992] A.C. 599.

Mens Rea. See *D.P.P.* v. *Morgan, ante,* p. 142, and next case.

R. v. Satnam and Kewel
(1983) 78 Cr.App.R. 149
Court of Appeal

S. & K. were convicted of rape and appealed on the ground of misdirection as to the meaning of "reckless."

BRISTOW J. (delivering the judgment of the court): The judge rightly pointed out that there was no dispute that sexual intercourse had in fact taken place. He went on to deal impeccably with the elements of consent by the girl and the knowledge of the appellants which was relevant to the counts on which they were acquitted. He then turned to the element of recklessness and said this: "Members of the jury, a person is reckless in this context: if there was an obvious reason, in the circumstances as the jury find them to be, if there was an obvious reason that the girl was not in fact willing to have sexual intercourse, that is to say, obvious to every ordinary observer, and the defendant either did not apply his mind to that reason at all, for whatever reason, or, applied his mind to the reason, but carried on having sexual intercourse with her, or trying to, that is recklessness." He then repeated that direction and gave no further direction as to the necessary elements to be proved in the crime of reckless rape.

Two grounds of appeal were relied on in this Court. (1) That the judge should have directed the jury that a genuine though mistaken belief that the girl was consenting offered a defence to a charge of reckless rape; (2) that the judge erred in referring to an "ordinary observer" in his direction as to recklessness, and that he should have directed the jury that it was necessary to prove that each appellant was actually aware of the possibility that the girl was not consenting before they could find him reckless.

So far as the first ground was concerned, it was accepted by Mr. Smith for the Crown that he could not support the summing up in the absence of a direction as to belief. In *R.* v. *Thomas* (1983) 77 Cr.App.R. 63 Lord Lane C.J. said, at p. 65: "In this particular case, the judge should have spelt out in terms that a mistaken belief that the woman was consenting, however unreasonable it may appear to have been, is an answer to the charge, and that it is for the prosecution to eliminate the possibility of such a mistake if they are to succeed. He should then have gone on to deal with the matters set out in section 1(2) of the 1976 Act. As it was the jury were left without any guidance on the matter." The same situation arose here. The jury were left without any guidance on the matter of belief and on that ground alone we would allow the appeal.

We turn now to consider the second ground, *i.e.* the direction as to recklessness. Strictly it may be said that this point has already been decided in *R.* v. *Bashir* (1983) 77 Cr.App.R. 59, 62 where Watkins L.J. said: "As recently as the fifth of this month, Lord Lane C.J. in *Thomas* restated the definition of 'reckless' as applied to the offence of rape. He said (1983) 77 Cr.App.R. 63, 66: 'A man is reckless if either he was indifferent and gave no thought to the possibility that the woman might not be consenting, in circumstances where, if any thought had been given to the matter, it would have been obvious that there was a risk she was not, or, he was aware of the possibility that she might not be consenting but nevertheless persisted, regardless of whether she consented or not.' He was in almost exact form repeating the definition of 'reckless' in relation to rape which he had provided in the case of *R. v. Pigg* (1982) 74 Cr.App.R. 352. . . . "

Mr. Tayler on behalf of the appellants submitted, in his able argument, that the use of the word "obvious" in its context in both *R. v. Pigg* and *R. v. Thomas* gives rise to a possible ambiguity. "Obvious" to whom? If it meant obvious to any reasonable person that would introduce an objective test, and Mr. Tayler submitted that the authorities properly understood do not warrant such a conclusion. He invited us in effect to clarify the situation which has developed since *R. v. Caldwell* (*ante*, p. 111) and *R. v. Lawrence* (*ante*, p. 117), as he said that judges up and down the country are now in a state of some confusion as to the state of the law. He submitted that the direction of recklessness in *R. v. Pigg* was in any event *obiter*.

[After quoting from *Elliott* v. *C.*, *ante*, p. 119]. The instant case, unlike *Elliott* is not concerned with the Criminal Damage Act 1971 but with the Sexual Offences (Amendment) Act 1976, and the Court is considering recklessness in the context of rape and not in the context of criminal damage. We feel we are therefore free to review the situation so far as it is governed by relevant authority, and accepting as we do that there is an ambiguity in the suggested direction in *Pigg*, which was in any event *obiter*.

Mr. Tayler took as his starting point *D.P.P. v. Morgan* (*ante*, p. 142), a decision of the House of Lords on the very question of rape, which was not overruled by either *Caldwell* or *Lawrence* and is binding on this Court. Lord Hailsham said at [1976] A.C. 215: "I am content to rest my view of the instant case on the crime of rape by saying that it is my opinion that the prohibited act is and always has been intercourse without consent of the victim and the mental element is and always has been the intention to commit that act, or the equivalent intention of having intercourse willy-nilly not caring whether the victim consents or no. A failure to prove this involves an acquittal because the intent, an essential ingredient, is lacking. It matters not why it is lacking if only it is not there, and in particular it matters not that the intention is lacking only because of a belief not based on reasonable grounds."

In the Report of the Advisory Group on the Law of Rape (The Heilbron Committee) Cmnd. 6352, 1975, the following "Recommendations for declaratory legislation" were made: "81. Notwithstanding our conclusions that *Morgan's* case is right in principle, we nevertheless feel that legislation is required to clarify the law governing intention in rape cases, as it is now settled. We think this for two principal reasons. The first is that it would be possible in future cases to argue that the question of recklessness did not directly arise for decision in *Morgan's* case, in view of the form of the question certified: to avoid possible doubts the ruling on recklessness needs to be put in statutory form. 82. Secondly, it would be unfortunate if a tendency were to arise to say to the jury 'that a belief, however unreasonable, that the woman consented, entitled the accused to acquittal.' Such a phrase might tend to give an undue or misleading emphasis to one aspect only and the law, therefore, should be statutorily restated in a fuller form which would obviate the use of those words. 83. We think that there would be advantage if this matter could also be dealt with by a statutory provision which would—(i) declare that (in cases where the question of belief is raised) the issue which the jury have to consider is whether the accused at the time when sexual intercourse took place believed that she was consenting, and (ii) make it clear that, while there is no requirement of law that such a belief must be based on reasonable grounds, the presence or absence of such grounds is a relevant consideration to which the jury should have regard, in conjunction with all other evidence, in considering whether the accused genuinely had such a belief."

There followed the Sexual Offences (Amendment) Act 1976, section 1.

[His Lordship read the section]. We think that in enacting those provisions Parliament must have accepted the recommendations of the Heilbron Committee, so that the provisions are declaratory of the existing law as stated in *D.P.P.* v. *Morgan.*

Any direction as to the definition of rape should therefore be based upon section 1 of the 1976 Act and upon *D.P.P.* v. *Morgan*, without regard to *R.* v. *Caldwell* or *R.* v. *Lawrence*, which were concerned with recklessness in a different context and under a different statute.

The word "reckless" in relation to rape involves a different concept to its use in relation to malicious damage or, indeed, in relation to offences against the person. In the latter cases the foreseeability, or possible foreseeability, is as to the consequences of the criminal act. In the case of rape the foreseeability is as to the state of mind of the victim.

A practical definition of recklessness in sexual offences was given in *R.* v. *Kimber* (*ante*, p. 153), where the Court was concerned with how far an honest belief in consent constituted a defence to a charge of indecent assault. The defendant said in evidence: "I was not really interested in Betty's" (the victim's) "feelings at all." Lawton L.J. said at [1983] 1 W.L.R. 1123: "We have already set out in this judgment the admissions which he is alleged to have made to the police and relevant parts of his own evidence. In our judgment a reasonable jury would inevitably have decided that he had no honest belief that Betty was consenting. His own evidence showed that his attitude to her was one of indifference to her feelings and wishes. This state of mind is aptly described in the colloquial expression, 'couldn't care less.' In law this is recklessness."

In summing-up a case of rape which involves the issue of consent, the judge should, in dealing with the state of mind of the defendant, first of all direct the jury that before they could convict of rape the Crown had to prove either that the defendant knew the woman did not want to have sexual intercourse, or was reckless as to whether she wanted to or not. If they were sure he knew she did not want to they should find him guilty of rape knowing there to be no consent. If they were not sure about that, then they would find him not guilty of such rape and should go on to consider reckless rape. If they thought he might genuinely have believed that she did want to, even though he was mistaken in his belief, they would find him not guilty. In considering whether his belief was genuine, they should take into account all the relevant circumstances (which could at that point be summarised) and ask themselves whether, in the light of those circumstances, he had reasonable grounds for such a belief. If, after considering those circumstances, they were sure he had no genuine belief that she wanted to, they would find him guilty. If they came to the conclusion that he could not care less whether she wanted to or not, but pressed on regardless, then he would have been reckless and could not have believed that she wanted to, and they would find him guilty of reckless rape.

Appeals allowed: convictions of rape quashed

Questions

Is the recklessness described above the same as *Cunningham* recklessness? See *ante*, p. 109.

2. How will the model summing up suggested by Bristow J. affect the case of the defendant who never gave a thought to the

question of consent? See the Law Commission's Commentary on the Draft Code, para. 15.12, below.

Draft Criminal Code Bill, clause 89

"Rape and related offences

1. A man is guilty of rape if he has sexual intercourse with a woman without her consent and—

(a) he knows that she is not consenting; or

(b) he is aware that she may not be, or does not believe that she is consenting.

2. For the purposes of the section a woman shall be treated as not consenting to sexual intercourse if she consents to it—

(a) because a threat, express or implied, has been made to use force against her or another if she does not consent and she believes that, if she does not consent, the threat will be carried out immediately or before she can free herself from it: or

(b) because she has been deceived as to—

    (i) the nature of the act; or

    (ii) the identity of the man."

Law Com. No. 177: Commentary on Draft Criminal Code Bill

"Para. 15.12. It is arguable that any man who is aware that a woman might not be consenting does not believe that she is consenting so that the cases in recommendation (b) [in clause 1(i)] could be covered by a provision that a man is guilty of rape if he does not believe that the woman is consenting. Indeed, such a provision covers everything in recommendation (a) as well ... We ... think it is useful to state expressly that awareness is a sufficient mental element. 'Is aware' and 'does not believe' are coupled in the same paragraph because they are both appropriate to describe reckless rape but the clause avoids the use of the word 'reckless'. There is no requirement that it be unreasonable for a man who is aware that a woman is not consenting, or does not believe that she is consenting, to take the risk that the woman may not be [see clause 18(1) on recklessness, *ante*, p. 139], the premise being that it is never reasonable to take that risk."

Note

See discussion in Mistake, *ante*, p. 142.

ii. Other Offences Involving Sexual Intercourse

Sexual Offences Act 1956

"2.—(1) It is an offence for a person to procure a woman, by threats or intimidation, to have unlawful sexual intercourse in any part of the world.

3.—(1) It is an offence for a person to procure a woman, by false pretences or false representations, to have unlawful sexual intercourse in any part of the world.

5. It is felony for a man to have unlawful sexual intercourse with a girl under the age of thirteen.

6.—(1) It is an offence, subject to the exceptions mentioned in this section, for a man to have unlawful sexual intercourse with a girl under the age of sixteen.

(3) A man is not guilty of an offence under this section because he has unlawful sexual intercourse with a girl under the age of sixteen, if he is under the age of twenty-four and has not previously been charged with a like offence, and he believes her to be of the age of sixteen or over and has reasonable cause for the belief.

In this subsection, 'a like offence' means an offence under this section or an attempt to commit one, or an offence under paragraph (1) of section five of the Criminal Law Amendment Act, 1885 (the provision replaced for England and Wales by this section).

7.—(1) It is an offence, subject to the exception mentioned in this section, for a man to have unlawful sexual intercourse with a woman who is a defective.

(2) A man is not guilty of an offence under this section because he has unlawful sexual intercourse with a woman if he does not know and has no reason to suspect her to be a defective.

8. [Repealed]

9.—(1) It is an offence, subject to the exception mentioned in this section, for a person to procure a woman who is a defective to have unlawful sexual intercourse in any part of the world.

(2) A person is not guilty of an offence under this section because he procures a defective to have unlawful sexual intercourse, if he does not know and has no reason to suspect her to be a defective."

Note

For the relationship between these offences and rape under section 1, see next case.

R. v. Williams
[1923] 1 K.B. 340
Court of Criminal Appeal

W., a singing master, had sexual intercourse with a pupil aged 16 by pretending to her that it was a method of training her voice. The girl made no resistance, as she believed him and did not know that he was having sexual intercourse with her. He was convicted of rape and appealed.

LORD HEWART C.J.: Mr. Gorst has today taken one point and one point only on behalf of the appellant—namely, that in view of the evidence the appellant ought not to have been convicted of the crime of rape. In support of that argument the attention of the court has been directed to *R. v. O'Shay* (1898) 19 Cox 76, and to the provisions of the Criminal Law Amendment Act, 1885. There is no doubt that before the passing of the Act of 1885 a man who by fraudulent pretence succeeded in obtaining sexual intercourse with a woman might be guilty of rape. For example, in *R. v. Case* (1850) 4 Cox 220, a medical practitioner had sexual connection with a girl of fourteen years of age upon the pretence that he was treating her medically and the girl made no resistance owing to a bona fide belief that she was being medically treated. It was held that he was properly convicted of an assault and might have been convicted of rape. In *R. v.*

Flattery (1877) 2 Q.B.D. 410 the same principle was affirmed. But it has been argued that the position has been changed by the passing of the Criminal Law Amendment Act, 1885. Mr. Gorst, when the question was specifically put to him, did not contend that that Act would prevent the laying of an indictment for rape in such a case as *R.* v. *Flattery*, but he said that that Act made an indictment for rape impossible in the present case. The argument is based upon the provisions of section 3, subsection (2), of the Act of 1885, which provides that "any person who ... by false pretences or false representations procures any woman or girl, not being a common prostitute or of known immoral character, to have any unlawful carnal connection, either within or without the Queen's dominions ... shall be guilty of a misdemeanour ... " It is obvious that those words go beyond a case of rape. It is easy to imagine a case which would come within the comprehensive scope of those words and yet fail to come within the charge of rape. No doubt in *R.* v. *O'Shay*, Ridley J. did appear to say that after the passing of Criminal Law Amendment Act *R.* v. *Flattery* was no longer law. ... It is, however, quite clear when one looks at the report of the case that the attention of the judge was not directed to section 16 of the Act of 1885. That section makes it plain that the provisions of the statute were not in the least intended to interfere with the liability of a person for an offence punishable at common law, but were intended to supplement the offences punishable at common law. In the opinion of this court the decision in *R.* v. *O'Shay* was given under a misapprehension.

Reference has been made in the course of the argument to *R.* v. *Dicken* (1877) 14 Cox 8, which was tried at the Stafford Assizes in 1877. In that case a man was charged with rape upon a girl above the age of twelve and under the age of thirteen years. Mr. C. J. Darling (as he then was) argued that the prisoner could not be convicted of felony. He said that the prisoner "was charged with rape. That offence consisted of his unlawfully and carnally knowing the girl against her will, *i.e.* without her consent. But such an offence was now defined in 38 & 39 Vict., c. 94, section 4, and thereby declared to be a misdemeanour. Consequently, with respect to girls between the age of twelve and thirteen the earlier statutes making that offence a felony were repealed." That argument depended upon the words in the statute: "whether with or without her consent." Mellor J., who was the judge trying the case, said: "The carnal abuse of children having excited the attention of the legislature, they have been specially protected by Acts of Parliament. 24 & 25 Vict., c. 100, section 51, enacted that "Whosoever shall unlawfully and carnally know and abuse any girl being above the age of ten years and under the age of twelve years, shall be guilty of a misdemeanour." Under this provision an offender was punishable, whether the girl did or did not consent to his act. In 1875 it was thought desirable that further protection should be given to young girls, and the limit of ten years was extended, by 38 & 39 Vict., c. 94, section 4, declaring that 'Whosoever shall unlawfully and carnally know and abuse any girl being above the age of twelve years, and under the age of thirteen, whether with or without her consent, shall be guilty of misdemeanour.' *Ex abundanti cautela* the words 'whether with or without her consent' were inserted in the later enactment; but, save in respect of the alteration in the age of the girl, the law remained exactly as it was previously—that is to say, if she consented, the prisoner might be convicted of the statutory misdemeanour; if she did not, *a fortiori* he might be so. But if she did not consent, his offence would amount also to a higher crime—the felony—of rape, and he might be indicted and tried for it quite irrespective of the modern statutes throwing special protection around children. The present indictment is for rape, and therefore if the girl consented to the carnal knowledge, the act was not done 'against her will,' and the crime is not made out. It would be preposterous to suppose that Parliament intended to repeal the law of rape as to girls of the very age during which extra statutory protection is cast over them, and I am clearly of the opinion that no such repeal has been effected." ...

In the present case the argument on behalf of the appellant must amount to this—if it be a sound argument at all—that after the passing of the Act of 1885 it is no longer possible to indict a man for rape in such cases as *R. v. Case* and *R. v. Flattery.* That is to say that inasmuch as there is a statute which makes the obtaining of carnal connection with a woman by false pretences a misdemeanour that offence can no longer be rape. That proposition cannot be the law, for the same reason as that stated by Mellor J. in *R. v. Dicken,* even if section 16 of the Act of 1885 be disregarded, but in view of that section the proposition is obviously untenable. Branson J. stated the law in the course of the summing-up in the present case in accurate terms. He said: "The law has laid it down that where a girl's consent is procured by the means which the girl says this prisoner adopted, that is to say, where she is persuaded that what is being done to her is not the ordinary act of sexual intercourse but is some medical or surgical operation in order to give her relief from some disability from which she is suffering, then it is rape although the actual thing that was done was done with her consent, because she never consented to the act of sexual intercourse. She was persuaded to consent to what he did because she thought it was not sexual intercourse and because she thought it was a surgical operation."

Appeal dismissed

Questions

1. In view of the meaning of consent given in *R. v. Olugboja, ante,* p. 633, what scope is there for the offences in sections 2 and 3?

2. Ought there to be a lower limit below which threats inducing intercourse are insufficient for the offence in section 2? If so, at what point should the line be drawn?

3. Is a bigamist necessarily guilty of an offence under section 3 if he has intercourse with his deluded "wife"?

4. While Alan is having consensual intercourse with Betty, aged 15, Cora, aged 15, acts as lookout to warn them of approaching strangers. Are Betty and Cora guilty as accessories to an offence under section 6? See *R. v. Tyrrell, ante,* p. 403? Are any of the three guilty of conspiracy to commit the offence in section 6? See section 2 of the Criminal Law Act 1977, *ante,* p. 460.

iii. Indecent Assault

Sexual Offences Act 1956

"**14.**—(1) It is an offence, subject to the exception mentioned in subsection (3) of this section, for a person to make an indecent assault on a woman.

(2) A girl under the age of sixteen cannot in law give any consent which would prevent an act being an assault for the purposes of this section.

(3) Where a marriage is invalid under section two of the Marriage Act, 1949, or section one of the Age of Marriage Act, 1929 (the wife being a girl under the age of sixteen), the invalidity does not make the husband guilty of any offence under this section by reason of her incapacity to consent while under that age, if he believes her to be his wife and has reasonable cause for the belief.

(4) A woman who is a defective cannot in law give any consent which would prevent an act being an assault for the purposes of this section, but a person is only to be treated as guilty of an indecent assault on a defective by reason of that incapacity to consent, if that person knew or had reason to suspect her to be a defective.

15.—(1) It is an offence for a person to make an indecent assault on a man.

(2) A boy under the age of sixteen cannot in law give any consent which would prevent an act being an assault for the purposes of this section.

(3) A man who is a defective cannot in law give any consent which would prevent an act being an assault for the purposes of this section, but a person is only to be treated as guilty of an indecent assault on a defective by reason of that incapacity to consent, if that person knew or had reason to suspect him to be a defective."

Notes

1. A maximum penalty of 10 years' imprisonment attaches to both of these offences: Schedule 2, as amended by section 3(3) of the Sexual Offences Act 1985.

2. Indecent assault is used where for some reason a charge involving sexual intercourse is inapplicable, *e.g.* where the accused is a boy under 14, or where a man under 23 has the statutory defence of reasonable belief that a girl under 16 is over that age: see section 6(3), *ante*, p. 645.

3. Both offences may be committed by a woman, and if a woman has sexual intercourse with a boy under 16, she is guilty of indecently assaulting him, at any rate if she does anything active which causes her body to come into contact with his: *R.* v. *Hare* [1934] 1 K.B. 354; *Faulkner* v. *Talbot* [1981] 3 All E.R. 468 (D.C.) As for when she remains completely passive, see next note.

4. There must be an assault, from which it follows that genuine consent by the victim may be a complete defence: see *ante*, p. 595. Both sections provide that a person who is under 16 or a defective cannot in law consent; but if D. remains passive and allows V. to touch his or her body, this cannot be an assault by D., whatever the age of V: see *Fairclough* v. *Whipp*, *ante*, p. 584. It may be an offence under the Indecency with Children Act 1960, if V. is under 14.

5. The assault must be indecent. There has been controversy over whether the assault must be objectively indecent, or whether a colourless act is indecent if D.'s motive for the assault is the obtaining of sexual gratification. For a summary of many authorities in this country and in other parts of the Commonwealth, see A. N. Mackesy, "The Criminal Law and the Woman Seducer" [1956] Crim.L.R. 529–542. But see next case.

R. v. Court
[1988] 2 All E.R. 221
House of Lords

D., a shop assistant, pulled a 12-year-old girl visitor to the shop across his knees, and smacked her 12 times on the buttocks outside her shorts for no apparent reason. Asked by the police why he had done so, he said "I don't know: buttock fetish." He pleaded guilty to assault, but denied that the assault was indecent and contended that his statement about his "buttock fetish" should be excluded as evidence because it was merely a secret motive which was not communicated to the victim and it could not make indecent an act which was not overtly indecent. The judge having refused to exclude the evidence, D. was convicted of indecent assault and appealed, ultimately to the House of Lords.

LORD ACKNER: ... It is particularly important to bear in mind that the essential basis of the appeal [in the Court of Appeal] was that the judge was wrong to admit the statement about the "buttock fetish" because, so it was contended, it was merely an admission of the appellant's secret motive, which had not been communicated to the victim of the assault and could not therefore make the assault an indecent one. It was argued that the cause of the wrongful admission of this damaging evidence was the judge's direction that the prosecution had to prove that the accused had an indecent intention in doing what he did. It was accordingly submitted by the appellant that no mental element is required with reference to the indecency ingredient of the offence. It was contended before the Court of Appeal, which contention was maintained before your Lordships, "that the mental element required for indecent assault is that required for common assault, namely that the offender intends to use force on the victim, or is reckless as to the infliction of force, without his or her consent."

As to the admissibility of the appellant's statement about the "buttock fetish," it is apparent from the judgment of the Court of Appeal ([1987] Q.B. 156) that the prosecution contended that, given that the circumstances of the assault were such that the jury *could* hold them to be indecent, then the uncommunicated purpose of the appellant should be taken into account by the jury in deciding whether the circumstances were indecent. It is not, however, apparent from the judgment what were the prosecution's submissions with regard to the mental element required for the proof of the offence. Before your Lordships, counsel for the Crown, consistent with his written case, has argued "that no more need be proved than for common assault, namely that the defendant intends to inflict force or the fear of force on the victim, or is reckless thereto, without the victim's consent" subject to the proviso expressed in these terms "that evidence of the defendant's state of mind is admissible in appropriate cases." This is a surprising submission since, not only does it not support the decision of the Court of Appeal, to which I shall refer hereafter but, in addition, the proviso is, for the reasons I give later, quite inconsistent with the substantive submission. ...

After considering [*R. v. Kilbourne* [1972] 3 All E.R. 545, and *R. v. Kimber*, *ante*, p. 153], Ralph Gibson L.J., giving the judgment of the Court of Appeal, said ([1987] Q.B. 156 at 162):

"On any view the submission for the appellant that no mental element is required with reference to indecency is impossible of acceptance having regard not least to *R. v. Kimber*. An indecent assault is an assault committed in circumstances of aggravation. It seems to us that at least it must be proved that the accused intentionally assaulted the victim with knowledge of the indecent circumstances or being reckless as to the existence of them."

As an illustration of the need to establish the accused's "knowledge of the indecent circumstances" the court gave the case of a person who used words which could constitute circumstances of indecency towards the person assaulted, but did so in a foreign language, not knowing that they were indecent, as a result of a malicious trick by a third party. It concluded that even though the words were, and were understood by the victim to be, indecent he could not be convicted of an indecent assault.

Although the Court of Appeal used the phrase "at least it must be proved," its final conclusion was that the essential mental element of an indecent assault was that the accused intentionally assaulted the victim with knowledge of the indecent circumstances or being reckless as to the existence of them. No proof of any further indecent intention was required.

As to the admission of the "buttock fetish" statement, which had stimulated the appeal, the Court of Appeal held that it did not follow from its decision that if evidence of the appellant's purpose or motive exists it must be excluded as irrelevant. Ralph Gibson L.J. said ([1987] Q.B. 156 at 164–165):

"It seems to us that the grabbing of a 12-year-old girl by a 27-year-old man, who placed her in his lap, face down, in order to smack her bottom over her shorts, is likely to vary in the nature of the act as it is done, and as it will seem to the child who suffers it, according to the purposes of the man. It may be the ordinary innocent rough play of an uncle and niece in which nothing indecent obtrudes. If the man is actuated by an indecent motive, it is likely in our view to affect the way in which he takes hold of the child and restrains her and then strikes her. The man may well explain that his secret motive in fact had no effect on his actions. In our view, in the rare case in which the prosecution has available evidence of an admitted secret motive which actuated the accused to commit the particular offence charged, it is open to the prosecution to call that evidence. It was in our view admissible in this case and we see no reason why the judge should have excluded it ... The jury were, as we have said, entitled to assess the nature of the appellant's acts by reference to his proved purpose."

However, in the view of the Court of Appeal the judge should have directed the jury "that the secret motive cannot turn into circumstances of indecency circumstances which without it the jury would not regard as indecent" (see [1987] Q.B. 156 at 165).

The Court of Appeal saw no ground for regarding the verdict as unsafe or unsatisfactory, and accordingly it dismissed the appeal but certified that it involved a point of law of public importance, namely:

"Whether it is correct that on a charge of indecent assault the prosecution must prove:—(a) That the accused intentionally assaulted the victim and (b) that he was aware of the indecent circumstances of what he did, or was reckless as to their existence; but that it is not necessary for the prosecution to prove in addition that the accused had an indecent purpose or intention."

On the hearing of the application for leave to appeal, counsel for both the appellant and the Crown were critical of the judgment of the Court of

Appeal and drew your Lordships' attention to the contrary views of certain well-known and respected academic writers expressed both before and following the decision. However, in granting leave your Lordships observed that the grant of leave should not be interpreted by the appellant as indicating that his prospects of his conviction being quashed were strong.

As previously stated, the appellant maintained his submission made to the Court of Appeal that no mental element is required with reference to indecency. Consistent with his written case counsel rejected the test propounded by the Court of Appeal arguing that "the requirement of proof of knowledge of or recklessness as to the circumstances of indecency is superfluous and confusing." As previously stated, counsel for the Crown adopted the same line, subject to the proviso that in appropriate cases the jury may have regard to the appellant's state of mind at the time of the assault, where such evidence is probative of the true nature of the circumstances accompanying the assault, adopting the very words of the Court of Appeal quoted above that "the jury were . . . entitled to assess the nature of the appellant's acts by reference to his proved purpose."

[His Lordship quoted section 14(1) of the Sexual Offences Act 1956, and dicta from *Sherras* v. *De Rutzen, ante,* p. 184, and *Sweet* v. *Parsley, ante,* p. 190]: It cannot, in my judgment, have been the intention of Parliament that an assault can, by a mere mistake or mischance, be converted into an indecent assault, with all the opprobium which a conviction for such an offence carries. To take one of the less imaginative examples discussed in the course of the arguments, it may be a common occurrence during travel on the London tube during rush hours for a person suddenly to realise belatedly that the train has stopped at the very station where he wishes to alight, without his having taken the wise precaution of getting close to its doors. Such a person may well in his anxiety to get out, rather than be carried on to the next stop, use unnecessary force in pushing his way through his fellow passengers. If he thus came into contact with a woman, then he would be guilty of having assaulted her. If something that he was carrying, such as an umbrella, became caught up, as it might well do, in her dress as he pushed past, thus tearing away her upper clothing, he would in my judgment be guilty only of an assault. He would not be guilty of an indecent assault. The contrary result would appear to be possible if the Court of Appeal's test was applied. It would certainly follow, if the submission made in their cases by counsel both for the appellant and the prosecution were right, that to establish the mental element in the offence of indecent assault no more need to be established than for common assault.

 . . . The judge in assisting the jury in his summing up as to the meaning of an *indecent* assault adopted, inter alia, a definition used by Professor Glanville Williams in *Textbook of Criminal Law* (2nd edn., 1983) p. 231: " 'indecent' " may be defined as 'overtly sexual.' " This is a convenient shorthand expression, since most, but not necessarily all, indecent assaults will be clearly of a sexual nature although they, as in this case, may have only sexual undertones. A simpler way of putting the matter to the jury is to ask them to decide whether "right-minded persons would consider the conduct indecent or not." It is for the jury to decide whether what occurred was so offensive to contemporary standards of modesty and privacy as to be indecent.

It also was common ground before your Lordships, as it was in the Court of Appeal, that, if the circumstances of the assault are *incapable* of being regarded as indecent, then the undisclosed intention of the accused could not make the assault an indecent one. The validity of this proposition is well illustrated by *R.* v. *George* [1956] Crim.L.R. 52. The basis of the prosecution's case was that the defendant on a number of occasions removed a shoe from a girl's foot and that he did so, as indeed he admitted, because it gave him a kind of perverted sexual gratification. Counsel for the prosecution submitted that an assault was indecent if it was committed to gratify an indecent motive in the mind of a defendant, even though there was no overt circumstances of indecency. Streatfeild J. ruled that an assault became indecent only if it was accompanied by circumstances of indecency towards the person alleged to have been assaulted, and that none of the assaults (the removal or attempted removal of the shoes) could possibly amount to an indecent assault.

Again it was common ground that if, as in this case, the assault involved touching the victim it was not necessary to prove that she was aware of the circumstances of indecency or apprehended indecency. An indecent assault can clearly be committed by the touching of someone who is asleep or unconscious.

As to the facts of this case, it is important to bear in mind that at the trial not only did the appellant admit that he was guilty of an assault but his counsel expressly conceded that what had happened *was capable* of amounting to an indecent assault. That concession was repeated in the Court of Appeal and accepted by the court as being a correct concession. Sensibly no attempt was made before your Lordships to withdraw this concession, for the sound reason that the explanation of this unprovoked assault could reveal that the assault was an indecent one, as indeed the girl's father suspected and as the jury so decided.

The assault which the prosecution seek to establish may be of a kind which is inherently indecent. The defendant removes, against her will, a woman's clothing. Such a case, to my mind, raises no problem. Those very facts, *devoid of any explanation*, would give rise to the irresistible inference that the defendant intended to assault his victim in a manner which right-minded persons would clearly think was indecent. Whether he did so for his own personal sexual gratification or because, being a misogynist or for some other reason, he wished to embarrass or humiliate his victim seems to me to be irrelevant. He has failed, ex hypothesi, to show any lawful justification for his indecent conduct. This, of course, was not such a case. The conduct of the appellant in assaulting the girl by spanking her was only *capable* of being an indecent assault. To decide whether or not right-minded persons might think that assault was indecent, the following factors were clearly relevant: the relationship of the defendant to this victim (were they relatives, friends or virtually complete strangers?), how had the defendant come to embark on this conduct and *why* was he behaving in this way? Aided by such material, a jury would be helped to determine the quality of the act, the true nature of the assault and to answer the vital question: were they sure that the defendant not only intended to commit an assault on the girl, but an assault which was indecent; was such an inference irresistible? For the defendant to be liable to be convicted of the offence of indecent assault, where the circumstances of the alleged offence can be given an innocent as well as an indecent interpretation, without the prosecution being obliged to establish that the defendant intended to commit both an assault and an indecent one, seems to me quite unacceptable and not what Parliament intended.

Much reliance was placed by counsel for the appellant on the definition of "indecent assault" in *Beal* v. *Kelley* [1951] 2 All E.R. 763 at 764 as approved by Lord Goddard C.J.: " ... an assault, accompanied with circumstances of indecency on the part of the prisoner." It was submitted to your Lordships that an indecent motive can only become "a circumstance of indecency" if it is communicated to the victim by means of words or gestures at the time of the assault. If the motive is not communicated it is not such a circumstance. However, the definition which Lord Goddard C.J. accepted has not the force of a statute. It was wholly appropriate to the facts of that case, where the defendant had indecently exposed himself to a young boy and, when the boy refused to handle him indecently, he got hold of the boy's arm and pulled him towards himself. In such a case and in many others cited to us the assault in itself was not indecent. It was the combination of the assault with circumstances of indecency that established the constituents of the offence. In the instant case, it is the assault itself, its true nature, an assault for sexual gratification, which was capable of amounting to an indecent assault.

The jury in their question to the judge were concerned with the position of a doctor who carried out an intimate examination of a young girl. Mars-Jones J. dealt with their point succinctly by saying (see [1987] Q.B. 156 at 166):

> "In that situation what is vital is whether the examination was necessary or not. If it wasn't necessary but indulged in by the medical practitioner it would be an indecent assault. But if it was necessary, even though he got sexual gratification out of it, that would not make it an indecent assault."

I entirely agree. If it could be proved by the doctor's admission that the consent of the parent, or if over 16 the patient, was sought and obtained by the doctor falsely representing that the examination was necessary, then, of course, no true consent to the examination had ever been given. The examination would be an assault and an assault which right-minded persons could well consider was an indecent one. I would not expect that it would make any difference to the jury's decision whether the doctor's false representations were motivated by his desire for the sexual gratification which he might achieve from such an examination or because he had some other reason, entirely of his own, unconnected with the medical needs or care of the patient, such as private research, which had caused him to act fraudulently. In either case the assault could be, and I expect would be, considered as so offensive to contemporary standards of modesty or privacy as to be indecent. A jury would therefore be entitled to conclude that he, in both cases, intended to assault the patient and to do so indecently. I can see nothing illogical in such a result. On the contrary, it would indeed be surprising if in such circumstances the only offence that could be properly charged would be that of common assault. No doubt the judge would treat the offence which had been motivated by the indecent motive as the more serious.

Our attention has been drawn to a number of cases, but they do not, except with one exception, focus sharply on the question of the mental element required to be established in this offence. The only exception is *R. v. Pratt* [1984] Crim.L.R. 41. That was a case tried in the Crown Court at Plymouth and presided over by Mr. Clive Nicholls Q.C. sitting as an assistant recorder. The facts were very strange. Two 13-year-old boys were engaged in night fishing when they were suddenly threatened by the defendant with a gun. As each boy was forced to undress, the other was obliged to shine a torch on him. The defendant stood some way from the boys and touched neither of them. He gave evidence that his sole motive in causing the boys thus to expose their private parts was to search for cannabis which he thought the boys had taken from him the previous afternoon. The prosecution submitted that the defendant's evidence could not provide a defence to the charges, since it was only necessary for the prosecution to prove a common assault and, having proved a common assault, for there to be circumstances of indecency. It was not relevant for the defendant's state of mind to be further considered. In short, the prosecution needed only to prove intention or recklessness as to the common assault and the jury could then find if there were circumstances of indecency accompanying the assault. The assistant recorder held that it was necessary for the prosecution to prove an indecent intention and he decided to admit the evidence. Contrary to the view taken by the Court of Appeal, I consider that the decision of the assistant recorder on the facts of the case was right. The defendant was entitled to put before the jury his explanation of his strange conduct in order to contend that the prosecution had not established that he intended to commit an assault which was indecent. If the jury thought that his explanation might be true, they might decide that right-minded persons would not think that what he had done in the circumstances was indecent.

I, therefore, conclude that on a charge of indecent assault the prosecution must not only prove that the accused intentionally assaulted the victim, but that in so doing he intended to commit an indecent assault, *i.e.* an assault which right-minded persons would think was indecent. Accordingly, any evidence which tends to explain the reason for the defendant's conduct, be it his own admission or otherwise, would be relevant to establish whether or not he intended to commit, not only an assault, but an indecent one. The doctor's admissions in the two contrasting examples which I have given would certainly be so relevant. The appellant's admission of "buttock fetish" was clearly such material. It tended to confirm, as indeed did the events leading up to the assault and the appellant's conduct immediately thereafter, that what he did was to satisfy his peculiar sexual appetite. It was additional relevant evidence. It tended to establish the sexual undertones which gave the assault its true cachet.

If, contrary to my view, the Court of Appeal correctly decided that, in addition to establishing the assault, all the prosecution had to do was to establish that the defendant was aware of the indecent circumstances of what he did or was reckless as to their existence, I cannot follow how his uncommunicated motive could have been relevant and therefore, as the Court of Appeal held, admissible evidence. As Professor Glanville Williams has pointed out in "What is an Indecent Assault?" (1987) 137 N.L.J. 870 at 872, since there was no evidence that the appellant did anything other than spank the girl as if he was chastising her, there was no evidential basis for suggesting that his explanation of his conduct was relevant because it was "likely to affect the way in which he takes hold of the child and restrains her and then strikes her." Counsel for the Crown has not sought to uphold the court's reasoning. He submits that in the no doubt rare cases where there is evidence of the accused's state of mind which discloses his motive, purpose or intention such evidence is admissible "as probative of the true nature and circumstances accompanying the assault." He submitted that "the defendant's motive is no less a circumstance of indecency towards the complainant, merely because it is secretive." This submission cannot stand side by side with the contention that no mental element is required to be proved with reference to indecency. If all that has to be proved is the intended assault, the evidence of the accused's state of mind relative to the indecent ingredient of the offence must be wholly irrelevant. However, the resolute determination shown by the Crown before your Lordships to establish the admissibility of such evidence underlines the obvious, that it would be an affront to common sense that if such evidence exists it must be concealed from the jury, who must thus be deprived of the answer to the vital question necessary for the proper evaluation of this accused's behaviour: why did he behave like that?

I would accordingly dismiss the appeal and answer the certified question as follows. On a charge of indecent assault the prosecution must prove (1) that the accused intentionally assaulted the victim, (2) that the assault, or the assault and the circumstances accompanying it, are capable of being considered by right-minded persons as indecent, (3) that the accused intended to commit such an assault as is referred to in (2) above. These requirements, as counsel for the Crown confirmed, should give rise to no difficulty or complication.

I would add that evidence, if any, of the accused's explanation for assaulting the victim, whether or not it reveals an indecent motive, is admissible both to support or to negative that the assault was an indecent one and was so intended by the accused.

LORD GOFF OF CHIEVELEY. ... What then is an indecent assault? The answer is that it is an assault (in the sense I have described) which is indecent. This appears always to have been the law. So in a case which attracted much attention in its time, *R.* v. *Baker* (1875) *The Times*, 31st July, Brett J. directed the jury as follows:

> "The defendant is charged, first, with an assault, and if without any ill-feeling in his mind he laid his hand upon her without her consent it is an assault. But he is charged next under a statute with an indecent assault, and as to that I have no right to tell you what particular act according to law will or will not amount to an indecent assault. The only definition I can give you is that, if a man assaults a woman in such a way that ordinary right-minded men would say it was indecent, then it is an indecent assault. I cannot lay down the law as to what is or is not 'indecent' beyond saying it is what all right-minded men, men of sound and wholesome feelings, would say was indecent."

It has, however, been established that, in considering whether or not an assault is indecent, it is appropriate to have regard not only to the nature of the assault itself, but also to the circumstances in which the assault took place. This was laid down in *Beal* v. *Kelley* [1951] 2 All E.R. 763; and it led Lord Goddard C.J. to describe an indecent assault as an assault which takes place in "circumstances of indecency" (at 764), a phrase which has, I understand, been regularly used in directing juries ever since. The expression could perhaps be said to be more appropriate in cases where the indecency arises from some circumstances apart from the nature of the assault itself; and I myself might have preferred to put the question as being whether the assault, taking into account the surrounding circumstances, would be regarded by ordinary right-thinking people as an indecent assault, the question of indecency being a matter for the jury. But I do not regard this criticism as important, since Lord Goddard C.J.'s expression appears to have created no difficulty in the past.

Does an indecent assault require any mental element different from a common assault? There are, I consider, two matters to be borne in mind. First, the requisite intention on the part of the defendant to commit the relevant act involves, in the case of an indecent assault, that the defendant should have intended to commit any part of that act which rendered the assault indecent. Second, especially since, in considering whether an assault is indecent, it may be appropriate to have regard to the surrounding circumstances, it is necessary that the defendant should have been aware of the existence of any circumstances which are relied on as rendering the assault indecent. These requirements have, of course, the effect of eliminating the possibility of a person being convicted of an indecent assault in any case of accident or mistake; they provide, therefore, the simple answer to the case, posed in argument, of a man forcing his way out of a crowded underground train and accidentally tearing off a woman's clothing, which nobody would regard as an indecent assault. I am bound however to say that both requirements are likely to be of theoretical rather than practical importance; and I have omitted any reference to recklessness because, although theoretically relevant, it is difficult to imagine circumstances where it would be relevant in practice (apart from cases such as *R.* v. *Kimber*).

It is, in my opinion, as simple as that. And, as I understand the position, especially following the decision of the Divisional Court in *Beal* v. *Kelley,* the law in this form has regularly been applied and acted on, no doubt in innumerable cases, without any difficulty at all.

However, in the present case the judge added a further mental element, viz. that the defendant should have had an "indecent intention." First of all, what did he mean by this? The expression is capable of bearing a number of different meanings. It may, for example, mean that the defendant intended to do an act which was in fact indecent; or it may mean that he intended to do an act for an indecent purpose of any kind; or it may mean that he acted with a particular indecent purpose, viz. with the motive of obtaining sexual gratification from his act. I infer, from the fact that the judge thought it right to admit the evidence of the appellant's statement to the police in the present case, that he intended to attribute the last of those three meanings to the expression "indecent intention," though he did not explain this to the jury.

Why did he add this extra requirement? He certainly did not do so on the basis of any previous authority; for it seems that the only previous reported case in which this direction has been given was the decision of an assistant recorder in the briefly reported *R.* v. *Pratt* [1984] Crim.L.R. 41. Your Lordships were, however, told that, during an adjournment in the course of the trial, the judge was provided with reading matter in the form not only of copies of the relevant authorities, but also of academic writings, including Professor Glanville Williams's *Textbook of Criminal Law* (2nd edn., 1983). It is almost certain, therefore, that the judge was persuaded to add the element of "indecent intention" to his direction by the work of the learned professor.

A requirement that the defendant must have acted from a sexual motive, which I understand to be from the motive of obtaining sexual gratification from his act, would, as Professor Glanville Williams recognises, exclude from indecent assault cases where a man undressed a woman in public but did so not from the motive of obtaining sexual gratification but because he was a mysogynist, or because he wanted to cause the woman embarrassment, or out of sheer mischief. I cannot think that this is right. In its judgment, the Court of Appeal referred to the case of an examination of a 15-year-old girl by a midwife or doctor for medical purposes, the point being that, by virtue of section 14(2) of the 1956 Act, a girl under the age of 16 cannot in law give any consent which would prevent an act being an assault for the purposes of the section. Professor Glanville Williams considers that such a case would not amount to an indecent assault because the doctor or midwife acted from a non-sexual motive. The Court of Appeal expressed its disagreement with this view, in the following passage from its judgment, ([1987] Q.B. 156 at 164):

"In our judgment it is not necessary to infer a requirement of proof of a sexual purpose, or of an indecent intention, for proof that a person has made an indecent assault, in order to protect from the theoretical risk of conviction for indecent assault the midwife or doctor who intimately examines a girl under the age of 16 without effective consent. If consent has been given by the parent or guardian there is, of course, no assault. If no such consent has been given, an intimate examination carried out for genuine medical purposes is, in our view, not indecent. Neither the girl examined, nor the right thinking members of society, would regard such an examination as an affront to the modesty of the girl or conduct which contravened normal standards of decent behaviour. So long as the examination is carried out for genuine medical purposes in a manner and in circumstances consistent with those purposes, then in our view the fact that the doctor or midwife happens to have some secret indecent motive, or happens to obtain some sexual gratification known only to himself from carrying out his legitimate work, cannot in our view render the circumstances indecent."

I entirely agree. As I see it, it is the fact that the assault is objectively indecent which constitutes the gravamen of the offence, which is to be found in the affront to modesty. This conclusion is consistent with the decision of Streatfeild J. in *R.* v. *George* [1956] Crim.L.R. 52. Furthermore, I accept the submission of both counsel that to introduce the requirement of indecent motive would be undesirable, in that it would create complications in what is at present treated as a relatively simple and straightforward offence. One has only to imagine a jury grappling with a case where a man has been charged with what anybody would call an indecent assault on a woman, and then claims (following the proposed change in the law) that he is not guilty on the ground that he committed the assault only because he is a misogynist. If there is any offence which should, so far as possible, be kept simple, this is it; and I strongly suspect that most of the examples used in argument are thoroughly unreal, and that jurors and magistrates are perfectly capable of recognising indecency when they are faced with it, and indeed that any gloss on the word "indecent" is more likely to do harm than good. I am, for example, content to leave it to juries, and to magistrates, to draw a sensible distinction between courtship and indecency; and I strongly suspect that any attempt to draw some hard and fast line between the two would more than likely land up in disaster.

I understand, however, that what has found favour with the remainder of your Lordships is neither the law as it has hitherto been understood, viz. an indecent assault is an assault committed in circumstances of indecency, nor the law as proposed by Professor Glanville Williams and adopted by the judge, viz. it is a necessary ingredient of indecent assault that the defendant should have acted with an "indecent intention," *i.e.* with the motive of obtaining sexual gratification from his act. The proposition, as I understand it, is that, where the act is "inherently indecent," it may constitute an indecent assault even though the defendant had no intention to obtain sexual gratification from his act, but, where it is only *capable* of constituting an indecent assault, then the question whether it is so or not may be resolved by ascertaining whether or not the defendant has such an intention. I am, with all respect, unable to accept this approach.

It seems to me that either the intention to obtain sexual gratification should be an ingredient of the offence or it should not. If (contrary to my opinion) it is, then it must be proved in every case, and without it the defendant must be acquitted, however objectively indecent the assault may be, with the effect that a man who forcibly undresses a woman in public because he is a misogynist, or because he wants to embarrass her, or because he is acting out of sheer mischief, would not be guilty of an indecent assault. If, however, it is not an ingredient of the offence, then in my opinion it must be generally irrelevant; it cannot, for example, be adduced in evidence by the prosecution to prove that an assault which was not objectively indecent was in fact indecent, or to prove that an assault which might or might not be thought to be objectively indecent was in fact indecent.

Of course, I am not saying that evidence of the motive of the defendant is never admissible. . . . In Smith and Hogan, *Criminal Law* (5th edn., 1983) p. 424 it is stated:

"While an indecent motive cannot convert an objectively decent act into an indecent assault, a decent motive may justify what would otherwise be an indecent act."

With that proposition, I respectfully find myself to be broadly in agreement, though I would myself (unaffected by the pressures on space in a textbook) express it rather more fully as follows. First, if the prosecution cannot establish that an assault is objectively indecent, they are not allowed to fortify their case by calling evidence of a secret indecent intention on the part of the defendant. Second, if an assault is prima facie indecent, the defendant may seek to show that the circumstances of the assault were not in fact indecent, and for that purpose evidence of his intention would be relevant and admissible.

It was on the basis that evidence of the appellant's secret intention was probative of the true nature of the circumstances accompanying the assault that counsel for the Crown submitted that it was admissible in the present case. With this submission, I am unable to agree. For on this basis the prosecution would be seeking, in my opinion illegitimately, to fortify what is assumed to be a doubtful case of an objectively indecent assault by calling evidence of a secret indecent intention on the part of the appellant. In truth, the evidence was admitted on the erroneous basis that an indecent intention is an ingredient of the offence, which, in my opinion, it is not; and the conviction cannot, in my opinion, be salvaged by defending the admissibility of the evidence on some other ground. . . .

In my opinion, evidence of the appellant's secret motive was, in the present case, inadmissible. I would accordingly allow the appeal and quash the conviction.

[Lords Keith and Griffiths delivered speeches in favour of dismissing the appeal. Lord Fraser agreed that the appeal should be dismissed]

Appeal dismissed

Questions

1. Lord Ackner said that if the circumstances of an assault are *incapable* of being regarded as indecent, the undisclosed intention of the accused could not make the assault an indecent one. But in his view, it was rightly conceded that Court's actions were *capable* of amounting to an indecent assault "for the sound reason that the explanation of this unprovoked assault could reveal that the assault was an indecent one, as indeed the girl's father suspected" (*ante*, p. 651). Could not the explanation of George's unprovoked assault by removal of shoes (see *ante*, p. 652) reveal that this assault was

an indecent one? What relevant distinction is there between forcibly removing shoes and spanking on the buttocks? Are the victim's father's suspicions relevant?

2. In the following cases, there being nothing in the circumstances to suggest indecency, is evidence of D.'s motive admissible on a charge of indecent assault?

(i) D. seized V. by the hand in the street. V. thought he was trying to rob her, but his object was to drag her into a nearby abandoned house and rape her.

(ii) D., a burglar, hit V. on the head. His object was to render her unconscious so that he could rape her.

(iii) D., a burglar, hit V.'s husband on the head. His object was to disable him so that he could rape V.

3. D., posing as a doctor, was pretending to treat F. in order to obtain money from him. At F.'s request, D. made an intimate examination of F.'s 8-year-old daughter V. On a charge of indecent assault, is it relevant that D.'s only motive for examining V. was to preserve his pretence of being a doctor?

4. Can the behaviour of the *victim* make a "colourless" assault on him or her indecent? See *R.* v. *Goss* (1990) 90 Cr.App.R. 400 (C.A.), where a grown woman D. gave a "motherly" hug to an underage girl V., while V. was sexually stimulating D. with her hand. *Held*: "the clearest evidence of an indecent assault by the woman."

Draft Criminal Code Bill

"111. **Indecent assault.** A person is guilty of an indecent assault if he assaults another in such a manner, of which he is aware, or in such circumstances, of which he is aware, as are—

 (a)   indecent, whatever the purpose with which the act is done; or
 (b)   indecent only if the act is done with an indecent purpose and he acts with such a purpose.

115. **Indecency with children under sixteen.** A person is guilty of an offence if he commits an act of gross indecency with or towards a child under the age of sixteen or if he incites a child under that age to commit such an act with him or another unless—

 (a)   he believes that he or that other is married to the child; or
 (b)   he believes the child to be aged sixteen or above."

Note

The rule that a child under 16 cannot consent is to disappear, but if the indecency is gross, clause 115 will make consented-to activity an offence. Gross indecency remains undefined.

CHAPTER 10

THEFT AND ROBBERY

	PAGE		PAGE
1. Theft	660	iv. "With the Intention of De-	
i. Appropriation	662	priving Permanently"	717
ii. "Property"	679	v. "Temporary Deprivation"	727
iii. "Belonging to Another"	692	vi. "Dishonestly"	733
		2. Robbery	744

1. THEFT

Notes

1. Before 1969, the law about dishonest acquisition of the property of another was contained in the Larceny Act 1916, which was a codification of a number of common law rules with certain piecemeal statutory amendments mostly occurring in the Victorian era. The principal offence was larceny, but it was a highly technical crime, too narrowly defined to cover certain quite common cases of dishonesty. The crime was tinkered with both by statute and by judicial innovation, but the basis of the crime was such that no amount of tinkering would enable it to cover the whole range of dishonest conduct involving the property of another. The basis of the offence was that the accused should take and carry away property in the possession of another; it therefore failed to cover an accused person who dishonestly misappropriated that of which he already had lawful possession, and the offences of embezzlement and fraudulent conversion had to be invented to fill some of this gap. Moreover, the law's insistence that the crime was a wrong against possession, not against ownership, meant that the law was complicated by the need to reflect the intricacies of the English law of possession. The offence of fraudulent conversion, which, in its modern form, was first created by statute in 1901, was tied neither to taking and carrying away by the accused, nor to possession as the invaded interest of the victim. It consisted essentially of the accused fraudulently converting to his own use or benefit or to the use or benefit of any other person the property of the victim. When it was decided to replace larceny, embezzlement and fraudulent conversion by a single new offence of theft, the offence of fraudulent conversion was the model taken for the new definition in section 1. See Criminal Law Revision Committee's Eighth Report, on Theft and Related Offences, Cmnd. 2977, paras. 15–39.

2. What might be called "swindling," *i.e.* obtaining by false pretences and certain other offences of fraud, was not swept into the new definition, and was treated separately by both the Report, § 38, and the Act, which contains a range of new offences of swindling, which have since been supplemented by additional

offences in Theft Act 1978. See next Chapter, which deals with offences of fraud. Various other offences against property—blackmail, handling, burglary—are also contained in the Theft Act 1968 (see Chaps. 12–14), but the Act does not deal with offences of damaging property (see Chap. 15).

3. So far as concerns theft and the other offences contained in the Theft Acts, the Acts are comprehensive and in one sense conclusive. There is nothing left of the old offences, which were all completely swept away. However, this does not mean that cases on the earlier law, and on other branches of the law such as property or contract, can be entirely ignored. Occasionally the Court of Appeal concludes that the draftsman must have had a particular decision in mind in choosing the words used in the Act (see, *e.g. post*, p. 712). Moreover, protecting as it does property interests, theft law cannot easily avoid using the technical terms found in and given meanings by the civil law, *e.g.* "proprietary right or interest," "obligation." But in general the Courts, taking the view that the object of the Theft Act was to simplify the law, resist the introduction of the complexities of the civil law into a trial for theft, and are loth to give the statutory words any technical meaning. The rules of property and contract have sometimes been disregarded in a cavalier fashion, and there has been an increasing tendency to categorise the words in the Act as "ordinary" words and to leave juries to say what they mean. The result is that the law of theft, which because of its subject matter could never be simple, has become more complicated than it need be and indeed, in some places, unprincipled and capricious. See, *e.g. post*, pp. 679, 700, 734.

4. Most of the offences in the Theft Acts appear in the Draft Criminal Code Bill. However, although the Law Commission (Law Com. 177, Commentary 16.4) recognise the existence of criticisms of the Acts and the case law on them, they content themselves with reproducing the Acts, without any changes of substance. An exception will be found, *post*, p. 846, on the subject of burglary with intent under section 9(1)(*b*), Theft Act 1968.

Theft Act 1968, section 1

"(1) A person is guilty of theft if he dishonestly appropriates property belonging to another, with the intention of permanently depriving the other of it; and 'thief' and 'steal' shall be construed accordingly.

(2) It is immaterial whether the appropriation is made with a view to gain, or is made for the thief's own benefit.

(3) The five following sections of this Act shall have effect as regards the interpretation and operation of this section (and, except as otherwise provided by this Act, shall apply only for purposes of this section)."

Note

The *actus reus* of theft is (i) appropriating (ii) property (iii) belonging to another. The *mens rea* is found in the expressions (iv) with the intention of depriving the other of it and (v) dishonestly. All five elements are given extended definitions by sections 2–6.

i. Appropriation

Theft Act 1968, section 3

"(1) Any assumption by a person of the rights of an owner amounts to an appropriation, and this includes, where he has come by the property (innocently or not) without stealing it, any later assumption of a right to it by keeping or dealing with it as owner.

(2) Where property or a right or interest in property is or purports to be transferred for value to a person acting in good faith, no later assumption by him of rights which he believed himself to be acquiring shall, by reason of any defect in the transferor's title, amount to theft of the property."

Glanville Williams, Textbook of Criminal Law (1st ed.), p. 726

"The phrase 'any assumption of the rights of an owner' [in section 3(1), *supra*] is a remarkable juristic invention. Except in special situations that the framers of the Act were probably not thinking of, it is impossible for anyone to 'assume the rights of an owner' by way of theft, in the sense of actually acquiring rights of ownership. Thieves do not normally acquire rights against the owner. One may steal a watch, but one cannot generally steal rights of ownership in the watch. The thief may act in a way that would be lawful *if* he had the rights of an owner, or *if* he were acting by authority of the owner; but he does not by stealing give himself those rights. Obviously the word 'assumption' in this context means, generally, a *usurpation* of rights. (The word 'usurpation' is given as one of the meanings of 'assumption' in the OED). What appears to be intended by this cloudy definition is that an appropriation is (or includes) anything done in relation to property by a non-owner that only the owner could lawfully do or authorise."

Notes

1. As Williams points out (*supra*), it is never necessary that the owner shall lose his rights to the property as a result of D.'s act (and in most cases he does not). In many cases, the owner loses *possession* to D. by the latter's act of appropriation, but even that is not necessary. Nothing is said about "possession" in section 3(1). It seems that if D. does something in relation to property which only the owner can do, *e.g.* offer it for sale, it is an appropriation even if the owner's rights are not affected in any way, or even put at risk. Thus if D. draws an unauthorised cheque on V.'s bank account, that is an appropriation of V.'s rights against the bank (see *R. v. Kohn, post,* p. 682), even though in law any debit entry on V.'s account which the bank might make on honouring the cheque is a complete nullity, so that V.'s rights against the bank remain exactly as before: *Chan Man-sin* v. *Att.-Gen. of Hong Kong* [1988] 1 All E.R. 1 (P.C.). Even if the cheque is never presented, the mere fact of drawing it (a thing which only the owner of the account can do) is an assumption of the rights of the owner and therefore "amounts to an appropriation": *Re Osman* [1989] 3 All E.R. 701 (D.C.). In truth, as Lord Oliver pointed out in *Chan Man-sin*, (at p. 3) the

definition of appropriation in section 3(1) is a completely artificial one.

It does not follow that where there is an appropriation there is a complete theft, because there must in addition be an intent to deprive the owner permanently. However, this concept also has an artificial meaning (see *post*, p. 726), and it can exist even if there is no intention that V. should be deprived of the property itself. On this see further, p. 727.

2. Glanville Williams's choice of the word "usurpation" as being what "appropriation" means in section 3(1) is no longer entirely appropriate. This is because it contains within it the idea of acting in a way not authorised by the owner. However, although what a thief does is usually unauthorised, it need not be so: see next case, which settled a long-standing conflict of authority.

R. v. Gomez
[1993] 1 All E.R. 1
House of Lords

D was assistant manager of an electrical goods shop. He was approached by B, who asked to be supplied with goods in exchange for two stolen building society cheques. D agreed and asked the shop manager G to authorise the transaction, without telling him the cheques were worthless. In response to G's enquiries on the point, D falsely told him the cheques "were as good as cash". G then authorised the handing over of the goods to B in exchange for the cheques, which were dishonoured. D was convicted of theft of the goods and appealed. His appeal was allowed and the prosecution appealed to the House of Lords.

LORD KEITH OF KINKEL: My Lords, this appeal raises the question of whether two decisions of your Lordships' House upon the proper construction of certain provisions of the Theft Act 1968 are capable of being reconciled with each other and, if so, in what manner. The two decisions are *Lawrence* v. *Metropolitan Police Commissioner* [1972] A.C. 626 and *R.* v. *Morris* [1984] A.C. 320. The question has given rise to much debate in subsequent cases and in academic writings.

[After reciting the facts] The respondent appealed to the Court of Appeal (Criminal Division) which on 22 April 1991 (Lord Lane C.J., Hutchison and Mantell JJ.) quashed the convictions: ([1991] 1 W.L.R. 1344). Lord Lane C.J., delivering the judgment of the court, after considering *Lawrence* and *Morris*, said at p. 1338:

"What in fact happened was that the owner was induced by deceit to agree to the goods being transferred to Ballay. If that is the case, and if in these circumstances the appellant is guilty of theft, it must follow that anyone who obtains goods in return for a cheque which he knows will be dishonoured on presentation, or indeed by way of any other similar pretence, would be guilty of theft. That does not seem to be the law. *Morris* decides that when a person by dishonest deception induces the owner to transfer his entire proprietary interests that is not theft. There is no appropriation at the moment when he takes possession of the goods because he was entitled to do so under the terms of the contract of sale, a contract which is, it is true, voidable, but has been avoided at the time the goods are handed over."

And later, at p. 1339:

"We therefore conclude that there was de facto, albeit voidable, contract between the owners and Ballay; that it was by virtue of that contract that Ballay took possession of the goods; that accordingly the transfer of the goods to him was with the consent and express authority of the owner and that accordingly there was no lack of authorisation and no appropriation."

The court later granted a certificate under section 1(2) of the Administration of Justice Act 1960 that a point of law of general public importance was involved in the decision, namely

"When theft is alleged and that which is alleged to be stolen passes to the defendant with the consent of the owner, but that has been obtained by a false representation, has (a) an appropriation within the meaning of section 1(1) of the Theft Act 1968 taken place, or (b) must such a passing of property necessarily involve an element of adverse inference with or usurpation of some right of the owner?"

The Crown now appeals, with leave granted here, to your Lordships' House.

[After quoting sections 1(3), 3(1), 4(1), 7 and 15(1) Theft Act 1968]: It is to be observed that by section 26 of the Criminal Justice Act 1991 the maximum sentence for theft was reduced from 10 to 7 years. The section 15(1) penalty was left unchanged.

The facts in *Lawrence*, as set out in the speech of Viscount Dilhorne, were these:

"The appellant was convicted on December 2, 1969, of theft contrary to section 1(1) of the Theft Act 1968. On September 1, 1969, a Mr. Occhi, an Italian who spoke little English, arrived at Victoria Station on his first visit to this country. He went up to a taxi driver, the appellant, and showed him a piece of paper on which an address in Ladbroke Grove was written. The appellant said that it was very far and very expensive. Mr. Occhi got into the taxi, took £1 out of his wallet and gave it to the appellant who then, the wallet being still open, took a further £6 out of it. He then drove Mr. Occhi to Ladbroke Grove. The correct lawful fare for the journey was in the region of 10s. 6d. The appellant was charged with and convicted of the theft of the £6."

The conviction was upheld by the Court of Appeal (Criminal Division) which in granting leave to appeal to your Lordships' House certified the following questions as involving a point of law of general public importance:

"(1) Whether section 1(1) of the Theft Act 1968 is to be construed as though it contained the words 'without the consent of the owner' or words to that effect and (2) Whether the provisions of section 15(1) and of section 1(1) of the Theft Act 1968 are mutually exclusive in the sense that if the facts proved would justify a conviction under section 15(1) there cannot lawfully be a conviction under section 1(1) on those facts."

Viscount Dilhorne, whose speech was concurred in by Lord Donovan, Lord Pearce, Lord Diplock and Lord Cross of Chelsea, after stating the facts, and expressing some doubts as to what Mr. Occhi had meant when he said that he "permitted" the taxi driver to take £6, continued, at p. 631:

"The main contention of the appellant in this House and in the Court of Appeal was that Mr. Occhi had consented to the taking of the £6 and that, consequently, his conviction could not stand. In my opinion, the facts of this case to which I have referred fall far short of establishing that Mr. Occhi had so consented.

"Prior to the passage of the Theft Act 1968, which made radical changes in and greatly simplified the law relating to theft and some other offences, it was necessary to prove that the property alleged to have been stolen was taken 'without the consent of the owner' (Larceny Act 1916, section 1(1)).

"These words are not included in section 1(1) of the Theft Act, but the appellant contended that the subsection should be construed as if they were, as if they appeared after the word 'appropriates.' Section 1(1) reads as follows: 'A person is guilty of theft if he dishonestly appropriates property belonging to another with the intention of permanently depriving the other of it; and 'thief' and 'steal' shall be construed accordingly.'

"I see no ground for concluding that the omission of the words 'without the consent of the owner' was inadvertent and not deliberate, and to read the subsection as if they were included is, in my opinion, wholly unwarranted. Parliament by the omission of these words has relieved the prosecution of the burden of establishing that the taking was without the owner's consent. That is no longer an ingredient of the offence.

"Megaw L.J., delivering the judgment of the Court of Appeal, said [1971] 1 Q.B. 373, 376 that the offence created by section 1(1) involved four elements; '(i) a dishonest (ii) appropriation (iii) of property belonging to another (iv) with the intention of permanently depriving the owner of it.'

"I agree. That there was appropriation in this case is clear. Section 3(1) states that any assumption by a person of the rights of an owner amounts to an appropriation. Here there was clearly such an assumption. That an appropriation was dishonest may be proved in a number of ways. In this case it was not contended that the appellant had not acted dishonestly. Section 2(1) provides, inter alia, that a person's appropriation of property belonging to another is not to be regarded as dishonest if he appropriates the property in the belief that he would have the other's consent if the other knew of the appropriation and the circumstances of it. A fortiori, a person is not to be regarded as acting dishonestly if he appropriates another's property believing that with full knowledge of the circumstances that other person has in fact agreed to the appropriation. The appellant, if he believed that Mr. Occhi, knowing that £7 was far in excess of the legal fare, had nevertheless agreed to pay him that sum, could not be said to have acted dishonestly in taking it. When Megaw L.J. said that if there was true consent, the essential element of dishonesty was not established, I understand him to have meant this. Belief or the absence of belief that the owner had with such knowledge consented to the appropriation is relevant to the issue of dishonesty, not to the question whether or not there has been an appropriation. That may occur even though the owner had permitted or consented to the property being taken. So proof that Mr. Occhi had consented to the appropriation of £6 from his wallet without agreeing to paying a sum in excess of the legal fare does not suffice to show that there was not dishonesty in this case. There was ample evidence that there was.

"I now turn to the third element 'property belonging to another.' Mr. Back Q.C., for the appellant, contended that if Mr. Occhi consented to the appellant taking the £6, he consented to the property in the money passing from him to the appellant and that the appellant had not, therefore, appropriated property belonging to another. He argued that the old distinction between the offence of false pretences and larceny had been preserved. I am unable to agree with this. The new offence of obtaining property by deception created by section 15(1) of the Theft Act also contains the words 'belonging to another.' 'A person who by any deception dishonestly obtains property belonging to another, with the intention of permanently depriving the other of it' commits that offence. 'Belonging to another' in section 1(1) and in section 15(1) in my view signifies no more than that, at the time of the appropriation or the obtaining, the property belonging to another, with the words 'belonging to another' having the extended meaning given by section 5. The short answer to this contention on behalf of the appellant is that the money in the wallet which he appropriated belonged to another, to Mr. Occhi.

"There was no dispute about the appellant's intention being permanently to deprive Mr. Occhi of the money.

"The four elements of the offence of theft as defined in the Theft Act were thus clearly established and, in my view, the Court of Appeal was right to dismiss the appeal."

In the result, each of the certified questions was answered in the negative.

It will be seen that Viscount Dilhorne's speech contains two clear pronouncements, first that it is no longer an ingredient of the offence of theft that the taking should be without the owner's consent and second, that an appropriation may occur even though the owner has permitted or consented to the property being taken. The answer given to the first certified question was in line with those pronouncements, so even though Viscount Dilhorne was of opinion that the evidence fell short of establishing that Mr. Occhi had consented to the taking of the £6 it was a matter of decision that it made no difference whether or not he had so consented.

Morris involved two cases of price label switching in a supermarket. In the first case the defendant had removed the price label from a joint of meat and replaced it with a label showing a lesser price which he had removed from another joint. He was detected at the check-out point before he had paid for the joint and later convicted of theft contrary to section 1(1) of the Theft Act. In the second case the defendant had in similar manner switched price labels on goods in a supermarket but was not arrested until after he had passed the check-out point and paid the lesser prices for the goods. He was charged with two counts of theft contrary to section 1(1) and one count of obtaining property by deception contrary to section 15(1). The jury convicted him on the counts of theft, but by directions of the recorder returned no verdict on the section 15(1) count. Appeals against conviction by both defendants were dismissed by the Court of Appeal (Criminal Division) and by this House. Lord Roskill, in the course of a speech concurred in by Lords Fraser of Tullybelton, Edmund-Davies, Brandon of Oakbrook and Brightman, at p. 331 referred to the *Lawrence* case with apparent approval as having set out the four elements involved in the offence of theft and as having rejected the argument that there could not be theft within section 1(1) if the owner of the property had consented to the defendant's acts. He observed that in *Lawrence* the House did not have to consider the precise meaning of "appropriation" in section 3(1) and continued:

"Mr. Denison submitted that the phrase in section 3(1) 'any assumption by a person of *the rights*' (my emphasis) 'of an owner amounts to an appropriation' must mean any assumption of '*all* the rights of an owner.' Since neither defendant had at the time of the removal of the goods from the shelves and of the label switching assumed *all* the rights of the owner, there was no appropriation and therefore no theft. Mr. Jeffreys for the prosecution, on the other hand, contended that *the* rights in this context only meant *any* of the rights. An owner of goods has many rights—they have been described as 'a bundle or package of rights.' Mr. Jeffreys contended that on a fair reading of the subsection it cannot have been the intention that every one of an owner's rights had to be assumed by the alleged thief before an appropriation was proved and that essential ingredient of the offence of theft established.

"My Lords, if one reads the words 'the rights' at the opening of section 3(1) literally and in isolation from the rest of the section, Mr. Denison's submission undoubtedly has force. But the later words 'any later assumption of a right' seem to me to militate strongly against the correctness of the submission. Moreover the provisions of section 2(1)(*a*) also seem to point in the same direction. It follows therefore that it is enough for the prosecution if they have proved in these cases the assumption by the [defendants] of *any* of the rights of the owner of the goods in question, that is to say, the supermarket concerned, it being common ground in these cases that the other three of the four elements mentioned in Viscount Dilhorne's speech in *Lawrence* had been fully established.

"My Lords, Mr. Jeffreys sought to argue that any removal from the shelves of the supermarket, even if unaccompanied by label switching, was without more an appropriation. In one passage in his judgment in *Morris's* case the learned Lord Chief Justice appears to have accepted the submission, for he said [1983] Q.B. 587, 596: 'it seems to us that in taking the article from the shelf the customer is indeed assuming one of the rights of the owner—the right to move the article from its position on the shelf to carry it to the check-out.'

"With the utmost respect, I cannot accept this statement as correct. If one postulates an honest customer taking goods from a shelf to put in his or her trolley to take to the checkpoint there to pay the proper price, I am unable to see that any of these actions involves any assumption by the shopper of the rights of the supermarket. In the context of section 3(1), the concept of appropriation in my view involves not an act expressly or impliedly authorised by the owner but an act by way of adverse interference with or usurpation of those rights. When the honest shopper acts as I have just described, he or she is acting with the implied authority of the owner of the supermarket to take the goods from the shelf, put them in the trolley, take them to the checkpoint and there pay the correct price, at which moment the property in the goods will pass to the shopper for the first time. It is with the consent of the owners of the supermarket, be that consent express or implied, that the shopper does these acts and thus obtains at least control if not actual possession of the goods preparatory, at a later stage, to obtaining the property in them upon payment of the proper amount at the checkpoint. I do not think that section 3(1) envisages any such act as an 'appropriation,' whatever may be the meaning of that word in other fields such as contract or sale of goods law.

"If, as I understand all your Lordships to agree, the concept of appropriation in section 3(1) involves an element of adverse interference with or usurpation of some right of the owner, it is necessary next to consider whether that requirement is satisfied in either of these cases. As I have already said, in my view mere removal from the shelves without more is not an appropriation. Further, if a shopper with some perverted sense of humour, intending only to create confusion and nothing more both for the supermarket and for other shoppers, switches labels, I do not think that that act of label switching alone is without more an appropriation, though it is not difficult to envisage some cases of dishonest label switching which could be. In cases such as the present, it is in truth a combination of these actions, the removal from the shelf and the switching of the labels, which evidences adverse interference with or usurpation of the right of the owner. Those acts, therefore, amount to an appropriation and if they are accompanied by proof of the other three elements to which I have referred, the offence of theft is established. Further, if they are accompanied by other acts such as putting the goods so removed and relabelled into a receptacle, whether a trolley or the shopper's own bag or basket, proof of appropriation within section 3(1) becomes overwhelming. It is the doing of one or more acts which individually or collectively amount to such adverse interference with or usurpation of the owner's rights which constitute appropriation under section 3(1) and I do not think it matters where there is more than one such act in which order the successive acts take place, or whether there is any interval of time between them. To suggest that it matters whether the mislabelling precedes or succeeds removal from the shelves is to reduce this branch of the law to an absurdity.''

The answer given to the question certified by the Court of Appeal was this:

"There is a dishonest appropriation for the purposes of the Theft Act 1968 where by the substitution of a price label showing a lesser price on goods for one showing a greater price, a defendant either by that act alone or by that act in conjunction with another act or other acts (whether done before or after the substitution of the labels) adversely interferes with or usurps the right of the owner to ensure that the goods concerned are sold and paid for at that greater price."

In my opinion Lord Roskill was undoubtedly right when he said in the course of the passage quoted that the assumption by the defendant of any of the rights of an owner could amount to an appropriation within the meaning of section 3(1), and that the removal of an article from the shelf and the changing of the price label on it constituted the assumption of one of the rights of the owner and hence an appropriation within the meaning of the subsection. But there are observations in the passage which, with the greatest possible respect to my noble and learned friend Lord Roskill, I must regard as unnecessary for the decision of the case and as being incorrect. In the first place, it seems to me that the switching of price labels on the article is in itself an assumption of one of the rights of the owner, whether or not it is accompanied by some other act such as removing the article from the shelf and placing it in a basket or trolley. No one but the owner has the right to remove a price label from an article or to place a price label upon it. If anyone else does so, he does an act, as Lord Roskill puts it, by way of adverse interference with or usurpation of that right. This is no less so in the case of the practical joker figured by Lord Roskill than in the case of one who makes the switch with dishonest intent. The practical joker, of course, is not guilty of theft because he has not acted dishonestly and does not intend to deprive the owner permanently of the article. So the label switching in itself constitutes an appropriation and so to have held would have been sufficient for the dismissal of both appeals. On the facts of the two cases it was unnecessary to decide whether, as argued by Mr. Jeffreys, the mere taking of the article from the shelf and putting it in a trolley or other receptacle amounted to the assumption of one of the rights of the owner, and hence an appropriation. There was much to be said in favour of the view that it did, in respect that doing so gave the shopper control of the article and the capacity to exclude any other shopper from taking it. However, Lord Roskill expressed the opinion that it did not, on the ground that the concept of appropriation in the context of section 3(1) "involves not an act expressly or impliedly authorised by the owner but an act by way of adverse interference with or usurpation of those rights." While it is correct to say that appropriation for purposes of section 3(1) includes the latter sort of act, it does not necessarily follow that no other act can amount to an appropriation and in particular that no act expressly or impliedly authorised by the owner can in any circumstances do so. Indeed, *Lawrence* is a clear decision to the contrary since it laid down unequivocally that an act may be an appropriation notwithstanding that it is done with the consent of the owner. It does not appear to me that any sensible distinction can be made in this context between consent and authorisation.

In the civil case of *Dobson* v. *General Accident Fire and Life Assurance Corporation plc* [1990] 1 Q.B. 274 a Court of Appeal consisting of Parker and Bingham L.JJ. considered the apparent conflict between *Lawrence* and *Morris* and applied the former decision. The facts were that the plaintiff had insured property with the defendant company against inter alia "loss or damage caused by theft." He advertised for sale a watch and ring at the total price of £5,950. A rogue telephoned expressing an interest in buying the articles and the plaintiff provisionally agreed with him that the payment would be by a building society cheque in the plaintiff's favour. The rogue called on the plaintiff next day and the watch and the ring were handed over to him in exchange for a building society cheque for the agreed amount. The plaintiff paid the cheque into his bank, which informed him that it was stolen and worthless. The defendant company denied liability under its policy of insurance on the ground that the loss of the watch and ring was not caused by theft within the meaning of the Act of 1968. The plaintiff succeeded in the county court in an action to recover the amount of his loss, and the decision was affirmed by the Court of Appeal. One of the arguments for the defendants was that there had been no theft because the plaintiff had agreed to the transaction with the rogue and reliance was placed on Lord Roskill's statement in *Morris* at p. 332 that appropriation

> "involves not an act expressly or impliedly authorised by the owner but an act by way of adverse interference with or usurpation of those rights."

In dealing with this argument Parker L.J. said, at p. 281:

> "The difficulties caused by the apparent conflict between the decisions in *Lawrence* and *Morris* have provided, not surprisingly, a basis for much discussion by textbook writers and contributors to articles to law journals. It is, however, clear that their Lordships in *Morris* did not regard anything said in that case as conflicting with *Lawrence* for it was specifically referred to in Lord Roskill's speech, with which the other members of the Judicial Committee all agreed, without disapproval or

qualification. The only comment made was that, in *Lawrence*, the House did not have to consider the precise meaning of 'appropriation' in section 3(1) of the Act of 1968. With respect, I find this comment hard to follow in the light of the first of the questions asked in *Lawrence* and the answer to it, the passages from Viscount Dilhorne's speech already cited, the fact that it was specifically argued 'appropriates is meant in a pejorative, rather than a neutral, sense in that the appropriation is against the will of the owner,' and finally that dishonesty was common ground. I would have supposed that the question in *Lawrence* was whether appropriation necessarily involved an absence of consent."

[After quoting other criticisms by Parker L.J. of Lord Roskill's speech in *Morris*, and noting Bingham L.J.'s suggestion that Viscount Dilhorne's ruling might be reconciled with the reasoning in *Morris* on the ground that in *Lawrence* the victim might not in fact have consented to the taxi-driver taking anything in excess of the correct fare]:

It was argued for the respondent in the present appeal that the case of *Dobson* was wrongly decided. I disagree, and on the contrary find myself in full agreement with those parts of the judgment of Parker L.J. to which I have referred. As regards the attempted reconciliation by Bingham L.J. of the reasoning in *Morris* with the ruling in *Lawrence* it appears to me that the suggested basis of reconciliation, which is essentially speculative, is unsound. The actual decision in *Morris* was correct, but it was erroneous, in addition to being unnecessary for the decision, to indicate that an act expressly or impliedly authorised by the owner could never amount to an appropriation. There is no material distinction between the facts in *Dobson* and those in the present case. In each case the owner of the goods was induced by fraud to part with them to the rogue. *Lawrence* makes it clear that consent to or authorisation by the owner of the taking by the rogue is irrelevant. The taking amounted to an appropriation within the meaning of section 1(1) of the Theft Act. *Lawrence* also makes it clear that it is no less irrelevant that what happened may also have constituted the offence of obtaining property by deception under section 15(1) of the Act.

In my opinion it serves no useful purpose at the present time to seek to construe the relevant provisions of the Theft Act by reference to the Report which preceded it, namely the Eighth Report of the Criminal Law Revision Committee (1966) Cmnd. 2977. The decision in *Lawrence* was a clear decision of this House upon the construction of the word "appropriate" in section 1(1) of the Act, which had stood for twelve years when doubt was thrown upon it by obiter dicta in *Morris*. *Lawrence* must be regarded as authoritative and correct, and there is no question of it now being right to depart from it. . . .

My Lords, for the reasons which I have given I would answer branch (a) of the certified question in the affirmative and branch (b) in the negative, and allow the appeal.

LORD LOWRY: . . . Under the law before 1968 the facts of this case would have led to charges, to which there would have been no defence, of obtaining goods by false pretences. Since the passing of the Theft Act 1968 the accused could equally well have been prosecuted successfully for obtaining property by deception contrary to section 15 of the Act. Under the old law they could not have been found guilty of larceny, because the seller agreed to transfer the property in the goods to Ballay, and the fact that the seller's agreement was obtained by a fraud does not affect that conclusion. Indeed, if the seller's consent could have been vitiated in that way, Parliament would never have needed to create the statutory offence of obtaining by false pretences. The accused in this case, however, were prosecuted for theft under section 1(1) of the Act and were convicted notwithstanding the submission of counsel for the defence to the effect that the crime for which the accused were indicted did not amount to theft because the seller had consented to sell the property, albeit consent had been obtained by fraud, as alleged. When Gomez appealed, the Court of Appeal upheld that submission and quashed his convictions. In order to restore those convictions, the Crown must say that the Theft Act has altered the law in such a way (among others) that anyone who, by a false representation such as worthless cheque, induces an owner to sell property is thereby guilty of stealing. . . .

Since the question turns on the meaning of the word "appropriates" in section 1(1) of the Theft Act 1968, the problem is therefore one of statutory interpretation and it will be helpful to start by setting out the immediately relevant provisions of the Act.

[His Lordship quoted sections 1–4, 5(1) and 15 Theft Act 1968]

To be guilty of theft the offender, as I shall call him, must act dishonestly and must have the intention of permanently depriving the owner of property. Section 1(3) shows that in order to interpret the word "appropriates" (and thereby to define theft), sections 1 to 6 must be read together. The ordinary and natural meaning of "appropriate" is to take for oneself, or to treat as one's own, property which belongs to someone else. The primary dictionary meaning is "take possession of, take to oneself, especially without authority", and that is in my opinion the meaning which the word bears in section 1(1). The act of appropriating property is a one-sided act, done without the consent or authority of the owner. And, if the owner consents to transfer property to the offender or to a third party, the offender does not appropriate the property, even if the owner's consent has been obtained by fraud. This statement represents the old doctrine in regard to obtaining property by false pretences, to which I shall advert presently . . .

Coming now to section 3, the *primary* meaning of "assumption" is "taking on oneself", again a unilateral act, and this meaning is consistent with subsections (1) and (2). To use the word in its secondary, neutral sense would neutralise the word "appropriation", to which assumption is here equated, and would lead to a number of strange results. Incidentally, I can see no magic in the words *"an* owner" in subsection (1). Every case in real life must involve *the* owner or *the* person described in section 5(1); "the rights" may mean *"all* the rights", which would be the normal grammatical meaning, or (less probably, in my opinion) "any rights": see *Morris.* For present purposes it does not appear to matter; the word "appropriate" does not on either interpretation acquire the meaning contended for by the Crown. Still looking at section 3(1), I point out that "any later assumption of a right to it" (that is, a right to the property) amounts to an appropriation of a right to it and that normally "a right to it" means a right *to* the property and not a right *in* it. Section 3(2) protects an innocent purchaser from an accusation of theft when, having bought in good faith from someone with a defective title, he later treats the property as his own.

[After noting sections 4(2) and 6(1) and that in 1991 the maximum penalty for theft (but not obtaining by deception) was reduced to 7 years]:—

Accordingly, reading sections 1 to 6 as a whole, and also taking into account sections 24(4) and 28(6) and the 1991 amendment, the ordinary and natural meaning of "appropriates" in section 1(1) is confirmed. So clear is this conclusion to my mind that, notwithstanding anything which has been said in other cases, I would be very slow to concede that the word "appropriates" in section 1(1) of the Theft Act is in its context ambiguous. But, as I have indicated, the Crown case requires that there must be ambiguity and further requires that the ambiguity must be resolved against the ordinary meaning of the word and in favour of the neutral meaning preferred and required by the Crown's argument. Therefore, my Lords, I am willing for the purpose of argument to treat the word "appropriates" as ambiguous in its context and, on that basis, ... I turn, for such guidance as it may afford, to the Eighth Report of the Criminal Law Revision Committee, "Theft and Related Offences" (1966) (Cmnd. 2977).

[After quoting extensively from the Report and concluding that the Committee intended that obtaining property by deception should not ordinarily be theft]

The conclusion from this comparison of the draft Bill and the Act is that Parliament has in all material respects adopted the Committee's approach and has thereby endorsed the Committee's point of view. While not forgetting the observations in *Black-Clawson International* [1975] A.C. 591 of Lord Reid at p. 614F, Lord Wilberforce at p. 629C-G and Lord Diplock at p. 637D, where he wisely warned against departing from the plain and natural meaning in favour of a strained construction, I am much impressed by the more adventurous but very logical pronouncements of Viscount Dilhorne at pp. 622C–623E and Lord Simon of Glaisdale at p. 646E-G. In particular, after stating the principles and citing authority, Viscount Dilhorne said at p. 623D:

"While I respectfully agree that recommendations of a Committee may not help much when there is a possibility that Parliament may have decided to do something different, where there is no such possibility, as where the draft Bill has been enacted without alteration, in my opinion it can safely be assumed that it was Parliament's intention to do what the Committee recommended and to achieve the object the Committee had in mind. Then, in my view the recommendations of the Committee and their observations on their draft Bill may form a valuable aid to construction which the courts should not be inhibited from taking into account."

... There are only three cases which I need to look at in detail, *Lawrence*, *Morris* and *Dobson*, a decision of the Court of Appeal in a case where a policy holder was insured against "loss or damage caused by theft." *Lawrence* is reported in the Court of Appeal (Criminal Division) at 1971 1 Q.B. 373, where the main contention of the defence, noted at p. 376H by Megaw L.J., who delivered the judgment of the Court, was that there must be implied into section 1(1) of the Theft Act a requirement that the dishonest appropriation must be without the consent of the owner of the property. Megaw L.J. then said at p. 377A–F:

"In our view, no such implication is justified. The words contained in the former definition of larceny, in section 1 of the Larceny Act, 1916, 'without the consent of the owner,' have been omitted, and, we have no doubt, deliberately omitted from the definition of theft in the new Act.
..."

My respectful view, for reasons which your Lordships will have noted, is that both the contention of the defence and the court's refutation of it were misconceived: the absence of consent on the part of the owner is already inherent in the word "appropriates", properly understood, and therefore the argument for the defence got off on the wrong foot and the counter-argument that the words specified by the defence cannot be read into section 1(1) did not assist the prosecution. And the observation, without further discussion, that the omission of the words "without the consent of the owner" is deliberate seems to have led directly to the erroneous conclusion that a supposed appropriation *with* the consent of the owner is one of the four ingredients which are required (and which suffice) to constitute theft. I do not propose to restate the facts of *Lawrence*. It is enough to recall that the Court of Appeal, accepting the defence submission on that point, regarded it as an example, according to the old law, of obtaining by false pretences; see p. 378B. But the court did not accept the legal conclusion which the defence sought to draw from that fact, since Megaw L.J. continued at p. 378C–E:

> "The court sees no ground for saying that, for present purposes, it makes the slightest difference whether under the old law the offence would have been false pretences or larceny by a trick. The old and unsatisfactory distinction is not to be unnecessarily perpetuated where the language of the Theft Act, 1968, does not so require. There is no magic in the word 'property' in section 1(1) in view of the definition in section 4(1) of the Act. In either case, the fact that a charge could have been brought under section 15(1), which covers both, in no way operates to prevent the charge being validly laid as theft under section 1(1) if the prosecution can prove what they must prove, as previously described, under that subsection. This is conceded in respect of an offence which would once have been larceny by a trick. It applies equally to what would once have been obtaining by false pretences, if, as is here the case, the requirements of section 1(1) are also satisfied. That submission also fails.
>
> "It may be that the result of our decision is that in any case where the facts would establish a charge under section 15(1) they would also establish a charge under section 1(1). The alternative, however, involves the writing back into section 1(1) of words which the legislature, no doubt deliberately omitted, and the reintroduction into the criminal law of the distinction between larceny by a trick and obtaining by false pretences."

It is true that it would make no difference whether under the old law the offence would have been false pretences or larceny by a trick, provided the charge was laid under section 15(1). It was, indeed, with the object of getting over that difference that the C.L.R.C. proposed their clause 12(1). But the "old and unsatisfactory distinction" continues to operate if the charge is laid under section 1(1) and this is due to the true meaning in that subsection of the word "appropriates". That is why section 15(1) is needed and why it is best to prosecute under that provision in cases where deception is alleged to have been practised. It can be seen that the entire reasoning of the passage I have just quoted is based on a misconception of the meaning of the word "appropriates", and that misconception springs from the misconceived argument and counter-argument at p. 377 of the judgment.

... In Chapter II of The Law of Theft, 6th edition, Professor J. C. Smith discusses the difference between larceny by a trick and obtaining by false pretences and continues at paragraph 38:

> "It may of course be perfectly proper for the court to put on the Act an interpretation different from that intended by the framers of it. The

question is one of the proper interpretation of the words enacted by
Parliament and it could be that the Act does what the Committee
thought was not practicable and what they did not intend to do. It is
submitted, however, that the right interpretation of the Act is that
intended by the Committee."

His further comment at paragraph 39 is also valuable, in my opinion:

"There is, however, a considerable degree of doubt about this matter,
because of the case of *Lawrence*. The Court of Appeal in that case
thought that the distinction between larceny by a trick and obtaining by
false pretences depended on the presence in the Larceny Act of the
words 'without the consent of the owner', and, as these words do not
appear in the definition of theft, the distinction is gone; all cases of
obtaining by deception, contrary to s.15, are also theft. This argument,
however, appears to give insufficient weight to the notion of
'appropriation' and to the words 'property *belonging to another*.' "

The report of the argument in this House in *Lawrence* shows that the
appellant, understandably from his own point of view, again approached
the case as one of false pretences. That basis would provide grounds for
an acquittal of the charge of theft if the word "appropriates" in section 1(1)
connotes an absence of consent by the owner, and the appellant presented
his argument on the meaning of that subsection (page 630A) in the same
way as in the Court of Appeal and with the same unsuccessful result. But
that was not all. Viscount Dilhorne at p. 631E-F, when reviewing the
evidence, expressed the opinion that the facts of the case fell far short of
establishing that Mr. Occhi, the Italian student who was the victim of the
taxi driver, had consented to the acquisition by the appellant of the £6, as
argued at p. 628C. On that footing the taxi driver could have been guilty of
larceny by a trick (in old-fashioned terms), so as to be guilty of theft under
any interpretation of section 1(1). ... What is important is the unequivocal,
but in my respectful opinion wrong, statement of the law made by
Viscount Dilhorne at p. 632A ... that Parliament by omitting the words
"without the consent of the owner" from section 1(1) of the Theft Act "has
relieved the prosecution of the burden of establishing that the taking was
without the owner's consent." He added "That is no longer an ingredient
of the offence" (scil. "of theft".) The reasoning which follows is based on
the opinion, already inseparable from what has been said, that
appropriation is a neutral expression and does not convey the sense of
taking property for oneself without the owner's authority. As in the Court
of Appeal, the defence argument was primarily directed towards implying
words into section 1(1), a difficult task at best, and only secondarily
towards the meaning of "appropriates" (see p. 631A). But the only speech
delivered did not consider this second point and the summary treatment of
the appellant's argument is reflected in the opinion expressed on p. 633
that the point certified and argued was scarcely worthy of their Lordships'
attention. My Lords, I have found nothing in *Lawrence* which affects my
view of the present appeal. ...

In *Morris*, the label-switching case, the facts to be considered by the jury
and subsequently by the Court of Appeal ([1983] Q.B. 587) were, like those
of many supermarket frauds, more complex than those of the present case.
There would have been no defence (just as in *Lawrence*) if the charge had
been laid under section 15(1) and, as in *Lawrence* and the present case, it
was the Crown's resort to section 1(1) which alone gave rise to a legal
problem. ...

Here again (understandably, since *Lawrence* was a decision of this House) the misconceived argument and refutation, which were related to the possibility of implying words into section 1(1), took precedence. ...

This House, having granted leave to appeal, affirmed the Court of Appeal's decision in *Morris*, but reached its conclusion by a different route, as explained in the speech of Lord Roskill, to which I have already referred. I would respectfully agree with his description, in relation to dishonest actions, of appropriation as involving an act by way of adverse interference with or usurpation of the owner's rights, but I believe that the less aggressive definition of appropriation which I have put forward fits the word as used in an honest sense in section 2(1) as well as elsewhere in the Act. The important feature, of course, which our definitions have in common is that the appropriation must be an act done without the authority or consent, express or implied, of the owner. I do not consider that it would help towards the solution of your Lordships' present problem for me to discuss further the points which arose in *Morris* ... I must, however, look at *Dobson*, which I referred to above. ... The Court of Appeal, dismissing the insurers' appeal, simply followed the *Lawrence* approach [a decision which] merely perpetuates what I would call the *Lawrence* fallacy and disregards the unilateral meaning of appropriation.

Parker L.J. then turned to the argument derived from *Morris* and said at p. 281C:

"The difficulties caused by the apparent conflict between the decisions in *Lawrence* and *Morris* have provided, not surprisingly, a basis for much discussion by textbook writers and contributors of articles to law journals. It is, however, clear that their Lordships in *Morris* did not regard anything said in that case as conflicting with *Lawrence* for it was specifically referred to in Lord Roskill's speech, with which the other members of the Judicial Committee all agreed, without disapproval or qualification."

It is true that *Morris* contains no disapproval or qualification of *Lawrence*, but, in my view, the main statements of principle in these cases cannot possibly be reconciled and the later case therefore must not be regarded as providing any support for the earlier.

[After noting that Bingham L.J. did not find it easy to reconcile Viscount Dilhorne's ruling in *Lawrence* with the reasoning in *Morris*]:—

I consider that the Lord Justice's rationalisation of the failure of *Morris* to disapprove of *Lawrence* is of some significance. ... In short, *Dobson* follows the erroneous interpretation which was endowed with authority by *Lawrence* and was therefore, in my respectful opinion, wrongly decided. I would refer with respectful approval to Professor Smith's note on *Dobson* at [1990] Crim.L.R. pp. 273–4.

The judgment in the Court of Appeal in this case, which was delivered by Lord Lane, C.J., is reported at [1991] 1 W.L.R. 1334. The matter is clearly put at p. 1338E:

"What in fact happened was that the owner was induced by deceit to agree to the goods being transferred to Ballay. If that is the case, and if in these circumstances the appellant is guilty of theft, it must follow that anyone who obtains goods in return for a cheque which he knows will be dishonoured on presentation, or indeed by way of any other similar pretence, would be guilty of theft. That does not seem to be the law. *Morris* decides that when a person by dishonest deception induces the owner to transfer his entire proprietary interests that is not theft. There is no appropriation at the moment when he takes possession of the goods because he was entitled to do so under the terms of the contract of sale, a contract which is, it is true, voidable, but has not been avoided at the time the goods are handed over."

Exception has been taken by some commentators to the words "*Morris decides*", but the proposition which is stated in the judgment of the court follows inevitably from Lord Roskill's statement as to the meaning of appropriation.

Having reviewed the judgment in *Dobson*, the Lord Chief Justice said at p. 1339H:

"We do not consider that the judgment in [*Dobson*] requires or allows us to disregard what we have earlier in this judgment sought to extract as the ratio of the decision in [*Morris*]. We therefore conclude that there was a de facto, albeit voidable, contract between the owners and Ballay; that it was by virtue of that contract that Ballay took possession of the goods; that accordingly the transfer of the goods to him was with the consent and express authority of the owner and that accordingly there was no lack of authorisation and no appropriation. In the absence of any charge under section 15 of the Theft Act 1968, this appeal must therefore be allowed and the conviction quashed."

I respectfully agree.

My Lords, to sum up, every indication seems to me to point away from adopting a neutral meaning of the word "appropriation". I would reinforce that view by recalling that in *George Wimpey & Co. Ltd.* v. *BOAC* [1955] A.C. 169 at p. 191 Lord Reid stated that if the arguments are fairly evenly balanced (not that I believe they are in this case), that interpretation should be chosen which involves the least alteration of the existing law.

. . .

If the change in the law of theft which is signalled by decisions such as that reached in *Dobson* has in reality occurred, the position of insurers in that field has in the result been prejudiced by legislation the effect of which was far from clear . . .

Accordingly, for the reasons already given, I would dismiss the Crown's appeal.

LORD BROWNE-WILKINSON: I have read the speech of my noble and learned friend Lord Keith of Kinkel with which I agree. I only add a few words of my own out of deference to the contrary view expressed by my noble and learned friend Lord Lowry and to consider the cases on thefts from companies to which we were referred in the course of argument.

In *Lawrence* Megaw L.J. in the Court of Appeal analysed the constituent elements of the offence created by section 1(1) of the Theft Act 1968 as being "(i) a dishonest (ii) appropriation (iii) of property belonging to another (iv) with the intention of permanently depriving the owner of it." This analysis was adopted and approved by this House and I do not intend to cast any doubt on it. But it should not be overlooked that elements (i) and (ii) (unlike elements (iii) and (iv)) are interlinked: element (i) (dishonest) is an adjectival description of element (ii) (appropriation). Parliament has used a composite phrase "dishonest appropriation". Thus it is not every appropriation which falls within the section but only an act which answers the composite description.

The fact that Parliament used that composite phrase—"dishonest appropriation"—in my judgment casts light on what is meant by the word "appropriation". The views expressed (obiter) by this House in *Morris* that "appropriation" involves an act by way of adverse interference with or usurpation of the rights of the owner treats the word appropriation as being tantamount to "misappropriation". The concept of adverse interference with or usurpation of rights introduces into the word appropriation the mental state of both the owner and the accused. So far as concerns the mental state of the owner (did he consent?), the Act of 1968 expressly refers to such consent when it is a material factor: see sections 2(1)(b), 11(1), 12(1) and 13. So far as concerns the mental state of the accused, the composite phrase in section 1(1) itself indicates that the requirement is dishonesty.

For myself, therefore, I regard the word "appropriation" in isolation as being an objective description of the act done irrespective of the mental state of either the owner or the accused. It is impossible to reconcile the decision in *Lawrence* (that the question of consent is irrelevant in considering whether this has been an appropriation) with the views expressed in *Morris*, which latter views in my judgment were incorrect.

It is suggested that this conclusion renders section 15 of the Act of 1968 otiose since a person who, by deception, persuades the owner to consent to part with his property will necessarily be guilty of theft within section 1. This may be so though I venture to doubt it. Take for example a man who obtains land by deception. Save as otherwise expressly provided, the definitions in sections 4 and 5 of the Act apply only for the purposes of interpreting section 1 of the act: see section 1(3). Section 34(1) applies subsection (1) of section 4 and subsection (1) of section 5 generally for the purposes of the Act. Accordingly the other subsections of section 4 and section 5 do not apply to section 15. Suppose that a fraudster has persuaded a victim to part with his house: the fraudster is not guilty of theft of the land since section 4(2) provides that you cannot steal land. The charge could only be laid under section 15 which contains no provisions excluding land from the definition of property. Therefore, although there is a substantial overlap between section 1 and section 15, section 15 is not otiose.

Turning to the company cases, the dictum in *Morris* has led to much confusion and complication where those in de facto control of the company have been charged with theft from it. The argument which has found favour in certain of the authorities runs as follows. There can be no theft within section 1 if the owner consents to what is done: *Morris*. If the accused, by reason of being the controlling shareholder or otherwise, is "the directing mind and will of the company" he is to be treated as having validly consented on behalf of the company to his own appropriation of the company's property. This is apparently so whether or not there has been compliance with the formal requirements of company law applicable to dealings with the property of a company and even to cases where the consent relied on is ultra vires: see *R.* v. *Roffel* [1985] V.R. 511; *R.* v. *McHugh* [1988] 88 Cr.App.R. 385.

In my judgment this approach was wrong in law even if the dictum in *Morris* had been correct. Where a company is accused of a crime the acts and intentions of those who are the directing minds and will of the company are to be attributed to the company. That is not the law where the charge is that those who are the directing minds and will have themselves committed a crime against the company: see *Attorney General's Reference (No. 2 of 1982)* [1984] Q.B. 624 applying *Belmont Finance Corporation Ltd.* v. *Williams Furniture Ltd.* [1979] Ch. 250.

In any event, your Lordships' decision in this case, re-establishing as it does the decision in *Lawrence*, renders the whole question of consent by the company irrelevant. Whether or not those controlling the company consented or purported to consent to the abstraction of the company's

property by the accused, he will have appropriated the property of the
company. The question will be whether the other necessary elements are
present, viz. was such appropriation dishonest and was it done with the
intention of permanently depriving the company of such property? In my
judgment the decision in *Roffel* and the statements of principle in *McHugh*
at p. 393 are not correct in law and should not be followed. As for the case
of *Attorney General's Reference (No. 2 of 1982)*, in my judgment both the
concession made by counsel (that there had been an appropriation) and
the decision in that case were correct, as was the decision in *R. v. Philippou*
(1989) 89 Cr.App.R. 290.

I am glad to be able to reach this conclusion. The pillaging of companies
by those who control them is now all too common. It would offend both
common sense and justice to hold that the very control which enables such
people to extract the company's assets constitutes a defence to a charge of
theft from the company. The question in each case must be whether the
extraction of the property from the company was dishonest, not whether
the alleged thief has consented to his own wrongdoing.

Lords Jauncey of Tullichettle and Slynn of Hadley agreed that the appeal
should be allowed for the reasons given by Lord Keith of Kinkel.

Appeal allowed. Conviction restored.

Glanville Williams: Appropriation: A Single or Continuous Act? [1978] Crim.L.R. 69

"A man steals a watch, and two weeks later sells it. In common sense and
ordinary language he is not guilty of a second theft when he sells it.
Otherwise it would be possible, in theory, to convict a thief of theft of a
silver teapot every time he uses it to make the tea.

This view is suggested also by several provisions of the Act. Section 3(1)
says that where a person comes by a thing *without* stealing it, a subsequent
assumption of right can be an appropriation, and so theft. This implies
that if he comes by the thing theftously no subsequent act by him in
relation to it can amount to theft. If Parliament had wished merely to say
that a person who is in possession of property, whether lawfully or not
can steal it, it could have said simply that.

The definition of robbery in section 8 is that a person "steals, and
immediately before or at the time of doing so, and in order to do so, he
uses force," etc. This implies that force used by the thief to defend his
possession after the theft is not robbery. Consequently, it implies that the
time of stealing does not extend into the time when the thief is in
possession of the article after the first appropriation.

The definition of handling stolen goods in section 22 excludes acts done
"in the course of the stealing." If a thief who, having taken goods, later
sells them to a receiver, is guilty of a continuous appropriation from the
taking to the sale, the receiver presumably receives the goods "in the
course of the stealing." But this was not the intention of the Act, and the
courts do not construe it in such a way. If a thief sells the property, even if
only a few seconds after the theft, the buyer can be convicted of handling.
(*R. v. Pitham, post*, p. 814.) This strongly implies that appropriation is a
single event, not a continuous proceeding.

The Criminal Law Revision Committee proposed that the former offence
of receiving stolen goods should be widened to include other people who
without receiving the goods, helped the thief to dispose of them, because
otherwise they might not be guilty of an offence. Hence the new offence of
handling, which appears in the Act. Now if later acts done by the thief

with the stolen goods could be regarded as new theftous appropriations, persons assisting him to do these acts would be accessories to the new thefts, and there would have been no real need to widen the old law of receiving. The fact that it was widened shows that the legislature like the Committee, assumed that there could be only one theftous appropriation ...

The arguments in favour of a continuous-appropriation rule turn on policy rather than authority. A single-appropriation rule might enable a person charged with theft at a stated time to defend himself impudently by showing that he had appropriated the article earlier. ... Another inconvenience of the single-appropriation rule may be illustrated as follows. D. steals an article in Germany (which would not be punishable by our law, being out of the jurisdiction). He brings the article to this country and sells it, appropriating the proceeds. On the single-appropriation rule he still cannot be touched in this country; and a recorder has so ruled (*R.* v. *Figures* [1976] Crim.L.R. 744). It would be convenient if he could be, but an amendment to the Act would be required to secure this result.

On balance, these arguments favour the view that the single-appropriation rule represents the present law, but that if the Theft Act comes to be reconsidered it might well be amended to adopt the concept of continuous appropriation. This might enable the offence of handling, with all its complexities, to be abolished."

Note

The implication of single appropriation in the words of section 8, referred to by Williams, was later rejected by the Court of Appeal, holding that, in robbery at least, appropriation is a continuous act: *R.* v. *Hale* (1978) 68 Cr.App.R. 415, *post*, p. 745. And see *R.* v. *Gregory* (1981) 77 Cr.App.R. 41, *post*, p. 816.

ii. "Property"

Theft Act 1968, section 4

"(1) 'Property' includes money and all other property, real or personal, including things in action and other intangible property.

(2) A person cannot steal land, or things forming part of land and severed from it by him or by his directions, except in the following cases, that is to say—

(a) when he is a trustee or personal representative, or is authorised by power of attorney, or as liquidator of a company, or otherwise, to sell or dispose of land belonging to another, and he appropriates the land or anything forming part of it by dealing with it in breach of the confidence reposed in him; or

(b) when he is not in possession of the land and appropriates anything forming part of the land by severing it or causing to be severed, or after it has been severed; or

(c) when, being in possession of the land under a tenancy, he appropriates the whole or part of any fixture or structure let to be used with the land.

For purposes of this subsection 'land' does not include incorporeal hereditaments; 'tenancy' means a tenancy for years or any less period and includes an agreement for such a tenancy, but a person who after the end of a tenancy remains in possession as statutory tenant or otherwise is to be treated as having possession under the tenancy, and 'let' shall be construed accordingly.

(3) A person who picks mushrooms growing wild on any land, or who picks flowers, fruit or foliage from a plant growing wild on any land, does not (although not in possession of the land) steal what he picks, unless he does it for reward or for sale or other commercial purpose.

For purposes of this subsection 'mushroom' includes any fungus, and 'plant' includes any shrub or tree.

(4) Wild creatures, tamed or untamed, shall be regarded as property; but a person cannot steal a wild creature not tamed nor ordinarily kept in captivity, or the carcase of any such creature, unless either it has been reduced into possession by or on behalf of another person and possession of it has not since been lost or abandoned, or another person is in course of reducing it into possession."

Notes

Section 4 replaces the common law definition of things capable of being stolen, which in general included only tangible moveable objects. There are, however, still some things which are not or not completely within the concept of stealable things.

1. *Land.* Land, and things attached to or growing on land could not in general be stolen, and although the Criminal Law Revision Committee were pressed to equate land with other property exactly, in the end they decided that the position should remain broadly as it was previously: Cmnd. 2977, paras. 44, 47.

Questions

1. Is theft involved in any of the following cases?

A. moves the fence between his own land and that of his neighbour B., so as to take in a strip of B.'s land.

C., a licensee of D.'s land, strips off some antique wooden panelling and sells it as firewood.

E., an outgoing tenant of F., purports to sell some antique panelling in the house to G., the incoming tenant.

H., tenant of J., cuts down a wood on the land and sells it as firewood.

K. enters L.'s land and uproots a Christmas tree growing wild, with intention of taking it home to decorate his own home.

M. is given £1. by N. to collect enough wild mushrooms from L.'s land to make a breakfast for N.

2. Is a charge of criminal damage available in any of these cases? Compare section 10(1) of the Criminal Damage Act 1971, *post*, p. 854.

2. *Wild animals*, while alive and free, were not the subject of larceny. Dead animals were larcenable but not, ordinarily, by the person who killed them; in other words, poaching was not larceny.

The Committee, on the grounds that poaching was not popularly regarded as stealing and that to make it theft would increase the maximum penalty too greatly, decided against equating wild animals with other things.

Various provisions making summary offences of taking deer and fish were contained in the Larceny Act 1861, which the Theft Act repeals entirely. In order to preserve these offences pending a comprehensive reform of the law of poaching, they were re-enacted substantially unchanged in Schedule 1 to the Theft Act. The provisions relating to deer were superseded by the Deer Act 1980. There are also other poaching statutes, *e.g.* the Salmon and Freshwater Fisheries Act 1975. Moreover, legislation not concerned with protecting anyone's property in the creatures involved protects wild birds, their nests and eggs (Protection of Birds Act 1954) and endangered species (Conservation of Wild Creatures and Wild Plants Act 1975). And see Wildlife and Countryside Act 1981, s.13.

Question

A rounds up wild ponies from the moorland where they are born and reared, in order to sell them at auction. B, who disapproves of this, releases them from the auction pen and one escapes. C captures it and refuses to return it to A or to pay for it. Can the actions of A or B or C amount to theft?

3. *Things in action and other intangible property.* Before the Theft Act, to be stealable, property had to be tangible. Other things of value, such as a legal right, could not be stolen, and a prosecutor was driven to such shifts as charging the stealing of the piece of paper which evidenced such a right. There is now no need to do that in many cases, as a result of the wide definition of property in section 4(1); but if a piece of paper is involved and changes hands, it may still be convenient to charge the theft of the paper, because the attempt in section 4(1) to widen the concept of stealable property is not without its difficulties.

3a. *Things in action.* A thing in action (or chose in action) is property which does not exist in a physical state, and cannot be enjoyed physically (looked at, listened to, eaten, worn, ridden, etc.), but can only be claimed by legal action. Examples are a debt, shares in a company, a copyright, a trade-mark, insurance cover. These things can be stolen by one who appropriates them with intent to deprive the owner permanently, *e.g.* a trustee or personal representative, the legal owner of shares beneficially owned by X, dishonestly assigning them to Y. A bank account is also a chose in action. The property rights involved in a bank account are often misunderstood.

Lord Goddard C.J. in *R.* v. *Davenport* [1954] 1 All E.R. 602, 603:

"Although we talk of people having money in a bank, the only person who has money in a bank is the banker. If I pay money into my bank, either by paying cash or a cheque, the money at once becomes the money of the banker. The relationship between banker and customer is that of debtor and creditor. He does not hold my money as an agent or trustee. ... When the banker is paying out, whether in cash or over the counter or whether by crediting the bank account of someone else, he is paying out his own money, not my money, but he is debiting me in my account with him. I have a chose in action, that is to say I have a right to expect that the banker will honour my cheque, but he does it out of his own money."

If a customer A has a credit of £500 in bank B, the only property is the chose in action, the right to call on B to honour cheques up to that amount. There is no particular sum in the bank vaults over which this right operates. The consequences are: (1) there is no question of a dishonest A stealing this thing in action from B, because by its nature it never could belong to B. Normally it belongs to A himself [but it may "belong to" someone else if another joint account holder is involved, or if it were obtained subject to an obligation to deal with it in a certain way, or by mistake with an obligation to restore: see section 5(3)(4) and *Att.-Gen.'s Reference (No. 1 of 1983)* [1984] 3 All E.R. 369, *post*, p. 717]. If A obtained the right to overdraw up to £500 by fraud, it is not theft by A, because this right (to call on B to honour cheques up to £500) never did or could belong to B: but see Obtaining Pecuniary Advantage by Deception, *post*, p. 776: (2) If A by fraud gets B. to honour his cheque by paying £500 to P, it is not theft. The £500 given to P. may be property, but A does not appropriate it by his fraud, since he does not assume the rights of ownership over any identifiable property; he merely causes B. to assume a duty to pay P. £500 out of B's general assets: *R. v. Navvabi* [1986] 3 All E.R. 102; but see Obtaining Services by Deception, *post*, p. 777.

But A's right to call on bank B may be stolen by *someone else*, as where, *e.g.* D. is A's cashier with power to draw cheques on A.'s account, and draws one dishonestly in favour of his own creditor Q. When this cheque is presented and met, A will have lost part of his debt against his banker B. See next case. And even if the cheque is not met, the act of presenting it for payment is an appropriation of one of the rights of the owner, A: *Chan Man-sin* v. *Att.-Gen. for Hong Kong* [1988] 1 All E.R. 1 (P.C.); *Re Osman* [1989] 3 All E.R. 701 (Div.Ct.).

See also Griew, "Stealing and Obtaining Bank Credits" [1986] Crim.L.R. 356.

R. v. Kohn
(1979) 69 Cr.App.R. 395
Court of Appeal

K. was a director of Panelservice Ltd., with authority to make payments on its behalf by drawing cheques against its bank account. He drew cheques against the account for his own purposes. He was convicted of theft of the things in action, which the cheques represented, and of the cheques themselves. He appealed.

GEOFFREY LANE L.J.: The way the indictment was drawn, broadly speaking, with one or two exceptions which need not concern us at this stage, was to allege each alleged defalcation by way of two counts. The first of the two counts in each case alleged the theft of a thing in action, namely a debt in the sum of £x owed by the National Westminster Bank Ltd. to Panelservice Ltd.; and the other of the two counts in each case alleged that the defendant on or about such and such a date stole a cheque No. so and so the property belonging to Panelservice Ltd.

The counts, as appears from what I have already stated, alleged these events on various dates and, not surprisingly, the state of the particular account at the National Westminster Bank varied from time to time, with the result, again as will emerge when one comes to examine the notice of appeal in detail, that some of the cheques were drawn or presented at a time when the account was in credit, some of the cheques were drawn or presented when the account was in overdraft but within limits of the overdraft facility, and there was one count, count 7, in which the cheque was drawn or presented at a time when the account was first of all in overdraft, and secondly beyond the agreed limit of the overdraft, that is to say the limit agreed between the bank and Panelservice. . . .

So far as the first situation is concerned, when the account is in credit, the prosecution say that, where an account is in credit the relationship of debtor and creditor exists between the bank and the customer. The customer is the creditor, the bank is the debtor. The debt is owing by the bank to the customer. That debt is something which cannot be physically handled, it is not a thing or chose in possession; it is a thing in action, namely something which can only be secured by action and, goes the argument, this is a case of a thing in action par excellence, and if it be proved that the defendant has stolen, in other words appropriated that thing in action, then the offence is made out. [After considering reported decisions on the meaning of "chose in action"]: So the prosecution start off with the advantage of the fact that that expression is plainly one which covers a multitude of matters and over the history of English law has spread really far beyond its original concept. So at first blush it would seem that the appellant's contentions on this point are a little difficult to sustain.

But what Mr. Tyrrell submits is this—since we are not sure we have followed the argument, we quote what he says verbatim: "The very act done which is relied on as interfering with the owner's rights destroys the subject matter of the theft and so there has been no appropriation. Nothing has ever come into the possession of the appellant." What he says, we think, is that the thing in action has been destroyed before any appropriation and therefore there has been no theft.

It seems to us that the argument is quite untenable. First of all, is there a thing in action, and the answer is undoubtedly yes. Secondly, has the appellant appropriated it? The answer is yes. Was the intention permanently to deprive the owner, and again there was ample evidence upon which the jury properly directed could come to the conclusion that it was. Was it dishonest? Again there was ample evidence on which the jury could come to that conclusion.

A submission was made at the close of the prosecution case similar to that made to us, which the judge rejected. We think that he was right to reject it.

Mr. Tyrrell has frankly said that his researches have brought to light no authorities which give any support to his proposition. In so far as there is authority it is against his contentions. It is contained in the writings of two eminent academic lawyers: first of all Professor Griew in his book *The Theft Acts 1968 and 1978* (3rd ed, 1978), paras. 2–11, where one finds this:

"The case of an employee (D.) who has authority to draw on his employer's (P.'s) bank account and who dishonestly draws on it for unauthorised purposes seem also to be theft (assuming the account to be in credit), D. has in some manner appropriated the debt owed by the bank to P. Although nothing in the transaction operates as an assignment of that debt to D., it would seem that D. has appropriated the debt or part of it by causing P.'s credit balance to be diminished, or at the very least taking the risk of such diminution. The case is analogous to the theft of a chattel by destruction."

The whole of that passage, and particularly the last sentence, if it is correct, as we think it is, sounds the death knell to this particular submission on behalf of the appellant. . . .

We now turn to the counts which cover the situation where the account was overdrawn, but the amount of the cheque was within the agreed limits of the overdraft. So far as this aspect of the matter is concerned, Mr. Tyrrell submits that the grant of facilities for an overdraft does not create a debt. [After considering authorities holding that specific performance is not possible on a contract to lend money, and holding that to that extent the contract does not constitute a debt] [But] if the account is in credit . . . there is an obligation to honour the cheque. If the account is within the agreed limits of the overdraft facilities, there is an obligation to meet the cheque. In either case it is an obligation which can only be enforced by action and therefore potentially a subject of theft under the provisions of the 1968 Act. The cheque is the means by which the theft of this property is achieved. The completion of the theft does not take place until the transaction has gone through to completion. . . .

[In] *William Rouse* v. *Bradford Banking Co. Ltd.* [1894] A.C. 586, 596, Lord Herschell L.C. said:

" . . . It may be that an overdraft does not prevent the bank who have agreed to give it from at any time giving notice that it is no longer to continue, and that they must be paid their money. This I think at least it does; if they have agreed to give an overdraft they cannot refuse to honour cheques or drafts, within the limit of that overdraft, which have been drawn and put in circulation before any notice to the person to whom they have agreed to give the overdraft that the limit is to be withdrawn. . . . "

Finally the passage of Sir John Donaldson P. in *Eckman* v. *Midland Bank Ltd.* [1973] Q.B. 519, 529 a decision of the National Industrial Relations Court, Sir John Donaldson sitting as President with two other lay members:

"If, however, a bank has contracted with the contemnor in terms which entitle him to draw on the bank up to a limit and that limit has not been reached, this facility is part of the property of the contemnor which the sequestrators are entitled to have transferred to them and which they can operate by authority of the writ of sequestration."

It seems to us, in the light of those authorities and in the light of the wording of the Theft Act 1968, that in this situation, when the order to the bank is within the agreed limits of the overdraft, a thing in action certainly exists and accordingly the judge was right in rejecting the submission. The appeal so far as those particular counts are concerned must fail.

That leads us to the third situation, which affects only count 7, that being, it will be remembered, the count which dealt with the cheque presented to the bank at the time when the account was over the agreed overdraft limit which had been imposed by the bank.

The situation here is that there is no relationship of debtor and creditor, even notionally. The bank has no duty to the customer to meet the cheque. It can simply mark the cheque "Refer to drawer." It can decline to honour the cheque. The reasons for that are obvious. If then a bank declines to honour a cheque, there is no right of action in the customer. If they do as a matter of grace—that is all it can be—honour the cheque then that is a course which does not retrospectively create any personal right of property in the customer and does not create any duty retrospectively in the bank. It seems, therefore, on that bald statement of principle, that this count which alleged a theft of a thing in action when the account was over the agreed limit must be quashed, unless some external reason can be found for saving it. . . .

We turn now to the next matter which has been urged before us, and that was a matter which was raised for the first time by a supplementary notice of appeal which has been placed before us. The supplementary grounds of appeal read as follows: "The appellant will seek leave to argue as a supplementary ground of appeal that the convictions on counts 4, 6, 8, 10, 12, 14, 16, 20 and 24 of the indictment (theft of cheques) were unsafe and unsatisfactory and proceeded on a misdirection of law. The case for the appellant is that it was not possible in law for him to steal the cheques as alleged in that: (a) he himself wrote and drew the cheques; (b) there was no possibility of Panelservice Ltd. being permanently deprived of the cheques in their character as pieces of paper since they had that character both before and after the appellant drew them; (c) there was no possibility of Panelservice Ltd. being permanently deprived of the cheques in their character as things in action since they did not acquire that character until the appellant wrote and drew them."

This point was not argued at the trial and one suspects this is the brainchild of Mr. Rose, who argued this matter before us and argued, if we may say so, most attractively. The way he put it is as follows: first of all he submits that if the cheque is treated as a piece of paper *simpliciter*, rather than in its character as a thing in action, it is not proved, he suggests, that there was any intention permanently to deprive the owner. It would be likely to go back to the company, and he submits that the provisions of section 6(1), which I have already read, do not in those circumstances bite. He submits that the decision of this Court in *Duru and Asghar* [1974] 1 W.L.R. 2 (*post*, p. 724) does not apply, because that case was dealing with a different section of the Theft Act 1968, namely section 15. Furthermore in that case the cheque, he suggests, was being treated in its capacity as a thing in action. He submits further that the defendant here in no way assumed the rights of an owner, if one is viewing the cheque simply as a piece of paper. He represented himself, so the argument goes, as agent of the company to draw a cheque and that is not acting as owner.

One of the difficulties in considering these arguments is that, by reason of the fact that the point was not raised in the Court below the issues never became crystallised. So that one has to search the transcript in order to try to discover the way in which, under these counts, the cheque was being viewed by counsel before the judge and consequently before the jury.

The matter seems to us to become reasonably clear so far as that is concerned, if one looks at p. 21 of the first volume of the transcript. Here the learned judge said to the jury: "What is represented by the cheque is, of course, the right of the person named in it, the payee, to receive the payment represented by that cheque. So far as that cheque itself is concerned, true it is a piece of paper but it is a piece of paper which changes its character completely once it is paid because then it receives a rubber stamp or, in this case, the perforated stamp saying that it has been paid and it then also ceases to be a thing in action. That is a bill of exchange which is a thing in action as I have told you. The cheque is the same thing. It ceases to be that or, at any rate, it ceases to be in its substance the same thing as it was before. That is an instrument on which payment falls to be made." It seems tolerably clear from that that the judge, counsel and the jury were not considering the cheque in its capacity as a piece of paper *simpliciter*, even if one can view a cheque properly in that light. They were looking at it as a negotiable instrument in the way that the judge described.

Even if that was the way the matter was being considered, said Mr. Rose, the drawing of a cheque in favour of a third party does not amount to treating oneself as an owner and therefore there is no appropriation sufficient to satisfy the requirements of section 1.

We do not consider that those submissions can be supported. The way in which the matter should be approached, we think is as Miss Goddard submitted to us, which was this. A cheque is not a piece of paper and no more. In no circumstances, in this type of situation, can it be so considered. It is a piece of paper with certain special characteristics.

The sequence of events in this case can be brought down to a simple series of facts. The defendant starts with a cheque book in his possession. It is the cheque book of the company and he is plainly in lawful possession of that book with cheques inside it. He apparently had the habit, as we have already indicated, at least occasionally, of removing blank cheques from the book, tearing out the cheque leaving the counterfoil in position, putting the cheque in his pocket and filling it in at a later stage. Still nothing wrong at all in that. He is still acting lawfully, although it may be somewhat unusual. He then makes up his mind to fill in a cheque with the amount, then the payee and the date and so on. The third party in whose favour the cheques were being made were *ex hypothesi* not entitled to those sums. The appellant was therefore using the company's cheques and the company's bank account for his own purposes. Miss Goddard suggests that there was a gradual appropriation as the events moved on in this way.

The next stage is this. He says to himself, "I am now going to make the cheque payable to E.P. or Happy Pets or whoever it may be." That action is unknown to Mr. Aust. It is *ex hypothesi* once again contrary to the interests of the company. It is contrary to the will of the company and it is dishonest. This is dealing with the cheque not as the agent of the company duly authorised, but is dealing with the cheque as if it were his own. That seems to us is sufficient to amount to an appropriation under the Act.

So when the writing gets on to the cheque, it becomes a bill of exchange and becomes a necessary demand upon the bank to honour the bank's obligations to the customer, which is the company. But that is being done for the defendant's own purposes, and when he sends it on to the company, to Happy Pets or to E.P., it has come to the point where he has made the cheque his own. For the purposes of the Theft Act he has appropriated the cheque, and given that the other elements of the crime are present, which one must assume for purposes of this argument, the offence is complete. Be it noted it is not a matter of what happens to the document thereafter.

Consequently for purposes of these counts, that is to say the even numbered counts, the "cheque" counts rather than the "thing in action" counts, it does not matter whether the account of the company is in credit, it does not matter whether it is within its overdraft limits, it does not matter whether it is outside the overdraft limits, the offence is nevertheless complete.

Now to deal with the further question of whether there is an intent permanently to deprive the owner? Here we would wish to do what the judge did, simply to cite the passage from Megaw L.J.'s judgment in *Duru and Asghar* [*post*, p. 724] "In the view of this Court there can be no doubt that the intention of both of these appellants, as would necessarily have been found by the jury if the matter had been left to the jury on a proper direction of law (a direction which would no doubt have been given if the pleas of guilty had not been entered), was permanently to deprive the Greater London Council of that thing in action, that cheque; that piece of paper, in the sense of a piece of paper carrying with it the right to receive payment of the sum of £6,002.50 which is the amount concerned in count 3. So far as the cheque itself is concerned, true it is a piece of paper. But it is a piece of paper which changes its character completely once it is paid, because then it receives a rubber stamp on it saying it has been paid and it ceases to be a thing in action, or at any rate it ceases to be, in its substance, the same thing as it was before: that is, an instrument on which payment falls to be made. It was the intention of the appellants, dishonestly and by deception, not only that the cheques should be made out and handed over, but also that they should be presented and paid, thereby permanently depriving the Greater London Council of the cheques in substance as their things in action. The fact that the mortgagors were under an obligation to repay the mortgage loans does not affect the appellant's intention permanently to deprive the council of these cheques."

Consequently so far as the counts involved in these supplementary grounds of appeal are concerned, particulars of which have already been detailed, the appeal must fail. The appellant was assuming the rights of the owner, that is to say the rights of the creditor vis-à-vis the bank, that is the rights of the company to demand that the bank should hand over the money. He is assuming the right to do what he likes with that part of the company's debt with which he is dealing.

The learned Lord Justice then dealt with the further grounds of appeal, discussed them and concluded: For the reasons which we have indicated it seems to us, apart from the conviction on count 7 which must be quashed, this appeal must be dismissed.

Conviction on count 7 quashed. Appeal dismissed on other counts

Notes

1. Although Geoffrey Lane L.J. (*ante*, p. 684) said that "the completion of the theft does not take place until the transaction has gone through to completion," this was held to be *obiter* in *Chan Man-sin* v. *A.-G. for Hong Kong* [1988] 1 All E.R. 1 (P.C.) and *Re*

Osman [1989] 3 All E.R. 701 (D.C); the giving of instructions to the bank to debit V.'s account is a usurpation of one of the rights of the owner of the account (V.).

2. The Court of Appeal holds that Kohn stole not only the right which Panelservice had against the bank to have their cheques met, but also the cheques themselves (the even-numbered counts). It is held that a cheque is not only a piece of paper but also a chose in action, a right in the drawee (Happy Pets) to be paid the amount of the cheque by Panelservice. Converting a blank cheque into a valid cheque is an appropriation of Panelservice's piece of paper, and so is sending it to Happy Pets; if done with intent to deprive, it is theft. The only question is, how does Kohn permanently deprive Panelservice of the appropriated property, *i.e.* the cheque which will eventually find its way back to Panelservices? One answer is to say that Panelserve has to "buy" it back, by meeting the cheque, by paying Happy Pets the amount specified in the cheque. It is clear that the owner of property is permanently deprived if he is only to get it back by buying it back [see, *post*, p. 720]. However the Court adopts another view (formulated in *R.* v. *Duru*), that what the owner, Panelservice, gets back is something entirely different from what was taken from it. What was taken was a thing in action, "a piece of paper carrying with it the right to receive payment of a sum of money," and what was returned was a mere piece of paper (a cancelled cheque). The inference is that it has been stripped of all or most of its value to Panelservice. It is not at first sight clear what has been removed from the cheque which is of value to Panelservice, since its obvious value is a duty in Panelservice to pay a sum of money to the payee. Removal of this "value" does not prejudice Panelservice. The answer appears to be that while it was a cheque, Panelservice could exchange it for goods or other value. Now it has only a worthless piece of paper. However it does not seem accurate to say that Panelservice is deprived of a thing in action, because that thing in action, being a right to sue Panelservice for money, could never have been owned by Panelservice.

3b. *Other intangible property*. Some intangible things can be valuable, without being a recognised thing in action. Examples are a patent, which is declared by statute to be personal property but not a thing in action: Patents Act 1977 s.30(1); and a trader's assignable export quota was held to be stolen by the person in the trader's organisation who was in charge of buying and selling such quotas when it was sold by him at a gross undervalue to a competitor: *Att.-Gen for Hong Kong* v. *Nai Keung* [1987] 1 W.L.R. 1339. Other examples are kinds of information: an idea, news, "know-how," a secret, especially a trade secret. Industrial espionage is rife nowadays, and such valuables are often "stolen," in popular parlance at least. However, it seems that information is not anyway comprehended in the statutory phrase "other intangible property."

Oxford v. Moss
(1978) 68 Cr.App.R. 183
Queens Bench Division

The facts appear in the judgment of Smith J.

SMITH J.: This is a prosecutor's Appeal by way of Case Stated.

On May 5, 1976, an information was preferred by the prosecutor against the defendant alleging that the defendant stole certain intangible property, namely, confidential information being examination questions for a Civil Engineering Examination to be held in the month of June 1976 at Liverpool University, the information being the property of the Senate of the University, and the allegation being that the Respondent intended permanently to deprive the said Senate of the said property.

The facts can be stated very shortly indeed. They were agreed facts. They are set out in the case and they are as follows. In May 1976 the defendant was a student at Liverpool University. He was studying engineering. Somehow (and this Court is not concerned precisely how) he was able to acquire the proof of an examination paper for an examination in Civil Engineering to be held in the University during the following month, that is to say June 1976. Without doubt the proof, that is to say the piece of paper, was the property of the University. It was an agreed fact, as set out in the case, that the respondent at no time intended to steal what is described as "any tangible element" belonging to the paper; that is to say it is conceded that he never intended to steal the paper itself.

In truth and in fact, and in all common sense, what he was about was this. He was borrowing a piece of paper hoping to be able to return it and not be detected in order that he should acquire advance knowledge of the questions to be set in the examination and thereby, I suppose, he would be enabled to have an unfair advantage as against other students who did not possess the knowledge that he did.

By any standards, it was conduct which is to be condemned, and to the layman it would readily be described as cheating. The question raised is whether it is conduct which falls within the scope of the criminal law.

The learned stipendiary magistrate at Liverpool was of the opinion that, on the facts of the case, confidential information is not a form of intangible property as opposed to the property in the proof examination paper itself, that is the paper and the words printed thereon. He was of the opinion, further, that confidence consisted in the right to control the publication of the proof paper and was a right over property other than a form of intangible property.

Finally, he was of the opinion that by his conduct the respondent had gravely interfered with the owner's right over the paper. He had not permanently deprived the owner of any intangible property. Accordingly, the learned stipendiary magistrate dismissed the charge.

The prosecutor appeals. The question for this Court, shortly put, is whether confidential information can amount to property within the meaning of the Theft Act 1968. By section 1(1) of the statute: "A person is guilty of theft if he dishonestly appropriates property belonging to another with the intention of permanently depriving the other of it ... ";

By section 4(1): " 'property' includes money and all other property, real or personal, including things in action and other intangible property."

The question for this Court is whether confidential information of this sort falls within the definition contained in section 4(1). We have been referred to a number of authorities emanating from the area of trade secrets and matrimonial secrets. In particular, we were referred to *Peter Pan Manufacturing Corporation* v. *Corsets Silhouette Ltd.* [1963] 3 All E.R. 402, to *Seager* v. *Copydex Ltd.* [1967] 2 All E.R. 415, to the case of *Argyll* v. *Argyll* [1965] 2 W.L.R. 790, and *Fraser* v. *Evans* 3 W.L.R. 1172.

Those are cases concerned with what is described as the duty to be of good faith. They are clear illustrations of the proposition that, if a person obtains information which is given to him in confidence and then sets out to take an unfair advantage of it, the courts will restrain him by way of an order of injunction or will condemn him in damages if an injunction is found to be inappropriate. It seems to me, speaking for my part, that they are of little assistance in the present situation in which we have to consider whether there is property in the information which is capable of being the subject of a charge of theft. In my judgment, it is clear that the answer to that question must be no. Accordingly, I would dismiss the Appeal.
(Lord Widgery C.J. and Wien J. agreed.)

Appeal dismissed

Questions

1. It was conceded that Moss never intended to steal the paper itself. On the agreed facts need this concession have been made? See s.6(1), *post*, p. 720, and J. R. Spencer, *The Metamorphosis of section 6 of the Theft Act*, *post*, p. 720.

2. It is not said how Moss obtained the proof. If he had used a collaborator in the University Registry, what would have been his offence? See, *ante*, p. 463.

Notes

The Court held that civil cases on protection of confidential information are of little assistance. Even if a right over something is protected by the law in some ways (*e.g.* by injunction, or by damages for its misuse) it does not follow that the right is intangible property, still less that it is intangible property for all purposes, *i.e.* that it ought to be protected by the criminal law, or by the law of theft specifically. In some areas theft is a blunt instrument where a discriminating tool is required.

R. v. *Stewart* (1983) 149 D.L.R. (3rd.) 583 turned on whether it was theft for an agent of a trade union wishing to organise the workforce in an hotel to arrange for the copying of a secret list of employees' names and addresses compiled by the employer. Under the Canadian Criminal Code, the subject matter of theft could be "anything whether animate or inanimate." The majority of the Ontario Court of Appeals, differing from *Oxford* v. *Moss*, held, on analogy with civil protection of confidence cases, that the information in the list was property capable of being stolen. Hammond, "Theft of Information" (1984) 100 L.Q.R. 252, 263, commented on the implications of this decision:

"Questions of entitlement to information will surface with increasing regularity in British Commonwealth courts in the next few years. These questions are themselves a reflection of fundamental changes in the economic and social structure of western societies. Resolution of these issues will involve a complex adjustment of several important public policy elements. The need to maintain the free and open transmission of ideas and information is the cornerstone of the western liberal tradition, and should be viewed as the overriding norm. Departures, or suggested departures, from this norm should be rigorously scrutinised and granted only in compelling cases, and then only in sufficient, but no more than sufficient terms. It may be, for instance, that a good case can be made out on economic grounds for improved civil remedies against misappropriation of trade secrets or other commercially valuable information of an intangible nature. Such an approach would add a third tier of statutory rights alongside patents and copyright. However, even where legal protection is, for reasons which are thought to be good and sufficient, extended to this kind of 'information,' such exceptions to the general principle may still have to be defeasible where there is an overriding 'right to know' in the public. These principles will probably have to be applied to a wide variety of fact situations with complex public policy assessments being made in each case to the likely social and economic costs entailed in granting or withholding protection. Information entitlement statutes may well become the industrial, health and welfare statutes of the future. The criminal law is too blunt an instrument for this task. It does not offer a 'quick fix' for the kinds of issues at stake. The solution to information issues lies in traditional legal methodology; the evolution and articulation of sound principles and their systematic, painstaking application on a situation by situation basis."

4. *Electricity.* This was not stealable at common law. It is not included in the definition of property in section 4 because the dishonest use or wasting or diverting of it is made a special offence in section 13. See *Low* v. *Blease* [1975] Crim.L.R. 513.

5. *Unspecific Property.* If A is charged with stealing a watch, he cannot be convicted of stealing an umbrella (see Cockburn C.J. in *R.* v. *McPherson* (1858) D. & B. 197, 200). He must be shown to have stolen the specific property he is charged with stealing, although not necessarily the whole of it.

Machent v. *Quinn* [1970] 2 All E.R. 255 (Q.B.D.). Q. was charged with stealing 35 shirts, nine pairs of trousers, four sweaters, two beach sets and two cardigans, to the total value of £199. It was proved that he stole four sweaters only, valued at £25. *Held,* he could be convicted as charged, (but his sentence was to relate to the four sweaters only).

It would be different if all that could be shown was that Q. had stolen some articles from the list, but not which articles. However if the articles are identical (or undifferentiated in the indictment, *i.e.* described as "goods"), it is no objection that the stolen ones cannot be identified.

R. v. *Tideswell* [1905] 2 K.B. 273 (C.C.C.R.). T. had permission to help himself to ashes in P.'s yard, paying for the weight taken. In collusion with P.'s servant, he took 32 tons 13 cwts., knowing that the servant had recorded the sale as of 31 tons 3 cwts. only. *Held* T. could be convicted on an indictment charging him with larceny of 1 ton 10 cwts.

And if it is impossible to show which particular articles A. stole and when, but only that goods or money to a certain total value was appropriated in a certain period (*e.g.* between two stock-takings), he may be charged with, and convicted of, stealing the general deficiency. *R.* v. *Tomlin* [1954] 2 Q.B. 274.

In charges of attempted theft, or burglary with intent to commit theft, it is not necessary to charge or prove that the accused had any particular property in mind: *Re A.-G.'s References* (*Nos. 1 and 2 of* 1979) [1980] Q.B. 180 (C.A.).

iii. "Belonging to Another"

Theft Act 1968, section 5

"(1) Property shall be regarded as belonging to any person having possession or control of it, or having in it any proprietary right or interest (not being an equitable interest arising only from an agreement to transfer or grant an interest).

(2) Where property is subject to a trust, the persons to whom it belongs shall be regarded as including any person having a right to enforce the trust, and an intention to defeat the trust shall be regarded accordingly as an intention to deprive of the property any person having that right.

(3) Where a person receives property from or on account of another, and is under an obligation to the other to retain and deal with that property or its proceeds in a particular way, the property or proceeds shall be regarded (as against him) as belonging to the other.

(4) Where a person gets property by another's mistake, and is under an obligation to make restoration (in whole or in part) of the property or its proceeds or of the value thereof, then to the extent of that obligation the property or proceeds shall be regarded (as against him) as belonging to the person entitled to restoration, and an intention not to make restoration shall be regarded accordingly as an intention to deprive that person of the property or proceeds.

(5) Property of a corporation sole shall be regarded as belonging to the corporation notwithstanding a vacancy in the corporation."

Notes

°1. A person can only steal what belongs to another. "Belonging to another" is given an extended meaning, and covers persons who have only minor interests in the property (possession, control, any proprietory right or interest). If B has such a minor interest in property, that property can be stolen from him by A, and it matters not whether A is also entitled to a minor (or indeed major) interest in the same property. Moreover, even if A is the entire owner, and B has no interest which the civil law will recognise, it may still be possible for A to steal the property if A got the property under an obligation.

2. Moreover a company is another person *vis-à-vis* its share-holders. Even if A owns all the shares in P. Ltd., the property is not his, but "belongs to another," *viz.* P. Ltd., and A can steal that property: *A.-G.'s Reference No. 2 of 1982* [1984] 2 Q.B. 624: *R.* v.

Philippou (1989) 89 Cr.App.R. 290. The fact that the defendant is in complete control of the company, and so able to secure its compliance with what he does, affords him no defence. His will is not that of the company when he is engaged in a crime against the company, and anyway the consent of the owner is irrelevant in theft, according to *R. v. Gomez*: see Lord Browne-Wilkinson, *ante*, p. 677.

3. The "belonging to another" factor, extended as it is, must exist at the time when the accused did the act which is said to be theft. If *before* he dishonestly does an act with regard to the property, it has ceased to belong to another and belongs to the accused, that act cannot be theft. See *Edwards* v. *Ddin*, below. But if the dishonest act *results* in the property belonging to the accused, because the victim consents to him becoming its owner, that act is nevertheless an appropriation of property belonging to another, and can be theft; it is sufficient if the property belonged to another at the time of the dishonest act: see *R. v. Gomez*, *ante*, p. 663 and particularly Viscount Dilhorne in *Lawrence*, *ante*, p. 666.

Edwards v. Ddin
[1976] 1 W.L.R. 942
Queen's Bench Division

The facts appear in the judgment of Croom Johnson J.

CROOM-JOHNSON J.: This is an appeal by way of case stated from the magistrates' court sitting at Amersham in which the defendant had an information preferred against him that he stole three gallons of petrol and two pints of oil together of the value of £1.77, the property of Mamos Garage, Amersham, contrary to section 1 of the Theft Act 1968.

On the facts as found by the justices the following things happened. The defendant arrived with a motor car and he asked for some petrol and oil to be placed in his car. Petrol and oil to the value as stated £1.77, was placed into the car at his request by the garage attendant. When he ordered the petrol and oil the defendant impliedly made to the attendant the ordinary representation of an ordinary customer that he had the means and the intention of paying for it before he left. He was not in fact asked to pay and he did not in fact pay, but the moment when the garage attendant was doing something else he simply drove away. The justices also found, as one would think was perfectly obvious, that whilst the petrol and oil had been placed in the car, either in the tank or in the sump, it could not reasonably be recovered by the garage in default of payment.

The questions therefore which have to be resolved in order to satisfy section 1 of the Act were two in number. First of all, was the defendant dishonest? It appears that the justices must have considered that that was so. Secondly, had he appropriated property belonging to another with the intention of permanently depriving the other of it? Upon that point the defence submitted successfully that at the time when the car was driven away the petrol and oil which had got into the tank or sump were in fact not the property of the garage any more but were the property of the defendant. On that basis the justices said that that particular essential ingredient of theft under section 1 of the Act had not been fulfilled and dismissed the information.

The whole question therefore was: whose petrol and oil was it when the defendant drove away? Property passes under a contract of sale when it is intended to pass. In such transactions as the sale of petrol at a garage forecourt ordinary common sense would say that the garage and the motorist intended the property in the petrol to pass when it is poured into the tank and irretrievably mixed with the other petrol that is in it, and I think that is what the justices decided.

But the prosecutor has appealed and has based his appeal on a consideration of the Sale of Goods Act 1893 and the provisions of that Act, and seeks a ruling that transfer of the petrol was conditional only and that therefore until payment the petrol remained the property of the garage.

But if one considers the provisions of the Sale of Goods Act 1893 one comes out at the same answer as common sense would dictate.

The prosecution argument went this way, that when the motorist arrives at the garage and says "will you fill me up, please?" or "will you give me two gallons?" then there is a contract for the sale of unascertained goods by description. In such circumstances when does the property in the petrol pass? Nothing will have been said between the motorist and the pump attendant about that, so one is thrown back on section 18 of the Sale of Goods Act 1893 and rules made under it in order to ascertain the intention of the parties.

By pouring the petrol into the tank the goods have been appropriated to the contract with the assent of both parties. If that is done unconditionally, then the property in the petrol passes to the motorist: rule 5(1). The prosecution argument then goes on that, however, there is a condition which is waiting to be fulfilled, namely, payment, and says that under section 19 of the Sale of Goods Act 1893 the garage reserves the right of disposal of the petrol until the payment has been made and that therefore the property has not passed under rule 5(1).

It is at this point that the argument breaks down. The garage owner does not reserve the right to dispose of the petrol once it is in the tank, nor is it possible to see how effect could be given to any such condition wherever petrol has been put in and is all mixed up with what other petrol is already there. Consequently one passes back to rule 5(2) of section 18, which says that where a seller delivers the goods to the buyer and does not reserve the right to dispose of them, he is deemed to have unconditionally appropriated the goods to the contract and in those circumstances the property has passed to the buyer in accordance with rule 5(1).

Reference was also made by the prosecutor to section 5 of the Theft Act 1968 which deals with one of the subsidiary definitions arising under section 1, which is the initial section dealing with theft. Section 5, which deals with but is not definitive of the expression "belonging to another," is concerned with all manner of interests in property. It was urged upon us that the motorist is under an implied obligation to retain his car with the petrol in its tank on the garage premises and not to take it away until such time as he has paid for it, and that until that has been done the garage owner retains some proprietary interest in the petrol in the tank.

The relevant part of section 5, which is in subsection (3), reads:

> "Where a person receives property from or on account of another, and is under an obligation to the other to retain and deal with that property or its proceeds in a particular way, the property or proceeds shall be regarded (as against him) as belonging to the other."

That section in my view is not apt to cover a case such as the present where there has been an outright sale of the goods and the property in the goods has passed and the seller is only waiting to be paid. Therefore the provisions of section 5 do not affect the conclusion in the present case.

I do not enter into any discussion for the purposes of this judgment of what might have been the position if the charge had been brought under some other section of the Theft Act 1968, or if the appropriation for the purposes of section 1 had been said to have arisen at an earlier stage of events which took place. On the facts as found and on the case as it was presented to the magistrates, in my view the magistrates reached a correct conclusion in law and I would dismiss the appeal.

Appeal dismissed

Questions

1. The Court leaves open the position if the appropriation had been said to have arisen at an earlier stage of the events. *Could* the appropriation have been said to have arisen earlier than the act of driving the car away? If yes, what difference should it have made to the result?

2. Would it have made any difference if the garage had *expressly* reserved the right of disposal pending payment? Consider the effect of the following condition of sale: "The seller supplies petrol on the understanding that from the moment of delivery until the amount supplied has been paid for, the whole of the petrol in the customer's tank shall be the property of the seller."

3. Of what offence could Ddin have been convicted if the facts had occurred in 1979? See, *post*, p. 784.

Notes

1. In *Davies* v. *Leighton* (1978) 68 Cr.App.R. 4, Lord Widgery C.J. regarded the law as well settled that in a supermarket sale the property in goods does not pass to the customer until he has paid for them, and he applied this rule to a case where the goods were not picked off the shelf by the customer but, being fruit, were weighed, bagged, priced and handed over by an assistant. See J. C. Smith's commentary on this case at [1978] Crim.L.R. 576 for discussion of many of the different problems which can arise out of shop sales.

2. The introduction of civil law contractual questions into trials for theft has been deprecated, *e.g.* by Lord Roskill in *R.* v. *Morris* [1984] A.C. 320. However, if the issue is whether the property the subject of an apparent sale "belongs to another" at the time of the alleged theft by D., such questions are inevitable.

R. v. *Walker* [1984] Crim.L.R. 112. V. bought a video recorder from D., which turned out to be defective. V. returned it to D. for repair and then, not getting any satisfaction, sued D. in the County Court for the return of money paid for defective goods. Two days after he was served with the County Court summons, D. sold the recorder to P. On D.'s trial for theft, the judge left it to the jury to decide on the evidence if the recorder belonged to V. at the time D. sold it to P. *Held*, this was not enough. "The relevant law, which was contained in the Sale of Goods Act 1979 was complicated but the judge had made no attempt to explain it. For centuries juries had decided civil actions on points arising under the law of sale of goods. There was no reason why this jury should not have had the relevant law explained to them and in the absence of such an explanation it was impossible for them to do justice in the case." *Appeal allowed*. [The relevant law is that recission of a contract of sale returns the property in the goods to the vendor, and the service of a summons for the return of the purchase price could have amounted to such a recission]

Questions

1. A in a pub approaches B, who works at a local garage, and says he will make it worth B's while if he "forgets" to ask for any money when he fills his vehicle with petrol. B consults his employer, who instructs B to pretend to play A's game and arranges for the police to be present. Next day, A asks B to fill his tank and when that has been done starts to drive off without paying, but is apprehended. Is this theft by A? See *R. v. Gomez, ante*, p. 663.

2. (i) A sees an old car parked on the hard shoulder of a motorway. It is the same model as A.'s car, for which he has found difficulty in obtaining spares. A. removes a part from the parked car, which A. thinks has merely broken down but which in fact has been abandoned there by B. Is this theft by A?

(ii) Is it attempted theft by A? See, *ante*, p. 424.

(iii) Would it make any difference if the car had been abandoned in Q.'s barn? See next case.

R. v. Woodman
[1974] Q.B. 758
Court of Appeal

A was the owner of a disused factory. He sold all the scrap metal in the place to B. B entered the factory and removed all the scrap metal which he could easily reach, but left some which was in such an inaccessible position as to be not worth the trouble of getting. A, who thought that all the metal had been removed by B, then put a barbed wire fence around the factory to exclude trespassers. W entered the factory and removed the remaining metal. He was convicted of theft, and appealed on the ground that no-one had possession or control of the metal.

LORD WIDGERY C.J.: ... [Theft Act 1968], Section 1(1) provides: "A person is guilty of theft if he dishonestly appropriates property belonging to another." I need not go further because the whole of the debate turns on the phrase "belonging to another." Section 5(1) of the Act expands the meaning of the phrase in these terms:

"Property shall be regarded as belonging to any person having possession or control of it, or having in it any proprietary right or interest ... "

The recorder took the view that the contract of sale between English China Clays and the Bird group had divested English China Clays of any proprietary right to any scrap on the site. It is unnecessary to express a firm view on that point, but the court are not disposed to disagree with that conclusion that the proprietary interest in the scrap had passed. The recorder also took the view on the relevant facts that it was not possible to say that English China Clays were in possession of the residue of the scrap. It is not quite clear why he took that view. It may have been because he took the view that difficulties arose by reason of the fact that English China Clays had no knowledge of the existence of this particular scrap at any particular time. But the recorder did take the view that so far as control was concerned there was a case to go to the jury on whether or not this scrap was in the control of English China Clays, because if it was, then it was to be regarded as their property for the purposes of a larceny charge even if they were not entitled to any proprietary interest.

The contention before us today is that the recorder was wrong in law in allowing this issue to go to the jury. Put another way, it is said that as a matter of law English China Clays could not on these facts have been said to be in control of the scrap.

We have formed the view without difficulty that the recorder was perfectly entitled to do what he did, that there was ample evidence that English China Clays were in control of the site and had taken considerable steps to exclude trespassers as demonstrating the fact that they were in control of the site, and we think that in ordinary and straightforward cases if it is once established that a particular person is in control of a site such as this, then prima facie he is in control of articles which are on that site.

The point was well put in an article written by no lesser person than Mr. Wendell Holmes in his book *The Common Law* (1881), at pp. 222, 223–224, dealing with possession. Considering the very point we have to consider here, he said, and I take the extract from *Hibbert* v. *McKiernan* [1948] 2 K.B. 142, 147:

> "There can be no animus domini unless the thing is known of; but an intent to exclude others from it may be contained in a larger intent to exclude others from the place where it is, without any knowledge of the object's existence. ... In a criminal case, the property in iron taken from the bottom of a canal by a stranger was held well laid in the canal company, although it does not appear that the company knew of it, or had any lien upon it. The only intent concerning one thing discoverable in such instances is the general intent which the occupant of land has to exclude the public from the land, and thus, as a consequence, to exclude them from what is upon it."

So far as this case is concerned, arising as it does under the Theft Act 1968, we are content to say that there was evidence of English China Clays being in control of the site and prima facie in control of articles upon the site as well. The fact that it could not be shown that they were conscious of the existence of this or any particular scrap iron does not destroy the general principle that control of a site by excluding others from it is prima facie control of articles on the site as well.

There has been some mention in argument of what would happen if in a case like the present, a third party had come and placed some article within the barbed-wire fence and thus on the site. The article might be an article of some serious criminal consequence such as explosives or drugs. It may well be that in that type of case the fact that the article has been introduced at a late stage in circumstances in which the occupier of the site had no means of knowledge would produce a different result from that which arises under the general presumption to which we have referred, but in the present case there was, in our view, ample evidence to go to the jury on the question of whether English China Clays were in control of the relevant time. Accordingly, the recorder's decision to allow the case to go to the jury cannot be faulted and the appeal must be dismissed.

Appeal dismissed

Questions

1. "In my judgment, it is quite clear that a person cannot be said to be in possession of some article which he or she does not realise is, or may be, in her handbag, in her room, or in some other place over which she had control": *per* Lord Parker C.J., in *Lockyer* v. *Gibb* [1967] 2 Q.B. 243, a prosecution for the offence of being in possession of a controlled drug. Is this dictum inconsistent with the decision in *R.* v. *Woodman*?

2. Suppose W., when stripping the factory of metal, had discovered and taken away a cache of controlled drugs abandoned there by X. If, consistent with Lord Parker's dictum English China Clays were held not to have possession of the drugs, could W. be convicted of stealing them?

Subsection 1: Possession, control or any proprietary right or interest

R. v. Bonner
[1970] 1 W.L.R. 838
Court of Appeal

B. took metal from the house of W., with whom he was in partnership as demolition contractors. B. said the metal was partnership property and he took it in order not to deprive W. of it permanently but hold it as security for what was due to him from W. out of the partnership profits. B. was convicted of theft but his appeal was allowed on the ground that the verdict was in all the circumstances unsafe and unsatisfactory. However the Court of Appeal thought it right to deal with the legal point certified by the trial judge, *viz.* whether the jury was misdirected on the law relating to the theft by a partner of partnership property. The direction in question is quoted in the judgment of Edmund-Davies L.J. below.

EDMUND DAVIES L.J.: ... Mr. Inglis-Jones has ... submitted that the circumstances of this case a mere taking away of partnership property, even with the intention of keeping the other partner permanently out of possession of it would not *per se* suffice to amount to theft; there would have to be something like destruction of the metal or its sale in market overt, which would have the effect (provided there was innocence in the buyer) of transferring a good title to him and so defeating the title of the deprived partner. Defending counsel summarised the matter by submitting that for there to be an "appropriation" within the Theft Act 1968, there must be a "conversion" of the property by one or other of the foregoing methods, neither of which was resorted to here. Therefore, so it is submitted, there was no theft.

Rejecting that submission, Judge Ranking directed the jury in these terms:

" ... even if you are satisfied that there was a full partnership between Webb and Bonner, a partner has no right to take any partnership property with the intention of permanently depriving the other of his share. Therefore, even if Bonner was a partner of Webb, if he took that lead, which was partnership property, intending to deprive Webb permanently of his share and when he did it, he knew perfectly well that he had no legal right to take it, then he is guilty of theft; he is guilty of the theft of the whole property and not just guilty of the theft of Webb's share, because the whole of it was partnership property and it had not been divided ... and if one partner takes it he is guilty of stealing the whole of it."

Was this a misdirection? This court is clearly of the opinion that it was not. Sections 1, 3 and 5 of the Theft Act 1968, are here relevant. Section 1(1) reads:

"A person is guilty of theft if he dishonestly appropriates property belonging to another with the intention of permanently depriving the other of it; and 'thief' and 'steal' shall be construed accordingly."

Section 3 defines the word "appropriates" in these terms:

"Any assumption by a person of the rights of an owner amounts to an appropriation ... " Section 5 defines the phrase, "belonging to another," used in section 1.

Mr. Inglis-Jones has boldly submitted that, since the basic requirement of theft is the appropriation of property belonging to another, there can be no such appropriation by one co-owner of property which is the subject matter of the co-ownership or partnership; and that there can be no "assumption ... of the rights of an owner" in a case like the present, where one is dealing with (as Bonner claims) property belonging to a partnership.

The whole object of the Theft Act 1968, was to get away from the technicalities and subtleties of the old law. Mr. Inglis-Jones has not repeated before us an interesting submission which he made below; but, since we are dealing with this topic, we think that it might be helpful if we resurrect it and attempt to dispose of it now. His submission below went something on these lines: The Larceny Act 1916, had a special provision (section 40(4)) that:

"If any person, who is a member of any co-partnership or is one of two or more beneficial owners of any property, steals or embezzles any such property of or belonging to such co-partnership or to such beneficial owners he shall be liable to be dealt with, tried, and punished as if he had not been or was not a member of such co-partnership or one of such beneficial owners."

The parent of that provision was the Larceny Act 1868, a one-section statute, and in *R.* v. *Jesse Smith* (1870) 1 C.C.R. 266 Bovill C.J. said, referring to the Larceny Act 1861, at p. 269:

"At the time that Act (Larceny Act 1861 (24 & 25 Vict. c.96)) was passed theft by a partner of the goods of the firm did not fall within the criminal law, either common or statute. This defect was supplied by the Larceny and Embezzlement Act 1868 (31 & 32 Vict. c. 116), which, after reciting that 'it is expedient to provide for the better security of the property of co-partnerships and other joint beneficial owners against offences by part-owners thereof, and further to amend the law as to embezzlement,' proceeds to enact, by the first section, that if a partner, or one of two or more beneficial owners, shall steal, etc., any property of such co-partnership or such joint beneficial owners, 'every such person shall be liable to be dealt with, tried, convicted, and punished for the same as if such person had not been or was not a member of such co-partnership, or one of such beneficial owners.' "

Mr. Inglis-Jones submitted that, there having been a special provision in the Larceny Act 1916, following upon the earlier Act, dealing with the position of a partner wrongfully treating partnership property, and there being no repetition of that statutory provision in the Theft Act 1968, the inference is that the law has been changed and that it is no longer theft for a partner to deprive a co-partner of any of the partnership property even if it be done dishonestly and intending permanently to deprive.

I said a little earlier that the object of the Theft Act 1968, was to get rid of the subtleties and, indeed, in many cases the absurd anomalies of the pre-existing law. The view of this court is that in relation to partnership property the provisions in the Theft Act 1968, have the following result: provided there is the basic ingredient of dishonesty, provided there be no question of there being a claim of right made in good faith, provided there be an intent permanently to deprive, one partner can commit theft of the property of another to whom he is a complete stranger.

Early though these days are, this matter has not gone without comment by learned writers. Professor Smith in his valuable work on the Theft Act 1968, expresses his own view quite clearly in paragraph 80 under the heading "Co-owners and partners" in this way:

"D. and P. are co-owners of a car. D. sells the car without P.'s consent. Since P. has a proprietary right in the car, it belongs to him under section 5(1). The position is precisely the same where a partner appropriates the partnership property."

In the joint work of Professor Smith and Professor Hogan, the matter is thus dealt with (Smith and Hogan's *Criminal Law*, (2nd ed. (1969), p. 361):

" ... D. and P. ... may ... be joint owners of property. Obviously there is no reason in principle why D. should not be treated as a thief if he dishonestly appropriates P.'s share, and he is so treated under the Theft Act."

We thus have no doubt that there may be an "appropriation" by a partner within the meaning of the Act, and that in a proper case there is nothing in law to prevent his being convicted of the theft of partnership property. But this *excursus* is of an academic kind in the present case for we have already indicated our view regarding the unsatisfactory and unsafe nature of the verdicts returned against each of these accused. In these circumstances, all four appeals are allowed.

Appeals allowed

[Three other men who had helped Bonner had been charged with him.]

R. v. Turner (No. 2)
[1971] 1 W.L.R. 901
Court of Appeal

T. took his car to a garage to have it repaired. Those repairs having been practically completed, the car was left in the road outside the garage. T. called at the garage and told the proprietor that he would return the following day, pay him, and take the car; instead he took the car, using his spare key, without paying for the repairs. Later he lied about the matter to the police. He was convicted of theft of the car.

LORD PARKER C.J.: The words "belonging to another" are specifically defined in section 5 of the Act, subsection (1) of which provides: "Property shall be regarded as belonging to any person having possession or control of it, or having in it any proprietary right or interest." The sole question was whether Mr. Brown [the garage proprietor] had possession or control.

This court is quite satisfied that there is no ground whatever for qualifying the words "possession or control" in any way. It is sufficient if it is found that the person from whom the property is taken, or to use the words of the Act, appropriated, was at the time in fact in possession or control. At the trial there was a long argument as to whether that possession or control must be lawful, it being said that by reason of the fact that this car was subject to a hire-purchase agreement, Mr. Brown could never even as against the defendant obtain lawful possession or control. As I have said, this court is quite satisfied that the judge was quite correct in telling the jury they need not bother about lien, and that they need not bother about hire purchase agreements. The only question was whether Mr. Brown was in fact in possession or control.

The second point that is taken relates to the necessity for proving dishonesty. Section 2(1) provides that: "A person's appropriation of property belonging to another is not to be regarded as dishonest (a) if he appropriates the property in the belief that he has in law the right to deprive the other of it, on behalf of himself or of a third person";

The judge said in his summing up: "Fourth and last, they must prove that the defendant did what he did dishonestly and this may be the issue which lies very close to the heart of the case." He then went on to give them a classic direction in regard to claim of right, emphasising that it is immaterial that there exists no basis in law for such belief. He reminded the jury that the defendant had said categorically in evidence: "I believe that I was entitled in law to do what I did." At the same time he directed the jury to look at the surrounding circumstances. He said this: "The prosecution say that the whole thing reeks of dishonesty, and if you believe Mr. Brown that the defendant drove the car away from Carlyle Road, using a duplicate key, and having told Mr. Brown that he would come back tomorrow and pay, you may think the prosecution are right." On this point Mr. Herbert says that if in fact you disregard lien entirely, as the jury were told to do, then Mr. Brown was a bailee at will and this car could have been taken back by the defendant perfectly lawfully at any time whether any money was due in regard to repairs or whether it was not. He says, as the court understands it, first that if there was that right, then there cannot be theft at all, and secondly that if and in so far as the mental element is relevant, namely belief, the jury should have been told that he had this right and be left to judge, in the light of the existence of that right, whether they thought he may have believed, as he said, that he did have a right.

The court, however, is quite satisfied that there is nothing in this point whatever. The whole test of dishonesty is the mental element of belief. No doubt, though the defendant may for certain purposes be presumed to know the law, he would not at the time have the vaguest idea whether he had in law a right to take the car back again, and accordingly when one looks at his mental state, one looks at it in the light of what he believed. The jury were properly told that if he believed he had a right, albeit there was none, he would nevertheless fall to be acquitted. This court, having heard all that Mr. Herbert has said, is quite satisfied that there is no manner in which this summing-up can be criticised, and that accordingly the appeal against conviction should be dismissed.

Appeal dismissed

Questions

1. A's car was taken by some person unknown. A few days later, A saw it standing locked on the drive of B's house. Using his spare key, he drove it away. Was this theft by A? Would it make any difference if he thought that the law gave him no right to repossess himself of the car but required him to report the matter to the police and leave them to take steps to get the car back? (Refer to the discussion of "legal impossibility" in regard to attempts, *ante*, p. 478).

2. Is the following case distinguishable from *R. v. Turner* (No. 2)?

> In *R. v. Meredith* [1973] Crim.L.R. 253, M.'s car was impounded by the police while he was at a football match and removed to the police station yard, where it was left locked. When M. went to the police station, he found it crowded and so, rather than wait, he took his car away from the yard without contacting any policeman. He was charged with stealing the car. Under the Disposal and Removal of Vehicles Regulations 1968, the owner was liable to pay the statutory charge of £4 if his car had been causing an obstruction. On going to the police he could (i) admit obstruction and pay £4, or (ii) refuse to pay and face prosecution for obstruction, or (iii) agree to pay and receive a bill for £4. In any event he would be allowed to take the car away for the regulations gave the police no power to retain it as against him. It was held by a Crown Court judge that M. had no case to answer.

Trust Property

Notes

1. A beneficiary under a trust clearly has a proprietory right or interest in the trust property, and a defaulting trustee may be guilty of stealing that property from him. The object of the special provision in section 5(2) (*ante*, p. 692) is to cover cases such as a charitable trust where there is no defined beneficiary, but the trust is enforceable by someone, *e.g.* the Attorney-General. The trust property "belongs to" that person for the purposes of theft.

2. As to constructive trusts, it was thought that the expression "proprietary interest" covered the interest of one entitled under such a trust (with the single stated exception of an equitable interest arising from an agreement to transfer or grant an interest). However there are divergent decisions of the Court of Appeal on whether to recognise interests under constructive trusts as proprietary interests within the meaning of subsection (1). In *A.-G.'s Reference (No. 1 of 1985)* (*post*, p. 707), a profit obtained by A. from the unauthorised use of his employer's premises and facilities was held not to make A. a constructive trustee of the profit; but the Court also held that, even if he was a constructive trustee, the trust did not give rise to a proprietary interest of the kind mentioned in subsection (1), because to convict a dishonest servant of stealing if he kept the profit would be far removed from ordinary notions of stealing. However, on the proprietary interest

remaining on one who hands over money or property by mistake, see next case.

R. v. Shadrakh-Cigari
(1988) Transcript by LEXIS
Court of Appeal

S was guardian of his nephew R, whose father in Iran arranged for money to be paid into R's bank account in the United States. By error at the bank, $286,000 was credited to the account instead of $286. The United States bank transferred the larger sum to R's account with the Midland Bank, Sutton Coldfield. S prevailed on R to sign an authority for the issue of bankers drafts in favour of S totalling £197,000. Midland Bank issued the drafts and delivered them to S, who cashed them for his own purposes. He was convicted of theft of the drafts and appealed on the ground that the drafts belonged entirely to him.

SAVILLE J. for the Court: ... In our judgment the error in these submissions lies in the assumption that the entire proprietary interest in the drafts existed and vested in the Appellant leaving the Midland Bank with no rights at all. The fact of the matter is that the drafts would not have been drawn and delivered to the Appellant at all but for the mistake made by the United States bank, which, in turn led the Midland Bank to believe that the amount in question had been duly transferred from the United States for the credit of the account of Ramin. As Mr. Phillips put it in evidence, a banker would not issue a banker's draft unless he himself was absolutely certain that he had received the money in payment and that in the instant case (having checked with London that the transfer had in fact been made and having credited the account of Ramin) he regarded the money as belonging to Ramin, who then authorised the issue of the drafts. It could hardly be suggested (and indeed it was not suggested) that if the Midland Bank had known the true position it would, nevertheless, have issued the drafts, since they would then be aware that there was, at the lowest, a substantial risk that the United States bank would be able to reclaim the funds. Indeed, we consider that the latter bank would have been able successfully to do so. See *Chase Manhattan Bank* v. *Israel-British Bank* [1981] 1 Ch 105. The mistake of the United States bank in the present case, therefore, totally undermined the basic assumption upon which the Midland Bank issued the drafts, namely that the funds which had been received could properly be dealt with as directed by the account holder.

In these circumstances, it seems to us that as between the Midland Bank and the Appellant, the transaction falls fairly and squarely within the principles of the law relating to mistake. In *Kelly* v. *Solari*, (1841) 9 M & W 54 and 58, Parke B stated the principle in the following terms:

> "I think that where money is paid to another under the influence of a mistake, that is, upon the supposition that a particular fact is true, which would entitle the other to the money, which fact is untrue, and the money would not have been paid if it had been known to the payer that it was untrue, an action will lie to recover it back, and it is against conscience to retain it."

It has been suggested in later cases that the principle is not, in fact, stated widely enough by Parke B. to cover all circumstances where money or property can be recovered after a mistake has been made, but this citation will suffice for present purposes, since in this context we can see no material distinction between money and the drafts in question.

As Lord Wright pointed out in *Norwich Union* v. *Price* [1934] AC 455 at
463, the mistake must be one in reespect of the underlying assumption of
the contract or transaction or as being fundamental or basic, but to our
minds that is clearly the case here. It is also probably the case that the
mistake must be one of fact rather than law, but again we consider that if
this is a requirement, it was satisfied in the present case.

The original mistake was clearly one of fact on the part of the United
States bank and so far as the Midland Bank were concerned, the latter to
our minds were clearly under the factual misapprehension that the former
truly intended to transfer and vest in Ramin the entire right, property and
interest in the amount remitted.

On this basis, it seems to us that the Appellant came under an
obligation to make restoration of the instruments in question on the basis
that the Midland Bank retained an equitable proprietary interest in the
drafts as a result of the mistake, as in *Chase Manhattan Bank* v. *Israel-British
Bank* (supra). The fact that the choses in action created by the drafts could
not be owned by the bank, since they were debts due from the bank, is in
our view irrelevant. The bank created the drafts and before delivery they
undoubtedly owned them, although at that stage, as promissory notes,
they were inchoate and incomplete (see Section 84 of the Bills of Exchange
Act 1882). Upon delivery under the mistake, the bank retained an
equitable interest in those instruments. It was not disputed that such an
equitable interest amounts to property within the meaning of Section 5 (1)
of the Theft Act 1968. To that extent, therefore, the drafts continued to
belong to the Midland Bank at all material times within the meaning of the
Theft Act 1968, so that the suggested difficulty in proving an appropriation
does not arise.

In our judgment this conclusion is not only supported by Section 5(4) of
the Theft Act 1968, but can be reached by another route through the
application of that subsection, which provides as follows:

> "Where a person gets property by another's mistake, and is under an
> obligation to make restoration (in whole or in part) of the property or its
> proceeds or of the value thereof, then to the extent of that obligation the
> property or proceeds shall be regarded (as against him) as belonging to
> the person entitled to restoration, and an intention not to make
> restoration is to be regarded accordingly as an intention to deprive that
> person of the property or proceeds."

It is clear from this sub-section that even if it cannot be said that the
property belongs to another in the sense of that other having proprietary
rights over the property itself, nevertheless (other things being equal) the
property is to be regarded for the purposes of theft as belonging to that
other even if the person getting it is only under an obligation to restore the
proceeds of the property or its value, as opposed to the property itself,
though the latter case is, of course, also covered by the sub-section.

We consider that the Appellant did come under an obligation to restore
the proceeds or value of the instruments to the Midland Bank on the basis
of the principles of civil law to which we have already referred.

On this aspect of the matter Mr. Brock submitted that neither an equity
in the drafts nor the right to claim their proceeds or value arose unless the
Appellant was shown to have been aware that he was not entitled to
receive the money in the form of the drafts. Mr. Brock cited *Att.-Gen.'s
Reference (No. 1 of 1985) post* p. 707 as authority for this proposition.

So far as the equitable proprietary remedy is concerned, (with which the
case cited did not deal) this proposition is clearly wrong, since it is settled
law that the beneficiary (i.e. the owner of the equitable interest) can claim

the property from an innocent volunteer who has taken it without notice of the equitable interest—see *Re Diplock* [1948] Ch 465 at 539.

So far as rights to claim the property or its proceeds or value on other grounds are concerned, the law is less certain. In the case cited by Mr. Brock, of course, the Lord Chief Justice was dealing with a case of theft, where knowledge is essential for another reason, namely to establish dishonesty, so that in that context it is hardly surprising that the Court made the observations upon which Mr. Brock places reliance.

We remain unpersuaded that knowledge on the part of the recipient is a necessary pre-condition to a civil obligation on his part to restore the property, its proceeds or value but for the purposes of this appeal we are prepared to make the opposite assumption in favour of the Appellant. Having done so, we take the view that the point is an academic one, for, in fact, the judge did leave this very question to the jury.

Appeal dismissed

Subsection 3: An obligation to retain and deal with the property or its proceeds in a particular way

R. v. Hall
[1973] 1 Q.B. 126
Court of Appeal

H., a travel agent, received money from certain clients as deposits and payments for air trips to America. He paid the money so received into his firm's general account. None of the projected flights materialised and none of the money was refunded. He was convicted of theft. He appealed on the ground that he had not, within the meaning of section 5(3), been placed under an obligation to retain and deal with in a particular way the sums paid to him.

EDMUND DAVIES L.J.: Two points were presented and persuasively developed by the appellant's counsel: (1) that, while the appellant has testified that all moneys received had been used for business purposes, even had he been completely profligate in its expenditure he could not in any of the seven cases be convicted of "theft" as defined by the Theft Act 1968; there being no allegation in any of the cases of his having *obtained* any payments by deception, counsel for the appellant submitted that, having received from a client, say, £500 in respect of a projected flight, as far as the criminal law is concerned he would be quite free to go off immediately and expend the entire sum at the races and forget all about his client ...

Point (1) turns on the application of section 5(3) of the Theft Act 1968, which provides: "Where a person receives property from or on account of another, and is under an obligation to the other to retain and deal with that property or its proceeds in a particular way, the property or proceeds shall be regarded (as against him) as belonging to the other."

Counsel for the appellant submitted that in the circumstances arising in these seven cases there arose no such "obligation" on the appellant. He referred us to a passage in the Eighth Report of the Criminal Law Revision Committee which reads as follows: "*Subsection* (3) provides for the special case where property is transferred to a person to retain and deal with for a particular purpose and he misapplies it or its proceeds. An example would be the treasurer of a holiday fund. The person in question is in law the owner of the property; but the subsection treats the property, as against him, as belonging to the persons to whom he owes the duty to retain and deal with the property as agreed. He will therefore be guilty of stealing from them if he misapplies the property or its proceeds."

Counsel for the appellant . . . submits that the position of a treasurer of a holiday fund is quite different from that of a person like the appellant, who was in general (and genuine) business as a travel agent, and to whom people pay money in order to achieve a certain object—in the present cases to obtain charter flights to America. It is true, he concedes, that thereby the travel agent undertakes a contractual obligation in relation to arranging flights and at the proper time paying the airline and any other expenses. Indeed, the appellant throughout acknowledged that this was so, although contending that in some of the seven cases it was the other party who was in breach. But what counsel for the appellant resists is that in such circumstances the travel agent "is under an obligation" to the client "to retain and deal with . . . in a particular way" sums paid to him in such circumstances.

What cannot of itself be decisive of the matter is the fact that the appellant paid the money into the firm's general trading account. As Widgery J. said in *R*. v. *Yule* [1964] 1 Q.B. 5, 10, decided under section 20(1)(iv) of the Larceny Act 1916: "The fact that a particular sum is paid into a particular banking account . . . does not affect the right of persons interested in that sum or any duty of the solicitor either towards his client or towards third parties with regard to disposal of that sum." Nevertheless, when a client goes to a firm carrying on the business of travel agents and pays them money, he expects that in return he will, in due course, receive the tickets and other documents necessary for him to accomplish the trip for which he is paying, and the firm are "under an obligation" to perform their part to fulfil his expectation and are liable to pay him damages if they do not. But, in our judgment, what was not here established was that these clients expected them "to retain and deal with that property or its proceeds in a particular way," and that an "obligation" to do so was undertaken by the appellant. We must make clear, however, that each case turns on its own facts. Cases could, we suppose, conceivably arise where by some special arrangement (preferably evidenced by documents), the client could impose on the travel agent an "obligation" falling within section 5(3). But no such special arrangement was made in any of the seven cases here being considered. It is true that in some of them documents were signed by the parties; thus, in respect of counts one and three incidents there was a clause to the effect that the People to People organisation did not guarantee to refund deposits if withdrawals were made later than a certain date; and in respect of counts six, seven and eight the appellant wrote promising "a full refund" after the flights paid for failed to materialise. But neither in those nor in the remaining two cases (in relation to which there was no documentary evidence of any kind) was there, in our judgment, such a special arrangement as would give rise to an obligation within section 5(3).

It follows from this that, despite what on any view must be condemned as scandalous conduct by the appellant, in our judgment on this ground alone this appeal must be allowed and the convictions quashed. But as, to the best of our knowledge, that is one of the earliest cases involving section 5(3), we venture to add some observations.

(A) It is . . . essential for the purposes of [s.2(1)(*b*) of the Act] that dishonesty should be present at the time of appropriation. We are alive to the fact that to establish this could present great (and maybe insuperable) difficulties when sums are on different dates drawn from a general account. Nevertheless, they must be overcome if the Crown is to succeed.

(B) Where the case turns, wholly or in part, on section 5(3) a careful exposition of the subsection is called for. Although it was canvassed by counsel in the present case, it was nowhere quoted or even paraphrased by the commissioner in his summing-up. Instead he unfortunately ignored it and proceeded on the assumption that, as the appellant acknowledged the purpose for which clients had paid him money, *ipso facto* there arose an "obligation ... to retain and deal with" it for that purpose. He therefore told the jury: "The sole issue to be determined in each count is this. Has it been proved that the money was stolen in the sense I have described, dishonestly appropriated by him for purposes other than the purpose for which the moneys were handed over? Bear in mind that this is not a civil claim to recover money that has been lost." We have to say, respectfully, that this will not do, as cases under section 20(1)(iv) of the Larceny Act 1916, illustrate. Thus in *R. v. Sheaf* (1927) 134 L.T. 127, it was held that whether money had been "entrusted" to the defendant for and on account of other persons was a question of fact for the jury and must therefore be the subject of an express direction. ...

(C) Whether in a particular case the Crown has succeeded in establishing an "obligation" of the kind coming within section 5(3) of the new Act may be a difficult question. Happily, we are not called on to anticipate or solve for the purposes of the present case the sort of difficulties that can arise. But, to illustrate what we have in mind, mixed questions of law and fact may call for consideration. For example, if the transaction between the parties is wholly in writing, is it for the judge to direct the jury that, as a matter of law, the defendant had thereby undertaken an "obligation" within section 5(3)? On the other hand, if it is wholly (or partly) oral, it would appear that it is for the judge to direct them that, if they find certain facts proved, it would be open to them to find that an "obligation" within section 5(3) had been undertaken—but presumably not that they must so find, for so to direct them would be to invade their territory. In effect, however, the commissioner unhappily did something closely resembling that in the present case by his above-quoted direction that the only issue for their consideration was whether the appellant was proved to have been actuated by dishonesty.

We have only to add that counsel for the Crown submitted that, even if the commissioner's failure to deal with section 5(3) amounted to a misdirection, this was a fitting case to apply the proviso. By point (1) successfully taken by defence counsel, is clearly of such a nature as to render that course impossible. We are only too aware that, in the result, there will be many clients of the appellant who, regarding themselves as cheated out of their money by him, will think little of a law which permits him to go unpunished. But such we believe it to be, and it is for this court to apply it.

Conviction quashed

Attorney-General's Reference (No. 1 of 1985)
[1986] 2 All E.R. 219
Court of Appeal

The facts appear in the opinion of the Court

LORD LANE C.J.: This is a reference under s.36 of the Criminal Justice Act 1972. The Court of Appeal is asked to give its opinion on the following points of law. (1) If an employee contracts with his employer to sell on his employer's premises only goods supplied by his employer and to retain

and deal with the proceeds of such sales for the benefit of his employer,
does he receive moneys on account of his employer within the meaning of
s.5(3) of the Theft Act 1968 when they are paid to him by customers on the
said premises for goods he had secretly obtained from someone other than
his employer and sold on the said premises to the said customers? (2) On
a charge of theft, where an employee has used his employer's premises
and facilities to make a secret profit, will that secret profit be subject to a
constructive trust in favour of the employer? (3) And, if so, does that
constructive trust give the employer of proprietary right or interest in the
secret profit within the ambit of s.5(1) of the Theft Act 1968?

The material facts of the case were these. A. and B. appeared before the
Crown Court charged on an indictment containing five counts. ... In the
remaining counts A alone was charged with stealing sums of money
belonging to his employer.

At the time of the alleged offences A was the salaried manager of a
"tied" public house and B was a barman employed by A. One of the terms
of A's employment was as follows:

> "All wines, liqueurs, beers, spirits and other excisable articles and all
> tobaccos, cigars and cigarettes and mineral waters and other non-
> alcoholic beverages required for sale or consumption on or off the
> premises will be supplied by or on account of the company to the
> manager and the company will also supply or cause to be supplied such
> other stock as may be required for sale and the manager may not
> purchase any of the before mentioned articles or stocks unless the
> company shall from time to time so direct."

A was under a duty to pay all the takings of the public house into an
account owned or managed by his employers. A and B were discovered by
the police transporting 18 barrels of beer to the public house at night. A
admitted to the police that he had bought the barrels of beer from a
wholesaler and intended to make a secret profit by selling the beer to
customers in the public house, a practice he had followed for some time.
...

At the close of the case for the Crown counsel for the defence made
submissions of no case to answer. Prosecuting counsel submitted that A
was in a fiduciary position *vis-à-vis* his employers, that a fiduciary who
makes a secret profit becomes in equity a constructive trustee of that
profit, that A's employers as beneficiaries of that constructive trust had a
proprietary right or interest in the secret profit within s.5(1) of the 1968
Act, that the sums of money in counts 3 to 5 (which were specimen counts
relating to secret profits allegedly made by A by selling barrels of three
different kinds of beer) were property belonging to A's employers. ...
Defending counsel conceded that equity gave the employers a right to
recover the secret profits in a civil action but contended that the criminal
courts had never recognised the existence of any proprietary right or
interest arising from a constructive trust, and that the secret profits did not
"belong to another" for the purposes of the 1968 Act.

The judge ruled that the submissions of defending counsel were well-
founded and withdrew counts 1, 3, 4 and 5 from the jury. ...

We were told at the outset of this hearing that this sort of behaviour by
managers of "tied" houses is becoming more prevalent. They do not, it
seems, appear to be deterred by the prospect of losing their job or of being
compelled by civil action to disgorge their illicit profit. An additional
deterrent, it is suggested, in the shape of a conviction for theft would not
be inappropriate. That is not a matter which concerns us. We have to
decide whether Parliament intended to bring such behaviour within the

ambit of the criminal law and in particular whether, as alleged by the Crown, the illicit profit obtained by A was "property belonging to another."

Counsel for the Attorney-General bases his submission on two of the subsections to s.5 of the 1968 Act. First of all s.5(3), which reads as follows:

"Where a person receives property from or on account of another, and is under an obligation to the other to retain and deal with that property or its proceeds in a particular way, the property or proceeds shall be regarded (as against him) as belonging to the other."

Although, goes the argument, at first sight the money which A receives from selling the beer which he bought seems to belong to him, the effect of this subsection is to make the profit element in the money notionally belong to the employers. Thus when A appropriates the profit, he is guilty of theft, assuming that he is acting dishonestly.

Whether that argument is correct or not depends on whether A can properly be said to have received property (*i.e.* the payment over the counter for the beer he has sold to the customer) "on account of the employers." We do not think he can. He received the money on his own account as a result of his private venture. No doubt he is in breach of his contract with the employers; no doubt he is under an obligation to account to the employers at least for the profit he has made out of his venture, but that is a different matter. The fact that A may have to account to B for money he has received from X does not mean necessarily that he received the money on account of B.

Although we appreciate that references to pre-1968 statutes and decisions are not always helpful, it does, we feel, cast some light on the meaning of s.5 if one looks at the provisions of the Larceny Act 1916 which s.5(3) sought to replace and simplify. Section 17 of the Larceny Act 1916 reads as follows:

"Every person who—(1) being a clerk or servant or person employed in the capacity of a clerk or servant—(*a*) steals any chattel, money or valuable security belonging to or in the possession or power of his master or employer; or (*b*) fraudulently embezzles the whole or any part of any chattel, money or valuable security delivered to or received or taken into possession by him for or in the name or on the account of his master or employer . . . shall be guilty of felony . . . "

That was designed to deal first with the case of the servant who dishonestly took goods belonging to his master of which he had the lawful custody and secondly, with the servant who dishonestly intercepted property handed to him to be delivered to his master and before it reached the master.

It seems to us that s.5(3) was designed to replace the old provisions relating to larceny by a servant and embezzlement by the simpler and all-embracing words of s.5(3), namely "who receives property from or on account of another. . . . " Section 17 of the 1916 Act was in almost identical terms to s.68 of the Larceny Act 1861. There is a decision on the meaning of that latter section which is in point, *R.* v. *Cullum* (1873) L.R. 2 C.C.R. 28. That was a case in which the defendant was the captain of a barge and in the exclusive service of its owner. His remuneration was half the earnings of the barge, and he had no authority to take any other cargoes except those appointed for him. It was his duty to account to his master for the proceeds of each voyage which he undertook. On one occasion, although he had been ordered to bring the barge back empty from a certain place, and forbidden to take a particular cargo, he nevertheless loaded such cargo in the barge and returned therewith, being paid by the freight owners for that service. He told his master that the barge had come back empty and he never accounted for the money which he had received. The question was whether the defendant was properly convicted of embezzlement. The Court for Crown Cases Reserved held that on those facts the defendant was not guilty. Bovill C.J. in the course of his judgment said (at 31):

"The facts before us would seem more consistent with the notion that the prisoner was misusing his master's property, and so earning money for himself, and not for his master. Under those circumstances, the money would not be received "for" or "in the name of," or "on account of," his master, but for himself, in his own name and for his own account. His act, therefore, does not come within the terms of the statute, and the conviction must be quashed."

Blackburn J. said (at 33);

"Now, in the present case, I cannot see how this was the master's property, or that the servant had authority to carry anything in this barge but the cargo he was directed to convey. He was actually forbidden to load this barge on the return voyage; he did load it, and very improperly earned money by the use of it; but in what sense he can be said to have received this sum for the use of his master I cannot understand. The test of the matter would really be this—if the person to whom the manure belonged had not paid for the carriage, could the master have said, "There was a contract with you, which you have broken, and I sue you on it?" There would have been no such contract, for the servant never assumed to act for his master, and on that ground his act does not come within the statute. I think that in no case could he have been properly convicted under the Act unless the money became that of the master."

The other three judges comprising the court agreed with those observations.

Counsel for the Attorney-General seeks to distinguish that decision on the grounds that the freight owners would imagine that the man with whom they were dealing, namely the defendant himself, was entitled to the money they paid, because they did not know of the existence of the master, whereas in the instant case the customers, he suggests, would think they were handing over their money to the employers. We doubt whether the customers would pause to consider the destination of their money or whether it would make any difference to the legal situation if they did. Alternatively it is submitted *R. v. Cullum* was wrongly decided. We disagree. The argument based on s.5(3) of the 1968 Act was a late addition to the reference. We think it is misconceived.

The reference as originally drawn relied solely on arguments based on s.5(1), which reads as follows:

"Property shall be regarded as belonging to any person having possession or control of it, or having in it any proprietary right or interest (not being an equitable interest arising only from an agreement to transfer or grant an interest)."

The argument of the Crown is that A. was a "constructive trustee" of the profit element in the money paid by customers over the bar for the "bought in" beer and that accordingly the money belonged not, as might seem at first, to A. but to the beneficiary of the trust, namely the employers. The result of that, it is said, is that when A. paid the money into his bank account or otherwise appropriated it, he was guilty of theft (assuming dishonesty).

(After referring to various authorities.) We find it impossible to reconcile much of the language used in these decisions. Two matters however do emerge. The first is that if the contentions of the Crown are well-founded, and if in each case of secret profit a trust arises which falls within s.5, then a host of activities which no layman would think were stealing will be brought within the 1968 Act. As this court pointed out in *Dip Kaur* v. *Chief Constable for Hampshire* [1981] 2 All E.R. 430 at 433, [1981] 1 W.L.R. 578 at 583:

" ... the court should not be astute to find that a theft has taken place where it would be straining the language so to hold, or where the ordinary person would not regard the defendant's acts, though possibly morally reprehensible, as theft."

The second matter is this. There is a clear and important difference between on the one hand a person misappropriating specific property with which he has been entrusted, and on the other hand a person in a fiduciary position who uses that position to make a secret profit for which he will be held accountable. Whether the former is within s.5, we do not have to decide. As to the latter we are firmly of the view that he is not, because he is not a trustee.

In *Reading* v. *A.-G.* [1951] A.C. 507, a sergeant of the R.A.M.C. used his uniform and position to facilitate lorry loads of drugs and/or spirits travelling to Cairo undetected and made large sums of money thereby. The Crown held the balance of the money after his conviction by court martial. The sergeant claimed return of the money. It was held that any secret profits made by a soldier by improper use of his uniform and the opportunities attaching to it were recoverable by the Crown. Lord Porter, commenting on the judgment of Denning J. at first instance, said (at 514):

"If this means, as I think it does, that the appellant was neither a trustee nor in possession of some profit-earning chattel, ... it is true, but, in my view, irrelevant."

We derive some support also from the decision in *Re Sharpe* [1980] 1 W.L.R. 219, although on the facts it was remote from the present case. An elderly lady, Mrs. J. had advanced moneys to enable S, her nephew, to buy a house. In return she was to live with S and his wife in the property and they were to look after her. A receiving order was made against S, and his trustee in bankruptcy, having twice written to Mrs. J. and having received no reply, contracted to sell the premises with vacant possession to P. It was held, *inter alia*, that the aunt's irrevocable licence was not merely a contractual licence but arose under a constructive trust and as such conferred on her an interest in the property binding on the trustee in bankruptcy. Browne-Wilkinson J. in the course of his judgment said (at 223):

"I turn then to the alternative claim that Mrs. Johnson is entitled to ... stay on the premises until the money ... has been repaid. This right is based on the line of recent Court of Appeal decisions which has spelt out irrevocable licences from informal family arrangements, and in some cases characterised such licences as conferring some equity or equitable interest under a constructive trust. I do not think that the principles lying behind these decisions have yet been fully explored and on occasion it seems that such rights are found to exist simply on the ground that to hold otherwise would be a hardship to the plaintiff."

Lord Wilberforce in *Tarling (No. 1)* v. *Government of the Republic of Singapore* (1978) 70 Cr.App.R. 77 at 110, said:

"[The transactions] . . . would appear, prima facie, to amount to a case of persons in a fiduciary capacity making a secret profit at the expense of their companies—conduct for which there exists classical remedies in equity. . . . Breach of fiduciary duty, exorbitant profit making, secrecy, failure to comply with the law as to company accounts . . . are one thing: theft and fraud are others."

Next there is the judgment of a powerful Court of Appeal in *Lister & Co.* v. *Stubbs* (1890) 45 Ch.D. 1. In that case Stubbs was employed by the plaintiffs who were silk spinners, as a foreman to buy for them certain materials which they used in their business. Stubbs corruptly took from one of the firms with whom he was so dealing (Messrs. Varley) large sums by way of commission, which he then invested in the purchase of land and other investments. Some of it was retained in the shape of cash. The plaintiff company sought to follow such money into the investments and moved for an injunction to restrain Stubbs from dealing with the investments, alternatively for an order directing him to bring the moneys and the investments into court. Cotton L.J. said (at. p. 12):

" . . . in my opinion this is not the money of the Plaintiffs, so as to make the Defendant a trustee of it for them, but is money acquired in such a way that, according to all rules applicable to such a case, the Plaintiffs, when they bring the action to a hearing, can get an order against the Defendant for the payment of that money to them. That is to say, there is a debt due from the Defendant to the Plaintiffs in consequence of the corrupt bargain which he entered into; but the money which he has received under that bargain cannot, in the view which I take, be treated as being money of the Plaintiffs, which was handed by them to the Defendant to be paid to Messrs. Varley in discharge of a debt due from the Plaintiffs to Messrs. Varley on the contract between them."

Lindley L.J. gave judgment in similar terms (at p. 15):

"Then comes the question, as between Lister & Co. and Stubbs, whether Stubbs can keep the money he has received without accounting for it? Obviously not. I apprehend that he is liable to account for it the moment that he gets it. It is an obligation to pay and account to Messrs. Lister & Co., with or without interest, as that of debtor and creditor; it is not of trustee and *cestui que trust*. We are asked to hold that it is—which would involve consequences which, I confess, startle me. . . . If by logical reasoning from the premises conclusions are arrived at which are opposed to good sense, it is necessary to go back and look again at the premises and see if they are sound. I am satisfied that they are not sound—the unsoundness consisting in confounding ownership with obligation."

Bowen L.J. concurred with those judgments.

It seems to us that the draftsmen of the 1968 Act must have had that decision in mind when considering the wording of s.5. Had they intended to bring within the ambit of the 1968 Act a whole new area of behaviour which had previously not been considered to be criminal, they would, in our judgment, have used much more explicit words than those which are to be found in s.5. Nor do we think it permissible to distinguish that decision by saying that bribes are in a different category from such transactions as those in the instant case. There is, in our view, no distinction in principle between the two.

Looking at the matter from a different angle, can it be said that the employers had a "proprietary right or interest" in the profit made by A? We are asked by counsel as *amicus curiae* to test the problem in the following way. Suppose that the transactions by A take place on credit, *i.e.* (i) A purchases the beer from the outside supplier in his own name and on credit, and (ii) A sells that beer on credit to customers in the public house. If A then defaulted in this obligation to pay the outside suppliers, it could scarcely be supposed that the latter could successfully sue the employers for the price of the beer. That is because the contract of sale was between A in his own name and the outside supplier, and secondly because the purchase was not only outside the scope of A's authority from the employers but was also in flagrant defiance of his authority and the terms of his employment. If that is right and the outside supplier could not have successfully sued the employers for the price, the employers can scarcely be said to have a proprietary interest in the beer. If they have no proprietary interest in the beer, why should they have a proprietary interest in the proceeds of the beer?

In the case of A's sale on credit to a customer of the public house, if the customer were to default, it is impossible to suppose that the employers could successfully sue the customer for the price of the beer, beer which did not belong to the employers and for which the employer could not be made to pay, beer moreover which was sold by A not only without the authority of the employers but in flagrant breach of the terms of his employment. If the employer is not in a position to sue the customer for the price of the beer, then it is difficult to see how he can be said to have a proprietary interest in the money or any part of it.

Assuming that, contrary to our views, s.5(1) does import the constructive trust into the 1968 Act, on the facts of the case the employers still obtain no proprietary interest. A trustee is not permitted to make a profit from his trust. Therefore if he uses trust property to make a profit from the trust, he is accountable for that profit. If and when such profit is identified as a separate piece of property, he may be a constructive trustee of it. However, until the profit is identifiable as a separate piece of property, it is not trust property and his obligation is to account only.

A used the employers' property and his own money to make a private profit in breach of contract. He received from customers sums of money which represented in part the cost of the beer he had bought and in part possible profit for which he was accountable to the employers. This profit element, assuming it existed, never became a separate piece of property of which A could be trustee. It remained part of a mixed fund. Therefore there never was a moment at which A was trustee of a definite fund. It follows that there never was a moment when the employers had any proprietary interest in any of the money. The money did not belong to another. There was therefore no theft.

No less difficulty would arise in the proof of dishonesty and guilty intent. A might very well say, and say truthfully, that he knew that he was breaking the terms of his contract, but the idea that he might be stealing from his employers the profit element in this transaction had never occurred to him. There are topics of conversation more popular in public houses than the finer points of the equitable doctrine of the constructive trust.

It is said in answer to that obligation that the employers could, by giving in advance the necessary warnings, instruct their servants what the true meaning of the 1968 Act is. That seems to us to be a good illustration of the objectionability of the proposition. If something is so abstruse and so far from the understanding of ordinary people as to what constitutes stealing, it should not amount to stealing.

For these reasons we think that the submissions based on s.5(1) likewise fail.

The answers to the questions posed in the reference are therefore these: (1) no; (2) if, which we do not believe, it is properly described as a trust, it is not such a trust as falls within the ambit of s.5(1) of the Theft Act 1968; (3) no.

Opinion accordingly

Notes

1. This subsection is to a large extent redundant, because in the vast majority of cases where there is an obligation to retain and deal with the property in a certain way, the person to whom the obligation is owed will have a proprietary right or interest in the property. Thus with a bailment, the property "belongs to" the bailor, and with a trust, the property "belongs to" the beneficiary, under subsection 1, and in the case of misappropriation by the bailee or trustee there is no need of subsection 3 to secure a conviction. There are so many difficulties involved in subsection 3 that it is unwise of a prosecutor to rely on it unless it is absolutely necessary to do so, which is rarely if ever the case.

2. It is said that the obligation must be a legal one, not a merely moral one (see *R.* v. *Gilks* [1971] 1 W.L.R. 1341: "In a criminal statute, where a person's criminal liability is made dependent on his having an obligation, it would be quite wrong to construe that word so as to cover a moral or social obligation as distinct from a legal one"). However, an obligation arising under a domestic arrangement of a sort which the civil law would say was not enforceable by action has been held to be enough (*R.* v. *Cullen* 1974, unreported: Smith § 75). Even if the accused is under an obligation at the moment of appropriation, he is not within the words of subsection 3 unless he received the property from or on account of the person to whom he now owes the obligation.

3. The obligation must be to retain and deal with *that property or its proceeds* in a particular way. This excludes an obligation to perform some service or do some act in return for being given the property, *e.g.* as in *R.* v. *Hall, ante,* p. 705, where B paid A money in return for A's promise to supply air tickets. A was not obliged to do anything *with* the money; his obligation was merely to perform his part of the bargain. It is the same, in most cases, if B lends A money. The only obligation in the borrower A is to repay the loan to B, not to do anything with the money lent. A owes B the amount of the loan, but a simple debtor-creditor relationship is not enough. A debtor who dishonestly puts himself in a position in

which he is unable to pay his creditor does not commit theft. "The essential notion is that D. must be under a fiduciary obligation with regard to the property which he receives. The idea of fiduciary obligation conveys accurately the essential requirement; the property, though it may be owned solely by D., must be earmarked in D.'s hands for certain purposes of P.'s": Smith and Hogan, p. 514.

The sort of situation which is within subsection 3 is illustrated by *Davidge* v. *Bunnett* [1974] Crim.L.R. 257 (D.C.). D. shared a flat with A, B & C, the expenses being shared. A gas bill having become due, A, B & C gave D. cheques for their shares, payable to D.'s employer, because she herself had no bank account. D. cashed the cheques, paid some of the bill, but spent most of the money on Christmas presents. *Held* D. was under an obligation to apply the proceeds of the cheques towards paying the bill and was guilty of theft of the money spent on Christmas presents. A, B & C were not the owners of the money received from cashing the cheques. On the other hand, in no sense could it be said that D. merely owed the money to them; what she owed them was a duty to use the fund to pay the gas bill. Similarly if A receives money on behalf of B, and merely has to keep an account of payments received and pay B an amount representing the total achieved, he is not bound to do anything with the money received and it does not belong to B: *R.* v. *Robertson* [1977] Crim.L.R. 629. *Aliter*, if he has a duty to keep the money separate from his own before paying it over to B: *R.* v. *Lord* [1905] 69 J.P. 467.

There are situations where B has the right to sue A in respect of some transaction involving the misuse by A of B's property, or the misuse by A of his position as B's servant or representative. The mere duty to account for an improper profit does not mean that the money A improperly received is property belonging to B. His duty to account is not the sort of obligation covered by subsection 3, and B's interest, if any, in the money, is not a proprietary right or interest referred to in subsection 1: *Att.-Gen.'s Reference (No. 1 of 1985), ante,* p. 707. The reason is said to be that the draftsmen of the Theft Act could not have intended such a large extension of the law of theft. "Breach of fiduciary duty, exorbitant profit-taking, secrecy, failure to comply with the law as to company accounts … are one thing; theft and fraud are others": Lord Wilberforce in *Tarling* v. *Singapore* (1978) 70 Cr.App.R. 77, 110, cited with approval, *ante,* p. 712.

4. "Whether or not an obligation arises is a matter of law, because the obligation must be a legal obligation": *R.* v. *Mainwaring* (1981) 74 Cr.App.R. 99, 107. Nevertheless, it was said at various places (including *R.* v. *Hall, ante,* p. 705) that although a judge could rule that any approved situation did *not* amount to a relevant obligation and direct an acquittal, he could not rule that it *did* amount to such, but must leave it to the jury to say whether the facts did amount to the sort of obligation covered by subsection 3. See also *R.* v. *Hayes* (1976) 64 Cr.App.R. 82. But in *R.* v. *Mainwaring*, the Court of Appeal, without reference to the previous

cases, said that the judge should direct "If you find such and such, then I direct you as a matter of law that a legal obligation arose to which section 4(3) applies." This is preferable in confining the jury to finding the facts, which indeed will be difficult enough in many cases. Except where a written document specifies the accused's obligation (which is a matter of construction for the judge), the jury must ask, did the payers *expect* the accused to retain and deal with the property in a particular way: see Edmund Davies L.J. in *R. v. Hall*, (*ante*, p. 705). In many cases, such as *R. v. Hall* itself where the payers were the multitudinous clients of a travel agency, it will be impossible to discover any general expectation, and any proved particular expectation by an individual client might be unreasonable and unassented to by the accused. The normal practice of traders in the accused's line of business would appear to be a better guide; but even if such were proved and was to the effect that clients' money was usually kept separate, it does not follow that the clients knew of the practice and expected the accused to follow it.

Subsection 4: Property got by another's mistake

Note

This subsection was passed in order to deal with a point highlighted in one particular case—*Moynes* v. *Coopper* [1956] 1 Q.B. 439. It was thought that if property was obtained by A from B by mistake in circumstances where B meant A to become the owner of it then, although A might be under a quasi-contractual obligation to restore the property or its value to B, in most cases B did not have any proprietary interest in the property, which belonged solely to A. The subsection provides that even if A is the only person with an interest in the property, the existence of the obligation to restore makes it theft if A dishonestly resolves not to restore. However, in 1979, it was held, apparently for the first time, in the case of *Chase Manhattan Bank* v. *Israel-London Bank* [1981] Ch. 105 (Goulding J.), that B has not merely a quasi-contractual right to sue A for the value, but an equitable interest in the property under a constructive trust. This principle was used in *R.* v. *Shadrakh-Cigari* (*ante*, p. 703) to convict A of theft when he dishonestly appropriated money given to him by mistake. The property belonged to B under subsection (1), and there was no need to have recourse to subsection (4). There is never a need to have recourse to that subsection. It is not every kind of mistake which gives rise to an obligation to restore, but if a mistake does have that effect, it gives rise to a proprietary interest in the person to whom the obligation is owed. There is one case where A is under an obligation to restore within the meaning of subsection (4) although B has no proprietary interest under subsection (1); that is when the property has become lost or consumed or otherwise untraceable under equity's rules. But in such a case, A's dishonest refusal to make good to B can never be theft, because there is no identifiable property for him to appropriate. He is no more than a defaulting debtor.

Although subsection (4) is not needed, it has been used to convict people who have got property by mistake: see *Att.-Gen.'s Reference (No. 1 of 1983)* 3 All E.R. 369.

iv. "With the Intention of Depriving Permanently"

Note

The definition of theft in section 1 requires that the appropriation should be with the *intention of permanently depriving the owner of it*. The italicised words are the same as those in the definition of larceny in section 1 of the Larceny Act 1916.

The intention to deprive must be a settled one at the time of the appropriation. As to an intention to deprive if and only if the goods on examination turn out to be what the taker wants, see next case.

R. v. Easom
[1971] 2 Q.B. 315
Court of Appeal

E. took a handbag, searched through it, found nothing to interest him, and left it with contents intact near the owner, who repossessed it. E. was convicted of theft of the bag and its detailed contents.

EDMUND DAVIES L.J.: This is an appeal by the appellant against his conviction at the Inner London Quarter Sessions last October on an indictment charging him with theft, the particulars of the charge being that, on December 27, 1969, he "stole one handbag, one purse, one notebook, a quantity of tissues, a quantity of cosmetics and one pen, the property of Joyce Crooks."

The circumstances giving rise to the charge may be shortly stated. In the evening of December 27, 1969, woman Police Sergeant Crooks and other plainclothes officers went to the Metropole cinema in Victoria. Sergeant Crooks sat in an aisle seat and put her handbag (containing the articles enumerated in the charge) alongside her on the floor. It was attached to her right wrist by a piece of black cotton. Police Constable Hensman sat next to her on the inside seat. When the house lights came on during an interval, it was seen that the appellant was occupying the aisle seat in the row immediately behind Sergeant Crooks and that the seat next to him was vacant. Within a few minutes of the lights being put out, Sergeant Crooks felt the cotton attached to her wrist tighten. She thereupon gave Police Constable Hensman a pre-arranged signal. The cotton was again pulled, this time so strongly that she broke it off. Moments later the officers could hear the rustle of tissues and the sound of her handbag being closed. Very shortly afterwards the appellant left his seat and went to the lavatory. The officers then turned round and found Sergeant Crooks's handbag on the floor behind her seat and in front of that which the appellant had vacated. Its contents were intact. When the appellant emerged from the lavatory and seated himself in another part of the cinema, he was approached by the police officers. When the offence of theft was put to him, he denied it.

... In every case of theft the appropriation must be accompanied by the intention of permanently depriving the owner of his property. What may be loosely described as a "conditional" appropriation will not do. If the appropriator has it in mind merely to deprive the owner of such of his property as, on examination, proves worth taking and then, finding that the booty is valueless to the appropriator, leaves it ready to hand to be repossessed by the owner, the appropriator has not stolen. If a dishonest postal sorter picks up a pile of letters intending to steal any which are registered, but on finding that none of them are, replaces them, he has stolen nothing, and this is so notwithstanding the provisions of section 6(1) of the Theft Act 1968. In the present case the jury were never invited to consider the possibility that such was the appellant's state of mind or the legal consequences flowing therefrom. Yet the facts are strongly indicative that this was exactly how his mind was working, for he left the handbag and its contents entirely intact and to hand, once he had carried out his exploration. For this reason we hold that the conviction of the full offence of theft cannot stand.

In so concluding, we have not overlooked that counsel for the Crown has, since the trial, altered his view of the case and now shares that expressed by the deputy chairman that the appellant should either have been convicted of the full offence charged or acquitted completely. Indeed he now submits that conviction for the full offence was justified. In support of this changed view we were referred to a passage in 1 Hale P.C. (1778 ed.), p. 533, which reads: "So if A without drawing his weapon requires B to deliver his purse, who doth deliver it, and finding but two shillings in it gives it to him again, this is a taking by robbery. 20 Eliz. Crompt. 34." But in our judgment counsel seeks to attach excessive weight to this short reference, and the true approach thereto is to be found in *Archbold's Criminal Pleading, Evidence and Practice*, 37th ed. (1969), p. 558 para. 1469, in the following words: "Returning the goods ... can be considered merely as evidence of the defendant's intention when he took them; for *if it appears that he took them originally with intent of depriving the owner of them, and of appropriating them to his own use*," [my italics] "his afterwards returning them will not purge the offence."

So once more, one is driven back to consider with what intention the appellant embarked upon the act of taking. This court, in *R.* v. *Stark* (unreported), October 4, 1967, quashed the conviction for larceny of a man caught in the act of lifting a tool-kit from the boot of a car, the judge having misdirected the jury by telling them: "Was Stark intending, if he could get away with it, and if it was worthwhile, to take the tool-kit when he lifted it out? If he picked up something, saying 'I am sticking to this—if it is worthwhile,' then he would be guilty." But does it follow from all this that the appellant (as to whose identity and physical acts the verdict establishes that the jury entertained no doubt) has to go scot-free? Can he not, as the Crown originally submitted, be convicted at least of attempted theft? Even though the contents of the handbag, when examined, held no allure for him, why was he not as guilty of attempted theft as would be the pickpocket who finds his victim's pocket empty (see *R.* v. *Ring* (1892) 61 L.J.M.C. 116). Does a conditional intention to steal count for nothing? In his *Criminal Law (The General Part)*, 2nd ed. (1961), p. 52, para. 23, Professor Glanville Williams says: "A conditional intention is capable of ranking as intention for legal purposes. Thus it is no defence to an apparent burglar that his intention was merely to steal a certain paper if it should happen to be there." He then cites the American Model Penal Code, s.2.02(6) (T.D. No. 4 pp. 14, 129), which states that: "When a particular purpose is an element of an offence, the element is established although such purpose is conditional, unless the condition negatives the harm or evil sought to be prevented by the law defining the offence."

But as to this, all, or, at least, much, depends upon the manner in which the charge is framed. Thus, "if you indict a man for stealing your watch, you cannot convict him of attempting to steal your umbrella" (*per* Cockburn C.J. in *R.* v. *M'Pherson* (1857) D. & B. 197, 200)—unless, of course, the court of trial has duly exercised the wide powers of amendment conferred by section 5 of the Indictment Act 1915. In our judgment, this remains the law and it is unaffected by the provisions of section 6 of the Criminal Law Act 1967. No amendment was sought or effected in the present case, which accordingly has to be considered in relation to the articles enumerated in the theft charge and nothing else. Furthermore, it is implicit in the concept of an attempt that the person acting intends to do the act attempted, so that the *mens rea* of an attempt is essentially that of the complete crime (see *Smith and Hogan*, *"Criminal Law*," 2nd ed. (1969), p. 163). That being so, there could be no valid conviction of the appellant of attempted theft on the present indictment unless it were established that he was animated by the same intention permanently to deprive Sergeant Crooks of the goods enumerated in the particulars of the charge as would be necessary to establish the full offence. We hope that we have already made sufficiently clear why we consider that, in the light of the evidence and of the direction given, it is impossible to uphold the verdict on the basis that such intention was established in this case.

For these reasons, we are compelled to allow the appeal and quash the conviction.

Appeal allowed

Notes

1. "What may be loosely described as a conditional appropriation will not do. If the appropriator has it in mind merely to deprive the owner of such of his property as, on examination, proves worth taking and then, finding that the booty is valueless to the appropriator, leaves it ready to hand to be repossessed by the owner, the appropriator has not stolen." For the subsequent history of this dictum of Edmund-Davies L.J. (*supra*), which caused difficulties in burglary with intent to steal, see *Att.-Gen.'s References (Nos. 1 and 2 of 1979)*, *post*, p. 839.

2. Usually, the crime of attempt is available to deal with cases of this kind. In *Att.-Gen.'s References, Nos. 1 and 2 of 1979*, Roskill L.J. (see *post*, p. 845) said of *Easom* "It seems clear from the latter part of Edmund Davies L.J.'s judgment that if he had been charged with an attempt to steal some or all of the contents of that handbag, he could properly have been convicted." In a case exactly like *Easom*—*R.* v. *Smith & Smith* [1986] Crim.L.R. 166 (C.A.)—just such a charge was preferred and the conviction was upheld on appeal. But since Easom was held not to intend to steal any of the listed contents of the bag, it seems odd to hold that he intended to steal "some or all" of the (unlisted) contents. Listed in the indictment or not, they were all rejected by him. What he intended to steal was something which was not there, *i.e.* something which he would have thought worth stealing. The fact that his attempt to steal something valuable was impossible is now no bar to his being

convicted of attempting to steal; and he is better dealt with by a charge of "attempted theft from a handbag," without any mention of the contents. See *R.* v. *Shivpuri, ante,* p. 485.

3. Edmund-Davies L.J. says (*ante,* p. 718) that his hypothetical dishonest postal sorter was not guilty of theft "notwithstanding the provisions of section 6(1) of the Theft Act 1968." Nevertheless, that section does apparently make theft of *some* cases of conditional intent to deprive permanently.

Theft Act 1968, section 6

"(1) A person appropriating property belonging to another without meaning the other to lose the thing itself is nevertheless to be regarded as having the intention of permanently depriving the other of it if his intention is to treat the thing as his own to dispose of regardless of the other's rights; and a borrowing or lending of it may amount to so treating it if, but only if, the borrowing or lending is for a period and in circumstances making it equivalent to an outright taking or disposal.

(2) Without prejudice to the generality of subsection (1) above, where a person, having possession or control (lawfully or not) of property belonging to another, parts with the property under a condition as to its return which he may not be able to perform, this (if done for purposes of his own and without the other's authority) amounts to treating the property as his own to dispose of regardless of the other's rights."

J. R. Spencer, "The Metamorphosis of Section 6 of the Theft Act" [1977] Crim.L.R. 653

"An 'intention to deprive' was, of course an element of the crime of larceny. Over the course of many years, the concept had been interpreted in numerous cases. Generally, an *intention* to deprive, rather than mere recklessness, was necessary. Thus abandoning another person's property knowing there was a risk that he would never get it back was not larceny, unless the person who did so actually desired the owner to lose it, or (presumably) foresaw the virtual certainty that he would do so. However, there were three judge-made extensions of 'intention permanently to deprive' where mere recklessness, or something like it, was sufficient. (a) There was the 'ransom principle,' whereby it counted as an intention permanently to deprive if the idea was to return the property to the owner only if he was prepared to pay for it. (b) There was the 'essential quality principle,' whereby it counted as an intention permanently to deprive if the idea was to return the property only after it had undergone some fundamental change of character: a live horse taken but a dead horse returned, a valid ticket taken but a cancelled ticket returned. And (c) there was the 'pawning principle,' where it counted as an intention permanently to deprive if a person pawned another's property without his consent, hoping to be able to redeem the pledge, but knowing he might be unable to do so. The Criminal Law Revision Committee heartily approved of 'intention permanently to deprive' as so elaborated by the courts, and it was the one element of larceny which the Committee thought could be transplanted into the new crime of theft without any alteration. The Committee assumed that the old case-law would automatically be applied if the phrase were enacted in the definition of theft without any attempt at further elaboration. It therefore opposed putting a section into the Theft

Act elaborating 'intention of permanently depriving,' and carefully omitted any such clause from the Draft Theft Bill which it appended to its Eighth Report. However, somebody who had the ear of the Government thought otherwise ... [after tracing the tangled Parliamentary history of the new clause]; Not surprisingly, the courts have so far failed to spot Parliament's real intention through the obscure verbiage in which Parliament has dressed it up. To date, they have been quite mystified by the section. ...

A fair summary of the Court of Appeal's interpretation of section 6 in [*R.* v. *Warner*] would be the following.

'The section was enacted to extend "intention permanently to deprive" beyond its previous interpretation; however, it was only meant to do so to some infinitesimal degree, and we are not prepared to say in which direction; any judge who drags section 6 into his summing-up can expect to be reversed on appeal.'

It has certainly not crossed anybody's mind that section 6 was designed to *preserve* the existing case law. In *Duru* [1974] 1 W.L.R. 2, the Court of Appeal applied the 'essential quality' principle, but did so without reference to section 6. And in *Easom* (*ante*, p. 717) Edmund Davies L.J. indicated that a conditional intention to deprive was insufficient for theft, notwithstanding section 6; whereas the 'pawning principle' and the 'ransom principle,' which section 6 was intended to preserve, are obvious instances of conditional intention.

Thus, as a result of section 6, the present meaning of 'intention of permanently depriving' in theft is doubly in doubt. The expression is thought to be extended beyond its literal meaning by section 6, but we do not know how far or in what direction. And we do not know, how far, if at all, the pre-1968 case law on 'intention permanently to deprive' can be relied on."

R. v. Lloyd
[1985] Q.B. 829
Court of Appeal

The facts appear in the judgment of the Court.

LORD LANE C.J. delivered the following judgment of the court: These are appeals against conviction by Sidney Douglas Lloyd, Ranjeet Bhuee and Mohammed Chaukal Ali. They come to this court by the certificate of the trial judge and the appeal arises in the following way.

On February 5, 1985 at the Central Criminal Court before Judge Hilliard and a jury, after a trial lasting about a fortnight, the appellants were convicted of conspiracy to steal and were sentenced to varying terms of imprisonment. ...

At all material times the appellant Lloyd was employed as chief projectionist at the Odeon Cinema at Barking. The other two appellants with whom we are concerned, namely Ali and Bhuee, were employed by a man called Mustafa, who was also named in the indictment and pleaded guilty to the charge of conspiracy to steal. They were employed at premises at 3, Plumstead Road, Barking. The case against the appellants was that over a period of months Lloyd had been clandestinely removing feature films which were due to be shown at the Odeon Cinema at Barking and lending them to his co-defendants, who had sophisticated equipment at their premises at 3, Plumstead Road. That sophisticated equipment enabled them to copy the feature films on to a master video tape, and, as a result of the preparation of that master video tape, they or others were enabled to produce a very large quantity of pirated versions of the film. The process of copying was done rapidly. The films were only out of the cinema and out of the hands of Lloyd for a few hours and were always back in time for their projection to take place at the advertised times to those people who attended the cinema to see them.

It was important that the film should be returned rapidly, because if it was not it would soon become apparent that the film had been illegally removed and steps would be taken to prevent a recurrence. The pirated copies prepared from the master tape would be put on the market to the great financial benefit of the pirates and the great financial detriment of the lawful owners, the film distributors and those who would derive money from the film enterprise. The detriment would occur in a number of different ways, and that indeed was proved before the jury. First of all it would occur through a lowering of cinema attendances to see the particular film, and secondly, through the legitimate sales of cassettes of the film being undermined by the sale of the pirated copies. The profits apparently, so it was stated in evidence, to the film pirates are enormous and the loss to the legitimate trade is potentially crippling. In the upshot the appellants were caught red handed in the process of copying a film called "The Missionary" on to the master tape.

The judge issued his certificate by posing the following question:

"Whether the offence of conspiracy to steal is committed when persons dishonestly agree to take a film from a cinema without authority intending it should be returned within a few hours but knowing that many hundreds of copies will be subsequently made and that the value of the film so returned will thereby be substantially reduced."

The complaint by the appellants is that the judge misdirected the jury first of all in leaving the question for them to decide whether the removal of a film in these circumstances could amount to theft, and secondly, in allowing them to consider section 6(1) of the Theft Act 1968 as being relevant at all in the circumstances of this case.

The point is a short one. It is not a simple one. It is not without wider importance, because if the judge was wrong in leaving the matter in the way in which he did for the jury to consider, it might mean, as we understand it, that the only offence of which a person in these circumstances could be convicted would be a conspiracy to commit a breach of the Copyright Act 1956. At the time when this particular case was being tried, the maximum penalties available for the substantive offence under the Copyright Act 1956 were minimal. Those penalties have now been increased by the provisions of the Copyright (Amendment) Act 1983, and in the light of that Act it can be said that although Parliament perhaps has not entirely caught up with this type of prevalent pirating offence, it is at least gaining on it.

We turn now to the provisions of the Theft Act 1968, the conspiracy alleged being a breach of that particular Act. Section 1(1) of that Act provides:

"A person is guilty of theft if he dishonestly appropriates property belonging to another with the intention of permanently depriving the other of it; and 'thief' and 'steal' shall be construed accordingly."

On that wording alone these appellants were not guilty of theft or of conspiracy to steal. The success of their scheme and their ability to act with impunity in a similar fashion in the future, depended, as we have already said, upon their ability to return the film to its rightful place in the hands of the Odeon Cinema at Barking as rapidly as possible, so that its absence should not be noticed. Therefore the intention of the appellants could more accurately be described as an intention temporarily to deprive the owner of the film and was indeed the opposite of an intention permanently to deprive.

What then was the basis of the prosecution case and the basis of the judge's direction to the jury? It is said that section 6(1) of the Theft Act 1968 brings such actions as the appellants performed here within the provisions of section 1. The judge left the matter to the jury on the basis that they had to decide whether the words of section 6(1) were satisfied by the prosecution or not. Section 6(1) provides:

"A person appropriating property belonging to another without meaning the other permanently to lose the thing itself is nevertheless to be regarded as having the intention of permanently depriving the other of it if his intention is to treat the thing as his own to dispose of regardless of the other's rights; and a borrowing or lending of it may amount to so treating it if, but only if the borrowing or lending is for a period and in circumstances making it equivalent to an outright taking or disposal."

That section has been described by J. R. Spencer in his article (*ante*, p. 720), as a section which "sprouts obscurities at every phrase," and we are inclined to agree with him. It is abstruse. But it must mean, if nothing else, that there are circumstances in which a defendant may be deemed to have the intention permanently to deprive, even though he may intend the owner eventually to get back the object which has been taken.

We have had the benefit of submissions by Mr. Du Cann in this case. His first submission is that the definition of "property" in section 4 of the Theft Act 1968 does not include value, and he submits that it was on the basis of loss of value or loss of virtue of the films that the prosecution of the case proceeded. In order to substantiate that submission, he referred us to the decision of the House of Lords in *Rank Film Distributors Ltd.* v. *Video Information Centre* [1982] A.C. 380. Relying upon that case he sought to demonstrate to us that the provisions of the Theft Act 1968 do not cover the stealing of copyright or kindred matters.

We are indebted to Mr. Du Cann for his careful arguments on this point, namely, to the effect that copyright is probably not a subject of theft, but we are not concerned with that proposition here, so it seems to us, except perhaps incidentally, because the allegation here was one of conspiracy to steal feature films, not the copyright in them, and the allegation that the defendants conspired together to steal feature films depends upon proof by the prosecution that that is the thing that they were conspiring to steal.

Mr. Du Cann next cites to us a series of helpful cases, and they are these. First of all *R.* v. *Warner* (1970) 55 Cr.App.R. 93. This was a case in which the judgment of the court was delivered by Edmund Davies L.J. Having cited the words in which the chairman directed the jury, Edmund Davies L.J. continued, at pp. 96–97:

"But unfortunately his direction later became confused by his references to section 6, the object of which he may himself have misunderstood. There is no statutory definition of the words 'intention of permanently depriving,' but section 6 seeks to clarify their meaning in certain respects. Its object is in no wise to cut down the definition of 'theft' contained in section 1. It is always dangerous to paraphrase a statutory enactment, but its apparent aim is to prevent specious pleas of a kind which have succeeded in the past by providing, in effect, that it is no excuse for an accused person to plead absence of the necessary intention if it is clear that he appropriated another's property intending to treat it as his own, regardless of the owner's rights. Section 6 thus gives illustrations, as it were, of what can amount to the dishonest intention demanded by section 1(1). But it is a misconception to interpret it as watering down section 1."

Those observations we must bear in mind, because that is a decision which of course is binding on this court.

Then Mr. Du Cann referred us to *R.* v. *Duru* [1974] 1 W.L.R. 2. That was a case involving cheques. The allegation was that the defendant had obtained certain cheques from the local authority by deception with the intention of permanently depriving the council of them. That was contrary to section 15(1) of the Theft Act 1968, but section 6(1) was equally applicable in that case as it would have been had the allegation been one simply of theft. Megaw L.J., delivering the judgment of the court, said, at p. 8:

"So far as the cheque itself is concerned, true it is a piece of paper. But it is a piece of paper which changes its character completely once it is paid, because then it receives a rubber stamp on it stating that it has been paid and it ceases to be a thing in action, or at any rate it ceases to be, in its substance, the same thing as it was before: that is, an instrument on which payment falls to be made. It was the intention of the defendants, dishonestly and by deception, not only that the cheques should be made out and handed over, but also that they should be presented and paid, thereby permanently depriving the council of the cheques in their substance as things in action. The fact that the mortgagors were under an obligation to repay the mortgage loans does not affect the defendants' intention permanently to deprive the council of those cheques. If it were necessary to look to section 6(1) of the Theft Act 1968, this court would have no hesitation in saying that that subsection, brought in by the terms of section 15(3), would also be relevant, since it is plain that the defendants each had the intention of causing the cheque to be treated as the property of the person by whom it was to be obtained, to dispose of, regardless of the rights of the true owner."

Finally Mr. Du Cann referred us to *R.* v. *Downes* (1983) 77 Cr.App.R. 260. That was a case similar in essence to *R.* v. *Duru.* The judgment in *R.* v. *Downes* was delivered by Nolan J. who said, at pp. 266–267:

"It is of some interest to note in *Duru* ... the Court was referred to the earlier case of *Warner*, which Mr. Lodge cited in support of the narrower reading of section 6(1) for which he contended. *Warner* ... does not however appear to us, as evidently it did not appear to this court in *Duru* ... to have any significant bearing on the point at issue. It follows that, for substantially the same reasons as those given by the learned judge, we consider that the charge of theft is made out, the vouchers having been dishonestly appropriated with the intention of destroying their essential character and thus depriving the owners, the Inland Revenue, of the substance of their property. In our judgment therefore the appeal must be dismissed."

In general we take the same view as Professor Griew in *The Theft Act 1968 and 1978*, 4th ed. (1982), p. 47 para. 2–73, namely, that section 6 should be referred to in exceptional cases only. In the vast majority of cases it need not be referred to or considered at all.

Deriving assistance from another distinguished academic writer, namely, Professor Glanville Williams, we would like to cite with approval the following passage from his *Textbook of Criminal Law*, 2nd ed. (1983), p. 719:

"In view of the grave difficulties of interpretation presented by section 6, a trial judge would be well advised not to introduce it to the jury unless he reaches the conclusion that it will assist them, and even then (it may be suggested) the question he leaves to the jury should not be worded in terms of the generalities of the subsection but should reflect those generalities as applied to the alleged facts. For example, the question might be: 'Did the defendant take the article, intending that the owner should have it back only on making a payment? If so, you would be justified as a matter of law in finding that he intended to deprive the owner permanently of his article, because the taking of the article with that intention is equivalent to an outright taking.' "

Bearing in mind the observations of Edmund Davies L.J. in *R. v. Warner*, we would try to interpret the section in such a way as to ensure that nothing is construed as an intention permanently to deprive which would not prior to the Act of 1968 have been so construed. Thus, the first part of section 6(1) seems to us to be aimed at the sort of case where a defendant takes things and then offers them back to the owner for the owner to buy if he wishes. If the taker intends to return them to the owner only upon such payment, then, on the wording of section 6(1), that is deemed to amount to the necessary intention permanently to deprive: see, for instance, *R. v. Hall* (1848) 1 Den. 381, where the defendant took fat from a candlemaker and then offered it for sale to the owner. His conviction for larceny was affirmed. There are other cases of similar intent: for instance, "I have taken your valuable painting. You can have it back on payment to me of £X,000. If you are not prepared to make that payment, then you are not going to get your painting back."

It seems to us that in this case we are concerned with the second part of section 6(1), namely, the words after the semi-colon:

"and a borrowing or lending of it may amount to so treating it if, but only if, the borrowing or lending is for a period and in circumstances making it equivalent to an outright taking or disposal."

These films, it could be said, were borrowed by Lloyd from his employers in order to enable him and the others to carry out their "piracy" exercise.

Borrowing is *ex hypothesi* not something which is done with an intention permanently to deprive. This half of the subsection, we believe, is intended to make it clear that a mere borrowing is never enough to constitute the necessary guilty mind unless the intention is to return the "thing" in such a changed state that it can truly be said that all its goodness or virtue has gone: for example *R. v. Beecham* (1851) 5 Cox C.C. 181, where the defendant stole railway tickets intending that they should be returned to the railway company in the usual way only after the journeys had been completed. He was convicted of larceny. The judge in the present case gave another example, namely, the taking of a torch battery with the intention of returning it only when its power is exhausted.

That being the case, we turn to inquire whether the feature films in this case can fall within that category. Our view is that they cannot. The goodness, the virtue, the practical value of the films to the owners has not gone out of the article. The film could still be projected to paying audiences, and, had everything gone according to the conspirators' plans, would have been projected in the ordinary way to audiences at the Odeon

Cinema, Barking, who would have paid for their seats. Our view is that those particular films which were the subject of this alleged conspiracy had not themselves diminished in value at all. What had happened was that the borrowed film had been used or was going to be used to perpetrate a copyright swindle on the owners whereby their commercial interests were grossly and adversely affected in the way that we have endeavoured to describe at the outset of this judgment. That borrowing, it seems to us, was not for a period, or in such circumstances, as made it equivalent to an outright taking or disposal. There was still virtue in the film.

For those reasons we think that the submissions of Mr. Du Cann on this aspect of the case are well founded. Accordingly the way in which the judge directed the jury was mistaken, and accordingly, this conviction of conspiracy to steal must be quashed.

Appeals allowed

Notes

1. Lord Lane C.J. said (*ante*, p. 723) that it might be that the only offence of which Lloyd and his collaborators could be convicted would be conspiracy to commit a breach of the Copyright Act. However, now section 12 of the Criminal Justice Act 1987, *ante*, p. 462, will allow a charge of conspiracy to defraud. See *Scott* v. *M.P.C.*, *ante*, p. 463.

2. Lord Lane's suggestion that a court should "try to interpret the section in such a way as to ensure that nothing is construed as an intention permanently to deprive which would not prior to the Act of 1968 have been so construed" (*ante* p. 725) appears to confirm Spencer's fear (*ante*, p. 721) that section 6 extends the law only minimally and obscurely, at least where a borrowing or a lending is involved. Nevertheless, since the decision in *Lloyd*, other cases have taken a less restricted view of the section's ambit; and the Court of Appeal in *R.* v. *Wille* (1988) 86 Cr.App.R. 296, and the Privy Council in *Chan Man-sin* v. *Att.-Gen. for Hong Kong* [1988] 1 All E.R. 1 read the section quite literally, and had no difficulty in holding that where D knew that V's bank account would not be diminished in any way by his drawing an unauthorised cheque on it, he was "nevertheless to be regarded as having the intention of permanently depriving" V, because he intended "to treat the thing (the bank account) as his own to dispose of regardless of the other's rights."

Question

V. carries on the business of dressing skins in his warehouse. V. buys undressed skins from A, paying him for the number delivered, and employs B to dress skins, paying him according to the number dressed. The practice is for A to dump skins in V.'s delivery room; when V. has credited them to A, V. moves them to the dressing room. Dressed skins, when B's work on them has been credited to him, are moved from the dressing room to the storage room. In order to be paid twice for delivered skins, A moves back a pile of undressed skins from the dressing room to the delivery room. In order to be paid twice for dressing skins, B moves back a pile of dressed skins from the storage room to the dressing room. What is the difference between the positions of A and B, so far as concerns a possible charge of theft?

See *R. v. Hall*, referred to *ante*, p. 725, and *R. v. Manning* (1852) Dears. 21, and compare *R. v. Holloway* (1849) 2 C. & K. 942.

Note

Smith & Hogan, pp. 504, 547, postulate a hypothetical case of D. "selling" the Crown jewels to a gullible tourist P. wandering near the Tower of London, in which the jewels are securely locked up, and consider whether this is theft. The act of selling property which does not belong to him means that D. appropriates it although he does not lay hands on it (see *ante*, p. 662); appropriation is an artificial concept. As a result of section 6(1) "intention to deprive" is also an artificial concept; and by "selling" the jewels, he treats them as his own to dispose of. It would seem ludicrous to hold that D.'s selling of the jewels to P. was theft, but section 6(1) is not permissive but mandatory; a person "*is* to be regarded" (not "*may* be regarded") as having the intention to deprive permanently when his intention is to treat the thing as his own to dispose of regardless of the other's rights. Perhaps a way out is to hold that, as the jewels remain safely locked up in the Tower of London, D. does not act "regardless" of the owner's rights when he "sells" them to a tourist in the street outside.

Of course, the victim of D.'s crime is P., not the owner of the jewels, and the obvious charge is that of obtaining the price from P. by deception (see *post*, p. 751), but the authorities sometimes fail to select the obvious charge: see, *e.g. Lawrence, Morris, and Gomez, ante*, p. 663.

v. "Temporary Deprivation"

Criminal Law Revision Committee's Eighth Report, Cmnd. 2977

§ 56 " ... We considered whether temporary deprivation of property in general should be included in theft or made a separate offence under the Bill. There is certainly a case for making temporary deprivation punishable in circumstances in which it may involve dishonesty comparable with that involved in theft and may cause serious loss or hardship. The taker gets the benefit of the property without payment, and the owner is correspondingly deprived. The property may be lost or damaged, or it may be useless to the owner by the time it is returned. ... But the committee generally are against extending theft to include temporary deprivation or creating a general offence of temporary deprivation of property. The former course seems to them wrong because in their view an intention to return the property, even after a long time, makes the conduct essentially different from stealing. Apart from this either course would be a considerable extension of the criminal law, which does not seem to be called for by any existing serious evil. It might moreover have undesirable social consequences. Quarrelling neighbours and families would be able to threaten one another with prosecution. Students and young people sharing accommodation who might be tempted to borrow one another's property in disregard of a prohibition by the owner would be in danger of acquiring a criminal record. Further, it would be difficult for the police to avoid being involved in wasteful and undesirable investigations into alleged offences which had no social importance. It is difficult to see how the provision could be framed in a way which would satisfactorily exclude trivial cases and meet these objections. If cases of temporary deprivation should become common, or if it should become too easy a defence to a charge of theft that the intention was to return the property in the end, it might be necessary, notwithstanding these formidable difficulties, to create an offence of temporary deprivation with a high enough maximum penalty for serious cases."

Note

The Committee nevertheless identified two particular cases where temporary deprivation should be an offence. They are articles in places open to the public, and conveyances. Special offences in relation to them appear in sections 11 and 12 of the Theft Act 1968 respectively.

For criticism of the details of both of these special offences, and of the general principle that temporary deprivation should not be theft, see, *post*, p. 730.

(a) *Removal of Articles from Places open to the Public*

Criminal Law Revision Committee's Eighth Report, Cmnd. 2977

§ 57 "A striking recent instance is the removal from the National Gallery of Goya's portrait of the Duke of Wellington. The portrait, before being returned, was kept for four years, during which there was evidence that the man who took it tried to make it a condition of his returning it that a large sum should be paid to charity. He was acquitted of stealing the portrait (but convicted of stealing the frame, which was never recovered and which, if his initial statement was true, he destroyed soon after taking it). In another case an art student took a statuette by Rodin from an exhibition, intending, as he said, to live with it for a while, and returned it over four months later. (Meanwhile the exhibitors, who had insured the statuette, had paid the insurance money to the owners, with the result that the statuette, when returned, became the property of the exhibitors.) Yet another case was the removal of the Coronation Stone from Westminster Abbey. There is obviously a substantial question whether conduct of this kind should be made criminal. Many people may think that taking in cases of these kinds should be punishable, if not as theft, then as a special offence. Churches, art galleries, museums and other places open to the public may contain articles of the greatest importance and value, many of them irreplaceable. They cannot always be protected as well as in private premises and, if removed, may easily be lost or damaged. Against this it can be argued that serious cases of the kind are rare and, judging from the cases mentioned, that offenders are more eccentric than genuinely criminal. Before the Goya case few people would have said that there was an evil unprovided for and serious enough to require the creation of a new offence: and there are objections to extending the criminal law because of isolated occurrences. There may also be the danger that the taker will be less likely to return the property eventually if he is liable to punishment for having removed it. We have come to the conclusion that the situation, especially in view of the Goya case, is serious enough to justify the creation of a special offence in spite of the possible objections. ... "

Note

The Committee felt that the offence ought to be designed as one of criminal damage, so did not draft a clause in their Bill. Nevertheless section 11 was inserted during the Theft Bill's passage through Parliament.

Theft Act 1968, section 11

"(1) Subject to subsections (2) and (3) below, where the public have access to a building in order to view the building or part of it, or a collection or part of a collection housed in it, any person who without lawful authority removes from the building or its grounds the whole or part of any article displayed or kept for display to the public in the building or that part of it or in its grounds shall be guilty of an offence.

For this purpose 'collection' includes a collection got together for a temporary purpose, but references in this section to a collection do not apply to a collection made or exhibited for the purpose of effecting sales or other commercial dealings.

(2) It is immaterial for purposes of subsection (1) above, that the public's access to a building is limited to a particular period or particular occasion; but where anything removed from a building or its grounds is there otherwise than as forming part of, or being on loan for exhibition with, a collection intended for permanent exhibition to the public, the person removing it does not thereby commit an offence under this section unless he removes it on a day when the public have access to the building as mentioned in subsection (1) above.

(3) A person does not commit an offence under this section if he believes that he has lawful authority for the removal of the thing in question or that he would have it if the person entitled to give it knew of the removal and the circumstances of it.

(4) A person guilty of an offence under this section shall, on conviction on indictment, be liable to imprisonment for a term not exceeding five years."

(b) *Taking Conveyances*

Note

If A took goods from B and later abandoned them in a position whence it would naturally be expected that B would eventually recover them, it was difficult to prove that the taking was with intent to deprive B. The fact that abandoned motorcars are invariably returned, through the system of universal registration of motor vehicles, to their registered owners, made it difficult to convict a "joy-rider" of larceny of the motor car. The legislature therefore invented a crime for motor vehicles (see section 217 of the

Road Traffic Act 1960) which could be described as larceny without intention permanently to deprive. Boats were covered by the Vessels Protection Act 1967, and the offence was widened still further by section 12 of the Theft Act, under which aircraft are covered for the first time.

Theft Act 1968, section 12

"(1) Subject to subsections (5) and (6) below, a person shall be guilty of an offence if, without having the consent of the owner or other lawful authority, he takes any conveyance for his own or another's use, or, knowing that any conveyance has been taken without such authority, drives it or allows himself to be carried in or on it.

(2) A person guilty of an offence under subsection (1) above shall be liable on summary conviction to a fine not exceeding level 5 on the standard scale (see scale on p. 581, *ante*) to imprisonment for a term not exceeding six months, or to both.

(3) Offences under subsection (1) above and attempts to commit them shall be deemed for all purposes to be arrestable offences within the meaning of section 2 of the Criminal Law Act 1967.

(4) If on the trial of an indictment for theft the jury are not satisfied that the accused committed theft, but it is proved that the accused committed an offence under subsection (1) above, the jury may find him guilty of the offence under subsection (1).

(5) Subsection (1) above shall not apply in relation to pedal cycles; but, subject to subsection (6) below, a person who, without having the consent of the owner or other lawful authority, takes a pedal cycle for his own or another's use, or rides a pedal cycle knowing it to have been taken without such authority, shall on summary conviction be liable to a fine not exceeding fifty pounds.

(6) A person does not commit an offence under this section by anything done in the belief that he has lawful authority to do it or that he would have the owner's consent if the owner knew of his doing it and the circumstances of it.

(7) For purposes of this section—

   (a) 'conveyance' means any conveyance constructed or adapted for the carriage of a person or persons whether by land, water or air, except that it does not include a conveyance constructed or adapted for use only under the control of a person not carried in or on it, and 'drive' shall be construed accordingly; and

   (b) 'owner' in relation to a conveyance which is the subject of a hiring agreement or hire-purchase agreement, means the person in possession of the conveyance under that agreement."

(c) *Criticism*

Glanville Williams: Temporary Appropriation Should Be Theft [1981] Crim.L.R. 129

"That the law of theft, taken by itself, would be inadequate is recognised not only by the survival of conspiracy to defraud but by the creation of special statutory offences. It is an offence under the Post Office Act 1953, s.53, unlawfully to take a postal packet in course of transmission by post, without any necessity for an intent to deprive the owner permanently. The same is true for the taking and concealment of judicial documents. It is an offence to take fish even though the angler throws them back immediately upon catching them. Blackmail for the purpose of making a temporary acquisition of property can be punished as blackmail (see *post*, p. 789) but a robbery for the same purpose is not robbery in law, this offence being dependent on the definition of theft. Better-known exceptions are those created by sections 11 and 12 of the Theft Act 1968 (the former inserted in response to the public indignation at the outcome of the *Goya* case). But the exceptions are rather arbitrary. Why should it be an offence to make off temporarily with a cart but not with a horse, or with a statuette from a public museum but not from an auction sale-room when the public have been invited to view the articles or from a private collection that specific people have been invited to view? Why should the statutory offence be committed by going off with a valuable duck from the grounds of a zoo if the zoo houses some of its exhibits in a building open to the public (*e.g.* a parrot-house) but not if the public are left entirely in the open air? Is a church a building 'where the public have access in order to view the building or part of it, or a collection or part of a collection housed in it,' or is it exclusively a place of worship? In *Barr* [1978] Crim.L.R. 244 it was ruled in the Crown Court that public access is given for devotional purposes only, and not 'in order to view.' If that is correct for the ordinary church, what about Westminster Abbey? It may be remembered that during the early hours of Christmas morning, 1950, some Glasgow students took the Stone of Scone from the Abbey, subsequently leaving it at Arbroath Abbey; so the point may not be wholly without practical importance.

The special offences do not mesh with other offences involving the concept of theft. For example, it is not burglary to break into a public museum to remove an exhibit for temporary enjoyment, or to break into a garage and take off a car for a temporary criminal purpose. . . .

Suppose that a person removes a small piece of sculpture from a private exhibition or a valuable book from a University library, and returns it after a year. During that time it has of course been lost to its owner; and both the owner and the police have been put to trouble. (If the owner has made a claim upon an insurer or bailee, and been compensated on the basis of total loss, he may even find that the insurer or bailee claims the right to sell the article when it is recovered, so that the owner loses it). The taker of the article may use it in such a way as to put it at risk, or he may make a profit from it, or he may return it in an impaired condition; and if he is a person of no substance the owner's civil remedy against him will be an insufficient penalty. . . .

As in the case of the missing Goya, the temporary removal of a thing may be done with the intention of causing loss to the owner, or with an intention that necessarily involves such loss. Another example of this relates to copyright and industrial espionage. It is not theft or any other offence to remove a paper that is due to be set in an examination in order to read it and then return it (See *Oxford* v. *Moss*, *ante*, p. 689) even though the result is that the examining body has to go to the expense of setting another paper. Nor is it an offence to remove a film unlawfully in order to make pirated copies, or to remove a secret document in order to copy it and sell the copy to a trade rival. A conspiracy to do these things may be punished as a conspiracy to defraud (see *Scott* v. *M.P.C.*, *ante*, p. 463), but is it right that the criminal law should take no notice of this behaviour by individuals? . . .

Yet it is not only a question of the risk of *losing* the article. When an article is unlawfully taken, even if only for a temporary purpose and without substantial risk of permanent loss of the article, the owner suffers an immediate loss, namely in respect of the use of it. . . .

One of the principal arguments for changing the law is that the value of articles lies in their use. More and more things are used by way of hiring, for longer or shorter periods, instead of by ownership. Many articles of use have comparatively short useful 'lives.' In a few years they wear out or become unfashionable or technically obsolete. Therefore, to deprive the owner of the article even for a short period is to deprive him of an appreciable part of its utility. Besides, the owner is in the dilemma of either being without the article for that time or putting himself to the expense of buying another—an expense that may turn out to have been unnecessary if the article is returned. The loss of the article will be particularly annoying if the owner has relied upon having the article for a particular purpose, which becomes frustrated. . . .

Particular trouble is caused to the police and others when dangerous articles are taken, as when in 1966 a Cobalt 60 isotope was taken from a factory by someone who broke in and then dumped it in a barrel of water in the factory area; shortly afterwards the same isotope was taken again. The fact that such a dangerous article is returned reduces but by no means eliminates the danger to the public and the nuisance of those responsible for the article when it is unlawfully carried off. . . .

Only two arguments against making the proposed extension of the Theft Act are worth consideration. The first, that it would be contrary to tradition, or that people would not recognise temporary appropriations as theft, can perhaps be answered by pointing to the legal systems that have this concept already. Many of the illustrations given in this article would, I think, readily be regarded as theft by many people. For example, it would, I am sure, generally be regarded as theft for a person to take a bicycle, use it for several weeks, and then abandon it on the street, even if the owner eventually recovers it. In the debate on the Theft Bill in the House of Lords, Viscount Dilhorne made the interesting point that none of the definitions of the word 'steal' in the *Oxford English Dictionary* required an intent to deprive the owner permanently; they spoke only of the dishonest taking or appropriating of the property of another. In one respect the definition of theft has always gone far beyond popular usage; the slightest moving of the article with the necessary intent is traditionally theft, though the ordinary man would not regard the theft as complete at that stage. Under the Theft Act it seems to be sufficient merely to touch the article, since touching is one of 'the rights of an owner' within section 3(1). It is strange to swallow this camel while straining at the gnat of saying that it is theft to decamp with someone's valuable article and to conceal it from him dishonestly for what may be a considerable period of time.

It may be that the reader, while accepting some of the arguments in this article, has throughout been afflicted by one other doubt. Is it seriously suggested that trivial cases of dishonestly using the property of another should be subject to prosecution as theft?

The argument about trivial cases is frequently used to oppose extensions of the law, but it is never conclusive in itself, because practically every offence covers *some* trivial matters. If an offence is needed to deal with serious misconduct, that is sufficient to justify it. Even the present law could be abused by prosecuting for trivial thefts, but in practice a sensible discretion is generally exercised. The Canadian experience bears out the view that a law of *furtum usus* is unlikely to be used oppressively. . . . The question has generally arisen in Canada in connection with people who walk off with articles of furniture from beer parlours or hotels; and I see no injustice or oppression in convicting them of theft, even though they aver, after being found out, that they were about to come back with the article. ...

My main legislative proposal is that the word 'permanently' should be repealed in section 1(1) of the Theft Act 1968. It should also be repealed in section 15(1), since it was put there only out of supposed logical necessity after being put in section 1(1). There is no reason of policy why a cheat who obtains the hire of a car by deception should not be guilty of obtaining property by deception. The fact that this conduct can now be brought, somewhat awkwardly, within the offence of obtaining services under the Theft Act 1978, s.1 is no argument for not making this change in the Act of 1968. ... "

vi. "Dishonestly"

Theft Act 1968, section 2

"(1) A person's appropriation of property belonging to another is not to be regarded as dishonest—

- (a) if he appropriates the property in the belief that he has in law the right to deprive the other of it, on behalf of himself or of a third person; or
- (b) if he appropriates the property in the belief that he would have the other's consent if the other knew of the appropriation and the circumstances of it; or
- (c) (except where the property came to him as trustee or personal representative) if he appropriates the property in the belief that the person to whom the property belongs cannot be discovered by taking reasonable steps.

(2) A person's appropriation of property belonging to another may be dishonest notwithstanding that he is willing to pay for the property."

Criminal Law Revision Committee, Eighth Report, Cmnd. 2977

§ 39 "The word 'dishonestly' in the definition in clause 1(1) is very important, as dishonesty is a vital element in the offence. The word replaces the requirement in 1916 section 1(1) that the offender should take the property 'fraudulently and without a claim of right made in good faith.' 'Dishonestly' seems to us a better word than 'fraudulently.' The question 'Was this dishonest?' is easier for a jury to answer than the question 'Was this fraudulent?' 'Dishonesty' is something which laymen can easily recognise when they see it, whereas 'fraud' may seem to involve technicalities which have to be explained by a lawyer. The word 'dishonestly' could probably stand without a definition and some members of the committee would have preferred not to define it. But we decided to include the partial definition in clause 2 in order to preserve specifically two rules of the present law. The first is the rule mentioned above that a 'claim of right made in good faith' is inconsistent with theft; this rule is preserved in different language in paragraph (a) of clause 2(1). The second is the rule in 1916 section 1(2)(d) that a finder of property cannot be guilty of stealing it unless he 'believes that the owner can be discovered by taking reasonable steps'; this rule is reproduced in slightly different language in paragraph [c] of clause 2(1)."

Note

Paragraph (*b*) of section 2(1) clarified what was not clear before, namely, that it is not an offence where the accused knows that he has no consent to what he is doing but believes that he would have been given consent if the owner had been asked.

Question

In *R.* v. *Thurborn* (1849) 1 Den. 387, T. found in the street a banknote with no means of identification on it. As soon as he picked it up, he resolved to appropriate it to his own use, but before he could spend it, he was told who the owner was. He nevertheless disposed of the note and was held not guilty of larceny, because he did not, at the time he found the note, know how the owner could be found. In view of sections 2(1)(*c*) and 3(1) (*ante*, pp. 733, 662) would T. today be guilty of theft? At what stage did he assume the rights of an owner?

Note

The definition in section 2 is not a complete one. The section instances three cases where the defendant's belief means that his appropriation is not to be regarded as dishonest, but is silent or inconclusive on other cases. One situation not covered is the case of a person who takes property (*e.g.* money) without any colour of right, knowing that the owner does not and would not consent, but intending to restore the equivalent (*e.g.* other coins to the value of the money taken). Section 2(2) covers the case but not conclusively, saying that such an appropriation *may* be dishonest. See next case.

R. v. Feely
[1973] Q.B. 530
Court of Appeal

F. was the manager of a bookmaker's betting shop. His employers wrote to all their managers stating that the practice of borrowing from tills was to stop. He nevertheless took £30 for his own purposes. He claimed that he always meant to return the money. He was convicted of stealing the money and appealed.

LAWTON L.J.: The appeal raises an important point of law, namely, can it be a defence *in law* for a man charged with theft and proved to have taken money to say that when he took the money he intended to repay it and had reasonable grounds for believing and did believe that he would be able to do so? The trial judge, Judge Edward Jones, adjudged that such a defence is not available. . . .

In section 1(1) of the Act of 1968, the word "dishonestly" can only relate to the state of mind of the person who does the act which amounts to appropriation. Whether an accused person has a particular state of mind is a question of fact which has to be decided by the jury when there is a trial on indictment, and by the magistrates when there are summary proceedings. The Crown did not dispute this proposition, but it was submitted that in some cases (and this, it was said, was such a one) it was necessary for the trial judge to define "dishonestly" and when the facts fell within the definition he had a duty to tell the jury that if there had been appropriation it must have been dishonestly done.

We do not agree that judges should define what "dishonestly" means. This word is in common use whereas the word "fraudulently" which was used in section 1(1) of the Larceny Act 1916, had acquired as a result of case law a special meaning. Jurors, when deciding whether an appropriation was dishonest can be reasonably expected to, and should, apply the current standards of ordinary decent people. In their own lives they have to decide what is and what is not dishonest. We can see no reason why, when in a jury box, they should require the help of a judge to tell them what amounts to dishonesty. We are fortified in this opinion by a passage in the speech of Lord Reid in *Cozens* v. *Brutus* [1973] A.C. 854, a case in which the words "insulting behaviour" in section 5 of the Public Order Act 1936, had to be construed. The Divisional Court had adjudged that the meaning of the word "insulting" in this statutory context was a matter of law. Lord Reid's comment was as follows, at p. 861: "In my judgment that is not right. The meaning of an ordinary word of the English language is not a question of law. The proper construction of a statute is a question of law. If the context shows that a word is used in a unusual sense the court will determine in other words what that unusual sense is. But here there is in my opinion no question of the word 'insulting' being used in any unusual sense. . . . It is for the tribunal which decides the case to consider, not as law but as fact, whether in the whole circumstances the words of the statute do or do not as a matter of ordinary usage of the English language cover or apply to the facts which have been proved."

When this trenchant statement of principle is applied to the word "dishonestly" in section 1(1) of the Theft Act 1968, and to the facts of this case, it is clear in our judgment that the jury should have been left to decide whether the defendant's alleged taking of the money had been dishonest. They were not, with the result that a verdict of guilty was returned without their having given thought to what was probably the most important issue in the case. . . .

Appeal allowed

Note

This case was thought by some to lay down a purely objective test of dishonesty, *i.e.* whatever the jury thought it was, without reference to what the defendant thought. That was felt to be too hard on the defendant, and inconsistent with the three specific cases of honesty in section 2(1), all of which are made to depend on the defendant's belief. On the other hand, making the test purely subjective (what view the defendant took of his own conduct) would be a charter of immunity for those with low or idiosyncratic moral viewpoints, *e.g.* Robin Hood seeing no wrong in robbing the rich to feed the poor. There followed discordant decisions, under which the meaning of dishonesty was held to be different depending upon which crime was involved or, in the case of obtaining by deception, which part of the crime was involved. See next case, which achieves a significant degree of reconciliation, but does not remove all problems.

R. v. Ghosh
[1982] Q.B. 2053
Court of Appeal

G., a consultant surgeon, obtained money by falsely pretending that it was owing as an anaesthetist's fee. He was convicted of dishonestly obtaining the money by deception, contrary to section 15, Theft Act 1968 (see, *post*, p. 751) and appealed.

LORD LANE C.J.: The grounds of appeal are simply that the judge misdirected the jury as to the meaning of dishonesty. What the judge had to say on that topic was as follows:

"Now, finally dishonesty. There are, sad to say, infinite categories of dishonesty. It is for you. Jurors in the past and, whilst we have criminal law in the future, jurors in the future have to set the standards of honesty. Now it is your turn today, having heard what you have, to consider contemporary standards of honesty and dishonesty in the context of all that you have heard. I cannot really expand on this too much, but probably it is something rather like getting something for nothing, sharp practice, manipulating systems and many other matters which come to your mind."

The law on this branch of the Theft Act 1968 is in a complicated state and we embark upon an examination of the authorities with great diffidence. When *R. v. McIvor* [1982] 1 W.L.R. 409 came before the Court of Appeal, there were two conflicting lines of authority. On the one hand there were cases which decided that the test of dishonesty for the purposes of the Theft Act 1968 is, what we venture to call, subjective—that is to say the jury should be directed to look into the mind of the defendant and determine whether he knew he was acting dishonestly: see *R. v. Landy* [1981] 1 W.L.R. 355, where Lawton L.J. giving the reserved judgment of the Court of Appeal said, at p. 365:

"An assertion by a defendant that throughout a transaction he acted honestly does not have to be accepted but has to be weighed like any other piece of evidence. If that was the defendant's state of mind, or may have been, he is entitled to be acquitted. But if the jury, applying their own notions of what is honest and what is not, conclude that he could not have believed that he was acting honestly, then the element of dishonesty will have been established. What a jury must not do is to say to themselves: 'If we had been in his place we would have known we were acting dishonestly so he must have known he was.' "

On the other hand there were cases which decided that the test of dishonesty is objective. Thus in *R. v. Greenstein* [1975] 1 W.L.R. 1353, the judge had directed the jury, see p. 1359:

" ... there is nothing illegal in stagging. The question you have to decide and what this case is all about is whether these defendants, or either of them, carried out their stagging operations in a dishonest way. To that question you apply your own standards of dishonesty. It is no good, you see, applying the standards of anyone accused of dishonesty otherwise everybody accused of dishonesty, if he were to be tested by his own standards, would be acquitted automatically, you may think. The question is essentially the one for a jury to decide and it is essentially one which the jury must decide by applying its own standards."

The Court of Appeal, in a reserved judgment, approved that direction.

In *R.* v. *McIvor* the Court of Appeal sought to reconcile these conflicting lines of authority. They did so on the basis that the subjective test is appropriate where the charge is conspiracy to defraud, but in the case of theft the test should be objective. We quote the relevant passage in full, at p. 417:

"It seems elementary, first, that where the charge is conspiracy to defraud the prosecution must prove actual dishonesty in the minds of the defendants in relation to the agreement concerned, and, secondly, that where the charge is an offence contrary to section 15 of the Theft Act 1968 the prosecution must prove that the defendant knew or was reckless regarding the representation concerned. The passage in my judgment in *R.* v. *Landy* to which we have referred should be read in relation to charges of conspiracy to defraud, and not in relation to charges of theft contrary to section 1 of the Theft Act 1968. Theft is in a different category from conspiracy to defraud, so that dishonesty can be established independently of the knowledge or belief of the defendant, subject to the special cases provided for in section 2 of the Act. Nevertheless, where a defendant has given evidence of his state of mind at the time of the alleged offence, the jury should be told to give that evidence such weight as they consider right, and they may also be directed that they should apply their own standards to the meaning of dishonesty."

The question we have to decide in the present case is, first, whether the distinction suggested in *R.* v. *McIvor* is justifiable in theory, and secondly, whether it is workable in practice.

In *R.* v. *Scott* [1975] A.C. 819, (*ante,* p. 463) the House of Lords had to consider whether deceit is a necessary element in the common law crime of conspiracy to defraud. They held that it is not. It is sufficient for the Crown to prove dishonesty. In the course of his speech Viscount Dilhorne traced the meaning of the words "fraud," "fraudulently" and "defraud" in relation to simple larceny, as well as the common law offence of conspiracy to defraud. After referring to *Stephen, History of the Criminal Law of England* and *East's Pleas of the Crown,* he continued, at pp. 836–837:

"The Criminal Law Revision Committee in their Eighth Report on 'Theft and Related Offences' (1966) (Cmnd. 2977) in paragraph 33 expressed the view that the important element of larceny, embezzlement and fraudulent conversion was 'undoubtedly the dishonest appropriation of another person's property'; in paragraph 35 that the words 'dishonestly appropriates' meant the same as 'fraudulently converts to his own use or benefit, or the use or benefit of any other person,' and in paragraph 39 that 'dishonestly' seemed to them a better word than 'fraudulently.'

Parliament endorsed these views in the Theft Act 1968, which by section 1(1) defined theft as the dishonest appropriation of property belonging to another with the intention of permanently depriving the other of it. Section 17 of that Act replaces sections 82 and 83 of the

Larceny Act 1861 and the Falsification of Accounts Act 1875. The offences created by those sections and by that Act made it necessary to prove that there had been an 'intent to defraud.' Section 17 of the Theft Act 1968 substitutes the words 'dishonestly with a view to gain for himself or another or with intent to cause loss to another' for the words 'intent to defraud.'

If 'fraudulently' in relation to larceny meant 'dishonestly' and 'intent to defraud' in relation to falsification of accounts is equivalent to the words now contained in section 17 of the Theft Act 1968 which I have quoted, it would indeed be odd if 'defraud' in the phrase 'conspiracy to defraud' has a different meaning and means only a conspiracy which is to be carried out by deceit.''

Later on in the same speech Viscount Dilhorne continued, at p. 839:

"As I have said, words take colour from the context in which they are used, but the words 'fraudulently' and 'defraud' must ordinarily have a very similar meaning. If, as I think, and as the Criminal Law Revision Committee appears to have thought, 'fraudulently' means 'dishonestly,' then 'to defraud' ordinarily means, in my opinion, to deprive a person dishonestly of something which is his or of something to which he is or would or might but for the perpetration of the fraud be entitled."

In *R. v. Scott* the House of Lords were only concerned with the question whether deceit is an essential ingredient in cases of conspiracy to defraud; and they held not. As Lord Diplock said, at p. 841B, "Dishonesty of any kind is enough." But there is nothing in *R. v. Scott* which supports the view that, so far as the element of dishonesty is concerned, "theft is in a different category from conspiracy to defraud." On the contrary the analogy drawn by Viscount Dilhorne between the two offences, and indeed the whole tenor of his speech, suggests the precise opposite.

Nor is there anything in *R. v. Landy* itself which justifies putting theft and conspiracy to defraud into different categories. Indeed the court went out of its way to stress that the test for dishonesty, whatever it might be, should be the same whether the offence charged be theft or conspiracy to defraud. This is clear from the reference to *R. v. Feely* (*ante*, p. 734), which was a case under section 1 of the Theft Act 1968. Having set out what we have for convenience called the subjective test, the court in *R. v. Landy*, continue:

"In our judgment this is the way *R. v. Feely* should be applied in cases where the issue of dishonesty arises. It is also the way in which the jury should have been directed in this case ... "

In support of the distinction it is said that in conspiracy to defraud the question arises in relation to an agreement. But we cannot see that this makes any difference. If A and B agree to deprive a person dishonestly of his goods, they are guilty of conspiracy to defraud: see *R. v. Scott*. If they dishonestly and with the necessary intent deprive him of his goods, they are presumably guilty of theft. Why, one asks, respectfully, should the test be subjective in the case of simple theft, but objective where they have agreed to commit a theft?

The difficulties do not stop there. The court in *R. v. McIvor* evidently regarded cases under section 15 of the Theft Act 1968 as being on the subjective side of the line, at any rate so far as proof of deception is concerned. This was the way they sought to explain *R. v. Greenstein*. In that case, after directing the jury in the passage which we have already quoted, the judge continued, at p. 1360:

"Now, in considering whether [the defendants] Green or Greenstein had or may have had an honest belief in the truth of their representations ... the test is a subjective one. That is to say, it is not what you would have believed in similar circumstances. It is what you think they believed and if you think that they, or either of them, had an honest belief to that effect, well then, of course, there would not be any dishonesty. On the other hand, if there is an absence of reasonable grounds for so believing, you might think that that points to the conclusion that they or either of them, as the case may be, had no genuine belief in the truth of their representations. In which case, applying your own standards, you may think that they acted dishonestly and it would be for you to say whether it has been established by the prosecution that they had no such honest belief ... "

The Court of Appeal in *R.* v. *Greenstein* appear to have approved that passage. At any rate they expressed no disapproval. In *R.* v. *McIvor* the court reconciled the two passages quoted from the judge's summing-up as follows, at p. 415:

"It seems clear that those two passages are concerned with different points. The first, which follows and adopts the standards laid down in *R.* v. *Feely*, is concerned with the element of dishonesty in section 15 offences. While the second is specifically concerned with the mental element in relation to the false representation the subject matter of the charge. Clearly, if a defendant honestly believes that the representation made was true the prosecution cannot prove that he knew of, or was reckless as to, its falsity."

The difficulty with section 15 of the Theft Act 1968 is that dishonesty comes in twice. If a person knows that he is not telling the truth he is guilty of dishonesty. Indeed deliberate deception is one of the two most obvious forms of dishonesty. One wonders therefore whether "dishonestly" in section 15(1) adds anything, except in the case of reckless deception. But assuming it does, there are two consequences of the distinction drawn in *R.* v. *McIvor*. In the first place it would mean that the legislation has gone further than its framers intended. For it is clear from paragraphs 87–88 of the Criminal Law Revision Committee's Eighth Report that "deception" was to replace "false pretence" in the old section 32(1) of the Larceny Act 1916, and "dishonestly" was to replace "with intent to defraud." If the test of dishonesty in conspiracy to defraud cases is subjective, it is difficult to see how it could have been anything other than subjective in considering "intent to defraud." It follows that, if the distinction drawn in *R.* v. *McIvor* is correct, the Criminal Law Revision Committee were recommending an important change in the law by substituting "dishonestly" for "with intent to defraud"; for they were implicitly substituting an objective for a subjective test.

The second consequence is that in cases of deliberate deception the jury will have to be given two different tests of dishonesty to apply: the subjective test in relation to deception and the objective test in relation to obtaining. This is indeed what seems to have happened in *R.* v. *Greenstein*. We cannot regard this as satisfactory from a practical point of view. If it be sought to obviate the difficulty by making the test subjective in relation to both aspects of section 15, but objective in relation to section 1, then that would certainly be contrary to what was intended by the Criminal Law Revision Committee. For in paragraph 88 they say:

"The provision in clause 12(1) making a person guilty of criminal deception if he 'dishonestly obtains' the property replaces the provision in 1916, section 32(1) making a person guilty of obtaining by false pretences if he 'with intent to defraud, obtains' the things there mentioned. The change will correspond to the change from 'fraudulently' to 'dishonestly' in the definition of stealing [contained in section 1]."

We feel, with the greatest respect, that in seeking to reconcile the two lines of authority in the way we have mentioned, the Court of Appeal in *R. v. McIvor* was seeking to reconcile the irreconcilable. It therefore falls to us now either to choose between the two lines of authority or to propose some other solution.

In the current supplement to *Archbold Criminal Pleading Evidence & Practice*, 40th ed. (1979), paragraph 1460, the editors suggest that the observations on dishonesty by the Court of Appeal in *R. v. Landy* can be disregarded "in view of the wealth of authority to the contrary." The matter, we feel, is not as simple as that.

In *R. v. Waterfall* [1970] 1 Q.B. 148, the defendant was charged under section 16 of the Theft Act 1968 with dishonestly obtaining a pecuniary advantage from a taxi driver. Lord Parker C.J., giving the judgment of the Court of Appeal, said, at pp. 150–151:

"The sole question as it seems to me in this case revolves round the third ingredient, namely, whether what was done was done dishonestly. In regard to that the deputy recorder directed the jury in this way: 'If on reflection and deliberation you come to the conclusion that this defendant never did have any genuine belief that Mr. Tropp [the accountant] would pay the taxi fare, then you would be entitled to convict him. . . . ' In other words, in that passage the deputy recorder is telling the jury they had to consider what was in this particular defendant's mind: had he a genuine belief that the accountant would provide the money? That, as it seems to this court, is a perfectly proper direction subject to this, that it would be right to tell the jury that they can use as a test, though not a conclusive test, whether there were any reasonable grounds for that belief. Unfortunately, however, just before the jury retired, in two passages the deputy recorder, as it seems to this court, was saying: you cannot hold that this man had a genuine belief unless he had reasonable grounds for that belief."

Lord Parker then sets out the passages in question and continues, at p. 151:

"the court is quite satisfied that those directions cannot be justified. The test here is a subjective test, whether the particular man had an honest belief, and of course whereas the absence of reasonable ground may point strongly to the fact that that belief is not genuine, it is at the end of the day for the jury to say whether or not in the case of this particular man he did have that genuine belief."

That decision was criticised by academic writers. But it was followed shortly afterwards in *R. v. Royle* [1971] 1 W.L.R. 1764, another case under section 16 of the Theft Act 1968. Edmund Davies L.J., giving the judgment of the court, said, at p. 1769:

"The charges being that debts had been dishonestly 'evaded' by deception, contrary to section 16(2)(a), it was incumbent on the commissioner to direct the jury on the fundamental ingredient of dishonesty. In accordance with *R. v. Waterfall*, they should have been told that the test is whether the accused had an honest belief and that, whereas the absence of reasonable ground might point strongly to the conclusion that he entertained no genuine belief in the truth of his representation, it was for them to say whether or not it had been established that the appellant had no such genuine belief."

It is to be noted that the court in that case treated the "fundamental ingredient of dishonesty" as being the same as whether the defendant had a genuine belief in the truth of the representation.

In *R.* v. *Gilks* [1971] 1 W.L.R. 1341, which was decided by the Court of Appeal the following year, the appellant had been convicted of theft contrary to section 1 of the Theft Act 1968. The facts were that he had been overpaid by a bookmaker. He knew that the bookmaker had made a mistake, and that he was not entitled to the money. But he kept it. The case for the defence was that "bookmakers are a race apart." It would be dishonest if your grocer gave you too much change and you kept it, knowing that he had made a mistake. But it was not dishonest in the case of a bookmaker. The judge directed the jury, at p. 1345:

> "Well, it is a matter for you to consider, members of the jury, but try and place yourselves in that man's position at that time and answer the question whether in your view he thought he was acting honestly or dishonestly."

Cairns L.J. giving the judgment of the Court of Appeal held that that was, in the circumstances of the case, a proper and sufficient direction on the matter of dishonesty. He continued, at p. 1345:

> "On the face of it the defendant's conduct was dishonest: the only possible basis on which the jury could find that the prosecution had not established dishonesty would be if they thought it possible that the defendant did have the belief which he claimed to have."

A little later *R.* v. *Feely* (*ante,* p. 734) came before a court of five judges. The case is often treated as having laid down an objective test of dishonesty for the purpose of section 1 of the Theft Act 1968. But what it actually decided was (i) that it is for the jury to determine whether the defendant acted dishonestly and not for the judge, (ii) that the word "dishonestly" can only relate to the defendant's own state of mind, and (iii) that it is unnecessary and undesirable for judges to define what is meant by "dishonestly."

It is true that the court said, at pp. 537–538:

> "Jurors, when deciding whether an appropriation was dishonest, can be reasonably expected to, and should, apply the current standards of ordinary decent people."

It is that sentence which is usually taken as laying down the objective test. But the passage goes on:

> "In their own lives they have to decide what is and what is not dishonest. We can see no reason why, when in a jury box, they should require the help of a judge to tell them what amounts to dishonesty."

The sentence requiring the jury to apply current standards leads up to the prohibition on judges from applying *their* standards. That is the context in which the sentence appears. It seems to be reading too much into that sentence to treat it as authority for the view that "dishonesty can be established independently of the knowledge or belief of the defendant." If it could, then any reference to the state of mind of the defendant would be beside the point.

This brings us to the heart of the problem. Is "dishonestly" in section 1 of the Theft Act 1968 intended to characterise a course of conduct? Or is it intended to describe a state of mind? If the former, then we can well understand that it could be established independently of the knowledge or belief of the accused. But if, as we think, it is the latter, then the knowledge and belief of the accused are at the root of the problem.

Take for example a man who comes from a country where public transport is free. On his first day here he travels on a bus. He gets off without paying. He never had any intention of paying. His mind is clearly honest; but his conduct, judged objectively by what he has done, is dishonest. It seems to us that in using the word "dishonestly" in the Theft Act 1968, Parliament cannot have intended to catch dishonest conduct in that sense, that is to say conduct to which no moral obloquy could possibly attach. This is sufficiently established by the partial definition in section 2 of the Theft Act itself. All the matters covered by section 2(1) relate to the belief of the accused. Section 2(2) relates to his willingness to pay. A man's belief and his willingness to pay are things which can only be established subjectively. It is difficult to see how a partially subjective definition can be made to work in harness with the test which in all other respects is wholly objective.

If we are right that dishonesty is something in the mind of the accused (what Professor Glanville Williams calls "a special mental state"), then if the mind of the accused is honest, it cannot be deemed dishonest merely because members of the jury would have regarded it as dishonest to embark on that course of conduct.

So we would reject the simple uncomplicated approach that the test is purely objective, however attractive from the practical point of view that solution may be.

There remains the objection that to adopt a subjective test is to abandon all standards but that of the accused himself, and to bring about a state of affairs in which "Robin Hood would be no robber": *R.* v. *Greenstein.* This objection misunderstands the nature of the subjective test. It is no defence for a man to say "I knew what I was doing is generally regarded as dishonest; but I do not regard it as dishonest myself. Therefore I am not guilty." What he is however entitled to say is "I did not know that anybody would regard what I was doing as dishonest." He may not be believed; just as he may not be believed if he sets up "a claim of right" under section 2(1) of the Theft Act 1968, or asserts that he believed in the truth of a misrepresentation under section 15 of the Act of 1968. But if he *is* believed, or raises a real doubt about the matter, the jury cannot be sure that he was dishonest.

In determining whether the prosecution has proved that the defendant was acting dishonestly, a jury must first of all decide whether according to the ordinary standards of reasonable and honest people what was done was dishonest. If it was not dishonest by those standards, that is the end of the matter and the prosecution fails.

If it was dishonest by those standards, then the jury must consider whether the defendant himself must have realised that what he was doing was by those standards dishonest. In most cases, where the actions are obviously dishonest by ordinary standards, there will be no doubt about it. It will be obvious that the defendant himself knew that he was acting dishonestly. It is dishonest for a defendant to act in a way which he knows ordinary people consider to be dishonest, even if he asserts or genuinely believes that he is morally justified in acting as he did. For example, Robin Hood or those ardent anti-vivisectionists who remove animals from vivisection laboratories are acting dishonestly, even though they may consider themselves to be morally justified in doing what they do, because they know that ordinary people would consider these actions to be dishonest.

Cases which might be described as borderline, such as *Boggeln* v. *Williams* [1978] 1 W.L.R. 873, will depend upon the view taken by the jury as to whether the defendant may have believed what he was doing was in accordance with the ordinary man's idea of honesty. A jury might have come to the conclusion that the defendant in that case was disobedient or impudent, but not dishonest in what he did.

So far as the present case is concerned, it seems to us that once the jury had rejected the defendant's account in respect of each count in the indictment (as they plainly did), the finding of dishonesty was inevitable, whichever of the tests of dishonesty was applied. If the judge had asked the jury to determine whether the defendant might have believed that what he did was in accordance with the ordinary man's idea of honesty, there could have only been one answer—and that is no, once the jury had rejected the defendant's explanation of what happened.

In so far as there was a misdirection on the meaning of dishonesty, it is plainly a case for the application of the proviso to section 2(1) of the Criminal Appeal Act 1968.

Appeal dismissed

Questions

1. Does this case dispose of the "Robin Hood defence," as Lord Lane suggests (*ante*, p. 742)? D, accused of stealing from his bookmaker, says in evidence "Bookmakers are a race apart; it would be dishonest if your grocer gave you too much change and you kept it, knowing that he had made a mistake. But it is not dishonest in the case of a bookmaker." (See *Gilks*, referred to, *ante* p. 741). Must he not be acquitted if (i) the jury think it is not dishonest to diddle bookmakers? or (ii) the jury do not think so but think that D may have thought that reasonable people may have thought so?

2. "Dishonesty is something which laymen can easily recognise when they see it" (C.L.R.C. § 39, *ante*, p. 733). Does this mean that 12 jurors will always agree in describing some transaction as honest or dishonest? and that successive juries dealing with similar transactions will agree in the same way? If so, do you agree? Is it possible to forecast the view of a jury on the honesty of, *e.g.* a taking of experimental animals in order to save them from vivisection? If juries did usually hold that such a taking was not theft, how could this be reconciled with the law which allows properly licensed vivisection?

3. Is (a) good motive, or (b) necessity, generally a defence to crime? See *ante*, Chaps. 3 and 5.

4. The judge needs to direct the jury to apply the double test of dishonesty laid down by Lord Lane (*ante*, p. 742) (was D.'s conduct dishonest by ordinary standards, and if so did he realise it was so?) only where dishonesty is a live issue, *i.e.* only where D. is in effect saying that he thought what he was doing was not dishonest. In other cases it is potentially misleading to direct on these matters: *R.* v. *Price* (1989) 80 Cr.App.R. 409.

5. In Victoria, under a statute in all material respects identical to the Theft Act, the Supreme Court, rejecting the reasoning in *Feely*, has held that the meaning of "dishonestly" is a matter of law for the judge, and that meaning is "with disposition to withhold from a person what is his right": *R.* v. *Salvo* [1980] V.R. 401, 432; *R.* v. *Brow* [1981] V.R. 738; *R.* v. *Bonollo* [1981] V.R. 633.

2. ROBBERY

Theft Act 1968, section 8

"(1) A person is guilty of robbery if he steals, and immediately before or at the time of doing so, and in order to do so, he uses force on any person or puts or seeks to put any person in fear of being then and there subjected to force.

(2) A person guilty of robbery, or of an assault with intent to rob, shall on conviction on indictment be liable to imprisonment for life."

Notes

1. *Theft*. Without a theft (or attempted theft in the case of assault with intent to rob) there is no robbery. Theft is complete as soon as there is an appropriation with intent to steal. See Appropriation, *ante*, p. 662, and *Corcoran* v. *Anderton* (1980) 71 Cr.App.R. 104 (D.C.), where it was held that wrestling with the owner for possession of an article is an assumption of the rights of the owner and therefore theft and, if accompanied by force, robbery.

In *R.* v. *Robinson* [1977] Crim.L.R. 173 (C.A.) it was held that the law as laid down in *R.* v. *Skivington* [1968] 1 Q.B. 166 had not been altered by the Theft Act. In *R.* v. *Skivington*, S. threatened with a knife his wife's employer in order to collect wages due to her which he had her authority to collect. The judge directed the jury that before S. could maintain a defence to a charge of robbery, they must be satisfied that he had an honest belief that he was entitled to take the money in the way in which he did take it. Lord Goddard C.J.: "In the opinion of this court the matter is plain, namely that a claim of right is a defence to robbery ... and that it is unnecessary to show that the defendant must have had an honest belief also that he was entitled to take the money in the way that he did."

Conviction quashed

Question

Is robbery involved in the following cases?

A is lent a lawnmower by his neighbour B. When B asks for its return, A drives him away with blows, saying he is going to keep it.

C, needing the use of a car to escape pursuit by the police, takes D's car from him at gunpoint.

E, needing the use of a car for a smash and grab raid on a shop, takes F's car from him at gunpoint. See below.

2. *Force immediately before or at the time of the theft*

Andrews, Robbery [1966] Crim.L.R. 524, 525

"Another advantage of the new definition is that the crime of robbery is not restricted to stealing from the person or in the presence of the person against whom force is used or threatened. ... However a problem does arise even under the new definition. Let us take the case of a defendant who assaults and binds someone and then proceeds to his victim's property some distance away where minutes or even hours later he steals. Is he guilty of robbery? The fact that the theft is away from the presence of the victim would no longer be a problem, but the new definition does restrict the scope of robbery to circumstances where the defendant 'immediately before or at the time of [stealing] wilfully uses force on any person or wilfully puts or seeks to put any person in fear of being then and there subjected to force.' Has the force been used 'immediately before' in our example? Does immediate mean seconds, minutes or hours? Presumably it is not intended to cover the situation where the violence precedes the stealing by a matter of days. Nor can one argue that the force or fear is a continuing factor if the victim remains under continuing fear or restraint, because what must be immediate is the wilful use of force not the continuing effect of it, or alternatively the putting of the person in fear or seeking to put him in fear must be immediate, not merely the continuing fear. The matter might be better put if the words 'immediately before or at the time of doing so' were left out of the definition. The crime of robbery would still be limited to where the person uses force or fear 'in order to [steal].' To further restrict it in terms of temporal proximity of force and theft is to make a defence of the criminal's divorcing in time the violence and the stealing and there seems no great reason in that. The real issue should surely be whether the force or threat of force was used *in order to steal*."

R. v. Hale
(1978) 68 Cr.App.R. 415
Court of Appeal

H. and M. entered the house of Mrs. C. wearing stocking masks. H. put his hand over her mouth to stop her screaming. M. went upstairs and came back with her jewellery box. They then tied up Mrs. C. and threatened harm to her child if she told the police within five minutes of their leaving. H. was convicted of robbery and appealed.

EVELEIGH L.J.: ... On behalf of the appellant it is submitted that the learned judge misdirected the jury in that the passages quoted above could indicate to them that if an accused used force in order to effect his escape with the stolen goods that would be sufficient to constitute the crime of robbery. In so far as the facts of the present case are concerned, counsel submitted that the theft was completed when the jewellery box was first seized and any force thereafter could not have been "immediately before or at the time of stealing" and certainly not "in order to steal." The essence of the submission was that the theft was completed as soon as the jewellery box was seized. . . .

Section 8 of the Theft Act 1968 begins: "A person is guilty of robbery if he steals. . . . " He steals when he acts in accordance with the basic definition of theft in section 1 of the Theft Act; that is to say when he dishonestly appropriates property belonging to another with the intention of permanently depriving the other of it. It thus becomes necessary to consider what is "appropriation" or, according to section 3, "any assumption by a person of the rights of an owner." An assumption of the rights of an owner describes the conduct of a person towards a particular article. It is conduct which usurps the rights of the owner. To say that the conduct is over and done with as soon as he lays hands upon the property, or when he first manifests an intention to deal with it as his, is contrary to common-sense and to the natural meaning of words. A thief who steals a motor car first opens the door. Is it to be said that the act of starting up the motor is no more a part of the theft?

In the present case there can be little doubt that if the appellant had been interrupted after the seizure of the jewellery box the jury would have been entitled to find that the appellant and his accomplice were assuming the rights of an owner at the time when the jewellery box was seized. However, the act of appropriation does not suddenly cease. It is a continuous act and it is a matter for the jury to decide whether or not the act of appropriation has finished. Moreover, it is quite clear that the intention to deprive the owner permanently, which accompanied the assumption of the owner's rights, was a continuing one at all material times. This Court therefore rejects the contention that the theft had ceased by the time the lady was tied up. As a matter of common-sense the appellant was in the course of committing theft; he was stealing.

There remains the question whether there was robbery. Quite clearly the jury were at liberty to find the appellant guilty of robbery relying upon the force used when he put his hand over Mrs. Carrett's mouth to restrain her from calling for help. We also think that they were also entitled to rely upon the act of tying her up provided they were satisfied (and it is difficult to see how they could not be satisfied) that the force so used was to enable them to steal. If they were still engaged in the act of stealing the force was clearly used to enable them to continue to assume the rights of the owner and permanently to deprive Mrs. Carrett of her box, which is what they began to do when they first seized it. . . .

Appeal dismissed

Compare C.L.R.C.'s Eighth Report, Cmnd. 2977, § 65: *infra,* and see *Appropriation: A Single or Continuous Act, ante,* p. 678.

3. *Force on any person*

Criminal Law Revision Committee, Eighth Report, Cmnd. 2977

§ 65 But the force will have to have been used for the purpose of stealing; force used only to get away after committing a theft does not seem naturally to be regarded as robbery (though it could be charged as a separate offence in addition to the stealing). We should not regard mere snatching of property, such as a handbag, from an unresisting owner as using force for the purpose of the definition, though it might be so if the owner resisted. In the case of robbery by putting in fear the draft requires the fear to be that of being then and there subjected to force. This seems to us to correspond to what should be the essence of the offence. A threat to accuse a person of an offence comes more naturally under blackmail than under property.

R. v. Dawson
(1976) 64 Cr.App.R. 170
Court of Appeal

D. and two others came alongside a sailor, and nudged him from side to side. While he was trying to keep his balance, one of the three was enabled to take his wallet. They were convicted of robbery and appealed.

LAWTON L.J.: Mr. Locke had submitted at the end of the prosecution's case that what had happened could not in law amount to the use of force. He called the learned judge's attention to some old authorities and to a passage in *Archbold* ... based on the old authorities, and submitted that because of those old authorities there was not enough evidence to go to the jury. He sought before this Court to refer to the old authorities. He was discouraged from doing so because this Court is of the opinion that in these cases what judges should now direct their attention to is the words of the statute. This had been said in a number of cases since the Theft Act 1968.

The object of that Act was to get rid of all the old technicalities of the law of larceny and to put the law into simple language which juries would understand and which they themselves would use. That is what has happened in section 8 which defines "robbery." That section is in these terms: "A person is guilty of robbery if he steals and immediately before or at the time of doing so, and in order to do so, he uses force on any person or puts or seeks to put any person in fear of being then and there subjected to force."

The choice of the word "force" is not without interest because under the Larceny Act 1916 the word "violence" had been used, but Parliament deliberately on the advice of the Criminal Law Revision Committee changed that word to "force." Whether there is any difference between "violence" or "force" is not relevant for the purposes of this case; but the word is "force." It is a word in ordinary use. It is a word which juries understand. The learned judge left it to the jury to say whether jostling a man in the way which the victim described to such an extent that he had difficulty in keeping his balance could be said to be the use of force. The learned judge, because of the argument put forward by Mr. Locke, went out of his way to explain to the jury that force in these sort of circumstances must be substantial to justify a verdict.

Whether it was right for him to put that adjective before the word "force" when Parliament had not done so we will not discuss for the purposes of this case. It was a matter for the jury. They were there to use their common sense and knowledge of the world. We cannot say that their decision as to whether force was used was wrong. They were entitled to the view that force was used.

Other points were discussed in the case as to whether the force had been used for the purpose of distracting the victim's attention or whether it was for the purpose of overcoming resistance. Those sort of refinements may have been relevant under the old law, but so far as the new law is concerned the sole question is whether the accused used force on any person in order to steal. That issue in this case was left to the jury. They found in favour of the Crown.

We cannot say that this verdict was either unsafe or unsatisfactory. Accordingly the appeal is dismissed.

Appeal dismissed

R. v. Clouden [1987] Crim.L.R. 56 (C.A.): C. was seen to follow a woman who was carrying a shopping basket in her left hand. He approached her from behind and wrenched the basket down and out of her grasp with both hands and ran off with it. He was charged in two counts with robbery and theft respectively and convicted on the first count of robbery. He appealed on the grounds (i) that there was insufficient evidence of resistance to the snatching of the bag to constitute force on the person under section 8 of the Theft Act 1968; and (ii) that the learned judge's direction to the jury on the requirement of force on the person was inadequate and confused.

Held, dismissing the appeal, the old cases distinguished between force on the actual person and force on the property which in fact causes force on the person but, following *Dawson*, the court should direct attention to the words of the statute without referring to the old authorities. The old distinctions have gone. Whether the defendant used force on any person in order to steal is an issue that should be left to the jury. The judge's direction to the jury was adequate. He told the jury quite clearly at the outset what the statutory definition was, though thereafter he merely used the word "force" and did not use the expression "on the person."

Questions

1. What exactly did *Dawson* purport to decide on the question of "force?" What did the Court in *Clouden* treat it as deciding?

2. If a pickpocket "lifts" a wallet, for it to be "force on a person" need the victim feel the movement? Need the pickpocket realise that the victim might feel the movement?

3. Is it justifiable to treat a "non-violent" removal of a bag from the victim's presence so much more seriously than simple theft if the victim is actually holding it at the time?

4. In view of the other offences necessarily involved in a robbery situation, do we need a separate crime of robbery at all?

CHAPTER 11

FRAUD

	PAGE		PAGE
1. Obtaining Property by Deception	751	iv. Dishonesty	774
i. Obtaining Property Belonging to Another with Intention Permanently to Deprive	751	2. Obtaining Pecuniary Advantage by Deception	776
		3. Obtaining Services by Deception	777
ii. Deception	751	4. Evasion of Liability by Deception	778
iii. The Obtaining must be by the Deception	762	5. Making off Without Payment	784

Note

The law of larceny did not, even in its latter-day expanded form, cover all offences of dishonesty connected with property. The law always drew a distinction between a thief and a swindler, the former being one who took the goods of another without any colour of consent and the latter being one who fraudulently persuaded the victim to make him (the swindler) the owner. The swindler was originally not punished by the common law at all in ordinary cases, and when statute invented the crime of obtaining by false pretences to cover him, it maintained a sharp distinction between the thief and the swindler, the former being in all cases a felon while the latter, except in cases where personation or forged documents were involved in the swindle, was guilty of misdemeanour only. By 1916, there was a range of offences covering various forms of swindling, see, *e.g.* the Forgery Act 1861, s.3; the Debtors Act 1869, s.13; the False Personation Act 1874, s.1, and the Larceny Act 1916, s.32, the principal offence being obtaining by false pretences under section 32(1) of the Larceny Act 1916.

Criminal Law Revision Committee's Eighth Report, Cmnd. 2977

"§ 38 The sub-committee for a considerable time proposed that the general offence of theft should be made to cover the present offence of obtaining by false pretences under 1916, s.32(1). It might seem appropriate to extend theft in this way in order to make it cover as many ways as possible of getting property dishonestly. But in the end the sub-committee gave up the idea (to the regret of some members), and the full committee agreed. In spite of its attractions, it seemed to the majority of the committee that the scheme would be unsatisfactory. Obtaining by false pretences is ordinarily thought of as different from theft, because in the former the owner in fact consents to part with his ownership; a bogus beggar is regarded as a rogue but not as a thief, and so are his less petty counterparts. To create a new offence of theft to include conduct which ordinary people would find difficult to regard as theft would be a mistake. The unnaturalness of including obtaining by false pretences in theft is

749

emphasised by the difficulty of drafting a satisfactory definition to cover both kinds of conduct. ... "

Notes

1. In spite of this declaration that theft and obtaining by deception are recognisably different, the scheme of the Committee's proposals, and of the Act which followed them, is that the two offences are equally reprehensible, and that in most situations it should make no difference whether the property was taken without any colour of right or by deceiving the victim into transferring it to the fraudulent person. Thus, the maximum penalty for theft and obtaining property by deception was to be the same (10 years' imprisonment—but since then the maximum for theft has been lowered to seven years: section 26 Criminal Justice Act 1991); for the purposes of handling, it makes no difference whether the goods were originally stolen or obtained by deception (s.24(4), *post*, p. 804); for the purpose of going equipped, it makes no difference whether the defendant has the article with him for use in a theft or an obtaining by deception (s.25(1), *post*, p. 848). Moreover there is nothing in the Theft Act making the offences mutually exclusive alternatives, *i.e.* it is no defence to a person charged with one crime to say that his offence is really the other. Indeed, as a result of the decisions in *R.* v. *Gomez, ante,* p. 663, in almost all cases of obtaining, a charge of theft would be equally appropriate; that case decides that where A by fraud induces B to make him the owner of the property, that is an appropriation of property belonging to another.

2. The principal crime is obtaining property by deception: see *infra.* The problem of how to deal with the swindler who obtains not property but some valuable service was a troublesome one for the law. After a false start largely represented by the offence in section 15(2)(a) of the Theft Act 1968 of obtaining pecuniary advantage by reducing or evading or deferring a debt or charge (now repealed), a range of offences was introduced by the Theft Act 1978. They overlap with each other, and also with section 15 of 1968 Act. For example, if A, intending never to pay, induces B to let him have some goods by dishonestly giving a worthless cheque, he obtains property by deception (section 15/1968), but also obtains services (the delivery of the goods) by deception (section 1/1978) and evades liability by inducing B to wait for payment (section 2(1)(b)/1978). Moreover, as a result of *R.* v. *Gomez,* he steals the goods under section 1/1968.

3. Apart from crimes in the Theft Acts, there is a wide range of offences in other Acts covering frauds involving forgery, trading by companies, misleading investors, revenue frauds and social security frauds. There is also the offence of conspiracy to defraud (*ante,* p. 463), covering all these and any other conceivable frauds, provided that more than one person is involved. A similarly wide general offence of fraud committable by one person has been mooted: Law Commission W.P. 104 (1987).

1. OBTAINING PROPERTY BY DECEPTION

Theft Act 1968, section 15

"(1) A person who by any deception dishonestly obtains property belonging to another, with the intention of permanently depriving the other of it, shall on conviction on indictment be liable to imprisonment for a term not exceeding ten years.

(2) For purposes of this section a person is to be treated as obtaining property if he obtains ownership, possession or control of it, and 'obtain' includes obtaining for another or enabling another to obtain or to retain.

(3) Section 6 above shall apply for purposes of this section, with the necessary adaptation of the reference to appropriating, as it applies for purposes of section 1.

(4) For purposes of this section 'deception' means any deception (whether deliberate or reckless) by words or conduct as to fact or as to law, including a deception as to the present intentions of the person using the deception or any other person."

Note

This is the principal swindling crime, and differs from the others dealt with in this chapter in that *property* is obtained *with intent to deprive permanently*.

i. Obtaining Property Belonging to Another with Intention Permanently to Deprive

Notes

1. By section 34(1) "property" in this offence is given the same meaning as that given by section 4(1) for the purposes of theft (*ante*, p. 679). The limitations and exceptions as to land and wild animals imposed by section 3(2)–(4) relating to theft have no application to the present offence. "Belonging to another" is given the same meaning as that given by section 5(1) for the purposes of theft (*ante*, p. 692). The remaining subsections of section 5 do not apply to the present offence.

2. On intention permanently to deprive, see *ante*, pp. 717–727. The need for this intention means that obtaining by lies the *loan* of an article which one intends to return is not an offence under this section. It is different with a loan of money, however, because there is usually no intention to return the precise coins or notes lent. In such a case the question of guilt will turn on what view the jury take of the accused's honesty. (See *post*, p. 774.)

ii. Deception

Note

Deception is needed for this crime, as it is also for obtaining pecuniary advantage (*post*, p. 776) obtaining services, and evasion of liability (*post*, p. 777). The definition in section 15(4) is made to apply to these other offences by the Theft Act 1968, s.16(3) and the

Theft Act 1978, s.5(1). The principal offence of obtaining pecuniary advantage was that contained in the Theft Act 1968, s.16(2)(a). This provision was repealed by the Theft Act 1978, s.5(5), a fact which must be borne in mind in considering some of the cases following, which are reproduced as authorities on deception and on the need for the deception to cause the obtaining.

Director of Public Prosecutions v. Ray
[1974] A.C. 370
House of Lords

R., and others, entered a restaurant and ordered a meal. R. did not have enough money to pay, but one of his companions agreed to lend him enough to pay. After eating the meal, while the waiter was still in the dining room, the men decided not to pay and to run out of the restaurant. Ten minutes later they did so while the waiter was absent in the kitchen. The Divisional Court quashed R.'s conviction for obtaining a pecuniary advantage by deception contrary to section 16(2)(a) of the Theft Act (since repealed). The prosecution appealed to the House of Lords.

LORD REID: . . . If a person induces a supplier to accept an order for goods or services by a representation of fact, that representation must be held to be a continuing representation lasting until the goods or services are supplied. Normally it would not last any longer. A restaurant supplies both goods and services: it supplies food and drink and the facilities for consuming them. Customers normally remain for a short time after consuming their meal, and I think that it can properly be held that any representation express or implied made with a view to obtaining a meal lasts until the departure of the customers in the normal course.

In my view, where a new customer orders a meal in a restaurant, he must be held to make an implied representation that he can and will pay for it before he leaves. In the present case the accused must be held to have made such a representation. But when he made it it was not dishonest: he thought he would be able to borrow money from one of his companions.

After the meal had been consumed the accused changed his mind. He decided to evade payment. So he and his companions remained seated where they were for a short time until the waiter left the room and then ran out of the restaurant.

Did he thereby commit an offence against section 16 of the Theft Act 1968? It is admitted, and rightly admitted, that if the waiter had not been in the room when he changed his mind and he had immediately run out he would not have committed an offence. Why does his sitting still for a short time in the presence of the waiter make all the difference?

The section requires evasion of his obligation to pay. That is clearly established by his running out without paying. Secondly, it requires dishonesty: that is admitted. There would have been both evasion and dishonesty if he had changed his mind and run out while the waiter was absent.

The crucial question in this case is whether there was evasion "by any deception." Clearly there could be no deception until the accused changed his mind. I agree with the following quotation from the judgment of Buckley J. in *In re London and Globe Finance Corporation Ltd.* [1903] 1 Ch. 728, 732:

"to deceive is, I apprehend, to induce a man to believe that a thing is true which is false, and which the person practising the deceit knows or believes to be false."

So the accused, after he changed his mind, must have done something intended to induce the waiter to believe that he still intended to pay before he left. Deception, to my mind, implies something positive. It is quite true that a man intending to deceive can build up a situation in which his silence is as eloquent as an express statement. But what did the accused do here to create such a situation? He merely sat still. . . . The magistrates stated that they were of opinion that

" . . . having changed his mind as regards payment, by remaining in the restaurant for a further 10 minutes as an ordinary customer who was likely to order a sweet or coffee, the appellant practised a deception."

I cannot read that as a finding that after he changed his mind he intended to deceive the waiter into believing that he still intended to pay. And there is no finding that the waiter was in fact induced to believe that by anything the accused did after he changed his mind. I would infer from the case that all that he intended to do was to take advantage of the first opportunity to escape and evade his obligation to pay.

Deception is an essential ingredient of the offence. Dishonest evasion of an obligation to pay is not enough. I cannot see that there was, in fact, any more than that in this case.

I agree with the Divisional Court [1973] 1 W.L.R. 317, 323:

"His plan was totally lacking in the subtlety of deception and to argue that his remaining in the room until the coast was clear amounted to a representation to the waiter is to introduce an artificiality which should have no place in the Act."

I would therefore dismiss this appeal.

LORD MACDERMOTT: . . . Two questions [are left] for consideration. First, do the facts justify a finding that the respondent practised a deception? And secondly, if he did, was his evasion of the debt obtained by that deception?

The first of these questions involves nothing in the way of words spoken or written. If there was deception on the part of the respondent it was by his conduct in the course of an extremely common form of transaction which, because of its nature, leaves much to be implied from conduct. Another circumstance affecting the ambit of this question lies in the fact that, looking only to the period *after* the meal had been eaten and the respondent and his companions had decided to evade payment, there is nothing that I can find in the discernible conduct of the respondent which would suffice in itself to show that he was then practising a deception. No doubt he and the others stayed in their seats until the waiter went into the kitchen and while doing so gave all the appearance of ordinary customers. But, in my opinion, nothing in this or in anything else which occurred *after* the change of intention went far enough to afford proof of deception. The picture, as I see it, presented by this last stage of the entire transaction, is simply that of a group which had decided to evade payment and were awaiting the opportunity to do so.

There is, however, no sound reason that I can see for restricting the inquiry to this final phase. One cannot, so to speak, draw a line through the transaction at the point where the intention changed and search for evidence of deception only in what happened before that or only in what happened after that. In my opinion the transaction must for this purpose be regarded in its entirety, beginning with the respondent entering the restaurant and ordering his meal and ending with his running out without paying. The different stages of the transaction are all linked and it would be quite unrealistic to treat them in isolation.

Starting then, at the beginning one finds in the conduct of the respondent in entering and ordering his meal evidence that he impliedly represented that he had the means and the intention of paying for it before he left. That the respondent did make such a representation was not in dispute and in the absence of evidence to the contrary it would be difficult to reach a different conclusion. If this representation had then been false and matters had proceeded thereafter as they did (but without any change of intention) a conviction for the offence charged would, in my view, have had ample material to support it. But as the representation when originally made in this case was not false there was therefore no deception at that point. Then the meal is served and eaten and the intention to evade the debt replaces the intention to pay. Did this change of mind produce a deception?

My Lords, in my opinion it did. I do not base this conclusion merely on the change of mind that had occurred for that in itself was not manifest at the time and did not amount to "conduct" on the part of the respondent. But it did falsify the representation which had already been made because that initial representation must, in my view, be regarded not as something then spent and past but as a continuing representation which remained alive and operative and had already resulted in the respondent and his defaulting companions being taken on trust and treated as ordinary, honest customers. It covered the whole transaction up to and including payment and must therefore, in my opinion, be considered as continuing and still active at the time of the change of mind. When that happened, with the respondent taking (as might be expected) no step to bring the change to notice, he practised, to my way of thinking, a deception just as real and just as dishonest as would have been the case if his intention all along had been to go without paying.

Holding for these reasons that the respondent practised a deception, I turn to what I have referred to as the second question. Was the respondent's evasion of the debt obtained by that deception?

I think the material before the justices was enough to show that it was. The obvious effect of the deception was that the respondent and his associates were treated as they had been previously, that is to say as ordinary, honest customers whose conduct did not excite suspicion or call for precautions. In consequence the waiter was off his guard and vanished into the kitchen. That gave the respondent the opportunity of running out without hindrance and he took it. I would therefore answer this second question in the affirmative.

I would, accordingly, allow the appeal and restore the conviction.

LORD MORRIS OF BORTH-Y-GEST: For a deception to take place there must be some person or persons who will have been deceived. "Deception" is a word which is well understood. As Buckley J. said in *In re London and Globe Finance Corporation Ltd.* (1903) 1 Ch. 728, 732:

> "To deceive is, I apprehend, to induce a man to believe that a thing is true which is false, and which the person practising the deceit knows or believes to be false."

In the present case the person deceived was the waiter. Did the respondent deceive the waiter as to what were his intentions? Did the respondent so conduct himself as to induce the waiter to believe that he (the respondent) intended to pay his bill before he left the restaurant whereas at the relevant time he did not so intend? ...

The situation may perhaps be unusual where a customer honestly orders a meal and therefore indicates his honest intention to pay but thereafter forms a dishonest intention of running away without paying if he can. Inherent in an original honest representation of an intention to pay there must surely be a representation that such intention will continue.

In the present case it is found as a fact that when the respondent ordered his meal he believed that he would be able to pay. One of his companions had agreed to lend him money. He therefore intended to pay. So far as the waiter was concerned the original implied representation made to him by the respondent must have been a continuing representation so long as he (the respondent) remained in the restaurant. There was nothing to alter the representation. Just as the waiter was led at the start to believe that he was dealing with a customer who by all that he did in the restaurant was indicating his intention to pay in the ordinary way, so the waiter was led to believe that the state of affairs continued. But the moment came when the respondent decided and therefore knew that he was not going to pay: but he also knew that the waiter still thought that he was going to pay. By ordering his meal and by his conduct in assuming the role of an ordinary customer the respondent had previously shown that it was his intention to pay. By continuing in the same role and behaving just as before he was representing that his previous intention continued. That was a deception because his intention, unknown to the waiter, had become quite otherwise. The dishonest change of intention was not likely to produce the result that the waiter would be told of it. The essence of the deception was that the waiter should not know of it or be given any sort of clue that it (the change of intention) had come about. Had the waiter suspected that by a change of intention a secret exodus was being planned, it is obvious that he would have taken action to prevent its being achieved.

It was said in the Divisional Court that deception under section 16 should not be found unless an accused has actively made a representation by words or conduct which representation is found to be false. But if there was an original representation (as, in my view, there was when the meal was ordered) it was a representation that was intended to be and was a continuing representation. It continued to operate on the mind of the waiter. It became false and it became a deliberate deception. The prosecution do not say that the deception consisted in not informing the waiter of the change of mind; they say that the deception consisted in continuing to represent to the waiter that there was an intention to pay before leaving.

On behalf of the respondent it was contended that no deception had been practised. It was accepted that when the meal was ordered there was a representation by the respondent that he would pay but it was contended that once the meal was served there was no longer any representation but that there was merely an obligation to pay a debt: it was further argued that thereafter there was no deception because there was no obligation in the debtor to inform his creditor that payment was not to be made. I cannot accept these contentions. They ignore the circumstance that the representation that was made was a continuing one: its essence was that an intention to pay would continue until payment was made: by its very nature it would not cease to operate as a representation unless some new arrangement was made. ...

The final question which arises is whether, if there was deception and if there was pecuniary advantage, it was by the deception that the respondent obtained the pecuniary advantage. In my view, this must be a question of fact and the magistrates have found that it was by his deception that the respondent dishonestly evaded payment. It would seem to be clear that if the waiter had thought that if he left the restaurant to go to the kitchen the respondent would at once run out, he (the waiter) would not have left the restaurant and would have taken suitable action. The waiter proceeded on the basis that the implied representation made to him (*i.e.* of an honest intention to pay) was effective. The waiter was caused to refrain from taking certain courses of action which but for the representation he would have taken. In my view, the respondent during the whole time that he was in the restaurant made and by his continuing conduct continued to make a representation of his intention to pay before leaving. When in place of his original intention he substituted the dishonest intention of running away as soon as the waiter's back was turned, he was continuing to lead the waiter to believe that he intended to pay. He practised a deception on the waiter and by so doing he obtained for himself the pecuniary advantage of evading his obligation to pay before leaving. That he did so dishonestly was found by the magistrates who, in my opinion, rightly convicted him.

I would allow this appeal.

LORD HODSON: ... The vital question is whether by sitting in the restaurant for 10 minutes after having consumed the meal the respondent was guilty of deception when he departed without paying. If he had no intention of paying at the outset cadit quaestio. If, on the other hand, his representation made at the outset was honest, I find it difficult to accept that the effect of the original representation continues so as to make subsequent failure to pay his creditor, automatically, so to speak, an evasion of debt obtained by deception.

Whether any evidence was given by a waiter is not disclosed. The case states that the waiter had gone to the kitchen and that durng his absence the respondent and his four companions ran out of the restaurant after having been there for nearly an hour and maintaining the demeanour of ordinary customers. Would the reasonable man say that a deception had been practised on him? Evade the debt the respondent did, but no more than any other debtor who, having originally intended to pay for a pecuniary advantage, subsequently changes his mind and evades his contractual obligation by not paying.

In order to succeed the prosecution must rely on the original representation honestly made by the respondent when he entered the restaurant as a continuing representation which operated and lulled the restaurant proprietor into a sense of security so that the respondent was enabled to leave as he did. I do not recollect that the prosecution put the case in this way but I think it is most formidable if so presented, for if the representation continued it was falsified by the change of mind of the respondent.

It is trite law and common sense that an honest man entering into a contract is deemed to represent that he has the present intention of carrying it out but if, as in this case, having accepted the pecuniary advantage involved in the transaction, he does not necessarily evade his debt by deception if he fails to pay his debt. Nothing he did after his change of mind can be characterised as conduct which would indicate that he was then practising a deception. To rely on breach of a continuous representation I suggest that in administering a criminal statute this is going too far and seems to involve that the ordinary man who enters into a contract intending to carry it out can be found guilty of a criminal offence if he changes his mind after incurring the obligation to pay unless he has taken a step to bring the change of mind to the notice of his creditor.

The appellant sought to support the argument, that there was a duty on the respondent to correct his original representation, by authority. *With* v. *O'Flanagan* [1936] Ch. 575 is good authority for the proposition that if a person who makes a representation, which is not immediately acted upon, finds that the facts are changing he must, before the representation is acted upon, disclose the change to the person to whom he has made the representation. That case concerned the sale of a medical practice. The seller, a doctor, represented that his practice was profitable. This was true when the representation was made but by the time the contract was signed the practice had dwindled to practically nothing. This was not disclosed to the purchaser who, on discovery, sought rescission. It was held that the statement made, though true at the time, had become untrue during the negotiations and that there was an obligation to disclose the fact to the purchaser.

The earlier case of *Traill* v. *Baring* (1864) 4 De G.J. & Sm. 318 was cited [1936] Ch. 575, 583. It contains the following passage from the judgment of Turner L.J., at p. 329:

"I take it to be quite clear, that if a person makes a representation by which he induces another to take a particular course, and the circumstances are afterwards altered to the knowledge of the party making the representation, but not to the knowledge of the party to whom the representation is made, and are so altered that the alteration of the circumstances may affect the course of conduct which may be pursued by the party to whom the representation is made, it is the imperative duty of the party who has made the representation to communicate to the party to whom the representation has been made the alteration of those circumstances; and that this court will not hold the party to whom the representation has been made bound unless such a communication has been made."

This authority does not assist the appellant as to continuity of representation generally. The position there taken was based upon a duty to communicate a change of circumstances which had occurred after a representation, true when made, had been falsified by the time the contract was entered into. Here no contract was entered into following a deception of any kind.

The respondent was in breach of his obligation to pay his debt but I agree with the conclusion of the Divisional Court that there was no evidence that he evaded it by deception.

I would dismiss the appeal.

LORD PEARSON: ... The essential feature of this case, in accordance with the magistrates' findings and opinions as I understand them, is that there was a continuing representation to be implied from the conduct of the respondent and his companions. By "continuing representation" I mean in this case not a continuing effect of an initial representation, but a representation which is being made by conduct at every moment throughout the course of conduct. The course of conduct consisted of: (i) entering the restaurant, sitting down at a table and probably looking at the menu; (ii) giving to the waiter an order for a main course to be served; (iii) eating the main course; (iv) remaining at the table for about 10 minutes. The remaining at the table for that time was consistent in appearance with continuing their conversation and deciding whether or not to order another course. In my opinion all those actions can properly be regarded as one course of conduct continuing up to but not including the running out of the restaurant without paying. That is where the course of conduct was broken off. Up to the moment of running out they were behaving ostensibly as ordinary customers of the restaurant, and the ordinary customers of such a restaurant intend to pay for their meals in the appropriate manner before leaving the restaurant. . . .

In my view, the magistrates could and did reasonably imply from the course of conduct a representation by the respondent that he had a present intention of paying for his meal before leaving the restaurant. It was a continuing representation in the sense that I have indicated, being made at every moment throughout the course of conduct. Insofar as it was being made before the decision to run out without paying, it was according to the magistrates' finding a true representation of the respondent's then present intention. Insofar as it was being made after that decision, it was a false representation of the respondent's then present intention, and of course false to his knowledge. That false representation deceived the waiter, inducing him to go to the kitchen, whereby the respondent with his companions, was enabled to make his escape from the restaurant and so dishonestly evade his obligation to pay for his meal. Thus by deception he obtained for himself the pecuniary advantage of evading the debt.

In my opinion, the respondent was rightly convicted by the magistrates. I would allow the appeal and restore the conviction and sentence.

Appeal allowed

Questions

1. Is the misrepresentation of a person in Ray's position (a) that he intends to pay for the meal, or (b) that his original representation that he would pay for the meal is still true? Can it ever matter which it is?

2. A, after consuming his meal, discovers that his wallet is empty and realises that he cannot pay. Is he under a duty at once to own up to the waiter? If not, how is he to be distinguished from Ray? If so, how is he to be distinguished from the ordinary man (referred to by Lord Hodson) who enters into a contract intending to carry it out but fails to take steps to bring the change of mind to the notice of his creditor?

3. Does it follow from *D.P.P.* v. *Ray* that failure to correct a mistaken impression in the other party before he transfers property to the accused counts as a deception? A, a private person, orders goods from P., a wholesaler, making no representation express or implied as to his own status. During the negotiations, he becomes aware that P. thinks that he (A) is a retailer and will only sell to retailers. A fails to correct the misapprehension. Is he guilty of obtaining the goods by deception?

Notes

1. Omissions in a statement which cause it to convey a false impression make the statement a false one: *R.* v. *Lord Kylsant* [1932] 1 K.B. 442. It has also been held that omission to make any statement at all is a deception if the situation is such that it is

incumbent upon D. to make a statement and failure to do so gives a false impression: *R.* v. *Firth* [1991] Crim.L.R. 326 (C.A.), which concerned evasion of liability, *post*, p. 778. See also *R.* v. *Shama* [1990] 2 All E.R. 602 (C.A.)—false accounting, where D. did not, as his duty required, fill in a blank form recording a transaction.

2. *Deliberate or reckless*: In *R.* v. *Staines* (1974) 60 Cr.App.R. 160 (C.A.), a case of A signing cheques on B's behalf not *knowing* that B's account was overdrawn, James L.J. said (at p. 162) "This Court accepts the contention put forward that in this section 'recklessly' does mean more than being careless, does mean more than being negligent, and does involve an indifference to or disregard of the feature of whether a statement be true or false."

Compare "recklessly" in other parts of the law, *ante*, pp. 109, 111.

Griew, The Theft Acts 1968 and 1978, 6th ed.

"§ 7.41 *Need P believe the representation?* 'To deceive is, I apprehend, to induce a man to believe that a thing is true which is false.' This well-known statement by Buckley J. in *Re London and Globe Finance Corporation* [1903] 1 Ch. 728 at 832, was cited with approval in *D.P.P.* v. *Ray* (*ante*, p. 752). It appears at first sight to state the obvious and require no elaboration. Yet there is, on reflection, a good deal of uncertainty attaching to the notion of 'believing that a thing is true'; and there has been no judicial consideration of what amounts to 'believing' for this purpose. It is submitted that, if indeed 'believing' is an appropriate word in this context, it should not be understood only in the sense of firmly accepting the truth of the statement in question. The deception offences can hardly be limited to cases in which P. is induced to hold a strong positive belief. P. may be well aware he does not know D, that there are rogues and liars abroad and that D. may be one of them. He may act 'on the strength' of D.'s assertion and in reliance upon it, but without any positive sense either believing or disbelieving it. If D. is lying, P. is surely 'deceived' for the purposes of section 15. It may in fact be better to abandon the word 'believe' and say that to deceive is to induce a man to act in reliance upon a false representation."

Note

The deception must be "as to fact or as to law." There were two kinds of representations which were not enough for the pre-1968 crime of obtaining by false pretences. One was the making of a false promise: *R* v. *Dent* [1955] 2 Q.B. 590 (C.A.). That is now covered by the words in subsection 4 "including a deception as to the present intentions of the person using the deception." The other was the expression of a dishonest opinion: *R.* v. *Bryan* (1857) D. & B. 265 (C.C.C.R.).

J. C. Smith: The Law of Theft, 6th ed., § 186

"[186] The Theft Act gives no guidance as to whether a misrepresentation of opinion is capable of being a deception. In principle there is no reason why it should not be, where the opinion is not honestly held. A vendor's description of his tenant as 'a most desirable tenant' when the rent was in arrears and, in the past, had only been paid under pressure was held by the Court of Appeal to be a sufficient misrepresentation to found an action in deceit.

'In a case where the facts are equally well-known to both parties, what one of them says to the other is frequently nothing but an expression of opinion. ... But if the facts are not equally well-known to both sides, then a statement of opinion by one who knows the facts best involves very often a statement of a material fact, for he impliedly states that he knows facts which justify his opinion.' *Smith* v. *Land and House Property Corporation* (1884) 28 Ch.D. 7, 15.

The way seems open to the courts, if they so wish, to hold that 'deception' extends to this kind of case. The use of that term frees them from the fetters of false pretences. A view of commercial morality very different from that of the majority of the judges in *Bryan* now prevails and deliberate mis-statements of opinion would today be generally condemned as dishonest, no less dishonest, indeed, than mis-statements of other facts—for whether an opinion is held or not is a fact—and the law should follow the changed attitude. It may, moreover, be a significant fact that at the time *Bryan* was decided, it was not possible for the prisoner to give evidence in his own defence.

Against this view, it might be argued that, since the Act has expressly removed one limitation on false pretences (representations as to intention) and has said nothing about this limitation, Parliament's intention is to allow it to continue. It is submitted that this would be a quite unjustifiable assumption. Parliament, in fact, has left it to the judges and, by the use of new terminology, given them a more or less free hand. The question now ought to be not 'Is it a matter of opinion?' but, 'If it is a matter of opinion, was it D's real opinion?' If the opinion is not honestly held there is, in truth, a misrepresentation of fact for the accused's state of mind is a question of fact. The Act indeed recognises this by holding false promises to be deception. If 'I intend ... ' (not intending) is a deception, is not 'I believe ... ' (not believing) equally a deception?''

R. v. Silverman
(1988) 86 Cr.App.R. 213
Court of Appeal

D. was known to two elderly sisters because he and his firm had done building work for their family for many years. On the occasions the subject of his prosecution, he grossly overcharged them for building work, and was convicted of obtaining the money they paid him by deception, namely by representing that the sum involved was a fair and reasonable charge for the work. On appeal:—

WATKINS L.J. for the Court: [Counsel for D.] has argued, first, that the appellant made no representations to the complainants. He has not shrunk from conceding that the appellant was dishonest. He has submitted that the appellant quoted the sisters for the work to be done but that it was open to them either to accept or reject the quotation upon such advice as they might seek and perhaps in the light of tenders by others, and that the appellant was in much the same position as anyone else who is asked to quote for work to be done. He has argued that it is a dangerous concept to introduce into the criminal law that an excessively high quotation amounts to a false representation under section 15(1) of the Theft Act 1968. In certain circumstances that submission may we think be well founded. But whether a quotation amounts to false representation must depend upon the circumstances.

It seems clear to us that the complainants, far from being worldly wise, were unquestionably gullible. Having left their former home, they relied implicitly upon the word of the appellant about their requirements in their maisonette. In such circumstances of mutual trust, one party depending upon the other for fair and reasonable conduct, the criminal law may apply if one party takes dishonest advantage of the other by representing as a fair charge that which he but not the other knows is dishonestly excessive.

In our view, the judge, in directing the jury, dealt with the matter accurately at the outset. At p. 3 of the transcript he said:

"So what are the essentials about which you have to be sure? Well, there are really four of them and they are these. First of all, the prosecution have got to prove that there was a deception, and the deception alleged here is a false representation that the said sum of £2,875 was a fair and proper charge for the work. The deception must operate on the mind of the person deceived, in this case the two sisters. The second essential is this, that the deception must be made dishonestly, and you, members of the jury, must be satisfied that it was in fact made dishonestly. Thirdly, the prosecution must prove that as a result of that deception the defendant obtained property belonging to another, in this case the cheque. Fourthly, it must be done with the intention of permanently depriving the others, that is to say, the sisters, of it. These are the four essentials which have got to be proved in respect of count 1, and the same four essentials have got to be proved in respect of each count."

The judge went on to advise the jury perfectly properly of what he stated was a sensible way of approaching the matter, and referred with equal propriety to the relationship that had obtained between the sisters and the appellant and the firm which had employed him over a very long period of time. He encouraged the jury, rightly, in our view, to regard the matter of establishing the four essentials with the background circumstances very well in mind.

As to directing the jury upon what the prosecution had to prove and the circumstances in which they might succeed, we find no fault whatever in the way in which the judge directed them. There was material for a finding that there had been a false representation although it is true that the appellant had said nothing at the time he made his representations to encourage the sisters to accept the quotations. He applied no pressure upon them, and apart from mentioning the actual prices to be charged was silent as to other matters that may have arisen for question in their minds.

On the matter of representation we have been referred to *D.P.P.* v. *Ray*, *ante* p. 752, which concerned someone leaving a restaurant without paying for a meal. At [1974] A.C. 379 Lord Reid said: "So the accused, after he changed his mind, must have done something intended to induce the waiter to believe that he still intended to pay before he left. Deception, to my mind, implies something positive."

Mr. Hopmeier submits that nothing positive was done in this case. Lord Reid continued (*ibid.*): "It is quite true that a man intending to deceive can build up a situation in which his silence is as eloquent as an express statement."

Here the situation had been built up over a long period of time. It was a situation of mutual trust and the appellant's silence on any matter other than the sums to be charged were, we think, as eloquent as if he had said: "What is more, I can say to you that we are going to get no more than a modest profit out of this."

There is, we think, no foundation for the criticism of the judge in the first ground of appeal nor any substance in this ground in law. ...

Appeal allowed on other grounds

iii. The Obtaining must be by the Deception

Note

It must be shown that the victim, because he was deceived, made the transfer complained of.

It appears from *Davies* v. *Flackett* [1973] R.T.R. 8 (D.C.) that deception needs a human victim, and it is impossible to practice a deception on a machine.

R. v. *Collis-Smith* [1971] Crim.L.R. 716 (C.A.) A. drove his private car into a service station and asked for petrol, which was put into his tank. The attendant then asked if he was paying for it, and A. said it was to be booked to his employer although, as A. well knew, he had no authority to pledge his employer's credit for petrol. He was convicted of obtaining the petrol by deception, the deception being that his employer would pay. His appeal was allowed; the petrol had already been obtained before the deception took place. The court emphasised that it was dealing with a particular situation where petrol had been put in the tank of a vehicle, and would be difficult to recover, and not with different situations, such as a person putting goods into a shopping basket and being stopped before leaving the shop.

Questions

1. Why would it make a difference if the property, instead of being petrol in the tank of a car, had been goods in a shopping basket in a shop? See *Edwards* v. *Ddin, ante,* p. 693.

2. If the deception alleged had been an implied representation that he (the defendant) would pay, might the result have been different?

R. v. *Mills* (1857) 8 Cox 263: (C.C.C.R.): M. claimed money from P. for work done which had not been done as M. well knew. P. also knew this but sent the money to M. for the purpose of entrapping him. Held, the representation was not what caused P. to send the money, but the desire to entrap M.

R. v. *Lince* (1873) 12 Cox 451 (C.C.C.R.): D. obtained a quantity of potatoes from P. after stating that he was the nephew of a man in P.'s employ (which was true) and that he lived at a certain beer house (which was false). P. said in evidence that both facts influenced him. Bovill C.J.: "It has long been settled that it is immaterial that the prosecutor was influenced by other circumstances than the false pretence charged. If that were not so, an indictment for false pretences could scarcely ever be maintained, as a tradesman is generally more or less influenced by the profit he expects to make on the transaction." *Conviction affirmed.*

R. v. *Laverty* [1970] 3 All E.R. 432 (C.A.): A. reconstructed an old car and substituted for the original number plates, plates from another car he had broken up. A. sold the car with the false plates to B. The deception alleged was that the car bore its original number plates. B. said in evidence that what induced him to part with his money was the representation that A. had a title to sell. Lord Parker C.J.: "The proper way of proving these matters is through the mouth of the person to whom the false representation is conveyed, and further it seems to the court in the present case that no jury could say that the only inference was that B. parted with his money by reason of this false representation. B. may well have been of the mind as he stated he was, namely that what operated on his mind was the belief that the appellant was the owner. Provided that the appellant was the owner it may well be that B. did not mind that the car did not bear its original number plates. At any rate, as it seems to the court, it cannot be said that the only possible inference here is that it actuated on B.'s mind." *Appeal allowed.*

Note

Laverty was a case where the victim's evidence did not support the prosecution's case. Often, in the nature of the case, there will be no evidence by any victim and the question of whether anyone was influenced will have to be decided by inference. The necessary inference was not drawn in *Laverty*, but see next case.

R. v. Doukas
[1978] 1 W.L.R. 372
Court of Appeal

D., a waiter at a hotel, was found with bottles of wine not of a type sold by the hotel. He admitted that he intended, when a customer ordered wine, to substitute his own bottle for his employer's, make out a separate bill and pocket the money paid by the customer. He was convicted of going equipped to cheat, contrary to section 25 of the Theft Act 1968. He applied for leave to appeal against conviction.

GEOFFREY LANE L.J.: ... The offence of going equipped to cheat is to be found in section 25 of the Theft Act 1968. It reads:

"(1) A person shall be guilty of an offence if, when not at his place of abode, he has with him any article for use in the course of or in connection with any ... cheat ... (5) For purposes of this section ... 'cheat' means an offence under section 15 of this Act."

Section 15 concerns obtaining property by deception. ...

Combining those two sections of the Theft Act—section 25 and section 15—which are apposite, one reaches this result: a person shall be guilty of an offence if, when not in his place of abode, he has with him any article for use in the course of or in connection with any deception, whether deliberate or reckless, by words or conduct, as to fact or as to law, for purposes of dishonestly obtaining property belonging to another with the intention of permanently depriving the other of it.

If one analyses that combined provision, one reaches the situation that the following items have to be proved. First of all, that there was an article for use in connection with the deception: here the bottles. Secondly, that there was a proposed deception: here the deception of the guests into believing that the proffered wine was hotel wine and not the waiter's.

Thirdly, an intention to obtain property by means of the deception, and the property here is the money of the guests which he proposes to obtain and keep. Fourthly, dishonesty. ... Fifthly, there must be proof that the obtaining would have been, wholly or partially, by virtue of the deception. The prosecution must prove that nexus between the deception and obtaining. It is this last and final ingredient which, as we see it in the present case, is the only point which raises any difficulty. ...

We have, as in the notice of appeal, been referred to the decision in *R.* v. *Rashid* [1977] 1 W.L.R. 298, which was a decision by another division of this court. That case concerned not a waiter in a hotel, but a British Rail waiter who substituted not bottles of wine for the railway wine but his own tomato sandwiches for the railway tomato sandwiches; and it is to be observed that the basis of the decision in that case was that the summing up of the judge to the jury was inadequate. On that basis the appeal was allowed. But the court went on to express its views obiter on the question whether in those circumstances it could be said that the obtaining was by virtue of deception, and it came to the conclusion, as I say obiter, that the answer was probably no.

Of course each case of this type may produce different results according to the circumstances of the case and according, in particular, to the commodity which is being proffered. But, as we see it, the question has to be asked of the hypothetical customer, "Why did you buy this wine, or, if you had been told the truth, would you or would you not have bought the commodity"? It is, at least in theory, for the jury in the end to decide that question.

Here, as the ground of appeal is simply the judge's action in allowing the case to go to the jury, we are answering that question, so to speak, on behalf of the judge rather than the jury. Was there evidence of the necessary nexus fit to go to the jury? Certainly so far as the wine is concerned, we have no doubt at all that the hypothetical customer, faced with the waiter saying to him: "This of course is not hotel wine, this is stuff which I imported into the hotel myself and I am going to put the proceeds of the wine, if you pay, into my own pocket," would certainly answer, so far as we can see, "I do not want your wine, kindly bring me the hotel carafe wine." Indeed it would be a strange jury that came to any other conclusion, and a stranger guest who gave any other answer for several reasons. First of all, the guest would not know what was in the bottle which the waiter was proffering. True, he may not know what was in the carafe which the hotel was proffering, but he would at least be able to have recourse to the hotel if something was wrong with the carafe wine, but he would have no such recourse with the waiter; if he did, it would be worthless.

It seems to us the matter can be answered on a much simpler basis. The hypothetical customer must be reasonably honest as well as being reasonably intelligent and it seems to us incredible that any customer, to whom the true situation was made clear, would willingly make himself a party to what was obviously a fraud by the waiter upon his employers. If that conclusion is contrary to the obiter dicta in *R.* v. *Rashid* then we must respectfully disagree with those dicta. ...

Application refused

Note

"It seems to us incredible that any customer ... would willingly make himself a party to what was obviously a fraud by the waiter on his employers." Although the inference that all customers are bound to be honest and unwilling to participate in fraud has not proved irresistable to all judges (see, *e.g.* *R. v. Rashid*, and Lord Bridge in *R. v. Cooke* [1986] A.C. 909, 921), the notion has proved useful in securing convictions in the not-uncommon case where A obtains things from B by proffering a cheque and cheque card, or a credit card, when the bank has withdrawn his authority to use the card. Since the giving of an ordinary unbacked cheque by A implies a representation that he has funds or an arrangement with his bank under which the cheque will be honoured, B will obviously rely on the representation of credit-worthiness in deciding whether to give A goods or credit. If he makes a mistake he will lose. The obtaining is thus clearly caused by the representation in all ordinary cases. But where a cheque and apparently valid cheque card, or an apparently valid credit card, is presented by A, B will be paid anyway whatever the state of A's finances, and it becomes difficult to say that B relies on the representation of credit-worthiness in giving A goods on credit. It is now recognised that the relevant representation in this sort of case is not as to credit-worthiness (which may well be a matter of indifference to B), but as to *authority to present the card*, which, so it is held in the next case, cannot be a matter of indifference to B.

R. v. Lambie
[1981] 2 All E.R. 776
House of Lords

L. obtained a credit card from a bank giving her credit facilities up to a limit of £200. The bank entered into contracts with retailers by which the bank guaranteed any purchase made with the credit card provided the retailer complied with certain conditions relating to the validity of the card. L., when well over her credit limit of £200, purchased goods from a shop using her credit card. The shop complied with the conditions of a credit card purchase and, since the amount involved was less than the amount for which special authorisation was required from the bank, made no enquiry of the bank as to L.'s credit standing. L. was charged with obtaining a pecuniary advantage by deception contrary to section 16(1) of the Theft Act 1968. The judge asked the jury whether the shop keeper relied on the presentation of an apparently valid credit card as being due authority to use the card. The jury convicted, L.'s appeal to the Court of Appeal was allowed, and the prosecution appealed to the House of Lords.

LORD ROSKILL: ... My Lords, at the close of the case for the prosecution, learned counsel for the respondent invited the learned judge to withdraw both counts from the jury on, it seems, from reading the learned judge's clear ruling upon this submission, two grounds, first, that as a matter of law there was no evidence from which a jury might properly draw the inference that the presentation of the card in the circumstances I have described was a representation by the respondent that she was authorised by the bank to use the card to create a contract to which the bank would be a party, and secondly, that as a matter of law there was no evidence from which a jury might properly infer that Miss Rounding [the departmental manager at Mothercare] was induced by any representation which the respondent might have made to allow the transaction to be completed and the respondent to obtain the goods. The foundation for this latter submission was that it was the existence of the agreement between Mothercare and the bank that was the reason for Miss Rounding allowing the transaction to be completed and the goods to be taken by the respondent, since Miss Rounding knew of the arrangement with the bank, so that Mothercare was in any event certain of payment. It was not, it was suggested, any representation by the respondent which induced Miss Rounding to complete the transaction and to allow the respondent to take the goods.

My Lords, the learned judge rejected these submissions. He was clearly right to do so, as indeed was conceded in argument before your Lordships' House, if the decision of this House in *Commissioner of Police for the Metropolis* v. *Charles* [1977] A.C. 177 is of direct application. In that appeal this House was concerned with the dishonest use, not as in the present appeal of a credit card, but of a cheque card. The appellant defendant was charged and convicted on two counts of obtaining a pecuniary advantage by deception, contrary to section 16 of the Theft Act 1968. The Court of Appeal (Criminal Division) and your Lordships' House both upheld those convictions. Your Lordships unanimously held that where a drawer of a cheque which is accepted in return for goods, services or cash, uses a cheque card he represents to the payee that he has the actual authority of the bank to enter on its behalf into the contract expressed on the card that it would honour the cheque on presentation for payment.

My Lords, I venture to quote in their entirety three paragraphs from the speech of my noble and learned friend, Lord Diplock, at pages 182 and 183 of the report, which as I venture to think, encapsulate the reasoning of all those members of your Lordships' House who delivered speeches:

"When a cheque card is brought into the transaction, it still remains the fact that all the payee is concerned with is that the cheque should be honoured by the bank. I do not think that the fact that a cheque card is used necessarily displaces the representation to be implied from the act of drawing the cheque which has just been mentioned. It is, however, likely to displace that representation at any rate as the main inducement to the payee to take the cheque, since the use of the cheque card in connection with the transaction gives to the payee a direct contractual right against the bank itself to payment on presentment, provided that the use of the card by the drawer to bind the bank to pay the cheque was within the actual or ostensible authority conferred upon him by the bank.

By exhibiting to the payee a cheque card containing the undertaking by the bank to honour cheques drawn in compliance with the conditions endorsed on the back, and drawing the cheque accordingly, the drawer represents to the payee that he has actual authority from the bank to make a contract with the payee on the bank's behalf that it will honour the cheque on presentment for payment.

It was submitted on behalf of the accused that there is no need to imply a representation that the drawer's authority to bind the bank was actual and not merely ostensible, since ostensible authority alone would suffice to create a contract with the payee that was binding on the bank; and the drawer's possession of the cheque card and the cheque book with the bank's consent would be enough to constitute his ostensible authority. So, the submission goes, the only representation needed to give business efficacy to the transaction would be true. This argument stands the doctrine of ostensible authority on its head. What creates ostensible authority in a person who purports to enter into a contract as agent for a principal is a representation made to the other party that he has the actual authority of the principal for whom he claims to be acting to enter into the contract on that person's behalf. If (1) the other party has believed the representation and on the faith of that belief has acted upon it and (2) the person represented to be his principal has so conducted himself towards that other party as to be estopped from denying the truth of the representation, then, and only then, is he bound by the contract purportedly made on his behalf. The whole foundation of liability under the doctrine of ostensible authority is a representation, believed by the person to whom it is made, that the person claiming to contract as agent for a principal has the actual authority of the principal to enter into the contract on his behalf."

If one substitutes in the passage at page 182G the words "to honour the voucher" for the words "to pay the cheque," it is not easy to see why *mutatis mutandis* the entire passages are not equally applicable to the dishonest misuse of credit cards as to the dishonest misuse of cheque cards.

But the Court of Appeal in a long and careful judgment delivered by Cumming-Bruce L.J. felt reluctantly impelled to reach a different conclusion. The crucial passage in the judgment which the learned Lord Justice delivered reads thus:

"We would pay tribute to the lucidity with which the learned judge presented to the jury the law which the House of Lords had declared in relation to deception in a cheque card transaction. If that analysis can be applied to this credit card deception the summing-up is faultless. But, in our view, there is a relevant distinction between the situation described in *Charles* and the situation devised by Barclays Bank for transactions involving use of their credit cards. By their contract with the bank, Mothercare had bought from the bank the right to sell goods to Barclaycard holders without regard to the question whether the customer was complying with the terms of the contract between the customer and the bank. By her evidence Miss Rounding made it perfectly plain that she made no assumption about the appellant's credit standing at the bank. As she said 'the Company rules exist because of the Company's agreement with Barclaycard.' The flaw in the logic is in our view demonstrated by the way in which the Judge put the question of the inducement of Miss Rounding to the jury:

'Is that a reliance by her, Miss Rounding of Mothercare, upon the presentation of the card as being due authority *within the limits as at that time* as with count one?'

In our view, the evidence of Miss Rounding could not found a verdict that necessarily involved a finding of fact that Miss Rounding was induced by a false representation that the appellant's credit standing at the bank gave her authority to use the card."

I should perhaps mention, for the sake of clarity, that the person referred to as the appellant in that passage is the present respondent.

It was for that reason that the Court of Appeal (Criminal Division) allowed the appeal, albeit with hesitation and reluctance. That court accordingly certified the following point of law as of general public importance, namely:

"In view of the proved differences between a cheque card transaction and a credit card transaction, were we right in distinguishing this case

from that of *Commissioner of Metropolitan Police* v. *Charles* [1977] A.C. 177
upon the issue of inducement?"

My Lords, as the appellant says in paragraph 9 of his printed case, the
Court of Appeal Criminal Division laid too much emphasis upon the
undoubted, but to my mind irrelevant fact that Miss Rounding said she
made no assumption about the respondent's credit standing with the
bank. They reasoned from the absence of assumption that there was no
evidence from which the jury could conclude that she was "induced by a
false representation that the appellant's credit standing at the bank gave
her authority to use the card." But, my Lords, with profound respect to
the learned Lord Justice, that is not the relevant question. Following the
decision of this House in *Charles*, it is in my view clear that the
representation arising from the presentation of a credit card has nothing to
do with the appellant's credit standing at the bank but is a representation
of actual authority to make the contract with, in this case, Mothercare on
the bank's behalf that the bank will honour the voucher upon
presentation. Upon that view, the existence and terms of the agreement
between the bank and Mothercare are irrelevant, as is the fact that
Mothercare, because of that agreement, would look to the bank for
payment.

That being the representation to be implied from the respondent's
actions and use of the credit card, the only remaining question is whether
Miss Rounding was induced by that representation to complete the
transaction and allow the respondent to take away the goods. My Lords, if
she had been asked whether had she known the respondent was acting
dishonestly and, in truth, had no authority whatever from the bank to use
the credit card in this way, she (Miss Rounding) would have completed
the transaction, only one answer is possible—no. Had an affirmative
answer been given to this question, Miss Rounding would, of course, have
become a participant in furtherance of the respondent's fraud and a
conspirator with her to defraud both Mothercare and the bank. Leading
counsel for the respondent was ultimately constrained, rightly as I think,
to admit that had that question been asked of Miss Rounding and
answered, as it must have been, in the negative, this appeal must succeed.
But both he and his learned junior strenuously argued that, as my noble
and learned friend, Lord Edmund-Davies, pointed out in his speech in
Charles at pages 192 and 193 of the report, the question whether a person
is or is not induced to act in a particular way by a dishonest representation
is a question of fact, and since what they claimed to be the crucial question
had not been asked of Miss Rounding, there was no adequate proof of the
requisite inducement. In her deposition, Miss Rounding stated, no doubt
with complete truth, that she only remembered this particular transaction
with the respondent because someone subsequently came and asked her
about it after it had taken place. My Lords, credit card frauds are all too
frequently perpetrated, and if conviction of offenders for offences against
sections 15 or 16 of the Theft Act 1968 can only be obtained if the
prosecution are able in each case to call the person upon whom the fraud
was immediately perpetrated to say that he or she positively remembered
the particular transaction and, had the truth been known, would never
have entered into that supposedly well-remembered transaction, the guilty
would often escape conviction. In some cases, of course, it may be possible
to adduce such evidence if the particular transaction is well remembered.
But where as in the present case no one could reasonably be expected to
remember a particular transaction in detail, and the inference of
inducement may well be in all the circumstances quite irresistible, I see no

reason in principle why it should not be left to the jury to decide, upon the evidence in the case as a whole, whether that inference is in truth irresistible as to my mind it is in the present case. In this connection it is to be noted that the respondent did not go into the witness box to give evidence from which that inference might conceivably have been rebutted.

My Lords, in this respect I find myself in agreement with what was said by Humphreys J. giving the judgment of the Court of Criminal Appeal in *R.* v. *Sullivan* (1945) 30 Cr.App.R. 132 at 136:

> "It is, we think, undoubtedly good law that the question of the inducement acting upon the mind of the person who may be described as the prosecutor is not a matter which can only be proved by the direct evidence of the witness. It can be, and very often is, proved by the witness being asked some question which brings the answer: 'I believed that statement and that is why I parted with my money'; but it is not necessary that there should be that question and answer if the facts are such that it is patent that there was only one reason which anybody could suggest for the person alleged to have been defrauded parting with his money, and that is the false pretence, if it was a false pretence."

It is true that in *R.* v. *Laverty* (*ante*, p. 762), Lord Parker C.J. said that the Court of Appeal Criminal Division was anxious not to extend the principle in *Sullivan* further than was necessary. Of course, the Crown must always prove its case and one element which will always be required to be proved in these cases is the effect of the dishonest representation upon the mind of the person to whom it is made. But I see no reason why in cases such as the present, where what Humphreys J. called the direct evidence of the witness is not, and cannot reasonably be expected to be available, reliance upon a dishonest representation cannot be sufficiently established by proof of facts from which an irresistible inference of such reliance can be drawn.

My Lords, I would answer the certified question in the negative and would allow the appeal and restore the conviction of the respondent upon the second count in the indictment which she faced at Bedford Crown Court.

Appeal allowed: Conviction restored

J. C. Smith: The Law of Theft, (6th ed.) § 164

"The tradesman accepting either type of card will usually do so simply because the conditions on the card are satisfied. He will neither know nor care whether the customer is exceeding his authority and using the card in breach of contract with the bank. He will get his money in any event—and that is all he is concerned with. This is neither immoral nor unreasonable. The whole object of these cards is to dispense the tradesman from concerning himself in any way with the relationship between the cardholder and the bank. The tradesman is perfectly entitled to take advantage of the facility which the banks offer him."

See also Williams, *Textbook*, p. 791.

R. v. Clucas
[1949] 2 K.B. 226
Court of Criminal Appeal

C. induced a bookmaker to bet with him by falsely representing that he was acting as agent for many people at his place of work. The bet was successful and C. was paid the winnings. C. was convicted of obtaining money by false pretences.

LORD GODDARD C.J.: The main point which arises in the case ... may be stated in this way: Does a man who induces a bookmaker to bet with him by making false pretences as to his identity or as to the capacity in which he is putting on the bets, obtain money by false pretences if he is fortunate enough, having made those pretences, to back a winning horse so that the bookmaker pays him? The case as it was argued originally before a court consisting of three judges raised this point, and the court showed when they adjourned the hearing, that there was not unanimity at that stage, consequently they adjourned it to be heard before a full court, for which reason five judges have now heard it.

In the opinion of the court it is impossible to say that there was an obtaining of the money by false pretences which were alleged, because the money was obtained not by reason of the fact that the people falsely pretended that they were somebody else or acting in some capacity which they were not; it was obtained because they backed a winning horse and the bookmaker paid because the horse had won. No doubt the bookmaker might never have opened an account with these men if he had known the true facts, but we must distinguish in this case between one contributing cause and the effective cause which led the bookmaker to pay the money.

The effective cause which led the bookmaker to pay the money was the fact that these men had backed a winning horse. ... Although these two men induced the bookmaker to bet with them by means of a false pretence, what the court cannot see is that the false pretence was the false pretence which led to the payment of the money. What led to the payment of the money was the fact that these men backed a winning horse by inducing the bookmaker to bet with them. They put themselves in the position that if they backed the horse and lost, they had to pay the bookmaker and if they backed the horse and won they were entitled to receive the money. In the opinion of the court, therefore, it cannot be said that the money was obtained by false pretences within the meaning of section 32, subsection (1), of the Larceny Act, 1916.

Mr. Boileau has called the attention of the court to certain cases, and no doubt the nearest case to this one and the only one which I think it is necessary to mention is *R. v. Button* [1900] 2 Q.B. 597. In that case the defendant, by representing that he was a person of the name Sims, who was a very moderate performer in athletic sports and was not known as a likely winner of races, managed to obtain from the committee of some athletic sports which were to be held in Lincoln a very substantial handicap in a race. He was in fact a man who had won a great many races and had the truth been known he would have received either no handicap at all or a very moderate handicap instead of the very substantial handicap which he obtained. Indeed, after the race was won by him he repeated the false pretence to the secretary and obtained a prize, but it was not only on account of the repetition of the false pretence that he obtained the prize. The court held that by falsely representing himself to be someone he was not, thereby obtaining a substantial handicap, he obtained the prize on false pretences because it was a matter directly connected with the winning or not winning of the prize. He obtained for himself a winning chance. He got the handicap which he would not otherwise have got, and thereby enabled himself to win the race. We think that that case on the facts is clearly distinguishable from this case.

Conviction on this count quashed

Note

In fact Button did not actually receive the prize and the charge was attempting to obtain property by false pretences.

The distinction between the two cases appears to be that in *Clucas* the placing of the bet was merely a *causa sine qua non* of the obtaining; without making the bet, he could not have received any winnings, but that applies equally to all sorts of other factors such as the fact that the bookmaker had a telephone which enabled C. to get in touch with him and place the bet; these are merely contributing causes; the *causa causans*, the one cause which above all others produced the payment of winnings was the fact that the horse that C. backed was first past the post. But in *Button*, the one effective cause, the *causa causans* was the fact that he had been given a big start in the race. Since the false pretences produced the *causa causans* it can be said that (had the crime been complete) the false pretence produced the handing over of the prize.

Questions

B by lies obtains a three yard start, wins by five yards, claims and is given the prize. Is B, on the view adopted in *Clucas*, guilty of obtaining the prize by deception? Is he guilty of attempting to gain the prize by deception?

R. v. King
[1987] 1 All E.R. 547
Court of Appeal

K. and S., falsely representing they were from a famous firm of tree surgeons, falsely represented to an elderly householder that it was necessary to remove trees on her property to prevent damage to gas mains and house foundations. They said the work would cost £470, and she agreed to them doing the work. The police arrested K. and S. before they could go any further, and they were subsequently convicted of attempting to obtain £470 from the householder by deception. They appealed.

NEILL L.J.: gave the judgment of the Court: In support of the appeal against conviction counsel for the appellants argued that the judge erred in rejecting the motion to quash the indictment, or alternatively the submission that there was no case to answer. The argument was developed on the following lines: (1) that, as the appellants were charged with an attempt, it was incumbent on the prosecution to prove that if the relevant conduct had been completed it would have constituted a criminal offence; (2) that if the appellants had received £470 for cutting down the trees they would have been paid by reason of the work they had done, and not by reason of any representation they had made to secure the work; (3) that since the decision in R. v. *Lewis* (January 1922, unreported) it had been generally recognised that conduct of the kind complained of in the present case did not constitute the criminal offence of obtaining property by false pretences or by deception because, as a matter of causation, the relevant property was obtained by reason of the work carried out rather than by reason of any representation or deception. Our attention was directed to statements on the subject in some leading textbooks ...

In order to examine these arguments it is necessary to start by setting out the particulars of offence as stated in the indictment, as amended. The particulars read as follows:

"David King and Jimmy Stockwell on the 5th day of March 1985 in Hampshire, dishonestly attempted to obtain from Nora Anne Mitchell, £470 in money with the intention of permanently depriving the said Nora Anne Mitchell thereof by deception, namely by false oral representations that they were from J. F. Street, Tree Specialists, Pennington, that essential work necessary to remove trees in order to prevent damage to the gas supply and house foundations would then have to be carried out."

... The argument advanced on behalf of the appellants on causation or remoteness was founded on the decision in *R. v. Lewis*, and on commentaries on that decision by academic writers. The report of the decision in *R. v. Lewis* is scanty and, as far as we are aware, is contained only in a footnote in *Russell on Crime* (12th ed., 1964), vol. 2, p. 1186, n. 66).

In that case (which was a decision at Somerset Assizes in January 1922) a schoolmistress obtained her appointment by falsely stating that she possessed a teacher's certificate. She was held to be not guilty of obtaining her salary by false pretences, on the ground that she was paid because of the services she rendered, and not because of the false representation.

It was submitted on behalf of the appellants that the principle underlying the decision in *R. v. Lewis* could be applied in the present case. It was further submitted that the authority of *R. v. Lewis* was implicitly recognised by the enactment of para. (*c*) of s.16(2) of the Theft Act 1968. Section 16 is concerned with the obtaining of a pecuniary advantage by deception; s.16(2) provides:

"The cases in which a pecuniary advantage within the meaning of this section is to be regarded as obtained for a person are cases where ... (*c*) he is given the opportunity to earn remuneration or greater remuneration in an office of employment ... "

It is to be observed, however, that Professor Glanville Williams in his *Textbook of Criminal Law* (2nd ed., 1983) p. 792 has this to say of the decision in *R. v. Lewis*:

"Yet *Lewis* would not have got the job and consequently her salary, if it had not been for the pretence. Her object in making the pretence was to get the salary. Assuming, as is likely, that her employer would not have made her any payment of salary if a lie had not been operating on his mind, there was certainly a factual causal connection between the lie and the obtaining of salary. Why should it not be a causal connection in law? We have seen that when the defendant produces a consequence intentionally, it is generally regarded as imputable to him. Why should it not be so here?"

Furthermore, the learned author of *Russell on Crime* p. 1187 (immediately after the footnote already referred to) continued:

"But it is submitted that cases of this kind could be placed beyond doubt if the indictment were worded carefully. The essential point in this crime is that in making the transfer of goods the prosecutor must have been influenced by the false pretence as set out in the indictment."

We have given careful consideration to the argument based on causation or remoteness and have taken account of the fact that some support for the argument may be provided by the writings of a number of distinguished academic lawyers. Nevertheless, we have come to the conclusion that on the facts of the present case the argument is fallacious.

In our view, the question in each case is: was the deception an operative cause of the obtaining of the property? This question falls to be answered as a question of fact by the jury applying their common sense.

Moreover, this approach is in accordance with the decision of the Court for Crown Cases Reserved in *R. v. Martin* (1867) L.R. 1 C.C.R. 56, where it was held that a conviction for obtaining a chattel by false pretences was good, although the chattel was not in existence at the time that the pretence was made, provided the subsequent delivery of the chattel was directly connected with the false pretence. Bovill C.J. said:

"What is the test? Surely this, that there must be a direct connection between the pretence and the delivery—that there must be a continuing pretence. Whether there is such a connection or not is a question for the jury."

The decision in *R. v. Martin* was referred to with approval in *R. v. Moreton* (1913) 8 Cr.App.R. 214, where Lord Coleridge J. said:

"*Martin* leaves the law in no doubt; it was held there that the fact that the goods were obtained under a contract does not make the goods so obtained goods not obtained by a false pretence, if the false pretence is a continuing one and operates on the mind of the person supplying the goods."

In the present case there was, in our judgment, ample evidence on which the jury could come to the conclusion that had the attempt succeeded the money would have been paid over by the victim as a result of the lies told to her by the appellants. We consider that the judge was correct to reject both the motion to quash the indictment and the submission that there was no case to answer.

For the reasons which we have set out, we consider that the appellants were rightly convicted in this case, and the appeals must therefore be dismissed.

Appeals dismissed

Questions

1. D, by using a false reference, obtained employment as a teacher. When the lie was discovered, she was dismissed and charged with obtaining her last month's salary by deception. Is it relevant

(i)   that since appointment she had been promoted?
(ii) she held the post for ten years but consistently performed her duties less well than would be expected if the reference had been genuine and true?

2. Is it an appropriate test (as suggested in *King*) that the property was transferred *as a result* of the deception. Griew, § 7.52 suggests that a more appropriate test would be whether at the time

of the transfer P was induced by D's earlier false statement to do so. What difference, if any, would the application of this test have made to the cases of *Button, Clucas, Lewis* and *King*?

Note

Nowadays persons in the position of Clucas and Lewis commit the offence of obtaining by deception a pecuniary advantage (the opportunity to win money by betting, to earn remuneration in an office or employment, respectively; see section 16(2), *post*, p. 776. This may be thought a more appropriate way of dealing with such cases, reflecting more accurately what it is which is got by deception. However section 16 only covers a few particular cases. It was conceded in *King* that the offence did not cover what happened there because King was not given an opportunity to earn remuneration "in an office or employment." [but see now *R.* v. *Callendar, post* p. 777] The C.L.R.C. proposed a general offence of dishonestly, with a view to gain, by deception inducing a person to do or refrain from any act, but this was rejected by Parliament as being too broad.

iv. Dishonesty

Criminal Law Revision Committee's Eighth Report, Cmnd. 2977

§ 88 "The provision in [section 15(1)] making a person guilty of criminal deception if he 'dishonestly obtains' the property replaces the provision in 1916, s.32(1), making a person guilty of obtaining by false pretences if he 'with intent to defraud, obtains' the things there mentioned. The change will correspond to the change from 'fraudulently' to 'dishonestly' in the definition of stealing which is discussed in § 39. (*Ante*, p. 733). 'Dishonestly' seems the right word to use in relation to criminal deception also. Owing to the words 'dishonestly obtains' a person who uses deception in order to obtain property to which he believes himself entitled will not be guilty; for though the deception may be dishonest, the obtaining is not. In this respect also the offence will be in line with theft, because a belief in a legal right to deprive an owner of property is for the purpose of theft inconsistent with dishonesty and is specifically made a defence by the partial definition of 'dishonesty' in [section] 2(1). The partial definition in [section] 2(1) is not repeated in [section 15(1)]. It would be only partly applicable to the offence of criminal deception, and it seems unnecessary and undesirable to complicate the Bill by including a separate definition in [section 15]). The fact that a claim of right will be a defence to a charge under [section 15(1)] is probably in accordance with the present law of obtaining by false pretences; for the existence of a claim of right to the property obtained is regarded as inconsistent with that of an 'intent to defraud' for the purpose of 1916, s.32(1)."

Notes

This desire to avoid complication in the Bill has resulted in "claim of right" not being a defence in law to a charge of obtaining. Once the question of dishonesty was held to be one of fact for the jury (see *R.* v. *Feely, ante*, p. 734, *R.* v. *Ghosh, ante*, p.

736), then with the failure of section 15 to include the three cases which in theft are legally not to be regarded as dishonest by section 2(1), there are no such cases in obtaining. The *Ghosh* directions are all that are needed in every case of obtaining in which honesty is in issue.

R. v. Woolven
(1983) 77 Cr.App.R. 231
Court of Appeal

D. was convicted of attempting dishonestly to obtain money by deception. In trying to withdraw money from a bank account he pretended to be the owner of the account. In evidence he admitted that most people would think his behaviour was dishonest, but insisted that he thought he was acting on the instructions of the owner of the account. The direction to the jury followed the guidelines in *Ghosh*, but contained no reference to claim of right.

LEONARD J.: In the judgment of this Court any direction based on the concept of claim of right as set out in section 2(1)(*a*), or otherwise, would have added nothing to what the learned judge in fact said. Indeed a direction based on *Ghosh* seems likely to us to cover all occasions when a section 2(1)(*a*) type direction might otherwise have been desirable.

Our attention was drawn to *R. v. Falconer-Atlee* (1973) 58 Cr.App.R. 348—a case of theft to which section 2(1)(*a*) therefore applied. A claim of right was raised by the evidence. The learned judge directed the jury as to the elements which the prosecution had to prove in order to establish the offence. In dealing with the element of dishonesty he said: "The all important word ... in those four elements is 'dishonestly,' but of course, it may well be that you may not have much difficulty in deciding that if somebody in circumstances such as are alleged here appropriated property belonging to another with the intention of permanently depriving the other of it, then it was done dishonestly, but that is a matter for you. It is for you to decide whether whatever was done was done dishonestly. If you are not satisfied that it was, then you could not convict. ... "

In delivering the judgment of this Court, Roskill L.J. (as he then was) said at p. 359: "To give the jury the limited direction which the learned judge gave, impeccable so far as it went in relation to 'dishonestly,' but on the facts of this case not to go on to tell them what section 2(1)(*a*) expressly provided was *not* to be regarded as 'dishonest' was to omit what was an extremely important direction."

In contrast, the summing-up in the present case clearly brought home to the jury that they must consider the appellant's own account of events and what he said about his state of knowledge and if, on that basis, they thought he might have regarded his actions as honest, they must acquit.

At pp. 32–33 the trial judge summarised the matters which were put forward by the appellant as part of his case. ... The jury, in all probability, considered them in the context of Roberts's [an accomplice] version which imputed some knowledge of the true state of affairs to the appellant.

The jury in the present case had the facts before them. The appellant eventually conceded that ordinary people would, on the basis of his own version, have found his behaviour to be dishonest. He maintained that he himself had not thought it to be dishonest at the time. In the view of this Court it was inevitable that the jury would disbelieve the last proposition, even if they believed the appellant's account otherwise.

There is in our view nothing unsafe or unsatisfactory about this conviction. Accordingly, for the reasons stated, the appeal is dismissed.

Appeal dismissed

Question

A and B both have what they think are justifiable claims to be paid £10 by P. A, by force, takes £10 from P B, by lies, gets P. to give him £10. Should there be, and is there, any difference in the way the issue of their honesty should be summed up to the juries who are trying them for theft and obtaining by deception respectively?

2. OBTAINING PECUNIARY ADVANTAGE BY DECEPTION

Theft Act 1968, section 16

"(1) A person who by any deception dishonestly obtains for himself or another any pecuniary advantage shall on conviction on indictment be liable to imprisonment for a term not exceeding five years.

(2) The cases in which a pecuniary advantage within the meaning of this section is to be regarded as obtained for a person are cases where—

(a) [repealed by Theft Act 1978, Section (5)]
(b) he is allowed to borrow by way of overdraft, or to take out any policy of insurance or annuity contract, or obtains an improvement of the terms on which he is allowed to do so; or
(c) he is given the opportunity to earn remuneration or greater remuneration in an office or employment, or to win money by betting.

(3) For the purposes of this section 'deception' has the same meaning as in section 15 of this Act."

Notes

No pecuniary advantage need in fact be obtained. If the situation comes within the two cases in subsection 2 a pecuniary advantage "is to be regarded as obtained." On the other hand, the two cases are exhaustive, and no other case of a *de facto* pecuniary advantage is comprehended in the offence. See *D.P.P.* v. *Turner* [1974] A.C. 357.

2. For "deception," "dishonestly," and the need for the deception to cause the obtaining, see *ante*, pp. 751–776.

Case (b)

R. v. *Waites* [1982] Crim.L.R. 369 (C.A.) W., who was issued with a cheque book and cheque card, but with no power to overdraw, wrote cheques to pay for purchases. By contract with the shopkeepers, the bank was obliged to meet the cheques, so that W.'s account went into overdraft to the extent of £850. *Held:* she was "allowed to borrow" in that she was allowed to use the card which carried the power (albeit in breach of contract with the bank) to commit the bank to meeting her cheques and thereby creating an overdraft.

Question

Did W obtain the *power to commit the bank* by deception?

R. v. Watkins [1976] 1 All E.R. 578 (Crown Ct.) D., as a result of lies, was granted overdraft facilities but did not draw on them.
Held: subsection 2(*b*) referred in its alternatives to the *granting* of facilities or improved facilities, not to the use of them. D.'s offence was complete.

Question

D, by lies, was given insurance cover over the phone. No policy was issued, or claim made, before D's lies were uncovered. Is he guilty of an offence under section 16(2)(*b*)?

Case (c)

R. v. Callender [1992] 3 All E.R. 51 (C.A.): D., by pretending to be a qualified accountant, obtained "employment" in helping small businessmen to prepare their tax and VAT returns. *Held*: "employment" was not limited to a master and servant relationship. The dictionary meaning, which covered D.'s situation, was what Parliament intended.

Note

The principal case of obtaining pecuniary advantage was until 1978 contained in section 16(1)(*a*). It was the case where "any debt or charge for which he makes himself liable or is or may become liable (including one not legally enforceable) is reduced or in whole or part evaded or deferred." This short passage caused such difficulties of interpretation that it was repealed by the Theft Act 1978. Its replacement, founded on the 13th Report of the Criminal Law Revision Committee, (Cmnd. 6733) but amended in Parliament, consists of the three offences mentioned below. The first two are punishable on indictment by imprisonment for 5 years, the third by imprisonment for 2 years.

3. OBTAINING SERVICES BY DECEPTION

Theft Act 1978, section 1

"(1) A person who by any deception dishonestly obtains services from another shall be guilty of an offence.
(2) It is an obtaining of services where the other is induced to confer a benefit by doing some act, or causing or permitting some act to be done, on the understanding that the benefit has been or will be paid for."

Notes

1. For "deception," "dishonestly" and the need for the deception to cause the obtaining, see *ante*, pp. 751–776; and on the offence generally see Smith, §§ 225–236, and Spencer, *"The Theft Act 1978"* [1979] Crim.L.R. 26–30.

2. The services provided can include the delivery of property, where a charge under section 15 of the 1968 Act is more appropriate. But it is an offence under this section also: *R. v. Widdowson* (1986) 82 Cr.App.R. 314, 318, (*ante*, p. 441).

3. There must be an understanding that the benefit has been or will be paid for. The deception need not be as to the payment; the reference to an understanding of payment is merely to exclude gratuitous conferment of benefit from the definition of services. But it is the doing of an act or causing or permitting an act to be done which must be on this understanding.

Questions

Are the following cases offences under section 1?

1. A, by pretending that his dog is an entrant for a championship dog show to be held next day, gets B, a vet, to examine and prescribe for it, for an agreed sum of £20, which A intends to pay.

2. B, by pretending to be a vet, gets A to allow him to examine and prescribe for his dog, for an agreed payment of £20.

3. A, by falsely pretending that he has no money with him, induces B, a taxi-driver, to give him a free ride. And see, section 2(1)(c) below.

4. A, a non-resident using the restaurant at a hotel, by representing that he is a resident guest, persuades a waiter to allow him to enter the television room and to watch the television, services which are available only to resident guests.

4. EVASION OF LIABILITY BY DECEPTION

Theft Act 1978, section 2

"(1) Subject to subsection (2) below, where a person by any deception—

(a) dishonestly secures the remission of the whole or part of any existing liability to make a payment, whether his own liability or another's; or

(b) with intent to make permanent default in whole or in part on any existing liability to make a payment, or with intent to let another do so, dishonestly induces the creditor or any person claiming payment on behalf of the creditor to wait for payment (whether or not the due date for payment is deferred) or to forgo payment; or

(c) dishonestly obtains any exemption from or abatement of liability to make a payment;

he shall be guilty of an offence.

(2) For purposes of this section 'liability' means legally enforceable liability; and subsection (1) shall not apply in relation to a liability that has not been accepted or established to pay compensation for a wrongful act or omission.

(3) For purposes of subsection (1)(b) a person induced to take in payment a cheque or other security for money by way of conditional satisfaction of a pre-existing liability is to be treated not as being paid but as being induced to wait for payment.

(4) For purposes of subsection (1)(c) 'obtains' includes obtaining for another or enabling another to obtain."

Note

For "deception," "dishonestly" and the need for the deception to cause the remission, inducement or obtaining, see, *ante*, pp. 751–776.

Spencer, The Theft Act 1978 [1979] Crim.L.R. 34

"There seems little practical need for 2(1)(a). Where it applies, D. has been fraudulent and dishonest, but his conduct is unlikely to have done P. any harm. In theory harm has been caused: P. used to own a debt against D.; by deceiving P. into waiving it, D. has deprived him of it. So, it may be said, D. ought to be punished just as if he had deprived P. of any other item of his property—his car, for example—by deception. But the analogy is false. Where D. obtains P.'s car by deception, P. once had a car, and is left with a civil remedy against D. which usually is worthless. Where D. secures the remission of a debt by deception, P. is also left with a probably worthless civil remedy. He can rescind the remission for fraud, and then enforce the debt—but D. probably has no assets with which to pay it. However, in this case what did P. have *before* D. deprived him of it by deception? Merely a debt—a right to sue D. for the money. It is possible that D. had the money to pay at the time of the deception, and spent it on beer after the debt was remitted; but this is most unlikely. Usually, the reason why D. deceived P. will be that D. had no money but lacked the effrontery to say so. Therefore, as a result of D.'s deception, P. is unlikely to be any the worse off. The only result of fining and imprisoning D. if he is caught will be to make P.'s civil remedy against D. worthless in the rare case where D. was, before the prosecution, worth powder and shot.

Section 2(1)(b) seems to have little more rhyme or reason to it. It is said to be aimed mainly at those who knowingly write dud cheques in purported settlement of existing liability—conduct which frequently does the creditor good rather than harm [because the creditor can sue on the cheque as well as on the debt]. It is harmful in only two ways. First, the payee may unsuspectingly draw against the cheque and so overdraw his own bank account. If this is the mischief aimed at, however, 2(1)(b) is too narrow, because the offence is only committed where D. intends never to pay, and P. is equally likely to overdraw whatever D.'s intentions. Secondly, tendering the cheque may enable D. to disappear without trace. However, the mischief here is only the same as that involved in 'making off without payment.' Why should running away after telling lies carry a sentence of five years' imprisonment under 2(1)(b), when running away without telling lies—which is more harmful, because D. is likely to be harder to trace—only carries a sentence of two years under section 3? Furthermore, as against any dubious benefits to society which 2(1)(b) may provide, there is the uncomfortable fact that because of it, anyone who, however innocently, tenders a cheque which is dishonoured, can be threatened with a prosecution which is likely to get past the committal stage.

The only part of section 2 which seems to strike accurately at an evil worthy of criminal sanction is 2(1)(c), which applies to the evasion of future liability by deception. Although originally intended partly to cover obtaining services cheap or free by deception, and now in that respect redundant, [because section 1 as finally enacted has a wider scope than clause 1 as proposed by the C.L.R.C.], it still covers conduct which is really harmful to the victim and amounts to no other criminal offence. Take for example the case of the council-house tenant who by deception has his rent halved by way of rent rebate. The council will thereafter fail to collect half his rent as it would otherwise have fallen due. If the fraud is not discovered for several years, the council may lose thousands of pounds. On discovery of the fraud, the council will have in theory a right to sue the tenant for the money, but whereas he could have paid it in instalments over the years, the chance of his ever finding it now—in addition to future rent at the proper rate—is remote. This sort of conduct surely does deserve a prosecution.

A final criticism of section 2 is that it is complicated. Long, expensive hours will be spent in the courts discussing arid procedural questions resulting from a failure to specify what the relationship between the three main clauses is, and whether they are three offences or one. It is an ill wind of legal change which blows no barrister any good."

Note

The gloomy prognostication in the last paragraph above has not been fully borne out. The cases below demonstrate that the Courts have a relaxed attitude about evasion of liability. Without going to the length of holding that it is all one offence, they are unsympathetic to appeals claiming that the wrong sub-paragraph was charged.

R. v. Holt and Lee
[1981] 2 All E.R. 854
Court of Appeal

The facts and charge appear from the judgment of the Court.

LAWSON J.: Victor Reginald Holt and Julian Dana Lee apply to the full court for leave to appeal against their convictions at the Crown Court at Liverpool at July 16, 1980 of attempting, contrary to common law, to evade liability by deception, that is to say, an attempt to commit an offence contrary to section 2(1) of the Theft Act 1978. This court granted leave to appeal and treated the hearing of the application as the hearing of the appeal.

The charge on which they were convicted was as follows. The statement of the offence was attempted evasion of liability by deception, contrary to common law. The particulars of the offence were that the appellants, on December 9 1979, by deception with intent to make permanent default on an existing liability, did attempt to induce Philip Parkinson, servant of Pizzaland Restaurants Ltd., to forgo payment of £3.65 by falsely representing that payments had been made by them to another servant of the said Pizzaland Restaurants Ltd.

From the use of the expressions "with intent to make permanent default" and "to induce (the creditor's agent) to forgo payment," it is clear that the attempt charged was one to commit the offence defined by section 2(1)(b) of the 1978 Act.

The facts of the case were that in the evening of December 9, 1979, the appellants consumed meals costing £3.65 in the Pizzaland Restaurant in Southport. There was a police officer off duty also having a meal in the restaurant and he overheard the appellants planning to evade payment for their meals by the device of pretending that a waitress had removed a £5 note which they had placed on the table. When presented with their bill, the appellants advanced this deception and declined payment. The police officer concerned prevented them from leaving the restaurant and they were shortly afterwards arrested and charged.

At the close of the prosecution case in the Crown Court counsel who has also conducted this appeal, made a submission which was overruled, the main point of which was that assuming the facts as we have recounted them to be correct, the attempt to evade thus emerging was an attempt to commit an offence not under section 2(1)(b) as charged but under section 2(1)(a) of the 1978 Act since, he submitted, had the attempt succeeded, the appellants' liability to pay for their meals would have been "remitted" and not just "forgone," to use the contrasting terms contained in the respective subsections.

Counsel further developed his submission before us. As we understand it, he submits that the vital differences between the two offences defined in the first two paragraphs of section 2(1) of the Act are that "remission" involves that, first, the creditor who "remits" the debtor's existing liability must communicate his decision to the debtor and, second, the legal consequence of the "remission" is to extinguish the debt, whereas the "forgoing of an existing liability," to use the words of subsection 2(1)(b), need not be communicated to the debtor and has not the consequence in law of extinguishing such liability. We find great difficulty in introducing these concepts into the construction of the subsection. We will later return to the matter.

Counsel further submitted that the effect of section 2(1) of the Act was to create three different offences but conceded that there could be situations in which the conduct of the debtor or his agent could fall under more than one of the three paragraphs of section 2(1).

The elements of the offence defined by section 2(1)(b) of the Act relevant to the present case are clearly these: first, the defendant must be proved to have the intent to make permanent default on the whole or part of an existing liability. This element is unique to section 2(1)(b); it has no application to the offences defined in section 2(1)(a) or (c). Second, given such intent, he must use deception. Third, his deception must be practised dishonestly to induce the creditor to forgo payment.

It must always be remembered that in the present case, whatever offence was being attempted, the attempt failed. The creditor was not induced by the dishonest deception and did not forgo payment. It is clear on the evidence that the appellants' conduct constituted an attempt to evade liability by deception, and the jury, who were properly directed, clearly concluded that the appellants' conduct was motivated by the intent to make permanent default on their supper bill. Thus, all the elements needed to enable an attempt to commit the offence defined in section 2(1)(b) were found to be present, so that the appellants were rightly convicted as charged.

Reverting to the construction of section 2(1) of the Act, as to which the commentators are not at one, we are not sure whether the choice of expressions describing the consequences of deception employed in each of its paragraphs, namely in paragraph (a) "secures the remission of any existing liability," in paragraph (b) "induces a creditor to forgo payment" and in paragraph (c) "obtains any exemption from liability," are simply different ways of describing the same end result or represent conceptual differences.

Whilst it is plain that there are substantial differences in the elements of the three offences defined in section 2(1), they show these common features: first, the use of deception to a creditor in relation to a liability, second, dishonesty in the use of deception, and third, the use of deception to gain some advantage in time or money. Thus the differences between the offences relate principally to the different situations in which the debtor-creditor relationship has arisen.

The practical difficulty which counsel's submissions for the appellants failed to confront is strikingly illustrated by cases of attempting to commit an offence under section 2(1)(*a*) or section 2(1)(*b*). If, as he submits, section 2(1)(*a*) requires communication of remission to the debtor, whereas section 2(1)(*b*) does not require communication of the "forgoing of payment" but, as the case is a mere attempt, the matter does not *end* in remission of liability or forgoing of payment, then the prosecution would be in a dilemma since it would either be impossible to charge such an attempt or the prosecution would be obliged to charge attempts in the alternative in which case, since any attempt failed, it would be quite uncertain which of the alternatives it was.

These appeals are accordingly dismissed.

Applications for leave to appeal granted. Appeals dismissed

R. v. *Jackson* [1983] Crim.L.R. 617 (C.A.) D. used a stolen credit card to pay for petrol. He was convicted of evading liability by securing the remission of an existing liability, contrary to section 2(1)(*a*). He appealed on the ground that he should have been charged under section 2(1)(*b*).

Held, dismissing the appeal, that although in *Holt, supra*, it was held that the element under section 2(1)(*b*) of an intent to make permanent default on the whole or part of an existing liability was unique to sub-paragraph (*b*), that judgment was not authority for the proposition that the elements in sub-paragraphs (*a*), (*b*) and (*c*) of section 2(1) were mutually exclusive. The transaction of tendering a stolen credit card and having it accepted by a trader who forthwith would look to the authority issuing the card for payment and not to the person tendering the card, meant that that person had dishonestly secured the remission of an existing liability. It was not necessary to consider whether a charge in respect of that transaction could be brought under section 2(1)(*b*). In the circumstances the matter was not wrongly charged under section 2(1)(*a*).

R. v. *Sibartie* [1983] Crim.L.R. 470 (C.A.) D. "flashed" at a ticket inspector a pass which did not cover the journey he was making. He was convicted of attempted evasion of liability by obtaining exemption from liability to make a payment, contrary to section 2(1)(*c*).

Held, dismissing the appeal that the correct method of approach was to ask whether, taking the words of section 2(1)(*c*) in their ordinary meaning, one would say that what the appellant was attempting to do fell within the ambit of the words. The jury by their verdict must have been satisfied that the appellant dishonestly used his season ticket, which did not in fact cover the journey he was making, in an attempt to persuade the ticket inspector that they did cover the journey. Did that amount to an attempt to obtain exemption from liability to make a payment for the journey he was making or had made? He was saying, albeit tacitly, by waving the supposed season ticket in the air that he was the holder of a ticket authorising him to be making the journey without further payment and consequently he was not under any liability to pay any more. In the ordinary meaning of words that was dishonestly obtaining an exemption from the liability to pay the excess which, had he been honest, he would have had to pay. There might be a degree of overlap between section 2(1)(*a*), (*b*) and (*c*), and the fact that what the appellant did might also have been an attempt to commit an offence under section 2(1)(b) was neither here nor there.

J. C. Smith, [1983] Crim.L.R. 471, commenting on this case: "If he was guilty of three offences, does not this look like a case of overkill on the part of the legislator? Some overlap of offences is reasonable and to be expected; but it must surely be assumed that Parliament intended each offence to have some function. If the broadest construction is put upon each offence there seems to be nothing for paragraph (b), in so far as it relates to forgoing payment, to do.

Paragraphs (a) and (c) do not require proof of an intent to make permanent default and, if they cover cases of forgoing payment, Parliament's evident intention, that one who merely induces a creditor to forgo payment should not be guilty unless he has an intent to make permanent default, is defeated. It is no answer to this argument that there was evidence of an intent to make permanent default in the present case. Such an intent was no part of the offence of which the appellant was convicted.

There is, however, an interpretation of the section which avoids this result, and which requires nothing more extravagant than a literal reading of the words of the section. Offence (a) is not committed unless the defendant "secures the remission" of a liability. Offence (c) is not committed unless the defendant obtains an "exemption from . . . liability to make a payment." Assuming again that the defendant had succeeded in deceiving the inspector in the present case, the inspector would have had no intention to "remit" an existing liability because he would have been persuaded that there was no liability to remit, nor would he in law have remitted any liability. The defendant's liability to pay the proper fare would unquestionably have continued unimpaired. Similarly, the inspector would not have intended to exempt the defendant from any liability to make a payment, existing or otherwise, being persuaded that there was no liability, and the defendant would not have been exempted from any liability. . . .

What the defendant would have succeeded in doing if he had deceived the inspector was to induce him to forgo payment of an unremitted, still existing liability to pay the full fare, from which no one intended to exempt him and from which he was not exempted."

R. v. *Andrews & Hedges* [1981] Crim.L.R. 106 (C.C.Ct.): Mr. Recorder Sherrard Q.C.: Defendants were charged with inducing creditors to wait for payment by deception contrary to section 2(1)(b) of the Theft Act 1978. The creditors had in the course of dealing supplied large quantities of meat to the defendants on credit terms of up to three weeks for which payments were duly made by cheques which were met. The dishonesty relied upon by the prosecution was that thereafter having obtained meat from suppliers in a later period the defendants issued cheques unsupported by funds in their bank account which were not met on presentation, and induced the creditors to wait for payment. The deception relied on in each case was the false representation that the cheque in question was a good and valid order and that in the ordinary course, the cheque would be met.

Held, there was no inducement to wait for payment where the parties had traded together previously and where credit terms had been allowed and where payment by cheque was accepted in the ordinary course of dealing between the parties; for section 2(1)(b) only applied where a creditor is induced to accept a cheque instead of cash, and only then did section 2(3) operate as a matter of law to treat the creditor as having been induced to wait for payment. There was no evidence that the creditors had asked for cash and no evidence that they had been induced to accept cheques or to wait for payment. Accordingly, there was no case to answer.

5. MAKING OFF WITHOUT PAYMENT

Theft Act 1978, section 3

"(1) Subject to subsection (3) below, a person who, knowing that payment on the spot for any goods supplied or service done is required or expected from him, dishonestly makes off without having paid as required or expected and with intent to avoid payment of the amount due shall be guilty of an offence.

(2) For the purposes of this section 'payment on the spot' includes payment at the time of collecting goods on which work has been done or in respect of which service has been provided.

(3) Subsection (1) above shall not apply where the supply of the goods or the doing of the service is contrary to law, or where the service done is such that payment is not legally enforceable.

(4) Any person may arrest without warrant anyone who is, or whom he, with reasonable cause, suspects to be, committing or attempting to commit an offence under this section."

Note

No deception is needed; only dishonesty. Nor is it material whether ownership of goods has been transferred to the defendant, nor whether he was dishonest before or after any goods were supplied or service done. Many difficulties in the way of a prosecution for theft or obtaining property by deception are thus avoided, but the wording of the present offence is not without its own difficulties, *e.g.* as to "on the spot," "goods supplied," "makes off" "without having paid."

Questions

1. A travels on a train without first buying a ticket, as the regulations require. When challenged at the exit barrier at his destination, he runs away. Is he still "on the spot" when he makes off? Yes, according to *Moberley* v. *Alsop*, (1991) *The Times*, Dec. 13 (D.C.).

2. A, in a self-service store, picks up an article, puts it in his pocket and dishonestly departs without paying for it. Can the article be described as "goods supplied?"

3. A, having eaten a meal at B's restaurant, persuades B to let him go without paying by falsely promising to return next day with the money. Is this "making off" by A? See *R.* v. *Brooks & Brooks*, *infra*.

4. On facts such as occurred in *R.* v. *Lambie*, *ante*, p. 765, where a credit card is dishonestly presented to a supermarket cashier, does the customer make off "without payment"?

5. A, having consumed a meal, absent-mindedly leaves without paying. On being followed out into the street by the waiter, he

realises his omission, but decides not to pay and runs away. Has A dishonestly made off? See *R. v. Brooks & Brooks, infra*.

6. A, having consumed a meal, discovers he has no money. To avoid a fuss, he slips out of the restaurant, intending to return next day with the money. Has A made off "with intent to avoid payment of the amount due"? See *R. v. Allen, infra*.

In *R. v. Brooks & Brooks* (1983) 76 Cr.App.R. 66, 68 (C.A.), the meaning of "makes off" was considered:

"We have been referred to a fuller examination of the definition of the offence which has been made in the academic field, notably by Professor Smith in 'The Law of Theft' (4th ed. 1979) paragraph 242 and Mr. J. R. Spencer in an article entitled 'The Theft Act 1978,' [1979] Crim.L.R. 24, in particular at p. 37 thereof. Thus Professor Smith comments that the words 'makes off' should be construed in a pejorative sense and includes both a sudden and secret departure but excludes departure consented to by means of a deception. Mr. Spencer relies upon one meaning given to the term 'makes off' in the Shorter Oxford Dictionary, namely 'to depart suddenly, often with a disparaging implication, to hasten away; to decamp.'

Pausing there, it is plain that the learned compilers do not suggest that the words must always be construed in the pejorative sense. In any case it is an unnecessary construction, for the words do not stand alone. The making off must be dishonest.

Mr. Spencer is of the opinion that the term suggest a sudden and unexpected departure. In so doing he fails to consider one of the alternatives given in the dictionary, namely to 'decamp,' which may be an exercise accompanied by the sound of trumpets or a silent stealing away after the folding of tents. Obviously, the term covers a wide variety of modes of departure. Nevertheless, we strongly deprecate the involvement of a jury in any philosophic study, however interesting it may be to lawyers and academics. Nor do we adopt the attitude feared by Mr. Spencer of simply saying it is 'all a question of fact for the jury.'

In our opinion, the words 'dishonestly makes off' are words easily understandable by any jury which, in the majority of cases, require no elaboration in a summing-up. The jury should be told to apply the words in their ordinary natural meaning and to relate them to the facts of the case. We agree with the decision in *R. v. McDavitt* [1981] Crim.L.R. 843 that 'making off' involves a departure from the spot where payment is required."

R. v. Allen
[1985] A.C. 1029
House of Lords

A, who had incurred a bill of £1286 at an hotel, left without paying. Two days later, he rang to explain that he was in financial difficulties, he expected to be able to pay soon, and offered to return and deposit his passport as security. When he did return he was arrested and charged with making off without payment. In answer to a question from the jury, the judge directed them that the intent to avoid payment in section 3(1) did not have to be permanent but need only apply to the date on which A had avoided the payment on the spot that had been required or expected from him by the hotel. His conviction having been quashed by the Court of Appeal, the prosecution appealed to the House of Lords.

LORD HAILSHAM OF ST. MARYLEBONE: Despite some (though not unanimous) text book opinions in an opposite sense ... I consider [the judge's] answer to be clearly erroneous. [His Lordship read section 3(1).]

The appellant's contention was that the effect of this section is to catch not only those who intend permanently to avoid payment of the amount due, but also those whose intention is to avoid payment on the spot, which, after all, is the time at which, *ex hypothesi*, payment has been "expected or required," and the time, therefore, when the "amount" became "due."

The judgment of the Court of Appeal, with which I agree, was delivered by Boreham J. He said [1985] 1 W.L.R. 50, 57:

"To secure a conviction under section 3 the following must be proved: (1) that the defendant in fact made off without making payment on the spot; (2) the following mental elements—(a) knowledge that payment on the spot was required or expected of him; and (b) dishonesty; and (c) intent to avoid payment [sc. 'of the amount due']."

I agree with this analysis. To it the judge adds the following comment:

"If (c) means, or is taken to include, no more than an intention to delay or defer payment of the amount due it is difficult to see what it adds to the other elements. Anyone who knows that payment on the spot is expected or required of him and who then dishonestly makes off without paying as required or expected must have at least the intention to delay or defer payment. It follows, therefore, that the conjoined phrase 'and with intent to avoid payment of the amount due' adds a further ingredient—an intention to do more than delay or defer—an intention to evade payment altogether."

My own view, for what it is worth, is that the section thus analysed is capable only of this meaning. But counsel for the appellant very properly conceded that, even if it were equivocal and capable of either meaning, in a penal section of this kind any ambiguity must be resolved in favour of the subject and against the Crown. Accordingly the appeal falls to be dismissed either if on its true construction it means unambiguously that the intention must be permanently to avoid payment, or if the clause is ambiguous and capable of either meaning. Even on the assumption that, in the context, the word "avoid" without the addition of the word "permanently" is capable of either meaning, which Boreham J. was inclined to concede, I find myself convinced by his final paragraph, which reads:

"Finally, we can see no reason why, if the intention of Parliament was to provide, in effect, that an intention to delay or defer payment might suffice, Parliament should not have said so in explicit terms. This *might* have been achieved by the insertion of the word 'such' before payment in the phrase in question. It *would* have been achieved by a grammatical reconstruction of the material part of section 3(1) thus, 'dishonestly makes off without having paid and with intent to avoid payment of the amount due as required or expected.' To accede to the Crown's submission would be to read the section as if it were constructed in that way. That we cannot do. Had it been intended to relate the intention to avoid 'payment' to 'payment as required or expected' it would have been easy to say so. The section does not say so. At the very least it contains an equivocation which should be resolved in favour of the appellant."

There is really no escape from this argument. There may well be something to be said for the creation of a criminal offence designed to protect, for instance, cab drivers and restaurant keepers against persons who dishonestly abscond without paying on the spot and without any need for the prosecution to exclude an intention to pay later, so long as the original act of "making off" could be described as dishonest. Unlike that in the present section, such an offence might very well, as with the railway ticket offence, be triable summarily only, and counsel for the appellant was able to call in aid the remarks of Cumming-Bruce L.J. in *Corbyn* v. *Saunders* [1978] 1 W.L.R. 400, 403 which go a long way to support such a view. But, as the Court of Appeal remarked, that decision was under a different statute and a differently worded section which did not contain both the reference to "dishonestly" and the specific intention "to avoid payment" as two separate elements in the *mens rea* of the offence. In order to give the section now under consideration the effect required the section would have to be remodelled in the way suggested by Boreham J. in the passage quoted above, or the word "and" in the ultimate phrase would have to be read as if it meant "that is to say" so that the required intent would be equated with "dishonestly" in the early part of the subsection.

Apart from a minor matter not relevant to the judgment there is nothing really to be added to the judgment delivered by Boreham J.

The minor matter to which I have just referred was the disinclination of the Court of Appeal to consider the 13th Report of the Criminal Law Revision Committee, Section 16 of the Theft Act 1968 (1977) (Cmnd. 6733), which led to the passing of the Act of 1978. In accordance with present practice, this, for the purpose of defining the mischief of the Act but not to construe it, their Lordships in fact have done. The "mischief" is covered by paragraphs 18 to 21 of the report and it is significant that the report was accompanied by a draft Bill, section 3 of which is in terms identical with section 3 of the Act, save that the proposed penalty was three years instead of two. Though we did not use it as an aid to construction, for the purpose of defining the mischief to be dealt with by the section, I consider it to be relevant. The discussion had originated from the decision in *D.P.P.* v. *Ray, ante,* p. 752, and the committee defined the mischief in the following terms (paragraph 18):

> "there was general support for our suggestion that where the customer knows that he is expected to pay on the spot for goods supplied to him or services done for him it should be an offence for him dishonestly to go away without having paid *and intending never to pay.*" (Emphasis mine.)

From this it is plain beyond doubt that the mischief aimed at by the authors of the report was precisely that which the Court of Appeal, construing the section without reference to the report, attributed to the section by the mere force of grammatical construction.

(Lords Scarman, Diplock, Bridge and Brightman agreed)

Prosecution's appeal dismissed

Note

Griew § 12.18, commenting on this case: " 'Section 3 turns out not to do the whole job it ought to do. In the case of sellers and suppliers of services who undertake very small transactions on the basis of immediate payment, the mischief to be controlled is the very act of making off. ... The decision in *Allen* threatens an increase in the number of contested cases as bilkers run bogus, but possibly just plausible, defences of 'I was going to go back and pay later.' "

CHAPTER 12

BLACKMAIL

	PAGE		PAGE
i. Demand with Menaces	789	iii. With a View to Gain, etc.	799
ii. Unwarranted	793		

Theft Act 1968, section 21

"(1) A person is guilty of blackmail if, with a view to gain for himself or another or with intent to cause loss to another, he makes any unwarranted demand with menaces; and for this purpose a demand with menaces is unwarranted unless the person making it does so in the belief—

(a) that he has reasonable grounds for making the demand; and
(b) that the use of the menaces is a proper means of reinforcing the demand.

(2) The nature of the act or omission demanded is immaterial, and it is also immaterial whether the menaces relate to action to be taken by the person making the demand.

(3) A person guilty of blackmail shall on conviction on indictment be liable to imprisonment for a term not exceeding fourteen years."

i. Demand with Menaces

Notes

Neither "demand" nor "menaces" is defined by the Act. "Menaces," where it was used in the statutory predecessor of the present section (*i.e.* section 29(1) of the Larceny Act 1916) had acquired a definite meaning, being exactly synonymous with threat.

Thorne v. *Motor Trade Association* [1937] A.C. 797: Lord Atkin (at p. 806), "If the matter came to us for decision for the first time I think there would be something to be said for a construction of 'menace' which connotes threats of violence and injury to person or property, and a contrast which might be made between 'menaces' and 'threats,' as used in other sections of the various statutes. But in several cases it has been decided that 'menace' in this subsection and its predecessors is simply equivalent to threat."

But "threat" was regarded as too wide by the draftsmen of the Theft Act 1978.

Cmnd. 2977, § 123: "We have chosen the word 'menaces' instead of 'threats' because notwithstanding the wide meaning given to 'menaces' in

Thorne's case ... we regard that word as stronger than 'threats' and the consequent slight restriction of the scope of the offence seems to us right."

R. v. Lawrence and Pomroy
(1971) 57 Cr.App.R. 64
Court of Appeal

L. and P. were convicted of blackmail in that on January 20, with a view to gain for themselves they made an unwarranted demand of £70 from T. with menaces. P. had done some work for T. T., not being satisfied with the work, had paid part only of the contract price and had indicated that the balance of £70 would be paid when the work was completed to his satisfaction. On January 16, P. had asked T. for the £70 and, on being refused, said that unless T. paid up, he had better look over his shoulder whenever he went out. On January 20, P. again visited T., this time in company with L., a big man. The conversation on that occasion is set out in the judgment of Cairns L.J., below. L. and P. appealed on the grounds that the judge failed to give (a) a definition of menaces and (b) a direction on proviso (b) of section 21(1).

CAIRNS L.J.: Detective Constable Walters said that in company with other officers he was concealed behind the door of Thorn's house when the appellants arrived on January 20. He heard a conversation about the £70 which ended with Lawrence saying: "Now listen, I've got an interest in the £70, see," and then after a pause: "Come out of the house and we'll sort this lot out now." Thorn said: "No" and Lawrence said: "Come on mate, come outside." The police officers then revealed themselves and Walters said that he saw the appellants outside the door. He said to Lawrence: "What is your name?" and Lawrence said: "Leave off, what do you want to know for?" Pomroy said: "Yes it's all right, we only want my money." Lawrence said: "Leave me out, I've only come to help my mate," and when asked gave his name to the police. The appellants were told that they were being arrested for demanding money from Thorn. After caution Lawrence said: "That's nice, we've been well set up." Pomroy said: "But he does owe me money. ... "

The first point we deal with is the contention that the judge gave the jury no definition of what constitutes a menace. It is said that they should have been directed in accordance with *R. v. Clear* [1968] 1 Q.B. 670, that they must consider what the effect would be in the mind of a reasonable man of the words and actions of the two defendants. The word "menaces" is an ordinary English word which any jury can be expected to understand. In exceptional cases where because of special knowledge in special circumstances what would be a menace to an ordinary person is not a menace to the person to whom it is addressed, or where the converse may be true, it is no doubt necessary to spell out the meaning of the word. But, in our view, there was no such necessity here. The judge made it abundantly clear that the issue for the jury was whether the two men had gone to Thorne's house merely to ask reasonably for payment, on Pomroy's part to ask reasonably for payment and on Lawrence's part merely as a companion, or whether they had gone to threaten and frighten him into paying. That was quite a sufficient explanation of what is meant by menaces.

Next, should the judge have directed the jury on the proviso to section 21(1)(b) of the Theft Act: that is to say, as to whether the accused believed that what they did was a proper way of enforcing the debt? Neither of them suggested at the trial that, if menaces were used by them, it was a proper means of enforcement. It is true that the police evidence was that when Pomroy's statement was read to him, Lawrence said: "That's about it, what's wrong with that?" but he repudiated that in his evidence and said that his reaction had been "It's a lot of nonsense."

Where on the face of it the means adopted to obtain payment of a debt is not the proper way of enforcing it and where the accused does not at his trial set up the case that he believed it to be, there is no need for any direction to be given on the proviso. . . .

Appeals dismissed

Note

As to the exceptional cases mentioned by Cairns L.J. where it is necessary to spell out the meaning of "menaces," the Court of Appeal in *R. v. Garwood* [1987] 1 All E.R. 1032, 1034 said:

> "It seems to us that there are two possible occasions on which a further directive on the meaning of the word menaces may be required. The first is where the threats might have affected the mind of an ordinary person of normal stability but did not affect the person actually addressed. In such circumstances that would amount to a sufficient menace: see *R. v. Clear* [1968] 1 Q.B. 670. The second situation is where the threats in fact affected the mind of the victim, although they would not have affected the mind of a person of normal stability. In that case, in our judgment, the existence of the menaces is proved providing that the accused man was aware of the likely effect of his actions on the victim."

R. v. Harry [1972] Crim.L.R. 32 (Crown Ct.): H. sent letters to 115 local shopkeepers asking them to buy immunity posters by contributing to a Student Rag Appeal in aid of charity. The purpose of the poster was to "protect you from any Rag Activity which could in any way cause you inconvenience." The poster read "These premises are immune from Rag '73 activities whatever they may be." In directing an acquittal of blackmail, Judge Petre said "Menaces is a strong word. You may think that menaces must be of a fairly stern nature to fall within the definition."

Treacy v. Director of Public Prosecutions
[1971] A.C. 537
House of Lords

T. wrote and posted in England a letter addressed to a woman in Germany, which letter contained a demand. T. argued that he was not triable in England, not having made the demand in England.

LORD DIPLOCK: . . . Arguments as to the meaning of ordinary everyday phrases are not susceptible of much elaboration. The Theft Act, 1968, makes a welcome departure from the former style of drafting in criminal statutes. It is expressed in simple language as used and understood by ordinary literate men and women. It avoids so far as possible those terms of art which have acquired a special meaning understood only by lawyers in which many of the penal enactments which it supersedes were couched.

So the question which has to be answered is: Would a man say in ordinary conversation: "I have made a demand" when he had written a letter containing a demand and posted it to the person to whom the demand was addressed? Or would he not use those words until the letter had been received and read by the addressee?

My answer to that question is that it would be natural for him to say "I have made a demand" as soon as he had posted the letter, for he would have done all that was in his power to make the demand. He might add, if it were the fact: "but it has not reached X yet," or: "I made a demand but it got lost in the post." What, at any rate, he would not say is: "I shall make a demand when X receives my letter," unless he contemplated making some further demand after the letter had been received.

I see nothing in the context or in the purpose of the section to indicate that the words bear any other meaning than that which I have suggested they would bear in ordinary conversation. . . .

As respects the purpose of the section, I see no reason for supposing that Parliament did not intend to punish conduct which is anti-social or wicked—if that word is still in current use—unless the person guilty of the conduct achieves his intended object of gain to himself or loss caused to another. The fact that what a reasonable man would regard as an unwarranted demand with menaces after being posted by its author goes astray and never reaches the addressee, or reaches him but is not understood by him, or because of his unusual fortitude fails to disturb his equanimity, as was the case in *R. v. Clear* [1968] 1 Q.B. 670, may be a relevant factor in considering what punishment is appropriate but does not make the conduct of the author himself any less wicked or anti-social or less meet to be deterred.

My Lords, all that has to be decided upon this aspect of the instant appeal is whether the appellant "made a demand" when he posted his letter to the addressee. In the course of the argument many other and ingenious ways in which a blackmailer may choose to send his demand to his victim have been canvassed, and many possible, even though unlikely, events which might intervene between the sending of the demand by the blackmailer and its receipt and comprehension by the victim have been discussed. These cases which so far are only imaginary may fall to be decided if they ever should occur in real life. But unless the purpose of the new style of drafting used in the Theft Act, 1968, is to be defeated they, too, should be decided by answering the question: "Are the circumstances of this case such as would prompt a man in ordinary conversation to say: 'I have made a demand'?"

For both the reasons which I have given I would dismiss this appeal.

Appeal dismissed

Notes

1. A possible danger in "the new style of drafting used in the Theft Act, 1968," is illustrated by the fact that of the five Law Lords concerned in *Treacy's* case, three thought that posting a letter containing a demand was making a demand, but two thought that no demand was made until the letter reached the addressee. A technical term at least has the merit that its meaning is precise and can be the subject of a precise direction to the jury.

2. Both demand and menaces may be implicit, rather than explicit. See next case.

R. v. Collister and Warhurst
(1955) 39 Cr.App.R. 100
Court of Criminal Appeal

C. and W., who were police officers, were charged with demanding money with menaces, under section 30 of the Larceny Act 1916. C. told W., in the presence of the prosecutor, that the prosecutor had been importuning him. The prosecutor protested, but W. said to him, "This is going to look very bad for you." They arranged to meet him on the next day, W. telling C. in the prosecutor's hearing to type out a report on the matter but to hold it up and use it only if the prosecutor failed to keep the appointment. When they met next day, W. asked the prosecutor whether he had brought anything with him, and the prosecutor handed over five one pound notes.

PILCHER J. directed the jury: What you have got to be satisfied with in this case is that these two men, working in concert, intended to convey, and did in fact convey, to Mr. Jeffries in the first place that they, being police officers, intended to take him to the West Central Police Station on a charge of importuning, or to put in a report about him, unless Jeffries then or later paid them money. That, I think, is putting it as simply as I can put it. You need not be satisfied that there was an express demand for money in words. You need not be satisfied that any express threats were made, but if the evidence satisfies you that, although there was no such express demand or threat, the demeanour of the accused and the circumstances of the case were such that an ordinary reasonable man would understand that a demand for money was being made upon him and that that demand was accompanied by menaces—not perhaps direct, but veiled menaces—so that his ordinary balance of mind was upset, then you would be justified in coming to the conclusion that a demand with menaces had been made. ...

They were convicted and on appeal this direction
was held to be perfectly proper

ii. Unwarranted

Criminal Law Revision Committee: Eighth Report, Cmnd. 2977

"§ 118 As to the illegality of making the demand we are decidedly of the opinion that the test should be subjective, namely whether the person in question honestly believes that he has the right to make the demand. This means in effect adopting the test of whether there is a claim of right, as in 1916, s.30, and not the test whether there is in fact a reasonable cause for making the demand, as in 1916, s.29(1)(i). Since blackmail is in its nature an offence of dishonesty, it seems wrong that a person should be guilty of the offence by making a demand which he honestly believes to be justified. Moreover to adopt the objective test seems to involve almost insuperable difficulty. It would be necessary either to set out the various kinds of demand which it was considered should be justified or to find an expression which would describe exactly these kinds but not others. The former course might in theory be possible; but the provision would have to be very elaborate, and it would involve the risk which attends any attempt to list different kinds of conduct for the purpose of a criminal offence—that of including too much or too little. Moreover there is much room for disagreement as to what kinds of demand should or should not be treated as justified. The latter course seems impossible having regard to the results which have followed from making liability depend on the absence of a 'reasonable and probable cause.' Any general provision would probably have to use some such uninformative expression, and it would be almost bound to cause similar difficulty and uncertainty.

§ 119 It is in relation to the question when it is permissible to employ threats in support of a demand that differences of opinion become most acute. Several situations are possible. A. may be owed £100 by B. and be unable to get payment. Perhaps A. needs the money badly and B. is in a position to pay; or perhaps A. can easily afford to wait and B. is in difficulty. Should it be blackmail for A. to threaten B. that, if he does not pay, A. will assault him—or slash the tyres of his car—or tell people that B. is a homosexual, which he is (or which he is not)—or tell people about the debt and anything discreditable about the way in which it was incurred? On one view none of these threats should be enough to make the demand amount to blackmail. For it is no offence merely to utter the threats without making the demand (unless for some particular reason such as breach of the peace or defamation); nor would the threat become criminal merely because it was uttered to reinforce a demand of a kind quite different from those associated with blackmail. Why then should it be blackmail merely because it is uttered to reinforce a demand for money which is owed? On this view no demand with menaces would amount to blackmail, however harsh the action threatened unless there was dishonesty. This is a tenable view, though an extreme one. In our opinion it goes too far and there are some threats which should make the demand amount to blackmail even if there is a valid claim to the thing demanded. For example, we believe that most people would say that it should be blackmail to threaten to denounce a person, however truly, as a homosexual unless he paid a debt. It does not seem to follow from the existence of a debt that the creditor should be entitled to resort to any method, otherwise non-criminal, to obtain payment. There are limits to the methods permissible for the purpose of enforcing payment of a debt without recourse to the courts. For example, a creditor cannot seize the debtor's goods; and in *Parker* (1910) 74 J.P. 208, it was held ... that a creditor who forged a letter from the Admiralty to a sailor warning him to pay a debt was guilty of forgery notwithstanding the existence of the debt.

§ 120 If it is agreed that some threats should make a demand amount to blackmail, the difficulty is to draw the line between different kinds of threats in a way which would be generally accepted. It may be thought that a threat to cause physical injury or damage to property should always be sufficient, even though one does not ordinarily think of such threats in connection with blackmail. A threat to injure a person in relation to his business, for example by cutting off supplies to a retailer if he will not pay a debt or persists in breaking an agreement, would probably not be regarded as rightly included in blackmail. Some might think that any threat to disclose a matter not connected with the circumstances giving rise to the debt should be included; but opinion may differ widely about threats to disclose some discreditable conduct which resulted in the debt being incurred. Probably most people would say that the offence should not extend to a threat to disclose the existence of a debt. For example, it is not blackmail to threaten to post the name of a betting defaulter at Tattersalls (see *Russell on Crime*, 12th edition, pp. 881–882). As in the case of demands, the possible courses seem to be to lay down a subjective test, depending on whether the person who utters the threat believes in his right to do so, or an objective test, whether by specifying the kinds of threats which should or should not be permissible or by means of a general provision to cover the latter. For reasons similar to those given in paragraph 118 concerning the demand we think that the only satisfactory course would be to adopt a subjective test and to make criminal liability depend on whether the person who utters the threat believes in the propriety of doing so.

§ 122 At first we proposed to include a requirement that a person's belief that he has reasonable grounds for making the demand or that the use of the menaces is proper should be reasonable belief. There would be a case for this in policy; for it may be thought that a person who puts pressure on another by menaces of a kind which any reasonable person would think ought to be blackmail should not escape liability merely because his moral standard is too low, or his intelligence too limited, to enable him to appreciate the wrongness of his conduct. The requirement might also make the decision easier for the jury; for if they found that the demand was unwarranted or that the menaces were improper, they would not have to consider whether the accused believed otherwise. But we decided finally not to include the requirement. To require that an honest belief, in order to be a defence, should be reasonable would have the result that the offence of blackmail could be committed by mere negligence (for example, in not consulting a lawyer or, as did Bernhard, in consulting the wrong kind of lawyer). [See *R. v. Bernhard* [1938] 2 K.B. 264.]"

Sir Bernard MacKenna, "Blackmail: a Criticism" [1966] Crim.L.R. 466

"5. A man's belief that he has reasonable grounds for making a demand depends on two matters:

(a)   his belief that the facts of the case are such-and-such; and
(b)   his opinion upon these facts that it would be reasonable to make the demand.

In a particular case one man's belief that there are reasonable grounds for making a demand may differ from another's because of a difference in their beliefs about the facts (one believing the facts to be X., the other to be Y.), or because of a difference in their opinions upon the same facts (one opinion that those facts give a reasonable ground for making the demand, the other that they do not).

6. 'Reasonable grounds' in [section 21(1)(a)] cannot be limited to such as are believed to give a legally enforceable claim. To many it would seem reasonable to demand satisfaction of a claim recognised by the law as valid though unenforceable by legal action for some technical reason, such as the want of a writing or the expiration of the period of limitation. To some it would seem equally reasonable to demand payment of a claim incapable in any circumstances of being enforced by action, such as the claim to be paid a winning bet. There may be many other cases in which a moral, as distinct from a legal, right would seem to some at least a reasonable ground for making a demand. On these questions there could be differences of opinion, particularly as to whether on the facts of the case the person demanding had a moral right to the thing demanded. There could be similar 'moral' differences about the propriety of using threats.

7. The Committee intend that the test shall be subjective in both the respects indicated in 5 above: (i) the facts shall be taken to be those which the defendant believed to exist, and (ii) his opinion as to whether those facts gave him a reasonable ground for making a demand (or made it proper for him to use threats) will be the only relevant one. His own moral standards are to determine the rightness or wrongness of his conduct. This

appears from a sentence in paragraph 122 where the Committee discuss (and dismiss) the possible objection to [section 21(1)(a)] that 'it may be thought that a person who puts pressure on another by menaces of a kind which any reasonable person would think ought to be blackmail should not escape liability merely because his moral standard is too low, or his intelligence too limited, to enable him to appreciate the wrongness of his conduct.'

8. That a sane man's guilt or innocence should depend in this way on his own opinion as to whether he is acting rightly or wrongly is, I think, an innovation in our criminal law.

9. The claim of right which excuses a taking that might otherwise be theft under section 1 of the Larceny Act 1916, may of course be a mistaken claim, and the mistake may be one of law or of fact. A man's mistaken belief that the rules of the civil law make him the owner of a certain thing is as good an excuse as his mistaken belief that the thing is X. when it is in fact Y. But [section 21(1)] goes further than this, and gives efficacy to the defendant's moral judgments whatever they may be. That is surely something different. It is one thing to hold that the defendant is excused if he believes the civil law to be X. when it is Y. It is another to excuse him in any case where he thinks that what he is doing is morally right, though according to ordinary moral notions he may be doing something very wrong."

R. v. Harvey
(1980) 72 Cr.App.R. 139
Court of Appeal

H. and others paid £20,000 to S. for what was thought to be a consignment of cannabis, but in fact was a load of rubbish. They kidnapped S.'s wife and small child and told S. they would maim and kill his family unless he gave them their money back. They were convicted of blackmail and appealed.

BINGHAM J.: The learned judge in his direction to the jury quoted the terms of the subsection and then continued as follows: "Now where the defence raise this issue, in other words, where they say that the demand is warranted and where they say they believe they had reasonable cause for making the demand and that the use of the menaces was a proper way of reinforcing the demand, it is for the prosecution to negative that allegation. It is not for the defendants to prove it once they have raised it. It is for the prosecution to prove that they had no such belief. Now is that clear? It is not easy and I do not want to lose you on the way. It has been raised in this case so you have got to ask yourself this. Has the prosecution disproved that these defendants or those who have raised the matter believed that they had *reasonable* grounds for making the demand? Certainly you may say to yourselves that they have been ripped off to the tune of £20,000. They had been swindled. ... As I say, on this question of reasonable ground for making a demand, you may say to yourselves: 'Well, they did have reasonable ground for making the demand in this sense, that they had put money into this deal, they had been swindled by Scott, and it was reasonable to demand the return of their money.' So you may say: 'Well, the prosecution have not negatived that but what about the second leg of the proviso, the belief that the use of menaces is a proper method of reinforcing the demand?' Now it is for you to decide what, if any, menaces were made, because that is a question of evidence.

If you decide that the threats or menaces made by these accused, or any of them, were to kill or to maim or to rape, or any of the other matters that have been mentioned in evidence—I mention about three that come into my mind—then those menaces or threats are threats to commit a criminal act, a threat to murder, a threat to rape, or a threat to blow your legs or kneecaps off, those are threats to commit a criminal offence and surely everybody in this country, including the defendants, knows those are criminal offences. The point is that this is a matter of law. It cannot be a proper means of reinforcing the demand to make threats to commit serious criminal offences. So I say to you that if you look at these two counts of blackmail and you decide that these defendants, or any of them, used menaces, dependent upon the menaces you decide were used, the threats that were used, but if you decide that these threats were made by these men to commit criminal offences against Scott, they cannot be heard to say on this blackmail charge that they had reasonable belief that the use of those threats was a proper method of reinforcing their demand."

Later, when prosecuting counsel drew attention to the learned judge's erroneous reference to "reasonable" belief, he added the following: "I do not think it affects the point I was seeking to make, that where the demand or the threat is to commit a criminal offence, and a serious criminal offence like murder and maiming and rape, or whatever it may be, it seems hard for anybody to say that the defendants had a belief that was a proper way of reinforcing their demand. That is the point."

For the appellants it was submitted that the learned judge's direction, and in particular the earlier of the passages quoted, was incorrect in law because it took away from the jury a question properly falling within their province of decision, namely, what the accused in fact believed. He was wrong to rule as a matter of law that a threat to perform a serious criminal act could never be thought by the person making it to be a proper means. While free to comment on the unlikelihood of a defendant believing threats such as were made in this case to be a proper means, the judge should nonetheless (it was submitted) have left the question to the jury. For the Crown it was submitted that a threat to perform a criminal act can never as a matter of law be a proper means within the subsection, and that the learned judge's direction was accordingly correct. Support for both these approaches is to be found in academic works helpfully brought to the attention of the Court.

The answer to this problem must be found in the language of the subsection, from which in our judgment two points emerge with clarity: (1) the subsection is concerned with the belief of the individual defendant in the particular case: " . . . a demand with menaces is unwarranted unless *the person making it* does so in the belief . . . " (added emphasis). It matters not what the reasonable man, or any man other than the defendant, would believe save in so far as that may throw light on what the defendant in fact believed. Thus the factual question of the defendant's belief should be left to the jury. To that extent the subsection is subjective in approach, as is generally desirable in a criminal statute. (2) In order to exonerate a defendant from liability his belief must be that the use of the menaces is a "proper" means of reinforcing the demand. "Proper" is an unusual expression to find in a criminal statute. It is not defined in the Act, and no definition need be attempted here. It is, however, plainly a word of wide meaning, certainly wider than (for example) "lawful." But the greater includes the less and no act which was not believed to be lawful could be believed to be proper within the meaning of the subsection. Thus no assistance is given to any defendant, even a fanatic or a deranged idealist, who knows or suspects that his threat, or the act threatened, is criminal, but believes it to be justified by his end or his peculiar circumstances. The test is not what he regards as justified, but what he believes to be proper. And where, as here, the threats were to do acts which any sane man knows to be against the laws of every civilised country no jury would hesitate long before dismissing the contention that the defendant genuinely believed the threats to be a proper means of reinforcing even a legitimate demand.

It is accordingly our conclusion that the direction of the learned judge was not strictly correct. If it was necessary to give a direction on this aspect of the case at all (and in the absence of any evidence by the defendants as to their belief we cannot think that there was in reality any live issue concerning it) the jury should have been directed that the demand with menaces was not to be regarded as unwarranted unless the Crown satisfied them in respect of each defendant that the defendant did not make the demand with menaces in the genuine belief both—(a) that he had had reasonable grounds for making the demand; and (b) that the use of the menaces was in the circumstances a proper (meaning for present purposes a lawful, and not a criminal) means of reinforcing the demand.

The learned judge could, of course, make appropriate comment on the unlikelihood of the defendants believing murder and rape or threats to commit those acts to be lawful or other than criminal.

On the facts of this case we are quite satisfied that the misdirection to which we have drawn attention could have caused no possible prejudice to any of the appellants. Accordingly, in our judgment, it is appropriate to apply the proviso to section 2(1) of the Criminal Appeal Act 1968, and the appeals are dismissed.

Appeals against conviction dismissed

Questions

1. On the C.L.R.C.'s proposal for a subjective test of propriety, Sir Bernard MacKenna comments: "That a sane man's guilt or innocence should depend this way on his own opinion as to whether he is acting rightly or wrongly is, I think, an innovation in our criminal law" (*ante*, p. 796). Has not the law reached this position with regard to theft? See *Ghosh, ante*, p. 736.

2. "No act which was not believed to be lawful could be believed to be proper within the meaning of the subsection. ... The test is not what he regards as justified, but what he believes to be proper":—Bingham J., above. Is this consistent with the subjective test of propriety proposed by the C.L.R.C., *ante*, p. 795, § 120?

3. Can mistake of law be relevant in this connection?

4. In the following cases, D, on trial for blackmail, contends that his request and threat were perfectly justified. How ought the judge to deal with the issue in his directions to the jury?

(a) D, with his entourage, arrives in England from a country where it is common for thieves to have their right hands cut off. D discovers that a member of his entourage, P, has been stealing money from him. He warns P that unless he returns the money, D will cut off his right hand.

(b) D, who uses his car daily to get to work, discovers that his road fund licence has expired. Not having the money to renew it, he asks P, his mother, for the money. When P refuses D says; "Driving an unlicensed car is a crime. Unless you give me the money, I will certainly commit this crime every day. You wouldn't want that on your conscience, would you?"

Note

Williams, Textbook, p. 837: "A factor of prime importance in a blackmail case will frequently be the secrecy or the openness of the transaction. A man who thinks he is acting properly in making a threat will not try to conceal his identity, and demand that money should be left in used pound notes at a telephone kiosk. Again, it is in practice impossible for a defendant both to argue that he did not utter the menaces and that if he did they were justified. So, if he chooses merely to deny the menaces, and the jury find against him and the menaces are prima facie improper, the judge need not direct the jury on the unscrupulous mental element."

iii. With a View to Gain, etc.

Theft Act 1968, section 34

" . . . (2) For the purposes of this Act—

(a) 'gain' and 'loss' are to be construed as extending only to gain or loss in money or other property, but as extending to any such gain or loss whether temporary or permanent; and

    (i) 'gain' includes a gain by keeping what one has, as well as a gain by getting what one has not; and

    (ii) 'loss' includes a loss by not getting what one might get, as well as a loss by parting with what one has."

R. v. *Parkes* [1973] Crim.L.R. 358 (Sheffield Crown Court). D. was charged with blackmail (*inter alia*). The evidence adduced by the prosecution showed that in one instance the money demanded was undoubtedly money owed to D. by the complainant and, indeed, long overdue. In the other instance there was some issue as to whether or not the money demanded was a debt but the submission was made and ruled upon the basis that it *was* a debt owing by the complainant to D.

It was submitted that to demand what is lawfully owing to you was not a demand "with a view to gain" within the meaning of section 21(1) of the Theft Act 1968, as interpreted by section 32(2)(a) of that Act. Judge Dean Q.C. ruled that by demanding money lawfully owing to him D. did have a view to "gain." Section 34(2)(a)(i) defines gain as including "getting what one has not"; by intending to obtain hard cash as opposed to a mere right of action in respect of the debt D. *was* getting more than he already had and accordingly the submission failed.

R. v. *Bevans* [1988] Crim.L.R. 236 (C.A.): D., suffering from osteoarthritis, went to a doctor's surgery, produced a gun and threatened to shoot the doctor if he did not give him an injection of a pain-killing drug. *Held*, upholding his conviction of blackmail, the drug was property; the demand involved gain for D.; the fact that his ulterior motive was relief from pain rather than economic gain was immaterial.

Note

If the immediate object is to get property, the motive for making an unwarrantable demand with menaces is irrelevant: see *Bevans, supra*. But if D's immediate object is to get a service rather than property or money, it may still be blackmail if his *motive* is financial. The words *"with a view to gain"* are capable of comprehending an ulterior motive of gain, *e.g.* D demands that V vote for him in an election for a company directorship, *so that* D will gain director's fees. See next case which concerned a different crime but one which also requires a view to gain or intent to cause loss.

R. v. Golechha and Choraria
(1990) 90 Cr.App.R. 241
Court of Appeal

G. and C. were convicted of falsification of accounts, contrary to section 17(1) Theft Act 1968, in that they dishonestly and with a view to gain for themselves or with intent to cause loss to another falsified certain bills of exchange. Their object was alleged to be to obtain a bank's forbearance to enforce against them certain other bills which had matured. On appeal:—

LORD LANE C.J. for the Court: " . . . When he came to sum up, the learned judge . . . directed the jury as follows:

"Going back to count one, you will see that after the word 'dishonestly' we get 'and with a view to gain for themselves.' Now you may not have thought that this required a great deal of your consideration, but there are certain things that have to be proved. The dishonest falsification, if you find that there was such a thing, must be with a view to gain for the person or persons who are doing the falsifying. As a matter of law I will tell you that the mere fact that Johnson Matthey credited the dollar current account of Berg [a company owned and ran by Golechha] with a sum which represented the discounted value of the bill does not amount to gain if you stop there. All that has happened is that there has been a paper plus put on the account and that does not amount to gain if you stop there. But if you decide that what the defendant Golechha and the defendant Choraria or either of them had in view—there is the word 'with a view to gain'—went further than just getting a credit, a paper plus on Berg's account, but that what they were after was that Golechha should be able to turn that credit to practical use by drawing on it, converting it to cash in order to raise hard finance to buy goods, confirm deals and so forth, if you come to that view or that decision I should say, and you decide that that was the view that these people or either of them had in mind, members of the jury, that would amount to gain. That is a matter of fact for you."

. . . Mr. Blair Q.C. for the Crown submitted, rightly in our view, that in the passage we have cited from the summing up the learned judge was . . . directing the jury [that] the mere crediting of the account . . . was not in law a gain; but if they concluded that the object of the defendants was to turn that paper credit, by drawing on it, to cash for the purposes of trade, that would amount to gain. Mr. Blair submits that the judge's interpretation of the section was perfectly reasonable and indeed correct. Parliament deliberately chose the words "with a view to gain"—a phrase plainly admitting of some flexibility—precisely in order to cover cases such as the present.

As to the distinct argument to the effect that a mere forbearance to sue cannot in any event constitute a gain, Mr. Blair contended that here too the judge was correct to regard his interpretation as affording an answer to it. He argued that even if all that was sought to be achieved by means of putting in place the last three bills was a forbearance on the part of the bank from suing on the earlier bills, the appellants were by that means trying to keep what they had in the sense that they were seeking to preserve a facility upon which they could in practice draw, whether or not it was enforceable in law.

In his reply to these submissions Mr. Marshall-Andrews for Golechha ... concentrated on two submissions only: first, that the judge's interpretation of section 17 is incorrect, and second that, even if it be correct, it does not meet the forbearance to sue point.

Mr. Marshall-Andrews developed the first point in this way. He argued that the words "with a view to gain" must refer to the gain sought to be obtained by the falsification. They were included so as to incorporate temporary gain and keeping what you have, but there was in truth no distinction between the expressions "with a view to gain" and the expression "with intent to obtain property." It was not legitimate to look at the property into which that which was obtained might be converted.
. . .

We see the attractions, from a practical common sense point of view, of the judge's interpretation of the section, while at the same time appreciating the force of Mr. Marshall-Andrews' argument against it. However we find it unnecessary in the present case further to examine or to seek to resolve this matter, because we have reached the clear conclusion that Mr. Marshall-Andrews' ... second answer to Mr. Blair's submissions is conclusive in favour of the appellants.

Put in its simplest form, the prosecution's argument on forbearance to sue amounts to this: that even if all that the appellants sought to achieve was forbearance on the part of the bank to enforce their rights under an earlier bill, they were seeking by that means to preserve the facility. This argument is superficially attractive, but fallacious. Even if it be assumed in favour of the Crown that the first two bills reflected genuine trade transactions—as to which there was no evidence one way or the other—all that had been brought into existence was a debt owed by Berg to the bank: a debt which existed at all times. To speak of "preserving the facility" by means of the placing of the falsified bills is to attribute to the facility characteristics which it does not possess. A debtor is not possessed of any proprietary rights: he does not have money, and the chose in action represented by the debt is owned by the creditor. Accordingly, while it may well be that the three falsified bills were falsified with a view to securing the bank's forbearance from enforcing their rights on the earlier bills, this did not and could not constitute falsification with a view to gain (that is gain by keeping money or other property). It was designed simply to postpone the enforcement of an obligation.

If it be accepted for present purposes that the learned judge's construction of the words "with a view to gain" was correct, and that it is therefore legitimate to see how funds sought to be obtained on the strength of a falsified bill would be used by the defendant, that cannot avail the prosecution in a case where all that the defendant had in view was the forbearance to enforce an existing indebtedness. If the desired forbearance is obtained, this neither gives to the defendant nor allows him to retain anything on which he can draw or which he can convert into cash or goods. Such a case is quite distinct from one in which the object in view is to obtain an advance.

If, which we do not, we had any doubts as to the correctness of this analysis, they would be dispelled by the reflection that section 16 of the 1968 Act or section 2 of the 1978 Act are entirely apt to found charges based on the sort of conduct we have been considering.

It follows that, since it was at the very least a distinct possibility that the appellants' object in falsifying the bills in question was merely to obtain the bank's forbearance, the judge's failure to invite the jury to consider whether that was the position and to direct them that if it was the defendants were not guilty of the offence charged was a misdirection.

Accordingly these appeals must on that ground be allowed.

Convictions quashed

Note

Blackmail is a sort of inchoate offence in that the making of the unwarranted demand with menaces is the full crime, even if the demand is not acceded to and no property is got as a result. If property *is* got as a result, then theft and robbery may also be committed. But blackmail is also a "fall-back" offence, in that if property is got but claim of right prevents a conviction of theft or robbery (see *R.* v. *Skivington, ante,* p. 744) it will be blackmail if the jury think D knew the menaces used were improper. As *Parkes, ante,* p. 799, shows, the fact that D is or thinks he is entitled to what he gets does not mean that he does not act "with a view to gain." Similarly if the menaces used do not amount to the use of force on a person or the putting or seeking to put a person in fear of imminent force, it cannot be robbery but can be blackmail.

CHAPTER 13

HANDLING

	PAGE		PAGE
i. Stolen Goods	804	iv. Knowing or Believing them to be Stolen Goods	822
ii. Otherwise than in the Course of Stealing	814	v. Dishonesty	826
iii. Forms of Handling	817		

Theft Act 1968, section 22

"(1) A person handles stolen goods if (otherwise than in the course of stealing) knowing or believing them to be stolen goods he dishonestly receives the goods, or dishonestly undertakes or assists in their retention, removal, disposal or realisation by or for the benefit of another person, or if he arranges to do so.

(2) A person guilty of handling stolen goods shall on conviction on indictment be liable to imprisonment for a term not exceeding fourteen years."

Note

The offence created by this section replaces the offence of receiving stolen goods contained in section 33 of the Larceny Act 1916 and section 97 of the Larceny Act 1861. The present offence is wider than the former. Receiving was confined to cases where a man took into his possession goods which he knew had been obtained unlawfully. Handling, however, "will punish not only receivers, but also those who knowingly convey stolen goods to any place after the theft, those who take charge of them and keep them on their premises or hide them on the approach of the police, those who negotiate for the sale of the goods and the like. The definition will also include a person who in the course of his otherwise innocent employment knowingly removes the goods from place to place, for example a driver employed by dishonest transport owners. If the driver knows that the goods are stolen and that in conveying them he is helping in their disposal, it seems right that he should be guilty of the offence. The fact that he is acting in the course of his ordinary employment may go in mitigation." (Cmnd. 2977, 128.)

If, as is often the case, what is done by any of the above persons is a dishonest appropriation of the property with intent permanently to deprive the owner (see Chap. 10), it will also be theft.

i. Stolen Goods

Theft Act 1968, section 24

"(1) The provisions of this Act relating to goods which have been stolen shall apply whether the stealing occurred in England or Wales or elsewhere, and whether it occurred before or after the commencement of this Act, provided that the stealing (if not an offence under this Act) amounted to an offence where and at the time when the goods were stolen; and references to stolen goods shall be construed accordingly.

(2) For purposes of those provisions references to stolen goods shall include, in addition to the goods originally stolen and parts of them (whether in their original state or not)—

(a)   any other goods which directly or indirectly represent or have at any time represented the stolen goods in the hands of the thief as being the proceeds of any disposal or realisation of the whole or part of the goods stolen or of goods so representing the stolen goods; and

(b)   any other goods which directly or indirectly represent or have at any time represented the stolen goods in the hands of a handler of the stolen goods or any part of them as being the proceeds of any disposal or realisation of the whole or part of the stolen goods handled by him or of goods so representing them.

(3) But no goods shall be regarded as having continued to be stolen goods after they have been restored to the person from who they were stolen or to other lawful possession or custody, or after that person and any other person claiming through him have otherwise ceased as regards those goods to have any right to restitution in respect of the theft.

(4) For the purposes of the provisions of this Act relating to goods which have been stolen (including subsection (1) to (3) above) goods obtained in England or Wales or elsewhere either by blackmail or in the circumstances described in section 15(1) of this Act shall be regarded as stolen; and 'steal,' 'theft' and 'thief' shall be construed accordingly."

Theft Act 1968, section 34

"(2) For the purposes of this Act—

(b)   'goods,' except in so far as the context otherwise requires, includes money and every other description of property except land, and includes things severed from the land by stealing."

Notes

1. It has to be shown that "goods" within the meaning of section 34(2)(*b*), were stolen (or obtained by blackmail or deception: s.24(4)) by someone (who may be the present defendant: see *post*); that the property the subject of the charge is either those goods or represents them (s.24(2)); and that, at the time of the alleged handling, the goods were still stolen goods (s.24(3)).

2. As to the definition of "goods," compare "property" in section 4(1), *ante*, p. 679. Things in action are not specifically mentioned in section 34(2)(*b*), but see next case.

Attorney General's Reference (No. 4 of 1979)
(1980) 71 Cr.App.R. 341
Court of Appeal

The facts appear in the Court's opinion

LORD WIDGERY C.J.: This reference by the Attorney-General arises out of a case in which the accused was indicted on one count which alleged that she dishonestly received certain stolen goods, namely a cheque for £288.53 knowing or believing the same to be stolen goods.

After a submission on behalf of the accused at the end of the prosecution case, the trial judge directed the jury to acquit. There was no issue as to the receipt by the accused of the cheque, nor was it in dispute that the person who paid the cheque had previously obtained sums of money by dishonest deception, but the judge ruled that there was no evidence that the cheque so paid to the accused was in law stolen goods.

The facts of the case were these. Over a period of six months in 1976 and 1977, a fellow-employee of the accused obtained by deception from their employer certain cheques. It is convenient, for brief reference, to refer to that fellow-employee as "thief." The thief paid those fraudulently obtained cheques into her bank account.

During the same period the thief also paid into her bank account other cheques which she had lawfully received from her employer and which represented, first, amounts earned by and due to fellow-employees which she was required to pay on to those employees; and, secondly, sums lawfully earned by the thief.

The total of the sums paid into the bank account by the thief as sums dishonestly obtained by deception from the employer was £859.70.

The thief had duly paid out to the other employees the amounts she had received for such payments.

On the date when the thief handed to the defendant the cheque for £288.53, the state of the thief's bank account was a credit balance of £641.32.

The total amount lawfully received into the account by the thief for payment to other employees, which had been paid out to them, exceeded that balance of £641.32. The total amount lawfully received by the thief in respect of her own earnings and paid into the account had also exceeded £641.32. The Court has no information as to the nature or purpose of other disbursements made from the account by the thief and assumes there was no evidence.

There was evidence that the defendant had admitted that she knew of the obtaining by deception of the £859.70 by the thief. It is said that there was evidence from which it would have been open to the jury to conclude that, for the continued deceptions of the thief to succeed, the co-operation, or at least acquiescence, of the defendant was necessary. Whatever the reason it was thought more appropriate to charge her with handling than with obtaining by deception.

The defendant was asked about the cheque paid to her by the thief. One question asked of her was this: "Was that your share?" She replied: "I suppose it was." She added, according to the evidence which the jury was invited to consider: "I suppose you could call it guilt but I haven't touched it."

The judge at trial was invited to rule that there was no evidence upon which the jury could conclude that the cheque given to the defendant by the thief amounted in law to stolen goods within the meaning of the Theft Act 1968.

Two points were taken on behalf of the defendant by counsel. First, that the offence of handling stolen goods could not be committed with reference to a stolen thing in action, or to a thing in action representing stolen goods; secondly, that on the evidence before the court the offence of handling stolen goods could not be proved.

As to the first point, the judge rejected the submission. As to the second, the judge ruled that since the thief's bank account had been fed by payments in the three categories described above, namely: (i) sums lawfully obtained for payment on to other employees; (ii) sums lawfully obtained as money earned by the thief; and (iii) the £859.70 dishonestly obtained by deception; it was impossible for the prosecution to prove vhat the payment made to the defendant was in law stolen goods.

In reaching his conclusion the judge said this: "I have to consider whether or not the cheque which the thief paid to the accused's account indirectly represents the stolen goods in the hands of the thief. It is very tempting to say that if the drawer of the cheque and the recipient of the cheque intend that the money represented by the cheque shall represent that part of the choses in action owed by the bank to the account holder which is stolen money that that is sufficient for these purposes. But in my view the Act does not say that. It does not imply it and I consider that as I have to construe this part and every part of the Act strictly that if Parliament had intended to provide for such a case it would have said so."

It is from this conclusion on the second point that the point of law referred to this Court arises. The point of law referred to us under section 36(1) of the Act of 1972 is as follows: "Where a payment is made out of a fund constituted by a mixture of money amounting to stolen goods within the meaning of section 24 of the Theft Act 1968, and money not so tainted, or of a bank account similarly constituted, in such a way that the specific origin of the sum paid cannot be identified with either portion of the fund, is a jury entitled to infer that the payment represented stolen goods within the meaning of section 24(2) of the Act, from the intention of the parties that it should represent the stolen goods or a share thereof?"

... We can begin the statement of our opinion upon the point of law referred to us by observing that the cheque which the accused was alleged to have received was, plainly, not part of the goods originally stolen or obtained. In order to succeed, therefore, the prosecution had to bring the case within the terms of section 24(2) of the Theft Act 1968, which defines the scope of offences relating to the handling of stolen goods. The relevant provisions are contained in section 24(2)(a), which reads as follows: " ... references to stolen goods shall include ... any other goods which directly or indirectly represent or have at any time represented the stolen goods in the hands of the thief as being the proceeds of any disposal or realisation of the whole or part of the goods stolen. ... " By section 24(4) the reference to "goods which have been stolen" includes goods which have been obtained by deception.

It was submitted that the language of section 24(2)(a) afforded some support for the first point made on behalf of the accused, namely, that a thing in action cannot be handled by receiving within section 22 of the Theft Act. By section 34(2)(b), however, the interpretation section of this

Act,"goods," except where the context otherwise requires, includes money and every other description of property except land and includes things severed from the land. Further by the combined effect of section 4(1) and section 34(2), "property" includes money and all other property real and personal including things in action.

In our judgment therefore it is clear from that extended definition of "goods" that a cheque obtained by deception constitutes stolen goods for the purposes of sections 22 and 24 of the Act.

Next, it is clear that a balance in a bank account, being a debt, is itself a thing in action which falls within the definition of goods and may therefore be goods which directly or indirectly represent stolen goods for the purposes of section 24(2)(a).

Further where, as in the present case, a person obtains cheques by deception and pays them into her bank account, the balance in that account may, to the value of the tainted cheques, be goods which "directly represent the stolen goods in the hands of the thief as being the proceeds of the disposal or realisation of the goods stolen ... ," within the meaning of section 24(2)(a).

If, however, the prosecution is to prove dishonest handling by receiving, it is necessary to prove that what the handler received was in fact the whole or part of the stolen goods within the meaning of section 24(2)(a). To prove that, the prosecution must prove (i) that at the material time, namely, at the time of receipt by the handler, in such a case as this, the thief's bank balance was in fact comprised, at least in part, of that which represented the proceeds of stolen goods; and (ii) that the handler received, at least in part, such proceeds.

In some cases no difficulty will arise. For example, if the thief opened a new account and paid into it only dishonestly obtained cheques, then the whole balance would constitute stolen goods within the meaning of section 24(2)(a). If then the thief transferred the whole balance to an accused, that accused would, in our opinion, have received stolen goods.

By the same reasoning if at the material time the whole of the balance in an account consisted only of the proceeds of stolen goods, then any cheque drawn on that account would constitute stolen goods within section 24(2)(a).

We have no doubt that when such a cheque is paid, so that part of such a balance in the thief's account is transferred to the credit of the receiver's account, the receiver has received stolen goods because he has received a thing in action which " ... directly represents ... the stolen goods in the hands of the thief ... as being the proceeds of ... realisation of the ... goods stolen. ... "

The same conclusion follows where the receiver directly cashes the cheque drawn on the thief's account and receives money from the paying bank.

The allegation in this case was that the defendant received stolen goods when she received the thief's cheque. Mr. Lee, in the course of argument, was disposed to accept a suggestion from a member of the Court that a cheque drawn by the thief, directed to her bank, and intended to enable the accused to obtain transfer of part of the thief's credit balance, or cash, might not itself be stolen goods within the meaning of section 24(2)(a). This point is not necessary for decision on the point of law referred to us and it has not been fully argued. It appears to us that there is much to be said in favour of the proposition that receipt of such a cheque, drawn in circumstances wherein it is plain that it must serve to transfer the proceeds of stolen goods, would constitute receiving stolen goods on the grounds that such a cheque would directly or indirectly represent the stolen goods within section 24(2)(a).

In the present case the prosecution sought such proof, as to the nature of the payment received by the defendant, from the statement which the defendant made as to her understanding and intention when the payment was made. She had said that she regarded the payment to her as "her share."

In our opinion, such an admission could not by itself prove either that part of the thief's bank balance did or did not represent stolen goods within section 24(2)(a), or that part of such stolen goods was received by the defendant. Her admission was, of course, plainly admissible on the issue of her knowledge that the payment represented stolen goods, and as to her honesty in receiving the money. On the issue of fact, however, as to whether the cheque received by her represented stolen goods, the primary rule is that an accused can only make a valid and admissible admission of a statement of fact of which the accused could give admissible evidence: see *Surujpaul* v. *R.* [1958] 1 W.L.R. 1050. It is not necessary in this case to examine the limits of, or the extent of any exceptions from, that primary rule.

In our opinion Mr. Nicholl was right in his submission when he acknowledged that the prosecution must, in such a case as this, prove in the first place that any payment out of a mixed account *could*, by reference to payments in and out, be a payment representing stolen goods. Unless she had personal knowledge of the working of the thief's account, the defendant could make no valid admission as to that.

It is to be noted that the point of law referred to us contains the words: "Is a jury entitled to infer ... from the intention of the parties. ... " The use of the plural "parties" is misleading. There was no direct evidence in this case of what the intention of the thief might have been, only of that of the receiver. It may perhaps be that a payment can be proved to have been a payment of money representing stolen goods, even where there was enough honest money in the account to cover the payment, if there is proof direct or by way of necessary inference of the intention of the paying thief to pay out the stolen money. That problem can be decided when it arises. It does not do so here. The prosecution did not advance their case on such a basis.

The only question arising on the facts here is whether a jury is entitled to infer that the payment represented stolen goods within section 24(2) from the intention or belief of the receiver that it should or did. The answer is "No."

Declaration accordingly

Question

A stole goods and deposited them in the warehouse of B, an innocent man. A delivered B's receipt for the goods to C, so that C, who knew the goods were stolen, could obtain them from B. Before C could present the receipt to B, he was arrested. Is he guilty of handling?

Note

Section 24(2) was explained by the C.L.R.C., § 138 as follows, "It may seem technical; but the effect will be that the goods which the accused is charged with handling must, at the time of the handling or at some previous time, (i) have been in the hands of the thief or of a handler, and (ii) have represented the original stolen goods in the sense of being the proceeds direct or indirect, of a sale or other realisation of the original goods."

Question

A, having stolen a car, sold it to B, an innocent man, for £10,000. B later sold the car to C, also innocent, for £8,000. A gave the £10,000 to D and B gave the £8,000 to E. Both D and E knew the full circumstances. Are they guilty of handling?

Attorney-General's Reference (No. 1 of 1974)
[1974] Q.B. 744
Court of Appeal

The facts appear in the Court's opinion

LORD WIDGERY C.J.: This is a reference to the court by the Attorney-General on a point of law seeking the opinion of the court pursuant to section 36 of the Criminal Justice Act 1972. . . .

The facts of the present case, which I take from the terms of the reference itself, are these:

"A police constable found an unlocked, unattended car containing packages of new clothing which he suspected, and which in fact subsequently proved to be stolen. The officer removed the rotor arm from the vehicle to immobilise it, and kept observation. After about ten minutes, the accused appeared, got into the van and attempted to start the engine. When questioned by the officer, he gave an implausible explanation, and was arrested."

Upon those facts two charges were brought against the respondent: one of stealing the woollen goods, the new clothing, which were in the back of the car in question and secondly and alternatively of receiving those goods knowing them to be stolen. The trial judge quite properly ruled there was no evidence to support the first charge, and that he would not leave that to the jury, but an argument developed as to whether the second count should be left to the jury or not. Counsel for the respondent in the court below had submitted at the close of the prosecution case that there was no case to answer, relying on section 24(3) of the Theft Act 1968. That provides as follows:

" . . . no goods shall be regarded as having continued to be stolen goods after they have been restored to the person from whom they were stolen or to other lawful possession or custody. . . . "

The rest of the subsection is not relevant and I do not read it. It was therefore contended in the court below on the facts to which I have already referred that by virtue of section 24(3) the goods had been restored to other lawful possession or custody, namely the custody or possession of the police officer before the respondent appeared on the scene and sought to drive the car away. If that argument was sound of course it would follow that there was no case for the respondent to answer, because if in fact the police constable had restored the stolen goods to his own lawful possession or custody before the act relied upon as an act of receiving occurred, it would follow that they would not be stolen goods at the material time.

After hearing argument, the judge accepted the submission of the respondent and directed the jury that they should acquit on the receiving count. That has resulted in the Attorney-General referring the following point of law to us for an opinion under section 36 of the Criminal Justice Act 1972. He expresses the point in this way:

> "Whether stolen goods are restored to lawful custody within the meaning of section 24(3) of the Theft Act 1968 when a police officer, suspecting them to be stolen, examines and keeps observation on them with a view to tracing the thief or a handler."

One could put the question perhaps in a somewhat different way by asking whether upon the facts set out in the reference the conclusion as a matter of law was clear to the effect that the goods had ceased to be stolen goods. In other words, the question which is really in issue in this reference is whether the trial judge acted correctly in law in saying that those facts disclosed a defence within section 24(3).

Subsection (3) is not perhaps entirely happily worded. It has been pointed out in the course of argument that in the sentence which I have read there is only one relevant verb, and that is "restore." The section contemplates that the stolen goods should be restored to the person from whom they were stolen or to other lawful possession or custody. It is pointed out that the word "restore" although it is entirely appropriate when applied to restoration of the goods to the true owner, is not really an appropriate verb to employ if one is talking about a police officer stumbling upon stolen goods and taking them into his own lawful custody or possession.

We are satisfied that despite the absence of another and perhaps more appropriate verb, the effect of section 24(3) is to enable a defendant to plead that the goods had ceased to be stolen goods if the facts are that they were taken by a police officer in the course of his duty and reduced into possession by him.

Whether or not section 24(3) is intended to be a codification of the common law or not, it certainly deals with a topic upon which the common law provides a large number of authorities. I shall refer to some of them in a moment, although perhaps not all and it will be observed that from the earliest times it has been recognised that if the owner of stolen goods resumed possession of them, reduced them into his possession again, that they thereupon ceased to be stolen goods for present purposes and could certainly not be the subject of a later charge of receiving based on events after they had been reduced into possession. It is to be observed that at common law nothing short of a reduction into possession, either by the true owner or by a police officer acting in the execution of his duty, was regarded as sufficient to change the character of the goods from stolen goods into goods which were no longer to be so regarded.

I make that assertion true by a brief reference from the cases to which we have been referred. The first is *R. v. Dolan* (1855) 6 Cox C.C. 449. The facts there were that stolen goods were found in the pocket of a thief by the owner. The owner sent for a policeman, and the evidence given at the subsequent trial showed that after the policeman had taken the goods from the thief, the thief, the policeman and the owner went towards the shop owned and occupied by the prisoner at which the thief had asserted that he was hoping to sell the stolen goods. When they got near the shop the policeman gave the goods to the thief, who then went on ahead into the shop with a view to selling the goods, closely followed by the owner and the policeman, who proceeded to arrest the shop keeper. It was held there

"that the prisoner was not guilty of feloniously receiving stolen goods; inasmuch as they were delivered to him under the authority of the owner by a person to whom the owner had bailed them for that purpose."

Put another way, one can explain that decision on the broad principle to which I have already referred: the goods had already been returned to the possession of the owner before they were then released by him into the hands of the thief in order that the thief might approach the receiver with a view to the receiver being arrested. The principle thus enunciated is one which, as I have already said, is to be found in the other authorities to which we have been referred.

The next one which is similar is *R. v. Schmidt* (1866) L.R. 1 C.C.R. 15. The reference in the headnote suffices:

"Four thieves stole goods from the custody of a railway company, and afterwards sent them in a parcel by the same company's line addressed to the prisoner. During the transit the theft was discovered; and, on the arrival of the parcel at the station for its delivery, a policeman in the employ of the company opened it, and then returned it to the porter whose duty it was to deliver it, with instructions to keep it until further orders. On the following day the policeman directed the porter to take the parcel to its address, when it was received by the prisoner, who was afterwards convicted of receiving the goods knowing them to be stolen, . . ."

And it was held by the Court for Crown Cases Reserved "that the goods had got back into the possession of the owner, so as to be no longer stolen goods and that the conviction was wrong." Again unquestionably they had been reduced into the possession of the owner by the hand of the police officer acting on his behalf. They had not been allowed to continue their course unaffected. They had been taken out of circulation by the police officer, reduced into the possession of the owner or of the officer, and it matters not which, and thus had ceased to be stolen goods for present purposes. . . .

Then there is a helpful case, *R. v. Villensky* [1892] 2 Q.B. 597. Again it is a case of a parcel in the hands of carriers. This parcel was handed to the carriers in question for conveyance to the consignees, and whilst in the carriers' depot it was stolen by a servant of the carriers who removed the parcel to a different part of the premises and placed upon it a label addressed to the prisoners by a name by which they were known and a house where they resided. The superintendent of the carriers on receipt of information as to this and after the inspection of the parcel, directed it to be placed in the place from which the thief had removed it and to be sent with a special delivery receipt in a van accompanied by two detectives to the address shown on the label. At that address it was received by the prisoners under circumstances which clearly showed knowledge on their part that it had been stolen. The property in the parcel was laid in the indictment in the carriers and an offer to amend the indictment by substituting the names of the consignees was declined. The carriers' servant pleaded guilty to a count for larceny in the same indictment. It was there held by the Court for Crown Cases Reserved "that as the person in which the property was laid"—that is the carriers—"had resumed possession of the stolen property before its receipt by the prisoners, it had then ceased to be stolen property, and the prisoners could not be convicted of receiving it knowing it to have been stolen."

On p. 599 there is a brief and valuable judgment by Pollock B. in these terms:

"The decisions in *Dolan*, and *Schmidt*, are, in my judgment, founded on law and on solid good sense, and they should not be frittered away. It is, of course, frequently the case that when it is found that a person has stolen property he is watched; but the owner of the property, if he wishes to catch the receiver, does not resume possession of the stolen goods; here the owners have done so, and the result is that the conviction must be quashed."

We refer to that brief judgment because it illustrates in a few clear words what is really the issue in the present case. When the police officer discovered these goods and acted as he did, was the situation that he had taken possession of the goods, in which event, of course, they ceased to be stolen goods? or was it merely that he was watching the goods with a view to the possibility of catching the receiver at a later stage? I will turn later to a consideration of those two alternatives.

Two other cases should, I think, be mentioned at this stage. The next one is *R.* v. *King* [1938] 2 All E.R. 662. We are now getting to far more recent times. The appellant here was convicted with another man of receiving stolen goods knowing them to have been stolen. A fur coat had been stolen and shortly afterwards the police went to a flat where they found the man Burns and told him they were enquiring about some stolen property. He at first denied that there was anything there but finally admitted the theft and produced a parcel from a wardrobe. While a policeman was in the act of examining the contents of the parcel, the telephone bell rang. Burns answered it and the police heard him say: "Come along as arranged." The police then suspended operations and about 20 minutes later the appellant arrived, and, being admitted by Burns, said "I have come for the coat. Harry sent me." This was heard by the police, who were hiding at the time. The coat was handed to the appellant by Burns, so that he was actually in possession of it. It was contended that the possession by the police amounted to possession by the owner of the coat, and that, therefore, the coat was not stolen property at the time the appellant received it. Held by the Court of Appeal: that the coat had not been in the possession of the police and it was therefore still stolen when the appellant received it. . . .

The most recent case on the present topic, but of little value in the present problems is *Haughton* v. *Smith* [*ante*, p. 479], in the House of Lords. The case being of little value to us in our present problems, I will deal with it quite briefly. It is a case where a lorry load of stolen meat was intercepted by police, somewhere in the North of England, who discovered that the lorry was in fact full of stolen goods. After a brief conference they decided to take the lorry on to its destination with a view to catching the receivers at the London end of the affair. So the lorry set off for London with detectives both in the passenger seat and in the back of the vehicle, and in due course was met by the defendant at its destination in London. In that case before this court it was conceded, as it had been conceded below, that the goods had been reduced into the possession of the police when they took possession of the lorry in the

North of England, so no dispute in this court or later in the House of Lords was raised on that issue. It is, however, to be noted that three of their Lordships, when the matter got to the House of Lords, expressed some hesitation as to the propriety of the prosecution conceding in that case that the goods had been reduced to the possession of the police when the lorry was first intercepted. Since we cannot discover on what ground those doubts were expressed either from the report of the speeches or from the report of the argument, we cannot take advantage of that case in the present problem.

Now we return to the present problem again with those authorities in the background: did the conduct of the police officer, as already briefly recounted, amount to a taking of possession of the woollen goods in the back seat of the motor car? What he did, to repeat the essential facts, was: that seeing these goods in the car and being suspicious of them because they were brand new goods and in an unlikely position, he removed the rotor arm and stood by in cover to interrogate any driver of the car who might subsequently appear. Did that amount to a taking possession of the goods in the back of the car? In our judgment it depended primarily on the intentions of the police officer. If the police officer seeing these goods in the back of the car had made up his mind that he would take them into custody, that he would reduce them into his possession or control, take charge of them so that they could not be removed and so that he would have the disposal of them, then it would be a perfectly proper conclusion to say that he had taken possession of the goods. On the other hand, if the truth of the matter is that he was of an entirely open mind at that stage as to whether the goods were to be seized or not and was of an entirely open mind as to whether he should take possession of them or not, but merely stood by so that when the driver of the car appeared he could ask certain questions of that driver as to the nature of the goods and why they were there, then there is no reason whatever to suggest that he had taken the goods into his possession or control. It may be, of course, that he had both objects in mind. It is possible in a case like this that the police officer may have intended by removing the rotor arm both to prevent the car from being driven away and to enable him to assert control over the woollen goods as such. But if the jury came to the conclusion that the proper explanation of what had happened was that the police officer had not intended at that stage to reduce the goods into his possession or to assume the control of them, and at that stage was merely concerned to ensure that the driver, if he appeared, could not get away without answering questions, then in that case the proper conclusion of the jury would have been to the effect that the goods had not been reduced into the possession of the police and therefore a defence under section 24(3) of the Theft Act 1968 would not be of use to this particular defendant.

In the light of those considerations it has become quite obvious that the trial judge was wrong in withdrawing the issue from the jury. As a matter of law he was not entitled to conclude from the facts which I have set out more than once that these goods were reduced into the possession of the police officer. What he should have done in our opinion would have been to have left that issue to the jury for decision, directing the jury that they should find that the prosecution case was without substance if they thought that the police officer had assumed control of the goods as such and reduced them into his possession. Whereas on the other hand, they should have found the case proved, assuming that they were satisfied about its other elements, if they were of the opinion that the police officer in removing the rotor arm and standing by and watching was doing no

more than ensure that the driver should not get away without
interrogation and was not at that stage seeking to assume possession of
the goods as such at all. That is our opinion.

Opinion accordingly

Note

It is not always a question of fact whether the owner or police
have reduced the goods into possession. In *M.P.C.* v. *Streeter*
(1980) 71 Cr.App.R. 113, the owner's security officer initialled the
goods and alerted the police, who kept watch and followed the
defendant when he picked up the goods. It was held by the
Divisional Court that the magistrates were wrong to conclude that
this was a reduction into the possession of the owner, and the case
was sent back with a direction to convict.

ii. Otherwise than in the Course of Stealing

R. v. Pitham and Hehl
(1986) 65 Cr.App.R. 45
Court of Appeal

P. and H. were charged with burglary along with M. M. was convicted
of burglary but P. and H. were acquitted, when it appeared that M had
invited them into the victim's house and offered them the victim's
furniture. They paid him for it and took it away. P. and H. were also
charged with handling stolen goods and were convicted of this. They
appealed on the ground that the handling was not "otherwise than in
the course of stealing."

LAWTON L.J.: . . . What was the appropriation in this case? The jury found
that the two appellants had handled the property *after* Millman has stolen
it. That is clear from their acquittal of these two appellants on count 3 of
the indictment which had charged them jointly with Millman. What had
Millman done? He had assumed the rights of the owner. He had done that
when he took the two appellants to 20 Parry Road, showed them the
property and invited them to buy what they wanted. He was then acting
as the owner. He was then, in the words of the statute, "assuming the
rights of the owner." The moment he did that he appropriated McGregor's
goods to himself. The appropriation was complete. After this appropriation
had been completed there was no question of these two appellants taking
part, in the words of section 22, in dealing with the goods "in the course
of the stealing."
    It follows that no problem arises in this case. It may well be that some of
the situations which the two learned professors envisage and discuss in
their books may have to be dealt with at some future date, but not in this
case. The facts are too clear.
    Mr. Murray suggested the learned judge should have directed the jury
in some detail about the possibility that the appropriation had not been an
instantaneous appropriation, but had been one which had gone on for
some time. He submitted that it might have gone on until such time as the
furniture was loaded into the appellants' van. For reasons we have already
given that was not a real possibility in this case. It is no part of a judge's

duty to give the jury the kind of lecture on the law which may be appropriate for a professor to give to a class of undergraduates. We commend the judge for not having involved himself in a detailed academic analysis of the law relating to this case when on the facts it was as clear as anything could be that either these appellants had helped Millman to steal the goods, or Millman had stolen them and got rid of them by sale to these two appellants. We can see nothing wrong in the learned judge's approach to this case and on that particular ground we affirm what he did and said. . . .

Appeal dismissed

Questions

1. Does it follow that Millman, the thief, was also guilty of handling? See forms of handling below.

2. If he was guilty, is that a satisfactory result? See *infra*.

Criminal Law Revision Committee's Eighth Report, Cmnd. 2977

"§ 131 [Justifying the phrase 'otherwise than in the course of the stealing'] Under the definition a thief may be liable for handling if, after the theft is complete, he does some of the things mentioned in the definition for someone else, for example if he helps a receiver to dispose of the goods. Since it might be thought too severe to make a thief guilty of handling in such a case, we thought of providing that a thief should not be guilty of handling by reason of doing any of the things mentioned in the definition in respect of goods which he has himself stolen. But we decided not to include the provision. If after the theft is complete the thief takes part in a separate transaction for the disposal of the goods, it seems right that he should be guilty of handling like anybody else involved in the transaction."

Notes

1. This compromise by the C.L.R.C. is not without its awkwardness in practice. The offences of theft and handling are not entirely mutually exclusive, in that D can be guilty of both if, after the theft is complete, he takes part in a separate transaction for the disposal of the goods. But apart from the difficult question of what is a separate transaction, as to which see *R. v. Pitham and Hehl, supra*, in practice in many cases where D is inferentially guilty of handling, by being in possession of goods which have recently been stolen by someone, there will be nothing to suggest one way or the other whether he was the thief and his possession arose out of the stealing. Although separate counts for theft and handling may be included in one indictment, the difficulty remains that the jury may well be sure that D is guilty of either theft *or* handling, but are not sure which. In such a case, they may not convict of either. Their duty is to consider the theft which made the goods stolen goods, and if they are satisfied that D committed it, to convict him of theft. If they are not so satisfied, they must acquit him of theft and go on to consider whether he handled the goods with guilty knowledge. They are not entitled to say, "We are

satisfied he committed one or the other," and then go on to convict of the offence which seems more probable: see *Att.-Gen. for Hong Kong* v. *Yip Kai-Foon* [1988] 1 All E.R. 153 (P.C.).

2. Of course many (though not all) acts of handling are themselves appropriations of property belonging to another with intent to deprive the owner permanently. Any handler who deals with the goods himself (as opposed to merely "arranging", or "assisting" someone else), commits theft when he does so, and if the alternative count for theft is drafted sufficiently widely to cover both the original taking and the subsequent dealing with the goods, then even if there is doubt about whether the original theft was by him and his act of handling was in the course of that theft, he may still, on a suitably careful direction, be convicted of theft in respect of the appropriation in the act of handling. See *Stapylton* v. *O'Callaghan* [1973] 2 All E.R. 782.

Question

Were Pitham and Heyl rightly acquitted of burglary? (See, *post*, Chap. 14.) When they took the goods from Millman, did not they dishonestly appropriate property belonging to the victim? Did they not enter the victim's house as trespassers with the intent to commit that theft? See next case.

R. v. *Gregory* (1981) 77 Cr.App.R. 41 (C.A.) The jury were allowed to convict D. of burglary if they thought that he had gone to V.'s house at the invitation of A. and B. with the intention of buying V.'s goods which they had stolen. D. appealed on the ground that since, according to *R.* v. *Pitham & Heyl*, the theft of the goods by A. & B. would have been complete by the time D. dealt with them, his offence was handling, not burglary. In upholding the conviction, the Court of Appeal distinguished *R.* v. *Pitham & Heyl* as being a case of "what might be called instantaneous appropriation. But not every appropriation ... need be or indeed is instantaneous."

[After quoting Eveleigh L.J. in *R.* v. *Hale, ante,* p. 745]

"Nor do we think that in a given criminal enterprise involving theft there can necessarily be only one 'appropriation' within section 3(1) of the Theft Act 1968. It seems to us that the question of whether, when and by whom there has been an appropriation of property has always to be determined by the jury having regard to the circumstances of the case. The length of time involved, the manner in which it came about and the number of people who can properly be said to have taken part in an appropriation will vary according to those circumstances. In a case of burglary of a dwelling-house and before any property is removed from it, it may consist of a continuing process and involve either a single appropriation by one or more persons or a number of appropriations of the property in the house by several persons at different times during the same incident. If this were not a correct exposition of the law of appropriation, startling and disturbing consequences could arise out of the presence of two or more trespassers in a dwelling-house. Thus a person who may have more the appearance of a handler than the thief can nevertheless still be convicted of theft, and thus of burglary, if the jury are satisfied that with the requisite dishonest intent, he appropriated, or took part in the appropriation, of another person's goods."

Question

To uphold the conviction, was it necessary to distinguish *R.* v. *Pitham & Heyl*?

iii. Forms of Handling

Notes

1. The offence is not confined to "receiving," as before 1968. It can be committed either by "receiving" or by "undertaking or assisting in the goods' retention, removal, disposal or realisation by or for the benefit of another person," or "arranging" to do any of these things.

2. If the goods are not in fact stolen goods when any of these forms of handling is done, it is not the full offence (see *Haughton* v. *Smith, ante*, p. 479), although it may be an attempt to handle (see *R.* v. *Shivpuri, ante*, p. 485). An "arrangement" to receive or to undertake or assist in the goods' retention etc. entered into before they are stolen, may well be conspiracy to handle, but it is not the full offence (see *R.* v. *Park* (1988) 87 Cr.App.R. 164 C.A.), unless, presumably, the arrangement is ratified or confirmed in some way after the theft has taken place.

3. Receiving, or arranging to receive, may be entirely on the accused's own account; but if the form of handling alleged is one of the other matters mentioned in section 22(1), it must be "by or for the benefit of another person." On the meaning of this expression, see *R.* v. *Bloxham, post*, p. 821.

R. v. Pitchley
(1972) 57 Cr.App.R. 30
Court of Appeal

P.'s son handed P. £150 in order that P. should look after it for him. According to P., he paid it into his post office savings account, and then later became aware that the £150 was stolen. Because he did not wish to give his son away, P. did nothing about the money in the account until he was interviewed some days later by the police. He was convicted of "dishonestly handling goods, namely the sum of £150 ... knowing or believing the same to be stolen goods." He appealed.

CAIRNS L.J.: The indictment ... simply charged handling stolen goods without specifying whether it was under the first limb or under the second limb, and if the latter, under which part of the second limb of section 22(1) of the Theft Act; but the case that was presented by the prosecution at the trial was clearly presented in the alternative, that it was either under the first limb of receiving, or under the second limb for assisting in the retention of stolen goods. ...

The main point that has been taken by Mr. Kalisher, who is appearing for the appellant in this court, is that, assuming that the jury were not satisfied that the appellant received the money knowing it to have been stolen, and that is an assumption which clearly is right to make, then there was no evidence after that, that from the time when the money was put into the savings bank, that the appellant had done any act in relation to it. His evidence was, and there is no reason to suppose that the jury did not believe it, that at the time when he put the money into the savings bank he still did not know or believe that the money had been stolen—it was only at a later stage that he did. That was on the Saturday according to his evidence, and the position was that the money had simply remained in the savings bank from the Saturday, to the Wednesday when the police approached the appellant. It is fair to say that from the moment when he was approached he displayed the utmost frankness to the extent of correcting them when they said it was £100 to £150 and telling them where the post office savings book was so that the money could be got out again and restored to its rightful owner.

But the question is: Did the conduct of the appellant between the Saturday and the Wednesday amount to an assisting in the retention of this money for the benefit of his son Brian? The court has been referred to the case of *Brown* (1969) 53 Cr.App.R. 527 which was a case where stolen property had been put into a wardrobe at the appellant's house and when the police came to inquire about it the appellant said to them: "Get lost." The direction to the jury had been on the basis that it was for them consider whether in saying: "Get lost," instead of helping the police constable, he was dishonestly assisting in the retention of stolen goods. This court held that that was a misdirection but there are passages in the judgment in the case of *Brown* (*supra*) which, in the view of this court, are of great assistance in determining what is meant by "retention" in this section. I read first of all from p. 528 setting out the main facts a little more fully: "A witness named Holden was called by the prosecution. He gave evidence that he and others had broken into the café and had stolen the goods, and that he had brought them to the appellant's flat, where, incidentally, other people were sleeping, and had hidden them there; and he described how he had taken the cigarettes out of the packets, put them in the plastic bag and hidden them in the wardrobe. Holden went on to say that later and before the police arrived he told the appellant where the cigarettes were; in other words, he said that the appellant well knew that the cigarettes were there and they had been stolen." There was no evidence that the appellant had done anything active in relation to the cigarettes up to the time when the police arrived. The Lord Chief Justice, Lord Parker, in the course of his judgment at p. 530 said this: "It is urged here that the mere failure to reveal the presence of the cigarettes, with or without the addition of the spoken words 'Get lost,' was incapable itself of amounting to an assisting in the retention of the goods within the meaning of the subsection. The court has come to the conclusion that that is right. It does not seem to this court that the mere failure to tell the police, coupled if you like with the words 'Get lost,' amounts in itself to an assisting in their retention. On the other hand, those matters did afford strong evidence of what was the real basis of the charge here, namely, that knowing that they had been stolen, he permitted them to remain there or, as it has been put, provided accommodation for these stolen goods in order to assist Holden to retain them." Having said that the direction was incomplete the Lord Chief Justice went on to say: "The Chairman should have gone on to say: 'But the fact that he did not tell the constable that they were there and said "Get lost" is evidence from which you can infer, if you think right, that this man was permitting the goods to remain in his flat, and to that extent assisting in their retention by Holden.' " In this present case there was no question on the evidence of the appellant himself, that he was permitting the money to remain under his control in the savings bank book, and it is clear that this court in the case of *Brown* regarded such permitting as sufficient to constitute retention within the meaning of retention. That is clear from the passage I have already read, emphasised in the next paragraph, the final paragraph of the judgment, where the Lord Chief Justice said (at p. 531): "It is a plain case in which the proviso should be applied. It seems to this court that the only possible inference in these circumstances, once Holden was believed is that this man was assisting in their retention by housing the goods and providing accommodation for them, by permitting them to remain there." It is important to realise that that language was in relation to a situation where there was no evidence that anything active had been done by the appellant in relation to the goods.

In the course of the argument, Nield J. cited the dictionary meaning of the word "retain"—keep possession of, not lose, continue to have. In the view of this court, that is the meaning of the word "retain" in this section. It was submitted by Mr. Kalisher that, at any rate, it was ultimately for the jury to decide whether there was retention or not and that even assuming that what the appellant did was of such a character that it could constitute retention, the jury ought to have been directed that it was for them to determine as a matter of fact, whether that was so or not. The court cannot agree with that submission. The meaning of the word "retention" in the section is a matter of law in so far as the construction of the word is necessary. It is hardly a difficult question of construction because it is an ordinary English word and in the view of this court, it was no more necessary for the Deputy Chairman to leave the jury the question of whether or not what was done amounted to retention than it would be necessary for a judge in a case where goods had been handed to a person who knew that they had been stolen for him to direct the jury it was for them to decide whether or not that constituted receiving.

We are satisfied that no complaint of the summing-up which was made can be sustained and that there is no ground on which this verdict could be said to be unsafe or unsatisfactory. The appeal is therefore dismissed.

Appeal dismissed

R. v. Kanwar
[1982] 2 All E.R. 529
Court of Appeal

K.'s husband brought home stolen goods. K., knowing they were stolen, used them to furnish the house. Later she told lies to police officers about the goods in order to persuade them that they were not stolen. She was convicted of handling stolen goods by dishonestly assisting in their retention, and appealed.

CANTLEY J.: In *R. v. Thornhill*, decided in this court on May 15, 1981 (unreported), and in *R. v. Sanders* (see *infra*), it was held that merely using stolen goods in the possession of another does not constitute the offence of assisting in their retention. To constitute the offence, something must be done by the offender, and done intentionally and dishonestly, for the purpose of enabling the goods to be retained. Examples of such conduct are concealing or helping to conceal the goods, or doing something to

make them more difficult to find or to identify. Such conduct must be
done knowing or believing the goods to be stolen and done dishonestly
and for the benefit of another.

We see no reason why the requisite assistance should be restricted to
physical acts. Verbal representations, whether oral or in writing, for the
purpose of concealing the identity of stolen goods may, if made
dishonestly and for the benefit of another, amount to handling stolen
goods by assisting in their retention within the meaning of section 22 of
the Theft Act 1968.

The requisite assistance need not be successful in its object. It would be
absurd if a person dishonestly concealing stolen goods for the benefit of a
receiver could establish a defence by showing that he was caught in the
act. In the present case, if, while the police were in one part of the house,
the appellant, in order to conceal the painting had put it under a mattress
in the bedroom, it would not alter the nature of her conduct that the police
subsequently looked under the mattress and found the picture because
they expected to find it there or that they caught her in the act of putting
it there.

The appellant told these lies to the police to persuade them that the
picture and the mirror were not the stolen property which they had come
to take away but were her lawful property which she had bought. If that
was true, the articles should be left in the house. She was, of course,
telling these lies to protect her husband, who had dishonestly brought the
articles there but, in our view, she was nonetheless, at the time,
dishonestly assisting in the retention of the stolen articles.

In his summing up, the judge directed the jury as follows:

> "It would be quite wrong for you to convict this lady if all she did was
> to watch her husband bring goods into the house, even if she knew or
> believed that they were stolen goods because, no doubt, you would say
> to yourselves, 'What would she be expected to do about it?' Well, what
> the Crown say is that she knew or believed them to be stolen and that
> she was a knowing and willing party to their being kept in that house in
> those circumstances. The reason the Crown say that, and we shall be
> coming to the evidence, is that when questioned about a certain number
> of items, [the appellant] gave answers which the Crown say were not
> true and that she could not possibly have believed to be true and that
> she knew perfectly well were untruthful. So, say the prosecution, she
> was not just an acquiescent wife who could not do much about it, she
> was, by her conduct in trying to put the police officers as best she could
> off the scent, demonstrating that she was a willing and knowing party
> to those things being there and that she was trying to account for them.
> Well, it will be for you to say, but you must be satisfied before you can
> convict her on either of these counts, not only that she knew or believed
> the goods to be stolen, but that she actively assisted her husband in
> keeping them there; not by just passive acquiesence in the sense of
> saying, 'What can I do about it?' but in the sense of saying, 'How nice
> to have these things in our home, although they are stolen goods.' "

In so far as this direction suggests that the appellant would be guilty of
the offence if she was merely willing for the goods to be kept and used in
the house and was thinking that it was nice to have them there, although
they were stolen goods, it is a misdirection. We have considered whether
on that account the conviction ought to be quashed. However, the offence
was established by the uncontradicted evidence of the police officer which,
looked at in full, clearly shows that in order to mislead the officer who had
come to take away stolen goods, she misrepresented the identity of the

goods which she knew or believed to be stolen. We are satisfied that no miscarriage of justice has occurred and the appeal is accordingly dismissed.

Appeal dismissed

R. v. *Sanders* (1982) 75 Cr.App.R. 84 (C.A.): A., who owned a garage, stole some equipment. It was found in the garage being used by D., the son of A., who was employed there. He admitted he knew it was stolen. *Held,* mere use of goods knowing them to be stolen was not enough to found a conviction of assisting in the retention of them; he must have concealed, disguised, or held the goods pending disposal.

R. v. *Coleman* [1986] Crim.L.R. 56 (C.A.): D. and his wife purchased a flat in their joint names with money the wife had stolen, as D. well knew. *Held,* the *actus reus* was assisting in the disposal of the money, not getting the benefit, and the fact that D. had benefited from what his wife did was no proof that he had assisted her. There had to be evidence of helping or encouraging. On a proper direction, the jury could properly have inferred that D. told his wife to use the stolen money or agreed that she should do so; but they were not so directed, and it was impossible to say whether they would have done so; they might have inferred that the wife acted without assistance.

Questions

1. A, after stealing a gold watch, deposits it in the potting shed of his friend B. Later B and C, another friend, notice the watch, recognise it as stolen, and guess that A will return and remove it when he has the opportunity. Because they do not wish to "shop" A, both B and C reply "Get lost" when asked by a policeman if they have seen the watch. On this evidence, can either of them be convicted of handling?

2. A gives a fur coat to his wife B. He later tells her that he had stolen it in a burglary, but she continues to wear it. Is B guilty of handling?

3. A gives a fur coat to his wife B. When he later tells B that he bought the coat with the proceeds of a burglary he had committed, B sells the coat to a friend. Does B undertake the disposal or realisation of the coat for the benefit of another? See next case.

R. v. Bloxham
[1982] 1 All E.R. 582
House of Lords

B. agreed to buy a car which, unknown to him, had been stolen. Several months later, he became convinced that it had been stolen, because his vendor failed to produce the registration documents. B. therefore sold the car to a man he did not know who was prepared to buy it without the documents. B. was charged with handling stolen goods contrary to section 22 of the Theft Act 1968. After a ruling by the trial judge that the sale was a dishonest realisation of the car for the benefit of another person, B. pleaded guilty. He appealed on the ground that the judge's ruling was wrong in law.

LORD BRIDGE OF HARWICH: The critical words to be construed are "undertakes ... their ... disposal or realization ... for the benefit of another person." Considering these words first in isolation, it seems to me that, if A. sells his own goods to B., it is a somewhat strained use of language to describe this as a disposal or realisation of the goods for the benefit of B. True it is that B. obtains a benefit from the transaction, but it is surely more natural to say that the disposal or realisation is for A.'s benefit than for B.'s. It is the purchase, not the sale, that is for the benefit of B. It is only when A. is selling as agent for a third party C. that it would be entirely natural to describe the sale as a disposal or realisation for the benefit of another person.

But the words cannot, of course, be construed in isolation. They must be construed in their context. ... The ... words contemplate four activities (retention, removal, disposal, realisation). The offence can be committed in relation to any one of these activities in one or other of two ways. First, the offender may himself undertake the activity *for the benefit* of another person. Second, the activity may be undertaken *by* another person and the offender may assist him. ... If the analysis holds good it must follow, I think, that the category of other persons contemplated by the subsection is subject to the same limitations in whichever way the offence is committed. Accordingly, a purchaser, as such, of stolen goods cannot, in my opinion, be "another person" within the subsection, since his act of purchase could not sensibly be described as a disposal or realisation of the stolen goods *by* him. Equally, therefore, even if the sale to him could be described as a disposal or realisation for his benefit, the transaction is not, in my view, within the ambit of the subsection. ...

Appeal allowed: conviction quashed

Question

What offence was committed by Bloxham if (i) the purchaser from him knew or believed that the car was stolen, (ii) the purchaser did not know or believe that?

iv. Knowing or Believing them to be Stolen Goods

Notes

1. *R.* v. *McCullum* (1973) 57 Cr.App.R. 645: M. was charged with handling by assisting in the retention of stolen guns and ammunition. The guns and ammunition were in a suitcase in her possession. Part of her case was that she did not know what was in the suitcase. A direction by the trial judge that knowledge or belief that the suitcase contained stolen goods without knowledge of the nature of the goods was sufficient, was upheld by the Court of Appeal, even though the indictment had specified the goods as guns and ammunition.

2. *R.* v. *Hulbert* (1979) 69 Cr.App.R. 243: (C.A.): H. was charged with handling stolen clothes. H. admitted to the police that she bought them at low prices in public houses from persons who told her they were stolen. *Held*, the information from the sellers was evidence that she knew they were stolen, but no evidence that they were stolen (being hearsay). However, her appeal was dismissed because the *circumstances*, admitted by her, (namely

purchases in public houses at low prices) were *prima facie* evidence that the goods were stolen. See also *A.-G.'s Reference* (*No. 4 of 1979*), *ante*, p. 805.

3. The previous law required the accused to receive "knowing" that the goods were stolen. The C.L.R.C., Cmnd. 2977 § 134, justified the addition of the alternative "or believing" as follows:

> "It is a serious defect of the present law that actual knowledge that the property was stolen must be proved. Often the prosecution cannot prove this. In many cases indeed guilty knowledge does not exist, although the circumstances of the transaction are such that the receiver ought to be guilty of an offence. The man who buys goods at a ridiculously low price from an unknown seller whom he meets in a public house may not *know* that the goods were stolen, and he may take the precaution of asking no questions. Yet it may be clear on the evidence that he *believes* that the goods were stolen. In such cases the prosecution may fail (rightly, as the law now stands) for want of proof of guilty knowledge. We consider that a person who handles stolen goods ought to be guilty if he believes them to be stolen. A purchaser who is merely careless, in that he does not make sufficient inquiry, will not be guilty of the offence under the new law any more than under the old."

4. *R.* v. *White* (1859) 1 F. & F. 665: W. was charged with receiving lead, he well knowing it to have been stolen. Bramwell B. (to the jury): "The knowledge charged in this indictment need not be such knowledge as would be acquired if the prisoner had actually seen the lead stolen; it is sufficient if you think the circumstances were such, accompanying the transaction, as to make the prisoner believe that it had been stolen." Since a receiver or handler can only rarely "know" about the history of the goods, this direction may be thought to be only common sense. The question is, what is added by the inclusion of the words "or believing" in section 22?

5. *Haughton* v. *Smith* [1975] A.C. 485 (H.L.) (*ante*, p. 479): Viscount Dilhorne, at p. 503: "It is, in my opinion, clear that section 22(1) of the Theft Act 1968 does not make the handling of goods which are not stolen goods an offence if a person believes them to have been stolen. The offence created by that section is in relation to goods which are stolen and it is an ingredient of the offence that the accused must know or believe them to have been stolen. The word 'believing' was, I think, inserted to avoid the possibility of an accused being acquitted when there was ample evidence that he believed the goods stolen, but no proof that he knew they were."

6. *R.* v. *Griffiths* (1974) 60 Cr.App.R. 14 (C.A.): James L.J., at p. 18: "To direct the jury that the offence is committed if the defendant, suspecting that the goods were stolen, deliberately shut his eyes to the circumstances as an alternative to knowing or believing the goods were stolen is a misdirection. To direct the jury that, in common sense and in law, they may find that the defendant knew or believed the goods to be stolen because he deliberately closed his eyes to the circumstances is a perfectly

proper direction." [On "Wilful blindness," see, degrees of knowledge, *ante*, p. 102.]

R. v. Hall
(1985) 81 Cr.App.R. 205
Court of Appeal

D. was discovered in his own flat examining stolen pictures and silver which had been brought there by A. and B. D. said that A. and B. had told him that the property was from a house clearance sale; but that when he saw the way the goods were wrapped he concluded that they were not from a house clearance in the ordinary sense (*i.e.* he suspected they had been stolen). He was convicted of handling the goods after a summing-up outlined in the Judgment below and appealed.

BOREHAM J.: (After disposing of another ground of appeal): That brings us to Mr. Owen's second submission. That is that the learned judge did not make clear to the jury what state of mind had to be proved if they were to convict of this offence, namely that the defendant either knew or believed that the goods were stolen. In particular, he contends that no clear distinction was drawn between belief and suspicion. He has reminded us, if reminder was necessary, that this has been a recurrent problem in this Court as a number of comparatively recent decisions of the Court demonstrate. With his encouragement we have concluded that the time has come for us to give some guidelines on this subject to those who have to direct juries upon it.

We think that a jury should be directed along these lines. A man may be said to know that goods are stolen when he is told by someone with first hand knowledge (someone such as the thief of the burglar) that such is the case. Belief, of course, is something short of knowledge. It may be said to be the state of mind of a person who says to himself: "I cannot say I know for certain that these goods are stolen, but there can be no other reasonable conclusion in the light of all the circumstances, in the light of all that I have heard and seen." Either of those two states of mind is enough to satisfy the words of the statute. The second is enough (that is, belief) even if the defendant says to himself: "Despite all that I have seen and all that I have heard, I refuse to believe what my brain tells me is obvious." What is not enough, of course, is mere suspicion. "I suspect that these goods may be stolen, but it may be on the other hand that they are not." That state of mind, of course, does not fall within the words "knowing or believing." As I understand it, Mr. Owen accepts those propositions.

The question remains whether the learned judge has, in substance, directed the jury in those terms. He commences this part of his summing-up (at page 58E) thus: "It is 'knowing or believing,' not knowing and believing, 'knowing *or* believing.' If you were to come to the conclusion in this case that the thieves made it perfectly plain to this Defendant that they had been out stealing that night and that they told him so, that is knowing, is it not, because he has been told so by the thieves themselves, so he knows and that would be an end of the case. But, members of the jury, the law has spread the net wider in pursuit of those who are dishonest with other people's property, it is knowing or believing. You cannot shut your eyes to the obvious. You know what believing means because we all believe things every day. We look at all the circumstances and we make up our minds about something, we come to a belief about them having looked at all the circumstances of the case and we say yes, everything points in that direction and I believe that such and such is the fact. We do it all the time and, members of the jury, it means exactly the same in this charge."

In our judgment, that is an impeccable direction to the jury so far as both knowledge and belief is concerned. At the end of the day I think that is not really disputed by Mr. Owen. He has two complaints to make. The first is this: that earlier in his summing-up the judge had spoken to the jury in such a way as may have given them the impression that it was not so much the appellant's attitude of mind, as what the jury thought would have been their attitude of mind had they been present, that was important. It is unnecessary to go into detail. It is clear, in our judgment, that in the passage quoted the learned judge was indicating to the jury their approach to the problem that they had to resolve, namely what was in the appellant's mind. Indeed, a little later in the summing-up, in a passage which follows almost immediately after that which I have just read, he emphasised to the jury that it was the appellant that they were trying, that it was his state of mind that was in issue and that they should consider not only those matters that he had previously suggested they might consider, but what sort of man this was, namely whether he was a man of acute perception or whether he was a dullard, whether he was a fool who would not recognise what most people would recognise before their two eyes and so forth. They had seen him, they should judge him: and of course that was entirely appropriate.

He then asked the question: "What was the evidence in front of him that morning? What was the evidence staring him in the face about those goods? Members of the jury, you then ask yourselves what did he believe?" In our judgment again, it was a proper, clear and accurate direction and a proper approach for the jury. But it did not stop there; he went on with these words: "The law says you cannot simply say it is perfectly obvious but I am not going to believe it. In other words, you cannot shut your eyes to the plain and obvious. You have got to make up your mind did he know or, if you say there is not enough evidence for us to find that he knew, in other words that the thief told him, did he on the other hand believe?" Again, in our judgment, that was an entirely appropriate and clear direction.

Mr. Owen's last complaint is that the expression "You cannot shut your eyes to the plain and obvious" is capable of being misunderstood by a jury unless a clear distinction is drawn for the jury's benefit between suspicion and belief, such a distinction as we have attempted to draw. We were referred to the case of *R.* v. *Griffiths* (1974) 60 Cr.App.R. 14. That too was a case of handling stolen goods and, of course, as in most cases, one of the central issues was the knowledge or belief of the defendant. The learned judge in that case had directed the jury at one stage in these terms: "It is a matter for you whether to decide at that moment that Mr. Griffiths came at that moment into the category of someone who did have real suspicion that the goods were stolen and deliberately shut his eyes to the circumstances. It is a matter for you to decide what you think." The difference—and the important difference—between what was said in *R.* v. *Griffiths* and what was said here is that the judge in *R.* v. *Griffiths* was referring to shutting one's eyes in the context of suspicion. That was not an error into which this learned judge fell. When he was talking of "shutting your eyes to the plain and obvious" he was still dealing with the matter of belief. In our judgment, as we have attempted to point out, in that context that is an entirely appropriate observation to make. There is no suspicion here that the jury may have been confused and thus may not have drawn the distinction between suspicion and belief.

At the end of the day and almost at the end of his summing-up the learned judge dealt with the question of suspicion and rightly directed the jury that that, of course, was not enough. He did not confuse the issue or the jury by referring to shutting one's eyes in that context. He had already dealt with that in its proper context. In those circumstances, this submission too must fail. . . .

Appeal dismissed

Question

After quoting the C.L.R.C. on their reasons for adding "or believing" to "knowing" in section 22 (see *ante*, p. 823), Spencer comments ("Handling, Theft and the *Mala Fide* Purchaser") [1985] Crim.L.R. 92: "Yet the courts with surprising perversity have interpreted 'knowing or believing' to mean 'knowing or knowing.'" Do you think that, after *R. v. Hall*, this charge is still sustainable against the judiciary?

v. Dishonesty

Notes

1. Dishonesty must exist at the time of the act alleged to constitute handling. On Dishonesty in Theft, see *ante*, p. 733.

2. In a case at York Assizes in 1971, it was held by Shaw J. that a person who, on instructions from the owner, arranged with the thieves for the return of the goods, was not guilty of *dishonestly* assisting in the goods' disposal. See Harvey, "What Does Dishonesty Mean?" [1972] Crim.L.R. 213. In *R. v. Roberts*, (1985) 84 Cr.App.R. 117, a case on dishonesty generally, one ground of appeal was that dishonest in section 22 meant dishonest in relation to the loser of the goods and not dishonest in a more general way. The Court of Appeal held that the York case was no authority for this, but as Roberts was not acting for the owner, the question of whether dishonesty must be *vis-à-vis* the owner did not really arise. But in the York case, D was acting throughout for the owner, who had recruited him for the purpose of recovering the goods. Smith comments, [1986] Crim.L.R. 123:

> "It is very difficult to see how the sole owner of the stolen property could be said to be dishonest for the purposes of handling; and, as the defendant was identified with her, it seems to follow that he could not be held to be dishonest either. The same act may frequently constitute [both theft and handling]. The House of Lords held in *Morris* (*ante*, p. 667) that theft 'involves not an act expressly or impliedly authorised by the owner but an act by way of adverse interference with or usurpation of the owner's rights.' Probably a similar principle ought to apply to handling. This suggests that the true test of dishonesty is whether there is dishonesty *vis-à-vis* the owner (or one of the owners, if there are more than one). Who else is there in respect of whom the act specified in section 22 could be dishonest? Since they are all acts of dealing with property, it seems that they could only be dishonest with respect to

someone with a proprietary interest. Perhaps the court has the public in mind but it is noteworthy that in the 1972 case Shaw J. did not find considerations of public policy to be of assistance. The public interest in matters of this kind is defended by the offences of perverting the course of justice and those contained in sections 4 and 5 of the Criminal Law Act 1967 as well as section 23 of the Theft Act 1968 (Advertising rewards for return of goods stolen or lost).''

Questions

1. In *R. v. Matthews* [1950] 1 All E.R. 137, M received what he well knew were stolen goods, intending to hand them over to the police. Later, he changed his mind and did not hand them over. It was held that this did not amount to receiving stolen goods. If a similar case arose today, would M be guilty of handling? See forms of handling, *supra*.

2. B owed A £10. Being short of cash, A broke into B's desk and helped himself to £10. He later admitted to the police that he knew he had no right to do this. A shared the money with C. C knew how A got the money, but thought that since B owed A £10, A was entitled to help himself. A was convicted of theft. Ought C to be convicted of handling?

CHAPTER 14

BURGLARY AND KINDRED OFFENCES

	PAGE			PAGE
1. Burglary	828	3.	Going Equipped	848
i. Entry	829		i. Has with him	848
ii. As a Trespasser	831		ii. When not at his Place of	
iii. Buildings or Parts of Buildings	838		Abode	849
iv. Intent to Commit an Offence			iii. Any Article	850
in the Building	839		iv. For use in the Course or in	
v. The Ulterior Offence	845		Connection with any Bur-	
2. Aggravated Burglary	846		glary, Theft or Cheat.	851

1. BURGLARY

Theft Act 1968, section 9, as amended by Criminal Justice Act 1991, section 26(2)

"(1) A person is guilty of burglary if—

(a) he enters any building or part of a building as a trespasser and with intent to commit any such offence as is mentioned in subsection (2) below; or

(b) having entered any building or part of a building as a trespasser he steals or attempts to steal anything in the building or that part of it or inflicts or attempts to inflict on any person therein any grievous bodily harm.

(2) The offences referred to in subsection (1)(a) above are offences of stealing anything in the building or part of a building in question, of inflicting on any person therein any grievous bodily harm or raping any woman therein, and of doing unlawful damage to the building or anything therein."

"(3) A person guilty of burglary shall on conviction on indictment be liable to imprisonment for a term not exceeding—

(a) where the offence was committed in respect of a building or part of a building which is a dwelling, fourteen years;

(b) in any other case, ten years.

(4) References in subsections (1) and (2) above to a building, and the reference in subsection (3) above to a building which is a dwelling, shall apply also to an inhabited vehicle or vessel, and shall apply to any such vehicle or vessel at times when the person having a habitation in it is not there as well as at times when he is."

Note

The range of conduct prohibited by this section was before the Theft Act distributed between the offences of burglary, housebreaking and sacrilege, and the law was found in sections 25, 26 and 27 of the Larceny Act 1916. There were many intricate and confusing differences between the different offences; burglary proper needed a dwelling-house, a breaking and entering, and an intention to commit a felony, and it had to be committed in the night. The present offence may take place at any time of day. Any kind of building is now covered, and vehicles and vessels are also covered provided they are inhabited. Burglary in such a vehicle or vessel, or in a dwelt-in building, attracts a higher maximum penalty.

i. Entry

Note

Breaking, round which a great number of technicalities clustered, is no longer necessary, but entry is still required. This, too, was a highly technical concept, and as entry is not defined in the Act, it remains a question to that extent the pre-existing meaning is still operative. In that meaning, the law made a distinction between entry by the defendant's body and entry by an instrument wielded by him.

R. v. Hughes
(1785) 1 Leach 406
Old Bailey Sessions

H. with intent to steal property from a house, inserted a centre bit into a door near the bolt. The end of the bit penetrated the door but no part of the prisoner's body entered the house. He was indicted for burglary. On the question of whether there was an entry:

COUNSEL FOR THE PRISONER: It has been held that the smallest degree of entry whatever is sufficient to satisfy the law. Putting a hand, or a foot, or a pistol over the threshold of the door, or a hook or other instrument through the broken pane of a window ... have been decided to be burglarious entries; but the principle of all these new determinations is, that there has been such a previous breaking of the castle of the proprietor, as to render his property insecure. ... And in those cases where an instrument has formed any part of the question, it has always been taken to mean, not the instrument by which the breaking was made, but the instrument, as a hook, a fork or other thing by which the property was capable of being removed, introduced subsequent to the act of breaking. ... In the present case, the introduction of the instrument is part of the act of breaking, but it is impossible to conceive that it was introduced for the purpose of purloining property, for it is incapable of performing such an office.

The prisoner was acquitted

Note

But the insertion of any part of the body was an entry, whether the purpose of the insertion was to commit the ulterior felony or merely to effect entry: see *R. v. Bailey* (1818) R. & R. 341. However, see now *R. v. Collins*, below, particularly the following remark of Edmund Davies L.J.: "Unless the jury were entirely satisfied that the defendant made *an effective and substantial entry* into the bedroom without the complainant doing or saying anything to cause him to believe that she was consenting to his entering it, he ought not to be convicted of the offence charged." (Italics supplied.) In *R.* v. *Brown* [1985] Crim.L.R. 212, (C.A.), it was held that the word "enter" in section 9 did not require that the whole of D's body be within the building. The use by Edmund-Davies L.J. in *R.* v. *Collins* of the words "substantial" and "effective" in relation to entry did not support that contention. "Substantial" did not materially assist in the matter, but a jury should be directed that, in order to convict, they must be satisfied that the entry was "effective."

Griew (§ 4.19) suggests that this word is not much more helpful. To achieve sensible results in some cases it would have to mean "more or less completely in," but in others it would have to mean "enough in to enable D to attempt the ulterior offence," *e.g.* in one case, the ulterior offence is intended to occur deep inside the building in an inner room but most of D's body is across the threshold; in another case, only a hand is in but that is enough to enable D to try to reach an article he intends to steal. Both cases ought to count as entry, but they can only do so if "effective" is given two different meanings. In practice however, all such cases could anyway be charged as attempted burglary, as could any doubtful "instrument" cases, as to which see *infra.*

Smith, The Law of Theft, §§ 344, 345

"§ 344 Even if the courts are willing to follow the common law in holding that the intrusion of any part of the body is an entry, they may be reluctant to preserve these technical rules regarding instruments, for they seem to lead to outlandish results. Thus it seems to follow from the common law rules that there may be an entry if a stick of dynamite is thrown into the building or if a bullet is fired from outside the building into it. What then if a time bomb is sent by parcel post? Has D. 'entered,' even though he is not on the scene at all—perhaps even abroad and outside the jurisdiction? Whether D. enters or not can hardly depend on how far away he is and the case seems indistinguishable from the others put. Yet this is hardly an 'entry' in the simple language as used and understood by ordinary literate men and women in which the Act is said to be written (*per* Lord Diplock, in *Treacy* v. *D.P.P.* [*ante*, p. 791]).

§ 345 There is, however, a cogent argument in favour of the common law rules which may be put as follows. If D. sends a child, under the age of ten, into the building to steal, this is obviously an entry by D, through an 'innocent agent,' under ordinary principles. Suppose that, instead of a child, D. sends in a monkey. It is hard to see that this should not equally be an entry by D. But if that point be conceded, it is admitted that the insertion of an animate instrument is an entry; and are we to distinguish between animate and inanimate instruments? Unless we are, the insertion of the hooks, etc., must also be an entry."

Question

Suppose D puts a child under 10 through a window, not to steal but to open a door and admit D who will himself steal. Is that entry by D?

ii. As a Trespasser

R. v. Collins
[1973] 1 Q.B. 100
Court of Appeal

C. was convicted of burglary with intent to commit rape in the circumstances outlined in the judgment below.

EDMUND-DAVIES L.J.: ... Let me relate the facts. Were they put into a novel or portrayed on the stage, they would be regarded as being so improbable as to be unworthy of serious consideration and as verging at times on farce. At about 2 o'clock in the early morning of Saturday, July 24, 1971, a young lady of 18 went to bed at her mother's home in Colchester. She had spent the evening with her boyfriend. She had taken a certain amount of drink, and it may be that this fact affords some explanation of her inability to answer satisfactorily certain crucial questions put to her at the trial.

She has the habit of sleeping without wearing night apparel in a bed which is very near the lattice-type window of her room. At one stage in her evidence she seemed to be saying that the bed was close up against the window which, in accordance with her practice, was wide open. In the photographs which we have before us, however, there appears to be a gap of some sort between the two, but the bed was clearly quite near the window.

At about 3.30 or 4 o'clock she awoke and she then saw in the moonlight a vague form crouched in the open window. She was unable to remember, and this is important, whether the form was on the outside of the window sill or on that part of the sill which was inside the room, and for reasons which will later become clear, that seemingly narrow point is of crucial importance.

The young lady then realised several things: first of all that the form in the window was that of a male; secondly, that he was a naked male; and thirdly, that he was a naked male with an erect penis. She also saw in the moonlight that his hair was blond. She thereupon leapt to the conclusion that her boyfriend, with whom for some time she had been on terms of regular and frequent sexual intimacy, was paying her an ardent nocturnal visit. She promptly sat up in bed, and the man descended from the sill and joined her in bed and they had full sexual intercourse. But there was something about him which made her think that things were not as they usually were between her and her boyfriend. The length of his hair, his voice as they exchanged what was described as "love talk," and other features led her to the conclusion that somehow there was something different. So she turned on the bed-side light, saw that her companion was not her boyfriend and slapped the face of the intruder, who was none other than the defendant. He said to her, "Give me a good time tonight," and got hold of her arm, but she bit him and told him to go. She then went into the bathroom and he promptly vanished.

The complainant said that she would not have agreed to intercourse if she had known that the person entering her room was not her boyfriend. But there was no suggestion of any force having been used upon her, and the intercourse which took place was undoubtedly effected with no resistance on her part.

The defendant was seen by the police at about 10.30 later that same morning. According to the police, the conversation which took place then elicited these points: He was very lustful the previous night. He had taken a lot of drink. ... He went on to say that he knew the complainant because he had worked around her house. On this occasion, during sexual intercourse—and according to the police evidence he added that he was determined to have a girl, by force if necessary, although that part of the police evidence he challenged—he went on to say that he walked around the house, saw a light in an upstairs bedroom, and he knew that this was the girl's bedroom. He found a step ladder, leaned it against the wall and climbed up and looked into the bedroom. He could see through the wide-open window a girl who was naked and asleep. So he descended the ladder and stripped off all his clothes, with the exception of his socks, because apparently he took the view that if the girl's mother entered the bedroom it would be easier to effect a rapid escape if he had his socks on than if he was in his bare feet. That is a matter about which we are not called upon to express any view, and would in any event find ourselves unable to express one.

Having undressed, he then climbed the ladder and pulled himself up on to the window sill. His version of the matter is that he was pulling himself in when she awoke. She then got up and knelt on the bed, she put her arms around his neck and body, and she seemed to pull him into the bed. He went on: "I was rather dazed because I didn't think she would want to know me. We kissed and cuddled for about 10 or 15 minutes and than I had it away with her but found it hard because I had had so much to drink."

The police officer said to the defendant: "It appears that it was your attention to have intercourse with this girl by force if necessary, and it was only pure coincidence that this girl was under the impression that you were her boyfriend and apparently that is why she consented to allowing you to have sexual intercourse with her." It was alleged that he then said, "Yes, I feel awful about this. It is the worst day of my life, but I know it could have been worse." Thereupon the officer said to him—and he challenges this: "What do you mean, you know it could have been worse?," to which he is alleged to have replied: "Well, my trouble is drink and I got very frustrated. As I've told you, I only wanted to have it away with a girl and I'm only glad I haven't really hurt her."

Then he made a statement under caution, in the course of which he said: "When I stripped off and got up the ladder I made my mind up that I was going to try and have it away with this girl. I feel terrible about this now, but I had too much to drink. I am sorry for what I have done."

In the course of his testimony, the defendant said that he would not have gone into the room if the girl had not knelt on the bed and beckoned him into the room. He said that if she had objected immediately to his being there or his having intercourse he would not have persisted. While he was keen on having sexual intercourse that night, it was only if he could find someone who was willing. He strongly denied having told the police that he would if necessary, have pushed over some girl for the purpose of having intercourse. ...

Now, one feature of the case which remained at the conclusion of the evidence in great obscurity is where exactly Collins was at the moment when, according to him, the girl manifested that she was welcoming him. Was he kneeling on the sill outside the window or was he already inside the room, having climbed through the window frame, and kneeling upon the inner sill? It was a crucial matter, for there were certainly three ingredients that it was incumbent upon the Crown to establish. Under section 9 of the Theft Act, 1968, which renders a person guilty of burglary if he enters any building or part of a building as a trespasser and with the intention of committing rape, the entry of the accused into the building must first be proved. Well, there is no doubt about that, for it is common ground that he did enter this girl's bedroom. Secondly, it must be proved that he entered as a trespasser. We will develop that point a little later. Thirdly, it must be proved that he entered as a trespasser with intent at the time of entry to commit rape therein.

The second ingredient of the offence—the entry must be as a trespasser—is one which has not, to the best of our knowledge, been previously canvassed in the courts. Views as to its ambit have naturally been canvassed by the textbook writers, and it is perhaps not wholly irrelevant to recall that those who were advising the Home Secretary before the Theft Bill was presented to Parliament had it in mind to get rid of some of the frequently absurd technical rules which had been built up in relation to the old requirement in burglary of a "breaking and entering." The cases are legion as to what this did or did not amount to, and happily it is not now necessary for us to consider them. But it was in order to get rid of those technical rules that a new test was introduced, namely, that the entry must be "as a trespasser."

What does that involve? According to the editors of *Archbold Criminal Pleading Evidence & Practice*, 37th ed. (1969), para. 1505: "Any intentional, reckless or negligent entry into a building will, it would appear, constitute a trespass if the building is in the possession of another person who does not consent to the entry. Nor will it make any difference that the entry was the result of a reasonable mistake on the part of the defendant, so far as trespass is concerned." If that be right, then it would be no defence for this man to say (and even were he believed in saying), "Well, I honestly thought that this girl was welcoming me into the room and I therefore entered, fully believing that I had her consent to go in." If *Archbold* is right, he would nevertheless be a trespasser, since the apparent consent of the girl was unreal, she being mistaken as to who was at her window. We disagree. We hold that, for the purposes of section 9 of the Theft Act, a person entering a building is not guilty of trespass if he enters without knowledge that he is trespassing or at least without acting recklessly as to whether or not he is unlawfully entering.

A view contrary to that of the editors of *Archbold* was expressed in Professor Smith's book on *The Law of Theft*, 1st ed. (1968), where, having given an illustration of an entry into premises, the author comments, at paragraph 462: "It is submitted that ... D. should be acquitted on the ground of lack of *mens rea*. Though, under the civil law, he entered as a trespasser, it is submitted that he cannot be convicted of the criminal offence unless he knew of the facts which caused him to be a trespasser or, at least, was reckless."

The matter has also been dealt with by Professor Griew, who in paragraph 4–05 of his work *The Theft Act* 1968 has this passage: "What if D. wrongly believes that he is not trespassing? His belief may rest on facts which, if true, would mean that he was not trespassing: for instance, he may enter a building by mistake, thinking that it is the one he has been invited to enter. Or his belief may be based on a false view of the legal effect of the known facts: for instance, he may misunderstand the effect of a contract granting him a right of passage through a building. Neither kind of mistake will protect him from tort liability for trespass. In either case, then, D. satisfies the literal terms of section 9(1): he 'enters ... as a trespasser.' But for the purposes of criminal liability a man should be judged on the basis of the facts as he believed them to be, and this should include making allowances for a mistake as to rights under the civil law. This is another way of saying that a serious offence like burglary should be held to require *mens rea* in the fullest sense of the phrase: D. should be liable for burglary only if he knowingly trespasses or is reckless as to whether he trespasses or not. Unhappily it is common for Parliament to omit to make clear whether *mens rea* is intended to be an element in a statutory offence. It is also, though not equally, common for the courts to supply the mental element by construction of the statute."

We prefer the view expressed by Professor Smith and Professor Griew to that of the editors of *Archbold*. In the judgment of this court there cannot be a conviction for entering premises "as a trespasser" within the meaning of section 9 of the Theft Act unless the person entering does so knowing that he is a trespasser and nevertheless deliberately enters, or, at the very least, is reckless as to whether or not he is entering the premises of another without the other party's consent.

Having so held, the pivotal point of this appeal is whether the Crown established that this defendant at the moment that he entered the bedroom knew perfectly well that he was not welcome there or, being reckless as to whether he was welcome or not, was nevertheless determined to enter. That in turn involves consideration as to where he was at the time that the complainant indicated that she was welcoming him into her bedroom. If, to take an example that was put in the course of argument, her bed had not been near the window but was on the other side of the bedroom, and he (being determined to have her sexually even against her will) climbed through the window and crossed the bedroom to reach her bed, then the offence charged would have been established. But in this case, as we have related, the layout of the room was different, and it became a point of nicety which had to be conclusively established by the Crown as to where he was when the girl made welcoming signs, as she unquestionably at some stage did.

How did the judge deal with this matter? We have to say regretfully that there was a flaw in his treatment of it. Referring to section 9, he said "There are three ingredients. First is the question of entry. Did he enter into that house? Did he enter as a trespasser? That is to say, was the entry, if you are satisfied that there was an entry, intentional or reckless? And, finally, and you may think this is the crux of the case as opened to you by Mr. Irwin, if you are satisfied that he entered as a trespasser, did he have the intention to rape this girl?

The judge then went on to deal in turn with each of these three ingredients. He first explained what was involved in "entry" into a building. He then dealt with the second ingredient. But here he unfortunately repeated his earlier observation that the question of entry as a trespasser depended on "was the entry intentional or reckless?" We have to say that this was putting the matter inaccurately. This mistake may have been derived from a passage in the speech of counsel for the Crown when replying to the submission of "no case." Mr. Irwin at one stage said: "Therefore, the first thing that the Crown have got to prove, my Lord, is that there has been a trespass which may be an intentional trespass, or it may be a reckless trespass." Unfortunately the judge regarded the matter as though the second ingredient in the burglary charged was whether there had been an intentional or reckless entry, and when he came to develop this topic in his summing up that error was unfortunately perpetuated. The judge told the jury: "He had no right to be in that house, as you know, certainly from the point of view of the girl's parent. But if you are satisfied about entry, did he enter intentionally or recklessly? What the prosecution say about that is, you do not really have to consider recklessness because when you consider his own evidence he intended to enter that house, and if you accept the evidence I have just pointed out to you, he in fact did so. So, at least, you may think, it was intentional. At the least, you may think it was reckless because as he told you he did not know whether the girl would accept him."

We are compelled to say that we do not think the judge by these observations made sufficiently clear to the jury the nature of the second test about which they had to be satisfied before this young man could be convicted of the offence charged. There was no doubt that his entry into the bedroom was "intentional." But what the accused had said was, "She knelt on the bed, she put her arms around me and then I went in." If the jury thought he might be truthful in that assertion, they would need to consider whether or not, although entirely surprised by such a reception being according to him, this young man might not have been entitled reasonably to regard her action as amounting to an invitation to him to enter. If she in fact appeared to be welcoming him, the Crown do not suggest that he should have realised or even suspected that she was so behaving because, despite the moonlight, she thought he was someone else. Unless the jury were entirely satisfied that the defendant made an effective and substantial entry into the bedroom without the complainant doing or saying anything to cause him to believe that she was consenting to his entering it, he ought not to be convicted of the offence charged. The point is a narrow one, as narrow maybe as the window sill which is crucial to this case. But this is a criminal charge of gravity and, even though one may suspect that his intention was to commit the offence charged, unless the facts show with clarity that he in fact committed it he ought not to remain convicted.

Some question arose as to whether or not the defendant can be regarded as a trespasser *ab initio.* But we are entirely in agreement with the view expressed in *Archbold,* again in paragraph 1505, that the common law doctrine of trespass *ab initio* has no application to burglary under the Theft Act, 1968. One further matter that was canvassed ought perhaps to be mentioned. The point was raised that, the complainant not being the tenant or occupier of the dwelling house and her mother being apparently in occupation, this girl herself could not in any event have extended an effective invitation to enter, so that even if she had expressly and with full knowledge of all material facts invited the defendant in, he would nevertheless be a trespasser. Whatever be the position in the law of tort, to regard such a proposition as acceptable in the criminal law would be unthinkable.

We have to say that this appeal must be allowed on the basis that the jury were never invited to consider the vital question whether this young man did enter the premises as a trespasser, that is to say knowing perfectly well that he had no invitation to enter or reckless of whether or not his entry was with permission. . . .

Appeal allowed

R. v. Jones and Smith
[1976] 3 All E.R. 54
Court of Appeal

J. and S. were convicted of burglary contrary to section 9(1)(*b*) of the Theft Act 1968. They had entered the house of S's father and stolen two television sets. S's father had reported the theft to the police at the time, but at the trial, he gave evidence to the effect that he had given S. unreserved permission to enter the house, stating that S. "would not be a trespasser in the house at any time." J. and S. appealed.

JAMES L.J.: The next ground of appeal relied on by Counsel for the appellants in his argument is that which is put forward in the first of each of the defendants' grounds. It is the point upon which Counsel had laid the greatest stress in the course of his argument. The argument is based upon the wording of the Theft Act 1968, section 9(1)(b) which is this:

"(1) A person is guilty of burglary if— ... (b) having entered any building or part of a building as a trespasser he steals or attempts to steal anything in the building or that part of it or inflicts or attempts to inflict on any person therein any grievous bodily harm."

The important words from the point of view of the arguments in this appeal are "having entered any building ... as a trespasser." This is a section of an Act of Parliament which introduced a novel concept. Entry as a trespasser was new in 1968 in relation to criminal offences of burglary. It was introduced in substitution for, as an improvement upon, the old law which required considerations of breaking and entering and involved distinctions of nicety which had bedevilled the law for some time.

Counsel for the appellants argued that a person who had a general permission to enter premises of another person cannot be a trespasser. His submission is as short and as simple as that. Related to this case he says that a son to whom a father has given permission generally to enter the father's house cannot be a trespasser if he enters it even though he had decided in his mind before making the entry to commit a criminal offence of theft against the father once he had got into the house and had entered that house solely for the purpose of committing that theft. It is a bold submission. Counsel frankly accepts that there has been no decision of the court since this Act was passed which governs particularly this point. He has reminded us of the decision in *Byrne* v. *Kinematograph Renters Society Ltd.* [1958] 1 W.L.R. 762, which he prays in aid of his argument. In that case persons had entered a cinema by producing tickets not for the purpose of seeing the show, but for an ulterior purpose. It was held in the action, which sought to show that they entered as trespassers pursuant to a conspiracy to trespass, that in fact they were not trespassers. The important words in the judgment are (at p. 776): "They did nothing that they were not invited to do. ... " That provides a distinction between that case and what we consider the position to be in this case.

Counsel has also referred us to one of the trickery cases, *R.* v. *Boyle*, [1954] 2 Q.B. 292, and in particular to a passage in the judgment of that case (at p. 295). He accepts that the trickery cases can be distinguished from such a case as the present because in the trickery cases it can be said that that which would otherwise have been consent to enter was negatived by the fact that consent was obtained by a trick. We do not gain any help in the particular case from that decision.

We were also referred to *R.* v. *Collins* [*ante*, p. 831], and in particular to the long passage of Edmund Davies L.J., where he commenced the consideration of what is involved by the words "the entry must be 'as a trespasser.' " Again it is unnecessary to cite that long passage in full; suffice it to say that this court on that occasion expressly approved the view expressed in Professor Smith's book on the Law of Theft, and also the view of Professor Griew in his publication on the Theft Act 1968 on this aspect of what is involved in being a trespasser.

In our view the passage there referred to is consonant with the passage in the well known case of *Hillen and Pettigrew* v. *I.C.I. (Alkali) Ltd.* [1936] A.C. 65 where, in the speech of Lord Atkin, these words appear:

"My Lords, in my opinion this duty to an invitee only extends so long as and so far as the invitee is making what can reasonably be contemplated as an ordinary and reasonable use of the premises by the invitee for the purposes for which he has been invited. He is not invited to use any part of the premises for purposes which he knows are wrongfully dangerous and constitute an improper use. As Scrutton L.J. has pointedly said (*The Calgarth, the Ontarama* [1927] P. 93 at 110) 'When you invite a person into your house to use the stair case you do not invite him to slide down the banisters.' "

The decision in *R.* v. *Collins* in this court, a decision on the criminal law, added to the concept of trespass as a civil wrong only the mental element of *mens rea*, which is essential to the criminal offence. Taking the law as expressed in *Hillen and Pettigrew* v. *I.C.I. (Alkali) Ltd.* and *R.* v. *Collins*, it is our view that a person is a trespasser for the purpose of section 9(1)(*b*) of the Theft Act 1968 if he enters premises of another knowing that he is entering in excess of the permission that has been given to him to enter, providing the facts are known to the accused which enable him to realise that he is acting in excess of the permission given or that he is acting recklessly as to whether he exceeds that permission, then that is sufficient for the jury to decide that he is in fact a trespasser.

In this particular case it was a matter for the jury to consider whether, on all the facts, it was shown by the prosecution that the appellants entered with the knowledge that entry was being effected against the consent or in excess of the consent that had been given by Mr. Alfred Smith to his son Christopher. The jury were, by their verdict, satisfied of that. It was a novel argument that we heard, interesting but one without, in our view, any foundation. . . .

Finally, before parting with the matter, we would refer to a passage of the summing-up to the jury which I think one must read in full. In the course of that the recorder said.

"I have read out the conversation they had with Detective Sergeant Tarrant and in essence Smith said, 'My father gave me leave to take these sets and Jones was invited along to help.' If that account may be true, that is an end of the case, but if you are convinced that that night they went to the house and entered as trespassers and had no leave or licence to go there for that purpose, and they intended to steal these sets and keep them permanently themselves, acting dishonestly, then you will convict them. Learned counsel for the prosecution did mention the possibility that you might come to the conclusion that they had gone into the house with leave or licence of the father and it would be possible for you to bring in a verdict simply of theft but, members of the jury, of course it is open to you do to that if you felt that the entry to the house was a consequence of the father's leave or licence, but what counts of course for the crime of burglary to be made out is the frame of mind of each person when they go into the property. If you go in intending to steal, then your entry is burglarious, it is to trespass because no one gave you permission to go in and steal in the house."

Then the recorder gave an illustration of the example of a person who is invited to go into a house to make a cup of tea and that person goes in and steals the silver and he went on:

"I hope that illustrates the matter sensibly. Therefore you may find it difficult not to say, if they went in there they must have gone in order to steal because they took elaborate precautions, going there at dead of night, you really cannot say that under any circumstances their entry to the house could have been other than trespass."

In that passage that I have just read the recorder put the matter properly to the jury in relation to the aspect of trespass and on this ground of appeal as on the others we find that the case is not made out, that there was no misdirection, as I have already indicated early in the judgment, and in those circumstances the appeal will be dismissed in the case of each of the appellants.

Appeals dismissed

Questions

1. Smith was not residing with his father at the time of the theft. Would it have made any difference if he had been so residing?

2. A knocks on the door of his neighbour, Miss B. Miss B, recognising him and thinking his call is purely social, invites him in, and he goes in. In fact A's intention is to rape Miss B. On the question of whether A is guilty of burglary, do the cases of *Collins*, and *Jones and Smith* give different answers?

3. Does it follow from *Jones and Smith* that an intending shoplifter necessarily commits burglary as soon as he walks through the door of the shop? Consider the following from Dawson J. in *Barker* v. *R.* (1983) 57 A.L.J.R. 426, 440 (High Court of Australia):

> "It is essential to recognise that the offence consists both of an intentional entry as a trespasser and an intent to steal at the time of entry. The distinction must be maintained because a person accused of burglary may enter premises with an intention to steal but nevertheless in the belief that he is entitled to enter. A person who enters premises with apparent consent but with intent to steal, such as an ordinary shoplifter, is likely to believe at the time he enters the premises that he has the same right of entry as other persons notwithstanding the criminal purpose for which he enters. If interrupted before attempting to steal anything, no doubt he would say that he had done nothing wrong and was entitled to be on the premises. And if he believed that to be so, as he very well might, the mental element required to prove entry as a trespasser would be lacking, notwithstanding evidence of that other aspect of intent required for burglary, an intent to steal at the time of entry. Before there can be a burglary there must be an entry as a trespasser with intent to enter as a trespasser as well as with intent to steal."

4. If A, while in a shop, forms the intent to steal, that is no offence. If he attempts to steal or actually steals, he is liable to 7 years imprisonment. But whether or not he steals or attempts to steal, if he formed the intent to steal before entering the shop, he is (subject to Dawson J.'s remarks above) liable to 10 years imprisonment. What policy of the law can be thought to demand this extra punishment?

iii. Buildings or Parts of Buildings

Notes

1. The word "building" in statute law has had many different meanings given to it. Under the Malicious Damage Act 1861, the word was held to cover a house which was unfinished but substantially complete and with a roof on; *R.* v. *Manning* (1871) L.R. 1 C.C.R. 338. In *Stevens* v. *Gourlay* (1859) 7 C.B. (N.S.) 99, the

C.C.C.R. held that both the ordinary meaning and the presumed intention of the legislature must be looked at. Thus a wooden structure intended as a shop was held to be a building for the purposes of the Metropolitan Building Act 1855, the court holding that an object of the Act was to prevent the metropolis from being covered by combustible structures. The ordinary meaning was held to require a structure of considerable size and intended to be permanent or at least to endure for a considerable time. This dictum was apparently used in *B. and S.* v. *Leathley* [1979] Crim.L.R. 314 (Carlisle Crown Court) to hold that burglary applied to a freezer container, 25 feet long with 7ft. square cross-sections, left standing in a farm yard for two or three years, notwithstanding that it was portable. It seems to be agreed that tents are not buildings (the C.L.R.C. did not envisage that they were: Cmnd. 2977, § 78), and that portability alone does not prevent a structure from being a building. Apart from that, little can be said with confidence, and puzzles such as a bandstand, or telephone kiosk, will have to be elucidated as and when cases arise.

2. Entry as a trespasser into a "part" of a building, *either* with intent to commit a relevant crime in that part, *or* followed by the commission of a relevant crime in that part is also burglary, even if there is no trespassory entry of the building as a whole. Most "parts" of buildings, *e.g.* rooms, cause no difficulty, but doubt might be caused by less differentiated areas, *e.g.* separate counters in a department store. It seems that there must be at least some physical demarcation for an area to be a "part" for the purposes of the law of burglary.

R. v. *Walkington* (1979) 1 W.L.R. 1169, 1175: W. was convicted of burglary by entering a part consisting of a movable three-sided enclosure round a till in a department store. On appeal: Geoffrey Lane L.J. One really gets two extremes, as it seems to us. First of all you have the part of the building which is shut off by a door so far as the general public is concerned, with a notice saying "Staff Only" or "No admittance to customers." At the other end of the scale you have for example a single table in the middle of the store, which it would be difficult for any jury to find properly was a part of the building, into which the licensor prohibited customers from moving.

Here, it seems to us, there was a physical demarcation. Whether there was sufficient to amount to an area from which the public were plainly excluded was a matter for the jury. It seems to us that there was ample evidence on which they could come to the conclusion (a) that the management had impliedly prohibited customers entering that area and (b) that this particular defendant knew of that prohibition.

iv. Intent to Commit an Offence in the Building

Attorney General's References (Nos. 1 and 2 of 1979)
[1980] Q.B. 180
Court of Appeal

The references arose out of two cases in each of which the judge directed an acquittal.

In Case 1, A. was discovered ascending the stairs to the private rooms above a grocer's shop, where he had no right to be. He said he was looking for money to steal. He was charged with burglary with intent to steal.

In Case 2, B. at 3.15 a.m. was discovered by a householder trying to force the french windows of her house. He said he wasn't going to damage anything, only to see if there was anything lying around. He was charged with attempting to enter the house with intent to steal therein.

ROSKILL L.J.: The matters arising for determination are of wide general importance for the administration of justice both in the Crown Court and in magistrates' courts. There appears from what we have been told by counsel and from an admirable memorandum prepared by the Law Commission for the assistance of the court on these references, to be a question of law which is causing and has caused considerable confusion, and has led to what would appear to be unjustified acquittals as a result of circuit judges or their deputies in the Crown Court and also magistrates' courts acceding to submissions that there was no case to answer, the submissions being based on a single sentence in the judgment of this court in *R.* v. *Husseyn* (Note) (1977) 67 Cr.App.R. 131, decided on December 8, 1977, the court consisting of Viscount Dilhorne, Lord Scarman and the late Cusack J. The Attorney-General has referred two such cases decided in the Crown Court to this court in order that a decision may be obtained whether the acquittals with which we are immediately concerned, and also certain other acquittals of which we have been told, were in fact justified.

The question referred to in Reference No. 1 is:

"Whether a man who has entered a house as a trespasser with the intention of stealing money therein is entitled to be acquitted of an offence against section 9(1)(a) of the Theft Act 1968 on the grounds that his intention to steal is conditional upon his finding money in the house."

The answer of this court to this question is "No." In the second reference the question is:

"Whether a man who is attempting to enter a house as a trespasser with the intention of stealing anything of value which he may find therein is entitled to be acquitted of the offence of attempted burglary on the ground that at the time of the attempt his said intention was insufficient to amount to 'the intention of stealing anything' necessary for conviction under section 9 of the Theft Act 1968."

The answer of this court to this question is also "No."

[His Lordship read section 9 (burglary) and section 1(1) (basic definition of theft) of Theft Act 1968]. How the present problem arises is told with admirable clarity in the Law Commission's memorandum. There are certain passages which I read in full, because it would be impossible, if I may say so, to improve upon them:

"10. In turning to the problems raised by these references, it is desirable to say something about the term 'conditional intention.' From the letter from counsel for the appellant in the July 1978 issue of the Criminal Law Review—[1978] Crim.L.R. 444–446—it appears that during argument in *R.* v. *Husseyn* Viscount Dilhorne expressed strong disapproval of the use of 'conditional intention.' This is certainly understandable. The content of the criminal law should be kept as clear and simple as is consonant

with reality and any development which required magistrates to think or
Crown Court judges to sum up to juries in terms of all the verbal
complexities which such pseudo-philosophical or psychological concepts
as conditional intent would involve could only be accepted if no other
way could be found of enabling a fair and accurate description of the
appropriate mental element in these crimes to be conveyed to those who
have to decide such questions of fact."

Thus far this court whole-heartedly and emphatically agrees.

"Nevertheless, it is a convenient term in which to describe collectively a
variety of mental states in argument before an appellate court, and its
use in the text books, in *R.* v. *Easom* (*ante*, p. 717) and *R.* v. *Husseyn*,
and academic discussion of these and subsequent cases and in the
present reference themselves necessitate the use of this term in this
memorandum. 'Conditional intent' is used here to describe any state of
mind falling short of an intention permanently to deprive a person of
property of his, which property at the time of the intention is specific
and identifiable in the mind of the accused. It means that the accused
does not know what he is going to steal but intends that he will steal
whatever he finds of value or worthwhile stealing."

We respectfully agree with Viscount Dilhorne's stated strong disapproval
of the phrase, but if it is to be used, it should only be used for that limited
purpose set out in the last sentence which I have read. In paragraph 13 the
paper goes on:

"The doctrine finds its first expression in the statement of Lord Scarman
in *R.* v. *Husseyn*, that 'it cannot be said that one who has it in mind to
steal only if what he finds is worth stealing has a present intention to
steal.' *R.* v. *Husseyn* was a case of attempted theft and, taken literally,
the statement means that a conditional intent to steal in the sense of an
intention to steal whatever the accused may find worth stealing or of
value is insufficent to ground a charge of attempted theft. It follows
from this that a charge or indictment for attempted theft must
necessarily be quashed as bad in law if it specifies the mental element as
'intending, at that time, to steal whatever he might find worth stealing
(or of value) therein.' Thus, wherever the prosecution has to establish
an intention to steal as one of the constituents of a theft-related offence,
it must prove a fixed and settled intention, contemporaneous with the
act forming the other (actus reus) element of the offence, on the part of
the accused permanently to deprive someone of a specified identifiable
object which either exists or is believed by the accused to exist in or near
the scene of his operations (or 'the target,' as the references aptly
describe it). This is self-evident in cases of completed theft or
'successful' burglary or robbery where, *ex hypothesi*, the accused is
charged with having appropriated a specific identifiable object. The
importance of the doctrine lies in the field of attempted theft or other
cases where, although an intention to steal is required, the relevant *actus
reus* does not postulate that anything should necessarily have been
appropriated. These offences include burglary, attempted burglary,
assault with intent to rob, or, as a suspected person, loitering with
intent to steal or rob."

Thus the so called doctrine of "conditional intention" is described.

It will be useful to go through some of the cases to show how this so
called doctrine has developed and to explain, as each member of this court
is satisfied is the position, that the whole problem arises from a

misunderstanding of a crucial sentence in Lord Scarman's judgment, which must be read in the context in which it was uttered, namely an indictment which charged an attempt to steal a specific object.

[His Lordship then considered *R. v. Stark* (unreported, October 5, 1967), *R. v. Easom* (*ante*, p. 717), *R. v. Husseyn*, and continued] Lord Scarman [in *R. v. Husseyn*] dealt with the law relating to attempts at p. 132 and said that in that respect there was no misdirection by the judge. But his Lordship then went on:

> "Very different considerations apply when one comes to consider the way the learned judge summed up the issue of intention. The learned judge said that the jury could infer that what the young men were about was to look into the holdall and, if its contents were valuable, to steal it. In the view of this court that was a misdirection. What has to be established is an intention to steal at the time when the step is taken, which constitutes or which is alleged to constitute, the attempt. Edmund Davies L.J. put the point in *R. v. Easom* [*ante*, p. 717]: 'In every case of theft the appropriation must be accompanied by the intention of permanently depriving the owner of his property. What may be *loosely* described as a "conditional" appropriation will not do. If the appropriator has it in mind merely to deprive the owner of such of his property as, on examination, proves worth taking and then, finding that the booty is valueless to the appropriator, leaves it ready to hand to be repossessed by the owner, the appropriator has not stolen.' The direction of the learned judge in this case is exactly the contrary. It must be wrong, for it cannot be said that one who has it in mind to steal only if what he finds is worth stealing has a present intention to steal."

We were asked to say that either that last sentence was wrong or that it was *obiter*. We are not prepared to do either. If we may say so with the utmost deference to any statement of law by Lord Scarman, if this sentence be open to criticism, it is because in the context it is a little elliptical. If one rewrites that sentence, so that it reads: "It must be wrong, for it cannot be said that one who has it in mind to steal only if what he finds is worth stealing has a present intention to steal *the specific item charged*," (our emphasis added), then the difficulties disappear, because, as already stated, what was charged was attempted theft of a specific object, just as what had been charged in *R. v. Easom* had been the theft of a number of specific objects.

[His Lordship then considered *R. v. Hector* (1978) 67 Cr.App.R. 224, and continued]. So we have these four cases: Stark, Easom, Husseyn and Hector. In each the charge related to specific objects and in each the conviction was quashed because there had been a misdirection or because the Crown was not in a position to prove that there was on the part of the accused person or persons at the relevant time an intent to steal or to attempt to steal the specific objects which were the subject of the charges or for both those reasons. None of those cases is authority for the proposition that if a charge is brought under section 9(1) of entering any building or part of a building as a trespasser with intent to steal, the accused is entitled to acquittal unless it can be shown that at the time he entered he had the intention of stealing specific objects.

The last case to which it is necessary to refer is *R. v. Walkington* [1979] 1 W.L.R. 1169. Mr. Tudor Price for the Attorney-General and Mr. Simon Brown, who has appeared as *amicus curiae*, both agree that if *R. v. Walkington* is right, as they submitted and as we think it clearly is, that decision is conclusive as to the answer in Reference No. 1, for the reasons given by Geoffrey Lane L.J. in giving the judgment of the court. ...

In *R.* v. *Walkington* the indictment was for burglary. At the beginning of his judgment Geoffrey Lane L.J. set out the indictment, at p. 1171:

"Statement of offence: Burglary, contrary to section 9(1)(a) of the Theft Act 1968. Particulars of offence: Terence Walkington on January 15th, 1977, entered as a trespasser part of a building known as Debenhams Store with intent to steal therein."

Be it noted there was no averment in those particulars of any intention to steal any specific or identified objects. Geoffrey Lane L.J., after dealing with the first point which is presently irrelevant, dealt with the second and relevant point, at p. 1176:

... "These submissions are based upon the decision of this court in *R.* v. *Husseyn*: if we may say so respectfully, a most powerful court, because it consisted of Viscount Dilhorne, Lord Scarman and Cusak J."

The Lord Justice then read the headnote and the passage in Lord Scarman's judgment upon which we have already commented. Geoffrey Lane L.J. said, at pp. 1177–1178:

"What Mr. Osborne suggests to us is that that last passage—the last two sentences—meets the situation in this case and that if the facts were that the defendant in this case had it in mind only to steal if what he found was worth stealing, then he had no intention to steal. That is the way he put it. First of all we would like to say that the particulars of offence in *R.* v. *Husseyn* were that the two men ... 'attempted to steal a quantity of sub-aqua equipment'. Plainly what considerations have to be applied to a charge of attempting to steal a specific article are different considerations from those which have to be applied when one is considering what a person's intent or intention may be under section 9 of the Theft Act 1968. That, we feel, is sufficient to distinguish our case from *R.* v. *Husseyn*."

Then the Lord Justice read what Lord Scarman himself had said about *R.* v. *Husseyn* in *D.P.P.* v. *Nock* [1978] A.C. 979. I will return to this shortly—and said, at p. 1178:

"In this case there is no doubt that the defendant was not on the evidence in two minds as to whether to steal or not. He was intending to steal when he went to that till and it would be totally unreal to ask oneself, or for the jury to ask themselves, the question, what sort of intent did he have? Was it a conditional intent to steal if there was money in the till or a conditional intention to steal only if what he found there was worth stealing? In this case it was a cash till and what plainly he was intending to steal was the contents of the till, which was cash. The mere fact that the till happened to be empty does not destroy his undoubted intention at the moment when he crossed the boundary between the legitimate part of the store and the illegitimate part of the store. The judge's direction which we have cited already covered that point, and the matter was accurately left to the jury.
It has again been pointed out to us, and it is right that we should make reference to it, that that decision in *R.* v. *Husseyn* has apparently been causing some difficulty to judges of the Crown Court."

The Lord Justice then referred to two cases reported in the Criminal Law Review and said that the brief report in the latter case would suffice to demonstrate the difficulties which had arisen. After reading that report Geoffrey Lane L.J. went on, at p. 1179:

"A reading of that would make the layman wonder if the law had taken leave of its senses, because, if that is the proper intepretation to be applied to section 9(1)(a), there will seldom, if ever, be a case in which section 9(1)(a) will bite. It seems to this court that in the end one simply has to go back to the words of the Act itself which we have already cited, and if the jury are satisfied, so as to feel sure, that the defendant has entered any building or part of a building as a trespasser, and are satisfied that at the moment of entering he intended to steal anything in the building or that part of it, the fact that there was nothing in the building worth his while to steal seems to us to be immaterial. He nevertheless had the intent to steal. As we see it, to hold otherwise would be to make nonsense of this part of the Act and cannot have been the intention of the legislature at the time when the Theft Act 1968 was passed. Nearly every prospective burglar could no doubt truthfully say that he only intended to steal if he found something in the building worth stealing.

So, whilst acknowledging that these recent decisions do provide difficulties which have been pointed out to us clearly by Mr. Osborne, it seems to us in the end that one must have regard to the wording of the Act. If that is done, the meaning, in our view, is clear."

I come back to what Lord Scarman himself said in *D.P.P.* v. *Nock* [1978] A.C. 979. The relevant passage is at pp. 999 to 1000. His Lordship, after referring to the decision of the House of Lords in *Haughton* v. *Smith* [*ante,* p. 479] said at p. 1000:

"We were invited by the Crown to express an opinion as to the correctness or otherwise of three decisions of the Court of Appeal, *R.* v. *Easom, Partington* v. *Williams* (1975) 62 Cr.App.R. 220 and *R.* v. *Husseyn*. *Easom* and *Husseyn* (to which I was a party) were, I think, correctly decided: but each, like every other criminal appeal, turned on its particular facts and on the way in which the trial judge directed the jury on the law. In *Easom* Edmund Davies L.J. emphasised that in a case of theft the appropriation must be accompanied by the intention of permanently depriving the owner of his property. This, of course, follows from the definition of theft in section 1(1) of the Theft Act 1968. All that *Husseyn* decided was that the same intention must be proved when the charge is one of attempted theft. Unfortunately in *Husseyn* the issue of intention was summed up in such a way as to suggest that theft, or attempted theft, could be committed by a person who had not yet formed the intention which the statute defines as a necessary part of the offence. An intention to steal can exist even though, unknown to the accused, there is nothing to steal: but, if a man be in two minds as to whether to steal or not, the intention required by the statute is not proved."

We venture to draw particular attention to the opening part of that last sentence: "An intention to steal can exist even though, unknown to the accused, there is nothing to steal. ... "

We had an interesting discussion, with the help of Mr. Tudor Price and Mr. Simon Brown, how, in these cases of burglary or theft or attempted burglary or theft, it is in future desirable to frame indictments. Plainly it may be undesirable in some cases to frame indictments by reference to the theft or attempted theft of specific objects. Obviously draftsmen of indictments require the maximum latitude to adapt the particulars charged to the facts of the particular case, but we see no reason in principle why what was described in argument as a more imprecise method of criminal pleading should not be adopted, if the justice of the case requires it, as for example, attempting to steal some or all of the contents of a car or some or all of the contents of a handbag. The indictment in *R.* v. *Walkington* is in no way open to objection. There is no purpose in multiplying further examples. It may be that in some cases further particulars might be asked for and if so the prosecution could in a proper case no doubt give them without difficulty. The important point is that the indictment should correctly reflect that which it is alleged that the accused did, and that the accused should know with adequate detail what he is alleged to have done.

Taking as an example the facts in *R.* v. *Easom*, plainly what the accused intended was to steal some or all of the contents of the handbag if and when he got them into his possession. It seems clear from the latter part of Edmund Davies L.J.'s judgment that, if he had been charged with an attempt to steal some or all of the contents of that handbag, he could properly have been convicted, subject of course to a proper direction to the jury.

It follows that this court respectfully and whole-heartedly adopts Geoffrey Lane L.J.'s judgment on the second question in *R.* v. *Walkington* which, as I have already said, is conclusive of the answer in the first reference.

So far as the answer in the second reference is concerned, it would, as Mr. Simon Brown very properly agreed, be very strange if a different answer had to be given in the second reference, which is concerned with attempted burglary, from that given in the first reference. In our view, notwithstanding the argument that Mr. Shepherd attempted to advance in the first of the two Divisional Court cases, it is impossible to justify giving different answers according to whether the charge is burglary or attempted burglary, theft or attempted theft or loitering with intent to commit an arrestable offence, which in most cases will be theft. In our view both principle and logic require the same answers in all these cases.

For those reasons the answers in the two references will be, as I have already indicated, "no" in the first and "no" in the second.

Opinions accordingly

Note

On conditional intent in theft, see *ante*, p. 717.

v. The Ulterior Offence

Notes

1. It will be noted that the list of possible ulterior offences is different according as whether the charge is entering with intent under section 9(1)(*a*) or entering and committing under section 9(1)(*b*). Thus if A enters B's house with the intention of quarrelling with B, and in the course of the quarrel he deliberately breaks B's priceless Ming vase, A is not guilty of burglary, but he *is* guilty of burglary if he punches B and breaks his nose. And he is guilty of burglary if, when he entered, he intended to do either of these two things.

2. The wording of section 9(1)(b) does not require that, after trespassory entry, D should commit the *offence* of inflicting grievous bodily harm on any person on the building, only that he should

inflict grievous bodily harm. It is thus possible on the wording for D to be guilty of burglary if he enters as a trespasser and *accidently*, even *lawfully*, inflicts grievous bodily harm. This was not intended, and the Draft Criminal Code Bill, cl. 147(b) puts right the mistake by requiring D to commit *an offence* of theft, attempted theft, or causing or attempting to cause serious bodily harm.

3. The only dishonest offence in either list is theft: fraudulent abstraction of electricity under section 13 of the Theft Act is not covered: *Low* v. *Blease* [1975] Crim.L.R. 513. Nor is obtaining property by deception, but, as a result of *R.* v. *Gomez, ante,* p. 663, most cases of obtaining are also theft.

2. AGGRAVATED BURGLARY

Theft Act 1968, section 10

"(1) A person is guilty of aggravated burglary if he commits any burglary and at the time has with him any firearm or imitation firearm, any weapon of offence, or any explosive; and for this purpose—

(a) 'firearm' includes an airgun or air pistol, and 'imitation firearm' means anything which has the appearance of being a firearm, whether capable of being discharged or not; and

(b) 'weapon of offence' means any article made or adapted for use for causing injury to or incapacitating a person, or intended by the person having it with him for such use; and

(c) 'explosive' means any article manufactured for the purpose of producing a practical effect by explosion, or intended by the person having it with him for that purpose.

(2) A person guilty of aggravated burglary shall on conviction on indictment be liable to imprisonment for life."

Notes

1. *"At the time."* The time is the time of the burglary charged. In the case of entry with intent under section 9(1)(*a*), it is the time of entry as a trespasser. In the case of ulterior offence after trespassory entry under section 9(1)(*b*), it is the time of the ulterior offence. In *R.* v. *Francis* [1982] Crim.L.R. 363 (C.A.), A and B banged on V's door with sticks, and then entered as trespassers. They discarded their sticks, but later stole articles in the house. The judge directed that the prosecution had to prove that they were armed when they entered. *Held,* if a person entered a building as a trespasser and stole under section 9(1)(*b*), he committed burglary at the moment he stole and he committed aggravated burglary only if he had with him a weapon of offence at the time when he stole.

Question

When D enters as a trespasser with intent to steal, he is not armed with a weapon of offence. Once inside the house, he picks up a golf-club in case he is disturbed by the occupier. Being disturbed by the occupier, he threatens him with the club and then steals a valuable clock. Is D guilty of aggravated burglary? See *R. v. O'Leary* (1986) 82 Cr.App.R. 341, and *R. v. Kelly, The Times,* Dec. 2, 1992.

2. *"Has with him"*: This means "knowingly" has with him: *R. v. Cugullere* [1961] 1 W.L.R. 858, and one who has forgotten that he has the article with him is not "knowing" for this purpose: *R. v. Russell* (1984) 81 Cr.App.R. 315 (*ante,* p. 105). It is an open question whether it must be shown that D, who knowingly has an article, also knows that it is a weapon of offence: see *R. v. Warner* [1969] 2 A.C. 256; *R. v. Pierre* [1963] Crim.L.R. 513, decided under different statutes, which suggest the answer "No." The words "has with him" do not require that D should be actually carrying the weapon of offence at the time of the offence: *R. v. Kelt* (1977) 3 All E.R. 1099, 1102 (C.A.); but, on the other hand, the fact that at that time he "possesses" it, *e.g.* at his home, is not enough: *ibid.* What is needed is that the weapon of offence be readily accessible to him, *e.g.* in his car parked outside the premises in which he is committing the offence: *R. v. Pawlicki & Swindell* [1992] 3 All E.R. 902 (C.A.). (Both cases decided under section 18, Firearms Act 1968:—"having with him a firearm with intent to commit an indictable offence.")

3. *"Made or adapted for use for causing injury or incapacitation"*: If D at the relevant time has with him such an article, it is immaterial whether he intends it for such use. As to whether an article is so made or adapted, if it is one about which a realistic question can arise, it is for the jury to decide: *R. v. Williamson* (1977) 67 Cr.App.R. 35 (C.A.), *e.g.* a sheath knife, where it would depend on the sort of knife in the sheath. But with a flick knife, the jury must take judicial notice that it is so made: *R. v. Simpson* [1983] 3 All E.R. 789 (C.A.).

4. *"Intended by the person having it with him for such use."* If an article is not made or adapted for use for causing injury to or incapacitating a person, it is nevertheless a weapon of offence if "intended by the person having it with him for such use." The intended use need not be with respect to the particular burglary D is engaged in: *R. v. Stones* (1989) 89 Cr.App.R. 26 (C.A.). If A has with him a coil of rope with which he intends to tie up a watchman on the premises, the rope is a weapon of offence and if burglary is involved it will be aggravated burglary. But suppose A has with him an article, not otherwise a weapon of offence, which he does not intend to use on this or any other occasion, for injuring or incapacitating, but which, perhaps on the spur of the moment, he does in fact use for such purposes. A has a rope which he intends to use to lower stolen goods out of a window, but on being surprised by a watchman B, uses the rope to tie B up. Does A have with him an article intended for such use? In *R. v. Kelly, The Times,* Dec. 2, 1992 (C.A.), it was held that it was sufficient that he had it with him at the time when he used it (distinguishing cases on similar wording in the Prevention of Crime Act 1953, s. 1).

3. GOING EQUIPPED

Theft Act 1968, section 25

"(1) A person shall be guilty of an offence if, when not at his place of abode, he has with him any article for use in the course of or in connection with any burglary, theft or cheat.

(2) A person guilty of an offence under this section shall on conviction on indictment be liable to imprisonment for a term not exceeding three years.

(3) Where a person is charged with an offence under this section, proof that he had with him any article made or adapted for use in committing a burglary, theft or cheat shall be evidence that he had it with him for such use.

(4) Any person may arrest without warrant anyone who is, or whom he, with reasonable cause, suspects to be, committing an offence under this section.

(5) For the purposes of this section an offence under section 12(1) of this Act of taking a conveyance shall be treated as theft, and 'cheat' means an offence under section 15 of this Act."

i. Has with him

Note

See the cases cited on similar wording in section 10(1) (aggravated burglary), *supra*.

Question

A and B are apprehended while trying to break into a warehouse at night. When B is searched he is found to possess a banker's credit card which does not apparently belong to him. There is no evidence that A knew that B was carrying this article. Are A and B guilty of an offence under section 25? Would it make any difference if the article was not a credit card, but a jemmy? See next case.

R. v. Lester and Byast
(1955) 39 Cr.App.R. 157
Court of Criminal Appeal

L. and B. were convicted of being found by night having in their possession implements of housebreaking. Most of the implements were found in the boot of a car owned and driven by B., but some were found on B.'s person. L was a passenger in the car. The police had seen both L. and B. in the act of stealing petrol from another car, but there was no evidence of joint participation on their part in any enterprise of housebreaking.

HALLETT J.: It seems to us that the housebreaking implements found in the boot of the car were found in the possession of Byast within the meaning of section 28 [of the Larceny Act 1916], and we would refer to what was said in *Thompson* (1869) 11 Cox 362, more particularly in the interpolations at p. 364, where Lush J. says, "Or if a burglar were to hire a little boy to carry his implements, could he not be convicted under [the relevant section]?" and Blackburn J. says, "Or if the implements were in a pannier on an ass's back, could the donkey be said to be in possession of them?" The case was decided by a very powerful court, and those two interpolations seem to us to indicate what the learned judges concerned would have thought to be the true view when the implements were being carried, not by a little boy or by an ass, but by the more modern method of a boot of a motor-car. ...

With regard to Lester, on the other hand, somewhat different considerations arise. As we understand it, the case made against him is twofold. In the first place it is said that the implements of housebreaking which were found in the car were in his possession as well as in the possession of Byast. There was, however, a distinction between the facts proved in the case of Byast and those proved in the case of Lester. Whatever suspicions may be entertained—and certainly strong suspicions can be entertained—the only evidence is that Lester was a passenger in the car belonging to and driven by Byast, in the cubbyhole of which were two pairs of gloves and a piece of celluloid, and in the boot of which were other housebreaking implements. In our view, the *mere* fact that a man is a passenger in a car which contains housebreaking implements is not sufficient to show that he is in possession of them, whatever may be the case as regards the owner and driver of the car.

The alternative ground on which it is suggested that Lester should have been found guilty is that he was a participant with Byast in a housebreaking expedition, and that in such a case, where one of the participants is found in possession of housebreaking implements, his possession can be attributed in law to the other participant also, the authority for that proposition being *Thompson, supra*. We do not doubt that, if a common participation in a housebreaking expedition had been established by the evidence, the principle of *Thompson, supra*, would apply and the conviction of Lester would be upheld on that ground. The difficulty which we all feel in this case is that ... there is ... a lack of evidence, ... that the common enterprise in which Lester was engaged with Byast was an enterprise of housebreaking. It may very well have been, but we can see no evidence to establish that it was.

Byast's appeal dismissed
Lester's conviction quashed

ii. When Not at his Place of Abode

R. v. Bundy [1977] 2 All E.R. 382 (C.A.). B was convicted under section 25 of the Theft Act, in respect of articles found in a car he was driving. He appealed on the ground that for several weeks he had been living in the car, which was therefore his place of abode.

LAWTON L.J. (at 384): We must construe the phase in the context in which it appears in section 25(1) of the Theft Act 1968. In that context it is manifest that no offence is committed if a burglar keeps the implements of his criminal trade in his "place of abode." He only commits an offence when he takes them from his "place of abode." The phrase "place of abode," in our judgment, connotes, first of all, a site. That is the ordinary meaning of the word "place." It is a site at which the occupier intends to abide. So, there are two elements in the phrase "place of abode," the element of site and the element of intention. When the appellant took the motor car to a site with the intention of abiding there, then his motor car on that site could be said to be his "place of abode," but when he took it from that site to move it to another site where he intended to abide, the motor car could not be said to be his "place of abode" during transit.

When he was arrested by the police he was not intending to abide on the site where he was arrested. It follows that he was not then at his "place of abode." He may have had a "place of abode" the previous night, but he was away from it at the time of his arrest when in possession of articles which could be used for the purpose of theft. It follows, in our judgment, that there is no substance in the point. ...

iii. Any Article

Smith, The Law of Theft, §§ 380, 381

The *actus reus* consists in the accused's having with him any article. Clearly the article need not be made or adapted for use in committing one of the specified offences. It is sufficient that the *mens rea* is proved in respect of the article, that is, that the accused intended to use it in the course of, or in connection with, one of the specified offences. Thus, it might be a tin of treacle, intended for use in removing a pane of glass; a pair of gloves to be worn so as to avoid leaving fingerprints; a collecting box marked "Oxfam" when the possessor did not represent that organisation; and so on. There may occasionally be difficulty in deciding what is an "article." Does it include blacking on the face to prevent recognition, or "Bostik" on the fingers to prevent fingerprints? Having regard to the mischief at which the section is aimed, it is arguable that a substance so applied to the body, remains an "article".

The offence is thus very wide in its scope. But there must be some limits. Thus D. can hardly be committing an offence because he is wearing his trousers when on his way to do a burglary. Yet he intends to wear them while he is committing the burglary and would not dream of undertaking such an enterprise without them. Similarly, he can hardly be committing an offence by wearing his shoes or any other item of everyday apparel. Yet it was suggested above that gloves for the avoidance of fingerprints would entail liability. This suggests that the article must be one which D. would not be carrying with him but for the contemplated offence. If it is something which he would carry with him on a normal, innocent expedition, it should not fall within this section. So there might be a difference between a pair of rubber gloves and a pair of fur-lined gloves which D. was wearing to keep his hands warm on a freezing night, even though he did intend to keep them on so as to avoid leaving fingerprints. The latter pair of gloves is hardly distinguishable, for this purpose, from D.'s overcoat which seems to fall into the same category as his trousers. If D is carrying a pair of plimsolls in his car to facilitate his cat-burgling, this seems a plain enough case; but what if he has simply selected his ordinary crepe-sole shoes for wear because they are less noisy than his hob-nails?

iv. For Use in the Course of or in Connection with any Burglary, Theft or Cheat

R. v. Ellames
[1974] 3 All E.R. 130
Court of Appeal

After a robbery had taken place, E. disposed of a bag containing articles used in the robbery, including a sawn-off shotgun, and ammonia in spray containers. He was charged under section 25 Theft Act. The judge directed that the fact that the theft was over did not prevent him from having the articles for the purpose of theft. E. was convicted and appealed.

BROWNE J.: In our judgment the construction of the section suggested by the Crown would produce many problems, anomalies and absurdities, and it is impossible to give it that construction having regard to the words used.

In our judgment, the words in section 25(1) of the 1968 Act: "has with him any article for use" mean "has with him for the purpose" (or "with the intention") "that they will be used." The effect of section 25(3) is that if the article is one "made or adapted for use in committing a burglary, theft or cheat," that is evidence of the necessary intention, though not of course conclusive evidence. If the article is not one "made or adapted" for such use, the intention must be proved on the whole of the evidence—as it must be in the case of an article which is so made or adapted, if the defendant produces some innocent explanation. We agree with the learned authors of Smith and Hogan's Criminal Law (3rd ed., p. 484) that section 25 is directed against acts preparatory to burglary, theft or cheat; that

> "Questions as to D.'s knowledge of the nature of the thing can hardly arise here, since it must be proved that he intended to use it in the course of or in connection with [burglary, theft or cheat]";

and that the *mens rea* for this offence includes "an intention to use the article in the course of or in connection with any of the specific crimes."

An intention to use must necessarily relate to use in the future. If any support is needed for this view, we think it is found in the recent decision of this court in *R. v. Allamby, R. v. Medford* [1974] 3 All E.R. 126, decided under the Prevention of Crime Act 1953. It seems to us impossible to interpret section 25(1) of the 1968 Act as if it read: "has with him any article for use or *which has been used* in the course of or in connection with any burglary, theft or cheat." Equally, it is impossible to read section 25(3) as if it said: "had it with him for *or after* such use."

In our judgment the words "for use" govern the whole of the words which follow. The object and effect of the words "in connection with" is to add something to "in the course of." It is easy to think of cases where an article could be intended for use "in connection with" though not "in the course of" a burglary, etc., *e.g.* articles intended to be used while doing preparatory acts or while escaping after the crime (see Smith and Hogan).

In our view, to establish an offence under section 25(1) the prosecution must prove that the defendant was in possession of the article, and intended the article to be used in the course of or in connection with some future burglary, theft or cheat. But it is not necessary to prove that he intended it to be used in the course of or in connection with any *specific* burglary, theft or cheat; it is enough to prove a general intention to use it for *some* burglary, theft or cheat; we think that this view is supported by the use of the word "any" in section 25(1). Nor, in our view, is it necessary to prove that the defendant intended to use it himself; it will be enough to prove that he had it with him with the intention that it should be used by someone else. For example, if in the present case it had been proved that the defendant was hiding away these articles, which had already been used for one robbery, with the intention that they should later be used by someone for some other robbery, he would be guilty of an offence under section 25(1).

It follows from our conclusion as to the true construction of section 25(1) that in our judgment the judge should have upheld the appellant's submission of no case on count 2 and that the conviction must be quashed.

We come to this conclusion with some regret. But our conclusion that a person who is in possession only after a burglary, theft or cheat of articles which had been used in the crime is not guilty of an offence under section 25(1) of the 1968 Act, does not mean that he cannot be guilty of some other offence—the obvious possibility is a offence under section 4 of the Criminal Law Act 1967 of impeding apprehension or prosecution. It may be that if this appellant had been charged under that section he could properly have been convicted, but he was not charged under that section.

Accordingly, this appeal must be allowed and the conviction quashed.

Appeal allowed; conviction quashed

Notes

1. "The prosecution must prove that the defendant was in possession of the article and intended the article to be used in the course of or in connection with some future burglary theft or cheat": Browne J., *supra*. However it has been held that if D comes into possession of the article after he has embarked on an offence and intends to use it in the course of that offence, that is enough: *Minor* v. *D.P.P.* (1987) 86 Cr.App.R. 378 (D.C.).

2. The offence in prospect must not be too remote. In *R.* v. *Mansfield* [1975] Crim.L.R. 101 (C.A.), D was in possession of a driving licence and other documents belonging to another, with intent to obtain a job which would give him the opportunity to steal. *Held* he did not have them with him "in connection with" the contemplated thefts.

3. Moreover, one who has not decided whether to use the article in the course of or in connection with any burglary theft or cheat does not have it with him for such use: *R.* v. *Hargreaves* [1985] Crim.L.R. 243. However, a conditional intent to use it (*e.g.* if the opportunity or need arises) ought to be enough.

4. For what must be proved if the contemplated offence is cheat, *i.e.* obtaining property by deception, see *R.* v. *Doukas* [1978] 1 W.L.R. 372, *ante*, p. 763, approved in *R.* v. *Cooke* [1986] A.C. 909, 934 (H.L.). These and other cases concentrate on whether the victim would be influenced to part with his property by D's deception, but the true question, it has been suggested [Griew 15.11, Smith 385], is whether D *intended* to influence the victim.

CHAPTER 15

CRIMINAL DAMAGE

	PAGE			PAGE
1. Destroying or Damaging Property	853	iv. Being Reckless as to		
A. The Simple Offence	857	whether any such Property		
i. Belonging to Another	857	would be Destroyed or		
ii. Without Lawful Excuse	860	Damaged.		867
iii. Intending to Destroy or		B. The Aggravated Offence		868
Damage any such Property	864	2. Other Offences		870

Note

The principle offences concerned with damage to property are contained in Criminal Damage Act 1971. The previous law was mostly in the Malicious Damage Act 1861, which made it an offence unlawfully and maliciously to commit any damage to a large number of specifically mentioned types of property. The Act of 1971 creates only a small number of wide, general, offences. The Draft Criminal Code Bill proposes no substantial changes, except as to "Lawful Excuse": see *post*.

1. DESTROYING OR DAMAGING PROPERTY

Criminal Damage Act 1971, sections 1 and 4

Section 1: "(1) A person who without lawful excuse destroys or damages any property belonging to another intending to destroy or damage any such property or being reckless as to whether any such property would be destroyed or damaged shall be guilty of an offence.

(2) A person who without lawful excuse destroys or damages any property, whether belonging to himself or another:

(a) intending to destroy or damage any property or being reckless as to whether any property would be destroyed or damaged; and

(b) intending by the destruction or damage to endanger the life of another or being reckless as to whether the life of another would be thereby endangered;

shall be guilty of an offence.

(3) An offence committed under this section by destroying or damaging property by fire shall be charged as arson."

Section 4: "(1) A person guilty of arson under section 1 above or of an offence under section 1(2) above (whether arson or not) shall on conviction on indictment be liable to imprisonment for life.

(2) A person guilty of any other offence under this Act shall on conviction on indictment be liable to imprisonment for a term not exceeding ten years."

Notes

1. If the damage or destruction is by fire, the offence must be charged as arson. Moreover, since a heavier penalty is provided, it is a different offence from criminal damage, and if arson is

charged, there can be no conviction on that indictment of criminal damage in either of its forms: see *R.* v. *Cooper & Cooper* [1991] Crim.L.R. 524 (C.A.)

2. As to criminal damage, there are two offences in section 1, a simple offence and an aggravated one. The differences between them are connected with the expressions "belonging to another" and "without lawful excuse" (see *infra*), and with the additional *mens rea* required for the aggravated offence. The common features are the destroying or damaging of any property. "Property" is defined in section 10, below, but neither "destroy" nor "damage" is defined. Destroy may be surplusage, since it is hardly possible to destroy property without damaging it.

Criminal Damage Act 1971, section 10

"(1) In this Act 'property' means property of a tangible nature, whether real or personal, including money and:

(a) including wild creatures which have been tamed or are ordinarily kept in captivity, and any other wild creatures or their carcasses if, but only if, they have been reduced into possession which has not been lost or abandoned or are in the course of being reduced into possession; but

(b) not including mushrooms growing wild on any land or flowers, fruit or foliage of a plant growing wild on any land.

For the purpose of this subsection, 'mushroom' includes any fungus and 'plant' includes any shrub or tree."

[Compare the definition of property in section 4 of the Theft Act 1968, *ante*, p. 679].

R. v. Whiteley
(1991) 93 Cr.App.R. 25
Court of Appeal

D. was a computer hacker, who gained unauthorised access to a computer network and altered data contained on discs in the system. Charged under Section 1(1) Criminal Damage Act 1971, he was convicted on counts in which the crown case was that he caused damage to the discs by way of alteration of the state of the magnetic particles on them so as to delete and add files. The discs themselves were not physically damaged, but the jury were directed that once the particles were written on the disc, they formed part of it and were therefore capable of sustaining damage. On appeal:—

LORD LANE C.J., for the Court: The evidence before the jury was that the discs are so constructed as to contain upon them thousands, if not millions, of magnetic particles. By issuing commands to the computer, impulses are produced which magnetise or demagnetise those particles in a particular way. By that means it is possible to write data or information on the discs and to program them to fulfil a variety of functions. By the same method it is possible to delete or alter data, information or instructions which have previously been written on to the disc. The argument advanced on behalf of the appellant, when reduced to its essence, seems to us to be this. That since the state of the magnetic particles on the disc is not perceptible by the unaided human senses, for instance of sight or touch, therefore the appellant's admitted activities only affected the "intangible information contained" on the disc itself. Even if the absence of such a perceptible change is not fatal to the prosecution, goes on the submission, interference with the particles cannot amount to damage in law.

It seems to us that that contention contains a basic fallacy. What the Act requires to be proved is that tangible property has been damaged, not necessarily that the damage itself should be tangible. There can be no doubt that the magnetic particles upon the metal discs were a part of the discs and if the appellant was proved to have intentionally and without lawful excuse altered the particles in such a way as to cause an impairment of the value or usefulness of the disc to the owner, there would be damage within the meaning of section 1. The fact that the alteration could only be perceived by operating the computer did not make the alterations any the less real, or the damage, if the alteration amounted to damage, any the less within the ambit of the Act.

We have been referred to a number of authorities which to a greater or lesser extent bear upon this problem. *Fisher* (1865) L.R. 1 C.C.R. 7: Here the defendant was convicted of damaging a steam engine. He had plugged up the feed-pipe and displaced other parts so as to render it temporarily useless and potentially explosive. There was no removal of any part, no cutting, no breaking and no lesion (as it was put). The conviction was upheld by the Court of Crown Cases Reserved. Pollock C.B. put the matter as follows at p. 9:

> "It is like the case of spiking a gun, where there is no actual damage to the gun, although it is rendered useless. ... Surely the displacement of the parts was a damage ... if done with intent to render the machine useless."

It should however be noted that the charge was brought under the Malicious Damage Act 1861 which provided by section 14 as follows:

> "Whosoever shall unlawfully and maliciously cut, break, or destroy, or damage with intent to destroy or to render useless, ... any machine or engine. ... "

In *Tacey* (1821) Russ. and Ry. 452, the allegation was that the defendant had mischievously damaged a frame used for stocking-making, by unscrewing and taking away a part of the machine, so rendering the whole useless. The judge reserved the point of whether mere removal of a part in these circumstances could amount to "damaging." It was held that it could. These two cases seem to demonstrate that no actual lesion to the tangible object is necessary. In *Henderson and Batley* (unreported, November 29, 1984), this Court had to consider the meaning of "damage" in section 1(1) of the 1971 Act. The property allegedly damaged was a development land site upon which the defendants had dumped 30 lorry loads of rubble, which the owners had to remove at a cost of some £2,000. The argument advanced by the defendants was that what they had done could not be said to have damaged the land. The trial judge ruled against them and his decision was upheld on appeal, on the grounds that damage can be of various kinds and that the definition found in the *Concise Oxford Dictionary*, (6th ed. p. 256) namely "injury impairing value or usefulness," was appropriate to cover the facts of the case. It was a question for the jury to decide whether damage had been proved.

That decision was cited by Stephen Brown L.J. in the Divisional Court decision of *Cox v. Riley* (1986) 83 Cr.App.R. 54, where the facts were not altogether dissimilar from those in the instant case. A disgruntled employee had erased from the printed circuit card a computer program which controlled a computerised saw belonging to his employers. The saw was thereby put out of action. He was charged with damaging the circuit card. It was contended on behalf of the prosecutor that by removing the information stored upon the card, the defendant had damaged the card within the meaning of section 1(1). On behalf of the defendant it was argued that the program in question did not exist in a tangible form and therefore was not property within the meaning of section 10(1), and secondly, that erasing a program from the printed circuit card did not amount to damage. "Damage," it was contended, should be given its "original meaning." This argument was amplified by counsel on the basis that because the program could not be seen or touched in the ordinary physical sense, the removal of the program could not amount to causing damage.

Stephen Brown L.J. in rejecting that argument in the course of his judgment at pp. 56, 57, 58, said this:

"It has to be observed that the property referred to in the charge was the plastic circuit card, which undoubtedly ... is property of a tangible nature ... the only possible argument which [counsel] could put forward is that there was no damage within the meaning of the Act. ... The defendant ... wished to put out of action, albeit temporarily, the computerised saw, and he was able to do that by operating the computer blanking mechanism in order to erase from the printed circuit card the relevant programs. That made it necessary for time and labour and money to be expended in order to replace the relevant programs on the printed circuit card. ... It seems to me to be quite untenable to argue that ... this ... did not amount to causing damage to property."

We respectfully agree with those conclusions. *Morphitis* v. *Salmon* [1990] Crim.L.R. 48 was another decision of the Divisional Court. The facts of the case are immaterial, but in the course of delivering his judgment, with which Lloyd L.J. agreed, Auld J., in the transcript of the judgment, having cited the decision in *Cox* v. *Riley* (*supra*), said this:

"The authorities show that the term 'damage' for the purpose of this provision, should be widely interpreted so as to include not only permanent or temporary physical harm, but also permanent or temporary impairment of value or usefulness."

The effect of those various decisions, in our judgment, is as follows: Any alteration to the physical nature of the property concerned may amount to damage within the meaning of the section. Whether it does so or not will depend upon the effect that the alteration has had upon the legitimate operator (who for convenience may be referred to as the owner). If the hacker's actions do not go beyond, for example, mere tinkering with an otherwise "empty" disc, no damage would be established. Where, on the other hand, the interference with the disc amounts to an impairment of the value or usefulness of the disc to the owner, then the necessary damage is established ...

Appeal dismissed

Note

This case remains of authority as to audio or video recorders or tapes, but as to computers, section 3(4) Computer Misuse Act 1990 provides that a modification of the contents of such shall not be regarded as damaging any computer or computer storage medium unless the modification affects or impairs the physical condition of the computer or storage medium. Persons like Whiteley or Riley would now be guilty of unauthorised modification of computer material: section 3(1) *ibid*.

See Wasik, "The Computer Misuse Act 1990" [1990] Crim.L.R. 767.

Roe v. *Kingerlee* [1986] Crim.L.R. 735 (Div.Ct.). D smeared the walls of a police cell with mud, which cost £7 to clean off. The Magistrates held that there was nothing amounting to damage, but on appeal by the prosecutor, *Held*: What constitutes criminal damage is a matter of fact and degree and it is for the justices, applying their common sense, to decide whether what occurred was damage or not. It is not necessary that the damage should be permanent before an act can constitute criminal damage. ... In the circumstances of the present case, what occurred so far as the walls of the cell were concerned could amount to criminal damage. The justices were wrong to take the view that as a matter of law it could not. ... The application of graffiti to a structure will not necessarily amount to causing criminal damage. That must be a question of fact and degree for the tribunal of fact.

A. The Simple Offence: Without Danger to Life

i. Belonging to Another

Criminal Damage Act 1971, section 10

"(2) Property shall be treated for the purposes of this Act as belonging to any person:

(a) having the custody or control of it;
(b) having in it any proprietary right or interest (not being an equitable interest arising only from an agreement to transfer or grant an interest); or
(c) having a charge on it.

(3) Where property is subject to a trust, the persons to whom it belongs shall be so treated as including any person having a right to enforce the trust.

(4) Property of a corporation sole shall be so treated as belonging to the corporation notwithstanding a vacancy in the corporation."

Note

Before the Act, a person was criminally responsible for destroying or damaging his or her own property, if he or she did so with the intention of defrauding anyone. But see next case, and *R.* v. *Smith, post*, p. 864.

R. v. Denton
[1982] 1 All E.R. 65
Court of Appeal

D, employed at a cotton mill, set fire to the mill and machinery in it because he thought his "employer" T. had asked him to do so, saying

"There is nothing like a good fire for improving the financial circumstances of a business." After submissions by him were rejected, he pleaded guilty, but appealed.

LORD LANE C.J.: The certificate given by the judge reads:

"As to Count 2 the defendant's defence was that he believed he had not only the permission but the encouragement of the proprietor of the business for which he worked, to set fire to the goods of that business with a view to obtaining insurance monies for that proprietor by fraud. After hearing submissions of Counsel at the conclusion of the evidence, I ruled that the word 'entitled' in section 5(2) the Criminal Damage Act 1971, despite the proprietorial basis of the Criminal Damage Acts, carried a connotation of general lawfulness in addition to private title. On the basis that the proprietor could not be said to be 'entitled' to consent to damage for a fraudulent purpose, the defendant changed his plea to guilty."

Section 1(1) of the Criminal Damage Act 1971 reads:

"A person who without lawful excuse destroys or damages any property belonging to another intending to destroy or damage any such property or being reckless as to whether any such property would be destroyed or damaged shall be guilty of an offence."

Section 5, which was the section round which the arguments and submissions revolved in the court below, reads:

"(1) This section applies to any offence under section 1(1) above and any offence under section 2 or 3 above other than one involving a threat by the person charged to destroy or damage property in a way which he knows is likely to endanger the life of another . . .
(2) A person charged with an offence to which this section applies shall, whether or not he would be treated for the purposes of this Act as having a lawful excuse apart from this subsection, be treated for those purposes as having a lawful excuse—(a) if at the time of the act . . . he believed that the person . . . whom he believed to be entitled to consent to the . . . damage to the property in question had so consented . . . "

It was agreed on all hands for the purpose of this case that T. was the person who, any evil motives apart, was entitled to consent to the damage. It was likewise conceded that the defendant honestly believed that T. occupied that position and was entitled to consent.

It is plain from the way that the judge put the matter in his certificate that he had come to the conclusion that the word "entitled" was in some way qualified by a word which does not appear in the section, namely "honestly." It is on that basis that counsel for the Crown here seeks to support the judge's direction.

In order perhaps to see what the scheme of the Criminal Damage Act 1971 entails, it is necessary to have regard to the earlier Act, namely the Malicious Damage Act 1861. Under that Act, certainly by section 3, and also by two other sections (sections 13 and 59), a man's right to do what he liked to his own property was restricted, and it was, amongst other things, an offence to set fire to certain buildings if there was an intent to injure or defraud, even if those buildings were in the possession of the defendant. It is very striking to observe that the words "with intent to injure or defraud" are absent from the terms of the 1971 Act which I have just read. It is quite apparent from that, indeed in this court it is not argued to the contrary, that in so far as the 1971 Act is concerned it is not an offence for a man to damage or injure or destroy or set fire to his own premises.

One therefore turns to see what the situation would have been had T. made a confession in the same, or similar, terms as that made by the defendant, and to see what would have happened on the Crown's argument if the two of them, T. and the defendant, stood charged under section 1(1) of the 1971 Act in the Crown Court. It is not an offence for a man to set light to his own property. So T. would have been acquitted. But if the Crown is correct, the defendant, the man who had been charged with the task of actually putting the match to the polystyrene, and setting the fire alight, would have been convicted.

Quite apart from any other consideration, that is such an anomalous result that it cannot possibly be right. The answer is this: that one has to decide whether or not an offence is committed at the moment that the acts are alleged to be committed. The fact that somebody may have had a dishonest intent which in the end he was going to carry out, namely a claim from the insurance company, cannot turn what was not originally a crime into a crime. There is no unlawfulness under the 1971 Act in burning a house. It does not become unlawful because there may be an inchoate attempt to commit fraud contained in it; that is to say it does not become a crime under the 1971 Act, whatever may be the situation outside of the Act.

Consequently it is apparent to us that the judge, in his ruling in this respect, was wrong. Indeed it seems to us, if it is necessary to go as far as this, that it was probably unnecessary for the defendant to invoke section 5 of the 1971 Act at all, because he probably had a lawful excuse without it, in that T. was lawfully entitled to burn the premises down. The defendant believed it. He believed that he was acting under the directions of T. and that on its own, it seems to us, may well have provided him with a lawful excuse without having resort to section 5.

The result is that the plea of guilty to count 2 in the indictment was based on a wrong view of the law by the judge. Consequently, despite the plea of guilty, the conviction on count 2 must be quashed and the appeal allowed.

Appeal allowed

Note

This case proceeds on the ground that T, who was variously described as D's "employer," and "the proprietor," was the owner of the mill. In fact the mill was owned by Leslie Fink & Co., Ltd. The assumption that T was the person who was entitled to consent to the damage was therefore of doubtful validity. In *R. v. Appleyard* (1985) 81 Cr.App.R. 319 (C.A.) a managing director charged with burning down a store belonging to the company was not allowed to use the assumption in *R. v. Denton* to argue that as managing director he was entitled to consent to the damage.

Questions

1. Ought not a person in Appleyard's position to be able to argue at least that he *thought* he was entitled to consent to the damage?

2. Is a person who damages his own property in order to
defraud his insurers guilty of attempt to obtain money from them
by deception? See *ante*, p. 441.

ii. Without Lawful Excuse

Criminal Damage Act 1971, section 5

"(1) This section applies to any offence under section 1(1) above and any
offence under section 2 or 3 above other than one involving a threat by the
person charged to destroy or damage property in a way which he knows is
likely to endanger the life of another or involving an intent by the person
charged to use or cause or permit the use of something in his custody or
under his control so to destroy or damage property.

(2) A person charged with an offence to which this section applies shall,
whether or not he would be treated for the purpose of this Act as having a
lawful excuse apart from this subsection, be treated for those purposes as
having a lawful excuse:

(a) if at the time of the act or acts alleged to constitute the offence he
believed that the person or persons whom he believed to be
entitled to consent to the destruction or damage to the property in
question had so consented, or would have so consented to it if he
or they had known of the destruction or damage and its
circumstances; or

(b) if he destroyed or damaged or threatened to destroy or damage the
property in question or, in the case of a charge of an offence under
section 3 above, intended to use or cause or permit the use of
something to destroy or damage it, in order to protect property
belonging to himself or another or a right or interest in property
which was or which he believed to be vested in himself or another,
and at the time of the act or acts alleged to constitute the offence
he believed:

(i) that the property, right or interest was in immediate need
of protection; and

(ii) that the means of protection adopted or proposed to be
adopted were or would be reasonable having regard to all
the circumstances.

(3) For the purpose of this section it is immaterial whether a belief is
justified or not if it is honestly held.

(4) For the purpose of subsection (2) above a right or interest in property
includes any right or privilege in or over land, whether created by grant,
licence or otherwise.

(5) This section shall not be construed as casting doubt on any defence
recognised by law as a defence to criminal charges."

Notes

1. All the offences in the Act must be committed "without lawful
excuse." But as to the simple offence (not the aggravated offence)
section 5 gives particular cases of beliefs which count as lawful
excuse. None of the beliefs need be reasonable, provided they are
generally held. But see *R.* v. *Hill*, below.

2. The definition of lawful excuse is not exhaustive: see section 5(5). Thus any other defence to the use of force will avail, *e.g.* duress, prevention of crime, arrest of offenders, self-defence. However these, as justifications for any crime, are only effective if the measures taken by D are objectively reasonable: see *ante*, p. 330. In *Lloyd* v. *D.P.P.* [1992] 1 All E.R. 982 (D.C.), D's car was parked unlawfully on V.'s land: V. applied a wheel clamp and demanded £25 for its release. D. damaged the clamp in order to free his car without paying the £25. It was held that whatever the position in civil law between D and V, D had no lawful excuse for damaging the clamp: he could have paid the £25 under protest and then sued for its return.

3. The fact that subsections 2 and 3 deal specifically with mistaken belief in consent of owner and mistaken belief in a right to be protected has been held to mean that such mistakes can ground a defence even though they arise as a result of self-induced intoxication: see *Jaggard* v. *Dickinson* [1980] 3 All E.R. 716. See *ante*, p. 268.

Question

D, whose trousered leg is being attacked by P's small dog, brains the dog with his walking stick. If D is prosecuted under the Act for killing the dog, what difference might it make whether D acted to prevent injury to his leg or to prevent damage to his trousers?

R. v. Hill
(1988) 89 Cr.App.R. 74
Court of Appeal

Hill was apprehended outside a U.S. Naval Base in Dyfed in possession of a hacksaw blade. She admitted that she intended to use it to cut the perimeter fence of the base. She was convicted of having the blade with intent without lawful excuse to use it to damage property belonging to another, contrary to Section 3 Criminal Damage Act 1971 (see *post*, p. 870). She said that she feared that the presence of the base would at some future time attract a nuclear strike by Soviet missiles, which would damage her property in the vicinity. The object of her proposed activity was to make the U.S. authorities close the base. She claimed that she was acting with lawful excuse in that her property was in immediate need of protection and that the means of protection proposed would be reasonable having regard to all the circumstances. The judge in effect directed the jury to convict. [Another woman was also convicted on the same charge in precisely similar circumstances]. On appeal:—

LORD LANE C.J. for the Court:— The learned judge ... directed the jury to convict on two bases. The first basis was this, that what the applicant did or proposed to do could not, viewed objectively, be said to have been done to protect her own or anyone else's property under section 5(2)(*b*) which I have just read. It is simply, he concluded, part of a political campaign aimed at drawing attention to the base and to the risks as she described them raised by the presence of the base in Pembrokeshire. It aimed further at having the base removed. He came to the conclusion that the causative relationship between the acts which she intended to perform and the alleged protection was so tenuous, so nebulous, that the acts could not be said to be done to protect viewed objectively.

The second ground was with reference to the provision that the lawful excuse must be based upon an immediate need for protection. In each case the judge came to the same conclusion that on the applicant's own evidence the applicant could not be said to have believed under the provisions of section 5(2)(b)(i) that the property was in immediate need of protection . . .

The judge in each case relied upon a decision of this Court in *Hunt* (1978) 66 Cr.App.R. 105. We have the advantage also of having that report in transcript. We also have before us a more recent decision of this Court in *Ashford and Smith* (unreported) decided on May 26, 1988, in which very similar considerations were raised to those which exist in the present case. It also has the advantage of having set out the material findings of the Court in *Hunt* which were delivered by Roskill L.J. I am referring to p. 4 of the transcript in *Ashford and Smith*, and it will help to set out the basis of the decision not only in *Ashford and Smith* but also in *Hunt* if I read the passage. It runs as follows:

"The judge relied very largely upon the decision of this Court in *Hunt* (1978) 66 Cr.App.R. 105. That was a case in which the appellant set fire to a guest room in an old people's home. He did so, he said, to draw attention to the defective fire alarm system. 'He was charged with arson, contrary to section 1(1) of the Criminal Damage Act 1971. He sought to set up the statutory defence under section 5(2) by claiming to have had a lawful excuse in doing what he did and that he was not reckless whether any such property would be destroyed. The trial judge withdrew the defence of lawful excuse from the jury and left the issue of recklessness for them to determine. The jury by a majority verdict convicted the appellant. On appeal, " 'Held, that, applying the objective test, the trial judge had ruled correctly because what the appellant had done was not an act which in itself did protect or was capable of protecting property; but in order to draw attention to what in his view was an immediate need for protection by repairing the alarm system; thus the statutory defence under section 5(2) of the Act was not open to him; accordingly, the appeal would be dismissed.'

'Giving the judgment of the Court Roskill L.J. said, at p. 108: 'Mr. Marshall-Andrews' submission can be put thus: if this man honestly believed that that which he did was necessary in order to protect this property from the risk of fire and damage to the old people's home by reason of the absence of a working fire alarm, he was entitled to set fire to that bed and so to claim the statutory defence accorded by section 5(2). 'I have said we will assume in his favour that he possessed the requisite honest belief. But in our view the question whether he was entitled to the benefit of the defence turns upon the meaning of the words 'in order to protect property belonging to another.' It was argued that those words were subjective in concept, just like the words in the latter part of section 5(2)(b) which are subjective. 'We do not think that is right. The question whether or not a particular act of destruction or damage or threat of destruction or damage was done or made in order to protect property belonging to another must be, on the true construction of the statute, an objective test. Therefore we have to ask ourselves whether, whatever the state of this man's mind and assuming an honest belief, that which he admittedly did was done in order to protect this particular property, namely the old people's home in

Hertfordshire? 'If one formulates the question in that way, in the view of each member of this Court, for the reason Slynn J. gave during the argument, it admits of only one answer: this was not done in order to protect property; it was done in order to draw attention to the defective state of the fire alarm. It was not an act which in itself did protect or was capable of protecting property.' "

Then the judgment in *Ashford and Smith*, delivered by Glidewell L.J. continued as follows: "In our view that reasoning applies exactly in the present case. *Hunt* is, of course, binding upon us. But even if it were not, we agree with the reasoning contained in it."

Now it is submitted by Mr. Bowyer to us that the decision in *Hunt* and the decision in *Ashford and Smith* were wrong and that the test is a subjective test. In other words the submission is that it was a question of what the applicant believed, and accordingly it should have been left to the jury as a matter of fact to decide what it was the applicant did believe.

We are bound by the decision in *Hunt* just as the Court in *Ashford and Smith* were bound, unless that case can be demonstrated to have been wrongly decided in the light of previous authority. Mr. Bowyer endeavoured to persuade us that the decision which I have read of Roskill L.J. flew in the face of the decision of the House of Lords in *Chandler* v. *Director of Public Prosecutions* (*ante*, p. 97.) [After rejecting this submission]

That leaves us with the fact that we are bound by the decision in *Hunt*. But we add that we think that *Hunt* was correctly decided, for this reason. There are two aspects to this type of question. The first aspect is to decide what it was that the applicant, in this case Valerie Hill, in her own mind thought. The learned judge assumed, and so do we, for the purposes of this decision, that everything she said about her reasoning was true. ... Up to that point the test was subjective. In other words one is examining what is going on in the applicant's mind.

Having done that, the judges in the present cases—and the judge particularly in the case of Valerie Hill—turned to the second aspect of the case, and that is this. He had to decide as a matter of law, which means objectively, whether it could be said that on those facts as believed by the applicant, snipping the strand of the wire, which she intended to do, could amount to something done to protect either the applicant's own home or the homes of her adjacent friends in Pembrokeshire.

He decided, again quite rightly in our view, that that proposed act on her part was far too remote from the eventual aim at which she was targeting her actions to satisfy the test.

It follows therefore, in our view, that the judges in the present two cases were absolutely right to come to the conclusion that they did so far as this aspect of the case is concerned, and to come to that conclusion as a matter of law, having decided the subjective test as the applicants wished them to be decided.

The second half of the question was that of the immediacy of the danger. Here the wording of the Act, one reminds oneself, is as follows: She believed that "the property ... was in immediate need of protection."

Once again the judge had to determine whether, on the facts as stated by the applicant, there was any evidence on which it could be said that she believed there was an immediate need of protection from immediate damage. In our view that must mean evidence that she believed that immediate action had to be taken to do something which would otherwise be a crime in order to prevent the immediate risk of something worse happening. ... The evidence given by this woman (and the evidence given by the other applicant was very similar) drives this Court to the conclusion, as they drove the respective judges to the conclusion, that there was no evidence on which it could be said that there was that belief ...

Appeal dismissed

Note

The provisions on lawful excuse are sorted out and extended to defence of person by clauses 184, 184 Draft Criminal Code Bill, below, which apply to the "simple" offences and not to the "aggravated" offences. The definition of "lawful excuse" is still not to be exhaustive; common law defences preserved by Clause 45(c), *ante*, p. 353, may apply.

Draft Criminal Code Bill

"**184**. A person does not commit an offence to which this section applies if—

(a) he knows or believes that the person whom he believes to be entitled to consent to the destruction or damage has so consented; or

(b) he believes that that person would so consent if he knew of the destruction or damage and its circumstances.

185.—(1) A person does not commit an offence to which this section applies by doing an act which, in the circumstances which exist or which he believes to exist, is immediately necessary and reasonable—

(a) to protect himself or another from unlawful force or injury; or

(b) to prevent or terminate the unlawful detention of himself or another; or

(c) to protect property (whether belonging to himself or another) from unlawful appropriation, destruction or damage.

(2) Section 44(3) (meaning of "unlawful") applies for the purposes of this section."

iii. Intending to Destroy or Damage any such Property

R. v. Smith
[1974] Q.B. 354
Court of Appeal

S., a tenant of a flat, installed some stereo equipment and, with the consent of the landlord, put in certain roofing, wall panels and flooring to mask the electric wiring. These fixtures thereupon belonged to the landlord by law, but S. did not know this. When he was given notice to quit he damaged the fixtures in order to remove the wiring. He said he thought he was damaging his own property. He was convicted of an offence under section 1(1) Criminal Damage Act 1971, and appealed.

JAMES L.J.: The appellant's defence was that he honestly believed that the damage he did was to his own property, that he believed that he was entitled to damage his own property and therefore he had lawful excuse for his actions causing the damage. In the course of his summing up the deputy judge directed the jury in these terms:

"Now, in order to make the offence complete, the person who is charged with it must destroy or damage that property belonging to another, 'without lawful excuse,' and that is something that one has got to look at a little more, members of the jury, because you have heard here that, so far as each defendant was concerned, it never occurred to them, and you may think, quite naturally never occurred to either of them, that these various additions to the house were anything but their own property. ... But members of the jury, the Act is quite specific, and so far as the defendant David Smith is concerned lawful excuse is the only defence which has been raised. It is said that he had a lawful excuse by reason of his belief, his honest and genuinely held belief that he was destroying property which he had a right to destroy if he wanted to. But, members of the jury, I must direct you as a matter of law, and you must, therefore, accept it from me, that belief by the defendant David Smith that he had the right to do what he did is not lawful excuse within the meaning of the Act. Members of the jury, it is an excuse, it may even be a reasonable excuse, but it is not, members of the jury a lawful excuse, because, in law, he had no right to do what he did. Members of the jury, as a matter of law, the evidence, in fact, discloses, so far as David Smith is concerned, no lawful excuse at all, because, as I say, the only defence which he has raised is the defence that he thought he had the right to do what he did. I have directed you that that is not a lawful excuse, and, members of the jury, it follows from that that so far as David Smith is concerned, I am bound to direct you as a matter of law that you must find him guilty of this offence with which he is charged."

It is contended for the appellant that that is a misdirection in law, and that, as a result of the misdirection, the entire defence of the appellant was wrongly withdrawn from the jury.

Section 1 of the Criminal Damage Act 1971 reads:

"(1) A person who without lawful excuse destroys or damages any property belonging to another intending to destroy or damage any such property or being reckless as to whether any such property would be destroyed or damaged, shall be guilty of an offence."

The offence created includes the elements of intention or recklessness and the absence of lawful excuse. There is in section 5 of the Act a partial "definition" of lawful excuse. ...

[After reading section 5(2), (3), (5), his Lordship continued]

It is argued for the appellant that an honest, albeit erroneous, belief that the act causing damage or destruction was done to his own property provides a defence to a charge brought under section 1(1). The argument is put in three ways. First, that the offence charged includes the act causing the damage or destruction and the element of *mens rea*. The element of *mens rea* relates to all the circumstances of the criminal act. The criminal act in the offence is causing damage to or destruction of "property belonging to another" and the element of *mens rea*, therefore, must relate to "property belonging to another." Honest belief, whether justifiable or not, that the property is the defendant's own negatives the element of *mens rea*. Secondly, it is argued that by the terms of section 5, in particular the words of subsection (2), "whether or not he would be treated for the purposes of this Act as having a lawful excuse apart from this subsection," and the words in subsection (5), the appellant had a lawful excuse in that he honestly believed he was entitled to do as he did to property he believed to be his own. This it seems is the way the argument was put at the trial. Thirdly, it is argued, with understandable diffidence, that if a defendant honestly believes he is damaging his own property he has a lawful excuse for so doing because impliedly he believes that he is the person entitled to give consent to the damage being done and that he has consented: thus the case falls within section 5(2)(a) of the Act.

We can dispose of the third way in which it is put immediately and briefly. Mr. Gerber for the Crown argues that to apply section 5(2)(a) to a case in which a defendant believes that he is causing damage to his own property involves a tortuous and unjustifiable construction of the wording. We agree. In our judgment, to hold that those words of section 5(2)(a) are apt to cover a case of a person damaging the property of another in the belief that it is his own would be to strain the language of the section to an unwarranted degree. Moreover, in our judgment, it is quite unnecessary to have recourse to such a construction.

Mr. Gerber invited our attention to *Cambridgeshire and Isle of Ely County Council* v. *Rust* [1972] 2 Q.B. 426, a case under section 127 of the Highways Act 1959, concerning the pitching of a stall on a highway without lawful excuse. The case is cited as authority for the proposition that in order to establish a lawful excuse as a defence it must be shown that the defendant honestly but mistakenly believed on reasonable grounds that the facts were of a certain order, and that if those facts were of that order his conduct would have been lawful. Applying that proposition to the facts of the present case, Mr. Gerber argues that the appellant cannot be said to have had a lawful excuse because in law the damaged property was part of the house and owned by the landlord. We have no doubt as to the correctness of the decision in the case cited. The proposition is argued here in relation to the appellant's contention that he had a lawful excuse and does not touch the argument based on absence of *mens rea*.

It is conceded by Mr. Gerber that there is force in the argument that the element of *mens rea* extends to "property belonging to another." But it is argued, the section creates a new statutory offence and that it is open to the construction that the mental element in the offence relates only to causing damage to or destroying property. That if in fact the property damaged or destroyed is shown to be another's property the offence is committed although the defendant did not intend or foresee damage to another person's property.

We are informed that so far as research has revealed this is the first occasion on which this court has had to consider the question which arises in this appeal.

It is not without interest to observe that, under the law in force before the passing of the Criminal Damage Act 1971, it was clear that no offence was committed by a person who destroyed or damaged property belonging to another in the honest but mistaken belief that the property was his own or that he had a legal right to do the damage. In *R.* v. *Twose* (1879) 14 Cox C.C. 327 the prisoner was indicted for setting fire to furze on a common. Persons living near the common had occasionally burned the furze in order to improve the growth of grass but without the right to do so. The prisoner denied setting fire to the furze and it was submitted that even if it were proved that she did she could not be found guilty if she *bona fide* believed she had a right to do so whether the right were a good one or not. Lopes J. ruled that if she set fire to the furze thinking she had a right to do so that would not be a criminal offence.

Upon the facts of the present appeal the charge, if brought before the Act of 1971 came into force, would have been laid under section 13 of the Malicious Damage Act 1861, alleging damage by a tenant to a building. It was a defence to a charge under that section that the tenant acted under a claim of right to do the damage.

If the direction given by the deputy judge in the present case is correct, then the offence created by section 1(1) of the Act of 1971 involves a considerable extension of the law in a surprising direction. Whether or not this is so depends upon the construction of the section. Construing the language of section 1(1) we have no doubt that the *actus reus* is "destroying or damaging any property belonging to another." It is not possible to exclude the words "belonging to another" which describes the "property." Applying the ordinary principles of *mens rea*, the intention and recklessness and the absence of lawful excuse required to constitute the offence have reference to property belonging to another. It follows that in our judgment no offence is committed under this section if a person destroys or causes damage to property belonging to another if he does so in the honest though mistaken belief that the property is his own, and provided that the belief is honestly held it is irrelevant to consider whether or not it is a justifiable belief.

In our judgment, the direction given to the jury was a fundamental misdirection in law. The consequence was that the jury were precluded from considering facts capable of being a defence to the charge and were directed to convict. ...

Appeal allowed

Questions

1. In *Jaggard* v. *Dickinson*, (*ante*, p. 268), the accused, because she was drunk, thought that the owner of the property had consented to her damaging it. It was held that since the case came under section 5(2)(a), she was entitled to be acquitted notwithstanding that her mistake was due to self-induced intoxication. But in *R.* v. *Smith*, the Court rejected the argument that his case came under section 5. Does this mean that if Miss Jaggard thought it was her *own* window she was breaking, her drunken mistake would not have saved her?

iv. Being Reckless as to Whether any such Property would be Destroyed or Damaged

See *R.* v. *Caldwell; Elliott* v. *C.; R.* v. *R., R.* v. *Sangha, ante*, pp. 111, 119, 122, 124 on recklessness.

Note

The Intention or Recklessness must be with regard to "any such property" (s.1(1), *ante*, p. 853), *i.e.* property belonging to another.

Question

Is the simple offence involved in the following cases?

(a) D intends to damage P's property and unexpectedly damages Q's property.
(b) D is reckless as to harm to P and unexpectedly damages P's property.

B. The Aggravated Offence: With Danger to Life

Note

See section 1(2), and *R. v. Caldwell, ante,* p. 111. Since the gravamen of the offence is danger to life, the property damaged need not belong to the accused. The extended meaning of "without lawful excuse" in section 5 does not apply, and in addition to the *mens rea* required for the simple offence he must intend to endanger the life of another or be reckless as to whether another's life is endangered.

R. v. Steer
[1988] A.C. 111
House of Lords

S. fired a shot through a window pane behind which Mr. & Mrs. G. were standing. The pane was broken by the shot, but they were not hurt. It was accepted that S. did not intend to endanger their lives. He was charged, *inter alia*, with damaging property being reckless whether the life of another would be endangered. On the judge's ruling against his submission that the endangering must by the damage to the window, not by the act which caused damage to the window, he pleaded guilty to the charge. His appeal against the ruling was allowed by the Court of Appeal. The prosecution further appealed.

LORD BRIDGE OF HARWICH: We must, of course, approach the matter on the footing, implicit in the outcome of the trial, that the respondent, in firing at the bedroom window, had no intent to endanger life, but accepts that he was reckless whether life would be endangered.

Under both limbs of section 1 of the 1971 Act it is the essence of the offence which the section creates that the defendant has destroyed or damaged property. For the purpose of analysis it may be convenient to omit reference to destruction and to concentrate on the references to damage, which was all that was here involved. To be guilty under subsection (1) the defendant must have intended or been reckless as to the damage to property which he caused. To be guilty under subsection (2) he must additionally have intended to endanger life or been reckless whether life would be endangered "by the damage" to property which he caused. This is the context in which the words must be construed and it seems to me impossible to read the words "by the damage" as meaning "by the danger or by the act which caused the damage." Moreover, if the language of the statute has the meaning for which the Crown contends, the words "by the destruction or damage" and "thereby" in subsection 2(b) are mere surplusage. If the Crown's submission is right, the only additional element necessary to convert a subsection (1) offence into a subsection (2) offence is an intent to endanger life or recklessness whether life would be endangered simpliciter.

It would suffice as a ground for dismissing this appeal if the statute were ambiguous, since any such ambiguity in a criminal statute should be resolved in favour of the defence. But I can find no ambiguity. It seems to me that the meaning for which the respondent contends is the only meaning which the language can bear.

The contrary construction leads to anomalies which Parliament cannot have intended. If A. and B. both discharge firearms in a public place, being reckless whether life would be endangered, it would be absurd that A., who incidentally causes some trifling damage to the property, should be guilty of an offence punishable with life imprisonment, but that B., who causes no damage, should be guilty of no offence. In the same circumstances, if A. is merely reckless but B. actually intends to endanger life, it is scarcely less absurd that A should be guilty of the graver offence under section 1(2) of the 1971 Act, B. of the lesser offence under section 16 of the Firearms Act 1968.

Counsel for the Crown did not shrink from arguing that section 1(2) of the 1971 Act had created, in effect, a general offence of endangering life with intent or recklessly, however the danger was caused, but had incidentally included as a necessary, albeit insignificant, ingredient of the offence that some damage to property should also be caused. In certain fields of legislation it is sometimes difficult to appreciate the rationale of particular provisions, but in a criminal statute it would need the clearest language to persuade me that the legislature had acted so irrationally, indeed perversely, as acceptance of this argument would imply.

It was further argued that to affirm the construction of section 1(2)(*b*) adopted by the Court of Appeal would give rise to problems in other cases in which it might be difficult or even impossible to distinguish between the act causing damage to property and the ensuing damage caused as the source of danger to life. In particular, it was suggested that in arson cases the jury would have to be directed that they could only convict if the danger to life arose from falling beams or similar damage caused by the fire, not if the danger arose from the heat, flames or smoke generated by the fire itself. Arson is, of course, the prime example of a form of criminal damage to property which, in the case of an occupied building, necessarily involves serious danger to life and where the gravity of the consequence which may result as well from recklessness as from a specific intent fully justifies the severity of the penalty which the 1971 Act provides for the offence. But the argument in this case is misconceived. It is not the match and the inflammable materials, the flaming firebrand or any other inflammatory agent which the arsonist uses to start the fire which causes danger to life, it is the ensuing conflagration which occurs as the property which has been set on fire is damaged or destroyed. When the victim in the bedroom is overcome by the smoke or incinerated by the flames as the building burns, it would be absurd to say that this does not result from the damage to the building.

Counsel for the Crown put forward other examples of cases which he suggested ought to be liable to prosecution under section 1(2) of the 1971 Act, including that of the angry mob of striking miners who throw a hail of bricks through the window of the cottage occupied by the working miner and that of people who drop missiles from motorway bridges on passing vehicles. I believe that the criminal law provides adequate sanctions for these cases without the need to resort to section 1(2) of the 1971 Act. But, if my belief is mistaken, this would still be no reason to distort the plain meaning of that subsection. ...

[Lords Griffiths, Ackner, Oliver and Goff agreed]

Appeal dismissed

Note

The damage by which D intended to endanger life or was reckless as to endangering life is the damage he intended to cause or was reckless as to causing, not the damage he actually caused. The fact that he was not intentional or reckless about the damage actually caused endangering life, and the fact that that damage involved no danger to life, are both immaterial: R. v. *Dudley* [1989] Crim.L.R. 57.

2. OTHER OFFENCES

Criminal Damage Act 1971, sections 2 and 3

"2. A person who without lawful excuse makes to another a threat, intending that that other would fear it would be carried out—

(a) to destroy or damage any property belonging to that other or a third person; or

(b) to destroy or damage his own property in a way which he knows is likely to endanger the life of that other or a third person;

shall be guilty of an offence.

3. A person who has anything in his custody or under his control intending without lawful excuse to use it or cause or permit another to use it—

(a) to destroy or damage any property belonging to some other person; or

(b) to destroy or damage his own or the user's property in a way which he knows is likely to endanger the life of some other person;

shall be guilty of an offence."

Notes

1. As with section 1, both of these sections have a pair of offences, a simple offence and an aggravated offence, *i.e.* one referring to danger to life (although the maximum penalties—10 years imprisonment—are the same). With the offences in sections 2(*a*) and 3(*a*), but not with the offences in sections 2(*b*) and 3(*b*), the lawful excuse provisions in section 5 apply, and the threatened property must belong to someone else.

2. There need be no intention to carry out the threat in section 2, merely an intention that the person to whom it is made would fear that it would be carried out. If there is such an intention, it makes no difference that such a fear is not aroused in that person.

3. For the offence in section 3, "in his possession" was rejected by the Law Commission on account of the difficulties centred round the question of when a person can be said to be in possession of something without knowing: see *Warner* v. *Commissioner of Police* [1969] A.C. 256.

Questions

1. That question can be said to be purely academic with regard to section 3. Why is this?

2. D, looking for a "squat" to sleep in, has in his custody a jemmy so that he can break into a suitable house if he cannot get in in any other way. Is he guilty of an offence in section 3? See

discussion of conditional intent in theft, *ante*, p. 717, and burglary, *ante*, p. 845, and *R.* v. *Buckingham* (1976) 63 Cr.App.R. 159 (C.A.).

INDEX

Abortion, 568
Absolute Offences. *See* Strict Liability.
Accessories,
  not convictable as principal, when, 402
  withdrawal by, 398
Accomplices. *See also* Degrees of
    Responsibility.
  aids, abets, counsels or procures, 374
  innocent agency, 368
  mens rea of accessories, 379
  principals and accessories, 366
Actus Reus, 12–63
  causation, 33–55
  co-incidence with *mens rea*, 56–63
  omissions, 18–31
  unconscious actions, 16
  voluntary conduct, 14
Aiding and Abetting. *See* Accomplices.
Arson. *See* Criminal Damage.
Assault and Battery. *See also* Assaults,
    Statutory.
  actus reus, 582
  consent in, 595
  justifications for, 587
  mens rea, 586
  necessity, as justifying, 587
Assaults, Statutory,
  malicious wounding, 622
  mens rea, 626
  occasioning actual bodily harm, 622
  proposals for reform, 630
  wounding with intent, 629
Attempts,
  actus reus of, 437
  Law Commission's Proposals on, 425,
    437
  impossible result, at, 478
  mental element in, 426
Automatism, 226
  proposals for reform, 237
  self-induced, 234

Blackmail, 789–802
Burglary, 828–852
  aggravated, 846
Butler Committee, 241, 273

Causation, 33
  alternative approach, an, 55
  imputability, 36
  sine qua non, 34
Causing Death by Driving, 576
Child Destruction, 568
Concept of Crime, 1–8

Conspiracy,
  common law, under, 462
  corrupt public morals, to, 467
  defraud, to, 463
  impossible end, to do, 490
  jurisdiction in, 467
  statute, under, 451
Corporations, 413
  manslaughter, and, 418
Credit Card,
  deception by using, 765
Crime,
  definition of, 1–4
  elements of, 12
Criminal Code, 10
Criminal Law Revision Committee, 9
Criminal Damage, 853–870
  destroying or damaging property, 853
  other offences of, 870

Deception,
  evasion of liability by, 778
  meaning of, 751
  obtaining by,
    pecuniary advantage, of, 776
    property, of, 751
    services, of, 777
Defences, 280–365
  duress, 281
  in general, 280
  necessity, 314
  proposals for reform, 353
  self-defence, 330
  unknown circumstances, and, 345
Degrees of Responsibility, 366–423
  accomplices, 366
  corporations, 413
  proposals for reform, 373, 407, 410, 421
  vicarious liability, 408
Diminished Responsibility. *See* Murder.
Draft Criminal Code, 10
Drunkenness. *See* Intoxication.
Duress, 281
  circumstances, of. *See* Necessity.
  murder, and, 292
  proposals for reform, 355

"Fault Element", 137
Fraud. *See also* Deception.
  conspiracy to defraud, in, 463
Form of English Criminal Law, 8–11

Going Equipped For Crime, 848

Handling, 803–827
Homicide, 495–580. *See also* Manslaughter;
       Murder.
   actus reus, of, 495
   causing death by driving, 576
   infanticide, 568
   reform of, 505–512, 577–580
   suicide, 575
House of Lords,
   Practice Statement (Judicial Precedent),
       489

Incitement, 473–478
   impossible result, to, 491
Inchoate Offences,
   attempts, 424–451
   conspiracy, 451–473
   impossibility in relation to, 478–494
   incitement, 473–478
   proposals for reform, 450, 461, 477
Insanity, 215
   disease of the mind, 219
   nature and quality of act, 223
   uncontrollable impulse, 226
Intention. *See* Mens Rea.
   attempts, in, 426
Intoxication, 246
   becoming intoxicated with intent, 265
   defences, and, 268
   proposals for reform, 273
   specific and basic intent, 246

Knowledge. *See* Mens Rea.

Larceny, 660
Law Commission, 9

Making Off Without Payment, 784
Malice. *See* Mens Rea.
Manslaughter,
   reckless, 557
   unlawful act, by, 546
   voluntary, 513–545
Mens Rea, 64–213
   intention, 70
   motive, contrasted with, 97
   knowledge, 102
 - malice, 109, 126
   meaning of terms, 68–140
   mistake, 140
   proposals for reform, 137
 - recklessness, 106
   requirement of, 64
   strict liability, 182
   wilfulness, 128
Mental Incapacity, 214–279
   automatism, 226
   insanity, 215
   intoxication, 246
   "mental disorder", 239
   proposals for reform, 237–246

Mistake,
   excusatory claim, as to, 164
   irrelevant, 169
   justificatory claim, as to, 154
   law, of, 172
   mens rea, negating, 141
   relevant, 141
   strict liability, and, 169
 - transferred malice, and, 175
Motive. *See* Mens Rea.
Murder,
   diminished responsibility,
      burden of proof, as to, 529
      intoxication, and, 539
      reform of, 542
      what amounts to, 530
   mental element in, 497
      malice, constructive, 498
      malice, implied, 499
         grievous bodily harm, by, 503
   penalty for, 497
   provocation, 513
      reasonable man in, 517
      self-induced, 526

Necessity, 314
   duress of circumstances, 319
   homicide, and, 321
   proposals for reform, 358
Non-Fatal Offences Against the Person.
      See Assault and Battery; Assaults,
      Statutory; and Sexual Offences.

Prevention of Crime, 334
Provacation. *See* Murder.

Rape, 632
   consent, in, 633
      fraud, as affecting, 638
   definition of, 632
   husband, by, 640
   mens rea, 641
Recklessness. *See also* Mens Rea.
   manslaughter, in, 557
Retribution,
   criminal theory, in, 6
Robbery, 744–748

Self-Defence and Kindred Defences, 330
   defence of others, 331
      property, 333
      self, 331
   duty to retreat, 342
   force,
      excessive, 350
      reasonable, 347
   mistake, 350
   offences, which, applying to, 346
   prevention of crime, 334
   pre-emptive strike, 339
   proposals for reform, 353, 360

Sexual Offences. *See also* Rape.
  defectives, with, 645
  indecent assault, 647
  procurement by threats or fraud, 644
  young girls, with, 645
Strict Liability, 182–213
  critique of, 206
  evolution of, 182
  mistake and, 169
  present uncertainty of, 183
  proposals for reform, 210
  public welfare offences, in, 202
  regulatory offences, in, 195
Suicide, 575

Theft, 660–743
  appropriation in, 662
  definition of, 661
  dishonesty in, 733

Theft—*cont.*
  information, of, 689
  intent to deprive in, 717
  land, of, 680
  property in, 679
    belonging to another, 692
    intangible, 688
    trust, 702
  temporary deprivation, by, 727, 730
    articles in a collection, of, 728
    conveyances, of, 729
  things in action, of, 681
  wild creatures, of, 680

Vicarious Liability, 408
  delegation principle, and, 411

Wilfulness. *See* Mens Rea.
Wounding With Intent, 629